DISTRIBUTED AUTOMOTIVE EMBEDDED SYSTEMS

Other SAE books in this series:

Infotainment Systems
(Product Code: PT-135)

Object Detection, Collision Warning and Avoidance Systems, Volume 2
(Product Code: PT-133)

Adaptive Cruise Control
(Product Code: PT-132)

Electronic Braking, Traction, and Stability Controls, Volume 2
(Product Code: PT-129)

Multiplexing and Networking, Volume 2
(Product Code: PT-128)

Automotive Software
(Product Code: PT-127)

Electronic Engine Control Technologies, Second Edition
(Product Code: PT-110)

Sensors and Transducers, Second Edition
(Product Code: PT-105)

Multiplexing and Networking
(Product Code: PT-78)

DISTRIBUTED AUTOMOTIVE EMBEDDED SYSTEMS

PT-136

Edited by
Ronald K. Jurgen

Published by
SAE International
400 Commonwealth Drive
Warrendale, PA 15096-0001
U.S.A.
Phone: (724) 776-4841
Fax: (724) 776-0790

For permission and licensing requests contact:

SAE Permissions
400 Commonwealth Drive
Warrendale, PA 15096-0001-USA
Email: permissions@sae.org
Tel: 724-772-4028
Fax: 724-776-3036

For multiple print copies contact:

SAE Customer Service
Tel: 877-606-7323 (inside USA and Canada)
Tel: 724-776-4970 (outside USA)
Fax: 724-776-0790
Email: CustomerService@sae.org

ISBN-13 978-0-7680-1966-7
Library of Congress Catalog Card Number: 2007935110

SAE Order No. PT-136

Printed in USA

INTRODUCTION

Distributed Embedded Systems: Key to Future Automotive Electronics

Automotive embedded systems are distributed throughout modern vehicles using multiple vehicle networks partitioned across a variety of different electronic modules. The need for such systems arises from the continuing proliferation of increasingly complex control systems with cross-functional system interactions. As more complex control systems are used in automobiles, more distributed automotive embedded systems will be needed.

Distributed embedded systems can be characterized in different ways. The following selected comments from papers in this book offer some of those characterizations:

- "An embedded control system is commonly used in the automotive industry to achieve complex and accurate control functionality. An embedded control system consists of three portions including a control object, i.e., the peripheral under control, a micro-controller and control software that is executed on the micro-controller." (2005-01-1430)

- "The low cost of microcontrollers makes them increasingly popular for electronic control of a wide range of embedded systems throughout the vehicle. An embedded mixed-signal or mechatronic system is one that uses a microcontroller to control some aspect of the physical system such as motion, speed, temperature, etc.... The added dimension of software presents a significant challenge to the design, integration and verification of this class of systems." (2004-01-0718)

- "In automotive embedded control systems, the available throughput in the controller is to be shared by the system application functions and the system safety functions. Achieving balance of both system safety and performance of these systems is critical in the success of the system design." (2006-01-0840)

- "The SIA [Semiconductor Industry Association] data show a roadmap toward 65 nanometers for high-performance automotive grade embedded processors by 2010 with 80–90 million transistors. With this increase in integration and shrinking geometries comes lower system voltages, while maintaining or slightly decreasing the power of the embedded processor." (2005-01-3690)

The 88 papers in this book, published from 2001 through 2007, address the many different aspects of distributed embedded systems. The papers are presented in seven categories. The first three—controller design/development, software design/development, and communication networks/systems—cover the basic components of distributed embedded systems. The fourth category—model-based hardware/software/network designs—contains papers highlighting the growing importance of the modeling approach to embedded systems design. Papers in the fifth category—systems testing/diagnosis—treat the many aspects of making certain that embedded systems perform as they were intended. Papers in the sixth category—implementation examples—focus on specific system developments, some for use in production automobiles. The final category—future trends—is self-explanatory.

Note that many of the papers herein cover more than one of these categories, and determining which category should include a particular paper can at times be a somewhat arbitrary decision. An obvious example is paper 2006-01-0170, "Hardware/Software Design and Development Process." It was placed in the controller design/development category but, arguably, could have been included with the software design/development papers.

The following are selected key insights from papers in the various groupings in this book:

- ". . . the authors propose the concept of a 'controller grid,' which enables a microcontroller in an automotive control system to borrow the required computing power from other microcontrollers connected to the network, guaranteeing the 'real-timeness' of control operations. By applying the controller grid, advanced control applications (which cause a single microcontroller to become overloaded) can be executed. Additionally, software developers will be able to write programs without having to consider which microcontroller each functional job runs, since the controller grid makes lots of distributed microcontrollers into one 'virtual real-time computer'." (2007-01-1615)

- "Once it is understood that code generation from models is as much of a process solution as it is a technical solution, the appropriate focus can be applied. It is from this concept of process focus, and problem space identification, that a practical method of transitioning from models to code can be achieved." (2007-01-1622)

- "Technology has reached the stage where parallel ANN [artificial neural network] implementations are available and suitable for embedded 'real-time' SOC [system on chip] solutions. Developing control systems for non-linear actuators based on ANNs is now a practical consideration. The ANN-based control system approach leads to rapid development by avoiding the need for a detailed analytical solution. Because the ANN creates a map of the non-linear transfer function of the system, it is able to provide both accuracy and flexibility. The flexibility provided by ANN control allows for changes to actuator operating profiles to be implemented simply by creating the desired demand profile." (2003-01-0359)

- "Embedded systems of today need to manage more data than ever before. The main reasons for the increase in number of data items are increased functional requirements on the software. With a larger amount of data to manage comes the problems of storing data and its meta-information, sharing between programmers which data items exist, and ensuring freshness and consistency requirements of the data items." (2006-01-0305)

- "The development of advanced safety-critical systems is driving the development of new tools and processes to help verify that these systems operate safely and that they are reliable and predictable. For these systems, product safety needs to be considered up front and addressed as part of the overall design process." (2005-01-0779)

- "It is estimated that the software which monitors the health of an ECU now takes up about 60% of the total ECU software code to monitor, diagnose, and announce the problems an ECU may have during its normal or abnormal operational modes." (2005-01-0327)

- "In recent years, automated code generation has become popular, particularly in rapid prototyping. Currently we see these tools moving from being utilized in prototyping only into software development processes for mass production. If these tools can take over most of the code generation and actually fill the gap between algorithm design and the executable file, the development process could be sped up dramatically." (2004-01-0702)

- "In today's vehicles there are mainly two networks: a high-speed network for the power train and a low-speed network for the body electronics. Since the complexity of the network is increasing and the demand for bandwidth is growing, future vehicles will require many partitioned networks. The partitioning of the networks will be done based on the locality as well as the functionality of the modules." (2005-01-1531)

- "FlexRay is a new communication standard for future in-vehicle controls. This protocol provides flexibility and determinism by providing scalable static and dynamic message transmission. Due to FlexRay's time-triggered features and its possible use in safety-critical applications, considerable software and developmental planning is required. Proper and optimal use of FlexRay in safety-critical applications requires construction of reliable embedded software." (2005-01-1279)

- "There is a clear sense of urgency among the automotive industry to cut the cost and time spent on all aspects of vehicle development, and move as much as possible towards virtual design practices. In the area of embedded engine control systems development, this move requires that the industry gradually accept a paradigm shift towards a rigorously model-based design practice." (2005-01-0320)

- "The objective of an embedded system is to have a predictable output for any combination of input sequences. If the operation of the embedded system is viewed as a big state diagram, testing verifies that the embedded system operates in acceptable states and that transitions between states are all known and predictable." (2006-01-1679)

- "Designing automotive chassis applications is becoming increasingly complex due to cross-functional system interactions and the inherent safety-critical nature of the systems involved. One consequence is the need for a rapid prototyping platform, targeted and tailored to meet the specific needs of the chassis domain.

  "This paper describes an example of such an architecture for a rapid prototyping system incorporating several Infineon TriCore embedded microcontrollers and Emulation Devices (ED), networked together by the Micro Link Interfaces (MLI). It also discusses how using such a development platform can lead to a significant reduction in the overall development time of a production intent chassis system." (2006-01-1657)

* * * * * * * * * *

This book and the entire Automotive Electronics Series are dedicated to my friend Larry Givens, a former editor of SAE's monthly publication, *Automotive Engineering International.*

Ronald K. Jurgen, Editor

TABLE OF CONTENTS

INTRODUCTION

CONTROLLER DESIGN/DEVELOPMENT

SOFTWARE DESIGN/DEVELOPMENT

COMMUNICATION NETWORKS/SYSTEMS

MODEL-BASED HARDWARE/SOFTWARE/ NETWORK DEVELOPMENTS

SYSTEMS TESTING/DIAGNOSIS

IMPLEMENTATION EXAMPLES

FUTURE TRENDS

CONTROLLER DESIGN/DEVELOPMENT

2007-01-1619

Power Saving in Body Applications at High Temperatures

Axel Freiwald
Infineon Technologies AG

ABSTRACT

The increasing requirements for body features - for greater memory size and better controller performance on the one hand, and for energy consumption on power down on the other - make new concepts necessary.

Higher performance and increasing features in semiconductor industries typically lead to the use of smaller structures. The latest structures being seen in automotive silicon devices are 0.18μ and 0.13μ. With these structures it is possible to achieve the requirements for performance and size of integrated memories.

The drawback of these technologies is a dramatic increase of leakage currents, especially when such devices are getting hot.

The paper will describe what can be done to get rid of such high leakage currents and how this was implemented in the latest 16/32 bit microcontroller family XC2000 from Infineon.

There are two ways to get rid of leakage current. The first is to lower the supply voltage and the second is to switch off the supply at parts of the device that are not needed in a power down mode.

The first samples that have implemented these new features are now available to serve the automotive industry for coming challenges.

INTRODUCTION

Most electronic control units (ECUs) in automotive body applications are challenged with power consumption issues.

Significant here is the very wide range over which power supply and power consumption has to be managed. A range of four magnitudes between full operation mode and power saving mode is a typical requirement.

A good starting point is to look into the main drains for electric power in such ECUs. These can be grouped into four categories:

Switching logic

- Clock distribution
- All gates used by the operation

Analog devices

- Voltage regulators and power supply including power distribution
- Sensors
- AD converters
- Clock generation like oscillators and PLLs

IO

- Drivers
- Pull up and pull down devices
- Display devices like LEDs, etc.

Leakage current

- Leakage within integrated devices, especially microcontrollers and memories
- I/O Leakage on drivers, signals and wires

These drains can be seen regardless of the level of integration, though typically it can be stated that the higher the integration level the lower the power dissipation.

INCREASING REQUIREMENTS FOR MICROCONTROLLERS IN BODY ECUS

Moore's law [1] is valid for microcontrollers in body ECUs, too.

In the same way as in computer industries this is not caused by the nature of the hardware but more by the increase of requirements on the hardware. It is the constantly growth of requirements that leads to greater demands on memory size and processor performance.

There are several factors driving this.

FEATURES

First of all, the number of features supported by body ECUs is increasing. Most of these features are located in the area of comfort. As an example here the feature interior light can be used. Whereas in the past it was globally just switched on and off, it is now slowly dimmed with some delay, controlled regarding which door is open, electronically checked and so on. All these features are mainly controlled by a microcontroller and some electronic switches. Any increase of features here ends up in additional control software, memory space and computing performance.

CHANGING PROGRAMMING STYLE

Second, the programming style is changing. Assembler has disappeared almost completely. The C language widely being used is now being replaced by automatic code generation.

MORE COMFORTABLE SW STRUCTURE

Third, the software organization is changing. In the past a typical operating system in a body ECU, including maintenance routines, did not have more than 10-50k bytes of code and the structure not more than 3 layers (drivers, operating system, application software). Especially the number of layers is now increasing. As an example with AUTOSAR it is increasing to 5 layers with the introduction of abstraction layers and service layers.

MORE MEMORY SPACE

More comfortable software structures, together with the new programming tools, rapidly increase the demand for code space. Though tools' suppliers are trying to say something different, in reality each of these steps more or less doubles the code size being generated. In addition, not only code size increases but also the requested memory size for data is increasing. The first results from AUTOSAR implementations are showing that both, code size and data size are increasing. Data size could increase by a factor of about three, while code size could increase by a factor of two, just by introducing this standard and not changing the programming style. This means the increase rate for data is higher than that for code.

MORE COMPUTING POWER

The required time to provide any of the features within a body application is not changing, but, as already mentioned, the features that are being added and the way they are being implemented is changing. Thus it is not astonishing that required computing power is increasing. Typically it is increasing linearly with both code space and number of features.

NEXT GENERATION OF MICROCONTROLLERS IN BODY APPLICATIONS

Microcontrollers with more than 1M bytes of integrated Flash memory for code and more than 80k bytes of SRAM are already being requested for new designs of body ECUs for year 2007 with up to 60 MIPS of performance. For 2009 it is 2M bytes of Flash.

Such memory sizes can no longer be efficiently produced in 0.25µ technologies. Most of the automotive microcontroller suppliers have already stepped up to 0.18µ or even 0.13µ like Infineon Technologies.

LESS POWER CONSUMPTION DURING POWER DOWN

One specialty for body electronics is the control of power down currents to assure car battery life while a car is parked.

These currents become more a challenge the higher the requirements for features during power down and wake up, and an increasing number of ECUs can no longer be switched off while the car is parked. Many of these ECUs are operating in a low power mode or are awakened periodically. Typical examples of such features are remote keyless entry and alarm systems.

Mainly caused by the increasing number of body ECUs, but also because of the attempt to reduce battery size, the automotive industries are requesting less power consumption per ECU. Typical values are a reduction of power down current from 250µA per ECU down to less than 100µA.

THE LEAKAGE CHALLENGE AT HIGH TEMPERATURES

So far, power down values are typically measured at room temperature, implying that this is the linear average temperature over a longer period. Unfortunately the influence of temperature on leakage currents is not linear.

Regardless of the technology, level leakage currents are increasing exponentially. This is a physical rule of semiconductors using silicon. As a rule of thumb there is an increase by a factor of 10 every 20° C . Thus if for example at 25°C the leakage is at 1µA, it is 1mA at 85°C.

Though temperatures for body ECUs are usually not in the same range as for others like ECUs in power train applications, their maximum temperature can get above 85°C, too.

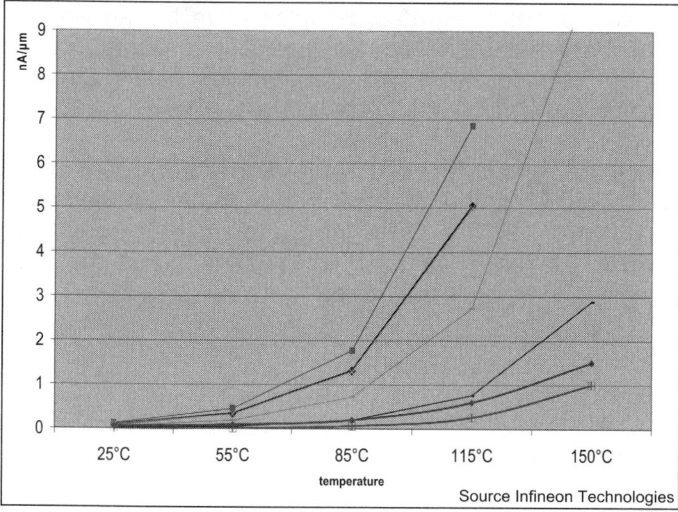

Figure1: Leakage current over temperature for several transistor types in different technology steps

The graph above shows how the leakage current is increasing over temperature for six different types of transistors. The values are standardized in terms of gate width. Transistor types differ in gate length and implantation.

For every semiconductor leakage currents are getting higher at higher temperatures. The absolute values are significantly depending on the technology step being used.

For microcontroller designs down to 0.09µ technologies leakage is still not significant at room temperature. Other power drains are still more dominant there. But at high temperatures this is no longer the case. This will be discussed shortly.

As soon as leakage currents enter the calculation, average power down currents can no longer be calculated at an average temperature of 25°C. For example, the temperatures inside a car standing in the sun in a parking lot are definitely much higher. Even though the sun will not heat up cars for 24 hours a day, the period when the car is hot has a significant influence on average power consumption in such ECUs. Significant leakage values within all semiconductors being powered will result.

It is not only the microcontroller that is contributing to this drain of power. All power supply devices, sensors and switches are contributing, too, to the overall consumption of a body ECU.

Car industries have noticed these facts and are pushing to achieve similar power down values at higher temperatures, too.

CHALLENGES FOR MICROCONTROLLERS IN TECHNOLOGIES BELOW 0.25µ

For body ECUs the new technologies have the same two advantages as for computer industries:

- It is possible to integrate more gates and memories on the same size of silicon
- The performance of the CPUs is increasing rapidly.

In compliance with Moore's law the next generations of semiconductor technologies are providing the solutions for memory size and CPU performance.

But there is one significant drawback. The smaller dimensions of the transistors do dramatically increase the leakage current. For a typical transistor with a regular voltage threshold the leakage increases by at least a factor of 50 going from 0.25µ to 0.18µ using regular voltage threshold transistors. It increases in the same range doing the next technology step to 0.13µ.

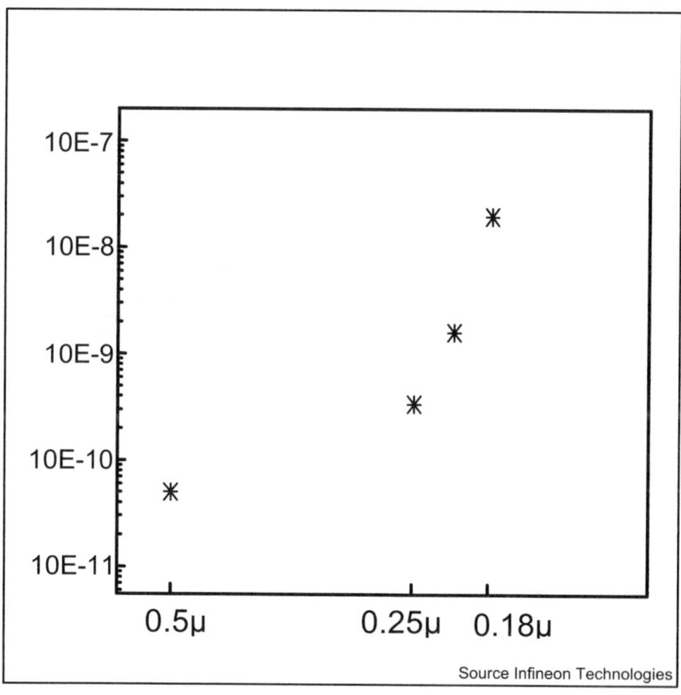

Figure2: Leakage current in A/µm of gate at 125°C for various technologies using regular voltage threshold

This graph shows how leakage current increases for transistors if the gate length is getting smaller. The values are given for 125°C and per gate width. In other words, it is given for devices having a comparable sum of gate width. In real designs doing the same function in a smaller technology the sum of gate width is getting less, too. Thus the effect is a bit smaller than the graph shows.

On the other hand, in more highly integrated devices the number of transistors is increasing, too, and each transistor counts for leakage.

Another way to reduce leakage is to increase the threshold voltage of a transistor, but this will reduce the performance. This will be discussed shortly.

One fact remains. With the new technologies the greatly appreciated high number of gates and memories is becoming a challenge for strategies to save in power down modes.

POWER SAVING STRATEGIES

The power consumption of a microcontroller consists of a linear value and a base value. Linear values go along with operating performance or operating frequency. Base values are put together of static IO currents, currents within a mixed signal or an analog module, and leakage current.

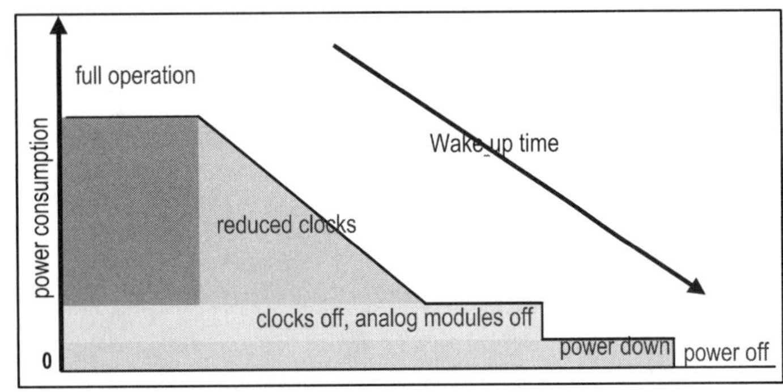

Figure 3: Reducing power consumption at microcontrollers

Each power drain group asks for its own strategy of how to save power.

SWITCHING LOGIC

- shut off or slow down the clock
- switch off clock distribution

Reducing the clock linearly reduces power consumption down to a base value. Switching off clock distribution will reduce the base value. Typically these methods can save a lot of power coming from the peak consumption at highest performance. Values are in the range of 90% to 99% of peak consumption.

ANALOG MODULES

- reduce accuracy when not needed (ADCs, band gaps,)
- use on chip modules with power control
- reduce voltage
- switch off power supply

In most cases integrated modules have the advantage, that there are more signals available to control power consumption in a smart way, and not just having them on or off.

Since any circuit has a different set of analog or mixed signal modules, the amount of current that can be saved is different. In any case, these measures again can reduce the base value of consumption and are less sensitive to high temperature.

IO

- switch off all drivers
- switch off displays

These two measures are basic for bringing current values down to a few micro amps.

LEAKAGE CURRENT

- use the technology that fits the performance requirements
- switch off power supply

Especially with technologies below 0.20µ and at higher temperatures, leakage is becoming the dominant drain of power. Transistors with a regular voltage threshold have higher leakage currents than high Vth transistors, but the maximum performance of such logic is decreasing, too. Typically the performance decreases by 25% while leakage can get reduced by 50% going from regular to high Vth. This is not enough to really reduce leakage. The only sure way to reduce leakage is to switch off the supply.

POWER SAVING MODES AND WAKE UP

All measures described above are in some way combined to form different power saving states. These power saving modes are for example named sleep mode, stop mode, stop over mode, standby mode, idle mode.

Power saving modes are measured by two parameters: the supply current in that mode, and how long it takes to wake up the system. Typically the lower the power down current in a certain mode the longer it can take to wake up.

Power saving modes should differ significantly in both parameters, at least as long as there are not other features that makes it hard to compare them.

If a power saving mode is to handle leakage reduction, then it must handle how to switch off the power supply.

SMART SOLUTIONS IN SWITCHING POWER OFF

There is no way to really save power at higher temperatures other than to switch off the supply.

If in a low power mode there is still some limited functionality required, then there are smart solutions necessary that just switch off power for those parts of the system where it is not really needed. ECUs are getting two or more power domains.

Today there are several systems being used with two power domains at the digital control level comprising two microcontrollers, a small one for power down features and a big one for the main application. The small microcontrollers are typically 8-bit controllers with just a few kilobytes of memory, while the big micros are 16-bit or 32-bit controllers with several hundred kilobytes of memory. The effort to control the power supply and power domains at the board level is quite high. Signals being used in two or more domains or crossing domains must get handled such that the system remains stable and safe while the power to one domain is switched off.

Realization is getting easier for the board level but more tricky on the silicon level as soon as systems are integrated in one piece of silicon, so-called "systems on a chip" (SOC).

Up to now most such SOCs are used in mobile solutions. For automotive microcontrollers this integrated approach is new.

The first microcontrollers offering this feature are the XC2000 microcontroller family from Infineon technologies. This family is implemented in a 0.13µ technology.

The core of the silicon is split into two power domains. Each power domain has its own power supply. The supply is generated by one voltage regulator for each power domain. Both domains are completely isolated and can principally get independently powered.

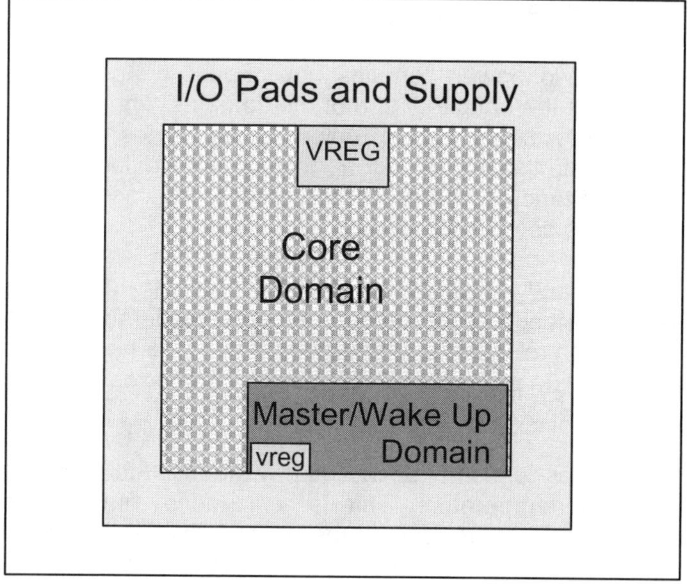

Figure4: Power domains within XC2000 microcontrollers

Both supplies are getting their power from the IO voltage supply that can be operated in the range of 3.0V to 5.5V.

POWER SUPERVISION

There are several circuits in place to supervise the different supply voltages.

Core supply watchdogs

The operating voltage of each domain is typically at 1.5V +/- 0.1V. The voltages of both domains are independently regulated and also supervised separately. If the voltage of one of the domains is getting too low, then the whole system is getting unstable. Normal operation can no longer be guaranteed. In this case a reset is automatically generated to bring the system into a known default state.

IO supply watchdog

The supply voltage for the regulators and thus for all IO pads is supervised, too. If the IO voltage is dropping below the specified minimum, the result for the microcontroller is not as dramatic as if the core voltage is too low. The CPU can still continue to execute code, but the micro might no longer be able to control external signals or communicate correctly. Thus the reaction to a low IO voltage is programmable. The default reaction is to generate a reset.

For several applications the other options, a high level interrupt or a trap, could be the smarter choice. Typically when voltage drops there is still some time left until the CPU really stops operation. This time can be used to store data in a non-volatile memory and to bring the system into a non-critical state.

NEW POWER DOWN MODE

Having two power domains now makes it possible to switch off the supply of one of the domains. Thus, on top of all previously known power down states, such a microcontroller is getting a new power saving mode, called Standby Mode. In Standby Mode one power domain is completely shut off.

Consequently the other domain contains all those features needed to control this Standby Mode and has all those control circuits integrated, which are needed for the wake up procedure. This domain can be regarded as the master domain, and is named accordingly.

The power consumption in Standby Mode is independent from the temperature. This is achieved by limiting the number of gates and transistors within the master domain. Leakage current is no longer dominant during Standby Mode.

Nevertheless all features are still available that are typically requested for body ECUs. There is an SRAM for data storage, there is an on chip oscillator, there is a timer for periodic wake up and real-time clock feature, there are functions to wake up the device through external events on pins and there are several registers and control bits to signal the CPU what happened during the standby state.

During the standby state the main part of the core is completely powered off. As a consequence all volatile data are lost. There is no longer any guarantee that any register contents or RAM contents are still valid. In reality it can take seconds until the contents change, but there would be an extreme overhead needed to check this, especially for all the registers.

Thus the wake up procedure for the main core only has one way to go. A full reset procedure has to be performed for the CPU and all registers in the main core. The master domain is excluded from this reset. The contents of the standby SRAM and registers are preserved.

This sounds like it is very time consuming, but with several design measures the effect could be limited in conjunction with a smart software program. For example, if a crystal oscillator is used for operation after wake up and the crystal was switched off during standby, then it typically takes 4 to 12 ms to restart the oscillation. This time can easily be used for a full initialization by running the system out of an internal clock source.

CONSEQUENCES FOR SOFTWARE DESIGN

Using a power down mode that switches off the CPU requires a special software system if periodic wake up is requested while a car is parked.

Such a software system must be able to handle short wake up periods without fully booting the system. Just the minimum operating system should be loaded that is needed to check to see if there is anything to which the system should respond. One reaction could be to fully wake up and boot the system.

Such low-level operating modes cannot use a standard real-time OS and standard drivers, but this is also not needed. After reading a few values and comparing them with values stored in the standby SRAM, in most cases the system will go back into standby mode. The power of the CPU is shut off again.

CONCLUSION

Within the next years microcontroller performance and memory size within body ECUs will increase. Along with this increase and with the new technologies being used leakage currents during power down states will become a challenge. Especially at higher temperatures leakage currents will get dominant for the overall power consumption as long as a device is powered. More advanced strategies have to be used in order to control these leakage currents. One method to do this, is to implement several power domains in one silicon and to switch off power in those domains that are not needed during a power down phase. The new XC2000 family of Infineon technologies has two power domains and can switch of most of the device going into an active standby mode.

REFERENCES

1. Moore's Law: Gordon Moore "Cramming more components onto integrated circuits", *Electronics Magazine* 19 April 1965.

CONTACT

Axel Freiwald Infineon Technologies AG, D-81726 Munich, Germany

Axel.freiwald@infineon.com,

Axel Freiwald works in Munich as manager in application engineering for microcontrollers at Infineon Technologies. He has a masters degree for electrical engineering from Technische Universität Munich.

DEFINITIONS, ACRONYMS, ABBREVIATIONS

ADC: analog to digital converter
AUTOSAR: automotive open system architecture
CPU: central processing unit
ECU: electronic control unit
IO: input output
OS: operating system
RAM: random access memory
SRAM: static RAM
SOC: system on chip
Vth: voltage threshold

2007-01-1615

Controller Grid: Real-Time Load Balancing of Distributed Embedded Systems

Akihiko Hyodo, Fumio Arakawa and Naoki Kato
Hitachi, Ltd.

ABSTRACT

The concept of a "controller grid", which makes effective use of computational resources distributed on a network while guaranteeing real-time operation, is proposed and applied to realize highly advanced control. It facilitates the total optimization of a plant control and achieves the high efficiency that is not acquired by individual plant optimization. To realize this concept, migration of a control task customized to be executed on one particular microcontroller to another microcontroller is necessary while strictly observing the required response time. Two techniques to meet this requirement are proposed: "task migration" for a control system and "real-time guaranteed scheduling of task migration and execution". The effectiveness of the controller grid is assessed by applying it in experiments with electronic-throttle-body (ETB) advanced control.

INTRODUCTION

As the age of ubiquitous computing approaches, microcontrollers are being embedded in all kinds of information appliances and connected with each other via networks (as shown in Fig. 1). As an example, recent automotive control systems contain over 100 microcontrollers connected by an automobile LAN such as a controller area network (CAN) [1], and it is expected that this number will keep increasing.

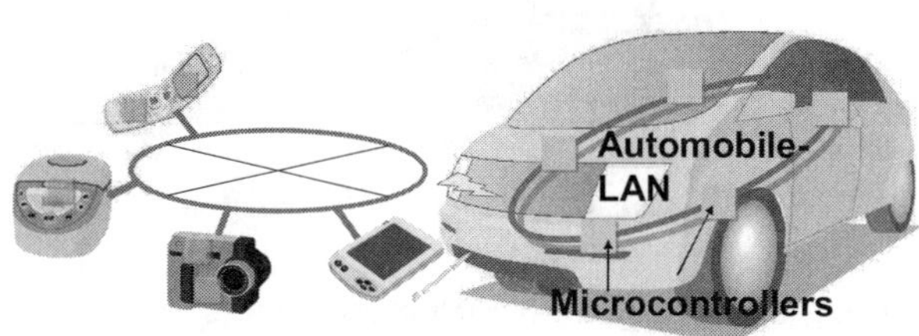

Fig. 1: Ubiquitous computing age

With this background in mind, the authors propose the concept of a "controller grid", which enables a microcontroller in an automotive control system to borrow the required computing power from other microcontrollers connected to the network, guaranteeing the "real-timeness" of control operations. By applying the controller grid, advanced control applications (which cause a single microcontroller to become overloaded) can be executed. Additionally, software developers will be able to write programs without having to consider which microcontroller each functional job runs, since the controller grid makes lots of distributed microcontrollers into one "virtual real-time computer".

FUNDAMENTALS OF A CONTROLLER GRID

MOTIVATION

Automotive control systems are getting more sophisticated year by year in order to satisfy passenger safety, comfort, and environmental needs. This trend has caused a rapid increase in the demand for performance (as shown graphically in Fig. 2). Consequently, it is projected that the performance demand will overtake actual microcontroller performance in the near future.

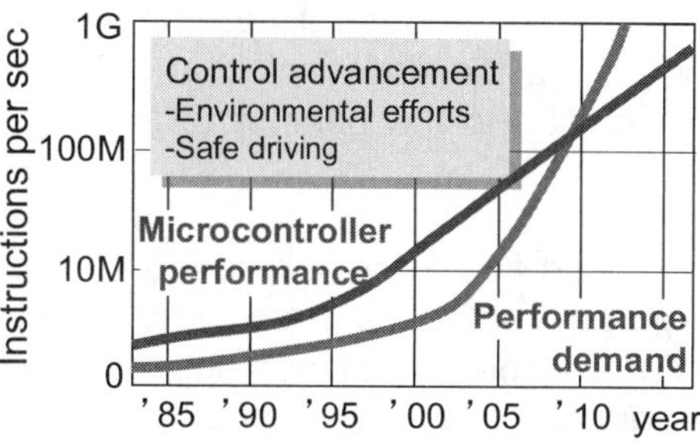

Fig. 2: Growth of performance demand in automotive applications

However, it is not necessary to take a pessimistic view of such a situation, because much computing power in a typical automotive control system is not fully exploited. In general, an individual microcontroller is designed to execute only a specific control program, with its processing performance corresponding to the peak workload. In this case, the microcontroller is not used for other programs when the plant (i.e., control target) is not operating or complex control is not needed. As a result, the operation efficiency of the microcontroller as a whole is not very high.

Though microcontrollers in an automobile control system have recently been designed to share data and coordinated operation through an automotive LAN, the approach of sharing computing resources has not been researched much. Accordingly, our controller grid aims to achieve performance far exceeding that of a single microcontroller by making optimum use of the resources available within the whole system.

COMPARISON WITH OTHER APPROACHES

In the following, other methodologies are compared with a controller grid from the viewpoint of the optimal construction of an automobile control system. The comparison is summarized in Table 1. Generally, system optimization of individual plants has taken the lead lately.

Table 1: System architecture options

APPROACH	Individual optimization		**Controller grid**
	Centralized	Distributed	
ADVANTAGES	Conventional extension	Simple wiring	Simple system
DRAWBACKS	Complex wiring	Inefficient CPU use	Consider whole system

The advantage of doing this is that a centralized control system (one kind of system optimization) is an extension of conventional technology and a certain amount of cooperative control is possible. On the other hand, the drawback is that the wiring of such a system is complicated.

As for a distributed control system (the other kind of system optimization), although it has the advantage of simple wiring, it has the drawback that CPU utilization becomes inefficient and the number of microcontrollers will increase.

In contrast to these two approaches, the controller grid can simplify an entire system and attain high performance at low cost by autonomous decentralization. On the other hand, it is a new technology and presents the difficulty of taking the entire system into consideration.

TECHNICAL ISSUES

In a general automobile control system, a microcontroller is assigned to each subcomponent of an automobile, such as the engine and brakes, and connected to other microcontrollers by a network. The controller grid dynamically reallocates a task, which is an individual program designed by categorizing its function purpose and timing, so that the task "migrates" from a heavily loaded microcontroller to lightly loaded microcontrollers through the network (as shown in Fig. 3).

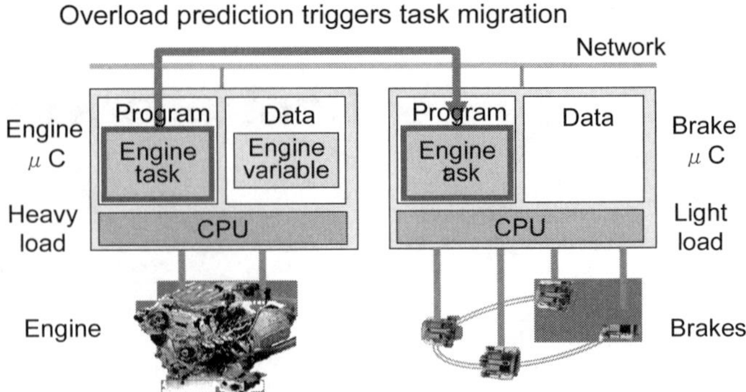

Fig. 3: Load balancing by a controller grid

In the following section, the features and restrictions of the controller grid are clarified by comparing them with those of grid computing used in business, science, and technology fields (which are called "information system grids" here).

Locality of control task processing

The tasks of the control system include a series of processing operations like sensor input, execution, and actuator outputs. Therefore, as shown in Fig. 4, it is difficult for the engine control task to be simply moved and executed on another microcontroller, such as the brake microcontroller, because it has a specific operation like I/O processing, in which it refers to internal valuables. This condition is called "locality of control task processing". To realize "load balancing" by the controller grid, it is necessary to side-step this issue of locality processing and construct a mechanism of control task migration instead.

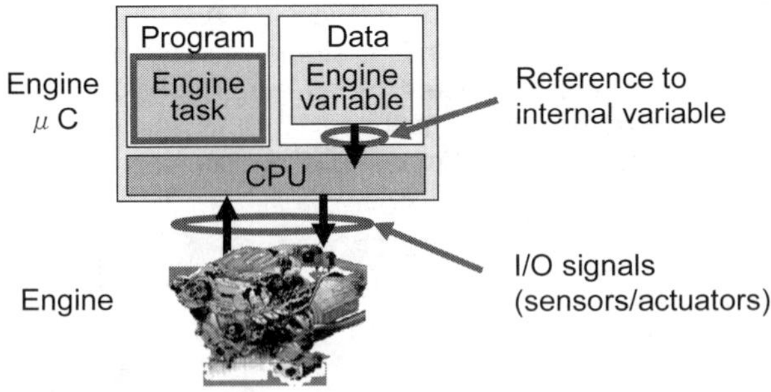

Fig. 4: Example of locality of control task processing

Real-time operation

Real-time operation means finishing a task operation within its time constraint. To control a plant correctly, the control task must output the calculation result in the required time. If this "real-timeness" is not satisfied, the plant goes out of control. In the case of a passenger car, as shown in Fig. 5, this outcome could cause extensive damage involving human lives.

Guaranteeing real-time operation

Lack of real-time response causes out-of-control engine

Network

Engine μC | Program | Data | Engine variable | Heavy load | CPU

Program | Engine task | Data | Brake μC | CPU | Light load

Engine may get broken | (No actuation) | Brakes

Fig. 5: Example of potential damage without guaranteeing real-time operation

The research topics regarding the controller grid in response to the above-mentioned requirements are as follows:

- Control-task migration
- Guarantee of real-time processing

The approaches to these topics are proposed in the next section.

REALIZATION TECHNIQUES

CONTROL-TASK MIGRATION

First, the problem of conventional technology related to the issue of "locality of control task processing" should be mentioned. Technology that enables I/O data and internal data of other microcontrollers to be accessed by way of a network is often applied in an information-system grid. To execute the migrated task, the receiver-side microcontroller thus accesses the sender-side microcontroller over the network for every application that needs to refer to I/O and variables.

Although this approach has the advantages that program modification is unnecessary and that software reusability is high, it requires several tens of milliseconds to migrate a task (assuming a conventional transfer rate on a control network). It therefore cannot satisfy the demand for millisecond-order response of control systems.

As an alternative approach, we propose "I/O divide migration (IDM)", which realizes control-task migration with sufficiently fast response for control systems. IDM has two key features: task pre-division and data batch transmission. As shown in Fig. 6, a control task is split into an I/O task and a calculation task, and only the calculation task is stored at a destination microcontroller in advance. The required data for calculation (such as sensor data and internal valuables) are all packed up and sent by the sender task of the source microcontroller. Similarly, the calculation results and updated internal data are packed up and sent by the sender task of the destination microcontroller. This process reduces the total number of transmissions and realizes task migration with fast response.

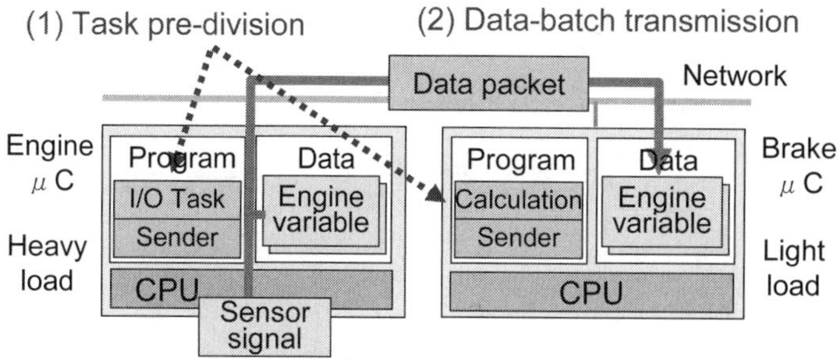

Fig. 6: Overview of IDM (I/O divide migration)

However, a lot of time is required to make this task division/data batch transmission program. We have thus developed an "auto-configurator", which automatically performs the division of a control task and generates the data batch transmission programs. As a result, it enables us to build the execution environment for IDM with less time and effort.

The flow of the IDM processing is described in detail here. First, Microcontroller 1 receives an input signal from a sensor; second, Microcontroller 1 sends the data required to be executed to Microcontroller 2; third, Microcontroller 2 performs the calculation on its CPU; fourth, Microcontroller 2 sends the calculation result to Microcontroller 1; and finally, Microcontroller 1 outputs the control signal to the actuator.

GUARANTEED REAL-TIME RESPONSE

To achieve task migration and execution guaranteeing the required response time, it is necessary to judge in advance whether a task can be finished within the deadline and whether to plan to migrate the schedule including the task. A conventional task scheduler only has a function to manage the sequence of tasks to be executed according to the priority level (which is determined before they are executed). On the other hand, the task scheduler required in the controller grid needs to add functions for checking whether the task completion is within the deadline before starting to execute the tasks and for "migrating" a task when a deadline is expected to be missed, as shown in Fig. 7.

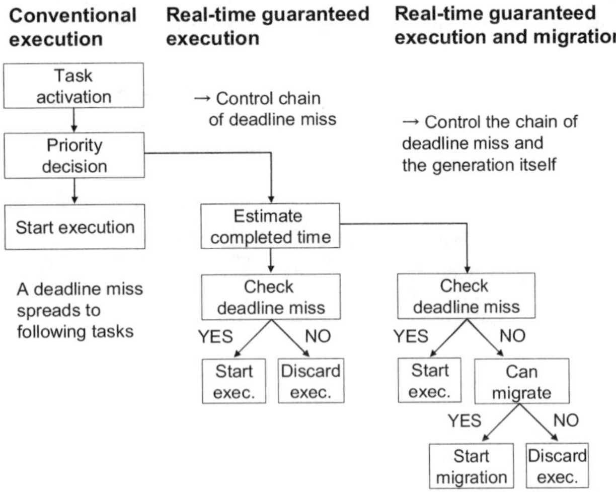

Fig. 7: Functions required by grid scheduler and its effects

There are methods for determining the execution order for a single microcontroller, such as EDF (earliest deadline first) [2], which gives high priority to an early task before the deadline. However, when such scheduling methods are applied for a grid scheduler, a problem arises: a deadline miss results from the delay in data arrival, as shown in Fig. 8. A delay time occurs until all the data of the IDM's batch transmission arrives, which cannot be disregarded. Therefore, even if the execution of the migrated task has already started, it is forced to stop and wait until the reference data arrives before it can finish, and the flowing tasks also miss the deadline.

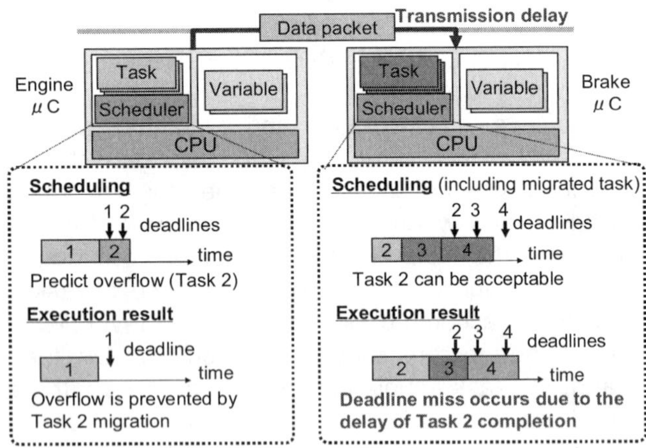

Fig. 8: Problem with EDF: Deadline miss caused by data transmission delay

To avoid this issue, we propose "migration predictive EDF" (MP-EDF)—which creates a forecasting schedule that considers the migrated tasks waiting for data arrival — and apply it to the grid scheduler. MP-EDF estimates in advance the time when execution becomes possible from the information on the transmission data size and transmittal overhead and gives a constraint that does not assign the CPU before that time. This prevents deadline misses from being generated by the transmission delay, as shown in Fig. 9.

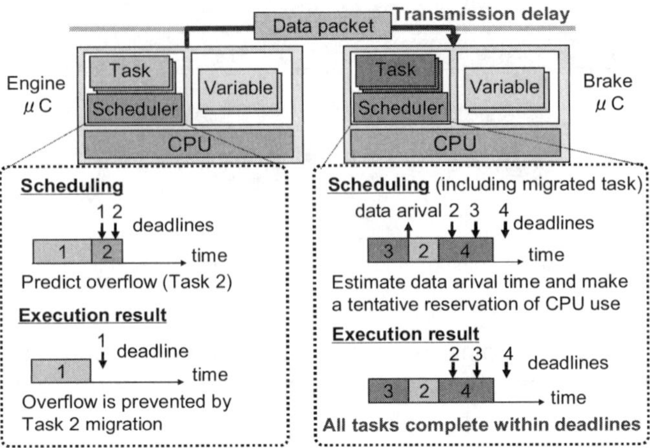

Fig. 9: Example of deadline-miss prevention by MP-EDF

The task processing flow performed by the grid scheduler is shown in Fig. 10. Whenever a task activation or a migration request is received, the grid scheduler performs forecasting scheduling via the MP-EDF, and it judges from the execution time whether each task will finish within the deadline. As for the migrated task, the pros and cons of acceptance are relayed to the source microcontroller. When a deadline miss is detected beforehand, the task to migrate is selected and an inquiry of migration is sent.

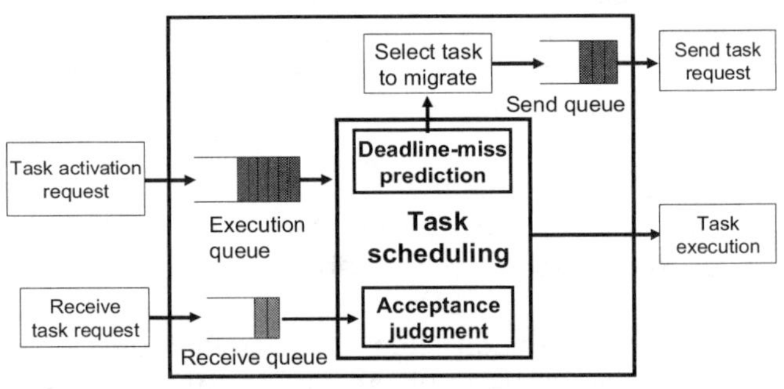

Fig. 10: Task processing flow of grid scheduler

EVALUATION BY ETB CONTROL

This section evaluates the effectiveness of the controller grid by applying it to the electronic throttle body (ETB) control system.

The ETB is an actuator that adjusts the amount of air flow into the engine. Since the control result influences fuel consumption directly, it is one of the parts expected to be enhanced by the control. We thus chose "model reference adaptive control" (MRACS), which precisely controls the ETB while following the deterioration of its mechanical properties over the years. Since its processing load is heavy, MRACS cannot be executed with a single microcontroller. It is therefore suitable for applications with the controller grid.

The microcontroller that controls the throttle can "migrate" a task to another microcontroller connected through the network. The response time of a task is 3 ms.

SIMULATION FLAMEWORK

To evaluate this controller grid system, we built a simulation environment for a microcontroller model described by SystemC (cycle accurate) and for an ETB model operating on the control system development tool "Matlab/Simulink". Figure 11 shows an overview of the evaluation environment.

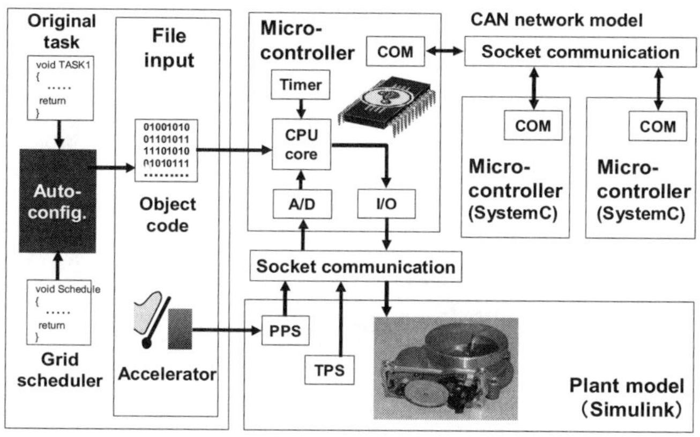

Fig. 11: Simulation environment for microcontroller and mechanical system

EXPERIMENTAL RESULTS

The results of valve control by ETB for repeatedly opening and shutting a throttle valve in the case with a single microcontroller and the controller grid are shown in Figs. 12 and 13, respectively. The CPU load exceeds 100% when MRACS is executed on a single microcontroller, and it can be seen that the control becomes unstable (Fig. 12). On the other hand, MRACS applying a controller grid realizes stable throttle control (Fig. 13) by migrating a task to other microcontrollers.

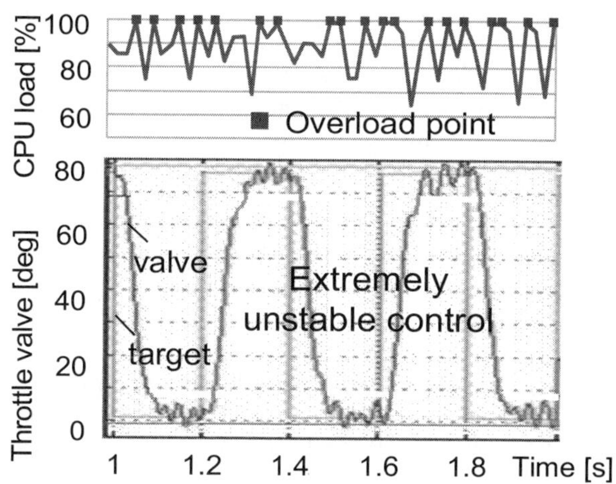

Fig. 12: Results of MRACS simulation on a single microcontroller

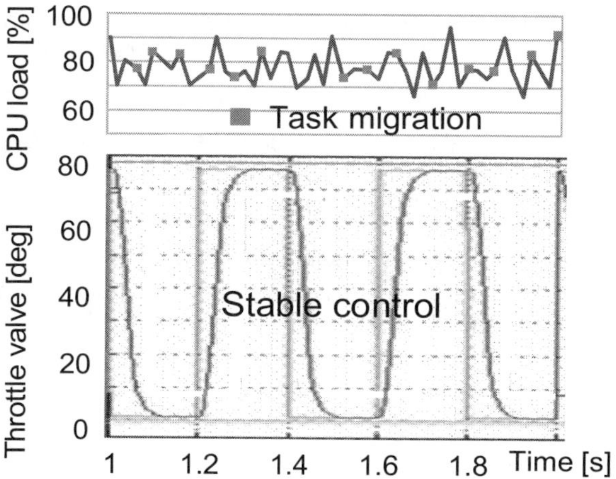

Fig. 13: Results of MRACS applying controller grid

These results confirm that a control task can be migrated between distributed microcontrollers and that the migration and execution of the control task can be performed strictly within the required 3 ms response time.

In automobile system software containing real-time OS, device drivers, etc., the workload must be reduced to 20% of the total workload or less. According to this simulation, the total workload of the system software including MP-EDF is 14%; thus, it is considered that the software can be applied to the automobile domain.

SUMMARY

A "controller grid" is proposed, which dynamically distributes the workload by migrating a control task while guaranteeing real-time operation. Moreover, requirements of the controller grid are clarified and satisfied by two techniques: I/O divide migration (IDM), which enables fast migration of a control task, and migration predictive EDF (MP-EDF), which enables task scheduling of both migration and execution while guaranteeing task completion within the deadline. Furthermore, it is demonstrated that an advanced control application which cannot be executed on a single microcontroller because of overloading can be executed by applying these two techniques.

REFERENCES

1. International Standards Organization: ISO11898. Road Vehicles – Interchange of digital information – Controller area network for high-speed communication, 1993.
2. CL. Liu and J. Lauland, "Scheduling Algorithms for Multiprogramming in a Hard Real-time Environment" ,Journal of the ACM, 20(1):46-61,1973

CONTACT

Akihiko Hyodo is Researcher of Hitachi Ltd., Central Research Laboratory. He can be reached at akihiko.hyodo.ay@hitachi.com

Fumio Arakawa is Senior Researcher of Hitachi Ltd., Central Research Laboratory. He can be reached at fumio.arakawa.vz@hitachi.com

Naoki Kato is Senior Researcher of Hitachi Ltd., Central Research Laboratory. He can be reached at naoki.kato.bh@hitachi.com

2006-01-0840

Controller Integrity in Automotive Failsafe System Architectures

Padma Sundaram and Joseph G. D'Ambrosio
Delphi Corporation

ABSTRACT

Embedded controllers and digital signal processors are increasingly being used in automotive safety critical control systems. Controller integrity is a significant concern in these systems. Over the past decade, several techniques have been published about controller safety and integrity verification. These techniques include: single processor with watchdog, dual processors, dual core processor, and asymmetric processor (intelligent watchdog). Each of these techniques have benefits, however, many new non-distributed safety-critical systems are applying the asymmetric processor technique to help verify controller integrity.

This paper discusses an overview of five controller integrity techniques, and then provides a detailed discussion of an asymmetric processor approach. This paper presents two different options within the asymmetric processor approach.

INTRODUCTION

Over the last decade there has been rapid growth of automotive safety-critical systems controlled by embedded software. Embedded controllers are used to achieve enhancements in vehicle comfort, feel, fuel efficiency, and safety. For those systems that are safety critical, software is handling key decision making related to controlling essential vehicle functions such as steering and braking independent of the driver. Although many of these systems help provide significant improvements in vehicle safety, potential unexpected interactions among the software, the hardware, and the environment could lead to potentially hazardous situations.

Software is a logical construct, and in isolation may not cause harm [1]. However, the components or systems that are controlled by software logic may have the potential to cause harm if not controlled correctly. Since software resides in a controller, any potential controller failure could affect the execution of the software, possibly leading to undesired system behavior. Thus, helping confirm controller integrity also helps confirm software and system safety.

By identifying potential controller hardware failure modes, it is possible to understand their effects on software execution and develop diagnostic techniques to detect and handle their occurrences. Some of the common controller hardware failures include memory cell failures in either the code space or variable space, Central Processing Unit (CPU) failures (Arithmetic Logic Unit (ALU), registers, op-codes) or peripheral failures (Analog to Digital Converter (ADC), Input Output (IO) ports etc). Memory cell failures can cause conditions where the software jumps to the end of a routine abruptly without completely executing the desired functionality. Interrupt failure modes like return of incorrect priority and failure to return, thereby blocking lower priority interrupts, can also be caused by memory corruption. CPU failures like ALU errors can cause incorrect calculations in the software potentially leading to incorrect output states. Peripheral failures like ADC and IO port failures can impact incoming or outgoing signals of the controller thus potentially impacting system behavior.

Generally, a controller integrity strategy selected for a specific system is such that it satisfies system safety requirements and does not compromise system performance requirements. In this paper, we review existing controller integrity techniques that have been applied in the automotive industry. Each of these techniques has benefits; however, many new non-distributed safety-critical systems are applying the asymmetric processor technique to help verify controller integrity. The remaining portion of the paper expands on the asymmetric processor approach. The different options that are possible within the asymmetric processor approach are briefly discussed. By combining these external controller diagnostics performed by a secondary controller, with complimenting primary controller's self-diagnostics, high confidence in controller integrity can be achieved.

OVERVIEW OF AUTOMOTIVE FAILSAFE CONTROLLER STRATEGIES

Over the past two decades, several strategies have been developed to satisfy the failsafe requirements of automotive embedded systems. For safety critical systems, the controller should provide deterministic behavior under conditions of failure. Typical criteria for selecting a specific strategy include:

Primary Criteria

1. Must satisfy system safety requirements. Failure management provided within the system safe response times. Meaning system transitioned to a safe state within the required safe fault response time.

Secondary criteria

1. Level of independent checking provided
2. Performance
3. Technology availability
4. Development effort

Generally system design is influenced by system safety requirements. Safety requirements provide guidance in the selection of the safety approach for the controller. Safety requirements prescribe the failure management and fault response needs under failure conditions of the system. In software intensive systems, failure management is typically handled by the controller. Failure management process requires that critical faults are detected and handled within the system's *safe fault response* time. This time is defined as the time that is available for the system to detect a critical fault and transition to a safe state before the fault could lead to a potentially undesirable system condition. This prescription of safe fault response times can guide the choice of an appropriate processor that can handle the safe fault response time requirements without compromising system performance needs.

In the following paragraphs the different approaches for fail-safe controller architectures are discussed, highlighting the benefits of each approach.

SINGLE-CONTROLLER STRATEGY

A single-controller failsafe strategy, as shown in Figure 1, consists of a single controller executing the target application software and self-checking diagnostics, along with a simple watchdog circuit. The watchdog provides a limited-level of independent checking of the primary processor. A watchdog typically requires the controller to periodically reset or toggle the watchdog. If such a reset is not performed within some time interval, the controller will reset itself. Thus, the watchdog detects conditions where the execution of software on the controller has hung up (e.g., endless loop) or where specified program flow has been interrupted (unwanted branch). A simple watchdog cannot detect other types of potential failures, such as incorrect output calculations.

To help verify high integrity operation for this failsafe controller strategy, the controller may implement internal hardware protection techniques (e.g., error detection circuits or error detection and correction circuits), or a significant portion of the processors throughput could be dedicated to self-checking diagnostics. For this approach, controller throughput and memory size must be adequate to handle both the control application and the self-checking diagnostics. By carefully combining hardware and software protection mechanisms, it may be possible to achieve high confidence in controller integrity using this controller strategy.

In summary, this controller strategy may be best for those applications where significant processor resources (throughput and memory) can be dedicated to self-checking diagnostics.

Figure 1: Single-controller strategy

SYMMETRIC-CONTROLLER STRATEGY

In this controller strategy, two symmetrical (identical) controllers are used for crosschecking controller operations (see Figure 2). Each controller executes the same application based on the same inputs. At specific time points, the controllers exchange key calculations and compare the results. If either controller detects a mis-compare, the system is assumed to have a fault. By checking for time-outs in communications, all the faults detected by a simple watchdog are guaranteed to be detected by this approach as well.

This strategy provides good coverage of hardware faults with minimal effort devoted to developing self-checking diagnostics. Any random hardware failure that influences key calculations can be detected (other than those failures that lead to common cause failures in both controllers). As a consequence, extensive self-checking diagnostics to detect random controller failures are not explicitly required. Software errors can also be detected if a diverse programming approach is followed, however, this typically requires significant investment in software development and verification activities.

One significant technical issue in implementing this controller strategy is maintaining synchronization between the two processors. Since each processor has its own clock, the two processors may not run at the exact same clock frequency, and care must be given to help confirm that the calculations being compared were performed at the same time. If comparisons are made between calculations based on different inputs (due to synchronization issues), two fully functional processors could produce calculations that mis-compare. If a design team is willing to invest in the additional costs associated with implementing a time-triggered architecture, the global clock synchronization services these architectures provide can help solve this problem.

In summary, the symmetric controller strategy provides a high-level of independent checking of the hardware. Depending on the level of synchronization, the fault detection time achievable by independent hardware checks may be fast. Extensive self-checking diagnostics are likely not required, reducing the demand on software development, processor throughput and memory requirements. The major limitations of the approach include the need to synchronize processors and the cost, size, power, etc. of adding a second processor.

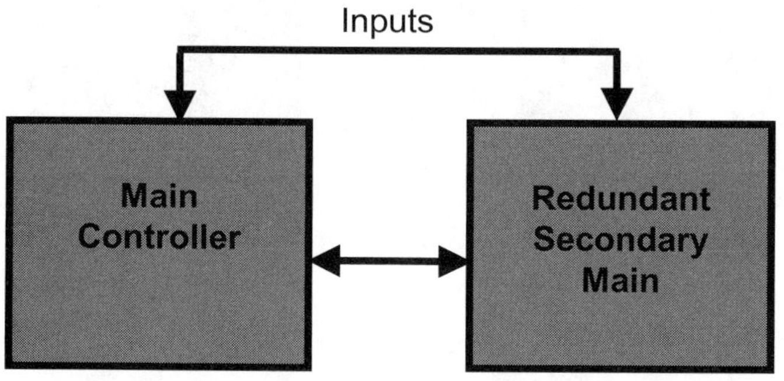

Figure 2: Symmetric controller strategy

DUAL-CORE CONTROLLER STRATEGY

In this controller strategy, the primary processor has a duplicate CPU (see Figure 3). The two CPUs receive the same data and control inputs, and the outputs of the CPUs are compared to detect discrepancies. This approach provides high coverage of random hardware failures that can occur in the central processing unit. Additional self-checking diagnostics (e.g., memory checks) along with a simple watchdog can be implemented to provide a high-integrity controller [2].

Typically, an overall bootstrapping strategy is followed to check the processor's resources for correct operation. Given that all CPU failures can be detected, the CPU is assumed to be reliable, and additional self-checking diagnostics rely on the correct operation of the CPU, and begin to verify correct operation of other controller resources. As each additional resource is tested for correct functionality, it then too can be trusted by the remaining diagnostics to be reliable.

This controller strategy can provide a higher level of independent checking than is provided by a single controller strategy, without the potential size, cost, etc. penalties associated with a symmetric processor strategy. CPU related failures can be detected immediately, but detection time of all types of controller failures in general depends on the execution time of the self-checking diagnostics that must be implemented. Given that non-CPU self-checking diagnostics are still required, software development effort, processor throughput and memory requirements are potentially less than that required by a single controller approach, but more than that required by a symmetric controller approach. One significant issue with a dual-core strategy is the availability of the technology: there are a limited number of processors that implement a dual core strategy, and as a consequence this strategy may not be an option depending on commercial issues.

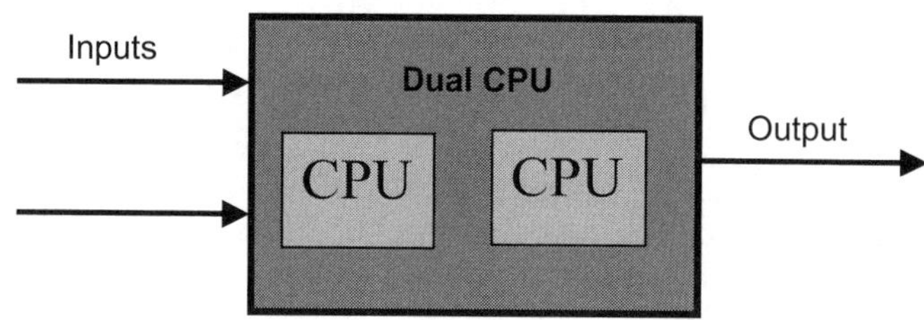

Figure 3: Dual CPU strategy

ASYMMETRIC-CONTROLLER STRATEGY

In this controller strategy, a simple, low cost secondary processor (or ASIC) is used as an intelligent watchdog to check the primary processor (see Figure 4). The strategy has the potential to provide a high level of independent checking at a lower cost compared to the symmetric processor strategy. Often, the secondary processor is an off-the-shelf purchased controller instead of an ASIC, as custom ASICs typically require more design time and may have higher cost depending on the volume produced.

To help detect hardware failures, the secondary processor periodically requests diagnostic checks by the primary processor to verify the integrity of the primary processor. This communication can occur either via a discrete line, or a serial communication line like for example, a Serial Peripheral Interface (SPI). Depending upon the design of the diagnostics architecture, it is possible to achieve good diagnostic coverage of the different sections of the processor (e.g., CPU, Memory, and Peripherals). Since an external processor is verifying the primary processor, confidence in the controller's integrity can be higher than that provided by self-checking diagnostics.

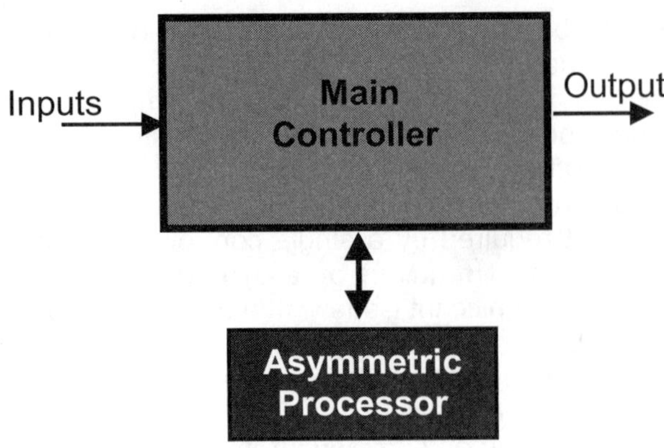

Figure 4: Asymmetric processor strategy

DISTRIBUTED-CONTROLLER STRATEGY

In this controller strategy, the primary controller is checked by another networked controller (see Figure 5). This approach supports a wide range of diagnostic options, including:

1. Independent redundant algorithm execution with voting.

2. Independent primary processor state of health checks.

The first option is very similar to the symmetric-controller strategy. Sensor input signals for the primary processor along with algorithm results are sent to a second controller on the network. The second controller executes the same algorithm as the primary controller, and compares its results against those of the primary controller. If there is a discrepancy, the second controller disables the primary controller (for failsafe applications).

The second option is very similar to the asymmetric-controller strategy. The primary controller receives a seed (i.e., input) from a second controller on the network. The primary controller performs a sequence of calculations, and returns the result to the second controller. The second controller compares the result with a pre-computed value, and if there is a discrepancy, the second controller disables the primary controller.

Both options and other variations depend on the ability of the second controller to disable the primary controller. If the primary controller is faulted, it may not be possible to rely on sending a shutdown command from the second controller to the primary over the network, because there is no guarantee that the faulted primary controller will be able to process the shutdown command. As a consequence, an independent means of shutting down the primary controller is needed.

Two possible options for shutting down the primary controller include: dedicated shutdown line, and shutdown by local network controller. For the first option, a dedicated wire is run from the second controller to the primary controller and hard wired to a local independent disable circuit. For the second option, the primary's local network communication controller has the ability to independently recognize the shutdown command and has the ability to activate a local disable circuit if such a command is received.

The selection of the specific approach for a distributed-controller strategy depends on a number of factors, including: available network bandwidth, fault response times, available controller throughput, synchronization issues, and controller sourcing decisions (i.e., single supplier vs. multiple suppliers).

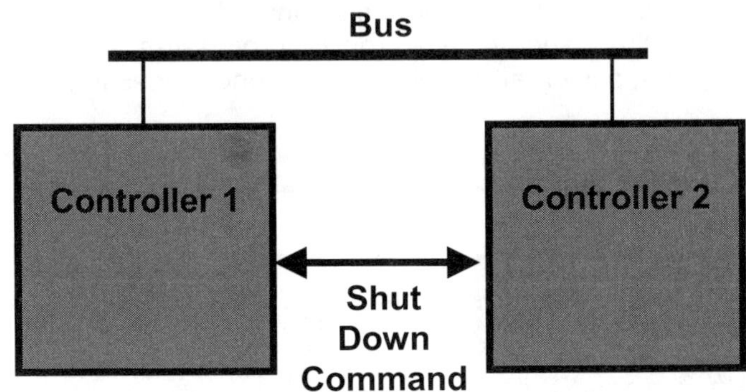

Figure 5: Distributed-controller strategy

Recently, a trend for implementing the asymmetric-controller strategy has begun to emerge for non-distributed controlled steering and braking applications. Early applications of the symmetric-controller strategy by automotive suppliers were abandoned, due in part to the difficulties in achieving tight processor synchronization and component cost. The dual-core strategy has seen significant application in steering and braking products, but this approach has not been possible for newer systems requiring more powerful processors, as dual core technology has not been available for these processor families. The single-controller strategy has been applied to occupant protection systems, as these systems have the ability to dedicate a significant amount of controller throughput to diagnostic checking, but this approach has not seen much application on controlled steering and braking products. As a consequence of the above, many new controlled steering and braking systems implement an asymmetric strategy.

As new technologies such as time-triggered networks and AUTOSAR [3] become practical for production applications, the distributed-controller strategy may become dominant. However, as previously discussed, much of the asymmetric strategy can be implemented within the context of the distributed strategy, and thus the asymmetric approach has significant value now and possibly in the future as well.

In this paper, asymmetric strategy appropriate for automotive domain applications is discussed. The paper highlights the different options within the asymmetric controller approach that can be implemented to achieve high ECU coverage, thus providing increased confidence in the primary processor's integrity.

ASYMMETRIC CONTROLLER APPROACH

Before the asymmetric approach is discussed, fundamentals of controller integrity checks are discussed. Figure 6, shows a typical high level structure of a processor. At a high level, typical controllers can be viewed as containing three major subsystems:

1. Central Processing Unit (CPU)
2. Peripherals including input/output devices and
3. Memory subsystem

The CPU includes data registers and data manipulators, which primarily include the ALU, the auxiliary registers, and the op-code/decode circuits, etc. Memory subsystem can include the RAM, FLASH, ROM, and EEPROM. Peripherals include the Timers, Event Managers, and Input/Output (I/O) subsystem. I/O subsystem can include peripherals like the Analog to Digital Converter (ADC), Controller Area Network (CAN), the Serial Peripheral Interface (SPI), Serial Communication Interface (SCI) etc [4,5]. Ensuring that the execution and control functions of the controller are healthy is the primary goal of any controller diagnostics approach. Once that is achieved, based on system safety requirements, the I/O and the memory subsystem of the controller may need to be verified either independently or by the primary CPU itself.

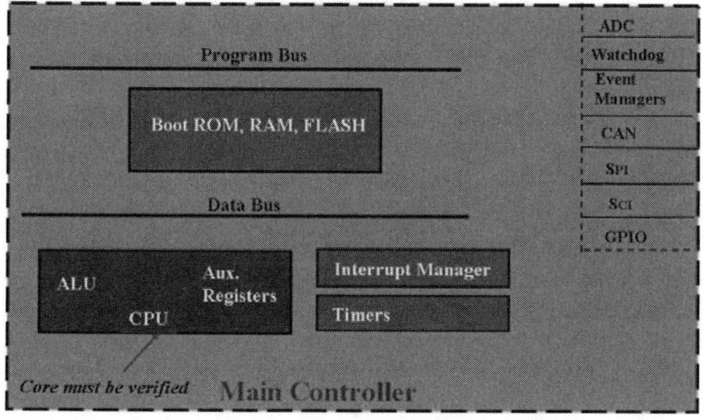

Figure 6: Typical processor components

The fundamental benefit of the asymmetric approach is the independent verification of the primary controller integrity by a secondary processor. The extent of independent verification can vary depending upon system safety requirements. Typically the quality and the quantity of the independent verification checks are chosen to satisfy individual system safety requirements. In this paper two approaches of using the asymmetric processor for controller integrity verification are discussed. First, a basic asymmetric approach which is a bootstrap approach based on independent CPU verification, is discussed. Following that an extended approach for independent verification of different controller components is presented.

BASIC ASYMMETRIC PROCESSOR APPROACH

In a basic asymmetric processor approach, the secondary processor is primarily used to verify the integrity of the primary processor's CPU. Figure 8 shows the general hardware layout of the basic Asymmetric approach.

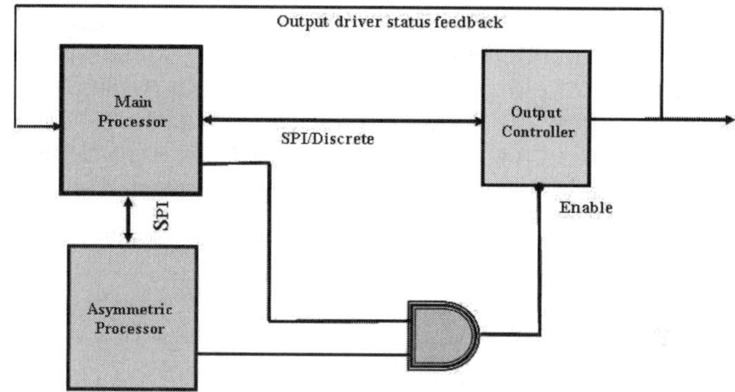

Figure 7: System architecture for a basic asymmetric approach

In this approach, the primary processor represents the processor whose integrity is being verified. ASP represents the Asymmetric processor that cross-checks the primary controller's CPU. The output controller represents any driver that controls the output from the primary. It could be a motor driver, a CAN controller or any power control circuit. The ASP physically resides on the same circuit board as the primary processor and continuously monitors the health of the primary processor's CPU as well as itself through various diagnostics. It communicates to the primary processor via a serial communication interface like for example, the Serial Peripheral Interface (SPI). The ASP controls one input of the enable gate of the output controller. The primary processor controls the other input of the enable gate. Either the primary processor or the ASP can disable the output controller on detection that the other processor is not responding or functioning correctly and also in response to detection of any local faults within the processor. The output controller will be enabled only when both the primary processor and the ASP send an enable signal to the output controller. Both the processors establish communication during controller initialization following an exchange of key diagnostic data. Further on successful startup, the ASP continues to monitor the primary processor's CPU health by exercising the different functions of the CPU during system runtime. In this approach the ASP provides increased confidence in the primary processor's CPU. The primary processor utilizes the CPU to self-check other parts of the controller including the memory and peripherals.

EXTENDED ASYMMETRIC APPROACH

The following sections discuss briefly some possible independent controller checks that can be performed by the asymmetric processor. Within an extended approach, the asymmetric controller can be used to independently check additional primary processor resources beyond the CPU. The specific amount of additional checking depends on a number of factors including: system safety requirements, processor capacity and throughput of the both the processors, communication throughput between the processors, and the amount of primary processor throughput available to support interactions between the two processors. The following are some of the checks that can be performed within the extended asymmetric approach.

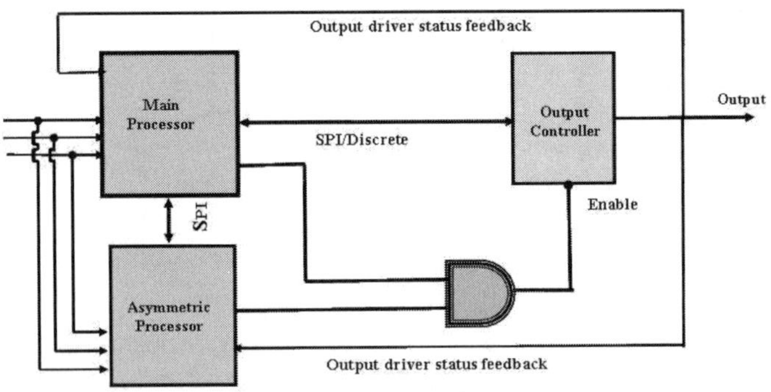

Figure 8: System architecture for an extended asymmetric approach

Integrity verification during system start up

During system initialization, correct operation of both the primary controller and the ASP can be confirmed using both processors to query the other. The queries can include memory integrity checks, CPU checks and overall system fail safe operability check. For example one way to achieve this is as follows: The primary processor and the ASP can exchange their respective memory checksum results during power-up handshake for cross verification against a pre-stored value in their memory. This can provide independent check on the memory integrity of the primary processor and the ASP. The ASP sends back the status of the verification checks to the primary processor. In addition to this, the primary processor can be used to confirm that the ASP is capable of monitoring the primary processor during normal operation mode and vice versa. This approach exercises the failsafe operation of the entire system. The primary processor and the ASP will transition out of the initialization state after the successful completion of tasks pertaining to that state. Lack of response by either processor within a specific time during message exchanges, can result in either communication driver to flag a fault condition (time out). This check will exercise the execution unit as well as the "Timer" functions within the processors [6].

Analog to Digital Converter (ADC) integrity verification

Sampling the same analog signals in both processors and comparing the sampled values can confirm the integrity of the ADC. The more ADC channels checked, the higher the confidence in ADC peripheral. This check requires achieving brief synchronization to sample the ADC signals at the same time. The sampled signal can be compared for any significant discrepancy which can signal problems with the ADC module within either of the processors.

CPU verification using program execution sequence and completion check

Software program flow monitoring can be embedded with a set of ALU calculations at specific points throughout the primary application program. This can confirm that the application executed in the proper sequence to completion. At the same time, program monitoring can also be used to exercise several components within the controller including the ALU, the addressing modes functions of the CPU, the event manager, and the clock function. By threading the program flow monitor through the sequence flow of the primary software program, including the interrupt service routines it is possible to detect any illegal invocations of interrupts or functions that were not intended to be executed by design.

To implement this approach, the ASP is used to inject several checks into the primary processor periodically and to check the primary processor's response. A fault is flagged if either processor fails to communicate within a specified time period or the ASP detects discrepancy in the primary's response to its query. Based on system safety requirements and throughput availability, the program flow monitoring can be applied at different levels of abstraction of the primary software. Based on the inquiry received from the ASP, the primary software can recognize the specific task to be checked, and can activate the monitoring of that task. As part of the verification of CPU, the primary processor can also be used to verify the integrity of the ASP. This can be achieved by forcing the ASP to exercise the CPU functions as it performs verification of the primary processor's responses to the queries. An example implementation of the program flow-monitoring algorithm is shown in Figure 9 below.

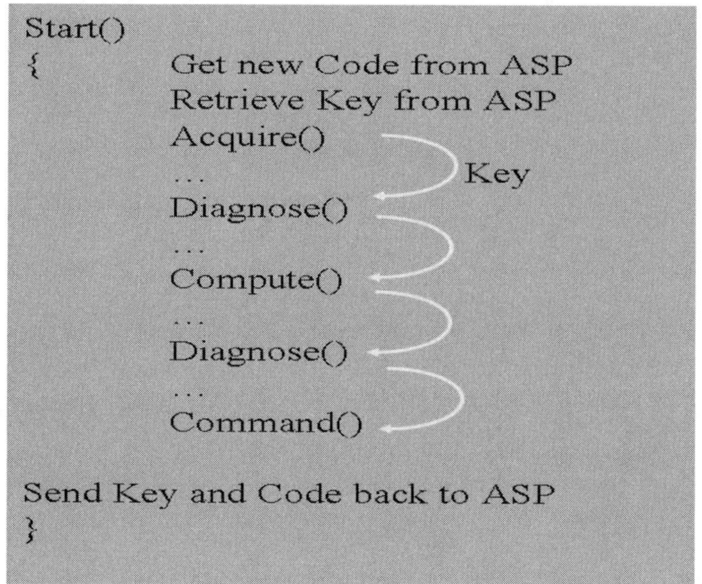

Figure 9: Example of program execution monitoring

Peripheral configuration integrity verification

Typically, the primary processor can have several peripherals like an Event manager (EVM), PIE Interrupt Manager, ADC, General Purpose Input-Output (GPIO), CAN, SPI, SCI, WATCHDOG etc. A peripheral's mode of operation is based on the configuration of the associated control register. The ASP can be used to verify that the assigned peripheral configurations are not corrupted by comparing it against stored values in its memory.

Application output sanity verification

The objective of this diagnostic is to perform a high-level sanity check of the application output of the primary processor. This type of diagnostic has the potential to detect a wide-range of processor failure modes, because producing a correct output typically depends on the proper functioning of the CPU, the peripherals, and the memory. In essence both the control unit and execution unit of the processor must be healthy to produce consistent healthy output. A simplified version of the overall application function can be executed periodically in the asymmetric processor, with similar inputs as that provided to the application in the primary processor. The outputs of both the simplified application and the full application can be compared for sanity. The ability to implement this type of safety function depends on the availability of simplified logic of the primary application, the capacity and throughput of the ASP and the primary processor.

In any controller safety approach, where a secondary processor is used to monitor the primary processor's health, communication integrity between the two processors has to be verified. Industry best practice techniques can be applied in ensuring the validity of the communication between the processors.

Implementing extensive monitoring of the primary processor using a secondary processor can be challenging in terms of development effort, throughput availability for diagnostics within both the processors and overall system performance requirements. The primary criterion is to choose techniques that can achieve balance of both functional safety requirements, and system performance requirements [7].

SUMMARY AND CONCLUSIONS

This paper summarized briefly five different safety strategies for failsafe controller architectures. Primarily, choice of a safety strategy for controllers is guided by individual system safety requirements. The paper discussed a basic and an extended option within the asymmetric controller safety approach. The various controller safety functions discussed are designed to confirm the health of the different components of the processor, including the CPU, memory, peripherals etc.

In automotive embedded control systems, the available throughput in the controller is to be shared by both the system application functions and the system safety functions. Achieving balance of both system safety and performance of these systems is critical in the success of the system design. Considering such limitations it is more desirable to have a reduced set of diagnostics that provides maximum coverage of utilized controller functions. By carefully combining independent controller verification diagnostics with complementing self-monitoring diagnostics of a processor, high coverage of controller functions is possible, thus providing increased confidence in the integrity of controller outputs.

REFERENCES

1. Leveson, N.G., Safeware: System Safety and Computers, ISBN 0-201-11972-2, 1995.
2. Terry Frueling, Delphi Secured Microcontroller Architecture, SAE# 2000-01-1052
3. AUTOSAR partnership, (2004). Automotive Software Architecture: An industry wide initiative to manage the complexity of E/E architecture. http://www.autosar.org
4. Sunil Jain, Alfred K.Susskind, Test Strategy for Microprocessors, 078-100X, 20th Design Automation Conference, IEEE 1983.
5. A.J.van de Goor: Testing Semiconductor Devices, Theory and Practice, ISBN 0-471-92586-1
6. IEC 61508-3, Functional Safety Of Electrical/Electronic Programmable Electronic Safety Related Systems – Part 3 Software Requirements First Edition, 1998-12.
7. FAA System Safety Handbook, Dec. 2000.

CONTACT

Padma Sundaram, Senior System Safety Engineer, Delphi Corporation, 12501 E. Grand River, Brighton, MI 48116, Phone: 810-494-2453, Facsimile: 810-494-4689, Email: padma.sundaram@delphi.com

Padma Sundaram works at the Delphi Innovation Center in the area of research and development of advanced vehicle dynamics systems. Her area of expertise is in the design analysis of safety critical systems. Her current research interests include: Systems architecting, advanced simulation and modeling techniques, advanced safety functions for vehicle dynamics, and high integrity controller strategies. Ms.Sundaram has a B.S. in Electrical & Electronics Engineering and M.S. in Computer Science and Engineering. She is currently pursuing a graduate program in Systems Architecture and Engineering at University of Southern California (USC). She is a member of the Society of Automotive Engineers (SAE).

Joseph G. D'Ambrosio, Ph.D., Manager, Systems & Safety Engineering, Delphi Corporation, 12501 E. Grand River, Brighton, MI 48116, Phone: 810-494-5885, Facsimile: 810-494-4689, Email: joseph.g.d.ambrosio@delphi.com

Dr. D'Ambrosio works at the Delphi Innovation Center in the area of development of advanced vehicle dynamic systems. He has worked in the automotive industry for 22 years. He has recently been involved in automotive steer- and brake-by-wire applications. D'Ambrosio received a Ph.D. degree in computer science and engineering from the University of Michigan. He is a member of the SAE and the System Safety Society.

2006-01-0310

A Design Approach using Seamless Development Environments, SILS/RCP, for Real-Time Control Systems

Jooyoung Ma, Jeamyoung Youn and Minsuk Shin
Graduate School, Hanyang University

Myoungho Sunwoo
Hanyang University

ABSTRACT

Computer Aided Control System Design (CACSD) tools are widely used in the development of embedded control systems. Automatic code generation for CACSD models is the subject of increasing interest. In this study, Software-in-the-Loop Simulation (SILS) and Rapid Control Prototyping (RCP) are proposed as a development framework for the design of real-time control systems. SILS is a simulation environment to consider functional behavior as well as temporal behavior of control systems. RCP supports seamless development from design to implementation through automatic code generation. SILS/RCP environments make it possible to design and analysis control systems under conditions similar to real execution during off-line simulation and to realize controllers in the early design phase.

INTRODUCTION

Embedded control systems generally have stringent real-time requirements. The controllers have to satisfy not only control specifications, but also temporal requirements. In other words, they should ensure functional correctness (the correct result is produced) and temporal correctness (the result is produced at the correct time). [1], [2] However, most Computer Aided Control System Design (CACSD) tools do not (or are hard to) support simulation of the temporal behavior of control systems.

Control systems are normally implemented using microcontroller units (MCUs). In many cases, computer based control theories assume equidistant sampling intervals and negligible or constant control delays which are the latency between the sampling of inputs to the controller and the generation of outputs. [3] These assumptions are not realistic and can not be achieved in practice. Therefore, as the undeterministic delays increase, the predictability of control systems decreases. Time delays are induced when a control system is implemented. The delays degrade performance and can even cause instability. The demands for simulation environments to consider temporal behavior have increased.

There were two approaches for the design of CACSD tools. One is a control engineering perspective. The other is a software and computer engineering perspective. From control engineering perspective, tools are designed in order to support functional simulation and mathematical analysis. A few of these tools can automatically generate software to implement specified control algorithms. From a software and computer engineering perspective, a number of tools are developed to perform mathematical analysis of temporal behavior. A few of these tools have been developed to support automatic software assembly that merges the system codes with a real-time kernel or a real-time operating system (RTOS). In the 1990's, an effort to integrate the two different environments began. ControlH and MetaH were introduced by Steve Vestal at Honeywell Technology Center. [4] ControlH was a language designed to support dynamical system modeling and control algorithm specification. [5] MetaH was designed to support specification and analysis of real-time, secure, fault-tolerant, and multi-processor computer system architectures. [6] This toolset offered the analysis of functional and temporal behavior and automatic code generation. However, ControlH and MetaH used two different platforms, so that control specifications and real-time specifications need to be described by each language in different environments. In order to design control systems using these environments, users needed to be familiar with each language and environment.

There have been several attempts to overcome the problem using different platforms for the system analysis including temporal behavior. They are RT/CS Co-design [7], DRTSS [8], STRESS [9], HaRTS [10], AIRES [1], and TRUETIME [3], [11], which make it possible to simulate the control algorithm in consideration of real-time characteristics in the same platform. Other studies have focused on automatic implementation combining control algorithms with a real-time kernel or a RTOS. These include RT-UML [12], AIDA [13], MIRCOS [14], and Giotto [15], which support the real-time control system analysis and implementation. Nevertheless, in the previous studies, the design and the implementation do not work under the identical platform.

In this paper, Software-In-the-Loop Simulation (SILS) and Rapid Control Prototyping (RCP) are proposed as a simulation environment and an implementation environment. SILS and RCP integrate separated environments into seamlessly connected environments under the identical platform. The simulation result of SILS holds temporal behavior, so that the result is affected by the functional behavior of the control logic as well as the temporal behavior related to real-time properties. The control system designed by SILS environment can be immediately transformed into executable binary code using the proposed RCP environment.

The concept and the realization of SILS/RCP environments are described. The feasibility and the effectiveness of SILS/RCP environments are considered with a case study.

SILS/RCP TOOLBOX

THE CONCEPT OF SILS/RCP

The design process of automotive Electronic Control Units (ECUs) requires multidisciplinary approaches which are related to the control engineering and the software engineering. The traditional development process can be represented as a V-shape model. [15]

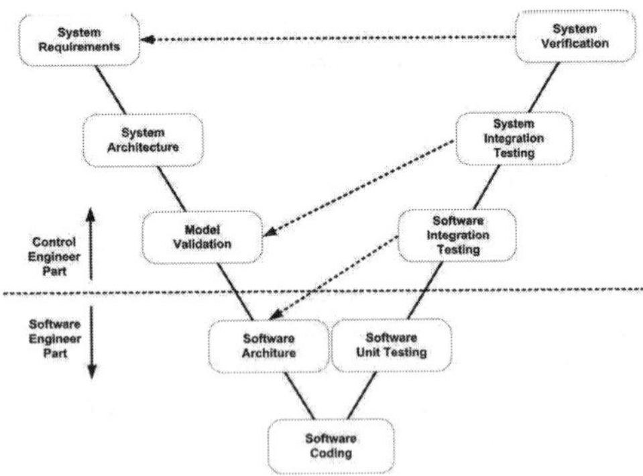

Figure 1. System Development V

In the system V development diagram shown in Figure 1, the whole process is clearly divided into two parts which are control engineering and software engineering. Control engineers are in charge of acquiring system requirements, analyzing system architecture, and building up the control logic. Software engineers play a role in forming the control algorithms into the software that will be embedded in MCUs. However, there are potential problems caused by unrealistic assumptions, differences between continuous and discrete time-domain, unconsidered real-time properties, and so on. As the result of that, the controller performance may not be consistent with the simulation results, so that the design process must be iterative. Additionally, in the waterfall models such as the V-shape model, software engineers can not apply the changes to the realization until control engineers finish modifying the algorithms completely.

In order to reduce the time-to-market and support greater performance-assured controller design, SILS/RCP environments are developed. SILS/RCP environments work under Matlab/Simulink® which is a representative CACSD toolset. SILS/RCP environments have several blocks that consider the temporal behavior of control systems such as the real-time kernel, the task representation, and the network induced effect. The blocks for the real-time kernel describe the scheduler's behaviors. Task concept is used for the scheduling unit. Time delay blocks of tasks are also considered for realistic simulation results. SILS/RCP environments support the simulation and realization of network based control systems for Controller Area Network (CAN) and Local Interconnect Network (LIN) which are most popularly applied protocols in the automotive engineering field.

In SILS, control engineers are able to achieve a simulation that is more similar to the execution on MCUs from the early design phase. RCP makes it easy to implement the control logic so that control engineers can validate the real performance of algorithms on MCUs, even though the design of whole systems may not be finished. The goal of our research is to build a development framework for real-time embedded control systems that is composed of a timing analysis environment (Response-time Analysis Tool: RAT) [17], SILS, RCP, and Hardware-In-the-Loop Simulation (HILS). By using the development framework, a modified development V-process is proposed as shown in Figure 2. [18], [19], [20]

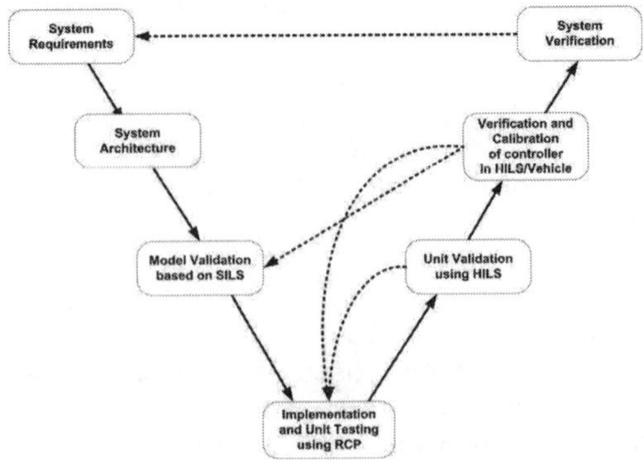

Figure 2. Modified System Development V

In the modified system development V, the design process is simplified and software engineers are not required because the software design and the implementation steps are integrated. Control engineers can develop the control law and verify the performance by themselves. Since the block representations are equivalent to the software realization using RCP, the reuse of the verified algorithm blocks may stand for the reuse of the reliable software. In many cases, the error of software is caused by error-prone hand-coding. The automatic code generation may be the one of the solutions for reliable system implementation.

SILS/RCP environments contribute toward seamless development process from design phases to implementation phases.

THE STRUCTURE OF SILS/RCP

SILS/RCP toolbox is shown in Figure 3 and 4.

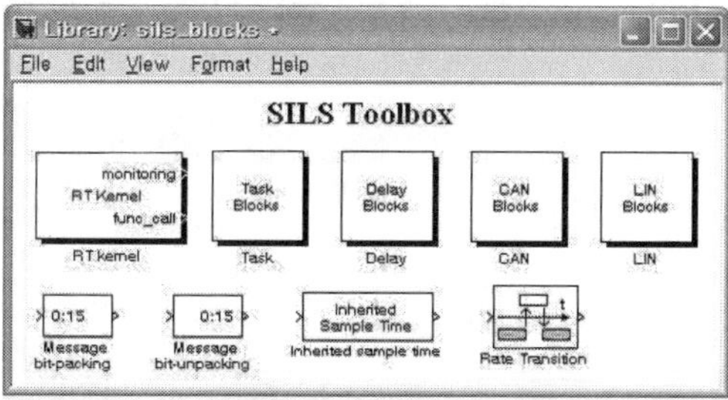

Figure 3. SILS Toolbox

In Figure 3, each subsystem is used for the real-time kernel configuration, the task representation, the system delay, and the in-vehicle network simulation.

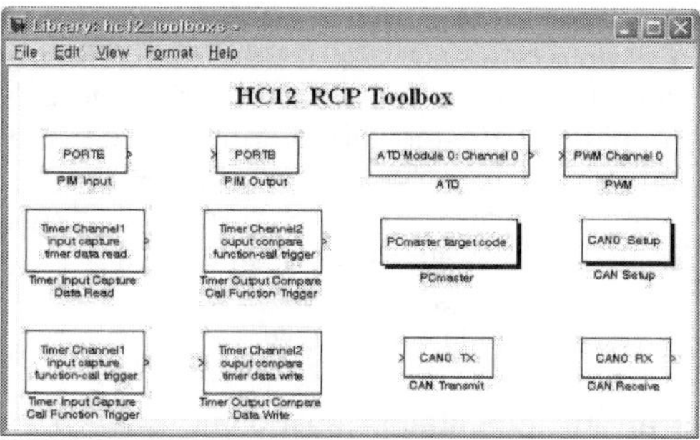

Figure 4. RCP Toolbox

Each block of RCP toolbox is related to the specific hardware modules of the target MCU. According to the required hardware modules such as digital I/O, Analog-To-Digital (ATD) converter, Timer, CAN, etc., control engineers should replace the inputs and the outputs of SILS models for the simulation with corresponding RCP blocks before the implementation.

REAL-TIME KERNEL

In Simulink®, the execution of models is managed by internal state transitions, according to the fixed or variable sampling rate. However, in this scheme, it is not easy to express the real execution on the MCU scheduled by a real-time kernel or a RTOS. In order to consider the influence of scheduling algorithms, the real-time kernel is supported in SILS. This scheduler uses the task for the scheduling unit. The real-time kernel is following the static cyclic scheduling policy. The attributes configured in SILS for the scheduler are succeeded by RCP, so that the scheduling properties are maintained after the implantation.

Figure 5 shows the block of the *Real-Time Kernel*, and Figure 6 shows the attributes of the *Real-Time Kernel*. The scheduler is periodically activated in each *Hyper period*. After the release time defined in the *Schedule release time table*, the scheduler releases the corresponding task listed in the *Schedule task table*. The task release is fulfilled by the *func_call* signal.

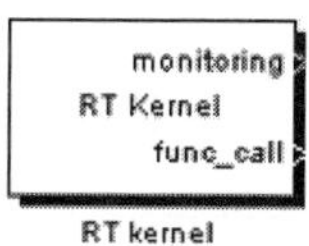

Figure 5. Real-Time Kernel based on static cyclic scheduling policy

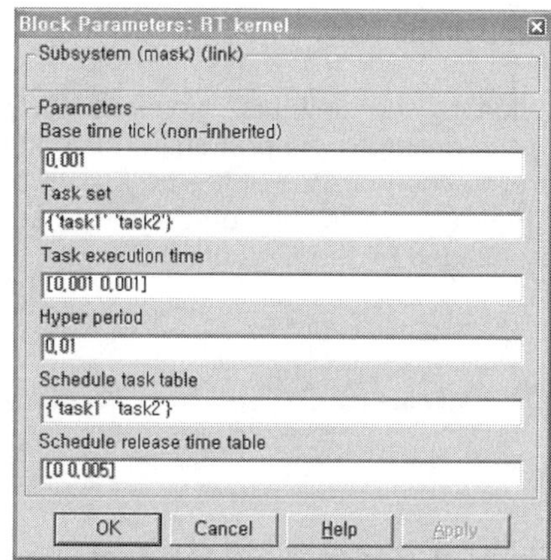

Figure 6. Real-Time Kernel configuration

TASK MODELING

In order to facilitate modularization, the concept of the task is adopted. The task is treated as a unit of function that is scheduled and executed by the system because

SILS is scheduled based on the static cyclic scheduling policy. [21] The task is defined as follows

- *Task – An encapsulated sequence of operations that executes independently of other tasks* [22]

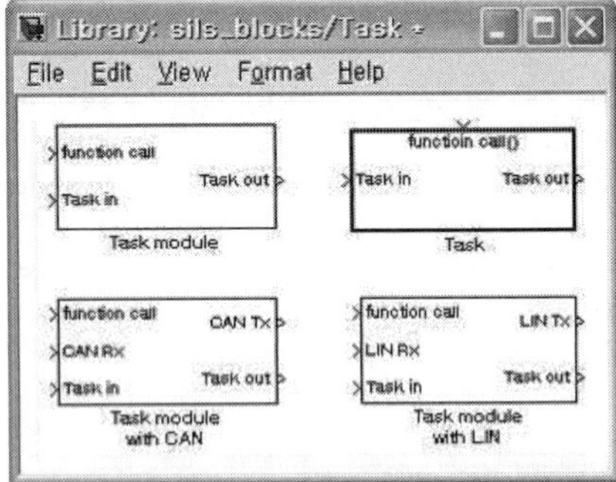

Figure 7. Task representation in SILS/RCP

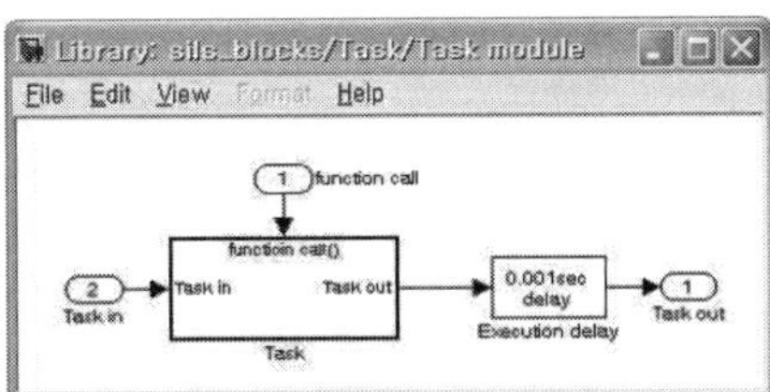

Figure 8. Subsytem of Task Module

The task model in SILS/RCP is shown in Figure 7. Figure 8 is the subsystem of the Task Module in Figure 7. The left block, *Task*, is related to the function of the task. The *Execution delay* block is the time delay for the execution time of the task.

The execution of the unit task consists of two parts: computation and output generation. The computations of the task are accomplished at the beginning of the task as shown Figure 9. The task output is generated after some delay defined by the *Execution Delay*.

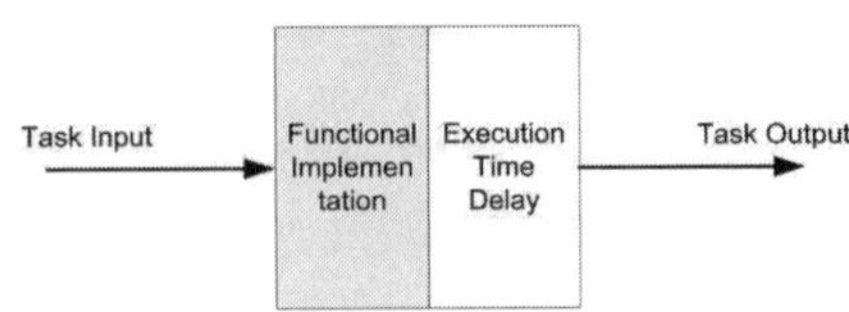

Figure 9. Concept of Task Execution

The execution time of the task should be measured as following definition.

- *Task execution time – The amount of time required to complete the execution of the task when it is executed alone and has all the resources it requires* [21]

In order to measure the execution time of the unit task, generated codes for a unit task from RCP are used. With following the definition of the task execution time, all interrupt sources except a timing module used by the scheduler are disabled and preemptions are not allowed.

NETWORK MODELING

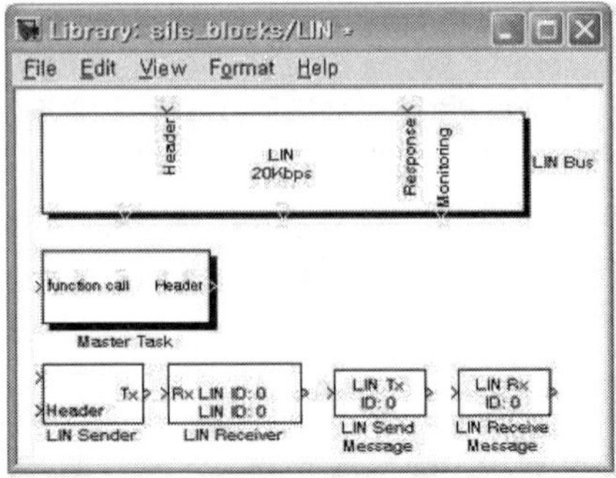

Figure 10. Network model of LIN protocol

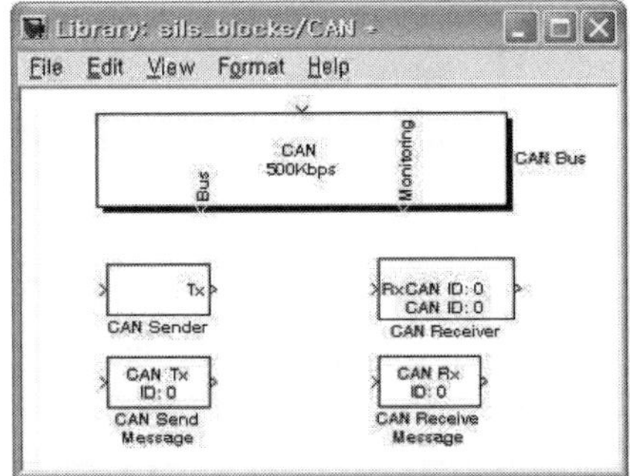

Figure 11. Network model of CAN protocol

SILS/RCP environments provide the simulation and the implementation of CAN and LIN network protocol. When control engineers design the distributed control system based on in-vehicle networks, SILS/RCP environments support the analysis of the performance degradation which is caused by network induced delays.

IMPLEMENTATION USING RCP

RCP is an implementation environment that generates executable codes from the models designed in SILS. RCP is realized using Real-Time Workshop Embedded Codder presented by Mathworks®, in order that proposed RCP is based on the identical platform to SILS and using the same block representations of Matlab/Simulink®. Embedded Codder creates only general C code, so additional work is required to connect Embedded Codder environment to the specific target processor. In this research, MC9SDP256B produced by freescale is selected as the target MCU. In order to connect Embedded Codder to the target,

HC(S)12 HAL[1] which is developed and distributed by ACE Lab[2] is used. [25], [26]

Since RCP provides the implementation environment, the performance verification on the MCU is available from the early design phase. As a result, the process from the design phase to the implementation phase can be simplified.

CASE STUDY: ELECTRONIC THROTTLE CONTROLLER DESIGN

In order to validate the feasibility and the effectiveness of SILS/RCP environments, the design process of an Electronic Throttle Controller (ETC) is described.

ETC MODELING IN SILS

An ETC model for SILS is shown in Figure 12. Figure 13 shows the controller of the ETC. A PID controller is used which is divided into three tasks: *Sensing_Task*, *Computation_Task*, and *Actuation_Task*. In the *Sensing_Task*, the throttle angle is computed from the sensing values of the ATD converter. In the *Computation_Task*, the control inputs are calculated from the differences between the current throttle angle and the reference angle. In the *Actuation_Task*, the PWM signal is generated based on the control input decided in the *Computation_Task*.

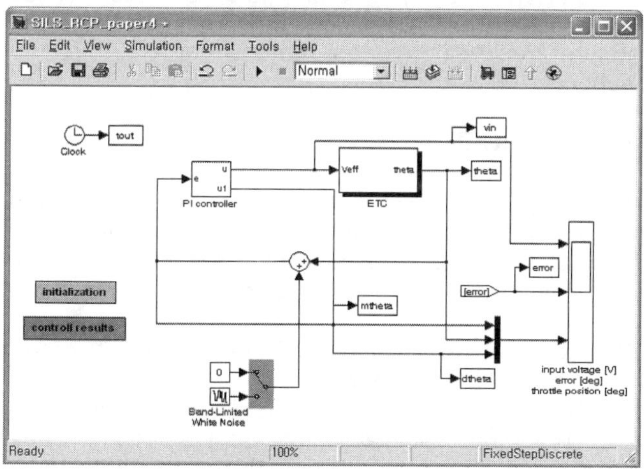

Figure 12. ETC model for SILS

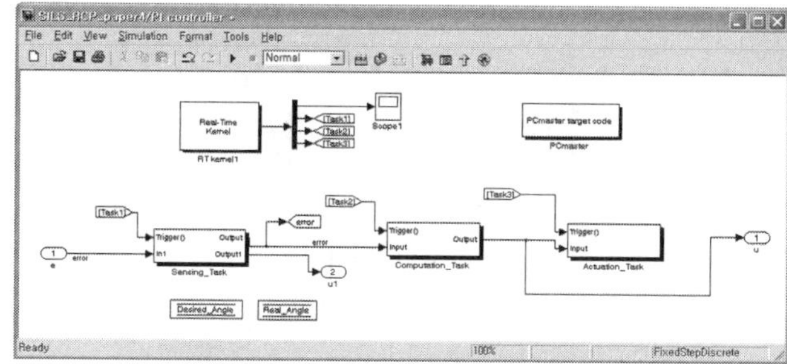

Figure 13. Controller of ETC for SILS

SIMULATION AND IMPLEMENTATION RESULT

The result from a simulation that does not consider temporal behaviors of the target system is shown in Figure 14.

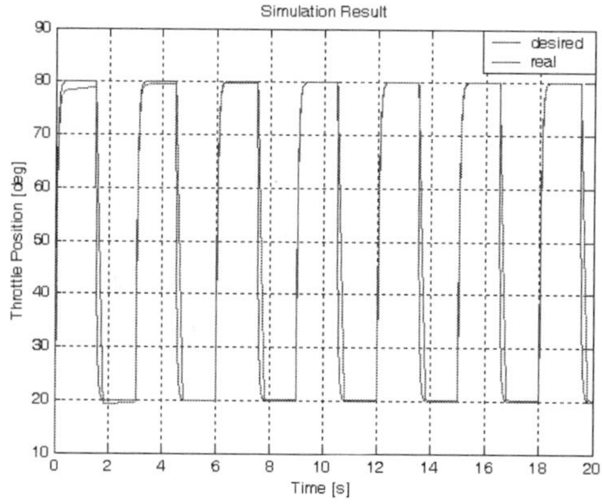

Figure 14. Simulation result without SILS

The controller models used in Figure 14 is transformed to the block diagram shown in Figure 13 using SILS environment. The control gains are fixed in order to compare the previous result to the result generated by SILS. The scheduling attributes which consist of the execution time and the release time are configured. The measured execution times of the *Sensing_Task*, *Computation_Taks*, and *Actuatioin_Task* are 1ms, 2ms, and 1ms, respectively. These execution times are measured according to the definition of the execution time. The release times of the tasks are 0ms, 1ms, and 4ms.

Figure 15 presents the simulation result in SILS environment. In this figure, overshoot, undershoot, and time delay in falling time are observed which are not seen in the simulation result generated without SILS. After gain tuning under SILS environment, the control performance is improved as can be seen in Figure 16.

---

[1] HC(S)12 Hardware Abstract Layer: http://www.acelab.org/HAL

[2] Automotive Control and Electronics Laboratory at Hanyang University in Seoul, Korea http://www.acelab.org

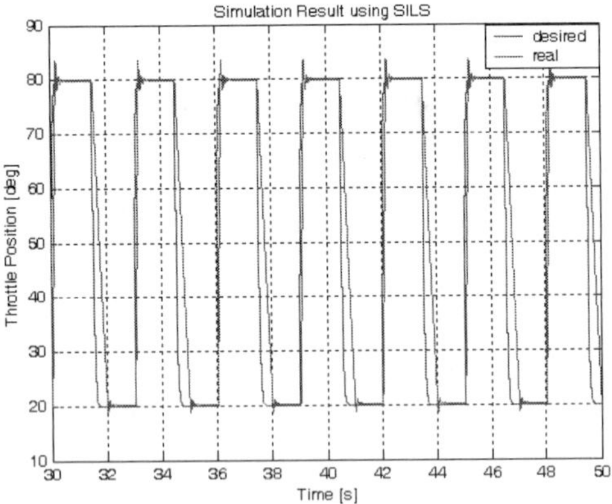

Figure 15. Simulation result with SILS

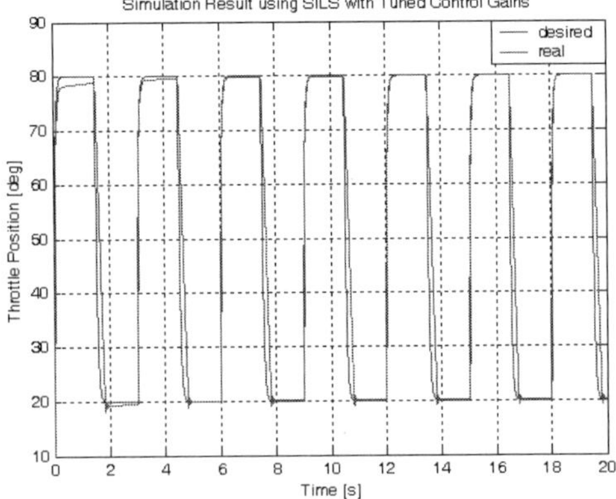

Figure 16. After gain turning with SILS

By applying the turned gain, executable code can be created by RCP. In Figure 17, the implementation result is shown.

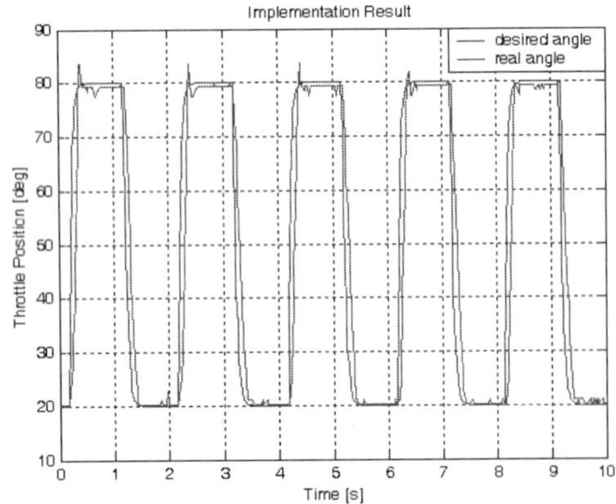

Figure 17. Implementation result using RCP

From the Figures 16 and 17, the implemented result is reasonable except for the overshoot in the rising time. The occurrence of the overshoot is caused by modeling uncertainties and nonlinearity around 80°.

CONCLUSION

In this paper, SILS/RCP environments are proposed to support a seamless development process from the design phase to the implementation phase. The feasibility of the environments is validated from the ETC design process.

Control engineers are able to obtain more realistic simulation results using SILS environment from the early design phase. RCP supports an immediate phase shift from the design phase to the implementation phase. The integrated development environment which consists of SILS and RCP can simplify the development process, reduce the time-to-market, and provide greater performance-assured design. Especially, control engineers develop the control algorithms and implement the controller to the MCU using identical platform and same models with SILS/RCP environments.

ACKNOWLEDGMENTS

This research is supported in part by MOST (Ministry of Science and Technology) under the National Research Laboratory program, and part of the project 'Development of Partial Zero Emission Technology for Future Vehicle'. We are grateful for their financial support.

REFERENCES

1. Zonghua Gu, Shige Wang, Jeong Chan Kim and Kang G. Shin, "Integrated Modelling and Analysis of Automotive Embedded control systems with Real-Time Scheduling," SAE International, p.115~p.122, 2004.
2. Hermann Kopetz, "Real-Time Systems," Kluwer Academic Publishers, 1997
3. Dan Henriksson, Anton Cervin, Karl-Erik Arzen, "TrueTime: Simulation of Control Loops Under Shared Computer Resources," 15th IFAC World Congress on Automatic Control, Barcelona, Spain, July 2002.
4. Steve Vestal, "Integrating Control and Software Views in a CACE/CASE Toolset," IEEE/IFAC Joint Symposium on Computer Aided Control System Design for Control Systems, Tucson, AZ, USA, pp.353~358, 1994.
5. Matt Englehart and Mike Jackson, "ControlH: A Fourth Generation Language for Real-time GN&C Applications," Proceedings of the 1994 IEEE Symposium on Computer Aided Control System Design, 1994.
6. E. E. L. Mitchell and J.S. Gauthier, "ACSL: Advanced Continuous Simulation Language - User

Guide and Reference Manual," Mitchell & Gauthier Associates, Concord MA, 1986.
7. Johan Eker, Anton Cervin "A Matlab Toolbox for Real-Time and Control Systems Co-Design"
8. M. F. Storch and J. W.-S. Liu. "DRTSS: A simulation framework for complex real-time systems," In Proceedings of the 2nd IEEE Real-Time Technology and Applications Symposium, pp.160~169, 1996.
9. N. C. Audsley, A. Burns, M. F. Richardson, J. Wellings, "STRESS: A Simulator for Hard Real-Time Systems"
10. Jiang Zhu, "Design and simulation of hard real-time applications," Proc. of 27th Annual Simulation Symposium, pp.217~225, 1994.
11. Anton Cervin, Dan Henriksson, Bo Lincoln, Johan Eker, KarlErik Årzén, "Analysis and Simulation of Controller Timing," IEEE Control Systems Magazine, 2003.
12. UML notation guide. Version 1.1. Object Management Group, doc. no. ad/97-08-05.http://www.rational.com/uml, 1997.
13. M. Törngren, O. Redell, "A modelling framework to support the design and analysis of distributed real-time control systems," Microprocessors and Microsystems 24, pp.81~93, 2000.
14. Sven Rebeschieß, "MIRCOS – Microcontroller-Based Real Time Control System Toolbox for use with Matlab/Simulink"
15. Thomas A. Henzinger, Christoph M. Kirsch, Marco A.A. Sanvido, Wolfgang Pree, "From Control Models to Real-Time Code Using Giotto," IEEE Control Systems Magazine, pp.50~64, 2003.
16. Steve Toeppe, Scott Ranville, Dave Bostic, Yanxin Wang, "Practical Validation of Model Based Code Generation for Automotive Applications," IEEE 10.A.3-1~10.A.3-14, 1999.
17. Myoungho Sunwoo, Jaebum Choi, Minsuk Shin, " DEVELOPMENT OF TIMING ANALYSIS TOOL FOR DISTRIBUTED REAL-TIME CONTROL SYSTEM, " KSAE Int. Journal of Automotive Technology, Vol. 5, No. 4, pp. 269 ~ 276, December 2004.
18. Wootaik Lee, Seungbum Park, Myoungho Sunwoo, "Towards a seamless development process for automotive engine-control system," Control Engineering Practice, Vol.12, pp.977~986, 2004.
19. M. Sunwoo, M. Shin, W. Lee, "Target-identical rapid control prototyping platform for model-based engine control", IMechE, Part D, Vol. 218, 2004.
20. Junghyun Song, Wootaik Lee, Myoungho Sunwoo, "Development of a Rapid Control Prototyping Platform for Engine Control System," Transaction of the Korean Society of Automotive Engineers, 2003.
21. Jane W.S. Liu, "Real-Time Systems," Prentice Hall, 2000.
22. Bruce Powel Douglass, "Doing Hard Time - Developing Real-Time Systems with UML, Objects, Frameworks, and Patterns," Addison-Wesley, 1999.
23. Target Language Compiler Reference Guide ver.4, MathWorks Inc.
24. Writing S-Functions ver.4, MathWorks Inc.
25. Grantley Hodge, Jian Ye and Walt Stuart, "Multi-Target Modeling for Embedded Software Development for Automotive Applications", World congress SAE international, In-Vehicle Networks and Software, Electrical Wiring Harnesses, and Electronics and Systems Reliability, 2004.
26. http://www.acelab.org/HAL

2006-01-0170

Hardware/Software Design and Development Process

Everett Lumpkin and Michael Gabrick
Delphi Corporation, Electronics and Safety Division

ABSTRACT

In today's extremely competitive, technically challenging and cost sensitive market place, the design process must be reviewed to shorten the design time and remove the expenses associated with building engineering development controllers. Embedded system software is steadily increasing in size and sophistication, as well as the complexity of the hardware and environmental interfaces which adversely impacts the Embedded Control Unit (ECU) time-to-market and quality. To remedy the increasing complexity, the trade-offs between software and hardware can now be investigated via concurrent development early in the design cycle. Virtual systems provide a method to evaluate the interaction of microprocessors, memories, peripheral devices as well as software prior to hardware realization. This paper discusses and demonstrates the productivity improvements that can be realized using new virtual system design tools and methodologies to enhance the traditional design process.

INTRODUCTION

Process and technology advancements in the semiconductor industry have helped to revolutionize automotive and consumer electronics. As Moore's Law predicted, the increase in complexity and operating frequencies of today's integrated circuits have enabled the creation of system applications once thought to be impossible. End systems such as camera cell phones, automotive infotainment systems, advanced powertrain controllers and handheld personal computers have been realized as a result.

In addition to the increases in process technology, the Electronic Design Automation (EDA) industry has helped to transform the way semiconductor integrated circuits (IC) and subsequent software applications are designed and verified. This transformation has occurred in the form of design abstraction, where the implementation continues to be performed at higher levels through the innovation of design automation tools.

An example of this trend is the evolution of software development from the early days of machine-level programming to the C++ and Java software written today. The creation of the assembler allowed the programmer to move a level above machine language, which increased the efficiency of code generation and documentation, but still tied the programmer to the underlying hardware architecture. Likewise, the dawn of C / C++ compilers, debuggers and linkers helped to move the abstraction layer further away from the underlying hardware, making the software completely platform independent, easier to read, easier to debug and more efficient to manage.

However, a shift to higher levels of software abstraction has not translated to a reduction in complexity or human resources. On the contrary, as integrated systems have become more feature rich, the complexity of the operating system and corresponding applications have increased rapidly, as have the costs associated with the software implementation and verification activities. Certainly the advancements in embedded software tools such as static code checkers, debuggers and hardware emulators have helped to solve some of the software verification problems, but software verification activities have become more time and resource consuming than the actual software creation. Time-to-market constraints have pushed software verification activities to the system-level, and led to a greater demand for production hardware to be made available earlier in the software development flow.

As with the software case, the semiconductor design community has made a very similar transformation in their design and verification strategies sparked by advances in the EDA community. Designs that were once implemented completely at the transistor level migrated to the gate-level implementation through the development of schematic capture tools. The creation of hardware description languages such as Verilog and VHDL and the corresponding compilers, simulators and synthesis tools allowed hardware designers to move away from the gate-level implementation to the register transfer level (RTL). The EDA community is now promoting even higher levels of abstraction, often under the banner of electronic system level design (ESL) [6]. Again, this represented a fundamental change in design abstraction, which allowed the designers to think in terms of overall functionality instead of the configuration of gates needed to implement the desired functionality.

As Application Specific Integrated Circuit (ASIC) design complexities have grown and the process geometry continued to shrink, the manufacturing and NRE costs for silicon has increased rapidly. For example, the cost for silicon mask sets range from $50,000 for a simple ASIC to greater than $1,000,000 for an advanced microprocessor or microcontroller [4]. The high costs associated with ASICs underscores the motivation of the hardware community to insure that the intended functionality is implemented correctly prior to taking a design to silicon. The EDA industry has helped this cause by providing sophisticated verification tools that prove the high-level design and the silicon implementation will function equivalently. However, even with these tools available, more than ½ of all IC and ASIC designs require a re-spin of silicon, where 70% of the re-spins are due to logic or functional errors that verification efforts should have caught [5]. With the huge investment required for each re-spin, system level verification is becoming a focus of the overall hardware verification strategies.

Although we have seen significant advancements in the processes of hardware and software design during the past two decades, surprisingly, there have been little advancements made at the system level. Today's system process consists of the paper study of the proposed hardware architecture, required functionality, microprocessor throughput, memory configuration, and the potential hardware migration paths. The process has remained relatively unchanged. Furthermore, the software implementation is typically held off until hardware prototype units are created, placing the software developers and system verification teams at a disadvantage. This current approach has many drawbacks including: slow adaptation to changes in customer requirements, drawn out hardware and software integration, limitations in system debugging, and difficulties meeting the time-to-market constraints.

This paper presents a new approach to system-level design through the creation of a virtual system, which allows for an early analysis of hardware and software interaction while removing many of the drawbacks plaguing traditional system development. This paper also presents a virtual automotive air-bag system implementation and explores the benefits of virtual system development.

PARADIGM SHIFT

The motivation for system level design and analysis is to significantly improve productivity through a paradigm shift that allows hardware and software to be designed concurrently rather than serially. Productivity is thus enhanced by the elimination of re-work, increased quality of the final system, improved verification, and shorter time-to-market.

As design trends continue to move to higher levels of abstraction, more emphasis will continue to be placed in verification activities at both the component and system level. The creation of a "virtual" system using accurate models of the hardware provides engineers with the following benefits: an architectural exploration of hardware and software functions, the creation of flexible prototype hardware, more accurate analysis of throughput and portability, software development earlier in the cycle, and rapid debugging through the instrumentation of the virtual hardware.

One of the primary advantages of a virtual system implementation is architecture exploration, which is the process of determining an optimum solution to a design space problem. Take for example the two-dimensional architectural space shown in Figure 1. The two design parameters shown (typically there are many design parameters) are power consumption and clock speed, with the ideal solution illustrated by the center of the target. In this simplified example, the yellow cross illustrates a hardware prototype ECU that exceeds the ideals for power consumption and fails to meet the clock speed ideals. Because of the time-to-market constraint, the system architecture continues to be based upon the initial hardware prototype without adequate exploration of alternative choices. The end result of a hardware based development process is a suboptimum product that may miss the design targets.

Conversely the green crosses show an alternative path to the optimum design solution. Several virtual systems are assembled and tested in the same time-to-market window. The final virtual system is on-target for the design parameters, and the resulting work products from the virtual system are quickly converted into the physical product. Models of the system are initially created at a high level of abstraction, and, through the model-based methodology, are driven to a full virtual implementation, then to an actual product.

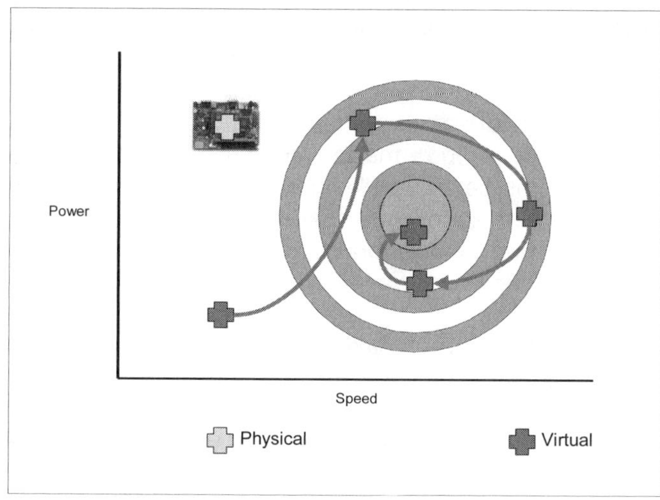

Figure 1 – Exploration of the design space using physical and virtual prototypes

The model-based methodology approach proposes the use of an architecture exploration tool to facilitate the rapid exploration of various CPUs, memories, and peripherals (system architecture). The system architecture is shown in the upper right of Figure 2 [7]. The upper left of Figure 2 shows early revisions of the functional models of the system, known as system behavior. The system behavior and system architecture are combined, and an optimal solution is achieved by iteratively comparing the performance of each partitioned alternative. The objective is to evaluate the various architectural and partitioning alternatives to gain a first order approximation of the optimum design.

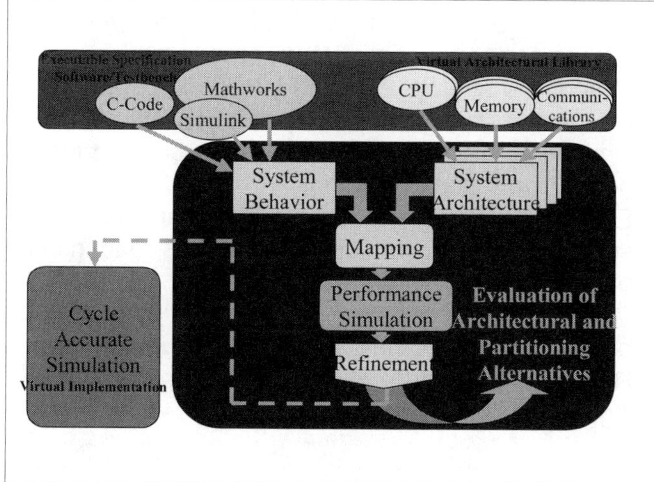

Figure 2 – Architecture exploration process

Some of the proposed EDA tools for architecture exploration [1] offer the ability to model microcontroller architectures in only a few weeks duration. The simulations for architectural simulation may be only 80% accurate, but that is believed to be good enough to make the first order choices of microcontroller, timer architecture and memory usages. Our evaluations of the architectural exploration tools, however, indicate that the industry has not yet focused on solving microcontroller selection in a general way. As this paper presents, there is a tradeoff between simulation accuracy, cost of the modeling effort, and the time to model a new architecture. We are awaiting further tool maturation before expanding beyond paper evaluations of architecture exploration.

The industry trend is toward building libraries of very accurate architecture models that execute the embedded software directly. A sufficient library of these detailed models can then be used to evaluate system architectures and also used for the final software development.

We have focused our efforts on the lower left box of Figure 2; the highly accurate and fast simulation of a virtual system known as cycle-accurate simulation. This portion of the co-design market has matured to the point that it is now feasible to simulate a moderate sized ECU, such as an air-bag deployment module, at about 1/15th the speed of the actual hardware. As additional models become available, these cycle-accurate simulations will be capable of solving much of the architectural exploration space as well.

Detailed and highly accurate simulation encourages evaluation of the system behavior on a proposed architecture. The models, as well as the target code, can be adapted to determine the optimum design solution. Full target software simulation is supported using a 32-bit CPU Virtual Processor Model (VPM), the microcontroller peripheral models, system ASIC models, and the environmental stimuli. The VPM is able to load and simulate the same executable image as used in traditional bench development. The models may be exported from CoMET to the lower cost METeor integrated development environment to provide a fixed platform (models cannot be changed) virtual product simulation.

SIMULATION SPEED AND ACCURACY

Before we begin discussing the system, it is important to present some background material that highlights the levels of modeling abstraction and how they are best applied.

In general, total simulation speed decreases as detail is added to the model. Functional models execute orders of magnitude faster than the models used during co-verification. The levels of abstraction used in product modeling include [3]:

- Functional Simulation – Very little to no timing accuracy of the real hardware.
- Timed Functional Simulation – Contains estimated execution time of individual modules.
- Cycle-Approximate – Timed functional simulation techniques applied to instruction set and cycle-accurate simulation.
- Instruction Set Simulation – Cross-compiled code executed on model of target CPU.
- Cycle-Accurate – Simulation is very similar (or identical) to hardware behavior.

The remainder of this section discusses each of these abstraction levels in greater detail.

FUNCTIONAL SIMULATION – Pure functional simulation is often faster than the actual product implementation due to the speed of the host platform compared to the embedded system. The behavior of the individual modules is modeled in a sequential manner. The system behavior model is then compiled and executed directly on the host platform, providing excellent simulation speed. This level of modeling is extremely useful for algorithm development. An example of functional simulation is a Matlab Simulink algorithm. Functional simulation is typically used to discover and refine the requirements of the system.

TIMED FUNCTIONAL SIMULATION – Adding timing constraints or "timing budgets" becomes a very powerful addition to the functional simulation model. Each module is assigned a timing constraint based on its estimated communication throughput, hardware complexity or software instruction throughput capability. The simulation kernel for this level of simulation has the capability to denote passage of time and detect overflow (over-budget) conditions. The accuracy of this simulation is near that of the final hardware, yet the simulation proceeds without continual context switching. This model has a reasonable tradeoff of simulation speed vs. accuracy for use in partitioning studies as well as software development. Timed functional simulation is used to evaluate system architecture and it's ability to support the desired system behavior.

Performance modeling (co-design) of the system is best conducted with this level of simulation. As timing estimates are added to the various modules, they are modeled together to insure that the timing assumptions do not violate the overall system performance budget.

INSTRUCTION SET SIMULATION – Instruction set simulators (ISS) use cross-compiled target code to automatically derive timing information. This information is used to interface the application software with cycle-accurate simulations of the hardware. The simulation speeds (when coupled with traditional Verilog simulations) are typically too slow for use in actual software development, as just a few seconds of product operation may require hours or days of simulation.

Through careful attention to detail, instruction set simulations can be made to execute at speeds acceptable for software development (10-1000 million instructions per second). Instruction set simulation is best used for the debugging and optimization of embedded code.

CYCLE ACCURATE – Cycle-accurate simulation means that the hardware or software is executed in a manner identical to the actual hardware. The logic associated with a clock cycle is executed every cycle, such as timers, counters, etc. This level of modeling often requires a simulation kernel that supports concurrent operations, such as a Verilog or VHDL simulator. The models are timing accurate (typically within tens of nanoseconds) and simulation will be slow. Cycle-accurate simulation is used for hardware development. We often use the term "cycle-accurate" to loosely describe the desired accuracy of a system level simulation, but the more appropriate term is cycle-approximate".

CYCLE APPROXIMATE – Cycle-approximate simulation attempts to combine the best of instruction set, timed functional and cycle-accurate simulations to achieve a simulation with the fidelity that appears to be cycle-accurate, yet approaches simulation speeds similar to timed functional simulation. The techniques used to increase simulation speed include:

- Execution of "pure software" in bursts until a specific latency or hardware register access is met
- Timed event delays rather than counting cycles
- Reduction of decision (if, switch) statements in the simulation models, often via the use of function pointers and state machines
- Execution of update logic only when necessary, such as when a communication path is read instead of every time it is written
- Condensing serial communication (bits) into a parallel transfer of the data at the appropriate time
- Removal of clocking signals and schemes
- Aggregation of discrete signals into buses or ports

For effective virtual system simulation, the primary modeling level is cycle-approximate, but uses the above techniques to replicate the accuracy of cycle-accurate modeling. The accuracy is effectively the same as cycle-accurate simulation (typically tens of nanoseconds). Cycle-approximate simulations are used to develop software against full models of the peripherals and ASICs, and can also be used for some architecture exploration activities. The virtual system described in this paper uses a combination of timed functional, cycle-accurate and cycle-approximate simulation.

AIR-BAG VIRTUAL SYSTEM

The air-bag virtual system has the equivalent functionality of a recent production air-bag ECU. The module consists of a 32-bit microcontroller coupled with 7 ASIC devices as shown in the right side of Figure 3.

The air-bag system software reads acceleration data directly from accelerometers within the ECU, and also receives acceleration/severity data from remote sensors that communicate to the ECU. The algorithms make a deployment decision based upon the acceleration "crash waveform" data as well as vehicle state information such as seat belt engagement, seat position and occupant detection. There are 5 different serial interfaces used by the target software. The software continuously communicates with the ASIC devices that control deployment, and executes various diagnostics on the deployment loops. In the event of a severe crash, the 32-bit microcontroller and a simple "safe-ing" microcontroller must agree and command the air-bag deployment loop via the deployment ASIC. The ECU also contains a serial EEPROM device that is used to record operating statistics such as ignition cycles as well as "event" information during deployment or near-deployment.

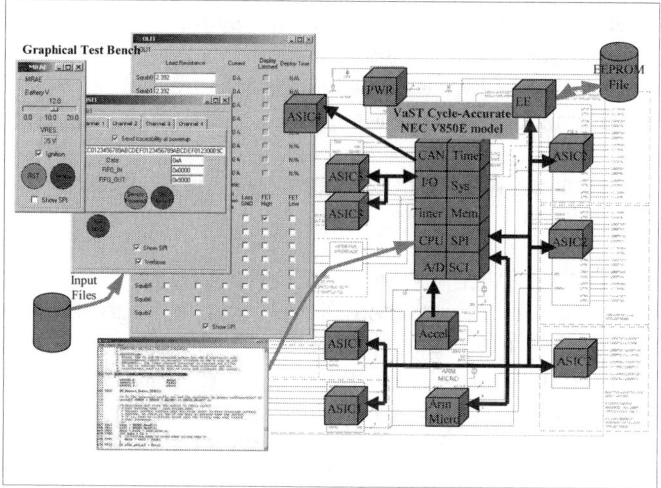

Figure 3 – Block diagram of an air-bag Virtual System

The 32-bit RISC based microcontroller includes various peripheral functions: less than 100 discrete I/O pins, DMA controller, interrupt controller, clock generator, 16-bit timers, watchdog timer, UART, serial peripheral interface, A/D and a CAN interface. As such it represents the medium complexity microcontroller commonly used in restraint and body functions of an automobile.

In the virtual system the microcontroller model loads the target executable image and symbol tables. The executable image is the same as used for bench development; even using the same compiler optimization flags and compile options. The microcontroller peripherals such as the A/D, timers, UART, SPI, and IO pins are also part of the simulation model, and are written as 'C' timed behavioral-level functional models. The models are interconnected using a subset of Verilog to describe the coherency and hierarchal portions of the design. The peripheral models were supplied in object form (no source code). Each model is accompanied by documentation showing interconnections; register map, embedded warning messages, and configuration options. Full interrupt capability of the peripheral models is supported, and a peripheral interrupt will cause the CPU model to take the exception and begin execution of the interrupt handler code, just as the hardware would behave. The models appear to be cycle-accurate, however some abstractions are applied to the behavioral models. For example a timer counter register may only be updated when the target software accesses the timer or when an interrupt occurs.

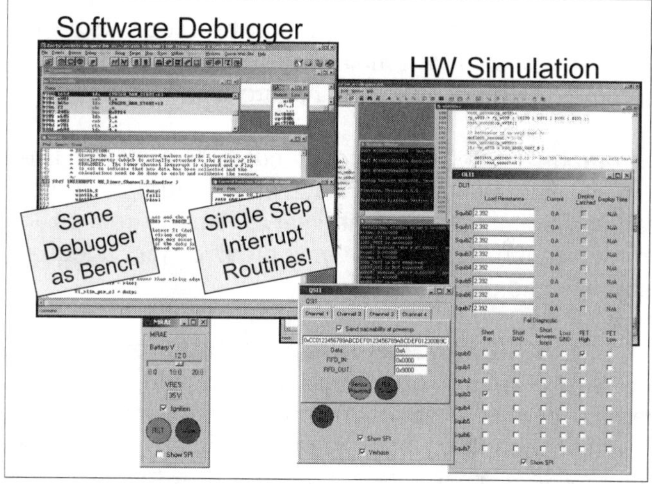

Figure 4 – Screen shot showing execution of the virtual system

The CPU model (also known as the Virtual Processor Model - VPM) executes the target instruction stream cycle-by-cycle, such that register and memory accesses occur just as in the actual hardware. An example of this execution is shown in Figure 4, where the virtual system simulates while the software and hardware are monitored by the debugger. The CPU model by itself executes extremely fast at nearly 100 million instructions per second (on a 2.2GHz Windows 2000 PC). Execution of the CPU and the peripherals slows the simulation to around 10 million instructions per second, which is within one order of magnitude the speed of the actual hardware!

The various ASIC devices range in complexity from a simple serial EEPROM to a deployment ASIC with a dozen control/status registers and an integrated state machine. The most complex device is described with a 60 page functional level specification. Almost all of the devices communicate to the microcontroller via an 8 or 16-bit SPI (Serial Peripheral Interface) synchronous communication. Behavioral level 'C' is used to interconnect the ASIC devices because they use analog voltages not easily represented by Verilog interconnections. Moreover, the ASIC models are connected to the microcontroller model via regular discrete time intervals and by "microcontroller pin events". The "pin events" can occur at any time within the discrete time intervals, and ASIC models process the events in the order they occur. Typically the events are discrete I/O such as chip selects, SPI transfers, and other control signal changes.

For the air-bag system the ASIC discrete time interval was chosen to be the same as the 10kHz sampled accelerometer data, (ie. 100us). The accelerometer model thus supplies a new data sample to the A/D pin of the microcontroller at each discrete time interval. Other ASICs update filtered analog voltages or execute timed events based upon the 100us discrete interval. The choice for the discrete interval can be modified by the end user but should remain less than the fundamental loop time (hundreds of us) of the target software.

The graphical user interface executes at a slower fixed interval. The exchange of data with the graphical user interface is limited to a 1ms interval time to reduce the communication overhead, yet provide for adequate response time of the display.

VIRTUAL SPI EXAMPLE – As described previously the models are written at a cycle-approximate level. An example of this abstraction is the combining of serial communication (bits) into a parallel transfer. The air-bag virtual system makes extensive use of a "SPI streams interface". The high level SPI protocols (such as phase and polarity) are checked but without the implementation of a bit-by-bit electrical interface as shown in Figure 5.

The SPI data is transferred with parallel transfers. The MOSI (Master Out Slave In) and MISO (Master In Slave Out) signals transfer the data bits in parallel. CS (Chip Select) is a normal discrete signal. The CONTROL signal contains several bit fields that allow error checking of the transfer including size, strobe, bit order, clock polarity and phase. This communication of the SPI protocol between the master and the slave devices allows the simulation to warn for miss-matches in the communication protocol. Note that the "Electrical" parameters such as setup and hold time are not communicated nor checked.

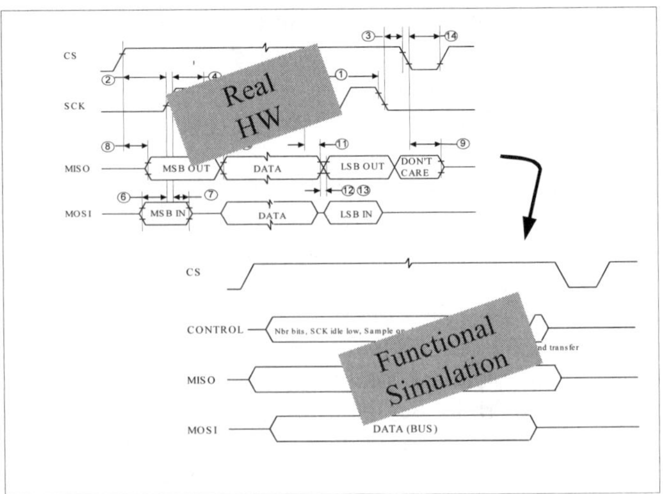

Figure 5 – Virtual SPI "streams interface"

BENEFITS

The air-bag virtual system offers several benefits for both hardware and software verification. Because the verification is conducted on a model (that can be easily changed), the feedback loop to improve the design is shortened. The following benefits have been realized for the air-bag virtual system:

- System level ASIC verification
- Software verification on a virtual system
- Sophisticated analysis tools
- Internal hardware visibility (observe-ability)
- Advanced test benches

This section will discuss each of these benefits in greater detail.

SYSTEM LEVEL ASIC VERIFICATION – ASIC verification at the system level has a high benefit compared to the modeling costs. Existing models may be combined to create entirely new designs. For example, while the original air-bag virtual system was developed to support software development, a relatively low incremental investment in ASIC models allowed the creation of new virtual systems. The new virtual system is then programmed with target (product) software to validate the requirements of the new ASIC prior to the mask set release. Within the environment the SW engineer has the ability to optimize the functionality of the proposed ASIC along with the software driver prior to ASIC design and fabrication.

SW VERIFICATION ON A VIRTUAL SYSTEM – Software verification on a virtual system is very similar to verification on a physical prototype. The simulator and the virtual processor model (VPM) integrate the same debugger used on the bench. The debugger is provided with full run-time control of the simulation as well the ability to set breakpoints, step through source level code, inspect memory and observe behavior of the microcontroller registers.

In simulation, the entire virtual system (including the test stimuli) is paused by the run-time control of the debugger. This allows the software developer to step into and out of interrupt routines while the software remains in synchronization with the test stimuli. This type of increased visibility is one of the reasons the software engineers often prefer the virtual bench for daily software development [6].

Within a system, "plant models" are the stimuli needed to test the ECU. When testing physical hardware, these plant models often consist of graphical interfaces and scripts that control hardware boxes interfaced to the product. The virtual system needs the same types of user interfaces; however, the hardware boxes can be eliminated because the plant models connect to the virtual system directly. The savings associated with virtual test benches (vs. hardware box driven test approaches) may be on the order of $100K per development station. It is, however, clearly understood that there will continue to be a need for a mix of "real benches" and "virtual systems" for product development. This is necessary to validate the actual physical products and to confirm that the virtual system matches the behavior of the physical product.

For a "physical test bench", emulators are typically used to provide the visibility inside the microcontroller. These emulators often require special silicon "bond-out" chips or Field Programmable Gate Array (FPGA) devices in order to make the internal registers visible to the software developer. As microcontrollers increase in complexity and frequency, extensive engineering is required to accurately replicate the microcontroller. In some cases the development of the emulator becomes technically un-feasible and the software engineer is left with only the "background debug mode" access to the silicon and registers or reduce functionality (or frequency) of the emulator. Verification on a virtual system allows visibility of the simulated registers and removes the difficulty of silicon bond-out chips and high frequencies.

ANALYSIS TOOLS – Software and hardware analysis tools can be applied to the simulation to measure system metrics. These metrics include: interrupt latency, stack depth, code coverage, data traces, bus or serial communication traffic. When ASICs often communicate via the serial peripheral interface (SPI), confirming communication messages on the bench requires use of a four-channel oscilloscope and manual observation of each message on a bit-by-bit basis. Simulations, however, are easily instrumented with a "SPI watcher" module that records the SPI transfers while a chip select is active. At the trailing edge of a chip select, the buffer is output with a simple print statement resulting in a display such as:

```
uP SPI to EE: 0x03 0x00 0x3C 0x00 0x00
EE SPI to uP: Hi-Z Hi-Z Hi-Z 0x9F 0xFF
```

A powerful non-intrusive extension to the simulation streams out details of the instruction path, register, memory and cache usage. A Windows DLL (Dynamically Linked Library) is added to the simulation to direct the tracing and profiling. This extension allows the capture of instruction traces, measure code execution time, measure interrupt latency, and monitor code coverage. Subsequent functions can then receive and process the output [2]. An example display is shown in Figure 6.

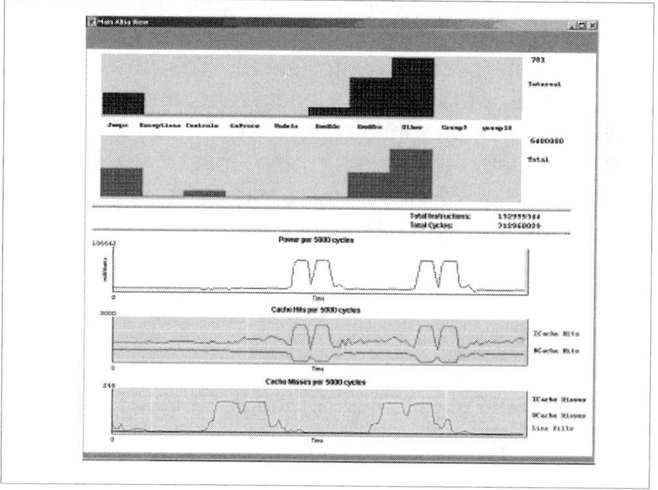

Figure 6 – Analysis of a virtual design using METrix; measuring design parameters such as interrupt service routine latency, cache hits/misses, bus transactions, and code profiling. Data can be filtered to graphics and files and triggers based on either hardware or software events

A minimally intrusive and simple instrumentation method allows a direct connection between the target and the host computer running the simulation. For example, the function `TspiHostPrintString()` can be added to the target code and provides print capabilities to the host (PC) software window.

One example of this instrumentation is a method to verify the target code implementation. The deployment algorithm is first developed on (and compiled for) a host computer with access to a large library of vehicle acceleration profiles. The host simulation records the algorithm variables every loop time while the acceleration profile is applied, similar to a strip chart. The record from the host computer is then compared to a record generated by the source code compiled for the target system. The record is simple to capture on the host system, but with physical bench equipment an extensive logic analyzer setup is required to capture the many target system variables. Because of the difficult setup, only a limited number of vehicle acceleration profiles may be captured on the bench. Using the direct connection between the target simulation and the host computer the target system can access the library of acceleration profiles directly facilitating a one-step regression process with the large library.

VISIBILITY OF THE HARDWARE – Another benefit of a virtual system is internal hardware visibility. The microcontroller and ASIC simulation models are built with extensive warnings that monitor the execution of the software. For example, the internal EEPROM peripheral model knows when it is in the "write" state and thus a subsequent "read" of the same EEPROM returns invalid data. Many internal EEPROMs are designed to supply high voltages to the internal memory cells during write sequences, and thus data reads are not possible during the several millisecond "write" state. The physical part offers no indication of this illegal (read during a write) condition, and an incorrectly written system may compute critical algorithms using invalid data. The model of the EEPROM is constructed to output a message under this invalid condition:

```
"WARNING: EEPROM1 data read from
address 0xXXXX while in the write
state".
```

This message alerts the software engineer of the specification violation.

An ASIC model may also embed warning messages. Take for example an output driver chip that provides for a current measurement, but while the ASIC is in the measurement state, the die temperature rise is increased. The design of the ASIC package allows for short duration current measurements on a single output driver. The model for that ASIC is built in a way that if the duration is exceeded or the number of measured channels is exceeded, a warning message is displayed to the software developer. In this manner, the assumptions about the usage of the chip are communicated and enforced throughout the development process. The software developer thus benefits from a "field application engineer in the box" that is constantly checking the software execution for correct interaction with the hardware design.

The number of warnings provided in a peripheral or ASIC simulation varies with the complexity of the model. Typically 2 to 20 warning messages are included in each microcontroller peripheral or ASIC model. Many of these warnings monitor subtle requirements and caution statements in the specification. Without these warnings, the target software drivers may be written in violation of the requirements, which may later result in a quality or field return issue.

Each ASIC model is created with "elements" or registers that provide visibility of the inner functionality. An element may be read only (allowing visibility) or read/write (allowing visibility and control). For example, an accelerometer model provides a writable element of acceleration to modify the force in units of gravity (G's). A power supply model, as shown in Figure 7, can display the contents of internal registers as well as visual indicators of the outputs of the ASIC.

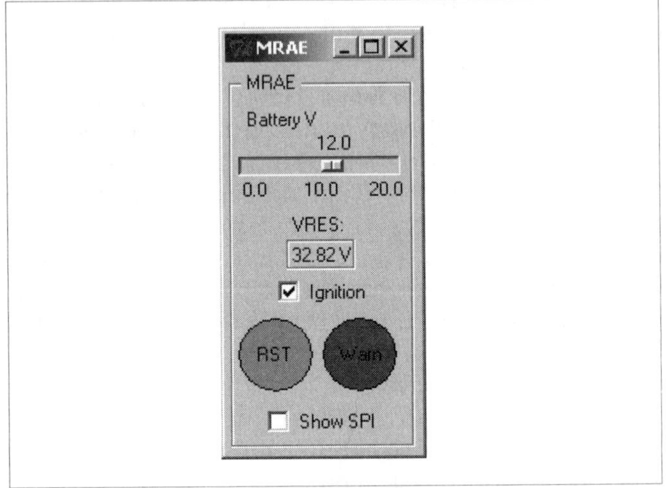

Figure 7 – Example of power supply ASIC showing control of the battery voltage and status of the charge pump (VRES), reset output and warning lamp output.

ADVANCED TEST BENCHES – The virtual system test bench provides the ability to view and control the simulation. A test bench can be as simple as a command line, a script interpreter, or even a full graphical interface. In Figure 3, the graphical interface for the air-bag system is shown on the left. The plant models include acceleration data files; external serial-communication based sensor models, as well as CAN communications. Because a virtual system can be tested without building hardware interface "boxes" it costs significantly less to instrument the virtual system than the actual product. In general, the visual and scripting capabilities of the test bench are shared with the actual bench, i.e. they use the same graphical and scripting environments. Automatic tests thus developed for the virtual test bench also execute without significant modification on a physical test bench.

Automatic regression and unit testing is the ability to regress the functional units of the system at every step of development, looking for unexpected changes introduced by recent modifications. The plant models, debugger, and the simulation share the same host computer system, which facilitates unit testing. Serial communication messages can be generated and intercepted via scripts. The software development team is thus provided with the tools to allow daily execution of the regression test suite. The tests also include the environmental stimuli needed to exercise the software and report a pass/fail upon completion of each test.

Another powerful capability of the test bench is the simulation of multiple models (or actual product) in parallel, with the same test stimuli and similar monitoring functions. For example a high level functional model ("golden model") of the system can by executed in synchronization with a detailed cycle-accurate model, as shown in Figure 8. The test bench can verify parameters of interest such as ignition response times, communication messages or air-bag deployment times by comparing the two models. Although the two models run at very different abstraction levels, their top-level functionality will match to verify implementation. One example is an OEM supplied "golden" model in Matlab, compared with the cycle-accurate target code on the microcontroller and hardware models.

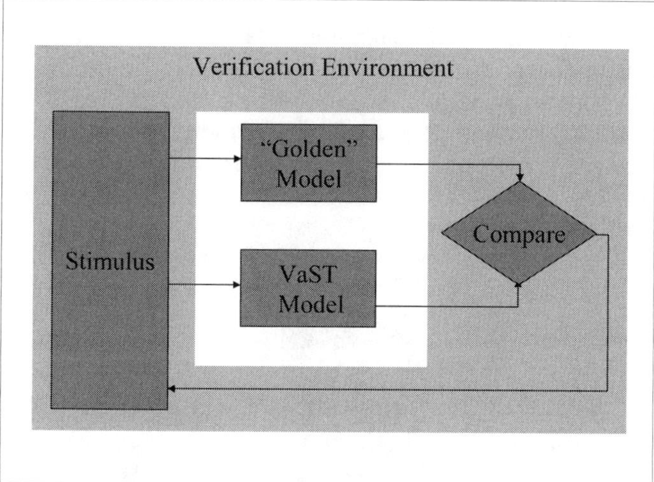

Figure 8 – Golden model comparison

Simulation of the hardware and software improves the quality of the overall system. The "field application engineer in the box" provides continuous enforcement of the proper usage of the hardware. The analysis tools allow visibility across the software/hardware boundary and generation of charts for throughput and code coverage. Elements provide for visibility inside the ASICs, deepening the hardware understanding. Finally the test benches facilitate automatic regression and unit testing.

LOGISTICS

Various logistical aspects must be managed in order to make effective use of product simulation. While it is beyond the scope of this paper to address rollout of these tools, it is important for the reader to see that tool availability, training, and model attainment must be considered.

Virtual systems are easily distributed to worldwide development sites. When intense bursts of software development resources need to be added, it is only a matter of minutes to make another copy of the development environment. A global floating license pool of simulators and models allows virtual system to be invoked worldwide and around the clock. Compilers/linkers and debuggers are the same as those used for the bench environment and can also benefit from widespread availability. Contrast the virtual system availability with the conventional development environment; it often takes a week or more to add a new development "bench".

The virtual system is easy to setup and use, and requires minimal training. We rely on an initial 2-hour individualized training/project start. In this training the basics of invocation and customization of the simulation are covered. That training is supplemented with 1-hour ad-hoc "classes" on detailed topics as well as on-line reference pages. For software engineers already familiar with the debugger, only minimal training is required to become proficient in the use of the simulator.

Clearly, the creation of a virtual system is a large undertaking and requires careful planning. Once the initial virtual system has been created, it will serve as the springboard for future derivative systems. The virtual system consists of microcontroller "core" (VPM and memory devices) microcontroller peripheral models (typically from the semiconductor supplier), ASIC models (typically developed internally) and plant models (typically re-using existing bench test apparatus).

The microcontroller VPM is verified against semiconductor vendor supplied test vectors to assure accuracy. The VPM can be built and verified in the duration of 6-20 weeks, depending on the complexity of the CPU. Microcontroller peripheral models such as the timers, SPI, and A/D are written in behavior level ANSI-C. The peripherals are interconnected to the VPM via one or more "virtual buses". The semiconductor vendor is in the best position to create and verify the peripheral models, as they have the best understanding of the specifications and intricate details

The system ASIC devices often contain company intellectual property. A core team familiar with the model generation tools and the abstraction level required creates the models from the functional specifications. For new devices, the design, source code for the model, and test cases may be shared with the semiconductor supplier as an executable reference. The intent is that the executable reference provides a "golden" model of the ASIC that has been tested in the system implementation. We are working with the various semiconductor vendors to integrate the executable reference model into their respective design flows. For reference, the average ASIC device of the air-bag system required approximately 6 man-weeks for the design, code and verification activities.

RESULTS

Embedded ECU's continue to increase in both software and hardware complexity. Even as transistor densities increase, the bulk of the system complexity will be added to software. In other words, if one compares the complexity of a 20K ECU to a 2M ECU, the complexity of the 2M software is 2 orders of magnitude larger than the 20K ECU, while the complexity of the hardware (CPU, peripherals and ASIC) may seem to be only 1 order of magnitude more complex [7]. A virtual system, once developed, can easily grow to match the memory size changes of the system. Moreover, we have shown the benefits of verifying software on a virtual system as opposed to a hardware platform in terms of time, effort and scalability.

Overall, the entire simulation of the air-bag system with the core, peripherals, ASIC models and test bench executes at a rate of about 1 million instructions per second, approximately 1/15th the speed of the actual hardware. This speed is significantly faster than what is achievable by the typical instruction set simulators and Verilog simulations. The speed is satisfactory for most software development, but may still be slower than desired for 24/7 repetitive regression testing of a system.

The following benefits have been realized during the air-bag product development, due to the use of the virtual system:

- Quickly gathered throughput data for a business decision on new product directions.
- Six hardware schematic issues were found and eliminated prior to board fabrication. Re-work was avoided.
- 27+ target SW issues were found, many of which may have been difficult to detect on the bench. Some examples:
    1. SPI data size changed w/o re-initializing SPI HW
    2. SPI TXE/RXE were modified while PWR=1 (specification violation)
    3. Inter-message communication gap (5ms) to ASIC violated
    4. CAN error interrupt handler did not handle all sources of interrupt
    5. Improper I/O port initialization order
    6. Improper A/D frequency (prescaler) selected causing incomplete conversion result
- Reduce the number of hardware test benches needed to verify the system.
- Demonstrated capability to reduce the design cycle time.

FUTURE VIRTUAL SYSTEMS

Once a baseline system has been modeled, it can then be quickly modified for future virtual systems. An example modification is given as a case study below.

The engineering design group planned for a next generation ASIC that combined two previous ASICs (See Figure 9). The new ASIC removed some diagnostics functionality such that diagnostics previously done in hardware are now implemented via software algorithms. This change impacts the target software because the diagnostics must be manually commanded and read via the microcontroller. While paper studies were conducted on this new approach, some lingering questions remained about the SPI traffic loading and the impact of the software diagnostics on the microcontroller throughput. Those questions were easily answered through the analysis of the application software on the virtual system.

The new ASIC specification was provided to the semiconductor supplier in February 2004. The hardware development schedule is about 10 months to create the actual ASIC, and 2-3 additional months to build the hardware prototype, write the software, and measure the impact.

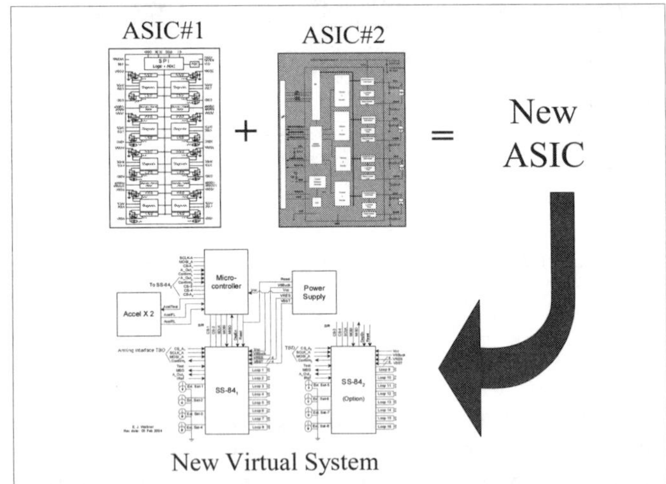

Figure 9 – Virtual system can measure a planned system change with significantly less expense than the development of hardware

In parallel with the ASIC design activity, we modeled the new ASIC and integrated it within the existing virtual air-bag system. Instead of the 10 months required for the silicon design, the modeling activity was completed in about 10 weeks. That is about the same time required to write and review the new software requirements for the device. Then, using the virtual system, the actual software drivers were implemented. The use of the virtual system during this development resulted in 8 target code design and coding error corrections and allowed for a 1-week integration/testing time of the silicon with the (already verified) target software.

The process of creating the ASIC model identified 9 functional changes that were implemented in the first pass silicon along with more than 30 specification corrections/ clarifications. Clearly, the addition of up-front modeling adds a rigor that improves the quality of the design as well as the time to market.

CONCLUSION

In this paper we have presented a virtual system ECU that encourages development and testing in an environment that significantly contributes to the quality. The virtual system executes the same code as used on the hardware bench, at approximately 1/15th the speed of the real system. Full functionality is supported, including the ASICs and various plant models to stimulate the system. The built-in "field application engineer in the box" warnings help the software engineer to identify various required target software changes.

The realized development time savings are associated with the elimination of design rework, such as:

- Evaluation of new ASICs prior to the expense of silicon development
- Development of driver software in parallel with silicon and board fabrication
- Detection of difficult to find software driver defects via: "field application engineer in the box"
- Comparison of a golden reference to a nearly fully implemented system
- Regression and unit testing as the ECU is being built rather than after it is complete
- Visibility into details of the hardware operation
- Analysis tools for system throughput, interrupt latency, code coverage and communication traffic
- Savings of bench costs through replacement of the pre-silicon emulator and equipment costs

In summary, the virtual system allows the software and hardware activities to be parallelized, resulting in less total manpower, and reduced time-to-market development cycle for the creation of a new ECU.

ACKNOWLEDGMENTS

We gratefully acknowledge the end users of the air-bag system simulation who provided near daily feedback and improved usability of the simulation.

REFERENCES

1. Cadence Virtual Component Co-Design (VCC) environment for engine control unit design: http://www.cadence.com/company/success_stories/magneti_ss.pdf
2. James Brogan "Guide to Creating a User METrix DLL for CoMET and METeor Toolsets", 22-Apr-2003, VaST Systems Technology.
3. Lennard, Chris; Mista Davorin; "Taking Design to the System Level", April 2005, http://www.arm.com/pdfs/ARM_ESL_final_checked(3)JC.pdf
4. "Maximizing Silicon ROI: The Cost of Failure and Success", Nassda White Paper WP020522-1A; http://www.nassda.com/ROI_WP_v062503.pdf
5. "The verities of verification", Bill Roberts, Electronic Business 01-Jun-2003; http://www.reed-electronics.com/eb-mag/article/CA301056?industryid=2112
6. Perrier, Vincent; "A look inside electronic system level (ESL) design", 26-Mar-2004, EETimes, http://www.eetimes.com/news/design/features/showArticle.jhtml?articleID=18402916
7. Winters, Frank; Mielenz, Carsten; Hellestrand, Graham, "Design Process Changes Enabling Rapid Development", Convergence 2004, http://www.vastsystems.com/notes/convergence20041018.pdf

CONTACTS

Everett R. Lumpkin (Simulation and Modeling) 765-451-3247; everett.r.lumpkin@delphi.com

Michael T. Gabrick (Digital IC design) 765-451-3056; michael.t.gabrick@delphi.com

DEFINITIONS, ACRONYMS, ABBREVIATIONS

ASIC – Application Specific Integrated Circuit

Co-Design – The process of exploring various CPU architectures and system partitioning. Also referred to as the simultaneous design of hardware and software.

Co-Verification – The process of verifying the correct operation of the system, including hardware, software and the timing effects of each, typically at the cycle-accurate or cycle-approximate level.

CPU – Central Processing Unit, usually used in the context of general microcontroller architecture without a specific embedded peripheral set.

Cross-compiled code – Use of a host computer to compile, link and locate code for a target computer.

Cycle-Accurate Simulation – Behavioral model of system hardware (CPU & peripherals) with timing steps equal to the fundamental bus frequency.

Cycle-Approximate Simulation – Behavioral model of the system hardware (CPU & peripherals) with timing that approximates the behavior of pipelining and cache effects.

ECU – Embedded Control Unit, sometimes also referred to as an Electronic Control Unit.

ESL – Electronic System Level design

Executable Specification – A host platform functional model of the system that allows customer and test interaction with the product.

GUI – Graphical User Interface

Golden Model – A reference model used to convey the functionality of the system. Used to compare with a more detailed model.

HDL – Hardware Description Language, i.e. Verilog or VHDL.

HLL – High Level Language, i.e. C/C++.

Host – Engineering workstation commonly using HPUX, Solaris or Windows operating system.

ISS – Instruction Set Simulator, a model of a CPU that is able to execute cross-compiled application software.

Module – Grouping of related functions to perform a requirement of the system. Also known as a block and may become either hardware or software.

NRE – Non-Recurring Engineering Costs

Plant – A portion of the model that simulates external stimuli such as sensors, actuators, or even a vehicle transmission.

Regression Test – A suite of tests executed against the product that can automatically determine if the product has "regressed" from a previous level of functionality due to additional detail/refinement added to the model. Sometimes known as test vectors.

RTL – Register Transfer Level, a level of abstraction of digital hardware designs that allows synthesis from HDL code to a gate level representation.

Target – Embedded CPU such as ARM, PowerPC, Star12, V850, or TriCore.

Test Bench – Simulation environment that surrounds the system model to supply input stimuli and displays behavior of the system. May support command line or graphical user interfaces.

Unit Test – A detailed test of a subsystem. Functional unit tests determine if a module is within the capabilities of the design. Structural unit tests (white box) determine of a module is correctly coded.

Verilog – A hardware description language

VHDL – VHSIC (Very High-Speed IC) Hardware Description Language

VPM – Virtual Processor Model

2006-01-0169

Custom Real-Time Interface Blockset Development in Matlab/Simulink for On-Target Rapid Prototyping

Oguz H. Dagci and Alan W. Brown
General Motors Corporation

ABSTRACT

In GM R&D Powertrain/Engine Control Group, rapid prototyping controller (RPC) systems with Matlab/Simulink are used extensively to design, simulate and implement advanced engine control algorithms and models. However, those RPC systems use powerful microprocessors with large amounts of RAM contrary to engine control modules (ECM) in production vehicles. Therefore, a thorough analysis on the comparatively much more complicated algorithms and models cannot be performed during the research stage, since there are not enough tools to enable the smooth transition from Matlab/Simulink to the production type processor. The Real-Time Interface (RTI) Blockset for a production like microprocessor would close the transition gap between rapid prototyping controller systems and production type microprocessors by leveraging the power and popularity of Matlab/Simulink in control engineering world and automatic code generation tools. Therefore, RTI Blockset with different customized functionalities for a production like microcontroller is developed in Matlab/Simulink in order to facilitate on-target rapid prototyping. Moreover, an engine control algorithm, which was developed before on a production like microcontroller via handwritten C-code is implemented on the same hardware using Matlab/Simulink Embedded Coder and the aforementioned RTI Blockset.

INTRODUCTION

In the last 10 years, with the advent of powerful and affordable microprocessors, rapid prototyping controllers have found wide usage in many disciplines especially in control engineering area. The reason why it is called rapid prototyping is the seamless transition from simulation to implementation. The automatic code generation tools integrated with simulation tools including peripheral configuration tools have driven the development of rapid prototyping controllers. Although rapid prototyping controller systems decreased the difficulty level of transitioning from design and simulation to implementation, it did not bring a thorough solution how to migrate the newly designed algorithm into the production hardware. The reason of this vacancy was the inefficiency of automatic code generation tools that necessitate hand written code for production after rapid prototyping stage. Moreover, because of this inefficiency, very powerful microprocessors that do not resemble production systems in terms of speed and capacity are utilized in rapid prototyping controllers.

In recent years, in addition to rapid prototyping controllers, there are interesting advancements in automatic code generation, where the quality of automatically generated code comes closer to the quality of hand written code in terms of code size and efficiency. It brings new revolutionary methods in software development since the standard V-chart in software development can be changed into a much less steep V chart or even straight line, which can cause considerable efficiency increases in software development processes. Many automotive OEMs and suppliers support these developments and adapt into their own processes. However, in these efforts, generally only some portion of software is generated automatically and then that code is migrated to the rest of software manually, which is not an efficient process and may lead to errors due to human intervention. This paper explains the efforts to combine the merits of rapid prototyping controller systems and efficient automatic code generation tools. The real time interface (RTI) blockset for a production microprocessor is developed in Matlab/Simulink that will be the bridge between control algorithms designed in Simulink and production like controller hardware. In order to test that blockset and show its functionality, we converted a previously designed controller algorithm for a V-8 engine in plain C code into a single Simulink model for full-pass on-target prototyping.

HARDWARE SELECTION

The hardware platform, for which blockset has been designed is Freescale MPC565, since this is one of the microcontrollers used in current production cars. Moreover, we have been using development boards with that type of microcontrollers for our other projects.

SOFTWARE ARCHITECTURE

To explain the necessary software architecture, the process to facilitate efficient full-automatic code generation should be presented first. As seen in Figure 1, the first step in full-automatic code generation is to develop a template make file, skeleton main C code and main tlc file. Main tlc file is the file, which Simulink Real Time Workshop/Embedded Coder (code generation machine of Simulink) looks for to learn how to generate code from Simulink blocks. That file tells whether the generated code will be in C or Ada format, which libraries are going to be used in code generation and which optimizations are going to be applied. It can be considered a guide, who tells the code generator what to do and where to branch. Main C file is the file that holds the main routine, which is a must in C applications. That file is independent from Simulink model names such that every Simulink model can use that file as its main code. It can hold the initialization routines, scheduling and background processes. Template make file is a specific file that directs the compiler and linker how to generate and upload the executable code. It is a generic file and during compile process, Simulink fills the necessary places in that file such as the name of the Simulink model from which code is generated.

The second layer in Figure 1 is related to the real-time interface blocks in the Simulink model, which provide an interface to processor peripheral control. These blocks are the vital ones to merge application model with the driver code of real hardware. In the next section, they are going to be explained in detail.

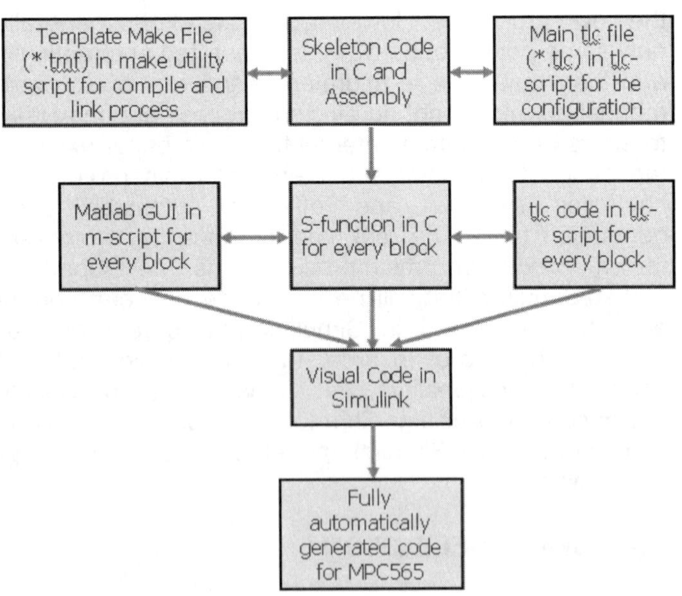

Figure 1. The development process of full automatic code generation

During code generation, Simulink Real Time Workshop/Embedded Coder takes the files in the first layer in Figure 1 as base files and then create C code from the Simulink native blocks, S-functions and the real-time interface blockset. Finally, it compiles the generated source codes based on the directions in template make file and if directed, uploads the executable to the target hardware.

The application specific content of the three files in the first layer of Figure 1 is summarized below. As mentioned before, these files are created to generate an executable file for a hardware target with Freescale MPC565 processor.

MAIN TLC CODE (*.TLC)

Using main tlc code, we added an extra pane to the RTW code generation options for the user. It asks to the user about which serial COM port and at which baud rate that port will be used to upload the executable file. Moreover, since we have been using different versions of MPC565 development boards, some of which have different types of RAMs, we put a user option to select different RAM types. All of these specific options are passed to makefile for compiling, linking and uploading tasks. We included our custom tlc files to the main tlc in order to execute them at the end of code generation process. They were crucial since these tlc files use the global information (selected options, number of setup blocks etc.) about the blocks used in the model and creates the necessary C structures. These C structures hold the initial configuration data for the microcontroller peripherals during boot up process.

MAIN C CODE TEMPLATE (*.C)

The purpose of the main C-Code template file is to provide an interface between the Matlab Simulink runtime environment and the MPC565 hardware resources during startup and runtime. In our case the file is “cmd565_ert_main.c”.

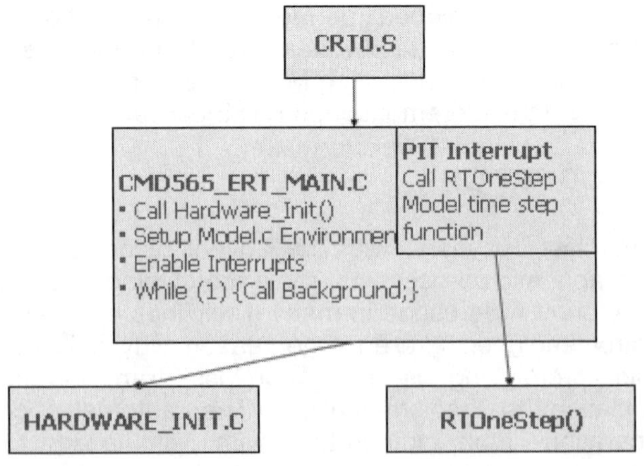

Figure 2. Main C Code Template

The code in file “cmd565_ert_main.c” is executed after the assembly code in file “crt0.S”, which is the low-level

C-runtime environment setup. “crt0.S” file’s task is to perform a basic set of board initializations such as stack allocation, memory chip selects, global variable initialization, eabi (Embedded Application Binary Interface) environment initialization for proper C-code execution.

After “crt0.S” is finished, it calls “cmd565_ert_main.c”, which then calls “Hardware_Init.c”. “Hardware_Init.c” is used to setup the MPC565 hardware I/O modules such as TPUs (Time Processor Units), MIOS14 (Multiple Input Output Submodule), CAN Controllers (Controller Area Network), QADC’s (Queued Analog to Digital Converters), PIT (Periodic Interrupt Timer – used by the Matlab Simulink Timer Scheduler), Interrupt Controller, SCI (Serial Communications Interface) and other specific MPC565 controller settings for the Matlab Simulink Model. This configuration is determined by the options selected via RTI blockset in Simulink model or by the default values if not used in the model or not desired to be used in the model.

During Simulink model execution for each time step, the PIT (Periodic Interrupt Timer) interrupt service routine calls “RTOneStep()” function, which is the Simulink model task scheduler. This is called at the smallest model time step. The scheduler in “RTOneStep()” takes care of scheduling other model tasks that may have different execution rates, which should be integer multiples of the smallest time step.

TEMPLATE MAKE FILE (*.TMF)

The template makefile is a compiler specific file used during final model build process. After converting the desired Matlab Simulink model to C-code, the makefile is invoked to compile, link and then download the executable to the MPC565 target.

The makefile also builds all the necessary C-support files, builds all required real-time function support libraries needed by the model, compiles all custom TPU microcode for TPU blocks mentioned later in this report and any other application specific files. There in affect will exist a unique template makefile for a given desired target board.

REAL-TIME INTERFACE BLOCKSET FOR MPC565

The RTI Blockset establishes the connection between application Simulink model and low-level driver code written in C and assembly. With the help of that blockset, the control engineer does not need to know the details how to program the target processor, since it is done automatically in the background based on options dictated by the user through graphical user interface (GUI).

That RTI blockset for MPC565 is developed in three steps. The first step is to write an S-function for each peripheral that needs to be configured. One S-function for each custom-made Simulink model is required due to the way Simulink is designed in order to perform simulations and pass user input during code generation. The second step is to design a GUI and to write an m-file for that GUI that processes the user input, saves it and transfers it to the S-function. Third step is to create a Target Language Compiler (tlc) file, which has the same name as the S-function name. That tlc file directs Real-Time Workshop how to create code from that Simulink model. It consists of tlc code (a special language) and peripheral control (driver) code in assembly or C. Based on the user inputs entered through GUI and directions in tlc code, the file that is going to be compiled and linked has been created at the end of tlc file. In fact, the entire process is much more complicated. The interested reader is referred to read [1].

Furthermore, we did not create blocks for every single peripheral in MPC565. For the ones we designed, we tried to keep them as flexible as possible without increasing the complexity of GUIs such that control engineers are not required to learn the intricacies of the MPC565 to implement their algorithms.

DIGITAL INPUT/OUTPUT BLOCKS

MPC565 has Modular Input/Output System (MIOS14) to handle digital input and outputs. That peripheral is used for digital input/output signal processing such as digital signal toggling, PWM signal generation and pulse and period measurements. We didn’t create any block to program pulse and period measurement tasks, since we use Time Processing Units (TPU) of MPC565 for these tasks in our software architecture.

DIGITAL INPUT/OUTPUT SETUP BLOCK

MIOS14 channels of MPC565 can be programmed as either digital input or digital output. Figure 3 shows digital input/output setup block used to interface application Simulink model with the target hardware. When the user double clicks on that block, digital input/output configuration GUI pops up. That GUI offers the user to assign input or output characteristics to each of the 16 digital channels. Moreover, the user can determine what the initial condition will be, if that channel is assigned to be an output channel. After the user configures that GUI and pushes OK button, the m-file running behind that GUI takes these selections and puts them into an array form to the parameter section of S-function. As a reminder, we have created an S-function for each RTI block in order to do simulation and to interface it to automatic code generation process. If the user pushes Cancel button, all the modifications are ignored and the configuration before block was double clicked is restored.

As seen in Figure 3, some channels are grayed out. The reason is to prevent the user to change the direction configuration of these channels, if they are used in the rest of the model. Before GUI is shown to the user, the background m-file searches the entire model to find any assignment to these 16 channels. If it finds any previously assigned channel, then it deactivates them. It is a kind of protection against user errors. Moreover, digital input/output setup block can be put in a Simulink model just once, since configuration of the system can be done once in our architecture. If two S-functions are put, our software creates an error message during automatic code generation and abandons code generation process.

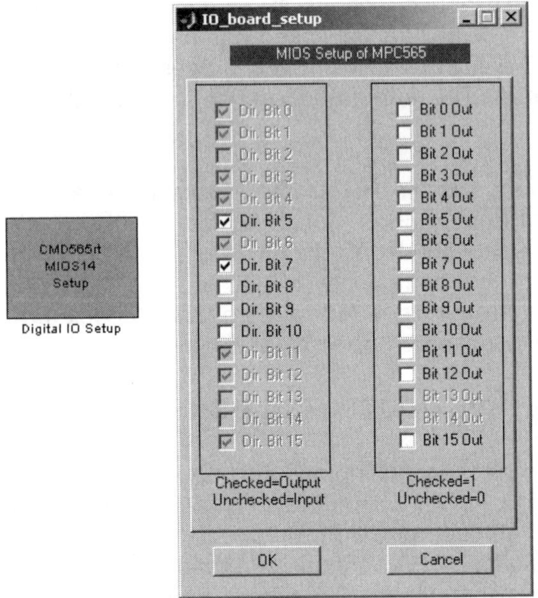

Figure 3: Digital Input/Output Setup Block for MPC565

DIGITAL OUTPUT BLOCK

Digital Output Block is used to connect signals coming from application layer to the MIOS peripheral of MPC565 such that values are converted to the real signals on the target hardware. The channels that are grayed out are either the channels that are not configured as outputs or the ones that are used at another place of the model. Two push buttons at the upper section of GUI are tabs to switch the appearance of GUI from the first set of 8 channels (Ch0-Ch7) to the second set of 8 channels (Ch7-Ch15). This configuration facilitates to put more information into the limited area of GUI.

The user can establish hysteresis logic by entering different numbers to Upper Threshold and Lower Threshold fields. If the number entered into these fields is a number without a fractional digit such as 2, 3, the code generated for the corresponding channel will have integer number comparison. If the number in that field has fractional digit such as 2.5, 2.0, then the code that will be generated will have single precision comparison. This convention gives the user the opportunity to select integer or floating-point code generation options for performance reasons. OK and Cancel buttons operate in the same way that Digital Input/Output Setup Block works.

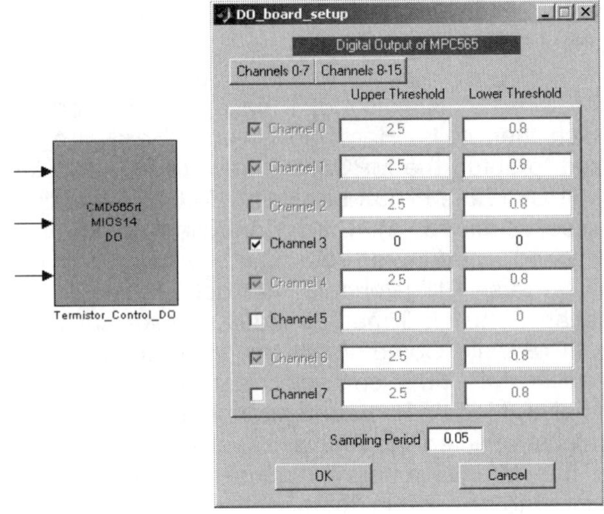

Figure 4: Digital Output Configuration Block

DIGITAL INPUT BLOCK

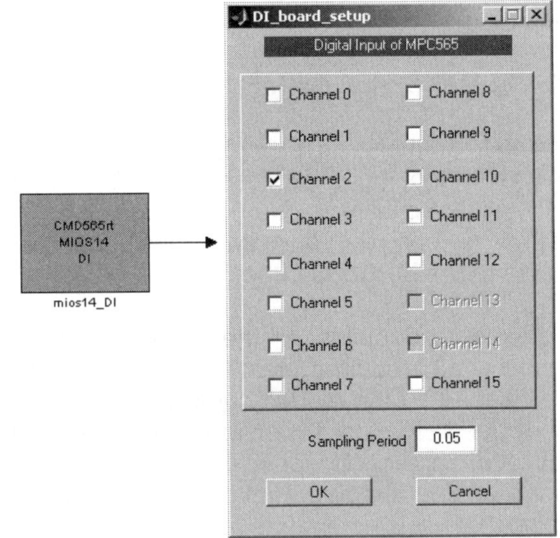

Figure 5: Digital Input Configuration Block

Digital Input Block is similar to Digital Output Block. The user selects which channels he/she wants to sample at which rate. Since MPC565 MIOS peripheral does not have hysteresis logic for the external digital signals, we did not put hysteresis configuration fields in digital input GUI. The channels 13 and 14 are grayed out as seen in Figure 5 and cannot be sampled, since these two channels are multiplexed in MPC565 to its CAN C unit's transmission and reception signal lines. Furthermore, contrary to digital output block, a digital input channel can be sampled many times at the different places of Simulink model, since that block is just a reading not a driver block.

PWM GENERATION BLOCK

PWM Setup Block is used to generate PWM signals out of MIOS peripheral of MPC565. As seen in Figure 6, there are total 8 channels reserved for PWM signal generation. Variable Frequency checkbox if checked creates an extra input for that channel at the input port of PWM S-function. That option provides PWM signal with varying frequency (frequency modulation). Frequency Field is valid in order to determine the frequency of PWM signal if Variable Frequency Checkbox is unchecked. Max. Frequency and Min. Frequency Fields are active if Variable Frequency checkbox is checked in order to limit the frequency input to the PWM S-function. The number in Initial Duty Cycle Field determines what the duty cycle of a PWM signal will be during start-up. Binary Bit Position determines what kind of code is generated and what kind of data types at the input port of PWM S-function is expected. If binary bit position is 0, PWM S-function expects 32-bit single precision floating point number. If binary bit position is different than 0, PWM S-function expects an integer number, whose radix point is the same as the number entered to that field. As a result, it gives the user the option of creating floating point or pure integer number code.

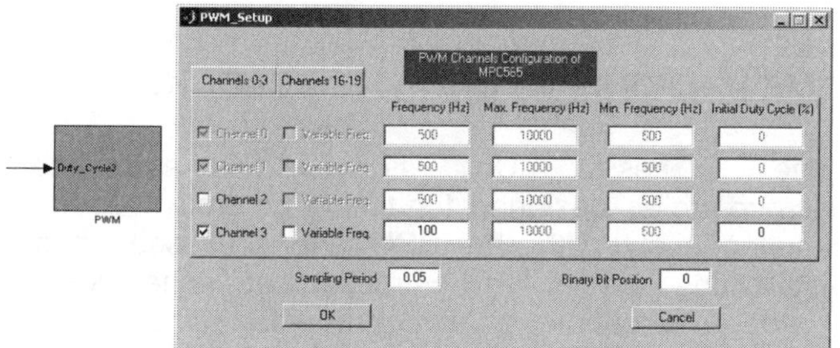

Figure 6: PWM Configuration Block

PWM Submodule of MPC565 has one common timer for all PWM channels and one separate timer for each PWM channel cascaded to that common timer. We developed an optimization algorithm in tlc code of PWM S-function that takes the frequency, max and min frequencies of each PWM channel and finds the optimum clock prescalers for each PWM channel such that the resolution of duty cycle step sizes for each channel is maximized. In that algorithm, first the prescaler value of common timer is optimized based on the numbers in frequency fields of PWM GUI. Then the prescaler value of each PWM channel's timer is calculated based on the determined prescaler value of common timer.

ANALOG-TO-DIGITAL CONVERTER BLOCKS

MPC565 has two queued analog-to-digital converter (QADC) modules that are 10-bit, unipolar, successive approximation converters with analog multiplexers. These modules are configured such that each module can access all 40 of the analog inputs.

QADCE SETUP BLOCK

QADCE Setup Block is for the configuration of analog-to-digital converter. Since there are two available modules in QADCE, the user can put at most two of these into Simulink model. If Module A is selected in one block, in the other block, Module A radio button is deactivated so that the same QADCE module is not configured in two separate blocks by mistake. Two queues can be established in each module, where the first queue has precedence over the second queue. Although different sampling modes can be set to each queue, we eliminated some sampling modes to be assigned in order to decrease the complexity of QADCE programming. As a result, the first queue has external triggered sampling and the second queue has two options, either external triggered sampling or continuous sampling. The radio buttons in QADCE Setup GUI assigns which pin is going to be used to feed external trigger signal. Queue Size field determines how big the size of sum of queue 1 and queue 2 will be. The next field called Start Queue for Queue 2 is to set where Queue 2 starts. That number should be less than queue size, if the user wants to setup a queue 2. If it is greater than queue size, there will be no queue 2 in QADCE. QADCE has an internal timer that determines sample-hold and conversion time. If the signal source that we want to measure has high impedance, we may have to sample and hold that signal longer in order to have enough time to charge the sampling capacitor in QADCE. In this case, clock prescaler should be set to a large number (max is 128). If we have a signal that has fast transient, then we may have to set clock prescaler to a small number (min is 2) in order not to miss any high frequency data. We have displays in GUI that show based on clock prescaler how many microseconds hold time would be. A checkbox is to set sampling mode of Queue 2. If that checkbox is selected, Queue 2 becomes in continuous scan mode where the channels in Queue 2 are sampled one by one without interruption. Rising Edge and Falling Edge radio buttons are to determine at which event the sampling is going to be performed if external triggered sampling mode is selected. There are four tabs to fit all queues total of 64. For each queue, there are two options. The first option is whether sampling is going to be paused until next trigger. The other option is whether hold time will be 2 QADCE clock periods or 16 QADCE clock periods. There is also complicated verification software in that GUI running at background that checks the consistency of selections done by the user. If it detects an inconsistency, the GUI gives an error message and returns to the state before that inconsistent selection was done.

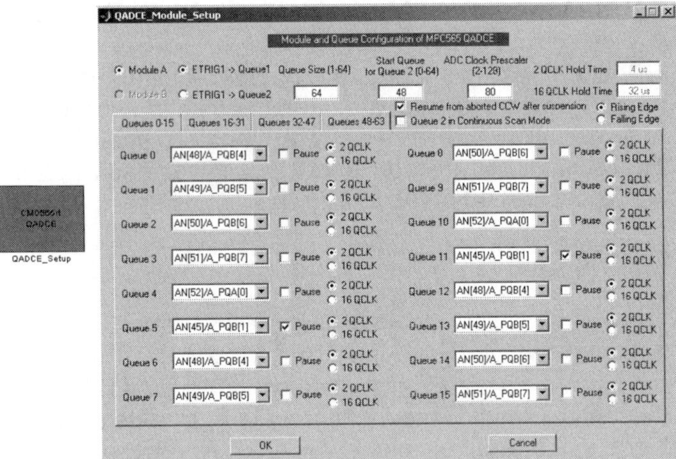

Figure 7: QADCE Configuration Block

QADCE RESULT READ BLOCK

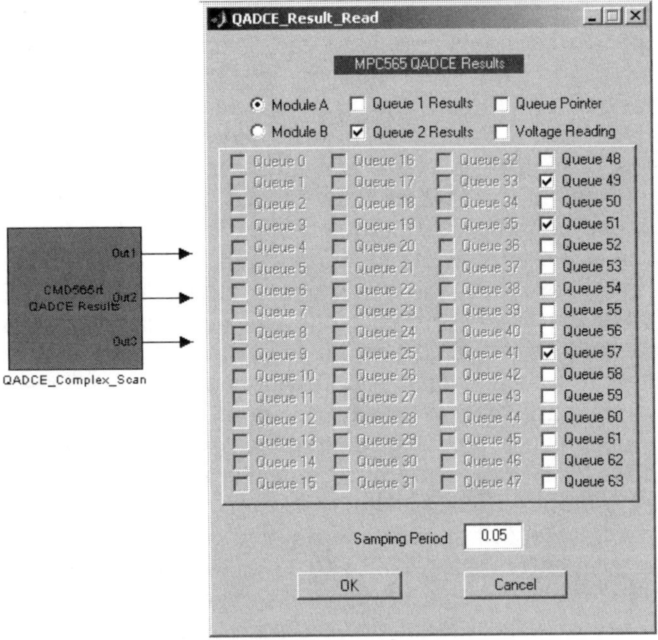

Figure 8: QADCE Result Read Block

QADCE Result Read Block is used to read the conversion results. The user selects the module and the queue. The code running at background enables the channels assigned to those module and queue. The user can also read the queue pointer, showing at which queue the analog-to-digital conversion takes place. If voltage reading is checked, the output of this block is the scaled value between 0 and 5V in single precision floating point format. If unchecked, the output of the block is raw data between 0 and 1023 counts in integer number format.

QADCE INTERRUPT BLOCK

QADCE Interrupt Block creates a function call signal at its output. The subsystem that is connected to that block becomes an interrupt service routine in the automatically generated code structure. The prospective events that will cause interrupts are End of Queue1, End of Queue2 and Pause events. The user can choose in GUI, which event he wants to create interrupt. In MPC565, there are 48 interrupt levels in total, where the smaller number has higher priority. The user assigns a priority to each interrupt for preemptive scheduling designed in software architecture. If the user chooses an interrupt level that has been chosen at another place of Simulink model, after OK push button is clicked, an error is generated explaining its reason.

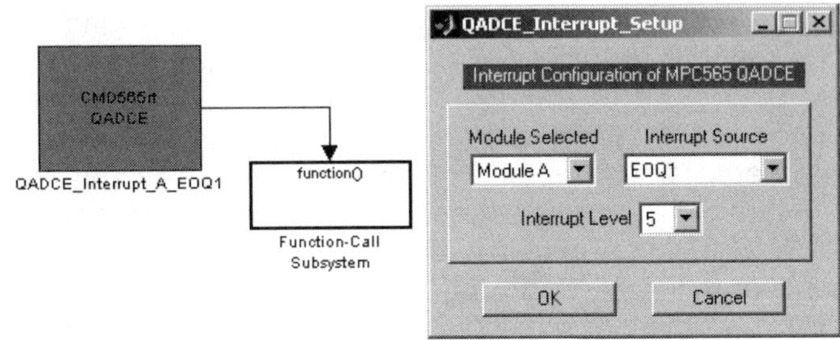

Figure 9: QADCE Interrupt Generation Block

TIME PROCESSOR UNIT (TPU) BLOCKS

Time Processor Unit is a semi-autonomous microcontroller designed for timing control. It operates simultaneously with the CPU and processes micro-instructions (special TPU instruction set), schedules and processes real-time hardware events, performs input and output operations and accesses shared data without CPU intervention. It can also create CPU interrupt or CPU can call TPU functions. As a result, CPU setup and service times are minimized or eliminated for timer related tasks. MPC565 contains three independent TPU's [2].

TPU CONFIGURATION BLOCK

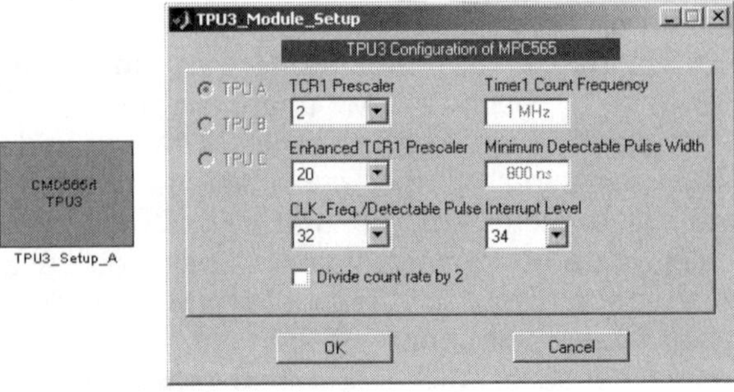

Figure 10: TPU Configuration Block

Since MPC565 has three TPU's, there are three radio buttons in GUI to select TPU. Since it is a configuration block, one block for each TPU is required. If the user puts a second configuration block, the radio button in the second block's GUI for the module that is selected in the first configuration block is disabled to prevent to check the same TPU in two different blocks. There are two drop-down boxes to adjust the frequency of the timer in TPU. A display shows the calculated frequency of TPU timer. The other option is to choose the minimum detectable pulse width in order to filter out spikes on the signals entering TPU channels. Moreover, interrupt level for the interrupts created by TPU is chosen in this GUI among 48 levels. As in QADCE Interrupt Block, the code running in the background checks the rest of the Simulink model whether there is a conflict of interrupt levels.

24X ENCODER SETUP BLOCK

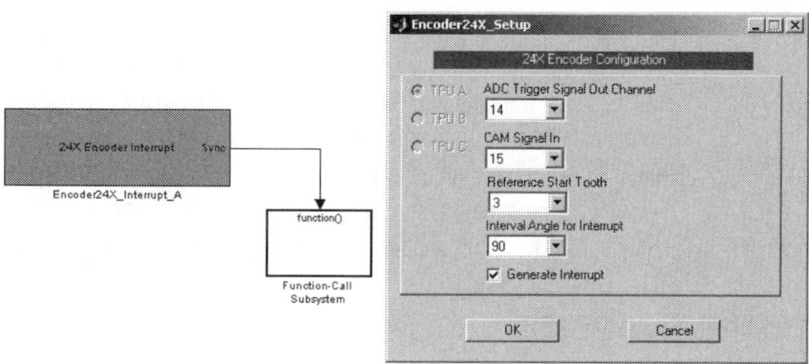

Figure 11: 24X Encoder Setup

24X Encoder Setup Block is used to resolve 24X encoder crank and CAM signals. If this block exists in Simulink model during code generation, TPU microcode is compiled and placed to the memory area reserved to TPU code in MPC565. Crank signal should be fed always to Channel 0 of the selected TPU. The channel for the CAM signal is determined by the user via a drop-down box. 24X Encoder code also generates a signal at the desired channel to trigger analog-to-digital conversion. Moreover, there is an interrupt generation option. If Generate Interrupt checkbox is checked, the 24X Encoder Block establishes a function-call output port that is going to be connected to the interrupt subroutine. The interrupt event is generated at user defined crank angles, which can be entered in a drop-down box, labeled Interval Angle for Interrupt in GUI. During TPU channel assignment, the code at background checks whether any channel is allocated to more than one signal in the entire Simulink mode. If it is, then the code generates an error message and does not allow the user to make that mistake.

24X ENCODER RESULT READ BLOCK

Since 24X Encoder TPU code resolves crank and CAM signals, 24X Encoder Result Read Block converts TPU timer readings into desired outputs. The major items that can be read are average and instantaneous rpm, crank position, synchronization state (sync or out-of-sync). Instantaneous period is the time passed between two consecutive teeth of the 24X encoder. Average 24X period is calculated between two consecutive crank angles defined by the user in the drop down box mentioned earlier. Here the sum of all encoder periods between teeth are summed then divided by the number of teeth encountered between the two crank angles. The granularity of the crank angles is 15deg.

Based on the number of selected parameters to be measured, the code running behind GUI creates output ports with the corresponding labels and data types.

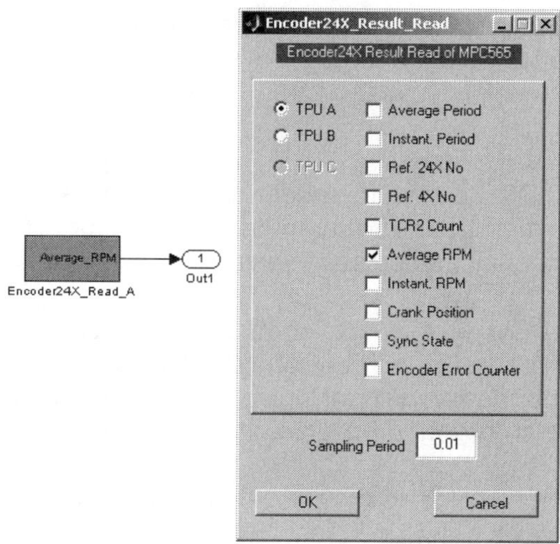

Figure 12: 24X Encoder Result Read Block

FUEL COMMAND BLOCK

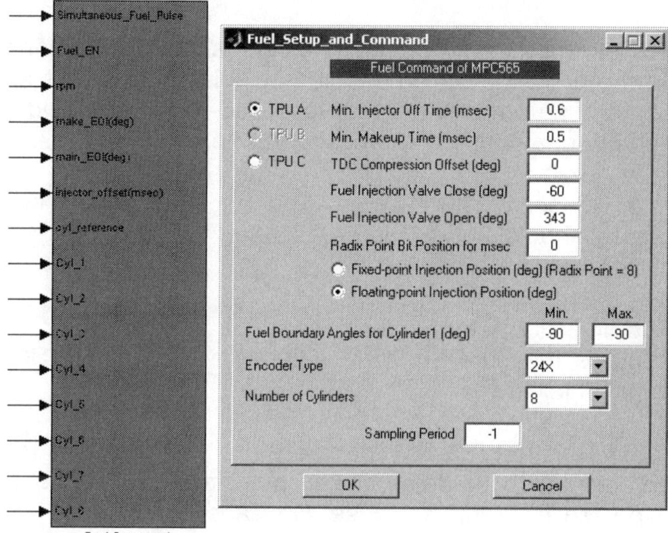

Figure 13: Fuel Command Block

Fuel Command and Spark Command Blocks are the most complex ones in terms of algorithm implementation in C and TPU microcode due to the extensive interaction between TPU, CPU and other parameters. Fuel Command Block takes the following parameters and measurements as inputs:

Simultaneous Fuel Pulse: During start up, simultaneous fuel pulsing may be necessary for an easy start by wetting the manifold walls with fuel.

Fuel EN: It is just to stop or start fueling.

rpm: rpm should come from 24X Encoder Result Read Block in rev/min.

make EOI and main EOI: Fuel is injected in two pulses, make and main for better drivability. These inputs are end of injection angles in deg from Cylinder 1 top dead center.

Injector Offset: Injector offset in msec is the minimum pulse width needed to open the fuel injector. This value is added to all fuel pulses injected (i.e. main, makeup).

Cyl_1 – Cyl_x: It is the width of fuel pulse in msec. x refers here to the number of cylinders since the number of input ports for cylinder pulse width changes based on the user selection in Fuel Command GUI.

The data fields in Fuel Command GUI can be summarized below:

Min. Injector Off Time: The amount of time that the injector must stay off after a fuel pulse is completed.

Min. Makeup Time: The minimum allowable difference between the desired fuel pulse width and the sum of all injected pulses in the current engine cycle before another fuel pulse is injected.

TDC Compression Offset: A fudge factor used to fine tune the global placement of fuel pulses such that an angle of zero coincides with top-dead-center of cylinder number one during compression stroke.

Fuel Injection Valve Close: The angle at which fuel pulses should not be delivered after during an engine cycle.

Fuel Injection Valve Open: The angle at which the SOI angle is measured from to determine the earliest SOI angle of injection.

Radix Point Bit Position for msec: This edit box uses the entered value to determine what kind of data type is expected from injector offset time and fuel pulse width input ports. If that value is 0, it means that single precision floating point data is expected for those inputs. If it is different than 0, it means that those inputs should be integer numbers, whose radix point starts from the bit position entered in this edit field. The purpose of doing such an arrangement is to be able to use fuel command block in both integer and floating point code generation.

There are also two radio buttons to determine whether integer numbers with radix point or floating point numbers are going to be used in the representation of position information (deg).

Fuel Boundary Angles for Cylinder 1: These angles make up the fuel injection window that all fuel pulses for a particular engine cycle must lye within.

Encoder Type: In order to be able to reuse this fuel command block with other types of crank signals, we added that option into GUI.

Number of Cylinders: Based on the number of cylinders in this drop down box, the number of input ports of Fuel Command Block is changed.

Furthermore, since each Fuel Block reserves one of the TPUs in MPC565 for its operation, in a Simulink model, Fuel Command Block cannot be assigned to the same TPU, which is used by a Spark Command Block or another Fuel Command Block. To prevent that kind of conflict, the GUI software running at background prevents the user to make such an unintentional mistake in a proactive manner.

SPARK COMMAND BLOCK

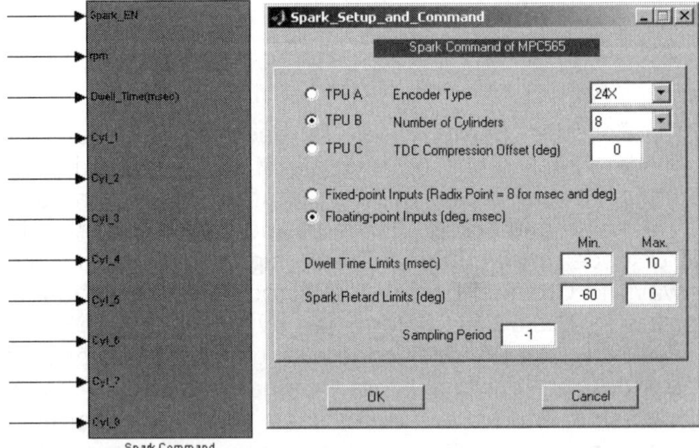

Figure 14: Spark Command Block

Spark Command Block is very similar to Fuel Command in terms of the items in GUI. Encoder Type, Number of Cylinders, TDC Compression Offset, Fixed or Floating Point Inputs serve the same purpose as those data fields in Fuel Command GUI. Additionally, there is a dwell time limit field to restrict dwell time input values and spark retard limit field to define a spark window.

FREQUENCY/PERIOD MEASUREMENT BLOCK

Frequency/Period Measurement Block is another TPU application to measure period or frequency of a digital signal without CPU intervention. Whether period or frequency is measured is determined in GUI. The user can select which TPU performs period/frequency measurement on which channel. The user can assign one of the three priorities (high, medium, low) to that task for preemptive scheduling if there are other TPU channels running in the same TPU. Moreover, measurement can be done based on rising or falling edge of the signal. The measured data can be in either single precision floating point number or integer number with a radix point.

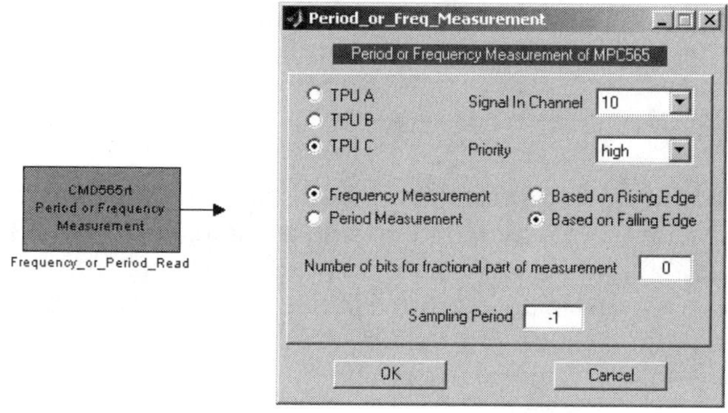

Figure 15: Frequency/Period Measurement Block

CONTROLLER AREA NETWORK (CAN) BLOCKS

CAN SETUP BLOCK

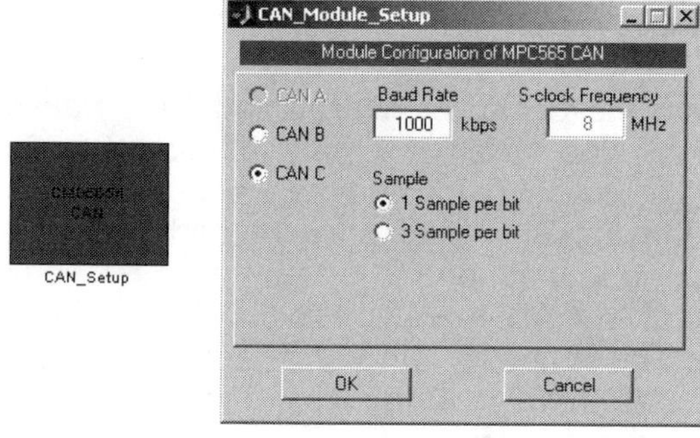

Figure 16: CAN Setup Block

CAN Setup Block is for the configuration of three CAN modules in MPC565. Since there are three available modules, the user can put at most three of these into a Simulink model. If CAN A is selected in one block, in the other block, CAN A radio button is deactivated so that the same CAN module is not configured in two separate blocks by mistake. The user can set the baud rate for each CAN. Not every baud rate is acceptable since CAN can be configured in a number of ways. Based on baud rate, the code running in the background calculates S-clock frequency, which is an internal clock in CAN module. One of the 1 sample per bit or 3 samples per bit options can be chosen by the user, where these two bit sampling methods are defined in CAN 2.0 protocol [3].

CAN TRANSMIT AND RECEIVE BLOCKS

CAN Transmit and Receive Blocks are almost the same. The only difference is input and output ports. Therefore, they are going to be explained in this subsection together. Each CAN Transmit/Receive Block corresponds to one CAN message with a unique ID and Mailbox number. These values are assigned in their GUIs as seen in Figure 17. If the same Message ID or Mailbox number is given in two separate blocks, error message during code generation with the explanation of the reason stops the process. Message Length Field determines the size of the message in terms of bytes. If message length is set to 2 Bytes, then the user has to populate message screen with the signals, whose length adds up to 2 Bytes. If not, during code generation and error message is given. The message frame can be either in standard or extended format, which are explained in [2]. The lower part of CAN Transmit/Receive Block GUI is for signal definitions. For every signal that is added on the signal list, the GUI program creates an input/output port. The user should define the signal length, its start bit in CAN message frame and its data type. Because integer numbers are sent via CAN messages, if a floating number is required to be transmitted, then the necessary scaling and offsetting may be needed. Factor and Offset Edit Fields play that role in the GUI. After the message structure is established with the signals, the user can change them anytime with Add, Modify, Clear and Delete buttons. When OK button is pressed, the number of input/output ports is adjusted according to the new message structure. During code generation, tlc code of that block calls specific data manipulation functions to fit the raw signals into the desired positions of the message.

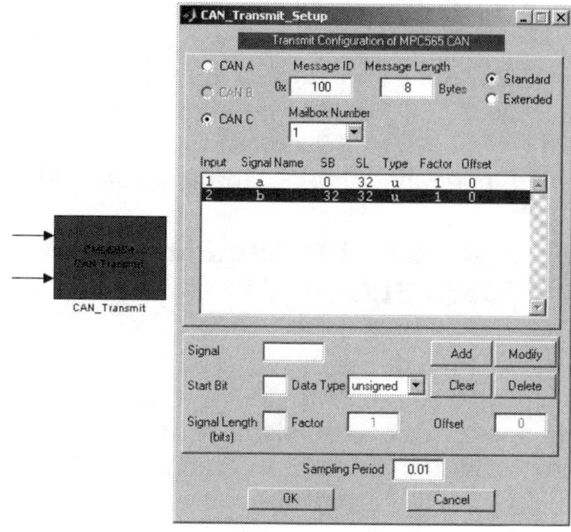

Figure 17: CAN Transmit Block

TASK EXECUTION TIME MEASUREMENT BLOCK

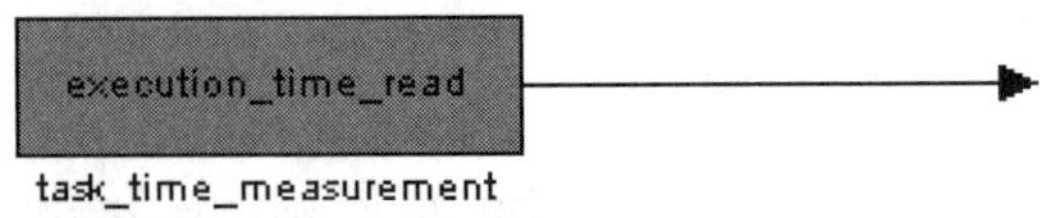

Figure 18: Task Execution Time Measurement Block

Task execution time measurement block is necessary in order to evaluate how much all or some portion of the code takes to be executed by MPC565 processor. It can measure task execution times of different timer tasks, function call subsystems, atomic subsystems, triggered and enabled subsystems.

Different from other blocks, execution time measurement block does not have any GUI since the user does not need to configure it other than sampling period.

When the user wants to measure task execution time of a subsystem, he/she should insert that block inside that subsystem with an inherited sampling period (-1). To measure execution time of a timer task, the user should put that block with the sampling period of that timer task.

The Task execution time measurement block places software hooks at the beginning and at the end of the code that is generated from a subsystem. The software hook at the beginning of the code reads a free running 32-bit timer value with 1μsec resolution. The hook at the end reads the same timer again and subtracts the first reading from the last reading to calculate execution time. The overhead of these hooks to the existing software is timer reading in assembly and integer math subtraction, which is a minor operation. The picture gets complicated for complex Simulink models with different timer tasks. The code generator machine of RTW divides the code of a timer task into different pieces and scatters them to some places between different timer task codes. To solve that problem, we added some intelligence to our code such that it understands whether the code is divided and scattered. If is so, the manipulation of timer readings is different and we add up the execution times of each piece of a scattered timer task to the accumulated value. At the end of the last piece of code, we calculate execution time for that specific task.

ENGINE CONTROLLER IMPLEMENTATION USING MPC565 BLOCKSET

Although we tested the functionality of each blockset individually with stimulating inputs, it was not enough to verify its operation and to demonstrate its capabilities. Therefore, we implemented an engine control algorithm in Simulink using Simulink native blocks and our blockset. That engine control algorithm had been implemented on MPC565 before with fully hand-written C-code. We can divide that implementation into three steps:

ADDITIONAL BLOCKS

In order to increase the efficiency of the automatic code generation, we had to create our own functional blocks for specific tasks. The blocks we first created were lookup tables. This gave us the opportunity to implement our own index search and interpolation algorithms in the automatic generated code. Moreover, in our control algorithm, there were state machines such as engine mode control or fuel state control that are written very efficiently by hand before. Therefore, we wanted to keep them in our automatic code. We created blocks with the necessary input and output ports for these algorithms that put hand-written C-code into the rest of the software during code generation.

SOFTWARE IMPLEMENTATION

In software implementation, we bring together each task of control algorithm into a single Simulink model. The algorithms are constructed using Simulink native blocks, our custom blocks for table lookups and state machine algorithms. Since our custom blocks are designed to be able to be operated in both simulation and code generation processes, we could verify the functionality of control algorithms offline except low-level actuator control. We gave test signals to the overall model and observed outputs for any anomaly. This eased our debugging stage significantly.

HARDWARE IMPLEMENTATION AND FINAL TESTING

We tested the final engine control model both on an engine dynamometer and vehicle. Since MPC565 boards were wired to these engines in the test benches before, it was easy to port our algorithms through our blockset to the hardware system.

To debug the controller, we utilized CAN transmit and receive blocks, which are part of our MPC565 block library. The critical outputs in the model are connected to CAN Transmit Blocks to observe and the parameters and command that need to be controlled by the user are connected to CAN Receive Blocks. As the interface to resolve and transmit CAN messages, we used the existing dSPACE Autoboxes, which were rapid prototyping hardware and software tools for advanced control algorithm implementations for those engines. As a result, without adding any extra hardware by just using existing components, we implemented and debugged a fully automatic generated engine control algorithm code on a production-like processor seamlessly.

CONCLUSION

The development of a hardware interface blockset for a production type microcontroller is a critical step to enable full automatic code generation, since it closes the gab between controller algorithm and actual hardware.

In this paper, we explained our first attempt to achieve the design of such a blockset and we showed two sample applications that tested and utilized the blockset for the realization of full automatic code generation.

REFERENCES

1. Real-Time Workshop User's Guide for Use with Simulink, The MathWorks, Inc.
2. MPC565/566 Reference Manual, Freescale Semiconductor, Inc.
3. CAN Specification Version 2.0, Robert Bosch GmbH.

2005-01-3690

Silicon Technology Enables the Modern Vehicle Systems

Ronald W. Stence
Freescale Semiconductor, Inc.

ABSTRACT

Embedded processors are incorporated into almost every type of electronic device. The automobile is no exception where the expectations for new features; system performance and increased reliability are increasing rapidly. Advances in engine technology and the eventual "Green Machines" will require new approaches to solving many of the current technology barriers of today. Semiconductors will play an increasing role in breaking through many of the electrical challenges with higher voltage power semiconductors, new memory technologies, increased performance of the embedded processor and improvements in timing control functions.

New semiconductor technologies will enable exciting opportunities toward solving existing technical barriers within the automotive electronics industry. Microcontroller's now contain over 30 million transistors and will push beyond 60 million transistors in 2008. As the system integration increases in the next few years, new techniques will be required to bring the semiconductor's full capabilities to increasingly complex systems.

The roadmap for the silicon industry will have an ever increasing impact on the automotive industry's ability to respond to current safety, technology and environmental challenges. The silicon industry is responding with new embedded processor architectures as a result of deep sub-micron system-on-a-chip products.

INTRODUCTION

The semiconductor industry has seen phenomenal growth in the area of integration in the past decades. 2005 marks the 40th anniversary of a publication that has since been coined Moore's Law. An example of the impact of applying the semiconductor industry paradigm to everyday life can be demonstrated with an example from the 2005 SIA Annual Report [1]. "In 1978, a commercial flight between New York and Paris cost $900 and took seven hours. If the principles of Moore's Law were applied to the airline industry, that flight would now cost about one penny and take less than a second."

The SIA data shows a roadmap toward 65nano meter for high-performance automotive grade embedded processors by 2010 with 80-90 million transistors. With this increase in integration and shrinking geometries comes lower system voltages, while maintaining or slightly decreasing the power of the embedded processor.

NEW CHALLENGES TO OLD PROBLEMS

The next century is full of new challenges for the automotive engineer. These challenges will require new approaches toward faster time to market, lower cost, higher reliability and an ever increasing number of features, forcing the engineering teams to adapt. In the automotive marketplace, embedded control for engine management has a very complex set of electro-mechanical system requirements. The change in engine management is being brought on by the increasing customer expectations and governmental regulations. Changes in engine technology toward lean burn engines, cam-less engines and electric hybrid vehicles will directly impact the powertrain electronics in the cars of the future. Continuously variable transmissions will likely play an important role in the powertrain

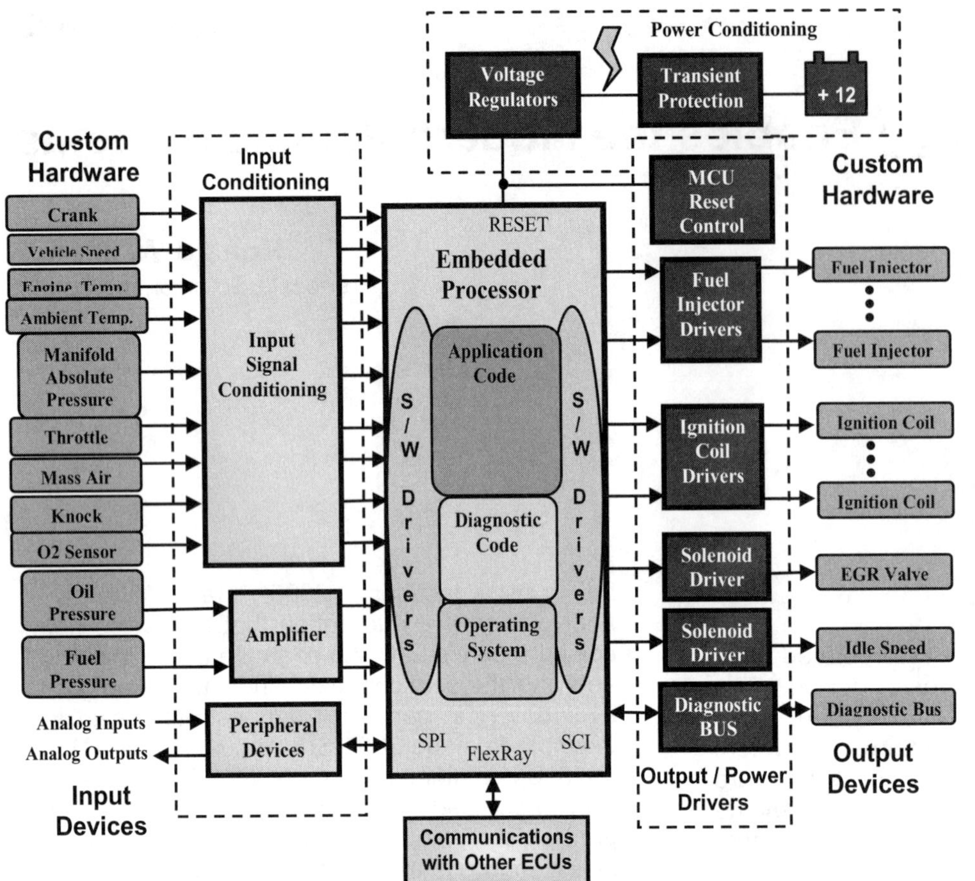

Figure 1: Engine Control Block Diagram

system of the future. New microcontroller techniques and silicon solutions will be a major portion of the advances to make new technologies a reality. The microcontroller selection can be very complex for any embedded design; however, the embedded processor selection for an automobile can be especially difficult. The powertrain embedded processor of today is moving beyond the 16-bit microcontroller to very complex 32-bit RISC microcontrollers. The 32-bit microcontrollers of the next generation will require an increasing amount of S/W written in high level languages. The H/W design is relying on integration and very complex S/W to solve the new problems in engine management.

Figure 1 demonstrates the complex nature of engine management. The block diagram is a typical engine control with multiple inputs and several output devices. The inputs will generate different levels of interrupts or exceptions depending on the impact to the system. The output device may be pulse-width-modulated (PWM), general purpose I/O or timed I/O.

SOFTWARE CONSIDERATIONS

Software has become the key to making the system behave in a particular way. When reusing assembly code that was written for another architecture, care must be taken to avoid architectural dependencies from the original code. This can be very difficult, since the person who wrote the original assembly code may not be on the project. One option is to re-write the algorithm in a higher level language and simulate the system effects on the new architecture. When migrating S/W from one system to another, there are three significant factors that are to often overlooked. The first factor is the microprocessor architecture. When changing from one architecture to another, understanding the microprocessor architecture in great detail is critical. This can be very true for the newer RISC processors, where features such as exception processing may be very different. Second, the compiler can impact many areas of the S/W. A different compiler on the same architecture can make differences in the size of the code and performance of the system by as much as 50%. Also, the change in the compiler can make re-compiling existing code difficult in many cases where there is a great deal of legacy code from several S/W engineers. Third, the system support modules can make dramatic impacts on the system performance and re-use of the original C code. Support modules might be serial communications, pulse-width-modulation (PWM), complex timers (i.e., Time Processor Unit) analog-to-digital (ADC) and digital-to-analog (DAC) converters.

The new engine algorithms of today are written in C or C++ programming languages or with an algorithm based tool. There are several types of high level algorithm based languages that are designed for different types of environments. There are algorithm languages that are designed to solve reactive control types of problems that have a significant number of inputs from real world events. Each of these events must be handled in a predictable amount of time. State diagram based algorithm tools are used to define a series of events that occur in a pre-determined order or sequence. Other algorithm tools can be used to generate efficient C or C++ code for use in production environments.

The requirement for new techniques to achieve better emissions and higher efficiency will drive the need for new approaches through software and hardware. One significant change will likely be in the engine management strategy code. The trend toward more model based algorithms will change the types of data manipulation and instruction mix. This will result in an increasingly difficult computational loading on the microcontroller in order to handle the larger software load. The microcontroller has to support the growing complexity in the engine control environment with more than just a faster processor. Intelligent I/O systems are an integral part of the solution for the future.

The algorithm tools of today have one feature in common: the increased use of floating point based math routines. High level algorithm based tools can generate code without the need for a hardware floating point unit onboard. However, there are a couple of additional things for the S/W engineers to consider when using these tools without a floating point unit on the embedded processor. First, the algorithms generated by these tools tend to generate large and very small numbers, which are more efficient to deal with in a floating point unit. Second, the algorithm based tools will rely on more complex calculations, where checking for boundary conditions on an integer number may become very microprocessor intensive. Third, the S/W engineer implementing the algorithm in a traditional control language like C or C++ can make an implementation error. A common error occurs when a number has been scaled and another program had not accounted for the scaled value, resulting in a computational error that may or may not be detected. Ideally, the original algorithm would be moved directly from the theoretical or R&D laboratory, to the production version of the S/W. This would greatly reduce the possibility that the original strategy is misinterpreted and/or error is incurred when being ported from an algorithm based tools to C or C++.

The need for new techniques to achieve higher efficiency will require new approaches to the software and hardware in embedded microprocessor systems. One significant change will likely be in the generation of engine management strategy code for powertrain applications with algorithm development tools. The trend will be toward using more model-based algorithm strategy code. This will result in an increasingly difficult computational requirement on the microcontroller in order to handle the larger software load. The microcontroller will need to support the growing complexity in the engine control environment with more than just a faster processor. Intelligent I/O systems are becoming a significant part of the solution for future powertrain systems.

DEBUG, CALIBRATION AND RAPID PROTOTYPING

Real time debug is critical when debugging and calibrating electromechanical systems which often cannot tolerate the embedded processor performance being altered or halted for interrogation by a development tool [2,3,4]. Today's systems engineer can take advantage of improvements of development tools that were not possible a few years ago.

The IEEE-ISTO Nexus 5001 Consortium, or Nexus Forum was created to solve the problem of real time data and instruction trace across multiple processor core types. The Nexus Forum released the original specification in 1999 and an update in 2003.

The Nexus 5001 specification includes standard features for setting breakpoints and watchpoints on data and instructions using non-intrusive debug techniques. The specification will deploy several unique features for tracking down the toughest S/W and H/W bugs. Some of these new features include ownership trace messaging, data trace, memory substitution, port replacement, program trace, overrun and error messaging. While many of these features have been deployed on microprocessors over the years, none have implemented all of these and a real time debug interface.

The past decade of calibration and debugging methodology has deployed a "must see every cycle" mindset for debug and calibration powertrain systems. The Nexus 5001 in methodology makes four assumptions about the debugging scenario that frees it from the "must see every cycle" mindset.

1. The source code and object code are available to the development tools. This allows the host based tools to track or make calculations as to the program flow without any direct address or data bus visibility.
2. Only change of flow instructions are required from the target system to the development tool. When the host calibration/debugging tool has access to the object code, proper synchronization can be maintained between the embedded processor and the host tool with just change of flow instruction addresses being transmitted over the debugging interface. The Nexus 5001 specification will send out a synchronization message if a change of flow has not forced a synchronization address within 255 instructions. This would be a rare event since most C compiled programs generally generate a change of flow once every 5 to 10 instructions for embedded processors systems.
3. Only a limited number of the data locations have to be displayed in real time, while most data values can be examined during a halted condition or updated due to a special event. The ability of the Nexus 5001 interface to trace on data values will be new for many engineers. Often this is accomplished with a powerful logic analyzer tracing the address bus and triggering on the data bus writes to a specific memory location. This is a very cumbersome task that is made nearly impossible with the advent of large data caches and system SRAM on-chip.
4. Fourth, if or when an error occurs, the user must be informed by the debugging environment. The Nexus 5001 specification provides for a variable sized FIFO buffer in the transmitter section. If the FIFO overflows, the interface will transmit an error condition. The user has the option to specify that when an overflow error condition occurs, to enforce a stale of the embedded processor or to continue with a new synchronization message.

Table 1 summarizes the basic Nexus features and characteristics by product class. [5,6]. Chip designs that might not need the full capabilities of the Nexus Specification, can chose from a variety of features grouped together in four Classes. The Class 3 provides for real-time instruction and data trace over a single port.

Feature	Class 1	Class 2	Class 3	Class 4
Read & write registers while in debug mode	✓	✓	✓	✓
Read & write memory while in debug mode	✓	✓	✓	✓
Enter debug mode from reset	✓	✓	✓	✓
Enter debug mode from user mode	✓	✓	✓	✓
Exit debug mode to user mode	✓	✓	✓	✓
Single-step instruction; reenter debug mode	✓	✓	✓	✓
Stop on breakpoint; enter debug mode	✓	✓	✓	✓
Set breakpoint or watchpoint	✓	✓	✓	✓
Device identification	✓	✓	✓	✓
Notify of watchpoint match	✓	✓	✓	✓
Monitor process ownership in real time (OTM)		✓	✓	✓
Monitor program flow in real time (program trace)		✓	✓	✓
Monitor data writes in real time (data trace)			✓	✓
Monitor data reads in real time			Optional	Optional
Read & write memory in real time			✓	✓
Execute program through Nexus port (memory substitution)				✓
Begin trace on watchpoint				✓
Begin memory substitution on watchpoint				Optional
Low-speed I/O port replacement		Optional	Optional	Optional
High-speed I/O port sharing		Optional	Optional	Optional
Transmit data-acquisition			Optional	Optional

Table 1: Nexus 5001 Features by Classification

The Nexus 5001 port can be configured based on the amount of information that is being captured by the development, hardware-in-the-loop or calibration tool. The Nexus 5001 specification has been deployed on multiple CPU architectures by several IC venders for a variety of applications from cell phones to automotive to hard disk drive controllers to video processors.

MULTI-CORE REAL-TIME INTERFACE

A multi-core real-time interface has been recently developed for the PowerPC® ISA compatible architecture to provide real time debug, calibration, rapid prototyping and hardware-in-the-loop capabilities over a single interface [7]. Figure 2 shows the block diagram for the 4 processing elements in the multi-core debug architecture based on the Nexus 5001 standard. The first version allows for a real time interface for four data processing elements. The four processing elements are the e500z PowerPC ISA compatible core, the dual Enhanced Timer

Processor Units (E-TPU) and Direct Memory Access (DMA) unit. With the single connection over the Class 3 Nexus 5001 interface, the host tool can collect data from any or all of the four processing elements simultaneously. In addition, the debug and calibration tool could establish breakpoints and/or watchpoints on any of the four processing elements for data and/or instructions. An example where this would be used is when the engineer is tracking an issue between a timed event over the E-TPU and the code running on the PowerPC ISA compatible Book-e processing core.

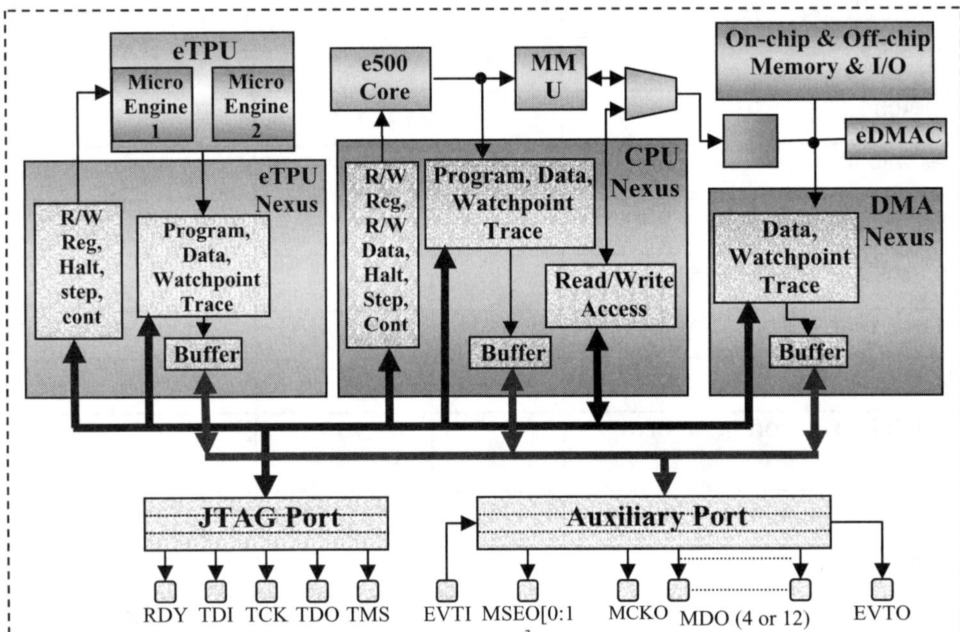

Figure 2: Nexus Block Diagram of a Multi-Processor Implementation

A 32-bit embedded processor can be implemented with a floating point unit and/or a Single Instruction – Multiple Data (SIMD) unit to assist with complex mathematical functions. The SIMD allows for one instruction to be performed on multiple data sets and is very useful in filter and array mathematical equations. The Nexus debug port allows for the monitoring of the data and instructions of the floating point and the SIMD.

The "PowerPC" name is a trademark of IBM Corp. and used under license.

ROADMAP TO ELECTRONICS

A luxury vehicle today can have 3 miles of wiring. A proper networked system can reduce and simplify much of the additional complexity, weight and cost from the point-to-point communications found in existing cars. FlexRay is being adopted as the networking solution of choice for many of the next generation of applications.

Graph 1 shows the growth rate of the silicon content in the vehicle over a decade. The dramatic growth of 16:1 is a result of the increased need for higher feature and functional content in the car. Also, the advances that electronics can bring in a cleaner vehicle that is safer and much more efficient.

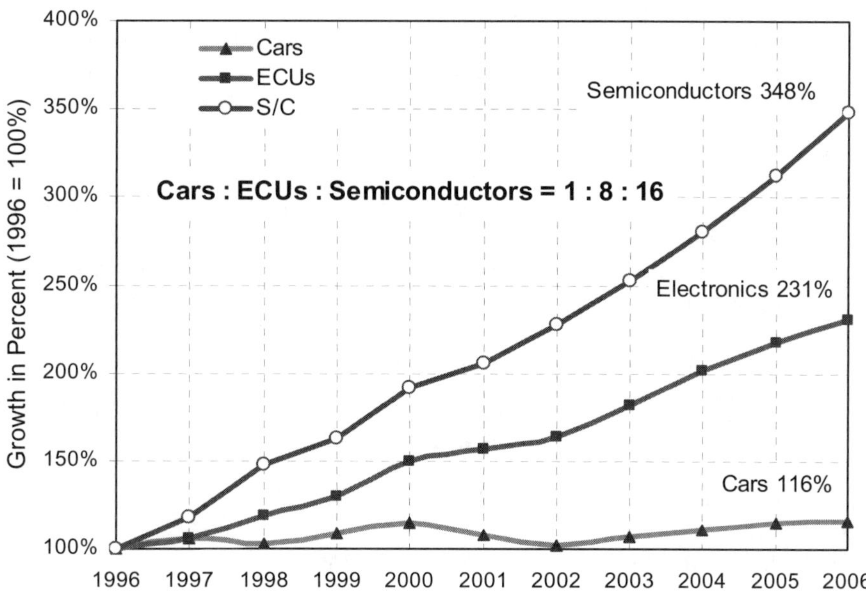

Source: ZVEI -Trendanalysis

Graph 1: Growth of vehicles : electronics : semiconductors in cars

The functionality that a high-speed, fault tolerant networked protocol can provide car manufactures will be a major enabling technology for new and safer vehicles in the next couple of years.

The road to a vehicle that is absolutely safe is still years off. There will be several near term advancements that can bring significant improvements with TCS, EPAS and adaptive cruise control culminating with an automated vehicle and highway system. All of these near term and future systems will require fault tolerant, deterministic and high speed networking communications protocol.

MODULE COMMUNICATION

CAN has served as the mainstay of ECU module communications for more than a decade [8,9,10]. However, CAN is limited is several major areas that would not provide solutions for mission critical applications. A new high speed automotive networking protocol has been architected specifically for mission critical communications, called FlexRay. The major features of FlexRay are:

- **Synchronous and asynchronous data transmission**
- **High net data rate of 5 Mbit/sec; gross data rate approximately 10Mbit/sec**
- **Deterministic data transmission, guaranteed message latency and message jitter**
- **Support of redundant transmission channels**
- **Fault tolerant and time triggered services implemented in hardware**
- **Fast error detection and signalling**
- **Support of a fault tolerant synchronised global time base**
- **Error containment on the physical layer through an independent "Bus Guardian"**
- **Arbitration free transmission**
- **Support of optical and electrical physical layer**
- **Support for bus, star and multiple star topologies**

FlexRay is a network communication system targeted specifically at the next generation "by-wire" automotive applications. The by-wire applications demand high-speed bus systems that are deterministic, fault-tolerant and capable of supporting distributed control systems. Major automotive OEM, Tier 1, independent S/W design firms and semiconductor suppliers are working together to develop and establish FlexRay as the standard for next generation applications.

The FlexRay protocol encompasses more than just being a fault tolerant communications protocol. FlexRay includes specifically designed high-speed transceiver and the definition of hardware and software interfaces between various components of a FlexRay 'node'. The FlexRay defines the protocol format and function of the communication process within an automotive networked system.

FlexRay is designed to meet key automotive requirements like dependability, availability, flexibility, and a high data rate to complement the major in-vehicle networking standards - CAN, LIN and MOST.

New applications requiring improved communication and higher data transfer rates between the vehicle's ECUs will drive by-wire applications to the forefront. FlexRay is initially targeted for a data rate of approximately 10Mbit/sec; however, the design of the protocol allows much higher data rates in the future.

FlexRay provides for a scalable communication system with both synchronous and asynchronous data transmission, or a mixture of both. The synchronous data transmission enables time triggered communication to meet the requirement of dependable systems. The asynchronous transmission technique has its fundamentals based on work from the Byteflight™ protocol which allows each node to use the full bandwidth for event driven communications.

When FlexRay is operated in a synchronous data transmission mode, the messages are deterministic with a message latency and message jitter guaranteed as built-in feature of the standard. The time base is controlled by a redundant, fault-tolerant synchronized clock. The FlexRay clock is used as a global time base to keep the schedule for all the network nodes within a tight, predefined precision window.

The physical layer acts as an independent bus guardian by insuring that no data collisions can occur even in the event of a fault in the communication controller. It is critical that by-wire applications can have the information in a distributed system linked by a communications protocol which guarantees that messages will transfer in a known timeframe.

FlexRay has been designed to support both optical and electrical physical layers, to provide for flexibility in the wiring system choices now and into the future. A FlexRay system supports networking from a single channel bus to dual channel multi-star topology with full redundancy.

For additional information on FlexRay visit the web site:

www.flexray.com

CONCLUSION

Balancing the electro-mechanical needs of the changing automotive market, and many other challenging requirements will stimulate new approaches from the hardware and software engineering team. Just over the horizon, are the emerging ultra clean power sources: electric vehicles, full hybrids and fuel cell powered vehicles. As we approach the new technologies, the emergence of new microcontrollers, I/O systems, development tools and methodologies will keep the automobile in the forefront of technology.

The embedded processors already in the market and coming to market over the next 12 months will make the traditional run-control debug methodology obsolete. The external address and data buses have virtually disappeared from the 8-bit processors of today. The 16-bit and 32-bit processors are reducing in many cases the external buses in favor of more specialized I/O functions while integrating the memory on-chip leaving little room for the external buses.

The Nexus 5001 consortium has published the current revision of the specification (version 2.0 2003) on the consortium Web site:

www.nexus5001.org

ACKNOWLEDGMENTS

The author wishes to thank the members of the Nexus 5001 Consortium. Special thanks to Gary Miller, Kevin Hall, Wayne Willis, Martin Elbs, Rudan Bettelheim, Alan Hutton, Randy Dees and Richard Collins for contributions to the development of the Nexus consortium and standard.

A special thanks to Gerrie Stence for tolerating the extra hours needed to get a worldwide standard off the ground and correcting so many papers over the years.

REFERENCES

1. Semiconductor Industry Association, "2020 is Closer Than You Think", SIA 2005 Annual Report
2. Miller, G. (Motorola), Hall, K. (Agilent Technologies), etal, "The Evolution of Powertrain Microcontrollers and it's Impact on Development Processes and Tools", http//www.ieee-isto.org
3. Allen, James (Delphi), "Calibration Development with Production Intent Electronic Control Units" SAE Paper 00P-487, 2000
4. Ronald Stence, "Real Time Calibration and Debug Techniques of Embedded Processors with the Nexus 5001 Interface" SAE Paper 03AE-144
5. Randy Dees, "Nexus Revealed, an Introduction to the IEEE-ISTO 5001 Nexus Debug Standard", Book from AMT Publishing
6. Jim Turley, "Nexus Standard Brings Order to Microprocessor Debugging", A White Paper www.nexus5001.org
7. Richard Soja and Munir Bannoura, "MPC5554 Revealed – Introduction to the MPC5554 Architecture and Programming", Book from AMT Publishing
8. Strategy Analytics, "Automotive Multiplexing Trends December 2002 - Viewpoint
9. Gabriel Leen (PEI Technologies), Donal Heffernan (University of Limerick), "In - Vehicle Networks: Expanding Automotive Electronic Systems", January 2002 IEEE 0018-9162/02
10. F. Bogenberger, A. Krüger (Motorola), "FlexRay–The Communication System for Advanced Automotive System for Advanced Automotive Control Systems Control Systems" SAE 2001

CONTACT

The author has worked in the electronics industry for 24 years. Most of this time he spent working in the semiconductor industry with Motorola Semiconductor, now Freescale Semiconductor, Inc. Prior to working for Motorola, Mr. Stence worked for Advanced Micro Devices (AMD) and Tellabs.

Mr. Stence has made significant contributions toward establishing the IEEE-ISTO Nexus 5001 Debug Interface as an industry wide standard and currently serves on the Steering Committee and is the Chairman of the Nexus 5001 Consortium. He has received 5 Motorola Corporation awards for his contribution to the Nexus 5001 standard.

Mr. Stence currently holds 9 U.S. Patents in the area of embedded processors and graduated from Texas A&M University in 1986 with a BS in Computer Science.

Email: ron.stence@freescale.com

DEFINITIONS, ACRONYMS, ABBREVIATIONS

BDM – BACKGOUND DEBUG MODE

A debug port that was deployed on Motorola embedded processors in the late 1980s. Provided run control and memory & register visibility with the processor in a halted mode.

DMA – DIRECT MEMORY ACCESS UNIT

Capable of transferring data from one location to another location without requiring intervention form the main CPU processor.

E-TPU – ENHANCED-TIMER PROCESSSOR UNIT

A complex timer originally designed to handle angle and time based systems on the M68332. The Enhanced TPU has new extensions and is assembly code compatible with the TPU found on multiple devices and architectures.

FLEXRAY

An emerging communications standard and consortium. The major advantages are the fault tolerate, time triggered communications and higher data rate over other protocols.

www.flexray.com

JTAG – JOINT TEST ACCESSS PORT

Originally defined as a boundary scan port under the IEEE 1149.1. Extended use as a slow speed run-control debug port.

NEXUS

Name of the IEEE-ISTO Nexus 5001 Consortium and Specification. The charter of Nexus is to develop a real time debug and calibration standard for multiple embedded processor architectures. More information and the specification are available on the web site

www.nexus5001.org

RISC – REDUCED INSTRUCTION SET COMPUTER

A processor architecture that has many attributes that defines it as a different type of processor core (i.e. DSP, CISC). The major attributes of a RISC processor are: 1) fixed length instructions, 2) load/store architecture, 3) single cycle execution of instructions 4) hard coded instructions, 5) high-level language support.

RUN CONTROL DEBUG

The basic run control (run, halt, download and upload data to and from memory and/or registers while the processor is stopped) debug mode found in many embedded processors. Operates over a dedicated debug port to provide basic run control and static memory, register information. Data is often serially transmitted from the target to a host development tool. Examples of Run Control ports include: BDM, ONcE and JTAG debug.

SIMD – SINGLE INSTRUCTION - MULTIPLE DATA

A CPU architecture that allows a single instruction to modify or manipulate more than one data value at a time. Used to quickly calculate multiple points of a curve or object, where the mathematical equation is the same with a finite number of data values to be calculated.

SOC – SYSTEM-ON-A-CHIP

A highly integrated embedded processor that is focused at a single market. Often contains the part or all of the system memory.

TCODE – TRANSFER CODE

Defined by the Nexus 5001 Specification as a defined command used to communicate between the target processor and the host tool.

2005-01-1309

Configuration Management for Electronics in Automotive Engineering

Olaf Kluge and Roman Klement
BMW AG, München, Germany

ABSTRACT

Today's automotive systems engineering focuses mainly on the design of components, e.g. ECU's. In the future functionality becomes increasingly more important than the component because the consumers do not order ECUs but functionality. This focus on functions gets even more important, as these functions are often realised by sets of components distributed all over the vehicle. A function can be realised in alternative sets of components and each of these components can realise parts of different functions.

A solid configuration management becomes crucial to perform the change from component based to functionality-oriented systems engineering as it ensures the integrity of all variants and releases of the system throughout its development. In this contribution the authors address how configuration management supports functionality-oriented system design with respect to the development of distributed embedded systems as found in modern cars.

INTRODUCTION

Consider a board net as a set of connected components with matching interfaces. Each of it has its own specification and – due to cost optimization – variants which are not only driven by hardware (memory, cpu, colour...) but also by their functionality. This means one ends up with variants of ECUs with each having its unique interface definition. Requiring free combination of any variant with any board net setting a huge set of combinations is inevitable. Without actuators and sensors a board net consisting of 70 ECUs – each having three variants – would allow more than $3.5 \cdot 10^{21}$ different combinations. Technical constraints may reduce this to at least 10 million useful combinations, still leaving too many possibilities.
This means, an alternative to the component driven approach is needed. Seeking the analogy with mechanical design where assemblies get tested according to their functionality regardless of the colour they have, we provide this approach for a board net: regard the different functionality regardless the device it is implemented.

Focusing on a function based approach offers a whole bunch of advantages:

- You can specify functionality once and reuse it for your component specification.
- You change the specification once and see the consequences on your components immediately.
- You test the functionality just once for each implementation and not once in each variant of a component.
- You are able to reuse your implementation on different devices once you have a matching infrastructure such as AUTOSAR [5] proposes.

It is then the task of configuration management to watch for valid system configurations – valid baselines and variants to receive the simplest yet working board net providing just the functionality chosen by the customer.

In the following sections we give a short introduction to the component-based systems engineering. Next we motivate the structural separation of function specification and its component realisation in systems engineering. Subsequently we discuss configuration management for automotive systems engineering and how it must change to support the functional approach.

SYSTEMS ENGINEERING: COMPONENT BASED APPROACH

Systems engineering starts usually with the capture of the requirements. Typically these requirements cover specific functional behaviour, descriptions of look and form of certain system parts as well as international and national standards and laws that the system must comply with. Typically these requirements can be assigned to a specific component, a subsystem or the system as a whole.

Product Data Management systems (PDM) are usually employed to manage the system in the engineering process. Thereby, the system is hierarchically decomposed into its subsystems and parts. The PDM systems employ a so-called product structure, which represent this hierarchy in a tree like notation. Many of today. used product structures are derived from a mechanical point of view representing an assembly structures.

Often alternative concepts for components or subsystems evolve during the development of the system. These alternatives can be represented as alternative branches in the product structure. PDM systems can then assist in the evaluation of these alternative concepts. Analogously variants and releases of components and subsystems can be managed. The properties of subsystems are handed down to all components in the according sub-tree. Thus the product structure represents all versions and variants of all components.

Throughout the system life cycle the configuration management (CM) has to maintain the data integrity of all product data. It has to ensure that when a system is build, then the right versions and variants off all components are chosen. In order to determine the right components each element of the product structure holds a set of attributes describing its version and variant. Many different approaches for the organisation of changes are known. Amongst them configuration by effectivity and baselining belong to the more common practices. For systems engineering with its highly connected and therefore dependant components, baselining seems to be more appropriate. A baseline represents the state of the system under development at a defined point in time and captures the elements as well as structural information. It serves as reference for further activities. Subsequently filters can be employed on the product structure to determine all components of a baseline of the system as well as of a system variant (of a baseline).

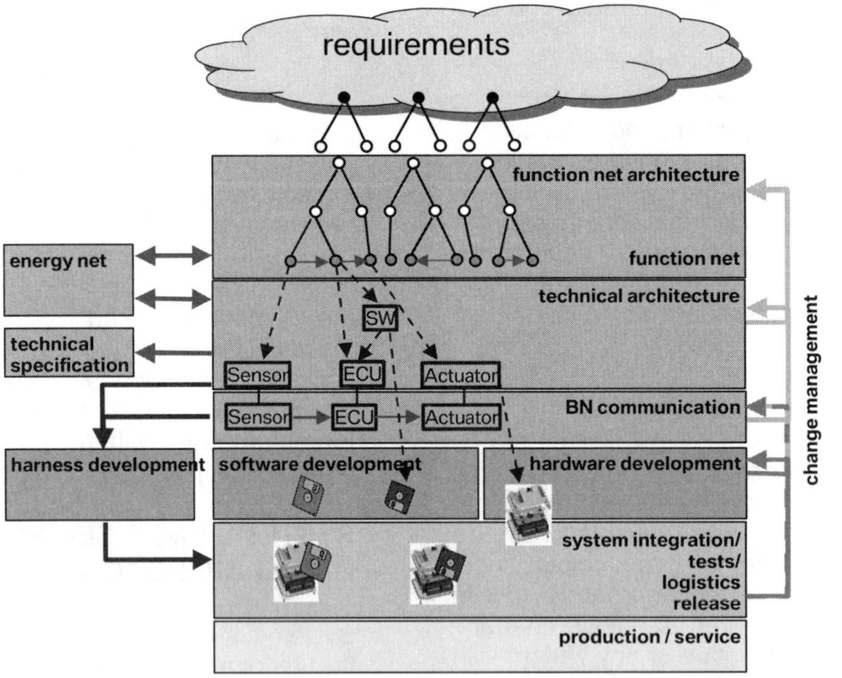

To ensure the consistency of the product structure all modifications of elements in the product structure must be managed in according processes and result in new versions of this element in the product structure.

Focusing on components is quite common in today's practice. Design methodologists provide abstract and formal methods since long. Throughout system development and life cycle this has the eminent advantage that ensuring data consistency is much easier. In the component-oriented world requirements and solution alternatives are attached to the same object in the product structure, i.e. component. If the component's requirements or solutions are changed, it is much easier to ensure that requirement and solution are consistent as just one object is directly affected.

However, as a requirement can apply to more then one component, a change of the requirements involves a propagation of this change to all affected components. Ensuring this consistency of the requirements in the product structure during the system development and life cycle becomes difficult and time-consuming. This is even more so as cars become increasingly complex and the number of dependencies between components grows exponentially.

Usually the elements of a system depend on each other. That is, if one element is changed, then many depending elements must be re-adjusted. In the geometric world Digital Mock-Up (DMU) serves as a means to ensure that all components fit to one another. Thereby, the consistency checking is usually performed with regard to variants and baselines.

While such geometric methods for checking dependencies are highly developed and provided by many IT-systems, the dependency checking for other aspects is still an open issue.

Figure 1: interaction and dependencies of product development processes

Especially in the development of highly distributed embedded systems it is necessary to keep track of dependencies that are not visible in the product structure. For example a function is realised with a sensor, an electronic control unit (ECU) and an actuator. These three components might be represented at different places in the product structure. Still these components depend on each other, i.e. the function is only provided by the correct function of the three components. A classical product structure, however, just allows modelling these dependencies via the application of appropriate configuration rules. Thus, the components can be tied together but the reason why got lost.

Another issue with embedded systems is that the developments of hardware and software have different characteristics. While hardware is not changed as often as

software it also needs more time to perform the modification. The change of the hardware usually requires the change of tools in its manufacturing which is time consuming and expensive. Additionally time is needed to get the hardware from its manufacturer to the assembly line. Contrary, a software change is much cheaper, does usually not need new tools and can fast and cheap be transported to almost every place in the world.
These facts lead to a change in systems engineering processes. On one hand the functionality gets into the focus throughout the system life cycle, on the other hand the development processes are adapted to the characteristics of the software and hardware development processes. The following section gives an overview of this functional approach to systems engineering.

SYSTEMS ENGINEERING: FUNCTIONAL APPROACH

As described in the previous section a function is often realised by the cooperation of several components. If the requirements, the functionality and the solution description are maintained at the component object in the product structure, it becomes difficult to ensure functionality of distributed functions especially when the requirements change over the life-cycle (fig. 1).

An approach to manage the distributed functionality in an easier way is to maintain different structures for the description of the functions and the components.

In addition to the product structure a function structure is maintained. Thereby, at first the function structure is designed. In a first step a set of high-level functions is defined. These high-level functions comprise functions, which are experience by the customer, as well as system-functions. Examples for such high-level functions are Adaptive Cruise Control (ACC) or Park Distance Control (PDC).

In a second step these high-level functions are hierarchically decomposed into low-level functions, which can be realised by a sensor, actuator or within an ECU. For example the PDC function could be decomposed into low-level functions measuring the distances at the front and the back of the car, for evaluating the distances and for communicating the distances to the driver. The signals being passed between the low level-functions are also represented in the low-level nets. Thus, a low-level function net is designed for each high-level function. Subsequently, merging the low-level function nets derives a so-called function net architecture (FNA). Thereby, similar low-level functions are united. For example several low-level nets contain a function for acquiring the vehicle speed, which instead can be provided by one function system wide. The result is a function net architecture representing the complete functionality of the system.

Concurrently to the function structure a product structure, i.e. the technical architecture, is designed. Then the components in the product structure are linked to the low-level function in the function structure. Creating this link, the so-called allocation, defines which component realises a low-level function. In order to allow different system variants a low-level function can be allocated to different components depending on the system variant. However, low-level functions cannot be distributed over several components. Thus for each variant a low-level function must be allocated to exactly one component. This approach is based on STEP AP 212 providing a data model supporting the relations mentioned above.

This way, the amount of devices assembled to a car can be reduced. E.g. the control for an automated gearbox might – if combined with a small 4-cyl. Engine – on the ECU of the engine, but if combined with a 6-cylinder engine reside in its own ECU. Or park distance control could be allocated on the lightning ECU, this way reducing one ECU.

Another positive side effect is that the requirements of a component are defined by the low-level functions, which are allocated onto this component.

A prominent big advantage of this approach is that functional dependencies between components can be easier detected. Following the decomposition and the allocation it is directly possible to determine the components, which are necessary to realise a high-level functionality. Furthermore, the components that are affected by a change of another component can be easier identified.

Nevertheless, this functional approach has the big disadvantage that in addition to the product structure the function structure and their links, i.e. the allocation, must be managed. As a result the configuration management becomes more complex and much more important.

The system requirements can be managed in the form of high-level functions. Another option for managing the system requirements is a requirement structure, which is linked to the function structure. However, this approach is not discussed in this paper. The consequences resulting from this separation into function and product structure for the configuration management are discussed in the following section.

CONFIGURATION MANAGEMENT IN SYSTEMS ENGINEERING

Configuration management has a long tradition in many industries. Many publications, books and standards can be found on configuration management ([1], [3], [4]). Unfortunately an automotive OEM cannot just take these standard approaches, which have been proven to be right many times and implement it into its organization [2]. is mainly driven from domains outside the automotive domain and does only partially fit the specific electric/electronic needs within the automotive domain. These specific needs make a different view on configuration management necessary, which is illustrated in fig. 2.

There are basically four building blocks of configuration management within the automotive domain [3]. These building blocks themselves are not considered to be automotive specific, while their content is considered to be.

(1) Configuration items and structure
(2) Configuration management processes
  a. Baseline management (planning, establishing, auditing, and releasing baselines)
  b. Variant management, i.e. deriving customer specific configurations
  c. Change management
(3) Configuration management organization
(4) Configuration management IT infrastructure

The following part of this section discusses mainly the configuration items and structure (1) and the related configuration management processes (2) as this presentation focuses on the differences of component and function oriented systems engineering. The IT infrastructure (4) manages the configuration items and structure and supports CM processes with automated workflows. Therefore the IT infrastructure depends fundamentally on the configuration structure and processes. CM organisation (3) deals with roles and organisational changes.

The configuration items comprise all elements and artefacts that occur in the development process and change over the life cycle. Examples are requirements, the specifications of components as well as bills of material (BOM). The configuration structure organises these configuration items and thus defines the contents of a baseline.

A baseline represents a freeze of the configuration management structure. It consists of three major steps:

- During planning the components, which should be part of the baseline, are determined.
- Afterwards the relevant versions of the previously chosen components are chosen
- Finally the baseline gets frozen and the contents gets evaluated and eventually released.

Managing product variants is another challenge. In classical configuration management each variant of the product usually gets its own baseline as a branch of the main baseline. Unfortunately this approach does not work for products with a very large number of possible variants, as it is impossible to manage a baseline for each variant. Therefore an attribute logic is employed to control for each item its validity in variants.

Finally change management controls and documents the changes of configuration items between baselines. Thereby it ensures the consistency of the configuration items within the baseline. This includes also the attributes for the variant management.

In component-oriented systems engineering the components are the main configuration items and requirement and variant control attributes are assigned to these com-

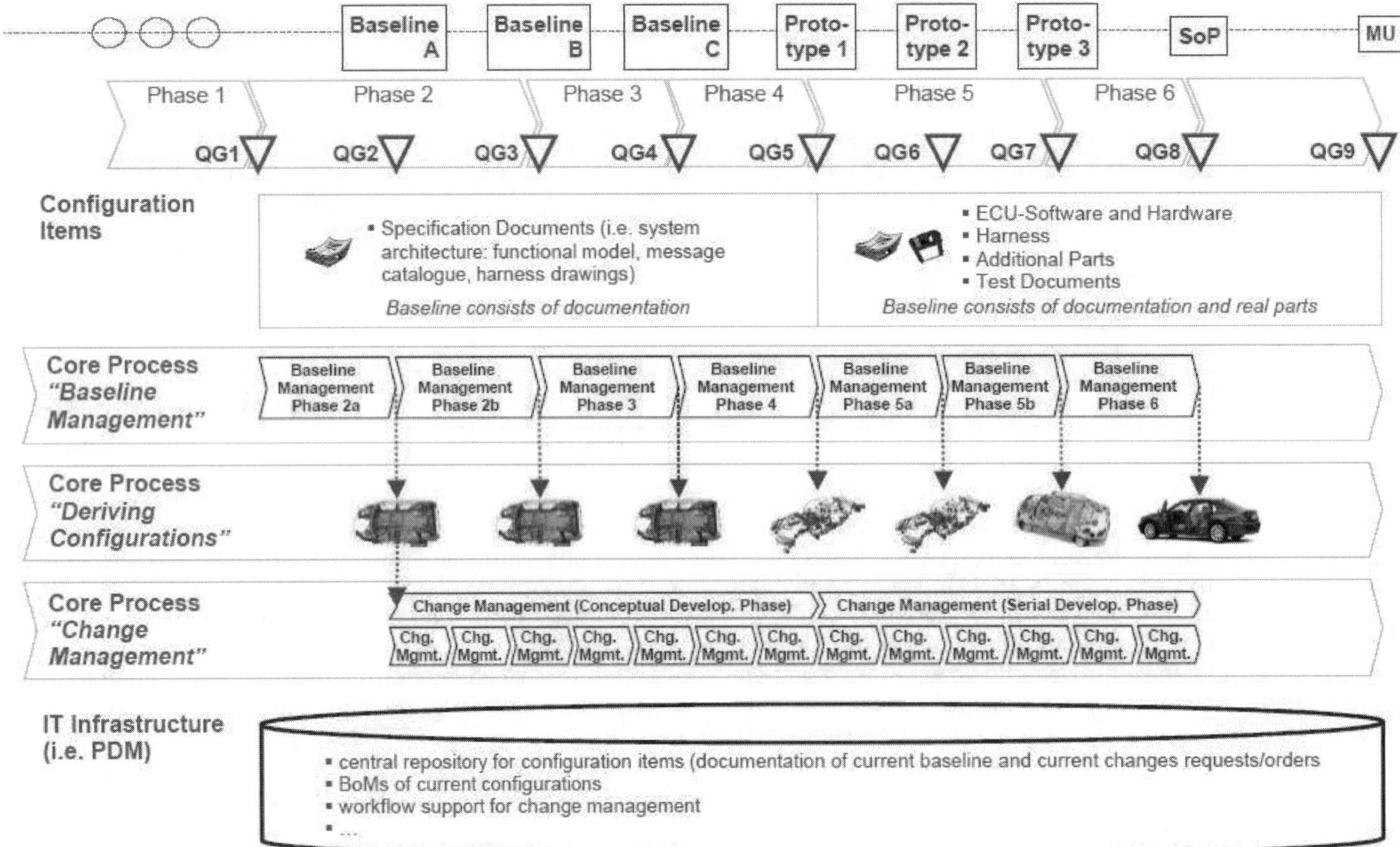

Figure 2: Overview – baselines during product development

ponents. This approach ensures data consistency for each single component. Unfortunately this is not the case on the system level, as it is very hard to manage the dependencies between the components.

The function-oriented approach helps considerably to manage functional dependencies on the system level. As a drawback, several linked configuration items in the function and the component structure define the component data. Also a baseline does not only contain the component structure, but also the function structure and the links between the structures.

However, maintaining consistency of the function and component structure can be easy. It is important to apply the change not only to the component in the component structure, but also to all affected items in the functional structure. Thus, dependent components can be easily identified and also changed.

This procedure is especially important for the variant configuration. To ensure a customer function in a product variant all necessary components must be valid for this variant. This component variant configuration can be easily derived from the function structure. Therefore, it is important not to change this configuration information on the component, but in the function structure or the allocation. In fact, it is much easier to control the variant configuration on the functional level then on the component level.

Fig. 3 illustrates the structures and dependencies with respect to a proposed IT infrastructure. The left side shows the hierarchical product structure as represented in a PDM system. The right side shows the function structure and the technical architecture which both reside in an E/E-PDM system. The technical architecture is the E/E view of the product structure, which is linked to the product structure. The function structure has also a link into the product structure thereby the high-level functions are assigned to product variants. The advantage of this infrastructure is that the link between function and product structure is not managed at the interface between IT-systems but in one system only. Still the product structure is the system where the product variants are defined. This separation enables a seamless transition from component oriented to function oriented systems engineering as some parts can be engineered in the old process while especially E/E components can employ the new one.

Managing the variant configuration in the function structure has many advantages. It allows for example to identify for each possible product variant which components are necessary to realise a function. For example in the system architecture design this helps optimising the variant configurations of the system. It is also easier to check if all component variants are tested in at least one prototype. As mentioned previously a change of the product variants can be easier managed on the component level.

This approach also supports the separation of software and hardware, whereby the function is realised in software while the hardware provides the necessary infrastructure. In this way a reduction of the up to now increasing number of ECUs in cars is possible as many software components can coexist on the same ECU. In

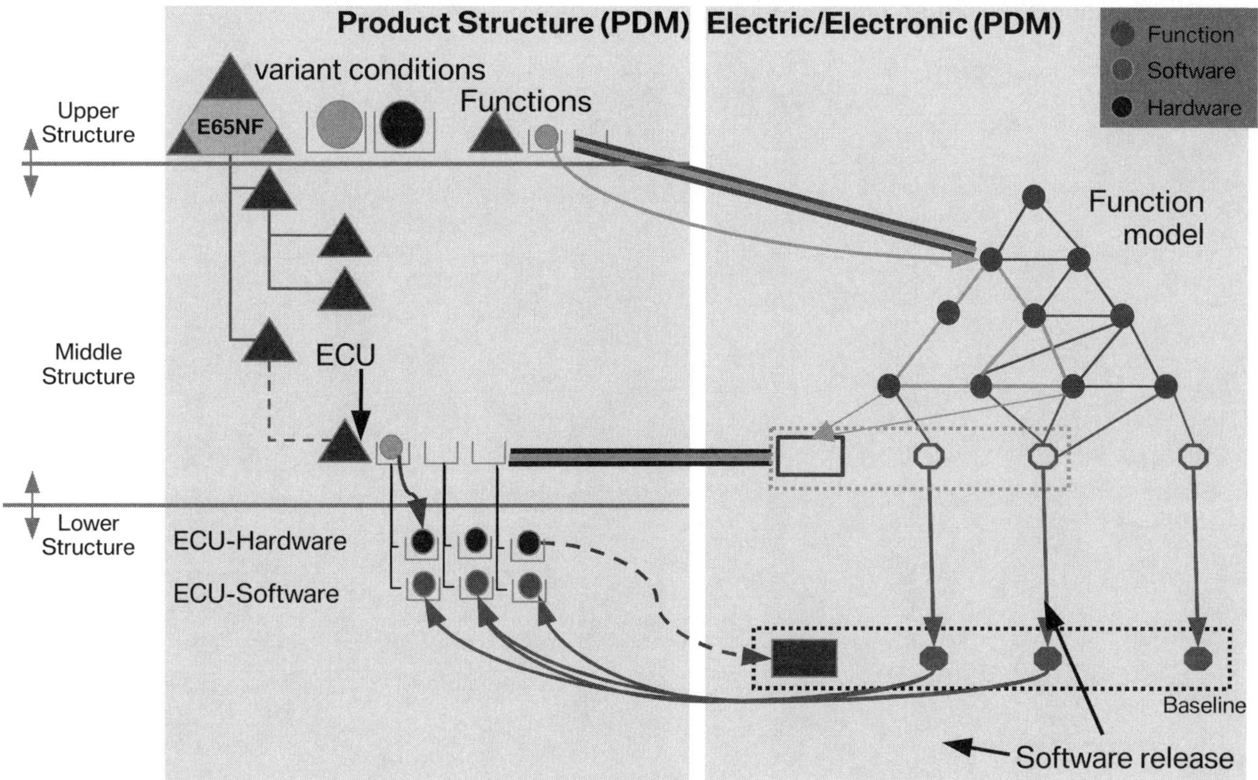

Figure 3: Interaction between product and function structure and configuration driven by functional dependencies

fact, this function-oriented approach is therefore essential to establish AUTOSAR [5].

Among many other advantages, managing compatibility of components is also simplified. Electronic parts have much shorter life cycles then cars. This and also bug fixes result in redesigns of components and whole subsystems over the car-projects life cycle. Therefore it is necessary to manage compatibility between old and new components. If a component is exchanged by another version, then it is necessary to know which dependent components must be also exchanged and which components must undergo a software update. Thereby it is much easier to manage compatibility on the functional level and inherit this information to the components. Again this information must be managed in baselines and controlled by a reliable change management.

CONCLUSION

Differentiating between functions and realising components in systems engineering has many advantages. Functional dependencies on the system level can be managed in the function structure and inherited to the component structure. Thereby, the correct implementation of functions distributed over several components and variants of components can be tested and ensured, although different suppliers develop the components and sometimes even software and hardware independently.

However, ensuring data consistency between the function and the component structure and the links is an additional challenge for configuration and change management. Changes of functions and functionality must be managed in the function structure and inherited into the component structure and the links. As a side effect dependent components can be easily identified and the component interfaces of different variants can be harmonised.

Thus, the function oriented systems engineering together with a robust configuration and change management offers many new chances to manage complexity and variance of products such as modern cars. Especially the support for the separation function and component in form of software and hardware helps to establish AUTOSAR.

REFERENCES

1. EIA 649 “National Consensus Standard on Configuration Management”, Electronic Industries Alliance, August 1998.
2. E. Knippel and A. Schulz “Lessons Learned from Implementing Configuration Management within Electrics/Electronics Development of an Automotive OEM”, Proceedings of INCOSE 2004, Toulouse, France, June 2004
3. MIL-HDBK-61 “Military Handbook – Configuration Management Guidance” Department of Defence Hand Book, USA, September 1997.
4. SEI “CMMI 1.02 Stage Representation” Software Engineering Institute, Pittsburgh, 2000.
5. AUTOSAR: www.autosar.org

2005-01-1285

A Framework for Optimized Allocation of Control Functions to a Distributed Architecture

Thomas Rambow and Uwe Kiencke
Institute of Industrial Information Technology, University of Karlsruhe (TH)

Rainer Schlör, Rainer Busch and Achim Seibertz
Ford Research Centre Aachen

ABSTRACT

In this paper we present the results of a project that concentrates on the design of distributed embedded systems for control-related applications. The OPTMAP (Optimal Mapping of Virtual Control Functions to a Distributed Architecture) framework supports the function allocation based on given constrains involving a feasible solution. The control systems we will consider use a time-triggered paradigm for sensor reading and event-driven behavior for inter-processor communication. Sensor values are read at fixed periods in time and data processing occurs after the control unit receives the proper message. The aim of the project is to get an optimized mapping which minimizes information traffic on the network and guarantees that all processing units are able to handle the distributed control functions in real time.

INTRODUCTION

In the automotive industry more and more functionality is being moved from traditional hardware to software on distributed computer systems. The functions, their performance and dependability requirements need to be considered when the distributed computer system is designed, especially when the system consists of heterogeneous distributed computers. It is necessary to analyze the requirements of all functions in an early design phase to establish a structure of the distributed computer system. There are several design tools, as for example Matlab®/Simulink®, that provide a model-based specification of the functionality, where analysis through simulation and early identification of design failures is possible. The use of rapid prototyping systems to verify the specification in a real-time environment is also supported. Unfortunately, an implementation of the functionality on a network of different distributed real-time computer systems is not included. There is an urgent need to provide a support for the design of distributed real-time systems, for which existent tools and models are insufficient.

DEVELOPMENT METHOD AND MODEL

The OPTMAP project concentrates on issues related to the design of distributed embedded systems for control-related applications. One of the main sources of complexity in current and future embedded systems is their highly heterogeneous nature, with hardware and software components from various sources. One key aspect of the project is to provide an open architecture, composed of formal specifications and tools, supporting the design methodology and automating it as far as possible. Given the complexity of such a task, only an adequate design environment can effectively support decisions leading to an acceptable and high performance solution. The OPTMAP environment is depicted in Figure 1. The following points characterize the essential parts of the tool design:

SOFTWARE ABSTRACTION

Structural model

A control algorithm is first divided into nodes. Each executing node is a self-contained software part. This opens up the possibility of developing a library of standardized control software functions encapsulated in reusable data flow components. The dataflow architecture of the functionality consists of a collection of components that communicate via data interfaces. Such a design can be depicted graphically. A node is a computational component, and an arrow is a directed communication between data interfaces.

Run-time model

In this step, the application characteristics of the structural model are used as a basis for partitioning and allocation approaches. The functionality of the structural model is decomposed into tasks. A task is the smallest distributable unit that must be allocated to one processor only. During execution a task first reads the incoming information, then performs its function and writes the result to its out-port before completion. There is no direct communication between tasks. Therefore tasks can be executed without knowledge of where the input data was produced or where the output data will be used. Each task also has a configuration containing its temporal properties, e.g., period time, deadline, release time and worst-case execution time. Each task has a function that implements its behavior and also a state, i.e. it can store data that will not be lost between calls to the task. Each task has temporal attributes, precedence relations, and communication settings. The run-time model supports the specification of the properties affecting the timing behavior of the system. For the task model used in this approach it is assumed that tasks are periodic and must execute within the time interval given by the period. Since fixed priority scheduling of all tasks is assumed, each task is assigned a priority. The application is modeled as a dataflow graph. The dataflow graph is a pair of vertices and edges $G=\{V, E\}$. The set of vertices $V=\{ (T_i, c_i^{min}, c_i^{max}, d_i, \pi_i, p_i) \mid 1 < i \leq n \}$ represents the real-time tasks $\tau_i \in V$ where T_i is the period c_i^{min} and c_i^{max} are the best- and worst-case execution times, d_i is the deadline, π_i the priority and p_i the processor to which τ_i is allocated. The directed edges $e_{ij}=(\tau_j, \tau_i)$ represent the communication between the tasks sent from task τ_j to τ_i.

HARDWARE ABSTRACTION

We consider a multiprocessor architecture with a set of schedulable processors $P=\{p_q: 1 < q \leq m\}$ connected by a set of communication links $L=\{l_v: 1 < v \leq m_l\}$. The processors are heterogeneous in terms of processing speed. This means that the amount of time it takes to execute a task depends on the processor. Communication links between the processing nodes are assumed to be a CAN bus (*Controller Area Network*). There can be an arbitrary number of stations connected to the bus. A station is a processor plus a special controller, which acts as an interface between the bus and the processor. The communication is assumed to be asynchronous in the network, as the communication is allowed to take place concurrently with the processor computation. Directed edges e_{ij} between different processing units p_i and p_j are mapped to messages $m_{ij} \in M=\{ (T_j, s_{ij}, \pi_{ij}, l_l) \mid p_i \neq p_j \}$ sent from task τ_j to τ_i over the CAN bus $l_{ij} \in L$. For each message we know its size s_{ij} and the period, which is equal to the period T_j of the sending task. The message priorities π_{ij} are based on the deadlines of the receiving task τ_i. The communication between tasks residing on the same processor is done by using shared memory, and its communication delay is assumed to be negligible.

PERFORMANCE DATA

The Performance data, for example the worst-case execution times of the tasks on the different hardware nodes, is provided by manual input. To generate this data automatically additional effort has to be made for the prediction of accurate time bounds of tasks on different hardware nodes. But this challange is assigned to a separate worst-case execution time analyzer.

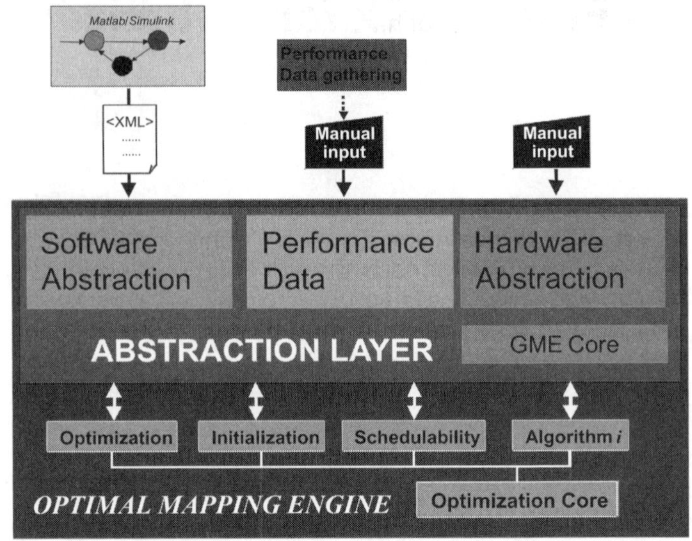

Figure 1: OPTMAP Environment

OPTIMIZATION FRAMEWORK

In this section we define the problem of automated allocation of control functions to a distributed architecture and the constraints used in the allocation framework.

PROBLEM DEFINITION

The application behavior relies on the requirements that are demanded from the system. The real-time system design is affected by functional requirements defining how the system reacts to events, timing requirements describing the demands on the timeliness of tasks in the system, and resource requirements stating the conditions the application has to keep for hardware and software resources. Constraints emerge from these requirements that will control the system design. Functional requirements are precedence constraints which synchronize the data exchange between tasks by the sending task. Timing constraints are the rate at which a real-time application requires computations to be performed and the time at which a real-time computation must end. The resource constraints are: a limited number of available resources, predetermined assignment of tasks to a resource and the utilization of the CAN bus as a critical performance bottleneck of the system.

Our system specification is in the form of a set of task graphs with the tasks as the basic atomic functional blocks. The allocation algorithm maps the functional objects to the system components of the hardware architecture. The allocation result is evaluated based on the given constraints and estimation of the optimization objectives.

THE ALLOCATION FRAMEWORK

An overview of our framework is given in Figure 2. First the type and number of hardware and software elements upon which the tasks will execute have to be defined. Then each task has to be assigned to a processing unit and each communication edge sent between different processing units is mapped to a communication link. A constructive approach builds the system from bottom up, incrementally mapping the components to the hardware architecture with the aim of maintaining the tasks' timing requirements and generating a feasible solution. An iterative approach starts with the solution obtained in the previous step and modifies the solution by attempting to improve the objective function. In each iteration step we obtain a global schedule and evaluate the system constraints such as bus utilization and real-time violations.

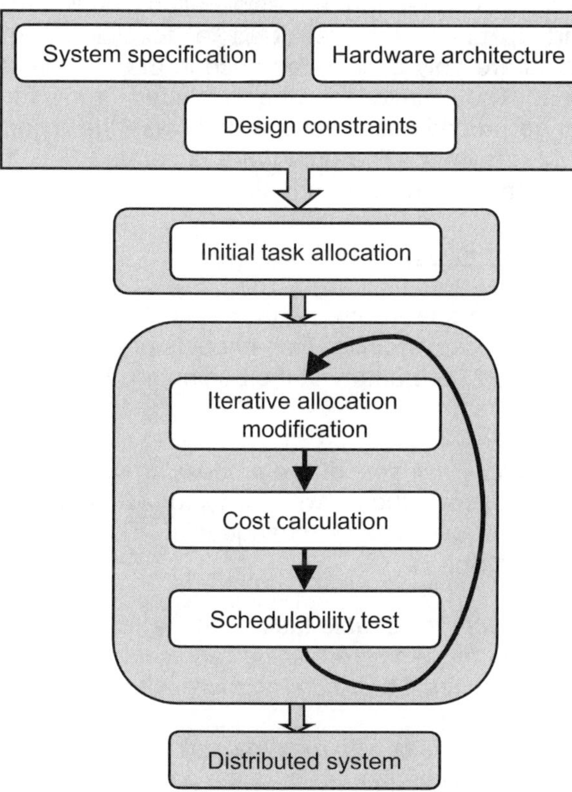

Figure 2: Optimization framework

MULTIPROCESSOR SCHEDULING

The knowledge of the worst-case execution time for each task allows early time verification before the actual implementation. The task set can be scheduled before the tasks are implemented and, assuming that the estimated time budget is not violated during implementation, the system is schedulable. Schedulability and timing analysis can, in this way, be performed early in the development. A multiprocessor schedule for a task set V and a multiprocessor architecture P is the mapping of each task $\tau_i \in V$ to a processor $p_q \in P$, provided that no processor executes two tasks at the same time and every task is executed exactly once during its period. In such systems, an application may execute sequentially on many different processors, as depicted in Figure 3. Each task in the system is activated by the arrival of a triggering event that may be generated by the external environment, a timer, or by the arrival of a message from another task. During the execution of the response to this event, several tasks may need to be executed in one or more nodes, and several messages exchanged in the network. Other timing requirements may also be imposed on individual actions. The response time of the application is measured from the release of its first subtask to the completion of its last subtask, and is called the end-to-end response time. A task set is schedulable if its end-to-end response time is never greater than the specified end-to-end deadline.

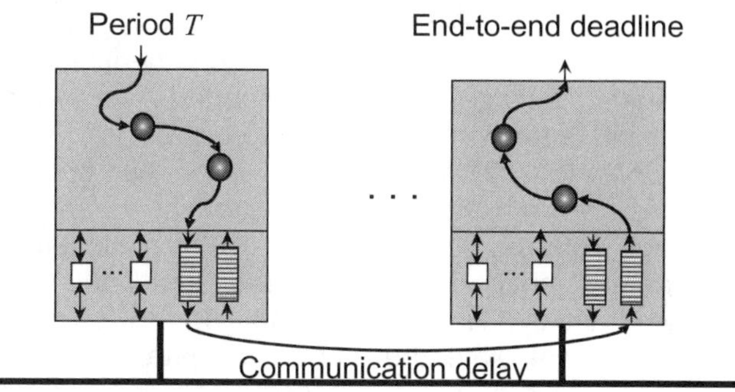

Figure 3: Multiprocessor system

FIXED PRIORITY SCHEDULING

Timing behavior is important to all computing systems. Thus it has become very important to develop models and theory that can be used to reason about the behavior of real-time systems. In order to make it possible to predict worst-case response times, it is necessary to schedule the activities in each processing node using an approach that allows processing activities with shorter deadlines before activities with longer deadlines. In our approach we concentrated on fixed priority scheduled systems. In fixed priority scheduling analysis the priorities of the tasks must be static and unique. One reason for this limitation is that the theory of fixed priority scheduling is well developed, and there is a large amount of research results that provides a solid base for this project. Furthermore, fixed priority scheduling is the industry standard for on-line scheduling of real-time systems. A large amount of theory enables analysis such that the feasibility of a fixed priority scheduled system, in terms of timing, can easily be verified.

SCHEDULABILITY ANALYSIS

To guarantee that all tasks are meeting their real-time conditions, a schedulability test has to be implemented. Altenbernd [1] presented a method for the response time analysis of multiprocessor systems that uses minimal and maximal offsets for the timing analysis. This method is used as a basic approach to calculate the worst case response times of tasks communicating with each other [6]. Tasks with precedence constraints can only start after the completion of their predecessors and the arrival of all incoming information. They can also be delayed or preempted by tasks belonging to other transactions with higher priorities. Given a certain priority assignment and an execution synchronization method, we compute the worst-case response time r_i^{wcrt} of each task τ_i, so that we can verify the schedulability of the system if each task terminates before its deadline d_i.

NETWORK ANALYSIS

Messages m_{ij} are used to describe the communication between tasks allocated to different processing units. For each message we know its size and the period that is equal to the period T_j of the sending task. The communication delay between tasks on the same processing unit is assumed to be negligible. For massages between tasks mapped to different processing units the CAN [2] protocol is used for communication. The CAN bus operates based on priorities, as massages with higher priorities in the message queue are sent first. We calculate the message priorities based on the deadlines of the receiving tasks. Tindell et al. [8, 9, 10] present an analysis to calculate the worst-case latencies of CAN messages. This analysis is based on the standard fixed priority response time analysis. The worst-case message response times implemented in the response time analysis of the system are the result of the CAN bus analysis.

ALGORITHMS FOR OPTIMIZED BUS UTILIZATION

BEST GAIN FIRST

The Best Gain First (BGF) allocation strategy is based on a heuristic search strategy, and was developed by J. Neumann [6]. We used this approach as a basis for a feasible task assignment with additional restrictions that support timing constraints for the entire system. The objective is to minimize communication between the tasks allocated on different processors. Therefore, highly communicating tasks are mapped to the same processor. First, the algorithm has to check to see if all tasks are initially allocated. In the next step the optimization process starts. The algorithm searches for the task whose transfer to another processing node results in the maximum decrease of the communication costs without violating the allocation constraints. Tasks with a fixed assignment are excluded from exchange.

Objective Function

As mentioned before, the main objective is the reduction of the bus load. If there is a connection between task τ_j to task τ_i with the tasks assigned to different processing units, a message m_{ij} is sent on the bus. The objective function specifies the communication costs for the message transmission resulting from the stationary transmission rate T_j^{-1} and the transmission delay C_{ij} of each message.

$$Cost = \sum_{m_{ij} \in M} \left(\frac{C_{ij}}{T_j} \right). \quad (1)$$

The transmission delay depends on the signal length s_{ij} in bits and the transmission speed of one bit on the bus τ_{bit}.

$$C_{ij} = s_{ij} \cdot \tau_{bit} . \quad (2)$$

It is obvious that keeping the timing restriction is more important than the optimisation goal, because a potential exchange is accomplished only if the resulting allocation is feasible. Provided that a feasible allocation is used as a starting point, the result is a feasible solution. Elements are only exchanged once in the context of an iteration. They have to be excluded from further exchange procedures, because otherwise the algorithm may not terminate. The procedure is iterated until there are no more initially exchangeable tasks left.

Algorithm structure

The algorithm starts with the task sets P_1 and P_2 on two different processing units. The amounts of exchangeable units X_1 and X_2 are empty at the beginning. The following steps are executed:

Step 1: Select task sets of two processing units
All tasks except those with a fixed assignment are assumed to be initial exchangeable. These are the partitions P_1 and P_2

Step 2: Select replaceable tasks
A search is made for remaining replaceable tasks. The algorithm finishes if there are no more left.

Step 3: Choose task with maximal gain
If there are replaceable tasks in the partitions P_1 and P_2, the one whose transfer creates the maximal reduction of communication costs is taken and put into the amount of possible exchangeable units X_1 or X_2 of the corresponding processing unit and deleted from P_1 or P_2.

Step 4: Check schedulability and replace tasks
The response times of all tasks and messages have to be calculated. In this situation different cases have to be considered:

Case 1: If the gain exceeds zero and the timing constraints are not violated, all tasks in the amount of exchangeable tasks are assigned to the new processing nodes. Once replaced units are not changeable anymore and therefore deleted from the amount of initial exchangeable tasks P_1 and P_2.

Case 2: If the transfer does not reduce the external communication, the tasks will not be replaced and the amounts of possible exchangeable units X_1 and X_2 will be deleted.

Case 3: If the timing restrictions are violated and there are exchangeable tasks left, the task with the next highest gain in the context of cost reduction will be taken into the amount of possible exchangeable units X_1 or X_2. If a transfer of this task does not improve the timing performance it is deleted again. This step will be repeated until there are sets of exchangeable tasks with a positive total gain. If the resulting allocation is feasible, the tasks of the exchangeable units X_1 and X_2 will be replaced and deleted from P_1 and P_2. Otherwise the tasks will not be replaced and the amounts of possible exchangeable tasks X_1 and X_2 will be deleted.

Step 5: Repeat
Steps 2 to 4 are repeated until there are no initial exchangeable tasks left in the task sets P_1 and P_2.

The algorithm is applied to all m over 2 pairs of processing units.

SIMULATED ANNEALING

Kirkpatrick et al. [4] introduced the concept of the physical annealing process in optimization problems where the set of feasible solutions is discrete, and the goal is to find the best possible solution. Annealing is known as a thermal process to obtain low energy states. The analogy between a physical system and a combinatorial optimization problem results from the following equivalence. The solution states in a combinatorial optimization problem are equivalent to states of a physical system, and the objective function value of a solution is equivalent to the energy of a state. The temperature controlling the whole annealing process is equivalent to a parameter that is called a control parameter in the simulated annealing algorithm. The principal elements of the simulated annealing algorithm are:

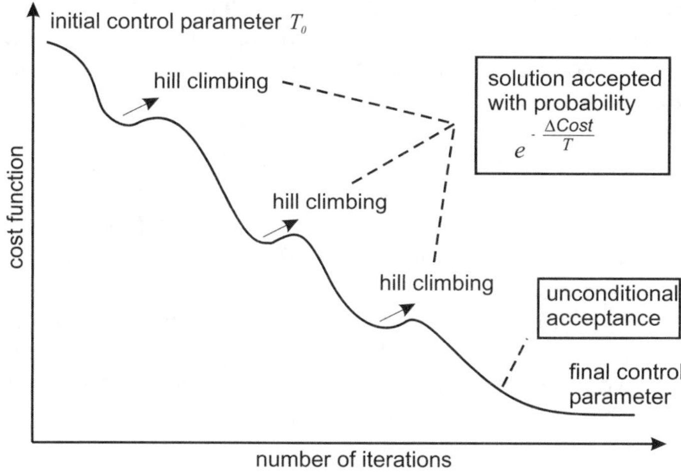

Figure 4: Simulated annealing

Acceptance criteria

The acceptance criteria

$$\exp\left(-\frac{\Delta Cost}{T}\right) > \text{rand}(0,1) \qquad (3)$$

determine whether to accept the new solution state as the new current solution state. Starting with a solution S as the current assignment of tasks to the different processing units, a neighbor solution S_i can be generated by moving one task to a different processing unit. Since the new allocation has an influence on the timing behavior of the whole system, the worst-case response times of all tasks have to be recalculated. If the worst-case response times are smaller than the deadlines, the system is schedulable. In the BGF algorithm the move from the current solution to the new solution is made only if the new solution has a better objective function value than the current solution. The simulated annealing algorithm uses a probability to ascertain a move so that it occasionally accepts the new solution state as inferior to the current solution in terms of the objective function value. In doing so, the algorithm is able to avoid getting stuck in a local optimum (see Figure 4).

Control parameter T

The control parameter T (also called "temperature"), besides the cost difference between the current solution state and new solution state, is the only factor in the acceptance criteria. The greater the control parameter is, the easier the acceptance criteria are met. Thus the control parameter T steers the whole simulated annealing process. At the beginning of the iteration process, the control parameter T is usually set to a large number so that most of the new solution states would be accepted. As the value of control parameter T decreases, only a few new solutions with better objective functions would be accepted. Finally, as the value of T approaches 0, no worse solution will be accepted at all, and only finding the better solution would lead to a transition of the current solution state to a new solution state. To design a proper simulated annealing algorithm, not only should the solution state generating mechanism be well well-designed, but more importantly, the cooling schedule should be well-designed also. For example a small decreasing rate of the temperature-control parameter is important for a good solution, but it greatly increases the computing difficulty.

Objective Function

The main goal of an objective function must be to measure the quality of a given solution. Objective functions are usually expressed as a sum of weighted costs or objectives, as follows:

$$Cost(S) = \sum_i w_i \cdot \frac{C_i(S)}{N_i} \quad (4)$$

where S is the solution under evaluation, $C_i(S)$ is the value of a particular objective or cost, w_i is the weight factor applied to this objective in the solution evaluation and N_i is a normalization parameter needed to sum relative values. But this expression has a clear drawback: optimum values can be found outside of the valid search space, since the violation of constraints either is not checked or it is performed modifying the control scheme. We propose the use of different correction terms to correctly guide the search in the design space.

We use barrier functions for design constraints that must be satisfied, because it ensures that the constraint will never be exceeded and therefore provides a clear boundary in the design space in such a way that the cost associated with a solution out of this region will be infinity.

When the system constraints are less restrictive, the use of penalty functions can be more suitable [5]. Penalty functions do not contribute to the cost function when the solution is in the allowed search space. This kind of function is not as restrictive as the barrier functions, since solutions around the border of the allowed exploration region can be accepted if they are really close.

The cost function tries to reduce the bus utilization for the allocation problem.

$$Cost_1(S) = \sum\nolimits_{m_{ij} \in M} \left(\frac{C_{ij}}{T_j} \right). \quad (5)$$

where C_{ij} is the transmission time of message m_{ij} and T_j the period of the sending task τ_j.

As there are additional constraints like keeping the response times r_i^{wcet} below the tasks deadlines d_i we add a penalty function according to how the constraints are violated.

$$Cost(S)_2 = 150 \cdot \sum\nolimits_{\tau_i \in V} \left(\frac{\max(0, r_i^{wcrt} - d_i)}{d_i} \right). \quad (6)$$

Assigning tasks with a fixed allocation to different processing units is not allowed. In this case a barrier function sets the objective function to infinity. The resulting objective function for the allowed solutions is

$$Cost(S) = Cost_1(S) + Cost_2(S). \quad (7)$$

Algorithm structure

Starting with an initial allocation, the algorithm performs the following steps:

Step 1: Initialize control parameter T
Initialize the control parameter T with a high value.

Step 2: Select neighbor solution S_i
Change the task allocation through a random move of one task to another processing unit. The resulting task assignment is the considered neighbor solution S_i.

Step 3: Calculate cost difference $\Delta Cost$
Calculate the change in the cost due to the move made.

Step 4: Accept or reject neighbor solution
Depending on the change in cost, accept or reject the move. The probability of acceptance is dependent on the current control parameter T.

Step 5: Update and repeat
After a defined number of moves lower the current control parameter T and go back to step 2.

Simulated Annealing Parameters

The decreasing rate of the control parameter T is one of the most important factors affecting the progression of the simulated annealing process. If the decreasing rate is too high, the process would be terminated quickly due to the stricter acceptance criteria, so a sufficient solution cannot be obtained. If the decreasing rate is too low, the simulated annealing would require a very long time to terminate to a desirable solution state.

The simulated annealing converges to the set of globally optimal solutions under the condition that the stationary distribution is obtained at each value of T, and the probability of finding an optimal solution increases uniformly with decreasing T. The number of iterations at each temperature step and its updating function determine whether the stationary distribution can be achieved or not. However, if the number is too high, it would lead to a very inefficient algorithm. To derive an adequate cooling schedule, the parameters of the simulated annealing algorithm are adapted by using an adaptive annealing approach.

1. Initial temperature T_0: The condition proposed by White [11] is used to determine the starting temperature. The temperature is considered to be high enough when $T >> \sigma$, where σ is the standard deviation of the cost function. Hence $T_0 = k\sigma$, where k is computed assuming a normal cost distribution. A temperature is selected that accepts a configuration whose cost is 3σ worse than the present one with a given probability P. This leads to

$$k = -\frac{3}{\ln P} \quad . \qquad (8)$$

With P=0,9 as a typical value we get k=28. First the configuration space is explored to determine the standard deviation σ of the cost function, and then the starting temperature is calculated. Starting from the current solution the cost values of all N neighbor solutions S_i and the mean cost value has to be calculated.

$$\sigma = \sqrt{\frac{\sum_{i=1}^{N}(Cost(S_i) - MeanCost(S_i))^2}{N-1}} \quad . \qquad (9)$$

2. Decrement of T: The annealing curve is used to guide the temperature decrease. The way in which we decrement our temperature is critical to the success of the algorithm. Theory states that we should allow enough iterations at each temperature so that the system stabilizes at that temperature. Unfortunately, theory also states that the number of iterations at each temperature to achieve this might be exponential to the problem size. Since this is impractical, we need to compromise. We can either do this by doing a large number of iterations at a few temperatures, a small number of iterations at many temperatures or a balance between the two. One way to decrement the temperature is a simple linear method. An alternative is a geometric decrement where $T = T\alpha$ where $\alpha < 1$.
   Experience has shown that α should be between 0.8 and 0.99, with better results being found in the higher end of the range. Of course, the higher the value of α, the longer it will take to decrement the temperature to the stopping criterion.

3. Number of iteration steps: This value determines the number of successful moves that will be considered at each temperature level. A larger value increases the optimization time, but tends to yield solutions near the global optimum. An obvious choice for L_k, the number of iterations at the k-th temperature step, is a value that depends on the size of the problem, so L_k is independent of k. Alternatively it can be argued that a minimum number of successful moves should be accepted at each temperature. However, as T approaches 0, moves are accepted with decreasing probability, so the number of trials required to achieve η acceptances approaches ∞. Thus, at each temperature level the algorithm is executed for

   a. L_k transitions or
   b. η acceptances,

whichever comes first, as a suitable compromise. With the parameter $L_k = nm$ we choose the size of the neighborhood, since the system should have the possibility of investigating all configurations of a given configuration. For the number of acceptances we take η=100.

COMPARISON OF THE HEURISTIC ALGORITHM WITH SIMULATED ANNEALING

In this section we compare the performance of the BGF algorithm with the simulated annealing technique. For this purpose we have implemented a software tool, written in C running on an Athlon 1.2Ghz PC, that can apply both methods using a parametric description of the real-time system. Example systems are generated with the program Task Graphs For Free (TGFF) [3]. TGFF is a program to generate pseudo-random task graphs for use in scheduling and allocation research. The task graphs generated by TGFF can be restricted by different user parameters. For periodic task sets, the user specifies a set of integer period-multipliers which determine the relative periods of the multiple task graphs in each case. Communication data size and worst-case execution times can be generated randomly. A set of different application examples has been generated to test the performance of the allocation algorithms.

	Tasks	Edges	Processing units
System 1	41	100	2
System 2	63	159	3
System 3	89	146	7
System 4	114	190	7
System 5	138	238	11
System 6	167	339	10
System 7	199	399	13
System 8	226	318	14
System 9	233	249	14
System 10	282	395	12
System 11	311	350	16
System 12	362	687	18
System 13	391	581	13
System 14	438	429	19
System 15	472	532	26

Table 1: Example systems

Figure 5 shows a comparison of the performance of both algorithms using the example systems of Table 1.

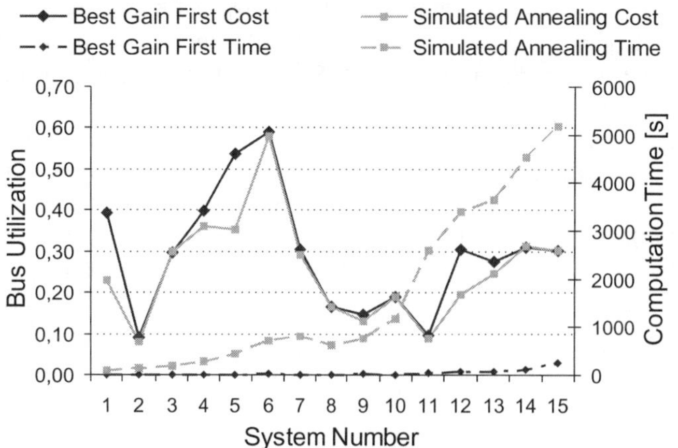

Figure 5: Comparison of the BGF algorithm with simulated annealing

The number of processing units has been chosen close to the limit where feasible solutions could be found.The graph shows the computation time and the resulting bus utilization for each algorithm. The simulated annealing algorithm performs better for the tested systems, but the optimized cost of the BGF algorithm does not differ very much from the SA algorithm. Simulated annealing is a nondeterministic algorithm and therefore needs more optimization steps to converge to the optimized task allocation. This results in larger computation times, as shown in Figure 4. As an example, the CPU time consumed by the two algorithms to generate the results of System 11 was:

Best Gain First: 49 s

Simulated Annealing: 2592 s

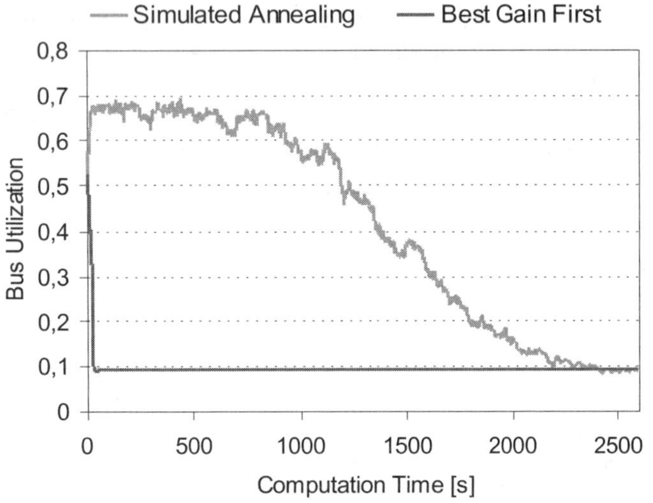

Figure 6: Optimization progress

The corresponding optimization progress is shown in Figure 6.

CONCLUSION

In this paper we propose a framework for the optimized allocation of real-time systems to a multiprocessor environment connected by a Controller Area Network. We have compared the BGF algorithm with simulated annealing as a general purpose discrete optimization algorithm. We adapted the simulated annealing parameters and the objective function to our problem. The analysis tool has been applied to examples and we compared the optimization results of the two algorithms. As a result of the comparison the difference in computation times between the BGF algorithm and simulated annealing is enormous, and the BGF algorithm finds solutions near the simulated annealing approach.

Given the good performance of the proposed heuristic algorithm additional constraints will be implemented in future work.

REFERENCES

[1] P. Altenbernd. Timing Analysis, Scheduling, and Allocation of Periodic Hard Real-Time Tasks. Dissertation, Paderborn, 1996.

[2] CAN Specification 2.0, Part-A and Part-B. CAN in Automation (CiA), Am Weichselgarten 26, D-91058 Erlangen. http://www.can-cia.de/, 2004.

[3] D. R. R. P. Dick and W. Wolf. Tgff: Task graphs for free. *Proc. Int. Workshop Hardware/Software Codesign*, pp 97-101, 1998

[4] S. Kirkpatrick, Jr. C. Gelatt and M. Vecchi: *Optimization by simulated annealing*. Science, Volume 220 (4598), pp. 498-516, 1983

[5] D. G. Luenberger. Linear and non-Linear Programming. Addison- Wesley, 1984.

[6] K.J Neumann. Partitionierung verteilter Echtzeitfunktionen in vernetzten Systemen. Dissertation, Universität Karlsruhe (TH), 1997.

[7] T. Rambow, R. Schloer, R. Busch, A. Seibertz and U. Kiencke: Timing Analysis and Scheduling of Distributed Control Functions. First IFAC Symposium on Advances in Automotive Control AAC04, April 2004, Salerno, Italy

[8] K. W. Tindell and A. Burns. Guaranteed Message Latencies for Distributed Safety-Critical Hard Real-Time Control Networks. Technical Report YCS229, Dept. of Computer Science, University of York, June 1994.

[9] K. W. Tindell, A. Burns, and A. J. Wellings. Calculating Controller Area Network (CAN) Message Response Times. Control Engineering Practice, 3(8):1163–1169, 1995.

[10] K. W. Tindell, H. Hansson, and A. J. Wellings. Analysing Real-Time Communications: Controller Area Network (CAN). Proceedings of RTSS'94 -IEEE Real-Time Systems Symposium, pp 259–265, December 1994

[11] S. R. White: Concept of scale in simulated annealing, IEEE International Conference of Computer Design, pp 646-651, 1984

CONTACT

Thomas Rambow can be contacted through the Institute of Industrial Information Technology, University of Karlsruhe (TH), Germany at +49 (721) 608-4519, or by email: rambow@iiit.uni-karlsruhe.de

2004-01-0278

Meeting the Challenges in a Collaborative OEM-Supplier Development of Distributed Embedded Systems

Roman Nossal
DECOMSYS

ABSTRACT

This paper gives a detailed description of a development process for distributed embedded systems, which is capable of handling a collaborative development of an OEM and several suppliers. The process comprises a set of development models, operations, which are the transitions from one model to the other, and contracts. Contracts define the interface between the OEM and the supplier.

INTRODUCTION

At the 2003 SAE World Congress DECOMSYS introduced the theoretical background for handling the OEM-supplier relationship, the so-called information domain model. In this paper we want to discuss the practical application of this model.

The paper deals with the challenges of developing distributed embedded systems, which have been identified in discussions and ongoing development projects with major players in the automotive industry. The paper addresses the challenges by devising a development process for distributed embedded systems, which are created in a collaborative effort between an OEM and a multitude of suppliers. Apart from the technical details like the system models involved in the process, the focus lies on organizational issues such as the information flow between the process participants.

CHALLENGES IN EMBEDDED SYSTEMS

OEM, SUPPLIER, SYSTEM INTEGRATOR

There is a lot of confusion about the terms OEM, supplier, and system integrator. A look at Table 1 reveals that these terms are by no means clearly distinguished and show substantial overlapping. The OEM can be the system integrator while at the same time acting as a supplier for an ECU or a function. Similarly, a supplier can just supply an ECU to a system or he can be the integrator of a system, which is then supplied to the OEM as an entirety. Thus, whenever we talk of an OEM in this paper, the same applies to any system integrator.

	OEM	Supplier
System Integrator	X	X
ECU/Function Supplier	X	X

Table 1: Roles In the Development of Embedded Systems

DISTRIBUTED INFORMATION

The organizational setting of automotive embedded system development creates a special situation regarding the possession of information by the process participants. While common projects, e.g., for commercial applications like supply chain systems, strive to provide all applicable knowledge to all process participants, the OEM as well as the suppliers must cope with incomplete information in automotive embedded systems.

The OEM possesses the knowledge of the intended function of the system. He also selects the system architecture and distributes the functionality among the ECUs in the system.

Suppliers, on the other hand, have detailed information about the functions their ECUs should perform. They are the experts regarding the software architecture, the control algorithms, and of course the implementation. They can specify the communication requirements on the input side, i.e., the data that must be provided by other functions executed on other ECUs. Similarly, they can define the communication offer on the output side, i.e., the data that can be provided by the functions executed on their ECUs. The latter two pieces of information should constitute an input for the OEM.

None of the process participants has the “full picture”, yet the ultimate goal is to create a working system. This leads to two issues to be handled by a development process: the exchange of requirements and the exchange of models.

Requirements Exchange

As discussed above, each process participant possesses certain pieces of information when the project starts. These pieces of information constitute requirements for other process participants. The distribution of functions to ECUs of the system, for example, forms a stringent requirement for the supplier when implementing the ECU.

Any useful development process must ensure that all relevant requirements are exchanged and made available to the other process participants.

Information and Model Exchange

In contrast to the requirements, which are known at project start and should be exchanged in early project phases, models and information like the communication timing are created in the course of the project. The communication timing, for instance, is a result of the communication scheduling done by the system integrator.

During the project the development process must take care that information that is created is passed on to all process participants, which need this information.

REUSE

OEMs do not only face the development of one specific car, but have to deal with several car series. The car series have some functions in common; other functions are implemented in only one series. Depending on the hardware architecture of a car series, the mapping of functions to ECUs is different, although the functions themselves are the same. The set of functions residing on an ECU thus is specific to the car series as well.

A similar situation is encountered at the suppliers. A piece of software code implementing a function is used not only once but should be the same for several projects. The combination of code pieces on a certain ECU, however, depends on the car series in which the ECU is used.

In both cases the goal obviously is reuse. OEMs want to reuse functions or entire ECUs in different car series; suppliers strive to reuse code for different ECUs and projects [3]. In order to facilitate reuse, two issues must be addressed: standardized architectures and interfaces and standardized ways of information exchange.

Standardized Interfaces

Standardizing interfaces for software means to provide one operating system API for the software to access communication as well as other resources like ADCs. Similarly, the hardware of a distributed system can have a standardized interface represented by an abstract description of the network communication. The implementation of a function or the realization of an ECU adhering to standardized interfaces need not be changed when the code or the ECU is reused in a new system. Adaptation to the new environment is confined to a potential change in the timing of the system.

Standardized Information Exchange

Commonly, the OEM and his suppliers agree on a set of tools to be used for each project. The development of pieces of code or an entire ECU is done with these tools. If the code or the ECU should be reused in another project, there might be an agreement to use a different set of tools. This substantially hinders the adaptation of the code and the ECU, as development data are not available for the new tools.

For the future the trend should be not to agree on specific tools but on an information exchange format, which all tools must understand. If functions should be reused in a new project, the tools can also be reused, provided the two projects use the same information

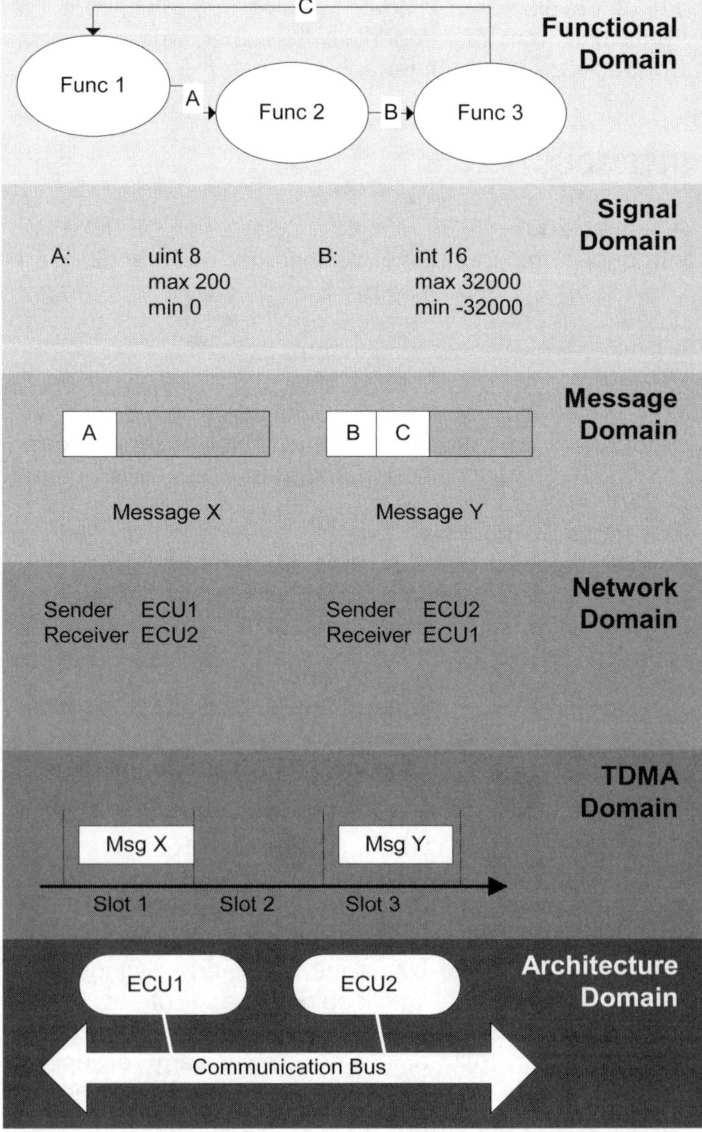

Figure 1: Network Information Domain Model

exchange format. Considering this, it is obvious that the industry would benefit from a standardized information exchange format that is agreed upon by the key players and that covers all information that might arise in development projects.

INFORMATION DOMAIN MODEL

At the 2003 SAE World Congress DECOMSYS introduced the so-called information domain model [2], which we use to classify information created or exchanged during the development process. The model focused on defining the communication system and did not take into account any ECU-internal aspects. We refer to this model as the *network information domain model*, which we will briefly sum up in the following. Subsequently, we will extend this model to cope with ECU-internal aspects such as software and dispatching. This extended model is called the *system information domain model*.

NETWORK MODEL

The network information domain model consists of 6 domains (see Figure 1):

The *functional domain* defines entities called functions and the communication relations between them. A communication relation starts at a sender function, connects the sender function with receiver functions, and has an assigned signal.

Signals are defined in the *signal domain*. A signal definition contains a signal name, the signal semantics, and the value range. Signals are assigned to messages. The *message domain* defines names of messages and the setup of the signals in the messages.

The *network domain* determines which ECU will send a frame containing a message.

The *TDMA domain* establishes the exact points in time when a frame is transmitted.

Finally, the *architecture domain* defines the physical structure of a system, with all ECUs, communication systems, and the connections of the ECUs to them.

SYSTEM MODEL

The system information domain model goes beyond the pure network model and adds two additional domains, which are positioned in parallel to the network model domains (see Figure 2). The two new domains are the process domain and the dispatching domain.

The *process domain* describes the software architecture of the system. It lists all processes and their interactions like mutual exclusion, as well as the assignment of processes to functions.

Processes are information processing units of an application. They have timing parameters assigned to them that define the period and the time offset of their execution.

The *dispatching domain* is the ECU counterpart of the TDMA domain. It determines the application timing, i.e., which process is executed at which point time. Implicitly, this also defines the preemption of processes, i.e., when a process is interrupted by the execution of another process.

CONTRACTS

Information from the above domains can be used to form contracts among the participants in the process. Much like a legal contract, a contract here defines certain pieces of information agreed upon by the contracting parties. The contract binds both parties. However, normally one of the parties is the principal, while the other is the agent.

The entire embedded system can be described by means of contracts. Obviously contracts must not contradict each other and they have to describe the system comprehensively. If the latter is not the case, i.e., if no set of contracts exists that represents the entire requirements or system specification, then the system is not defined sufficiently.

OEM-SUPPLIER PROCESS

In the section on challenges we have identified the need to exchange requirements and development information among the process participants. This section introduces a development process for an OEM-Supplier collaborative project, which meets this need. The process comprises a set of development models, operations, which are the transitions from one model to the other, and contracts, which define the interface between the OEM and the supplier.

The proposed development process is divided into an OEM part and a supplier part (see Figure 3).

OEM DEVELOPMENT PROCESS

The OEM bases the development on two models, which are normally available as a result of the requirements process and the vehicle architecture. The *Functional Model*[1] is a description of the functions, which the embedded system should perform. Apart from the definition of the functionality itself, the Functional Model deals with the specification of external inputs and outputs, i.e., sensor values and values sent to actuators, as well as the interaction between the functions. Obviously, the Functional Model belongs to the functional domain of the information domain model.

---

[1] A more detailed description of the models and their purpose is given in [1].

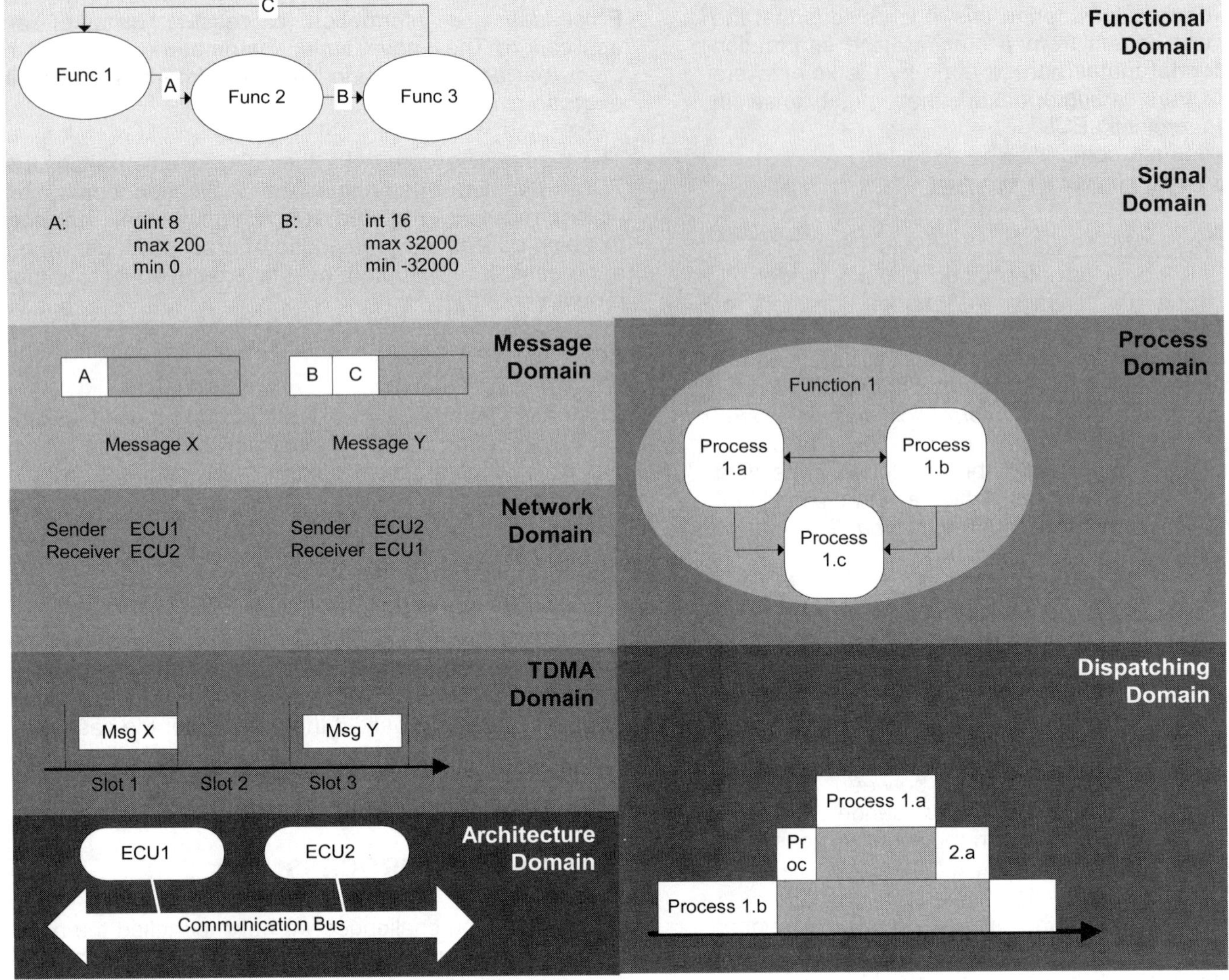

Figure 2: System Information Domain Model

A Functional Model can be as rough as just describing "high-level" functions such as steer-by-wire or gear determination or it can be much more refined, breaking up the high-level functions into subfunctions. Which level of detail is used depends on the OEM's amount of information and his intentions. A more detailed approach enables the OEM to allocate only small portions of a function to a certain supplier, while in a rough model the allocation must be based on entire functions.

The *Hardware Model* constitutes the second starting point of the OEM's development flow. The Hardware Model, which is part of the architecture domain of the information domain model, describes the number of ECUs present in the system, their technical details such as the CPU, and their interconnection via one or more communication networks and possibly gateways.

The interested reader might note a difference between the above approach and the approach commonly taken in today's cars. Normally each ECU has a certain function or a certain set of functions. The functions are always linked with the specific ECU and not considered independently. We feel, however, that in the future the increased need of reuse will require the above distinction. Looking at functions and hardware architecture independently facilitates reuse of the functional model (and later of its implementation) by remapping the Functional Model to a different Hardware Model.

The first operation performed on the two initial models is *function partitioning and mapping*. For each function or part of it (subfunction) the OEM has to decide which ECU should carry out this function. The partitioning and mapping process results in the *Distributed Functional Model*. The Distributed Functional Model is a crossover between two information domains, the functional domain as it still describes functions and the signal domain, because the partitioning and mapping to different pieces of hardware implicitly defines the signals that are exchanged between ECUs.

Once the partitioning is performed the OEM can carry on with *communication scheduling,* which creates the *Network Configuration*. This single step actually covers three information domains. Firstly, signals are combined to messages, i.e., packages, which are transmitted together. This defines the message domain. Secondly, the senders and receivers of a message are determined in the network domain. Depending on the hardware allocation of the sending and the receiving function, the sending and receiving ECU of a message varies. Finally, the TDMA domain comprises the timing or schedule of the communication system.

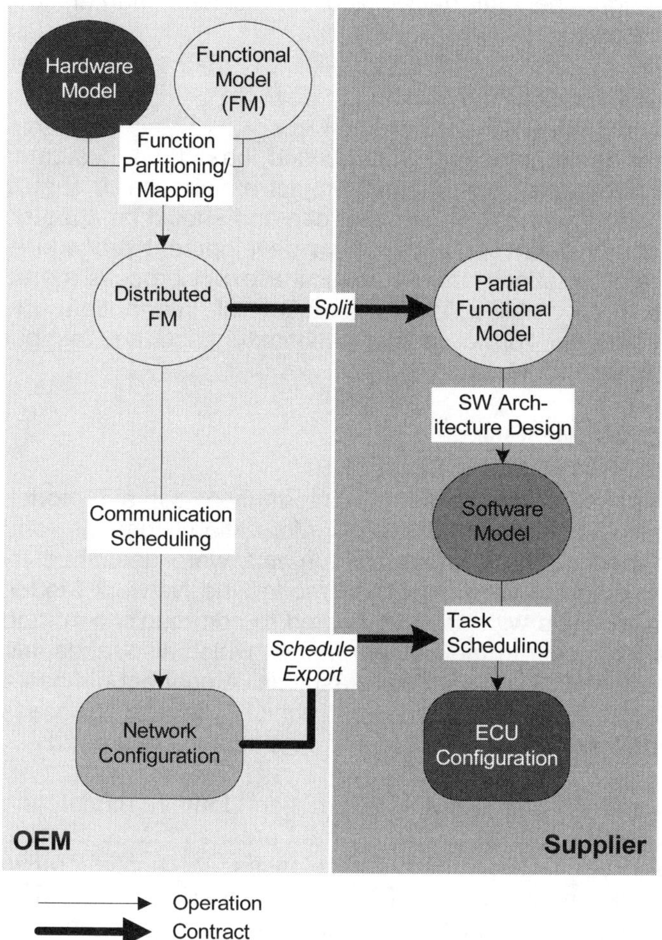

Figure 3: OEM-Supplier Development Process

SUPPLIER DEVELOPMENT PROCESS

The suppliers' development flow starts from the *Partial Functional Model*, which is a subset of the Distributed Functional Model used by the OEM. It comprises those functions that belong to one ECU, which is the supplier's responsibility.

The derivation of the Partial Functional Model from the Distributed Functional Model is called *Split*. The Split constitutes two contracts, one located in the functional domain and the other in the signal domain. The contract of the functional domain governs the functions to be delivered by the ECU. It comprises all functions and subfunctions that are allocated to the ECU. For each function or subfunction the OEM also provides a response time requirement, which is derived from the overall response time of the function. During ECU development the supplier must guarantee that this response time is met by the implementation.

The functional contract is complemented by a signal contract, which governs the incoming communication needed and the outgoing communication offered by the ECU. As mentioned above, when the Functional Model is partitioned and mapped to hardware, the signals crossing ECU boundaries are identified.

The supplier carries out the *software architecture design* on the Partial Functional Model, thus creating the *Software Model*. Unlike a functional model, which focuses on functions and subfunctions, the Software Model deals with tasks and processes, i.e., the units of execution of the operating system. A process can either implement exactly one function, a part of a function, or (parts of) several functions. There is not necessarily a one-to-one mapping between functions and processes. Furthermore, the relations between processes are part of the Software Model. Processes might be independent or they can have relations such as communication, precedence, and mutual exclusion. Process relations play an important role during task scheduling (see below). The Software Model is part of the process domain of the information domain model.

Although the Software Model describes the architecture of the software, it does not deal with the execution timing. The supplier calculates this and determines the configuration of the ECU in the course of *task scheduling*. Based on the knowledge of the Partial Functional Model and the Software Model, in particular parameters like function repetition periods, worst-case execution times of processes, and process relations, the supplier seeks to find an optimal schedule for all processes of the ECU.

Apart from the above parameters, task scheduling is constrained externally by the OEM. The *Schedule Export* consists of three contracts on the message, the network, and the TDMA domain. They describe the packaging of signals to messages, who sends and receives these messages, and the timing of message transmission, respectively. The contracts set the constraints for the supplier. When calculating the process timing, the supplier must strive to meet the timing conditions set forth in the global communication schedule and the response time requirements of the functions. Assume, for example, a case where the supplier implements an ECU for actuator control. The TDMA contract defines when the latest set point value arrives at the ECU. In the functional contract of the Split operation, the response time between value arrival and output to the actuator is defined. Thus the implementation of the function and the scheduling must guarantee that all ECU-internal steps are finished between the reception of the set point value and the reception time plus the required response time (see Figure 4).

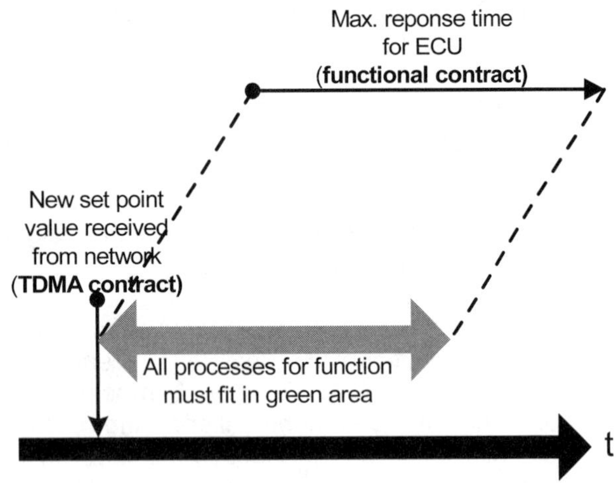

Figure 4: Task Scheduling Constraints by Contracts

All results of the OEM's development steps are considered to be *global information*, since they are common to all ECUs within a network and have an influence on the entire system. On the other hand, all results of the suppliers' development steps are so-called *local information*. They determine the behavior of a single ECU, but do not influence other ECUs. The global information constitutes strict boundary conditions for the degrees of freedom of a supplier. Whatever design decisions are taken by the supplier, he must never violate any global information.

TOOL SUPPORT

From the amount of information created in the process as well as from the number of operations to be performed, it is quite clear that the process must be implemented by development tools, which help and guide the developer. We do not want to promote any particular tool, but we do want to give a brief outline of which features a tool supporting the above process should provide:

- It should have an integrated "data base" for development data, i.e., the models.
- It should implement operations such as task scheduling or support for function partitioning and mapping.
- It should provide a means to implement OEM-supplier contracts.
- It should provide information hiding and security. For example, the supplier must not be able to locally change the communication schedule, i.e., the TDMA contract.

Probably there won't be any single tool, which covers all process areas. The participating companies should rather agree on a set of tools that they want to apply. In order to guarantee the interoperability of these tools, standardized information exchange formats are gaining in importance. Any tool, which is able to read or write an exchange format, can interoperate with any other tool capable of the same format. A step in the right direction has been taken by the FIBEX (Field Bus Exchange Format) initiative in Europe. FIBEX, which has lately become part of the ASAM consortium[2], is an XML-based definition of a system description that covers functions, hardware architectures, and communication.

We feel that open exchange formats – aside from their interoperability advantages – are an important driver for the tool market. Developing new tools becomes more attractive if those tools interact with well-established tools through open interfaces and thus closed markets get opened up again.

PROCESS ADAPTATION

The above process was defined based on customer requirements and practical project experience. It should be used as a role model that can and should be adapted to meet each company's own development procedure. The adaptations should cover the exact process steps, the responsibility for the creation of information, the amount and format of information exchange, and last but not least the tools.

CONCLUSION

This paper presented the information domain model, which consists of several information domains and contracts. The information domains were described by two different versions of the model, the Network Model, which deals with aspects related to communication, and its extension to the System Model, which also takes into account ECU and software aspects. A contract defines a piece of information, on which several process participants, i.e., an OEM and suppliers, have agreed.

Based on the system information domain model, the paper introduced a development process that is suitable to cope with the particularities of collaborative development by an OEM and several suppliers. The process pays particular attention to the interaction between the OEM and the suppliers, the information exchanges between them, and the constraints resulting from the exchanged information.

A brief definition of requirements for tools supporting the development process concludes the paper.

It is important to be aware of the role model character of the described process. If it is to be employed in a real project, the process participants must make several process decisions before actually starting the development in order to adapt the process to other processes already used in the organizations involved.

REFERENCES

1. R. Nossal, R. Lang. Model-Based System Development—An Approach to Building X-by-Wire Applications. IEEE Micro, July/August 2002, pp. 56-63.

---

[2] Association for Standardization of Automation and Measuring Systems (www.asam.net)

2. R. Nossal, D. Millinger. Dealing With the OEM-Supplier Relationship in the Development of Embedded Software. Paper No. 2003-01-1198, 2003 SAE World Congress, March 2003.
3. D. Lederer, G. Heling, J. Fetzer, and T. Beck. Der Schlüssel zum Erfolg (The Key to Success; in German). Elektronik Automotive, June 2002, pp. 42-46.

CONTACT

Please direct questions or comments about this article to Roman Nossal at DECOMSYS - Dependable Computer Systems, Hardware und Software Entwicklung GmbH, Stumpergasse 48/28, A-1060 Vienna, Austria; nossal@decomsys.com; www.decomsys.com

DECOMSYS is a development partner of the FlexRay® consortium.

Roman Nossal is product manager at DECOMSYS. He has a PhD in computer science from the Vienna University of Technology and an MBA in General Management from Danube University in Krems, Austria.

2005-01-0322

A Fault-Tolerant Processor Core Architecture for Safety-Critical Automotive Applications

Emmanuel Touloupis, James A Flint and Vassilios A Chouliaras
Loughborough University

David D. Ward
MIRA Ltd

ABSTRACT

The introduction of drive-by-wire systems into modern vehicles has generated new challenges for the designers of embedded systems. These systems, based primarily on microcontrollers, need to achieve very high levels of reliability and availability, but also have to satisfy the strict cost and packaging constraints of the automotive industry. Advances in VLSI technology have allowed the development of single-chip systems, but have also increased the rate of intermittent and transient faults that come as a result of the continuous shrinkage of the CMOS process feature size. This paper presents a low-cost, fault-tolerant system-on-chip architecture suitable for drive-by-wire and other safety-related applications, based on a triple-modular-redundancy configuration at the processor execution pipeline level.

INTRODUCTION

The number of electronic components in vehicles has been continuously increasing in recent decades. With the development of drive-by-wire applications such as steer-by-wire and brake-by-wire, computers are beginning to replace existing mechanical systems, thus taking over those safety-related functions of the vehicle that have a high Safety Integrity Level (SIL). This means that the design of such computer systems must incorporate all the appropriate techniques for achieving high reliability levels and tolerating faults. The strategies adopted in aerospace applications and fly-by-wire systems in airplanes at the hardware level include the use of radiation-hardened components and large-scale redundancy. These techniques may not be directly applicable to the automotive industry, where stringent cost and packaging constraints exist.

The advantages of embedded VLSI technology allow single-chip solutions to be designed that integrate large redundant structures relatively cheaply. Furthermore, the continuous shrinkage of CMOS geometries and the associated increase in the silicon real estate can provide a key integrated solution to the package constraints of the automotive industry. The challenge for embedded systems designers is to successfully adapt traditional hardware fault-tolerant techniques into system-on-chip (SOC) solutions.

FAULTS IN DIGITAL VLSI SYSTEMS

Semiconductor materials are by nature sensitive to radiation exposure. Very high radiation levels can actually damage the structure of the semiconductor material, thus causing a permanent fault that is usually referred to as a hard fault. Another cause of permanent faults is electromigration. Electromigration in an IC is the movement of metal ions as the result of the flow of electrical charge through the metal wires of the chip. This unwanted ion movement may create metal gaps in some parts of the wires, and build up metal at other sites, which can lead to open-circuits and short-circuits [1]. Open-circuits and short-circuits are initially manifested as intermittent faults. The rate of permanent faults in CMOS microprocessors and static and dynamic memories has significantly decreased over the last decades due to improvements in manufacturing techniques. As geometries shrink, the wire cross-section decreases, thus increasing the sensitivity to electromigration, although the use of copper interconnects provide better protection against this phenomenon [2].

Unlike intermittent and permanent faults, that occur after several months of the circuit's operation and can be removed by replacing the faulty circuit, transient faults occur at the same rate in all cases. These faults affect the stored charges that represent data inside the chip and can generate an error that can possibly lead to a system failure. The main sources of such faults are the following [3, 4]:

- Electrical noise from external sources.
- Electromagnetic coupling (crosstalk) between the chips' interconnects.
- The decay of radioactive material that exists in small amounts in the semiconductor material

and the surrounding package that generates alpha particle emission.

- Neutron particles that originate from extraterrestrial cosmic rays that bombard the earth's surface constantly.

Some of these problems can be minimized by carefully selecting the CMOS process materials, following strict decontamination procedures and utilizing radiation-hardening technology. In practice these solutions are expensive for commercial applications.

Transient faults caused from radiation are at the moment a problem that mostly occurs at high altitudes. Future sub 100 nm technologies will suffer from the same problem at ground level, since the stored electrical charge that represents data decreases as layout dimensions shrink. The transient faults appear as single or multi-bit flips (change of the contents of a storage cell) but they can also affect combinational circuits. They are also referred to as single event upsets (SEU). Several other factors will increase the occurrence of transient faults: 1) the lower power supplies decrease noise margins, 2) increased density brings interconnects on the chip closer together, which increases the crosstalk between them, 3) higher clock frequencies generate ground bounces (voltage spikes on the ground).

DESIGNING A LOW-COST FAULT-TOLERANT PROCESSOR

In order to satisfy the low-cost requirements of automotive and other commercial safety-critical applications, designing a processor should focus on detecting and masking, or correcting the errors induced by radiation and coupling disturbances rather than preventing them. This can be achieved by carefully designing each part of the processor based on redundancy, error detection and correction, and system reconfiguration as shown in Figure 1. Previous research has focused on developing error detection and correction techniques for those memory elements (data and instruction cache, register file, internal RAM, etc.) that are considered to be more susceptible to transient faults. Some typical examples include the use of parity bits, or error correcting codes [5, 6, 7].

In this work we have used an open source configurable processor, which is described using the VHDL hardware description language. It is a 5-stage pipeline processor that implements the SPARC V8 [8] instruction set and is equipped with various peripherals that interconnect through two types of the AMBA bus (AHB and APB) [9]. We have implemented an architecture that protects the pipeline unit against SEUs. The motivation behind this work was that the pipeline consists of several memory elements and parts of combinational logic that are both sensitive to SEUs. Considering the fact that the pipeline unit is the "heart" of the processor and is responsible for its correct and continuous reliable operation, we come to the conclusion that its adequate protection against faults is essential for real-time and safety-critical applications. The details of this implementation are discussed in the following sections of this paper. The main objective of this work is to develop a very reliable processor that is portable and can be implemented in any semiconductor technology.

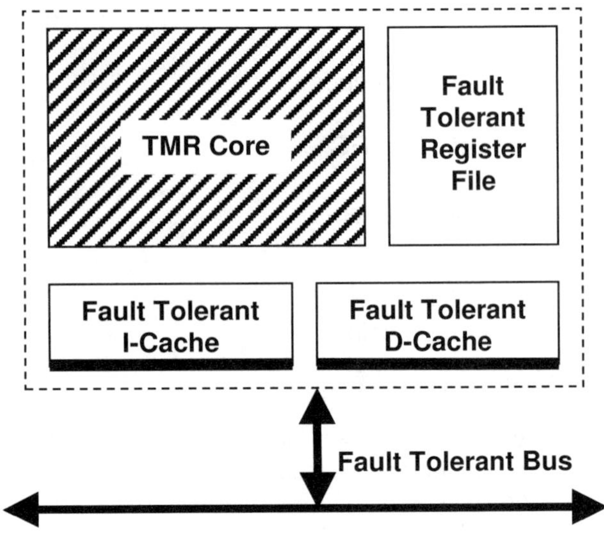

Figure 1: A fault-tolerant processor architecture. The shaded part is the area this work is targeting

SAFETY ANALYSIS

It is a requirement of system safety standards (e.g. [10], [11]) that safety analysis be performed on systems to identify SIL and safety requirements, select an appropriate design process and to confirm that the implemented system meets the safety requirements. Therefore any drive-by-wire system will be subject to a safety analysis. The normal procedure is for a preliminary analysis to be performed at the start of the design, often at the concept stage. More detailed analysis is then performed in an iterative fashion as the design progresses.

In designing the TMR processor core, we considered what the implications would be for system safety analysis. A preliminary analysis would not be concerned with architectural issues, and indeed the approaches typically adopted (see [13]) would be difficult to apply to the on-chip architecture. However, detailed safety analyses of the design would need to consider architectural decisions that may affect (either beneficially or detrimentally) the achieved SIL of the system. We therefore considered what safety analysis method could be applied to a design of this nature in order to confirm its suitability for use in a safety-related system.

Initially, we considered a generic steer-by-wire system such as the one described in [12] and performed a preliminary safety analysis (PSA) [13]. For the detailed structure of the embedded architecture we chose to perform a hazard and operability study (HAZOP) [14]. This is a powerful and flexible technique that has the advantage that it can be carried out before, during and after each design stage of the system. The HAZOP process is based on a series of structured questions using "guide words" to explore potential deviations from the intent of the design. We found that specific tailoring of the guide words would be needed to apply HAZOP to VLSI technology, but that the technique was eminently suitable to help build up the overall safety case for a system based on the proposed TMR architecture.

TMR CORE ARCHITECTURE

A novel TMR arrangement has been selected for the pipeline level that offers several advantages. We chose this configuration despite the additional hardware required, since the silicon overhead is minimal in state-of-the-art system-on-chip designs. Our design triplicates the entire execution pipeline, including the combinational parts of the circuit, thus offering greater protection against permanent hardware faults. It eliminates the possibility of a common mode fault - a fault that causes the redundant modules of a fault tolerant design to fail under identical conditions - which results from an error on the combinational circuit, something that is a significant drawback of a solution that uses triplicated flip-flops only (see Figure 3).

Finally, a TMR arrangement offers the possibility of physically separating the three pipelines during the floor planning of the final chip layout, in this way reducing even more the probability of a common mode fault. The internal architecture of the TMR core is shown in Figure 2. The three pipelines work concurrently executing the same code and utilizing common instruction and data caches and a single register file. All the outputs of the pipelines are passed through voters. These signals include the interface of the processor core with instruction cache memory, data cache memory, register file, co-processor, error and interrupt signals, etc. The outputs of the voters go to the TMR control module that decides which pipeline produces fault-free results and drives the multiplexer appropriately.

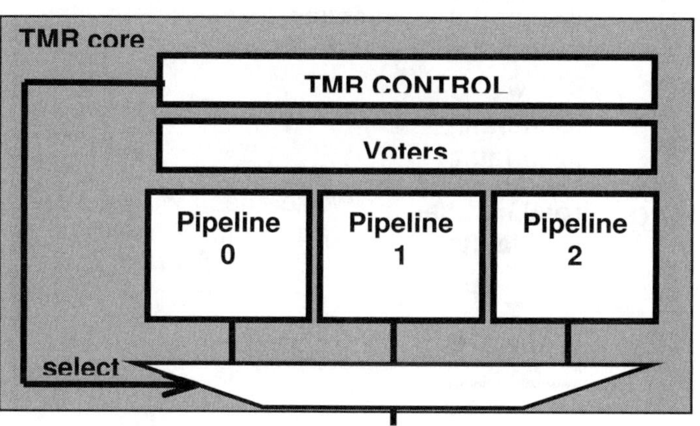

Figure 2: Architecture of the TMR Core

The traditional approach of digital TMR systems in terms of voting is to use simple majority voting circuits on the outputs of the triplicated modules, like the one shown in Figure 3. In case of multi-bit signals, conventional TMR systems use majority voting performed on a bit-by-bit basis. As illustrated in [15], this scheme may produce faulty outputs if there are two faults on two of the three modules. This is treated in [15] by the use of an extra signal as voter output that indicates this erroneous condition where no majority exists. In our design we have modified the voters to have the following outputs:

- A 'disagreement' signal that is active when one or more pipelines produces different outputs from the others.
- A 3-bit 'disagreement vector' where each bit corresponds to one pipeline and becomes 'high' when the pipeline in question disagrees with the other two.
- A 3-bit 'match vector' where each bit represents one pipeline pair and becomes 'high' when the respective pair produces the same outputs. This output is used when the system reconfigures its architecture when a fault is detected.

The voters have no actual data outputs. The reason for this is that voters in TMR (or NMR) systems are single points of failure. With this arrangement a transient fault on one of the voters would drive the TMR control module to change the default pipeline for a few cycles with no actual reason, something that has no implications on the whole system's output.

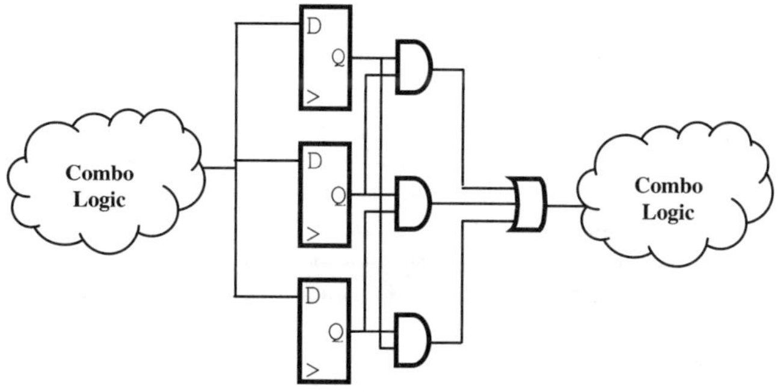

Figure 3: TMR flip-flop Arrangement

The TMR control module is a simple state machine that is driven by the outputs of the voters. When a fault is detected, the faulty pipeline is dynamically removed and the system reconfigures itself into a standby spare arrangement [16] for a specified number of clock cycles. This transition is performed with virtually no interruption of the processor's operation. The TMR-control stops the pipelines, cache memories and coprocessor for one cycle through a global hold signal, as depicted in Figure 4, which means that in a worst case scenario this transition will cause a delay of one clock cycle. In the example shown in Figure 4, a fault in Pipeline 0 causes the disagreement and disagreement_vector[0] signals to become 'high'. This results in the activation of the global hold signal (that has negative logic) for one clock cycle. In the next rising edge of the clock the system has switched into a standby spare arrangement between Pipelines 1 and 2. When the system switches into standby spare the TMR control module is checking the appropriate bit of the match vector to make sure that the outputs of the remaining cores agree. If a disagreement is detected, a warning signal is activated that can either trigger a trap [8], or a global reset. During this period all the registers of the removed pipeline are updated with correct data from the respective registers of one of the "healthy" pipelines. When this "state transfer" is performed successfully, which means that all three pipelines agree and no other faults were detected during the transfer, the removed pipeline is reintroduced into the system, which switches back to a TMR arrangement on the fly. This strategy guarantees that individual cores remain fail-silent, but it also maintains a high level of availability for the system as a whole. In the case where an external source causes multiple faults in more than one pipeline, the system can again generate a trap or a global reset.

The architecture described above enhances the reliability and availability levels of very vital parts of the processor, such as its pipeline unit. Application-specific strategies can be adopted through software by defining the appropriate trap handler. It must also be noted that the exact same concept can be applied to use more than three pipelines without important modifications, and generate an NMR system that switches into (N-1) modular redundancy if a fault is detected in one of the pipelines.

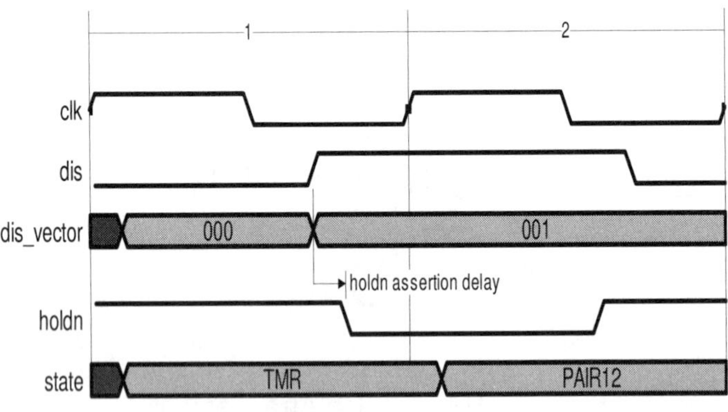

Figure 4: Timing of the system's transition

FAULT INJECTION

In order to test the system during design stages, and also to validate and demonstrate the effectiveness of its fault-masking capabilities, it is necessary to perform fault injection. When the target system is implemented on real hardware, such as an FPGA, software-based fault injection [17] can be used. Software-based fault injection has limited capabilities in the case of a pipelined processor, since not all the pipeline registers are accessible through the processor's instruction set. This meant that for the purposes of this work we developed a simulation-based fault injection strategy, by using the concept of saboteurs, as described in [18]. A saboteur is a VHDL component that alters the value of one or several signals when activated.

The VHDL module that injects faults into the simulation model is also responsible for the following:

1. It generates the fault by picking a bit at random out of the total bits that form the registers of the pipelines. It also picks a random time of injection in clock cycles.
2. It monitors specific signals that indicate the processor's status.
3. It halts a simulation when its execution time exceeds a specified number of clock cycles.
4. It generates a report with data concerning the fault that was injected and the implications it had on the program execution.

The faults can be injected in all the pipeline registers. When the time of injection is reached, the fault injector alters their inputs and this change is latched in the following rising edge of the clock. The system practically simulates faults on the circuit that generates the input of each register, but the effect of a direct bit-flip on the register would be the same.

Each set of fault injection simulation runs is controlled by the simulator, which also accumulates the results that are produced and generates the final experiment results. The basic steps of a fault-injection simulation run are shown in Figure 5.

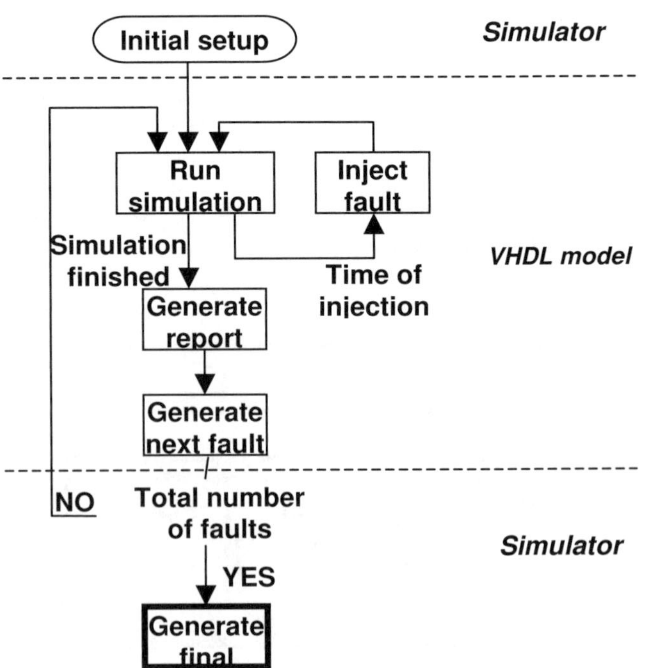

Figure 5: The steps of a fault injection simulation run

RESULTS

For our fault injection experiments we used a simple 4x4 matrix multiplication program. We first considered a single core implementation where no fault-tolerant mechanism was present in order to compare its behavior after injecting faults with the TMR core version presented in this paper. The faults were injected one per program execution and their effects are classified as follows:

1. *Timed Out (TO):* In this case the processor was not able to produce any results after a pre-specified period of time, and the simulation was terminated externally.
2. *Wrong Results (WR):* In this case the execution of the program terminates normally, but the results produced are not correct.
3. *Error Mode (EM):* In this case the processor enters into error mode [8] before reaching the end of the program, and no results are generated.
4. *Correct Results (CR):* In this case the program terminates normally, and the results that are produced are correct.

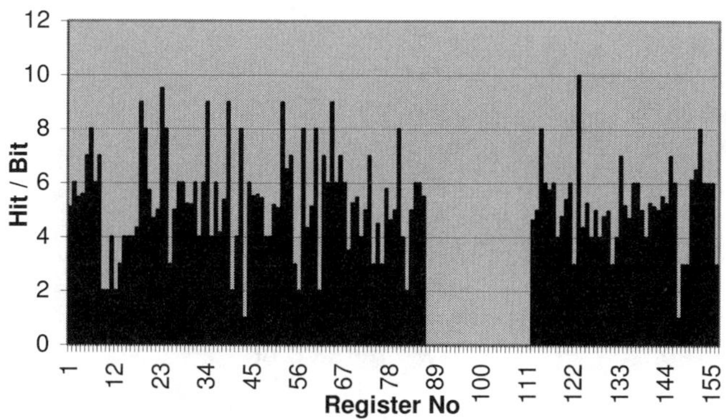

Figure 6: Number of faults per bit in each register

We injected 5000 faults into all the pipeline registers of a single core configuration. The average number of faults injected per bit in each register is shown in Figure 6. The gap in this graph is explained by the fact that we did not inject faults in the registers associated with the floating-point unit, since the architecture we simulated did not include one. The results obtained showed that in 42 (0.84%) of the cases the processor timed out, in 2569 (51.38%) the processor produced wrong results and in 1076 (21.52%). In 1313 (26.26%) the results generated were correct.

Under the same conditions, we injected 15000 faults in the TMR core configuration and the results showed that none of the faults caused the processor to time out, while the percentage of correct results was 99.37%. This confirms the effectiveness of the design. A comparison between the two fault injection campaigns is shown in Figure 7.

The most malicious effects of faults are the ones that generate wrong results, since there is no indication to the system outside the boundaries of the processor that the results are faulty apart from software-based acceptance tests [16]. The cases where the processor is driven to enter error mode are safer in this sense, but they have severe effects on the system's response, since they usually cause a reset that is time consuming, not a desirable action in hard real-time systems.

The results presented in this paper are preliminary. We are currently investigating the causes of the few failures that were observed during the fault injection in the TMR core configuration. Further fault injection experiments will test the behavior of the system in cases of multiple faults. Furthermore, the design of a hardware-based fault-injection system on an FPGA prototype board will permit more intensive tests of the processor's behavior.

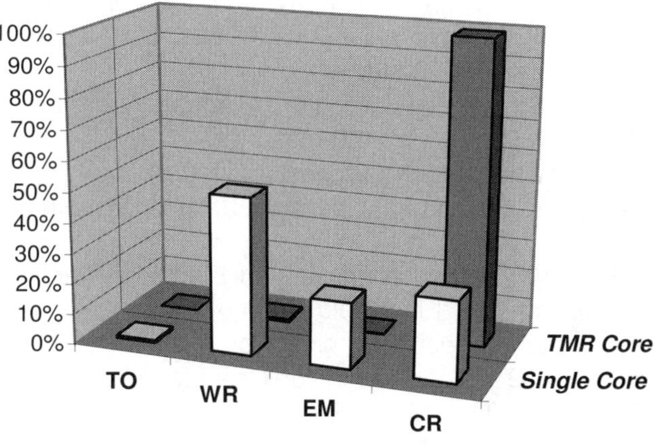

Figure 7: Fault injection results

CONCLUSION

In this paper we presented a fault-tolerant architecture that protects the execution pipeline of a RISC processor against SEUs and permanent faults. It is based on a TMR arrangement with low level voting, and allows dynamic self-reconfiguration in the event of a fault in order to maintain high levels of reliability and availability. Preliminary results of fault-injection simulations show vast improvement in fault-tolerance compared to normal processor architecture.

ACKNOWLEDGMENTS

The authors wish to thank the management of MIRA Ltd for funding this research and for permission to publish this paper.

REFERENCES

1. Ping-Chung Li and T. K. Young, "Electromigration: the time-bomb in deep-submicron ICs", IEEE Spectrum, Vol. 33, Nr. 9, pp. 75-78, Sep. 1996.

2. C. Constantinescu, "Trends and Challenges in VLSI Circuit Reliability", IEEE Micro, Vol. 23, No. 4, pp.14-19, Jul.-Aug. 2003.
3. J. F. Ziegler et al., "IBM experiments in soft fails in computer electronics (1978-1994)", IBM Journal of Research and Development, vol. 40, no. 1, pp. 3-18, Jan. 1996.
4. E. Dupond, M. Nicolaidis and P. Rohr, "Embedded Robustness IPs for Transient-Error-Free ICs", IEEE Design & Test, Vol. 40, No. 3, pp. 56-70, May 2002.
5. C. L. Chen and M.Y Hsiao, "Error-Correcting Codes for Semiconductor Memory Applications: A State-of-the-Art Review", IBM Journal of Research and development, Vol. 28, No. 2, pp. 124-134, Mar. 1984
6. J. Gaisler, "A Portable and Fault-Tolerant Microprocessor Based on the SPARC v8 Architecture", in Proc. of the International Conference on Dependable Systems and Networks, 2002, pp. 409-415.
7. N. Quach, "High Availability and Reliability in the Itanium Processor", IEEE Micro, Vol. 20, No. 5, pp. 61-69, Sep.-Oct. 2000.
8. "The SPARC Architecture Manual Version 8", SPARC International, Inc., (http://www.sparc.org/standards/V8.pdf).
9. "AMBA Specification, version 2.0", ARM Limited, 1999.
10. "IEC61508: Functional Safety of Electrical Electronic Programmable Electronic Safety-Related Systems", International Electrotechnical Commission, 1999.
11. "MISRA: Development Guidelines for Vehicle Based Software", The Motor Industry Software Reliability Association, 1994.
12. S. Amberkar et al., "A System-Safety Process For By-Wire Automotive Systems", SAE 2000-01-1056, 2000.
13. P. H. Jesty, K. M. Hobbley, R. Evans and I. Kendall, "Safety Analysis of Vehicle-Based Systems", in Proceedings of the 8th Safety-Critical Systems Symposium, 2000, pp. 90-110.
14. F. Redmill, M. Chudleigh and J. Catmur, System Safety: HAZOP and Software HAZOP. Wiley, 1999.
15. S. Mitra and E. McCluskey, "Word-Voter: A New Voter Design for Triple Modular Redundant Systems", in Proceedings of the IEEE VLSI Test Symposium, 2000, pp. 465-470.
16. N. Storey, Safety-Critical Computer Systems, Addison Wesley Longman, 1996.
17. G. A. Kanawati, N. A. Kanawati and J. A. Abraham, "FERRARI: A Flexible Software-Based Fault and Error Injection System", IEEE Transactions on Computers, Vol. 44, No. 2, pp. 248-260, Feb. 1995.
18. E. Jean, J. Arlat, M. Rimén, J. Ohlsson and J. Karlsson, "Fault Injection into VHDL Models: The MEFISTO Tool", in Proceedings of the 24tth Annual International Symposium on Fault-Tolerant Computing, 1994, pp. 66-75.

CONTACT

Dr. David D Ward
MIRA
Watling Street
Nuneaton
Warwickshire
CV10 0TU
UK

Tel: + 44 24 7635 5430
Fax: + 44 24 7635 8430

E-mail: david.ward@mira.co.uk
Internet: http://www.mira.co.uk/

2004-01-0718

Using VHDL-AMS as a Unifying Technology for HW/SW Co-verification of Embedded Mechatronic Systems

Thomas R. Egel
Mentor Graphics

Norman J. Elias
Consultant

ABSTRACT

The low cost of microcontrollers makes them increasingly popular for electronic control of a wide range of embedded systems throughout the vehicle. An embedded mixed-signal or mechatronic system is one that uses a microcontroller to control some aspect of the physical system such as motion, speed, temperature etc... The added dimension of software presents a significant challenge to the design, integration and verification of this class of systems.

This paper will discuss how the VHDL-AMS language can be used to describe the behavior of the physical hardware along with the controlling software algorithm together in a unified system model. This unifying technology can provide invaluable insight to the embedded system designer during the system design, integration, verification and debugging phases.

INTRODUCTION

Created in response to industry demand for a non-proprietary modeling language and approved by the IEEE in 1999, VHDL-AMS is the only industry standard, open-source hardware description language[1] capable of modeling diverse systems consisting of both electrical and non-electrical components. Being a superset of the all-digital VHDL language also makes it highly capable for controller hardware and software modeling. The analog and mixed-signal extensions (AMS) provide the enabling technology that allow the engineer to take the "next step" in HW/SW co-verification with the inclusion of both electrical and non-electrical hardware in the system model.

As system requirements become more complex and demanding, the use of microcontrollers continues to increase. Current system integration methods, which rely on the availability of the actual hardware, occur very late in the design cycle. Any problems that arise at this time often result in expensive design or schedule changes. Having a VHDL-AMS system model that incorporates both the hardware and software can allow a "virtual" system integration phase to begin well before the actual hardware is available. Such a model can help the system designer detect unforeseen integration issues and allow alternatives to be explored much earlier in the design cycle.

EMBEDDED MECHATRONIC SYSTEM DESIGN CHALLENGES

While the core of any embedded system is the microcontroller, the design of embedded mechatronic systems is further complicated by the inclusion of heterogeneous technologies. Figure 1 represents a typical embedded mechatronic system consisting of sensors to convert a physical quantity (such as position, temperature or speed) to an electronic signal for digital processing by the microcontroller.

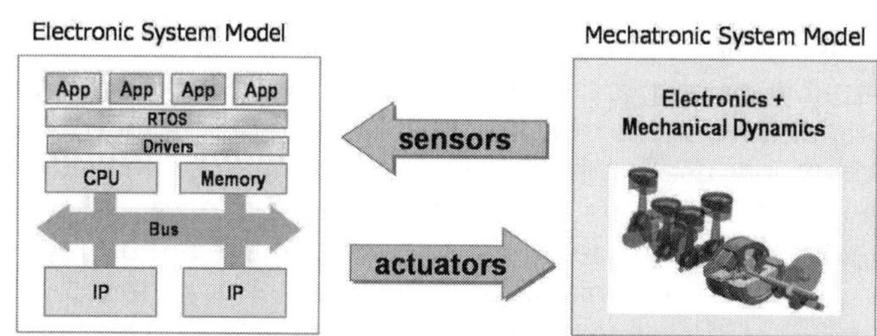

Figure 1 - Embedded Mechatronic System

Actuators receive the electronic signal from the controller and produce a physical output (such as mechanical motion). A powertrain control system, for instance, is comprised of hydraulic valves and actuators, moving mechanical gear sets, all precisely controlled electronically by an embedded microcontroller. A cruise control system processes information from sensors to determine the vehicle speed and adjust the throttle as needed. Even a "simple" voltage regulation system can use sophisticated current and temperature sensing techniques for precise voltage control.

VHDL-AMS is a powerful language capable of modeling all aspects of these embedded mechatronic systems. Design engineers can use the language to create detailed math-based hardware models of the individual components. System engineers can combine these models to perform "virtual" system integration. The following section describes in more detail how VHDL-AMS can be applied to solving the unique problems that embedded mechtronic systems present.

HARDWARE MODELING WITH VHDL-AMS

To be useful for system design, integration and verification, a modeling language must provide constructs that facilitate both top-down and bottom-up design methods. For system simulation to be effective, detailed device models must co-exist with high-level abstract models. In addition, a mechanism must exist allowing the user to easily select the appropriate level of detail for the analysis task at hand.

VHDL-AMS provides the ability to describe a system component at the appropriate level of abstraction allowing optimal model detail to be included at any stage of a top-down or bottom-up design process. In the early stages of a top-down design process, high-level models can be used to verify the system performance will meet the desired specifications. Here modeling the details of the technical interactions may be postponed until further definition becomes available. As the design progresses, technology-specific models can be inserted as they are defined. Towards the end of the design cycle, bottom-up verification techniques can be used to verify the entire system complete with multiple technologies. The result is the ability to perform successive verification in an orderly fashion as the design definition progresses.

Unlike other system modeling methods, VHDL-AMS is capable of both signal flow and conservative modeling. Signal flow or transfer function modeling techniques are commonly used in high-level block diagrams. Individual blocks have inputs and outputs and the data "flow" is unidirectional. While useful for verifying system behavior at a high level, this approach is extremely limited for modeling physical hardware interactions. Conservative modeling techniques, however, apply the laws of conservation at the connection points between models. Here data flow is bi-directional, automatically accounting for hardware interactions, such as loading effects. As a result, the conservative approach is more "hardware oriented" in that models can be developed to behave like the actual hardware without any special modeling considerations. Conservative models can also be easily created to accommodate parameters that directly correlate to the physical hardware. The ability to combine both modeling techniques within a single system model is one of the strengths of the VHDL-AMS language. In addition, the multi-technology constructs in VHDL-AMS provide the ability to model analog and digital electronics interacting with non-electrical components in the context of a complete system. As such, it is uniquely positioned to address the needs of engineers designing today's complex mechatronic systems.

The structure of a VHDL-AMS model[2] consists of an *entity* and one or more *architectures*. The entity defines the physical connection points along with any parameters needed for characterization. The architectures describe how the device operates using equations, algorithms or even extracted device data.

The sections that follow will provide some example models to illustrate how the VHDL-AMS language provides a unifying technology with the power and flexibility needed to solve complex system design and analysis tasks.

HIGH-LEVEL MODELING

In the early stages of a top-down design process, high-level modeling techniques can provide useful insight into the overall system performance. VHDL-AMS provides constructs to create transfer function models in both the s-domain and z-domain. An example of a simple lead-lag block modeled in the s-domain is shown in Figure 2.

This model has an input, output and parameters for the gain, pole and zero frequencies. It would typically be

```
entity q_LeadLag is
 generic (
   K  :  real := 1.0;      -- gain
   Fp :  real := 20.0e3;   -- pole frequency (in Hz)
   Fz :  real := 1.0e6;    -- zero frequency (in Hz)
   );
 port (
   quantity input  : in  real;
   quantity output : out real);
end entity q_LeadLag;

architecture s_dmn of q_LeadLag is
  constant wp  : real := math_2_pi*Fp;  -- Pole freq (in radians)
  constant wz  : real := math_2_pi*Fz;  -- Zero freq (in radians)
  constant num : real_vector := (1.0, 1.0/wz); -- Numerator
  constant den : real_vector := (1.0, 1.0/wp); -- Denominator
begin
  output == K * input'ltf(num, den);   -- Laplace transform of input
end architecture s_dmn;
```

Figure 2 - VHDL-AMS Lead-Lag Model

used with other signal flow models in a block diagram system model during the early stages of design definition as shown in Figure 3.

The power of VHDL-AMS is that these high-level blocks can eventually be replaced by physical hardware models and verified within the context of a complete system. The advantage of this will be clear as our discussion continues.

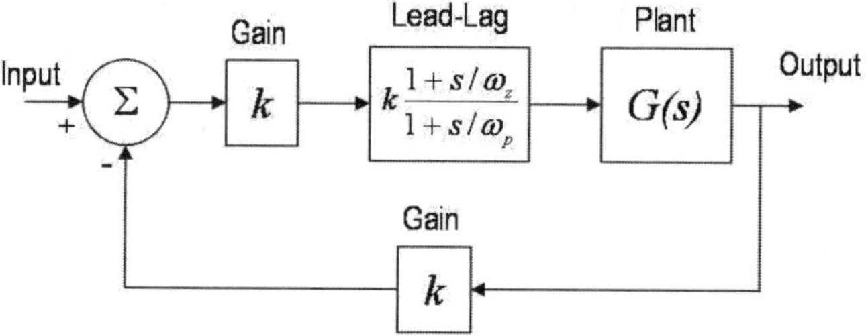

Figure 3 – Block Diagram System Model

ANALOG, DIGITAL AND MIXED-SIGNAL MODELING

In a typical mechatronic embedded system, the electronic hardware is often a combination of analog and digital circuitry, each of which requires significantly different modeling techniques. The electro-mechanical plant is primarily analog but the controls are often digital. Unlike continuous analog quantities, digital signals assume discrete values as determined by the control algorithm. Digital signal transitions constitute events that occur in a time sequence. This concept of event-driven digital signals is an essential element of a system modeling language. VHDL is a well-established digital hardware description language fully capable of modeling all aspects of digital electronics. The AMS extensions incorporate the necessary analog constructs making VHDL-AMS the unifying "glue" that links these distinctly different domains. Figure 4 shows examples of analog and digital waveforms created from a VHDL-AMS simulation.

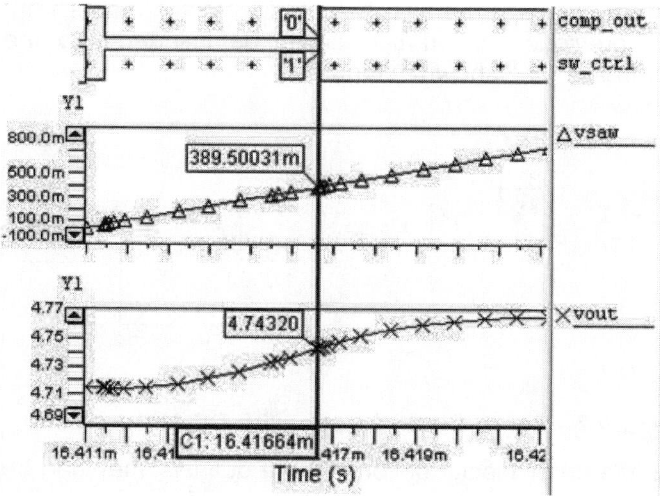

Figure 4 - Analog and Digital Signals

The analog waveforms (*vout* and *vsaw*) are continuous in the Y-axis and are calculated by the simulator using variable time steps (as indicated by the symbols). The digital signals (*sw_ctrl* and *comp_out*) have discrete Y values (0 and 1), which are assigned by the simulator when events occur. You can see that the analog "activity" increases during digital transitions. The VHDL-AMS language includes constructs to ensure that the analog and digital signals stay synchronized during a simulation. VHDL-AMS is unique in that analog and digital behavior can be modeled and synchronized within a single industry standard language. As we will see, this is a crucial requirement when modeling embedded mechatronic systems.

MIXED-TECHNOLOGY MODELING

To fully understand an embedded mechatronic system, the non-electrical components like sensors and actuators must be taken into account. Sensors convert some physical quantity (i.e. speed or temperature) into an electrical signal for processing. Actuators convert an electrical command signal from the processor into some physical phenomena (i.e. motion). Only with accurate models of these non-electrical devices interacting with the electronics entirely in a closed loop system can proper analysis be achieved. Using VHDL-AMS, system integration can begin before actual hardware is available by creating a system model that incorporates a combination of the various technologies. They may include the mechanical, magnetic, hydraulic, thermal effects or any other technology that can be described using algebraic differential equations.

VHDL-AMS has distinct advantages over traditional system modeling methods for modeling hardware of various technologies. To illustrate this let's examine the model development process for a simple DC motor. The starting point for any model is the equations that describe the behavior of the component or system. A DC motor is a mixed-technology (electromechanical device) governed by the following device equations[4]:

$$T = -K_t \cdot i_a + D \cdot \omega_m + J \cdot \frac{d\omega_m}{dt} \qquad (1)$$

$$V = K_e \cdot \omega_m + i_a \cdot R + L \cdot \frac{di_a}{dt} \qquad (2)$$

Where T is the motor torque at the shaft and V is the voltage across the electrical terminals.

The typical block diagram modeling approach would be to develop a transfer function model. This involves taking the Laplace transform of these equations and solving for the appropriate variables. After much manipulation, the following equation relating the voltage (V) torque (T) and angular velocity (Ω) is derived:

$$\Omega_m(s) = \frac{A}{\tau \cdot s + 1} V_a(s) + \frac{B}{\tau \cdot s + 1} T_q(s) \qquad (3)$$

Where:

$$\tau = \frac{J(R + sL)}{D(R + sL) + K_e K_t} \quad \textit{(Time Constant, sec)}$$

$$A = \frac{Kt}{D(R+sL)+K_e K_t}$$ *(Voltage Gain, rad/volt-sec)*

$$B = \frac{(R+sL)}{D(R+sL)+K_e K_t}$$ *(Torque Gain, rad/N-m-sec)*

Further manipulation is required to represent this in block diagram format, as shown in Figure 5, so it can be included as part of the overall system model

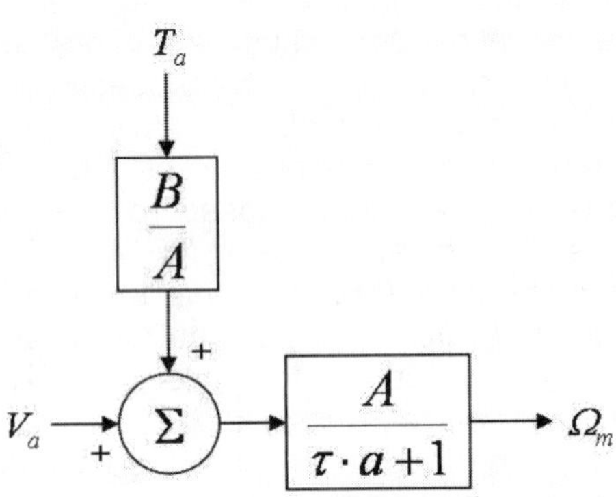

Figure 5 - Block Diagram DC Motor Model

Even for this relatively simple device, the generalized transfer function approach results in a significantly obfuscated model. The original device equations are nowhere to be found and the device parameters are buried within the transfer function coefficients. Furthermore, any change in the original equations will require significant rework to derive the new transfer function.

By contrast, the VHDL-AMS model for the same DC motor is shown in Figure 6. Here the original device equations (1) and (2) are preserved within the architecture of the model and device parameters are clearly identified and passed in through the entity declaration.

```
entity DCMotor is
  generic (
    r_wind : resistance;    -- Motor winding res [Ohm]
    kt  : real;             -- Torque coeff [N*m/Amp]
    ke  : real;             -- Back emf coeff [V/rad/sec]
    l   : inductance;       -- Winding induc [Henrys]
    d   : real;             -- Damp coeff [N*m/(rad/sec)]
    j   : moment_inertia); -- Inertia [kg*meter**2]
  port (terminal p1, p2 : electrical;
        terminal shaft_rotv : rotational_velocity);
end entity DCMotor;

architecture basic of DCMotor is
  quantity v across i through p1 to p2;
  quantity w across torq through shaft_rotv to ref;
begin
  torq == -1.0*kt*i + d*w + j*w'dot; -- Torque Equation
  v    == ke*w + i*r_wind + l*i'dot; -- Voltage Equation
end architecture basic;
```

Figure 6 - VHDL-AMS DC Motor Model

Any changes in the original device equations or parameters can be directly implemented in the model with minimal effort. In addition, this model can be shared among other team members with little or no additional documentation.

MODELING ABSTRACTIONS

Another key requirement for effective system modeling is to have the ability to describe the components at various levels of abstraction. This allows the engineer to focus on the details of a specific part of the system, while maintaining its context within the overall system design. This is particularly useful for top-down design methods, where the detail is added as the system design progresses. During the system definition stage, block diagram or signal flow methods are often used to describe the major aspects of the system. These methods are effective for system partitioning, but fail to completely account for interactions among the blocks. VHDL-AMS provides the ability to use block diagram methods for high-level modeling while selectively substituting physical hardware models as desired. Additionally, higher-level models can be incorporated when using VHDL-AMS for bottom-up verification to optimize the simulation speed and accuracy. Also known as "checkerboard verification", this is only possible with a modeling language capable of both signal flow and conservative modeling. In addition, VHDL-AMS provides this capability using the concept of multiple architectures which can be selected at simulation run time.

As an example, when designing a speed or position control system, the VHDL-AMS DC motor model from the previous section can easily be inserted into the control loop as shown in Figure 7.

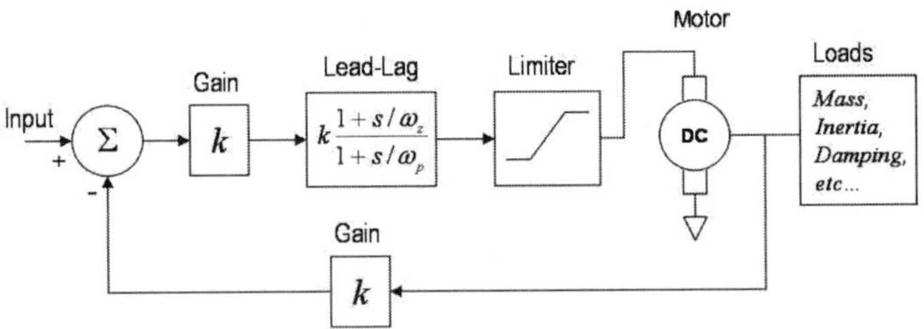

Figure 7 - Servo Control Loop with DC Motor

As the other blocks become more defined, they can be replaced by more detailed hardware models. During this verification process, realistic loads can be attached to the motor to examine the effects of loop stability. VHDL-AMS provides the ability to create models of varying degrees of fidelity and include them at any stage of the design process.

As we have shown, VHDL-AMS provides engineers with a modeling language for all physical aspects of a mechatronic system at arbitrary levels of abstraction. For an embedded mechatronic system, it is also necessary to incorporate the software algorithm into the system simulation to verify the overall system performance. The remainder of this paper explores how VHDL-AMS can be used for hardware/software co-verification of this class of systems.

MODELING THE MICROCONTROLLER

For an *embedded* mechatronic system, "virtual" integration of hardware and software requires a model of the microcontroller executing the software instructions that control the overall system performance. The challenge is to incorporate the software algorithm into the flow of the simulation.

MICROCONTROLLER MODELING ABSTRACTIONS

During system integration the microcontroller can be modeled as an algorithmic block. A single VHDL architecture can be constructed to model the software algorithm and verify its performance in a simulation at the block diagram level.

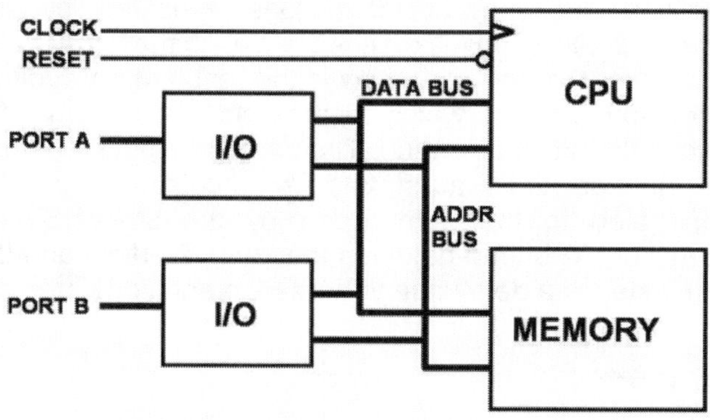

Figure 8 - Microcontroller Core

However, the algorithmic model is inadequate at more advanced design stages. Interactions between the physical hardware and the embedded software can only be properly analyzed if the software timing is accurately modeled. A gate level or RTL model of the microcontroller structure will model software timing to the precision of the system clock but is prohibitively complex and slow. A more realistic approach is to model the microcontroller as a finite–state machine that executes software instructions in sequence producing the correct pin outputs at accurate time intervals. Such a model is referred to as an *Instruction Set Model* [3] of the microcontroller.

INSTRUCTION SET MODELING

As shown in Figure 8, the core of a microcontroller is comprised of a CPU for interpreting and executing software instructions, memory for storing the instructions and data, and I/O controllers for feeding data into and out of the microcontroller.

VHDL architectures of the I/O and memory are straightforward applications of digital modeling. The CPU model, however, is much more complex in concept. Its task is to execute the software instructions which are stored in memory as a sequence of binary numbers.

For each instruction, the specific tasks involved are as shown in Figure 9, namely:

1. Decode the sub-sequence of numbers stored in the memory for that instruction.

2. Locate and read all data values required to execute the instruction.

3. Execute the instruction to determine the results.

4. Synchronize timing to match instruction delays.

5. And finally store those results after all of the above processing is complete.

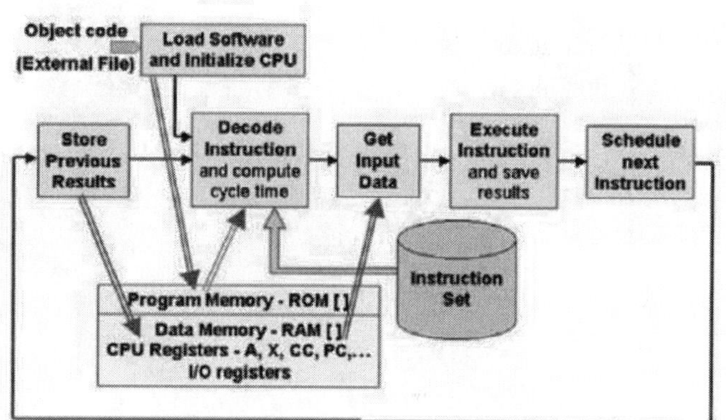

Figure 9 - Sequence of CPU Operations

The physical CPU takes a finite amount of time to complete these operations. The time required varies, depending on the instructions, and is determined by the number of CPU clock cycles required to perform the operations. To accurately simulate system performance the CPU model must account for these delays. The VHDL model can do so by simply counting the required number of clock cycles before storing the results of each instruction. VHDL provides a "wait" statement that is a natural mechanism for implementing this CPU scheduler.

Microcontroller reference manuals published by the manufacturer universally include descriptions of the complete instruction set. The data provided for each instruction is public information and is readily incorporated into the CPU model as a database for interpreting the control software.

PROGRAMMING THE MODEL

A requirement for any instruction set model must be the ability to read the software. In the real device, the software is embedded in the hardware by compiling or assembling the source code and subsequently burning the resulting object code into the microcontroller memory. An accurate simulation requires that the microcontroller model execute that exact same object code. This is accomplished by incorporating an object code file reader into the model which loads the compiled software into the simulated memory. As with the physical system, different versions of the software can be simulated by recompiling and loading the modified code. But, unlike the physical system, the simulation can quickly test numerous software variations without repeatedly burning code into chip samples and thereby consuming stockpiles of chips. Moreover, the "virtual" CPU is safe from the hazard of destructive failures. Figure 10 illustrates the compilation process for both the real microcontroller and simulation model.

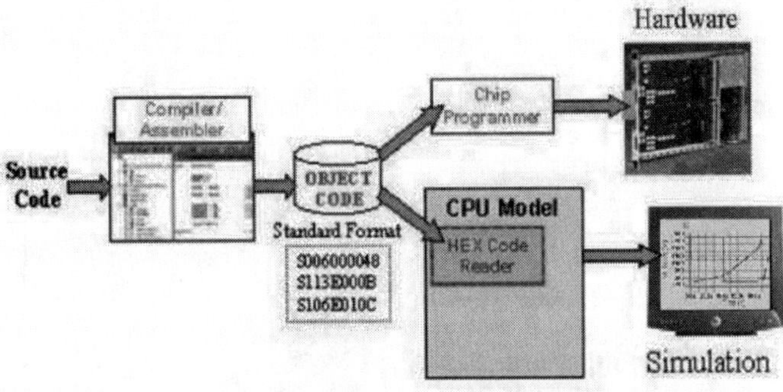

Figure 10 - Compilation Process

As you can see, the same compiled code used by the actual chip programmer can also be read by the VHDL CPU model. This provides extra assurance that when a prototype system is finally built, it will behave as expected due to the analyses performed using the system model.

PROBING THE MODEL

Another advantage of having a VHDL instruction set model of the processor is the ability to probe not only the input and output signals but also the internal software "signals". Figure 11 shows an example of these signals from a simple test circuit created to exercise some of the CPU instructions.

As you can see, an analog output (*out_val*), digital carry signal and the status of the internal accumulator can all be viewed together and values compared over time. Closer examination reveals, the analog ramp increasing in discrete steps but with an apparent negative step at about 86us. To explain this we can look at the microcontroller internal signals. The carry bit seen at the time of the step indicates a numerical overflow, however, the overflow appears to precede the step by a fraction of a microsecond.

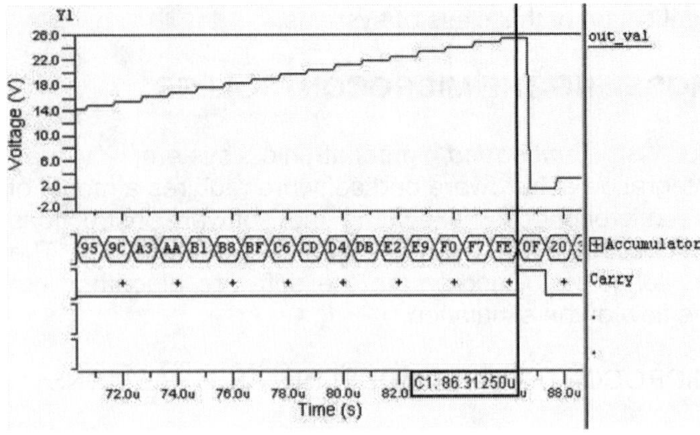

Figure 11 - Microcontroller Signals

Probing deeper still into the actual software operations, illustrates the full power of the instruction set model. The waveforms in Figure 12 include a software "signal" that identifies the specific instructions executed by the microcontroller. This expanded view of the time scale shows that the carry overflow is the result of an *addition* instruction (ADDA) which increments the Accumulator beyond its maximum value. The analog output step does not appear until after this Accumulator signal is propagated to the output port by the *store* (STAA) instruction. The time between the carry overflow and the output step is a delay due to hardware and software.

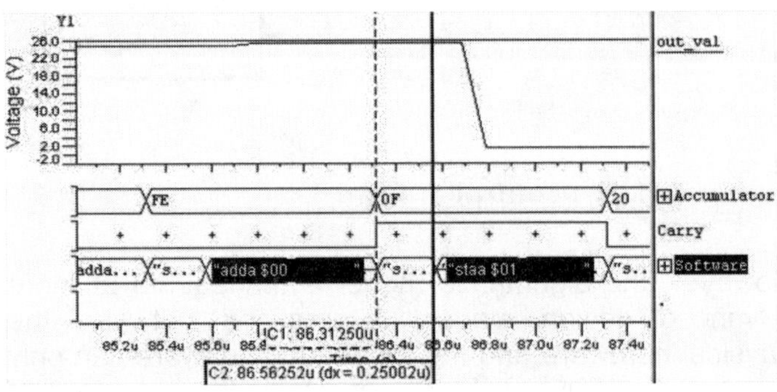

Figure 12 - Hardware and Software Details

Using simulation of the instruction set model for HW/SW co-verification allows us to identify this behavior qualitatively and to analyze it quantitatively. Access to the internal registers of the instruction set model is not possible using a physical processor. This added access can provide invaluable insight into the performance of the processor with the overall system

SUCCESSIVE VERIFICATION METHODOLOGY

One of the challenges in designing embedded mechatronic systems is the difficulty in debugging and verifying the operation of the software within the context of the complete system. Typically, the true system performance is not known until the first physical prototype is built. System integration at this late stage in the design cycle often results in problems due to unanticipated interaction between the hardware and software.

This final section will discuss how VHDL-AMS can be used for successive verification at critical stages of the system design, ranging from specification through final certification and beyond into the introduction and release of design updates. The DC motor servo loop example will be used to illustrate how to apply successive verification techniques using VHDL-AMS.

SERVO POSITION CONTROL LOOP EXAMPLE

Here we will revisit the servo control loop in Figure 7. This control system can represent any number of subsystems within the vehicle where a DC motor is used for position control. Some examples include power mirrors, power seat, and headlamp applications. The individual blocks were initially modeled as transfer functions in the S-domain, but as the design progresses, a decision must be made whether to implement each block in hardware or software.

It has been already shown that VHDL-AMS can sufficiently model any hardware implementation. Here we will explore the additional aspect of including software in the loop. To begin this let's revisit the lead-lag compensator. To implement a function in software, a 4 step design progression can be utilized with VHDL-AMS to perform successive verification as the design evolves:

1. Implement the lead-lag function in the s-domain and verify loop stability.
2. Convert to the z-domain and explore effects of sample clock frequency on loop stability
3. Convert to difference equations and verify system performance
4. Implement difference equations in C-Code and perform final system verification with instruction set microcontroller model.

For step 1, the VHDL-AMS model in Figure 2 was created using the Laplace transform operator (*'ltf*) to implement equation (4).

$$\frac{Y(s)}{X(s)} = k \cdot \frac{s+a}{s+b} = k \cdot \frac{1+s/\omega_z}{1+s/\omega_p} \tag{4}$$

Where Y(s) is the output and X(s) is the input. The pole and zero locations are passed into this model as parameters, allowing loop stability to be easily examined as a function of pole/zero locations. For step 2, a bilinear transform is performed by making the substitution for the Laplace variable s as shown in equation (5).

$$s \Rightarrow \frac{2}{T}\left(\frac{1-z^{-1}}{1+z^{-1}}\right) \tag{5}$$

This is typically a manual process, but can be easily automated within a VHDL-AMS model using the z-domain transform operator (*'ztf*) as shown in Figure 13.

```
entity q_LeadLag is
 generic (
  K      : real := 1.0;         -- gain
  Fp     : real := 20.0e3;      -- pole frequency (in Hz)
  Fz     : real := 1.0e6;       -- zero frequency (in Hz)
  Fsmp : real := 10.0e3         -- For Z-dmn only: Sample freq (in Hz)
  );
 port (
  quantity input  : in real;
  quantity output : out real);
end entity q_LeadLag;

architecture z_dmn of q_LeadLag is
 constant T   : real := 1.0/Fsmp;              -- Sample period
 constant wz  : real := math_2_pi*Fz;          -- Zero freq (in radians)
 constant wp  : real := math_2_pi*Fp;          -- Pole freq (in radians)
 constant n0  : real := wp*wz + 2.0*wp/T; -- z^0 num coeff
 constant n1  : real := wp*wz - 2.0*wp/T;  -- z^-1 num coeff
 constant d0  : real := wp*wz + 2.0*wz/T;  -- z^0 den coeff
 constant d1  : real := wp*wz - 2.0*wz/T;  -- z^-1 den coeff
 constant num : real_vector := (n0, n1);     -- numerator
 constant den : real_vector := (d0, d1);     -- denominator
begin
 output == K*input'Ztf(num, den, T); -- Z-domain transfer function
end architecture z_dmn;
```

Figure 13 - Z-Domain Lead-Lag VHDL-AMS model

Again this model can be characterized simply by supplying the pole and zero frequencies. The constants n0, n1, d0 and d1 then become the z-domain transfer function coefficients as shown in equation (6). An additional model parameter *Fsmp* represents the sampling frequency which can be varied over a range of values to examine its effects on system performance.

$$\frac{Y(z)}{X(z)} = k \cdot \frac{n_0 \cdot z^0 + n_1 \cdot z^{-1}}{d_0 \cdot z^0 + d_1 \cdot z^{-1}} \tag{6}$$

To illustrate the advantage of this approach, the system in Figure 7 was simulated at various clock frequencies. The resulting error signal in Figure 14 highlights the effects of the clock on the system error. As the frequency decreases, there is a visible increase in error and loop instability. This analysis determined that a minimum clock frequency of 10kHz is needed to meet the acceptable error criteria.

The *'ztf* operator also allows you to perform a final frequency analysis to verify the pole and zero locations will satisfy the system stability criteria. This is important because once the model takes on the form of difference equations, the analysis will be limited to the time domain.

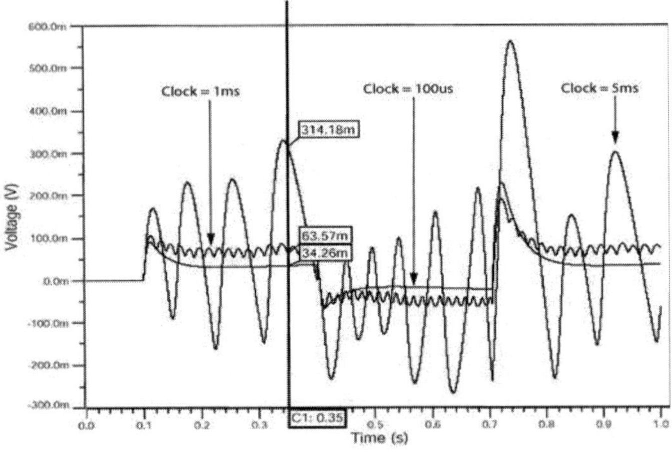

Figure 14 - Effect of Clock Freq on System Error

Step 3 in the process involves converting the z-domain transfer function into to difference equations[2,5]. This is a simple algebraic manipulation resulting in an equation in the form of (7).

$$Y(k) = a_0 X(k) + a_1 X(k-1) + a_2 Y(k-1) \qquad (7)$$

This difference equation can be easily modeled in VHDL-AMS, but more importantly, it can also be directly written in C-code. This leads us to the design goal of implementing the lead-lag block in software using a microcontroller. The successive verification approach outlined here provides the ability to debug the control algorithm as the design progresses. This approach provides a systematic method of ensuring successful system integration well before the prototype stage. Step 4 in this process of successive verification involves implementing the actual C-code and compiling it to a target processor. The combination of an instruction set CPU model and realistic hardware models, provides the engineer with a powerful system model useful for troubleshooting and final verification.

TROUBLESHOOTING

While performance verification is an analysis function, the corresponding design function is troubleshooting. A few of the important troubleshooting tasks that can be performed using simulation are:

1. Analyze destructive and non-destructive failures.
2. Analyze and verify hardware/software interactions.
3. Determine critical timing paths.
4. Guide the optimization of system performance.

The ability to probe internal signals is a powerful aid to failure analysis. Simulation plays an especially critical role in analyzing destructive failures because:

- No hardware is actually damaged.
- The failure is completely repeatable.
- Internal signals can be probed to diagnose the problem.

As we have shown, in using a VHDL-AMS system model to troubleshoot embedded mechatronic systems both the hardware and software details can be probed. Hardware performance can be displayed by viewing signals throughout the electro-mechanical plant and the digital controller. Signals internal to the microcontroller can be displayed to trace the state of the CPU registers. Additionally, the memory buses can be probed to monitor digital data transitions. As a further aid, the simulation model can print a full or partial dump of memory contents at any "time point" in the simulation. It can also print a run-time trace of software instructions to relate hardware events to the progress of the software.

Timing is a critical factor in the integration of embedded software into a hardware environment. The control algorithm has to complete critical functions quickly enough to respond to changes in the physical environment. Excessive software delays can render the system unstable. The capability of the simulator to probe internal signals and trace software execution enables the designer to calculate and analyze control delays. The simulation can distinguish between hardware and software delays and analyze the software delays down to the contribution from each instruction executed. This capability lets the designer expose the critical timing paths and introduce modifications to optimize system performance.

FINAL VERIFICATION

As we have shown, simulation serves a valuable function in verifying system performance at all stages of the design process. This brings us to the final verification step, before a prototype system is assembled for test. The ability to verify the operation of the software running on the CPU within the context of the complete system using successive verification methods, allows the engineer to ensure overall system performance. More importantly, this can be initiated before the hardware is available. As an example, Figure 15 shows a performance aspect of our position control system. The graph compares the final motor shaft position with the input voltage command signal. The system model used here includes the lead-lag filter difference equation implemented in software and compiled to an HC12 microprocessor instruction set model. This model is connected to VHDL-AMS hardware models for the DC motor and mechanical loads. A qualitative (visual) analysis indicates good tracking under static load conditions. Once the nominal operation is verified, additional test benches can be easily created to exercise the model under varying load conditions.

Furthermore, this system model also serves as a vehicle for maintaining design integrity as new features are added to the design. A series of simulation test benches can be defined to test existing features. The simulation commands and parameters can then be saved along with a database of expected results. As new features are added, these simulations can be repeated to serve as a regression test guaranteeing design integrity.

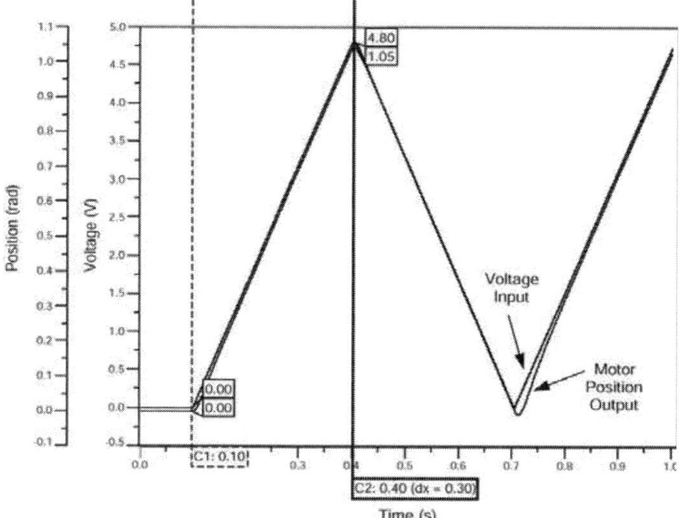

Figure 15 - Voltage Command and Motor Position

CONCLUSION

The combination of software used to control mixed technology hardware in an embedded mechatronic system presents a unique set of challenges for the engineering team. A successful design depends on an understanding of how these technologies interact within the context of the complete system. These interactions are often only fully realized during the system prototype stage, and unfortunately problems uncovered this late can be difficult and costly to correct. The VHDL-AMS modeling language provides a unifying technology for the design and integration of embedded mechatronic systems. The power and flexibility of VHDL-AMS make it superior to existing block diagram methods or circuit simulation techniques for both top-down and bottom-up design processes. This paper has described how a VHDL-AMS system model can be used during all phases of the hardware and software design, from system specification and concept exploration to software debugging, helping to ensure a successful system integration and product launch.

ACKNOWLEDGMENTS

Many thanks to R. Scott Cooper of Mentor Graphics for his guidance and research on this topic.

All simulations were performed using SystemVision™ by Mentor Graphics.

REFERENCES

[1] IEEE-SA Standards Board, "IEEE Standard VHDL Analog and Mixed-Signal Extensions" (Language Reference Manual), IEEE March, 2002.

[2] P.J. Ashenden, G.D. Peterson, D.A.Teegarden, "The System Designer's Guide to VHDL-AMS", Morgan Kaufmann Publishers, 2002.

[3] N.J. Elias, "Instruction Set Modeling of Micro-Controllers for Power Converter Simulation", APEC 2003.

[4] Franklin, G.F., Powell, J.D., Emami-Naeini, A., "Feedback Control of Dynamic Systems", Fourth Edition, Prentice Hall, 2002.

[5] Cooper, R. S., "The Designer's Guide to Analog and Mixed-Signal Modeling", Avant! Corp, 2001.

CONTACTS

Tom Egel is a Technical Marketing Engineer at Mentor Graphics specializing in automotive application development using VHDL-AMS. Previously employed by Analogy, Inc., Tom has over 15 years of experience with various hardware description languages and simulation methods. For more information on this topic, he can be contacted at tom_egel@mentor.com.

Norm Elias is an independent consultant specializing in simulation and modeling of automotive and other mixed-signal, mixed-technology systems. Over a 30 year career including research positions at Bell Laboratories and Philips Electronics, Norm has pioneered simulation technologies for statistical design and for modeling embedded software. For more information on these topics, he can be contacted at norm.elias@ieee.org.

2003-01-0359

Artificial Neural Network Based Control Systems

N. Lightowler and H. Nareid
AXEON Ltd

ABSTRACT

This paper reports on an Artificial Neural Network (ANN) based approach to the design of controllers. The system is developed from a truly parallel hardware implementation of a Self-Organizing Map (SOM) type network resulting in a controller suitable for embedded 'real-time' non-linear applications. Both open and closed loop control are described with the aid of their application to Active Valve Train (AVT) control. The utilization of such ANN based systems has been found to reduce development time and lead to increased system flexibility, thereby increasing the application opportunities. These advantages come about due to the nature of SOM based systems which enable controllers to be developed without requiring an analytical solution to be derived. Instead, these SOM based systems learn by example and create a map of a non-linear transfer function.

INTRODUCTION

As the control of non-linear engine management subsystems is becoming more prevalent and the requirements for more accurate control of such systems is increasing, traditional PID controllers are facing increasing challenges. While PID control structures are well known and accepted in the engine control arena, they have the disadvantage of requiring significant effort to calibrate making it difficult to achieve suitable control accuracy for non-linear control applications.

Several studies have shown that Artificial Neural Networks (ANNs) offer suitable solutions to many non-linear applications including control of non-linear systems [1]. However, until recently the use of ANNs in 'real-time' control applications was severely limited by the requirement to implement ANNs in software on traditional processor architectures such as DSP's. The limitation of implementing these parallel systems on a serial processor are significant and as a consequence few 'real-time' applications utilizing ANNs in an embedded system were ever developed.

As silicon fabrication processes have improved and feature sizes decreased single chip parallel microprocessor architectures have been realized [7]. As improvements in process have continued, component integration has followed resulting in the System On-Chip (SOC) approach. Technology has now reached the stage where it is possible to generate SOC solutions which include parallel computer architectures. Consequently, it is now possible to use a truly parallel implementation of ANNs within an SOC solution in order to address embedded 'real-time' non-linear applications that were previously inaccessible.

ANN BACKGROUND

There are two main training paradigms used by ANNs, supervised and unsupervised learning. Supervised learning involves presenting a network with an input and the corresponding desired output for each training step. Unsupervised learning requires only inputs, frequently referred to as input vectors, to be presented to the network during training. The most prominent of the supervised training networks is the Multi-Layer Perceptron (MLP) using back-propagation learning. The most popular unsupervised training network is the Self-Organizing Map (SOM) proposed by Kohonen [4]. While many in industry are familiar with the MLP algorithm, its advantages and shortcomings, few appear fully conversant with SOM type algorithms. Bearing the above statement in mind and to further assist in what follows a brief overview of the SOM and in particular the variant used for the work reported in this paper is presented below, however, a fuller account can be found in [3,6].

During training a SOM network creates a 2-dimensional map of the original N-dimensional input space. These maps can be useful as visualization tools, but SOMs are commonly used as classification engines or for function estimation. Figure 1 shows an example of a network trained and labeled for a classification application with four classes. The relationship between classes has been preserved on the surface of the network. It can be seen, for example, that the first and second classes abut each other while there is a clear boundary between the first and fourth classes. The maps are created during network training which is when network organization occurs. After the network has been trained each neuron is assigned a label denoting the meaning of its output. While training does not require desired output to be known, labeling does requires a small data set of known input type. Once a network is trained and labeled it is ready to be used in an application, this is its operational phase. In some applications it is also helpful for the network to continue to learn, or adapt to parameters that change over time, e.g. to allow for component wear.

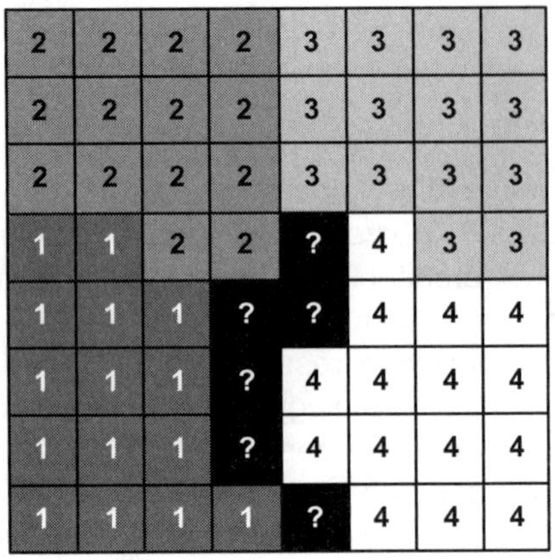

2	2	2	2	3	3	3	3
2	2	2	2	3	3	3	3
2	2	2	2	3	3	3	3
1	1	2	2	?	4	3	3
1	1	1	?	?	4	4	4
1	1	1	?	4	4	4	4
1	1	1	?	4	4	4	4
1	1	1	1	?	4	4	4

Figure 1. Map of a 64 neuron SOM showing class labels.

The underlying operation of a SOM network is conceptually rather simple. When an input vector is presented to the system all neurons in the network receive a copy. Each of these neurons has a local reference vector which it compares with the current input vector. The neuron with greatest similarity between input and reference vector then becomes the active neuron. During training the reference vector of the active neuron, and other neurons within the current neighborhood (i.e. close to the active neuron) modify their reference vectors to bring them closer to the current input. Both the current neighborhood size and the extent of the update applied to reference vectors are monotonically decreasing with time.

During the learning process several interesting factors emerge. The reference vectors tend to approximate various distributions of input vectors and the resulting order always reflects properties of the probability density function P(x), (see Luttrell [5] for further details). While reference vectors are tending to describe the density function of inputs, local interactions between neurons tend to preserve continuity on the surface of the map. A combination of these opposing forces causes the vector distribution to approximate a smooth hyper-surface in the pattern space with optimal orientation and form that best imitates the overall structure of the input vector density. i.e. The outcome of training is that the multidimensional Euclidean input space is mapped in a non-linear manner to a two dimensional output space (the surface of the network).

While the SOM algorithm appears simple at first glance no formal mathematical proof has yet been derived, the most comprehensive mathematical analysis currently available is that by Luttrel [5]. However, its performance has been shown to be valid many times [3]. What makes such mathematical formalism difficult is primarily the time varying nature of parameters during training.

ANN BASED CONTROL

A control system based on a SOM type network can be created by utilizing the ability of this network type to create 2-dimensional maps of non-linear systems. Both open and closed loop control are possible using such an approach. One network is required to generate the actuator signal, the nature of which is dependent on the actuator type, both electrical voltages and currents are frequently used. A second network is also used with a closed loop system for evaluating a merit function associated with the actuator response and providing feedback to the system.

OPEN LOOP CONTROL

In order to generate a suitable control signal the network requires to be trained on data which captures the essence of the control problem to be addressed. Consequently, both environmental and operational parameters which influence actuator response are required. Environmental parameters would include anything which may significantly influence actuator performance, e.g. hydraulic pressure. Particular emphasis should be placed on parameters which display a strong non-linear influence on actuator behavior. Operational parameters would normally include the desired actuator response and corresponding control signal.

A representative data set in line with the above description is collected over the operating envelope of the actuator. While it is not necessary to capture every possible combination of data values, it is important that the entire operating envelope of the actuator is covered. This can be achieved without the need for an existing control system. What is required is the generation of an actuator signal over the valid input range of the actuator, which may be achieved in a variety of ways, e.g. with systems such as signal generators.

Once an appropriate data set has been captured it is used to train the network. When the network has completed its training phase the network outputs are associated with appropriate control signal values. This is achieved by presenting data to the network together with corresponding output signals, this process is referred to as labeling. After training and labeling are complete the network can be used in operational mode, i.e. the feed forward part of a control system is complete.

Figure 2 shows an example of the surface of a trained network mapping for a non-linear actuator. It can be seen from this map that similar control signal values are close together which corresponds to neurons that are close together in the network. It should also be noted that control signal values increase gradually moving across the map surface. In this instance the actuator did not show discontinuities in its transfer function.

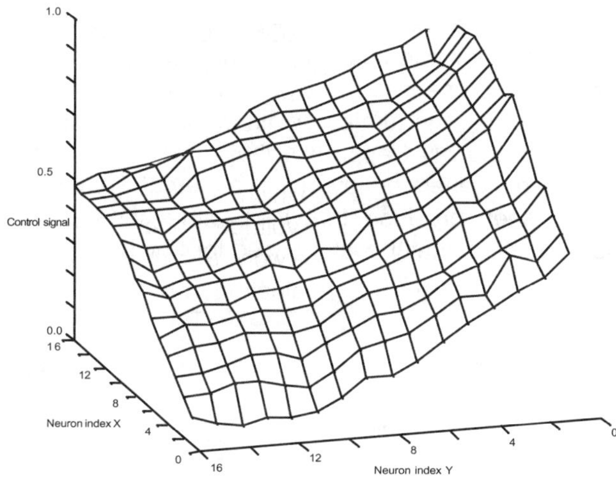

Figure 2. 3-dimensional plot of a 256 neuron SOM trained on a control application. Plot shows X, Y neuron positions against Control value.

In operational mode the network is able to provide the control signal for an actuator with arbitrary non-linearities. This is achieved by presenting the desired system response to the network along with the operational and environmental parameters used in training. There is no requirement for the actuator movement pattern to be cyclical or set to any particular movement pattern, however, the desired response input must be within the actuators operating envelope as used in network training.

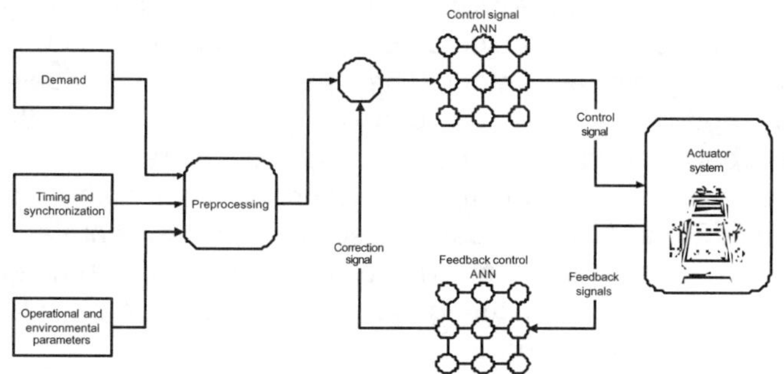

Figure 3. Schematic diagram of ANN based closed loop control system.

CLOSED LOOP CONTROL

In order to evaluate actuator performance a quantitative method (merit function) is required to describe deviation from optimum performance. The merit function would utilize parameters such as deviations from desired timing, position or velocity of the actuator response. These parameters would then be combined to form an input vector to the network. By using a SOM in this part of the control system it is possible to utilize multi-dimensional merit functions thereby taking account of several aspects of actuator performance. The network is then trained on a representative set of merit function data, in some cases this data set may be derived from that used to train the feed-forward component of the control system. After training, the network is labeled with appropriate correction factors. The output from this network is then combined with input to the network forming the feed-forward component of the control system. While such a control system uses two ANNs, these may in many cases be implemented on a single ANN device using multitasking.

APPLICATION TO ACTIVE VALVE TRAIN

Active Valve Train (AVT) is one of the terms used to describe the operation of inlet and exhaust valves on an internal combustion engine by way of an actuator system instead of the traditional camshaft. The 'camless' engine has the potential for significant improvements in engine efficiency and emission reduction [2]. These improvements are primarily due to the increased flexibility introduced by replacing the direct link between camshaft and valve with a variable control via an actuator system. The removal of this direct link allows for changes in valve opening times and lift profiles in order to achieve the optimum for each speed and load profile.

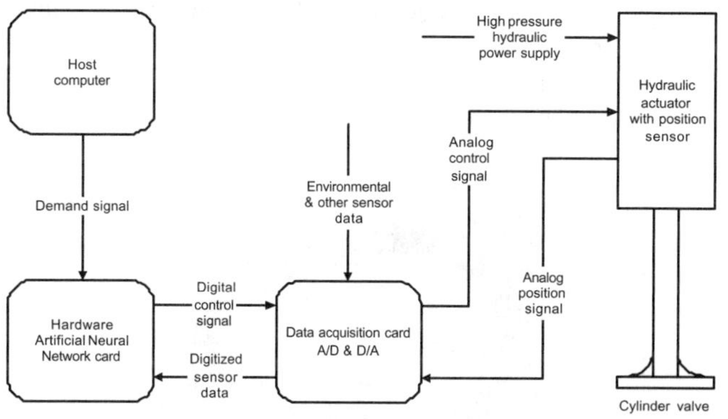

Figure 4. Schematic diagram of AVT experimental setup.

Investigations into AVT control were carried out using a research grade system similar to that detailed in [2]. An overview of the system used is also shown in figure 4. To maximize flexibility and minimize development time a host PC system was used with an ANN applications development system. The development system included a hardware ANN accelerator card containing a parallel hardware ANN integrated circuit to allow 'real-time' application investigations. The flexibility of the development system also enabled a standard Data Acquisition (DAQ) card to be integrated into the control mechanisms. The DAQ provided interfacing between controller, actuator system and environmental data sources.

The development system based approach allowed data for network training to be gathered directly. Training data was required to specify the desired system response, crank angle, time and environmental parameters such as temperature, hydraulic pressure etc. Data from all parameters believed to affect actuator response were gathered while the whole of the actuators operating envelope was explored, approximately 10 minutes operation in total.

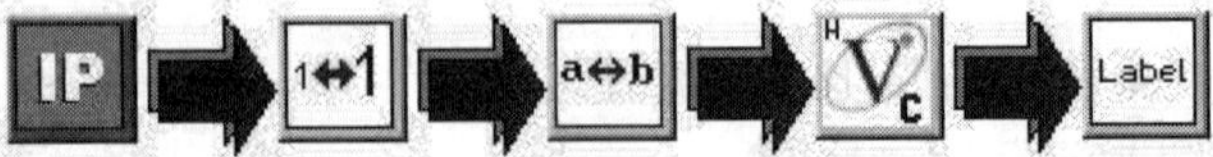

Figure 5. Example of a process sequence developed in the ANN applications development system. Blocks show data input, scaling, type conversion, ANN and label output.

In this particular instance the actuator used showed significant non-linearities over some regions of its operation, these non-linearities were further exacerbated by non-linear relationships between actuator operation and the environmental parameters of pressure and temperature. The non-linearities in the system make it difficult to provide an accurate control signal using the traditional PID control approach. When actuator velocity is plotted as a function of position and control signal with all other parameters fixed a non-linear relationship was noted. A linear relationship between control signal and actuator velocity would plot as a flat plane, but the plot in figure 6 shows variation due to valve position. Further investigation also showed the actuator exhibited both a delayed and damped response.

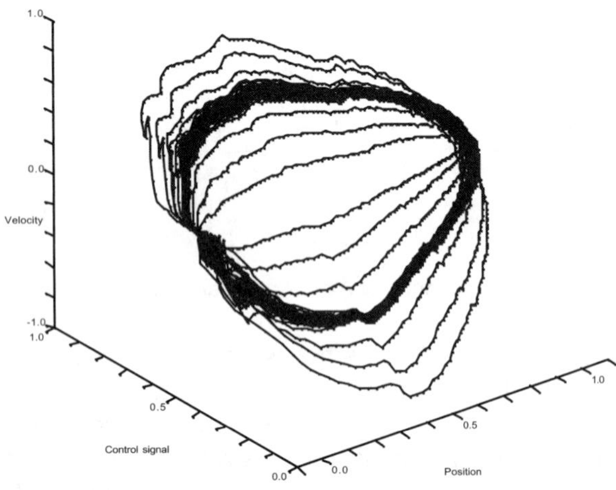

Figure 6. Plot showing control signal V actuator velocity and position.

After the data were evaluated and unnecessary parameters removed along with errored data approximately 100,000 training vectors, each of 6 dimensions were suitable for training a neural network. All data pre-processing, post-processing, network configuration and control structure were determined within the development system. In this instance a network of 256 neurons was used for the open loop control component. This network was trained and labeled using the data that had been gathered. The output from the network (open loop component) is the control signal for an electro-hydraulic actuator. A typical control signal for this application is shown in figure 7. It can be seen that non-linearities are present in the signal which are especially noticeable around the turning points in the curve. Such is the nature of the ANN approach that an accurate control signal can be generated even for a demand curve not previously seen provided that it is within the operating envelope of the actuator system used for training.

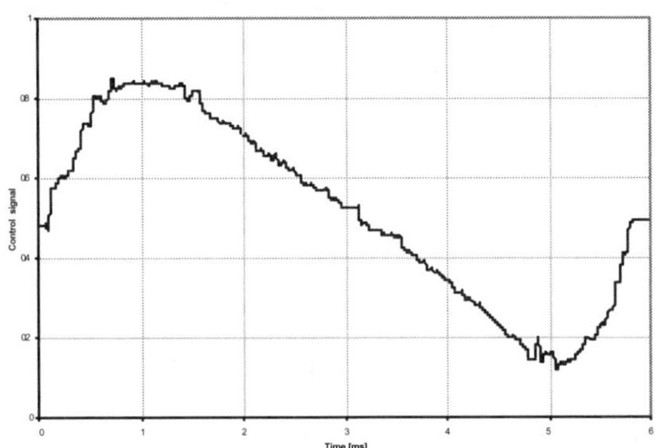

Figure 7. Plot of ANN generated control signal value V time.

Feedback is determined from desired response and actual response, the latter being provided by a position sensor fitted to the actuator. Using a subset of data gathered for initial training of the ANN generating the control signal, a network was trained to provide feedback control. This network contained only 64 neurons and used 5 dimensional input vectors. Due to the significant delay introduced by the actuator system used in this case it was not practical to modify the control signal in response to feedback during its current cycle. Instead, the feedback for all variations during a cycle were utilized in the following cycle to improve accuracy. As members of the family of ANN processor used in this instance are able to provide outputs at intervals of less than a microsecond, feedback correction during the current cycle is realistic for most applications [8].

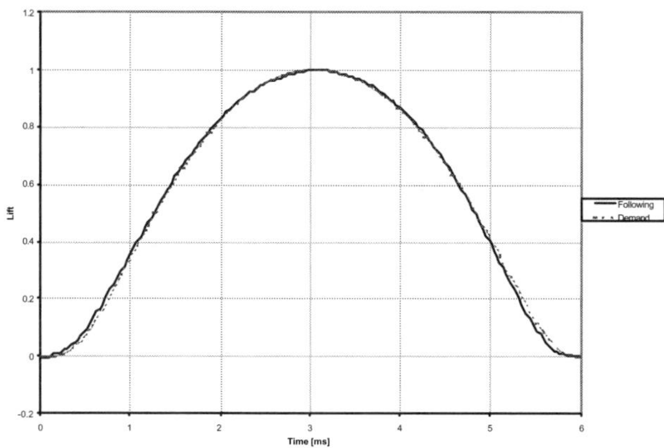

Figure 8. Plot of demand profile and actuator response for ANN based Closed loop control system.

When the ANN based control system was used to control a live actuator it was found that an accurate system response could be achieved. The non-linearities present in the control signal were not present in actuator response, further supporting the notion that the ANN has mapped the non-linear transfer function of the actuator. It was also noted that the system was able to provide suitable control for varying valve lift profiles, even when the system had not been trained on the specific profile being requested. In order to change valve lift profile or engine RPM only the demand curve input was required to be changed, no other parameter changes were required.

CONCLUSION

Technology has reached the stage where parallel ANN implementations are available and suitable for embedded 'real-time' SOC solutions. Developing control systems for non-linear actuators based on ANNs is now a practical consideration. The ANN based control system approach leads to rapid development by avoiding the need for a detailed analytical solution. Because the ANN creates a map of the non-linear transfer function of the system, it is able to provide both accuracy and flexibility. The flexibility provided by ANN control allows for changes to actuator operating profiles to be implemented simply by creating the desired demand profile.

ACKNOWLEDGMENTS

The authors would like to thank Steve Kenchington and Kevin Driscoll of Lotus Engineering for their assistance during the experimental AVT work presented in this paper.

REFERENCES

1. S Meyer and A Greff "New Calibration Methods and Control Systems with Artificial Neural Networks" SAE paper 2002-01-1147, World Congress 2002.
2. J Allen and D Law "Production Electro-Hydaulic Variable Valve-Train for a new Generation of I.C. Engines" SAE Paper 2002-01-1109, World Congress 2002.
3. T Kohonen "Self Organizing Maps" Springer-Verlag, Germany 1995
4. T Kohonen "Analysis of a simple self-organizing process" Biological Cybernetics, 44(2):135-140, 1982
5. S P Luttrell "A Bayesian analysis of Self-Organising Maps" Neural Computation, 6(5):767-94, 1994
6. N Lightowler, C T Spracklen and A R Allen "A Modular Approach to Implementation of the Self-organising Map" Proceedings WSOM 97, pp 130 - 135.
7. N Lightowler, A R Allen, H Grant, D C Hendry and C T Spracklen "The Modular Map" Neural Networks, IJCNN 99 Vol 2, pp 851-856.
8. "Summary Data Sheet for the VindAX Processor", AXEON Ltd, 2001.

CONTACT

Both authors are with Axeon Ltd, Aberdeen, Scotland. See www.axeon.com

2003-01-0031

When to Integrate or Not to Integrate - A VVA System Decision

Steven N. Ernest
Jacobs Vehicle Systems

ABSTRACT

Virtually all production engines today have some level of electronic control. As features have been added over the years, some of these Electronic Control Units (ECU's) have grown significantly in complexity, size and cost. As Variable Valve Actuation (VVA) systems evolve from simple, mechanically operated systems such as cam phasers to full VVA systems, electronic systems will also need to evolve to control them. This evolutionary path forces many system-level questions to be considered. Some global questions that will need to be considered as the industry continue on this path, are:

"What is the optimal level of electronics integration?"

"At what point should a distributed engine control system be considered?"

There are several key points that need to be considered to properly make these decisions, many of which will be addressed in this paper. A process for how these decisions might be made for a given system will be discussed. This process will then be applied to an engine control scheme for an engine utilizing a VVA system.

INTRODUCTION

Each time a new subsystem that requires electronics is added to a vehicle, the question arises: "Should these new electronics stand alone or should they be integrated into the existing controls?"

The simplistic view is "One box is cheaper than two, therefore, let's keep it all in one box." You sure can't beat the simplicity of the block diagram – See Figure 1.This typically seems like a rational and logical approach to all parties except those who have to actually do this integration.

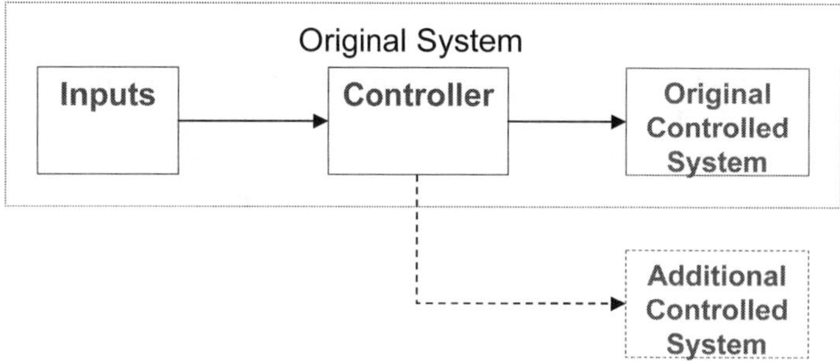

Figure 1. First-Cut Simplistic Control Scheme

Further analysis of the problem, however, reveals that there are several aspects that need to be considered. Among them are: system complexity, software complexity, available development time, available engineering resources, technology limitations, development costs, percent of systems using this new feature, production costs, system reliability, field service and warranty costs. While not an all-inclusive list, these certainly are among the key considerations.

As we will see, these considerations are not always mutually exclusive and therefore trade-offs will inevitably need to be made to get to an optimal system for any particular application.

DESCRIPTION OF THE ISSUES

At the start of any project there are several things that are known, generally in the area of what is available to the project team. These include what engineering resources and funding are available, the timeframe for completion and the target production cost.

More loosely defined are the goals regarding system and software complexity, warranty costs, and field failure rate. Clearly, all of these are to be minimized, -but not at *any* cost. When, and where to make the appropriate tradeoffs can determine the success or failure of the system design effort.

AUTOMOTIVE-SPECIFIC ISSUES

In the automotive world, there are additional issues one must consider: Electronic devices are allotted a minimum amount of space. In the case of the Valve Control Unit

(VCU), space is at a particular premium as the device must, in some cases, be capable of being mounted on the engine. This means that power dissipation and vibration handling capabilities are key to its long-term reliability.

Reliability is crucial to the Heavy-Duty (HD) engine customer. HD engines are used in commercial vehicles and are expected to last a very long time under harsh conditions with minimal downtime.

LOOKING AT THE WHOLE COST PICTURE

Cost is a key consideration in the automotive world. Any electronic device can be broken down into 3 components: packaging, infrastructure, and features. Features are what the customer cares about and for which he will pay. Unfortunately he can't have the features without the other two components.

If several devices can share the packaging and infrastructure, it can make sense to combine them. If the packaging or infrastructure need to be modified significantly at a potential cost penalty, this decision needs to be evaluated more closely.

The cost of two simple systems may be more than the cost of one more complex system that performs both tasks. A new, more complex device, however, will be statistically more likely to fail than either of the previously separate modules. If only one part of the new module fails and the entire module needs to be replaced, it will cost more than replacing one of the previously separate modules. This could have the unintended effect of increasing warranty costs. If the increase in warranty costs exceed the piece-cost savings of the combined module, ultimately the system cost has gone up leading to an unsatisfied customer.

If the new system requires electronic hardware modifications that are not going to be used by all customers, the choices are:

1) Produce separate electronics for customers using the feature
2) Integrate the electronics into a single ECU forcing all customers to share the cost burden of the additional electronics, even when they are not using them
3) Develop and stock 2 separate ECU's, one with the feature and one without

The *total* cost of each choice needs to be determined and compared. Typically engine OEM's don't like option 3 due to the increase in inventory carrying costs and tracking of additional part numbers etc. A good rule of thumb signaling the transition between 1 and 2 is when the feature will be used by more than 80% of the customers.

One has to be mindful of the myriad of things that help make up the "true" cost of a system. If, one is a bit too zealous in the rush to integrate in order to decrease the piece cost, the resulting true costs could overwhelm these savings by a surprising amount.

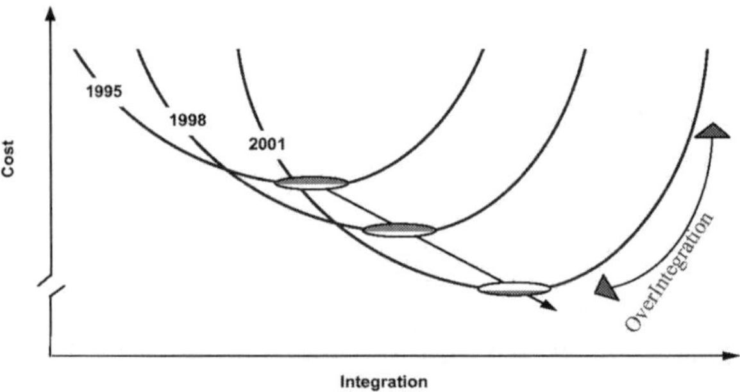

Figure 2. Finding the least-cost point of integration [1]

Figure 2 shows the relationship between integration and cost as technology improves year after year. At any point in time, the technology is such that there is an optimal level of integration. As technology improves, this point increases integration and lowers cost. Trying to "push the envelope" on this curve, however, is not always wise due to the reasons previously cited.

LEAST COST SOLUTION – A MOVING TARGET

Clearly everyone wants to design the least cost, maximum performance system. This optimal solution is, unfortunately, a moving target. The fast-paced world of electronics exerts its force on any system using semiconductors. Every month we hear of new electronic devices being introduced that out-perform the previous model by some large percentage. While this is true, it is also true that these latest devices are unproven and can cost plenty more than the last model. Wait a year or so, however, and these devices have more history, are shipping in larger quantities and probably have some competition. This allows -and forces- them to cost much less than when introduced. Figure 3 shows projected cost over time as new devices are introduced and they progress along their life cycle.

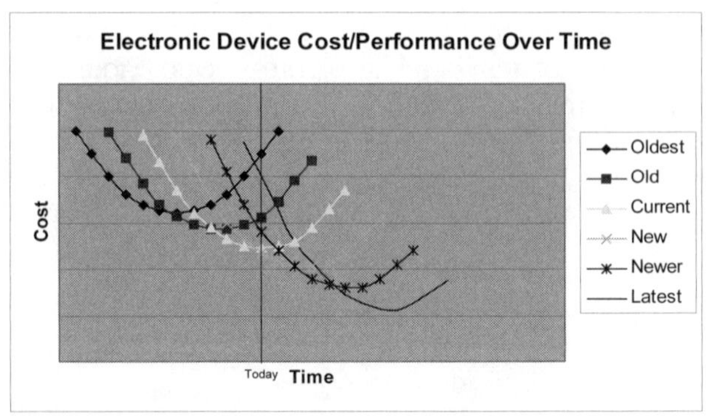

Figure 3. Electronic Device Cost Over Time

An example of this is Flash memory. Some older models with less capacity can actually cost *more* than newer, larger capacity devices. The processes to make the new parts may be less expensive or more efficient than that of the old part. Also, as products get older, the quantities produced are reduced as we all jump to purchase the latest device. The trick is to choose devices and system architectures that will be near the bottom of the cost/performance parabola either at product introduction or shortly thereafter. If one is very careful -and lucky-, the new product's life cycle ends before its components increase significantly in price as they near obsolescence.

A similar case can be made for the level of electronics integration on a given application. At some point in time, the sum of the cost of all the devices in a system will be at a minimum. If this were the only consideration in minimizing system cost, the problem would be tedious, but not necessarily difficult to solve. What makes this a truly interesting problem is dealing with all of the other issues mentioned above. Each of these issues has a cost, though not so easily calculated as the Bill Of Material.

LESS COMPLEX = LESS DEVELOPMENT TIME = HIGHER RELIABILITY

It is a well-known and accepted engineering rule of thumb that there is an inverse relationship between system complexity and system reliability. Simple systems work the best. They have less to break and so they break less.

In the book The Art of Designing Embedded Systems [2], Jack Ganssle claims "The most important rule of software engineering is also the least known: *Complexity does not scale linearly with size*." He sites data from hundreds of IBM projects showing that as project complexity and size increase, development time increases due to the extra size and a decrease in programmer *productivity*. Keeping track of the increased complexity and the additional testing required reduce the ultimate amount of software produced in a given amount of time.

Dr. Barry Boehm of the USC Center for Software Engineering has developed a Constructive Cost Model (COCOMO II) used by software development firms all over the world. While an explanation of the model is far beyond the scope of this paper, Ganssle suggests it can be simplified to:

Effort to Create a project = C x $(\text{KLOC})^M$

KLOC = thousands of lines of code

C and M are values derived from a large set of cost drivers, which depend on the mode of development, and they are always greater than one. The modes of development used for COCOMO II calculations are:

Organic Mode: Characterized by a familiar environment with a small group of very experienced developers working on a small, simple project where requirements are flexible.

Semi-detached Mode: Teams of mixed experience levels working on larger, more complex systems where some requirements are rigid and others may be more flexible.

Embedded Mode: Characterized by projects of high complexity, typically with more than one processor and various peripherals. Requirements for both hardware and software are rigid.

Ganssle claims that with embedded real-time systems, typically $C \geq 3.6$ and $M \geq 1.5$.

Again, the scope of this paper limits the explanation of this theory further, so let's focus on the *magnitude* of the values between an integrated and a distributed system:

An Example:

Two devices take 1000 lines of code each to perform their relative functions.

Effort for both devices = $2(3.6 \times 1000^{1.5}) = 113{,}842$

If they can be combined into one module and use 2000 lines of code (2 x 1000 lines)

Effort for integrated device = $3.6 \times 2000^{1.5} = 321{,}994$

Nearly a 3-fold increase in effort to integrate!!!

Both the previous points suggest that a statistically more reliable system can be made in a shorter amount of time by keeping each of the pieces of the system small and less complicated.

INTEGRATION – A CUSTOMER'S PERSPECTIVE

When a system requiring controls is offered for sale with the controls, customers generally assume that these controls have been optimized for that system. Since the designer of the system manufactures or at least specifies all system components, hopefully he has given great thought to the total system operation.

When this is true, the customer benefits greatly. First; the system does work optimally. Second; when the system malfunctions or otherwise works sub-optimally, the customer only needs to make one call. There is no finger pointing, (at least not visible to the customer), no blaming of other system component companies or other obfuscation, and the customer can get their problem corrected without getting deeply involved in the details.

Engineering development time and costs for new electronic modules can be significant. As discussed previously, development time and costs increase as the physical size and complexity of the module increases. While some customers prefer to have everything under their control, if they leave some control to their subsystem suppliers, they are rewarded with not having to revise their ECU each time the supplier makes a subsystem change. Also, when they do need to make an ECU change that will not affect their supplier's subsystem or other module, they can do this without worry, because the electronics are truly separate.

If the supplier is able to sell a more "generic" form of their product to multiple customers, the supplier's development costs can be spread out over a larger production volume, allowing all customers to benefit from the lower cost.

INTEGRATION – A SUPPLIER'S PERSPECTIVE

Clearly a subsystem supplier adds value to his products by providing a subsystem to the customer that has all the integration issues resolved. The controls work with the mechanical actuation system and the customer has minimal development time before being able to realize the benefits of the system.

For this added value, the supplier is able to charge more for their products than the cost of the commodity components it contains. The customer, in order to not incur increased engineering development time and the associated costs, is better served to pay the system integrator's price and leave the problems to the experts on that subsystem

If control system changes need to be made in a supplier's subsystem, those changes can be made without having to work through his customer's supply chain. This decreases the time it takes to make the change and increases the likelihood that it is made correctly.

If there are areas of operation that will cause subsystem damage or stress, the supplier has the capability of limiting operation in those areas or at least recording that the operation in that high-stress region occurred.

A DECISION FLOW CHART

Figure 4 shows an integration decision flow chart. Clearly this is a very simplified view of the topics I have discussed. It does, however, illustrate the steps and can help to clarify the data required in making the integration decision.

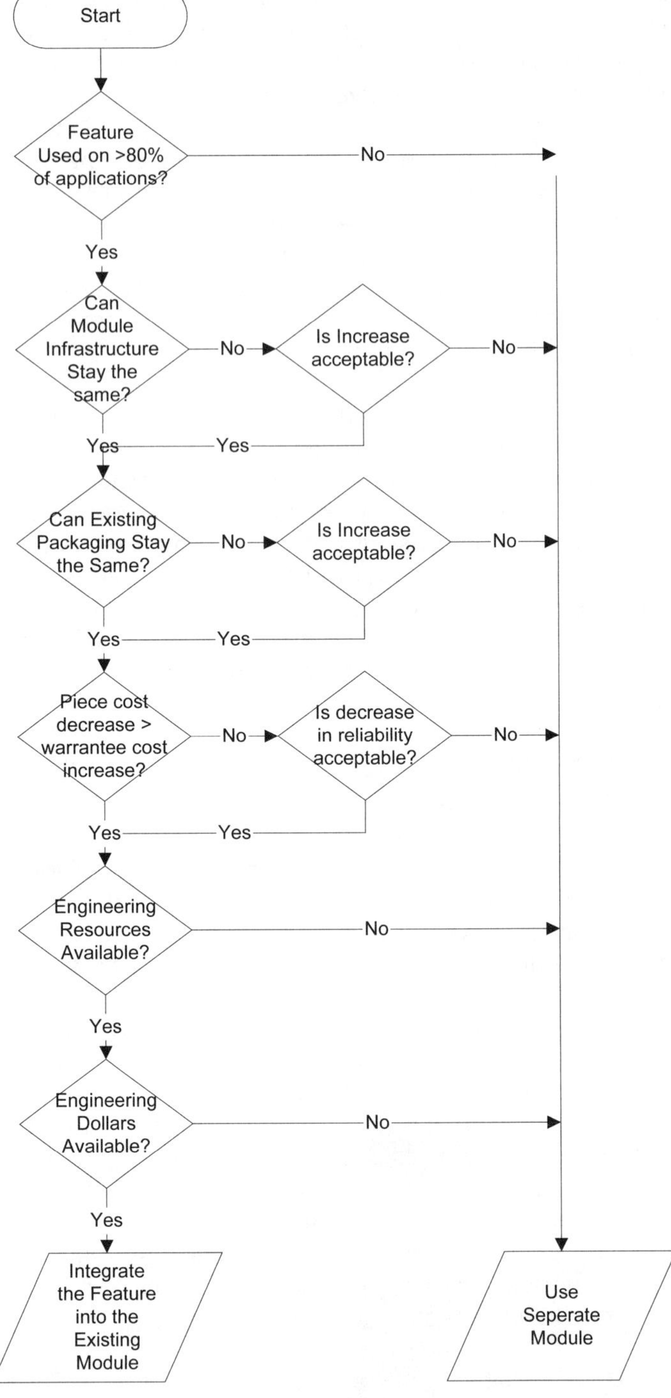

Figure 4. Integration Decision Flow-Chart.

A CASE STUDY – INTEGRATING THE VALVE CONTROL AND THE ENGINE CONTROL

The Valve Control Unit for a given six-cylinder diesel engine has 12 to 24 high current solenoid drivers to control the intake and exhaust valves. There may also be various other sensors and solenoids used specifically for controlling valve motion.

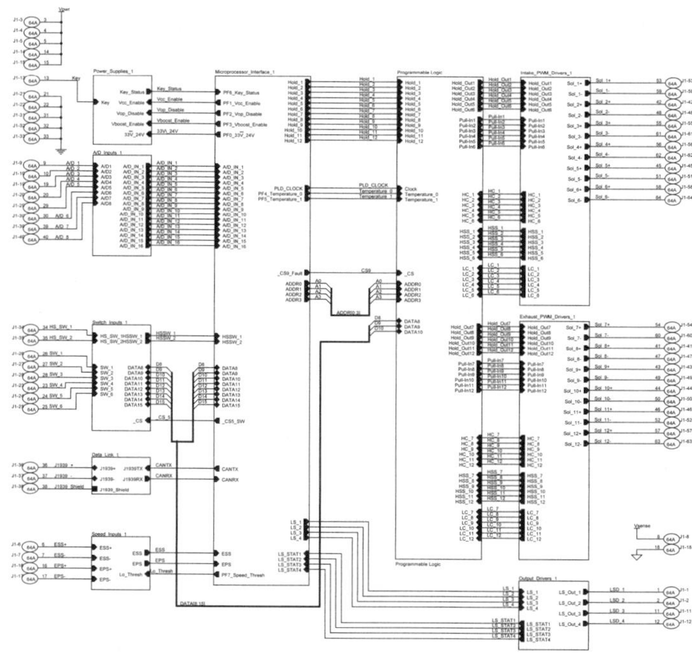

Figure 5. VCU Top Level Block Diagram

The complexity and size of the VCU is clearly not a trivial matter, as can be seen in figures 5 and 6. Compared to the fuel control events in the ECU, the valve timing events can have a very long duration. This means that the power supply needs to be able to support long duration, high current events. It also means that these events can, and do overlap, increasing the power supply current requirement significantly depending on calibrated tables.

Figure 6. Jacobs Vehicle Systems VCU

While the power supply is an issue, the real difficulty comes in the software complexity. In an ECU, the injection events are short and don't (usually) overlap, so the software doesn't need to track the location and duration of multiple events simultaneously. Each event happens near that cylinder's Top Dead Center (TDC).

The VCU software must keep track of multiple events on each valve and the length and duration of each event. These valve events nearly always overlap from cylinder to cylinder. Add to this the fact that there are always at least two and sometimes three or four valves to control per cylinder and you can clearly see that the VCU software complexity is more than firing a few extra solenoids.

The ECU for the same 6 cylinders has 6 and sometimes 12 high current drivers to control the amount and timing of fuel injected into the engine. It monitors a myriad of sensors and actuates drivers to control fan clutches, air conditioning, water pumps, Power Take-Off units and any other application-specific input or output.

The ECU has traditionally needed to absorb any and all new electronic features of each engine family. Thus it needs to be modified for each application or, at minimum, have features turned on and off via a calibration depending on the application. This has so far been successful, when the features are small, but it also causes each application to bear the cost of features that it doesn't use. Figure 7 shows a Siemens engine control.

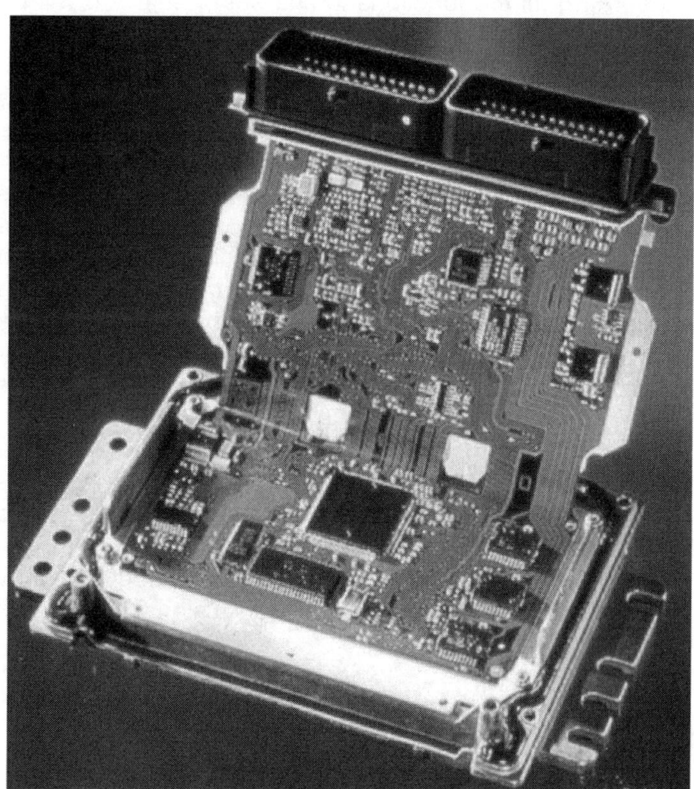

Figure 7. Siemens ECU

The VCU does have a significant advantage over the ECU. It is a "slave" module to the ECU, in the respect that the ECU is the device that responds to the vehicle operator's commands and has to deal with controlling engine speed and load. The VCU monitors and responds to the commands of the ECU.

The VCU for a given number of valves remains the same whether it is used on a vehicle, generator set or marine application. It's configuration and complexity remain basically the same, with calibration changes, regardless if the engine is a two or twenty-liter engine. There will be calibration differences between application and fuel types, but the basic VCU operation and function remains the same.

ECU designers generally agree that the typical ECU approaches 90 – 95% of throughput capacity at engine introduction. This does not leave much room for field upgrades or additional features.

Current automotive-grade microprocessors are just beginning to have the capability to drive the number of outputs required for all the valves, injectors and other solenoids required to control an engine with all of these features. It remains to be seen if processors have the bandwidth to accommodate the software to do all the functions. Certainly this technological capability will be available at some point. However, even when this capability exists, a study will have to be made to determine if the increased software complexity required to perform all the functions in one set of software will be worth the time for it to be developed.

One final issue is to determine the increase in ECU size required to integrate the VCU functions. ECU's are currently quite large, - ask any engineer responsible for mounting one on an engine! A conservative estimate would be that the VCU features would increase the size of the ECU by 50% due to the additional drivers and power supplies needed. It may very well be an even larger increase. An increase in size of 50% or more would likely not be tolerated. The vibration and power dissipation considerations would almost certainly put this out of consideration.

The current state of engine control technology indicates that the valve control function should not be integrated into the engine control. Revisiting this topic at the planning stage for each new product introduction may prove beneficial, to see if the conclusion changes as parameters change and new technology becomes available.

CONCLUSION

A process for determining whether a new electronic feature set should be integrated into existing controls is described. Careful consideration of the questions posed in the process development, will result in a sound decision at any given time and for any given electronic system.

The integration of the Valve Control Unit Function and the Engine Control Unit function, as an example, currently is not a workable solution, but this may change as technology improves, electronics get cheaper and perhaps software gets easier to write.

ACKNOWLEDGMENTS

Support for this work by Jacobs Vehicle Systems is greatly appreciated by the author. The author would also like to thank teammates Raymond Gosselin and Andrew Brzoska for their contributions to this project. Special appreciation goes to Dr. Zhou Yang, Frank Stawski and Adish Jain for their review of this paper.

REFERENCES

1. Randy Frank – On Semiconductor, "Vehicle Integration of Electronics and Semiconductors", PowerPulse.Net – June 18, 2001

2. Jack G. Ganssle – The Art of Designing Embedded Systems Published by Butterworth-Heinemann 1999.

3. Abts, C., Bailey, B. and Boehm, B (1998), "COCOTS Software Integration Cost Model: An Overview," Abts, C., Bailey, B. and Boehm, B., Proceedings of the California Software Symposium, 1998.

4. Boehm, B. (1981), Software Engineering Economics, Boehm, B., Prentice Hall, 1981.

Advanced Electronic Solutions for Highly Dependable Systems

Ross Bannatyne and Kevin Klein
Motorola Transportation Systems Group

ABSTRACT

This paper will discuss advances in electronic component technology that has been developed specifically for failsafe and fault-tolerant automotive systems such as braking and chassis control systems. These systems need to be highly dependable, and exhibit predictable behavior in the event of a system fault.

Such systems often perform many real-time self-checking operations to detect the occurrence of a fault. Integrated on-chip hardware can be used in such systems to help ensure that the dependable system can provide a 'fail-safe' operating mode. There are many different configurations of hardware used in such embedded systems to realize the fail-safe methodology, each having its own unique characteristics in terms of fault coverage, costs, complexity and performance. Hardware implementations, as opposed to software plausibility checks by a watchdog, are often advantageous and require less systems development effort. This paper will discuss such on-chip systems that lead to optimized 'failsafe' microcontrollers.

INTRODUCTION

There are an increasing number of systems for various applications that require highly dependable operation, often in safety critical applications. One of the latest areas to experience significant growth in this requirement is the automobile. In fact, automotive anti-lock braking systems have included such technology for many years. This technology is continually being enhanced as well as used in other areas such as electronic based steering and suspension control.

As electronics continues to become a larger part of the design of a new vehicle, systems are performing many more functions under the control of microprocessors and consequently mechanical and hydraulic systems are being replaced by 'by-wire' configurations of sensors, microprocessors and actuators.

Figure 1 illustrates a roadmap that highlights the main electronically controlled functions for a vehicle chassis, and highlights how they are being amalgamated under electronic controls. The goal is to achieve the 'automated highway', vehicles that will autonomously drive in infrastructures which support higher traffic throughput with less accidents.

REDUNDANT CPU CONFIGURATIONS

Each of these types of systems require failsafe operation. Traditionally, this function has been facilitated using two microprocessors. There are two common configurations - when two identical microprocessors are used, the configuration is known as symmetric redundancy, and when a smaller less powerful 'watchdog' microprocessor is used, the configuration is known as asymmetric redundancy. These configurations are shown in Figure 2.

FIGURE 1 - DEVELOPMENT OF DEPENDABLE SYSTEMS FOR AUTOMOTIVE CHASSIS CONTROL

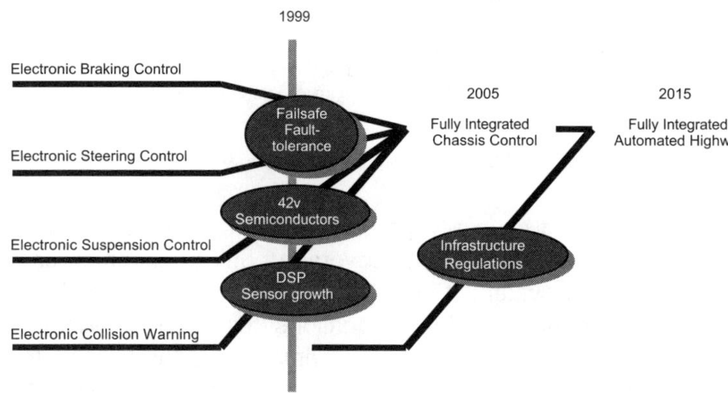

Although each configuration has its own advantages and disadvantages, the symmetric approach is becoming more popular, particularly when both of the Central Processing Units (CPUs) are integrated onto a monolithic silicon chip. The symmetric single-chip solution is popular on account of reduced physical size, increased reliability that results from reduced number of system interconnections and better electromagnetic compatibility performance. This last attribute results from having fewer high speed signals connected to the 'outside world'. Another benefit of having fewer communications links between several chips is the difficulty in synchronizing the operations of the two CPUs.

FIGURE 2 - REDUNDANT MICROPROCESSOR CONFIGURATIONS

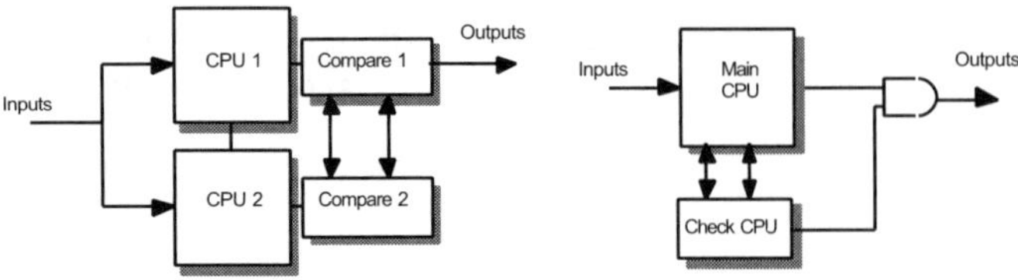

An advantage of using two separate microcontrollers (rather than two CPUs on a single die) is that there is more choice to select from many different devices which are available 'off-the-shelf'. It is also possible to introduce redundancy into the software by using two different routines.

FIGURE 3 - ASYMMETRIC REDUNDANCY

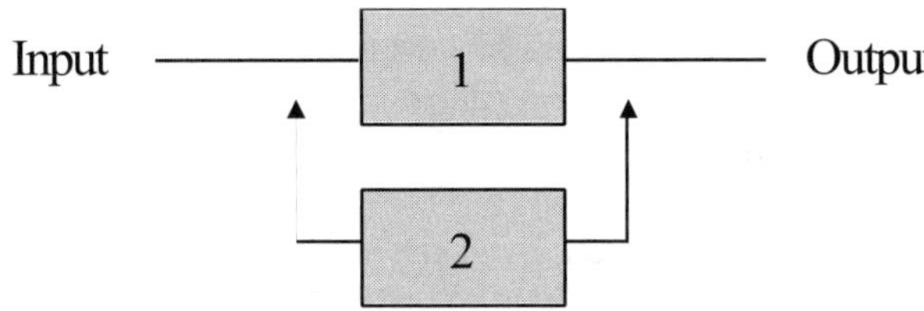

$$R(t) = R1(t) + [1 - R1(t)]C1R2(t)$$

* C1 is the fault coverage of R1(t) by R2(t).
* Note that Reliability is also a function of time
* Only if C1(t) approaches 1 does R(t) approach that of a parallel system

Source: 'Techniques for achieving dependability', Design for safety, Storey, University of Warwick, 1999.

From a fault coverage perspective, it is considered easier to optimize the fault coverage on a symmetrically redundant system. Figure 3 and Figure 4 illustrate block diagrams and reliability equations for each category of system. For Figure 3, asymmetric redundancy, the reliability is also a function of time. This increases the importance of the synchronization between the operations of both CPUs. The term C1 is the fault coverage of block 1 that is accomplished by block 2. Figure 4 illustrates the symmetric system. The diagram shows that this approach can expanded into a highly parallel configuration. Analysis of the respective reliability equations for each type of system illustrates that the asymmetric approach can only begin to achieve the same level as the symmetric approach if the term C1, fault coverage, approaches unity. This is quite a significant factor in favor of using a symmetric approach.

These considerations on the implementation of redundant systems have led to the popularity of using a symmetrically redundant approach in many cases. Examples of such products with two CPUs could be used in 'failsafe' systems.

FIGURE 4 - SYMMETRIC REDUNDANCY

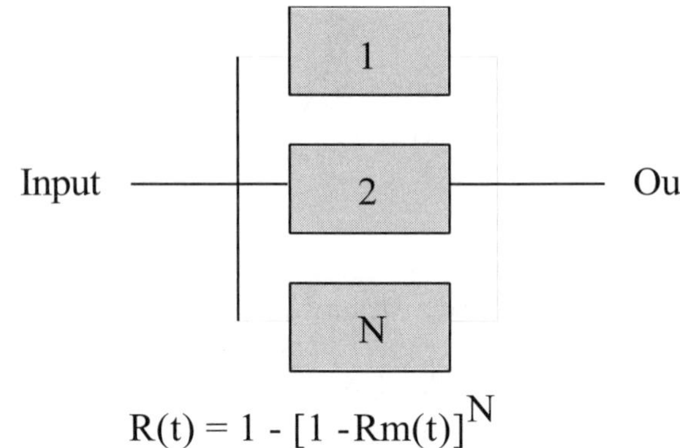

$$R(t) = 1 - [1 - Rm(t)]^N$$

* System will function correctly provided at least one module is operational

Source: 'Techniques for achieving dependability', Design for safety, Storey, University of Warwick, 1999.

There is an important difference between fail-safe systems and fault-tolerant systems. Today's Antilock Braking Systems are fail-safe: if an electrical system error is detected, the ECU switches to a safe 'off' mode, allowing the foundation hydraulic brakes to operate without the faulty ABS system interfering. A fault-tolerant system must not only recognize that an electrical fault has occurred, but must continue to operate safely with the existing known fault. Antilock braking systems use redundancy to facilitate a fail-safe system. Typically the CPU at the heart of the system supervises the continual testing of all the major system components. The CPU can only validate these components however, if the CPU itself is known to be 'sane'. Hence a second, redundant CPU is used to validate the sanity of the first CPU. A redundant CPU can either be implemented as a second standalone microcontroller or as an error detection CPU with comparison logic on the same microcontroller. This type of dual CPU configuration is shown in Figure 5. If the two CPU's disagree over result of an instruction execution, the 'fault' signal will be enabled and an interrupt will initiate a sequence of events to switch the control unit into the safe 'off' mode. Dual CPU microcontrollers will increase their popularity in automotive safety critical applications such as steering and airbags, as well as ABS.

Both CPUs are fed with the same inputs, although only one of them (Main CPU) is used to control the chip functions. The Complementary CPU is used only as a check to ensure that the output is exactly the same as the Main CPU. In the event that a fault is detected, an interrupt can be generated which will indicate that the system should deploy its 'failsafe' state of operation.

FIGURE 5 -DUAL CPU CONFIGURATION

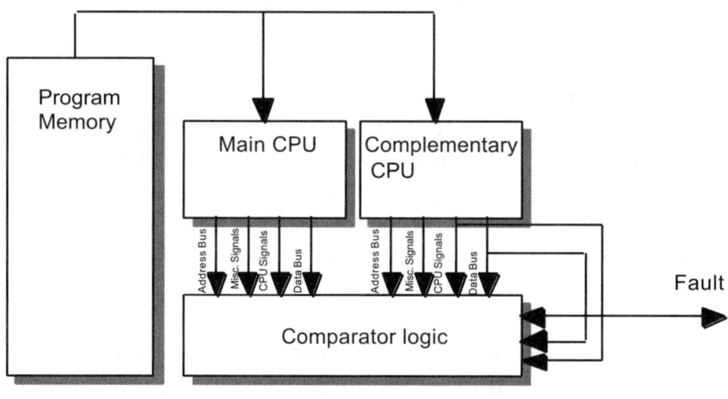

MEMORY VALIDATION TECHNIQUES

There are other on-chip systems that may be required to satisfy dependability requirements; one might be the ability to verify the contents of on-chip memory. This may be a requirement if a dual CPU is system is used with only one memory array. Therefore something is needed to provide a check on the memory contents. There is a possibility that a memory bit may be flipped (it is after all, impossible to discount the possibility of an alpha particle hitting a memory cell and flipping a bit...).

The configuration illustrated in Figure 6 illustrates a module which is connected to the internal bus structure of the device. The module will look for free cycles on the address / data bus, and when the bus is not in use, a word will be fetched from memory. This word will be fed into a signature analyzer. The process repeats until the entire memory contents have been fetched sequentially and a signature representing the memory contents has been generated. This signature is then compared to a previously generated value that is representative of the known correct memory contents. On CISC machines, there are usually lots of free cycles (often at least one every five cycles). On RISC based machines, there are less free cycles, although it is possible to set the memory validation up such that it will 'steal' a cycle if no free cycle is available. This allows deterministic validation time. If the signature matches, there is no need to generate any interrupts so the validation process is basically invisible and will be performed whilst the CPU is executing a control algorithm at full speed.

The memory system in future automotive microcontrollers may be enhanced in certain cases to allow simplified memory verification. In a safety critical system, it may be desirable to check that memory contents are stable and have not been corrupted during the course of operation. There are several techniques that can be implemented to validate memory contents, each having its own merits and problems. The most straightforward way is to implement a parity bit on the entire memory array. Whenever a byte is written to memory, a parity generator adds an extra bit and whenever a byte is read from memory a parity checker will ensure that a parity error has not occurred.

FIGURE 6 - MEMORY VALIDATION MODULE

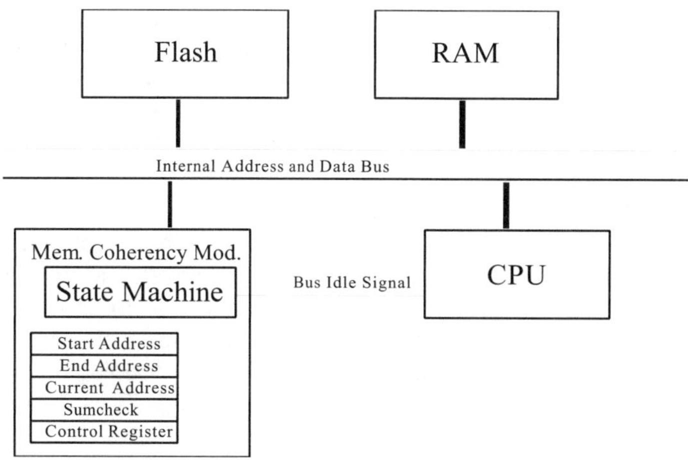

One shortfall of the memory validation approach is that it becomes very difficult to use this approach on the contents of RAM, which changes often. Unless the CPU can stop executing the control algorithm for a RAM check exercise (very unlikely in highly dependable real time embedded control systems), another method is required to ensure dependability of this array. There are two obvious approaches which can both be employed. The first is to add a redundant RAM array. This can be expensive though as RAM requirements may be large. The other approach is to add a parity scheme to the RAM such that each byte of RAM has an associated parity bit. A parity RAM generator is required to add these bits when the data is written to memory. When the data is fetched from memory, a parity checker is required to decode the parity and ensure that the data which is retrieved is the same as that which was written. Unless the RAM array is very small, the parity scheme is likely to be more inexpensive than using a redundant RAM array.

ADDITIONAL FUNCTIONS

In addition to these schemes for validating that the CPU and memory arrays are operating correctly, there are several features which are common on most families of microprocessors for fault detection. Bus Errors are usually generated if a non-implemented or reserved address is specified. Clock monitors are used to detect slow or irregular system clocks, and illegal opcode traps are useful to flagging faults that may occur in memory, software faults and dynamic or static bus faults.

FLEXRAY PROTOCOL FOR HIGHLY DEPENDABLE SERIAL COMMUNICATIONS

Future automotive systems will continue to see significant growth in multiplexed serial communications. One difference will be that the number and type of multiplexed networks in the vehicle will increase. Unfortunately, a single communications protocol that can cost-effectively address every automotive application does not exist. Instead a number of different communications subsystems will be integrated together in a modern vehicle. For example, highly dependable time-triggered' Class C' communication networks will be implemented to handle applications such as Steer / Brake / Drive by-wire, and lower speed, lower cost, serial communications systems are used for auto body systems.

Fault tolerant systems are set to become a growth area in the not too distant future, particularly in the automotive world, as brake-by-wire and steer-by-wire systems are set to become a reality in the next few years. In order to address the fault tolerant aspects of such communications systems, the network topology will support two buses to broadcast information. Thus if one bus system malfunctions, the second bus will still be available. This double bus system is illustrated in Figure 7.

FIGURE 7 – DOUBLE BUS SYSTEM

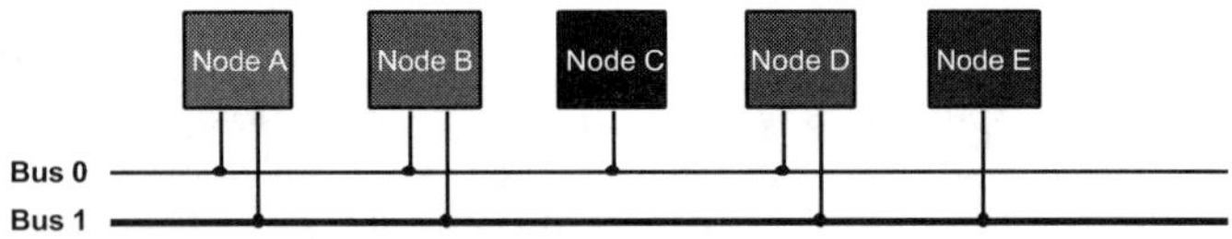

Such systems must be 'fail-operational' as they are deemed safety critical; if the system develops a fault, it could have catastrophic consequences. 'By-wire' systems transfer electrical signals down a wire instead of using a medium such as hydraulic fluid to transfer muscular energy. A conventional Antilock Braking System (ABS) is considered 'fail-silent'; if a fault in the electronic control system is detected, the control system is switched off, leaving the manual hydraulic back-up still operational. If no such hydraulic back-up is available (as in the case of a 'by-wire' system), the system must continue to function in the event of a fault occurring.

The unsuitability of the existing communications protocols is mainly due to the fact that they are 'event-triggered'. A precise moment in time when a message will be received is not specified. A communications protocol can only be predictable if worst case transmission time and jitter are known at the time of the design and meet the requirements of the application. The time delay between presenting a message to be transmitted at the senders interface and receiving the message at the receivers interface is known as the transmission time. Jitter is defined as the variability of this transmission time (maximum transmission time - minimum transmission time).The maximum jitter depends on the longest message that it is possible to transmit. Real-time control applications are very sensitive to jitter and it is an important parameter for developing real-time distributed systems.

The FlexRay serial communications protocol has been developed for use in such systems. FlexRay is a new protocol that supports bus, star and multiple star topologies and will initially provide a net data rate of up to 5Mbit/sec. The unique characteristic of FlexRay is its ability to support both event-triggered and time-triggered media access management.

Time triggered and event triggered systems operate very differently. For a time triggered system, control signals are derived from the progression of time, whereas in event triggered systems, control signals are derived from the occurrence of an event (i.e. an interrupt). Time triggered systems use state information which is obtained from the condition that exists for a defined period of time, like the value of a sensor reading. This differs from event information in that the event is an occurrence such as a sensor being triggered above or below a pre-defined threshold. Usually state information is transmitted to several recipients who do not consume the message upon reception. Event messages are usually deposited at a recipient who will queue the information or will activate an interrupt service routine to take the appropriate action which is merited by the event occurrence.

In summary, time triggered communication offers high predictability and easier testing for timeliness but it is inflexible in that additional nodes cannot be added to the system after it has been defined without a-priori knowledge. Event triggered communication systems are much for flexible with regard to adding nodes but are more unpredictable and require thorough testing to ensure that an overload condition does not occur when many events occur and the bus bandwidth is assaulted. One of the attractive characteristics of the FlexRay class C serial communications protocol is that it will support both static (time triggered) and dynamic (event triggered) media access. The bus access operation is illustrated in Figure 8.

FIGURE 8 -FLEXRAY BUS ACCESS

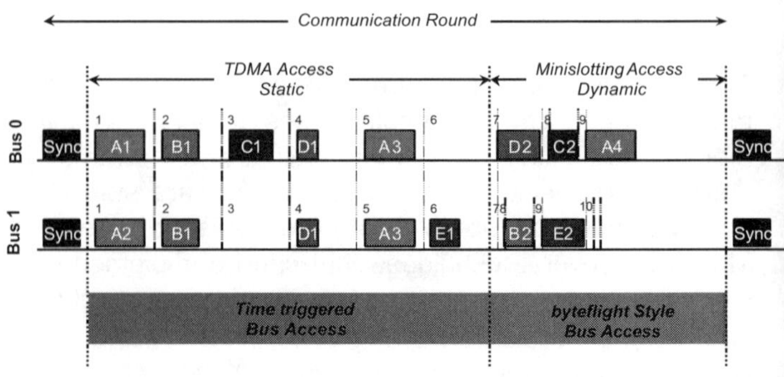

The time triggered bus access is shown on the left hand side of Figure 8, corresponding to the 'TDMA Access' portion of the communication round. The 'Minislotting access' portion, which is dynamic in nature, is based on the existing 'byteflight' serial communication protocol that will be used in BMW automobiles.

By definition, a real-time control system is a system in which the physical instant of time at which information is available at a receiving node is very important. As certain types of systems, such as those that are being developed for the automobile, require highly dependable real-time communications networks, there is becoming more interest in 'Hard' real-time communications. Hard real-time communications systems guarantee that all messages are delivered within their specified deadlines. A Time Triggered solution using a TDMA scheme addresses this requirement well.

In event-triggered systems there is a ubiquitous problem known as the babbling idiot failure. This occurs when a faulty node continually broadcasts a message which takes over the bus. The regularity of time based systems makes it possible to provide a mechanism which can guard against the babbling-idiot node. This is illustrated in Figure 9.

The faulty node is shown to retransmit its message continually. A bus guardian, an independent hardware unit with its own clock system is connected between the transmitting node and the bus. At the nodes pre-defined broadcasting slot, the bus guardian will 'open the gate' such that the bus signal which is transmitted will only be available for the correct duration of time in the appropriate time slot. The bus guardian can be viewed upon as a logical 'AND'ing operation with the nodes packet of information.

FIGURE 9 - BABBLING IDIOT AVOIDANCE

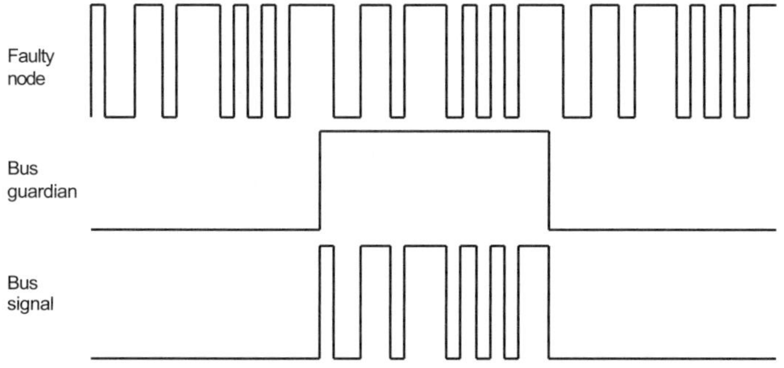

A FlexRay controller unit is illustrated in Figure 10. The diagram shows a host microcontroller that would be used to run the application. For example, in a braking control system, this would run the anti-lock braking algorithm. The host controller is linked to the FlexRay controller via a parallel bus interface. The FlexRay controller directs the flow of data to and from the host microcontroller and packages this data into the frame required for the bus access. The data frame is shown in Figure 11.

The bus guardians, used to protect against the 'babbling idiot' fault, are positioned between the FlexRay controller and the physical bus medium. These bus guardians are implemented as analog ASIC devices and have their own clock source, independent of the FlexRay controller in order to prevent common mode failures.

FIGURE 10 – FLEXRAY CONTROLLER

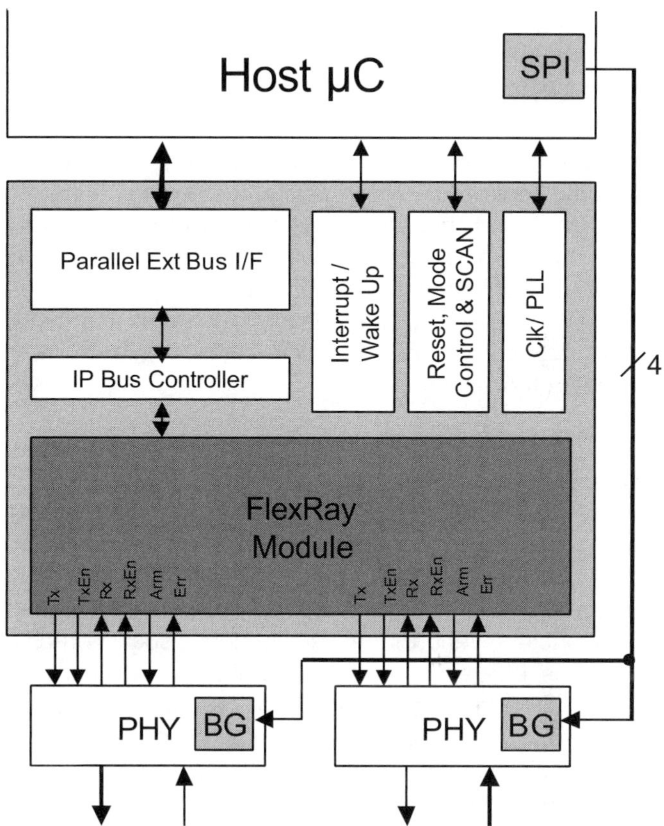

Although the first FlexRay controller devices will are standalone chips, it is expected that this functionality will be integrated onto 'standard' off-the-shelf microcontroller devices as a functional module. This integration is a logical step (just as CAN, J1850 and other serial communications protocol controller are now common functions on microcontrollers) and will reduce the overall chipcount and system cost.

FIGURE 11 – FLEXRAY FRAME FORMAT

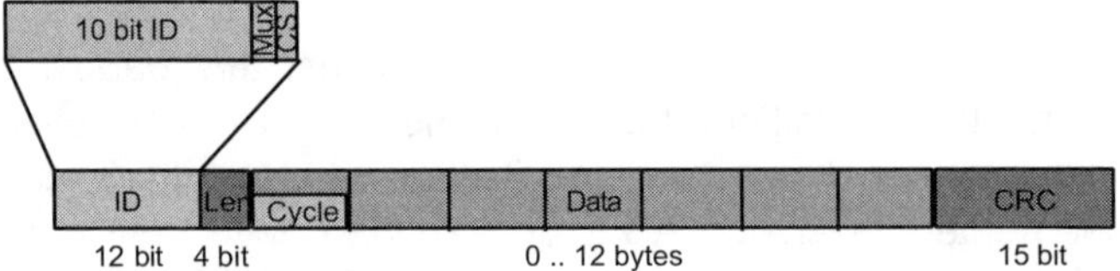

- 12 bit header
  - 10 bit ID
  - 1 clock sync (CS) bit
  - 1 multiplex bit
- Cycle count (uses first data byte)
- 12 data bytes (11 if cycle count is transmitted)
- 15 bit CRC - same polynomial as CAN and byteflight

CONCLUSION

This paper has discussed several of the key areas where microcontrollers are being enhanced to be better suited to applications which require a high degree of dependability or the ability to diagnose faulty operation. Until only recently, such functionality was almost always implemented at the system level, as there has been limited availability of semiconductor devices with appropriate functionality.

The number of applications that require such capabilities is increasing significantly. The automotive marketplace is only one example in the growth of highly dependable system operation, but has been influential in driving progress through its high volume appeal. The low cost requirements in this market has also helped lead semiconductor vendors to implement such on-chip systems as efficiently as possible. The same approach can be reused in other application areas that require the flexibility and performance of an 'off-the-shelf' popular microcontroller family, but with specific features added to ensure high dependability.

ACKNOWLEDGEMENTS

The authors would like to acknowledge Henrik Larsson for all the inspiration.

REFERENCES

Automotive Electronics Handbook, Jurgen, R. K., McGraw-Hill Book Company, New York, N.Y., 1999.

Using Microprocessors and Microcomputers, Wray, Greenfield, Bannatyne, Prentice Hall, New Jersey, 1999.

Automotive Microcontrollers, Jurgen, R. K., SAE Progress in Technology Series PT-75, 1998.

Electronic Braking, Traction, and Stability Control, Jurgen, R. K., SAE Progress in Technology Series ,PT-76, 1998.

SOFTWARE DESIGN/DEVELOPMENT

2007-01-1618

Writing Software Specifications Using Interface Matrix

Dev Raheja
Design for Competitiveness, Inc.

ABSTRACT

Software intelligence in most products is a function of several systems working together to produce properties and behavior different than those of components. The disciplines of gathering such intelligence are often missing. That is why typical software has many missing and ambiguous requirements. The purpose of this paper is to show how to capture unknown requirements through an interactions matrix based on a system-of-systems concept.

INTRODUCTION

Approximately 80% of the dollars that go into software development are spent on finding and fixing failures.[1] This is very inefficient and costly. For a robust design, the opposite is required, that is, 80% of dollars should be spent on preventing failures so that life cycle costs are dramatically reduced. The need for a cost reduction is obvious, because a fault fixed during the concept stage costs only a small fraction compared to the warranty costs and the cost of downtime for fixing it later. This technique allows the product development teams to see the forest from the trees by capturing the complexity of software requirements. Lack of this macro vision is bound to result in many costly failures that sneak up on you

PROGRESS TO DATE

There are three types of risks: the risk of the known, the risk of known unknowns, and the risk of unknown unknowns. The known risks are understood through past history and customer statements of needs. Unfortunately customers are not aware of over 60% of the potential requirements. This is the experience of this author working with many Fortune 100 organizations. They recognize the need for a requirement only after they "don't get it". This is particularly true for software specifications. Many companies attempt to make use of lessons learned,, but most do not have formal and verifiable protocols. Some known risks can be identified through tools such as Failure Mode and Effects Analysis, Fault Tree Analysis, and Even Tree Analysis. Therefore some progress is being made in handling the known risks. The other two risks are significant, but there is no significant progress.

RISK OF KNOWN-UNKNOWNS

These risks are known somewhere, but not known to the specification writer. They can be found in the checklist such as the one in Chapter 9 of this author's book[2]. The data on a major airline below at a FAA/NASA workshop[3] shows the extent of unpredicted failures:

- Problems reported confidentially: About 13,000
- Number actually in airline files: About 2% or 260
- Number known to FAA: About 1% or 130

The author, while working with the Baltimore Mass Transit System could not come up with more than 200 requirements in the specification. He interviewed train drivers, technicians, and passengers and discovered a list of about 3000 concerns. At least 500 of them were added to the Baltimore requirements.

RISK OF UNKNOWN-UNKNOWNS

These risks are usually unpredictable with the tools we have today. The reason is that the systems are too complex. No longer are we dealing with one mechanical system which can perform and stand alone. The software typically interacts with several systems, resulting in millions of possible interactions for an aircraft system and some automotive applications. A typical software program, such as for cruise control, deals with internal as well as external systems. The internal systems include the Hydraulic System, Fuel System, Chassis System, Air Bag Restraint System, Steering System and complex Electronic System. The external systems can be a human system (driver, service technician, and bystander in the path of an accident), a highway intelligence system, a braking system, an engine system, an OEM Interface, a communication system and an environmental system (A recent recall included door locks that opened but refused to close in the cold weather, because the rain water intruded in the locks). The key point is that we are dealing with a system made up of several systems. The interactions are unbounded. We cannot know how the system-of-systems will behave by knowing only the behavior of individual systems. Tweaking one system without the knowledge of inter-system behavior is doomed to failure. The unknown -unknown risks are the result of lack of knowledge of the interactions and associated behavior of the system-of-systems. Altering the behavior of any part affects other parts and connecting systems.

We need to capture macro-level interactions before we write the software specification. This view comes from the System Performance Specification, which is then translated into an interactions matrix as explained in this paper. A cross-functional team from interconnecting systems must be involved in writing the specification.

METHODOLOGY

In order for software requirements to be comprehensive, the system requirements have to be comprehensive. The system requirements in turn need the understanding of a system which is an open set with complementary properties, capabilities and behavior resulting from interactions of parts and other systems. In principle all systems are comprised of subsystems that are themselves systems. Every system, therefore, is a system of systems. The categories in the system specifications should include[2]:

- Application environment
- Functions
- Active safety
- Reliability
- Durability
- Serviceability/maintainability
- Human factors requirements
- Logistics requirements
- Input interface requirements
- Output interface requirements
- Installation requirements
- Shipping/handling requirements

The author suggests performing System Functions FMEA, System Hazard Analysis, and Use/Misuse Analysis to identify many missing system requirements. These tools are explained in the author's book in the reference section (pages 444 – 446.

The next step is to develop an interactions matrix consisting of all the system requirements (these are all technically the functions of the system) in rows and different interacting systems in columns as shown in Figure 1. The columns should be for each system, but sometimes we have to be specific so it is not misunderstood. For example: one of the columns is "Clutch System". Ideally it could be "Mechanical System", but it is difficult to make sure the teams will brainstorm the functions of the clutch - a safety-critical system.

Function	Driver	AMT	Power-train	Hydraulics	Clutch System	X/Y Shifter	Trans. Harness	ECU	CAN Bus	OEM Interface
Engage Clutch	X	X	X	X	C	X	X	C	X	X
Engage Gear	X	X	X	X	X	X	C	C	X	X
Isolate Fault	X	X	X	X	X	X	X	X	X	X
Reduce No Fault Founds	X	X	X	X	X	X	X	X	X	X
Smooth shifting	X	X	X	X	X	X	X	C	C	X
Starting the engine	X	X				X	X	X		
Acceleration	C	X	X	C	X	X	X	X	X	C
No unintended Motion		C	X	C	X	X	C	X	C	X
Robust OEM communication	X	X		X	X	X	X	X	X	X
Reliability Centered Maintenance	X		X	X	X					
Speed control on grade	C	X	C	X	X	C	X	C	X	X
PTO Operation	X	X	X	X		X		C	C	
Maneuverability	X	C	X	X		X	C	X	X	
Low Temperature Operation		C	X	X			X	C	C	X
Speed Control (Cruise)	X	C	X		X	X		C	X	
Diagnostics		X	X		X	X	X	X	X	X

Figure 1. System-of-systems Interactions Matrix

The symbol X in the matrix refers to a certain state each system has to be in to perform that function. For example, to engage the clutch (first row), all systems have to be active in their own certain state. However, to start the engine (sixth row), only five systems have to be active during that function. Therefore this matrix shows the relation between each function and its interactions with various systems.

We are still at the system level. However this level has to be right for a software specification to be right. Each interaction has to be allocated either to software or to hardware. No function should be allocated to both. This can create conflicting requirements. Of course, many functions will have to be partly performed by both, but the primary owner should be one. The owner has the responsibility to keep the system in the desired mode in the event of the failure of the partner. For example, if an air bag deployment function is allocated to software, then software has the responsibility to make sure that the hardware works all the time. It also has the responsibility to take the appropriate action in the event of hardware malfunction or failure.

WRITING SOFTWARE REQUIREMENTS

Each interaction allocated to software becomes a software function. The composite of all the functions then becomes the "Software Performance Specification." Such a specification describes "what" the software system will do, not "how." The "how" portion belongs to the next level, which is "Software Design Specification." Note that the software performance specification includes reliability, maintainability, durability (the air bag software has to survive over 20 years), the driver interface, prognostics requirements, diagnostics requirements, and response to unusual requests by the user.

CHARACTERISTICS OF A SOFTWARE REQUIREMEN

Figure 2 shows what each function description (software requirement) should contain.

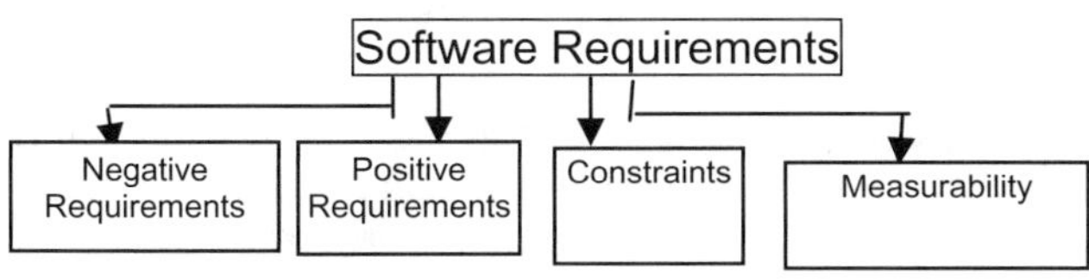

Figure -2. Composition of a software requirement

Positive requirements

Positive requirements are those that come from the interface matrix. Included are also non-requirements that may require historical reference and maintenance of the data base and structure. Requirements should have clarity so that they are not subject to interpretations. A cruise control function may be subject to interpretation when defined as: "The cruise control shall keep the car at a constant speed by controlling the throttle position after the user sets the desired speed. The user should be able to increase and decrease the desired speed. Activating the brake must disable the system safely until the "resume" command is selected by the user." This looks clear, but is not. It does not specify constraints on speed such as "not less than" and "not greater than". The quality of acceleration also is subject to interpretation. Missing also is how the cruise control is going to interact with external systems, such as braking and engine.

Another example is indicating the miles per gallon on the dashboard for a luxury car. It gave a reading anywhere from 18 to 70 miles per gallon. Obviously this would be very inaccurate and useless information. This happened because the sensors registered erroneous data from the car being driven over potholes on the road. The specification did not contain information on the accuracy of reporting.

Negative requirements

These describe the dangerous things that the system must not execute. Example: there shall be no sudden acceleration at any time; the cruise control shall never get stuck at any speed, or the cruise control shall never engage when not desired. One may say that this is common sense. It should be obvious to every software engineer. Wrong! The system requires a lot of thinking to prevent the software from going into these failure modes. Special tests are required to make sure such events cannot happen. If the requirements were obvious, the automotive industry would not be recalling cars for such events almost every year. A software fault in the Audi 5000 allowed cars to accelerate to 70 miles per hour when some drivers engaged the gear in reverse. On August 1, 2005 A Malaysian Airlines Boeing 777 plane climbed to 3,000 feet and almost stalled. The pilots were able to disengage the autopilot but the auto throttles refused to disengage. As the pilots tried to land, the primary flight display gave a false low air speed warning. The display also warned of a non-existent wind shear[4]. Some Toyota Prius cars also stalled after they reached the speed of about 50 mph. Such is the nature of unknown-unknowns. By clearly identifying the negative requirements in each interaction, the risk of unknown-unknowns is lowered.

If there are hundreds of interactions, a likely scenario, it will be prudent to at least identify safety critical interactions based on knowledge of safety critical functions. Such interactions can be color coded, such as a red X or as a letter C, as shown in the matrix. It is wise to group safety critical functions and require a firewall around them. Such a partitioning prevents corruption from interfacing systems. If possible, the hardware in which the software is embedded should also be partitioned.

Negative requirements must include how the system should behave in events such as the loss of electrical power, a sudden loss of communications, failure of the hardware, a loose harness and even sabotage. Testing should include these negative events. Such testing is called negative testing.

The constraints

Constraints are just as important. These are boundaries for safety, reliability, modifiability, fault recovery, and operational limits. A wind tunnel experimental lab at a University of Maryland facility was totally destroyed because a student entered 200 psi pressure on the keyboard instead of 20. There was no constraint on input pressure. Other constraints include precedence for priority tasks, criteria for interrupts, limits on outputs, interface criteria, and limits from interacting systems. In addition, there should be brainstorming with questions such as:

How should the system respond to false, invalid,and the absence of inputs?
Should a critical function be clock-driven or event-driven?
Limits on waiting for input and processing

Brainstorming should include the conditions under which the software can

- Fail to perform a function reliably
- Fail to perform a function safely
- Fail to perform a function when needed
- Perform a function when not needed, such as deploying an air bag in a car when there is no accident
- Perform functions that are not in the specification
- Fail to stop a task at the right time
- Lose input or output
- Fail to execute a function or a task
- Have intermittent behavior
- Get corrupted from an operating system
- Fail from an incorrect request by a user
- Have incomplete execution
- Be unable to execute critical interruptions
- Be unable to fail safely
- Be unable to respond safely when hardware fails (a recall included cars in which the door would open but not close in cold temperatures. Should software limit the speed in such conditions?)

Brainstorming on interactions should also include the system response to situations such as:

- EMI/RFI
- Coding errors
- Logic errors
- Input/output errors
- Data handling
- Definition of variables
- Interface failure
- Failed hardware
- Communication failure
- Power outage
- Omissions in the specification
- Corrupted memory
- Insufficient memory
- Operational environment
- Loose wires and cables

Measurability

This includes the ability to verify and validate before the product is sold in the market. A requirement such as "the software reliability shall be higher" is not verifiable, nor can it be validated before a product is released. The industry has simply not developed good accelerated testing tools to predict reliability during the product development phase. Also, since the software specifications often miss over 60% of the potential requirements (you will discover this quickly when you brainstorm on the interactions of the system-of-systems), does it make sense to predict reliability? A current reliability test for a new design such as measuring fault density (for example: the number of software bugs per thousand lines of code) is invalid, because the test is incomplete. The test is incomplete because many requirements are missing. If we need higher reliability, then we need to specify the qualitative features that will improve reliability, such as a top-down software structure, modularity, fault-tolerant architecture, and defensive programming. Their effectiveness can be measured qualitatively such as assigning a value in beauty contests.

Generally validation implies testing. The quality of the test determines the quality of the validation. Verification refers to indirect measurement or assessment. Each requirement must be verifiable or capable of being tested. Verification may consist of:

- Demonstration: A functional verification by observing events through the random exercise of software. It includes appropriate drivers, interrupts, or integrated hardware to verify that all requirements are met safely.

- Inspection: Visual examination of code or the logic design to verify the absence of mistakes and develop confidence in meeting the requirements.

- Analysis: Verification may be accomplished through tools such as Software Failure Mode and Effects Analysis, Fault Tree Analysis, Software Sneak Circuit Analysis or brainstorming.

- Simulation: Includes mathematical models, and random responses through tools like Monte Carlo simulation

- Similarity: Consists of satisfying verification requirements that are previously satisfied through other programs.

CONCLUSION

Writing software requirements cannot be accomplished without a comprehensive system specification. The system-of-systems interactions have to be understood and creative brainstorming has to take place. The project is likely to be ahead of schedule because fixing multiple requirements once takes less time than fixing one requirement at a time.

REFERENCES

1. NIST (National Institute of Standards and Technology), Planning Report 02-3, *The Economic Impact of Inadequate Infrastructure for Software Testing,* May 2003.
2. Raheja, Dev, *Assurance Technologies Principles and Practices,* Wiley, 2006.
3. Speech: Dr. Douglas R. Farrow, Fifth International Workshop on Risk Analysis and Performance Measurement in Aviation sponsored by FAA and NASA, Baltimore, August 19-21, 2003.
4. Jayaswal Bijay, and Patton Peter., *Design for Trustworthy Software,* Prentice Hall, 2007.

AUTHOR

Dev Raheja, President
Design for Competitiveness, Inc.
9811 Mallard Drive, Suite 213
Laurel, MD 20708 (USA)
draheja@aol.com
(301) 483-4525

Dev Raheja is an international design assurance consultant to many Fortune 100 companies and founder of the Design for Competitiveness, Inc. A former executive at Booz-Allen & Hamiliton, Inc. and General Electric, he is the author of the books: *Assurance Technologies: Principles and Practices* (Wiley 2006) and *Zen and the Art of Breakthrough Quality Management.* He served as Associate Professor at University of Maryland for its PhD program in Reliability Engineering during 1995-99, and teaches “Designing for Safety” and “Practical Reliability Engineering” courses for SAE. He is credited with turning unprofitable companies into market leaders. He has received several awards, including the Scientific Achievement Award from the System Safety Society for developing Software FMEA for safety critical applications. He is the Chairman of IEEE Design for Reliability Committee.

2006-01-1557

Using UML 2.0 to Create Executable Code from Requirements Capture and Consistent Requirement Specifications for Real-Time Automotive Software Development

Brendan Jackman
Waterford Institute of Technology

Shepherd Sanyanga
Ford (Europe), United Kingdom.

ABSTRACT

The development of vehicle control systems has evolved to become an exercise in the design and integration of complex, distributed hardware and software components. The various components are typically developed by geographically dispersed, multi-cultural teams from both OEMs and suppliers.

This paper gives a brief overview of using the Unified Modelling Language (UML) as a means of capturing the requirements of real-time distributed systems in a graphical notation shared by all team members. UML is commonly used to model system concepts, albeit typically as system "sketches" without any formal definition of the model's semantics. This paper specifically addresses the additions to the latest version of UML that supports higher levels of abstraction, model-based development, executable models and the specification of non-functional requirements. These improvements to UML make it more semantically complete, which means that a UML model can unambiguously describe a system, resulting in simpler automatic model verification and automatic code generation. The modelling of automotive network management requirements in a typical vehicle application is used to illustrate the benefits of the UML model development approach.

INTRODUCTION

UML has its origins in the early object-oriented analysis and design methodologies of Grady Booch (the Booch Methodology), James Rumbaugh and associates (Object Modeling Technique) and Ivar Jacobson (Objectory). After many years of working in parallel, these three approaches converged to become the first version of UML, resulting in UML V1.1 being standardized by the Object Management Group (OMG) in 1997. Since then UML has become the *de facto* standard for software and system modeling. The widespread use of object-oriented development languages (Java, C++, C#) and platforms (J2EE, COM+, .NET) in mainstream computing has increased the requirement for a semantically-rich modeling notation that supports component- and model-based development. The latest version of UML, UML 2.0, addresses the shortcomings of previous versions by providing additional support for expressing system structure, constraints and behavior. These latest enhancements also address the limitations of previous versions of UML in describing real-time distributed systems.

VEHICLE SYSTEMS SPECIFICATION

The requirements specifications for today's vehicle systems are usually expressed in natural language, perhaps supplemented with some informal diagrams such as state transition diagrams and flowcharts. The problem with these documentation methods is that they can be ambiguous, inconsistent and incomplete. When modules of a system are being developed by different organizations, much development and testing time is wasted trying to resolve differences in understanding of what the system requirements are.

A common approach to the management of complexity has traditionally been standardization, the use of interchangeable parts that provide compatible interfaces and services. The use of standard modules and protocols also helps the requirements specification effort because standard implementations also imply a commonly understood reusable specification.

There has been a move to model-based development in recent times which has brought with it a range of diagramming and modeling notations that developers can use instead of natural language specifications. To be effective however, the modeling notations used must have well-defined semantics and be more than just an informal diagramming notation. UML is a well-defined modeling notation that can be used to document system requirements.

UML SYSTEM VIEWS

UML currently has over a dozen different diagrams to model various aspects of a system. Fortunately not all of them need to be used in a development project. Developers are free to select the models that best express the important aspects of their system. While each diagram expresses either a behavioral or structural aspect of the system, it is useful to organize the models into a 4+1 view of the system, that is, there are four distinct views of a system, plus one view that describes how the overall system fits together. These views are shown in Figure 1.

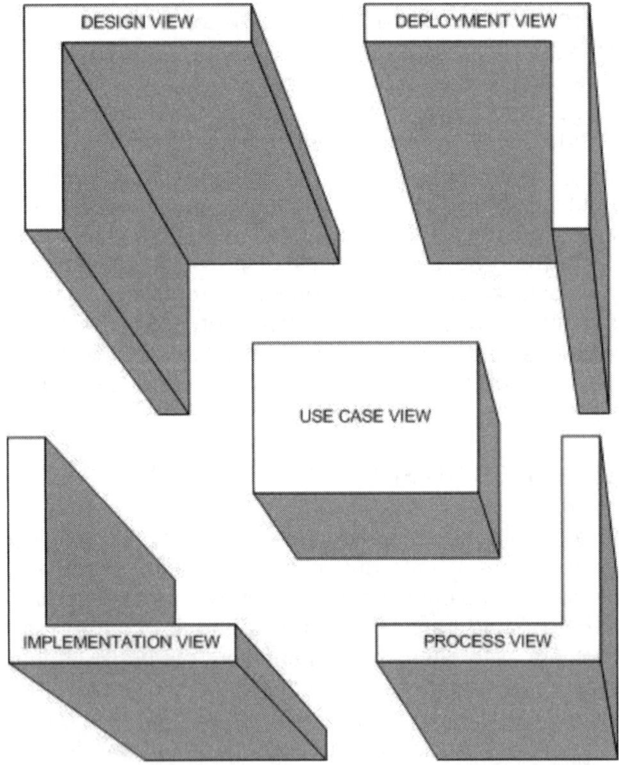

Figure 1. System Views

USE CASE VIEW

In UML the overall system functionality required by the users is described by a Use Case diagram. Use Cases are pieces of functionality that are invoked by Actors, which can be end-users, or in the case of real-time systems, external sensors or other system components. Use Cases can have dependencies on other Use Cases, allowing functions to be reused. Use Cases can also be special cases of other Use Cases using generalization or inheritance. This allows standard functions to be tailored to suit special requirements. Figure 2 shows a Use Case diagram for a power window system.

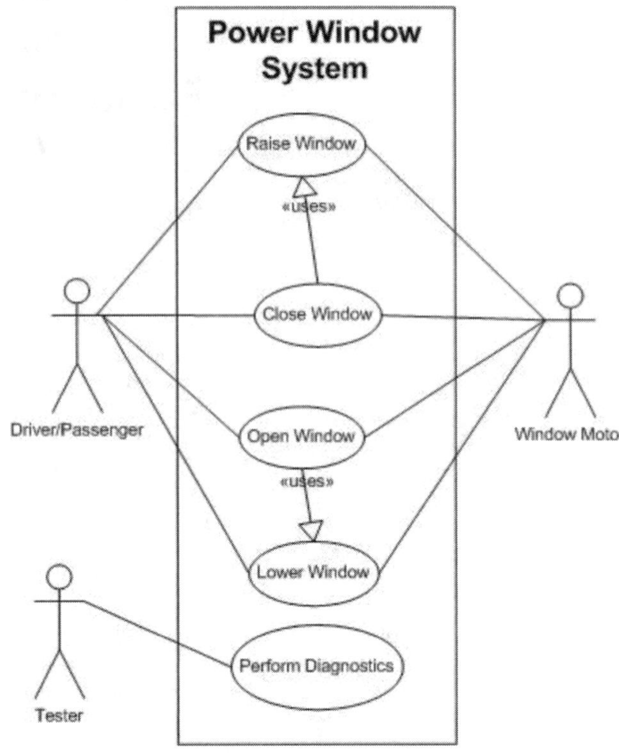

Figure 2. Use Case Diagram

Use Case requirements can be expressed in any suitable format. Traditionally this has been natural language, although such requirements can be incomplete, inconsistent and ambiguous. The availability of standard templates and requirements management tools has eased some of these problems. UML 2.0 also allows Use Cases to be expressed in terms of other UML models, most commonly Activity diagrams and Sequence diagrams. This hierarchical view of system requirements supports requirements traceability and automated consistency checking.

DESIGN VIEW

The design view describes the software elements and their interactions necessary to realize the functionality of the system. The design view provides the logical structure and behavior of the software without addressing how the software elements are distributed across the hardware platform. The UML diagrams that support the design view are

- Class diagrams
- Object Diagrams
- Activity Diagrams

- Composite Structure Diagrams
- Sequence Diagrams

DEPLOYMENT VIEW

The deployment view captures the details of how a system is configured and installed on physical hardware architectures. It can illustrate aspects of the system architecture such as network configuration and redundancy. The deployment view can be illustrated with the following UML diagrams

- Component diagrams
- Deployment diagrams
- Interaction Diagrams

IMPLEMENTATION VIEW

The implementation view is concerned with the configuration management of the system. It shows which source files implement which classes and the dependencies between system components. Implementation views can be expressed using the following diagrams

- Component diagrams
- Interaction diagrams
- Composite Structure diagrams
- Statechart diagrams
- Package diagrams

PROCESS VIEW

The process view illustrates the concurrency among the software elements and can be used to express performance and scalability requirements. The process view is expressed with the following UML diagrams

- Interaction diagrams
- Activity diagrams
- Timing diagrams

USING UML

As can be seen, individual UML diagrams can serve many purposes, supporting different views of a system. Many developers tend to use just a few UML diagrams to provide rough sketches of the system functionality. The Class diagram, Interaction diagram and Package diagrams tend to be the most commonly used models in this regard. To get the maximum benefit from UML, it needs to be regarded as more than just a diagramming notation. The semantics of UML 2.0 have been strengthened so that UML can now be considered a development language. New extensions to UML and tool support means that it is possible to create executable models of a system using UML. This allows for earlier verification of system functionality and support for model-based development at higher levels of abstraction.

In the latest version of UML, Each system requires a Use Case View that expresses the required system functionality. Once the requirements have been determined, the Design View is used to describe the fundamental components of the system and how they work together to realize the functionality of the system.

The developer can decide to use one or more of the other system views to highlight important requirements and design decisions. Non-functional requirements, for example performance constraints and software deployment, are sometimes expressed in natural language, but could be more clearly described using the Implementation, Deployment and Process view diagrams. With tool support it is possible to automatically verify these non-functional requirements when expressed as UML models.

UML FUNDAMENTALS

This section gives a brief overview of the main UML diagrams. The intention is to give the reader an idea of what is possible with UML. The reader is referred to the UML standard [ref] and some of the many UML books [ref] for a thorough treatment of the subject.

CLASS DIAGRAM

The Class diagram is the most fundamental of all the UML diagrams. A Class diagram describes the basic software elements that make up a system and the static relationships between them. A Class represents a set of things that have a common set of data (called attributes) and behavior (called methods). For example, in Figure 3 the class "Car" represents the general set of all cars. Its attributes might include details such as Make, Model, Model Year, Owner and Color. Its methods might include getColor(), getVIN() and changeColor(). Even though UML is fundamentally object-oriented, it can be used to model non-object-oriented (procedural) systems. The main thing to remember is that a Class can represent any important system <u>concept</u>, not just an object-oriented class in Java or C++. Classes can represent software components which encapsulate their own data (attributes) and behavior (methods). The Class diagram specifies the *interface* to the class and not its *implementation*. The class could be implemented in a procedural language such as C or even as a Simulink block. This flexibility in the interpretation of classes allows class diagrams to be used to describe both the system requirements in terms of domain concepts, as well as the subsequent realization of the requirements in terms of software elements. Developers distinguish between Analysis Class Diagrams, which contain only domain-level concepts, and Design Class Diagrams, which additionally contain software-specific classes to describe concepts such as data structures and data access protocols.

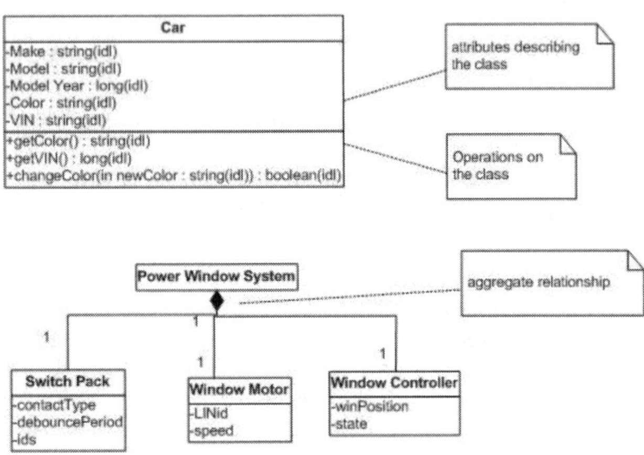

Figure 3. Class Diagram

Figure 3 illustrates the relationships between the class Car and some of the other system concepts. UML provides a shorthand notation for commonly used aggregate (assembly-subassembly) and inheritance (generalization-specialization) relationships.

During the requirements analysis phase the emphasis is on identifying the main system concepts/classes and the relationships between them. At the software design stage methods are assigned to each class to represent the responsibilities of the class in terms of the functionality that it provides. It is best to leave the assignment of methods to the design phase, since discovering a good, stable structure of system elements is the most important factor in architectural design. The assignment of responsibilities to the system elements tends to fall naturally out of a good system structure.

Class diagrams illustrate the general structure of the system in terms of similar software elements. They are static diagrams and so they do not show the run-time behavior of the software elements. At run time the classes are instantiated as individual objects which interact by calling each other's methods to execute system functionality.

SEQUENCE DIAGRAM

Sequence diagrams are used to show the order of method calls made by objects of each class. A particular class may be responsible for providing certain functionality, but sometimes it must delegate parts of that functionality to other classes in the system, in the same way that managers in an organization delegate certain tasks to subordinates. Objects of a class call the methods of other objects to invoke their behavior. Sequence diagrams chart chronologically, from top to bottom, the method calls required to implement a piece of functionality. Messages in a sequence diagram can be either synchronous (with solid arrow) or asynchronous (with open-ended arrow). The basic format of a Sequence diagram is shown in Figure 4.

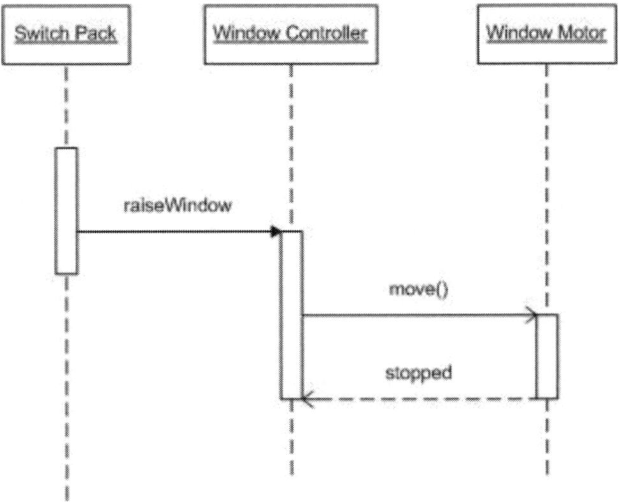

Figure 4. Sequence Diagram

STATECHART DIAGRAM

Statechart or State Transition diagrams capture the internal state transitions of UML elements such as a Class, subsystem or the whole system. They are very useful in describing the operation of event-driven real-time embedded systems. The Statechart notation has been enhanced in UML 2.0 to allow for easier expression of hierarchical state machines, reusable states, composite states for parallel processing and high-level transitions. In addition there is some new notation for emphasizing transitions and associated input/output signals that would be very useful in ECU modeling. Figure 5 provides an example of a Statechart showing some of the new features.

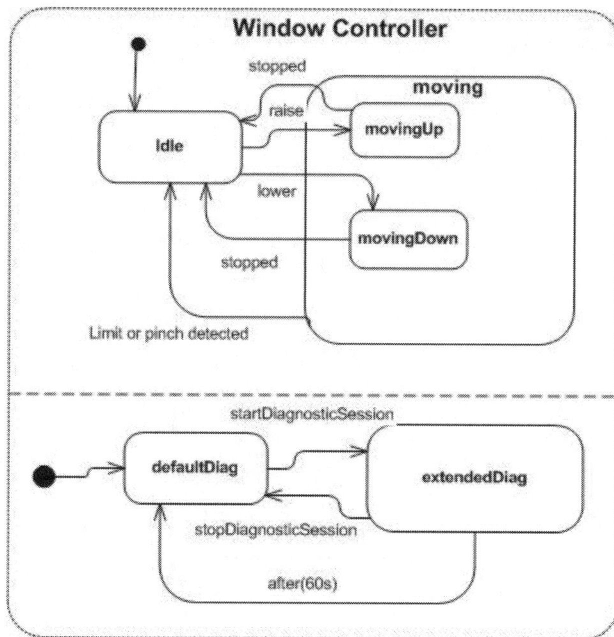

Figure 5. Statechart Diagram

COMPOSITE STRUCTURE DIAGRAM

Modern vehicle control systems are usually implemented by a combination of cooperating hardware and software components. Each component provides a well-defined interface and functionality to client components. Components are a fundamental method of reuse, whether they are hardware components, software modules or Java/C++ classes. UML now has a Composite Structure diagram that provides both black-box and white-box views of a component and its interfaces. The white-box view allows the implementation of a component to be specified in terms of other basic components, providing a hierarchical resolution of a system or component.

Components can have both *provided interfaces* and *required interfaces*. Provided interfaces represent the functionality implemented by the component in question. Required interfaces represent functionality that the component expects other components in turn to supply to it so that it can carry out its activities. UML provides the concepts of ports and connectors to enable components to be interconnected at interfaces. Figure 6 is an example of a black-box component showing both provided and required interfaces.

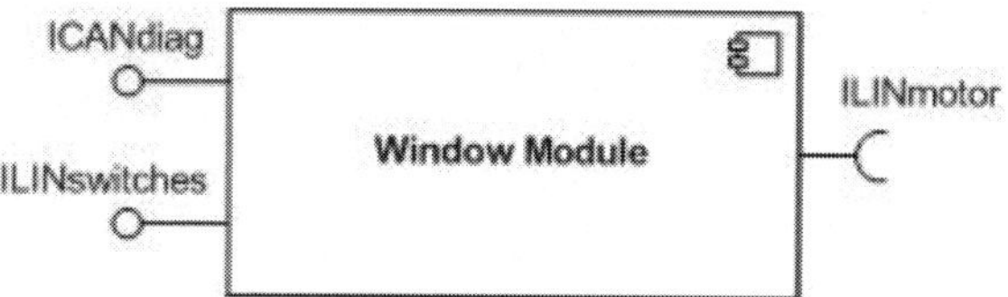

Figure 6. Black-Box Component View

The white-box view of a component can be used to show the classes that work together to provide the functionality at the component interfaces. Ports can be connected to internal classes to show which classes provide the functionality at component interfaces. In this way the end-to-end flows through system components can be documented. An example of a white-box component realization is shown in Figure 7.

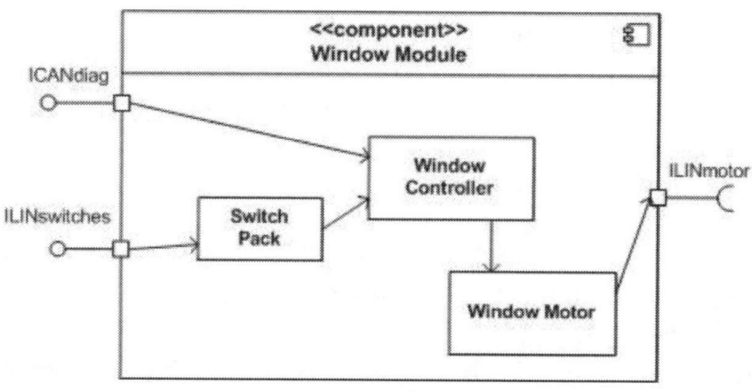

Figure 7. White-Box Component View

Classes can also be broken down in the same way to show how internal functionality is achieved using other delegate classes. These Composite Classes are new to UML 2.0 and provide both a hierarchical structuring of classes and an illustration of the end-to-end flows within a class.

ACTIVITY DIAGRAM

Sometimes the best way of describing a piece of system functionality is by using a procedural approach; a sequence of steps, much like traditional flowcharts. UML now has an Activity diagram that uses a mixture of control and data flow notation to describe system behavior. There is support for decision-making, concurrency and synchronization modeling using Activity diagrams. Figure 8 is an example of an Activity diagram.

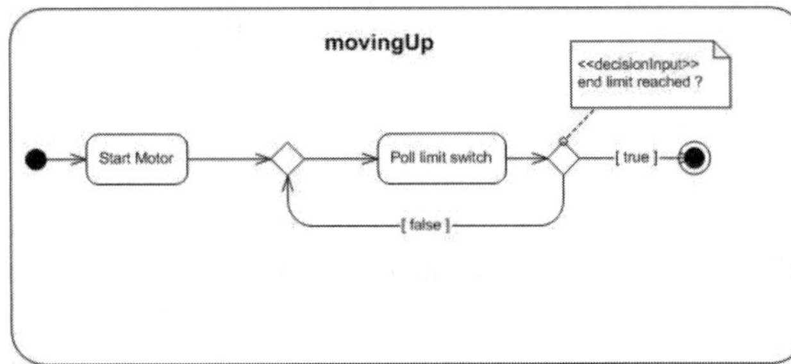

Figure 8. Activity Diagram

REAL-TIME SYSTEM MODELING

Real-time system development has to address the following concerns as part of the analysis and design phases.

- System deployment to distributed hardware and software components
- Concurrency
- Constraints on system resources
- Performance requirements

The enhancements found in UML 2.0 provide good support for the above concerns, making UML more suitable than ever for real-time system modeling. The gap between systems engineering and software engineering has been bridged with UML 2.0, providing a single modeling technique that can be used to model system architecture and subsequently refine this to software implementation models of each system component.

FUNCTION DEPLOYMENT

Composite Structure diagrams can be used to break down the system into a set of cooperating hardware and software components with clearly defined interfaces. Deployment diagrams can be used to show the allocation of software components to networked Electronic Control Units (ECUs) together with the network topology details. An example of a Deployment diagram is shown in Figure 9.

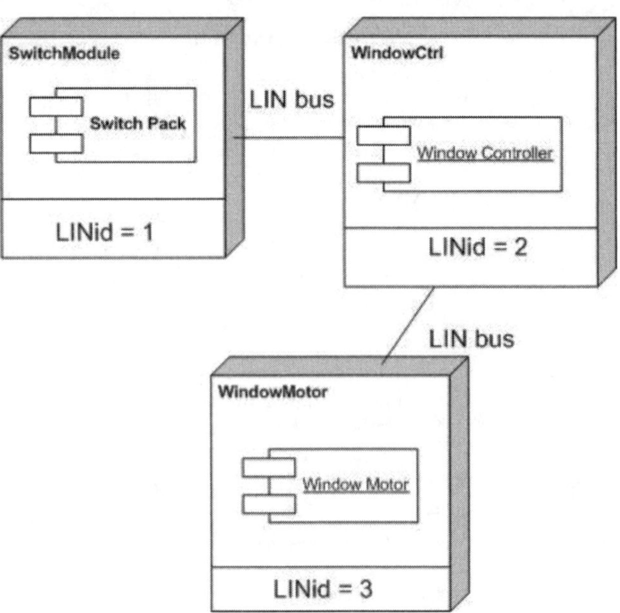

Figure 9. Deployment Diagram

CONCURRENCY

In addition to the concurrency implied in the Deployment diagrams, UML can represent parallel activities using composite states on Statecharts as shown in Figure 5.

An enhancement to Sequence diagrams allows for sets of method calls to be executed in parallel as shown in Figure 10.

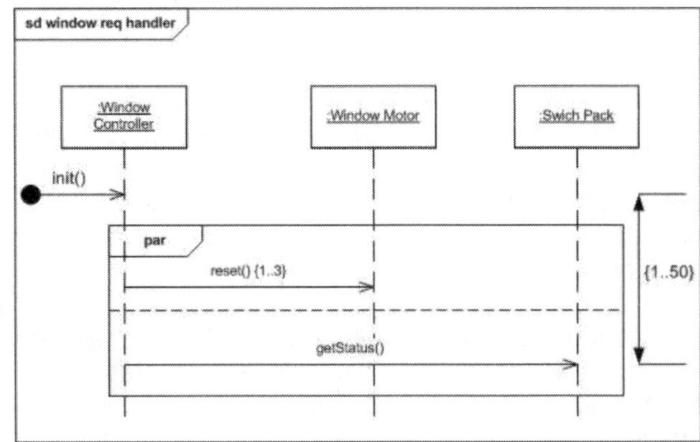

Figure 10. Enhanced Sequence Diagram

UML 2.0 allows portions of a timeline to be broken down, providing a hierarchical organization of sequence diagrams. This solves the problem with previous UML sequence diagrams which did not scale very well for use in large complex systems. UML now supports *Interaction Occurrences* on Sequence diagrams which allow common sequences of messages to be reused in many different Sequence diagrams.

CONSTRAINT MODELING

The Object Constraint Language is a declarative language that can be used to express constraints or invariants on any aspect of a UML model. OCL has its own set of keywords and operators, just like any other language. A developer can use OCL to express constraints on such things as the allowed range of values for a class attribute, a pre-condition for executing an action on a Statechart or allowed network bit rates on a deployment diagram. There are considerable benefits from using OCL to specify non-functional requirements as part of a Use Case. For a start, OCL expressions are unambiguous and can also be automatically checked for consistency with the help of some tools.

PERFORMANCE MODELING

There are a number of ways in which the performance aspects of a system can be specified in UML models. The Statechart notation includes the transition keyword *after,* which specifies the maximum allowed time before a transition will occur. This is useful for describing timeout conditions in state machines. An example of this is shown in Figure 5. The Sequence diagram can also be annotated to show the maximum allowable execution times for a method, as well as the time allowed for the method call itself. Examples of these notations are given in Figure 11.

UML has a Timing diagram that is used to show the effects of method calls on objects as time progresses. The Timing diagram can be used to show timing constraints on method calls and the sequencing of method calls. Figure 11 is an example of a Timing diagram, showing that the window should begin moving up within 10 milliseconds of receiving a raise command.

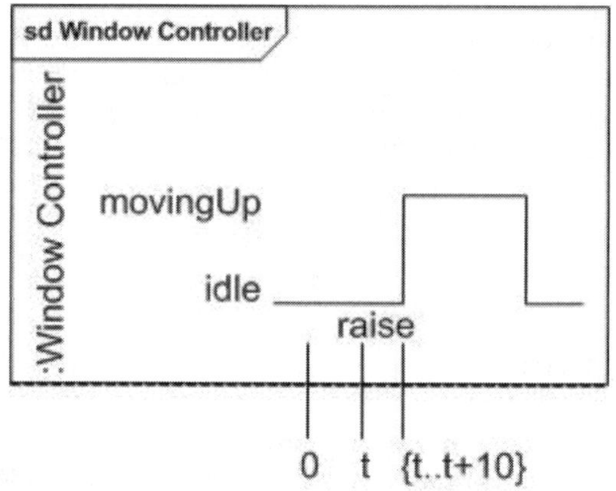

Figure 11. Timing Diagram

SYSTEM INTEGRATION SUPPORT

The effects of poor system requirements definition become apparent at the system test and integration phase. In the global automotive industry, where many cooperating system components are developed by geographically dispersed teams, the effects of poor interface definition are exacerbated. With UML 2.0 there is now a widely-used modeling notation that is comprehensive enough to span both the system modeling and software modeling domains. The use of a common notation by both system developers and software designers allows models from both domains to be synchronized earlier in the development process to avoid any major integration problems later on. The well-defined semantics of UML 2.0 together with the use of OCL provide better tool support for activities such as architecture validation and test case generation.

EXECUTABLE CODE SUPPORT

UML 2.0 is an extensible modeling environment. UML *profiles* can be used to extend the notation to support domain-specific concepts and implementation platforms. For example, an OSEK profile can be defined which is essentially a Class diagram describing OSEK concepts and the relationships between them. The profile defines a set of *stereotypes* which are the names of the OSEK concepts or classes and *tagged values*, which are used at design time to influence the configuration of stereotypes. When a developer is describing an automotive application to be implemented on OSEK the application classes can be further labeled with stereotypes (roles) such as <<Task>>, <<Alarm>> or <<Message>> instead of the generic label *class*. The purpose of the stereotypes is to give additional information to readers about the intended use of a class. However, tools such as code generators can also use the stereotypes to guide the generation of code and configuration details for the software element. A class with a <<OSEKtask>> stereotype is shown in Figure 12.

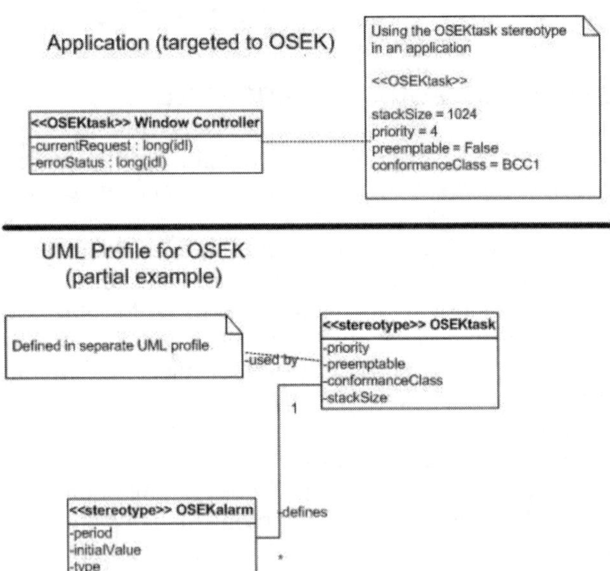

Figure 12 OSEK Task Stereotype

By adorning the UML models with appropriate stereotypes to indicate the intended implementation and defining suitable implementation profiles it is possible to automatically generate executable code from the UML models.

EXAMPLE – NETWORK MANAGEMENT SPECIFICATION

The Gateway module which is normally the electronic cluster has the basic task of transferring normal messages and generating pseudo gateway messages. The normal messages are transferred from one network to the other. The pseudo messages are generated based on internal information within the electronic cluster.

There are a number of network dependencies associated with gateways such as:

- management of the network when one bus is asleep and another is awake, therefore deciding what messages are transferred;

- Management of the network rings when both buses are asleep and how the rings wake up and are established once again. In all the above situations the gateway has to ensure there is no negative impact on both buses in terms of invalid faults such as missing messages and entering false limp home modes.

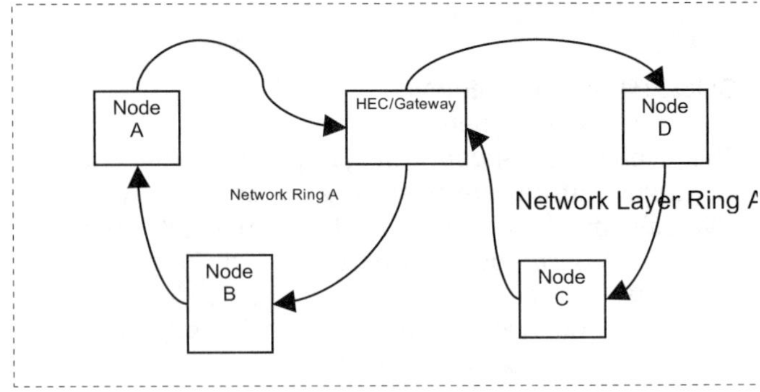

Figure 12. Example Logical Ring Architecture for Two Buses

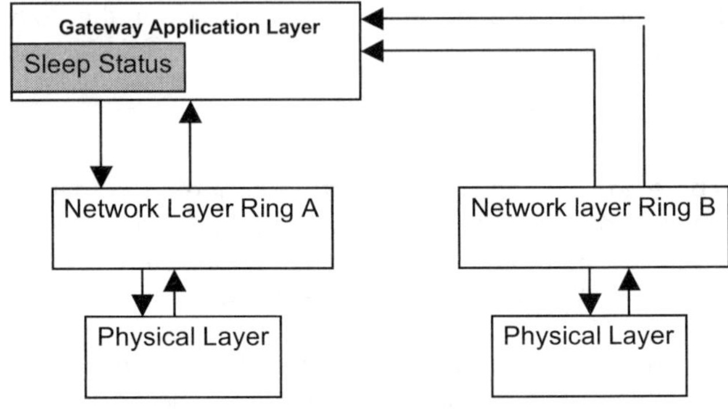

Figure 13. A Gateway module trying to match two networks into sleep mode

The problem of matching both network into a particular network state can best described using UML especially since the OSEK documentation is too detailed and cumbersome for the ordinary system engineer to understand properly.

The OSEK/VDX network management concept and application programming interface documentation does not show how to link two buses properly so that when one goes to sleep the other will do the same via sleep indication bits within network management messages. Using UML Statecharts and Sequence Diagrams to describe these scenarios would allow network management component developers and integrators to better understand and correctly implement this functionality.

CONCLUSION

This paper presented an overview of UML notation with an emphasis on new UML 2.0 features to support the modeling of real-time embedded systems such as those found in automotive applications. UML has developed into a comprehensive system and software modeling language that is semantically rigorous enough to provide tool support for development activities such as architecture validation, model-driven development and automatic code generation. A significant development has been the expansion of UML notation to support better integration of system modeling and software modeling.

REFERENCES

1. www.omg.org
2. UML 2.0 in a Nutshell. Dan Pilone. O'Reilly Media, 2005.
3. Applying UML and Patterns. Craig Larman. Prentice Hall PTR, 1998.

CONTACT

Brendan Jackman B.Sc. M.Tech.

Brendan is the founder and Leader of the Automotive Control Group at Waterford Institute of Technology, where he supervises postgraduate students working on automotive software development, diagnostics and vehicle networking research.. Brendan also lectures in Automotive Software Development to undergraduates on the B.Sc. in Applied Computing Degree at Waterford Institute of Technology. Brendan has extensive experience in the implementation of real-time control systems, having worked previously with Digital Equipment Corporation, Ireland and Logica BV in The Netherlands.

Email: **bjackman@wit.ie**

Website: **http://www.wit.ie/automotive**

Shepherd Sanyanga (BEng BSc MSc PhD CEng EurIng MIEE)

Shepherd has worked for United Nations in Africa in infrastructure development programs, worked for some years in the Aerospace Industry developing military electronic systems and then worked for a number of Tier One Automotive Suppliers (Lucas Electronics (UK), Sagem (France) TRW (UK). He is currently involved in a joint project between Ford Motor Company (Europe), Johnson Controls (France) and Takosan (Turkey). In his spare time he is also an external examiner on a masters degree automotive programme in a university in Ireland.

Email: **ssanyan2@ford.com**

2006-01-0599

Developing Safe Software Solutions for X-By-Wire Applications

Ireri Ibarra Alvarado, Richard K. Stobart and Rudi Lutz
University of Sussex

ABSTRACT

A promising technology for active safety is "X-by-Wire", where mechanical and electromechanical components are replaced by electronic functions. One of the reasons for this is to have more than the driver input in the command chain, and also include some degree of intervention by the control system in case the driver behaviour is likely to put the car at risk.

The adoption of a small number of computing nodes is a clear trend in vehicle design. A wide range of functions that are now distributed in the form of separate modules will instead be integrated. This approach will overcome the physical constraints of electrical and mechanical components and the costs of many separate electronic modules with their own power supplies. However this new arrangement can introduce hazards if the software contains flaws, the nature of these flaws comes in two types: omission (failing to adhere to a requirement) and commission (doing something that should not be done at all, not observing timeliness or violating a sequence) [1].

This paper presents a comprehensive safety approach to the development process of automotive software systems focusing on X-by-Wire applications. A modification to the traditional V-model Development Process is proposed as well as the use of the Rapid Object-Oriented Development Process for Embedded Systems. The system and controls are modelled in UML and then, as part of the safety assurance, can be analysed using hazard analysis techniques such as HAZOP, FMEA or Fault Trees.

The use of UML introduces a better communication between the different stakeholders of the project, as well as increasing the possibilities for reuse, and reliability; reducing development and systems integration time and costs.

In particular this paper describes the use of HAZOP as part of a systematic approach to develop complex software for embedded systems in safety-related applications.

INTRODUCTION

There is an increasing trend towards having computer controlled functions in vehicles. Software is moving from an auxiliary to a primary role in providing critical services. Object-Oriented technologies have been present as a powerful solution to complex IT problems for some time; however this is quite a new approach for automotive embedded systems [2].

Challenges for the development of new and enhanced systems are increasing rapidly without a change in the design approach. Current solutions using model based design employ graphical tools such as ASCET-SD or MATLAB/Simulink. MATLAB is a quasi standard for the conceptual phase of modelling, simulation and rapid prototyping mainly because the automotive sector is very conservative regarding the use of new technologies. These tools are not standardised as they change with every version released, leaving the designers facing new problems; these graphic notations are not based on a standard language, which makes reuse difficult; the notations are very suitable for control algorithms but not for low level software [3]. However in this era of vehicles with several embedded systems that combine safety related tasks with other tasks, software implementation and integration has to be considered in a more cohesive fashion.

One factor in ensuring safety is the development process, it can promote a more systematic approach to tackle the complexities in the development of software for embedded systems, as well as produce a system of consistent quality.

X-by-Wire applications demand very sophisticated engineering solutions; amongst X-by-Wire requirements we have high reliability and safety, some degree of failure management (including fault tolerance) and distribution of control units, which involves timely communication. The most effective way of eliminating hazards is to ensure a "safe design" rather than added safety measures latter in the design life-cycle.

In our research we are proposing a change to the traditional development process for automotive embedded systems by integrating explicit hazard identification procedures, supported by the ROPES (Rapid Object-Oriented Process for Embedded Systems) which uses the standard UML (Unified Modeling Language) meta-model for its semantic framework and notation . The UML models produced will be examined with adapted hazard analysis techniques, which in turn, will be reformulated for software use. The example applications we are proposing for this development framework are XbW (X-by-Wire) systems and in particular SbW (Steer-by-Wire).

A Hazard analysis is a process that produces a documentary record of faults, resulting hazards and the hazard control measures. A hazard analysis is carried out using one or several techniques; two will be explained in the following section.

The purpose of HAZOP is to identify what potentially hazardous variations from the design intent could occur in components and in the interactions between components of a system. A HAZOP study is performed by a team of people with different expertise that should be reflected in the safety analysis of the project, supported by the use of guidewords to conduct the analysis. This technique is of great use from very early design stages, to more mature designs.

FMEA is a technique used more in reliability analysis since all faults hazardous and non-hazardous are considered. FMEA is a systematic method for identifying and preventing product and process problems before they occur. FMEA is a qualitative reasoning which delivers a quantification of the probability of failure. This approach is best suited for reviews of systems in a more advanced design stage [4].

RELEVANT SAFETY STANDARDS

The most influential safety standards for our research are DEF STAN 00-55 [5], DEF STAN 00-58 [6] and MISRA C [7]. Using them as guidelines we were able to establish important safety features in our design process, such as constraining the C language to avoid unexpected behaviour of the application and using HAZOP to analyse the high-level system models.

The UK MoD DEF STAN 00-55 was heavily modified in December 2004. As a result of the modifications, the UK MoD DEF STAN 00-58 was cancelled and 00-56, left in interim status; however, we decided to carry on using the fundamentals of the previous issue as its original premise of assuring safe operation of programmable systems was unchanged.

AIMS

Based on the problems recently observed regarding software in vehicles [3, 8-10], current software development practices need to be adapted to give a competitive answer to the demands in the automotive market. This work explores the use of HAZOP on UML diagrams used in the analysis and design phases of the development lifecycle.

HAZOP was originally intended to find hazards arising from the interaction of components in chemical plants, mainly by analysing flows of substances. Our approach is to analyse the interaction of diagram elements, by examining message flows, represented by relationships defined by the UML standard.

Our main aim is the explicit incorporation of hazard analysis in the development process itself. This allows us to have a more systematic approach to tackling the complexities in the development of software for automotive embedded systems, as well as producing a system of consistent quality.

The objective of this research is to develop a set of guidelines on how to perform hazard analysis where models of both system and controls are developed in UML following the ROPES process. By using UML we establish a common language to be used by the different designers involved in the project. This is due to the multidisciplinary nature of automotive systems, where engineers with very different backgrounds are going to be contributing to the development of these systems. UML is also used in the different stages of the development process, from analysis to implementation.

SAFETY AND THE DEVELOPMENT PROCESS

In the automotive domain, the traditional V-model Development Process for electronic and software systems, does not explicitly incorporate analysis for safety in its phases; in our proposed development process we use the traditional V-model [4] as a basis, but we add a branch to incorporate safety procedures as a fundamental part of the whole system development see Figure 1.

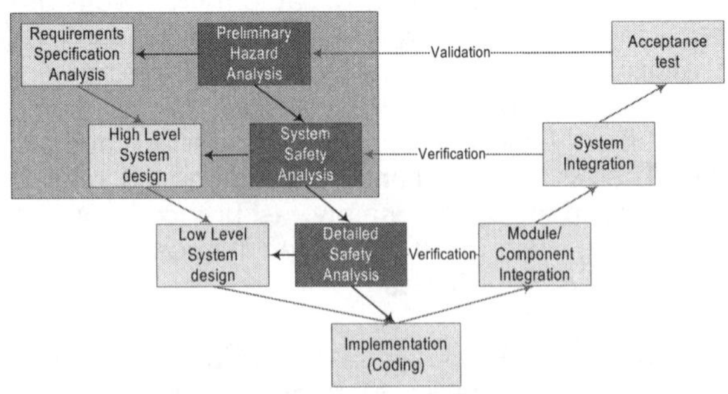

Figure 1. Modified V-model Development Process, incorporating safety procedures.

The objective of this addition is to make sure that the safety assessment is consistent throughout the development lifecycle.

Since the V-model is of generic nature, we use a well established Software Development Process for Real-Time embedded systems in parallel to design the architecture of the XbW system and controls. This is the means to incorporate safety processes to the traditional V- model.

Together with the development process, a model based design using systematic refinement including early validation by simulation and hazard analysis, can mitigate the risks of error-prone software developed using traditional methods (code and fix for example).

Our technique applies the HAZOP guidewords with suitable interpretations to elements of the UML diagrams used to model the system and controls. At an initial stage we have the UCD (Use Case Diagram) and the CD (Class Diagram). The elements incorporated in the analysis are those that could be subject to deviations leading to meaningful results. This systematic use of HAZOP applied to the UML diagrams has as main goals to explore, elicit and improve safety aspects.

SBW SYSTEM MODEL AND HAZARD ANALYSIS

From our point of view, the two most important diagrams to achieve a system model comparable to the system itself are the UCD and the CD. At the highest level of abstraction, the UCD captures and groups the requirements and the master CD maps these requirements to represent the interactions between subsystems without differentiating hardware and software. As we move from higher to lower levels of design, the CD becomes more detailed, and other diagram types (such as Statecharts and Sequence Diagrams) may be introduced to include an element of time and dependency of events.

Safety Lifecycle

The first phase of the safety lifecycle starts with a PHA (Preliminary Hazard Analysis) which involves an initial risk assessment in order to identify safety critical components and functions and then reflect them in the requirements.

PHA is performed on the UCD and CD to check that they contain enough information to roughly match the system requirements. This procedure is implicit to a degree, in the analysis process to build the diagrams and design reviews, in order to produce a highly abstract set of diagrams to be used in the next phase of the development lifecycle, which is the system safety analysis, where it is planned to use HAZOP.

As the traditional context for a HAZOP analysis is the chemical industry, in the DEF STAN 00-58, the guidewords were modified to be suitable for the analysis of programmable electronics systems. See [11] for a comparison of the standard set of guidewords and the one in DEF STAN 00-58. The general approach of our work is to use these guidewords with a very clear interpretation for each attribute under analysis; some examples for analysing requirements are shown in Table 1. It is very easy to introduce defects through a poor understanding of the specified requirements and thereby to introduce hazards.

For the System Safety Analysis (SSA) a HAZOP study is performed on the master CD, here we anticipate that we will verify that it adheres to the requirements. If flaws are found at this stage, these constitute potential faults which are being identified and corrected. We try to ensure that defects are fixed, since a "*defect is the evidence of the existence of a fault*" [12]. However two main things are evaluated with this strategy - the first is how close the model is to the requirements and the second is the completeness and accuracy of the requirements from a safety perspective. These feedback paths make it difficult to differentiate the first two stages of the safety lifecycle. We will discuss this in a later section of the paper.

Element: Requirement

Guideword	Interpretation
NO	complete failure to fulfil the requirement
MORE	a parameter related to the requirement is larger than normal.

Table 1. Example of guideword interpretation for Requirements

From these two phases of the safety lifecycle we can see that the focus on the diagrams changes according to the inherent detail in each phase of the development lifecycle.

In the Detailed Safety Analysis (DSA) that corresponds to the low level system design phase (see Figure 1) we plan to have a much more detailed CD and Statecharts and to use a different hazard analysis technique than HAZOP.

We have to bear in mind that not all hazard analysis techniques will be suitable to match the type of information provided by each diagram.

THE HAZOP STUDY

Our case study is a Steer-by-Wire System, an overview of which is shown in Figure 2. This is a true SbW system without mechanical backup - the input is given by the driver through the steering wheel, the steering angle is calculated by the SbW Controller considering the vehicle speed and then the result is sent to the Steering Actuator and Feedback Motor. The system also has sensors to measure the actual angle in the wheels.

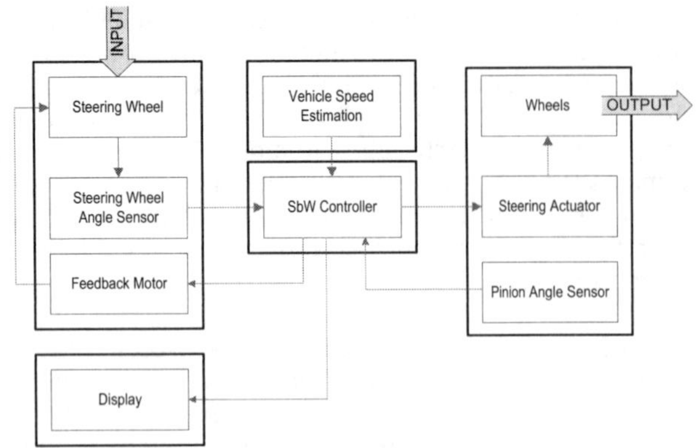

Figure 2. Steer-by-Wire System.

Once we had produced an initial set of diagrams a HAZOP study could be conducted. The diagram set was composed of the master CD and the UCD.

The HAZOP team consisted of: The Chairman, experts in the areas of automotive systems and software, the system designer and a secretary.

The highlighted area in Figure 1 represents the lifecycle phase where this HAZOP study actually fits, since at least in this application the analysis and design phases are very much interlinked, so distinguishing between the two is not straightforward in practice. This is mainly because once the master CD has been drawn some degree of design is implicit in it, especially regarding the hardware. The HAZOP study delivered valuable insights, such as taking account of particular safety and operability issues, e.g. potential improvements to investigate and additional features to include in future designs, information which could ultimately be fed back to the requirements analysis phase. These feedback paths make it difficult to perform the study in the analysis stage only. This leads to the HAZOP study being performed on both analysis and high level system design stages simultaneously.

During the HAZOP analysis we focused on the master CD, using the requirements list as the basis to determine if the information there was mapped adequately to the master CD. Two things are important to note here:

- A HAZOP study is not a design review. The master CD must be mature enough to be used in the HAZOP, making sure that it represents the designer's most refined representation of the system. Although informal design reviews were previously carried out between some members of the HAZOP team, a different perspective was brought up in the HAZOP meeting, such as a design change that needed to be considered for safety reasons, e.g. supplying additional information in the master CD such as redundancy for sensors and actuators.
- The master CD at this stage represents a combination of hardware and software, and the hardware at least needs to be represented as accurately as possible, since it constitutes a major design decision even at this early stage.

The changes to the master CD, that were suggested actions in the HAZOP study, were mainly adding either classes and their respective relationships, or just relationships between some classes. Other actions that were not reflected as changes in the master CD, were mainly about time management, such as delays introduced by the communications network; special road conditions that needed to be considered as part of the mechanisms to deal with disturbances; how to cope with faults in sensors and actuators making explicit the incorporation of redundancy; faults in the on board diagnosis (OBD) system that could lead to hazardous conditions and finally measures to protect the system from user modifications.

There were a total of 10 changes in the class diagram, they account for additions and deletions of inheritance and association relationships, and addition of classes. The nature of the changes in the CD that resulted from the HAZOP study, address specific safety concerns that were either not seen during the design reviews or that the requirements did not explicitly state.

For example, it was not enough to have only one class for the *steering wheel angle sensor*, since some degree of redundancy is required to meet the reliability criteria; and the strategy for redundant sensors is that they are based on different physical principles; each one of these sensors should have a class of its own. Another relevant example of the utility of the HAZOP study from a safety perspective was the addition of the class: *steering actuator disengage*, which provides a mechanism to decouple the steering actuator in case it is locked.

We are investigating metrics to evaluate the effectiveness of the HAZOP analysis. However our expectations are to find most of the hazards through a more detailed version of the CD in the second phase of the HAZOP analysis.

Relation to other Work

This paper is based on a combination of the fundamentals first explored in the work [13], [14] and the standard [11] and represents a starting point to combine UML and HAZOP.

The idea to integrate hazard analysis into the development lifecycle has been looked at before by [13], where they propose an individual analysis first and at a later stage a team meeting, instead of a pure team approach for HAZOP analysis. They also propose to change the traditional HAZOP guidewords. Nevertheless we think that the guidewords' main objective is to elicit discussion, so the relevant strategy is the interpretation of these guidewords when applied to attributes.

In [14] the authors provide a set of guidelines to perform HAZOP on UML models, focusing on software architecture. The application of this technique is considered for requirements analysis; however we suggest a number of changes in this matter, as they only consider a subset of UML elements. One of our aims is to produce a standard set of guideword-interpretations to perform HAZOP analysis for each type of UML diagram, based on the definitions given in the specification of UML 2.0 [15]. This step has been completed for the UCD and CD, but at this stage of our work remains to be done for the other diagrams.

FUTURE WORK

In the intermediate phase of the safety analysis, we intend to use the CD to verify its internal functionality, for this purpose a second HAZOP study will be performed.

The more detailed safety analysis still has to be completed along with the design of the SbW system, the code produced has to be deployed to the target hardware and then the testing stage can be achieved. It is out of the project scope to build a complete SbW system in a vehicle. However implementing a prototype of the system is feasible, where a comprehensive set of disturbances can be simulated and the software can be running in appropriate target hardware.

CONCLUSION

HAZOP appears to be a useful technique for the initial phases of the safety lifecycle, due to its inherent level of abstraction. Nonetheless, in a later phase a more detailed safety analysis will be performed using a different technique, such as FMEA (Failure Modes and Effects Analysis) expecting that it will allow the quantification of the probability of failures.

It is important to measure the impact of the hazard analysis in each phase of the development lifecycle, in order to put together a framework to work with safety-related embedded systems, and come out with the set of guidelines to design this type of systems. This aspect will be analysed in more detail as well as incorporate real data from manufacturers' studies.

REFERENCES

1. Leveson, N., *Software Safety: Why, What and How.* ACM Computing Surveys, 1986. **18**(2).
2. Grimm, K. *Software Technology in an Automotive Company - Major Challenges*. in *25th ICSE*. 2003.
3. Furst, S. *Autocoding in Automotive Software Development, Qualification Aspects Of ACGs*. in *Automotive Electronics Conference*. 2005.
4. Leveson, N., *SAFEWARE - System Safety and Computers*. 1995, USA: Addison Wesley.
5. MoD, *Defence Standard 00-55: Requirements for Safety Related Software in Defence Equipment, Parts 1 and 2, Issue 2.* 1997.
6. MoD, *Defence Standard 00-58: HAZOP Studies on systems containing programmable electronics*. 2000.
7. MISRA, *Guidelines for the Use of the C Language in Vehicle Based Software.* 1998.
8. Benz S., D., E., Dieterle, W., Muller-Glasser, K. *2004-01-1665 A Design Methodology for Safety Relevant Automotive Electronic Systems*. in *SAE World Congress*. 2004. USA.
9. Wilwert C., Charlois, A. *2004-01-0705 Impact of Fault-Tolerance Mechanisms on X-By-Wire System Dependability*. in *SAE World Congress*. 2004. USA.
10. Krueger, A., Kant, D. and Buhlmann, M. *2003-01-1288 Software Development Process and Software Components for X-By-Wire Systems*. in *SAE World Congress*. 2003. USA.
11. MoD, *Defence Standard 00-58: HAZOP Studies on systems containing programmable electronics, Parts 1 and 2, Issue 2,*. 2000.
12. Conte, S.D., Dunsmore, H.E., Shen, V.Y., *Software Engineering, Metrics and Models*. 1986: Benjamin/Cummings.
13. McDermind, J.A., Nicholson, M., Punfrey, D.J. and Fenelon, P.year. *Experience with the application of HAZOP to computer-based systems*. in *COMPASS '95*. 1995.
14. Hansen, M., Wells, L. and Maier, T. *HAZOP Analysis of UML-Based Software Architecture Descriptions of Safety-Critical Systems*. in *2nd NWUML*. 2004.
15. Rumbaugh, J., Jacobson, I. and Booch, G., *The Unified Modeling Language, Reference Manual*. Second ed. 2004: Addison-Wesley.

CONTACT

Ireri Ibarra Alvarado, University of Sussex, Dept. of Engineering and Design. Falmer, Brighton, BN1 9QT, England. eii20@sussex.ac.uk

DEFINITIONS, ACRONYMS, ABBREVIATIONS

CD: Class Diagram

DEF STAN: Defence Standard

FMEA: Failure Mode and Effect Analysis

HAZOP: Hazard and Operability

MISRA: Motor Industry Software Reliability Association

ROPES: Rapid Object-Oriented Development Process for Embedded Systems

SbW: Steer-by-Wire

UC: Use Case

UCD: Use Case Diagram

UK MoD: United Kingdom Ministry of Defence

UML: Unified Modeling Language

XbW: X-by-Wire

PHA: Preliminary Hazard Analysis

SSA: System safety Analysis

DSA: Detailed Safety Analysis

OBD: On Board Diagnosis

2006-01-0305

Database Functionality in Engine Management System

Thomas Gustafsson
Department of Computer and Information Science, Linköping University

Jörgen Hansson
Department of Computer and Information Science, Linköping University
Software Engineering Institute, Carnegie Mellon University

Anders Göras
Mecel AB

David Holmgren and Jouko Gäddevik
GM Powertrain Sweden

ABSTRACT

Embedded systems of today need to manage more data than ever before. The main reasons for the increase in number of data items are increased functional requirements on the software. With a larger amount of data to manage comes the problems of storing data and its meta-information, sharing between programmers which data items exist, and ensuring freshness and consistency requirements of the data items.

In this work we focus on efficient data management in embedded systems, and develop a database for such systems. The database has support for transactions, snapshots, and data freshness. We argue that the software maintenance efforts can be reduced using a database, and our performance results show that the performance can be increased without affecting consistency of data values.

INTRODUCTION

With the advent of devices with the availability of larger amount of memory and more computational power, the software development has moved from assembly programming to using high-level programming languages such as C and C++. High-level programming languages can abstract data into structures and classes. Using high-level programming languages, programs may be programmed in a modular way, where data can be global and accessible from all modules, or local and only accessible by functions within a specific module. Global data can be used for communication between modules. This division of data into global and module-specific data, complicates the way one can get a view of existing data items and their usage. COMET project and other projects claim that using a database in an embedded system leads to reductions in development costs, improvements in software quality, and increased maintainability of the software (see also the appendix) [22].

In an embedded system we have studied, an engine control software, the software is divided into applications with certain responsibilities, e.g., calculating fuel and diagnosing the system. Each application consists of tasks that perform calculations. The calculations take inputs forming a subset of all available data and derive results composing a subset of the available data. Furthermore, some of the data items are subject to freshness constraints, meaning that they might be stale as the external environment changes. The freshness constraints are ensured by deriving the data items often enough, i.e., the data values never get older than what is dictated by a worst-case scenario. By storing data decentralized, it is easy to introduce duplicates of data items—since it is hard to get a picture of which data items exist—and update data items multiple times only to be sure the freshness requirements are fulfilled. Hence, excess memory and CPU resources might be needed, which is an undesirable consequence of the data management technique that is used.

An important aspect of the deterioration of data values as external environment changes is that a calculation should get a consistent view of its input data. This means that the input data must be sufficiently correlated in time. One way to achieve this is to freeze the input data and let the calculation read the frozen, unchanged, data [21]. The frozen data is denoted a snapshot. Data freshness issues can also be handled by deriving period times on calculations such that freshness of data items and timeliness of the calculations are guaranteed [13, 14, 17, 23]. However, these techniques do not change the way data is stored and fetched, and, thus, cannot help in the data maintenance effort. Also, calculations are always carried out in these techniques which might waste resources if values of data items change within some bounds, then the calculations would produce the same results that are already stored in the system. In essence, we would like a system that makes software maintenance easier and uses available resources efficiently, e.g., the CPU.

Olson describes different criteria for choosing a database for an embedded system [19]. He classifies databases into client-server relational databases, client-server object-oriented databases, and, finally, embedded library databases. The embedded library databases are explicitly designed for embedded systems. The embedded database links directly into the software, and there is no need for a query language such as SQL. Existing client-server databases are not appropriate for real-time systems, because transactions cannot be prioritized. Nyström et al. identify that there are no commercial alternatives of embedded databases suited for embedded real-time systems [22]. Further, it is pointed out that most database systems use two-phase locking to ensure concurrent transactions do not interfere with each other [19]. Two-phase locking is an approach to concurrency control that guarantees the consistency of the data [6]. However, for some applications the consistency can be traded off for better performance [18]. This trade-off is not possible if only two-phase locking is available.

In the engine management system (EMS) software, the merits of using a database instead of storing data globally and locally in modules are that all data and data maintenance programming code are concentrated to one place in the software. In this way, the data maintenance code can easily be changed since it is hidden behind the API. Furthermore, the database can have functionality that would be hard to implement using data structures spread out in the software, e.g., the database takes care of updating data items that are needed by a calculation. Such functionality is not present in current database systems (see the surveys [19, 22]), so we have developed a database suited for embedded systems, **D**ata **I**n **E**mbedded **S**ystems ma**I**ntenance **S**ervice (DIESIS), with support for transactions, data freshness, consistent views of data, and reduced consistency requirements giving higher performance but still correct results. Our performance results achieved by using DIESIS in engine control show that the number of calculations needed to keep data items fresh with respect to changes in the external environment can decrease considerably compared to methods normally used in embedded systems, which are updating data items periodically.

The outline of this paper is as follows. In the next section we state our problem formulation. Section "Description of DIESIS" describes DIESIS and the algorithms being used. Section "Performance Evaluations of DIESIS" shows results from conducted simulations, and section "Conclusions" concludes this paper.

PROBLEM FORMULATION

Figure 1 shows a calculation using module-specific and global data. We have seen in the section "Introduction" that how the data is stored clearly affects the maintainability of the software. Having data items stored decentralized, i.e., spread out in different modules, makes it hard to overview which data items exist, what are their timing and freshness requirements, and whether these requirements are fulfilled. In figure 1, it is impossible to see if, e.g., `globalData3`, is up-to-date when the calculation reads it.

The following bullets exemplify problems that are hard to solve using unsupervised storage of data, i.e., where data is fetched and stored uncontrollably to different memory areas.

```
/* code in a calculation */
/* local data */
int v1, v2, v3, result;
v1 = structName1.dataItem1;
v2 = globalData3;
/* perform calculations */
result = v3;
```

Figure 1: An example of a calculation accessing data from global and local data.

- For instance, let us denote the calculation in figure 1 as c_1, and assume another calculation, c_2, changes `structName1.dataItem1` to an intermediate value during its execution. Then there could be an interleaving of c_1 and c_2 such that c_1 reads the intermediate value of `structName1.dataItem1`. This, unwanted, effect is called *ghost update* (see the appendix for three other undesirable effects that can arise).
- Assume c_1 gets interrupted by some other calculations after the assignment `v1 = structName1.dataItem1`. Then if any of the calculations being executed before c_1 continues to execute updates `globalData3`, then the variables `v1` and `v2` can have values from different system states. This can affect the quality of the value of `v3`, and, thus, the end result of c_1.

Thus, the following problems exist when maintaining data in embedded systems:

- The effort of maintaining embedded software is large because data is spread out in different modules.
- Memory and CPU resources might be ineffectively used due to duplicate data items and unnecessary updating of data items.
- Calculations need to get a consistent view of its input data in order to control the external environment effectively.
- Calculations need to be controlled such that no unwanted and wrong results are stored and further used by other calculations.

We believe a wide range of embedded system software, e.g., all embedded systems doing any kind of control of the external environment, have the following properties. The embedded system:

- Makes readings of the external environment by using sensors or reading values arriving on communication links.
- Derives data items directly or indirectly from sensors or values arriving on communication links.
  - All data items are known before the system starts, i.e., functionality for adding and removing data items is not needed.

  - Data items have specified freshness requirements that are measurable in the value domain of the data item.
  - Calculations deriving data items often require values that are derived from the same system state, e.g., actuator signals.
- Starts calculations in response to external events, e.g., a clock tick of a periodic timer.
  - The calculations have soft deadlines (see the appendix).
  - Calculations can be assigned fixed priorities without affecting the intended functionality of the system.
- Has data that is volatile in the sense that all data is re-initialized at system startup. This means that calculations are independent from results produced in previous executions of the software.

We envision that using a database makes it easier to maintain the software in an embedded system. We have seen in the introduction that there are no available databases that address these problems. We believe that specializing a database for systems fulfilling the properties above can increase the performance compared to using a general database. Furthermore, by adopting an approach of central storage and maintenance of data implies that we have a global view of all data and its current status. This knowledge should be possible to exploit to effectively utilize available CPU-resources. Using a database for storing data, it would be easier to spot duplicate data items since they are stored in a central repository. Moreover, the database could have functionality that is difficult to implement using an unsupervised storage approach, e.g., concurrency control and data freshness insurance.

DESCRIPTION OF DIESIS

This section contains a description of the functionality of DIESIS. The section is divided into a description of the functionality and interface of DIESIS (section "Application Programming Interface"), and descriptions of the freshness and consistency functionality that are used in sections "Data and Transaction Model", "Data Freshness", "Updating Algorithms", and "Concurrency Control".

APPLICATION PROGRAMMING INTERFACE

DIESIS is written in the programming language C, and it is built to work with the real-time operating systems Rubus [1] and μC/OS-II [16]. DIESIS uses the notion of transactions. Transactions are atomic units of computational work, and, thus, do not see intermediate results from each other (an elaborate description can be found in the appendix). The operations that are allowed on data items are reading and writing.

Figure 2 shows a transaction. Every transaction is a C-function, since in this way the transaction is easily accessed by a function pointer. To register a transaction with DIESIS, the `BeginTransaction` function is called. The transaction is

```
void TD9(s8 mode, void *arg)
{
    s8 transNr=TRANSACTION_START;
    DB_Data dbd,dbd0,dbd1,dbd2;
    while(BeginTransaction(&transNr, 10000, 200,
          LOW_PRIORITY_QUEUE, mode, D1))
    {
        UpdateDB(&transNr,D9,2500);
        ReadDB(&transNr, D6, &dbd0);
        ReadDB(&transNr, D7, &dbd1);
        ReadDB(&transNr, D8, &dbd2);
        /* Calculation of new value */

        WriteDB(&transNr,D9,dbd,&TD9);
        CommitTransaction(&transNr);
    }
}
```

Figure 2: A transaction deriving one value.

wrapped in a loop to model the possible occurrence of a transaction needing to be restarted. The only possible cause for a transaction to restart is that the operations of two concurrent transactions conflict meaning that at least one of them produce a wrong result. This is further discussed in section "Concurrency Control".

As is discussed in section "Introduction", the values of data items need to accurately reflect the state in the external environment. The function `UpdateDB` schedules data items needing to be updated before the current transaction continues deriving values (the scheduling is described in section "Updating Algorithms"). A value of a data item is read from DIESIS by using the `ReadDB` function. The values are enumerated with an enum type, e.g., `D6`, and the read value is stored in `dbd0`. A value is written to DIESIS using the `WriteDB` function. Finally, last in the loop, the `CommitTransaction` function should be called. This function checks if the values read by the transaction are consistent (this is further described in section "Concurrency Control"), and if that is the case the transaction can commit. The function registers the transaction as completed and `BeginTransaction` returns zero, which jumps out of the loop.

DATA AND TRANSACTION MODEL

This section describes the data and transaction models derived from the properties stated in section "Problem Formulation".

Data Model

Embedded systems that monitor a natural environment can represent the set of data items as *base items*, i.e., data items that are read from sensors or communication links, and *derived data items*, i.e., data items that are calculated from a set consisting of base items and derived data items. In our work, we divide the data items into a set B of base items, and a set D of derived data items.

The values a calculation produce depend on values derived by other calculations. Hence, there are precedence constraints on the calculations, and these can be described in a directed acyclic graph (DAG). The DAG is denoted *data dependency graph*, G, and an example of a data dependency graph is figure 3. Base items have zero in-degree, and nodes representing actuator values have zero out-degree. The read set of a data item d_i, i.e., the data items that are read and used when deriving d_i, is denoted $R(d_i)$. Furthermore, if a calculation derives a value of only one data item then there exists a simple mapping from precedence constraints in a DAG to calculations to data items.

By a snapshot at time t we mean that the values of data items in the database are frozen at t, and these values are read by a calculation [21]. By an up-to-date snapshot at time t we mean a snapshot at t where all values are *up-to-date*, i.e., all data items that are affected by changes in values of other data items are updated.

Transaction Model

Transactions are divided into *sensor transactions (STs)* that are periodically executed updating the base items, *user transactions (UTs)* that are started by applications in the software, and *update transactions* or *triggered updates (TUs)* that are started by DIESIS to update data items before a user transaction starts to execute. Every transaction updates one data item, and, thus, there exists a mapping via the data dependency graph G and a function pointer to a transaction.

The transaction in figure 2 is an update of data item `D9` in figure 3. The transaction is a user transaction when it is invoked by the software. The transaction is an update transaction if the data item `D9` has been scheduled by a user transaction, and determined to be necessary to be executed. Whichever of these two cases that apply is regulated with the argument `mode` to the function `TD9`.

DATA FRESHNESS

With the notion data freshness we mean a way to decide if a value of a data item is a correct reflection of the state of the external environment. As we saw in section "Introduction", in the EMS software, data freshness is implemented using aging of data items. When a data item d_i is too old it is considered to be stale, i.e., $|ct - t_{d_i}| > a_{d_i}$, where ct is current time, t_{d_i} is the time when the value of d_i was calculated, and a_{d_i} is the maximum allowed age on the value of d_i [20]. However, when a value of d_i is stale it may still be unchanged or close to the old value. We can reason about the *similarity* of two values instead of reason about their ages [9–12, 15]. Two values are said to be equal if they are similar according to a similarity relation. An example of a similarity relation is the one-dimensional distance between two values. If the distance is less than a specified bound then the values are similar, and, thus, equal.

In this work, the data freshness that is specified on every data item is a *data validity bound (DVB)* giving the allowed distance, e.g., using a data validity bound of 9 of data item `D3`, the two values 50 and 58 of data item `D3` are similar since the distance $|50 - 58|$ is less than 9.

UPDATING ALGORITHMS

In this section we describe an algorithm, On-Demand Top-Bottom with relevance check (ODTB), which is part of DIESIS, that creates a schedule of data items needing to be updated [11]. The algorithm is executed as a response to the start of a user transaction. The algorithm needs to find the data items that must be updated, and it needs to schedule these in the correct order, i.e., fulfilling the precedence constraints.

First, we discuss how ODTB can decide which data items need to be updated. The algorithm uses similarity to measure data freshness. Since similarity uses the value domain of data items to define their freshness, the freshness of a data item, d_i, only needs to be reconsidered at an update of any of its ancestors, i.e., a member of $R(d_i)$. Hence, the execution of calculations can be data-driven, meaning that during periods when the external environment is in a steady state fewer calculations need to be executed compared to during periods when the external environment is in a transient state. Using periodic invocations of calculations, it is difficult to adapt to such changes in the external environment. For instance, consider the following.

1. Data item b_7 in the DAG in figure 3 has changed such that its new value is dissimilar to its previous value.

   A value becomes dissimilar when $|nv_{b_7} - ov_{b_7}| > dvb_{b_7}$, where nv_{b_7} and ov_{b_7} are the new and the old values of b_7 respectively, and dvb_{b_7} is the data validity bound of b_7.
2. Data item d_5 must be recalculated to reflect the new value of b_7.
3. Data items d_8 and d_9 might as well need recalculations, but that depends on the new value of d_5.

Using periodic updating of d_5, it is updated even though b_7 has not changed.

Recalculations of data items can be done at different moments in time. The two extremes are:

- recalculate a data item as soon as a data item the calculation reads is found dissimilar, and
- recalculate when the data item is requested by DIESIS.

The first approach is denoted *updates first*, and the latter *on-demand* [3]. The on-demand approach is found to use less CPU time than updates first [3]. In the implementation of DIESIS, recalculations are executed on-demand. Thus, there must be a way to postpone recalculations and start a subset of them in response to the starting of a user transaction. In DIESIS there is a scheme, *affected updating scheme (AUS)*, that marks a data item as affected when any of its immediate parents in the DAG changes to a dissimilar value. Returning to figure 3, when b_7 becomes dissimilar data item d_5 is marked as affected by this change. The scheme does the following:

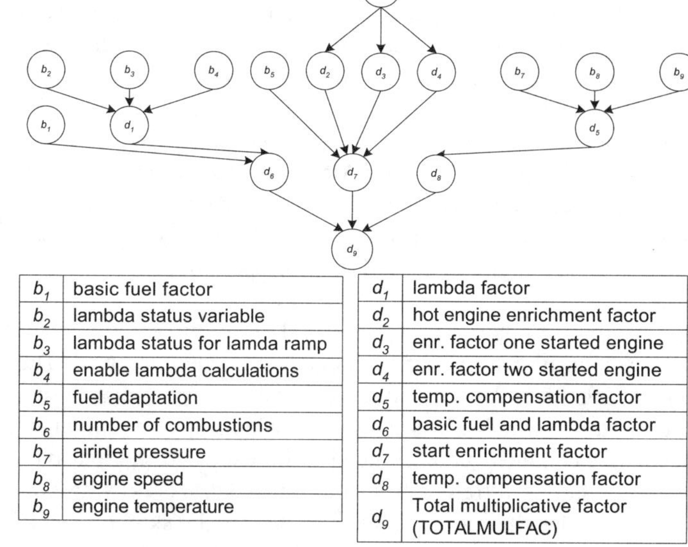

b_1	basic fuel factor	d_1	lambda factor
b_2	lambda status variable	d_2	hot engine enrichment factor
b_3	lambda status for lamda ramp	d_3	enr. factor one started engine
b_4	enable lambda calculations	d_4	enr. factor two started engine
b_5	fuel adaptation	d_5	temp. compensation factor
b_6	number of combustions	d_6	basic fuel and lambda factor
b_7	airinlet pressure	d_7	start enrichment factor
b_8	engine speed	d_8	temp. compensation factor
b_9	engine temperature	d_9	Total multiplicative factor (TOTALMULFAC)

Figure 3: An example of a DAG.

- keeps base items up-to-date by periodically updating them, and
- marks immediate children of d_i as affected when a recalculation of d_i finds the new value to be dissimilar to the old.

The marking may be a binary value, marked or not marked, but on rare occasions this approach can lead to missed updates. The marking can be a timestamp indicating with a timestamp greater than zero if the data item is changed or not. See [9] for a more detailed discussion.

Using AUS there is a way to decide which data items are affected by changes in data items. Thus, to schedule the data items needing to be updated, the DAG can be searched for data items that are marked as affected by a change. However, we must take the pessimistic approach and assume that a data item with a changed value renders descendant data items stale. This means that if a user transaction deriving data item d_9 starts, and data items d_4 and d_5 are marked as changed, then d_7 and d_8 need to be scheduled for being updated. The order these updates should be executed is first d_4 and d_5, and then d_7 and d_8, since there is no meaning in executing d_8 before d_5 because it will then read an old value of d_5.

To find data items to schedule for being updated, the DAG can be traversed from base items toward the data item d' being derived by the user transaction. When a data item d is found to be marked, all other data items that are on paths[1] from d to d' in G must also be put in the schedule.

One representation of the data items and the precedence constraints that allows for easy access is a depth-first order of the DAG. The algorithm in figure 4 is run on a DAG with an added bottom element resulting in the schedule S_{total}. Executing depthfirst(S,d_9) on the DAG in figure 3 yields the following schedule: $[d_1, d_6, d_2, d_3, d_4, d_7, d_5, d_8, d_9]$.

[1]Remember that there is a one to one mapping from data items to nodes in graph G.

```
depthfirst(schedule s, dataitem d)
  for all x ∈ R(d)\B do
    add x first to s
    depthfirst(s, x)
  end for
```

Figure 4: The depth-first algorithm.

For every data item there exists a subschedule of S_{total} that represents the data item and all its ancestors. Hence, only one schedule, S_{total}, needs to be stored together with information of where in S_{total} the subschedules, one for each data item, are located [11]. The storage requirements for the schedule and the location information is low, e.g., a graph consisting of 45 base items and 105 derived data items has 246 elements in S_{total} requiring 592 bytes of ROM.

The scheduling algorithm is executed on-demand, i.e., when a user transaction starts, and it traverses the subschedules of the read set for changed data items. The algorithm is denoted On-Demand Top-Bottom with relevance check (ODTB) and is presented in figure 5 [11]. This algorithm produces a schedule with data items that need to be updated. For each data item in the schedule a corresponding update transaction is triggered and executed.

```
ODTB(schedule s)
  for all x ∈ R(d)\B do
    for all u in top-bottom order of a depth-first subschedule
      of x do
      if data item u is marked then
        Copy u and the remainder of subschedule to s
        break
      end if
    end for
  end for
```

Figure 5: The On-Demand Top-Bottom with relevance check algorithm.

CONCURRENCY CONTROL

In a database there is normally functionality to handle concurrent transactions. DIESIS supports different concurrency control algorithms, and the algorithm is chosen at compile time. In this section we elaborate on problems of concurrently executing transactions and describe one solution.

A database has a set of integrity constraints (see the appendix)—e.g., a fuel compensation factor TOTALMULFAC that should be calculated from, say, two sensor readings that are at maximum 200 ms old—that defines what states the database can be in. Concurrency control, which maintains some of the integrity constraints, is intimately connected with the ACID properties of transactions (see the appendix). The purpose of having transactions with these properties is that committed transactions always write values that correctly reflect an environment the database models. For instance, in a banking application, transactions must have the ACID properties in order to have the correct balance on accounts that are touched by a money transaction.

Naturally, there are different integrity constraints for every database application. This means that some of the ACID properties can be loosened. The effects are that the throughput of the database, i.e., the number of committed transactions per time unit, increases compared to using full support for the ACID properties. Furthermore, the properties stated in section "Problem Formulation", that the system resets all values at a system startup, simplify the concurrency control algorithms, because there is no need to make sure committed results persist in the event of a system failure. Hence, the durability property is not needed.

Two well-established concurrency control algorithms that support the ACID properties are two-phase locking (2PL) and optimistic concurrency control (OCC) [6]. Two-phase locking has been extended to work in real-time databases, e.g., high-priority two-phase locking (HP2PL) [2], and OCC works correctly unchanged in real-time systems, provided fixed priority scheduling of calculations is used, i.e., the priority of the calculation never changes during the execution of it. Lee and Park present a database consistency denoted statewise consistency [18]. They claim that as long as transactions produce results equivalent to results from transactions executed one at a time, conflicting interleavings of operations do not matter. As we recall from section "Problem Formulation", data items can have freshness requirements measurable in the value domain. This implies that values on data items can take a range of values for a specific state in the external environment, and as long as conflicting operations for a data item produce results within the range of the data item, the conflicts do not matter. Hence, we can conclude that well-established concurrency control algorithms are too strict for the kind of embedded systems we focus on, and similarity provides necessary conditions wielding a loosened consistency that can improve performance.

We can infer, for databases for embedded systems, that the concurrency control algorithm should be similarity-aware since such an algorithm can increase the performance. Moreover, the database should be able to present a snapshot (section "Problem Formulation"), from a specific time, of up-to-date data items to a transaction. To achieve this, the updating algorithm and the concurrency control algorithm can be combined.

In DIESIS there is a multiversion timestamp ordering concurrency control algorithm using similarity (MVTO-S) [10], that ensures that transactions read an up-to-date snapshot of data items.

Next is an outline of the MVTO-S algorithm given (more details are in [10]). Every transaction gets a unique timestamp, and data items can have several versions where the versions are annotated with a timestamp. The timestamp on a version written by a transaction is the maximum of the timestamps on read versions by the transaction. The rationale behind using the maximum is that a version is valid when all members of the read set are valid, and they are all valid from the mentioned time. A transaction reads the latest version of a data item that is older than or as old as the transaction. Such a version is denoted a *proper version*. Hence, DIESIS is restricted to read values that were valid when a transaction starts. There are no guarantees that these values are valid when the transaction commits. We think this is not a drawback, since this is the functionality that is normally requested in the EMS software we have studied. Furthermore, when there are active but preempted transactions in the system, then written values result in new versions, since the old values might be needed by preempted transactions.

To ensure up-to-date values the ODTB algorithm (section "Updating Algorithms") is used to schedule needed updates. The scheduling of updates is done atomically when a user transaction starts, which gives a view of which updates might be needed. Scheduled updates need to be executed if input data to the update is different from the input data an existing version of the data item used. Thus, updates can be skipped due to that the value already exists in a version. This check is done by comparing the values of the read set members of the update to the corresponding values of a proper version. If all values are similar, then the update is not needed.

The MVTO-S algorithm is an abstract algorithm that can be implemented in different ways. The next subsection describes three implementations.

Description of Implementations of MVTO-S

The MVTO-S algorithm uses a memory pool to store versions of the data items. The amount of memory available for versions is limited, and therefore there are three implementations of MVTO-S, which each requires different amount of memory for storing a version. The algorithm MVTO-S^{UV} stores the value of each member of $R(d_i)$ when deriving d_i in the version. This strengthens the possibilities to make a similarity check. The MVTO-S^{UP} implementation, on the other hand, stores no values from members of $R(d_i)$, but these values are instead looked-up in the pool. The version size gets smaller, but the possibility to do a similarity check depends on if the values of members of $R(d_i)$ can be found in the pool. When the pool becomes full, versions are removed from it, and affected transactions are restarted. The implementation MVTO-S^{CRC} constructs versions with the same information as MVTO-S^{UV} but they are reduced in size because the values of members of $R(d_i)$ are condensed into a cyclic redundancy check (CRC) value. The CRC is calculated by taking an interval number (IN) for the value of each member of $R(d_i)$ by, e.g., dividing the value with 64, and calculating a CRC from these interval numbers. We assume these interval numbers can be represented as an 8-bit or 16-bit integer, and that the CRC of two versions are equal if and only if the used values are similar. For instance, let us denote two versions that the transaction in figure 2 has produced as v_1 and v_2, and the values the versions used are:

Data item	Used values				Data validity bounds
	v_1	IN	v_2	IN	
D6	11	2	13	2	5
D7	10	2	10	2	5
D8	5	1	6	1	5

From the table above we can easily see that used values on D6, D7, and D8 have the same interval numbers, and, thus, the same CRCs, which means that v_1 and v_2 are similar.

PERFORMANCE EVALUATIONS OF DIESIS

This section describes performance evaluations of DIESIS in two settings. One setting using DIESIS in an EMS connected to an engine simulator is described in section "Performance Evaluation using EMS". The other setting using DIESIS together with the real-time operating system μC/OS-II on top of Windows 2000 is described in section "Performance Evaluation of MVTO-S".

PERFORMANCE EVALUATION USING EMS

In many cases an embedded and real-time system is installed in a dynamically changing environment meaning that the system has to respond to these changes. Since tasks use data that should be fresh, state changes in the environment also affect the need to update data. This experiment treats steady and transient states and the number of required updates in each state. The number of updates is contrasted between an updating algorithm using value domain for data freshness and periodic updates.

We evaluate the algorithms on the EMS using the implementation of DIESIS. In the performance evaluations, we use the engine simulator to adjust engine speed. The EMS reacts upon the sensor signals as if it controlled a real engine. The performance evaluation shows how the updating algorithms react on state changes (transient and steady states).

The derived data item TOTALMULFAC is requested periodically by a task in the EMS software (see data item d_9 in figure 3). The request is transformed into a user transaction that arrives to DIESIS (see figure 2). ODTB is used in the EMS software, i.e., relevance checks are done if calculations are needed based on specified data freshness. This means that the data items d_1–d_8 in figure 3 are updated when needed, but not more often than the periodicity of TOTALMULFAC. In this experiment, the HP2PL concurrency control algorithm is used.

Recalculations of TOTALMULFAC are needed when the engine speed changes. Figure 6 shows how the requests for calculations are serviced only when the system is in a transient state, i.e., when the engine speed is changing. The plots in the bottom graph show the cumulative numbers of requests. The number of requests (dashed line) is increasing linearly since the requests are periodic and in the original EMS software each such request is processed. However, when using ODTB only some of the requests need to be processed. The number of serviced requests (solid line) shows how many of the requests need to be processed. In steady states, none of the requests need to be processed, and the stored value in DIESIS can be used immediately (e.g., the steady state in the time interval 2–7). Hence, during a steady state a considerable amount of requests can be skipped. Notice also that the data validity bounds allow DIESIS to accept a stored value if changes to the engine speed are small (in this case ± 50 rpm). This can be seen in the time interval 17-22, where the small changes in engine speed do not result in recalculations of the TOTALMULFAC variable. The number of serviced requests does not increase in this interval.

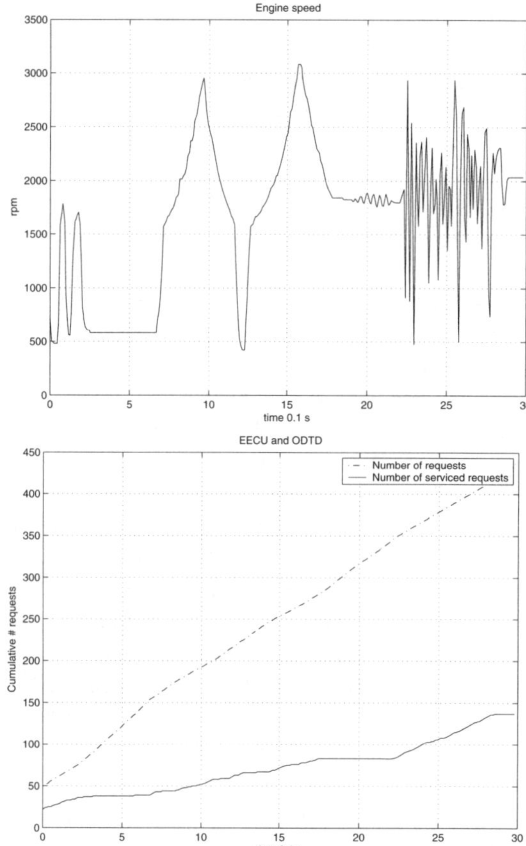

Figure 6: Number of requests of calculation of fuel compensation factor in EMS.

PERFORMANCE EVALUATION OF MVTO-S

The performance evaluations are conducted using DIESIS running on a real-time operating system that can be used in an embedded system. The operating system is μC/OS-II [16], and it provides the same functionality as Rubus we used in the EMS software in the experiments described in previous section. The simulations simulate periodic tasks invoking transactions from a database with similarity-aware updating and concurrency control algorithms. The base items are changing rapidly to model a transient state, where, as we saw in the previous section, the system needs to execute the most updates, i.e., the workload used in the simulator typifies a worst-case workload in a real-life system. The simulations run in a DOS command window in Windows 2000 Professional with servicepack 4. The computer is an IBM T23 with 512 Mb of RAM and a Pentium 3 running with 1.1 GHz.

The results show that using implementations of MVTO-S greatly improves performance and the number of transactions that commit within their deadlines, compared to using single version concurrency control algorithms.

Simulation Setup

Five tasks are executing periodically, and they invoke UTs that execute with the same priority as the task. The tasks are prioritized according to rate monotonic (RM), where a task gets a priority proportional to the inverse of its frequency [7]. The base period times are: 60 ms, 120 ms, 250 ms, 500 ms, and 1000 ms. These period times are multiplied with the ratio $32/arrival\_rate$, where 32 is the number of invoked tasks using the base period times, and $arrival\_rate$ is the arrival rate of UTs. The data item a UT derives is randomly determined by taking a number from the uniform distribution U(0,$|D|$). In the experiments, a database with 45 base items and 105 derived items has been used. The graph is constructed by setting the following parameters: cardinality of the read set ($|R(d)|$), ratio of $R(d)$ being base items, and ratio being derived items with only base item parents. The cardinality of $R(d)$ is set randomly for each d in the interval 1–8, and 30% of these are base items, 60% are derived items with only base item parents, and the remaining 10% are other derived items. These figures are rounded to nearest integer. The number of derived items with only base item parents is set to 30% of the total number of derived items. We believe a database of 150 data items represents the storage requirements of a hotspot of an embedded system, e.g., in the EMS 128 data items are used to represent the external environment and actuator signals. Further, we believe the data dependency graph G is broad (in contrast to deep), and that a data item does not depend on many other data items.

Every sensor transaction executes for 1 ms and every user transaction and triggered update executes for a time repeatedly taken from a normal distribution with mean 5 and standard deviation 3 until it is within $[0, 10]$. A simulation runs for 150 s with a specified arrival rate. Every simulation is executed 5 times and the showed results are the averages from these 5 runs. The user transactions are not started if they have passed their deadlines, but if a transaction gets started it executes until it is finished.

Every write operation creating the most recent version is adding a value from the uniform distribution U(0,350) to the previous most recent version. The data validity bounds are set to 400 for all data items. The creation of versions by the multiversion concurrency control algorithm involves taking values of the two closest versions, one older and one newer, and then randomly derive a value that is between the versions. The memory pool for storing versions holds 300 versions where 150 versions are reserved for the current value of each data item. Base item updates have a priority higher than UTs and execute on average every 100 ms, i.e., the period time is 50 ms and for every base item there is a 50% chance that the item is updated.

The updating algorithm used is the ODTB algorithm except in the OD-HP2PL simulation where periodic updates of data items is used. Table 1 shows the concurrency control algorithms that are used in the simulations. The algorithm MVTO is MVTO-S without a relevance check. OCC-S is OCC where the validation phase has been extended with a check whether the conflict involves similar values or not [9]. This extension of OCC is in line with the stepwise consistency (see section "Concurrency Control") that considers that as long as transactions produce end results correctly reflecting the external environment, then all conflicts are acceptable. By using a similarity check in the validation phase of OCC, it is possible to allow small errors in values that do not affect end results. The RCR implementations of OCC and OCC-S are restarting transactions until they are able to read a snapshot of DIESIS [9]. The on-demand updating and using HP2PL for concurrency control (OD-HP2PL) algorithm [4] triggers updates based on time instead of similarity, and in our test platform setup the allowed age on data items is set to 400 ms which is a good estimate on how long time a sensor value lives, since the average period time of sensors are 100 ms and it requires, on average, 3 updates to change outside a validity bound giving that values live 300–400 ms. The algorithm no concurrency control (NOCC) does not use any concurrency control, and is used as a baseline.

Table 1: Concurrency control algorithms used in simulations.

Algorithms		
MVTO-S^{UV}	MVTO-S^{UP}	MVTO-S^{CRC}
OCC-S	HP2PL	OCC
OD-HP2PL	RCR-OCC	RCR-OCC-S
NOCC	RCR-NOCC	

Simulation Results

The experiment investigates the number of committed user transactions within their deadlines. The no concurrency control scheme is used as a baseline. Figure 7 shows the performance of the algorithms.

First the benefit of using similarity can be seen in figure 7(a) studying the difference in performance between HP2PL and OD-HP2PL. In figure 7(b), MVTO-S^{UV} outperforms the single-version concurrency control algorithms at all arrival rates. The difference is most notable at higher loads where MVTO-S^{UV} performs significantly better than HP2PL, OCC, and NOCC. MVTO-S^{UP} cannot perform as good as MVTO-S^{UV} because less transactions are skipped [10]. MVTO-S^{UP} performs better than single-version algorithms at high arrival rates, but for small arrival rates OCC-S performs better.

Using multiple versions there are in total fewer restarts of transactions, i.e., less unnecessary work of transactions is done, compared to algorithms using restarts as resolving conflicts. Moreover, more transactions can be skipped since updates do not overwrite each other results because old values are stored in new versions. A transaction that derives an old version of a data item can benefit from versions from almost the same point in time that might exist in DIESIS, because a relevance check checks against such a version and not the most recent version as in single-version concurrency control algorithms. Table 2 shows the percentage of the total number of UTs and TUs that restart and can be skipped. The multiversion timestamp ordering algorithms have considerably fewer restarts than single-version algorithms. Every restart for MVTO, MVTO-S^{UV}, MVTO-S^{UP}, and MVTO-S^{CRC} is due to a full memory pool, whereas for single-version algorithms restarts are due to conflicts among concurrent transactions.

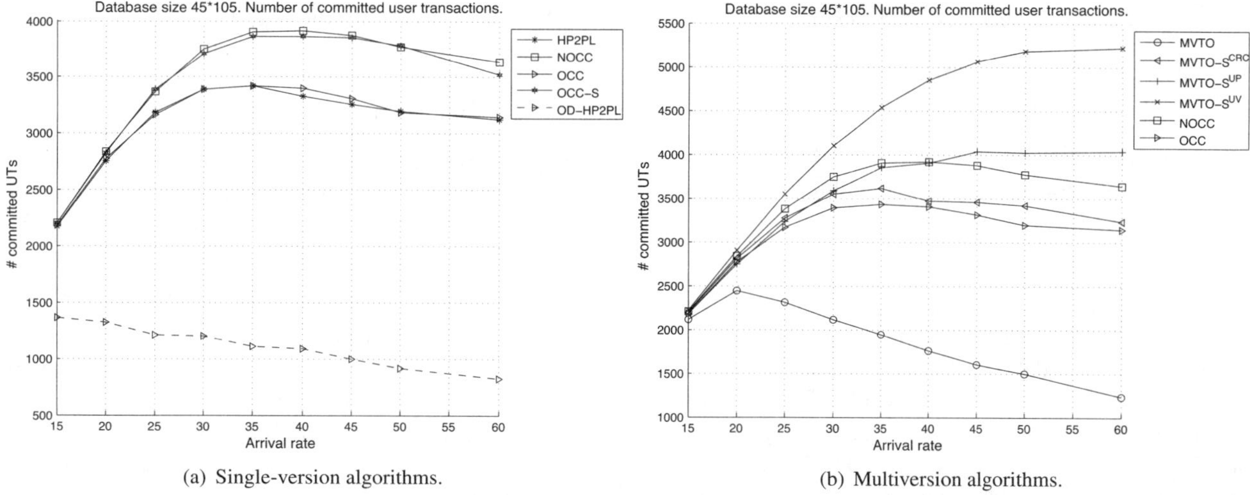

(a) Single-version algorithms.

(b) Multiversion algorithms.

Figure 7: Experiment 1: Performance evaluations of single-version and multiversion concurrency control algorithms.

Table 2: Experiment 1: Percentage of total number of UTs and TUs that restarts, and percentage of skipped transactions.

Alg.	Restarts	Skipped transactions
HP2PL	9.32%	16.2%
OD-HP2PL	9.46%	0%
OCC	9.03%	16.0%
OCC-S	0.96%	15.0%
NOCC	0%	14.5%
MVTO	0.24%	7.03%
MVTO-S^{UV}	0.039%	55.7%
MVTO-S^{UP}	0.15%	38.5%
MVTO-S^{CRC}	0.23%	39.6%

In figure 7(a), we see that using OCC-S gives the same number of UTs can commit as for NOCC. However, NOCC cannot guarantee the consistency of results produced by transactions since transactions read and write uncontrollably to DIESIS, but OCC-S produces consistent results. Table 2 shows that using similarity in OCC-S compared to using no similarity as in OCC, the percentage of restarts drops from 9.03% (OCC) to 0.96% (OCC-S). This indicates that conflicts among transactions often involve similar values since many of these conflicts cause restarts in OCC but not in OCC-S. Thus, a considerable amount of conflicts that do occur do not need any concurrency control. This is in line with observations made by Graham [8].

The implementations of MVTO-S guarantee that a transaction reads an up-to-date snapshot of DIESIS. The single-version concurrency control algorithms can guarantee this by restarting transactions until they read data items that are from the same external state. These algorithms are prefixed with RCR for relative consistency restarts. Figure 8 shows the performance using restarts to enforce relatively consistent read sets. The MVTO-S implementations are performing better than the single-version algorithms with restarts since values needed for deriving snapshots for transactions are stored in memory, therefore new updates to data items cannot destroy a snapshot for a transaction. Using a RCR algorithm, an update to a data item can be read by a preempted transaction which may destroy the derivation of a snapshot.

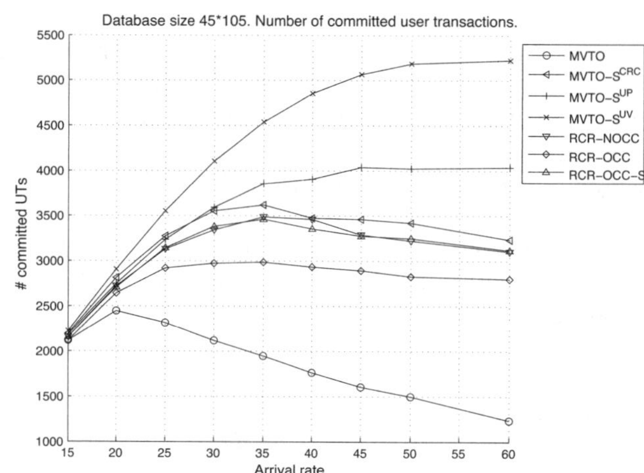

Figure 8: Experiment 1: Performance of relative consistency restarts algorithms.

CONCLUSIONS

In this paper we have described a database implementation aimed at being used in embedded systems—**D**ata **In E**mbedded **S**ystems ma**I**ntenance **S**ervice (DIESIS)—and specifically in an electronic engine control unit. The following is found to justify the usage of a real-time database in an embedded system:

- Software is built as modules that naturally divide data into different areas, but this makes it difficult to overview existing data and their freshness and time requirements. Using a database, data is instead stored in one central repository which is easier to overview. Moreover, it is possible to add meta-information of data items to the database.
- Data read by a transaction should correlate to the same state of the external environment. Using a database, the internal functions of the database can ensure that transactions read such data. This is hard (or even impossible) to guarantee if not having a global knowledge of all data.

The contribution of this work is incorporating functionality in DIESIS that:

- ensures data items have a specified data freshness,
- automatically adapts the frequency of executing transactions to the current state of the system, and
- guarantees a transaction reads values of data items that were valid when the transaction started and they correlate to the same state of the external environment.

These functionalities are transparent to the user which means it is easier to use the system for the programmer since he can focus on other things than data freshness and consistent values. Moreover, these functionalities are evaluated in both a real-life system, an electronic engine control unit, and in a simulator setup. The performance evaluations show that using an on-demand updating algorithm that is similarity-aware, i.e., defines data freshness in the value domain of data values, can greatly reduce the number of transaction invocations when the system enters a steady state compared to periodically recalculating data. Moreover, using a similarity-aware snapshot algorithm not only guarantees transactions see a consistent view of data values, but it also improves performance since calculations can be skipped to a larger extent compared to well-established concurrency control such as HP2PL and OCC.

For future work we intend to study an admission control of transactions in DIESIS to reduce the workload in the event of an overload.

REFERENCES

[1] Arcticus AB homepage. http://www.arcticus.se.

[2] Robert K. Abbott and Hector Garcia-Molina. Scheduling real-time transactions: a performance evaluation. *ACM Transactions on Database Systems (TODS)*, 17(3):513–560, 1992.

[3] B. Adelberg, H. Garcia-Molina, and B. Kao. Applying update streams in a soft real-time database system. In *Proceedings of the 1995 ACM SIGMOD*, pages 245–256, 1995.

[4] Quazi N. Ahmed and Susan V. Vbrsky. Triggered updates for temporal consistency in real-time databases. *Real-Time Systems*, 19:209–243, 2000.

[5] Paolo Atzeni, Stefano Ceri, Stefano Paraboschi, and Riccardo Torlone. *Database Systems Concepts, Languages and Architectures*. The McGraw-Hill Companies, 1999.

[6] Philip A. Bernstein, Vassos Hadzilacos, and Nathan Goodman. *Concurrency control and recovery in database systems*. Addison-Wesley Publishing Company, 1987.

[7] Giorgio C. Buttazzo. *Hard Real-Time Computing Systems*. Kluwer Academic Publishers, 1997.

[8] Marc H. Graham. How to get serializability for real-time transactions without having to pay for it. In *Proceedings of the Real-Time Systems Symposium 1993*, pages 56–65, 1993.

[9] Thomas Gustafsson. Maintaining data consistency in embedded databases for vehicular systems. Linköping Studies in Science and Technology Thesis No. 1138. Linköping University. ISBN 91-85297-02-X.

[10] Thomas Gustafsson, Hugo Hallqvist, and Jörgen Hansson. A similarity-aware multiversion concurrency control and updating algorithm for up-to-date snapshots of data. In *Proceedings of the 17th Euromicro Conference on Real-Time Systems*. IEEE Computer Society Press, 2005.

[11] Thomas Gustafsson and Jörgen Hansson. Data management in real-time systems: a case of on-demand updates in vehicle control systems. In *Proceedings of the 10th IEEE Real-Time and Embedded Technology and Applications Symposium (RTAS'04)*, pages 182–191. IEEE Computer Society Press, 2004.

[12] Thomas Gustafsson and Jörgen Hansson. Dynamic on-demand updating of data in real-time database systems. In *Proceedings of the 2004 ACM symposium on Applied computing*, pages 846–853. ACM Press, 2004.

[13] Shao-Juen Ho, Tei-Wei Kuo, and Aloysius K. Mok. Similarity-based load adjustment for real-time data-intensive applications. In *Proceedings of the 18th IEEE Real-Time Systems Symposium (RTSS '97)*, pages 144–154. IEEE Computer Society Press, 1997.

[14] Y.-K. Kim and S. H. Son. Supporting predictability in real-time database systems. In *2nd IEEE Real-Time Technology and Applications Symposium (RTAS '96)*, pages 38–48. IEEE Computer Society Press, 1996.

[15] Tei-Wei Kuo and Aloysius K. Mok. Application semantics and concurrency control of real-time data-intensive applications. In *Proceedings of IEEE 13th Real-Time Systems Symposium*, pages 35–45. IEEE Computer Society Press, 1992.

[16] Jean J. Labrosse. *MicroC/OS-II The Real-Time Kernel Second Edition*. CMPBooks, 2002.

[17] Chang-Gun Lee, Young-Kuk Kim, S.H. Son, Sang Lyul Min, and Chong Sang Kim. Efficiently supporting hard/-soft deadline transactions in real-time database systems. In *Third International Workshop on Real-Time Computing Systems and Applications, 1996.*, pages 74–80, 1996.

[18] Kyuwoong Lee and Seog Park. Classification of weak correctness criteria for real-time database applications. In *Proceedings of the 20th International Computer Software and Applications Conference 1996 (COMPSAC'96)*, pages 199–204, 1996.

[19] Michael A. Olson. Selecting and implementing an embedded database system. *IEEE Computer*, 2000.

[20] Krithi Ramamritham. Real-time databases. *Distributed and Parallel Databases*, 1(2):199–226, 1993.

[21] Håkan Sundell and Philippas Tsigas. Simple wait-free snapshots for real-time systems with sporadic tasks. In *Proceedings of the 10th International Conference on Real-Time and Embedded Computing Systems and Applicatins (RTCSA04)*, 2004.

[22] Aleksandra Tešanović, Dag Nyström, Jörgen Hansson, and Christer Norström. Embedded databases for embedded real-time systems: a component-based approach. Technical report, Department of Computer Science, Linköping University, 2002.

[23] Ming Xiong and Krithi Ramamritham. Deriving deadlines and periods for real-time update transactions. In *Proceedings of the 20th Real-Time Systems Symposium*, pages 32–43. IEEE Computer Society Press, 1999.

CONTACT

Thomas Gustafsson
e-mail: thogu@ida.liu.se
phone: +46 (0)13281426
address: Thomas Gustafsson
Department of Computer and Information Science
Linköping University
SE-581 83 Linköping
Sweden

Jörgen Hansson
e-mail: jorha@ida.liu.se
e-mail: hansson@sei.cmu.edu
phone: +1 412 268 6733

Anders Göras
e-mail: anders.goras@mecel.se
phone: +46 (0)53262120

Jouko Gäddevik
e-mail: jouko.gaddevik@se.gm.com
phone: +46 (0)855377078

David Holmberg
e-mail: david.holmberg@se.gm.com
phone: +46 (0)855377086

APPENDIX

REAL-TIME SYSTEMS

A real-time system consists of tasks, where some/all have time constraints on their execution. It is important to finish a task with a time constraint before its deadline, i.e., it is important to react to an event in the environment before a predefined time.

The correct behavior of a real-time system depends not only on the values produced by tasks but also on the time when the values are produced [7]. A value that is produced too late can be useless to the system or even have dangerous consequences. A task is, thus, associated with a deadline relative to the start time of the task. Note that a task has an arrival time when the system is notified of the existence of the ready task, and a start time when the task starts to execute. Tasks are generally divided into three types:

- *Hard real-time tasks*. The missing of a deadline of a task with a hard requirement on meeting the deadline has fatal consequences on the environment under control. For instance, the landing gear of an aeroplane needs to be ejected at a specific altitude in order for the pilot to be able to complete the landing.
- *Soft real-time tasks*. If the deadline is missed the environment is not severely damaged and the overall system behavior is not at risk but the performance of the system degrades.
- *Firm real-time tasks*. The deadline is soft, i.e., if the deadline is missed it does not result in any damages to the environment, but the value the task produces has no meaning after the deadline of the task. Thus, tasks that do not complete in time should be aborted as late results are of no use.

Scheduling algorithms determine the order tasks are executed. Two well-known real-time scheduling algorithms are rate-monotonic (RM) and earliest deadline first (EDF). Using RM means that a task is assigned a priority that is proportional to the inverse of its invocation frequency. This means that tasks with high frequency get higher priority than tasks with low frequency. The priority of a task, using EDF, is commensurate with the distance to the deadline, and the shorter the distance the higher the priority.

DATABASE

The following benefits of using a database for data storage are given in database textbooks [5]: (i) data storage is centralized, (ii) data storage is hidden behind an API or query language, and the data storage details are hidden for the users of the database, (iii) the database can seamlessly handle data freshness and concurrency control, (iv) meta-information, e.g., timestamps and deadlines, can be stored with the data, and (v) the relationships among data items can be stored in the database.

TRANSACTIONS

We define a transaction as computational work carried out in the database, e.g., a calculation. The database has integrity constraints on the data, and transactions must be executed such that the constraints are always fulfilled. In some applications, e.g., in bank applications moving money between accounts, the execution of transactions must conform to the following properties [5]:

- *Atomicity.* All operations of a transaction are reflected in the database, or none of them are.
- *Consistency.* The execution of transactions preserves the consistency of the database.
- *Isolation.* Each transaction is unaware of other transactions executing in the database system.
- *Durability.* The results of a committed transaction persist even in the course of system failure.

Transactions should avoid the four effects of conflicting operations that are described below.

- *Lost update,* where a transaction overwrites the result of another transaction, and, hence, the result from the overwritten transaction is lost.
- *Dirty read,* where a transaction reads and uses a result of a transaction that is aborted later on, i.e., the transaction should not have used the results.
- *Inconsistent read,* a transaction reading the same data item several times gets, because of the effects of concurrent transactions, different values.
- *Ghost update,* where a transaction only sees some of the effects of another transaction, and, thus, consistency constraints do not hold any longer. For example [5], consider two transactions, τ_1 and τ_2, and the constraint $s = x + y + z = 1000$. The operations are executed in an order such that the value of s in τ_1 at commit time is 1100 since τ_1 has seen intermediate results from τ_2.

Consistency constraints can be constructed for the following types of consistency requirements: internal consistency, external consistency, temporal consistency, and dynamic consistency. Below each type of consistency is described [15].

- *Internal consistency* means that the consistency of data items is based on other items in the database. For instance, a data item Total is the sum of all accounts in a bank, and an internal consistency constraint for Total is true if, and only if, Total represents the total sum.
- *External consistency* means that the consistency of a data item depends on values in the external environment that the system is running in.
- *Temporal consistency* means that the values of data items read by a transaction are sufficiently correlated in time.
- *Dynamic consistency* refers to several states of the database. For instance, if the value of a data item was higher than a threshold then some action is taken that affects values on other data items.

2005-01-1290

Standard Software Modules - One Key for Future Distributed Systems

Roman Nossal and Thomas M. Galla
DECOMSYS

Jochen Olig
3SOFT

ABSTRACT

The key to the required level of quality and safety in future distributed systems is a comprehensive standardized ECU (Electronic Control Unit) software architecture and infrastructure.

INTRODUCTION

The number of electronic systems in cars is continuously growing. Electronic systems account for up to 30% of a modern car's worth. Consequently, software plays an ever more important role, both for the implementation of functions and the infrastructure. The functional software heavily depends on the actual system and is a discriminating factor of competitive importance. This, however, does not apply to the software infrastructure. The software infrastructure, which is comparable to the BIOS or the operating system of a PC, does not influence competition – it is merely the foundation on which functions that are relevant for competition are built.

Keeping this in mind, the obvious approach is to standardize this software infrastructure for the sake of cost-effectiveness, reliability, and interoperability. This paper will provide a brief overview of the current status with respect to software infrastructure. This will be followed by a definition of goals to be achieved, as well as some insights into the AUTOSAR initiative [1], whose purpose is to define and standardize a comprehensive software infrastructure. The paper concludes with the introduction of TimeCore, a set of standard software modules for use in series applications.

STATE OF THE ART

Historically, if an ECU had some software infrastructure at all, it used to be some proprietary implementation. This was different for every ECU – not even parts, which were independent from the actual hardware, would be reused in another ECU.

Of course ECU suppliers – especially those with higher volumes and many different types of ECUs – discovered the inefficiency of this approach. As a result, they started to implement some platform software that was used in an entire family of ECUs. Hardware drivers and similar modules became company standards by this approach. This solution eased the implementation of new ECUs for the supplier considerably, yet it did not provide any gains for the system integrator, be it the OEM or a system supplier.

Consequently, OEMs and system suppliers took the next step. They no longer wanted to accept a company-specific platform, but to have one common software platform for all ECUs of a system. Thus the OEMs started to implement their own software infrastructure and to demand that their suppliers use this basic software in any ECU supplied to them. While this improved the situation for the OEMs, it diminished the advantages of platform software for the suppliers. They could no longer reuse the software for different OEMs.

Both developments, the platform software and the OEM-specific infrastructure, show that a standardization driven by either of the two main groups in the automotive industry will not be able to achieve the goal and provide benefits for all participants. Any standardization that does not involve the entire industry will have some obvious drawbacks:

- The software failure rate is high, because software has to be re-implemented more often than necessary. A supplier cannot reuse his implementation for another OEM, but instead has to implement it again to match this OEM's software infrastructure. Similarly, OEMs or their software infrastructure providers have to develop a specific implementation for each OEM, thus diminishing the effects of reuse.

- For the same reason, it is more or less impossible to argue that the implementation is field-proven, an important fact in safety-relevant systems.
- Interoperability is threatened. Integrating ECUs from different suppliers with different software platforms always carries the risk of incompatibilities at the interfaces.
- Most important of all, any reimplementation of the same functionality is inefficient. All the more so if it is not even relevant to competition.

To overcome these problems the automotive industry has one answer – industry-wide standardization.

OBJECTIVES

Standardization ensures a known, fixed functionality together with a stable API. The advantages are obvious:

- Standardization allows the re-use of functions and infrastructure.
- Standardization facilitates exchangeability on the OEM as well as on the supplier side.
- Standardization ensures interoperability. A service that has been standardized has a well-defined interface, which will be accessible by any other standard-conforming implementation.

RE-USE

Standardized software modules provide for better re-use than their proprietary counterparts. OEMs can easily re-use the functional software in different product lines if they apply the same software infrastructure in them. No porting is required as long as the functional software components can access an unaltered interface.

Suppliers, on the other hand, can re-use their software for different OEMs. Assuming that all OEMs agree on a common software architecture, the suppliers' software modules will use the same interfaces for each of the OEMs, so no porting is required.

Finally, the software and tool vendors can also re-use the software infrastructure they have implemented and sell it to several OEMs and suppliers.

Apart from the increased efficiency of re-using existing software, there is also a consideration of quality. Software that is used in several applications can claim to be field-proven. All applications that use the same piece of software can be considered field tests for this software. Thus, the more widely the same software is used, the better is its test coverage. The probability that there are dormant errors in the software decreases with each application. Likewise, the confidence in the quality of a specific software module increases with each application, whether it is part of the software infrastructure or the functional software.

EXCHANGEABILITY

With the possibility to re-use code there is a certain degree of exchangeability. OEMs are no longer bound to a specific software vendor. Any vendor who is able to apply the standardized software infrastructure can supply this to the OEM.

The OEM, however, also becomes exchangeable for the software vendors. As mentioned above, the vendors can provide the same implementation to several different OEMs.

INTEROPERABILITY

A service that has been standardized offers a well-defined interface. Hence, any other standard-conforming implementation can use this service without any alterations to the implementation.

For this reason, in order to be fully effective, the standardization needs to cover all aspects of an infrastructure: the operating system, hardware drivers, interface layers, communication drivers, and service layers like Network Management, a Transport Layer etc.

INITIATIVES

HISTORICAL OVERVIEW

In the recent years there have been several consortia, initiatives, and funded projects with a common goal – to standardize software infrastructure or at least parts of it. There are OSEK/VDX, HIS, and the EASIS project, to name but a few. The OSEK/VDX consortium [2] took action to standardize an operating system (OSEK OS) for embedded real-time applications. A communication access layer (OSEK COM) and a Network Management service (OSEK NM) complement the operating system. HIS [3] went a step beyond this, took the results of the OSEK/VDX consortium and added important software modules such as hardware drivers for input and output.

A somewhat different approach is taken in the EASIS project [4], which is funded by the European Commission. In this project a group of OEMs, suppliers, and tool vendors have gathered with the objective to define a common software architecture that is suitable for use in safety applications in vehicles.

The most recent development in this respect is the AUTOSAR initiative, which will be dealt with in the next section.

THE AUTOSAR INITIATIVE

The AUTOSAR initiative pursues the goal of establishing an open standard for automotive E/E architecture that will serve as a basic infrastructure for managing functions. This comprises the standardization of basic system functions and functional interfaces, the ability to integrate and transfer functions and to substantially improve software updates and upgrades over the lifetime of the vehicle.

The objectives of AUTOSAR are [1]

- Management of E/E complexity associated with growth in functional scope
- Flexibility for product modification, upgrade and update
- Scalability of solutions within and across product lines
- Improved quality and reliability of E/E systems.

AUTOSAR will provide a common software infrastructure for automotive systems in all vehicle domains based on standardized interfaces for the different layers shown in Figure 1.

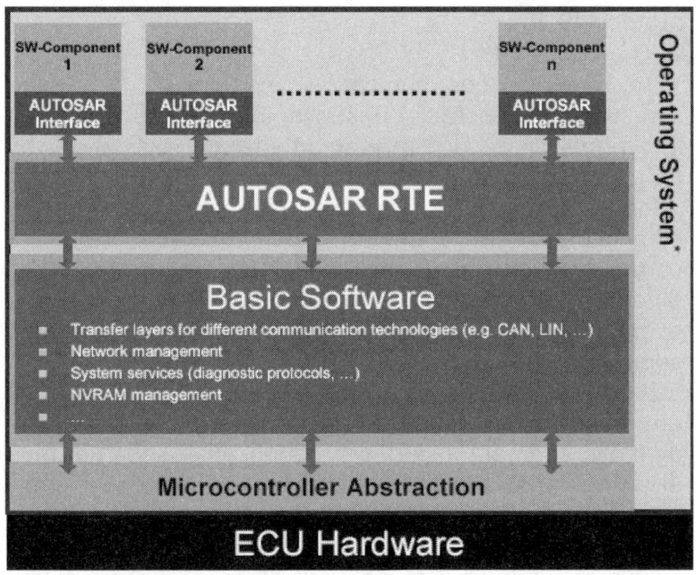

Figure 1: AUTOSAR Software Architecture (Source: www.autosar.de).

The scope of AUTOSAR is the entire software infrastructure of an ECU. It covers all layers, from the abstraction of the actual hardware, over the so-called "basic software", the AUTOSAR Run-Time Environment (RTE), to the interfaces for the functional software components.

TIMECORE

While an AUTOSAR-compliant software infrastructure is still a product of the future, there is a solution available. With their joint product called TimeCore, 3SOFT and DECOMSYS present a software kit that contains a wide variety of standardized software modules. TimeCore offers a software infrastructure similar to the intended coverage of AUTOSAR.

The following paragraphs provide an overview of the main constituents of the TimeCore package. While the description naturally highlights certain features contained in the TimeCore product, the modules presented and their functionality are valid for any software infrastructure in an automotive ECU.

OSEKTIME OS

OSEKtime OS is designed as a time-driven single chip operating system for distributed applications like X-by-Wire systems, which need to have synchronized access to various ECUs.

OSEKtime executes functions either as interrupt service routines or as tasks. Interrupt service routines (ISRs) are triggered by interrupts and execute interrupt-related services. Tasks on the other hand are started at defined points in time. They can have one of three states. In the *running state*, the CPU is assigned to the task and its commands are executed. The *preempted state* is reached by a task that has been in the running state and was preempted by another task that is to be activated. A task can leave the preempted state only if the preempting task changes into the suspended state. An inactive task that can be activated is in the *suspended state*. These state changes are shown in Figure 2.

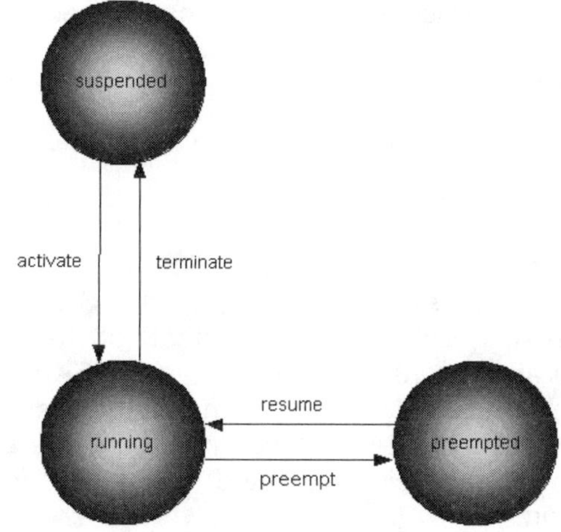

Figure 2: OSEKtime Task States

The activation times of the tasks are stored in a so-called dispatcher table during system configuration. A dispatcher uses the information stored in this table to activate the tasks according to their activation times. The dispatcher itself is usually triggered from a non-maskable interrupt.

The dispatcher table is processed cyclically. If a time-driven task is still in the *running state* when the activation time of another time-driven task is reached, the first task passes over to the *preempted state* and stays there until the interrupting task is finished. This kind of scheduling is called stack-based scheduling; no priorities are assigned to the tasks - only the activation times define the precedence between different tasks. The later a task is started the less likely it is that another task can interrupt it while it is being executed.

Depending on the design of the application, a dispatcher round can include times during which no tasks or interrupt service routines are active. A task named ttIdleTask is assigned to the CPU during these idle times. This task is provided by the OS, has no entry in the dispatcher table and no deadline assigned. Its sole purpose is to take up CPU time otherwise unused.

The occurrence of interrupts is also supervised and controlled by the operating system. An interrupt source is only switched on through an entry in the dispatcher table. After an interrupt is raised, its interrupt service routine will be executed. Then the operating system switches off the interrupt source and it can only be switched on again by a new entry in the dispatcher table. In this way, the whole dispatcher round can be divided into unconnected time intervals where a particular interrupt can occur at most once within one of these intervals.

The dispatcher's sole duty during run time is to cyclically execute the dispatcher table. It does not check for any task constraints etc. The configuration of the distributed system has to take care of these issues. Besides information about existing constraints between tasks, e.g., a mutual exclusion due to access to a common resource, the knowledge of the worst case execution time (WCET) [5,6,7,8] of every task and interrupt service routine is essential to plan the course of a dispatcher round.

OSEK/VDX SUBSYSTEM

If an application consists of a time-critical part and a more complex, non time-critical part, then OSEKtime offers an interesting solution for it: Instead of the idle task described above, one can integrate an OSEK/VDX subsystem. This OSEK/VDX subsystem acts as the idle task for the OSEKtime OS. Whenever the OSEKtime OS is idle, i.e., no task is being executed, the OSEK/VDX subsystem is run.

OSEK/VDX is a standard for an operating system that was designed for applications in the area of car body electronics or power train. It provides the user with system services like tasks, interrupt service routines, counters, alarms, and resources. It also offers an event mechanism for the signaling between tasks and interrupt service routines.

OSEK/VDX is a configurable and static system. Since every system service that an application wants to use must be defined and configured before compile time, there is no dynamic management of system resources. This results in an operating system kernel that is tailored to the needs of the corresponding application and that can therefore be highly optimized.

OSEKTIME FTCOM

FTCom (Fault Tolerant Communication) [2] provides all associated ECUs with a global time to which they synchronize their local time base. Furthermore, it is responsible for the fault tolerant sending and receiving of messages between the distributed communication partners in a temporally deterministic way.

The fault tolerant mechanisms of FTCom consist of the replication and reduction of messages. On the sender's side, the FTCom layer replicates a single application message into several instances and transmits these via redundant communication paths (e.g. on different communication channels). On the recipient's side, FTCom reduces the several instances of the received message to a single application message that is provided to the application.

FLEXRAY

In order to achieve the above-mentioned determinism at the communication level, OSEKtime FTCom in TimeCore uses the FlexRay time-driven communication protocol [9,10].

The FlexRay communication medium is accessed synchronously in a slot-based manner. Time is divided into equally sized slots that are owned exclusively by ECUs for transmitting their data. Slot assignment is done off-line during the system planning stage, thus eliminating any on-line competition for the communication medium. FlexRay integrates two different communication paradigms, time-driven and event-driven media access. In the so-called static segment, communication access follows a TDMA scheme with equally sized slots. In the dynamic segment an event-driven minislotting scheme is applied. The dynamic segment includes a prioritization scheme, thus enabling variable bandwidth distribution during run time.

Both segments strictly adhere to the above-mentioned exclusive ownership of slots providing a key foundation for an important FlexRay feature, composability. As each ECU owns slots exclusively, it is possible to develop ECUs autonomously and to integrate them later without side effects.

FlexRay also supports fault-tolerant clock synchronization and provides a global time base to OSEKtime FTCom.

FLEXRAY NETWORK MANAGEMENT

Network management (NM) in the automotive area handles the controlled startup and shutdown of the communication across a shared communication infrastructure. In particular, Network Management coordinates the common view of the network where each node can initiate a shutdown or a wakeup of the communication system during normal system operation. In TimeCore, NM is based on the FlexRay communication system.

FLEXRAY TRANSPORT LAYER

In general, a transport layer supports the transmission of messages whose length is greater than the maximum payload length of the underlying communication system. On the sender's side, the Transport Layer will split such long messages into packets that the underlying communication system can handle. The transport layer reassembles these packets on the receiver's side.

The support of direct addressing (sending a message to a specific node), broadcasts (sending a message to all nodes in the network), and multicasts (sending a message to a specific subset of nodes) is also implemented in the Transport Layer. Consequently the Transport Layer provides a unique address to every node addressable via the Transport Layer, addresses for groups of nodes, and a broadcast address.

CAN DRIVER AND CAN TRANSPORT LAYER

A CAN driver is also included in TimeCore. The driver can be operated in interrupt and polled mode. The number of message objects is user-definable, and a priority based message queue is also supported.

The working principle of the included CAN transport layer is similar to the transport layer for FlexRay.

KWP2000

KWP2000 is a standard for a diagnostic layer. It describes a set of functions with which an ECU can be diagnosed from a tester tool. The diagnostic layer is based on the Transport Layer. Within TimeCore, the KWP2000 layer can be accessed via CAN and FlexRay.

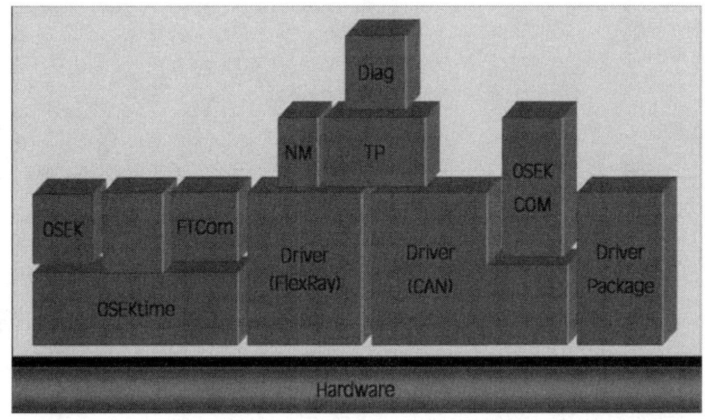

Figure 3: TimeCore Architectural Overview

TOOLING

All components of TimeCore require configuration before run time. The software modules are set up to match the requirements of the application exactly. Services that are not used by the application are not configured into the run-time software of TimeCore. This leads to highly optimized code with respect to execution time and memory consumption.

To configure TimeCore the development engineer can make use of the comprehensive toolset from DECOMSYS and 3SOFT, which is included in TimeCore. The DECOMSYS::DESIGNTOOLS tool suite with its graphical user interface allows the user to design the architectural model of his distributed system. Based on this model, the DECOMSYS::DESIGNER configures the FlexRay communication system and builds a communication schedule. Finally it generates FTCom code, which takes the particularities of each signal into account. *tresos*, a configuration tool that is used to configure OSEK/VDX, OSEKtime and all CAN components, is also part of TimeCore. During configuration, *tresos* resolves inter-component dependencies automatically. For example, an interrupt service routine used by the CAN Driver will be added automatically to the OSEK/VDX configuration. Both tools, DECOMSYS::DESIGNER and *tresos*, are well-integrated and thus support the user in configuring all modules during the development cycle.

CONCLUSION

This paper has stated the case for a standardized software infrastructure in automotive ECUs. We have argued that the objectives of re-use, exchangeability, and interoperability can only be achieved if all players in the automotive market, OEMs and suppliers alike, agree on one standard for software modules that are to be used in any ECU.

With its joint product TimeCore, DECOMSYS and 3SOFT deliver a set of software modules that meets all requirements of automotive applications. TimeCore comprises a time-driven as well as an event-driven operating system, communication layers, network management service, etc.

While TimeCore is readily available, several automotive companies have teamed up in the AUTOSAR consortium with the goal of standardizing the software infrastructure for automotive electronics. As soon as a set of AUTOSAR standards becomes available, DECOMSYS and 3SOFT will provide an updated, AUTOSAR-compliant version of TimeCore.

REFERENCES

1. AUTOSAR Website. www.autosar.org
2. OSEK/VDX Website. www.osek-vdx.org
3. HIS Website. www.automotive-his.de
4. EASIS Website. www.easis-online.org
5. P. Puschner. Timing Analysis for Real-Time Programs. PhD thesis, Technische Universität Wien, Institut für Technische Informatik, Treitlstraße 3/3/182-1, 1040 Vienna, Austria, 1993
6. Raimund Kirner. Extending Optimising Compilation to Worst-Case Execution Time Analysis. PhD thesis,

Technische Universität Wien, Institut für Technische Informatik, Treitlstraße 3/3/182-1, 1040 Vienna, Austria, May 2003
7. C. Y. Park and A. C. Shaw. Experiments with a Program Timing Tool based on a Source-Level Timing Schema. IEEE Computer, 24(5):48–57, May 1991
8. P. Puschner and A. V. Schedl. Computing Maximum Task Execution Times – A Graph-Based Approach. The Journal of Real-Time Systems, 13:67–91, 1997
9. FlexRay Consortium Website. www.flexray.com
10. A Manager's Guide to FlexRay. Automotive Design and Production, September 2002. http://www.flexray.com/publications/a_manager_guide.pdf

CONTACT

Please direct questions or comments about this article to Roman Nossal at DECOMSYS - Dependable Computer Systems, Hardware und Software Entwicklung GmbH, Stumpergasse 48/28, A-1060 Vienna, Austria; nossal@decomsys.com; www.decomsys.com

DECOMSYS and 3SOFT are development members of the FlexRay® consortium.

Roman Nossal is product manager at DECOMSYS. He has a PhD in computer science from the Vienna University of Technology and an MBA in General Management from Danube University in Krems, Austria.

Thomas M. Galla is the technical coordinator of all DECOMSYS developments. He has a PhD in computer science from the Vienna University of Technology.

Jochen Olig is senior software engineer with 3SOFT GmbH. He has studied engineering at the University of Erlangen-Nuernberg.

Jochen Olig can be contacted at

3SOFT GmbH Frauenweiherstrasse 14, D-91058 Erlangen, Germany. Jochen.Olig@3SOFT.de

2005-01-0779

Survey of Software Failsafe Techniques for Safety-Critical Automotive Applications

Eldon G. Leaphart, Barbara J. Czerny, Joseph G. D'Ambrosio, Christopher L. Denlinger and Deron Littlejohn
Delphi Corporation

ABSTRACT

A requirement of many modern safety-critical automotive applications is to provide failsafe operation. Several analysis methods are available to help confirm that automotive safety-critical systems are designed properly and operate as intended to prevent potential hazards from occurring in the event of system failures. One element of safety-critical system design is to help verify that the software and microcontroller are operating correctly. The task of incorporating failsafe capability within an embedded microcontroller design may be achieved via hardware or software techniques. This paper surveys software failsafe techniques that are available for application within a microcontroller design suitable for use with safety-critical automotive systems. Safety analysis techniques are discussed in terms of how to identify adequate failsafe coverage. Software failsafe techniques are surveyed relative to their targeted failure detection, architecture dependencies, and implementation tradeoffs. Lastly, certain failsafe strategies for a Delphi Brake Controls application are presented as examples.

INTRODUCTION

Delphi has been involved with development and production of numerous vehicle systems that may be classified safety critical with respect to their operation on the vehicle. Technological advances associated with these systems may require corresponding advances in techniques to help verify safe operation of these systems. One such technological advancement is the inclusion of electronics to aid in the control and safety aspects of vehicles. Such systems as Throttle-by-wire, Controlled Braking, Controlled Steering, and Supplemental Inflatable Restraint systems are commonly recognized as being integral to the safety aspects of the vehicle. These systems have advanced tremendously in their capabilities and application across a wide number of vehicles. As these types of systems continue to evolve, Delphi has been involved with helping to determine the proper methods and techniques for evaluating these systems and understanding the safety and reliability aspects at all levels of the design – be it within the whole system, a sub-system, or at a component level.

In the overall consideration of available techniques, the product teams need to understand the trade-offs between utilizing these techniques within their system hardware designs, and more and more commonly, within their software designs. With today's systems, a particular concern may be addressed by any of these design methods or by a combination of design methods. The software techniques and analysis methods described here do not represent an exhaustive list when compared to all techniques available within the broader embedded controls community, but they do represent sound methods that design teams may choose to utilize for their products.

ANALYSIS METHODS FOR IDENTIFYING NEEDED FAILSAFE TECHNIQUES

Software failsafe techniques are primarily developed to detect potential Electronic Control Unit (ECU) or peripheral hardware failures, thus enabling the system to initiate a transition to a safe state if any such potential failures occur. These techniques are important for safety-critical systems, because system developers must help verify that potential failures will not lead to any potential system hazards. There are many possible techniques to apply in helping to identify potential failures and needed failsafe techniques, but of these, fault tree analysis (FTA) and failure modes and effects analysis (FMEA) are the most commonly applied. In this section, we review these methods, as well as two others that we have found useful: preliminary hazard analysis (PHA) and fault coverage matrix.

A PHA is a high-level hazard analysis performed during the early stages of development to help identify the potential high-level hazards of the system, and to identify the potential risks of the high-level hazards. During PHA, the potential hazards are identified and described, potential worst-case mishap scenarios are determined, potential causes are identified, and the risk associated with the potential hazards and mishap scenarios is determined.

For potential high-risk items, the design team identifies ways to eliminate or mitigate the potential hazards. The mitigating actions become safety requirements for the system and may be implemented in hardware, in software, or in both. The safety requirements identified by the PHA are typically high-level, and as a result, don't necessarily identify individual failsafe techniques. Instead, these high-level requirements often provide direction on identifying an overall ECU integrity strategy. The strategy may include specific ECU hardware features to support high integrity operation and an initial list of software failsafe techniques appropriate for the targeted ECU integrity strategy. This initial list of software failsafe techniques would be primarily based on past development experience with similar ECU integrity strategies.

FTA is a deductive analysis method used to identify the specific causes of potential hazards, rather than to identify potential hazards. The top event in a fault tree is a previously identified potential system hazard, such as unwanted apply of the brakes. The goal of a FTA is to work downward from this top event to determine the potential credible ways in which the undesired top-level event could occur, given the system operating characteristics and environment. The fault tree is a graphical model of the parallel and sequential combinations of faults that could result in the occurrence of the top-level hazard. FTA uses Boolean logic (AND and OR gates) to depict these combinations of individual faults that can lead to the top-level potential hazard.

Each of the specific potential failures or classes of potential failures identified by a FTA is reviewed, and if necessary, appropriate hardware and software mitigation techniques are identified to reduce the likelihood that the top-level potential hazard will occur. One possible output of this activity is a list of software failsafe techniques needed to mitigate the identified potential hazards. While developing the fault tree, the initial list of software failsafe techniques, identified by the PHA, can be included in the analysis. Development of the fault tree can also identify additional software failsafe techniques that may be necessary as well as eliminating unnecessary techniques that add no value. If the initial list is based upon previously developed failsafe techniques, then the revised list will mostly likely be made up of well-understood techniques that require little development effort.

FMEA is an inductive analysis method used to:

- Identify and evaluate potential failure modes of a product design and document their system effects
- Determine actions or controls which eliminate or reduce the risk of the potential failure
- Document the process.

FMEAs are widely used in the automotive industry where they have served as a general-purpose tool for enhancing reliability, trouble-shooting product and process issues, and analyzing potential hazards.

Each of the potential failures or classes of failures identified by the FMEA is reviewed, and similar to FTA, appropriate hardware and software mitigation techniques are identified. Thus, a possible output of FMEA is a list of software failsafe techniques needed to mitigate those potential failure modes that may lead to potential system hazards.

Since FTA focuses on only those potential failures related to known potential hazards and FMEA considers all potential failures independently, it is probable that the FMEA will generate a larger set of potential failures to consider. However, the FTA may also contain potential failures or combinations of failures that are not identified by the FMEA process.

Another tool that may be used to determine necessary software failsafe techniques is a fault coverage matrix. The focus of this analysis is on determining the best set of controls (e.g., software failsafe techniques) to cover an identified set of failure classes (e.g., ECU hardware failure classes such as ALU miscalculations, and memory errors) such that adequate coverage is provided for each failure class.

The analysis can be performed using a spreadsheet similar to the one shown in Table 1.

Table 1: Fault Coverage Matrix

	Selected.	**Potential Failure 1**	**Potential Failure 2**	**...**	**Potential Failure N**
Potential Risk		*Critical*	*Moderate*		*Low*
SW FS Tech. 1	Yes	H	H		H
SW FS Tech. 2	No	M	H		N
...					
SW FS Tech. n	Yes	L	N		L
Coverage Metric		M	H		H

Known potential failures and associated risk levels are captured across the top of the spreadsheet. A list of known controls (e.g., failsafe methods) relevant to the potential failures is captured in the first column of the spreadsheet. The spreadsheet is filled out such that the coverage (e.g., High, Medium, Low, None) provided by each control for each of the potential failure classes is specified in the cells of the matrix. The controls that are currently selected for implementation are identified in the second column of the spreadsheet. The spreadsheet sums up the coverage level for each potential failure based on the coverage provided by each of the controls selected for implementation. The coverage metric depends on the potential risk associated with a potential hazard, such that high risk implies that higher coverage is required.

A significant advantage of a fault coverage matrix is that all failsafe techniques are considered at the same time, instead of individually, as is typically the case with FTA or FMEA. This global view helps verify that the best set of overall techniques is selected. Taken together, the PHA identifies the initial list of techniques, FTA and FMEA provide complementary detailed analysis to help verify that identified failsafe techniques cover all faults, and fault coverage matrix helps identify a final optimized set of failsafe techniques.

SOFTWARE FAILSAFE TECHNIQUES

This section provides information about different software failsafe techniques. For each technique a description, discussion of the major failures a given test will detect, and design limitations are given. In general, each of the techniques described may detect multiple types of failures. In some cases, the root cause of the failure may not be determined. However, detection of a failure is sufficient to trigger the appropriate failsafe action for the system. Eleven techniques are described in total. Table A1, found in the appendix, provides a comprehensive summary of these methods.

COMPLEMENT DATA READ/WRITE

Complement data read/write is useful for assuring the integrity of data being stored to memory (RAM). The data that is to be retained is stored as the actual value in one part of memory. The one's complement of the data is calculated and then stored in a separate part of memory. For example, if the data to be retained is 0xB136, then 0xB136 is stored in one part of memory, and 0x4EC9, the one's complement, is stored in a different part of memory. When the data is to be used, the two stored values are summed. If the summation is not zero, then a degradation in the memory has occurred.

Specific data storage errors that can be detected using this method include individual bits that are hard stuck to a value, and values that decay over time. Since this test is run prior to a value being used, even the long-term decay of values can be detected.

The major limitation on implementing the complement data method is memory size. If every data value is stored with its complement, the amount of RAM needed would double. To address the size requirements, data values can be partitioned into safety-critical data and non-safety-critical data. Only those variables identified as safety critical are stored as complements. In addition to the size limitation, if the complement values are stored in close physical proximity in memory, then a failure to a section of memory could cause both values to fail. A solution to this problem can be to store the complements in different physical locations, either on different pages of memory, if available, or in physically separated areas of the memory structure.

CHECKSUM COMPARES

The basic idea behind the checksum technique is to verify the integrity of program or calibration memory (ROM / Flash). The checksum method sums all of the data in memory, then truncates the sum to give the checksum value. The one's complement of the sum may be taken for easier comparison, however, two's complement or other formats are also common. When the checksum is verified, the data is again summed, and the original checksum value is added to the new sum of the data. A successful test results in zero. The length of a checksum can vary. In some applications words are used, and in other applications bytes are used.

A checksum test can be done at various times during program execution. One common time is at initialization. An initialization checksum test may be implemented in two ways. One of these is done mainly in ROM where the code will not change from cycle to cycle. In the original coding, the checksum values are calculated, stored, and then compared with the value calculated during initialization. For memory that will change from cycle to cycle, like EEPROM, a checksum can be calculated and stored at shutdown after all of the new values are written, then compared with the value calculated at initialization.

A ROM checksum may also be verified during runtime. This test may be done as a background task that takes many loop-times to test the entire code. Since verifying the entire ROM may take many loop-times, an error may persist for many control cycles before it is detected. To reduce the likelihood that an error in a safety-critical section of the code persists beyond a certain time, a separate checksum can be performed at a faster rate for the safety-critical code portions. This is called a fast compare.

The fast compare method detects failures in the ROM and EEPROM. Checksums are able to detect permanent errors in memory, such as flipped bits, and other changes in values. Since the calculation of the checksum requires the use of the ALU, this method also provides some fault detection coverage for the ALU.

The largest limitation related to checksum tests is time. During runtime, the background test may be too slow to detect all errors in time to prevent a failure from leading to a potential hazard. Therefore, the code may be partitioned into safety-critical and non-safety-critical code, and the fast compare method may be used for the safety-critical code sections. This method helps confirm that a fault occurring in the safety-critical code is detected fast enough to prevent a failure from leading to a potential hazard. Since the tests performed during runtime are executed in a background task, there is typically not a large burden on the CPU resources.

REDUNDANT CODING

Redundant coding, or dual path software, is a methodology to store critical code in the program memory identically in 2 different memory areas. During runtime, both sets of code are run using the same inputs and the results are compared. The two results should be the same (or within some specified tolerance), so that a difference indicates an error. One method to improve redundant coding is to store the different pieces of code on separate pages of program memory. This way, if there is a failure on a particular page of memory, the failure will not manifest itself in the second copy of the code.

This technique can detect changes in memory (either ROM, RAM or EEPROM), and intermittent faults in the ALU, such as faults caused by EMI.

The largest limitation for redundant coding is it doubles the amount of code and processor time needed to implement a function. Another limitation is only transient or intermittent faults in the ALU can be detected.

REDUNDANT "ORTHOGONAL" CODING

Orthogonal coding is a process where safety-critical code is implemented two times using different processes or processor resources for each implementation. Orthogonal coding may be done using a different algorithm for the calculation, using the same hardware resources, or using a different algorithm and different hardware resources. Since the orthogonal coding method relies on the use of different methods of calculations, the two results may not be exactly equal to each other. Therefore, when a comparison is done, a tolerance may be required to determine if the results match.

The major failures that can be detected by orthogonal coding are failures in memory or the ALU. Orthogonal coding may be effective at detecting a number of ALU failures depending on how it is implemented; for example, using different instructions of the ALU or using different hardware.

This orthogonal coding method may be memory intensive as it doubles the amount of memory required to implement a function. It may also double the amount of CPU time required. In addition, this method requires more development time since two different algorithms have to be created and maintained throughout development. Finally, the tolerances must be validated to help confirm that they are not too constrained, thereby leading to false positives, and that they are not too unconstrained, resulting in false negatives (i.e., no failures are identified, when a failure actually exists.)

Redundant "Orthogonal" Coding Example: MAC vs ALU

An Arithmetic Logic Unit (ALU) in parallel with a Digital Signal Processor (DSP) peripheral is one example of the redundant "orthogonal" coding technique appropriate for providing coverage of arithmetic intensive control algorithms. The ST Microelectronics ST10 processor features a Multiply and Accumulate (MAC) DSP peripheral in combination with the ALU within the CPU core. The configuration of the CPU core and MAC peripheral within the ST10 microcontroller is shown in the block diagram given in Figure 1.

The MAC and ALU have different instruction sets for mathematical operations. Several operations are possible within the MAC, however the unit is designed to optimize multiply, accumulate, and digital filtering operations.

A strategy has been developed for use within brake control applications to perform fixed point multiply instructions in parallel both in the ALU and in the MAC for each usage of the multiply operation. The products from the MAC and ALU are compared and should always be equivalent. A detected error indicates an issue in one of the peripherals. The basic data flow of this strategy is shown in Figure 2.

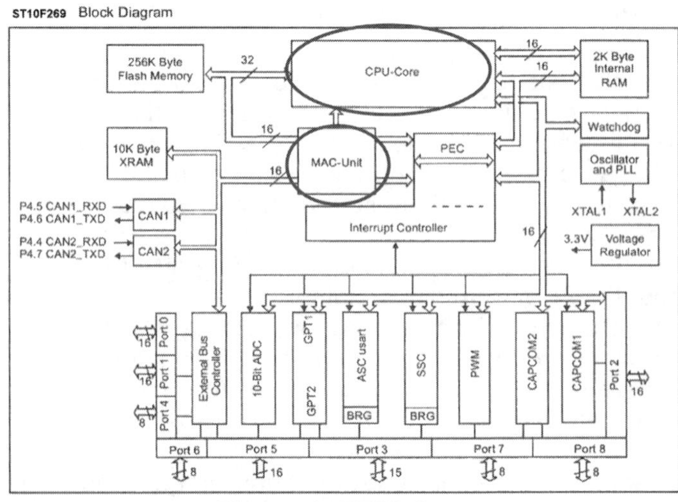

Figure 1: ST10 Core

The coverage of this strategy may be evaluated by identifying the number of multiplication operations used within an algorithm per execution loop. The MAC vs ALU compare will occur for each multiplication operation or macro that is executed. For a typical embedded controls fixed-point implementation, several types of multiplication macros may be used. A coverage matrix may be developed to identify which functions make use of certain multiply operations and how many multiplies are required per execution loop. Failsafe coverage is provided for the ALU during each usage of the MAC vs ALU compare. The redundant coding technique may be combined with other techniques to maximize the overall system failsafe coverage.

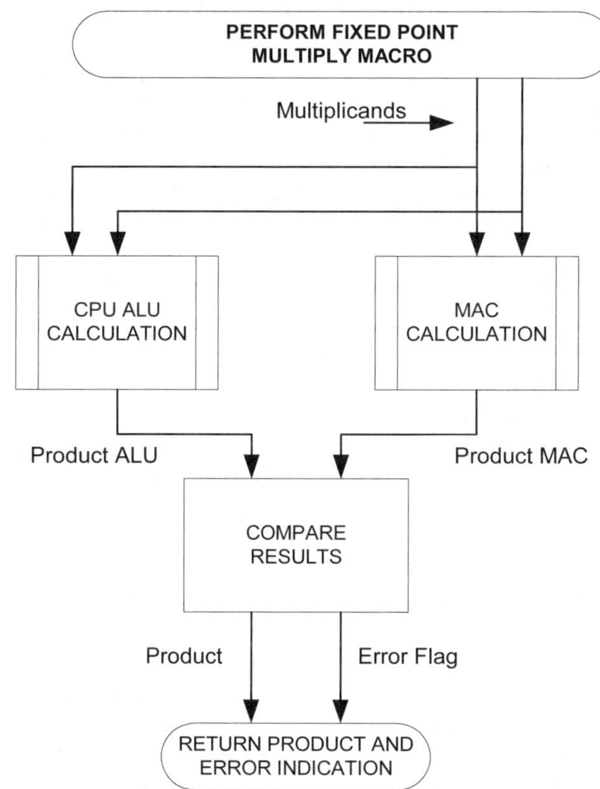

Figure 2: MAC vs ALU Compare

PROGRAM FLOW MONITORING

Program flow monitoring (PFM) or process sequencing, is a technique to include a specific seed (initial key value) and key (final value/result) process within the program function to assure that the program execution has completed the major parts of the program, and that it has completed them in the correct order. Typically, the program being monitored will contain specific update points throughout the program flow. The update points are specific functions that operate on a parameter being supplied to them. This parameter may be referred to as the key value. At regular update points, or at the end of the program execution, the resultant key value is compared to the pre-calculated acceptable value. If a mismatch is discovered, then a program execution error has occurred. PFM may be implemented in two ways: application independent or application dependent.

The application independent method works by having a PFM update point between each function call. A consequence or side effect of this approach is that the point can be updated without the function having actually been called. However, this approach also provides greater flexibility and opportunity for re-use. For example, assume there are common functions A, B, C, and D across applications, and that for a particular application only functions A and D are needed. Using the application independent implementation allows the program flow monitoring code to be used without modification across both applications.

The application dependent implementation is more tightly integrated into the program execution. The actual PFM update points are coded within the functions themselves. This approach helps assure that all of the functions are called and that they are called in the correct order.

If specific functions need to be called within a certain window of time in relation to other functions, the application independent or application dependent methods of PFM may be enhanced to help verify the correct timing requirements. This enhanced method is known as time dependent PFM. This method helps confirm not only that the functions are called and that they are called in the correct order, but also that they are called within the required window of time. This task is accomplished by requiring the PFM update to occur at a specific time during the program execution. A flow chart showing the differences in the implementation is shown in Figure A1 of the appendix.

At each update point in the program execution, a function is executed to update the PFM variable. Various algorithms can be utilized for updating the key value. A simple version of an update function is:

PFM_key=PFM_key+PFM_ID
PFM_key=PFM_key*PFM_ID

- PFM_key is the value carried throughout the loop that becomes the key
- PFM_ID is the ID of the update point. If there were four update points, then they would be numbered 1 to 4.

Therefore, as long as all of these updates or entry points, are run in the right order, the key will be correct. It is also beneficial to have multiple seed and key pairs so that the test cannot be passed merely because the key value is stuck at the correct value, or just never rewritten.

There are multiple ways to design PFM. One of these ways is with a single microprocessor design. The microprocessor can check the value of the PFM key at the end of a loop. This is equivalent to having the microprocessor check itself, and thus, not all failures related to PFM will be detected. Another design strategy uses an asymmetric microprocessor. An illustration of PFM data flow for an asymmetric design is shown in Appendix Figure A2. The monitoring microprocessor can query the main microprocessor every other loop for the PFM key. Since the monitoring microprocessor is an independent piece of hardware, it will be able to pick up most failures related to PFM. Another design strategy can be used if the controller is part of a distributed system. One of the other controllers in the system can take the place of the monitoring microprocessor in querying the main controller.

PFM can detect process errors such as the program skipping an important part of the program calculation. The extent to which program flow monitoring can detect errors is dependent on how many update points there are in the program and where the updates occur within the program (i.e., within the functions, or between function calls).

The biggest limitation for program flow monitoring is the amount of processor time consumed by the technique. If there are many PFM updates within a program performing a number of calculations, the amount of processor time PFM requires can be significant. Consequently, there is a trade-off inherent with PFM; the deeper the updates or thread depth, the better the detection ability of the method, but the more processor time is required.

Another design decision is which type of PFM to use. The benefit of an application independent approach is increased flexibility; the PFM code may be used over multiple applications. However, the coverage is limited and provides less confidence that a skipped function will be detected. Using an application dependent approach allows for better coverage and more confidence that a skipped function will be detected, but requires more maintenance as different applications may require a different set of functions to be used requiring all of the PFM routines to be reworked for each application. The time dependent approach used in conjunction with the application independent or application dependent methods helps assure that the program is flowing within the desired time frame, however, this method may not be feasible for applications with interrupts, since the interrupts may disrupt the timing.

RAM TESTS

RAM tests may be performed at initialization or during system runtime. A RAM initialization test is typically a set of tests to determine if the RAM of the microprocessor is functioning correctly before any application program tasks are started. On initialization, the RAM is tested to make sure that it can be written to and that it can hold a value for a short period of time. This is accomplished by writing a specific value or pattern to all RAM locations and then reading it back and comparing the read values to the written values. This operation is done twice using different values each time. Typically, the hex numbers 0xAA and 0x55 are used. These numbers are chosen so that all bits will have a '1' and then a '0' written to them. Other methods, such as "walking ones" method, where a single bit is systematically written and cleared are also commonly used.

There are two major failures of RAM that can be detected with this test: bits stuck as either a '1' or a '0', and decaying RAM cells. Some decaying faults may still pass depending on how long it takes the value to decay.

RAM tests may also be performed during system runtime. This test method is similar to the test at initialization, where a specific pattern is written and read to RAM values. The runtime test must be designed as to not interfere with normal operation of the system since test values written to RAM, if read and used by the application during the test, could cause improper operation. This can be accomplished by performing the test during a background task or disabling other system resources while performing the test. The runtime test will take longer to check all RAM than the test at initialization. During runtime, RAM must be checked in small segments incrementally per application loop in order to minimize impact on system resources.

POWER UP/DOWN MEMORY WRITE TESTS

Power up/down memory write tests are used to determine if a controller has shut down properly. Information critical to the proper operation of the system may need to be stored in nonvolatile (NVM) or "keep-alive" (KAM) memory between ignition cycles. Typically, this information is stored during the shutdown sequence of the controller.

During controller initialization, a specific data pattern is written to a NVM location (e.g. 0x55). During the shutdown sequence of a controller a different pattern is written to the same NVM location (e.g. 0xAA). A compare of the memory location is made at the next initialization sequence. If the data matches the data pattern written at the previous shutdown (e.g. 0xAA) then the test indicates that the controller had shutdown properly. A data read of the initialization pattern (e.g. 0x55) indicates that the controller had not gone through shutdown properly.

The power up/down sequence is effective in identifying when the controller has been abnormally reset or when system power is lost prior to completion of a shutdown sequence. Safety-critical processes or data may need to be reinitialized upon detecting an abnormal shutdown sequence. The design of a power up/down memory sequence must be coordinated with the overall power moding and software task execution of the controller design. In addition, NVM or KAM hardware resources must be present in the hardware design.

TEST CASES

Test cases or test vectors are used to exercise the instructions of the ALU to detect ALU faults. Independent hardware is required to perform the test cases. Either an asymmetric processor or a secondary processor in a distributed system can be used to perform test cases.

The ALU operations are tested using an algorithm written to access all of the ALU instructions used in the main program. This algorithm is called by the independent hardware using a seed and the output is compared to an output key. The seed is the initial starting value to be input into the test case calculation. There are multiple seed values. After all of the test calculations are completed, the output should be equal to the key that is appropriate for the given seed.

The algorithm can be split into multiple parts. Each part can be called at different times during a loop execution or the different parts may be called over multiple loops. Ideally the algorithm will cover all of the instructions of a microprocessor, but since the instruction set may be large (over 200 instructions for a Motorola HC12), including only those instructions used in the program is generally acceptable.

There are two ways to implement test cases. One is to have a sequenced query, such that the order of the seeds is the same every time the program is run. Another method is to have a random query. In the random query, the monitoring unit has the ability to vary the order of the test cases.

The major types of ALU failures that can be detected using test cases include register failures and individual instruction failures.

The test case method requires independent hardware to perform the test cases, so it can only be used in a design that will have either a monitoring unit or multiple processors as in a distributed system. Since the majority of safety-critical automotive software is written in higher level languages such as C, C++, Modula, etc., it is useful to know which low-level instructions are used to implement the high-level instructions, so these instructions can be adequately tested. If the program changes and new instructions are utilized, then the test cases will need to be modified to include the new instructions.

COMPUTER OPERATING PROPERLY (COP) WATCHDOG TIMER

A watchdog timer is a device that helps assure that the microcontroller is operating properly. A watchdog timer may be internal or external to the system. It is a mechanism that begins to count down once it has been initiated. The device needs to be toggled / refreshed by software within a certain period of time to prevent a microcontroller reset. For an internal watchdog timer implementation, the counter and refresh circuitry are built into the microprocessor chip. For an external implementation, the counter and refresh circuitry are external to the microprocessor chip. An external watchdog timer is typically built using an external RC circuit to perform the timing function. The external timer is toggled or refreshed via an output line from the microprocessor, and a reset is triggered via a reset input to the microprocessor in the event the timer function reaches the pre-set watchdog time.

Watchdog timers are useful for detecting failures such as timing delays, infinite loops, and hung interrupts. Depending on the implementation (i.e., the toggle values or refresh mechanism), watchdog timers may also trigger a reset if the program skips certain steps; i.e., if the toggle values are sent out of order.

If a watchdog is to be used, a key decision is whether an external or internal watchdog should be selected. External watchdog timers are more robust than internal watchdog timers in that they can detect more failures. For example, an internal watchdog timer will not continue to function, and thus will not reset the microprocessor, in the event that the system clock malfunctions. This could happen if the power is reduced to a level that does not cause the micro to reset, but that causes it to cease to function properly. In this situation, an external watchdog would still trigger a reset of the micro. However, external watchdogs require additional hardware which must be designed to interface with the micro. Application and customer safety requirements, as well as other failsafe design methods must be considered in determining which type of watchdog timer is feasible.

COMPONENT/PERIPHERAL TESTS

Software techniques may be used to determine if a specific hardware peripheral or driver is operating properly. For example, a controller output may be driven during a specific initialization sequence and monitored for correct operation. Another example is the comparison of data from two redundant peripherals, where an invalid comparison within a magnitude and/or time tolerance will indicate a failure.

Component/peripheral tests are specific to a hardware design. Often, redundant components are needed for a sufficient failsafe strategy. The design strategy may use additional tests beyond a compare of two inputs to isolate the exact component that is faulty. Synchronization and detection tolerance issues must be taken into account to help assure that the test is accurately identifying failed components.

REASONABLENESS TESTS

Reasonableness tests are methods in which a simplified model is developed for a control variable. The simplified model receives system inputs and determines an estimate of the expected output value. The actual value is compared to the expected value. If the two values differ by some pre-specified tolerance, then it is assumed that there is an error somewhere in the process.

These tests are high-level process checks. They do not detect a specific fault, but rather detect a problem in a calculated output value. They detect that the actual value is out of range with respect to the expected or estimated value. In general, this method provides a sanity check of the overall process.

This method is application dependent; therefore the limitations of this method depend on the specific application.

EXAMPLE REFERENCE: DELPHI ELECTRIC BRAKE SYSTEM 3.0 DESIGN

This section illustrates the application of certain hazard analysis and software failsafe techniques as applied to the Delphi Electric Brake System 3.0 design.

DELPHI ELECTRIC BRAKE 3.0 ARCHICTECTURE

Appendix Figure A3 shows a system mechanization of the Delphi Electric Brake (DEB) 3.0 system. The DEB 3.0 system is a hybrid braking system that contains 2 electric calipers, one on each rear wheel of the vehicle, while the front brakes maintain a conventional hydraulic apply system. The electric calipers receive commands from the brake system controller via a CAN link. The system controller receives all the inputs to the system, and provides the controls for the front hydraulic modulator as well as the processing for all the higher order functions (Anti-Lock Braking, Traction Control, Electronic Stability Control, etc.).

Figure A4 in the appendix shows a mechanization for the controller that is attached to the electric caliper. This controller receives commands from the system controller and provides the positioning of a brushless motor to actuate the rear brake. In addition to the control of the motor/actuator, a park brake mechanism is included in the brake that is controlled by the electric caliper controller. For design space and cost imperatives, each rear controller contains a single microcontroller. It was important during the design of this system that the safety implications of independent electronic control of each rear brake be managed appropriately.

DEB SYSTEM AND SOFTWARE ANALYSIS

Several of the system analysis methods discussed throughout this paper have been applied to the development phase of the DEB controller. Specifically Preliminary Hazard Analysis (PHA) and Fault Tree Analysis (FTA) were used to identify potential hazards and causes of these potential hazards for the DEB system. A coverage matrix was developed to consider which software failsafe techniques would be appropriate to detect potential controller failures that have the possibility of leading to hazards.

Table A2 in the appendix provides an example portion of the PHA. Failure to provide acceleration consistent with driver intent has been identified as a high level potential hazard within the DEB system. Several possible mishap scenarios are described which could result from the occurrence of this potential hazard. One item listed as a cause for such a potential hazard is that of controller failure.

To investigate effectiveness of strategies to detect possible controller failures a coverage matrix was developed. Potential severity and likelihood to occur were assessed for various types of potential controller failures such as memory failures, CPU failures, software processing errors, interface failures and communication failures. Proposed software failsafe techniques were considered for each controller failure category to determine if the coverage is strong (probable) or weak (less effective). Items identified as strong coverage would be considered as part of the failsafe software design. Table A3 shown in the appendix illustrates an abbreviated example of a portion of the coverage matrix.

FTA was used to identify causes of potential hazards of the rear electric brake system. A false apply of the DEB was analyzed to determine its possible causes. A DEB false apply was defined as too much caliper apply. The goal of this analysis is to work the graphical fault tree down to sufficient levels of detail that would identify undesirable causes for failures within the software design. Once these areas were identified, the appropriate software failsafe techniques were applied in order to diagnose these conditions and take the appropriate failsafe action.

A simplified example of a FTA diagram for the DEB 3.0 brake system is shown in Figure 3. It should be noted that this could be expanded to several more levels of detail, however, a general example is shown here. Several causes are identified as factors that given a potential failure could lead to a DEB false apply. Items represented by a transfer symbol (triangle) represent areas that may be further detailed on a separate page of the Fault Tree. Two areas identified as functional elements that could cause a false brake apply are improper behavior of the CAN transceiver and associated software, and improper behavior of the DEB controller software in its entirety.

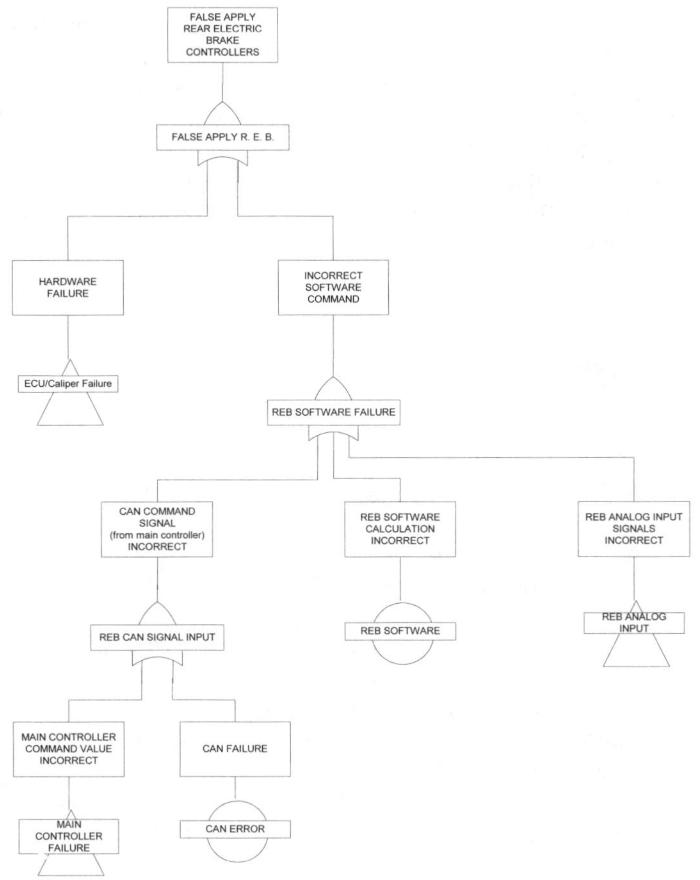

Figure 3: DEB False Apply Fault Tree Analysis

To mitigate the risk of these elements causing a false brake apply, Program Flow Monitoring and Reference Model Reasonable Tests are applied to the design. The following sections describe the tests that were applied to the DEB system.

PROGRAM FLOW MONITORING EXAMPLE

Given that DEB 3.0 is a distributed system, the PFM strategy for this application was to use the multiple controllers to crosscheck program flow. As the two rear controllers run the same software, the primary check is between these two controllers. Every other loop, a rear controller will query the other rear controller to request the key. A rolling seed is used, such that if the key received by the second controller is correct, the controller then sends the next seed. If the second controller thinks there is a problem, instead of shutting down both of the rear controllers, and thus shutting down the rear brakes, the controller will send back a message indicating that the key is wrong. At this time the system controller, which monitors all PFM communications, compares the key of the controller with what it believes the key should be. If the system controller does not agree with the key value, then the controller being tested will fail PFM and appropriate action will be taken. If the controller finds that the key is correct, the controller that initiated the query will fail PFM. The flow of events is summarized in Figure 4.

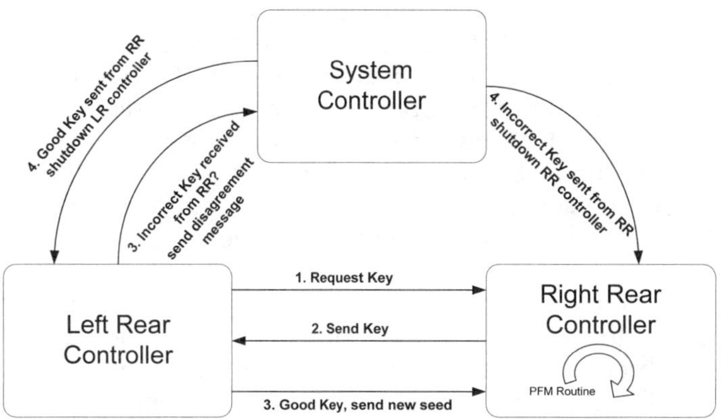

Figure 4: PFM Communications for DEB 3.0

The algorithm for PFM implements test cases to integrate the two techniques. Prior to this application the only experience with program flow monitoring known within Delphi had been using an asymmetric design. Therefore, to work out the exact procedure of the program flow monitoring, a computer simulation was created. The simulation consisted of three computers connected over a CAN link with the CAN traffic being monitored. Each computer simulated a different controller in the system. The goal of the simulation was to develop the messages that were needed to implement PFM and make sure that the idea would work over a CAN bus. To make the program easier to work with, the algorithm implemented for this test was a simple addition and multiplication routine instead of a comprehensive test algorithm.

The simulation demonstrated that the process could detect bit errors as long as they occurred in the correct loop. Since the key is only checked every other loop, it is possible for bit errors, such as a stuck bit, to go undetected by this test. Permanent bit errors were detected during the testing. The simulation program was also able to demonstrate the capability of PFM to detect program execution out of its intended sequence.

FORCE TO POSITION REFERENCE MODEL

For DEB 3.0 system, the output position of the motor is the physical variable that is controlled. The desired position of the motor is based on the force command given by the system controller. The entire process entails the performance of numerous calculations, thus, there are many places for errors to occur. To provide broad coverage of the entire process, a reasonableness test was developed for the position output.

The reasonableness test is set up so the system controller takes its force command and uses a non-linear lookup table to find the desired position. Next it uses a set of second order transfer functions to estimate the actual output of the motor. The transfer functions are used to model the dynamics of the motor. The output of these transfer functions is then compared to the actual motor position sent by the rear controller.

The system controller is only able to get an estimate for the motor position, so the comparison needs to have a tolerance. This tolerance needs to be based on the worst part of the model, which is a step-input for the force. Since the slope of the position curve is so high, a small error in time creates a large error in position. The output of the simulation and the error is presented in Figure 5.

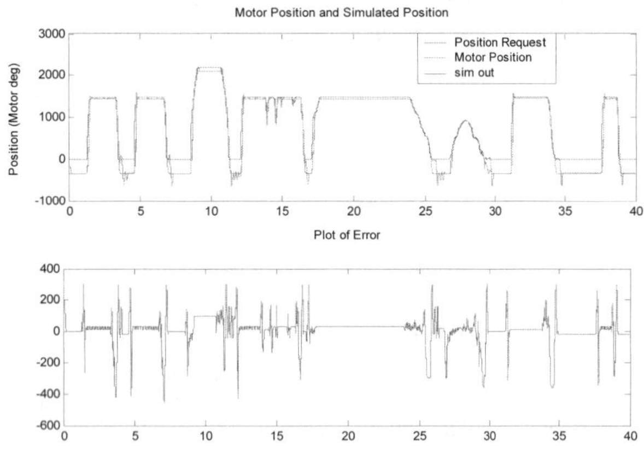

Figure 5: Plot of actual and simulated position with a plot of the error

From the simulation it was concluded that significant errors in position would be caught prior to these errors leading to a potential hazard.

CONCLUSION

The development of advanced safety-critical automotive systems is driving the development of new tools and processes to help verify that these systems operate safely and that they are reliable and predictable. For these systems, product safety needs to be considered up front and addressed as part of the overall design process. This paper summarizes many of the available techniques to help analyze and implement a safe embedded system design. Based on our application experience, the analysis and failsafe techniques described here may be considered sound and beneficial. These techniques will continue to evolve as new technological challenges are recognized and addressed.

REFERENCES

1. Delphi Secured Microcontroller Architecture SAE# 2000-01-1052
2. A Safety System Process For By Wire Automotive Systems SAE# 2000-01-1056
3. A Comprehensive Hazard Analysis Technique for Safety-Critical Automotive Systems SAE#2001-01-0674
4. Diagnostic Development for an Electric Power Steering System SAE# 2000-01-0819
5. The BRAKE Project – Centralized Versus Distributed Redundancy for Brake-by-Wire Systems SAE# 2002-01-0266
6. Delphi ETC Systems for Model Year 2000; Driver Features, System Security, and OEM Benefits . . . SAE# 2000-01-0556
7. Standardized EGAS Monitoring Concept Ver 1.0
8. SW FMEA Methodology Presentation
9. B. J. Czerny, J. G. D'Ambrosio, Paravila O. Jacob, et. al. *A Software Safety Process for Safety-Critical Advanced Automotive Systems,* Proceedings of The International System Safety Conference, August 2003.

CONTACT

Eldon G. Leaphart, Engineering Manager – Diagnostics, Communications & System Software / Controlled Brakes, Delphi Corp., 12501 E. Grand River, MC 483-3DB-210, Brighton, MI, 48116-8326 Phone: (810)-494-4767, Fax:(810)494-4458 email: eldon.g.leaphart@delphi.com

APPENDIX

Table A1: Summary of Software Failsafe Techniques - Criteria Selection Matrix (Part 1)

	Memory Failures	CPU Failure	Software Processing Errors	Interface (I/O) Failures	Communication Failure	System Failsafe
Complement Data R/W Duplicate storage of variables as data and complement value. Complement values are checked for correctness prior to data usage	✓ Memory intensive. Will require duplicate memory allocation for each parameter. Also increases CPU time load for complement check routine.	✓ Generally targeted toward memory failures, however, miscompare could indicate CPU failure to access data correctly	X n/a	X n/a	X n/a	Possible input to fail action decision
Checksum Compares Add sections of memory together to get the checksum value. When checked memory readded and sums compared.	✓ Could be slow to catch a fault depending on method chosen: Continuous background (slower) vs Fast compare. Fast compare requires specific placement of data.	X n/a	X n/a	X n/a	✓ Checksum methods used to verify serial data integrity between processors / controllers	Possible input to fail action decision
Redundant Coding Run a duplicate copy of a section of code and compare the answers prior to using.	✓ Memory intensive. Requires twice as much memory to implement a function.	✓ Doubles the amount of processing time to implement a function	✓ Incorrect result could indicate software processing error within a single path	X n/a	X n/a	Possible input to fail action decision
Redundant Orthogonal Implement a section of code using a different method or processor resources. Run both sections of code and compare answers prior to using.	✓ Memory intensive. Requires twice as much memory to implement a function.	✓ May doubles the amount of processing time to implement a function. Could be hardware or micro architecture dependent.	Incorrect result could indicate software processing error within a single path	X n/a	X n/a	Possible input to fail action decision
Program Flow Monitoring Uses a thread imbedded in important functions to assure all of the functions were called and in the right order. Implies asymetrical or symetrical hardware architecture.	X n/a	✓ Thread algorithm should be designed to have minimal effect on CPU load. Assumption that CPU failure may impact normal sequence of code execution.	✓ Effective method for identifying some synchronization code issues. Coverage of execution sequence is a function of thread "depth".	X n/a	✓ Depending on architecture employed, could indicate issues with interprocessor synchronization	Possible input to fail action decision
Initialization Test RAM or ROM test at initialization	✓ Fast check of memory resources during initialization. Application must take into consideration system startup timing requirements	X n/a	X n/a	X n/a	X n/a	Possible input to fail action decision
Power Up/Down R/W Write a pattern to memory for proper shutdown, and then write a different pattern at start-up	✓ Keap-Alive (KAM) or Non Volatile (NVM) memory required as part of design.	✓ n/a	✓ Effective method for showing that orderly shutdown was obtained. Should be coordinated with overall system moding strategy.	X n/a	X n/a	Possible input to fail action decision
Test Cases Give the controller a set of calculations to test the ALU. Implies asymetrical or symetrical hardware architecture.	✓ Provides some coverage of memory locations assuming that test case memory access failure would impact computed result.	✓ Test cases must be designed to consume a minimal amount of time relative to application. Test cases should be representative of methods / machine instructions used throughout application. Difficult to guarantee 100% coverage.	X n/a	X n/a	✓ Depending on architecture employed, could indicate issues with interprocessor synchronization	Possible input to fail action decision
COP Watchdog Timer that will cause a reset if it is allowed to zero	X n/a	X n/a	✓ Effectice in identifying software / task execution errors. Analysis required to choose watchdog frequency relative to system failure requirements.	X n/a	X n/a	Possible input to fail action decision

Table A1: Summary of Software Failsafe Techniques - Criteria Selection Matrix (Part 2)

	Memory Failures	CPU Failure	Software Processing Errors	Interface (I/O) Failures	Communication Failure	System Failsafe
Peripheral Test Software routine designed to monitor output	X n/a	X n/a	X n/a	✓ Dependent on hardware architecture of system. Implies checking redundant inputs or monitoring output feedback. Synchronization of comparison or tolerances must be considered	X n/a	✓ Typically includes mechanism to provide actuator failsafe for system
Reasonableness Test Uses a simplified model of the controlled variable to assure that the variable is in a reasonable area.	X n/a	X n/a	X n/a	✓ May need to determine regions of operation where model is valid prior to usage. Apply to variables driving controlled output	X n/a	Possible input to fail action decision

Table A2: Example Section - Delphi Electric Brakes 3.0 Preliminary Hazard Analysis

Concept									Projected System					
Num.	**Hazard**	**Major**	**Minor**	**Accident Scenario**	**Causes**	**Sev.**	**Lik.**	**Haz. Risk**	**Hazard Controls**	**Causes**	**Sev. w/ Cntl.**	**Lik. w/ Cntls**	**Hazard Risk of System**	**Recommendations and Comments**
HAZ-01.0	**Failure to Provide Desired Acceleration**	Vehicle does not provide acceleration consistent with driver intent						High					Moderate	
HAZ-01.1		*Total Loss*	Park brake fails to release	Driver attempts to drive vehicle with locked park brake, pulls out into traffic resulting in a minor collision	Bad PB Switch (D), wiring, connectors, or failed controller (D); failed PB motor (D)	III	E	Low	Fault Tolerant PB Switch; Actuator Diagnostics; Driver warning		III	E	Low	
HAZ-01.2		*Total Loss*	Failed interlock signal prevents driver from shifting into gear when desired	Driver unable to move vehicle after emergency stop at intersection or railroad crossing, vehicle hit by on coming vehicle or train	Failed brake determination (D)	I	E	Moderate	Redundant & diverse sensors w/ diagnostics; Driver Warning	Failed Pedal Travel sensor (E)	I	E	Moderate	
HAZ-01.3		*Degraded*	Reduced accleration capability due to undesired apply of braking system	Brake system inadvertantly applied while vehicle stopped, driver attempts to pull out into traffic, resulting in severe collision	Bad PB switch (D), common mode controller fault (D)	I	D	High	Redundant & diverse sensors w/ diagnostics; Fault Tolerant PB Switch; Driver warning;	Bad PB switch (mechanically faulted) (D), common mode controller fault (D)	I	E	Moderate	
HAZ-01.4		*Degraded*	Reduced accleration due to undesired traction control request	Vehicle does not accelerate as expected during a passing manuever; Vehicle unable to accelerate through an intersection	Improper Wheel Speed signals (D), specific controller failure (E)	II	D	High	Command voting; Redundant & diverse sensors w/ diagnostics; Watchdog; Fail silent components; Driver Warning	Improper Wheel Speed signals (D), controller failure (E)	II	E	Moderate	
HAZ-01.5		*Unwanted*	Undesired acceleration (e.g., negative vehicle acceleration (roll back) on incline due to loss of hill hold capability)	Vehicle is stopped on a hill, driver releases brakes to depresses the gas pedal, vehicle rolls back into another vehicle	Loss of higher level functions (controller failure (D))	III	E	Low	Command voting; Redundant & diverse sensors w/ diagnostics; Watchdog; Fail silent components; Driver Warning	Loss of higher level functions (controller failure (E))	III	E	Low	

Table A3: Coverage Matrix for DEB Controller

	Used?	Memory Failures	CPU Failure		Software Processing Errors
Potential Severity					
Likelihood to Occur					
Safety metric Code					
Program Flow Monitoring	yes	weak	strong	. . .	strong
Internal watchdog	yes		weak	. . .	strong
External watchdog	no		strong	. . .	strong
Flash checksummed during runtime and startup	yes	strong	weak	. . .	
Safety critical code fast checksum	no	strong	weak	. . .	
Software well written and verified	yes			. . .	strong
Key ROM locations tested at start-up	no	strong	weak		
.					
.					
.					
EEPROM checksummed at startup	yes	strong	weak		
Algorithm using complement values for safety critical values	yes	strong	weak		

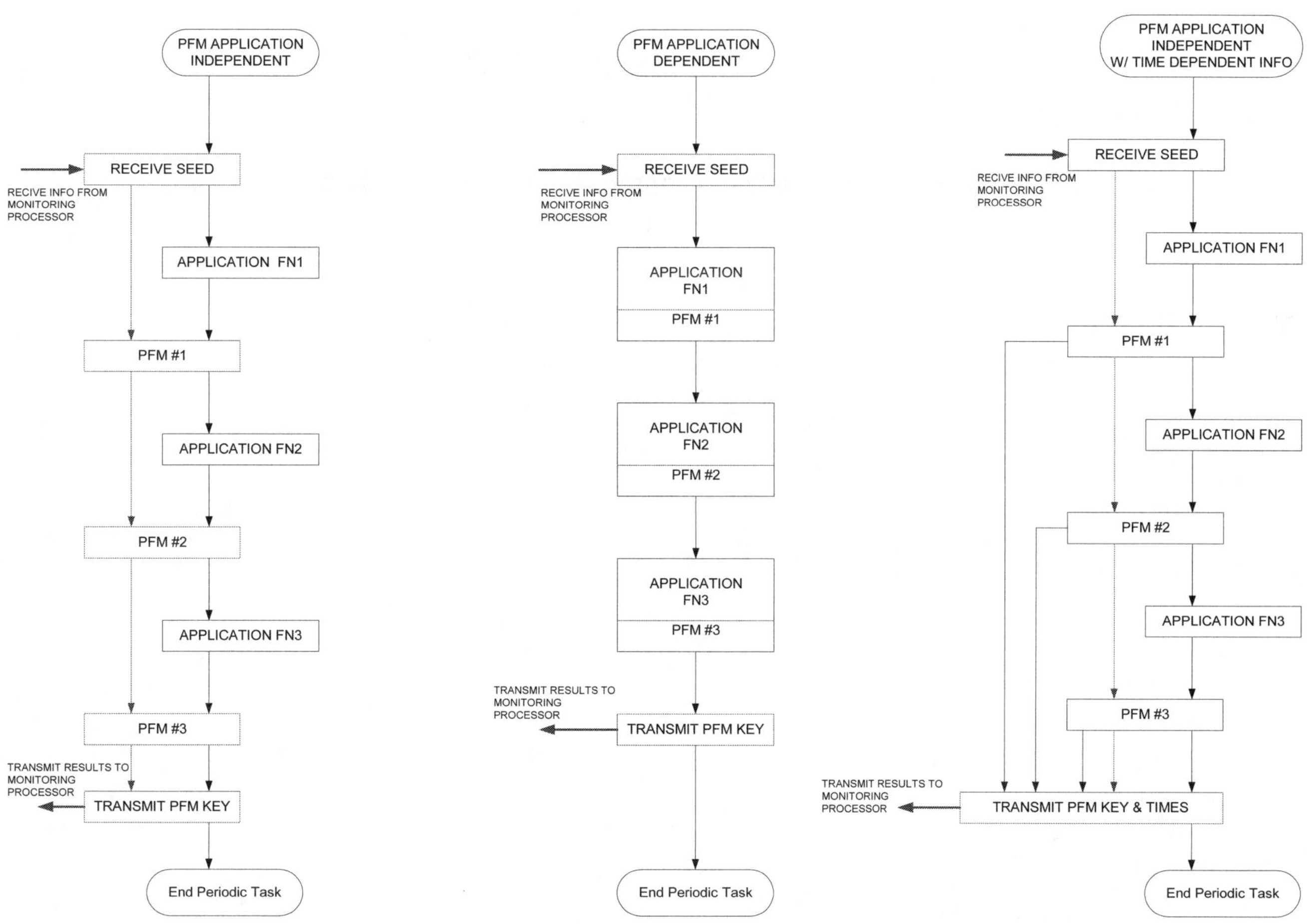

Figure A1: Example of Program Flow Monitoring Data Flow

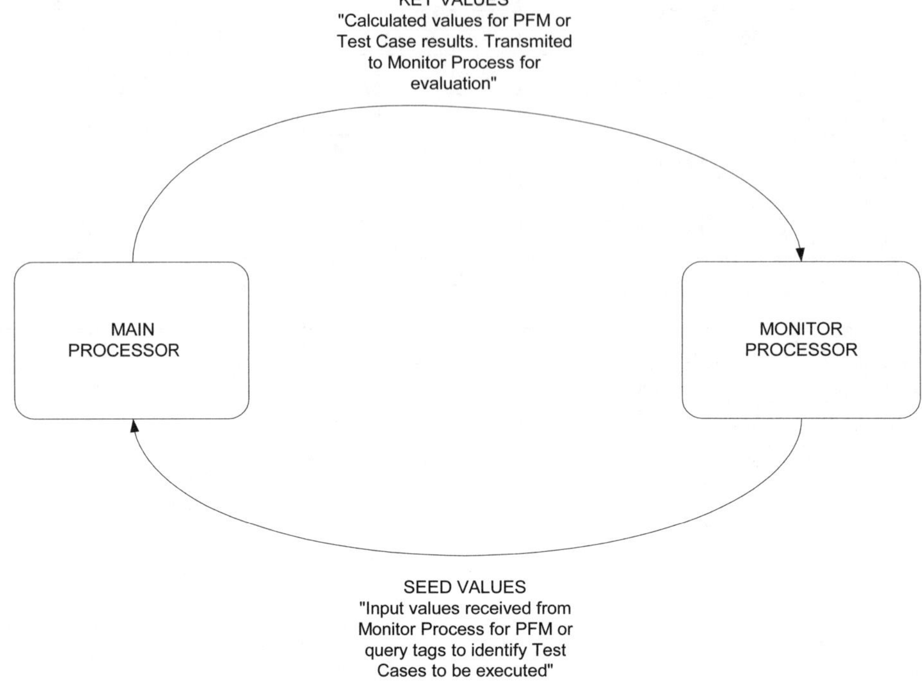

Figure A2: Example of Program Flow Monitoring Data Flow

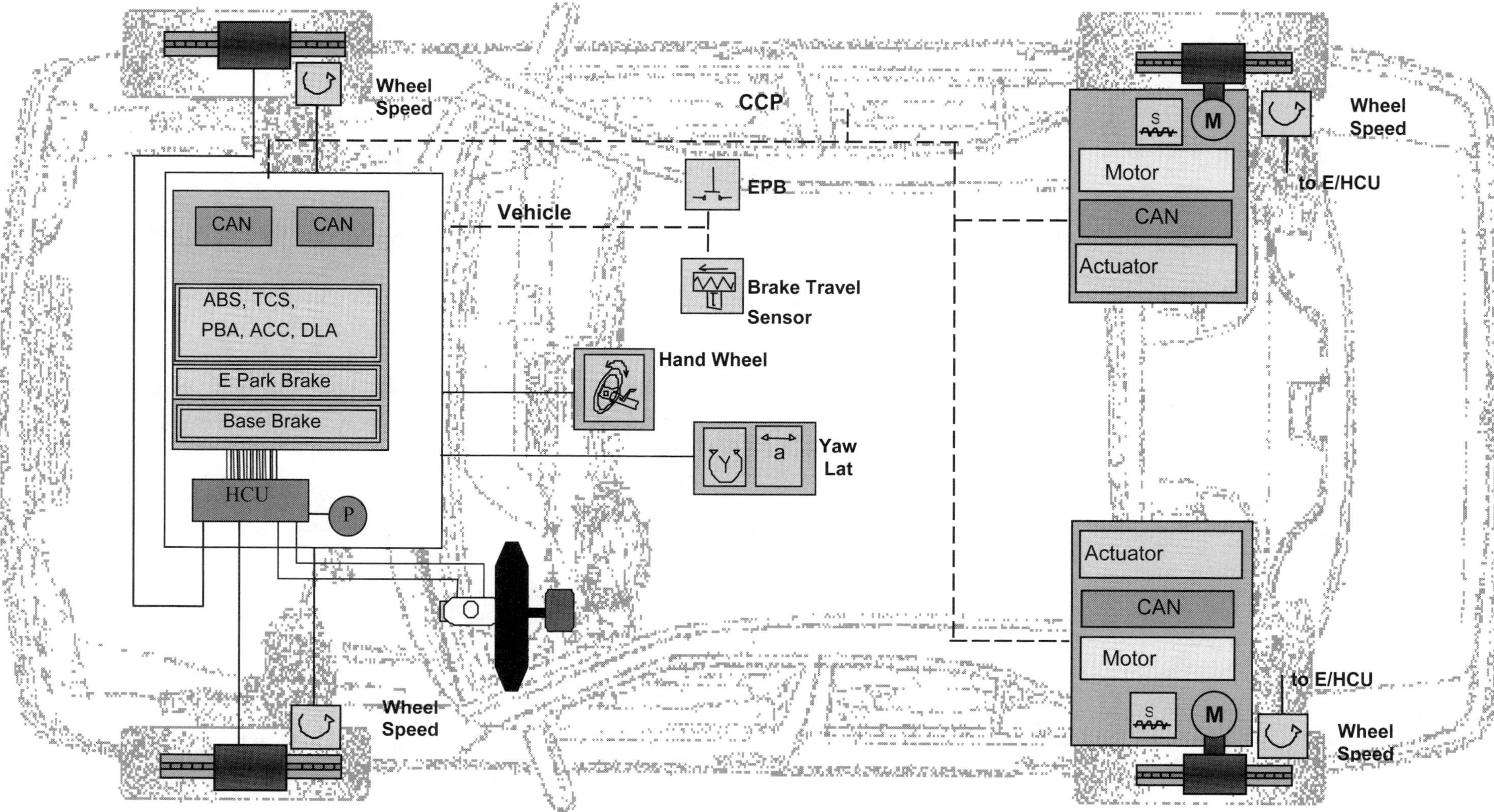

Figure A3: Delphi Electric Brakes 3.0 System Mechanization

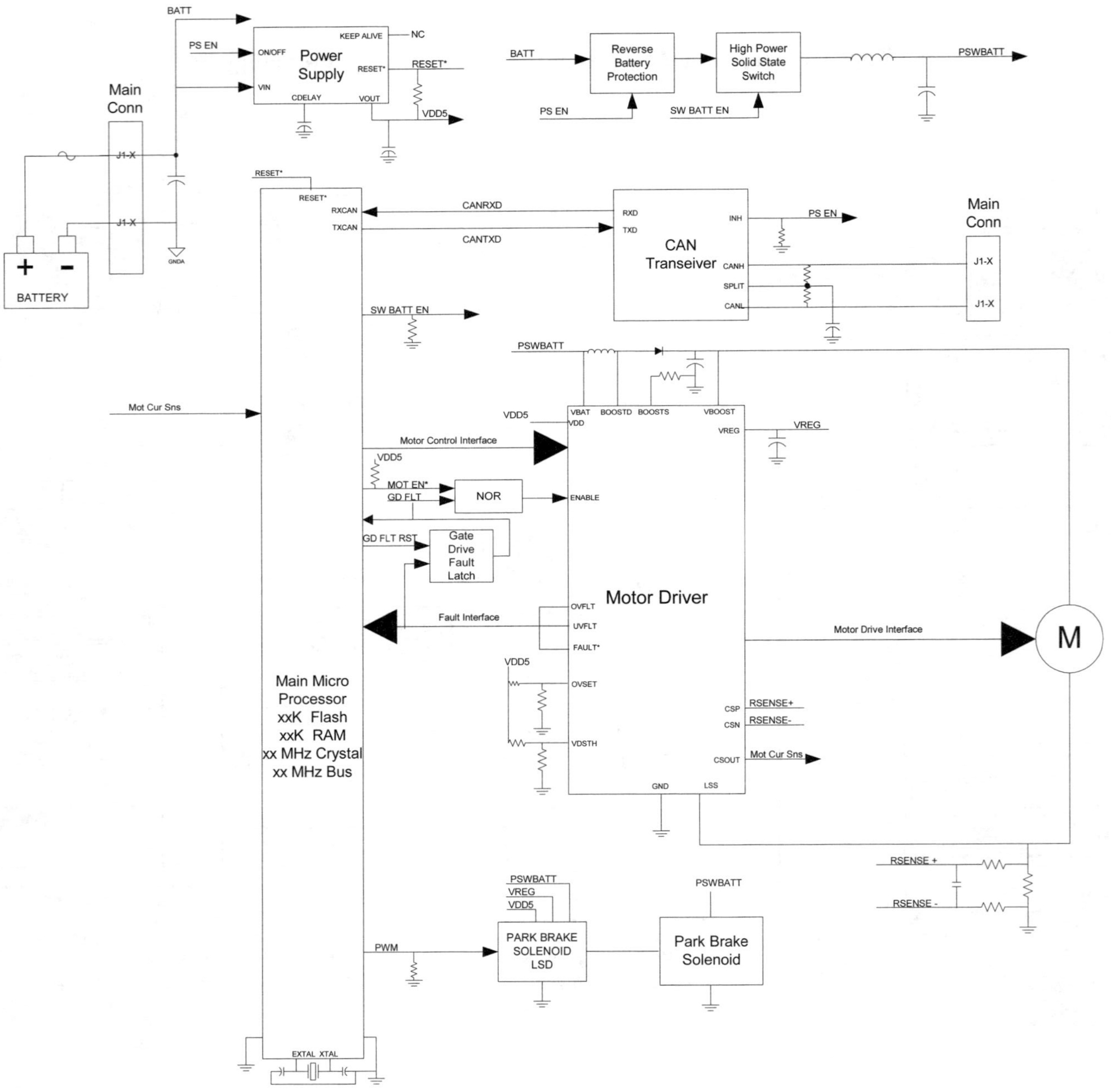

Figure A4: Delphi Electric Brakes 3.0 Controller Mechanization

2005-01-0327

A Software Component Architecture for Improving Vehicle Software Quality and Integration

Brendan Jackman
Centre for Automotive Research, Waterford Institute of Technology

Shepherd Sanyanga
TRW Automotive

ABSTRACT

It is estimated that the software which monitors the health of an ECU now takes up about 60% of the total ECU software code to monitor, diagnose and announce the problems an ECU may have during its normal or abnormal operational modes. It is the abnormal operation of the system which is the constant problem for vehicle OEMs because this side of the system operation is not easily defined or simulated. The integration of Failure Mode and Effects Analysis (FMEA) to normal design is now becoming central to tackling these issues head-on, such that FMEA is now used as part of the integration process. Having between 10 and 20 different ECUs on a vehicle network still leaves the integration of software from many different suppliers a difficult task. The main issues are incompatible interfaces, misunderstandings of vehicle OEM internal software requirements and a general lack of time to carry out rigorous and methodological integration testing at the Data and Physical Layers before proper vehicle production commences.

The vehicle OEMs have attempted to alleviate these problems by specifying common ECU infrastructures, providing standard outsourced software modules to their suppliers and by taking part in standardisation efforts such as OSEK/VDX and AUTOSAR. However due to location, perception and language differences, this has not reaped the benefits that were being sought and has created a new set of problems.

This paper describes an object-oriented component-based approach to vehicle software development to try to better solve the above issues. The work of the Object Management Group (OMG) is examined, and it is shown how the Object Request Broker (ORB) concept can be applied to existing real-time embedded automotive software systems to ease integration and simulation. The Object Request Broker concept has been successful in enabling reusable software components in the commercial software world. An ORB architecture supports integration and reuse of legacy software by separating component interfaces from their definition.

INTRODUCTION

Figure 1 depicts the typical information flow between a vehicle manufacturer and Tier 1 supplier during the development of an ECU subsystem. Due to the fact that early-on during the development of a vehicle the OEM is still unclear on what the final vehicle architecture will be in terms of requirements, the requirements will continuously evolve as the program progresses. This tends to be problematic for suppliers, since they need a static view of the vehicle architecture in order to give realistic system quotations and time scales for their ECU development. To manage this situation, most suppliers take a snapshot of requirements and quote based on that version of requirements. However this still does not mitigate the suppliers' costs in the development phase, so budget over-runs are common.

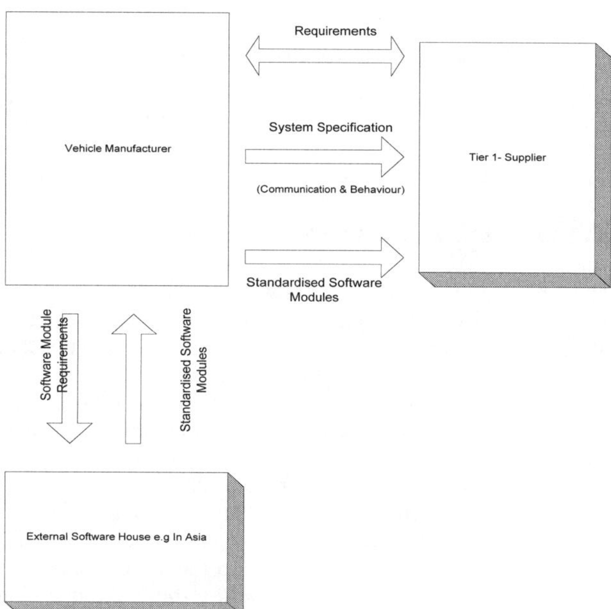

Figure 1. Information Flow and Interaction between OEMs and Supplier.

These budget overruns happen because most suppliers follow a methodological approach to their ECU system design process. This is usually called the 'V' cycle mode of ECU development, and is shown in Figure 2. It is after the architecture partition phase that suppliers identify where the standardized OEM software modules are going to be co-located in their subsystem design. It is at the module testing stage that inconsistencies between operational requirements and the OEM supplied modules are first seen. This also includes problems related to interface links to the supplier's proprietary code. To resolve these conflicts and to implement these amended requirement changes, suppliers end up expending extra resources to ensure that all parts of the design are updated with these final agreed code changes. In most systems with the OEM the cost implication of these changes can be potentially under-estimated in the agreed piece cost of the ECU subsystem.

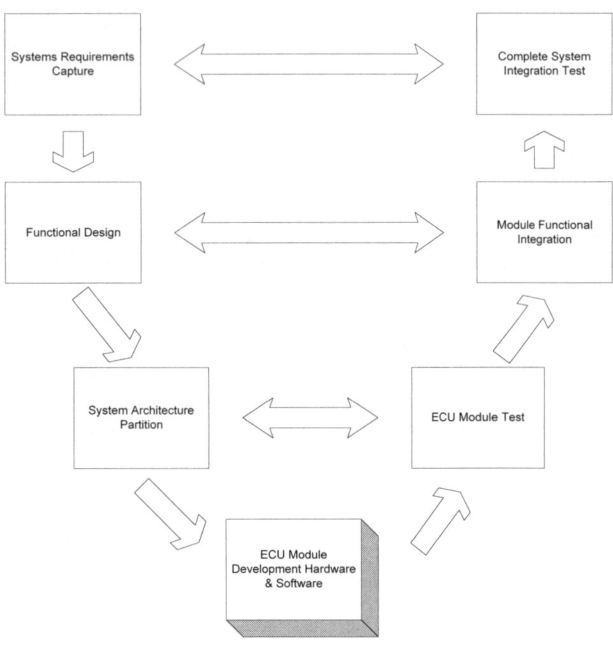

Figure 2. "V Cycle" ECU Subsystem Development Process.

SYSTEM INTEGRATION

The vehicle OEM usually builds what is termed a bench car. This is the electrical & electronic architecture representation of the final vehicle with all the electrical components that will exist on the real vehicle. This bench car integrates all ECU subsystems on every network communication on the target vehicle platform. This is the first time that the vehicle manufacturer is able to see how each ECU on the vehicle will interact with its neighbour and hence serves as an a early warning system to program teams of vehicle system problems. This bench car is very important, especially for suppliers, since it is used to develop the ECU subsystem software for the different ECUs before the pre-production prototype vehicles become available, as well as provide a platform for suppliers to really test their software in a real vehicle environment.

Due to the complexity of the vehicle architecture network and its interaction with its operating environment, it is here where the majority of vehicle system-wide problems are detected and solutions are sought. These problems may take the following form: Interface compatibility issues due to distributed functions; timing and data latency problems caused by incorrectly coded OEM supplied standardized software modules; harness connectivity issues; data corruption issues due to current and voltage distortion slew rates; ECU software configuration issues due to ECUs with the wrong level of software functionality on a network; vehicle ignition start-up and shut-down issues due to incorrect implementation of network management procedure requirements and ignition after-run requirements.

AUTOMOTIVE SOFTWARE INITIATIVES

The rapid increase in software functionality and additional ECUs being added to vehicles brings additional complexity to the system integration process. System integration can be eased by managing the complexity of the distributed vehicle control system. A common approach to the management of complexity has traditionally been standardization, the use of interchangeable parts that provide compatible interfaces and services. OEMs have usually standardized aspects such as the choice of microprocessors, ROM/RAM size, development tools and programming languages to simplify ECU application development and facilitate software reuse between ECUs and vehicle variants. ECU component standardization has also meant big cost reductions for suppliers.

Various industry-wide attempts at standardization have been initiated over the past decade with varying degrees of success. The widespread use of Matlab/Simulink as an application modeling and development tool has been a large factor in the proliferation of vehicle software functions. Matlab/Simulink allows engineers to model new applications graphically and therefore more productively than using conventional programming languages. Matlab/Simulink is well supported by Hardware in the Loop (HIL) tools and automatic code generators, allowing production ECU code to be generated directly from the application models. Furthermore, Simulink models can be easily shared and reused between applications.

The use of high- and low-speed CAN as a standard vehicle network has allowed for the easy exchange of data between ECUs that were previously interconnected with OEM proprietary serial point-to-point protocols such as ISO9141 (equivalent to K-line), UBP (UART-Based Protocol). Higher levels of vehicle control are now possible by exchanging data between several existing subsystems. For example, Vehicle Stability Control (VSC) systems depend on the interactions between Traction Control, ABS and Engine Management systems for successful operation.

In 1993 some major German automotive companies formed the OSEK group [1] with the purpose of defining a common software standard for ECU operating systems and associated network interfaces. The idea was to specify an open system standard that software vendors can comply with. OSEK essentially provides a set of microprocessor-independent services to ECU application software. Services include a real-time task scheduling system, interrupt handling, Alarm/Event handling and an inter-task communications mechanism that allows tasks on the same or different ECUs to exchange data. OSEK has been widely adopted in Europe and has significant support from independent software vendors. OSEK is also addressing the need for fault-tolerant and time-triggered services in subsequent versions of the standard.

The biggest weakness in the OSEK concept has been the lack of hardware device driver standards. A lot of ECU application code is required to interact with microprocessor peripherals, and this is still the biggest differentiating factor among microprocessors. So although OSEK goes a long way towards increasing the portability and reusability of ECU application software, the onus is still very much on the software designer to decouple the device handlers from the application code. The success with which this is done determines the level of application portability and reuse.

The ASAM group [2] has been successful in defining a set of standards for implementing measurement, calibration and diagnostic systems. The CAN Calibration Protocol (CCP) and its successor XCP is widely used for calibration and flash programming of vehicle ECUs. Standards such as these help the system integration process by providing a single data exchange format for calibrating and diagnosing all ECUs in a distributed vehicle control system.

The International Standards Organization (ISO) has provided a set of standards for retrieving diagnostic data from ECUs across K-Line, LIN and CAN networks. The most widely used standards are KWP2000 (ISO 14230, 1-4) and Diagnostics on CAN (ISO 15765, 1-4).

The latest standardization initiative is AUTOSAR [3], founded in 2003, which is made up of some of the largest OEMs and a whole host of Tier-1 suppliers. The goal of AUTOSAR is to establish an open standard for automotive Electrical/Electronic architecture. AUTOSAR intends to provide a complete run-time environment for ECU application software that will provide complete hardware independence. This run-time environment will be compatible with and make use of established automotive standards such as OSEK and CAN. One of the most significant aspects of the AUTOSAR proposal is the development of software interface standards for all functional aspects of a vehicle. For example, there will be a set of predefined software interfaces for powertrain control functions. This will ensure a high level of compatibility between different suppliers' systems and simplify the interchange and integration of these software systems. The first validation tests for AUTOSAR are expected in 2006.

These standardization efforts have brought the advantages of simplification and cost reduction to many OEMs and suppliers. However, the integration of co-operating ECUs on a distributed vehicle network is still a major issue in terms of network message interpretation, bus loading, and proper handling of system failure modes. The AUTOSAR standardization effort holds much promise, but widespread agreement and tool support for the standard, if successful, cannot be realistically expected until the end of the decade. In the meantime OEMs and suppliers cannot stand still in the face of increasing vehicle software complexity driven by customer demand and hence must look to alternative approaches to contain the integration problems.

AUTOMOTIVE SOFTWARE ARCHITECTURE

One of the main causes of integration problems has been the piecemeal development of system ECUs in isolation from one another. The vehicle control systems are usually partitioned into a set of networked ECUs early on in the vehicle design cycle before the complete software system requirements are known and properly understood. This early decision on hardware configurations has a detrimental constraining effect on the resulting software architecture. In effect, the choice of hardware predetermines the software architecture, since it influences the functional partitioning across the available ECUs and therefore dictates the network communications requirements. The emphasis is currently on hardware module design rather than software function design. While the hardware design costs have to be restrained because of the large volumes involved, there is a growing realization among OEMs that software costs are more significant than hardware costs. What must be considered is not just the software development cost alone, but the total software cost across the life cycle of the vehicle. This should include test and calibration costs, reprogramming/flashing costs, warranty costs and the potential cost of poor customer satisfaction caused by software failures. Surveys increasingly show that the majority of vehicle breakdowns are caused by software or electronic faults, not mechanical failures. The goal therefore must be to achieve a high level of robustness in the vehicle software/electronic systems.

What many OEMs lack is a software architecture for their vehicles. While they may have an Electrical/Electronic (E/E) Architecture, this is not quite the same thing. In the first instance, E/E architectures are not completely portable between different vehicle variants because of differences in body types and vehicle features. If software functions are closely coupled to individual ECU hardware, and a specific ECU cannot be fitted to a vehicle variant, then all associated software functions are lost to that vehicle variant. Usually some of the software functionality is required, which the supplier then tries to integrate onto a different ECU with resulting cost and integration problems. If the software architecture is completely independent of the hardware architecture, then none of these problems would arise. The OEM would just choose the subset of software functions to be delivered on the vehicle variant and partition the functions across whichever vehicle ECUs are available. For this scheme to work there must be a software infrastructure available to decouple the software functions from the ECU hardware and vehicle network. The remainder of this paper outlines ideas for such a software infrastructure based on existing software standards.

OBJECT-ORIENTED DEVELOPMENT

Most automotive software is developed using structured or procedural approaches (usually written in C) which view the software as a collection of separate code functions that share some common data. These code functions tend to be tightly coupled to the shared data and to each other so that any requirements change has a significant impact on the structure of the software.

Object-Oriented development is the process of developing software systems by considering the system to be made up of a set of co-operating *objects*. An object contains a set of data values called attributes that describe the object, together with a set of methods or services that can be invoked on the object.

Objects invoke the methods of other objects to carry out the functionality of the system. The overall system functionality is thus shared among the various objects in much the same way that work is shared among the employees of a company. Objects are a natural, intuitive way to view software systems, particularly systems that interact with real world objects. Software objects can be developed to represent each real world object being manipulated. For example, an engine control ECU could have a separate object for each fuel injector being controlled. Each fuel injector object would have attributes detailing the injector firing angles and duration, plus methods to fire and switch off the injector. The methods are in effect the responsibilities of the object. It should be noted that an object represents a specific instance, so that a fuel injector object represents a specific fuel injector. If an engine ECU is controlling four fuel injectors, then it would have four Fuel Injector objects, one for each physical injector. Object-Oriented methodologies use the concept of a class to generalize about objects, so the fuel injector class would represent the common traits (attributes and methods) of all fuel injector objects. Another way of looking at it is that classes represent the static structure of the system, whereas objects provide a dynamic, run-time view.

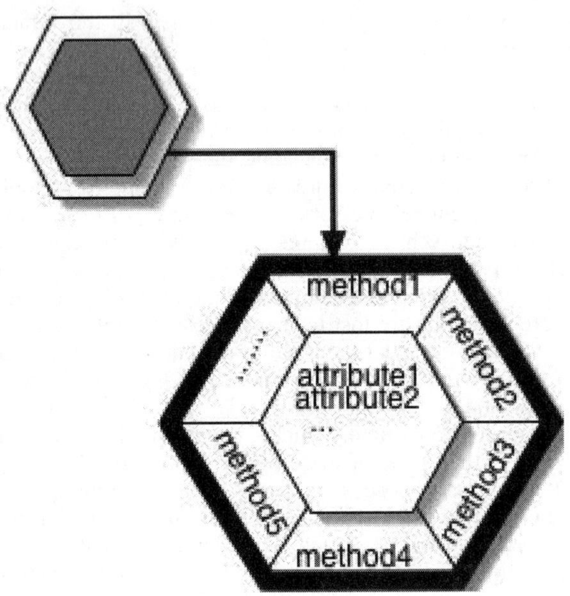

Figure 3. Object Structure and Method Invocation

The Unified Modeling Language (UML) is widely used for object-oriented modeling of systems. The use of object-oriented modeling techniques for automotive real-time systems has been investigated by Volvo [4] and DaimlerChrysler [5]. A detailed treatment of UML and object-oriented software development can be found in the many books available on the subject, such as the one by Craig Larman [6]. Figure 4 shows an example of how the fuel injector class would be modeled in UML.

Fuel Injector
startAngle : float duration : int currentlyOn : Boolean
int fire(duration : float) int stop() Boolean isOn()

Figure 4. UML Class Representation.

ENCAPSULATION

Objects support the idea of encapsulation or information hiding. This means that an object's attributes are not directly accessible by other objects. An object's attributes may only be read from or written to by the methods of that object. This provides a complete separation of interface from implementation, allowing the data types of attributes and the implementation algorithms of methods to be modified without affecting client objects that invoke an object's methods. As long as the method interface remains unchanged the client object remains unaffected. This powerful mechanism allows software objects to be easily upgraded without impacting the rest of the system. The objects are very much self-contained and loosely coupled with one another.

INHERITANCE

When defining systems in terms of objects it is quickly realized that many objects are very similar to other objects. The concept of inheritance allows one class to be specified in terms of another class. The new class is known as a subtype of the existing base class and only additional attributes and methods over and above those in the base class need to be specified for the new class. This is a powerful technique for describing variants in ECUs and vehicles.

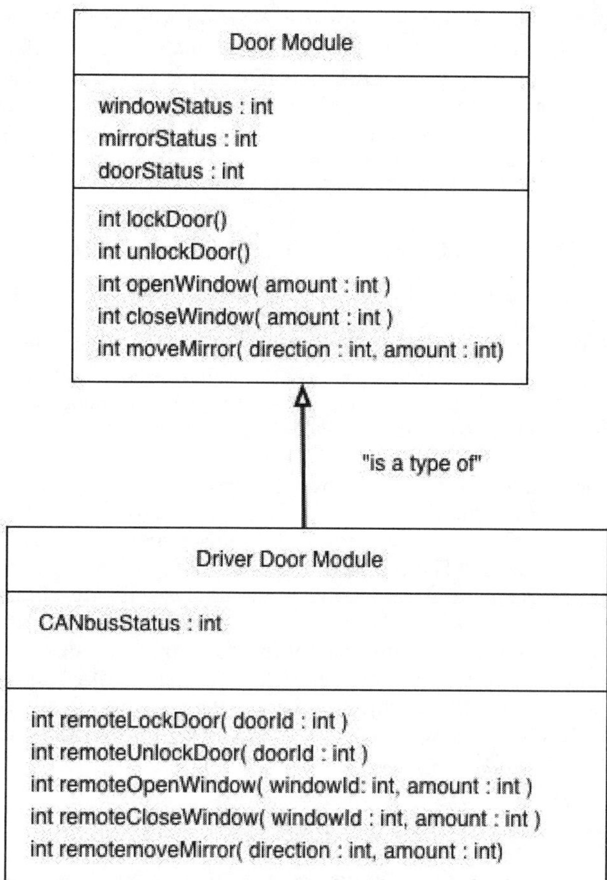

Figure 5. Inheritance between UML Classes.

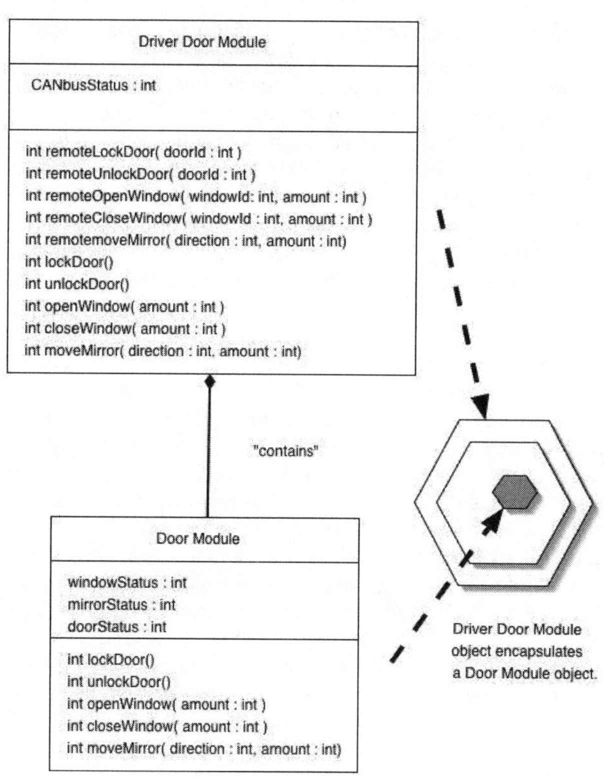

Figure 6. Aggregation between UML Classes.

In Figure 5 UML notation is used to show that a driver's door module is a specialization of a standard door module. Inheritance is an easy way to reuse software objects. Only the additional functionality needs to be added to the subclass. In the Driver Door Module example, when developing the Driver Door Module class just the additional functionality over and above the Door Module class needs to be implemented.

AGGREGATION

Aggregation is the process of using existing objects in the implementation of new objects. It is an alternative to inheritance for reusing objects. Aggregation is similar in concept to an assembly-subassembly type structure. Aggregation has the advantage over inheritance as a reuse mechanism because the reused objects are completely encapsulated within the new object and are not exposed to any client objects. With inheritance the methods of any inherited class may also be called by client objects, even if that is not the intention. Figure 6 illustrates the use of aggregation in UML, where the Driver Door Module class contains an instance of a Door Module class. Notice how the Driver Door Module class now needs to have a more comprehensive interface, since it no longer inherits the interface of the Driver Door Module class.

POLYMORPHISM

Polymorphism is a feature of object-oriented systems that allows the same method name to be used in more than one class of object. For example, the method *stop* could be used with various classes such as Motor, Engine, Fuel Injector and so on. Polymorphism allows the name *stop* to be used with all of these classes. The correct piece of code is executed based on the class of object in question.

Polymorphism has a number of advantages for the software developer. First of all, meaningful names can be given to methods regardless of whether the name has already been used. Secondly, the developer can generalize methods in the base class of an inheritance hierarchy without knowing in advance what subtypes may be defined. This makes the resulting objects more reusable.

SOFTWARE COMPONENTS

Component-based software extends the object-oriented concept to software applications as a whole. It is at a higher level of granularity, such that a single software user function exhibits the same characteristics as a software object. That is, it has certain well-defined interfaces that can be invoked, and it is possible that multiple instances of the software component exist. It should be emphasized that even though a software component has an object-oriented behavior it does not have to be implemented using an object-oriented programming language. The internal implementation could be in a language such as C or even Simulink code such as S-functions.

The Object Management Group (OMG) [7] is an industry consortium whose goal is to define a set of interfaces for interoperable software. It has been in existence since 1989 and has specified the Common Object Request Broker Architecture (CORBA) that defines a high-level facility for distributed computing. CORBA uses an object-oriented approach to hide the differences in programming languages, operating systems and object location in a distributed application. It provides an open distributed computing environment that facilitates component integration and reuse.

The central component of CORBA is the Object Request Broker (ORB) which works as a software bus that transparently relays object requests across the various implementation technologies. Application objects interact only with the ORB in a client-server fashion. A client object locates the required server object, invokes operations on it and is notified of the occurrence of any errors through a standard exception handling mechanism. The ORB is responsible for routing the request from the client object to the server object and returning any results. CORBA can handle both synchronous and asynchronous requests. A component may act as both a client and server simultaneously. The ORB implementations include code stubs and skeletons known as Object Adaptors that map the object interfaces to specific implementation languages. Figure 7 shows the structure of a CORBA-based software application.

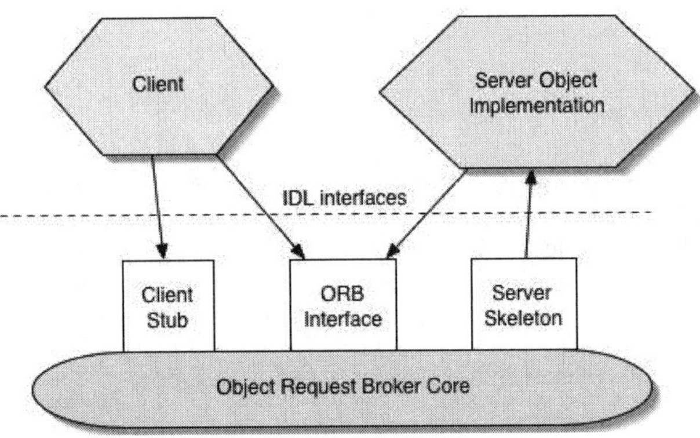

Figure 7. CORBA Distributed Application Structure.

The OMG has defined a range of object interfaces for commonly used services such as Object Location and Naming, Event Notification, Persistence, Concurrency, Transactions etc. These are known as CORBAservices and are provided by ORB vendors. CORBAservices are similar to many of the services provided by operating systems. There is also a set of object standards called CORBAfacilities that define functionality that would be common across many types of application. Examples are Printing, Task Management and User Interface. There are also standards known as CORBAdomains that define objects that would be useful in specific vertical markets. Some of the domains currently addressed include Air Traffic Control, Telecommunications, Data Acquisition and Computer Aided Design.

The key to integrating application objects is the specification of standard interfaces using the Interface Definition Language (IDL). The IDL is the mechanism that separates interface from implementation, and it provides for communication between objects that is independent of programming language, hardware platform, networking protocols and physical location.

INTERFACE DEFINITION LANGUAGE (IDL)

The IDL is a notation for defining application programming interfaces. It is independent of programming languages and defines the boundary between client code and object implementations of services. The IDL is a fundamental part of OMG standards and provides platform-independent definitions of software interfaces.

The OMG has defined standard language bindings for the IDL that enable an automatic translation of IDL specifications to programming languages such as C, Java, C++, Ada etc. The IDL is a pure specification language and does not dictate the implementation of the software object. The object may be implemented as a library function on the same computer as the client object, or may even be implemented on a remote networked computer. As long as the client and server objects adhere to the IDL specifications, communication will be successful. The following is an example of IDL for the door module objects.

```
module VehicleDoorSystems {

   interface Door_Module {

       // attribute declaration
       attribute unsigned long windowStatus;
       attribute unsigned long mirrorStatus;
       attribute unsigned long doorStatus;

       // possible exceptions that may be
       // raised when executing methods

       enum Faults { DoorFaultDetected,
             mirrorFaultDetected };

       // method declaration
       unsigned long lockDoor();
          raises ( DoorFaultDetected );
       unsigned long unlockDoor()
          raises ( DoorFaultDetected );
       unsigned long openWindow (
          in unsigned long amount );
       unsigned long closeWindow (
          in unsigned long amount );
       enum Direction {UP, DOWN, LEFT, RIGHT};
       unsigned long moveMirror (
          in Direction directionToGo,
          in unsigned long amount )
          raises ( MirrorFaultDetected );
   }

   // define Driver Door Module to be a subtype
   // of the basic Door Module

   interface Driver_Door_Module : Door_Module {

       // additional attributes to basic door
       // module
       attribute unsigned long CANbusStatus;

       // additional methods
       enum DoorType { PASSENGER, DRIVER, ALL };
       enum WindowType ( PASSENGER, DRIVER, ALL,
             BACKLEFT, BACKRIGHT };
       unsigned long remoteLockDoor(
             in DoorType door )
          raises ( DoorFaultDetected );
       unsigned long remoteUnlockDoor(
             in DoorType door )
          raises ( DoorFaultDetected );
       unsigned long remoteOpenWindow (
          in WindowType windowed,
          in unsigned long amount );
       unsigned long remoteCloseWindow (
          in WindowType windowed,
          in unsigned long amount );
   }
}
```

The example illustrates the use of enumerated types in IDL to define allowable values for items such as door types and windows types. Using enumerated types in the IDL definitions provides greater clarity on the expected usage of parameters. IDL also has an exception handling mechanism that allows methods to raise exceptions when an operational error occurs. The client application is notified of server or ORB exceptions synchronously through the calling interface.

The use of IDL provides a hardware-independent interface between the software functions and thereby simplifies the task of integrating software components. The quality of the IDL designs is very important for ensuring that the components are interoperable with one another and are widely reusable. For example, although the IDL will define the number and types of method parameters, the client and server objects must both agree on the semantics of how the parameters are used. CORBA and IDL do give the immediate advantage of hardware independence for the vehicle software architecture. Even ECU device drivers could be given an IDL object interface to make them part of the software architecture, free to be implemented on the appropriate ECU. The principles of high cohesion and loose coupling between IDL-defined objects will ensure greater reusability. Design patterns for use with object-oriented technology are well documented [6].

AUTOMOTIVE OBJECT REQUEST BROKER

The CORBA standards grew out of a need to provide seamless interfaces between the heterogeneous technologies used to implement enterprise-wide applications. The use of the internet and client-server computing paradigms as a means of implementing distributed applications motivated the design of the platform-independent CORBA architecture. CORBA has been hugely successful in the enterprise computing domain, and it has delivered on the promises of reusability, portability and simplified integration.

The CORBA specifications were originally designed with network servers and a PC environment in mind, but this does not mean that the concepts are not applicable to real-time distributed computing applications. Indeed, there is a subcommittee of the OMG tasked with the application of CORBA to real-time applications. The result is two additional specifications; the Minimum CORBA specification and the Real-Time CORBA specification. The Minimum CORBA specification describes the basic features needed to implement CORBA on resource-limited systems such as embedded systems. The Real-Time CORBA specification describes an implementation of CORBA on systems where end-to-end request timing constraints must be met and where real-time task scheduling policies are used. Although these specifications are a step in the right direction for showing how CORBA can be used in automotive applications, currently available real-time ORBs such as Borland's VisiBroker-RT [8] seem to be limited to the real-time Linux, Windows CE and VxWorks operating systems. As such they are not directly usable with OSEK systems that are typically used on vehicle ECUs. They might however be useful for vehicle infotainment and telematics applications where more computing power is usually available.

The key feature that underpins CORBA is the IDL specification. The authors suggest that most of the benefits of simplified integration and portability can be achieved by using IDL to specify software interfaces. Vehicle software components can be defined at a subsystem level using IDL early on in the design process. The structure and interactions among components can be verified functionally at an early stage using IDL and object-oriented specification methodologies without regard to the communication mechanisms. The software components could be functionally simulated on a PC using stub components. Once the OEM is satisfied, the subsystems can then be further decomposed into sets of software components (also specified in IDL) to be allocated to suppliers. The result is that the interactions among the components have already been functionally verified and failure mode responses explored before the supplier implements the software component. As long as the IDL interfaces remain unchanged, the process of integrating the finished components should be much easier. Using IDL as part of the requirements specification process removes much of the ambiguity of natural language specification, since the IDL is a compilable notation. The IDL can be supplemented with UML sequence diagrams that indicate the dynamic use of the software components. Software modules delivered by suppliers can be verified against the IDL specification using software test harnesses.

Once the overall software requirements have been defined and expressed using IDL, the next step is to map the software components to the hardware architecture. Some components may have to be mapped to a specific ECU because of sensor or other hardware requirements. Techniques such as cluster analysis [9] can be used to map remaining software modules to available ECUs. In this way the allocation of software to ECUs is neither predetermined nor constrained.

The issue of mapping IDL calls to specific implementation languages and tools needs to be addressed. The main problem to be overcome is the mapping of the dynamic run-time ORB operation to the static run-time operation of automotive ECUs. The Object Request Broker normally includes facilities to dynamically locate server objects, to invoke additional server objects to deal with increased loading and to dynamically prioritize client requests. Sufficient computing resources do not exist for this highly dynamic mode of operation in an automotive environment. On the other hand, the software components to be used in an automotive system are static and are defined during the software design phase, so the client-server object interactions are also known in advance. This prior knowledge allows the Object Request Broker implementation to be hard-coded to optimize the use of resources. This can be accomplished using a software configuration process prior to the final software build, in the same way that OSEK systems are statically configured at build time using the OSEK Implementation Language (OIL) file. This process is summarized in Figure 8.

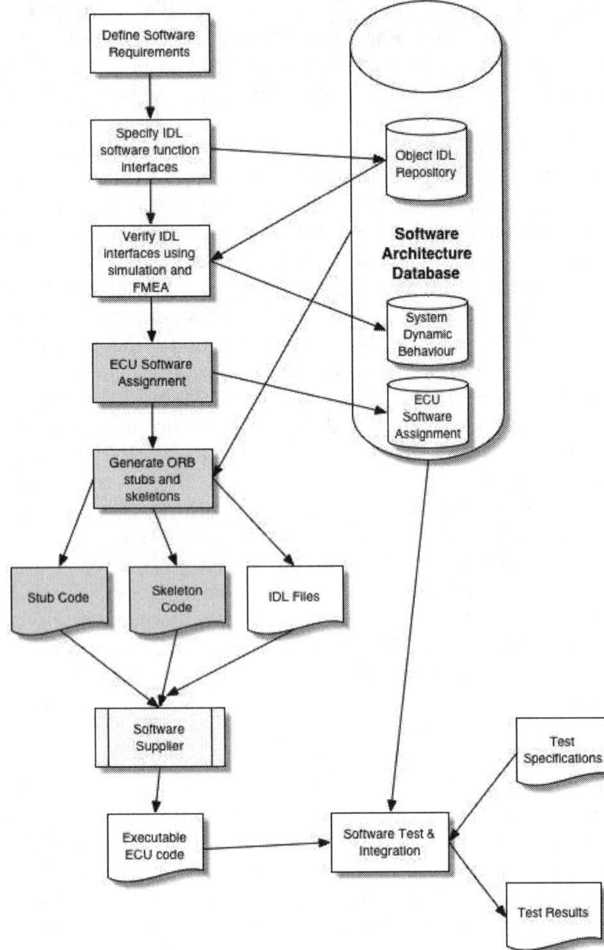

Figure 8. Development Process using CORBA/IDL.

The process of configuring the Object Request Broker consists of the following activities

1. ECU software assignment. The assignment of individual software functions to ECUs must be carried out first so that the system generation process knows whether each IDL call is to a server object on the same ECU or to a different ECU on the network. The actual client and server source code does not need to be changed as a result of reassigning software functions to different ECUs because the following process steps will take care of the interfacing details. Thus a significant simplification of ECU software integration can be realized using IDL interfaces.

2. Client Stub generation. CORBA IDL calls contained within client application code must be replaced with appropriate stub code that converts the IDL call to a proper call of the server object code. This works like a normal pre-compilation process by replacing IDL references in application code with appropriate stub routine calls. In a full-featured ORB the standard stub would call the ORB library, which would in turn locate and call the server object. In a custom static automotive implementation the configuration tool would generate code based on the target server object identification, the server object location and the desired communication mechanism. For example, if the server object is on the same ECU as the client, then a simple library call might be sufficient. If the server is located on another ECU then the stub would have to map the IDL call to a network message using OSEK COM or direct CAN messages, transmit the request to an ORB request handler on the remote ECU, and wait for a response before returning control to the client application. The mapping of CORBA requests to CAN messages has already been addressed in existing research [10].

3. Server Skeleton generation. The server side of the ORB implementation consists of code that unpacks the IDL parameters from remote CAN-based requests or else maps IDL parameters from local client requests to the correct calling interface for the server code. The skeleton code is responsible for returning any results to the client object according to the IDL specification. Various approaches may be taken to implement server code. Where only one instance of an object exists, the implementation can exist as a library routine in ROM. Where more than one instance of an object exists, the methods of the object could be implemented as reentrant routines in ROM with object-specific attribute values and other data stored in RAM. Techniques for mapping UML object-oriented designs to procedural C code have been described by James Rumbaugh [11]. The server object methods may be implemented in any suitable language. The skeleton code does the mapping from the object-oriented IDL interface to the ECU-specific implementation.

4. Target system build. The generated client stubs and server skeletons are linked with the application software functions for each ECU in the vehicle. The vendors of CORBA technology normally provide implementations of CORBAservices and CORBAfacilities with their ORB implementations. While most of these services are of little use in an automotive environment, one that is quite useful is the Event Notification service. This provides a publish-and-subscribe type interface between event sources and event consumers. It provides both push and pull type interfaces to event sources and event consumers. This service could be developed as a custom implementation based on the CAN bus. The result of doing this would be a hardware-independent distributed event notification service that would further decouple software functions in a predominately event-driven environment. A description of a CAN-based CORBA Event Notification service is described by Finocchiaro et al [12].

The OMG has specified a standard mapping of IDL to C and provides basic implementations of stubs and skeletons (Object Adaptors) that can be used as the basis for custom implementations.

CONCLUSION

This paper has examined the problems of software integration of ECUs on a vehicle network. Most of the problems are due to the tight coupling between the software functions and ECU hardware. The integration problems are compounded by the fact that the integration between ECUs currently takes place at the CAN network layer by means of message transfer. Integration testing occurs at a very low level, i.e. at the Physical Layer, which is in turn constrained by what information can be deduced, mapped and translated to the higher level network layer faults. This is further hampered by the fact that the Physical Layer has its own inherent problems due to its electrical characteristics in terms timing, transmission errors, latency problems, so it is difficult to debug and understand the problems at the higher layers due to the masking effect of these lower level issues. Using the techniques suggested in this paper, the integration process can be moved up to a higher application level where ECU software interactions take the form of client-server requests and responses. At this level the software design is easier to understand and debug. In addition, the intended operation of the system can be simulated and the failure mode operation analyzed and understood prior to programming. Using object-oriented modeling techniques for designing the software architecture will help achieve more flexible and reusable vehicle software functions.

It is hoped that the suggestions described in this paper for implementing CORBA technology in an automotive environment might be considered for future AUTOSAR and OSEK standardization, thereby bringing the associated benefits to a wider group of automotive software developers.

REFERENCES

1. http://www.osek-vdx.com. OSEK Specifications.
2. http://www.asam.de. ASAM Specifications.
3. http://www.autosar.org. AUTOSAR group details.
4. Axelsson, J., "Holistic Object-Oriented Modelling of Distributed Automotive Real-Time Control Applications". IEEE 1999. Proceedings of 2nd IEEE Symposium on Object-Oriented Real-Time Distributed Computing.
5. http://www.dc-cc.com. Automotive UML. DaimlerChrysler Competence Centre.
6. Larman, C. (2002). Applying UML and Patterns. Prentice Hall PTR. ISBN 0-13-092569-1.
7. http://www.omg.org. OMG, CORBA, IDL information and specifications.
8. http://www.borland.com/visibroker. VisiBroker-RT ORB product information.
9. Rushton, G., Zakarian, A. and Grigoryan, T. "Development of Modular Electrical, Electronic, and Software System Architectures for Multiple Vehicle Platforms". SAE paper 2003-01-0139.
10. Lankes, S., Jabs, A. and Bemmerl, T. "Integration of a CAN-based Connection-oriented Communication Model into Real-Time CORBA". IEEE Proceedings of the International Parallel and Distributed Processing Symposium 2003.
11. Rumbaugh, J. et al. Object-Oriented Modeling and Design. Prentice Hall. ISBN 0-13-630054-5.
12. Finocchiara, R., Lankes, S. and Jabs, A. "Design of a Real-Time CORBA Event Service customised for the CAN Bus". IEEE Proceedings of the 18th International Parallel and Distributed Processing Symposium 2004.

CONTACT

Brendan Jackman B.Sc. M.Tech.

Brendan is the founder and Director of the Centre for Automotive Research at Waterford Institute of Technology, where he supervises postgraduate students working on automotive software development, diagnostics and vehicle networking research.. Brendan also lectures in Automotive Software Development to undergraduates on the B.Sc. in Applied Computing Degree at Waterford Institute of Technology. Brendan has extensive experience in the implementation of real-time control systems, having worked previously with Digital Equipment Corporation, Ireland and Logica BV in The Netherlands.

Email: bjackman@wit.ie

Website: http://www.wit.ie/car

Shepherd Sanyanga (BEng BSc MSc PhD CEng EurIng MIEE)

Shepherd is a Technical Specialist in the design of Subsystem Communication Protocols & Diagnostics and the verification of such systems at TRW Automotive in the United Kingdom, working with the major OEMs in Europe and North America. He has had extensive experience in the system design of real-time embedded control systems for safety critical and comfort applications in both the Automotive and Aerospace industry. He has worked in organizations such the United Nations, Lucas Aerospace Systems, Sagem Automotive and Ford Motor Company. He is also an external examiner at an automotive research establishment in Ireland which runs MSc research courses for the automotive industry.

Email: shepherd.sanyanga@trw.com

2005-01-0323

Wireless Multicasting for Remote Software Upload in Vehicles With Realistic Vehicle Movements

Radovan Miucic and Syed Masud Mahmud
Electrical and Computer Engineering Department, Wayne State University

ABSTRACT

Future vehicles will have many features that include, but are not limited to, drive-by-wire, telematics, pre-crash warning, highway guidance and traffic alert systems. From time to time the vehicles will need to have their software modules updated for various reasons, such as to introduce new features in vehicles, the need to change the navigation map, the need to fine tune various features of the vehicles, etc. A remote software update has a number of advantages, such as it does not require consumers to take their vehicles to the dealers, and the dealers do not need to spend time on vehicles on an individual basis. Thus, remote software updates can save consumers' valuable time, as well as cost savings for the vehicle manufacturers.

Since wireless links have limited bandwidth, uploading software in thousands of vehicles in a cost-effective and timely manner is a challenge. Another major issue related to the remote software update is the security of the update process. In another paper, we addressed the security issue of the update process. In this paper, we present a wireless multicasting technique for uploading software in vehicles. Since the servers that will be broadcasting the software are located in some permanent places, and the vehicles are located all over the country, the software upload process has to depend on an infrastructure such as the cellular infrastructure. We have developed simulation models to determine the performance of our proposed wireless multicasting technique for remote software uploads. We simulated hundreds of vehicles distributed around a city area. In the simulation model, we assumed realistic speeds for the vehicles depending upon where the vehicles were located. The vehicles transfer the software from a buffer to an electronic control unit (ECU) when their ignition is off. Our simulation results show that if the multicast technique is used instead of the unicast technique (one vehicle at a time), then the software can be updated in a very cost-effective manner. The paper will give a detailed description of our technique and provide numerous results of the simulations collected for various distributions of the systems and vehicles.

INTRODUCTION

Today, most of the electronic controller units (ECUs) have in-vehicle programming (IVP) capabilities. Some of the ECUs in the modern vehicle are IC (instrument cluster), ABS (antilock brake system), ECM (engine control module), PCM (power control module), BCM (body control module), HVAC, infotainment systems, radio, MP3 player, DVD, On Star, door module, seat module, airbag module, navigation module, etc.

Sometimes software needs to be updated for various reasons, such as: calibration update, a problem with the existing software in modules, a recall of the vehicle due to software error, a new implementation, or the addition of new features. Some component suppliers only have a limited time to develop their products, and sometimes products go into production with very little testing. Such components are at high risk of unacceptable behavior later on, and it is very useful to have a cost-effective reprogramming system in place. Nowadays, if there is a need for a software update, a customer usually goes to the dealer, and the technician reprograms the module by physically plugging a programmer into the connector that has access to the intervehicele bus or busses such as CAN, LIN, J1850, UBP, SCP, etc. The programmer then uploads software into the vehicle's modules. Technicians at a dealership upload new software into vehicles one vehicle at a time. If there is a vehicle recall due to software error, dealers would have to reprogram hundreds of thousands of vehicles. The process of uploading software into each vehicle is an inconvenience for both the dealers and the customers. The car manufacturers lose money and the customers lose confidence because of this process. For each module to be programmed, it will take time for setup and actual servicing, including taking the customer's time to make the appointment, physically bringing the vehicle to the dealer, and spending time while the vehicle is being serviced. In addition, it takes months to update the software in all the vehicles, and there is no guarantee that all customers will bring in their vehicles for service.

Our motivation is to bring down the cost of updating modules by broadcasting the software that will be updated in particular modules in vehicles. Cellular towers are currently located in cities, towns and near major roads where the most vehicles are located. Car manufacturers can jointly work with major cellular companies to have some channels reserved for their needs, or lease the channels when needed. Software can be updated in vehicles by using either a unicast or a multicast process. In a unicast process, the vehicles will receive software on an individual basis, but in a multicast process, all vehicles within the range of a tower will receive software in parallel. However, updating software using the multicast process will need significantly less bandwidth than that needed by the unicast process.

Security of the transferred software is an important aspect of multicast programming. A vehicle network must have a cost-effective security system. The desired level of security needs to have a good balance of cost and extensiveness [3]. We will mainly focus on the wireless update process and leave security issues for another paper. This paper presents simulation models for performing remote software updates in vehicles. The simulation results show that updating software using the multicast process is very cost-effective compared to using the unicast process.

RELATED WORK

Rooftop networks, proposed in [1], provide an alternative to wired networks. The rooftop network is not mobile. In this network, antennas are mounted on building roofs, and several can be installed in metropolitan areas. The antennas are placed in line-of-sight orientation to their neighbors. The routing algorithm for rooftop networks proposes self-configuration for hundreds of thousands of such nodes in a metropolitan area. However, the routing algorithm faces significant scalability and security challenges.

GeoMote [2] developed a routing algorithm for TinyOS (Operating System for Tiny Networked Sensors). Low-cost, densely placed networked sensors with limited available memory, power and processing resources are called "motes". Every mote must know its own location in order to participate in the network. Three types of motes: GeoRouters, GeoGateways and GeoHosts are used in the networks. GeoRouters run routing algorithms to decide how the messages are to be routed based on the geographical locations.

OnStar, Vetronix and Networkcar have remote diagnostics programs. If remote diagnostics programs prove to be successful, OEMs will be sure to invest more to exploit remote diagnostics [4].

SOFTWARE SIMULATION DESCRIPTION

Our software consists of the simulation of three major elements: a map, the towers and the vehicles. These elements interact with each other. The vehicle movement and the tower broadcast are represented on a map, as shown in Figure 1.

The map, shown in Figure 1, is an array representing city blocks. City blocks consist of empty spaces and roads. In our simulation model, a vehicle cannot exist in an empty space - it can only be on a road. Roads intersect with each other. Software simulation considers situations in which a vehicle can travel east or west, north or south, and north, west, south, and east at intersections (see Figure 2).

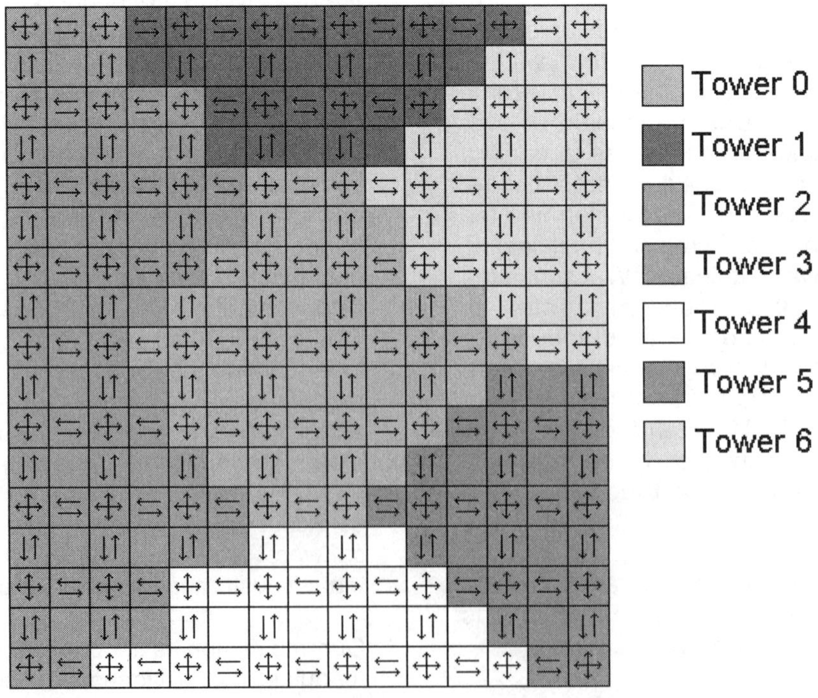

Figure 1: Map of the city blocks and towers' coverage areas

The towers are represented on the map. Each city block is under some tower coverage. Only the tower coverage of the roads is of interest to us. The towers broadcast software to their coverage area. For simplicity, we have assumed that there are no overlaps of the coverage areas of the towers. Assuming there is no overlap of tower coverage areas is reasonable, because a vehicle receiver can have a signal strength detector and the detector may be set to only accept the strongest signal.

Vehicles are simulated to be traveling on these roads. The vehicle position and direction is determined in the initialization phase of the simulation software. A vehicle may change direction when it reaches an intersection. When a vehicle enters an intersection, it randomly decides to change or not to change its current direction. For simplicity, if a vehicle reaches a boundary of the map, it reverses its direction. The vehicle receives software packets from the tower while it is moving. The vehicle may miss receiving a packet due to a weak signal and noise, or due to a change in the coverage area.

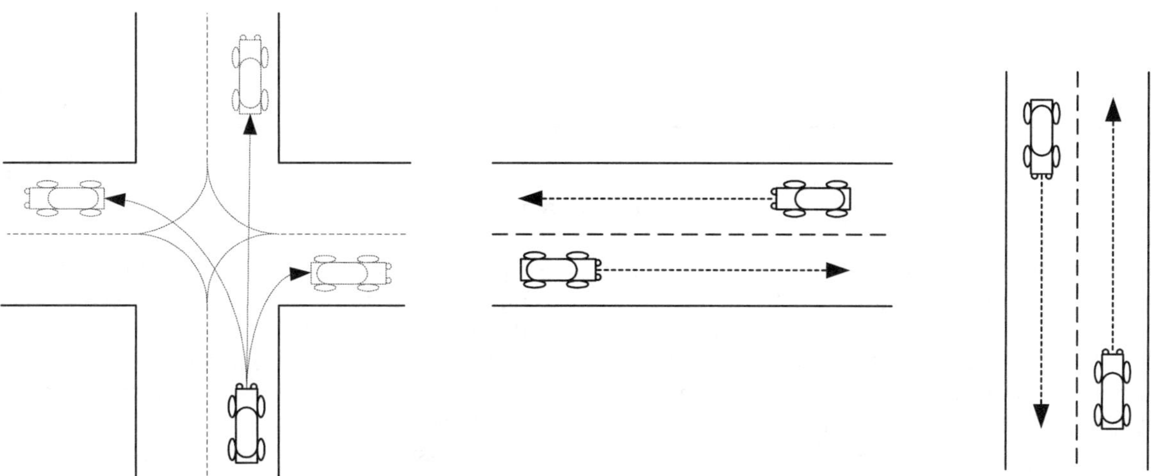

Figure 2: Possible vehicle movement in the simulation model

The original equipment manufacturer (OEM) or the supplier decides that a certain ECU needs an update. The OEM sends the software for a target ECU to the central server (CS). The CS uploads the software to the nearest tower, and the tower starts broadcasting the software to the vehicles within its coverage area. The tower also sends the software to its neighboring towers. The software must contain information about the vehicle model and year and about the ECU. The vehicle must recognize if the software that is being received is targeting one of its ECUs. If the software is targeting an ECU on the vehicle, the vehicle will buffer the received software. If the software is not targeting an ECU of the vehicle, the vehicle will ignore that software. The received software must contain version control information. The vehicle will compare the ECU's current software version with the received software version. The vehicle accepts received software only if the version of the broadcast software is newer than the version of the software currently available in the ECU. The strategy of matching the new software with the current software in the target ECU will be the topic of a different paper. In our simulation, we will only consider vehicles that have an ECU in need of an update.

Software Packets: The software is divided into smaller pieces of code, called packets. A tower sends packets sequentially, from the first packet to the last. Vehicles accept software packets that are being wirelessly sent from the tower. A vehicle may fail to receive a packet for various reasons, such as the presence of noise, transition from one tower to the next tower, etc. If a vehicle starts receiving a packet and does not receive the next packet for some time, or if it receives the last packet sent but some prior packets are missing, then it will start sending periodic "complain" messages indicating that the vehicle's target ECU has not been programmed. After a tower has sent all of the software packets it waits for some time to determine whether any vehicle sends a message indicating that the target ECU has not been programmed. We use the symbol VNP for any message that indicates that a vehicle has not been programmed, and the symbol WP to indicate the time during which the vehicle waits for the VNP message. A VNP message will identify what software is missing from a vehicle. If a tower receives a VNP message during the period WP, it starts transmitting the entire software all over again. If a vehicle exits and stays out of the coverage area after the WP period it will not be updated: the software will remain in the tower's buffer during the WP period. If a tower does not receive the VNP message, the tower flushes its buffer to make it free for other activities. If the tower receives a VNP message after the WP period, it will request the software from the central server, and the entire process of broadcasting the software is then repeated. Figure 3 shows the broadcasting timeline. The entire process includes the following steps, as shown in Figure 3:

1) The tower starts broadcasting the software.
2) The tower finishes broadcasting the software.
3) The tower waits in the WP state.
4) The tower receives a VNP message.
5) The tower starts broadcasting the software.
6) The tower waits in the WP state and does not receive any VNP message.
7) The tower deletes the software from its buffer.

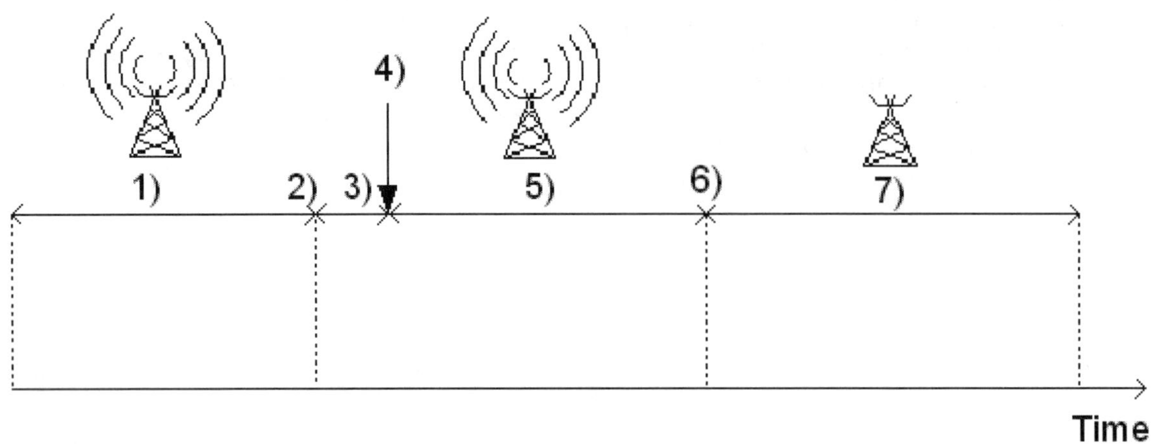

Figure 3 – Broadcasting timeline

There must be a dedicated device in the electrical architecture of the vehicle, perhaps a new ECU (WECU – Wireless ECU) which is capable of wireless communication. The vehicle will have a buffer large enough to store memory of the largest ECU in the vehicle's network architecture. The vehicle will receive the software via the WECU and save it in its buffer. The target ECU is reprogrammed from the buffer when it becomes convenient, i.e. safety critical ECUs may be updated when the vehicle stops and the ignition is off. Other ECUs may be updated on the fly. The WECU will determine if it is safe to update the target ECU. The designated ECU will check the battery condition and other target-specific conditions. Updating a vehicle without the customer's consent can pose problems. For example, the vehicle owner has memorized his/her favorite seat position. Their saved seat information will be lost during the software update, and the customer will notice the difference.

Simulation Process – Our software simulation executes in loops. Each loop takes the smallest time interval, here called time instance TI. In our simulation, the value of TI is 12.5 ms. The entire packet has been broken down in the simulation program into many small packets, and the size of each packet is 1KB (kilobytes). We assumed that a vehicle needs 8 time instances (TI) to receive a packet. In other words, the speed of the wireless communication is 10 KB/sec.

Broadcast Delay - The delay between a pair of neighboring towers is one hop. We consider one hop delay to be equal to one packet delay, or 8-TI delay. We assumed that tower T0 is the closest tower to the server. Since different towers are located at different hop distances away from Tower T0, different towers start broadcasting the software after a different length of delay, as shown in Figure 4. Tower T0, which is closest to the server, has no delay in broadcasting the software.

Signal Strength – The wireless signal is the strongest in the immediate vicinity of a tower. The signal strength of the broadcast in a city block depends on the distance from the city block to the broadcasting tower. We have defined four levels of signal strength. The city blocks closest to the tower have the strongest signal. The strongest signal is represented by using four fully colored bars, as shown in Figure 5. The city block that is farthest from the broadcasting tower has the weakest signal and it is represented with one fully colored bar, as shown in Figure 5. The vehicle in the city block with the strongest signal has the highest probability of receiving broadcasted packets. The vehicle in the city block with the weakest signal has the least probability of receiving broadcasted packets.

RESULTS

We ran our simulation with various input parameters. Figure 6 shows the outcome of the simulation. The cost, which is the number of times the towers had to rebroadcast the entire software, is shown on the Y-axis. The size of the software in packets is shown on the X-axis. The average cost to rebroadcast the software increases with the number of vehicles on the roads. As we mentioned earlier, packets may be lost due to low signal strength or due to movements of the vehicles from one tower region to another.

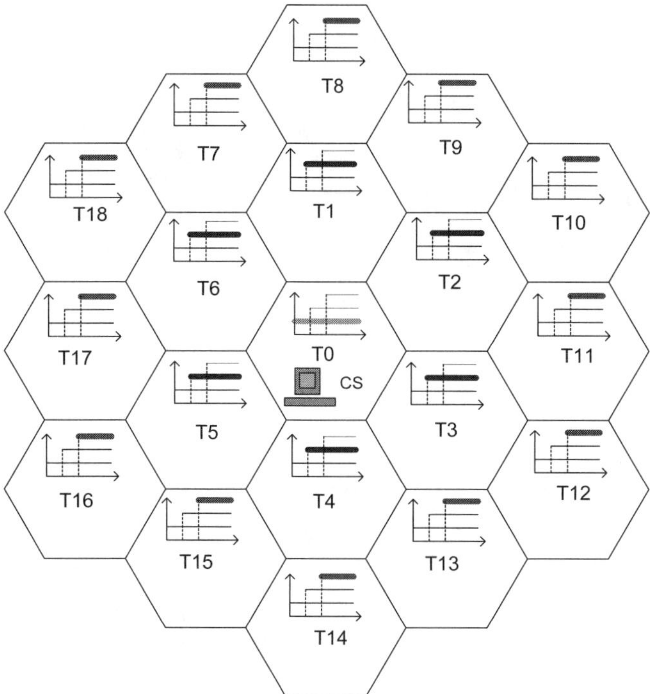

Figure 4 – Towers' broadcast delays.

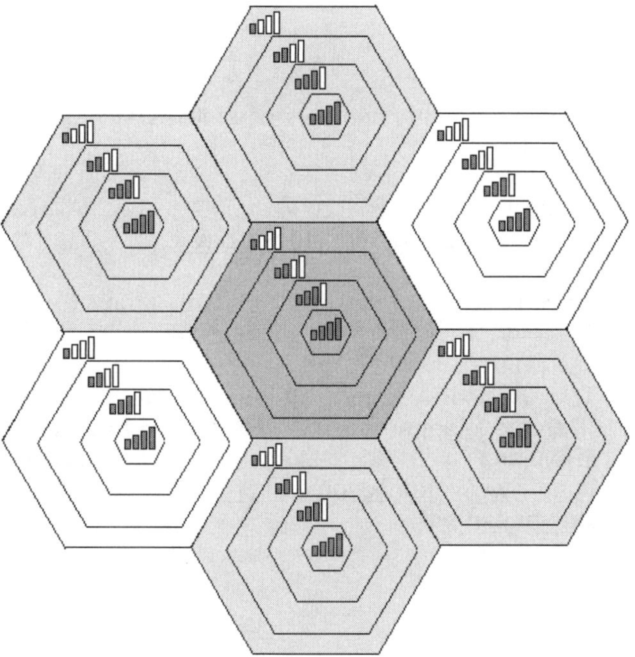

Figure 5 - Towers' signal strength

We assumed east-west and north-south roads connecting two intersections to be 800 meters long. Also, we assumed the length of the intersection to be 50 meters. Let's say that the bandwidth of the wireless link is 10 KB/sec. If a vehicle is moving at 100 km/hour it will travel 0.347 meter per time instance (12.5 ms). For simplicity, the simulation program updates the vehicle's position on the map after every 10 meters.

(Number of packets) x (number of instances per packet) x (time instance) = time for 1 software broadcast

For example, software containing 1500 packets will need 1500x 8 x 12.5 x 10^{-3} s = 150 sec to be uploaded in vehicles.

The signal strength at a vehicle depends on its distance from the nearest tower. In our simulation, a vehicle has to be in the coverage area during a software broadcast for 8 consecutive time instances in order for it to receive a complete packet. There is a possibility that the vehicle may receive corrupted data in any of the 8 time instances while a packet is being received, resulting in the loss of the packet. Figure 6 shows the results of the simulation runs for the following parameters.

- The probability of losing a packet is 10% in a region where the signal strength is the weakest (signal where only one bar is green, as shown in Figure 5)
- The probability of losing a packet is 5% in a region where the signal strength is nearly the weakest (signal where two bars are green, as shown in Figure 5)
- The probability of losing a packet is 2.5% in a region where the signal strength is nearly the strongest (signal where three bars are green, as shown in Figure 5)
- The probability of losing a packet is 0.01% in a region where the signal strength is the strongest (signal where all four bars are green, as shown in Figure 5)

Figure 6 is divided into two parts. The bottom part of Figure 6 shows the result for the case which assumes that the vehicles only lost packets because they were moving from one tower region to another. More specifically, this means that while a vehicle was receiving a packet it did not stay within the coverage of the tower from which it was receiving the packet for eight time instances (TI). For this case, the towers only broadcast the software a couple of times. The top part of Figure 6 shows the result for the case which took into consideration the vehicle movements and signal strengths. Figure 6 shows that the vehicles lost some packets mostly due to weak signals rather than due to vehicle movement. Thus, when signal strengths were taken into consideration, the towers had to broadcast the software significantly more times than when we were just considering vehicle movement. Figure 6 shows that the towers had to broadcast the software containing 1500 packets 18 times to load it into 500 vehicles. However, had the vehicles been uploaded one at a time instead of all 500 vehicles in parallel, then the towers would have been broadcasting the software 500 times. Thus, there is significant bandwidth saving when a group of vehicles is uploaded in parallel. This means that when compared to the unicast technique, a software upload using the multicast technique will result in significant cost savings.

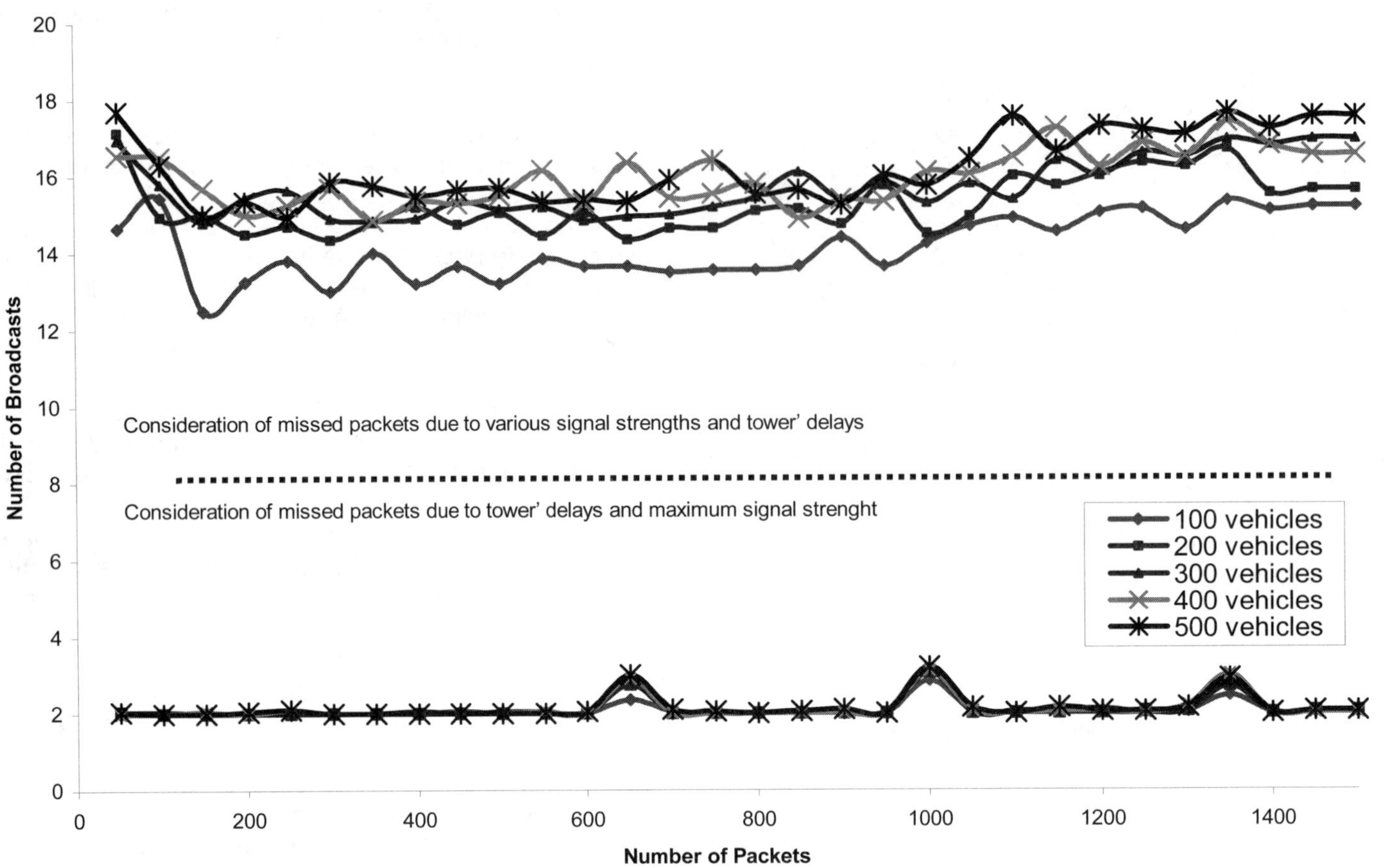

Figure 6 – Number of Broadcasts versus Number of Packets for various numbers of vehicles.

CONCLUSION

A study has been done to evaluate the effectiveness of software updates in vehicles using the multicast technique. We did a simulation assuming vehicles would move as predicted on city block maps. As the vehicles move from one city block to the next, they also move from one tower region to another tower region. According to the simulation results, updating software in vehicles using the multicast process is very cost-effective compared to that using the unicast process. Since the software can be updated using existing cell phone networks, no additional infrastructure is necessary for updating software in vehicles.

REFERENCES

1. Thanos Stathopoulos, John Heidemann, and Deborah Estrin. A Remote Code Update Mechanism for Wireless Sensor Networks. Technical Report CENS-TR-30, University of California, Los Angeles, Center for Embedded Networked Computing, November, 2003. http://www.isi.edu/~johnh/PAPERS/index.html

2. Peter Broadwell, Joseph Polastre, and Rachel Rubin, "GeoMote: Geographic Multicast for Networked Sensors." Class Project Paper 2001. 21 March 2004. Available: http://www.cs.berkeley.edu/~pbwell/

3. Mark Krage and Laci Jalics. "The Many Faces of Security," SAE, 2004-01-0236, 2004.

4. The Hansen Report on Automotive Electronics. "Remote Diagnostics— the Next OEM Frontier" dec. 2003/jan. 2004 Available: http://www.vetronix.com/pdf/press/vtx_2004-01-xx_hansen.pdf

CONTACT

Radovan Miucic received a B.S. degree in Electrical Engineering from Wayne State University, Detroit, in 2001 and his M.S. degree in Computer Engineering from Wayne State University, Detroit, in 2002. Currently he is working on his PhD degree, and as a software engineer in the automotive industry.

Email: radovanmiucic@hotmail.com

Syed Masud Mahmud, Ph.D.
Associate Professor
Department of Electrical and Computer Engineering
Wayne State University, Detroit, MI 48202
Phone: (313) 577-3855
Fax: (313) 577-1101
Email: smahmud@eng.wayne.edu

DEFINITIONS, ACRONYMS, ABBREVIATIONS

ECU – Electronic control unit.

CS – Central server. A computer repository for software to be broadcasted.

OEM – Original equipment manufacturer.

SFTE – Software for targeted ECU

VNP – The vehicle's targeted ECU is not programmed. A message from a vehicle to the tower indicating that some packets are missing in the vehicle's buffer.

TI –Time instance. This is the smallest time unit in the software simulation of loop time.

WP – Wait for VNP. The period of time the tower waits for a VNP message after a broadcast.

WECU – Wireless ECU.

2004-01-1735

Correct-By-Construction Methods for the Development of Safety-Critical Applications

Bernard Dion
Esterel Technologies

ABSTRACT

In this paper, we will describe how synchronous methods form the scientific basis for the creation of a correct-by-construction methodology required for safety-critical embedded systems. We will show how they are applied to software design, validation, and implementation through a process of high-level rigorous specifications from which we can create *correct-by-construction* embeddable implementation.

The synchronous methods we know today have more than 20 years of scientific research plus ten years of successful industrial application. This paper will explore the basic conceptual model of embedded computation supported by three underlying prerequisites: high-level rigorous graphical and textual languages, compiling algorithms for correct-by-construction implementation, and formal testing and verification techniques.

Lastly, we will show how a specialized specification to C compiler automated methodology can create embeddable C code that is automatically correct and certifiable to avionics guidelines DO-178B Level A and that makes low-level testing of generated C code unnecessary. Functional testing can be done at graphical specification level and the generated embeddable C code is automatically correct and certifiable.

INTRODUCTION

Synchronous methods are a global methodology to address embedded software and hardware design, validation, and implementation. The overall idea is to generate *correct-by-construction* embeddable implementation from high-level rigorous specifications, increasing quality while dramatically decreasing design and validation costs.

The methodology is supported by the SCADE (software) and Esterel Studio™ (hardware) integrated tool suites from Esterel Technologies, which ensure and automate the associated processes. In this paper, we will only describe the software methodology, the tools for which are SCADE Suite™ (avionics) and SCADE Drive™ (automotive). The very same concepts are applied to hardware circuit design with Esterel Studio; this solution is currently in early adoption use by major semiconductor companies for System-on-Chip design. The synchronous methodology is rooted in more than 20 years of scientific research [1, 2, 3, 5] and 10 years of successful industrial application. It is based upon a unified conceptual model of embedded computation backed by three strong technical cores: specific high-level rigorous graphical and textual languages, compiling algorithms for correct-by-construction implementation, and formal testing and verification techniques.

Source code development is based upon the SCADE graphical block-diagram notation familiar to control engineers, complemented by hierarchical Safe State Machines to describe state- or mode-oriented computations. These specification-level notations have precise semantics. Besides making software development more rigorous, they ease communication between engineers and between suppliers and customers. A key tool within the process is *KCG*, a SCADE-to-C automatic code generator qualifiable at Level A of the DO-178B guidelines for avionics [8]. The use of KCG makes low-level testing on generated C code unnecessary. Functional testing can be done at block-diagram level and the generated embeddable C code is automatically correct and certifiable.

Synchronous methodology, and the associated processes and tools, are particularly well-suited to the development of critical embedded software: fly- or drive-by-wire, engine control, power control, alarm handling, etc. They are currently used by market leaders such as Honeywell, Airbus, Dassault Aviation, Eurocopter, Hispano-Suiza, Pratt & Whitney and Audi. In critical avionics, for which processes must adhere to the DO-178B avionics guidelines, the methodology is yielding up to 50% cost reduction compared to older techniques. Business-critical applications where error or delay to market is intolerable also benefit from these technologies by reducing the validation cost, which today represents more than 60% of the total development cost. Since the implementation is automatically generated, there are no errors introduced at the implementation phase.

The rest of the paper is organized as follows: Section 2 presents the SCADE block-diagram and state-machine formalisms. Section 3 discusses the intuitive and formal semantics. Section 4 presents verification issues. Section 5 presents the software design and verification cycle associated with SCADE in a DO-178B context. We conclude in Section 6.

THE SCADE FORMALISMS

Embedded software applications are very different from classical IT applications. Instead of dealing with data files, they deal with the control of physical phenomena through specific sensor-actuator feedback loops and man-machine interfaces. Programs are implementations of control algorithms, with many parts acting concurrently, but in a deterministic way. This calls for very specific description formalisms close to the ones used in Control Engineering and Systems Engineering to design such algorithms. Classical programming tools used by most software engineers are not adequate for this purpose. Concurrency techniques used in Operating Systems and classical languages imply undesirable behavioral non-determinism, further studied in Section 3.2 below.

SCADE Suite and SCADE Drive use two specification formalisms familiar to control engineers: block diagrams for continuous control and state machines for discrete control. What the Synchronous Model adds is a very rigorous view of these well-known but often insufficiently defined formalisms. This view includes a precise definition of concurrency and a proof that all SCADE programs behave deterministically.

BLOCK DIAGRAMS FOR CONTINUOUS CONTROL

By continuous control, we mean sampling sensors at regular time intervals, performing signal-processing computations on their values, and outputting values often using complex mathematical formulae. Data is continuously subject to the same transformation. In SCADE, continuous control is graphically specified using block-diagrams such as the one depicted in Figure 1 below.

Boxes represent computation of mathematical functions, filters, and delays, while arrows denote flows of data between the boxes. Data flows continuously between blocks that continuously compute their outputs from their inputs. All blocks compute concurrently, and the blocks only communicate through the flows. To add some flexibility in functioning modes control, some flows may carry Boolean or discrete values tested in computational blocks or acting on flow switches or multiplexors.

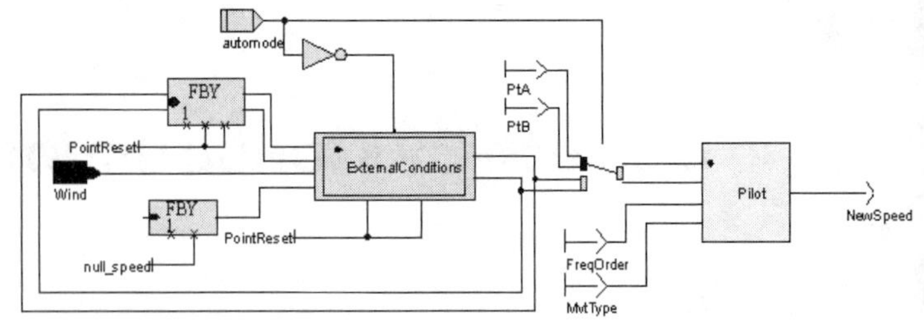

Figure 1: a SCADE Block Diagram

SCADE blocks are fully hierarchical: blocks at a description-level can themselves be composed of smaller blocks interconnected by local flows. In Figure 1, the ExternalConditions block is hierarchical, and one can zoom into it with the editor. Hierarchy makes it possible to break design complexity with a divide-and-conquer approach and to design reusable library blocks. Because of support for hierarchy, the set of primitive blocks can remain very small: there is no need to write complex blocks directly in C or ADA, since defining them hierarchically from smaller blocks is semantically better-defined, much more readable, and just as efficient. Compared to other block-diagram formalisms, hierarchy in SCADE is purely architectural and does not imply complex hierarchical evaluation rules: a hierarchical block occurring in a higher-level block is simply replaced by its contents, conceptually removing its boundaries.

SAFE STATE MACHINES FOR DISCRETE CONTROL

By *discrete control* we mean changing behavior according to external events originating either from discrete sensors and user inputs or from internal program events, e.g. value threshold detection. Discrete control is when the behavior continually changes, a characteristic of modal human-machine interface, alarm handling, complex functioning mode handling, or communication protocols.

Adding mode-control Boolean flows to block diagrams becomes messy rapidly when discrete control is non-trivial, and one must resort to another well-known formalism: *state machines*. A state machine is pictured in Figure 2 below. It is also composed of boxes, arrows, and names, but with a different meaning: boxes mean states, arrows mean transitions between states, and names denote signals exchanged with the environment: in transition label ``I/O", I denotes an input signal and O denotes an output signal. If the start state of the transition is active and I occurs, the transition is fired and O is emitted.

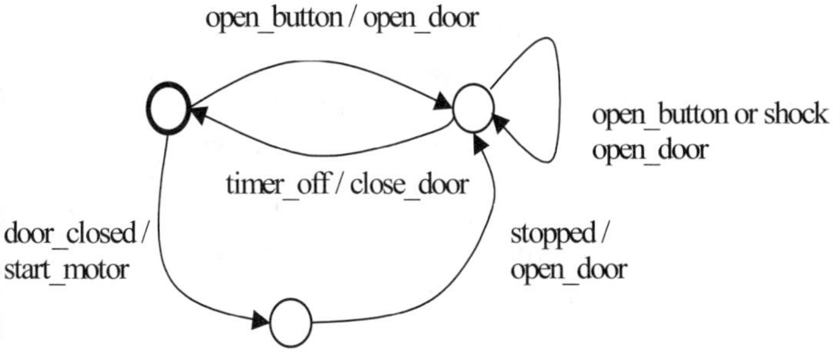

Figure 2: a Conventional State Machine

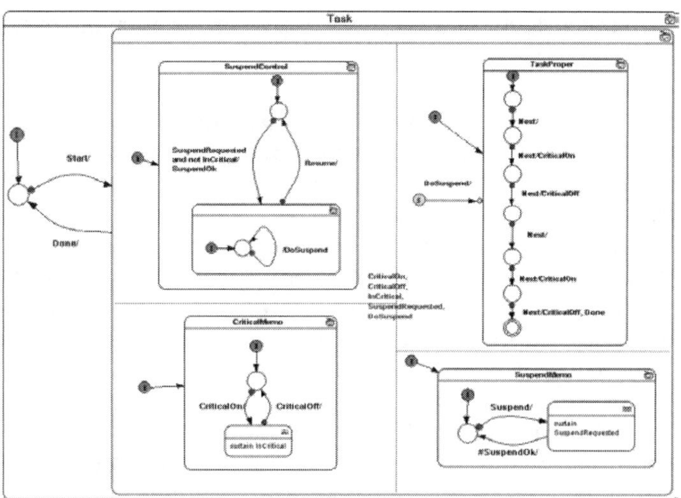

Figure 3: a Hierarchical and Concurrent Safe State Machine

State machines have been very extensively studied in the last 50 years, and their theory is well understood. However, in practice, they are not adequate even for medium-sized applications, since their size and complexity tends to explode very rapidly. For this reason, the richer concept of hierarchical state machines has been introduced, the initial one being Statecharts [6]. The Esterel Technologies hierarchical state machines are called Safe State Machines (SSMs), see Figure 3 for an example. These evolved from the Esterel programming language [2] and the SyncCharts state machine [1] model. SSMs have proved to be scalable to large avionics and automotive systems.

SSMs are hierarchical and concurrent. States can be either simple states or macrostates, themselves recursively containing a full SSM or a concurrent product of SSMs. When a macrostate is active, so are the SSMs it contains. When a macrostate is exited by taking a transition out of its boundary, the macrostate is exited and all the active SSMs it contains are preempted, whichever state they were in. Concurrent state machines communicate by exchanging signals, which may be scoped to the macrostate that contains them.

The definition of SSMs carefully forbids dubious constructs found in other hierarchical state machine formalisms: transitions crossing macrostate boundaries, transitions that can be taken halfway and then backtracked, etc. These are non-modular, semantically ill-defined, and very hard to figure out; hence, inappropriate for safety-critical designs. Their use is usually not recommended by methodological guidelines anyway.

HYBRID CONTINUOUS / DISCRETE CONTROL

Large applications contain cooperating continuous and discrete control parts. SCADE Suite and SCADE Drive make it possible to seamlessly couple both data flow and state machine styles. Most often, one includes SSMs into block-diagram designs to compute and propagate functioning modes. Then, the discrete signals to which a SSM reacts and which it sends back are simply transformed back-and-forth into Boolean data flows in the block diagram. The two computation models are fully compatible.

THE SCADE SEMANTICS

The semantics of a textual or graphical formalism define the meaning of programs written in it. At first glance, the SCADE block or state-machine diagrams look similar to those included in various specification and simulation tools, but their semantics are much more rigorously defined. Typically diagrams are meant to be read by experienced human users and to drive system simulations, with constraints far less stringent than for safety-critical embedded code. They are most often imprecise, locally ambiguous, and partly non-deterministic, which is unacceptable for critical applications: a program cannot be better-defined than the formalism it is written in. SCADE diagrams are completely precise and well-defined, without being heavier in practice.

INTUITIVE VS. FORMAL SEMANTICS

There are two orthogonal levels of semantics, both indispensable: the *intuitive level*, where semantics must be natural and easy to understand, and the *formal level*, where the semantics must be rigorously defined and fully non-ambiguous. Thanks to 40 years of progress in the field, defining language semantics in a mathematical way has matured into a robust technology. Both semantics levels must agree, and implementation must conform to them.

SCADE and SSMs have clear intuitive semantics based on the *cycle-based* traditional computation model. Their mathematical semantics have been extensively studied over the last 20 years, see [3, 5]. The match between intuition and semantics is perfect: programs mean what they say and do what they mean. The user definitely does not need to refer to the mathematical semantics for everyday programming, but these act as the *tables of the law* in any case of doubt.

Having formal semantics for the languages also makes code generators much easier to develop and verify. The translation process from concurrent source code to C code is based upon scientifically proven algorithms that the code generators directly implement. Object code is simple and uses no unsafe feature of the target language. All optimizations available in code generators can be proved correct. Furthermore, SCADE object code is fully traceable to the source specification, which is a mandatory requirement of DO-178B guidelines, and also w.r.t. language semantics, which is an additional safeguard.

KEY REQUIREMENTS: DETERMINISM AND PREDICTABILITY

We emphasize that *determinism* is a key requirement of most embedded applications. A system is deterministic if it always reacts in the same way to the same inputs occurring with the same timing. On the contrary, a non-deterministic system can react in different ways to the same inputs, actual reaction depending on internal choices or computation timings. It is clear that determinism is a must to drive a car or a plane: internal computation timings should not interfere with the driving algorithms.

Another important practical requirement is *performance predictability*. It is important to check that object code is fast and regular enough for the same application. Predictability is never an easy subject, in particular because of caching and pipelining in recent microprocessors. But, of course, any form of non-determinism makes it even harder.

Non-determinism is not a bad concept *per se*: an Internet connection behaves in a non-deterministic way, and there is nothing wrong with that. In the same way, a car entertainment system may have some local non-deterministic behavior. But the core driving algorithms must be deterministic and predictable. Therefore, *determinism should be preserved by the program whenever it is an essential feature of the specification.* SCADE specifications are deterministic by construction, and the SCADE tools do preserve determinism all along the specification-to-implementation chain.

THE CYCLE-BASED INTUITIVE COMPUTATIONAL MODEL

Cycle-based computation is a traditional model introduced many years ago to deal with embedded computation. It consists of performing a continuous loop of the form pictured in Figure 4 below. In this loop, there is a strict alternation between environment actions and program actions. Once the input sensors are read, the program starts computing the cycle outputs. During that time, the program is *blind to environment changes*. When the outputs are ready, or at a given time determined by a clock, the output values are fed back to the environment, and the program waits for the start of the next cycle.

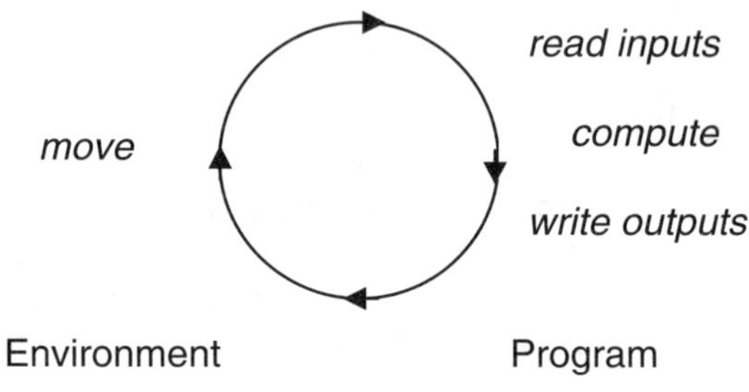

Figure 4: the Cycle-based computation model

Things are very similar to player interaction in a two-game play: players play in strict alternation and each player does not interfere with the other player's thinking. The cycle-based model is a direct computer implementation of the ubiquitous sampling-actuating model of Control Engineering.

In the implementation, there are several ways to control the cycle: *time-triggered* computation starts the cycle on a regular basis; *polling* consists of restarting the cycle as soon as it is over; and *event-triggered* computation consists of starting the cycle whenever some event occurs.

In a SCADE block diagram specification, each block has a cycle and all blocks act concurrently. Blocks can all have the same cycle, or they can have different cycles, which subdivide a master cycle, to realize undersampling calculations. At each of its cycles, a block reads its inputs and generates its outputs. If two connected blocks A and B have the same cycle, the outputs of A are used by B in the same cycle, unless an explicit delay is added between A and B. This is the essence of the *synchronous semantics* detailed in [5]. SSMs have the very same notion of a cycle. For a simple state machine, a cycle consists of performing the adequate transition from the current state and outputting the transition output in the cycle, if any. Concurrent state machines communicate synchronously with each other, receiving the signals sent by other machines and possibly sending signals back.

Finally, block diagrams and SSMs in the same design also communicate synchronously at each cycle. Within a cycle, communications amount to a chain reaction, in which blocks and SSMs exchange data tokens. The chain reaction remains fully predictable since it is blind to environment changes once started. Even if some internal communication orderings may change, the whole reaction is well-defined and deterministic.

IMPLEMENTING A CHAIN REACTION BY CYCLE FUSION

In the implementation, the conceptual chain reaction is realized in a very simple manner by *cycle fusion*, as shown in Figure 5. Each concurrent block generates sequential code statements, and the cycle-fusion process merges the statements of different blocks into a single sequential cycle. Communication between the individual tasks is performed implicitly, by an adequate interleaving of the statements that respects intra-cycle communication dependencies. To summarize, cycle fusion goes across concurrent blocks and across the hierarchy, yielding a single sequential code from a network of block diagrams and SSMs. Notice that there is *no overhead for communication*, which is internally implemented using well-controlled shared variables without any context switching.

Large-scale cycle fusion is unfeasible by hand but it is a relatively easy task for an automatic code generator. SCADE fully automates it and guarantees correct access to the shared memory. Finally, cycle fusion can be extended to handle under-sampling and it supports full separate compiling of blocks under some output-delay conditions not detailed here.

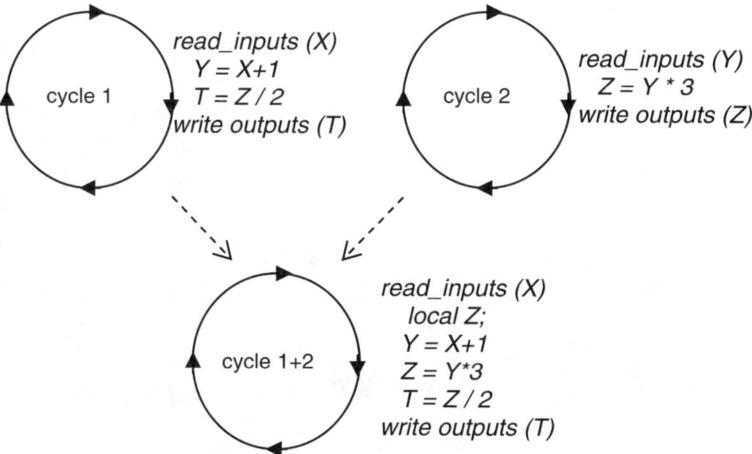

Figure 5: Cycle Fusion

This cycle-based computation model carefully distinguishes between *logical concurrency* and *physical concurrency*. The application is described in terms of logically concurrent activities, block-diagrams or SSMs. Logical concurrency applied to a large scale makes the designer's work much easier by breaking complex tasks into simple ones that communicate in a simple way. But concurrency is resolved at compile-time by cycle fusion, and the generated code remains standard sequential and deterministic C or ADA code, all contained within a very simple subset of these languages. What matters is that *the final sequential code behaves exactly as the original concurrent specification*, which can be formally guaranteed.

Cycle fusion makes the cycle-based model preserve the fundamental determinism requirements of embedded systems *by construction*. Implementation predictability analysis is also made easier by the straightforward nature of the generated code. For these reasons, the cycle-based model has been used early and extensively for safety-critical systems in avionics and nuclear systems (this is where the development of SCADE started) and is now proliferating to critical embedded software applications in the automotive industry. The synchronous approach extends the traditional cycle-based model into a fully precise *synchronous computation model*. The synchronous model makes it possible to rigorously *compute on programs* in the same way as one computes on control algorithms. This idea is central to this approach of critical systems: instead of ad-hoc and poorly justified compiling and verification algorithms, the SCADE and SSM compilers and verifiers rely on scientifically proven program transformation and analysis algorithms.

LOGICAL VS. PHYSICAL TIME

In the synchronous approach, one counts logical time only in terms of I/O cycles, just as in the mathematical system of equations. Synchrony simply states that events occurring in the program are viewed as logically *synchronous* if and only if they occur in the same cycle. One only distinguishes between computations occurring in the same cycle and computations occurring in successive cycles. Therefore, at SCADE specification level, *the physical time it takes to perform an addition or a division is temporarily ignored.* This is a basic *separation of concerns* principle: high-level specifications need not care early on about performance-related issues.

Ultimately, performance issues are essential in practice. Many systems must be fast and most of them require predictable performance. In this approach, performance analysis is done at the object code level once the SCADE specification has been compiled into a classical target language such as C or ADA. SCADE itself provides no tool for this, but we remind that cycle fusion makes the problem much easier.

PROGRAM VALIDATION

Validation of an embedded system consists in checking that the system fulfills its requirements. For the software part of the system, one usually runs a series of tests. Test cases are generated by the designers themselves, by specific test teams, or by extracting embedded code local inputs when running full system simulation. Using the SCADE high-level formalism makes test design easier: one can concentrate on real functional properties, ignoring implementation details which are correct-by-construction since the KCG code generator has been qualified.

One of the key issues is to characterize what is tested and what is not. One never knows for sure when testing should stop. In particular, it is important to detect corner cases or unexpected input sequences that can lead to catastrophic situations. Unfortunately, human beings are not good at discovering these bad behaviors, which are often completely counter-intuitive and hard to predict (How could I have thought of *that* input sequence?). Formal verification tools complement human–directed testing in the areas where it is weak. There are two benefits. First, in bug-chasing mode, these tools excel at finding nasty bugs by building sequences that lead to unwanted events, if any exist. Second, they can also automatically prove some safety program properties such as "regulation is active if in on state and if speed is between 30 and 130 km/h". Formal verification techniques originated from hardware where they are now of routine use. They are also applicable to embedded systems, and particularly to cycle-based applications that closely resemble hardware applications.

SCADE incorporates *Design Verifier,* a formal verification system based on symbolic Boolean and numerical technology developed by Prover Technologies. The properties themselves are expressed in the SCADE and SSMs formalisms, technically as Boolean flows that should never become false. The user need not learn specific property-definition languages to use the verifier. Counter-examples for false properties are automatically generated.

Formal verification techniques may disappoint users who would so much like their verification problem to magically disappear. It is definitely not a magical technique but its abilities complement human abilities very well. In particular, formal verification is very useful in finding nasty bugs that escape conventional testing but do show up in production systems. We believe that formal verification engines will continue making constant progress in the future and will become among the most efficient anti-bug weapons.

IMPACT ON THE SOFTWARE DEVELOPMENT AND VERIFICATION CYCLE

SCADE is not only a set of tools, it is a full design and validation process for certified software. SCADE simplifies and shortens the usual development / validation cycle. We will now describe how it has been used in the context of DO-178B certification for the development of avionics software.

MODEL-BASED DEVELOPMENT WITH SCADE IN THE DO-178B CONTEXT

The following Figure 6 depicts the system and software development cycles as they are required both by ARP 4754 [7] at system level & DO-178B [8] at software level:

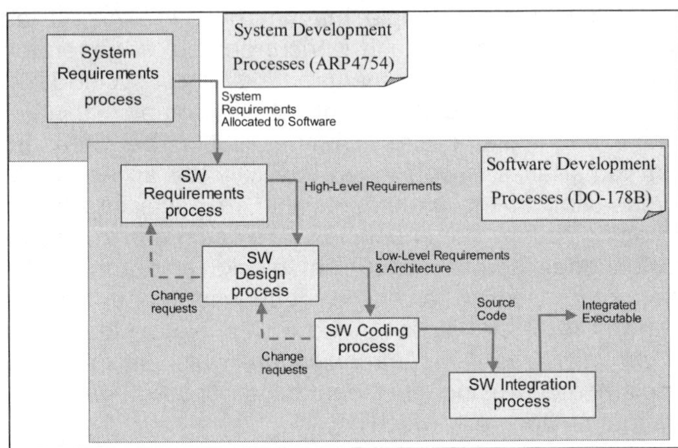

Figure 6: the ARP 4754 / DO-178B Development Cycle

Software development starts from System Requirements Allocated to Software. The role of the Software Requirements and Design processes is to completely define the Software Requirements (High and Low-level) together with the architecture of the software. Once this is done, the role of the Coding process is to produce the Source Code that is finally integrated to produce the Executable Code.

We now turn to the question of verifying the various development steps that we just described. In DO-178B, verification consists of reviews, analyses and tests. In the following Figure 7 we compare the use of SCADE vs. the use of a traditional manual method to develop embedded software:

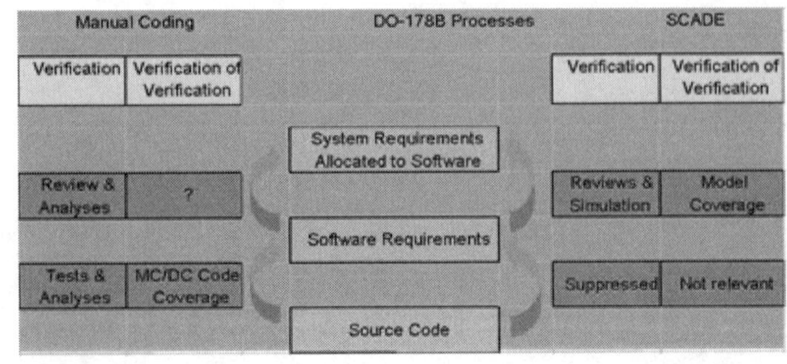

Figure 7: the Use of SCADE vs. the Use of Manual Coding

In both cases, we first follow the development steps in the middle of Figure 7, producing Software Requirements from System Requirements and then the Source Code. In a traditional setting, Source Code is manually written. In the case where SCADE is used, Source Code is automatically generated from the SCADE model (containing the Software Requirements) by using KCG, the qualifiable automatic C code generator. We now turn to the verification steps of DO-178B.

Let us first go upwards on the left of Figure 7 to follow the manual case. We must verify that Source Code agrees to Software Requirements: this is achieved by performing low-level tests that must be Software-Requirements-based. Moreover, when a verification activity is performed, there has to be a verification of this verification activity. As far as testing is concerned this means that two things have to be verified: tests must cover all Software Requirements (a manual activity) and the tests must achieve structural coverage of the Source Code, MC/DC in the case of Level A software, usually an activity that is supported by a tool.

Let us now go upwards on the right of Figure 7 to the case when SCADE is used. We do not have to verify that the Source Code matches the Software Requirements. This is guaranteed by construction and by qualification of the automatic code generator KCG as a software development tool at Level A (guideline DO-178B, Section 12). Since the verification of this activity can be suppressed, the verification of the verification of this activity is no longer relevant. In particular, we have eliminated the very costly need for MC/DC coverage analysis of the Source Code. We then have to verify that the Software Requirements truly implements the System Requirements Allocated to Software. Now, considering the fact that the Software Requirements are made of a SCADE model, it is possible to rely on simulation of SCADE models to prepare the required test-scenarios. This will allow us to verify that the expected output is obtained, and to measure the appropriate level of structural coverage of the SCADE model itself.

The question of verifying that there are no errors that can be introduced by the C compiler or the linker is not addressed in this paper but is detailed in the paper number [9] sited in the references at the end of this document.

By applying the processes described, we have moved most of the development and verification activities up one level, thus achieving true *Model-Based Development* with SCADE and creating substantial savings in the overall software development costs, as illustrated in the next Section.

THE SCADE Y DEVELOPMENT AND VERIFICATION CYCLE

The classical software development cycle is often called "the V cycle". Development flows down from Systems Requirements to embedded code, while validation flows up from embedded code low-level tests to system-level functional tests. Three steps are particularly difficult and expensive in this cycle: the precise specification of Software Requirements in a specification language; their precise coding in an executable language; and the low-level testing phase, which is usually the most costly. For embedded software development, the SCADE process and tools help in three ways:

- At the specification level, the transition from mathematical simulation tools to fully precise programs suited for a certifiable software flow is much more direct than with classical executable language hand-coding.
- Embeddable code is automatically generated from specification-level descriptions by the KCG code generator, which is qualifiable at Level A (the highest level) w.r.t. DO-178B guidelines. The object code can be considered correct by construction since the code generator itself is qualified with the very same process as the full application is certified. No low-level testing is needed.
- Verification is eased by the use of Design Verifier, which is able to find the nasty bugs that escape manual testing.

The SCADE process and automation results in important savings, in particular because KCG suppresses code testing w.r.t. specification, i.e. one of the most expensive parts of the whole development cycle. The V cycle is transformed into a Y cycle as pictured in Figure 8. Validation can concentrate on the highest level of the Y, i.e. on functionality. There are also additional savings in the lower part of the development cycle: we already mentioned that performance analysis is made easier.

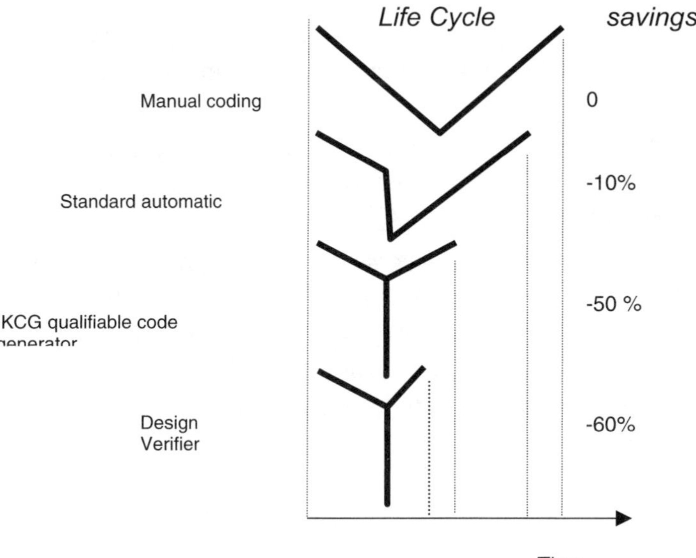

Figure 8: from a V to a Y Software Development Cycle

CONCLUSION

We have presented the SCADE process and tools, which are based on the powerful, well-defined and proven synchronous computation model for embedded systems. SCADE addresses the design flow from precise specification to embedded code generation. It is used in major industrial programs to generate DO-178B qualifiable implementation code from high-level block diagrams and state machines familiar to control engineers. This implies a dramatic cost reduction in one of the most difficult and error-prone part of systems development cycle. The use of SCADE also makes the upper and lower part of the whole cycle easier: the input formalism is close to classical notations used in high-level modeling. The simplicity of the generated code makes verification and implementation performance analysis much more efficient and productive.

REFERENCES

[1] C. André, *Representation and Analysis of Reactive Behaviors: A Synchronous Approach*, proc. CESA'96, IEEE-SMC, Lille, France (1996).

[2] G. Berry, *The Foundations of Esterel*. In “Proofs, Languages, and Interaction, Essays in Honour of Robin Milner”, G. Plotkin, C. Stirling and M. Tofte, ed., MIT Press (2000).

[3] G. Berry, *The Constructive Semantics of Pure Esterel*. Book available from www.esterel-technologies.com (download section).

[4] S. Edwards, *Languages for Digital Embedded Systems*. Kluwer, Boston, Mass (2000).

[5] N. Halbwachs, *Synchronous Programming of Reactive Systems*. Kluwer (1993).

[6] D. Harel, *Statecharts: a Visual Approach to Complex Systems*. Science of Computer Programming, vol. 8, pp. 231-274 (1987).

[7] *ARP 4754: Certification considerations for highly integrated or complex aircraft systems*, Society of Automotive Engineers (1996).

[8] *DO-178B: Software Considerations in Airborne Systems and Equipment Certification*, RTCA (1992).

[9] J.L. Camus, B. Dion, *Efficient Development of Airborne Software with SCADE Suite*, Esterel Technologies, see www.esterel-technologies.com (2003).

CONTACT

Bernard Dion, Vice President Strategy and Technology
Esterel Technologies
bernard.dion@esterel-technologies.com

Bio:

Bernard Dion received a Ph.D. in Computer Sciences from the University of Wisconsin, Madison (1978).

In the fall of 1999, Bernard Dion co-founded Esterel Technologies and has since been in charge of both product engineering and the development of methodologies of use for the products.

Prior to Esterel Technologies, Mr. Dion was part of the Simulog Group beginning in 1993, where he was first the Technical Director of Connexite; a subsidiary devoted to the development of programming systems for the Fortran language. He joined Simulog as Deputy CEO in 1995, developing a specific branch of the company with software engineering expertise for scientific and technical computing. He then became Simulog's Senior Executive Vice President from 1997 to 2000.

2004-01-0702

Analysis and Comparison Of 3 Code Generation Tools

Jayakumar Nair, Ning Lu, Pradeep Atraya and Johannes Reuter
IAV Automotive Engineering Inc.

ABSTRACT

In recent years, automated code generation has become popular, particularly in rapid prototyping. Currently we see these tools moving from being utilized in prototyping only into software development processes for mass production. If these tools can take over most of the code generation and actually fill the gap between algorithm design and the executable file, the development process could be sped up dramatically. IAV has been using autocode generation tools for several years in medium and large-scale projects, and is experienced in all aspects of using them. This includes also the integration of an RTOS and of BIOS and legacy code written in C.

In this paper we focus on three tools: ETAS ASCET-SD, dSPACE TargetLink and Realtime Workshop/Embedded Coder from The MathWorks. The tools have been used to generate complete application layer code for two Engine-Management systems and a Fuel Cell Application. The aspects considered in the paper are the modeling process, code quality, ease of integration with existing BIOS code and legacy code, as well as user friendliness and interaction with Real-Time Operating Systems. Further, the capabilities to generate ASAP2 files for calibration tools as well as the handling of State Machines has been investigated.

INTRODUCTION

The auto-code generation tools under consideration have been used by IAV in several recently developed engine control and fuel cell control projects. ASCET-SD 4.2.2 and TargetLink 1.3p2 have been used separately to generate code for a Motorola MPC565 platform for engine management functionality, while RTW 5.0/Embeddded Coder 3.0 and, for comparison, TargetLink 1.3p2 have been used for code generation for the fuel cell project. The target controller for the latter project was a MPC555. Since more than one tool was used to independently develop similar applications, objective comparisons could be made and valuable conclusions could be drawn. All projects used an OSEK compliant RTOS that had to be integrated into the tool-chain. For the engine controller, four time-triggered tasks and one event triggered task were implemented, while for the fuel cell project, four time-triggered tasks were required. The duration of the projects encompassed several months to more than a year. It was observed that the quality of the generated code heavily depended on the knowledge and experience of the user. This is especially true for tools that do not automatically guide the modeling style close to the code generation process, or do not inherently take care of data consistency.

ASCET-SD

The Advanced Simulation and Control Engineering Tool for Software Development (ASCET-SD) by ETAS is a tool used to develop control software for embedded systems automatically from diagrams. The tool claims to provide abstraction, simplicity and speed. ASCET-SD comes with a built in OSEK compatible operating system ERCOS. It is compatible with ETAS developed tools for testing and validation. Target hardware specific configuration and executable code generation is provided by an add-on package called Target Integration Package (TIP).

Modeling Options

Algorithms can be modeled in ESDL (Embedded Systems Description Language), C language or block diagrams. The Block Diagram Editor commonly referred to as the BDE comes with an array of basic building blocks similar to Simulink. ETA also provides a class library that contains additional components not available with the standard BDE menu.

The C/ESDL editors come in handy in two cases; to integrate legacy code, and to integrate hardware dependent BIOS code. Thus, while ASCET is intended for use mainly with the BDE, it provides enough flexibility to integrate existing code.

The biggest advantage is in program re-use, especially application programs. We found that the control strategy that was used for a Infineon C167 controller could be translated into the MPC 565 environment with minimum effort. The ease with which this migration can be done increases when the models are built in BDE rather than C or ESDL editors. Another visible advantage was that no special effort was needed to ensure data consistency. Because of the messaging technique adopted in ASCET SD, all tasks retain the value of every data element until a particular task is completed. Global data are written into only at task boundaries. However the models are not version compatible. An ASCET model generated in a lower version can be viewed only in current and higher versions; and once the model has been opened in a higher version, it cannot be reopened in a lower version

General Modeling Style

Software modeling is done using classes and modules. Classes contain methods, and modules contain processes. When compared to conventional programming languages, methods are similar to functions and processes to tasks. A class can be reused any number of times. The methods in a class work like re-entrant functions. A process contains a piece of code that is executed sequentially. The Scheduler or Operating System can invoke a process during program execution. A collection of modules and the associated processes along with the Scheduler forms a project.

When ASCET models become too big to be comprehended in a single viewing window, the hierarchy feature allows the user to encapsulate a larger model in a smaller viewing window. This is useful when one wants to keep a large control algorithm in a single class or module. Once the programming is completed, a basic offline test can be done on the model to check the logic by using the Physical Experiment Window in the tool.

Modeling of State Machines

ASCET provides a convenient way to model state machines. The capabilities provided by ASCET were more than sufficient for state machines used in the projects. Powerful modeling constructs like hierarchical state machines and junctions provide great flexibility in designing state machines. The tool flags an error on common mistakes like the absence of a start state (or initial state). There is also a priority for transitions, which resolves ambiguity in state transitions.

Version Management

ASCET 4.2.2 does not come with an inbuilt version management system. It does not directly support popular version management systems like PVCS and Clearcase. However it is possible to add user defined functions and integrate ASCET with external version management systems. The tool also provides convenient features to import from and export to external version management systems.

Task Scheduling and Interrupt Configuration

The tool provides a convenient graphical user interface to the task scheduler. Tasks, which run at periodic intervals or interrupt driven tasks can be created or modified with ease. It is possible to provide a 'Deadline' and 'Minimum Period' for two consecutive executions of a particular task. The 'Deadline' guarantees that two consecutive executions do not exceed a certain time difference. The 'Minimum Period' ensures that two consecutive task activations do not fall below a certain time difference.

The IAV Engine controller needed several periodic and interrupt driven tasks. Adding and scheduling tasks was straightforward but adjusting the priorities was not. Making target specific adjustments for the processor used (MPC 565) required manual editing of files provided by ETAS. The application mode feature that provides support for different run time modes like Startup, Normal Operating Mode, Shutdown, Diagnosis, etc. was not used but it appears to be an interesting feature.

Compiling and Code Generation

Compiling and linking the application was a tedious process and several attempts were needed to compile the application. The generated C-code is not meant to be readable. Variable and function names are mostly cryptic and do not indicate their origins in the model. This made standard debugging techniques, like bench testing using a debugger, insufficient to catch errors in the application.

Generation of ASAP2 files

ASAP2 files are needed to work with certain calibration tools. An ASAP2 file generator is included in the ASCET environment. The graphical environment also provides means, to specify variables and parameters that should be considered as measurements or characteristics in the a2l file. Nevertheless, a post processing of the generated file sometimes is necessary if a calibration tools from vendors other than ETAS are used.

REALTIME WORKSHOP /EMBEDDED CODER

The Realtime Workshop from The MathWorks comes as an additional toolbox with the simulation program Simulink. Simulink is proven to be a powerful tool for simulation and system modeling. The implementation of the model is based on so called S-functions, which represent the instantiation of a graphical block. These functions are called from the simulation frame with different parameters (flags) to perform the desired action such as initializing, updating, generation of the block output, or computing a state at a certain time instance for the ODE integrator. The RTW is used to generate C-code from the graphical model. The code generation process is based on tlc files. These files can be customized to control the style of the generated C- code. For the use of fixed-point values, i.e. integer arithmetic, a special toolbox is provided allowing us to even simulate the effects of quantization.

General Modeling Style

In principle there are no restrictions on how the model, from which code is generated, has to be designed. Thus, the user is responsible for properly implementing the model, especially if a Preemptive Multi-Tasking OS is used. This requires a detailed investigation and specific knowledge of the RTOS. Therefore, company styleguides have been developed to enable less experienced users to work with this tool. Types and classes of variables (signals) are specified in a Data Explorer. Special classes are provided for variables and parameters that need to be put into ASAP2 files.

Modeling of State Machines

With the toolboxes StateFlow and Stateflow Coder, The Mathworks provides a powerful instrument to graphically design State Machines. Code generated from these blocks, results in an easy to read if cluster. An additional feature is provided which circumvents the need to fully code every condition. Specifying the order, in which the conditions are evaluated as being counterclockwise, starting at 12 o'clock, does this. Nevertheless this feature seems to be undocumented.

Version Management

Like ASCET, there is no built-in version management tool. However a certain menu is provided to connect the Simulink environment to various version management tools. Special care needs to be taken when merging changes made by different developers. The merging on ASCII level only works under certain conditions.

Code Generation

The structure of the code generated by RTW/Embedded Coder is still based on the S-function concept. Some lines of code are generated to support simulation, but do not serve any purpose on an ECU. A framework for running the code is generated that is not clearly separated from the actual application code. Thus the efficiency of the code lags. Different switches determine the style and efficiency of the code.
Customizing the style, e.g. adding pragmas etc. requires detailed knowledge of the tlc style and is somewhat tedious. It should only be done by expert users.
Another point that needs to be considered is the order of execution of blocks from the Simulink model. Stateflow charts or demultiplexers driven by a function call block need to be used to ensure a determined execution order that otherwise might not be forced by the model. The readability of the code depends somewhat on the configuration used, however, debuging at the source code level seems to be easier than debugging with the code generated by ASCET.

RTOS integration

Unlike ASCET, the RTW is not inherently tied to an RTOS. To combine the generated code with an OSEK compliant OS, users are forced to create their own interfaces, and an OSEK specific Blockset. At IAV the Blockset consists of Task blocks, allowing to conveniently configure the RTOS by GUIs. Further blocks for OSEK- resources and Alarms have been designed. However, due to the open interface tlc files, even m-scripts can be used to generate the desired code. Again, the user is responsible to ensure data consistency.

Including BIOS and legacy code

Legacy code as well as device drivers can be integrated by including them in the tlc framework. However special care needs to be taken if the code also consists of states and global storage variables. The code can be used in the pure simulation framework as well, when it is integrated in an s-function.

Generation of ASAP2 files

RTW/Embedded Coder provides files to support the generation of a2l files from the generated code. However, this process has to be customized by tlc programming to generate a2l files for different calibration tools.

TARGETLINK

The production code generator TargetLink also uses the Simulink environment for modeling the controls functionality. However, special TargetLink blocks, provided by a Blockset, need to be used. These blocks consist of additional parameters to customize and optimize the code. The code generated is not based on the s-function principle, allowing the code to be more efficient and closer to the typical embedded style.
Since the modeling is based on a Simulink model, many properties mentioned for the Embedded Coder also hold good for TargetLink.

General Modeling Style

The TargetLink version used for these projects imposed some modeling restrictions on the user. The use of Simulink blocks, signal buses and the interfaces between functions requires a restrictive usage of guidelines. The phase for learning about these rules revealed a deep insight in the code generation mechanism. TargetLink provides special-blocks referred as Inport and Outport to declare variables and specify interfaces. The connections of blocks, especially the interfaces between subsystems, defined as functions (interfaces), are based on a binding by name strategy. Thus, regardless of the Simulink signals that are connected to a block, the code is generated assuming the name binding. If this is not taken into account it can lead to code that does not reflect the actual Simulink signal flow. TargetLink also provides tools to adjust, optimize and verify the fixed-point scaling process, required for code using integer arithmetic. This tool allows for a detailed analysis and automated adjustment of normalization constants.

Modeling of State Machines

Most of what was said for the RTW/Ecoder holds for TargetLink as well. However, we found that the 12 o'clock and counter clockwise evaluation does not hold here. This means, all conditions need to be fully coded.

Version Management

What was stated for RTW/Embedded Coder above holds for TargetLink.

Code- Generation

TargetLink offers plenty of opportunities to adjust the code regarding style and efficiency. It is even possible to choose call methods for function parameters such as by name or by reference calling. The code generated by TargetLink is easy to read, thus providing convenient debugging capabilities. The generated code has been error free throughout the project, as long the modeling style exactly follows the rules that were established during the training phase.

RTOS integration

For the TargetLink version used for this project an preliminary OSEK interface was provided by the vendor. This interface consists of different blocks to support OSEK elements such as alarms, resources and other API calls. Tasks are modeled by a subsystem, where particular parameters of the task, such as priority, preemptive/ non-preemptive, etc. can be selected by writing a particular string in the GUI.
A MATLAB m-script is provided to generate the OSEK implementation language file (oil-file). However the user is still responsible to ensure data consistency. The protection of the copy process into local copies or global messages is done through an OSEK resource. In our case the 'Resource' Block assures that the code inside a subsystem is embraced by proper OSEK API calls to occupy and release the resource. It is expected that future version will allow a more inherent use of an OSEK RTOS, similar to ASCET-SD.

Including BIOS and legacy code

For this purpose TargetLink provides a so called "Custom code" block. In a way, similar to the tlc script of RTW, code can be used for simulation as well. However, in TargetLink, the custom code template provides an easier environment to integrate existing code into the generated code.

Generation of ASAP2 files

TargetLink provides several opportunities to generate ASAP2 files suitable for different calibration tools. Since the ASAP2 file generation framework is based on MATLAB m-scriptsAdjustments and customizing as well as adapting to the company build process are straightforward.

DIRECT COMPARISON

The table on the next page summarizes the features presented.

FEATURE	ASCET	RTW	TARGET-LINK
Modeling options and style	Graphical blockdiagram s,ASCET specific ESDL, C-code. Very restrictive modeling	Graphical blockdiagrams, Matlab specific M scripts, C-code. Free modeling	Graphical blockdiagrams and TargetLink specific blocks, C-code, Moderately restrictive modeling
Code-Generation	Code not meant to be readable, difficult to compile and debug. Code functionality intuitively similar to model. Very efficient code	Code readability depends on configuration, easy to compile and debug. Code functionality not intuitively similar to model. Code is traceable to its origins in the model Code not as efficient as ASCET-SD or TargetLink	Code easily readable, easy to compile and debug. Code functionality not intuitively similar to model. Code is traceable to its origins in the model Code very efficient
RTOS Integration	Built in RTOS is very easy to configure and work with. Target specific modifications need training	No built in RTOS , need to create interface. Target specific modifications need training	Separate OSEK interface provided. Target specific modifications need training
Including legacy code	Straightforward to include legacy code	Special care should be taken while including legacy code,	Straightforward with the Custom Code block
Fixed-point support	Built-in support, automatic selection of data types, no autoscaling	Specific blockset required, automatic fixed-point scaling available, based on simulation results	Automatic scaling available, based on simulation results

Generation of ASAP2 files (Used by some calibration tools)	In built support provided. Easy to generate, but not usable without post processing in non ETAS calibration tools,	In built support provided. Some customization needed for the use with different calibration tools	Support provided to generate ASAP2 files for different calibration tools.
Statemachines	Powerful modeling constructs available	Powerful modeling constructs available	Powerful modeling constructs available
Version Management Support	Basic support for version management tools through API	Basic support for version management tools through M-scrip API	same as RTW

CONCLUSIONS

We conclude that ASCET-SD has its strength in the inherent RTOS awareness during modelingas well as in the reliability of the code that is generated. However it lacks interfaces, flexibility and code tracing capabilities. The tools based on MATLAB/Simulink are less restrictive in the modeling style. This means special knowledge is required to design models suitable for production code generation. The code generation process using RTW/EmbeddedCoder seems to be still not very mature.TargetLink, although it has its drawbacks especially since a special block sets is needed and the use of busses is restricted, seems closer to generating mass production code than RTW.

It has to be stressed that all tools require specific knowledge and practical experience to create production ready code. Consequently, the quality of training, technical support and user documentation are further points to pay attention to. For the development of complex systems, engineers with special software design experience are still required (and will be required in the future) to guide the function development and modeling engineers to a proper implementation. This is particular true for the Simulink based code generators.

CONTACT

Johannes Reuter
IAV Automotive Engineering Inc.
4110 Varsity Drive
Ann Arbor, MI 48108
United States of America

Phone: +1 (734) 971-1079 ext.199
Fax: +1 (734) 971-0570
e-mail: johannes.reuter@iavinc.com
web: http://www.iavinc.com

DEFINITIONS, ACRONYMS, ABBREVIATIONS

1) ESDL --- Embedded Systems Description Language
2) RTW – Real Time Workshop
3) ERCOS – OSEK compliant operating system provided by ETAS
4) TIP – Target integration package used to configure target specific options in ASCET
5) M-script – Matlab specific programming script files
6) a2l , ASAP2 file – Files needed by calibration tools
7) BIOS – Basic Input Output System

REFERENCES

[1] ASCET-SD V4.2 Users guide, *ETAS GmbH, Stuttgart, 2002*

[2] ASD TipEXP V4.3 Users guide, *ETAS GmbH, Stuttgart, 2002*

[3] Matlab/Simulink Users guide , The MathWorks, Inc., 2001

[4] TargetLink Users guide , dSPACE GmbH, Paderborn,1999-2001

2004-01-0280

Distributed Safety Architecture for OSEK Control Units

Melanie Cossy
STZ Softwaretechnik

ABSTRACT

This paper presents a distributed software architecture for safety-related embedded systems in modern automobiles. The safety architecture ensures that software and hardware faults are treated correctly and consistently by a distributed system that consists of various control units connected by a bus. This is especially important for safety-related vehicle applications.

The general design of the architecture as well as its concrete implementation will be described. It will be shown how the abilities of the OSEK operating system and its standardized components are used to seamlessly integrate distributed control units in such a way that the behavior of the different individual control units ensures the safety of the vehicle.

INTRODUCTION

The general structure of the functional software is similar in most vehicle applications. The functional software is built on top of basic software modules that offer some kind of run-time environment and interfaces to the hardware. The basic software modules are application-independent. There are committees that try to standardize these software modules.

STRUCTURE OF THE FUNCTIONAL SOFTWARE

The functional software in an embedded control unit can be decomposed into three main execution modules: *Input*, *Control* and *Output*. Figure 1 shows the information flow through such an embedded system.

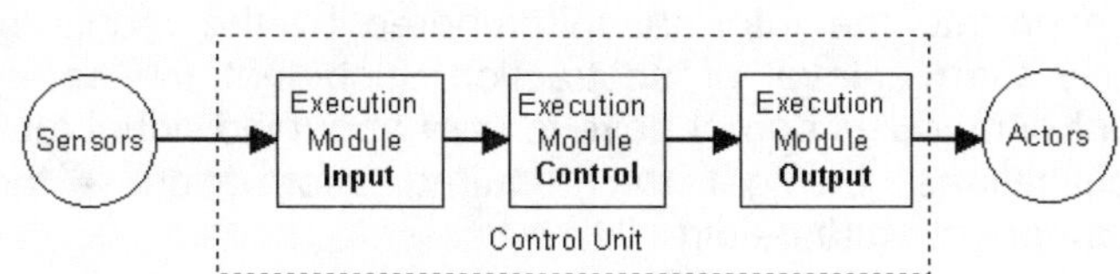

Figure 1 Execution modules of a control unit

If a functionality is implemented as a distributed system that involves various control units, the execution modules *Input* and *Output* not only communicate with sensors and actuators that are directly connected to the control unit, but also with other control units via a bus. A bus that is widely used in automobiles is controller area network (CAN), defined by ISO 11898.

The execution modules of a system run cyclically. In an electronic throttle control system, for example, the execution module *Control* calculates a new throttle position every 12.5ms and the execution module Output, which generates a pulse-width modulated signal for the direct-current motor that moves the throttle, runs every 2ms [1]. In this example the execution modules require different cycle times, and very often they must be executed with different priorities. To ensure this, a run-time environment is necessary that organizes the different execution modules into tasks.

STANDARD SOFTWARE MODULES

Standard software modules for distributed control units in vehicles have been defined in a joint project between German and French automotive companies. The industry standard is called OSEK[1] /VDX[2] and comprises the following three areas:

- Operating System:
  OSEK OS[3] is a real-time, multitasking operating system for the software in electronic control units and forms the basis for the other modules [2].
- Communication:
  OSEK COM[4] is a software module that facilitates data exchange between tasks within a control unit as well as between different control units [3].
- Network Management:
  OSEK NM[5] is a software module that determinates and monitors the network configuration [4].

---

1 Open Systems and the Corresponding Interfaces for Automotive Electronics
2 Vehicle Distributed eXecutive
3 Operating System
4 Communication
5 Network Management

The standard software modules have been designed to avoid high and recurring expenses for the development of software modules that are not application-related. Another important factor was the goal to achieve compatibility of control units even if they are made by different manufacturers. This goal has been achieved by standardizing interfaces and protocols.

OSEK OS constitutes the basis for the integration of automotive applications made by various manufacturers by standardizing the API[6] of the operating system. It ensures the portability and reusability of software modules and hides the hardware-specific implementation details. In addition, the operating system ensures that all real-time requirements of the different applications can be met. The API of OSEK OS covers the following areas:

- Task management:
  Interfaces to activate, terminate and switch tasks.
- Resource management:
  Interfaces to control the access of various software modules to jointly used data and program memory sections.
- Event management:
  Interfaces to synchronize activities and tasks.
- Interrupt management:
  Interfaces that can be used for interrupt processing.
- Error management:
  Interfaces that standardize error handling.
- Alarm management:
  Interfaces to handle relative, absolute, static and dynamic alarms.

OSEK COM implements the general communication functionality. It offers interfaces to transfer data between tasks and/or interrupt service routines. OSEK COM hides the differences between internal and external communication. This means that for the application programmer it is transparent whether the communication takes place between tasks that reside in the same control unit (internal communication) or whether different control units are involved (external communication).

OSEK NM provides services related to networks of communicating control units. It coordinates global operation modes, such as for example the network start-up or a network wide sleep mode to save energy. It also helps to monitor the operating states of the different network nodes.

CONCEPT OF THE SAFETY ARCHITECTURE

The standardized interfaces of the OSEK/VDX software modules allow the specification of a distributed safety architecture that is independent from the underlying hardware and that can be used to coordinate the applications of various suppliers. The safety architecture is built on top of the standard software modules and uses the application program interfaces offered by OSEK OS, OSEK COM and OSEK NM.

SAFETY ARCHITECTURE MODULES

The safety architecture structures the safety-related software, which is required in addition to the functional software, to ensure that possible failures are detected and handled correctly. The safety-related software consists of three types of modules: monitors, safety interface modules and safety control modules [5]. Figure 2 shows the information flow between the modules of the safety-related software and the functional software.

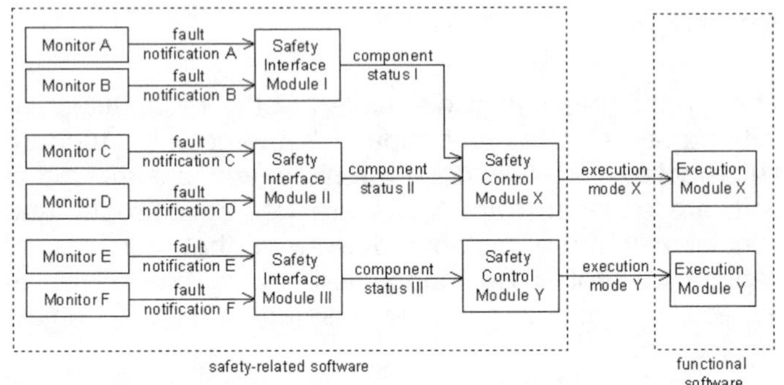

Figure 2 Safety architecture

Monitors are used to detect failures of hardware and software components. Embedded systems in vehicles normally consist of many sub-components. To detect all possible failures it is necessary to implement a huge number of monitors, which are executed in the tasks and interrupts of the control unit. Some of them are executed cyclically every x milli-seconds, while others are only activated in certain situations.

Safety interface modules are used to represent the hardware and software components that are important to ensure the safety of the system. They determine and trace the current status of the components by analyzing the fault notifications of the monitors used to check the component. If a new, safety-related component is added to a system, new monitors and a new safety interface module have to be implemented.

The main objective of the safety interface modules is to concentrate the information gathered by the monitors. They form a level of abstraction such that the safety control modules do not have to care about individual fault notifications, but get the required information – the component status – directly.

Safety interface modules are specified as state machines (see Figure 5). The active state of the state machine corresponds to the current state of the component represented. A safety interface module changes its internal state if one of its input monitors generates a fault notification.

[6] Application Program Interface

Safety control modules ensure that only correctly working components are used and degrade the functional software if a required component fails. Every execution module has its dedicated safety control module that uses the status information of the required components to determine how the execution module has to fulfill its function. The purpose for separating the execution modules that implement the system functionality from the safety control modules which control safety-related activities is to separate the functional software from the safety-related software.

Similar to the safety interface modules, the safety control modules are also specified as state machines. A safety control module changes its state if it is notified by a safety interface module about a failure of a component that is relevant for the controlled execution module.

DESIGN OF THE SAFETY ARCHITECTURE

The conceptual idea behind the safety architecture can be applied to different kinds of embedded systems. In the following it will be explained how the safety architecture can be implemented on communicating control units that use OSEK OS as the operating system. It will be shown how the API of OSEK COM facilitates the realization of a distributed safety architecture.

COLLABORATION BETWEEN THE MODULES

Figure 3 shows a collaboration diagram of the safety architecture. Each module of the safety architecture is represented as an object and the information flow is realized with the help of synchronous and asynchronous method calls between the objects.

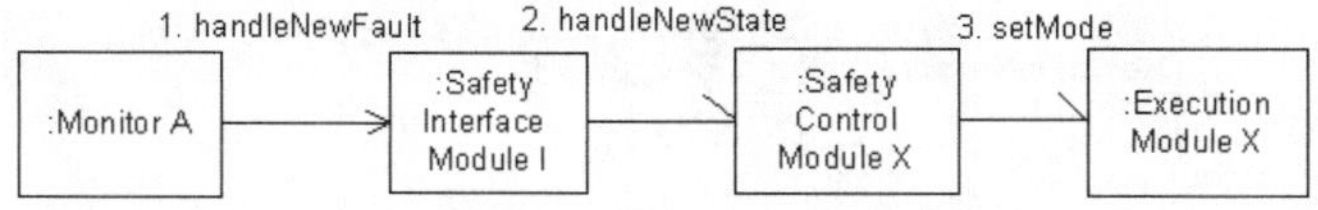

Figure 3 Collaboration diagram

Monitors are objects that implement methods to check the correctness of hardware or software components. If a monitor detects a failure it calls the synchronous method `handleNewFault` of the safety interface module representing the component. The method `handleNewFault` has the input parameter `monitorID`, which is a unique identifier of the calling monitor. In the method the safety interface module analyzes the identifier and changes its state if necessary. Then the method returns.

Normally the state machines of the safety interface modules are simple (no hierarchy) and the time needed to process a new fault notification is short. Therefore using a synchronous method call is possible – even if the calling monitor is running inside an interrupt service routine. Synchronous method calls have the advantage that their implementation is simple and efficient, because the use of communication services is not necessary.

Various monitors that may run concurrently in different tasks or interrupt service routines can call the method `handleNewFault` of a safety interface module. Therefore it is necessary to protect the code of the method as a critical section – e.g. by using the OSEK resource mechanism.

Every safety control module is implemented as a separate high-priority task. Tasks are used to protect the memory and stack sections of the safety control modules. The high task priority ensures that the safety control modules are executed in time. Compared to the safety interface modules, the safety control modules are more complex, and the processing of the method `handleNewState` can take some time. Therefore this method is called asynchronously to avoid that the calling safety interface module – and indirectly the calling monitor – has to wait until the method has been processed. Message queues provided by OSEK COM are used to implement the asynchronous method calls.

In situations, in which no new failures are detected and the component states remain unchanged, the safety control modules wait, without requiring any run time. If a monitor detects an error, it calls the method `handleNewFault` of its safety interface module. The safety interface module changes its active state and sends the OSEK message `handleNewState` to the interested safety control modules. The safety control modules that receive the message are automatically woken up and process the new state.

The main advantage of using OSEK message queues is that they facilitate the communication between different control units. This is necessary if a safety control module is interested in the state of a remote component (see Figure 4). A disadvantage of the OSEK message queue mechanism is that the messages are always processed in first-in-first-out order. Messages have no priority.

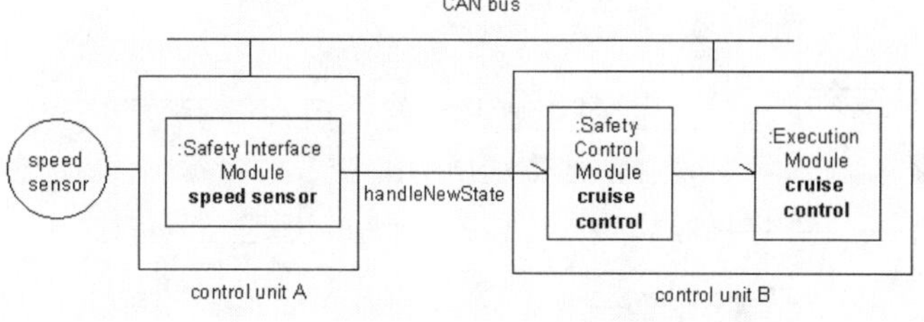

Figure 4 Remote safety interface module

The execution modules are executed cyclically – they are not event triggered like the safety control modules. Every time a new execution cycle begins, the execution module checks its execution mode. Then it fulfills its function according to the current mode. The safety control module of an execution module sets its current execution mode through the method `setMode`. OSEK offers two mechanisms how a safety control module can define the mode of an execution module that is running in a different task. The safety control module can send an un-queued message to the execution module or it can write the new mode into a global memory section protected by a resource. The message has the advantage that the safety control module does not depend on the correct resource handling of the execution module.

IMPLEMENTATION OF THE SAFETY INTERFACE AND SAFETY CONTROL MODULES

The safety interface and safety control modules are implemented as state machines. There are various well-known approaches how the state machines can be implemented:

1. Nested switch
2. State event table
3. State machine class

The safety interface modules can be implemented easily by using the *nested switch* or the *state event table* approach. For the more complicated safety control modules that are specified as hierarchical state machines the *state machine class* is used. In the following sections examples for the different implementations will be given and the advantages and disadvantages of the different approaches will be discussed.

Nested switch

Figure 5 shows a graphical representation of the state machine of a safety interface module that represents a pressure sensor (PS). The C code that implements this state machine with the help of a nested switch construct is shown in Figure 6.

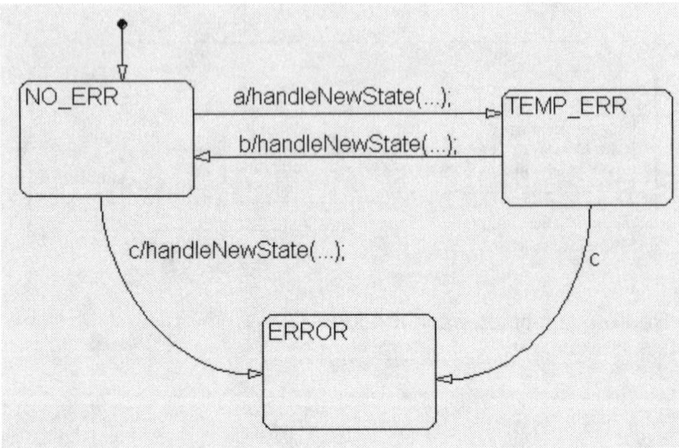

Figure 5 State machine of a safety interface module of a pressure sensor

```
void cPS_handleNewFault(cPS *me, unsigned const id) {
    switch (me->state__) {
    case NO_ERR:
        switch (id) {
        case a:
            handleNewState(...);
            cPS_Tran(me, TEMP_ERR);
            break;
        case b:
            handleNewState(...);
            cPS_Tran(me, ERROR);
            break;
            }
        break;
    case TEMP_ERR:
        ...
    case ERROR:
        ...
    }
}
```

Figure 6 C implementation of the nested switch approach

The main advantage of the *nested switch* approach is that it requires only the memory for a scalar state variable. A disadvantage of the approach is that the time needed to process a fault notification is not constant. The time depends on the switch branch in which the fault is processed. Another disadvantage is that the C code cannot be reused. Every state machine needs its own nested switch-case constructs.

State event table

In the *state event table* approach the state machine is transformed into a table that is stored in the permanent memory of the control unit (see Figure 7). Every table cell contains a function pointer that defines which actions must be executed and a constant that indicates the next state.

```
static Tran const cPS_Table[MAX_STATE][MAX_SIG] = {
    {{handleNewStateX, TEMP_ERR},
     {DoNothing, NO_ERR},
     {handleNewStateX, ERROR}},
    {{DoNothing, TEMP_ERR},
     {handleNewStateY, NO_ERR},
     {DoNothing, ERROR}},
    {{DoNothing, ERROR},
     {DoNothing, ERROR},
     {DoNothing, ERROR}},
};
```

Figure 7 State event table

The function `handleNewFault` (see Figure 8) is generic and can be used for all safety interface modules. Only the tables depend on the actual structure of the state machine.

```
void handleNewFault (cSIM *me, unsigned const id) {
    Tran const *t = me->table__ + me->state__*me->nSignals__ + id;
    (t->action)(me);
    me->state__ = t->nextState;
}
```

Figure 8 Generic `handleNewFault` function

Advantages of this approach are that the method handleNewFault can be reused and that the time needed to process the method is constant. Disadvantages are that the approach requires more memory to store the state event table and that – to avoid bugs – tool support should be used to modify the topology of the state machines. If for example the safety interface module of the pressure sensor must handle a new fault notification, three new lines must be added to the table shown in Figure 7. Another disadvantage is that it is necessary to implement a function for every transition action.

The implementation of hierarchical state machines by using state event tables is difficult. With the *nested switch* approach hierarchical state machines can be implemented by nesting more switches, but for complex hierarchical state machine the code gets chaotic. With both approaches entry and exit actions must be transformed into transition actions. This may cause additional code because the actions that belong to a state must be implemented for every transition entering or leaving the state again.

<u>State machine class</u>

For the specification of the safety control modules both hierarchy as well as entry and exit actions are used. Therefore the *state machine class* approach is used to implement the safety control modules. Every safety control module is derived from a generic class called `Statemachine` (Figure 9). Safety interface modules call the method `handleNewState` to inform the safety control module about a changed component state. The states of a safety control module are represented as methods implemented by the derived safety control module. In the attribute `myState` of the generic class `Statemachine` a function pointer to the method that represents the currently active state is stored. The method `handleNewState` (Figure 10) executes the function that is stored in `myState`.

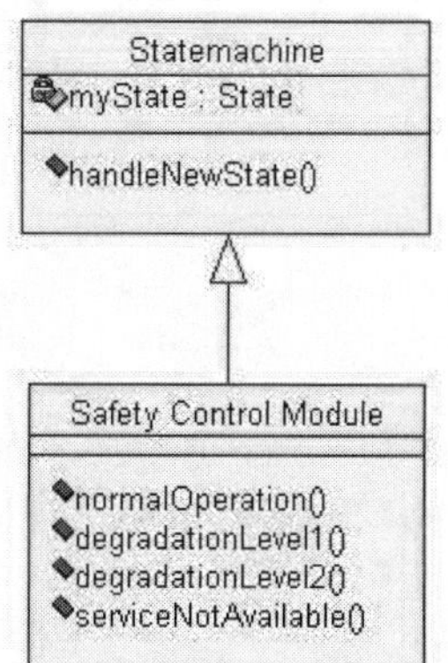

Figure 9 *State machine class*

```
CLASS(Statemachine)
   State myState__;
METHODS
   #define handleNewState(me_, e_) (*(me_)->myState__)((me_), (e_))
   ...
END_CLASS
```

Figure 10 `handleNewState` function

The advantage of the *state machine class* approach is that hierarchical state machines can be implemented easily by encapsulating the complexity of handling the hierarchy into the generic Statemachine class [6]. Another advantage is the reusability of the Statemachine class.

RESULTS

The state machines of the safety interface and safety control modules are normally defined with graphical tools such as Stateflow from MathWorks. The code generators integrated into these tools enable persons that are unfamiliar with C programming to generate C code from the specification. Writing the C code manually requires more time, and it is hard to avoid bugs, even if it is clearly defined how the state machines and all additional features like parallel and hierarchical state machines or history junction have to be implemented.

After analyzing the different possibilities of how the software modules of the safety architecture may communicate and how the safety interface and safety control modules can be implemented, an adequate code generator must be found. There are many code generators that very often use the *nested switch* approach to generate code from the specified state machines, but none of them can generate code that can be directly integrated into a distributed safety architecture that consists of software modules running on different control units. Until now it is necessary to manually write wrappers around the generated code, because the code generators offer no support for communication and distribution. This may change with the new version of the tool TargetLink (dSPACE) that will have a close integration with OSEK OS [7].

However, before any code generator can be used for the generation of safety-related software a general requirement must be fulfilled. A code generator for safety-related systems must either have a certificate of validation to a recognized national or international standard or it must be assessed to establish its fitness for its purpose (IEC61508 Part 3 Section 7.4.4.3a).

REFERENCES

1. Costin, M./ Schaller, R./ Maiorana, M./ Purcell, J./ Simon, R./ Bauerle, P./ Stockbridge, J.: An Architecture for Electronic Throttle Control Systems. SAE World Congress 2003. Paper 2003-01-0098

2. OSEK/VDX Operating System Specification (Version 2.2.1).
   http: //www.osek-vdx.org
3. OSEK/VDX OSEK Communication Specification (Version 3.0.1).
   http: //www.osek-vdx.org
4. OSEK/VDX OSEK Network Management Concept and Application Programming Interface (Version 2.5.2).
   http: //www.osek-vdx.org
5. Cossy, M.: Software-Sicherheitsarchitektur für Steuergeräte im Fahrzeug. Entwicklerforum Kfz-Elektronik Design & Elektronik (2003)
6. Samek, M.: Practical Statecharts in C/C++ Quantum Programming for Embedded Systems. CMPBooks (2002)
7. Köster, L./ Thomsen, T./ Stracke, R.: Von Simulink nach OSEK: Automatische Codegenerierung fuer Echtzeitbetriebssysteme mit TargetLink (2003) http: //www.dspace.de

CONTACT

Melanie Cossy is a system designer at *STZ Softwaretechnik* (Germany) and provides consulting services related to the development of embedded systems. Starting with the software design for a digital signal processor, Melanie has been engaged in a wide range of development activities in the recent years – examples are requirement management and test automation processes, the integration of standard components and the development of software architectures. She earned her MSc in *Distributed Computing Systems* at the *Brunel University* (West London) where she designed an Extensible Framework for testing Distributed Object-Oriented Systems. At present Melanie develops software safety architectures for safty-related embedded control systems on behalf of a large automotive company. This work is part of her dissertation research activities at the *Eberhard-Karls University* in Tübingen, Germany. Melanie has presented at the *SAE 2003 World Congress* in Detroit and the *DESIGN&ELEKTRONIK* Conference in Germany, and has written for *Automotive Electronics* magazine. e-mail address: melanie.cossy@stz-softwaretechnik.de web address: www.cossy.de/melanie.

2003-01-1198

Dealing With the OEM-Supplier Relationship in the Development of Embedded Software

Roman Nossal and Dietmar Millinger
DECOMSYS

ABSTRACT

Embedded electronic systems play an increasingly important role in the automotive field. Since they are the key to innovations and are the basis of most new functions, this paper deals with how to develop them. The first part identifies the problems that to a large extent arise from the particular organizational structure of the automotive industry. The second part of the paper describes an approach to how to control the complexity of the process. Information domains are introduced for this purpose. Contracts in these information domains between the process participants define the actual system behavior.

INTRODUCTION

In recent years SAE has published a number of papers dealing with the development of distributed embedded automotive software. Most of those papers addressed the development life cycle in general or related technical issues, e.g., the V-model or tools and their interoperability. While these topics are important for any type of embedded system, automotive or not, there is a characteristic about automotive software that requires special attention: Automotive industry OEMs collaborate with a multitude of suppliers. Each of these organizations contributes a part to the embedded system.

This organizational situation raises a number of problems to be tackled. When several organizations participate in the same project, information must be exchanged between the companies involved. On the other hand, each company strives to protect its proprietary know-how as far as possible.

It is obvious that in the first place there is a process question to be answered rather than a technical one. How the organizations collaborate must be defined, i.e., where interfaces between organizations are located in the development process and which information has to be shared among the process participants across these interfaces.

Only in the second place should the problems be approached from a technical point of view. The exact content and format of the data to be exchanged has to be specified at each step in the development process. Information hidden from other companies, "black-boxes", must be described in a way for others to accomplish their development tasks. The development tools must support data exchange, as well as information hiding and the handling of incomplete information, i.e., the "black boxes".

This paper works out the problems to be solved and the questions to be answered. It then outlines an information model that can be used to define various development processes for distributed embedded systems, in which several companies participate.

CHALLENGES IN EMBEDDED SOFTWARE

AUTOMOTIVE ELECTRONICS

Embedded systems play an increasingly important role in today's and tomorrow's vehicles. While innovations in mechanical systems seem to have leveled off, 90% of all innovations in a vehicle are in electronics. 80% of all new functions are based on electronics. It is estimated that the value of all electronics in a car will increase from $4000 today to $8000 in 2010 [2].

A new safety-critical class of applications is appearing on the embedded systems horizon. X-by-wire systems will change traditional cars significantly. They will replace mechanical systems by electrically driven, electronically controlled ones, e.g., the hydraulic brakes will be replaced by a brake-by-wire embedded system. Electronics for x-by-wire applications will take over the core functionality of a vehicle for the first time. This will have a direct impact on safety.

An important observation in this context is that embedded systems are evolving from centralized, stand-alone boxes to distributed systems consisting of several ECUs that are interconnected by a communication system.

ORGANIZATIONAL STRUCTURE

The automotive industry has a very distinct organizational structure. Several different companies cooperate and collaborate on projects together. On the one hand the organizations involved can be distinguished by the tier they belong to. Once this distinction has been made, one can identify the OEM, first tier suppliers, second tier suppliers, and so on. The system is comparable to shells with the OEM at the core (see Figure 1).

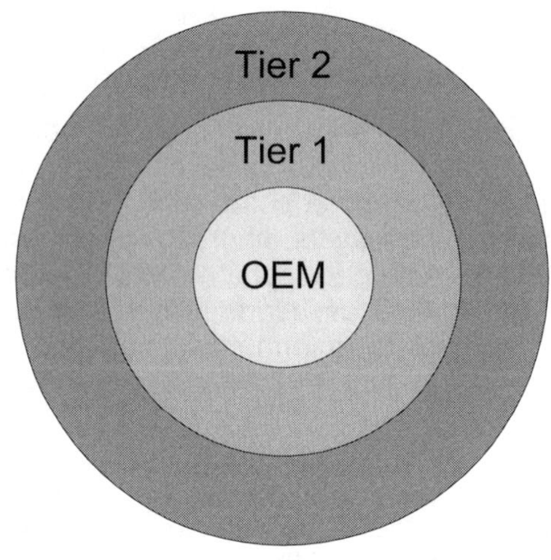

Figure 1: Supply Chain Shells

A second distinction relates to the function performed in the development process. There is a system integrator who has the responsibility for the overall system functionality. He/She[1] defines the system functionality and its distribution to ECUs. This also defines who the suppliers are. The suppliers produce the parts of the system functionality that have been assigned to them. Finally the system integrator assembles the parts developed by the various suppliers.

Unfortunately, the two distinctions are not well separated from each other. The system integrator, for example, can be the OEM, but could just as well be a supplier who delivers a complete system to the OEM.

To further complicate the situation, the setting is ambiguous. The system integrator can also build ECUs and thus act like a supplier. In this case the interface between the system integrator and the supplier is intra-organizational.

Finally, OEMs attempt to extend their know-how into traditional areas of supplier knowledge. As electronic systems in general and software in particular play an ever more important role in the car, they start to become distinctive features, which contribute to a car's "personality". From this perspective it is understandable that OEMs want to develop functions on their own.

[1] To improve the readability "He" will be used instead of "He/She" in the remainder of this paper.

KNOWLEDGE DISTRIBUTION

The organizational setting determines the roles that certain organizations play in the development process. Each role comes with a specific responsibility and requires a specific amount of knowledge.

The system integrator possesses the knowledge of the intended function of the system. He also selects the system architecture and distributes the functionality among the ECUs in the system.

Since suppliers have detailed information about the function their ECUs should perform, they can specify the communication requirements on the input side, i.e., the data that must be provided by other functions executed on other ECUs. On the other hand, the supplier can define the communication offer on the output side, i.e., the data that can be provided by the functions executed on his ECU.

OBJECTIVE

Figure 2: Development Process Objective

It is the main goal of the development process to coordinate the exchange of knowledge between the participants and to ensure that

- Each participant has all the information needed to develop assigned functions, and that
- Each participant does not have any information that is not needed and which might be the proprietary know-how of another participant.

A properly designed information exchange enables the transformation of knowledge into functions.

OPEN QUESTIONS

All questions to be identified and answered arise from the organizational setting described before and from the need to transfer distributed knowledge into the desired function according to a set of technical, quality, economic, legal, organizational and even social constraints.

ORGANIZATIONAL SETTING

The initial questions relate to assigning roles to the active members in a specific setting.

Who defines the roles of project members in the project setting? The project leader naturally wants to do this while the members want to place themselves in particular roles according to their special interests. However, possibly conflicting interests must be resolved and the roles clearly assigned and communicated to all members before the project starts; otherwise the processes are doomed to fail.

TRANSFORM KNOWLEDGE TO FUNCTION

In the previous section we mentioned that the transformation of knowledge to function requires a well-defined process. This process attaches operations to the roles in a project setting. The operations can either be information source, information transformation or information sink. The basic questions regarding the process are:

1. Are the operations well defined?
2. Does every role have operations assigned? Roles without operations are an indicator of inefficiency in the process.
3. Is every operation assigned to exactly one role? In case of an ambiguous assignment, operations may be left out or executed multiply leading to unexpected results.

Obviously, a fourth question about the process itself has to clarify which operations are to be used and which information is to be exchanged between roles and operations.

CONSTRAINTS

Apart from the questions about the basic operation of the processes, there are numerous questions, which come up as a result of restrictions hidden in the organizational setting and the environment of a project. Most obvious are technical constraints that result from the fact that inconsistently or incorrectly configured distributed applications are unlikely to work at all, but they certainly will not work according to the specification. Inconsistencies result either from badly designed processes (see above) or from contradicting requirements coming from different information sources. Thus it is important to find out how contradictions and inconsistencies in the information can be resolved and faults can be removed.

This issue is also important for setting up a structured process for change management. It is of utmost importance to manage change by finding out if there are ways to restrict the impact of changes to small sections in the information distributed and to ensure consistent distribution among the affected roles.

Vital economic interests like the protection of knowledge of participants leads to secrecy restrictions regarding the information exchanged between the roles. This raises the question, how can information be selectively hidden from other participants without limiting the processes?

Along with economic are legal issues that raise questions regarding the liability of the system integrator and the suppliers.

1. Which part of the information is relevant to the liability of a process participant?
2. Is there sufficient information available to base any liability on this information?

More questions arise from the process of information passing itself, since it is not certain that the receiver of information will interpret the information in the same way as the source. Thus it is important to clarify how to avoid misunderstandings between information sources and sinks, which can be members of different organizations, companies, and countries.

The following sections will describe a concept that answers many of these questions.

PROCESS

PROCESS ENTITIES

From a process point of view the second categorization of involved organizations is important. Three participants can be identified in the process:

1. System Integrator: The system integrator is the project leader. He is in charge of the overall system functionality, distributes the functions to different ECUs, and finally integrates the ECUs.
2. Supplier: The supplier is bound to the constraints set by the system integrator. However, the system integrator can define these constraints in cooperation with the supplier. The supplier provides an ECU performing a certain function.
3. Contractor: At the lower end of the hierarchy is the contractor, who does some implementation work for either a supplier or the system integrator. Other than a supplier, the contractor is not involved in defining constraints, i.e., is not part of the contract mechanism (see below).

INFORMATION MODEL

The information exchanged in the process can be assigned to different domains. This assignment forms an information model, which will be used in subsequent discussions.

The *functional domain* defines entities called functions and the communication relations between them. Functions are information processing units of an application. They have timing parameters assigned to them that define the period and the time offset of their execution. A communication relation starts at a sender function, connects the sender function with receiver functions, and has an assigned signal.

Signals are defined in the *signal domain*. A signal definition contains a signal name, the signal semantics,

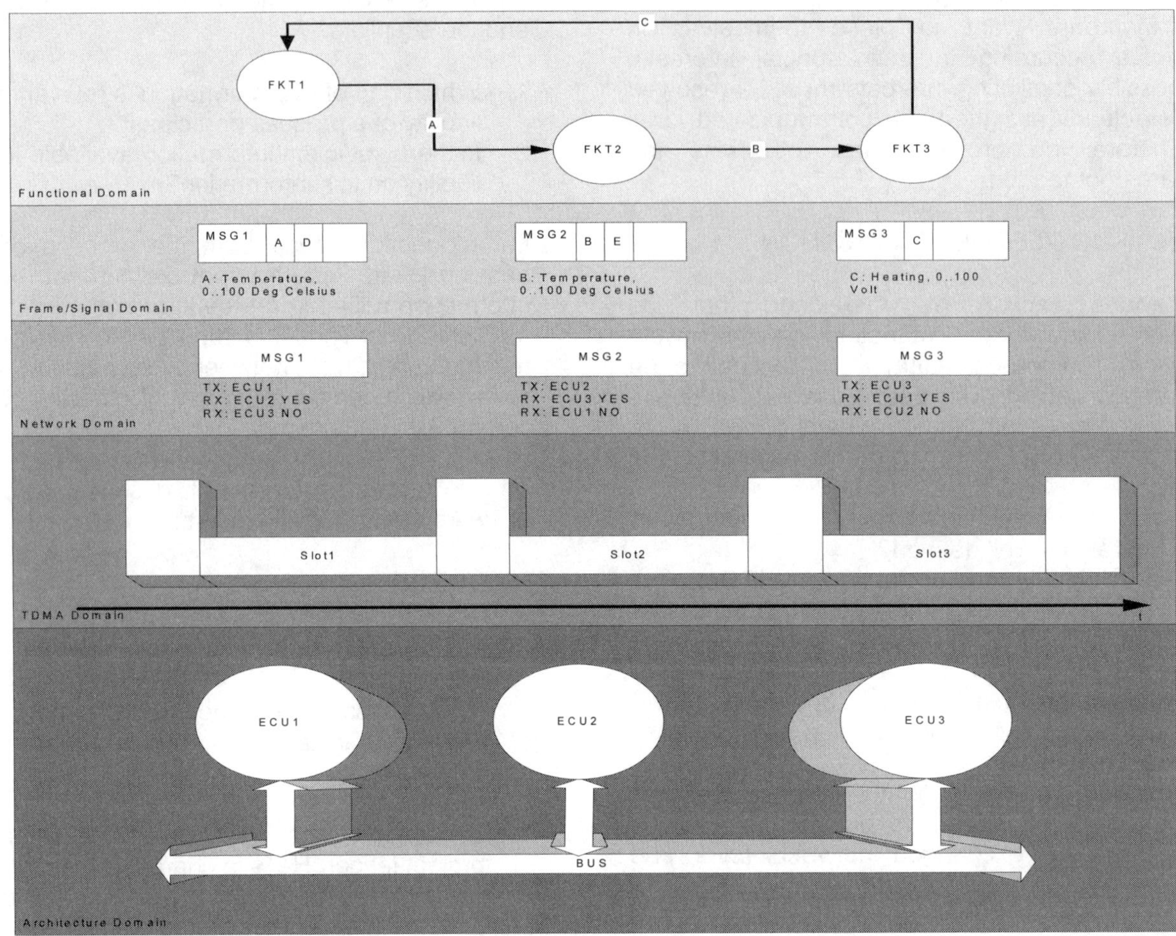

Figure 3: Information Domains

and the value range. Signals are assigned to frames. The *frame domain* defines names of frames and the setup of the signals in the frames.

The *network domain* determines which ECU will send a frame and the transmission slot of the frame in a TDMA access scheme.

The *TDMA domain* establishes the exact points in time when the transmission slots of a time-triggered communication system start and stop.

Finally, the *architecture domain* defines the physical structure of a system, comprising all ECUs, the communication systems, and the connections of the ECUs to these communication systems.

Information from these domains can be used to form contracts among the participants in the process. Much like a legal contract, a contract here defines certain pieces of information agreed upon by the contracting parties. The contract binds both parties. However, normally one of the parties is the principal, while the other is the agent.

The entire embedded system can be described by means of contracts. Sets of contracts that are merged form the requirements specification or the system specification. It is obvious that the contracts must not contradict each other and that they have to describe the system comprehensively. If the latter is not the case, i.e., if no set of contracts exists that represents the entire requirements or system specification, then the system is not defined sufficiently.

There are various types of contracts that can be made from the information within a domain or from a combination of information from more than one domain. In other words, a contract can deal with a row in Figure 3 or it can cover several rows. Assume, for example, an ECU delivered by a supplier, which should transmit a particular frame with defined and public signals at a particular point in time. This can be described using a frame contract for listing the signals contained in the message, a signal contract for describing the signals, a network contract for determining the sender and the transmission slot, and a TDMA contract, which defines the slot timing. In case the signals are not public, the signal contract can be omitted.

PROCESS INSTANTIATIONS

The general model that has been introduced in the previous section lays the groundwork for concrete process definitions. The model elements can be instantiated in many different ways, resulting in very different processes. All of these processes are guided by the principles of information exchange by means of contracts between those participating in the process. In the following we will present two process instantiations that are common in automotive electronics.

The first process (see Figure 4) assumes that the supplier already has detailed knowledge of the function to be delivered or — more likely — has already delivered a similar function to another system integrator. He defines the communication requirements of his function on the input side as well as the communication offer on the output side. The system integrator merges this information with similar information obtained from other suppliers. The result of this merge defines the communication schedule, which is the rule for integrating the ECUs (see the following subsection for more details on system integration via the common communication system). The schedule is given to the suppliers and is one of the factors limiting function development.

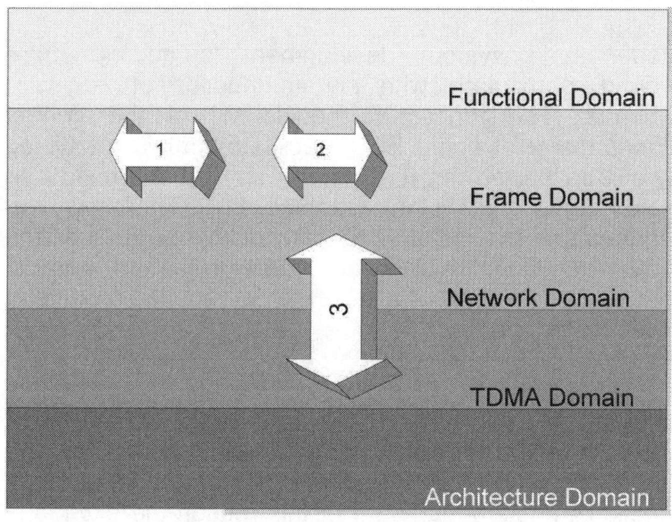

Figure 4: Contracts of Process Instantiation 1

In this process we make use of three information domains: the TDMA domain, the network domain, and the frame/signal domain. There are at least three contract types between these domains:

1. The contract governing the communication requirements of the supplier, which is entirely located in the frame domain. If the integrator fulfils this contract, then the supplier must be able to implement his assigned function. Optionally, the frame contract can be complemented by a signal contract that further describes the frame content.
2. The contract governing the communication offered by the supplier, which is part of the frame domain as well. This contract obligates the supplier to deliver the specified information as other suppliers might rely on it. Again, the frame contract can optionally be enhanced with a signal contract.
3. The contract defining the communication schedule, the basis for communication. This contract, which belongs to the TDMA and the network domain, sets the constraints for all suppliers, but also limits the system integrator. Any change in the distribution of functions or the schedule affects all suppliers. If all suppliers fulfill this contract, the system integrator can integrate the parts without side effects or incompatibilities.

For reasons of clarity we have omitted the contracts required for the definition of the system architecture etc.

The second process instantiation is more suitable for entirely new systems, for which none of the suppliers has knowledge from previous implementations. In this case the system integrator defines the system function, its distribution to ECUs, and the resulting communication requirements. He then develops the communication schedule and distributes it to the suppliers.

Again, there are three information domains used in this type of process: the TDMA, the network, and the frame domain. This simpler process only uses two types of contracts:

1. The communication schedule, which governs the timing behavior of the communication system and is the basis for integration. This contract is part of the TDMA and the network domain.
2. Closely tied to the TDMA/network contract is the frame contract that describes the communication inputs provided to each supplier and the communication required from him. Note that compared to the first process example, in this case the two sides - the requirements and the communication offer by the supplier - are exactly reversed.

From these two examples we can conclude that the domain model and the contract mechanism provide a practical way to cover a large number of processes. Note, however, that the contract mechanism is just a way to organize things. When setting up a real process, this technique has to be implemented in a specific technical way.

ADVANTAGES OF TIME-DRIVEN SYSTEMS

This section shows the advantages of a time-driven system architecture for system integration.

Time-driven systems [10] exhibit a characteristic called composability. Composability addresses the fact that parts of the system that have been developed autonomously can be integrated without unintended side effects. Obviously, this is what we want.

The composability of time-driven systems originates from the particular control strategy, i.e., how system services such as the transmission of a frame are activated. In a time-driven system all services are activated by the progression of global time, meaning that each service has a predefined point in time when it is activated. The sum of all activation times of a certain service type is called the schedule of the service.

If the system integrator performs fault-free scheduling, then all services, e.g., frame transmissions in a TDMA pattern, have compatible activation times. If — bound by the TDMA contract — all suppliers stick to their given activation times, then system integration can be done by simply plugging the parts together.

TECHNICAL ISSUES

In addition to all the process requirements there are, of course, a number of technical questions to be answered. These issues in particular are a matter of debate, as technical know-how is the main competitive advantage of companies involved. We are aware of the necessity to preserve this advantage, but we are also convinced that the most important technical issues can be settled without endangering any advantageous position. What is more, a proper definition of technical cooperation guidelines for basically competing organizations is a prerequisite for maintaining a competitive advantage. A mechanism for model exchange, for example, can be the basis for cooperation if it ensures that functional "black boxes" can be exchanged.

In the following we will raise those questions that from our point of view are the focus of the development process.

REQUIREMENTS EXCHANGE

Any system development project begins by defining requirements. These requirements are passed on from the system integrator, who decides on the system functionality, to the suppliers that contribute parts to that functionality. Just as important is the information flow in the opposite direction. Since suppliers provide ECUs to different OEMs and normally have a great deal of knowledge about the function to be performed, they also set requirements, which the system integrator must take into account.

The issue is to define a format that allows requirements to be described in an unambiguous way but is still readable and understandable. If the format also enables automatic consistency checking, the ideal has been reached.

SYSTEM ARCHITECTURE

Cooperation between organizations in the development process would substantially benefit from a common standardized system architecture. A standardized architecture would provide standardized interfaces where the parts of the system delivered by the suppliers could be integrated. From the OEM's point of view this integration process would be independent of the particular supplier. On the other hand, the supplier could provide its ECU to various OEMs without adapting the interface.

Contradicting Lederer et al. in [3], we feel that a thoroughly defined system architecture is not a competitive issue. Depending on where the interfaces are set, there is ample room for each participating company to use its strengths effectively to achieve its purpose. In our opinion the real competitive issue are the functions in an ECU or the overall system functionality that is realized by the interaction of ECU functions. The special feeling of an electronic power-steering system is mainly determined by the control algorithms and their application data, rather than by the type of communication interface used for integration.

Some steps have already been taken in the direction of a standardized architecture, e.g., the OSEK/VDX initiative that strives to standardize an operating system (OSEK OS) [4], a Communication Layer (OSEK COM) [5], and a Network Management Layer (OSEK NM) [6] for traditional automotive systems. Moreover, this initiative has been extended to cover safety-critical systems with a dedicated operating system (OSEKtime) [7,9] and an appropriate Fault-Tolerant Communication Layer (FTCom) [8].

MODEL EXCHANGE

Model-based system development is gaining more ground, particularly with the introduction of x-by-wire systems. The functional models [1] of the control algorithms or of entire ECUs facilitate virtual prototyping by simulation, so the functionality can be improved and tested before the system is actually built. This, however, requires that the system integrator is able to simulate the system functionality using the models of all of the parts. Similarly, the testing of a certain ECU requires models of other system parts.

At this point we obviously encounter a problem of competition. While it is desirable to have the most accurate models of the system, there is at the same time the demand to hide the detailed information about a function's implementation. For this reason the exchange of models between companies must support so-called "black boxes" that exhibit the correct behavior of the function at the interface without revealing the implementation details.

INTERFACE DEFINITIONS

The most important issue in a distributed development process is of course how to define interfaces. The section on the process has covered contracts as a form of process interface. This paragraph deals with technical interfaces.

Technical information is exchanged at various points in the process. In the beginning requirements are passed back and forth between the system integrator and the suppliers. In the specification phase the system integrator distributes the descriptions of the interfaces, which are to become the points where the system parts developed by suppliers are integrated. If modeling and simulation are used, models or parts of those models have to be exchanged in order to enable simulation (see also previous subsection). Finally, the suppliers deliver the object code of their functions or entire ECU modules to the system integrator.

A format at the interface must be defined for each of these information exchanges. The exchange format depends on the purpose of the interface and the details of the information. Standardized formats should be applied, because the exchange format is not of vital interest to OEMs and suppliers. The advantages of standardization in this area are the interoperability of the tools involved and an easier reuse of existing information.

Three questions should be asked whenever an interface is defined:

1. What is the purpose of the interface?
2. Which information has to be exchanged for this purpose?
3. How can information of competitive value remain confidential?

The third question relates to the second focal issue in the technical process definition. The process itself and as a consequence the technical interfaces must ensure that the vital competitive interests of the companies involved are not endangered. Any internal information on the implementation of functions or the architecture of an ECU delivered by a supplier must be hidden. At the same time, of course, the goal of everyone involved to build a system meeting the requirements must not be put at risk.

CONCLUSION

This paper gave a comprehensive overview of the particularities of the development of embedded systems in the automotive industry. The problems and questions were presented, which arise from the organizational setting of OEMs and suppliers cooperating in system development. The main part of the paper dealt with an information model consisting of information domains and contracts, which should provide everything needed to address the questions. A contract defines pieces of information from one or more domains, which have been agreed upon by the contracting parties, i.e., the OEM or suppliers.

The model presented in the paper has to be instantiated to represent a particular process. For each process type certain contracts are of importance while others are not used at all. A technical implementation of the abstract contract mechanism also has to be found in order to apply the model.

REFERENCES

1. R. Nossal, R. Lang. Model-Based System Development—An Approach to Building X-by-Wire Applications. IEEE Micro, July/August 2002, pp. 56-63.
2. Source: Automotive Business, February 2002.
3. D. Lederer, G. Heling, J. Fetzer, and T. Beck. Der Schlüssel zum Erfolg (The Key to Success; in German). Elektronik Automotive, June 2002, pp. 42-46.
4. OSEK/VDX. Specification of the OSEK/VDX Operating System, Version 2.2. Available from www.osek-vdx.org.
5. OSEK/VDX. Specification of the OSEK/VDX Communication, Version 2.2.2. Available from www.osek-vdx.org.
6. OSEK/VDX. Specification of the OSEK/VDX Network Management, Version 2.5. Available from www.osek-vdx.org.
7. OSEK/VDX. Specification of the OSEK/VDX Time-Triggered Operating System, Version 1.0. Available from www.osek-vdx.org.
8. OSEK/VDX. Specification of the OSEK/VDX Fault-Tolerant Communication, Version 1.0. Available from www.osek-vdx.org.
9. A. Krüger, Y. Domaratsky, B. Holzmann, A. Schedl, C. Ebner, R. Belschner, B. Hedenetz, E. Fuchs, A. Zahir, S. Boutin, E. Dilger, T. Führer, R. Nossal, B. Pfaffeneder, S. Poledna, M. Glück. OSEKtime: A Dependable Real-Time Fault-Tolerant Operating System and Communication Layer as an Enabling Technology for By-Wire Applications. SAE 2000 Congress, March 2000.
10. H. Kopetz. Event-Triggered versus Time-Triggered Real-Time Systems. In A. Karshmer and J. Nehmer, editors, Proceedings International Workshop on Operating Systems of the 90s and Beyond, pp. 87-101, Berlin, Germany, 1991, Springer Verlag.

CONTACT

Please direct questions or comments about this article to Roman Nossal at DECOMSYS - Dependable Computer Systems, Hardware und Software Entwicklung GmbH, Stumpergasse 48/28, A-1060 Vienna, Austria; nossal@decomsys.com; www.decomsys.com

DECOMSYS is a development partner of the FlexRay® consortium.

Roman Nossal is a team manager at DECOMSYS. His research interests include time-driven systems, scheduling, and the development process. Nossal has a PhD in computer science from the Vienna University of Technology.

Dietmar Millinger is one of the managing directors and owners of DECOMSYS. His research interests include the development process for distributed embedded systems in the automotive area with a focus on organizational requirements. Millinger has a PhD in computer science from the Vienna University of Technology.

2001-01-1221

Effective System Development Partitioning

Patrick Leteinturier
Infineon Technologies AG

Guenter Gromeier and Johannes Wagner
ETAS GmbH

ABSTRACT

In terms of modern technical systems, the automotive sector is characterized by escalating complexity and functionality requirements. The development of embedded control systems has to meet highest demands regarding process-, time- and cost-optimization. Hence, the efficiency of software development becomes a crucial competitive advantage. Systems design engineers need effective tools and methods to achieve exemplary speed and productivity within the development phase. To obtain such tools and methods, semiconductor manufacturers and tool manufacturers must work closely together. Within the joint efforts of ETAS and Infineon, the software tool suite ASCET-SD was enhanced to generate efficient C code for Infineon's TriCore architecture mapped on ETAS's real-time operating system ERCOS^{EK}. The processor interface to application & calibration tools was realized using the ETK probe based on a JTAG/Nexus link at very high bandwidth.

INTRODUCTION

To support a dynamic software design process, ETAS provides a complete tool suite optimized for the new generation Infineon processors. Starting from an initial idea, the first system specification or system design respectively, the entire process is supported step by step to the final control unit software or in-vehicle calibration. In every stage of this process reusable models can be generated, tested, alternated and improved in a timely and cost-effective way. Thus, increased productivity is possible despite growing complexity of the development process.

DEVELOPMENT OF EMBEDDED CONTROL SYSTEMS

Many details need to be considered when designing embedded control systems. Usually the control unit must incorporate numerous signals. Additionally, the physical relationships between the signals are highly complex. If the development engineer wants to obtain results quickly, he needs methods and tools that keep additional difficulties away from him when implementing the control unit on the microprocessor. By abstracting the task and shifting it to the physical plane, it is possible to reduce complexity to an acceptable level. Furthermore, the design can be made easier. As an example, we can have in mind the development of a complete traction control system.

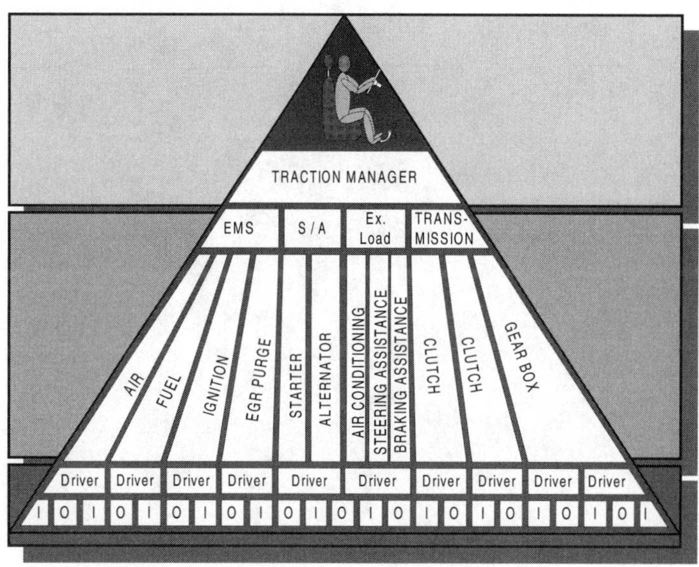

Figure 1: Traction Control Architecture

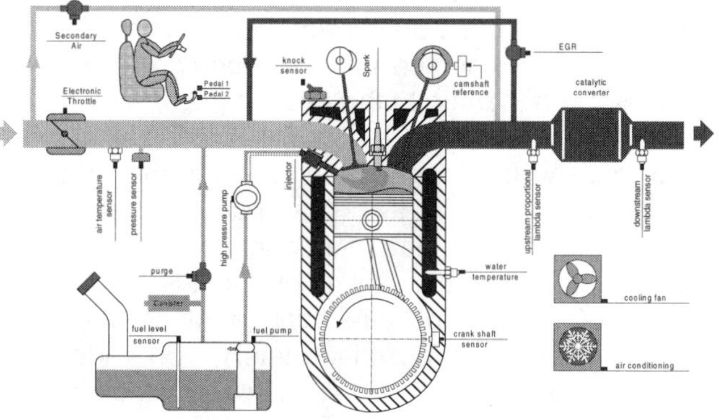

Figure 2: Engine Management Schematic

DEVELOPMENT ENVIRONMENT ASCET-SD – This tool suite meets the requirements for abstraction, simplicity and speed. It enables engineers to fully concentrate on the physics of the embedded control system, to design the control unit in an abstract and simple way, to test and improve it in order to finally automatically generate production code.

Embedded control systems implement complex control circuits. Sensors precisely record information on the current state of the controlled system. These signals are acquired and processed with previous data. The result is the output of control information via corresponding actuators.

To provide the design engineer with the necessary description options for control algorithms, the basic tool package contains a number of specification possibilities, such as block diagrams, state machines, text specifications and C-interfaces. Even the operating system is configured graphically and can therefore be set up quickly and simply. The following sections concentrate on the technical characteristics of the development environment.

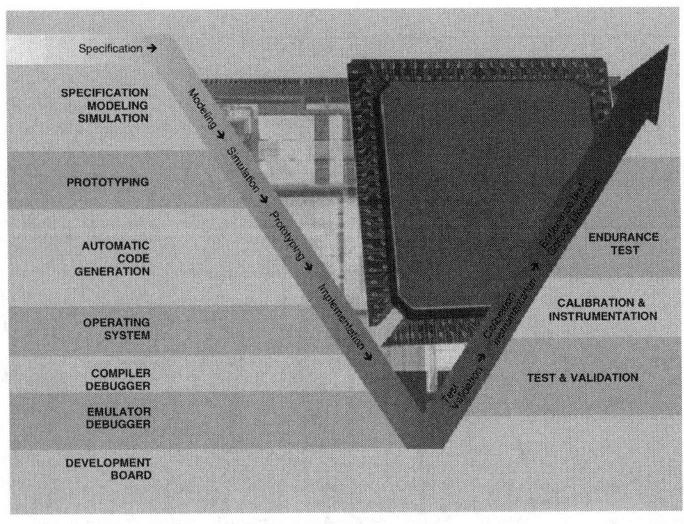

Figure 3: V development cycle

SPECIFICATION OF THE EMBEDDED CONTROL SYSTEM – While development processes are usually company-specific, there are many general requirements, such as efficiency, cost, quality and flexibility that should also ultimately be reflected in the supporting tools. The tool suite is more than up to this challenge.

The high quality development tool ensures the reuse of existing components. Its graphical development environment allows target-independent functional specifications. This tool suite offers the automatic generation of control software from graphical methods (which are going to be described later), target identical prototyping and the ability to test in every stage of the development cycle. The final result is a reusable specification from which target-specific executable production code can be easily generated.

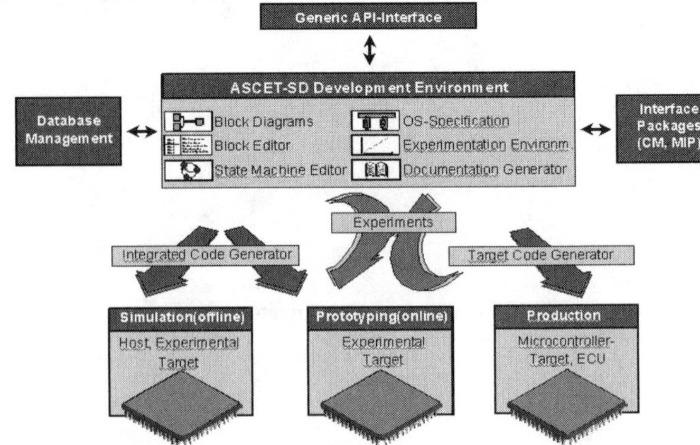

Figure 4: Development Environment

It is possible to define data records for your model. By assigning a certain data record, you can, for example, perform experiments for different engine variants, or generate code for different controller implementations. The algorithm itself remains unchanged.

The software development environment provides a powerful user interface to handle both the modeling of the software behavior and the specification of the respective data (parameters, tables, etc.) in an integrated manner. Data sets can be changed easily without changing the behavior at any stage of the development process. The development system handles the complete management of the software description, including the physical description, data and additional implementation information at any time. When generating code the respective data structure is generated according to the corresponding model. In a further step, the development tool generates a hex-file as well as an ASAP2-file, which can be processed for calibration and measuring with the integrated calibration and application tool INCA.

For the realistic simulation of embedded control systems, the tool suite offers a new quality standard. With the help of target identical prototyping, new control strategies can be tested and adapted under realistic conditions in the early phases of the development process. Based on the target system behavior, the complete functional and timing behavior is specified, simulated, optimized and executed on the development system with great accuracy. This results in impressive process optimization when developing control units.

The specification of control algorithms must be based on the design engineer's viewpoint. Use is made of tried and tested graphical methods for block diagrams and state machines.

The specification consists of a number of dependent elements. The executable specification or the operating system configuration is continuously managed in a project. Projects consist of a number of modules and tasks. These elements again contain several processes, which are specified in the modules and scheduled for execution in the tasks. Modules encapsulate several class instances as objects, and they only occur once. Each instance has precisely one class, which contains the related methods. As opposed to a module, a class can have several instances. Methods differ from processes in that they contain arguments and return values. Inter-process communication is provided by messages.

Both classes and modules can be implemented by block diagrams or text specifications. C-code modules and classes are also offered. State machines are treated as classes.

Block diagrams - The block description of control systems is based on interfaces in the control process. This approach is supplemented by the element of encapsulation, which is known from object-oriented programming languages. ASCET-SD blocks represent objects, which encapsulate items of information and are interconnected by interfaces. Object-based presentation ensures that they can be re-used easily and reliably. The block diagrams contain a purely physical presentation of control algorithms. Implementation information is easy to add to the elements using the block diagram by means of editors.

In addition, typical data flow elements (e.g. variables, characteristics, arithmetic operators) block diagrams contain control flow elements such as branches. Separate line and link types show the control flow in a well-arranged presentation. Furthermore, it is possible to specify the processing order of block operations directly by assigning block attributes to the graphic. Complex algorithms can at last be presented precisely in graphic form by means of sequencing and control flow elements.

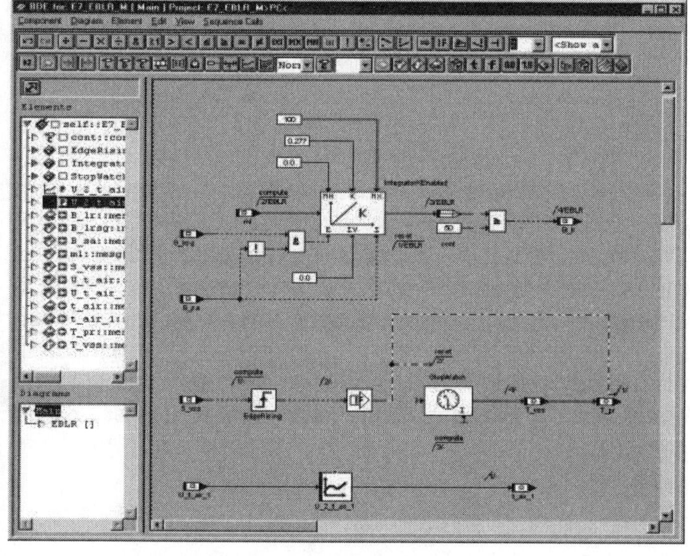

Figure 5: Example of Control Algorithm

To ensure know-how protection for cross-company work, an application-related view concept is provided. The user defines in a number of different views what blocks can be displayed or concealed in the documentation. At module and project levels, the tool suite also lets you define password-protected access rights at class, module and project levels.

State machines - Hierarchical state machines are in widespread use in control systems. This modeling method is especially of interest for systems where different control strategies are required depending on the working point. The tool enables the user to display contents of state machines for immediate understanding. This type of representation of open state hierarchies ensures unrestricted standard conformity of the tool suite when modeling state machines.

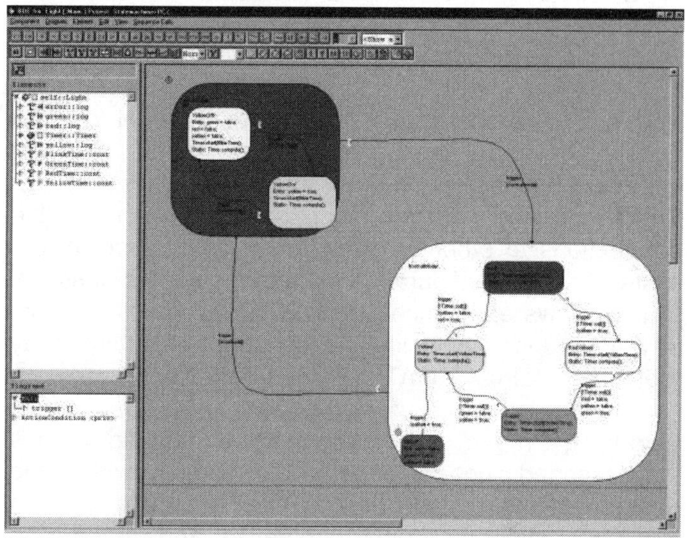

Figure 6: Example of State Machine

Text specification in ESDL – Contrary to the development of C-Code, the text specification of control algorithms in ESDL is a portable physical description. Instances are also encapsulated in classes and modules, which can be enriched with target-specific implementation information.

Specifications in ESDL, state machines and block diagrams can be mixed in any combination, i.e. a class may contain some instances in block diagram form or others as text specifications in ESDL. As opposed to C, ESDL requires no pointer arithmetic since all the objects can be directly addressed. There is no dynamic instantiation. In other words, all objects are fixed at compilation time. This allows an early consistency check of the control unit programs and shows that the available memory is indeed sufficient.

Operating system configuration – The operating system interface is located in the project. Priorities are assigned for tasks, which are vital for scheduling the processing order, e.g. whether they are cooperative or preemptive, whether they are cyclical or whether they are started at an external event or only initially. The operating system is then configured on this basis. The processes invoked in the tasks communicate by means of messages. Messages from various modules are linked by identical names. In the code generator, this information is checked for consistency (use of messages at several points, handling global variables, etc.).

The operating system is configured visually in a simple editor. This provides the design engineer with a continuous overview over the total system. Changes can be made to scheduling very easily and quickly. Finally, this is also supported by the fact that the operating system ERCOS^{EK} has a pre-translated library. As a result, hardly any effort is required when making changes to the operating system configuration except for the link process.

MODELING THE CONTROL PROCESS – Specifying complex control algorithms without modeling the related process is no longer conceivable today.

The control process and the process model can be developed in the same system. Furthermore, the tool suite also has the openness of integrating other systems. With a generic API interface, the tool makes flexible connections to other programs such as system design, system test or configuration management tools possible. It also allows easy access to ASCET-SD functions from any application, including the connection to third party tools (e.g. MatrixX®, MATLAB®/Simulink®).

Operating system and components – Planning various tasks (scheduling) is based on priorities, which the design engineer stipulates. The operating system ERCOS^{EK} supports both cooperative and preemptive scheduling and is used whenever severe real-time requirements and valuable memory space ask for extreme efficiency. The main task of the operating system is to transfer consistent data between processes by using messages.

Drivers for HW components only belong partly to the operating system since microprocessor peripheries can differ depending on the application. The abstraction of the functionality in the form of a data interface can be kept relatively general and categorized according to peripheral types. Above the operating system and HW encapsulation plane, there are drivers and protocols for application and measurement, diagnostics, etc. Together with the operating system, they are grouped as Automotive Services.

ERCOS^{EK} for the AUDO TC1775 features some remarkable facts:

- Highly efficient scheduling due to sophisticated ICU
- Resource consumption: 2 timers of any GPTU + 1 SRN
- Kernel ROM requirement: 3.5K (min) / 9K (typ.)
- Kernel RAM requirement: 224Bytes (min) / 400Bytes (typ.)
- Preemp. SW task activation + switch: <4.5µs @ 40MHz
- Hardware task activation + switch: <0.5µs @ 40MHz
- Memory protection (stack overflow / stack underflow)
- OIL based configuration tool: 'ESCAPE'
- Debugging with RTOS awareness (ORTI)

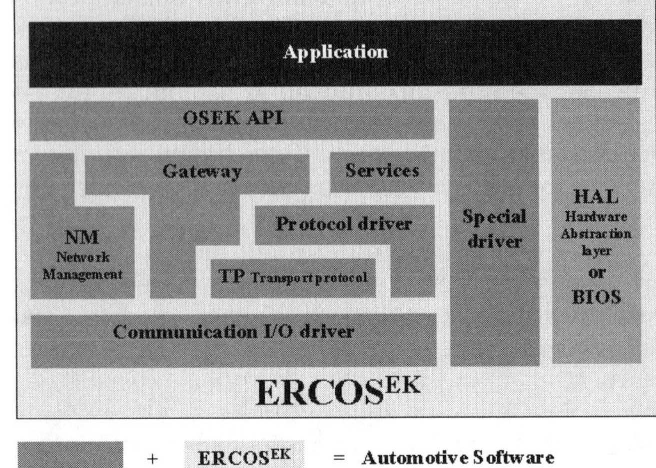

Figure 7: Example of Software Architecture

IMPLEMENTATION AND CODE GENERATION – Automatic code generation for production control units is the key to an efficient development methodology. Operating system interfaces must be configured for fix point arithmetics as well as for floating point processors. Memory management must be optimized and hardware encapsulation must be integrated. The following graph shows an overview to the principle of automatic code generation, featuring the inputs.

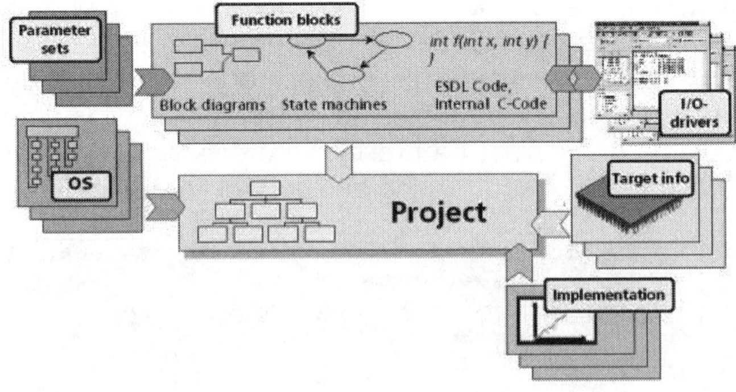

Figure 8: Code Generation flow

The implementation consists of the data types, value ranges and memory storage information. Conversion equations form the link between these implementation levels and the physical data description. At any place in the model highly optimized user defined code can be used. This option is typically used with controller or filter algorithms.

Basics of Integer Code Generation - The most essential task of implementation code generation is the automatic transformation of the arithmetics in the physical model (floating point arithmetic) into the quantized arithmetics for the target implementation. Necessary conversions and correction factors are generated and overflows avoided or corrected automatically. In the traditional manual coding process, this step has proven to be unreliable. Thus, a reliable automatic generation improves software quality.

The main goal of the implementation code generation is the semantically correct transformation of the physical specification while considering the implementations given by the user. Numerical errors are inevitable due to quantization and integer division. However, these errors are minimized. The generated code is robust, e.g. no overflows occur at run-time.

Code generation possibilities for TriCore – Mapping a functional model on executable program code is the main challenge in developing embedded control systems. While physical modeling is expected to be graphical, hardware-independent, reusable and supporting physical data types (floating point arithmetic), it should also be easy to understand through the use of block diagrams and state machines so that design engineers can use the documentation as a reference during the application phase. At control unit level, the code is expected to be specially optimized to the existing microprocessor with the appropriate memory devices. The code size and the runtime are the prime parameters. The data types are normally integer (fix point arithmetic).

Regarding Infineon's AUDO TC1775, current code generation possibilities include plain ANSI-C coding and ANSI-C with TriCore specific extensions and inclusion of optimized libraries. Furthermore, future code generation possibilities include intrinsic macros and assembly code generation.

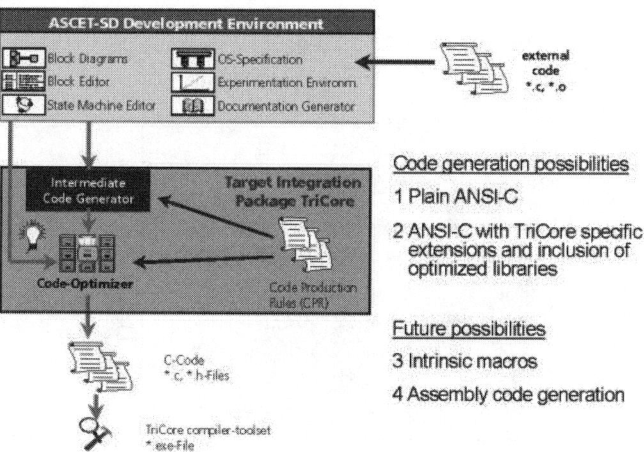

Figure 9: Automatic Code Generation steps

To implement the functionality developed with ASCET-SD in production code, a Target Integration Package (TIP) for the AUDO TC1775 is used. This TIP includes all necessary descriptive files and code generation rules for fixed-point code expansion.

Therewith, target-specific executable production code can be generated at the touch of button.

AUTOMOTIVE DRIVER SOFTWARE

To allow efficient and fast development time, a special automotive driver software was developed. This development was already the object of an SAE paper in 2000, "2000-01-0554: Automatic Code Generator for Automotive Configurable I/O System". The following drivers are available and used for the described platform concept:

Sensors
- angle position measurement (crankshaft + camshaft)
- PWM measurement
- analog measurement

Actuators
- injection actuation
- ignition actuation
- stepper motor actuation for air bypass or EGR
- PWM actuation

Communication Sockets
- serial synchronous interface
- serial asynchronous Interface
- network interface (CAN, J1850, ...)

In addition to this automotive driver software, many low level drivers are available. This allows an easy use of the new microcontroller peripherals. Standard interfaces for serial communications such serial synchronous, asynchronous or CAN are used in the platform concept. Several libraries are already available for the Infineon C16x at ETAS. The methodology used makes them easily portable to meet the requirements of the next generation microprocessors.

AUDO ARCHITECTURE

AUDO is designed to fulfill automotive embedded real time applications; the architecture fits the new development cycle perfectly. The application software is developed on the main processor "TriCore" using automatic code generation techniques, the driver software is done by an independent processor called PCP "peripheral control processor". The peripherals guarantee the time, analogue, and busses functions.

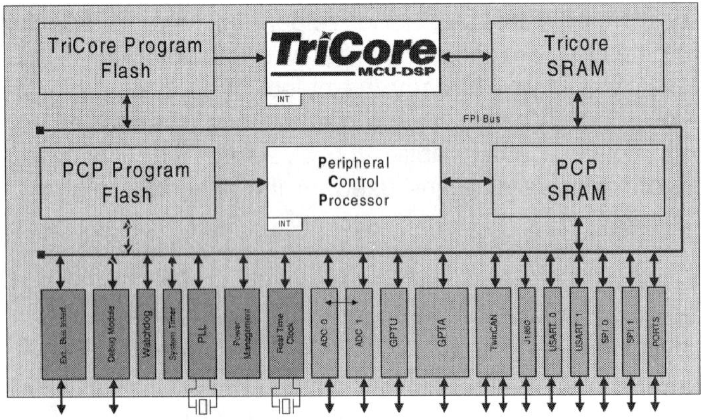

Figure 10: AUDO architecture

Tricore

TriCore is the first single-core 32-bit micro-controller-DSP architecture optimized for real-time embedded systems. TriCore unifies the best of 3 worlds – the real-time capabilities of micro-controllers, number crunching of DSPs, and highest performance/price implementations of RISC load-store architectures. The instruction set architecture (ISA) supports a uniform 32-bit address space, with memory-mapped input/output. It allows for a wide range of implementations, ranging from simple scalar to superscalar. Furthermore, the ISA is capable of interacting with different system architectures, including those with multiprocessing. This flexibility at the implementation and system levels allows for different trade-offs between performance and cost at any point in time.

Figure 11: TriCore architecture

To support TriCore implementations with 32-bit instructions and simplified instruction fetching, the entire architecture is represented in 32-bit instruction formats. In addition, the architecture includes 16-bit instruction formats for the most frequently occurring instructions. These instructions significantly reduce code space, lowering memory requirements, system costs, and power consumption. Real-time responsiveness is largely determined by interrupt latency and context-switch time. The high-performance architecture minimizes interrupt latency by avoiding long multicycle instructions and by providing a flexible hardware-supported interrupt scheme. Furthermore, the architecture supports fast context switching.

Tasks and contexts

The term "task" refers to an independent thread of control. There are 2 types of tasks: software-managed tasks and interrupt service routines. Software-managed tasks are created through the services of a real-time kernel or OS, and dispatched under the control of scheduling software. Interrupt service routines are dispatched by hardware in response to an interrupt. In this architecture, the term "interrupt service routines" refers only to the code that is invoked by the hardware directly. Software-managed tasks are sometimes referred to as user tasks, assuming that they will execute in user mode. Each task is allocated its own permission level. The individual permissions are enabled/disabled primarily by I/O mode bits in the program status word. There is a set of state elements associated with any task collectively known as the task's context. The context is all the processor needs to know in order to define the state of the associated task and enable its continued execution. It includes the CPU general-purpose registers that the task uses, the task's program counter, and its program status information. The TriCore architecture efficiently manages and maintains the tasks' contexts through hardware.

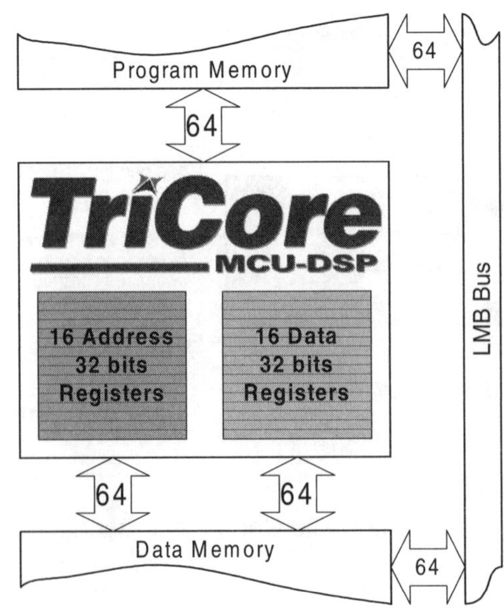

Figure 12: TriCore architecture

Fast context switching

The methods from customer to customer are different, some work with a large number of interrupts, others prefer to use the operating system's service. The aim is nevertheless the same for everybody: Make the software as predictable as possible. The ideal case would be to reserve a time slot for every task, and replace the event driven application by a time triggered application. This type of architecture will require huge performance and cost overheads. It is possible to reduce the impact of random events on the behavior of the application. The critical tasks must be identified and the execution must be guaranteed by the architecture of the machine. In any case, the right support can be provided to quickly identify the priority of the task to perform and switch the context without the machine losing too much performance. The interrupt system and/or the operating system will use these two mechanisms.

To increase performance, the architecture implements a uniform context-switch mechanism for function calls, interrupts, and traps. In all cases, the task's upper context is automatically saved and restored by hardware; saving (and restoring) the lower context is left as an option for the new task. Fast context switching is further enhanced by the TriCore's unique memory subsystem design, which allows transfers of up to 16 data words between processor registers and memory, therefore allowing a complete upper or lower context to be saved in 1 operation requiring 4 cycles.

Interrupt system

In this context a service request is defined as an interrupt request from a peripheral, a DMA request, or an external interrupt. For simplicity, a service request may also be referred to as an interrupt. The entry code for the interrupt service routine is a block within a vector of code blocks. Each code block provides an entry for one interrupt source. Each source is assigned a priority number. All priority numbers are programmable. The service routine uses the priority number to determine the location of the entry code block. The prioritization of service routines enables nested interrupts. A service request can interrupt the servicing of a lower priority interrupt. Interrupt sources with the same priority cannot interrupt each other.

Super-scalar architecture

TriCore is a super-scalar machine running up to three instructions in parallel: load store, arithmetic, and loop management. TriCore uses a four-step pipeline using the instructions fetch, decode, execution and write back.

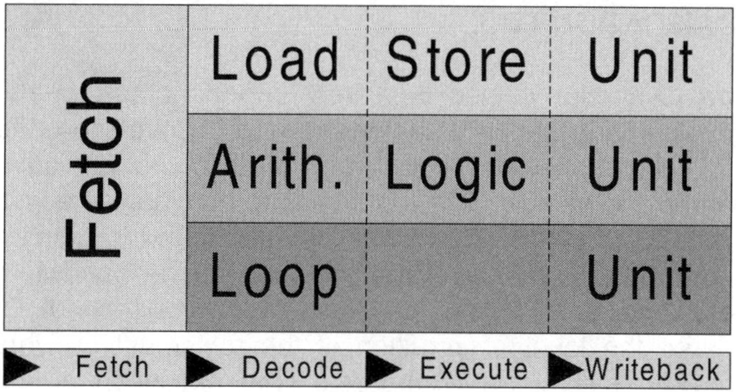

Figure 13: Super-scalar architecture

PCP peripheral control processor

The peripheral control processor (PCP) combines in one unit: a DMA controller and a micro-controller for interrupt service routines. It could easily be considered as the host processor's first line of defense as an interrupt-handling engine. The PCP can off-load the TriCore from having to service time-critical interrupts.

PCP allows clear independence between application software (running on TriCore) and driver software. The driver software is the interface between the specific implementation of the µC peripherals and the application software. The software modules will be connected using the standardized operating system EROS[EK]. To allow an easy integration procedure, it is required that any addition of new modules does not impact on the real time behavior of already validated software.

PCP has the same interrupt arbitration as TriCore, and a very fast context switch. It has dedicated instructions to optimize DMA transfers, and to run state machines.

PCP instruction set overview

DMA primitives	Efficient DMA channel implementation
Load/Store	Transfer data between memory and the general purpose registers, as well as move or exchange values between registers
Arithmetic	Add, subtract, compare and complement
Divide/Multiply	Divide and multiply
Logical	And, or, exclusive or, negate
Shift	Shift right or left, rotate right or left, prioritize
Bit Manipulation	Set, clear, insert and test bits
Flow Control	Jump conditionally, jump long, exit
Miscellaneous	No operation, Debug

CALIBRATION TOOL

The calibration phase is a very important part of the development, at this time the software is developed and the calibration values must be tuned to the particular engine and vehicle. The tool needs to communicate with the ECU to modify the calibration values and to monitor some internal values of the application. The bandwidth could reach 16 values of 32bits every millisecond. Of course the level of intrusion of the tool must be very small to still guaranty the real time execution of the application.

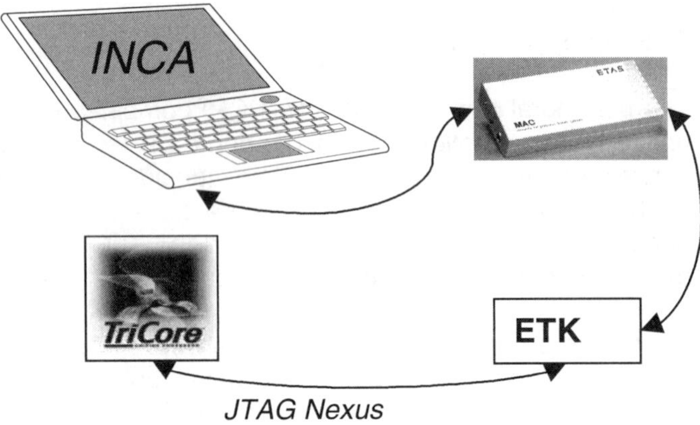

Figure 14: Calibration Tool connection

To fulfil these requirements ETAS developed a serial emulator probe called ETK to communicate with TriCore. The link used is the JTAG Nexus port running at 20 MHz. The ETK transfers the controller information to an external data acquisition box called MAC through a high-speed serial bus. The MAC box itself is linked to the PC using the parallel port. On the PC the software INCA is running to manage the calibration tasks.

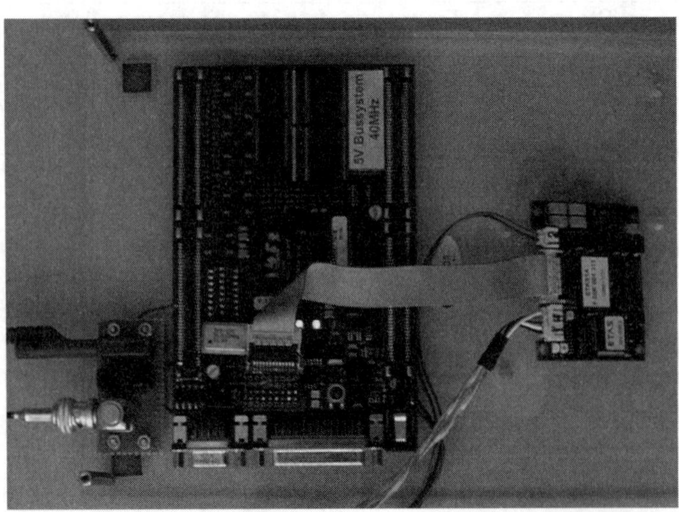

Figure 15: Connection of the ETK to TriCore

POWERTRAIN DEMONSTRATOR

To demonstrate the effectiveness of the combination of the tool suite ASCET-SD and the processor AUDO TC1775 a typical powertrain application was realized. The application software was developed using the high level language possibilities of ASCET-SD. The code was automatically generated and mapped on the operating system ERCOS^{EK}. This software was downloaded to TriCore. In addition driver software was developed to measure the flywheel information and to generate ignition and injection signals. These drivers were developed for the PCP peripheral control processor. The calibration and data monitoring was performed with the calibration tool INCA using the ETK JTAG Nexus interface.

Figure 16: Flywheel of the system

CONCLUSION

The ASCET-SD tool suite is the solution for most requirements regarding software development for electronic control units. The innovative technology of this tool suite is successful in improving the factors of time, costs, quality and flexibility. The control process can be modeled and included in the development. A continuous database supports cross-project reuse. The operating system ERCOS[EK] and the automatic code generation for TriCore processors are already up and running. The calibration & application steps were performed using the latest technology innovation based on the JTAG Nexus link to guaranty the real time operation of the application. Therefore, the close technical partnership between Infineon and ETAS is leading to a remarkable efficiency in the reduction of time and resources when developing embedded control software.

CONTACTS

Patrick Leteinturier
Infineon Technologies
Automotive System Definition
St.-Martin.-Str. 76
81609 Munich, Germany
Tel.: (49) 89 234 83828
Fax: (49) 89 234 81029
Email: patrick.leteinturier@infineon.com

Guenter Gromeier
ETAS GmbH
Embedded Control Development Systems
Borsigstraße 10
70469 Stuttgart, Germany
Tel.: (49) 711 89661 221
Fax: (49) 711 89661 273
Email: guenter.gromeier@etas.de

Johannes Wagner
ETAS GmbH
Embedded Control Development Systems
Borsigstraße 10
70469 Stuttgart, Germany
Tel.: (49) 711 89661 267
Fax: (49) 711 89661 273
Email: johannes.wagner@etas.de

REFERENCES

1999-01-0203 Enhanced Engine Position Acquisition & Treatment; Leteinturier Patrick

2000-01-0144 TwinCAN A new milestone for inter-network communication; Barrenscheen Jens

2000-01-0554 Automatic Code Generator for Automotive Configurable I/O System; Westerholz Karl

2000-01-0390 A Cost-Effective Calibration and Debug Interface for Automotive Controllers According to the www.NEXUS-STANDARD.org; Martin Gerhard

2000-01-0459 High pincount packages under automotive conditions; Dr. Alexandra Atzesdorfer

2000-01-1240 GPTA - A Flexible New Timer Approach for Automotive Applications; Benning Joseph

2001-01-0027 Distributed Automotive Safety System

2001-01-0065 Seamless Solutions for LIN

2001-01-0808 Flexible and Modular Telematics Demonstrator with Considered Network Topologies of Cars

DEFINITIONS, ACRONYMS, ABBREVIATIONS

API	Application Program Interface
DMA	Direct Memory Access
DSP	Digital Signal Processing
ECU	Electronic Control Unit
EGR	Exhaust Gas Recirculation
ESDL	System Design Language
ETK	Calibration Probe (Emulator TastKopf)
FFT	Fast Fourier Transform
GPTA	TM for General Purpose Timer Array
INCA	INtegrated Calibration & Application tool
ISA	Instruction Set Architecture
MAC	Measuring & Application unit Compact
PCP	Peripheral Control Processor
TIP	Target Integration Package
TM	Trade Mark
TriCore	TM for 32-bit Core

2001-01-1218

Sophisticated CAN on Embedded Microcontrollers for Smart In-Vehicle Real-Time Control Systems

Shigeo Uno, Naoyuki Hirayama, Akihiko Watanabe and Fumio Tsuchiya
Semiconductor & Integrated Circuits Group Hitachi Ltd.

ABSTRACT

In the past 10 years there have been a drastic evolution in car electronics. Most mechanically operated systems as like an engine control for example has switched to an electronic system to have more precise method to control the system and in some cases more cost effective. Due to the implementation of electronically controlled systems more and more information could be handled within these systems, and with more and more information there is a turning point that there is a large benefit to have a common use of the information. Now in-vehicle network is playing a major part in car electronics. CAN(Controller Area Network) is one of the most popular candidate for real time communications between the systems

This paper will describes the development concept of our new CAN module for embedded microcontrollers targeting automotive applications. Currently CAN have been used as one of the most popular control network systems. Due to expansion of data transactions via CAN, data handling by the module or by the controller has been a major subject. We have developed a method to handle the large amount of data with the least CPU(Central Processing Unit) overhead to provide maximum performance of the CPU. This will be shown with a simulation result in comparison of the new CAN module and the conventional CAN module, along with an example to show the efficiency in a application such as ACC(Adaptive Cruise Control) system. And furthermore this new CAN module will have the capability to cooperate with the latest requirements of the CAN specification such as the time triggered CAN of the ISO(International Organization for Standardization) standard.

INTRODUCTION

In the past decade there has been great progress in automotive control systems. The biggest motivation of the progress is the close-up on environmental preservation. And the biggest step forward was the introduction of electronic controlled systems. Sensors and actuators that are operated by ECU(Electronic Control Unit)s give the big advantage of more precise control and cost efficiency compared to the conventional mechanical control systems.

In today's high class passenger vehicles there are more than 50 ECUs existing to control each system. Each of these ECUs handles a certain amount of information to control the system. Although each ECU has a different role in the control system, there is lots of common information handled within the system. Therefore now in the current systems, data communication between the ECUs is playing a major role for advanced vehicle control systems. For data communication CAN has become the standard real time network system which supports the data transactions up to the speed of 1Mbits/s. Many real time network system have adapted the CAN because of its high speed capability and more over the high reliability of the data communication.

In the early stages of the CAN implementation, very few nodes (for example 2 to 3 nodes) were connected to the CAN bus, and also during these phases communication data that was transferred between the nodes were very few and not very frequent. But as the control systems grows and the control precision required in the systems gets higher, the data information increases and the data transaction speed will expand.

To solve these problems and cooperate with the expanding requirements the controller of the ECU needs to higher performance and in cases more intelligent data handling methods.

SYSTEM INTEGRATION TRENDS

As the vehicle control systems enhance, the information that is handled by the ECUs will automatically expand to achieve higher performance and higher precision. Introduction of additional sensors and actuators will expand the system and a large amount of common information to operate the additions above will exist within several systems. This common information could be utilized by centralizing the system. Figure 1 shows an example of the system integration for a powertrain control module. This is consisted by the engine management, automatic transmission and electronic throttle control.

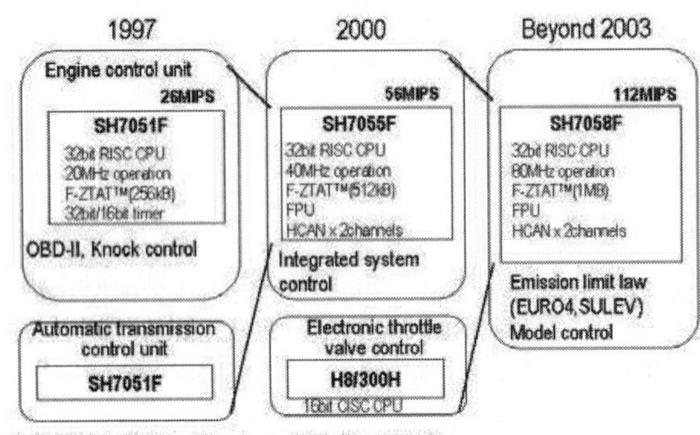

Figure 1 System integration of a powertrain control module

Integration of ECUs has been the major trend due to handling common information from the sensors and actuators in the 1990's. This integration will allow reducing the number of parts used in the total solution and also the reduction of the physical mounting area, which is also another critical factor in the limited space of an automobile.

But as the control systems and information expands, to harmonize lots of control applications such as engine management, AT control, ABS, ACC, etc. there is a point where system integration may not be the most effective solution. Figure 2 shows the trend of system integration and system distribution in control network. While common information continues to increase, the system integration advances and due to the help of advanced technology of semiconductors and peripheral components. One of the largest factors for the transition of system integration to distribution is the introduction of the now standardized network named CAN. CAN has been in the market for more than 15years and it's reliability has been proven on the market. CAN have become one of the major real time network systems. Figure 3 shows the trend of network nodes existing in one vehicle. As shown in this figure the increase of control application and information leads to more node connection for more interactive communication.

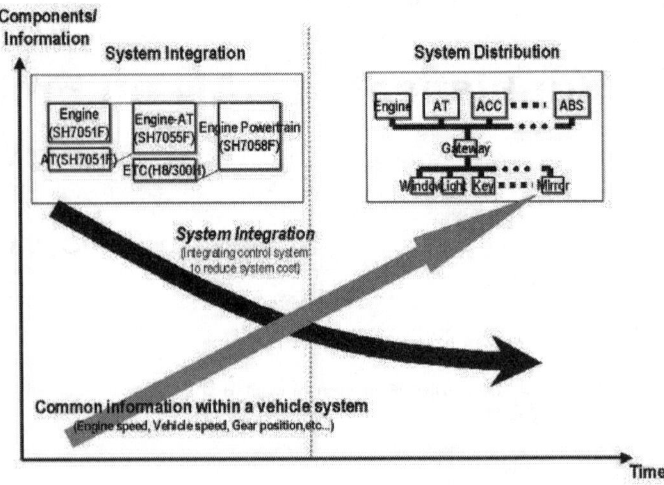

Figure 2 System integration & distribution

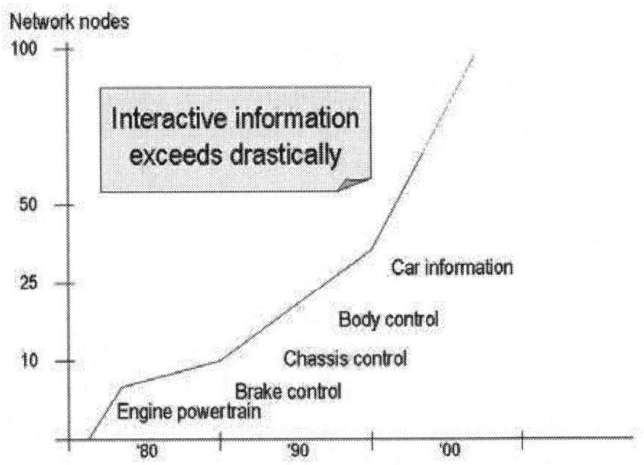

Figure 3 Number of network nodes in 1 vehicle

IMPLEMENTATION REQUIREMENTS

In recent real time applications, as mentioned above CAN is now a standard for car networking systems. Large numbers of information transactions are done via the CAN and currently in high class vehicles may have up to several hundreds of messages to obtain the high precision control of the vehicle and comfort. From this vast expansion, more and more performance is required for the CAN controller as well as the microcontroller. There are 3 key issues to drastically increase the performance of the microcontroller to gives the performance to concentrate on other control methods.

The 3 key implementations are :

- Sophisticated receive message handling

- Time triggered message transmission

- Time stamp functionality

Our newly developed HITCAN module will have the functionality of the 3 key items mentioned above. This will allow the microcontroller to handle a large amount of data with the least CPU overhead to provide the maximum performance of the CPU. Furthermore several other implementations have been done to give the user the opportunity to have the optimized functionality for real time applications. Table 1 shows the summary of the CAN implemented features and Figure 4 shows the hierarchical structure of our new HITCAN module.

Other key implementations:

- Thirty-two transmit/receive message mailboxes

- Non-read message overwrite function

Automatic re-transmission stop functionality

Table 1 HCAN implementation features

Functions		HCAN	HITCAN(New CAN)
Mailbox	Numbers	16 mailboxes	32 mailboxes
	Transmit/Receive programable	Available	Available
Transmit functions	Message completion flag	Available(Each mailbox)	Available(Each mailbox)
	Message abort	Available(Each mailbox)	Available(Each mailbox)
	Time triggered data transmission	-	Available(Each mailbox)
	Time stamp at data transmission	-	Available(Each mailbox)
	Automatic remote frame respons	-	Available(Each mailbox)
	Automatic re-transmission stop	-	Available(Each mailbox)
Receive function	Filtering	1 LAFM	32 LAFM(Each mailbox)
		16 bit wise filtering	32 bit wise filtering
	Message overwrite detection	Available(Each mailbox)	Available(Each mailbox)
	Message overwrite abort	-	Available(Each mailbox)
	Time stamp at data reception	-	Available(Each mailbox)
Others	Time base counter	-	16bit free running counter
	Global sychronization	-	ID compare match register to clear timer counter

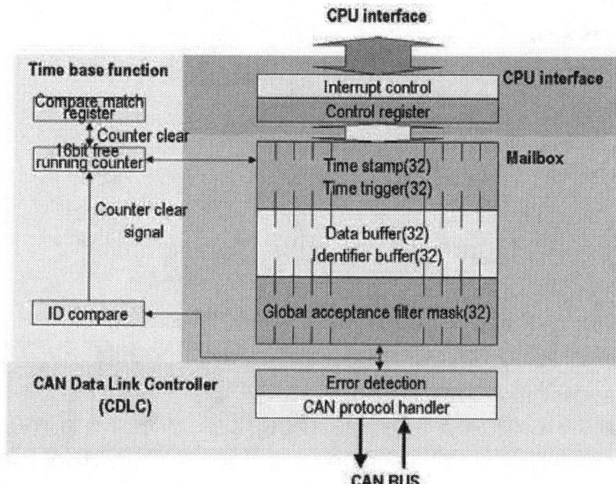

Figure 4 Hierarchical structure of the new HITCAN

SOPHISTICATED RECEIVE MESSAGE HANDLING

As number of messages handled within the CAN bus system increases, It is necessary to reduce the CPU process power to the minimum by having a sophisticated method to handle the receiving messages. Figure 5 shows the block diagram of how the HITCAN receives messages and stores it into the appropriate mailbox. Our HITCAN controller will provide 32 mailboxes which is capable to program receive or transmit on the fly. Each mailbox contains an independent identifier(standard & extended) area and data area for maximum 8 bytes. Furthermore each mailbox has its independent receive message filtering function with the full identifier range.

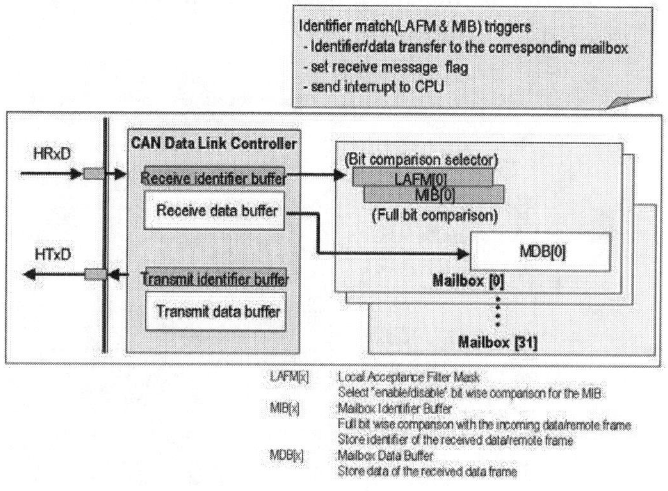

Figure 5 Block diagram of receive messages

For message receive a global mask filter and a bit wise filter is common. This HITCAN gives 2 filtering functionality for each of the 32 mailboxes. The first filter is called the Local acceptance filter and this allows setting the corresponding bit to be matched with the identifier buffer or not. For example if this is set to "1" this would mean a "must match" for the corresponding identifier buffer bit. And if "0" was set the receive identifier does not have to match the identifier buffer bit. This allows to receive a group of messages in certain mailboxes.

Once the identifier matches the condition of the LAFM and the identifier buffer this will trigger the transfer of the data value which is in the receive data buffer into the data buffer automatically. If the receive identifier structure is set to be optimized this will allow to have the minimum CPU load which could be used for other control which could be very important for real-time applications.

TIME TRIGGERED DATA TRANSMISSION

In the past, data transmission from the CAN has been realized by software tasks via the CPU. The bus arbitration will go into affective as soon as there is a request by the CPU. This method is very useful when the transferred message amount is fairly low and the data transaction system structure is an event driven system. But since the message transfer needs to be handled by the CPU, when the message amount increases and the data transaction system structure shifts to time base driven, this will directly effect the performance of the CPU. The performance will reduce drastically. Also as the side effect, if there is a necessity to transmit message in a critical time, on an event request and the CPU has other critical tasks or if the CPU load were heavy there would be a possibility to miss the critical time slot.

One solution to solve this problem is the introduction of the time trigger data transmission. Figure 6 shows the block diagram of the time triggered functionality.

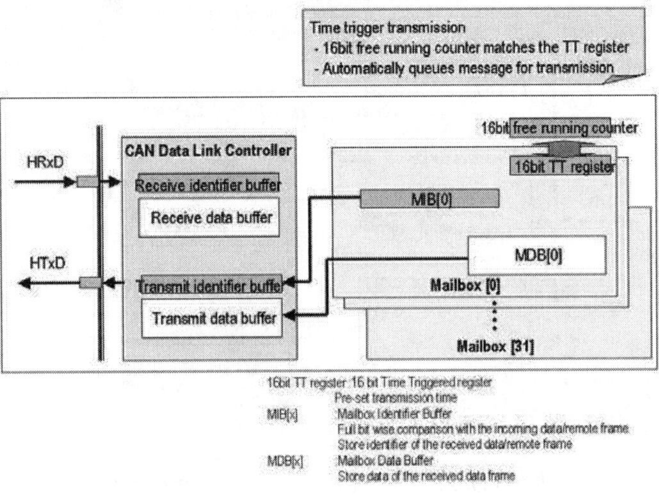

Figure 6 Time triggered function block diagram

This function consists of a independent 16bit free running counter which counts up on a internal clock which creates the time base, and in addition each individual mailbox has a register that consist of a compare match register. This compare match register determines the time when the corresponding mailbox is set for transmission. If the counter matches the compare match register the corresponding mailbox will be queued for transmission. At this point the information(identifier, DLC, data, etc.) which is stored in the mailbox previously is automatically queued for transmission. Therefore to update data which is set for periodic transmission at a pre-determined time slot, the CPU only needs to update the new data (DLC + data only) based on a task which does not have to relate to a CAN transmission task. This will allow the CPU to be free from a CAN transmission task and could perform other important tasks.

Also to secure the complete update of the new message content (to prevent half-new data and half-old data transmission) there is a secure bit which will indicated if the message is currently being updated or not. If this indication bit is inactive, if the compare match occurs this postpones the transmission queue and will be delayed until the next compare match occurs.

Along with this feature, this module has a register, which contains an identifier compare register. This register is dedicated to allow a global synchronization. When a message with a specific identifier which matches the identifier compare match register this will send a reset signal to the free running counter. This will also allow a global base time and is possible to synchronize without any CPU intervention.

By this methodology, it is able to achieve data transmission request with the least CPU overhead as well as an accurate periodical message transmission via the CAN bus.

TIME STAMP FUNCTIONALITY

Time trigger functionality is previously known functionality as a timekeeper to identify when the message has been transmitted or when it has been received.

This functionality could also be implemented using the 16bit free running counter. Figure 7 shows the methods of the time stamp functionality.

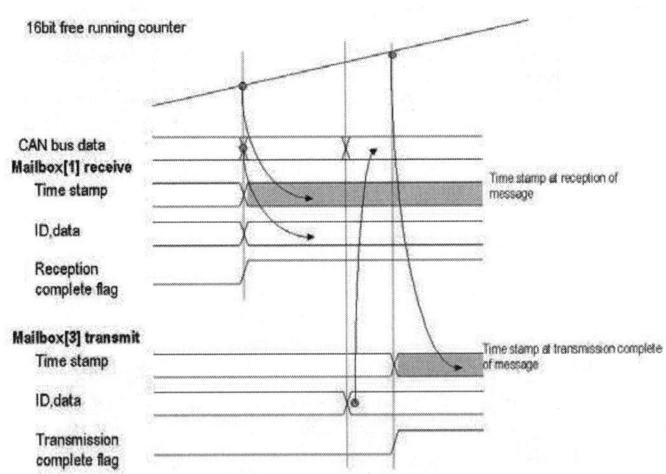

Figure 7 Time stamp functionality

Each individual mailbox has a 16bit register to store the counter value for the time stamp functionality.

As for time stamp for data reception, when the message is received the timer counter value is stored in the time stamp register of the corresponding mailbox. This allows to identify if the received data stored in the mailbox is up to date or not. This functionality would be useful when the CPU has a critical task other than the control of the CAN and polls the received data in the mailbox.

For data transmission, when the message is actually transmitted the timer counter value is stored in the time stamp register of the corresponding mailbox. This will also be useful to identify when the data actually has been sent on the CAN bus. In addition to this feature, if the data length of the message(data frame) is less than 6 bytes you have the possibility to capture the 16bit timer counter value to the last 2 bytes when the message is set for transmission queue. If the CAN system has been globally synchronized the receiver could identify when the data was queued for transmission and could possibly calculate the latency of the CAN. This functionality could be very useful in time critical systems.

IMPLEMENTATION EXAMPLES ON ACC

Here is an example of our HITCAN(Hitachi Intelligent Time triggered CAN) simulated in a real time application called ACC(Adaptive Cruise Control) which is a system that requires real time control. Figure 8 shows the diagram of the ACC control system.

ACC is a system to advance the conventional cruise control which controls the vehicle at a constant vehicle speed. In addition to the conventional cruise control, this new system detect the distance to the object ahead using a radar sensor system and gives command to the powertrain system (engine control, AT control and electrical throttle valve control) as well as the ABS system to control the vehicle to avoid collision with the object ahead or even acceleration to keep a certain distance with the obstacle ahead. The control information within this system is all transmitted or received via the CAN network which is the current trend of system distribution. This ACC system main processing unit runs on a 32bit RISC SH-2 microcontroller(40MHz) with a CAN interface with our new HITCAN.

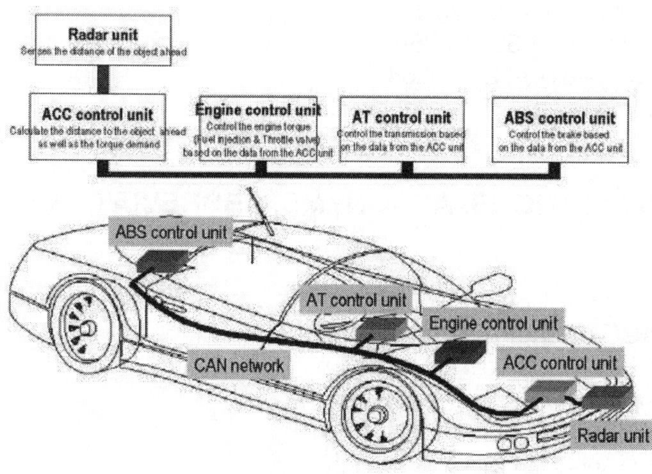

Figure 8 ACC control system diagram

The sequence of the control is based on every 20ms event to control the system. The ACC unit measures the desired driving speed via the radar by calculating the distance of the obstacle ahead which is located at the front of the vehicle. After the application program inside ACC calculates the desired drive force and the ACC sends desired drive force to the engine control unit via the CAN network. The engine control unit invokes the corresponding controls to the brake control system or the throttle control system via the CAN network again. The time the brake system or the throttle system will start the execution every 20ms.

PERFORMANCE EVALUATION

Since the system needs to use a various number of messages within the CAN system, the CAN will need to handle data with the least CPU overhead. One of the most efficient methods to handle the incoming messages would be to use the message filtering method mention previously. As the new HITCAN has an individual Local Acceptance Filter Mask, it is capable to compare the identifiers of the receive messages without CPU intervention. Once the message has passed the LAFM it will be stored in the corresponding mailbox which is to reduce the times of compare to identify which message has been received.

For example, if it is able to group the identifiers to distribute the identifier comparison equally this could give the minimum average comparison time.

LAFM settings = message numbers / receive mailbox numbers

Using 16 of the 32 mailbox as receive, and group the messages of 128 to the 16 mailboxes, this would give approximately 90% reduction compared to the conventional HCAN method which you needed to compare the identifiers with a single LAFM mailbox. Figure 9 shows the simulated performance difference with the number of LAFMs.

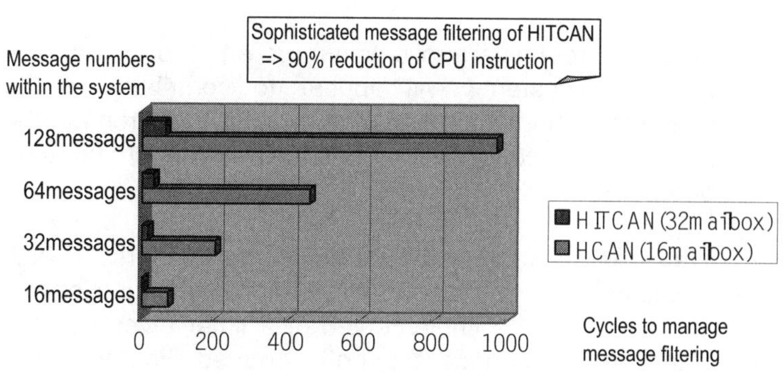

Figure 9 CPU load for message reception

As well as data reception, data transmission is also critical. To control the system accurately and give the driver immediate response of the transactions, the data transmission to the control systems via the CAN needs to time triggered rather than event driven. Figure 10 shows the periodic data transmission using the time triggered function. Using this functionality this will allow the CPU to run tasks independent to the 20ms data transmission to control the ACC system. To update a mailbox would take roughly 1.5us/message (using extended ID with 8 bytes of data) which the CPU load for would be approximately be 0.008%(Based on a 40MHz operation device).

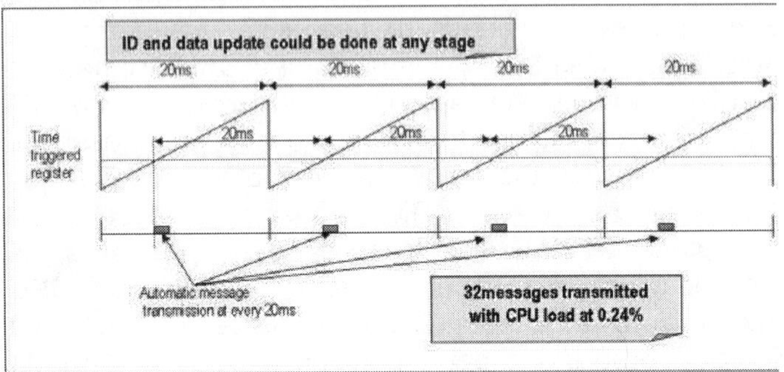

Figure 10 Time triggered function timing chart

This shows that the HITCAN will be capable to handle up to 32 messages keeping the CPU load down to 0.24%. This will allow the CPU to be 99.76% free and more than sufficient to handle the main application and other tasks.

Other than this control application, the CPU load is an inverse proportion to the task control frequency. As for a system with 5ms, 10ms task the CPU load would be 0.48% and 0.96%. As this shows a real-time network system could be operated without a large CPU overhead.

CONCLUSION

In vehicle real time application more and more electronic controlled systems will appear to contribute to the technology innovation. Networking is and will remain the key factor for control systems and CAN will remain state of the art.

The new developed HITCAN module offers a high functionality because of the 32 mailboxes functionality and also with the implemented of a timer gives you the capability to manage the new required time triggered CAN applications.

As simulation results using HITCAN in a real-time application, the CPU load for data reception was reduced 90% to the conventional HCAN and for data transmission the CPU load was held down to 0.24% in 32 message/20ms task application. This shows a very low CPU load of handling messages both data receive and data transmission and is suitable for real-time control network applications.

ACKNOWLEDGMENTS

This HITCAN module is planned to be lined up with our 32bit high performance SH microcontroller along with the 16bit H8S microcontrollers and provides a wide range of products to meet vehicle real-time control network application requirements.

REFERENCES

1. S. Suzuki, W. Nagaura, T. Imai, S. Kuragaki, T. Yokoyama, "A Distributed Control System Framework for Automotive Powertrain Control with OSEK Standard and CAN Network" in SAE 1999-0-1276
2. ISO 11898-1:Road vehicles – Interchange of digital information – Part 1: Controller area network data link layer and medium access control
3. ISO 11898-2:Road vehicles – Interchange of digital information – Part 2: High-speed medium access unit and medium dependent interface
4. CAN specification V2.0, 1991 Robert Bosch GmbH
5. S. Tanaka, M. Kaneyasu, A. Kodama, K. Matsubara "A New RISC Microcontroller with On-chip FPU to Introduce Adaptive Control into Powertrain Management" in SAE 1999-01-0865

CONTACT

Shigeo Uno
Hitachi Ltd.,
Automotive Semiconductor Marketing Department
Semiconductor & Integrated Circuits Group
Nippon Bldg., 6-2 Otemachi 2-chome
Chiyoda-ku, Tokyo Japan
Tel : +81-3-5201-5056
Fax : +81-3-3270-6254
E-mail : suno@denshi.head.hitachi.co.jp

DEFINITIONS, ACRONYMS, ABBREVIATIONS

ABS : Antilock Brake System
ACC : Adaptive Cruise Control
AT : Automatic Transmission
CAN : Controller Area Network
DLC : Data Length Code
HCAN : Hitachi CAN
HITCAN : Hitachi Intelligent Time triggered CAN
ID : Identifier
ISO : International Organization for Standardization
LAFM : Local Acceptance Filter Mask
RISC : Reduced Instruction Set Computer

2001-01-0022

Foundations for Rapid Embedded Development

Joseph J. Lemieux
EDS Embedded Solutions

ABSTRACT

When an architect designs a building, the foundation is designed first, then the structure, and finally the details of the building. In embedded development, the foundation is the basic software upon which the program is built, such as the startup code and operating system. The walls and the details are similar to the actual software application and user interface. In order to build embedded applications rapidly, a standard foundation must be in place. This allows the application developers to focus their creative energies on how the application will "look and feel". This paper will describe the methods for building a software foundation to streamline embedded systems development.

INTRODUCTION

Building the software application is like building a house. If you start with a good foundation, the rest of the building will be sound. On top of the foundation is built the actual product business specified by the customer.

When building a house, the customer primarily defines the upper levels of the house, how it looks, and how it feels. They will specify the colors, shapes, sizes, etc. The same is true when a customer specifies a software application. Usually, the customer is only concerned with how the total application functions, and does not specify how that application is developed. It is up to the application developer to make decisions such as the microcontroller used, the language in which the application is developed, and the architecture of the actual software application.

Why should a good software foundation be developed for an organization? Many benefits are realized with a good software foundation. The primary benefit is increased reuse of code. The entire foundation is reused with every application, which is typically 20 to 25 percent of the entire code. In addition, since a standard foundation is used by the entire organization, software components written for one application may be reused in a different application using the same foundation. Another benefit that is a direct result of increased reuse is a shorter development cycle, since the time to develop an application is proportional to the number of lines of code written for the application. If the foundation is developed properly, benefits such as simplified testing and increased quality are realized by utilizing the functions provided in the foundation. A reduction in training of new software engineers, or software engineers changing departments, will also be realized. The end result will be decreased cost in the total development of the system.

This paper will discuss the different attributes of a good software foundation, and provide some of the parameters that need to be addressed while the foundation is being built. The discussion of each attribute will include a list of options to meet the needs of an attribute, along with the pros and cons of each option. The intent of the paper is to provide a high level overview of some of the decisions required in creating foundation software.

FOUNDATION ATTRIBUTES

There are many attributes of a good foundation that need to be defined when specifying and developing the foundation. The attributes that will be covered in this paper are shown in the following list:

- System startup
- Exception handling
- Program flow control
- Hardware abstraction
- Network communication
- I/O system
- Diagnostics
- Debug/Development

A graphical description using a layered architecture with each of these attributes is shown in figure 1. This four-layer model is only one way of realizing a foundation. Many other realizations are possible. As with any layered model, each layer communicates only with the layers above and below.

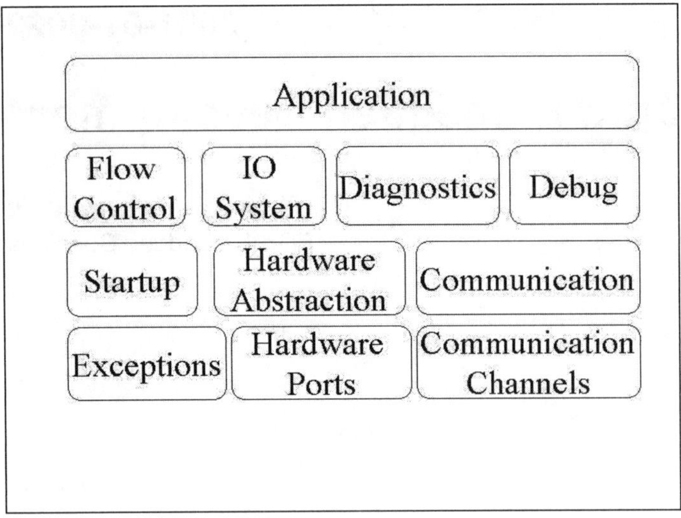

Figure 1 – Four Layer Model

SYSTEM STARTUP

System startup is initiated by an exception that forces the system to start from the beginning, in contrast to an exception that can be handled by the running application. Examples of these major exceptions include a power on reset, a hard reset, a soft reset, and a watchdog failure. The difference between a hard and a soft reset is that a hard reset is defined as a reset that is asserted by a device external to the microprocessor, and a soft reset is forced by the operating software. Not all microprocessors and microcontrollers support soft resets.

When system startup occurs, a number of steps have to be taken to put the system in a state in which it is ready to execute the application. The first step, which is optional, is to determine which type of exception occurred to force a system startup. Once determined, this value may be saved and/or passed to the application when it is started. The application may then take certain actions to recover gracefully from a major exception.

The second step during startup is to perform memory initialization. This is a required step and will be handled differently for different classes of applications and for different microprocessors or microcontrollers. At this point, the developer of the software foundation must decide how to handle memory during the startup. Some of the parameters that need to be decided are:

- Memory Testing Requirements
- Memory Integrity Check
- Memory Initialization Value

Memory testing requirements vary in complexity from no testing to a complex test to verify that all bits are fully functional and that nothing within nonvolatile memory has changed. Memory tests are divided into two types-volatile or RAM memory check and non-volatile or ROM memory check.

The volatile memory check usually consists of writing data to the memory followed by an immediate read of what was just written. The simplest and quickest check is to write all zeros to memory and then write all ones. This verifies that no individual cell within the memory block is shorted to either 0 or 1. The next level writes a bit pattern of hexadecimal AA and then 55. This test verifies that there are no shorts between individual bits of the memory block. The most complex test is a test in which the entire block is set to 0, then a single 1 is written to every bit location within the memory block, one bit at a time. The entire block is then verified to insure that only one bit is actually set to 1. This test verifies that there are no shorts anywhere in the memory block, and that every memory bit can be set to either 0 or 1.

The nonvolatile memory check is usually accomplished using a check sum or Cyclic Redundancy Check (CRC). The check sum can vary in size (8, 16, 32-bit) and in calculation (straight check sum, one's complement, two's complement). The two's complement check sum is the quickest to calculate since the algorithm just adds all of the memory in the block and the result will always be 0 if the memory passes the check. The CRC check is the most robust check, however it is also the most complex and time-consuming check. Other variations of the nonvolatile memory check include multiple check blocks where partial system operation can still occur if one block has failed.

The memory integrity check is a method to determine if the volatile memory has been corrupted. This integrity check may be made at the beginning of system startup and allow the system to bypass the memory tests when an exception occurs. Again, memory integrity checks take a number of different forms. The simplest form is one word in memory that is set with a predefined pattern, usually hexadecimal AA55. This location is checked upon startup and periodically throughout operation of the program to insure that the memory has not been compromised. A variation of this is to have multiple locations throughout the memory that are used for memory integrity checks. Another memory integrity check is to check sum a critical section of memory and to constantly update the check sum whenever memory is written. The system will constantly monitor the block of memory and verify that nothing has changed. This block of memory will usually be handled as a file system.

If upon startup the memory integrity has been compromised and the subsequent memory testing passes, volatile memory is typically initialized to some predefined value. This may be a value as simple as 00 or FF, or a special value that allows the foundation software to trap the runaway program that starts operating within the volatile memory. This special value could be a software interrupt or an illegal opcode.

The final step that is performed during system startup is to initialize the hardware registers to a predefined state that is assumed by the application. Some registers may actually have to be initialized prior to performing the memory checks in order to allow access to the memory. Other registers, such as I/0 configuration registers, can safely be initialized just prior to starting the application.

As can be seen in this section, there are many options available for system startup code. The developer of the foundation software must work with the organization to determine the best way to start up the system and put it into a state that is expected by applications developed for the organization.

EXCEPTION HANDLING

The next area to be addressed in development of the foundation software is the handling of exceptions, a.k.a. interrupts. There are many different methods of handling interrupts, from a simple interrupt service routine that performs the complete interrupt function, to a complex mechanism in which the interrupt service routine provides minimal processing and cues information for later processing by a task.

The simplest handling of exceptions is performed by a single interrupt service routine that is invoked by a vector. This vector may be hard coded into the ROM memory, programmed into a register, or a specific memory location hard coded into the CPU hardware, depending upon the specific microcontroller. This interrupt service routine performs all of the functions required to totally process the interrupt. The benefit is that this routine is very simple to develop. However, the drawback is that longer interrupt service routines increase the latency of handling other exceptions.

Another form of exception handling is where the interrupt service routine processes the critical information first, then re–enables the interrupts so another exception can occur. The interrupt service routine then continues processing the data until complete. The advantage of this method is lower interrupt latency. However, the interrupt service routine must be reentrant and may take a lot of stack space if the processor saves the entire context on the stack.

The final form of exception handling that will be discussed in this paper is where the interrupt service routine is very small, and only provides critical processing at the interrupt level. This usually entails saving some information, possibly in a FIFO queue, activating an operating system task, clearing and re-enabling the interrupt, and then exiting. The task itself will pull the information from the queue and perform the final processing. This task may not run immediately after the interrupt occurs due to the operating system priority and preemption. The advantage of this method is that interrupt latency is minimized. The disadvantage is that the system is much more complex, and it is possible due to priority for one interrupt to still be queued when a second interrupt occurs.

PROGRAM FLOW CONTROL

After developing the foundation software for starting up the system and handling exceptions, the next step is to determine how the foundation will handle program flow control. Flow control usually takes on the form of either an executive or a more traditional real-time operating system. Three types of flow control can be chosen for the foundation software: round-robin, time sliced, and multitasking real-time operating system.

Round-robin flow control consists of a list of tasks which are typically void functions with void parameters. The flow control consists of starting at the beginning of the list, executing each function once, and then going back to the beginning and starting again. Some variations of the round-robin flow control method include waiting for a set time between executions of the list, multiple lists depending upon the state of the system, and more complex function prototypes to allow passing of parameters and return of status.

The second form of flow control is called time sliced. A time sliced executive is similar to a round-robin in that multiple lists of functions are executed during equally spaced time slices. Each time slice executes a round-robin list and then returns control to the executive, which waits until the next time slice is ready to run. The number of times a task appears in the round-robin lists determines the execution rate of that task. For example, a time sliced executive may have slices of five milliseconds. A task that is executed in every time slice is executed at a rate of five milliseconds, in every other time slice is executed at a rate of 10 milliseconds, etc.

The final form of flow control is a multitasking operating system, a.k.a. an RTOS. There are many different RTOS programs and methods in existence today. In addition to the numerous flavors of commercial RTOS's, many companies have developed their own proprietary systems. Each RTOS has its own features and functions that many times makes it unique. Recently, a number of standards have arisen that define the API for a compatible RTOS. Some of these standards are: POSIX, OSEK/VDX, and ITRON.

Some of the more common features of an RTOS is the ability to define a task that may or may not execute continuously, timers that can allow a task to go to sleep for a predefined period of time, and a method to communicate between separate tasks. Tasks may be configured to execute periodically, or may only execute when a defined event occurs. This ability to only execute under certain situations allows the RTOS to maximize the usage of the processor cycles.

The decision on the type and format of program flow control for the foundation software is dependent upon the needs of a particular organization and a particular application. Small applications that are very memory constrained and do a small number of things often would benefit best from a small, efficient round-robin scheduler. If an application requires very strict timing of task execution as is usually found in a closed loop control system, the time sliced flow control mechanism would probably be better. Finally, an application that does a lot of different functions based on aperiodic events and works within a system that is constrained in the amount of processor time available, would work best within an RTOS. Figure 2 below shows a comparison of each type of program flow control and the amount of CPU utilization compared to the resource requirements.

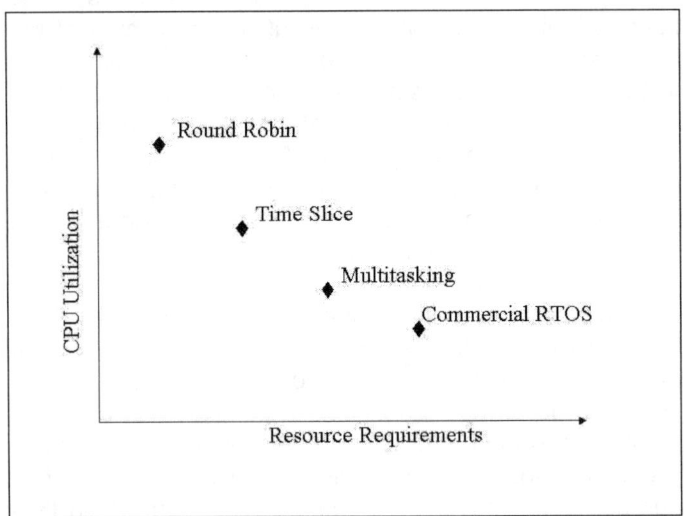

Figure 2 - Comparison of Different Types of Program Flow Control.

HARDWARE ABSTRACTION

After the functional software has been designed to get the system up and running, and the method of flow control has been decided, the designer of the foundation software must address how the system hardware is going to be handled. Many methods exist for abstracting hardware from the application, both within embedded systems and more traditional computing systems. As with the previous sections, there are many different ways of handling hardware abstraction. The three types of abstraction that I will discuss in this paper are: macro abstraction, API interface abstraction, and OS messaging abstraction.

Macro abstraction is a method of using the macro capability of the preprocessor of the C compiler to generate very efficient assembly language code to access the peripherals of the controller or other hardware. This method typically uses extensive global variables from which the actual value of the input is derived. The advantage, as previously mentioned, is a small, fast execution of the macro. The disadvantages, however, include the difficulty in debugging macros, the amount of effort required to write the macros every time the hardware changes, and the possibility of uncontrolled use of global variables.

API interface abstraction eliminates some of the disadvantages of using macros. Software is extensively reused, debugging of the software is easier due to lack of macros, and global variables are eliminated since all variables are encapsulated within the abstraction layer. A well-designed API interface abstraction can actually reduce the amount of memory used by the system since all code is defined in one location and optimization of shared functions can be greater. A drawback of this type of hardware abstraction is that access to the data requires a function call, which is inherently longer than accessing global variables directly.

The final method of abstracting hardware is to use the messaging characteristics of the operating system, if available. Most RTOS systems provide some method of interprocess communication in which data can be passed between tasks asynchronously. This method requires that a task or set of tasks are dedicated to determining the values of the inputs and then sending messages to the actual application, which in turn takes actions based upon the valuables inputs. The same is true for outputs. Messages are sent to the output tasks which control the hardware.

Figure 3 below shows a comparison of the different hardware abstraction types with respect to the setup time, debug time and the resource requirements and portability of each type.

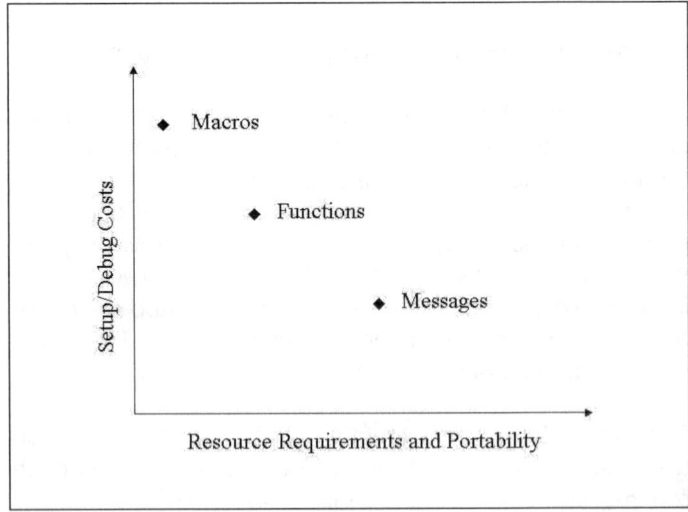

Figure 3 - Comparison of Different Types of Hardware Abstraction

NETWORK COMMUNICATION

In addition to abstracting hardware ports, the network or networks in an embedded device are many times extracted from the application. Like hardware abstraction, the network communication system provides a single interface for all of the networks.

The network communication system is typically realized using a network API. This API abstracts the lower layers of the networking protocol stack from the application. The number of layers abstracted in the network communication software varies between implementations. The software can abstract just the hardware drivers at the driver level, can abstract details of the message format for the particular protocol, or can abstract the data completely from the message.

Software that abstracts just the driver layer requires that the complete message is formatted by the application, including the headers and check sums. The next level of abstraction is at the message level, where the message data is passed to the networking software which is responsible to build the actual protocol dependent message. Finally, at the data level of network abstraction, the networking software extracts data from the message and presents the data independent of the message or the message structure to the application. This is typically used in a small control system type of environment where data is sent packed in the messages and where each data component is independent of the other components within the same structure. An example is in the automotive industry were messages tend to have small chunks of data. Figure 4 shows a graph comparing the different levels of abstraction in a network communication system and the effect on the flexibility and the complexity of the application required to support that software.

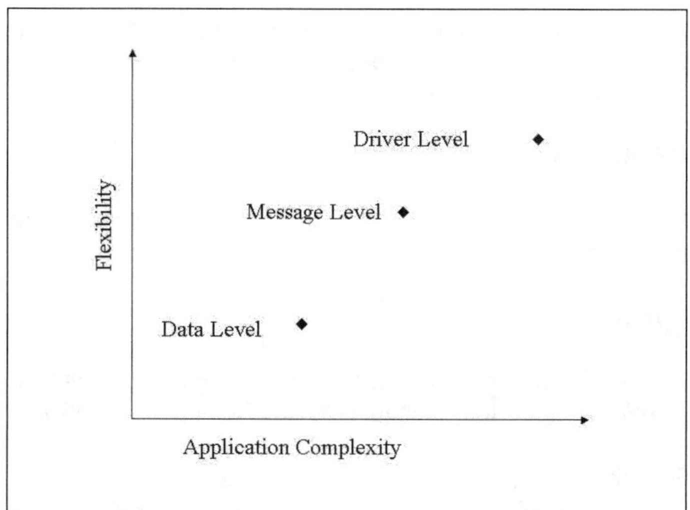

Figure 4 - Network Abstraction Methods Affect on Applications

Depending upon the type of network that is being implemented, commercial network operating systems or network protocol stacks are available. The drawback of many of these commercial network operating systems is that the API is many times unique to the particular operating system. Most TCP/IP protocol stacks provide a socket interface that is somewhat standard. However, the software available for smaller network protocols such as CAN usually have a proprietary interface. The OSEK/VDX communication standard defines a standard API for smaller systems.

The developer of the foundation software may have to create another interface layer between the application and the network operating system in order to truly abstract not only the networking hardware but also the networking protocol.

I/O SYSTEM

As mentioned in the previous section, the foundation software may have to provide another layer of abstraction between the application and the hardware and network. This is typically implemented using an I/O system where the I/O system is responsible for routing the data from the application to either the network or the hardware or both. The purpose of this layer is to provide true abstraction to the application as to the source and destination of the data. By truly abstracting this data, reuse of application modules is greatly increased.

Similar to hardware abstraction, the I/O system can be realized using macros, and API, or the OS messaging system. The advantages and disadvantages of all three types of abstraction are also true in the I/O system.

DIAGNOSTICS

Another section of the foundation software is the diagnostics capability. These diagnostics can range from very simple diagnostics to much more complex diagnostics dictated by the customer or government regulation. All sections of the foundation software should support the diagnostic environment with interfaces that can be invoked by the diagnostics subsystem.

The diagnostics subsystem should have the ability to read the raw data from any of the inputs and override any of the outputs. In addition, the operating mode of the system should be able to be changed by the diagnostic system. This operating mode would then be recognized by the flow control system and the other application modules to modify the workings of the application. Example operating modes include a diagnostics mode, an end of line mode for manufacturing, and possibly multiple levels of fail safe or fail soft modes.

Interfaces that may be required of a module by the diagnostics subsystem include the ability to query the state or values of a module, to force the module into a particular state or output value, and to partially modify the operation of that module.

DEBUG/DEVELOPMENT

In addition to a diagnostic system, it may be desirable to provide development support and field test support within the foundation software. This may be as simple as a small program that allows data to be queried or overridden by an external device, and may be as complicated as a full debug subsystem that allows the program to be stopped, restarted, memory changed, and execution of single tasks.

The simplest form of development support that should be included in any foundation software would be the ability of the developer to query data within the system, and to be able to force outputs to certain values in order to test the system. This small development support system would utilize the same interfaces that the diagnostic system uses to query and control application modules. A small amount of code would be required to either obtain data from or send data over some form of communication channel such as an RS 232 or other networking protocol.

If the embedded device has some other method of obtaining data and displaying data such as a small display, a minimal development support system could be expanded to obtain data from the device's inputs and display the current results on the device display.

Some of the bigger bells and whistles that can be added to the system include the ability to stop the system and enter into a monitor mode, profiling ability to determine CPU and memory usage, stack overrun detection, manual function and task execution, and breakpoint capability.

Another level of development and debug support is usually provided by the flow control mechanism. Hook routines can be called just prior to and/or just after a task is invoked. These hook routines can be used to determine the time that a task executes, how often the task executes, and the ordering of task execution. At an extreme, the task can be cancelled.

A final level of debug and development support is error detection and recovery. This may be an integral part of the diagnostics capability, or may be a part of the development support package. Error support typically involves the support of errors detected by the application with services such as logging errors, posting errors to an external device, and checking if any error has occurred.

The level of development support will have to be determined by the creator of the foundation software. The examples of development support included in this section are only a few of the possible types of support that are used in the embedded industry. In any event, the foundation software should still be robust enough to allow additional development support in the future.

CONCLUSION

This paper has attempted to outline some of the major decisions required in developing foundation software for use by an organization. Development of this foundation software is strongly encouraged to any organization that wishes to implement a strong reusable software system. As in the development of a building, without a good foundation, the whole structure will soon collapse.

The architect of the foundation software must make sound decisions in the following areas: System Startup, Exception Handling, Program Flow Control, Hardware Abstraction, Network Communication, I/O Subsystems, Diagnostics, and Debug/Development Support. These decisions should not be made in a vacuum but should leverage the acquired knowledge of the organization to develop the most robust foundation software system available.

CONTACT

Joseph Lemieux is a Senior Applied Specialist with EDS Embedded Solutions in Troy Michigan. He received his BSEE from General Motors Institute, and his MSEE and MBA from the University of Michigan. He may be contacted at joe.lemieux@eds.com.

ADDITIONAL SOURCES

"Component Software: Beyond Object Oriented Programming" by Clemens Szyperski. Addison-Wesley Publishing Co., 1998. ISBN 0201178885

Additional information on the standard APIs discussed in this paper can be obtained from the respective organizations as follows:

OSEK/VDX

Documents are available on the web site at http://www.osek-vdx.org.

ITRON

Some documents are available on their web site at http://tron.um.u-tokyo.ac.jp/TRON/ITRON/home-e.html.

POSIX

The POSIX specification can be purchased from the Institute of Electrical and Electronics Engineers. Please contact them for more information.

DEFINITIONS, ACRONYMS, ABBREVIATIONS

OSEK/VDX:
OSEK is a German acronym that translates approximately as "Open Standards and the Corresponding Interfaces for Automotive Electronics" and VDX is "Vehicle Distributed Executive".

ITRON:
ITRON is an acronym for "Industrial TRON". TRON is an acronym for "The Realtime Operating system Nucleus".

POSIX:
POSIX is an acronym for "Portable Operating System Interface"

COMMUNICATION NETWORKS/SYSTEMS

2007-01-1625

Formalized Design Procedure for Networked Control Systems

Minsuk Shin
ACE Lab, Hanyang University

Jaehyun Han and Jeamyoung Youn
Graduate School, Hanyang University

Myoungho Sunwoo
Hanyang University

ABSTRACT

In this paper, we proposed a formalized design procedure for networked control systems (NCSs). In a conventional development of NCSs, well-designed control algorithms do not result in the intended control performance after an implementation due to time delays, such as network-induced delays and controller computation delays. The proposed design procedure shows how to minimize the degradation of the control performance caused by the time delays. The design procedure was verified by designing a network-based traction control system (TCS). The designed TCS was realized and tested by using a rapid control prototyping (RCP) platform and a hardware-in-the-loop simulation (HILS) environment.

INTRODUCTION

The use of networked control systems (NCSs) is rapidly increasing because of its advantages, such as the reduction of development cost, ease of system diagnosis and maintenance, and enhanced sub-control system modularity and flexibility. However, time delays such as network-induced delays and the computation time delay of the controller may degrade the control performance of an NCS and may cause system instability as well. Therefore, temporal behaviors of the NCS should be considered during NCS design. The design aspect of the NCS is multi-disciplinary. For NCS design, control engineers usually deal with the development of control algorithms by considering the dynamic characteristics of the NCS, while real-time system engineers handle the implementation of developed control algorithms by considering temporal behaviors of the NCS. Hence, the design methodologies and procedures should consider the design issues faced by control and real-time system engineers [1].

Recently, many studies have investigated several approaches to reduce the gap between these two different perspectives by considering system performance and real-time characteristics of NCSs at the same time in the design phase [2-5]. Ref. [2] was one of the first references to address the relationship between the control performance and the schedulability of the control system. In this study, a model for selecting control periods for a set of control loops was proposed by using a performance index (PI) which is approximated by an exponential function. However, the PI did not consider the effects of time delays, even though they significantly affect control performance. In previous studies, time delays were defined as lumped delays, in which sensor-to-controller delays and controller-to-actuator delays are lumped and network-induced delays were not considered. Therefore, there are limitations to directly applying the proposed approaches determining design parameters (period and priority) for implementing NCSs. In this paper, a formalized design procedure is proposed to determine these design parameters. To verify the efficiency of the design procedure, we applied the procedure to a design of a network-based traction control system.

DESIGN PROCEDURE FOR NCS DEVELOPMENT

A formalized design procedure is proposed for NCS development that takes into consideration the viewpoints of both control engineers and real-time engineers. The design procedure is summarized as follows.

1. Design a control law.
2. Calculate the performance degradation using the temporal behavior of an NCS and the definition of a new performance index (PI), J.
3. Assign priorities and periods to tasks and messages by using an optimization methodology.

In this procedure, the new PI, J, is defined as the difference between a performance measure of a continuous time domain to design a control law, J_C, and

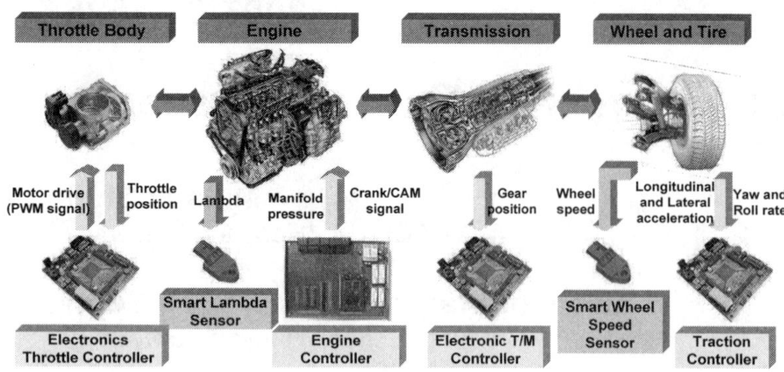

Figure. 1 Architecture of a traction control system

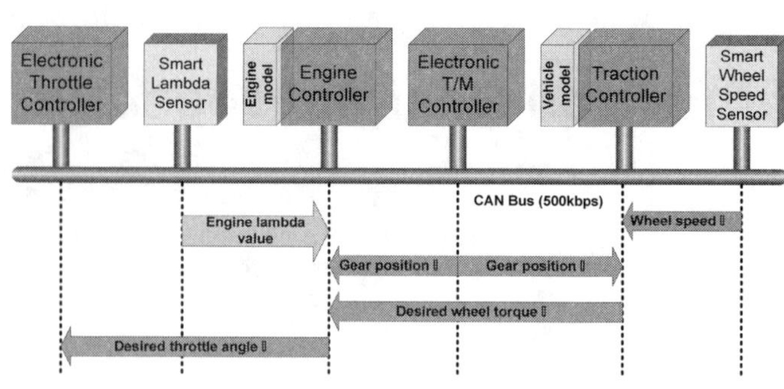

Figure. 2 Network configuration

a performance measure of the discretized system with time delays caused by implementation, $J_{\mathrm{D/w}}$ delays. In Step 1, a control law is designed to optimize the control performance J_{C} of an NCS in a continuous time domain without any consideration of time delays. In Step 2, the performance degradation of the NCS, caused by network induced delays and computation delays, is calculated. A set of available control periods and maximum delay bounds between sensor-to-controller and controller-to-actuator are used in the calculation. In this step, the proposed PI, J, is represented as a function of control periods and time delays. In Step 3, the PI is applied to an optimization methodology to assign priorities and periods to tasks and messages. At this time, the worst-case response times (WCRT) of tasks and messages belonging to the NCS are analyzed for many sets of priorities and periods [6]. Computed WCRTs are translated in terms of time delays and substituted into the PI obtained in Step 2. Then the fitness for each set of priorities and periods can be evaluated. Finally, the optimization approach can find a close-to-optimal set of priorities and periods to minimize the PI by using the fitness. In order to obtain the desired set of periods and priorities, considering the coupled effect of the two design parameters simultaneously, a genetic algorithm (GA) is applied [7].

TRACTION CONTROL SYSTEM

An automobile can unexpectedly go into a skid on wet, slippery roads, not only when braking but also when accelerating. Moreover, excessive slip of the drive wheels can occur during acceleration on slippery road surfaces. As a result, the friction coefficient between the tire and the road surface decreases, with a corresponding increase in wheel slip. This makes controlled steering impossible. The traction control system helps out in dangerous situations like this. The objective of traction control is to maximize tire traction by preventing the wheels from spinning during acceleration. In this study, a network-based traction control system that maintains slip at a desired value by controlling the throttle angle is considered. The traction control system is designed according to a proposed design procedure.

SYSTEM ARCHITECTURE OF A TRACTION CONTROL SYSTEM

The traction control system considered consists of four components which are connected with a CAN communication system. These components are the electronic throttle body, engine, transmission, and wheels, and each component has an individual ECU: electric throttle controller (ETC), transmission controller (TMC), engine management system (EMS) and traction controller (TCS) as shown in Fig. 1. Smart sensors for measuring wheel speed and air-to-fuel ratio (AFR) are used, and they have a network module which allows them to communicate with other devices through the network. Fig. 2 depicts how messages between ECUs and smart sensors are communicated through the CAN bus.

DYNAMIC MODELS AND CONTROLLERS

To validate the control algorithm and evaluate the performance of the traction control system, we need to construct an overall model that configures all of the drive-train components.

Engine model and lambda controller

The engine model adopted in this study is taken from [8]. This engine model is represented by three input values (throttle position, ignition timing, and fuel flow) and three state values (intake manifold pressure, fuel mass of fuel film, and engine rotational speed) and one disturbance (load torque).

To reduce tail-pipe emissions using a three-way catalytic converter, the AFR should be controlled very precisely in both the steady state and transient engine operations. In order to regulate the AFR, a feedforward control scheme and oxygen sensor feedback is used [9]. For the most complete combustion, gasoline usually needs to be burned at an AFR of 14.7. This AFR is called stoichiometric or lambda = 1. The feedforward term is calculated by engine RPM, manifold pressure, and a desired lambda (stoichiometric AFR). A proportional integral controller is applied as a feedback controller which uses a current lambda value transmitted from the lambda sensor via a network bus. The lambda controller determines the injection duration. It is assumed that the engine always operates at MBT (Minimum spark advance for Best Torque).

Vehicle chassis model and traction controller

In order to validate the performance of the traction control algorithm, the vehicle model with eight degrees of freedom (DOF) is used [10]. In addition, the tire model by Pacejka, which is sufficiently accurate to be used in a traction control system, is adopted in the vehicle model [11]. It is assumed that the vehicle is front-wheel-driven and the road is flat.

The traction controller is designed as a two-level controller that uses a sliding mode control method to decide the desired throttle angle for maintaining the desired slip [12]. In this study, we used a desired slip of 0.125. In the first control stage, a slip controller calculates the desired wheel torque using a sliding mode control algorithm. The first sliding surface is defined as a function of wheel slip to obtain the desired traction torque. At the second control stage, an engine torque controller determines a throttle-opening angle that generates the engine torque corresponding to the desired wheel torque. The desired throttle position is decided by the throttle characteristic equation, where the second sliding surface is defined as a function of the intake manifold air pressure.

EXPERIMENTAL ENVIRONMENTS FOR THE TRACTION CONTROL SYSTEM

A hardware-in-the-loop simulation (HILS) environment is used for evaluating the performance of the developed traction control system. A distributed HILS platform is used for the traction control system model. It distributes simulated models into several computing systems to perform parallel processing. The HILS environment supports a function for communication between real controllers. That is, it is a network-based HILS (Net-HILS) environment, as shown in Fig. 3 [13]. The platform consists of a widely used PC and commercial off-the-shelf I/O boards. This environment can be integrated seamlessly into the modern development process, including rapid control prototyping (RCP) [14]. These features make the HILS equipment more cost-effective and flexible.

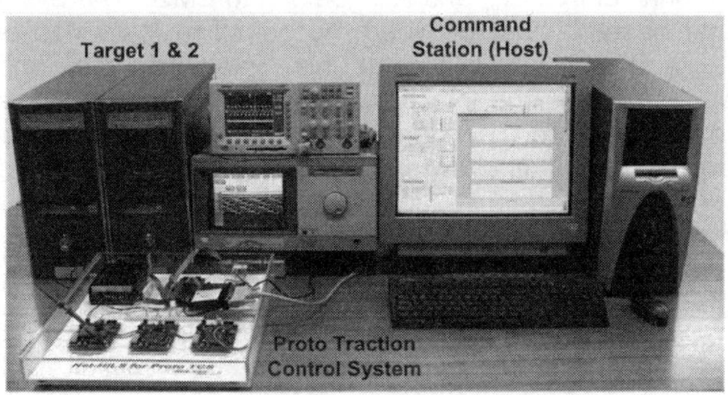

Figure. 3 Net-HILS environment

A PERFORMANCE INDEX FOR THE TRACTION CONTROL SYSTEM

A PI can be set according to the characteristics and objectives of the control applications. For example, in engine control, a PI can represent the aggregate effect on overall fuel consumption and emissions that would occur due to engine operation at all operating points. The objective of a traction control system is to prevent the wheels from spinning during acceleration. Wheel slip is the difference between the vehicle speed and the wheel speed normalized by the vehicle speed for braking and the wheel speed for acceleration. Wheel slip was chosen as the controlled variable for most of the traction control algorithm because of its strong influence on the driving force between the tire and the road. The most effective way to accelerate a vehicle without spinning is to regulate the wheel slip where the friction coefficient attains its peak value [15]. Therefore, the principal purpose of a traction control system is to provide maximum driving force under given driving conditions by keeping the slip value within a desired range. In our traction control system, there are two control loops to maintain the slip ratio at a desired value. One is a slip control loop and the other is a lambda control loop. In this study, the performance J_C of the traction control system is evaluated by the sum of slip errors and lambda errors for each desired value. Then, J_C can be expressed as (1), where the desired slip ratio is 0.125 and the desired lambda is equal to one.

$$\begin{aligned} J_c &= J_{slip\_c} + J_{lambda\_c} \\ &= \int_0^{t_f} \left[|slip\ ratio - desired\ slip\ ratio| + |lambda - desired\ lambda| \right] dt \end{aligned} \tag{1}$$

DESIGN OF PERIODS AND PRIORITIES FOR THE TRACTION CONTROL SYSTEM

Description of control loops for the traction control system

Fig. 4 shows a schematic diagram of the simulation models for the traction control system. There are two control loops: the slip control loop and the lambda control loop.

The slip control loop consists of four nodes: a smart sensor for sampling wheel speed, a throttle controller for the actuation of the electronic throttle body, and two distributed controller nodes for traction control, as shown in Fig. 5. The throttle controller, which is an actuator node, is assumed to be activated by a message for the desired throttle angle from the EMS node. The lambda control loop consists of a smart sensor and a controller, as shown in Fig. 6. The control network is only inserted between the sensor and the lambda controller, i.e. the lambda controller is directly connected to the plant.

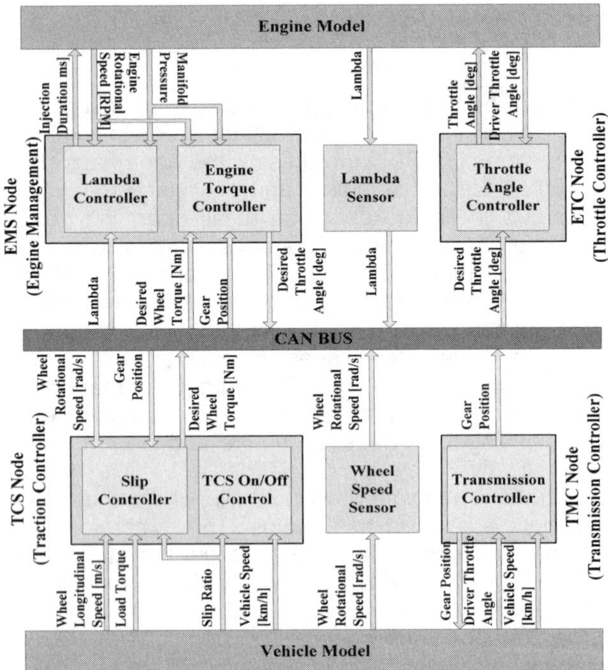

Figure. 4 Schematic diagram of a simulation model for the traction control system

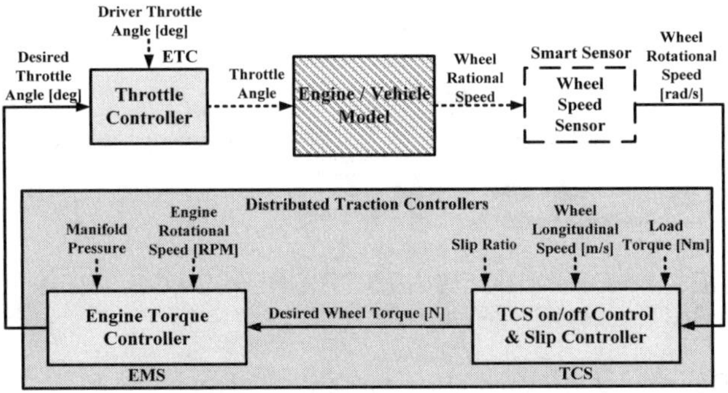

Figure. 5 Slip control loop

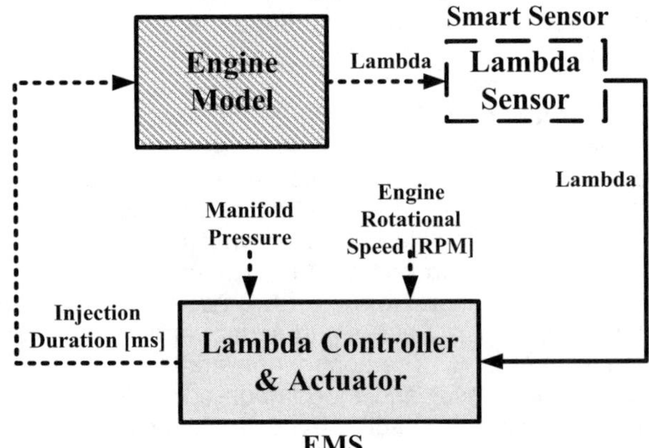

Figure. 6 Lambda control loop

The detailed assumptions used in this section are as follows:

1. Every message transmission occurs at the end of task execution.
2. An available set of periods for tasks and messages is given.
3. Sensor-to-controller time skews of two control loops are 3 ms.
4. A task execution delay τ_{exe} is equal to its worst-case execution time (WCET).
5. The maximum allowable delay bound for each control loop is 50 ms.
6. A priori overheads are negligible.
7. Allowable utilization of CPUs and a network bus is 0.8.

Time components used in this study, such as time skew, several delays, offset, and so on, refer to [16].

Each sensor and actuator node have only one task. The TCS and EMS nodes are assumed to have two dummy tasks to put virtual loads on each node. The CAN protocol with 500 kbps is used as a communication network.

Table 1 shows temporal attributes of the traction control system; the unit is milliseconds (ms). Sensor tasks (S_{ws} & S_{lam}) are periodically activated and transmit sensor data to each controller. In the slip control loop, the C_{tcs_on} task in TCS checks the wheel speed information transmitted from S_{ws} and the slip ratio and decides whether the traction control system is to be turned on or off. When the traction control system is turned on, the C_{slip} task computes the desired wheel torque to keep the slip ratio within the traction control area and sends the value to the C_{tqr} task in the EMS node via the network bus. Then C_{tqr} evaluates the desired throttle angle to generate an engine torque corresponding to the desired wheel torque. The computed desired throttle angle is transmitted to the ETC node by a network message. The A_{etc} task in the ETC node is immediately activated and operates the throttle body after a message from the C_{tqr} task arrives. In the lambda control loop, the tasks for lambda control, C_{lam} and A_{lam}, belong to EMS. There is a time offset (2 ms) between the sampling instances of C_{lam} and A_{lam}. C_{lam} calculates the injection duration and A_{lam} generates the injection signal according to Clam's command. The precedence relationship of each control loop is defined as shown in Table 2. An available period set of tasks and messages which implement the traction control system is given as h=[10 20 30 40 50] ms.

Off-line simulation to calculate the performance degradation caused by control periods and time delays

In order to derive a PI applied to the design of periods and priorities, we have to analyze the performance degradation caused by the control periods and time delays for the traction control system. In this study, we derived the performance measure of a discretized system with time delays $J_{D/w}$ delays for each control loop

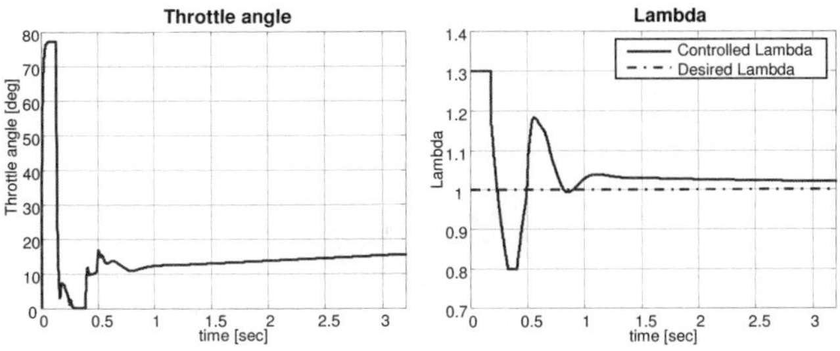

Figure. 7 Throttle angle and lambda for acceleration in a split road condition

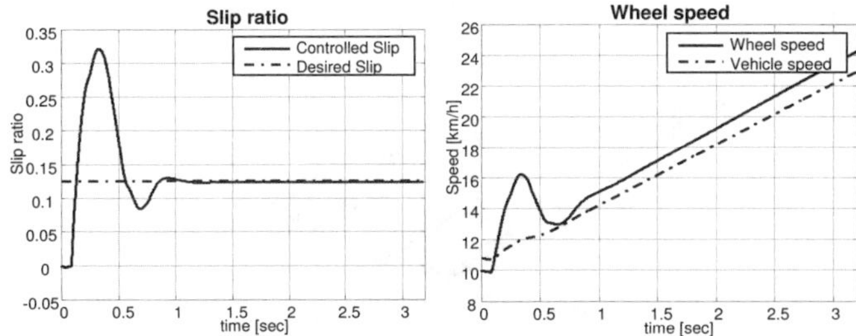

Figure. 8 Slip ratio and wheel speed for acceleration in a split road condition

Table 1
Temporal attributes of the traction control system

EMS	WCET	D	Offset	TCS	WCET	D	Offset
C_{lam}	1.5	50	0	C_{tcs_on}	0.5	50	0
A_{lam}	1	50	2	C_{slip}	3	50	0
C_{tqr}	3	50	0	D_{tcs1}	5	50	0
D_{ems1}	2	50	0	D_{tcs2}	2	50	0
D_{ems2}	2		0				0

ETC	WCET	D	Offset	TMS	WCET	D	Offset
A_{etc}	1	50	0	C_{gp}	2	50	0

WS_Sen	WCET	D	Offset	Lam_Sen	WCET	D	Offset
S_{ws}	1	50	0	S_{lam}	1	50	0

CAN_NW	D	Length	Signals	Tx node	Rx node
M_{ws}	50	1	Wheel speed (rps)	Sensor	TCS
M_{lam}	50	1	Lambda (AFR)	Sensor	EMS
M_{dTrq}	50	2	Desired wheel torque (Nm)	TCS	EMS
M_{dTA}	50	1	Desired throttle angle (deg)	EMS	ETC
M_{gp}	50	1	Gear position	TMC	TCS

Table 2
Precedence relationships of two control loops

Name	Precedence relationship
Lambda	S_{lam} ➔ M_{lam} ➔ C_{lam} ➔ A_{lam}
Slip	S_{ws} ➔ M_{ws} ➔ C_{tcs_on} ➔ C_{slip} ➔ M_{dTrq} ➔ C_{tqr} ➔ M_{dTA} ➔ A_{etc}

Table 3
Timing components in the traction control system

	Description
h_{slip}	Control period of the slip control loop
h_{lambda}	Control period of the lambda control loop
J_{sc_slip}	From the sampling instant of S_{slip} to the sampling instant of C_{slip}
J_{ca_slip}	From the sampling instant of C_{tcs_on} to the actuation instant of A_{etc}
J_{sc_lambda}	From the sampling instant of Slam to the sampling instant of C_{lam}
J_{ca_lambda}	From the sampling instant of Clam to the actuation instant of A_{lam}

from iterative simulations under several conditions for control periods and time. The timing components changed are summarized in Table 3. Fig. 7 and Fig. 8 show the results of an off-line simulation for two control loops.

Simulation was performed for acceleration under split road conditions where the wheels on one side of the vehicle passed over a slippery road. It was assumed that the friction coefficients of the right and left side wheels were 0.3 and 0.8 respectively and that the driver fully pushes the accelerator to the 77 ° throttle position at initial start-up. If the traction control system does not operate under this situation, there is a difference in traction force of the two tractive wheels. Specifically, the traction force on the unslippery side is much higher than on the slippery side, and so a yaw moment is generated on the vehicle. The vehicle speed may decrease because unintended lateral force occurs, and the unintended lateral force may cause lateral instability.

In Fig. 7 (a), the traction control system ignores the driver's intent and regulates the throttle position between 10 ° and 20 °. By regulating the throttle angle, the wheel slip ratio is controlled at a target value (slip ratio= 0.125), as demonstrated in Fig. 8 (a). Fig. 8 (b) shows the difference between wheel speed and vehicle speed. At this time, the lambda value is controlled near the desired value (lambda= 1), as shown in Fig. 7 (b).

A PI J is defined as a weighted sum of the difference between J_C and $J_{D/w}$ delays normalized by the desired slip ratio and the desired lambda for two control loops as follows:

$$
\begin{aligned}
J &= J_{slip} + J_{lambda} \\
&= \sum_{n=0}^{n-1} \int_{kh}^{(k+1)h} \left[\frac{\left| (slip\ ratio)_C - (slip\ ratio)_{D/w\_delay} \right|}{(slip\ ratio)_{desired}} \times w_{slip} \right] dt \\
&+ \sum_{n=0}^{n-1} \int_{kh}^{(k+1)h} \left[\frac{\left| (lambda)_C - (lambda)_{D/w\_delay} \right|}{(lambda)_{desired}} \times w_{lambda} \right] dt
\end{aligned}
\tag{2}
$$

where, J_{slip} and J_{lambda} are performance degradation factors derived from the slip and lambda control loop, respectively, and w_{slip} and w_{lambda} are weighting factors for slip errors and lambda errors. In this example, the weighting factors are 8 and 1, respectively.

Fig. 9 shows the values of J_{slip} and J_{lambda} for some available periods and various delays. The simulation results are used as a criterion to select the control periods and priorities of tasks and messages where

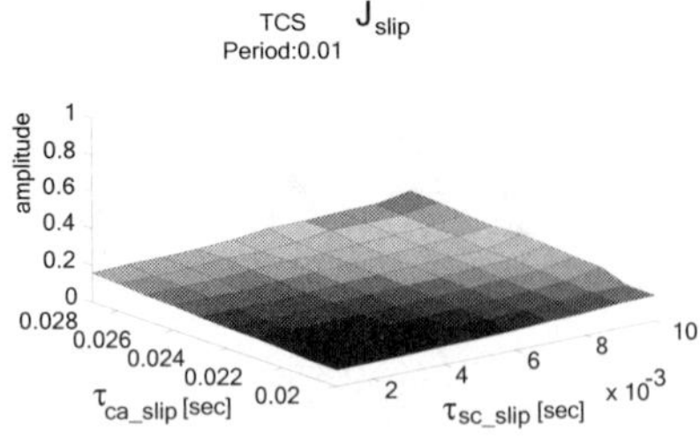

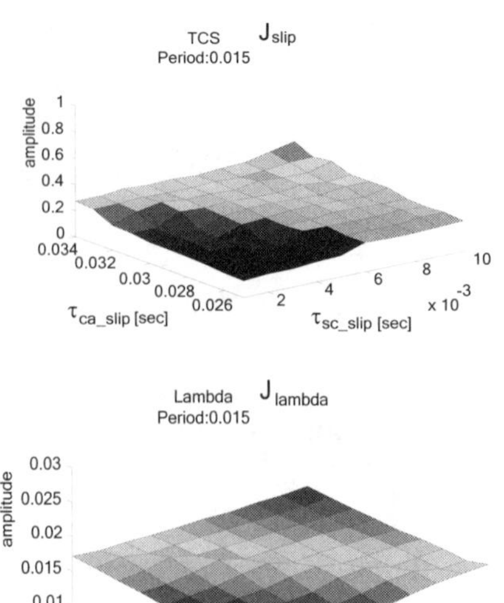

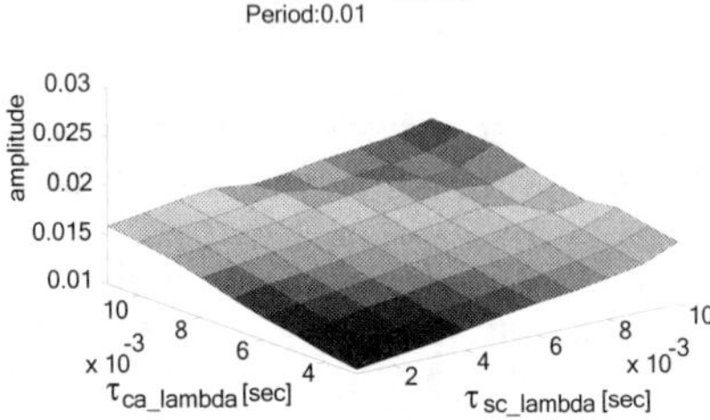

Figure. 9 Performance indices J_{slip} and J_{lambda} of the traction control system for several conditions

constraints are derived from the deadline requirements, dependent relationships of tasks and messages, and to select allowable resource utilization to guarantee the schedulability of the system in a design phase. Now, we can apply the approach proposed in [7] using the GA where the simulation results shown in Fig. 9 are used as the PI. Tables 4 and 5 show the sets of priorities and periods for tasks and messages acquired from the analysis. The time delays and PIs are given for each set in Table 6.

Table 4
The priority and period sets of tasks

	S_{ws}	S_{lam}	C_{lam}	A_{lam}	C_{tqr}	D_{ems1}	D_{ems2}	C_{tcs_on}	C_{slip}	D_{tcs1}	D_{tcs2}	A_{etc}	C_{gp}
P	1	1	2	3	1	4	5	1	2	4	3	1	1
T	10	10	10	10	10	20	20	10	10	20	20	10	10

Table 5
The priority and period sets of messages, (P, T)

M_{ws}	M_{lam}	M_{dTrq}	M_{dTA}	M_{gp}
(3,10)	(4,10)	(1,10)	(2,10)	(5,10)
(3,10)	(5,10)	(1,10)	(2,10)	(4,10)
(4,10)	(3,10)	(1,10)	(2,10)	(5,10)
(4,10)	(5,10)	(1,10)	(2,10)	(3,10)
(5,10)	(3,10)	(1,10)	(2,10)	(4,10)
(5,10)	(4,10)	(1,10)	(2,10)	(3,10)

Table 6
Delays and performance indices for two control loops

	Slip control loop	Lambda control loop
$(h, \tau_{sc}, \tau_{ca})$	(10, 3, 22.376)	(10, 3, 8.5)
J_i	1.623145	0.016119
$J = J_{slip} + J_{lambda} = 1.639264$		

From these results, we can see that tasks belonging to two control loops have higher priorities than those of dummy tasks, and the shortest periods of the available periods and messages for actuation have higher priorities than those of sensor messages. This is reasonable, because dummy tasks do not participate in any control loops and the maximum sensor-to-controller travel delays are smaller than sensor-to-controller time skews for each control loop. In other words, by assigning the lowest priorities to dummy tasks and messages related to sensor inputs, the optimal method tries to reduce performance degradation caused by other tasks which do not belong to control loops.

SIMULATION RESULTS

We implemented ECUs for the traction control system based on the periods and priorities for tasks and messages obtained using the RCP platform [14, 17]. The ECUs were evaluated on the HILS environment for the traction control system in a simulation performed for acceleration under split road conditions. In addition to the designed case (GA case), Tables 7 and 8 show two different conditions (Case 1 & Case 2) of periods and priorities for tasks and messages. For Case 1, the performance degradation of the traction control system is caused by the interference of dummy tasks because they have higher priorities than the other control tasks. The results of Case 2 show the effects of control periods on the control performance.

Table 7
The priority and period sets of tasks for Case 1 & 2

	S_{ws}	S_{lam}	C_{lam}	A_{lam}	C_{tqr}	D_{ems1}	D_{ems2}	C_{tcs_on}	C_{slip}	D_{tcs1}	D_{tcs2}	A_{etc}	C_{gp}
Case1	1	1	5	3	4	2	1	3	4	1	2	1	1
	10	10	10	10	10	20	20	10	10	20	20	10	10
Case2	1	1	2	3	1	4	5	1	2	4	3	1	1
	30	20	20	20	30	20	20	30	30	20	20	30	30

Table 8
The priority and period sets of messages (P, T) for Case 1 & 2

	M_{ws}	M_{lam}	M_{dTrq}	M_{dTA}	M_{gp}
Case1	(1,10)	(2,10)	(4,10)	(5,10)	(3,10)
Case2	(3,30)	(4,20)	(1,30)	(2,30)	(5,30)

In Fig. 10 (a), the traction control system ignores the driver's intent and oscillates the throttle position between 0 ° and 20 °. According to the oscillation, the lambda value varies around 1, as shown in Fig. 10 (b). Fig. 10 (c) shows that the wheel slip ratio is controlled close to the target slip ratio. These results indicate the GA case shows better control performance than that of other cases. From the results, we can see that the lambda control loop is more sensitive than the slip control loop because the variation of lambda is larger than that of the slip ratio under the same throttle conditions.

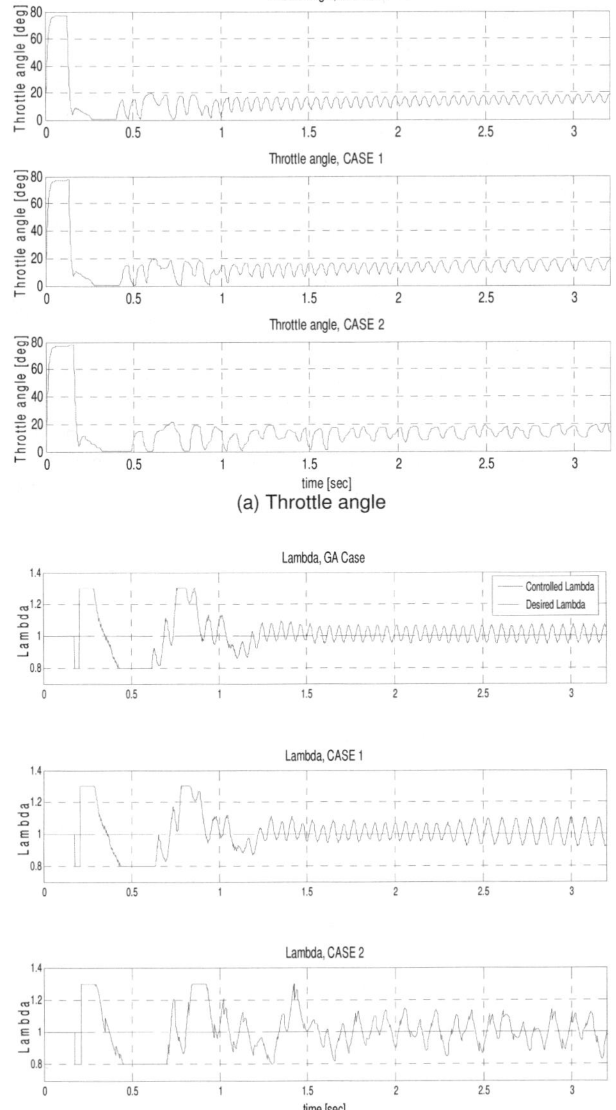

(a) Throttle angle

(b) Lambda

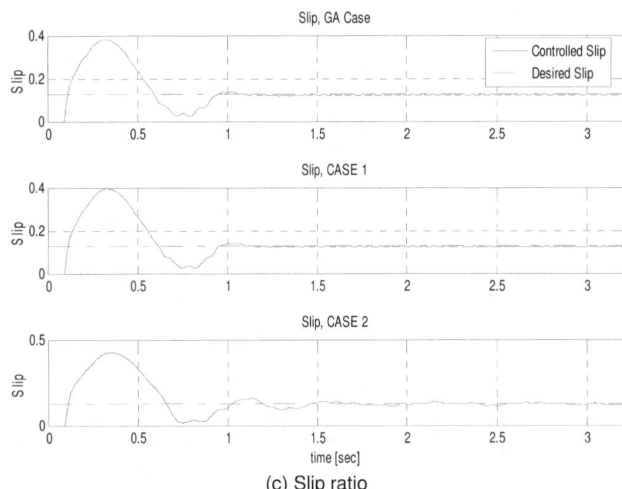

(c) Slip ratio

Figure. 10 Simulation results for three (P, T) sets

CONCLUSION

A formalized design procedure was proposed for designing a Networked Control System (NCS). According to the proposed procedure, a network-based traction control system was designed. In this study, the performance of the traction control system was evaluated by the sum of the slip error and the lambda error for each desired value. Through iterative simulations, we derived performance degradation of the traction control system caused by control periods and time delays. The simulation results were used as a PI to assign periods and priorities to tasks and messages subject to temporal constraints. We designed a close-to-optimal set of priorities and periods to minimize the PI by using the optimization method. Finally, the designed control system was implemented and tested using the RCP platform and the HILS environment. The simulation results show that the performance of controllers which are implemented by the proposed design procedure is closer to optimum than other implementations.

Through the design procedure, we derived a close-to-optimal implementation satisfying real-time constraints such as deadlines, allowable utilization limits, and precedence relationships and minimizing performance degradation caused by implementation. Consequently, it can be said that the proposed design procedure and the PI reflect the perspectives of both control engineers and real-time system engineers.

ACKNOWLEDGMENTS

This research is supported in part by MOST (Ministry of Science and Technology) under the National Research Laboratory program.

REFERENCES

1. M. Törngren, "Modelling and Design of Distributed Real-Time Control Applications," Ph.D. Thesis, Department of Machine Design, Royal Institute of Technology, Stockholm, Sweden, 1995
2. D. Seto, J. P. Lehoczky, L. Sha, and K. G. Shin, "On Task Schedulability in Real-Time Systems," Proceedings RTSS 96, 13-21
3. M. Ryu, S. Hong, and M. Saksena, "Streamlining real-time controller design: From performance specifications to end-to-end timing constraints," Proceedings of Real-Time Applications and Technology Symposium, June, pp. 192-203
4. B. Kim, "Task scheduling with feedback latency for real-time control systems," Real-time computing systems & applications Proceedings 5th International Conference, pp. 37-41
5. H. Rehbinder, and M. Sanfridson, "Integration of Off-Line Scheduling and Optimal Control," Proceedings of the 12th European Conference on Real-Time Systems, Stockholm, Sweden, pp. 137-143
6. K. Tindell, and J. Clark, "Holistic Schedulability Analysis for Distributed Hard-Real-Time Systems," Microprocessing & Microprogramming – Euromicro Journal, vol. 50, nos. 2-3, pp. 117-134, 1994
7. M. Shin, and M. Sunwoo, "Optimal period and priority assignment for a networked control system scheduled by a fixed priority scheduling system," International Journal of Automotive Technology, in press.
8. P. Yoon, and M. Sunwoo, "A nonlinear dynamic engine modelling for controller design," KSAE, vol. 7, no. 7, pp. 167-180, 1999.
9. P. Yoon, S. Park, W. Lee, and M. Sunwoo, "Robust Nonlinear Control of Air-to-Fuel Ratio in Spark Ignition Engines," International Journal of Automotive Technology, vol. 15, no. 6, pp. 699~708, 2001.
10. D. Smith, and J. Starkey, "Effects of Model Complexity on the Performance of Automated Vehicle Steering Controllers: Model Development, Validation, and Comparison," Vehicle system dynamics, Vol. 24, pp. 163-181, 1995.
11. E. Bakker, H. Pacejka, and L. Lidner, "A New Tire Model with an Application in Vehicle Dynamics Studies," SAE Paper 890087, pp. 439-451, 1989.
12. S. Kang, M. Yoon, and M. Sunwoo, "Traction control using throttle valve based on sliding mode control and load torque estimation," Proceedings of Institution of Mechanical Engineers, Part D, vol. 219, pp. 645-653, 2005.
13. J. Ryu, M. Yoon, and M. Sunwoo, "Development of a network-based traction control systems, validation of its traction control algorithm and evaluation of its performance using Net-HILS," International Journal of Automotive Technology, vol. 7, no. 6, pp. 687-695. October 2006.
14. W. Lee, M. Shin, and M. Sunwoo, "Target-identical rapid control prototyping platform for model-based engine control," Proceedings of Institution of Mechanical Engineers, Part D, vol. 218, pp. 755-765, 2004.
15. M. Kabganian, and R. Kazemi, "A new strategy for traction control in turning via engine modeling," IEEE Transaction on Vehicular Technology, vol. 50, no. 6, November 2001.
16. M. Shin, S. Ryu, and M. Sunwoo, " Modeling a time delay model to analyze network-induced delays for networked control systems," KSAE Spring Conference Proceedings, vol.Ⅲ, pp.1478-1485, June 2006
17. J. Ma, J. Youn, M. Shin, I. Hwang, and M. Sunwoo, "Integrated development environment from modeling to implementation for automotive real-time embedded control systems," International Journal of Automotive Technology, vol. 7, no. 3, pp. 345-351, May 2006.

2007-01-1621

A Hierarchical Flexray Bus and Task Scheduler

Sri Kanajan
General Motors Research

ABSTRACT

Flexray is widely expected to be the next generation in-vehicle communication bus protocol that will satisfy high-determinism, high bandwidth and safety-critical automotive requirements. The deployment of Flexray into the automotive architecture will require a paradigm shift from a development process and tools perspective relative to the legacy CAN-based development process and tools. One of the key aspects of this shift is in the concept that task and bus message schedules are deterministically decided during design time. This paper provides a scheduling framework that would enable a designer to schedule systems in a hierarchical fashion based upon an iterative refinement concept. The idea is to iteratively refine the schedule from the top level application cycle down to the communication cycle definition and finally to include the TDMA slot definition. This approach is amenable to the decoupling of task from message scheduling and further to enable the decoupling of the top level schedule from the protocol detail. The concept has been implemented as a tool in Microsoft Excel using a List Scheduling optimization scheme. Initial results from a case study based upon an active safety subsystem indicate the advantages and disadvantages of this approach to scheduling.

INTRODUCTION

The in-vehicle electrical content is increasing at an exponential rate. The cost contribution from electronics and software as a percentage of the cost of the entire vehicle has increased from 15% in 1990 to 37% in 2000 [1]. The number of nodes in the vehicle now can exceed 70 independent ECUs interconnected by up to five vehicle[1] CAN busses. Naturally, the serial data bandwidth requirements have also proportionally increased especially with the burgeoning of cross-subsystem features such as lane keeping, automatic collision preparation, and predictive powertrain management. Furthermore, safety critical requirements are starting to emerge, such as throttle, braking and steering systems that are augmented by automatic electronic controls. So what are OEMs doing to address these architectural issues? One of the key architectural element's that is meant to address these requirements is the Flexray protocol.

FLEXRAY PROTOCOL

The vision of the Flexray Consortium is to provide a protocol that can support high determinism and dependable and high bandwidth communication in a cost-efficient manner. Flexray is a time-triggered, distributed clock synchronized protocol that provides a global time base by which communication and computation can be statically scheduled.

However, along with its benefits, Flexray introduces significant change into the traditional CAN-based system design flow. Firstly, the approach of describing interfaces[2] with just a set of CAN messages and their corresponding IDs, will no longer be sufficient. In Flexray, a component interface will include a larger set of protocol parameters such as communication cycle, slot size, and the slot position in the cycle. Secondly, the notion of a global time synchronized computation and communication may cause a temporal coupling between receiver and transmitter that is unlike the traditional approach where transmitter and receivers along the bus are completely decoupled except they remain linked through a CAN identifier.

Both of these issues imply that scheduling communication and computation becomes a critical part in the design flow in a Flexray-based system. Although the general scheduling theory is a well explored field [4,5], Flexray scheduling approaches are still a relatively rich area of research especially since the protocol has just been released. As the reader will see in this paper, Flexray scheduling brings about its own interesting nuances and complexity that is unique in the field of scheduling.

Protocol Description

The most important part of the Flexray protocol, relative to bus and task scheduling, is its timing hierarchy. The time base is decomposed into different levels as reflected in Figure 1.

[1] Vehicle CAN bus here is meant to reflect that these busses are not private to a specific subsystem.

[2] This is assuming that the interface is described at the level of a physical component; e.g., a supplier provides a off-the-shelf component to the OEM.

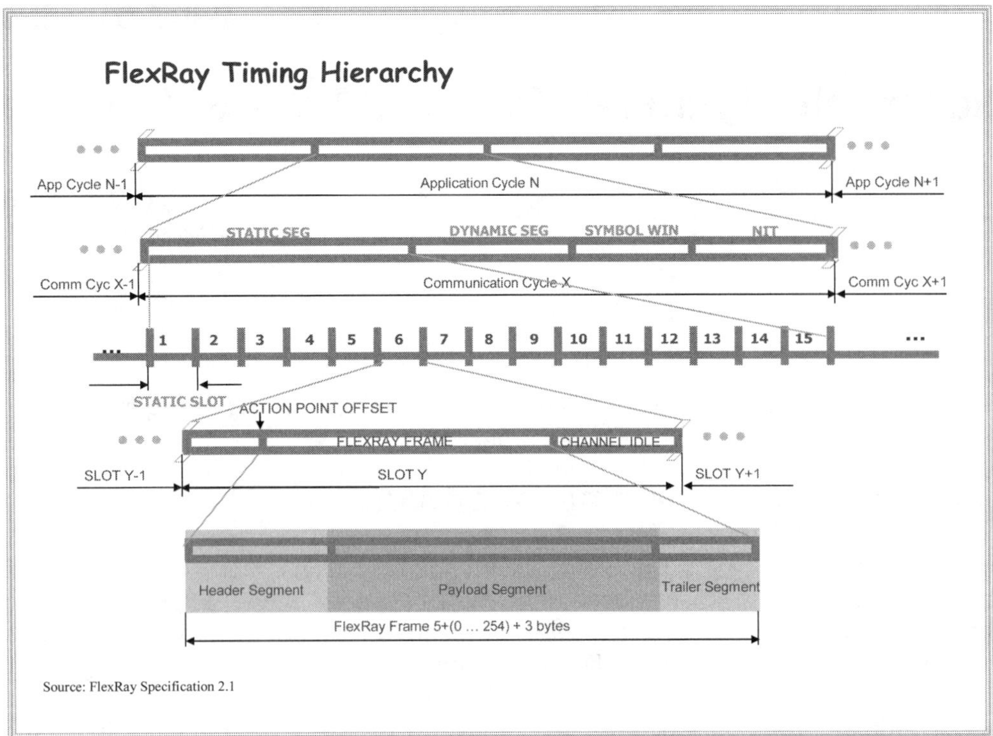

Figure 1: Flexray Timing Hierarchy [3]

At the top level all tasks and messages are statically scheduled throughout the application cycle which is defined as the least common multiple of all the unique periods of tasks and messages. The application cycle then consists of an integer number of communication cycles. Each communication cycle is in turn comprised of a static segment, dynamic segment, symbol window and network idle time (NIT). For the purposes of this paper, the schedule of the static segment is the only one that will be explored. Each static segment is comprised of an integer number of equal sized slots, in which each slot is sized to fit a message. An additional constraint is that each slot is owned by a specific node and that ownership must be maintained across all communication cycles.

CONTRIBUTION

The main concept that this paper presents is the idea of scheduling bus messages and operating system tasks in a hierarchical fashion relative to the global time base definition. In addition to this concept, this work has also focused on analyzing the Flexray protocol stack to derive key protocol parameters that would impact the schedule and some of its trade-offs.

The benefits of this approach are that the top level scheduling is decoupled from any protocol details. Hence, this approach can be extended to account for multiple busses with heterogeneous time synchronized protocols such as Flexray, TTP, and TTCAN. In addition, there can be different optimization metrics at the different levels of the hierarchy. For example, at the application cycle level, maximizing slack between the schedulable elements may be the most important metric, while at the communication cycle and slot level, maximizing effective bandwidth utilization may be the most appropriate.

However, there are drawbacks to this approach. The obvious one is that it is a form of heuristic to solve a complex optimization problem. The final schedule is guaranteed to be never better than any global optimization approach where all the degrees of freedom and constraints are considered together. Another drawback is that it is a purely top-down design flow. In a practical environment, the supplier could provide constraints to the entire schedule such as the slot size and communication cycle length, or the OEM could have a legacy implementation which must be preserved due to reuse constraints while the new entities have to be scheduled around them. This framework could be extended to go towards a "meet-in-the-middle" approach, but this paper will not address this.

RELATED WORKS

Flexray scheduling is a relatively new area of research in comparison to other well-known protocols such as TTCAN and TTP. The predominant development tool vendor for Flexray systems, DECOMSYS, does not yet have a full-fledged scheduling synthesis engine for Flexray. There have been research papers such as [6] that provide solutions. However, the approach in [6] does not address the slot sizing problem and assumes a periodic rate of the entities to be a harmonic of the communication cycle. Our framework provides a general solution to any multirate system[3] and considers the slot sizing issue.

Another piece of interesting work has come from Paul Pop [4,5,8] where the idea was to synthesize schedules of time-triggered systems using an optimization goal that would minimize the impact of an incremental design flow. The protocol used in that work was TTP, but recent work has moved towards the Flexray protocol. Their recent work on Flexray [8] does not address the issue of the sizing of the communication cycle and slot size, and assumes these parameters are an input to their optimization problem. They do, however, synthesize a schedule for both the dynamic and the static segment, whereas our approach focuses on the schedule for just the static segment.

The earlier work on TTP [7] at a high level is similar since both are time-triggered, TDMA protocols. However, there are a few key differences that make the scheduling synthesis problem for TTP very different from Flexray:

1. The communication cycle and slot size durations are variable in TTP, whereas in Flexray, they have to be the same.

2. Flexray has the constraint that node ownership of slots are preserved across all communication cycles. In TTP, a slot can be multiplexed[4] across multiple nodes.

3. TTP has the constraint that each node can only transmit once within a communication cycle, while Flexray allows multiple transmit slots within a cycle to be owned by the same node.

ARCHITECTURE DESCRIPTION

The architecture dealt with in this work consists of two types of physical components – the ECU and the Flexray bus. The topology is defined as a set of nodes interconnected with one or many communication busses.

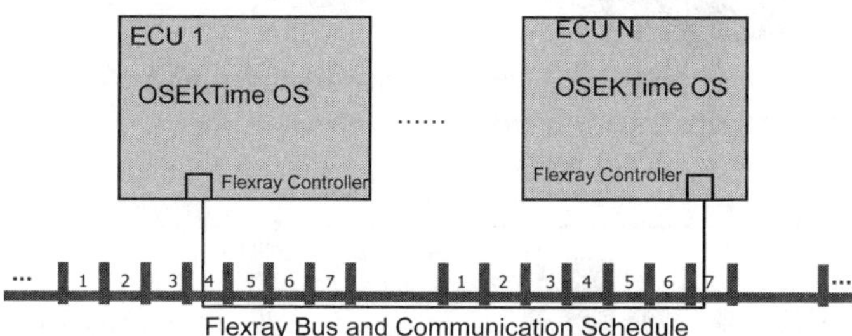

Figure 2: ECU and Flexray Bus Architecture

Electronic Control Unit (ECU)

The attributes of the ECU that are relevant to the scheduling framework in this paper are as follows:

1. The operating system is assumed to be an OSEKTime-based operating system. In short, the OSEKTime scheduler is a time-triggered scheduler that allows for fixed priority preemption or a "last in first out" preemption policy[5]. Figure 5 indicates a scenario where T4 preempts T3 until it completes its execution, since it was dispatched during T3's execution window.
2. The Flexray controller allows for a limited set of transmit and receive buffers. There will be a more detailed discussion on the Flexray message buffer configurability later in the paper.
3. There is an on-chip Flexray controller that abides by the Flexray protocol specification.

Flexray Bus

The Flexray bus in this paper is considered to be a single channel bus or a dual redundant[6] channel bus. However, the framework can be easily extended to consider multiple parallel channels and even heterogeneous channels such as a mixed CAN and Flexray topology. This is because the bus is treated like an ECU at the top level of the timing hierarchy. Having more than one bus simply means that there is a more parallelism in the architecture.

There are a few key Flexray protocol parameters relevant to scheduling that will be either assumed as an input or synthesized as part of the optimization process in this paper. They are described in Table 1.

Flexray Parameter Name (Unit)	Short Description	Input/Output[7]
gdCycle (msec)	Communication Cycle duration	Output
gdStaticSlot (MT)	Static Slot Size	Output
gdMacrotick (uS)	An interval of time derived from the cluster wide clock synchronization algorithm.	Input
ActionPointOffset (MT)	The offset between the start of a static slot and the start of transmission of data	Input

[3] Though, as will be indicated later in the paper, a harmonic rate system provides some nice scheduling benefits over non-harmonic rate systems.

[4] For example, in TTP, Node A can transmit in Slot 10 in Cycle 1 and Node B can transmit in Slot 10 in Cycle 2.

[5] This can be characterized as preemption off the stack, not dissimilar from a function call.

[6] I.e. the message schedules are exactly the same on both busses.

[7] This column delineates whether the parameter is considered an input or an output of this optimization process.

BaudRate (bps)	The bus bandwidth	Input
gPayloadLengthStatic (bytes)	The size of payload length of a frame to be transmitted	Output
gdNIT (MT)	Duration of Network Idle Time	Input
gdSymbolWindow (MT)	Duration of the Symbol Window in the cycle	Input
gNumberOfMiniSlots (int)	Duration of the dynamic segment	Input
gdTSSTransmitter (bits)	Number of bits before transmitting actual frame data.	Input

Table 1: Flexray Parameters Relevant for Scheduling

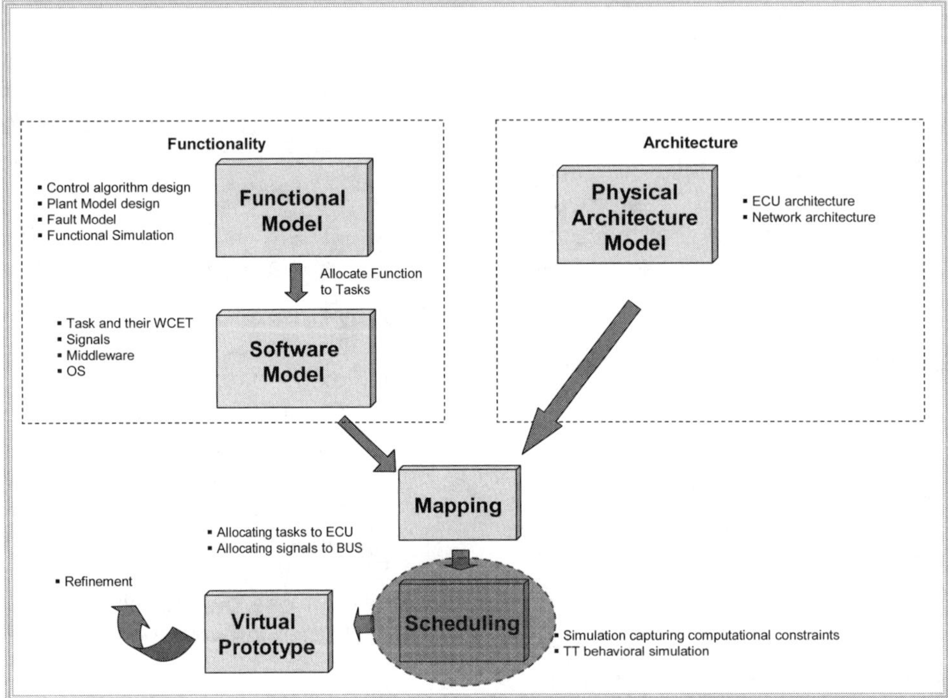

Figure 3: Architecture Design Flow Characterization

Each of these parameters has a constraint and some mathematical relationship between each other. This is specified within the protocol specification.

SCHEDULING THEORY

This section will describe the main mathematical constructs that define the scheduling framework.

Application Model

The application model is meant to refer to how the functions and the logical communication between functions are defined. In this paper, the functional model is described as a directed acyclic graph where the edges represent precedence constraints between functions/vertices. The function is triggered when **all** its inputs have arrived. For example in Figure 4, we see that T3 can only execute when the data from T1 **and** T2 arrives at its input. In this particular example, the functions/tasks are in a multirate configuration, with T3 running every 4 msec and T1 and T2 executing every 2msec. There will be a more detailed discussion on how multirate systems are treated later in this paper.

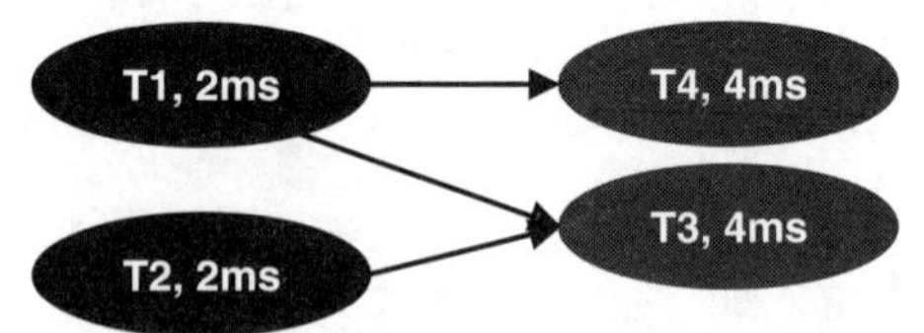

Figure 4: Functional Model[8] with Precedence Constraints and Periods

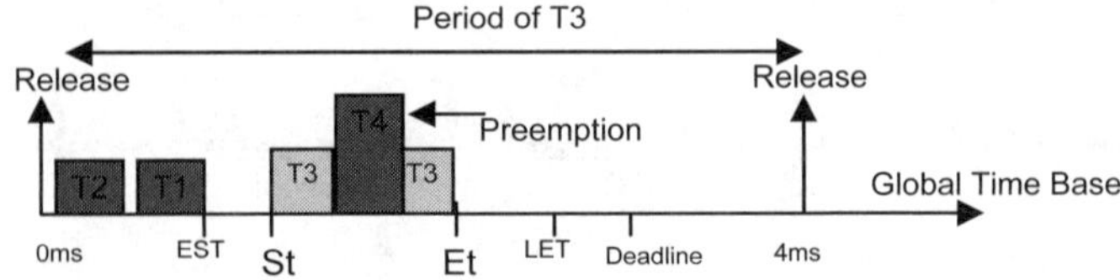

Figure 5: Graphical Description of Task Parameters of T3

[8] The difference in color is meant to reflect the mapping onto different ECUs.

We will refer to tasks and messages as schedulable entities in this paper.

Each schedulable entity[9] is annotated with some timing property. In this paper we consider the following properties: (Please refer to Figure 5 for a graphical description of some of these parameters.)

1. Release time (Rt)
2. Deadline (D)
3. Start Time (St)
4. Earliest Start Time[10] (EST)
5. End Time (Et)
6. Latest End Time[11] (LET)
7. Execution time/Message size (U)
8. Period (P)
9. Root Entity[12] (M)

Table 2: Parameter Set

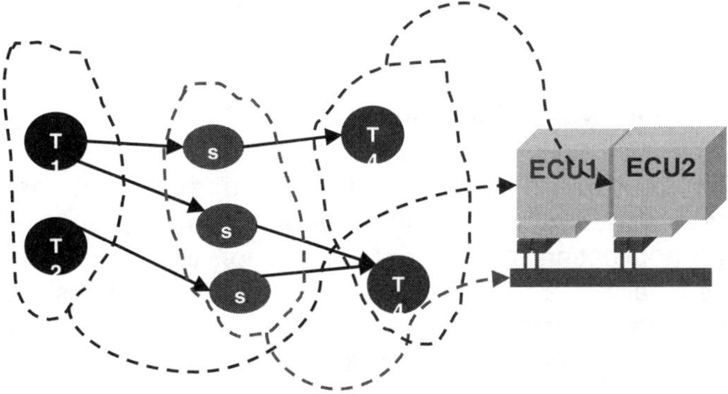

Figure 6: Functional Model Mapped onto the Architecture Model

A short summary of the notations used in the formulation are as follows:

[9] The entities are assumed to be defined after the task graph expansion process which will be described later.

[10] EST is a parameter that would be governed by constraints such as the **latest** completion time of any of the task's **reverse** precedence constraints.

[11] LET is a parameter that would be governed by constraints such as the **earliest** start time of any of the task's **forward** precedence constraints.

[12] A root entity is to indicate the entity's original identifier prior to the task graph expansion. This is to reflect that multiple entities could have the same root entity, but are instantiated at different times since the application cycle is greater than the entity's periodicity.

Sets

$Components ::= \{i : \mathbb{N} \mid 1 \le i \le L\}$
where L is the total number of ECU's and busses in the system.

$T_i = \{j : \mathbb{N} \mid 1 \le j \le N_i\}$ where N_i is the total number of schedulable entities (includes both tasks and messages)
in component i. i is of type Components.

$O_{ij} : Rt_{ij} \times D_{ij} \times St_{ij} \times EST_{ij} \times Et_{ij} \times LET_{ij} \times U_{ij} \times P_{ij} \times M_{ij}$
where i,j are the index to the
component i and the schedulable
entity j within component i.
The tuples are defined in Table 2 and illustrated in Figure 5.

Application_Cycle = Least common multiple of all unique periods, P_i in the system

$$CommunicationCycleSet = \{CC : \Re \mid (i : \{j : \mathbb{N} \mid 1 \le j \le 63\} \bullet CC = \tfrac{A_c}{i}) \wedge CC \le 16\}$$

where A_C refers to the application cycle length. There is a protocol constraint which says that the communication cycle duration cannot be longer than 16 ms.

SlotSizeSet = $\{SS : \Re \mid 4 \le SS \le 659\}$, where the units are in Macroticks.

HIERACHICAL SCHEDULING FRAMEWORK

This section will describe how the framework is defined. The high-level framework is described in Figure 7.

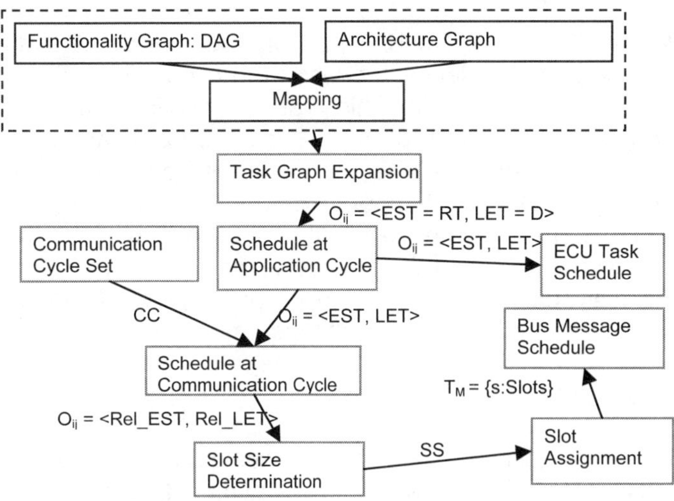

Figure 7: Hierarchical Scheduling Framework

In a nutshell, the approach goes as follows:

1. Schedule bus messages and tasks relative to the application cycle. Provide an abstract time window for messages and tasks.
2. Refine the previously derived message schedule to consider the Flexray communication cycle. Introduce protocol constraints related to the communication cycle such as symbol window, and NIT. Now the time window is discretized to the level of the communication cycle.
3. Refine the previous schedule again to consider the Flexray slot size and the protocol constraints related to it. The time window becomes an explicit offset which is represented by the slot identifier.

The following will describe the mapping of this description to the procedures reflected in Figure 7.

Task Graph Expansion

This part of the framework essentially takes a multirate functional model and converts it into a single rate functional model where the rate of all the elements is normalized into the application cycle.

Taking the example described in Figure 4 and expanding that task graph, the following schedulable entity attributes are derived (assuming an application cycle of 4 ms):

Entity Root ID	Entity Instance[13]	Period (ms)	Release Time (ms)	Deadline (ms)	Precedence (instance)
T1	0	2	0	2	T3(0),T4(0)
T1	1	2	2	4	T3(0),T4(0)
T2	0	2	0	2	T3(0)
T2	1	2	2	4	T3(0)
T3	0	4	0	4	-
T4	0	4	0	4	-

Table 3: Expanded Task Graph Description

As is clear from Table 3, the precedence constraints also need to be delineated when the expansion occurs. In the general case, this has implications on the behavioral semantics of the application. For example, a sensor task may be executed 3 times before a voting task gathers the temporal redundant data. In the expansion, the voting task should be executed at the completion of the 3 sensor tasks; however, this is not explicitly expressed in the initial pre-expanded model. Hence, this part of the process may not be entirely automatic and may require some analysis before the actual expansion can be derived.

As a note, it is recommended to have a harmonic[14] set of task rates since the communication patterns for a harmonic task chain are regular; that is, the number of instances of the transmitter in the receiver's cycle is the same and vice versa, independent of which cycle they are in. Mathematically, this implies the following:

$S = \mathbb{P}$ { All pairwise entities $(O_{ij} \times O_{ij})$ that have a precedence constraint between them }

$$\begin{array}{|l} R : S \\ \hline R = \{(O_{ij}, O_{ij}) : S \mid \frac{O_{ij}.P}{O_{ij}.P} \in \mathbb{N} \wedge O_{ij}.P \leq O_{ij}.P\} \end{array}$$

The entities O_{ij} represent the unique task or bus message. The set of "regular" tasks/entities is defined by the set R. It essentially says that if pairwise tasks with precedence constraints are of harmonic rates, then the interaction pattern is regular which in turn means that the graph expansion can be repeated deterministically[15] for any of the cycles of the pairwise tasks.

Constraints: None

Schedule within Application Cycle

This procedure essentially takes the expanded task graph and schedules each schedulable entity relative to the application cycle. The output of this procedure essentially is an abstract time duration that defines the earliest start time (EST) and latest end time (LET) of the entity. The sizing of this window is beyond the scope of this paper[16].

Constraints: Functional graph precedence constraints. Deadline constraints.

Communication Cycle Set

This part of the framework enumerates all the possible communication cycle durations. The scheduling procedures beyond the application cycle can be repeated to explore all possible communication cycle options in order to find the most optimal[17] setting.

Constraints: Communication_Cycle_Set =

$\{CC : \Re \mid (i : \{1 \ldots 63\} \bullet CC = \frac{A_C}{i}) \wedge CC \leq 16\}$, where

A_C refers to the application cycle length and i is the set of integers ranging from 1 to the 63[18]. In addition, there is a protocol constraint that says that the communication cycle duration cannot be longer than 16 ms.

[13] This is the instance of that schedulable entity in the application cycle.

[14] A harmonic rate is defined as a rate that is an integer multiple of the base rate for a specific interacting task chain.

[15] This behavior could improve the likelihood that the system is schedulable.

[16] The current tool implementation of this framework derives this window based on the metric of minimizing end to end latency.

[17] The optimality criterion is up to the user of the framework. It will be touched upon in this paper, but not explicitly.

[18] 63 is the maximum number of communication cycles as defined in the protocol specification.

Schedule within Communication Cycle

Given the EST and LET of each entity, now the next step is to discretize the application cycle to its individual communication cycles. The EST and LET will correspondingly be converted from an offset within the application cycle to an offset within a communication cycle. The output parameter will be referred to as Relative EST and Relative LET.

Constraints: No static slot transmission is allowed during NIT, symbol window and dynamic segment of the cycle. Duration of NIT, symbol window and dynamic segment are assumed to be inputs to this framework.

Slot Size Determination

The slot size is a key parameter in the Flexray schedule. It is a global parameter that defines the largest possible message frame length that can be transmitted within a static slot. One of the major trade-offs between having a large slot size vs. a small slot size is the degree of effective utilization that can be achieved. Since in Flexray all slots have to be of equal length, the choice of a slot size impacts all messages. If the slot size is large, then it favors large messages, but is poorly utilized for small messages. On the other hand, if the slot size is small, then large messages incur an overhead depending on how many slots to which that message is partitioned to. The actual optimization approach of the slot size determination is beyond the scope of this paper.

Constraint: The slot size must be between 4 and 659 Macroticks in duration. The slot size must account for the various protocol overheads such as frame formatting overhead and action point offsets.

Slot Assignment

Since all the Flexray parameters have been decided at this point, the final step in the framework is to actually assign slots to messages. The assignment policy affects the number of empty slots available for future growth. A policy that allows messages from the same node to be multiplexed together within the same slot has the benefit that it reduces the number of slots used, but has the drawback that it could cause reuse issues in the future, since slots are owned by specific nodes.

Constraint: Slot assignment must meet relative LET and relative EST requirements coming from the previous procedure. The ownership of slots to ECUs must be maintained across all communication cycles[19]. Frame mapping constraints are such that certain signals cannot be mapped together into the same slot due to reuse or receipt atomicity constraints.

[19] This is a fairly significant constraint that leads to the cycle crowding effect which will be discussed in detail further.

ECU and Flexray Bus Message Schedule

This is the final result where all the bus messages are assigned slots and the ECU tasks are assigned either an offset or a time window of execution. All the protocol parameters have been decided. Conceptually, this schedule can then be input into a code generator to form the actual dispatch tables that would be flashed into the ECU or bus controller.

FRAMEWORK IMPLEMENTATION

The framework described in this paper is a conceptual framework that does not prescribe a specific optimization approach for each of the refinement steps. In order to evaluate this concept, the framework has been implemented using a list scheduler with an end to end latency minimization heuristic optimization approach for the generation of the schedule. Other approaches such as genetic algorithms or mathematical programming could also be used to implement this framework.

Figure 9 illustrates the main design capture input into the tool. The worksheets represent the different views of the system that are impacted by the scheduling process. The ECU and bus description provide the relevant scheduling-related parameters of these components. For example, the ECU is described by its message buffers and its context switching time, while the Flexray bus is described by the parameters delineated in Table 2. The viewer worksheet as described in Figure 10 is a visualization of the entire time-triggered schedule of the distributed system. The scheduling synthesis worksheet captures the results of the optimization algorithm.

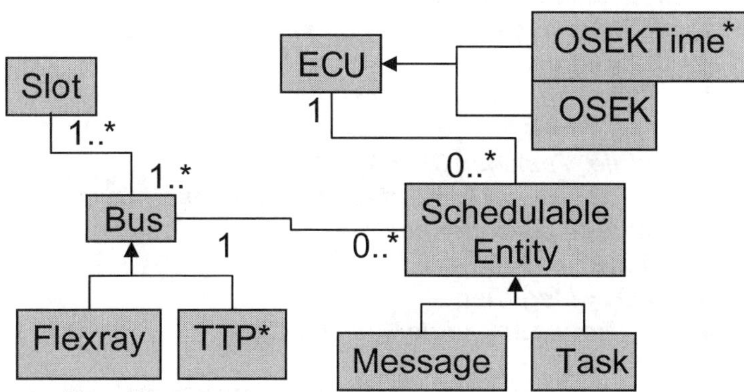

Figure 8: Class Diagram of the Elements Within the Framework[20]

[20] Classes postfixed with * have not yet been implemented.

List Scheduling

The implementation of this framework uses a list scheduling heuristic that minimizes the end to end latency of a task chain. The following is the algorithm in pseudo code[21]:

List_Scheduler () {

1. G(v,e)= Build_Graph // where v are the vertices and e are the edges represented by tasks or messages
2. G'(v,e) = TaskGraphExpansion(G(v,e))
3. CC = CommCycleSet()
4. R_L = InitializeReadyList (G(v,e))
5. while (R_L ∠ 0) {
6. O_{ij} = PickTaskMsgObj(R_L)
7. Schedule_TaskMsgObj (O_{ij},CC)
8. R_L' = R_L / O_{ij}
9. } // Schedule graph from source to sink
10. SS = SlotSize(G(v,e),CC)
11. SlotAssignment(G(v,e),SS,CC)
12. DisplayResults()

}

TaskGraphExpansion (G(v,e)) {

1. // Expand every schedulable instance, O_j by $\frac{AppCycle}{O_j.P}$ times. Assume that the forward precedence is always with the latest instance of the corresponding preceding task within the cycle instance[22] of O_{ij} .

}

PickTaskMsgObj(R_L) {

1. // Picks based on an earliest deadline first heuristic

}

Schedule_TaskMsgObj (O_{ij},CC) {

1. O_{ij}.EST = O_{ij}.RT or Latest end time of all O_{ij} 's reverse precedences
2. O_{ij}.LET = O_{ij}.D
3. If O_{ij} = Msg then
4. RefineScheduleMsg(O_j,CC)
5. Else if O_{ij} = Task then
6. RefineScheduleTask[23](O_{ij},OSEKTIME[24])
7. End if

}

RefineScheduleMsg(O_{ij},CC) {

1. // Discretize time window relative to CC definition. Create relative time window.
2. // Resolve comm. cycle "crowding" effect
3. O_{ij}.EST = Relative_EST
4. O_{ij}.LET = Relative_LET

}

SlotSize(G(v,e)) {

1. // Derive slot size based on message sizes. Pick slot size to be at least as big as the max message size[25].
2. Return Max_Message_size + Overhead

}

SlotAssignment(G(v,e),SS,CC) {

1. // Assign slots as early as possible in the time window (no cycle multiplexing)
2. OR
3. // Assign slots in order to minimize the number of used slots (cycle multiplexing)

}

The task graph expansion uses a heuristic that resolves ambiguity in the precedence constraint choice resulting from the expansion. It will always choose the latest instance of the receiver as the forward precedence constraint relative to the transmitter instance's time window. However, as mentioned earlier, this decision should be validated by the functional designer in order to ensure consistent semantics.

---

[21] Zed notation is used.

[22] Cycle instance is the cycle within the application cycle where O_j's instance executes. For example a 2ms task in a 4ms application cycle, executes two instances – one between 0ms and 2ms, and the other between 2ms and 4ms.

[23] This function will not be detailed further since it is similar to the Msg schedule function except without the effect of the discretization of the time window.

[24] Refine the schedule to account for the preemption policy allowed by OSEKTime.

[25] Ideally, this procedure should be an optimization problem by itself, but due to time constraints and since it isn't the focus of this paper, the slot size optimization scheme has not been implemented yet.

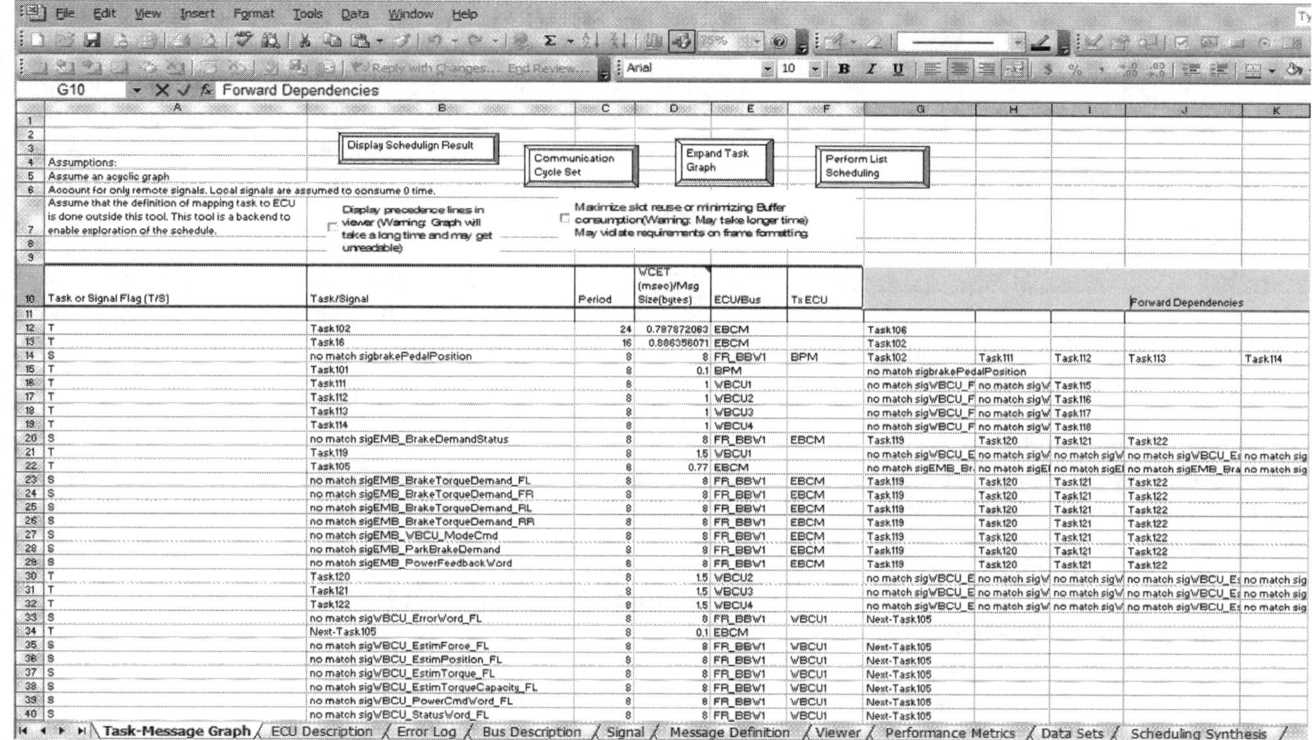

Figure 9: Main Worksheet of the Scheduling Tool Implementation of this Framwork

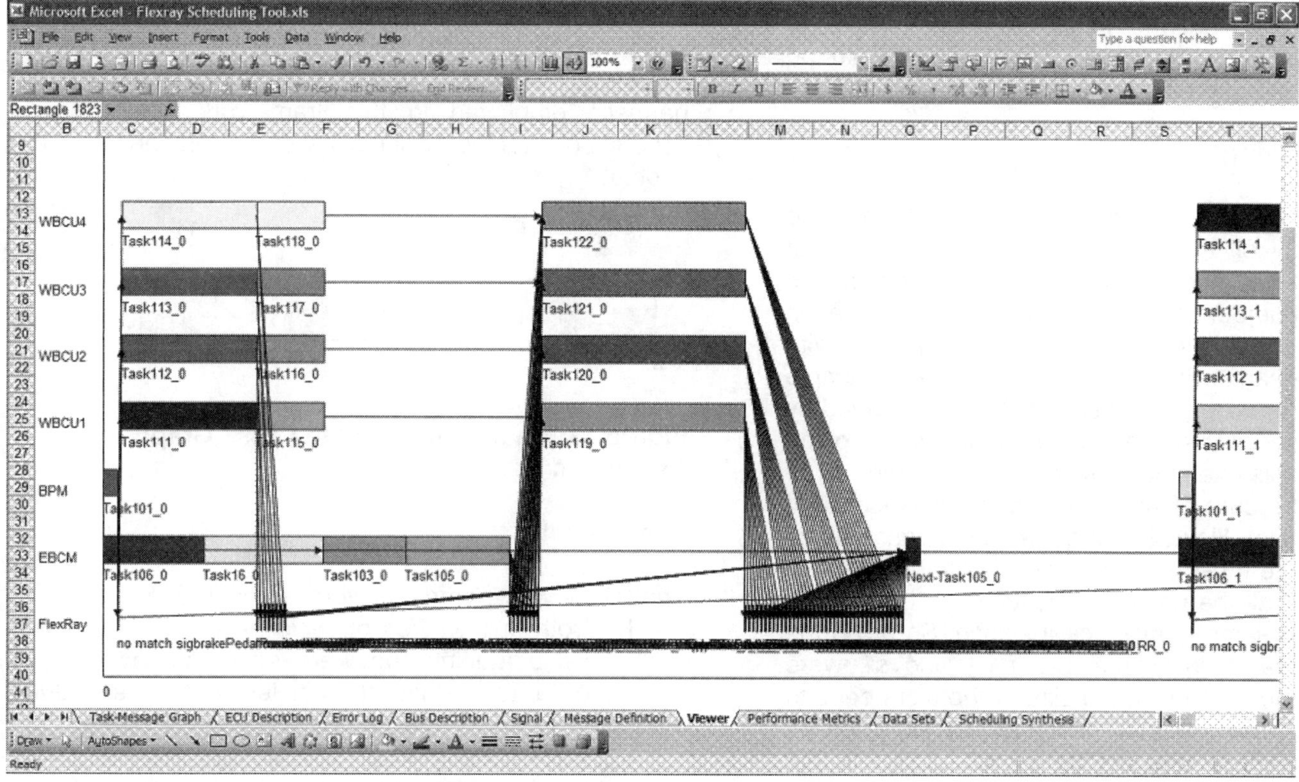

Figure 10: Graphical View of Scheduling Synthesis Results

Communication Cycle "Crowding" Effect

One of the constraints imposed by the Flexray protocol is that the ownership of slots by ECUs must be consistent through every communication cycle. For example, if ECU A transmits in Slot 1 in communication cycle 1, then no other ECU can transmit in that slot no matter which communication cycle it is.

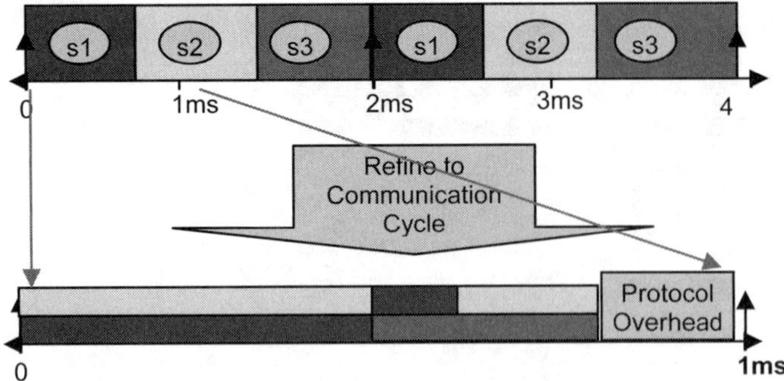

Figure 11: Illustration of the Cycle Crowding Effect Assuming a 1ms Communication Cycle

This constraint causes the time windows that go across cycle boundaries to overlap with other time windows. For example, in Figure 11 we see that s2 has a time window that crosses the 1ms communication cycle. This causes it to overlap with both s1's and s3's time window.

In general, this becomes an issue in a framework such as this, where the time window is allocated before the communication cycle has been decided. Hence, a time window allocation that is feasible at the time of the application cycle can easily become unschedulable once the communication cycle is taken into account. In addition to this, a task graph expansion that has an irregular communication pattern relative to the communication cycle further exacerbates the likelihood of the system being unschedulable.

Cycle Multiplexing

One of the observations made during the implementation of this framework was the fact that improving the likelihood of scheduling the system and reducing the number of used slots in the communication cycle could be achieved if slots were multiplexed with multiple messages. Hence, taking the example illustrated in Figure 11, the overlap is simply resolved by mapping s1 and s2, s2 and s3 or s1 and s3, into the same slot. In this example, this would require the slot to be sized to the sum of all the message instances that appear in the slot. However, in general, the constraint is that the slot size must be more than or equal to the sum of the sizes of all the unique[26] messages that appear in that slot at the same global time instance. So using the example illustrated in Figure 11, if s1 and s2 were mapped into the same slot, the size of the slot needs to be larger than the greatest message size between s1 and s2. This is due to the fact that s1 will be sent in that slot during Cycle 1 and s2 can be sent in the same slot during Cycle 2.

The current framework implementation allows the user to choose between either minimizing the number of slots used through the use of cycle multiplexing or to minimize the end to end delay with no cycle multiplexing.

[26] The message should not have the same root message. If it does, then its simply an instance of an existing message in that slot.

CASE STUDY

The case study involves scheduling a set of tasks and messages for a by-wire system. The architecture of this system is reflected in Figure 12. There were 57 messages and 19 tasks. In addition, it was a multirate system with 3 unique periods – {8, 16, 24} ms. The application cycle is then 48 ms. All the messages had a period of 8ms while 2 of the tasks had a period of 16 and 24ms respectively. The communication cycle set derived was {6, 8, 12, 16}.

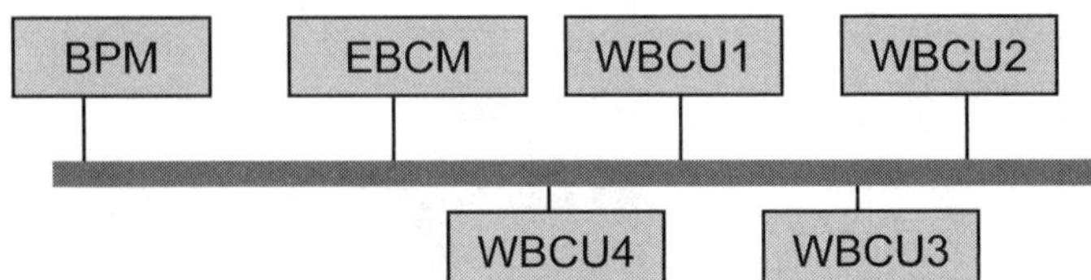

Figure 12: Case Study: By-Wire Systems Architecture

The task graph expansion portion of this framework implements a simple heuristic in order to resolve ambiguity in precedence choices. It essentially always picks the latest instant of the receiver task within the time window of the transmitter task. This assumes a specific semantic. Hence verification steps need to be performed by the designer relative to the behavior of this expanded functional graph. Figure 13 illustrates the heuristic employed in this framework where T1 is scheduled after both instances of T2 instead of in the middle.

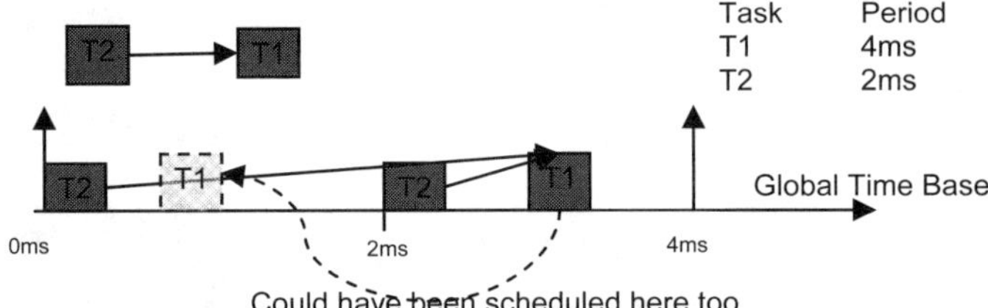

Figure 13: An Illustration of the Task Graph Expansion Heuristic

Experiments

The following experiments were conducted:

1. Both approaches of cycle multiplexing and non cycle multiplexing were experimented with, in order to evaluate the efficiency of the scheduler in terms of the number of slots or buffers that were consumed on a node-by-node basis. Try this for communication cycle durations of 8 and 16ms.
2. Communication cycle durations of {8, 12, 16} were evaluated to see the effect of cycle "crowding". Assume a cycle multiplexing approach.

RESULTS

For the first experiment (1), the results are reflected in Table 4.

	Communication Cycle = 16ms			
ECU	With Cycle multiplexing		No Cycle multiplexing	
	Number of TX Buffers[27]	Number of RX Buffers	Number of TX Buffers	Number of RX Buffers
EBCM	24	127	48	247
BPM	6	0	6	0
WBCU1	35	30	69	54
WBCU2	31	30	62	54
WBCU3	29	30	58	54
WBCU4	26	30	52	54
TOTAL	151		295	
	Communication Cycle = 8ms			
ECU	With Cycle multiplexing		No Cycle multiplexing	
	Number of TX Buffers	Number of RX Buffers	Number of TX Buffers	Number of RX Buffers
EBCM	25	82	48	154
BPM	6	0	6	0
WBCU1	25	31	49	54
WBCU2	21	31	42	54
WBCU3	19	31	35	54
WBCU4	11	31	22	54
TOTAL	107		202	

Table 4: Results from Experiment 1

The results from Experiment 1 match intuition since:

1. The cycle multiplexing procedure almost halved the number of slots used, relative to the non-cycle multiplexing approach.
2. The longer the communication cycle duration, the more slots that are used. This may not be always be the case, since it depends on the time window allocation for the entities. However, since this framework allocates time windows independently of the communication cycle, we expectedly observe a 44 slot reduction and 93 slot reduction for the cycle multiplexing scheme and non-cycle multiplexing scheme respectively.

For experiment 2, the following results were observed:

16 ms – All entities were **schedulable**.

[27] The number of transmit buffers and the number of slots is synonymous assuming a single buffer per slot.

12 ms – 13 entities were **unschedulable**.
8ms – All entities were **schedulable**.

The results from Experiment 2 indicate that the cycle duration has a very significant impact on the likelihood of the system being schedulable. Intuitively, it may seem that the longer the communication cycle, the more slots are available, and hence the more likely the scheduler is to find a feasible solution. However, it turns out that the time window allocation at the application cycle level can cause differing levels of cycle crowding depending on the communication cycle duration. Since the time window allocation was independent of the communication cycle, the 12ms cycle duration seemed to exhibit a larger amount of cycle crowding than the 16 or 8ms alternatives. Furthermore, all the messages in the system were run at a 8ms period which made the 16 and 8ms cycle lengths exhibit a more regular communication pattern where slots could be multiplexed.

CONCLUSION

A hierarchical scheduling framework for a distributed Flexray system has been presented. An implementation of this framework in an Excel environment indicates some of the advantages and disadvantages of this framework relative to a framework that has no hierarchy (i.e., a global optimizer).

The key advantages are as follows:

1. A hierarchical framework allows for different optimization concerns to be addressed at each level of the refinement. The implementation indicates how this is accomplished relative to the time window allocation at the application cycle level and Flexray slot sizing.
2. The problem size at each level of the hierarchy is much smaller than the problem size for a global optimization. This makes it more amenable to mathematical programming approach.

The key disadvantages are:

1. Since the hierarchical approach by definition solves the problem by decoupling, it does not provide a global optimal solution.
2. Analysis indicates that the decoupling of the application cycle and the communication cycle can exhibit cycle crowding that could easily lead to infeasible solutions. With a global optimal scheme, a feasible solution could have been found.

Further work is required to better understand what optimization metrics are relevant to the automotive industry relative to Flexray scheduling. In addition to this there is an interesting topic relative to what is the effective utilization of a Flexray link and approaches on

ACKNOWLEDGMENTS

The author would like to acknowledge Wei Zheng, Claudio Pinello, Thomas Fuhrman and Paolo Giusto for providing both parts of the implementation and conceptual advice on this work.

REFERENCES

1. Alberto Sangiovanni-Vincentelli, GSRC Presentation, 2004
2. Wei Zheng, Jike Chong, Sri Kanajan, Claudio Pinello, Alberto Sangiovanni-Vincentelli, Extensible and Scalable Time Triggered Scheduling, ACSD 2005
3. Flexray communications system specifications 2.1, 2005.
4. P. Paul. Analysis and synthesis of communication intensive heterogeneous real-time systems. Ph. D. optimizing the effective utilization.
   Thesis No. 833, Dept. of Computer and Information Science, Linkoping University, June 2003.
5. P. Pop, P. Eles, T. Pop, and Z. Peng. An approach to incremental design of distributed embedded systems, pages 450–455, 2001.
6. Shan Ding, Naohiko Murakami, Hiroyuki Tomiyama and Hiroaki Takada, A GA-Based Scheduling Method for FlexRay Systems, EMSOFT 2006
7. TTP Plan, scheduling synthesis tool, TTTech
8. Timing Analysis of the FlexRay Communication Protocol, Traian Pop, Paul Pop, Petru Eles, Zebo Peng, Alexandru Andrei, IEEE 2006
9. OSEKTime Specification V1.0, www.osek-vdx.org

CONTACT

Sri Kanajan is a senior research engineer at General Motors Research, Warren, MI, 48088 USA. (e-mail: sri.kanajan@gm.com).

2007-01-1614

TOYOTA Electronic Architecture and AUTOSAR Pilot

Kenji Nishikawa and Kazuhiro Kajio
TOYOTA MOTOR EUROPE NV/SA

ABSTRACT

This paper describes current engineering approaches to Electronic Architecture by TOYOTA and shows how systems are implemented with basic technologies such as Software Platform and In-Vehicle Networks. In addition, AUTOSAR Pilot and its analysis are introduced, showing actual software performance and indicating foreseen benefits and drawbacks introduced by AUTOSAR. A possible migration scenario from legacy architecture to AUTOSAR architecture is also presented.

INTRODUCTION

Automotive Electronics has been getting vastly complicated over the last decades due to innovative functionalities and cooperative and integrated control systems to meet market requirements for Environment, Safety and Comfort. Under these circumstances, the AUTOSAR Initiative has been formed to manage electronic system complexity and reduce the system cost, and also to achieve software reusability and maintain software quality. TOYOTA joined the AUTOSAR Partnership in January 2004 as a Core Partner.

MAIN SECTION

1. COMPLEXITY OF ELECTRONIC SYSYEM

1.1 ELECTRONIC SYSTEM

Fig.1 shows the history of TOYOTA Electronic Systems. After the late 70s we introduced several state-of-the-art technologies to meet safety demands of the market and several emission-related regulations such as EURO-04. In the late 90s, each electronic system was controlled independently, but around 2000 integration of systems from different domains began and several systems such as THS (Toyota Hybrid System), NAVI-AT Cooperative System and VDIM (Vehicle Dynamics Management System) that centrally manage Engine, Steering and Brakes were launched into the market.

1.3 IN-VEHICLE NETWORK ARCHITECTURE

Fig.2 shows the network architecture of current LEXUS models, and the number connected ECUs is increasing in proportion to the number of electronic systems and now in LEXUS models more than 70 ECUs are connected to multiplex communication buses.

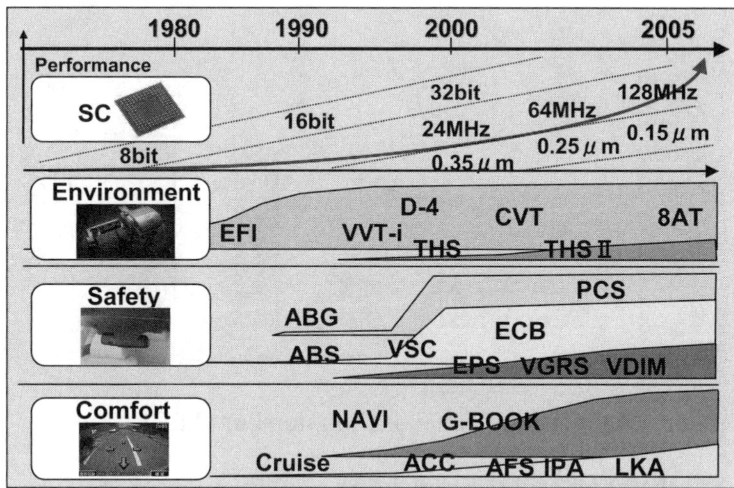

Fig.1 Automotive SC and Vehicle Electronic Systems

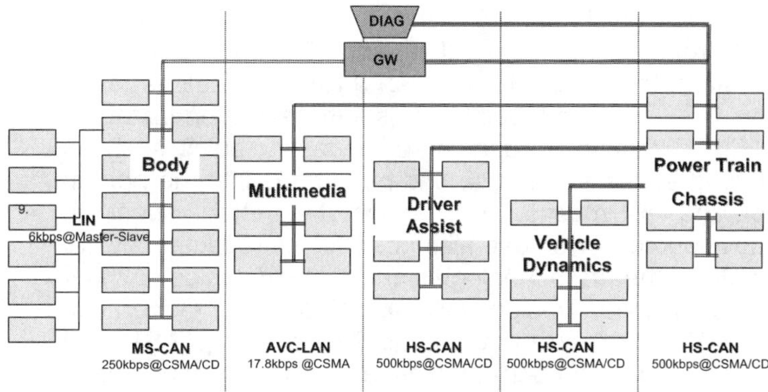

Fig.2 In-Vehicle Network Architecture (Image)

1.2 IN-VEHICLE SOFTWARE

Fig.3 shows the volume of developed in-vehicle software and Fig.4 shows the bus traffic on CAN communication and the number of ECUs on the vehicle. In proportion to the increase of the number of electronic systems, the volume of software and also bus traffic are increasing exponentially, and the total amount of in-vehicle code is more than 7 million steps in LEXUS models.

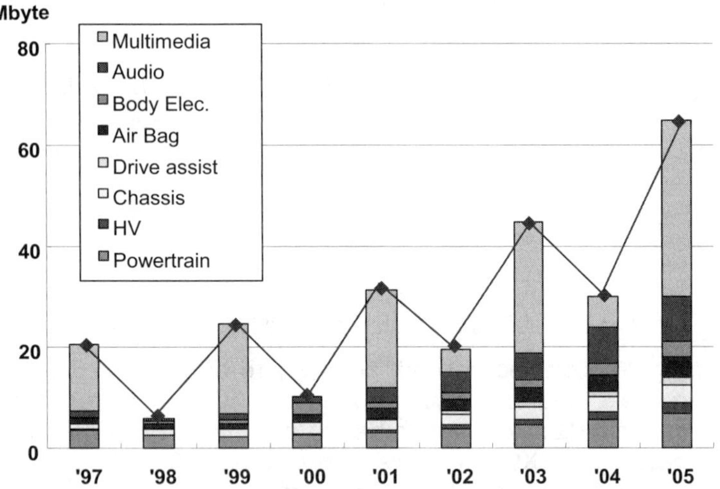

Fig.3 Development Volume of In-Vehicle Software

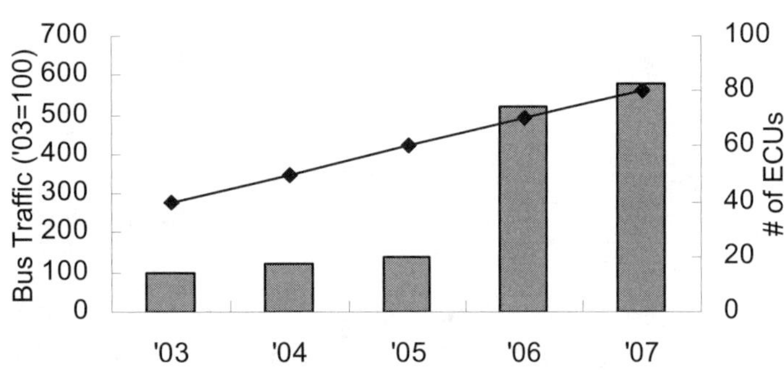

Fig.4 CAN Bus Traffic and the number of ECUs

1.4 DEVELOPMENT PROCESS

To manage electronic complexity and keep its quality, TOYOTA has introduced a unified process to develop electronic systems. Fig.5 shows a typical V-Process for electronic system development. Depending on the system, the coverage range of the process steps taken by TOYOTA and suppliers is different. For instance, TOYOTA develops leading-edge technologies such as hybrid systems in-house and penetrates into the bottom of the V-Process. To reduce the effort spent in development, we have also positively introduced several state-of-the-art technologies and methodologies such as Model-Based Design (MBD), Auto-Code Generation (ACG), Hardware-In-the-Loop-Simulation (HILS) and Software-In-the-Loop-Simulation (SILS) and have standardized Software Platform that is generally called Basic Software.

1.5 STANDARDIZTION OF E/E ARCHITECTURE

To cope with such electronic complexities, OEMs and suppliers have introduced several countermeasures, but with overwhelming requirements and demands on the electronics, it is getting difficult to meet such requirements within a single OEM or supplier. The AUTOSAR initiative has been formed by international OEMs and suppliers to manage E/E system complexity.

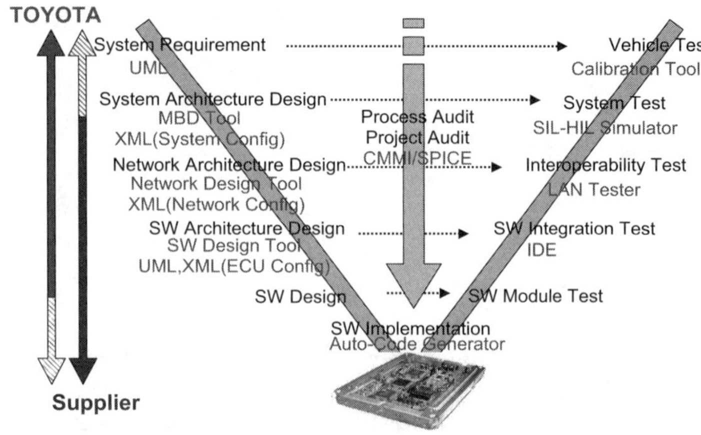

Fig.5 V-Process and Tools

2. AUTOSAR PILOT

TOYOTA joined the AUTOSAR partnership in January 2004 as a Core Partner. The partnership released AUTOSAR BSW/RTE R2.0 specification in 2006 to the public through the AUTOSAR official website. AUTOSAR concept is validated in AUTOSAR Validator, but focusing on AUTOSAR communication stacks, TOYOTA launched Pilot Project with following objectives. We integrated AUTOSAR BSW/RTE modules from 4 different Implementers on 2 different MCUs (Fig.6).

1) Refinement of AUTOSAR Specifications
   - APIs and Call Sequences
   - Buffer Structure
   - State Machine
2) Feature Test
   - Inter/Intra-ECU Communication
   - Wakeup/Sleep
   - Startup
3) Performance Evaluation
   - CPU Load
   - ROM/RAM Consumption
   - Runtime, End-to-end Latency
4) SW-C Portability Validation based on Virtual Functional Bus (VFB) Concept

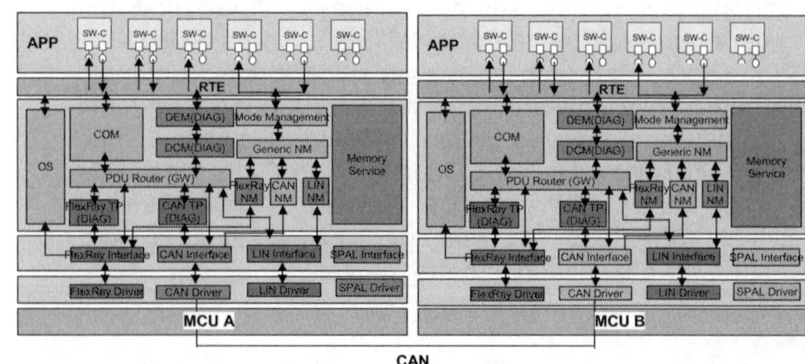

Fig 6. System Configuration of AUROSAR Pilot

2.1 SYSTEM ARCHITECTURE DESIGN

We adopted AVENSIS outer mirror control for a pilot implementation. For SW-C designing, we used DaVinci System Architect (Fig.7, Fig.8). When we design the system architecture in series production, we take the following items into account.

1) Function Design (Model-Based Design)
   - Control Logic Design
   - SW-C Design
   - SW-C Mapping on ECUs
2) I/O Design
   - Data Type, Length, LSB, Offset, Range, Unit
3) HW Requirement
   - MCU Performance
   - Peripherals
4) Functional Reliability and Safety

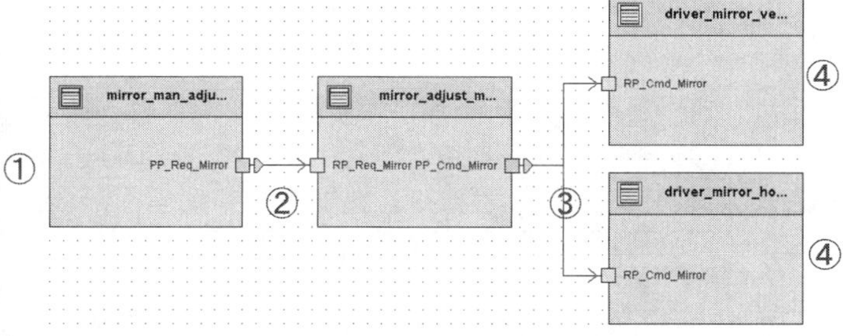

Fig.7 SW-C Design based on VFB Concept (DaVinci System Architect)

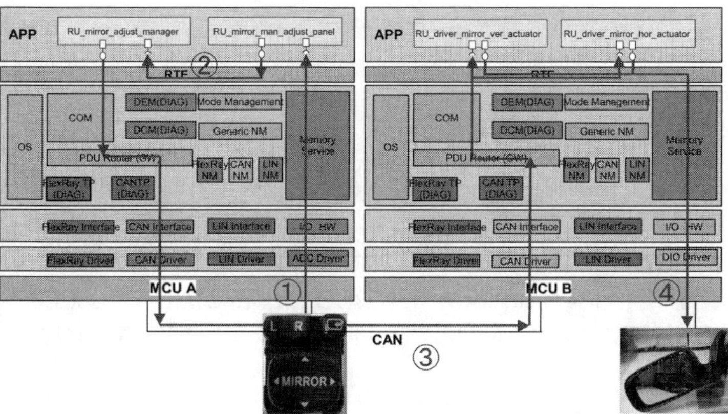

Fig.8 AVENSIS Outer Mirror Pilot Implementation

2.2 NETWORK ARCHITECTURE DESIGN

Based on the system configuration from Section 2.1, we designed a CAN matrix with DaVinci Network Designer from Vector (Fig.9). When we design the network architecture in series production, we have to take the following items into account to make sure that the in-vehicle network works and meet system requirements (ex: Timing Requirement). As for the wiring design, we normally design trunks and stubs of the topology based on TOYOTA Wiring Guidelines, but if necessary, we execute network simulation (SPICE, VHDL-AMS) to validate the integrity of the signal on the bus.

1) CAN Matrix Design (XML)
   - Bus Load
   - Data Consistency
2) Timing Analysis
   - Propagation Delay
3) CAN Wiring Simulation and Design
   - Trunk and Stub Length
   - Termination Points
   - Signal Integrity (Reflection, Attenuation)

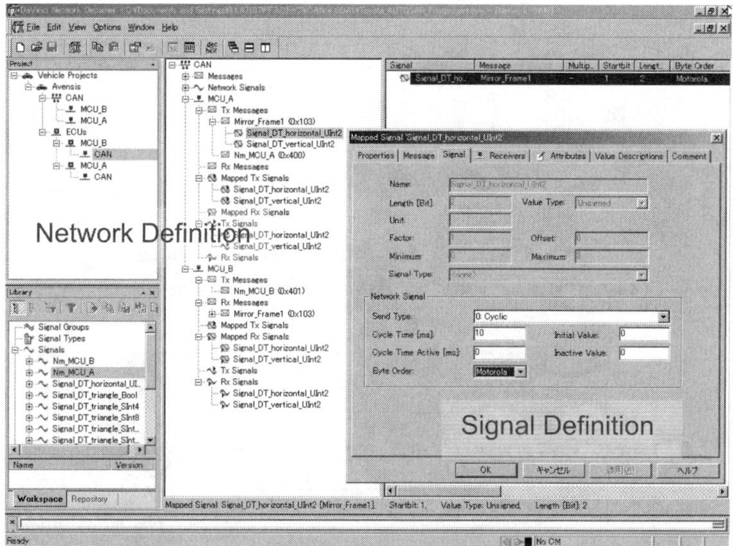

Fig.9 CAN Network Design (DaVinci Network Designer)

2.3 SOFTWARE ARCHITECTURE DESIGN

Based on the system configuration from Section 2.1 and the network configuration from Section 2.2, we refined AUTOSAR BSW /RTE architecture in detail using UML models. When we design the software architecture in series production, we take following items into account.

1) Application and Platform SW Design (UML)
   - Sequence Design
   - Configuration Design
   - Task/ISR Scheduling
   - Stack Size
   - Buffer Structure
2) Timing Analysis
   - SW Jitter
3) Electronic Reliability and Safety
4) Error Handling

2.3.1 Inter-ECU Communication Sender/Receiver Tx

Fig.10 shows the sequence of the inter-ECU communication transmission (Tx) sequence. In the pilot we adopted RTE TimingEvent to trigger Tx Runnable entities. In Periodic Transmission mode, RTE and BSW are decoupled. If there is any concern that Tx mailbox on CAN Controller might be overwritten and the system needs to avoid transmission PDU loss, a PDU transmit buffer at the CAN Interface and CAN Tx ISR should be configured as shown in Fig.11.

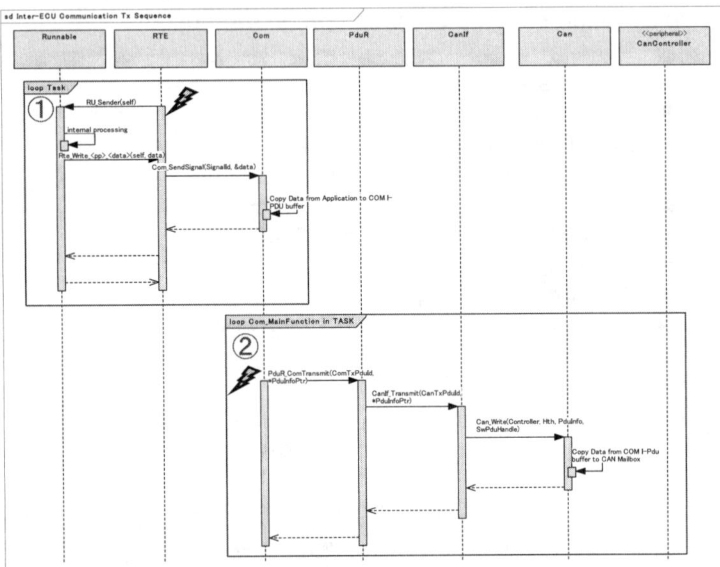

Fig.10 Inter-ECU Communication Tx Sequence (Explicit Write, TimingEvent, Periodic, w/o CAN Tx ISR)

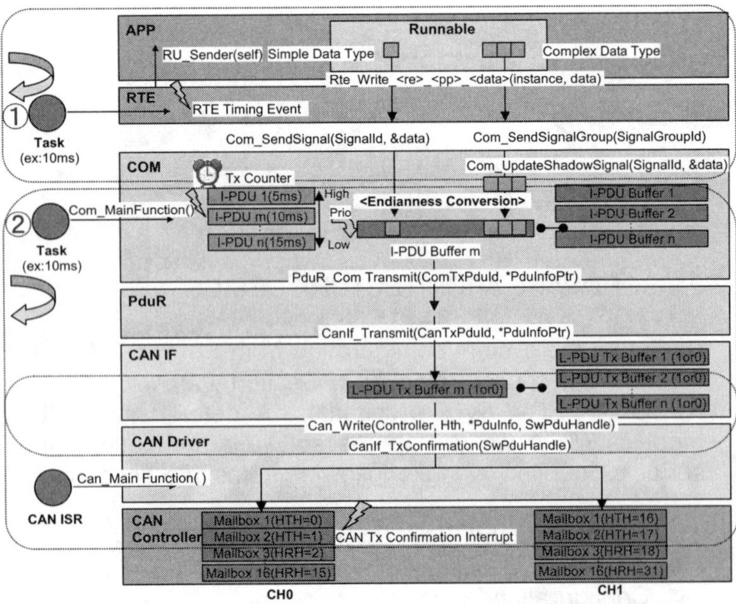

Fig.11 Tx Data Flow with PDU/Signal Buffer Structure (Implicit Write, TimingEvent, Periodic, w/ CAN Tx ISR)

2.3.1 Inter-ECU Communication Sender/Receiver Rx

Fig.12 and Fig.13 show the sequence of reception and the basic buffer structure. In the pilot we adapted the RTE TimingEvent and DataReceivedEvent to trigger Rx Runnable entities. In both cases, RTE and BSW are decoupled and if SW-C needs the latest signal as soon as possible, RTE DataReceivedEvent should be applied instead of RTE TimingEvent.

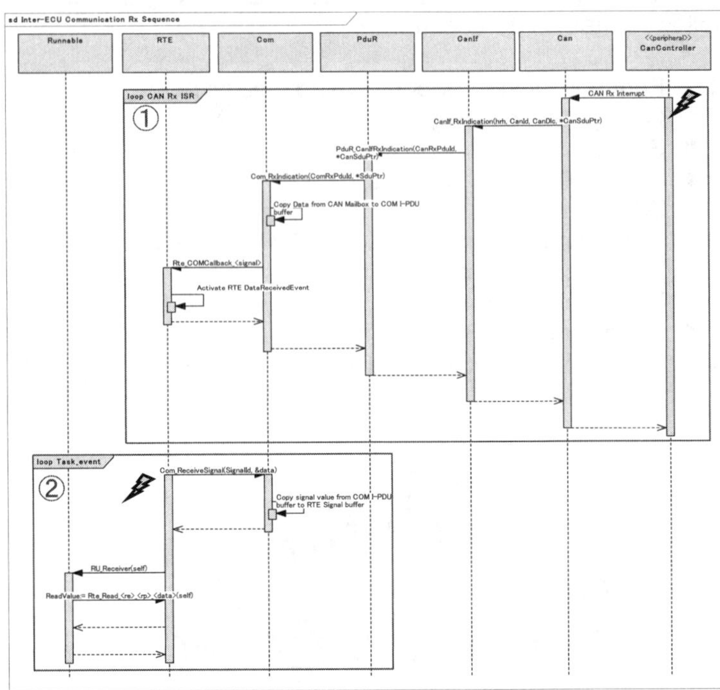

Fig.12 Inter-ECU Communication Rx Sequence (Implicit Read, DataReceivedEvent, CAN Rx ISR)

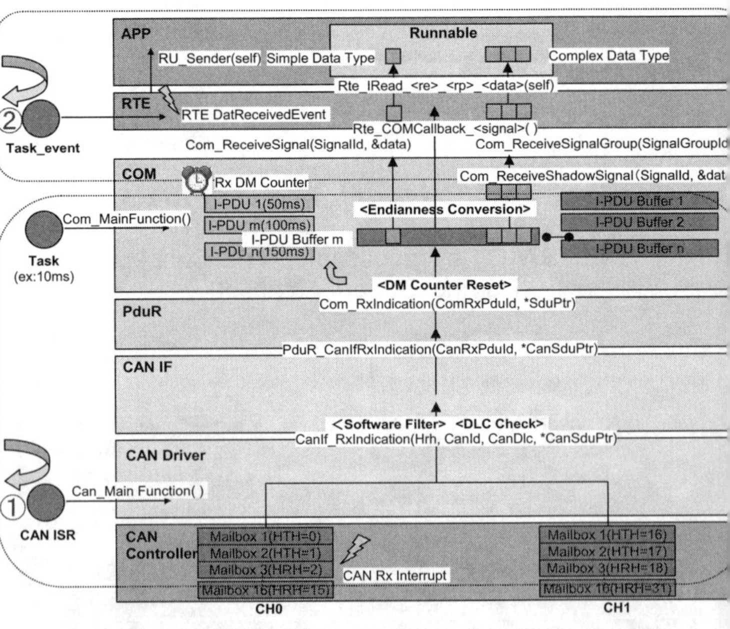

Fig.13 Rx Data Flow with PDU/Signal Buffer Structure (Implicit Read, DataReceivedEvent, CAN Rx ISR)

2.4 SW INTEGRATION TEST

In order to measure the practical performance of BSW/RTE, we simulated AUTOSAR BSW/RTE based on two different ECUs configuration. One is Body ECU with AUTOSAR Network Management (NM) and the other is VSC (Vehicle Stability Control) ECU without NM.

2.4.1 Body ECU

During the software integration test, several performance tests were executed. Fig.14 and Fig.15 show ROM/RAM consumption with Body ECU configuration with AUTOSAR NM (Wakeup/Sleep). Fig.16 shows the CPU load caused by AUTOSAR BSW/RTE based on Body ECU configuration. Interesting point is that the performances are so different between 2 different implementations on different HW platforms, though they are implemented referring to the same AUTOSAR specifications.

2.4.1 VSC ECU

In order to estimate more practical performance in the ECU which has rigorous requirements on the run-time and CPU load, we simulated AUTOSAR BSW/RTE based on the VSC configuration. Fig.16 also shows the CPU load based on the VSC ECU configuration without AUTOSAR NM. Tasks and BSW Main functions are called at the same period as the series project. Since the number of Tx/Rx signals and frames is much larger than that of Body ECU, CPU load of VSC ECU is much higher than that of Body ECU.

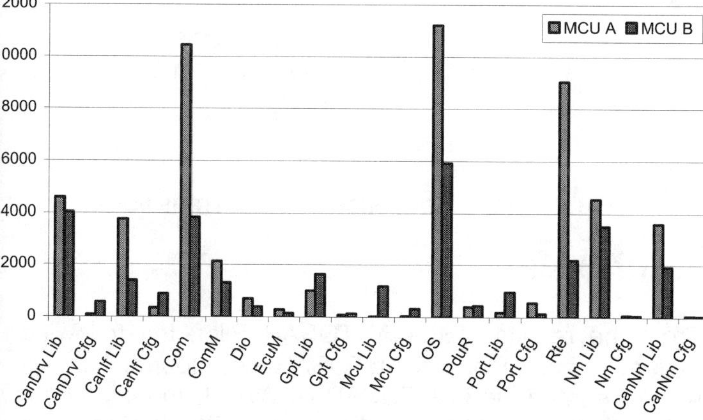

Fig.14 ROM Consumption (Total:A:54Kbyte, B:31Kbyte)

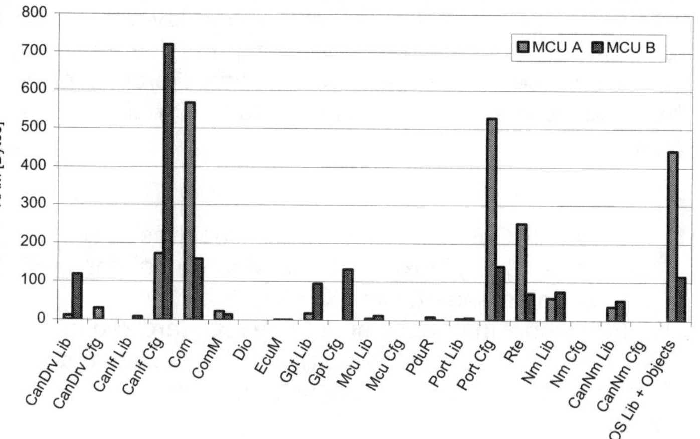

Fig.15 RAM Consumption (Total:A:2.4Kbyte, B:3.1Kbyte)

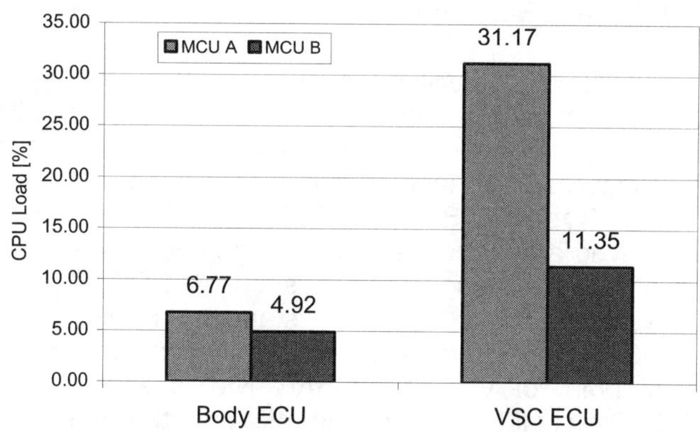

Fig.16 CPU Load by BSW/RTE
(A: RISC MPU 64MHz, B: CISC MPU 32MHz)

2.5 INTEROPERABILITY TEST

2.5.1 End-to-End Latency Measurement

In the interoperability test, several tests were executed. For instance, end-to-end latency was measured (Fig.17, Fig.18). Due to software jitter at the sender and receiver side and communication latency on the bus, the fluctuation of the latency was observed. When SW-C is integrated in series production, this kind of latency has to be taken care of to meet system-timing requirements and the most suitable configuration parameters have to be selected.

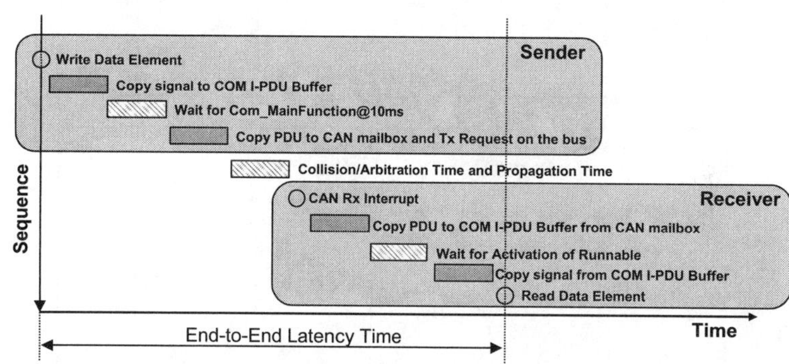

Fig.17 Concept of End-to-End Latency

Sender: MCU A ->MCU B	Min [ms]	Mean [ms]	Max [ms]
Tx:RU@100ms Rx:DataReceivedEvent CAN ID=10Bh, Periodic @100ms	1.06	1.12	1.18
Tx:RU@100ms Rx:DataReceivedEvent CAN ID=10Eh, Mixed @100ms, mindelay = 20ms	1.13	1.48	3.55
Tx:RU@100ms Rx:DataReceivedEvent CAN ID=111h, Direct	3.14	3.22	3.33
Sender: MCU B ->MCU A	**Min [ms]**	**Mean [ms]**	**Max [ms]**
Tx:RU@100ms Rx:DataReceivedEvent CAN ID=102h, Periodic @100ms	10.96 (1.15)	11.47 (1.62)	12.76 (2.05)
Tx:RU@100ms Rx:DataReceivedEvent CAN ID=105h, Mixed @100ms, mindelay = 20ms	0.7	1.18	2.47
Tx:RU@100ms Rx:DataReceivedEvent CAN ID=108h, Direct	1.67	2.37	2.94

Fig.18 End-to-End Latency Measurement

2.5.2 Wakeup/Sleep Validation

AUTOSAR Wakeup/Sleep sequences (Fig.19, Fig.20) were also measured and evaluated in the interoperability test. Active/Passive Wakeup and Sleep sequences were observed and investigated with 3 nodes (Node A, Node B, Node C). Basically AUTOSAR BSW modules are derived and enhanced by adding new features from and onto an existing standard such as OS/COM from OSEK and CAN TP from ISO standard. However, the AUTOSAR NM algorism is a quite new concept. From a logical point of view AUTOSAR NM is simpler than OSEK Direct NM, which is currently adopted by several OEMs and the total code size may be smaller.

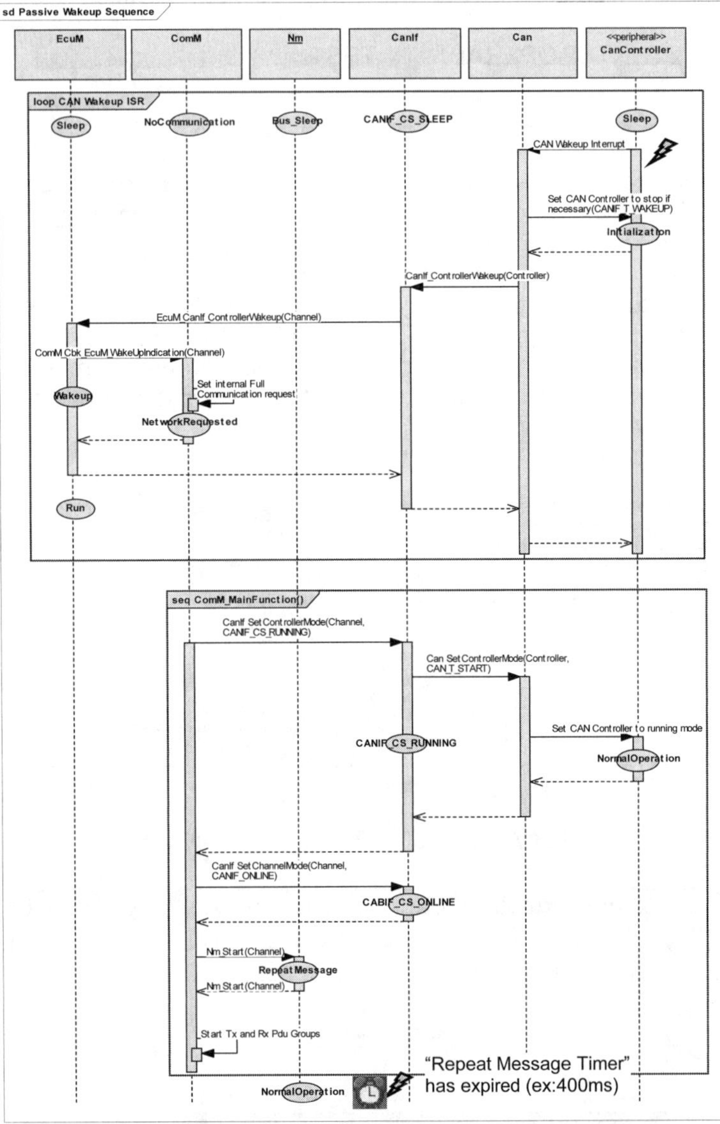

Fig.19 Passive Wakeup Sequence & State Transitions

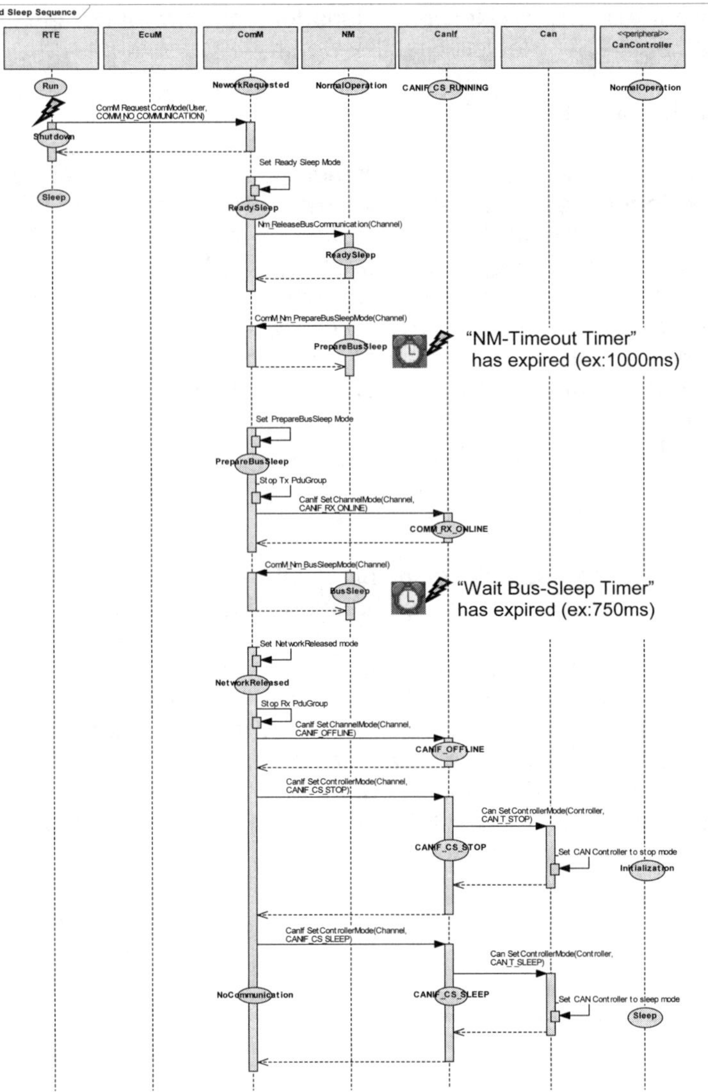

Fig.20 Sleep Sequence & State Transitions

3. ANALYSIS

From the results of the AUTOSAR Pilot, the following major Pros and Cons of AUTOSAR were found. Actually when we integrated AUTOSAR BSW/RTE modules from different implementers on the same HW platform, we encountered hundreds of bugs and drawbacks. As to the BSW/RTE specifications, the completion level and their configuration concept have to be improved. Afterwards we can foresee the exploitation in series production in the near future, as we experienced with the OSEK Standard.

Pros

1) AUTOSAR Communication Stack supports major protocols (CAN, FlexRay, LIN), which is not case with an existing standard like OSEK COM.
2) If Functional interfaces should be standardized in certain gratuity, Application (SW-C) portability and reusability shall be much easier than today.

Cons

1) Overhead on Run-time and ROM/RAM is still high especially for the ECU, which does not need the service of OS/RTE.

2) SW quality and migration risk is rather high since the specification is still under development.

CONCLUSION

TOYOTA Electronic Architecture was introduced and AUTOSAR Pilot driven by TOYOTA was presented. Based on the results of the pilot, Pros and Cons were analyzed and shown from TOYOTA's perspective.

REFERENCES

[1] www.autosar.org Official website of the AUTOSAR partnership

[2] Harald Heinecke etc: AUTOSAR – An industry-wide initiative to manage the complexity of emerging Automotive E/E-Architectures. Convergence 2004, International Congress on Transportation Electronics, Detroit, 2004

[3] Thomas Scharnhorst etc: AUTOSAR – Challenges and Achievements 2005. Electronic Systems for Vehicles 2005, VDI Congress, Baden-Baden, 2005

[4] Helmut Fennel etc: AUTOSAR – Achievement and exploitation of the AUTOSAR development partnership. Convergence 2006, International Congress on Transportation Electronics, Detroit, 2006

2007-01-1613

A Process Membership Service for Active Safety Systems

Carl Bergenhem
SP Swedish National Testing and Research Institute

Johan Karlsson
Chalmers University of Technology

Hakan Sivencrona
Mecel – Automotive Systems

ABSTRACT

This paper describes a process membership protocol for distributed real-time systems that use both time-triggered and event-triggered message passing for communication between its processing nodes (ECUs). TTCAN and FlexRay are examples of communication networks that support such systems. The membership protocol supports redundancy management in architectures where distributed applications such as braking, stability control, and collision mitigation share a common set of processing nodes. We assume that each such application consists of several processes executing on different nodes and that each node executes processes belonging to different applications. The protocol allows a group of co-operating processes to establish a consistent view of each other's operational status, i.e. whether they function correctly or not.

INTRODUCTION

A research trend within automotive electronics is fewer and more complex nodes (ECUs) that support several applications [1]. This ongoing trend will change how the system is organized. It can be summarized as a shift from a federated design to an integrated architecture. A federated system design is characterized by applications that are distinctly divided and are implemented separately; each application has a dedicated subsystem and is only loosely coupled to the subsystems of other applications. In an integrated architecture multiple applications are supported on a common distributed computing platform. The platform consists of interconnected nodes with its system services such as communication and the operating system.

A disadvantage of the federated design is that sharing of resources, such as computing nodes and networks is complex, since this would conflict with the federated design strategy. An incentive for the move towards an integrated architecture is the fact that applications in modern vehicles are becoming increasingly complex and require tight cooperation across several functions. Examples of these are braking, stability control, and collision mitigation. These are inherently distributed.

The research assumption in this paper is that a "distributed task", an application, consists of several communicating processes that execute on different nodes. Also, each node executes processes belonging to different distributed tasks. Examples of the trend towards integrated architectures in the automotive domain are AUTOSAR [2] and DECOS [3] initiatives. Both initiatives acknowledge the importance of a service for achieving data consistency, which indicates that a protocol that realizes a membership service will be required.

The goal of a membership agreement protocol is to achieve a consistent view of the status among a group of cooperating entities in a distributed system. The status, whether the entity is in the membership group or not, reflects its operational status. A survey of membership protocols can be found in [4]. It is of great importance for a distributed task to keep track of e.g. its constituent processes to support redundancy management. We expect that this information will be provided through a membership service in the platform.

This paper describes a new process membership protocol for use as a system service in an integrated architecture. We assume that a time-triggered communication system such as TTCAN [5] or Flexray [6] is used. These two have in common that the communication cycle is divided into two main parts: A prescheduled static segment for time-triggered messages and a dynamic segment for event-triggered messages. TTCAN and FlexRay both lack a built-in membership protocol, in contrast to TTP/C [7]. The TTP-membership protocol focus is on entire nodes and is tightly coupled to the communication of the node. If a node falls out of membership then communication is not

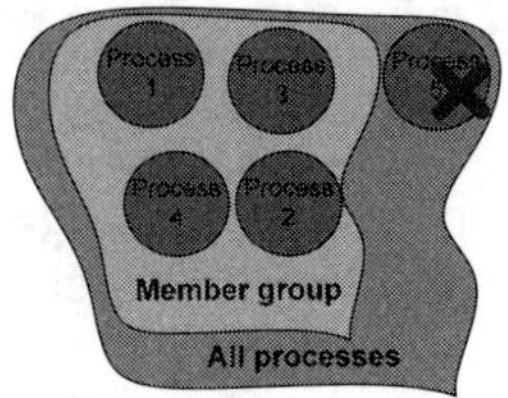

Figure 1: Definition of the membership group.

possible. In contrast to this, our protocol deals with processes and is implemented in the host instead of the communications controller. We expect that this gives added flexibility to the system.

The rest of this paper is organized as follows. A general system model with assumptions is presented. Next, the membership protocol is described. Finally conclusions are drawn.

SYSTEM MODEL

This section describes the system model and sets the scene for the proposed protocol. The system model contains a description of basic assumptions, communications network, a definition of distributed tasks, the requirements that the protocol must fulfill, and the fault model for the protocol.

BASIC ASSUMPTIONS

The test system consists of a number of nodes and processes. Each node hosts at least one process, which constitutes part of a distributed task. The node offers a membership service which all processes are part of. During run time, processes may be failed or correct; member or not member, see Figure 1. During run-time, processes may move to and from the Members group due to failures and then reintegration. If a process has experienced a failure then it is not member. This implies that it is outside the Membership group.

The nodes will broadcast data from each hosted process once during each cycle in the designated slot, i.e. all nodes are expected to broadcast at least once during a cycle. Each process is thus associated with one of the static slots during the cycle. Since the node may host several processes, it may be associated with several slots. Cycles are periodically repeated and contain a fixed schedule of static slots of known length and ownership. The broadcasted message contains process data that functions as a "heartbeat". Processes are assumed to fail in such a way that failure can always be detection by the membership protocol. Hence, a missing heartbeat message implies a failure in the associated process.

COMMUNICATIONS NETWORK STRUCTURE

The nodes of the system are interconnected via communication controllers to a bus or star network. We assume that the network (both topologies) can offer both time-triggered and event-triggered scheduling of

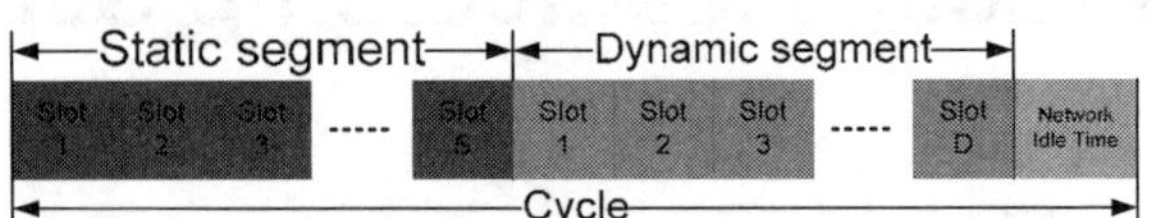

Figure 2: A communication cycle with both event- and time-triggered slots.

messages. Communication in the network is tightly synchronized by a clock synchronization algorithm that is part of the communication controller. Therefore, each node has a common time base of known precision, provided by the network.

We assume that the network provides a reliable broadcast service. A message that is broadcast by a node will be received by all other nodes during fault-free situations. The proposed protocol takes advantage of the following assumed properties of the network (under fault-free conditions). In a real implementation, these assumptions must be ensured by additional communication mechanisms.

- Static messages are broadcast and will be received at all destinations, within a known and bounded time.
- Dynamic messages are broadcast and will be received at all destinations.
- Messages are delivered in the same order as transmitted and no masquerading can occur.
- All nodes have knowledge of the network schedule.

The communication cycle is divided into two segments; a static and a dynamic segment, see Figure 2. The static segment contains slots, each of which is exclusively owned by exactly one process. The process produces data that is sent in the slot according to the time-triggered cyclic schedule. Since a node may contain several processes, it can thus be associated with several slots, one slot for each process. The status of a process is reflected in the slot. Membership protocol messages are sent during the dynamic segment. Here, access to the network is controlled with arbitration according to priority of the message. Priorities are allocated so that membership protocol messages have precedence over other messages. At the end of the cycle there is network idle time, where network operations such as clock synchronization are performed. During network idle time, the membership protocol may be executed in each node.

In the description of the membership protocol in this report, we assume that structural and temporal redundancy mechanisms of the network are not used. We assume that the network is based on a single non-redundant bus without time-redundant transmission of messages. Nodes are not replicated, so value failures are not handled. The protocol can be extended later to take advantage of structural redundancy and handle e.g. value failures.

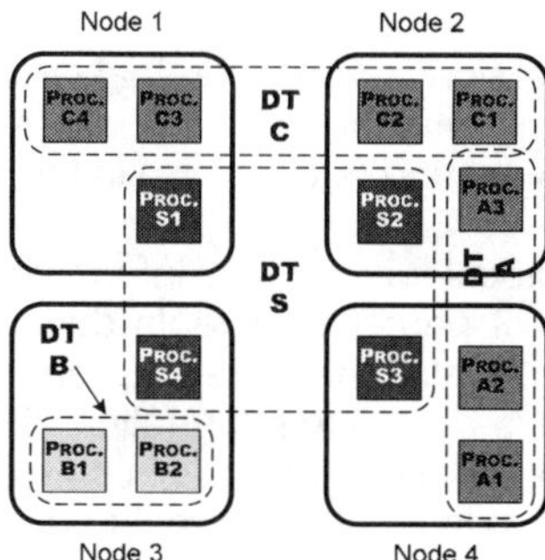

Figure 3: Several processes in different nodes constitute a distributed task (DT).

DISTRIBUTED TASKS

In this research we will deal with distributed applications that consist of several co-operating processes. To emphasize this fact we will refer to such an application as a distributed task (DT). A DT consists of a number of processes, potentially distributed throughout several nodes. Each node also executes processes belonging to different DTs. The processes of a DT may communicate with each other over a network, e.g. if they are situated in different nodes. Processes from different DTs cannot communicate unless specified to do so during the design of the system. An example of a DT is a distributed brake-by-wire function. It has a process running on nodes situated at each wheel, as in "DT S" in Figure 3. A DT requires information about the status of its constituent processes to adapt itself to the situation, i.e. redundancy management pending a failure of process or node. This information is provided through a membership agreement service.

FAULT MODEL

This section describes the types of fault that may occur in the system and the fault hypothesis, i.e. number and types of faults that may occur. We assume that faults can occur in the following items in the system: processes, nodes, and their in- and outgoing links. We also assume that failures of all other possible devices in a real system, such as power supply, network, etc., can be mapped onto the stated items. With this fault model we therefore assume that e.g. the network is free of failure. That is, we only handle failures in the stated items since we assume that these will cover failures in any other device. This simplifies design of the algorithm. The fault model is summarized in Table 1.

A node may experience failure of the incoming link and can thus transmit but not receive any messages for the duration of the failure. This will cause inconsistency, which must be handled by a membership protocol. The challenge is to distinguish whether a failure is local or remote, e.g. whether an expected message is not received due to an incoming link fault at the receiver or an outgoing link fault at the sender or whether the sending node or process is in fact fail-silent. A membership protocol is needed to draw this conclusion, in contrast to other failures where self assessment is sufficient. A cause of inconsistency is e.g. a marginal disturbance on the network interface. EMI may cause some nodes to correctly receive a correctly sent message while others do not. The failure may be due to slight differences of sensitivity in the receivers in nodes. In this case the result is incoming link failures of multiple nodes. An investigation of EMI in X-by-wire systems can be found in [8].

In general, faults may also be categorized according to their duration. We assume that a transient failure only affects one message. If, due to e.g. EMI disturbance, several consecutive messages suffer failure (consistently or inconsistently) during several slots, then this is considered as multiple transient failures. A permanent failure of an item remains in the system until repaired. Depending on which item we are concerned with, the failure may be categorized in a combination of permanent or transient duration and inconsistent or consistent manifestation. The membership protocol must handle all combinations of failures.

A node or process is considered faulty at the detection point. This point in time is when it is expected to manifest itself with a heartbeat message in a slot or a membership protocol message. The detection point can thus be later than the actual time of failure. The node performs the membership protocol and hosts the process. In our model, nodes and processes fail independently from each other, i.e. a failed node does not affect any other node and conversely for processes. We also assume that processes can fail independent of the hosting node, but not vice-versa, i.e. a failed node affects all hosted processes.

We assume that nodes and their processes are fail-silent, i.e. either a correct message is broadcast or nothing is sent. If the process falls fail-silent, then this will be detected by a missing heartbeat in the associated slot. Despite the failure of a hosted process, the node will be unaffected and will still participate in other communication and perform the membership protocol. Failure of the entire node also affects messages for the membership protocol, etc. A node falling fail-silent is similar to the failure of an outgoing link at a node. In the latter case, the node will continue to receive messages and process membership, etc. In this case, a membership protocol is needed to force the faulty node to halt.

An enabling technology to support the independence and fail-silent behavior of processes could be a

Failed item:	Type of faults that the item may introduce:
Node(consistent) (i.e. dead node)	Fail-silence of all hosted processes
Node incoming link (inconsistent)	Failure of all incoming messages
Node outgoing link (consistent)	Failure of all outgoing messages
Process (consistent)	Fail-silence of associated messages.

Table 1: The fault-model

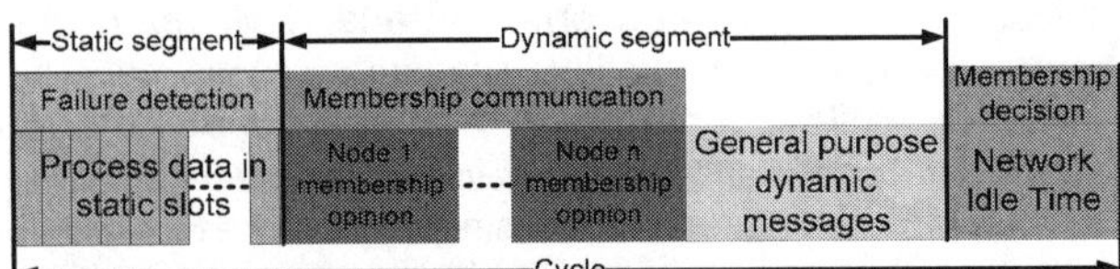

Figure 4: A network cycle with a static and a dynamic segment and idle time at the end. The three phases of the protocol are shown: Failure detection, Membership communication and Membership decision.

combination of memory management hardware and a suitable operating system. We expect such technology also in embedded automotive systems [1]. For the case of independence between nodes, we assume that fault propagation over the network is prevented by e.g. bus guardians.

REQUIREMENTS OF THE MEMBERSHIP PROTOCOL

The membership protocol must have essential properties that can be proven to hold in all situations. We consider the essential properties that the protocol must have are:

- Agreement: All correct nodes compute the same membership
- Timeliness:
  1. A faulty process will be removed from membership in a bounded time.
  2. Correct processes, of a correct node that attempts to reintegrate, will be added to membership in a bounded time.
  3. A faulty node will halt in a bounded time

These requirements will be used when the protocol is verified. Each requirement must hold in all situations as long as the fault-model is not violated, i.e. faults are introduced in the system that are outside the assumptions. Observe that "halt" in the third timeliness requirements implies that a faulty node will cease participating in any membership protocol activities and must not transmit any messages with a detectable heartbeat. Since we assume that processes fail independently from nodes, there may be a situation where all hosted processes of a node have failed. We require such nodes to halt, hence the third timeliness requirement.

THE MEMBERSHIP PROTOCOL

The membership protocol is presented in steps. All extensions build on the base protocol.

1. The base membership protocol. It does not support reintegration of processes and requires sending of membership protocol data during every cycle.
2. Support for reintegration of processes is added. This extends the base protocol to allow processes which were previously removed due to some fault to reintegrate back into membership.
3. Then a version is presented that does not require sending any membership protocol messages unless there is a change (e.g. failure) in the system.

The base protocol functions by informing all nodes of the local opinion of perceived events during the last cycle. When this information has been disseminated, all correct nodes will have complete information about the opinions of all nodes. Based on this complete information, consistently available at all correct nodes, a decision can be made about the status of processes in the last cycle. The membership protocol is executed once per cycle.

An overview of the protocol is found in Figure 4. Observe that the actions in the illustration are not drawn to scale. This scheme is used in all versions of the membership protocol. The illustration describes the phases of the protocol in conjunction with the two communication modes of the network: time and event-triggered (static and dynamic segments). The operation of the membership protocol is divided into three phases. The failure detection (FD) phase is performed during the static segment of the cycle. The membership communication (MC) phase is performed during the dynamic segment of the cycle. In this phase, membership protocol data is sent consisting of node opinions. It is assumed that the highest priority dynamic slots (event-triggered) are allocated for membership protocol data. Observe that these may be reused by other best-effort messages if no membership protocol data needs to be sent, as in Step 3. Finally the decision function is applied to the opinions from all nodes. This gives a new consistent state of membership in the system. It is performed in the membership decision (MD) phase, during network idle time of the cycle. Step 3 of the membership protocol describes an addition that allows the MC and MD phases to be performed only if there is a change in the system. After the membership protocol data has been sent in the dynamic segment, other general purpose dynamic messages may be sent. A similar scheme of dividing protocol operations is presented by Rosset et al. in [9].

The number of faults that can be tolerated during a communications round depends on the decision function. With majority voting, any number of faults may occur as long as at least more than half of the nodes are OK (and host at least one member process) during two communication cycles.

BASIC MEMBERSHIP PROTOCOL

During the FD phase, heartbeats (broadcasts of static messages) are noted by all nodes in the membership group. Each node has a pre-scheduled static message allocation for the network and it is assumed that nodes will broadcast consecutively in one slot during the cycle. Deviation from this will be known by the end of each slot. The result of the heartbeat (status of the message) in a slot is noted in a local opinion vector of nodes. A position in the opinion vector states whether a process is considered to be either member or not member. The

Network	Line speed	Frame overhead	Max. payload	Required frames	Total overhead	Ratio	Notes
TTCAN	500 kbit/s	4-6 bytes	8 bytes	2	2*(6+8)*100*8/1024 =21,9kbit/s	4,4%	Disregarding the effects of bit-stuffing
Flexray	10 Mbit/s	8 bytes	254 bytes	1	1*(8+16)*100*8/1024 =18,8kbit/s	0,18%	
Ethernet	100 Mbit/s	26 bytes	1500 bytes	1	1*(8+16)*100*8/1024 =18,8kbit/s	0,018%	Assume that there is a time triggered scheme

Table 2: Comparison of the basic membership protocol overhead in different networks

latter status indicates that the message was not received correctly, e.g. because of fail-silence of the sending node, a CRC error or other failure. Due to inconsistent failures, the opinion vector may differ between nodes.

Nodes will perform the MC phase when static data messages have been sent. Each node will broadcast a message containing its local opinion which is received by all nodes. These messages are sent during the dynamic communication segment. The dynamic segment is configured such that the protocol messages are guaranteed to be sent. Each node will assemble the received opinion messages into an opinion matrix, where each row contains the opinion from a specific node. At the end of the dynamic segment, all nodes will have had an opportunity to broadcast. If there are no failures, then the opinion matrix will be fully populated with opinions from all nodes.

To achieve a consistent view of the status of processes, the decision function is applied to each process in the system in the MD phase. The opinion matrix is processed column by column to account for all views about a particular process. It is of vital importance that the decision function gives a consistent result and can handle undefined situations such as ties or missing opinions. The decision function also requires an upper bound for the number of correct nodes in the system. This is basically the number of nodes that are expected to send their opinions. If more than half of the expected number of opinions are missing, then there cannot be any majority for either member or not member. This is hence an undefined situation and node that experiences this situation must halt. This removes all hosted processes from membership. The node will stop executing the membership protocol and stop sending any messages, in the same cycle that the fault occurred. The membership protocols described here all use majority voting as decision function.

We do not give a particular proof or argue formally that the protocol satisfies the requirements, but leave this to future work. Informally, argumentation for the correctness of the protocol and fulfillment of the requirements rests mainly on the assumption that more than half the nodes remain non-faulty during two cycles. Each correct node sends its opinion about processes in the system. Majority voting masks faulty opinions. To correctly handle incoming link failures, two cycles of membership processing may be required. Here, the faulty node must realize that it has a failure and halt, by listening to the opinions of other nodes during two cycles. Conversely, the correct node will receive confirmation that the faulty node in fact had suffered the (incoming link) failure. The argumentation for correctness follows the same lines as described in [13].

Protocol analysis of base protocol

The base protocol is analyzed for overhead. Protocol information must be sent during every cycle, i.e. the MC and MD phases must be executed regardless of whether or not there is a change in the system. The drawback is thus constant communications overhead for sending the opinion messages. However, the general trend in communication networks is increasing speed. This is also true for embedded systems [1]. The amount of overhead in the membership protocol scales with the number of nodes and processes, not the network line speed, thus the overhead ratio decreases, see Table 2.

In the analysis we assume 10 nodes (N) and a total of 128 processes (P) in the system, a cycle length of 10 ms. which includes static and dynamic segments and network idle time. The membership protocol will thus run and will exchange data at 100Hz. Each opinion message contains status data (1 bit) for each process P. The message may be split over several frames if it is larger that the maximum payload. The membership protocol thus requires N * (P+O) bits to be transmitted at the end of each cycle. These assumptions result in 128 bits (16bytes) of membership protocol data per node. Note that the total overhead accounts for the frame overhead, required payload, number of frames and data rate.

MEMBERSHIP WITH PROCESS REINTEGRATION

For the membership protocol to be practical it must also not only allow for reintegration of repaired processes and nodes but also non-faulty processes and nodes that were excluded due to a transient fault. The basic protocol is modified to handle reintegration. A node that wishes to join will indicate this by broadcasting a join message during FD and will then participate in MC and MD phases as if it were a member of the group. Since the state of the reintegrating node may not be in agreement with the correct nodes, the opinion of a reintegrating node will be handled differently in the MD phase. Every node must also broadcast its upper bound for number of nodes in addition to its opinion (in the MC phase), so that an integrating node can correctly perform the decision function.

It is assumed that the reintegrating node knows its own static transmission schedule and that of other nodes and is clock synchronized with the rest of the network. The same decision function is used as before. The algorithm also assumes that a node will only try to reintegrate if all of its hosted processes are functional. All processes of a reintegrating node will thus be set to 'member'. The delay for a process that wishes to join membership is at worst two cycles.

MEMBERSHIP USING DYNAMIC SCHEDULING FOR PROTOCOL OPERATIONS

The two previous versions of the membership protocol both require MC and MD phases to be performed during every cycle. The former phase involves sending messages and thus consumes network capacity in the dynamic communications segment. The goal behind this version is to only perform the MC and MD phases when there has been a change of status in the membership group, e.g. failure or reintegration.

When a change is detected by a node, it will signal this to other nodes in the FD phase. This includes other correct nodes that may not have perceived the change. Correct nodes will hence perform the MC and MD phases. The phases must also be executed again in the cycle following a cycle where processes were removed in the MD and MC phases. This allows for handling of faults occurring in these phases. As before, faults may be detected locally, but a node must determine whether it experienced an incoming link fault or the sending node or outgoing link was faulty.

Two states are added in this version. M-request is used to signal to non-faulty nodes that membership phases must be executed. It is included in the heartbeat message. Nodes must keep track of the "generation" of the membership group as perceived at each node. It is included together with the opinion and upper bound of number of nodes, sent in the MC phase. Each time the MD phase is performed (i.e. there has been some change), the local generation is incremented.

CONCLUSION

A background is presented to the area of embedded real-time systems which motivates the need for a membership agreement service. Such a protocol is proposed for use in a system that uses a communication network with scheduling of both event-triggered and time-triggered messages. The protocol supports reintegration of processes. It also takes advantage of event-triggered communication so that membership protocol messages need only be sent when there is a change in the system. During periods of no failures or reintegration of processes, the protocol will introduce virtually no communication overhead. The protocol can handle failures as long as at least a majority of nodes are non-faulty during two consecutive cycles. It will reach consensus about status in the system after at worst two cycles after the last failure. The delay for a process that wishes to join membership is at worst two cycles.

We are currently developing a test setup. It consists of a number of processing nodes that are interconnected with a FlexRay network. The membership protocol will be implemented to verify its properties and measure performance in a realistic environment. We also plan to verify the properties with formal methods.

ACKNOWLEDGMENTS

This research is conducted within the project CEDES, Cost Efficient Dependable Embedded Systems, which is funded by the Swedish industry and government joint research program IVSS - Intelligent Vehicle Safety Systems.

REFERENCES

[1] N. Navet, Y. Song, F. Simonot-Lion, and C. Wilwert, "Trends in automotive communication systems," *Proceedings of the IEEE*, vol. 93, pp. 1204-1223, 2005.

[2] "AUTOSAR, An industry-wide initiative to manage the complexity of emerging Automotive E/E-architectures," in *Vehicle Electronics to Digital Mobility: The Next Generation of Convergence*, vol. SAE/P-387, *International Congress on Transportation Electronics*, 2004, pp. 325-332.

[3] P. Peti, R. Obermaisser, F. Tagliabo, A. Marino, and S. Cerchio, "An integrated architecture for future car generations," Seattle, MA, United States, 2005.

[4] C. Bergenhem, "Survey of Membership Agreement Protocols," Chalmers dept. of computer science and engineering, Gothenburg, Sweden, Technical report 05-19, 2005.

[5] T. Führer, B. Müller, W. Dieterle, F. Hartwich, R. Hugel, and M. Walther, "Time Triggered Communication on CAN (Time Triggered CAN-TTCAN)."

[6] *FlexRay Communications System Protocol Specification Version 2.1*: FlexRay Consortium, 2005.

[7] H. Kopetz and G. Grunsteidl, "TTP-a protocol for fault-tolerant real-time systems," *Computer*, vol. 27, pp. 14-23, 1994.

[8] C. Wilwert, F. Simonot-Lion, Y. Song, and F. Simonot, "Quantitative evaluation of the safety of X-by-Wire architecture subject to EMI perturbations," Catania, Italy, 2005.

[9] V. Rosett, P. Souto, and F. Vasques, "A group membership protocol for communication systems with both static and dynamic scheduling," presented at Workshop on factory communications systems, 2006.

2006-01-1024

Assessment of FTT-CAN Master Replication Mechanisms for Safety-Critical Applications

Ricardo Marau, Luís Almeida and José A. Fonseca
DET/IEETA. Universidade de Aveiro, Portugal

Joaquim Ferreira
DETI/EST, Inst. Politécnico Castelo Branco, Portugal

Valter F. Silva
ESTGA/IEETA. Universidade de Aveiro, Portugal

ABSTRACT

The operational flexibility of distributed embedded systems is receiving growing attention because it is required to support on-line adaptation to varying operational conditions, either due to changes in the environment or to faults in the system. However, flexibility makes dependability more difficult to achieve, because there is less a priori knowledge. One protocol that favors flexibility and is widely used in embedded systems, particularly in automotive and robotic systems, is CAN, but some claim that it is not adequate to support safety-critical applications. We argue that CAN, deployed with an adequate overlay protocol, can provide the required support for dependability and flexibility. One such overlying protocol is Flexible Time-Triggered CAN (FTTCAN), that enforces a global notion of time and a global periodic schedule by means of specific messages issued by a master node. In this paper we assess the FTT-CAN master replication mechanisms implemented in a distributed robot control system. Above all, we provide experimental results that show the robustness of such mechanisms.

INTRODUCTION

Distributed embedded systems (DES) have been widely used in the last few decades in several application fields, ranging from industrial machinery to avionics and automotive systems. In some of these application domains the dependability requirements are of utmost importance, since failing to provide services in a timely and predictable manner may cause important economic losses or even put human life at risk [10]. The adoption of the best practices when designing distributed embedded systems does not fully avoid the occurrence of faults arising from the non-deterministic behavior of the operational environment. Thus, fault tolerance mechanisms need to be included in the DES to prevent possible faults from causing system failure. To be effective, fault tolerance mechanisms require *a priori* knowledge of correct system behavior to be capable of distinguishing it from erroneous behaviors.

Many safety-critical embedded systems used today, e.g. in transportation systems, are distributed and rely on a fieldbus network that interconnects sensors, actuators and controllers in a reliable and timely way. One popular network access control paradigm used in many of these applications is the master-slave paradigm, in which a single node controls the traffic on a bus using a cyclic traffic dispatching table. Several examples can be pointed out, such as WorldFIP [8] and TCN [7], largely used in train control systems, as well as MIL-STD-1553B [6], which has been used for a long time in the USA for distributed hard real-time applications. Master replication is, of course, essential to avoid the single point of failure and achieve fault tolerance during standard operation mode. Master-slave networks are naturally synchronized with the master, since this node explicitly tells each slave when to transmit. This feature also supports increased operational flexibility, allowing online changes to traffic parameters because such parameters are concentrated on the master node only. This simplifies controlling the admission of change requests and reduces the reaction time with respect to distributed alternatives. With this type of flexibility, one can turn on and off the transmission of message streams or vary the respective transmission rates according to the run-time needs of the system. This results in greater efficiency of network utilization, freeing bandwidth that can be used to serve more streams or to facilitate error recovery. However, the fact that communication requirements can vary on-line increases the difficulty in assuring synchronization between active and backup masters.

In this paper we address the effectiveness of the master replication mechanisms of a dynamic master-slave architecture based on the FTT-CAN protocol [1]. The experimental setup is a robot, namely a CAMBADA soccer robot [16], with a distributed system that supports a few feedback control loops. The rest of the paper is organized as follows. The next section briefly presents the FTT-CAN protocol, while Section III describes the basic design decisions made to provide fault tolerance in FTT-CAN. Section IV addresses the replication of the FTT-CAN master node. Section V presents the robotic soccer agent's architecture, while section VI addresses the experimental assessment of FTT-CAN master replication mechanisms. Finally, section VII presents the concluding remarks.

FTT-CAN: A BRIEF PRESENTATION

The FTT-CAN protocol (Flexible Time-Triggered communication on CAN) [1] has been developed with the main purpose of combining a high level of operational flexibility with timeliness guarantees and high efficiency in bandwidth utilization. It uses the dual-phase elementary cycle concept for isolated time and event-triggered communication. The time-triggered traffic is scheduled on-line and centrally in a particular node called a master, facilitating on-line admission control of requests, thus being managed in a flexible way, under guaranteed timeliness. The protocol relies on a relaxed master-slave medium access control in which the same master message triggers the transmission of messages in several slaves simultaneously (master/multi-slave). The eventual collisions between slave messages are handled by the native distributed arbitration of CAN.

FTT-CAN slots the bus time in consecutive Elementary Cycles (ECs) with fixed duration. All nodes are synchronized at the start of each EC by the reception of a particular message known as an EC trigger message (TM), which is sent by the master node. Within each EC the protocol defines two consecutive windows, asynchronous and synchronous, that correspond to two separate phases (see Figure 1). The first is used to convey event-triggered traffic, here called asynchronous because the transmission requests can be issued at any instant. The second is used to convey time-triggered traffic, herein called synchronous because its transmission occurs synchronously with the ECs. The synchronous window of the nth EC has a duration that is set according to the traffic scheduled for it. The schedule for each EC is conveyed by the respective EC trigger message (see Figure 2). Since this window is placed at the end of the EC, its starting instant is variable and it is also encoded in the respective EC trigger message.

The sequence of asynchronous windows maintains the real-time native properties of CAN [9], namely the arbitration mechanism, despite the interruptions caused by the intermixing with the synchronous windows. The strict temporal isolation between windows is enforced by preventing the start of transmissions that could not complete within the respective window.

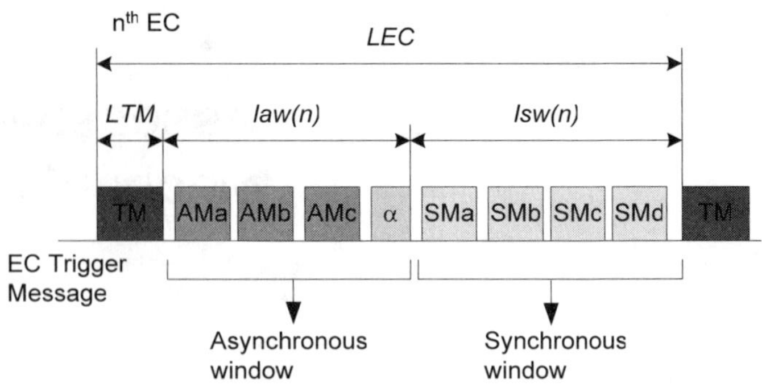

Figure 1 - The Elementary Cycle (EC) in FTT-CAN

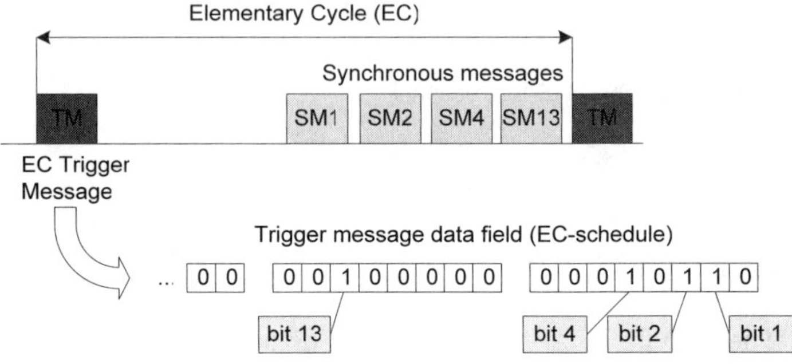

Figure 2 - Master/multislave access control and EC-schedule coding scheme

The communication requirements are held in a database located in the master node [13], the System Requirements Database (SRDB). This database holds several components, one of which is the Synchronous Requirements Table (SRT), that contains the description of the periodic message streams. Based on the SRT, an on-line scheduler builds the synchronous schedules for each EC (EC schedules). These schedules are then inserted in the data area of the appropriate EC trigger message (see Figure 2) and broadcast with it. Due to the on-line nature of the scheduling function, changes performed in the SRT at run time will be reflected in the bus traffic within a bounded delay, resulting in flexible behavior.

ACHIEVING FAULT TOLERANCE IN FTT-CAN

When addressing fault tolerance in FTT-CAN, the most obvious issue that must be dealt with is the single point of failure formed by the master holding the SRT and the traffic scheduler. In fact, if the master node fails, no more trigger messages with EC schedules are transmitted and thus communication is disrupted. This can be prevented by using replication, with one or more similar nodes acting as backup masters. However, all master replicas must be synchronized so that they can replace the active one without any discontinuity of the traffic schedule. When on-line adaptation is allowed, this synchronization is more difficult, because the communication requirements can evolve over time.

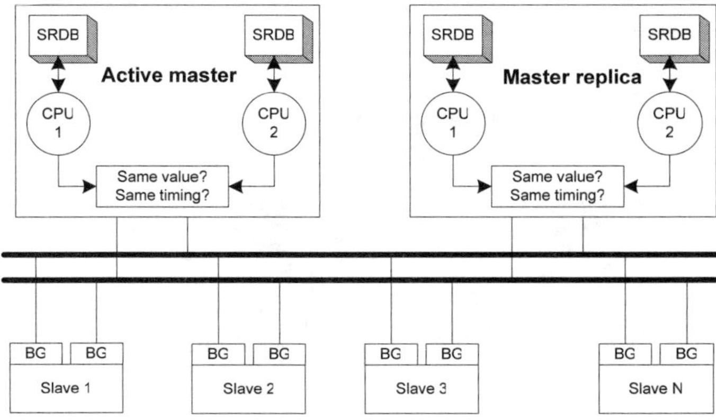

Figure 3 - Fault-tolerant FTT-CAN architecture based on a replicated broadcast bus, master replication and bus guardians

To facilitate the task of designing mechanisms that enforce masters synchronization, we consider that nodes are fail-silent. The mechanisms that enforce this property, as well as those used to synchronize the master replicas, are described in [5]. In this paper we focus on the master replacement scheme, on the protocol to synchronize starting or restarting backup masters by transferring the current SRT, and on the protocol that ensures consistent SRT updates for change requests. We briefly present these mechanisms and discuss their application and experimental assessment in a real setup.

The bus itself is another single point of failure and thus replication of the transmission path is essential to tolerate its physical partition. However, bus replication is outside the scope of this paper. An interesting possibility would be the use of a replicated star solution as described in [11]. Given these considerations, the proposed fault tolerant FTT-CAN architecture is shown in Figure 3.

MASTER REPLICATION

In order to achieve a successful master replication, so that a master backup takes over bus scheduling in case the currently active master fails to transmit the trigger message, it is mandatory that all replicas maintain synchronization with the current active master. In our case, the replica that assumes the role of primary master must have the same knowledge of the faulty master, i.e., they must be replica determinate. The master nodes are replica determinate if, starting from the same initial conditions (same SRT) and fed by identical inputs (SRT update requests), they produce the same result (EC schedule) at the same time (every EC).

Replication is a common way to provide fault tolerance, and it is used, for example, in TT-CAN to cope with failures of the time master. However, master replication in FTT-CAN includes an extra complexity which results from the dynamic nature of the SRT. Since the system requirements, replicated in all masters' SRTs, are flexible and may evolve over time, there is a potential for inconsistency in the replicated SRT images, compromising the replica determinism requirement. Two situations are particularly relevant:

1) During an asynchronous startup/restart a master node may lose the contents of its SRT. This calls for the definition of a protocol to transfer the SRT from the active master to the unsynchronized one.

2) During the processing of an SRT update request, it must be ensured that all replicas process the same request, in the same order, and commit the request synchronously. This calls for the definition of an adequate protocol to enforce consensus, preventing a master from accepting a request while others reject it or preventing different masters from transmitting a request at different instants.

Apart from these situations, there are no reasons for the replicas to diverge during standard operation mode. To cope with these issues, the master node replication in FTT-CAN is addressed by four mechanisms:

- A master replacement mechanism that acts upon active master failure.
- A policing mechanism to allow backup masters to detect loss of synchronization.
- A synchronization protocol to allow out-of-sync master backups to re-synchronize in a short interval.
- An agreement protocol to handle SRT updates to minimize the potential for loss of synch.

MASTER REPLACEMENT MECHANISM

Master replication and replacement is required to tolerate permanent failures of the master node. Recall that the master node is fail-silent and so when it fails it stops transmitting.

The master failure detection and replacement technique consists in making the backup masters try to transmit the TM after a short delay, the replacement delay (Figure 4), after the expected start of the TM transmission by the active master. The masters use a single shot transmission by issuing an abort request immediately after the transmit one. If the active master is already transmitting a trigger message on the bus, the abort request is successful. Otherwise, if the backup master effectively started transmitting the TM, the abort request fails and the trigger message produced by the backup master is effectively transmitted. In the former situation, the backup master detects a CAN receive interrupt and stays in the same state. In the latter situation the backup master allows a CAN transmit interrupt and changes its state to active.

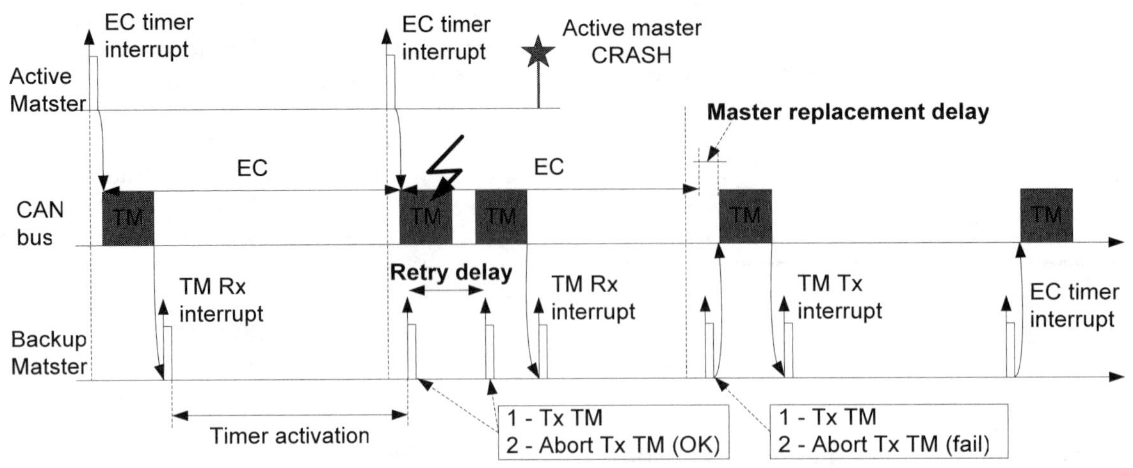

Figure 4 - Master replacement process

If there are several backup masters present in the network, the situation is similar, since possible backup master competition is handled by the native CAN arbitration. This implementation is quite efficient, since the master replacement delay is a fraction of the trigger message duration, and so the induced jitter due to master replacement is low (see the measurements further on).

In case of error during the transmission of the TM, all masters, active and backup, retry transmitting it in single shot mode after a short delay called the retry delay (Figure 4).

This controlled retry mechanism gives all masters the time required to check the reception of a TM before attempting to send it. Consequently, only one TM is successfully transmitted in each EC.

SYNCHRONIZATION POLICING

All master replicas in the system constantly scan their own copy of the SRT and build EC schedules. As long as they are synchronized, the EC schedules received in the trigger message should equal the ones generated locally. Therefore, when a mismatch is detected between the received and local EC schedules, a backup master declares itself as out-of-sync and issues a synchronization request to the active master using a special high-priority asynchronous message. Notice that with this approach the view of the active master prevails, assuring consistency in synchronous traffic scheduling.

MASTERS SYNCHRONIZATION PROTOCOL

Whenever the active master receives a synchronization request it starts to download its current SRT and scheduler state as necessary to resume scheduling synchronously [4] [12]. This data is transferred using high-priority asynchronous messages. The process may take a few ECs, depending on the size of the SRT and on the current network utilization. This is a time-critical process, since modifications to the SRT are not allowed during its execution and the synchronizing master is not yet capable of replacing the primary in case of failure.

The timeline of the synchronization process is shown in Figure 5. It begins with a backup master detecting inconsistency in the received EC schedule (A) and issuing a synchronization request (MST_DATA_QRY message) to the active master (B). This causes the active master to download the scheduling data in two rounds. The first round comprises the transmission of the static portion of the SRT (MST_DATA_MSGPROP), namely IDs, periods, deadlines and lengths. This data is fragmented in a set of CAN messages and transmitted in the asynchronous windows of several consecutive ECs.

In the second round the active master transmits the scheduling state data (MST_DATA_SCHINF). This comprises the relative phases of all messages and their respective states. Because this transmission may cover more than one EC, the data actually sent to the backup master is a snapshot of the phases and message scheduling states, just before the start of this round (C).

At the end of this round (D) the active master sends a special message containing the dynamic data transfer interval (DDTI), which is the count of the number of elapsed ECs since the scheduler state was captured. This number tells the backup master the scheduling delay (in ECs) relative to the active master. Since the backup master scheduler is now updated with the scheduling data just received from the primary, the backup master scheduler just needs to generate that number of consecutive EC schedules (fast forward). After that, the backup master is synchronized (E).

Note in Figure 5 that the backup master synchronizes only one EC after the reception of the DDTI message. This is to guarantee that the backup master has enough time (at least one EC long) to generate the required number of EC schedules specified in the DDTI message, even when this message arrives late in the EC. The worst-case synchronization time can be upper bounded under certain assumptions [4] [12] [5].

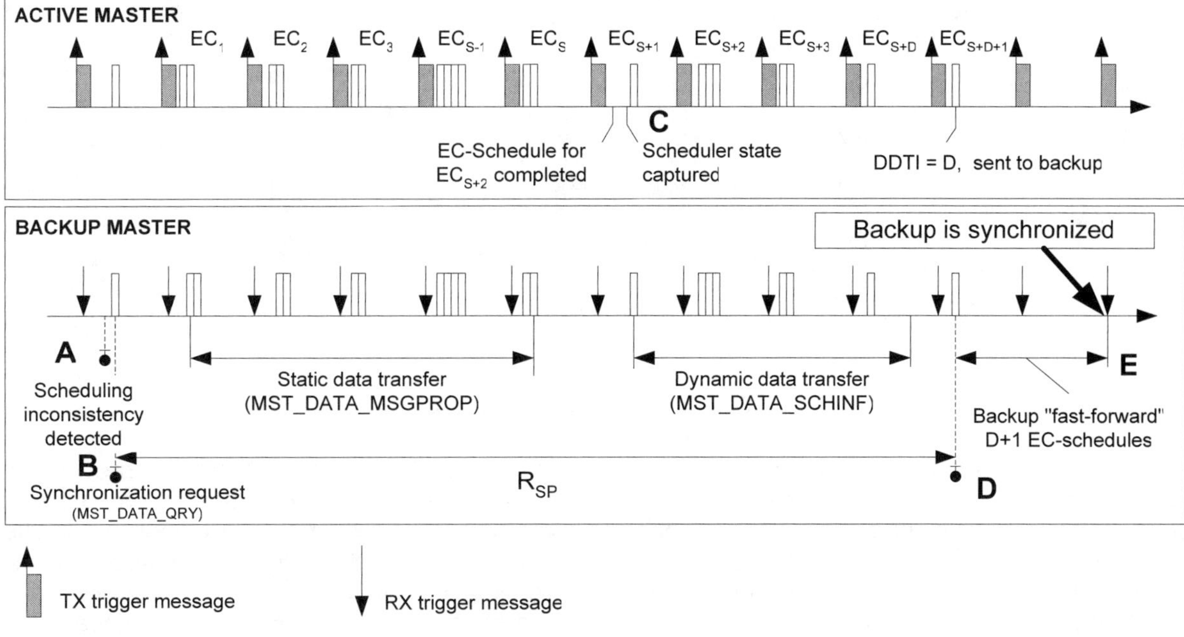

Figure 5 - Master synchronization protocol timeline

SRT UPDATE PROTOCOL

There is only one master operation which may modify the local copy of the SRT, i.e., the processing of an update request. Therefore, as long as each request is consistently processed by all the masters, the consistency of their SRT copies is preserved. In particular, if more than one request is received, then these requests must be processed in the same sequence. However, inconsistent channel errors, e.g. inconsistent omissions [15], turn out to impair this consistency because they may cause different masters to process requests in a different order.

This problem has been addressed previously from different perspectives and for different scenarios. A new agreement protocol was proposed in [14] for the specific case of FTT-CAN. In order to eliminate inconsistencies among masters, the active master assumes the role of *leader*, and the backup masters assume the role of *followers*. Instead of using specific messages, the active master uses the TM to broadcast its state. In particular, the TM conveys the identifier of the request that is being processed as well as the protocol state. Whenever a backup master is not able to follow the active master (e.g. because it did not receive the request to be processed), it considers itself as being unsynchronized, and initiates re-synchronization.

Figure 6 illustrates how the SRT update protocol works in the absence of channel and node faults. The whole process is divided into three phases: **request**, **admission control** and **reply**. In the **request** phase, the slave broadcasts an update request using a specific asynchronous message. If there is no pending request with higher priority, the active master changes its state to **admission control** and piggybacks the request ID and the protocol state on the next TM. Notice that the request ID is the FTT-CAN ID of the message the request refers to, taking 6 bits. The protocol state takes the other 2 bits. After receiving this TM, all the masters, active and backup, wait until the end of the asynchronous window (following the one of the initial request) and start the admission control test. This delay is used to guarantee that slaves have at least a full asynchronous window to retransmit a request in case of error, reducing the probability of inconsistent omission.

As soon as the admission control test concludes, the active master broadcasts the result. Again, the result of the admission control and the new protocol state are piggybacked on the TM. This phase is called the **reply** phase. At the end of this phase, all nodes (both masters and slaves) know which request has been processed as well as the result of the admission control test. Therefore, each master can update its local replica of the SRT according to the request. Once an update request has been processed and the result of the admission control has been broadcast, the active master is ready to process another request.

A potential problem of a leader-follower approach like the one described is that an inconsistent transmission of the TM might cause inconsistency among the backup masters. However, the active master knows whether the transmission of its TM has been inconsistent [3] and takes advantage of this feature by keeping the same protocol state in the following TM. In this way, the delayed leader delays all followers. The result is similar if the active master crashes while processing an update request. If this happens, the backup that takes over relays the same protocol information received in the last TM to enforce its consistency, thus delaying the protocol.

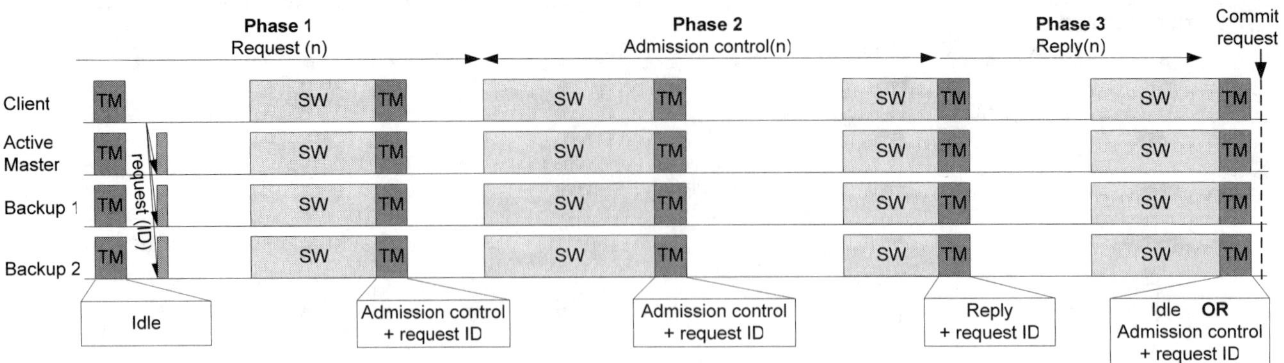

Figure 6 - Phases of the SRT protocol

Therefore, although replicated masters could face transient inconsistencies, such inconsistencies would be eventually solved after a consistent transmission of the TM. Thus, channel errors may enlarge the protocol execution but do not jeopardize consistency. In [14] we present a partial formal validation of this protocol using a PROMELA model and the SPIN model checker.

EXPERIMENTAL PLATFORM

The FTT-CAN protocol was recently implemented in the CAMBADA soccer robots [16], being an opportunity to assess the master replication mechanisms in a real platform. These robots have a two-tiered architecture with a higher-level coordination layer implemented on a PC running Linux/RTAI and a distributed low-level sensing/actuation system based on the FTT-CAN protocol that interconnects the robot physical actuators and low-bandwidth sensors to the coordination layer (Figure 7).

The low-level nodes are based on the PIC microcontroller 18Fx58 operating at 40MHz while the CAN network operates at a bit rate of 250Kbps. At this level there are 3 DC motors with controllers plus an extra controller, all of which provide independent rotation and translation capabilities to the robot. Each motor has an incremental encoder that is used to obtain speed and displacement information. Another node is responsible for combining the encoder readings from the 3 motors and building coherent displacement information that is then sent to the coordination layer. Moreover, there is a node responsible for the kicking system that consists of a couple of sensors to detect the ball in position and trigger the kicker. This node also monitors battery voltage. Finally, the low-level control layer is interconnected to the coordination layer by a gateway attached to the serial port of the PC which is configured to operate at 115 Kbaud. From the perspective of the low-level control layer, the higher coordination layer is hidden behind the gateway, and thus we will refer to the gateway as the source or destination of all transactions arriving from or sent to that layer.

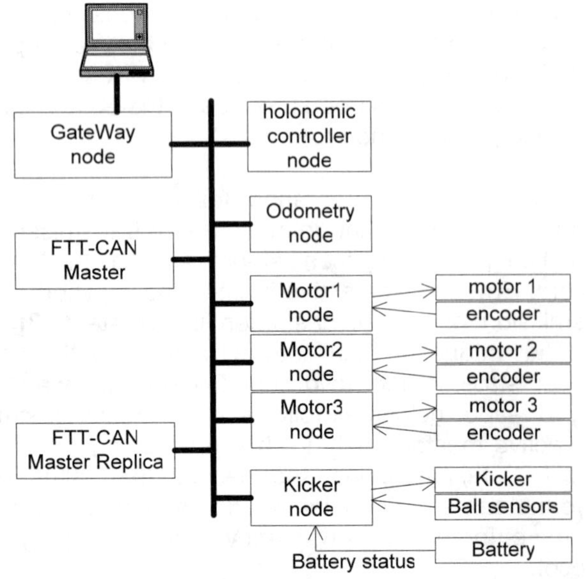

Figure 7 - Hardware architecture of the low-level control layer

The communication requirements representing the mapping of the low-level control layer over the hardware architecture are summarized in Table 1.

In this specific application and apart from the Odometry function, all the communication requirements are static. The Odometry function covers 4 nodes, the 3 motor controllers plus a 4th node that combines the individual encoder readings into coherent displacement information sent up to the higher layer. The encoder readings are the same as those used by the closed-loop motor speed control, and thus they are sampled every 5ms. This sampling should be carried out synchronously in all three motors. However, depending on the desired precision in constructing the robot displacement information, these readings can be sent with a periodicity that varies from 5ms to 20ms (higher to lower precision). During the execution of certain high level behaviors the odometry information is not needed, e.g. when tracking the ball, and thus it can also be temporarily switched off. Three messages are used to convey the encoder readings (M3.1-M3.3). When these messages are received the odometry node calculates the robot position and orientation, taking approximately 4ms, and sends it to the higher layer every 50ms, using 2 messages (M4.1, M4.2). This period is compatible with the cycles used by the processes running within the higher layer. The Odometry function also includes a pair

ID	Source	Target	Type	Period/mit (ms)	Size (B)	Short description
M1	Holonomic ctrl	Motor node[1:3]	Periodic	30	6	Aggregate motor speeds set points
M2	Kicker	Gateway	Periodic	1000	2	Battery status
M3.1-M3.3	Motor node [1:3]	Odometry node	Periodic	5 to 20	3*3	Wheels encoder values
M4.1-M4.2	Odometry node	Gateway	Periodic	50	7+4	Robot position + orientation
M5.1-M5.2	Gateway	Odometry node	Sporadic	500	7+4	Set/reset robot position + orientation
M6.1-M6.2	Gateway	Holonomic ctrl	Periodic	30	7+4	Velocity vector (linear+angular)
M7	Gateway	Kicker	Sporadic	1000	1	Kicker actuation
M8-M12	Every node	Gateway	Sporadic	1000	5*2	Node hard reset

Table 1 – Low-level control layer communication requirements

of sporadic messages (M5.1, M5.2) received from the higher layer to set or reset the current robot position and orientation information in the odometry node. These messages are not expected to be generated within less than 500ms intervals (minimum inter-arrival time - mit).

EXPERIMENTAL ASSESSMENT FTT-CAN MASTER REPLICATION MECHANISMS

To assess the feasibility and correctness of the proposed schemes, some experiments were carried out in the network shown in Figure 7. The EC duration was set to 5*ms,* which is the shortest period among all periodic activities and messages, i.e., the closed-loop motor speed control period. For a trigger message with 5 bytes, the communication overhead is lower than 8.4% (420μs/5ms), while the computing overhead is around 1.5% (76μs/5ms). These values were considered admissible, given the application load. Particularly, the communication load according to Table 1 is close to 27% of the bus bandwidth at 250Kbps. The maximum duration of the synchronous window was set to 2.5ms (corresponding to an asynchronous window of 2.1ms)

ASSESSMENT OF THE MASTER SYNCHRONIZATION PROTOCOL

Apart from the synchronous messages, asynchronous ones (M5.1, M5.2, M7, M8.1, M8.2, M8.3 and M8.4) were also injected onto the bus but with lower priority than those involved in the master replication mechanisms.

Table 2 shows the system SRT, including both synchronous messages and synchronization events. The periodic message set is related to the synchronous traffic requirements. The synchronization events are mapped in the SRT to manage the distributed applications synchronization. The initial phase of messages and events are chosen to reduce the application end-to-end delay and to spread the messages over the available bus time to reduce the interference jitter. The reader should refer to [16] for further details concerning the translation of the requirements expressed in Table 1 to the FTT-CAN SRT presented in Table 2.

As referred to in previous sections, in this case the static scheduling data consists of the message identifier, data size, period and deadline, while the scheduling state data consists only of the ID plus the relative phasing of the messages at the beginning of the next plan. All these properties are encoded in one byte each, resulting in an SRT occupying 126 bytes (accounting also for the instantaneous values of the periods, deadlines and relative phasing). Under these conditions, the worst-case synchronization time is $ST_{WC} \approx 48.1$ms [5].

FTT-CAN ID	Period (# ECs)	Deadline (# ECs)	Initial Phase (# ECs)	Size (bytes)
0	6	6	5	6
1	200	200	1	2
2	1-4	1-4	2	3
3	1-4	1-4	2	3
4	1-4	1-4	2	3
5	10	10	4	7
6	10	10	4	7
7	6	6	0	7
8	6	6	0	4
9	1	1	0	0
10	2	2	1	0
11	2	2	3	0
12	10	10	3	0
13	6	6	1	0
14	6	6	6	0

Table 2 – Synchronous Requirements Table - SRT

In order to assess both the accuracy of the worst-case synchronization time estimation and the reliability of the master replica re-synchronization scheme, a software routine injected an inconsistency in the backup's master SRT table and measured the elapsed time until the backup master became synchronized with the active master. Measured values ranged from 40.2ms to 45.4ms. This variation can be explained with the different synchronous scheduling in each EC which directly interferes with the FTT-CAN asynchronous window size, that is often larger than 2.1ms (minimum asynchronous window size). Thus, if more room is available in the asynchronous windows, the SRT is transferred faster.

ASSESSEMENT OF MASTER REPLACEMENT

To test this mechanism in our experimental setup, the active master was unplugged from the network several times. The backup master took an average time of 310μs, measured with an oscilloscope, to replace the active master (Figure 8).

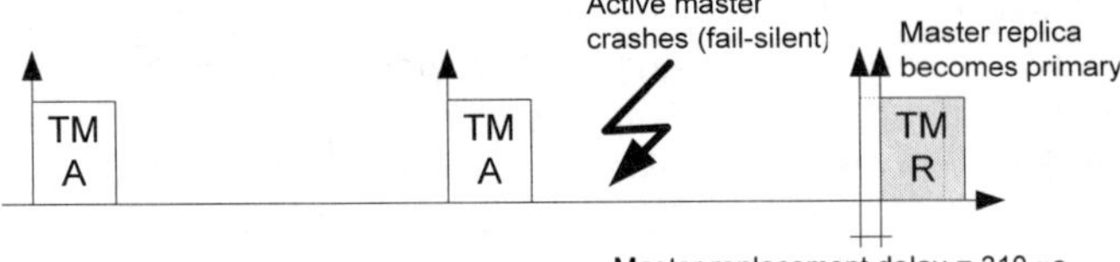

Figure 8 - Master replication delay

Notice that this value depends on the bit stuffing of the trigger messages. In fact, the replacement timer of the backup masters is triggered when the previous TM is received, which is affected by bit stuffing. When trigger messages have 5 data bytes, the number of stuff bits ranges from 0 to 15 [2]. This corresponds to a maximum variation of 60μs.

ASSESSMENT OF THE SRT UPDATE PROTOCOL

In order to assess the SRT update protocol, the high level robot control application issued several update requests to the master node in order to change the sampling period of the wheel encoder values according to the robot dynamics, i.e., to increase the sampling rate when the robot speed is high and decrease it when the robot speed is low. The response time of each SRT update request ranged between 15.8ms and 19ms, as expected (between 3 and 4 ECs).

CONCLUSIONS

In this paper we addressed the issue of combining operational flexibility with high dependability. In particular, we addressed the case of FTT-CAN and its fault tolerance mechanisms, which were developed to provide the referred combination. FTT-CAN is a dynamic master-slave protocol that requires master replication to achieve high dependability. In this work we evaluated the FTT-CAN master replication mechanisms using a real implementation on autonomous mobile robots. These mechanisms included master replacement and synchronization, synchronization policing and a protocol to support online adaptation of the communication requirements (SRT update protocol). The system included 9 nodes and used an elementary cycle of 5ms. The experimental results confirm the proper operation of the referred fault tolerance mechanisms, supporting the desired combination of operational flexibility with high dependability.

We are currently investigating the use of FTT-CAN in automotive applications to support novel adaptive approaches to X-by-wire systems, for example online adaptation to environmental, traffic and driving conditions.

REFERENCES

1. L. Almeida, P. Pedreiras, and J. A. Fonseca. The FTT-CAN Protocol: Why and How. IEEE Transactions on Industrial Electronics, 49(6), 2002.
2. CiA. CAN physical layer. http: // www. can-cia.de/ CANdll. pdf ; accessed September 28, 2005, 1999.
3. J. Ferreira, L. Almeida, J. Fonseca, G. Rodríguez-Navas, and J. Proenza. Enforcing Consistency of Communication Requirements Updates in FTT-CAN. Proceedings of the Workshop on Dependable Embedded Systems, held in conjunction with the 22nd Symposium on Reliable Distributed Systems (SRDS 2003), pages 7–12, October 2003.
4. J. Ferreira, P. Pedreiras, L. Almeida, and J. Fonseca. Achieving fault tolerance in FTT-CAN. Proceedings of the 4th Workshop on Factory Communication Systems (WFCS 2002), 2002.
5. Joaquim Ferreira. Fault-Tolerance in Flexible Real-Time Communication Systems. Phd thesis, University of Aveiro, 2005.
6. N. Haverty. MIL-STD 1553 - a standard for data communications. Communication & Broadcasting, 10(1):29–33, 1986.
7. IEC. IEC International Standard 61375-1 Electric railway equipment - Train bus - Part 1: Train Communication network. International Electrotechnical Committee, 1999.
8. IEC. IEC International Standard 61158: Fieldbus standard for use in industrial control systems – Type 1: Foundation Fieldbus H1; Type 3: PROFIBUS; Type 7: WorldFIP. International Electrotechnical Committee, 2000.
9. International Standards Organisation. ISO 11898. Road Vehicles—Interchange of digital information—Controller area network (CAN) for high speed communication, 1993.
10. H. Kopetz. Real-Time Systems: Design Principles for Distributed Embedded Applications. Kluwer Academic Press, 1997.
11. Julian Proenza M. Barranco, L. Almeida. Re-CANcentrate: A replicated star topology for CAN networks. Proceedings of ETFA'2005 10th EEE International Conference on Emerging Technologies and Factory Automation, September 2005.
12. Ernesto Martins, J. Ferreira, L. Almeida, P. Pedreiras, and J. Fonseca. An Approach to the Synchronization of Backup Masters in Dynamic Master-Slave Systems. Proceedings of the WiP Session of 23rd IEEE International Real-Time Systems Symposium (RTSS), 2002.
13. Paulo Pedreiras. Supporting Flexible Real-Time Communication on Distributed Systems. PhD thesis, University of Aveiro, Portugal, July 2003.
14. G. Rodríguez-Navas, J. Proenza, J. Rigo, J. Ferreira, L. Almeida, and J. Fonseca. Design and Modeling of a Protocol to Enforce Consistency among Replicated Masters in FTT-CAN. Proceedings of the 5th Workshop on Factory Communication Systems (WFCS 2004), pages 229–238, 2004.
15. J. Rufino, P. Veríssimo, G. Arroz, C. Almeida, and L. Rodigues. Fault-tolerant broacast in CAN. Digest of Papers, 28th International Symposium on Fault Tolerant Computer Systems, pages 150–159, 1998.

16. L. Almeida J. Ferreira M. Calha P. Pedreiras V. Silva, R. Marau and J. Fonseca. Implementing a distributed sensing and actuation system: The CAMBADA robots case study. Proceedings of ETFA'2005 10th EEE International Conference on Emerging Technologies and Factory Automation, September 2005.

ACKNOWLEDGEMENTS

This work was partially supported by the Portuguese Government (FCT) under grant PRODEP 2001-200.019 and by the European Union through the NoE ARTIST2, contract IST-2-004527.

CONTACT

Ricardo Marau, marau@det.ua.pt
Luis Almeida, lda@det.ua.pt
José A. Fonseca, jaf@det.ua.pt
Electronic Systems Lab, IEETA, Dep. de Electrónica e Telecomunicações, Universidade de Aveiro, Aveiro (PORTUGAL)

Joaquim Ferreira, jjf@est.ipcb.pt
Dep. de Eng. das Tecnologias da Informação, EST, Instituto Politécnico de Castelo Branco, Castelo Branco (PORTUGAL)

Valter Silva, vfs@estga.ua.pt
Esc. Sup. de Tecnologia e Gestão de Águeda, Universidade de Aveiro, Aveiro (PORTUGAL)

2005-01-4144

Analysis of Communication Requirements in Automotive Buses

Fernando Henrique Ataíde
Departamento de Engenharia Elétrica – UFRGS

Fabiano Costa Carvalho
Instituto de Informática – UFRGS

Carlos Eduardo Pereira
Departamento de Engenharia Elétrica – UFRGS

Max Mauro Dias Santos
Laboratório de Sistemas de Tempo Real – UnilesteMG

ABSTRACT

Distributed Control Systems (DCS) are becoming widely used in several areas of application, including automotive embedded systems. Many of these applications have severe timing constraints and are considered safety-critical, requiring predictable behavior in relation to both logical result and timing even in presence of faults. In such cases, a graceful degradation of service delivery that fulfils safety requirements can be tolerated. Especially in the automotive area, which is considering the possibility of replacing the major part of mechanical and/or hydraulic systems for electronic systems, the importance of reliable communication services plays a key role. To cover automotive DCS requirements, it is necessary to explore fault-tolerant techniques. In this context, this work presents an analysis on communication requirements in the automotive embedded system domain. In addition, a simulated analysis comparing a CAN and a TTP/C DCS is presented.

INTRODUCTION

For several years, communication between electronic devices has been treated as a topic of fundamental importance in design of electronic embedded systems. Computer assisted monitoring and software-based control loops are implemented with intelligent components physically distributed around the environment under control (e.g. a vehicle). In such cases, there is an intrinsic characteristic of special distribution of computational elements that imposes the utilization of an interconnection structure with relative low cost and enough support to meet application requirements of performance and timing. On account of the great quantity and heterogeneity of those intelligent devices, communication through shared bus has been considered the most reasonable solution due to cost restrictions of dedicated circuitry for each logical communication channel.

Nowadays, there is a strong interest in the automotive industry toward the production of popular vehicles with electronic driving control, where conventional mechanic and hydraulic systems are replaced by electrical actuators and sensors looking for weight diminution, cost and power consumption savings. In the scientific literature, these applications are also denoted as safety-critical applications because they are strictly involved with either integrity of people or expensive equipment. In view of that, today's designers of automotive buses and embedded applications face a new problem. On the one hand, it is state of art the development of new communication architectures to support the growing demands for performance, determinism and reliability of these emerging "audacious" applications. Further, as automotive buses become more complex, there is a need to understand the new concepts they adopt in order to profit all benefits associated.

The objective of this paper is to provide an analysis of communication requirements in automotive buses. First, a brief description of SAE's current classification of automotive applications is given. Second, the different communication paradigms for DCS are presented. Third, issues on fault-tolerance in automotive buses are discussed.

Fourth, a simulated case study analysis of a CAN and a TTP/C DCS is presented. Finally, some concluding remarks are made.

AUTOMOTIVE APPLICATIONS

The SAE (Society of Automotive Engineers) has defined three basic categories of automotive DCS applications with regard to safety requirements [1]. In the following items, each one is individually described:

CLASS A – Basically, class A encompasses non-critical applications with low bandwidth and relaxed safety requirements, e.g., electronic body applications. Examples are lighting systems (head, tail, brake and flash light control), seat positioning, mirror positioning, power-window and door-lock control, etc. A common characteristic of all these applications is that the payload length of messages is very short and the updating rate is relatively low. LIN [2] and TTP/A [3] are considered suitable protocols for class A applications.

CLASS B – Class B includes applications like air conditioning control, information display and fuel level, which demands higher bandwidth. The most important to note is that neither class A nor class B applications are directly involved with human's safety. CAN [4] is the most typical example of a protocol for class B.

CLASS C – Class C includes applications that are intrinsically involved with vehicle dynamics and driving control (e.g. steering and breaking active electronic systems, gearbox control). In such systems, the update rate of information is about 1 to 10ms and the payload field length of messages is larger if compared to class A and B applications. Moreover, class C applications are said to be safety-critical because a system failure can lead to disastrous consequences hence there are high demands of predictability, performance and reliability. In order to fulfill these requirements, enhanced communication platforms are needed. It must be someway guaranteed that applications executed over them can trust its services in a justifiably manner. Currently, TTP/C [5] and FlexRay [6] are examples of protocols for class C applications.

COMMUNICATION PARADIGMS FOR DCS

An intense debate on requirements of communication in DCS has been established and two conceptually distinct models have been identified, named event-triggered and time-triggered. These two models define particular characteristics related to the execution behavior of both application software and platform communication primitives. This section presents these two and discusses some issues related to design of distributed applications.

In an event-triggered system all actions are triggered due to the occurrence of a significant event or state change. With respect to communication, only transmitter nodes have knowledge about the exact instant a message will be sent, that is, each node has only its own view of the physical time. The major advantage of an event-triggered bus is its better responsiveness to asynchronous external events (e.g. an alarm condition) at low communication load. System reaction is fast since the transmission times of messages are not under the control of the platform architecture, that is, a node is able to try for media access whenever it needs. The problem is that depending on the collision resolution mechanism of the protocol, collisions will have direct impact on response times of communication services. In addition, event-triggered distributed systems are more flexible. The total bandwidth of the channel is shared among the nodes which mean that it automatically readapts when nodes are removed or included even if there is ongoing communication (hot-plug). Nonetheless, in event-triggered systems the response times of data transmission deteriorates as communication load increases. In truth, even at low loads the communication behavior will experiment quite large latency variations, which has negative impact on the control performance. For many years, CAN has been a de facto standard event-triggered protocol for chassis control systems and power train communications.

A time-triggered distributed system is characterized by its regular, deterministic time behaviour. All transmission times of messages are defined in a global schedule at design time, prior to deployment. The communication controller is responsible for every communication activity (transmission and reception of messages) and operates independently from the host computer.

The most appointed shortcoming of the time-triggered paradigm is its lack of flexibility. For every node inclusion that was not previously predicted, the whole system must be reprogrammed. On the other hand, an important advantage is that time-triggered based protocols offer cyclical data communication services with fixed latencies. The bandwidth is partitioned into dedicated time slots inside which only one node can transmit at a time hereby collisions never occur under normal operation. If there are no collisions, the transmission of messages defined in the global schedule is never delayed. This is the Time-Division Multiple Access (TDMA) arbitration mechanism.

Moreover, time-triggered systems have a very attractive property from the point of view of embedded system design which is named composability, that is, the possibility to develop two subsystems independently with prior guaranty that the integration will not jeopardize timing and other functional characteristics that were individually defined. Time-triggered buses are composable because communication media access is multiplexed, that is, each node has its own portion of bandwidth that will never be snatched by another node under normal conditions.

An interesting assumption for a time-triggered system is that every node has approximately the same view of time. Error detection is performed inside the controllers by verifying if every message was received within its expected time window. This facility providing intrinsic means to verify a node crash. When comparing design complexity, the implementation of time-triggered systems is indeed more complicated. For all those benefits of composability and predictable behaviour there is a price to be paid. Within each node it must be ensured that the application layer follows the communication scheme correctly. This means that the worst-case execution time (WCET) of all tasks in a node must be carefully estimated in order to avoid inconsistencies in the values that are used by actuators to interact with the system under control. During system design, not only the communication schedule but also the schedule of all control tasks must be defined.

Today, there are two emerging time-triggered solutions claiming being able to fulfil the rigorous requirements of class C in-vehicle applications. The first one is the TTP/C protocol and its Time-Triggered Architecture (TTA) [7], which is the result of many years of work started in 1979 at the Technical University of Berlin with the MARS project. The other one is the FlexRay Communications System developed by the FlexRay Consortium formed by a group of strong companies in the automotive area.

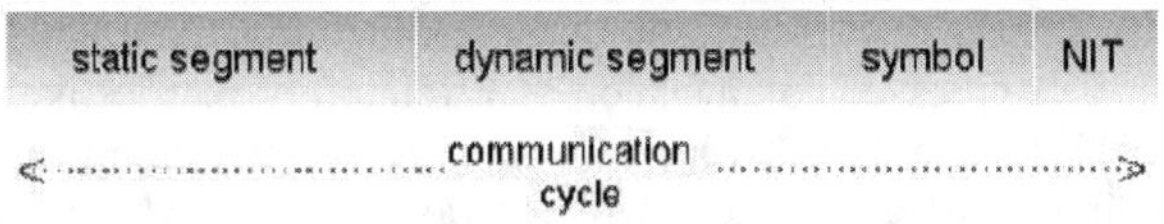

static segment	dynamic segment	symbol	NIT

Figure 1. FlexRay Communication Cycle.

It is noteworthy that the two paradigms are not mutually exclusive in practice but one of them always prevails against the other. Both FlexRay and TTP/C architectures provide event-triggered services in addition to their strictly regular time-triggered communication. The FlexRay's communication cycle (Figure 1) is divided into four different time windows: a static segment, an optional dynamic segment, a symbol window and the network idle time (NIT).

All communication services are handled within the static and dynamic segments. Therefore, this protocol prioritizes time-triggered traffic as the static segment is mandatory and the dynamic is optional. The former segment is used for time-triggered traffic while the other is shared among the nodes for asynchronous transmissions. Reaction to external events can be quite slow because of the static segment's presence. Consider for example that an asynchronous transmission request arrives at the end of the idle time. In this case, the transmission will be delayed at least by the entire duration of the static segment. In TTP/C, there is no time window reserved to handle asynchronous requests, event-triggered services are implemented over the time-triggered scheduled using empty slots (if any). Having all that in mind, it is clear that in an inherent time-triggered system, the cyclical traffic is always prioritized.

Table 1 summarizes the issues presented in this section.

Table 1. Comparison of Paradigms.

paradigm	***Event-triggered***	***time-triggered***
reaction to external events	*fast*	*slow*
control traffic latencies	*variable*	*fixed*
channel bandwidth	*shared*	*dedicated*
design complexity	*low*	*average*

Event-triggered and time-triggered concepts do not have a direct relationship with synchronous and asynchronous communication model present in traditional distributed system theory. An asynchronous model refers to the application processing in a distributed environment, which has no notion of time at all, whereas the event-triggered paradigm refers basically to the fact that each node in the DCS has its own notion of time.

Research on embedded DCS has recognized the time-triggered communication model as the most adequate design paradigm for safety-critical applications [8]. Bus architectures derived from the time-triggered model have some desirable properties like low communication jitter, predictable transmission delays, composability and efficient support for fault-tolerant techniques.

FAULT-TOLERANCE IN AUTOMOTIVE BUSES

In late years, automotive buses have become a fundamental component of in-vehicle electronic systems, providing functionality enhancement together with cost reduction. At first glance, the term "bus" may understate its complexity if one considers that it refers to the network topology only. In fact, automotive buses encompass several building blocks and represent the core of any safety-critical system. They are defined as the ensemble consisting of physical channel, communication protocol and host interface.

Bus architectures have a major advantage that communication services and hardware resources can be shared among distributed nodes, in opposition to the federated deployment approach, where each control function is implemented as a dedicated subsystem, which has minor access to information from other parts of the whole system and does not share resources. Having in mind that in a bus the physical media is shared, the most obvious problem that comes into play is the need to implement a contention resolution mechanism in the kernel of the protocol, to ensure that nodes gain access to the media in a mutually exclusive way. Moreover, this contention mechanism must be deterministic since embedded applications execute control functions with deadlines to be respected. The CAN protocol copes with the problem of contention using a CSMA bitwise arbitration based on priority of messages. A transmission can start at any time at any node. When two or more messages begin to be transmitted at the same instant, the highest priority message wins arbitration and does not perceive that a collision has occurred. CAN is the most popular example of an event-triggered protocol.

Another example of deterministic automotive protocol is byteflight [9]. This protocol avoids contention by means of a flexible time division multiple access (FTDMA) arbitration scheme. The channel bandwidth is partitioned in communication cycles, which are periodically triggered by the master's synchronization pulse. Inside each cycle, time is again partitioned into slots of variable length. If no transmission takes place at the beginning of a slot its length will be equal to a short reception window (minislot), else the duration of the slot is dynamically adjusted to fit the message transmission time. Despite the fact that all nodes are synchronized to the master's time base at each synchronization pulse, the byteflight is also considered an event-triggered protocol because transmission instants of messages are not statically define inside the communication cycles.

Both CAN and byteflight protocols provide efficient solutions in terms of costs, deterministic time behavior and flexibility due to the fact that the total bandwidth can be shared among all nodes. Nevertheless, as distributed embedded systems became more involved with human safety, other issues and challenges appear beyond these typical ones. In class C applications for instance, an unexpected failure can lead to disastrous consequences, probably resulting in live losses, large financial penalties or both. It follows that, in addition to timing and budget constraints, the design specification of those safety-critical systems has also rigorous requirements on reliability that must be fulfilled by means of combining fault-prevention and fault-tolerance.

Traditional theoretic studies on reliable distributed systems adopts a simplified fault model where only node processors are prone to failure and do not address the problem o faults in the communication link. It is assumed that if both sender and receiver are non-faulty then all messages transmitted are correct delivered. Unfortunately, this model is not sufficient for designing distributed embedded system. In hazardous environments, communication link faults due to electromagnetic disturbances, vibration, overheating and rapid temperature shifts can cause messages to be lost during transmission, so, more practical fault models are needed.

The definition of a fault model with all potential faults that can affect the system is a primary step prior to the implementation phase. As a result of a meticulous evaluation of runtime environment conditions and architecture characteristics, all faults that may cause a system failure are identified and included in the fault model. Before deployment, the system must be simulated, tested, formally verified and justifications on design decisions must be presented in order to prove that the system will be able to provide reliable services even in the presence of those faults defined in the model. In other words, the system must be able to deliver services that can be justifiably trusted. That is the current definition of dependability [10].

To achieve dependability, it is necessary that bus architectures be dependable themselves. They must provide fault-tolerant low level services and efficient implementation support for high level techniques of fault masking otherwise it is unfeasible or at least extremely expensive to attain a solution with the minimal qualitative or quantitative degree of dependability required for safety-critical missions. A quantitative dependability requirement can be expressed for instance as a reliability metric like a MTTF (Mean Time-to-Failure) rate, or as a minimum time of uninterrupted service delivery (availability) whereas a qualitative requirement can be a careful justification about the systems' ability to mask some kinds of faults.

Traditional protocols like CAN and byteflight are not suitable mainly because of their inherent event-triggered nature that limits the implementation of fault-tolerance. On the other hand, communication architectures based on the time-triggered paradigm have some particular properties that can be explored to design completely integrated dependable systems. In the following paragraphs, the most important features related to fault-tolerance support in time-triggered architectures are described.

FAULT ISOLATION – In order to apply fault-tolerant techniques in a distributed system, the establishment of error boundaries and the definition of fault containment units are of utmost importance. It must be ensured that the effect of a fault does not propagate in an unrestricted manner. The federated approach provides inherent error isolation since there is no resource sharing. In this case, fault-tolerance is introduced by means of resource redundancy without care about intercommunication conflicts. However, in bus architectures, errors may propagate through the physical media and disrupt communication between non-faulty components, so, each component or subsystem must be logically isolated when faults occur. Whenever arbitrary faults are considered in the fault model, there is a risk that a node assumes a babbling idiot behavior and hence tries to monopolize the media by sending spurious messages at any time. This problem is quite difficult to overcome in event-triggered systems because message transmission times are unpredictable by definition. On the other hand, babbling idiot failures in time-triggered systems are easily inhibited using the old concept of bus guardians (Figure 2). Since each node has its own time slot, all instants a node accesses the media are known before runtime. Therefore, the communication pattern of the whole system can be loaded into the guardians that behave like intelligent switches to grant access to the node only when it is allowed to transmit. Furthermore, in time-triggered systems the guardians can be implemented independently with respect to the logical behavior of the host. The internal state of the host is irrelevant to the guardian so, there is no need to communicate with the guardian to ensure that it will not deny access when the node is non-faulty. Strictly speaking, this bus protection mechanism is totally transparent to the application level.

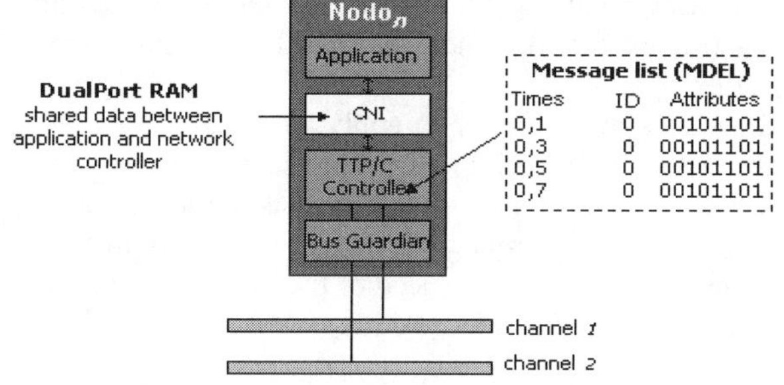

Figure 2. Example of a Time-Triggered Architecture.

A practical limitation of bus guardians is that it is very difficult to implement them as totally independent fault containment units in bus topologies. In theory, bus guardians are both logically and physically independents of the host, that is, they have their own clock, power supply and encapsulation in order to ensure that a fault will never affect the host and guardian at the same time. Start topologies represent a very attractive alternative to overcome this difficulty. In this case, a totally independent bus (start) guardian control unit can be included in the central hub.

CLOCK SYNCHRONIZATION – By having the nodes synchronized on a common time base, it is possible to apply redundancy at the application level with minimal side effects in distributed control loops. Time-triggered architectures have an inherent clock synchronization service that is tightly coupled with the TDMA arbitration scheme so, if application task scheduling is performed using the bus clock then all activations instants, periods and deadlines expressed as bus clock units are indeed the same. A straightforward solution for fault masking is to use replicated channels and to configure two nodes to perform the same calculation prior to send the result at the same time through different paths (Figure 3). Moreover, the use of other fault-tolerant mechanisms like spare is also facilitated thanks to the possibility to know in advance many (if not all) transmission times of messages with a precision close to $1us$. The detection of a failure (e.g. an omission failure) can be accomplished extremely fast with reduced effort.

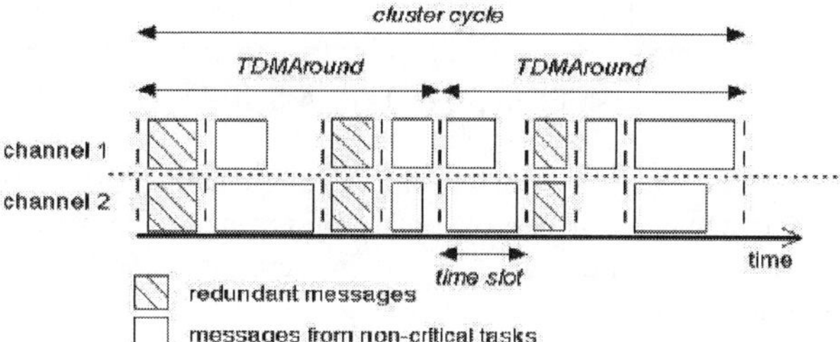

Figure 3. Communication Through Replicated Channels

Clock synchronization in event-triggered bus architectures can be implemented by means of rounds of message exchanges to send explicit clock values. An obvious inconvenience is the extra traffic overhead associated, which diminishes the percentage of channel bandwidth for control application data. On the other hand, in time-triggered systems there is no need to send messages with clock values due to the static nature of the communication pattern. At every message transmission the receiver can infer the state of the sender's clock by taking a snapshot of its local clock and comparing this value with the correspondent (expected) transmission time that was defined offline.

PREDICTABLE BEHAVIOR OF CONTROL TRAFFIC – In a DCS, control traffic means all information flow related to process variables, e.g., input sensor data for control loops and output data to actuators, which are characterized by fixed activation periods. During normal operation, the control performance deteriorates if these periods experiment variation, an undesirable effect that is also called jitter. From the bus architecture point of view, jitter is a consequence of timing faults that affect communication by delaying (casually advancing) transmission of messages. In time-triggered systems, timing faults (of control traffic) are excluded by definition. Consider the scenario in Figure 4 where a simple example of a TDMA schedule is shown. There are 3 messages with periods equal to 1, 2 and 4ms that are sent by different nodes. It can be observed that response time is fixed and jitter is near zero since transmissions of messages are never delayed. Using priority based event-triggered protocols, a possible undesirable situation is for instance when all messages are ready to be transmitted at the same time. This is possible due to the fact that the nodes are not synchronized (the host's time primitives are derived from the local clock source) so the periods Pmsg1, Pmsg2 and Pmsg4 run freely one from another at runtime. Furthermore, considering that arbitration is priority based, the lowest priority message would be delayed by at least the amount of time needed to transmit all higher priority messages.

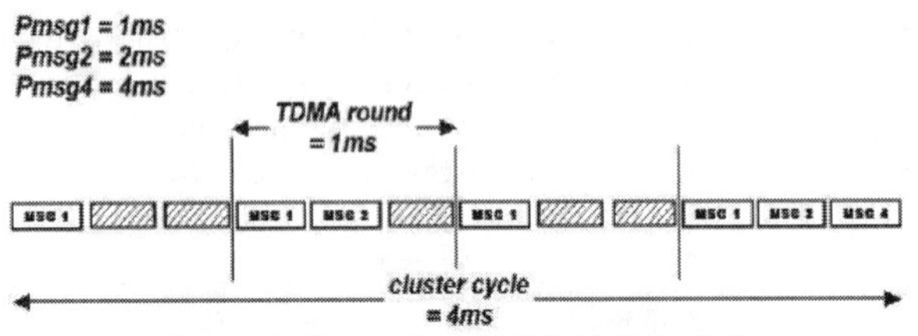

Figure 4. Example of TDMA Schedule.

The next section explores this characteristic of regular behavior of control traffic by means of simulation where a CAN and a TTP/C system were simulated in the Simulink environment.

CASE STUDY AND SIMULATION RESULTS

With objective to compare the temporal behaviours of a CAN and a TTP/C system, steer-by-wire model was simulated using the Matlab/Simulink with the TrueTime simulator [11]. The simulation was performed at the MAC level of the protocols in order to take into account the collision resolution control mechanism. Faults in the bus architecture were not included.

The model has five nodes: a node located at the steering wheel, which is responsible for transmitting steering angle information and controlling the feedback force to the driver and other four nodes each node located close to one road wheel, which are responsible for actuating in the road drivers according to information sent by the steering node. The road nodes also provide information to the steering node for feedback force control. Figure 5 shows the complete steer-by-wire model implemented in the Matlab/Simulink environment. Three different steering modes are considered: 4-wheel steering, parallel steering and 2-wheel steering.

To represent the driver's intention, a trajectory was previously defined to be the input information to the steering node. Throughout simulation time, the steering node broadcasts the trajectory information to all road wheel nodes to provide input data for the control algorithm that is executed inside each one of them.

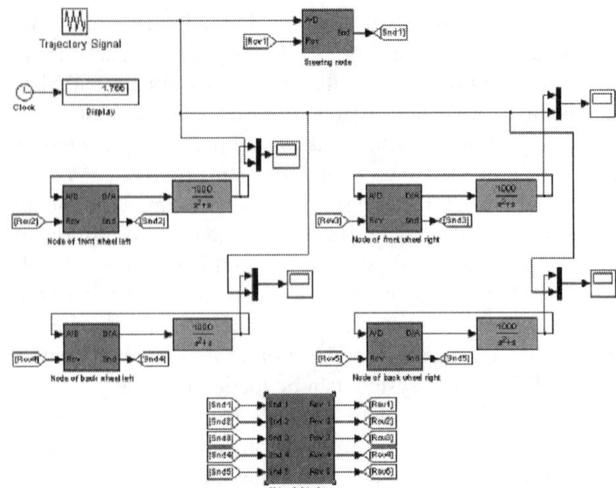

Figure 5. Steer-by-wire Model.

RESULTS UNDER THE CAN SYSTEM – The CAN system was simulated at 500kbps. Figure 6 presents the temporal behaviour control traffic.

The steering node sends a message with the steering mode information with a period of 100ms (Figure 6 (a)) while the steering angle information is sent with a period of 10ms (Figure 6 (b)). When each road wheel node receive the steering angle information, it runs the control algorithms and actuates in the driver to apply the desired force at the road wheel. The wheel nodes in turn sent road wheel status data back to the steering node that runs the feedback force algorithm. The left front wheel node is the only that sends information related to the speed of the vehicle in addition to the road wheel status (Figure 6 (d)).

The event-triggered behaviour of the CAN system is clearly distinguished. Once the steering node's message is received by the wheel nodes, they all execute internally and became ready to transmit almost at the same time hence competing for bus access. As a consequence, the arbitration mechanism determines that messages are sent in priority order as depicted in the grey areas of Figure 6.

RESULTS UNDER THE TTP/C SYSTEM – The results obtained from the TTP/C system are shown in Figure 7. The same control traffic load, bitrate and node placement

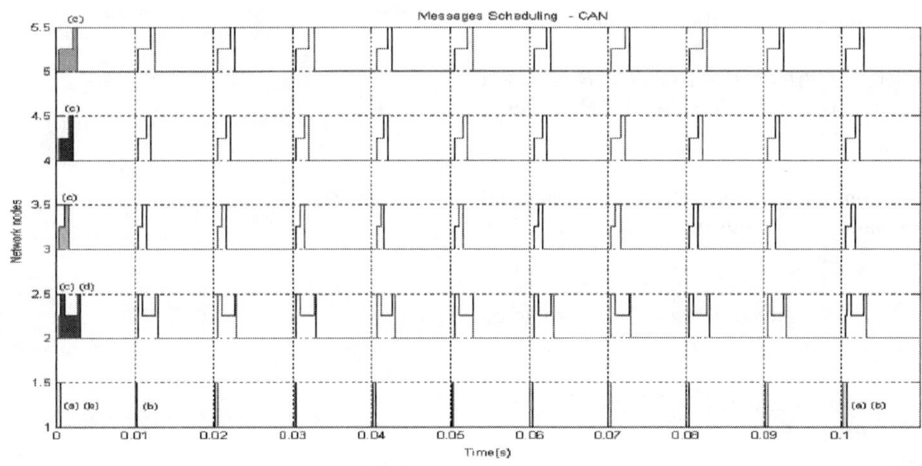

Figure 6. Control Traffic in CAN.

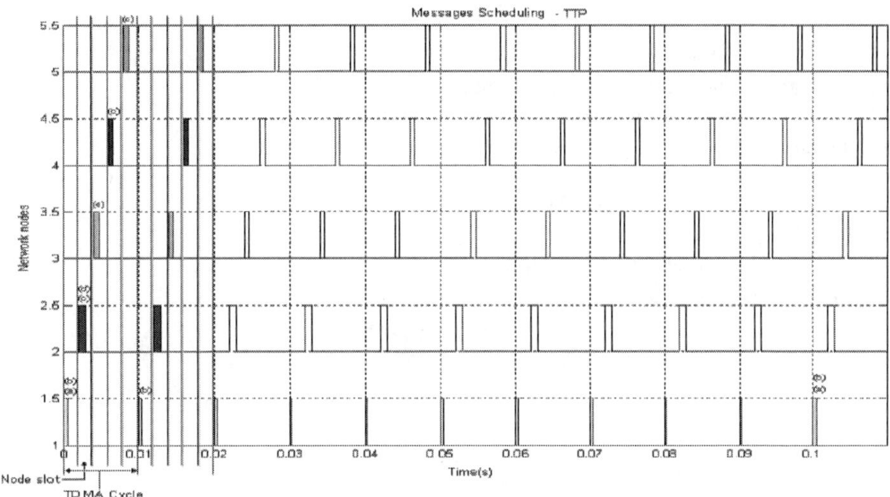

Figure 7. Control Traffic in TTP/C

is considered. It can be observed that there is no contention because messages are transmitted in dedicated slots according to the TDMA scheme.

CONCLUDING REMARKS

This paper presented a general overview on current challenges related to the design of embedded DCS by discussing the properties of different communication paradigms proposed for bus architectures and then by analyzing the dependability goals for the emerging class of safety-critical applications. Besides that, a case study was provided to show the difference with respect to time behavior between the event-triggered and time-triggered communication paradigms.

As the rigorousness of requirements grows new protocols became necessary. In this context, TTP/C and FlexRay are the most imminent solutions to be adopted by the automotive industry. However, the authors consider that the construction of other hybrid bus architectures (to handle asynchronous events and control traffic), and the development of new software-assisted design tools are interesting research areas in the embedded distributed system domain.

REFERENCES

[1] Wolfhard Lawrenz. *CAN System Engineering: From.Theory to Practical Applications*. Springer, 1st Edition, October 1997.

[2] LIN Consortium. LIN Specification Package. Revision 2.0. September 2003.

[3] Herman Kopetz et al. Specification of the TTP/A Protocol V2.00. September 2002.

[4] CAN in Automation, CAN Specification 2.0.

[5] Time-Triggered Protocol TTP/C High-Level Specification Document Protocol Version 1.1. November 2003. TTA Group.

[6] FlexRay Communications System Protocol Specification Version 2.0. Copyright c2004 FlexRay Consortium.

[7] Kopetz, H. Event-Triggered versus Time-Triggered Real Time Systems. Research Report Nr. 8/91. 1991.

[8] John Rushby. Bus Architectures For Safety-Critical Embbeded Systems. Proceedings of EMSOFT, 2001.

[9] Copyright-c BMW AG. byteflight Specification Version 0.5

[10] Algirdas Avizienis et al. Basic Concept and Taxonomy of Dependable and Secure Computing, Proceedings IEEE Transactions on Dependable and Secure Computing, January 2004.

[11] Henriksson, D.; Cervin A.; Arzén, K. TrueTime: Simulation of Control Loops Under Shared Computer Resources. 15th IFAC World Congress on Automatic Control, Barcelona, Spain 2002.

2005-01-1540

An Adaptive Data-Reduction Protocol for the Future In-Vehicle Networks

Praveen R. Ramteke and Syed Masud Mahmud
Electrical and Computer Engineering Department, Wayne State University

ABSTRACT

The demand for drive-by-wire, pre-crash warnings, telematics and many new features will require very high bandwidth from future in-vehicle networks. One straightforward solution to satisfy the bandwidth requirements of future vehicle networks would be to use a higher bandwidth bus or to use multiple busses. However, the use of a higher bandwidth bus would increase the cost of the network. Similarly, the use of multiple busses would increase the cost and the complexity of the wiring. Another option would be the development of a higher layer protocol to reduce the amount of data to be transferred. This paper presents an adaptive data-reduction algorithm based on the CAN (Controller Area Network) protocol.

INTRODUCTION

As automakers are incorporating more and more advanced features into vehicles, there is a growing need for enhanced processing power. S. Channon and P. Miller [1] estimate that the number of microprocessors per vehicle will increase exponentially and by the end of year 2010, the number of microprocessors in any high-end vehicle will be 250. Also, the application areas that demand more processing power are active safety systems, infotainment (TV, Video, gaming and navigation systems), and drive-by-wire systems. Additionally, functional integration of individual sensors will be necessary for applications such as collision avoidance. These additional functionalities can be achieved by increasing the number of nodes or Electronic Control Modules (ECM's), sensors and actuators that can exchange data among various other nodes in the network. However, the data traffic over the high-speed communication bus, like CAN, will increase significantly with the increase in the number of ECM's. Another important requirement would be to communicate data between the various ECM's in real time for safety-critical applications. Failure to communicate data within a given period of time may lead to degradation in system performance and may put the occupant's life in danger.

In order to address the bandwidth concerns and eliminate message latencies, data-reduction (DR) techniques have been developed which communicate large amounts of data in a short period of time, consuming very less bandwidth. DR techniques have been applied extensively for the task of image compression (e.g. MPEG, JPEG), data compression and digital data transmission.

Due to the safety-critical nature of automotive multiplexing system, selection of an optimum data-reduction technique is imperative to ensure proper system performance. An optimum DR technique can be characterized as the one that consumes the least network bandwidth and has zero message latency. Many DR techniques have been proposed for automotive multiplexing environment. Kempf *et al.* [2] and Michael *et al.* [3] recognized six data reduction algorithms, which could be applied to automotive multiplexing environment. The major drawback of all the DR techniques was that they could only be applied to text-data classes in automotive body electronics [3].

Misbahuddin *et al.*[4] proposed a generalized data-reduction algorithm that could be applied to all data classes found in automotive multiplexing environment. The algorithm is based on the SAE J1939 protocol [5]. This algorithm uses the fact that some of the bytes in the data field of the J1939 message remain constant over a period of time and that many of them change slowly [6]. For example, car speed, wheel speed, gas level, gear position etc. Also, these messages are sent at periodic intervals of time. For example, wheel speed data may be sent every 5 milliseconds and gas level may be indicated every 500 milliseconds. The bit reserved by SAE for future use or *R* bit in the protocol data unit (PDU) within the J1939 message is used to indicate data compression. The *R* bit is set to "1" and "0" to indicate compression and no compression, respectively. Each intelligent control module (ICM) in the multiplexing system consists of a transmit buffer (T_BUF) and a receive buffer (R_BUF). Each ICM keeps a copy of the most recently transmitted message in the T_BUF and a copy of the most recently received message in the R_BUF. Suppose an ICM transmits a message *ri* every *t* time units. The transmitting ICM keeps a copy of message *ri* in its T_BUF. The next time the ICM transmits a message *ri* after *t* time units, the ICM compares the data field of the previous *ri*, saved in the T_BUF, with the current message being transmitted. In the event that two or more of the data bytes of the current transmitted message are of same magnitude as of the message in T_BUF, the transmitting ICM realizes that few of the data bytes have been repeated. The transmitter then initiates a series of steps outlined below, to implement data compression.

1. The transmitter sets the *R* bit or data compression bit (DCB) in the PDU to "1".

2. The transmitter prepares a compression code (CC) to indicate repeated bytes in the recently transmitted message.

3. Each bit in the CC indicates a data byte in the message. The bits in the CC are set to "1" or "0" to indicate a repeated byte or non-repeated byte in the message, respectively. For example, if byte 3 in the message is repeated then bit 3 in CC is set to "1" and so on.

4. The non-repeated bytes are concatenated after the CC in the data field of the message being transmitted over the bus.

At the receiver, the ICM keeps a copy of the most recently received message in its R_BUF to perform decompression. The following steps are involved in data decompression process at the receiving end.

1. The receiver checks the DCB of the received message.

2. If DCB is "1", then the receiver treats the first byte in the data field of the received message as the CC.

3. The receiver retrieves the repeated data bytes by indexing through the R_BUF and fetching bytes whose corresponding bits in the CC have a value "1". For example, byte 3 is fetched if bit 3 in CC is "1".

4. The entire message is recreated using the repeated bytes from R_BUF and non-repeated bytes from the received message.

This algorithm works very well when data bytes within the message remain constant with high probabilities. However, in real life situations, one or more parameters in the message may fluctuate at low rates. For example, during braking, car speed may decrease at a constant rate say 8 miles/sec^2, or during acceleration the speed may increase at 4 miles/sec^2. Under such conditions, the above protocol would transmit the entire length of the data bytes used to represent the particular parameter even though the change in value of the parameter is very less. In the worst-case scenario, if all the parameters in the message change by small amounts, the algorithm would transmit all the eight bytes of the message without leading to any DR. This is highly undesirable since it would lead to high bus utilization and consumption of unnecessary bandwidth.

To overcome this drawback of the previous DR algorithm, we present an Adaptive Data-Reduction (ADR) algorithm. The algorithm is designed to be compatible with the CAN protocol since CAN is the standard protocol used in many present-day automobiles [7]. However, the algorithm can be applied to any SAE J1939 protocol with slight changes in the software. The following section presents the details of the adaptive-data reduction algorithm.

PROPOSED DATA REDUCTION ALGORITHM

The proposed ADR algorithm consists of two parts

- Non-Adaptive data-reduction
- Adaptive data-reduction

The ADR algorithm encompasses some of the desirable features of the DR algorithm presented in [4] with some notable changes.

1. The *R* bit or DCB is ignored.

2. The data field of CAN message is divided into signal fields of varying lengths instead of data bytes. This means that individual signal values in the messages can cross byte boundaries or can be contained in less than one byte.

Point 2 above springs from the fact that all signal values in a message cannot be contained in one byte. For example, on the one hand, engine RPM requires 16 bits and on the other hand, gear position can be indicated using just 3 bits. A clear understanding of the data field format of the CAN message can be obtained from Figure 1. The engine control module generates this message. Engine speed or RPM occupies two data bytes within the message and gas level occupies 7 bits. The following sections explain the details of the ADR technique.

DATA REDUCTION TECHNIQUE

An automotive multiplexing system consists of many nodes interconnected between each other using a high-speed bus. The nodes contain sensors, which periodically communicate to send the change in some parameter values to the Electronic Control Unit (ECU), which in turn ensures optimum operation of the entire vehicle by actuating certain precise operations based on the input parameter values. Additionally, each node transmits and receives a fixed set of messages [8]. We have made the following assumptions for the DR algorithm.

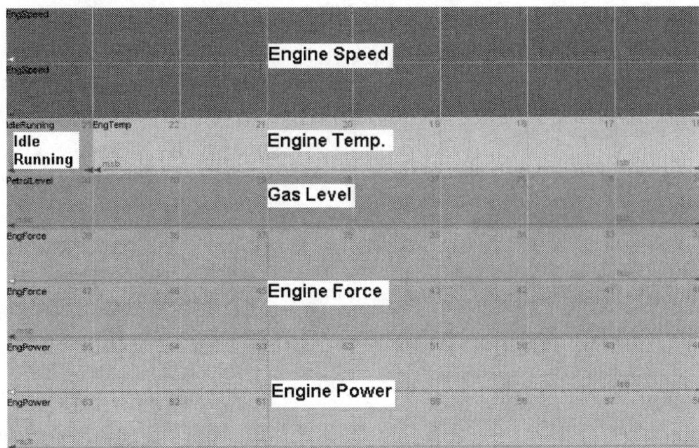

Figure 1. Data field of a CAN message showing various signal fields within the message. Each row indicates a data byte and each column indicates a bit. Some signals within the data field occupy more than a byte where as some others occupy one byte or less.

1. All messages in the system have their compressed version whose individual signal field lengths (in bits) are predefined based on the periodic message transmission rate and rate of change of the signal parameter.

2. The identifiers of the compressed messages differ from the identifiers of their original counterparts by a value of minus one. For example, if the identifier of a normal CAN message is 20, then the identifier of its compressed version would be 19.

3. Each CAN node in the network consists of two buffers called TX_BUF and RX_BUF to store the transmitted and received messages respectively. The TX_BUF and RX_BUF consist of two fields. One field stores the 11-bit (or 29-bit) identifier of the CAN message and another stores its 8-byte data field.

Data Compression

Each CAN node in the network transmits messages at fixed intervals of time depending on the nature of the message being sent. Let us assume that the transmitting unit of each node transmits messages every *t* time units where value of *t* may vary depending on the specific application. A safety critical message will have a very low value for the period *t* when compared to a non-safety critical message.

Assume that a CAN node transmits a message *ci* at time *m.* At time *m,* a copy of the sent message *ci* is stored in the TX_BUF of the transmitting node. When the next *ci* is being transmitted at time *m* + *t* time units, a comparison is made between the data fields of the message stored in TX_BUF at time *m* with that of the current message being transmitted at time *m* + *t.* Depending on the content of the new message, two types of DR techniques can be applied.

1. Non- adaptive DR

2. Adaptive DR

Let us explore the two techniques further.

Non-Adaptive Data-Reduction

This technique is applied for the case when none of the bytes in the data field of the new message *ci* at time *m* + *t,* change their value since their previous transmission at time *m*. In such a situation, the entire message at time *m* + *t* is not transmitted. The receiving node in the network assumes the most recent value of the message *ci* as the current value of the message. However, this technique has a drawback. In the event that none of the signal fields in the message *ci* change their value over a long period of time, the transmitting node will not transmit the message *ci* until it changes its value. To overcome this shortcoming, a copy of the most recent message *ci* is transmitted to the receiving node at every *y* intervals of time where *y>>t*. The value of *y* again depends on the safety-critical nature of the message. In the event of sudden and rapid changes in value of the signals, for example, during hard braking or hard acceleration, normal transmission of CAN messages over the bus resumes till a steady state is reached.

Adaptive Data-Reduction

Adaptive DR is based on the technique of delta modulation or differential pulse code modulation (DPCM) [9] that is widely used in the area digital communications. It is based on the principle that instead of sending the absolute value of a signal at each time instant, only the changes in the signal values from one time instance to another (delta) are transmitted.

To achieve data reduction, the first byte in the data field of the CAN message is used to indicate delta compression. This byte is called the delta compression code (DCC). In the ADR technique, if one or more signal fields in the message *ci* transmitted at time *m* + *t* change their value since their previous transmission at time *m*, the transmitting node executes the following series of steps.

1. The transmitting node computes a delta compression code (DCC). A value of “1” in the DCC indicates the delta change in the value of the signal rather than the absolute value. A value of “0” in DCC indicates no change in the value of the signal.

2. Since a copy of the message transmitted at time *m* is stored in TX_BUF, the transmitting node computes differences (deltas) in the value of the corresponding signals in TX_BUF at time *m* with that at time *m* + *t.*

3. The compressed version of the original CAN message having an identifier whose value is one less than the value of the identifier of the original message is encoded with the delta signal values.

4. The delta-compressed CAN message carrying the delta signals is sent over the CAN bus to the receiving node.

5. In the event that the value of a delta signal exceeds the length of the assigned field, the absolute values of all the signals (i.e. the original CAN message) are transmitted rather than the delta-compressed version of the message. This assumption is based on the fact that a drastic change in the value of a particular signal could reflect a critical condition in which case it would be necessary to communicate absolute values of all signals within the message.

The entire data-compression process is depicted using the flow chart of Figure 3.

Figure 2 shows the format of the data field of the delta-compressed message of Figure 1. The engine module generates this particular message. The first eight bits of the data field are the DCC. The signals within the delta-compressed message occupy half the number of bytes when compared to the original message of Figure 1.

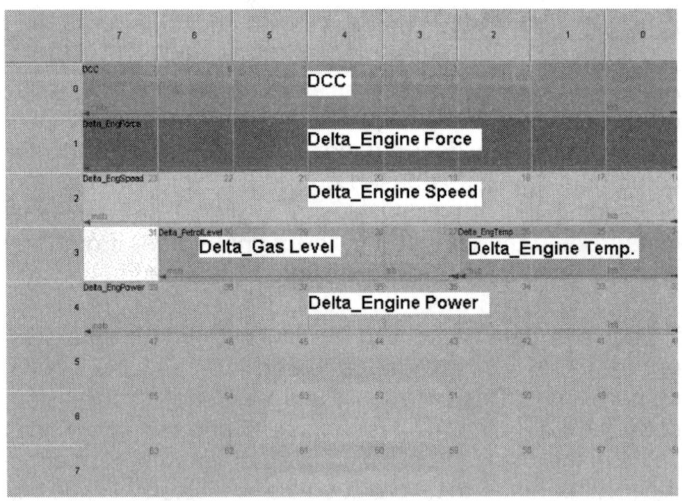

Figure 2. Data field format of delta-compressed message of Figure 1.

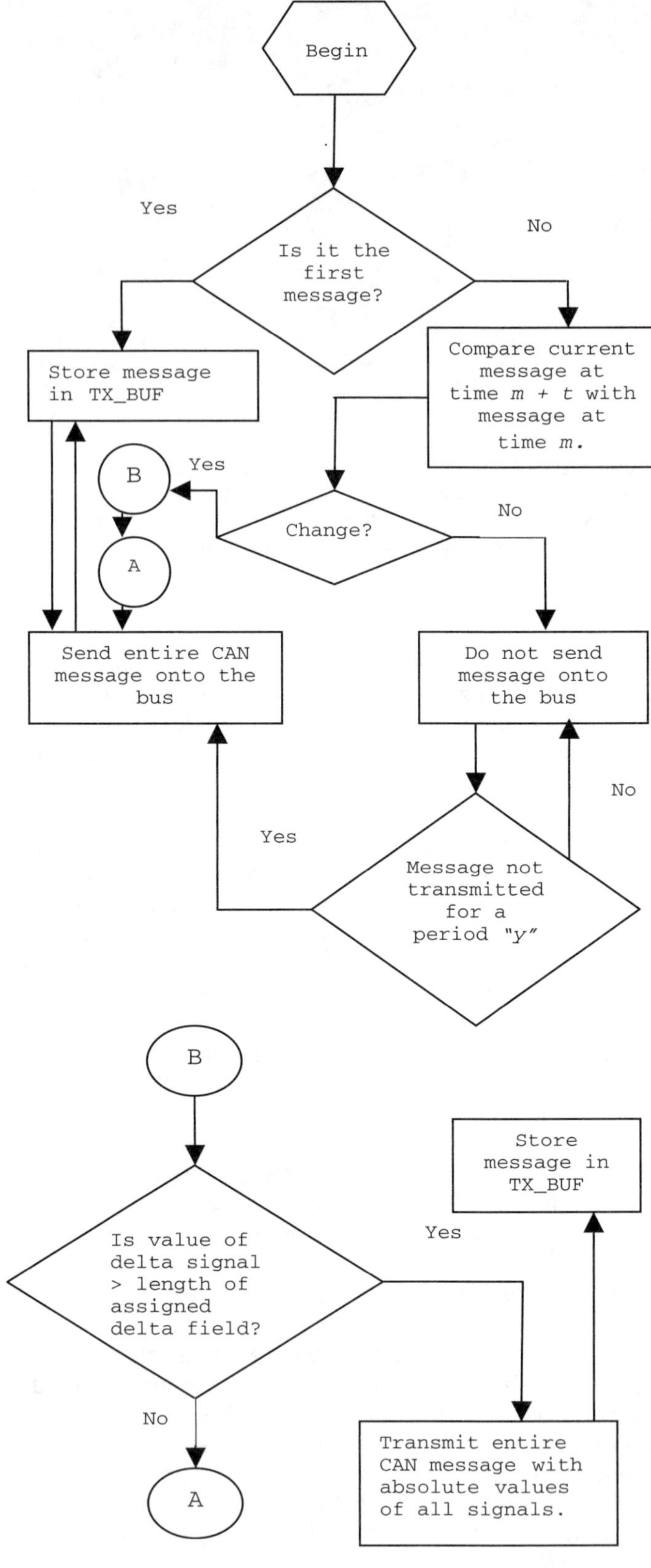

Figure 3. Adaptive data-reduction algorithm

Data-Decompression

The receiving node in the system decompresses the delta-compressed CAN message sent by the transmitter. The following series of steps are executed to perform

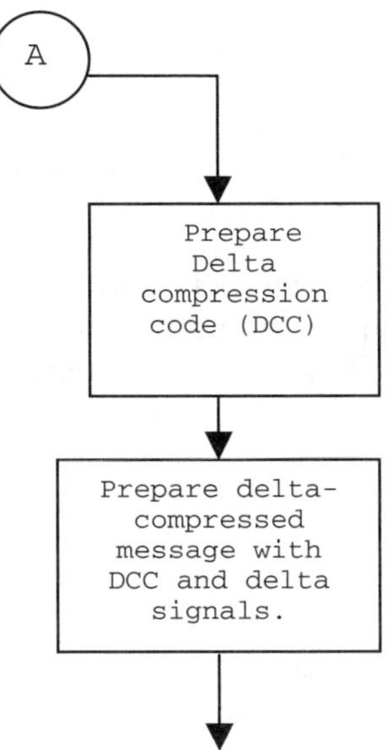

Figure 3. Adaptive data-reduction algorithm continued.

data-decompression. Assuming that a delta-compressed message *Dci* is received,

1. The receiving node checks the identifier of the CAN message *Dci*. If the message is a delta-compressed message, the first byte in the data field of the message is treated as the DCC.

2. The receiver then fetches a copy of the most recently received *ci* from the RX_BUF.

3. The DCC acts as an index to the corresponding signal fields within the delta-compressed message. For example, a value of "1" in the first bit position of the DCC means that the first signal field within the message is a delta signal of the first signal field within the message *ci* from RX_BUF. This delta signal is either added to or subtracted from the corresponding signal field within the message *ci* from RX_BUF to get the new value of the signal.

4. A value of "0" in the DCC means that the corresponding signal has not changed its value since the previous transmission. The absolute value of this signal is fetched from the previous *ci* in RX_BUF.

5. The receiver reconstructs all the signals within the message in a similar fashion.

6. The receiver then updates the RX_BUF with this new message, overwriting the previous *ci*.

The data-decompression process is illustrated graphically below.

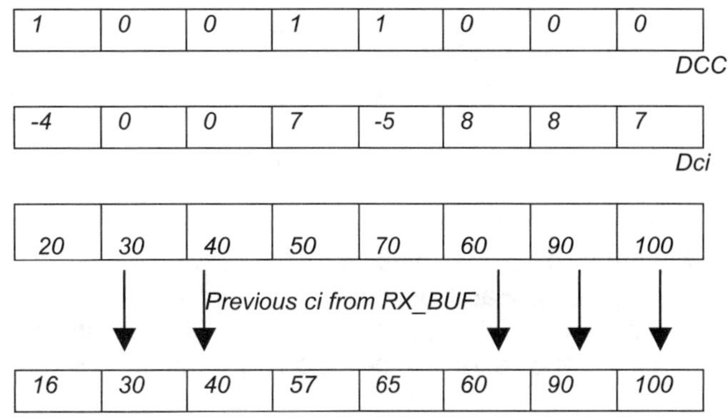

Figure 4. Data-decompression process.

The first row shows the mapping of the bits in the DCC of the received delta-compressed message. The second row is the delta-compressed message *Dci,* which holds delta values of all signal fields within any given message. Third row is the most recent copy of the message *ci* from the RX_BUF. A value of "1" in DCC indicates that the corresponding fields of *Dci* contain the delta values. In this example, delta signals corresponding to a "1" in DCC are -4, 7 and -5. These delta values are then added to the corresponding signal fields of the previous message *ci* in RX_BUF. All other signal fields within the new message retain previous values from the *ci* in RX_BUF. The RX_BUF is then updated with this new message.

The entire data decompression process is depicted in the flow chart of Figure 6. The following section presents simulation results for the presented ADR algorithm.

RESULTS AND DISCUSSIONS

A simulation program has been developed to analyze the performance of the adaptive DR algorithm. The main performance parameters considered are the bus load, message transmission rate (MTR) and the average length of messages (ALM). The simulation model consists of five CAN nodes each of which transmits a predefined set of messages. The distribution of messages among the five nodes is shown in Table I. Their corresponding periodic transmission rates are also included.

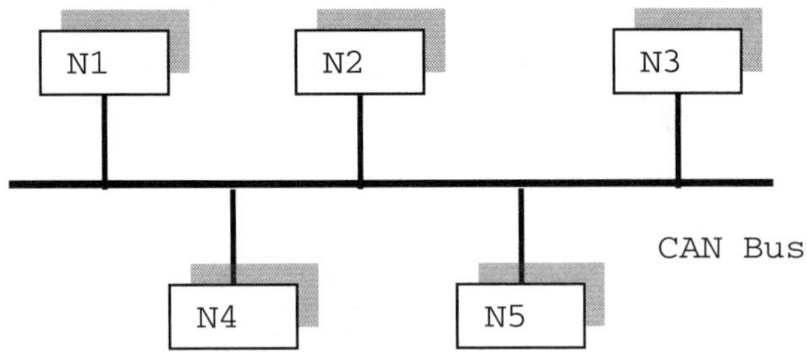

Figure 5. Simulation model consisting of 5 CAN nodes.

The simulation model consisting of 5 CAN nodes is shown in Figure 5. Each of the nodes numbered N1 to N5 consists of the TX_BUF and the RX_BUF to store the transmitted and received messages, respectively.

Table I. Distribution of messages among nodes in the simulation model.

Node Number	Message ID's	Periodic transmission rate (in milliseconds)
1	99 and 100	5
	101 and 102	5
2	200 and 201	5
3	1019 and 1020	50
4	1050 and 1051	500
	1052 and 1053	500
5	272 and 273	500

All message ID's on the left of the message ID column are the ID's of the delta-compressed message. The simulation has been developed to monitor the behavior of the system during three operating conditions.

1. During transient operation of the system i.e. during engine start and acceleration.

2. During steady-state operation i.e. under cruise control, and

3. During hard braking or deceleration.

We will further analyze the performance of the system under these three operating conditions. For the sake of comparison, we will consider the cases when no DR was applied and when non-adaptive and adaptive data-reduction techniques were applied under the three operating conditions. Bus-load, the number of data frames per second or MTR and the average length of messages or ALM have been monitored to evaluate the performance of the ADR algorithm. We will first analyze the system performance under the transient and steady-state conditions.

CASE 1: TRANSIENT AND STEADY-STATE OPERATION

The graphs of Figure 7 through Figure 9 compare the simulation results for the system under transient and steady-state, with no DR and when non-adaptive DR is applied. The variation of different signals within a message (in this case engine data) during transient and steady state is shown in Figure 10. The variation in the MTR is compared in Figure 7.

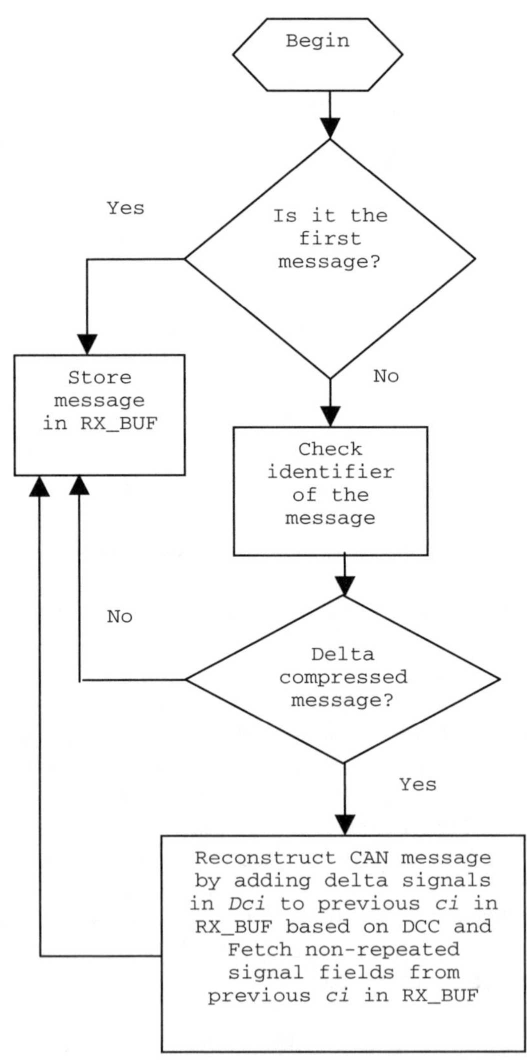

Figure 6. Data-decompression algorithm.

In the transient state, which lasts for sixty seconds after start of simulation, the MTR reaches a peak value of 138 frames/second at time T1 for both the cases, i.e. when no DR is performed and when non-adaptive DR is performed. After the transient period, the system reaches the steady state where all the signals reach a constant value. During the steady state, there is a considerable decrease in the MTR for the case when non-adaptive DR is applied. The MTR falls to 44 frames/second at time T2 reducing the number of message transmissions by 50 in comparison to the case where no DR is used. This gives a compression ratio of 53% over the case when no DR was applied.

The variation in the bus-load is compared in Figure 8. During the transient state, the variation in bus-load is the same for the cases when no DR is performed and when non-adaptive DR is performed. Notable gain in the parameter is made during the steady-state operation where majority of the signals do not vary rapidly from one instance to another and hence the message is not repeated unless there is significant change in its value since the previous transmission. During the steady-state operation, the peak bus-load at time T2 reduced from 18.55% to 7.98% giving a total bandwidth saving of 56% when compared to the case where no DR was applied.

Figure 9 compares the average lengths of the messages (ALM) transmitted between various nodes during the simulation. The ALM remained constant over majority of the simulation run for the two cases when no DR was applied and when non-adaptive DR was applied. However, as the system approached the steady state, minute reductions in the ALM were observed for the case when non-adaptive DR was applied. This is due to the fact that as the system reached the steady state, the small variations in the signals were transmitted in the delta-compressed messages.

CASE 2: HARD BRAKING OR DECELERATION

The performance of the ADR algorithm during the condition of hard braking or deceleration can be analyzed from the graphs of Figure 11 through Figure 13. The variation in MTR during hard braking with no DR and with ADR is compared in Figure 11. During hard braking, the behavior of the system is similar to the behavior during the transient state. The MTR reaches its peak value of 138 frames/second and 137 frames/second at the instance when the brake is applied at time T2, when no DR and when ADR is applied, respectively. There is no significant reduction in the MTR for the case when ADR is applied since the periodic rate of transmission of the delta-compressed messages is similar to the transmission rates of their uncompressed counterparts. After the period of braking, the system again goes to the steady state. The variation of the various signals within a message (in this case engine data) during the application of the brake is shown in Figure 14.

The variation in bus-load is compared in Figure 12. The application of brake leads to the transmission of the delta-compressed messages and hence, the peak bus-load at time T2 increases slightly to a value of 16.97%. A total bandwidth saving of 43% was gained in comparison to the case where no DR was applied.

Figure 13 compares the ALM for the cases when no DR is applied and when ADR is applied. There is a decrease in ALM when ADR is applied since the delta-compressed messages having a smaller duration are transmitted during the application of brakes. The ALM decreases to a value of 0.2 ms at time T2 when brakes are applied giving a total reduction of ((0.30-0.20)/ 0.30)*100= 33% in the ALM when compared to the case when no DR was applied. Table II summarizes the percentage gain in the values of various performance parameters with the application of non-adaptive and ADR algorithms.

Table II. Gain in the values of performance parameters in comparison to the case when no DR was applied to the system.

	% decrease in bus load	% decrease in MTR	% decrease in ALM
Non-adaptive DR	56%	53%	0%
Adaptive DR	43%	0%	33%

CONCLUSION

The performance of an adaptive data-reduction algorithm for future in-vehicle networking applications has been presented. The algorithm is based on the CAN protocol and uses the fact that some of the signals within a CAN message do not change their value from one transmission time instance to another. Another observation is that some of the signal values change by small amounts i.e. during cruise control or deceleration. The algorithm exploits the above two observations to decrease the amount of data traffic to be transmitted over the CAN bus. In the first case, the algorithm refrains from transmitting the repeated messages during successive transmitting instances and in the second case, the algorithm transmits only the delta-change in the value of signals from one transmitting instance to another. The adaptive data reduction (ADR) algorithm generates a delta compression code (DCC) to indicate signals whose corresponding delta values have been transmitted. A dynamic event-based simulation has been developed to analyze the performance of the presented ADR algorithm. The simulation of the algorithm has shown promising results in terms of the reduction in the values of important parameters like message transmission rate (MTR), bus-load and average length of messages (ALM). The reduction in the values of these parameters enables us to cater to the bandwidth requirements of new nodes into the network to provide advanced features like infotainment and active safety etc., without increasing the overall cost of the system.

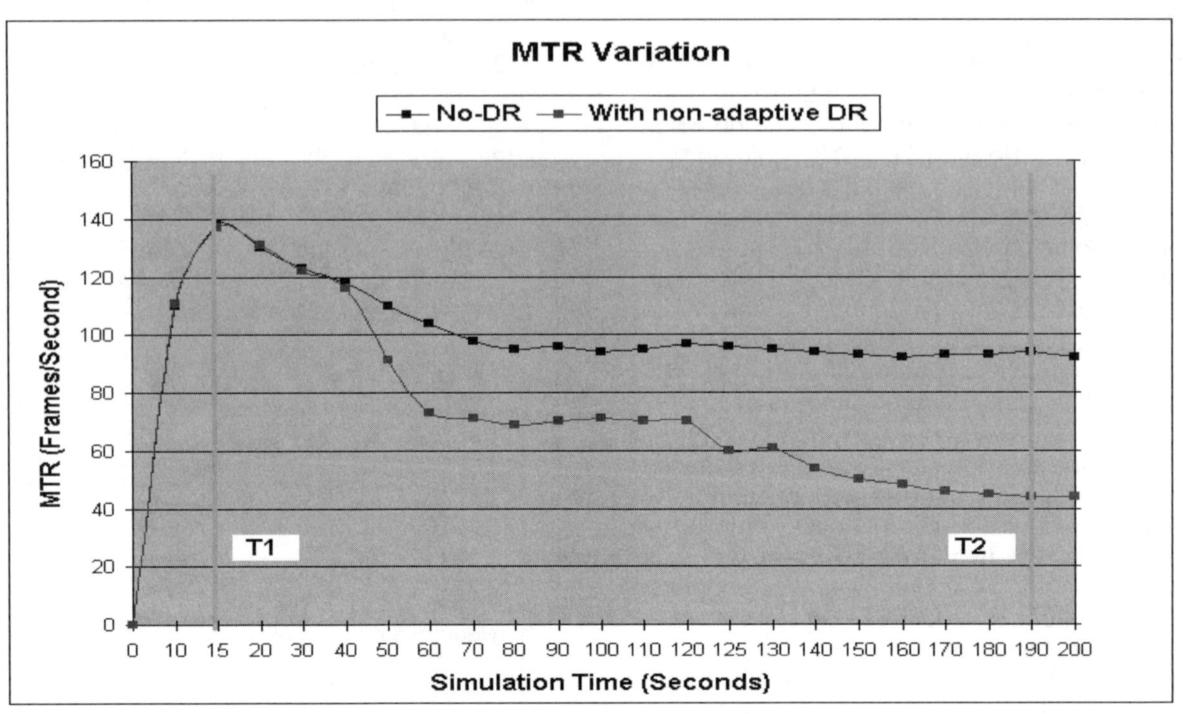

Figure 7. Message transmission rate (MTR) comparison.

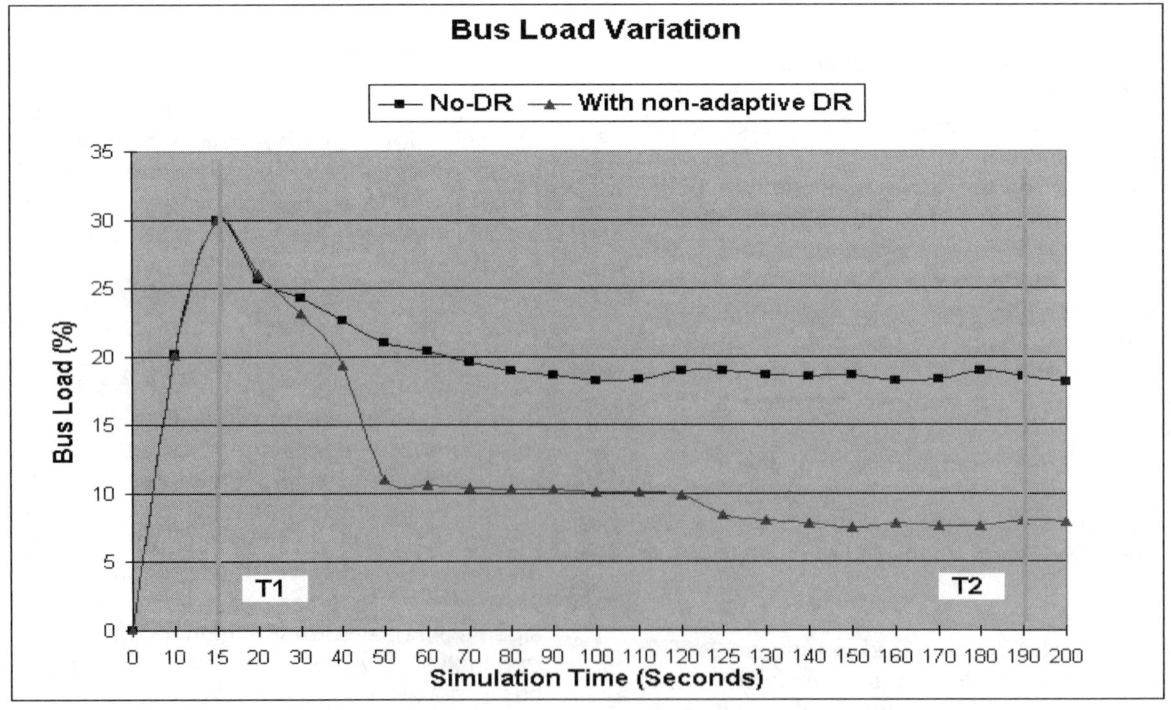

Figure 8. Bus load Comparison.

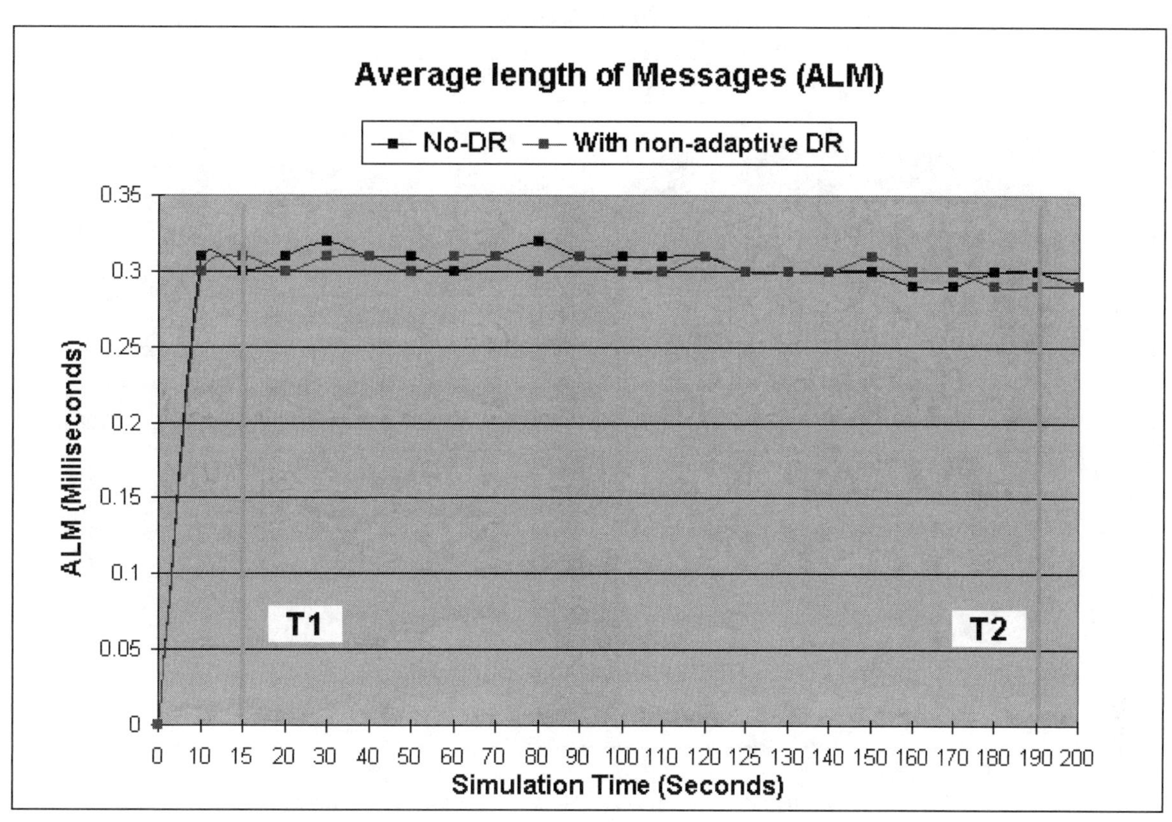

Figure 9. Average message length (ALM) comparison.

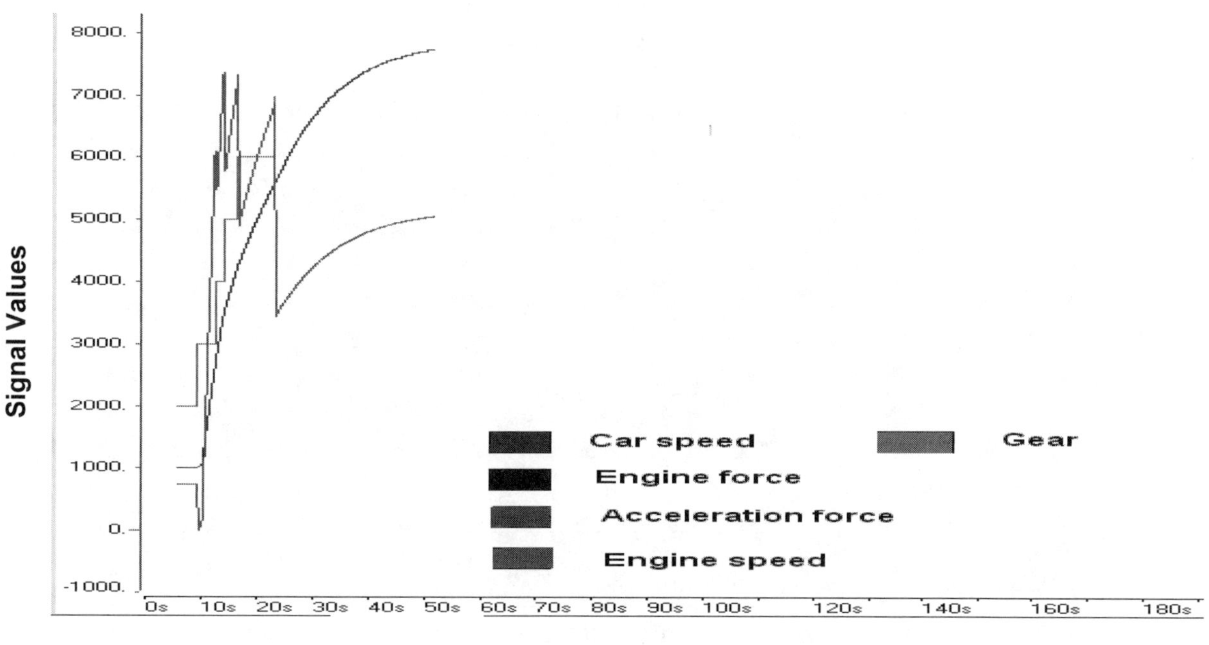

Figure 10. Variation of different signals during transient and steady state.

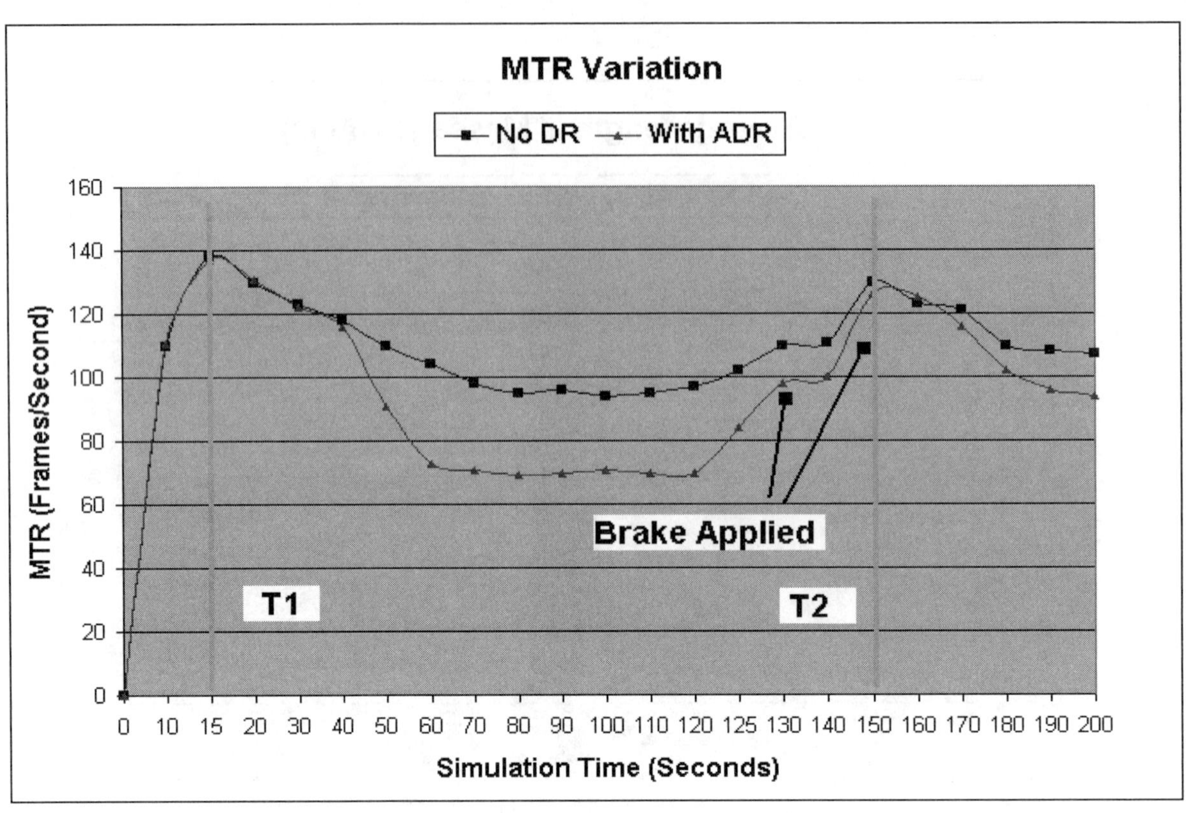

Figure 11. Message transmission rate (MTR) comparison during hard braking.

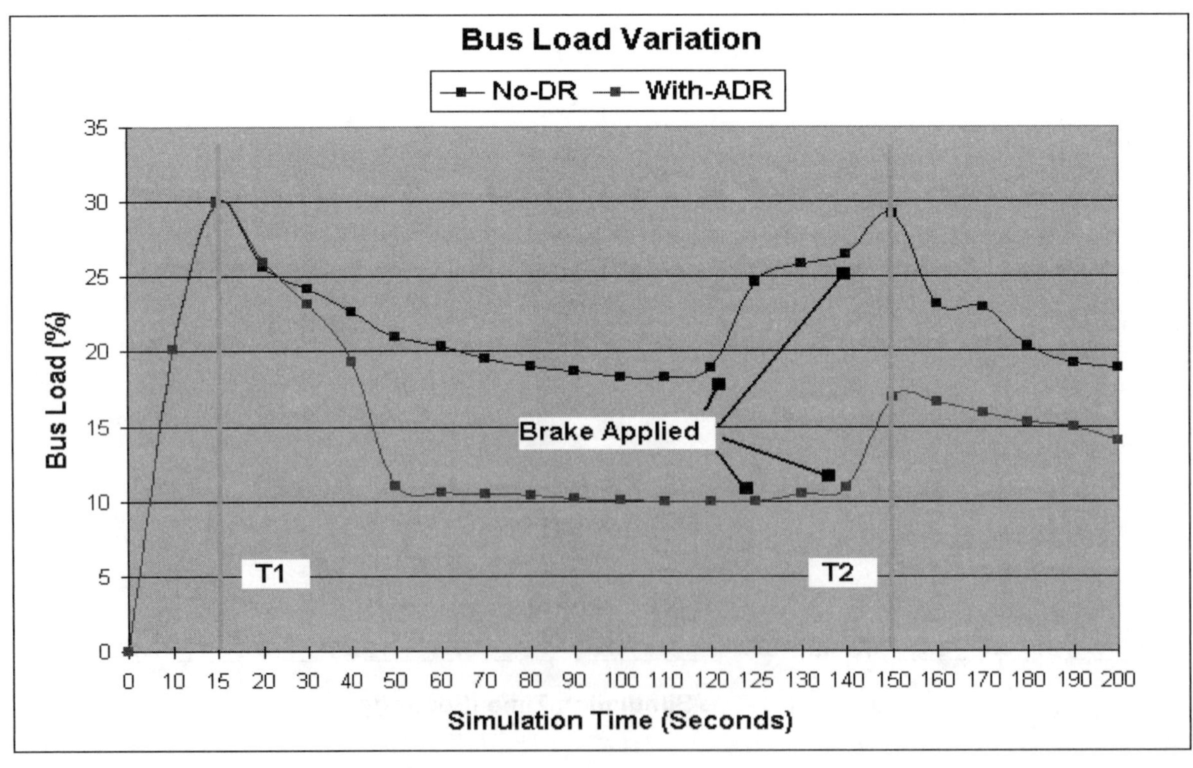

Figure 12. Bus load comparison during hard braking.

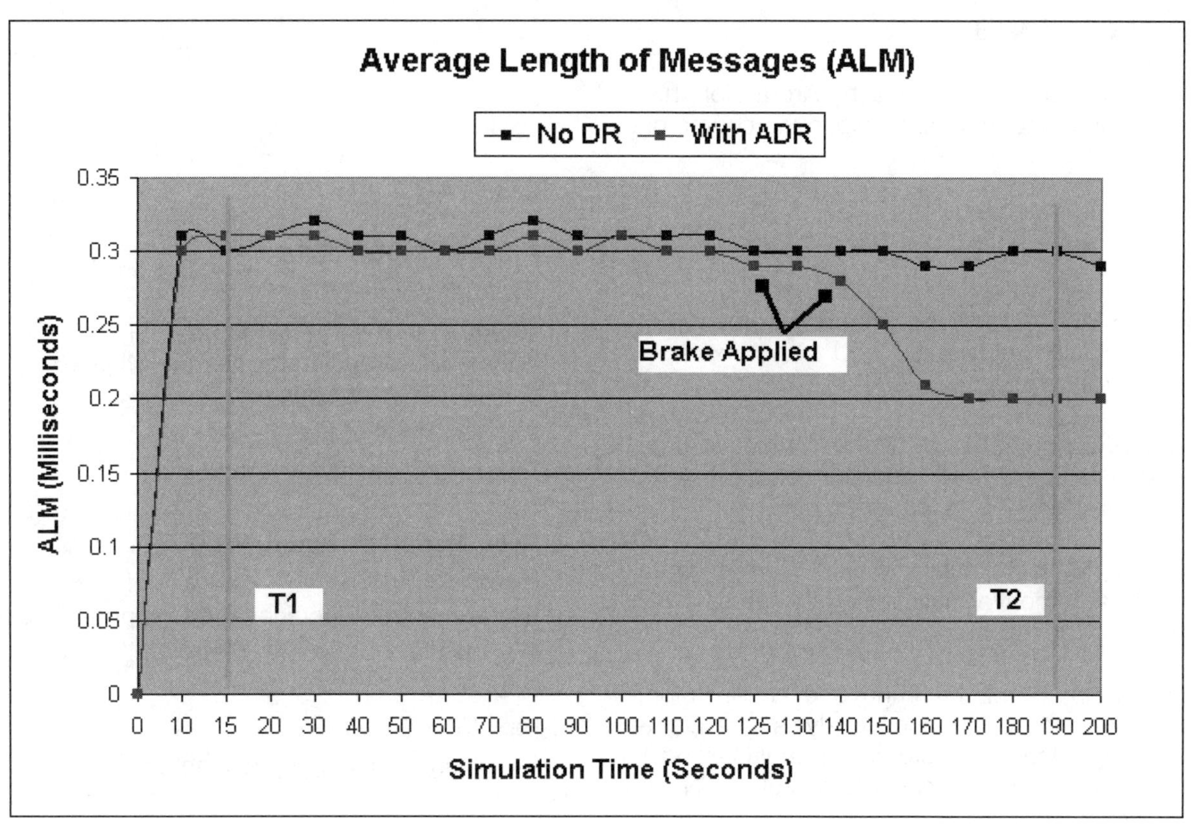

Figure 13. Average message length (ALM) comparison during hard braking.

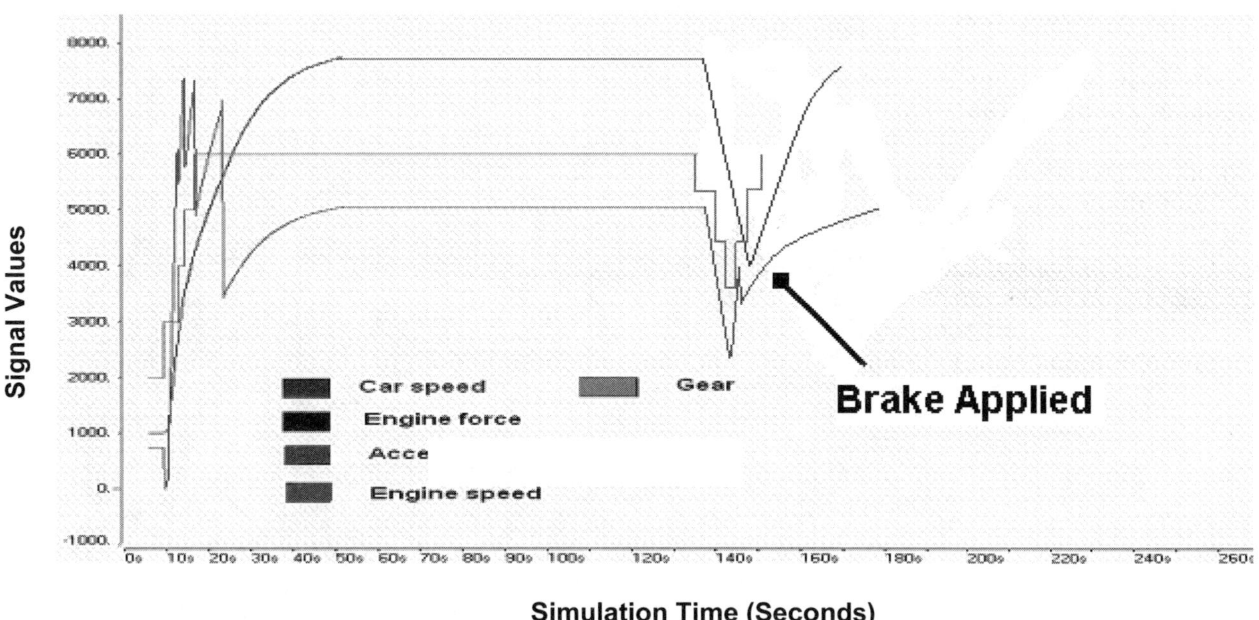

Figure 14. Variation of different signals during transient state, steady state and during hard braking or deceleration.

ACKNOWLEDGEMENTS

I would like to thank Mr. Aakash Arora for his constructive criticism and immense help in the course of this work.

REFERENCES

1. S. Channon and P. Miller, "The requirements of future in-vehicle networks and an example implementation," SAE paper 2004-01-0206.

2. G. G. Kempf and K. Strenzl, "Robust adaptive data compression for peak-load reduction in automotive multiplexing systems," SAE paper 941 658, pp. 1-5.

3. G. G. Kempf, M. J. Eckrich, and O. J. Rumpf, "Data reduction in automotive multiplexing systems," SAE paper 940 135, pp. 45-50.

4. S. Misbahuddin, S. M. Mahmud and N. Al-Holou, "Development and performance analysis of a Data-Reduction algorithm for automotive multiplexing,", *IEEE Trans. on Vehicular Technology,* Vol. 50, No.1, pp. 162-169.

5. "Recommended practice for serial control and communications vehicle network (Class C)," SAE draft J1939, 1939.

6. SAE recommended practice, "Vehicle application layer,", SAE J1939/71, Aug. 1994.

7. Bosch, "CAN specification Ver 2.0," Robert Bosch GmbH, Stuttgart, Germany, 1991.

8. R. Masaki *et al.,* "Development of class C multiplex control IC,",SAE paper 930 003, 1993.

9. Bill Waggener, "*Pulse Code Modulation Techniques: With Applications in Communications and Data Recording (Electrical Engineering)*," Kluwer Academic Publishers, 15 January, 1995.

CONTACT

Praveen R. Ramteke
Graduate Student
Department of Electrical and Computer Engineering
Wayne State University, Detroit, MI 48202
Phone: (313) 577-3855
Fax: (313) 577-1101
Email: ramteke@wayne.edu

Syed Masud Mahmud, Ph.D.
Associate Professor
Department of Electrical and Computer Engineering
Wayne State University, Detroit, MI 48202
Phone: (313) 577-3855
Fax: (313) 577-1101
Email: smahmud@eng.wayne.edu

2005-01-1534

Development and Verification of In-Vehicle Networks in a Virtual Environment

Thorsten Gerke
Synopsys, Inc.

Carsten Schanze
Volkswagen AG

ABSTRACT

Due to the increase in demand for comfort and safety features in today's automobiles, the internal vehicle communication networks necessary to accommodate these features are very complex. These networks represent a heterogeneous architecture consisting of several ECUs exchanging information via bus systems such as CAN, LIN, MOST, or FlexRay buses. Development and verification of internal vehicle networks include multiple design layers. These layers are the logical layer represented by the software application, the associated data link layer, and the physical connection layer containing bus interfaces, wires, and termination. Verification of these systems in the early stages of the design process (before a physical network is available for testing) has become a critical need. As a result, the need to simulate these designs at all their levels of complexity has become critically important. Internal vehicle networks can be simulated on many different abstraction levels using various model levels and modeling technologies. Early in the development process, analyses can be performed without having available any detailed models from the chip manufacturer or component supplier. Later in the development process, more accurate models can be integrated into the simulation process, including those provided by suppliers and chip manufacturers. This paper demonstrates a portion of the development and verification process of the physical layer of an internal vehicle CAN bus at Volkswagen using the Saber simulation environment. This paper also demonstrates the integration of portions of the logical layer into simulation so both logical and physical layers can be analyzed together.

INTRODUCTION

Today's automotive networks are very complex and combine a couple of networks together into one heterogeneous network environment. Figure 1 illustrates one portion of such a network where powertrain, body and infotainment system represent separate networks connected together via a gateway. Each sub- network might use different protocols or similar protocols with different transmission rates. Over the past 10 years CAN has become the standard in the automotive industry for applications like powertrain, comfort and infotainment. CAN belongs to the group of serial field bus systems, meaning that all nodes within one network are connected in parallel to every other node in the network. Figure 2

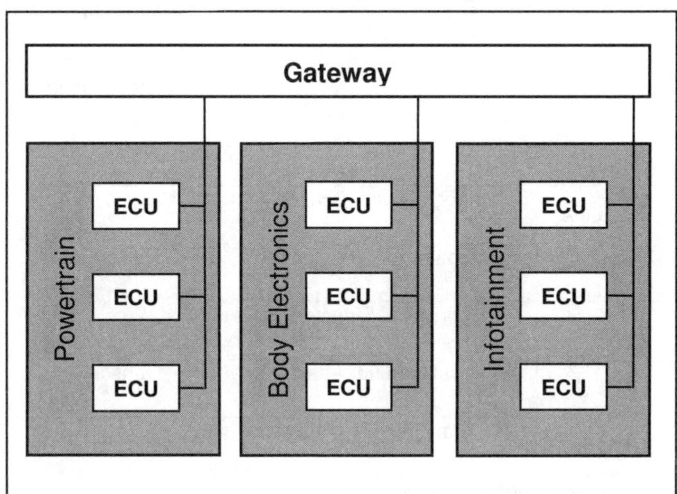

Figure 1 *Vehicle communication architecture*

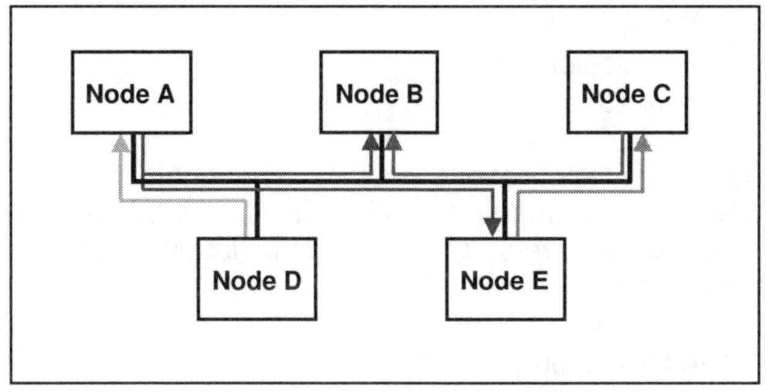

Figure 2 *CAN bus architecture*

shows the general structure of such a CAN bus network architecture with five nodes.

CAN is a multi master network as all network nodes can act as master or slave. During one message frame only one node acts as master and all remaining nodes act as slaves and listen to the bus. The Multi-Master ability of CAN is enabled through a CSMACD+CR (Carrier Sense, Multiple Access/Collision Detection + Collision Resolution) methodology that determines the node that can send its full message frame to the bus via bitwise arbitration. The generic structure of the network architecture, including its applications, is specified in the ISO/OSI layer representation. Every communication system can be described using this standardized 7-layer representation, shown in Figure 3. Only the first two layers are defined for CAN: the first layer describes the physical architecture and the second layer describes the data link layer for CAN.

OSI Layer		Implementation
Application Layer (7)		Microcontroller
:		
Data Link Layer (2)	Logical Link Control	CAN controller
	Medium Access Control	
Physical Layer (1)	Physical Signaling	
	Physical Medium Attachment	Transceiver
	Medium Dependent Interface	
Transmission Medium		

Figure 3 ***ISO/OSI layer***

The physical layer is specified in ISO 11898 and describes the requirements for the physical behavior in order to transmit signals across the CAN network. It specifies, for example, the voltage levels applied for the appropriate bus states. A complete CAN bus network contains the following components:

- CAN node
- Transmission line
- Termination

Usually the applications require additional circuitry in order to ensure immunity against EMC effects. As shown in Figure 4 every CAN node includes four main components:

- CAN transceiver
- CAN controller
- µ-controller
- Interface to sensors and actuators

The CAN transceiver is the interface between the transmission line and the CAN controller. Its task is to transform the logical signals, coming from the CAN controller, into the physical bus levels specified in ISO 11898. It also converts the analog signals received from the bus into logical signals that can be understood by the CAN controller. The CAN controller, also named protocol engine, coordinates the communication between the µ-Controller and the bus via the transceiver. It generates the CAN message frame containing the information that should be submitted to the bus. When the CAN node acts as receiver during a message frame, it reads the message frame and prepares this information for the µ-controller.

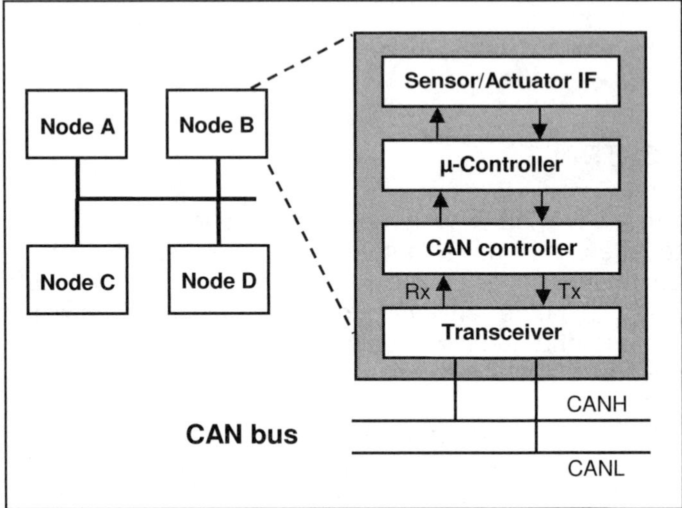

Figure 4 ***Structure of a CAN node***

Whereas the µ-controller runs the appropriate application e.g. the combustion engine control algorithm.

The physical layer of a CAN bus network contains the transmission medium (wire harness), transceiver, the physical signaling of the CAN controller and any additional circuitry necessary to achieve acceptable EMC behavior. This article describes how to model and simulate this physical layer.

PROBLEMS WHEN VERIFYING THE PHYSICAL LAYER OF A CAN NETWORK

The problem of verifying the physical layer of a CAN bus network is to guarantee sufficient signal integrity in order to ensure that the CAN controller always samples the correct bit value representing the current state on the bus.

SIGNAL INTEGRITY

Unlike the digital controller signals (Tx, Rx), signals on the physical layer (CANH, CANL) are analog quantities. The integrity of these analog signals depend on several factors:

- Network topology
- Interface between the transmission lines and the transceiver
- Transceiver

The topology includes the structure of the network (e.g. a star architecture or a linear bus with stubs), the number of ECUs and the length of the transmission lines. The minimum and maximum number of ECUs are fixed for the specific vehicle platform. However the number between minimum and maximum depends on the configuration of the individual vehicle. The interface between the ECUs and the transmission lines consists of passive elements like capacitors, ESD protection (e.g. varistors), termination resistors and common mode chokes. Each of these elements is affected by tolerances due to manufacturing inaccuracies or temperature dependencies.

BIT TIMING CONFIGURATION

Bit timing configuration is one of the important tasks of the verification process. It specifies when the CAN controller samples the bus and determines the transmission rate in the network. It significantly affects the performance of the CAN bus network since a poorly configured bit timing can force a CAN node to go into the error passive state during an arbitration phase. Unlike the digital signals of the controller the signal behavior on the bus is analog. Figure 5 shows this fact.

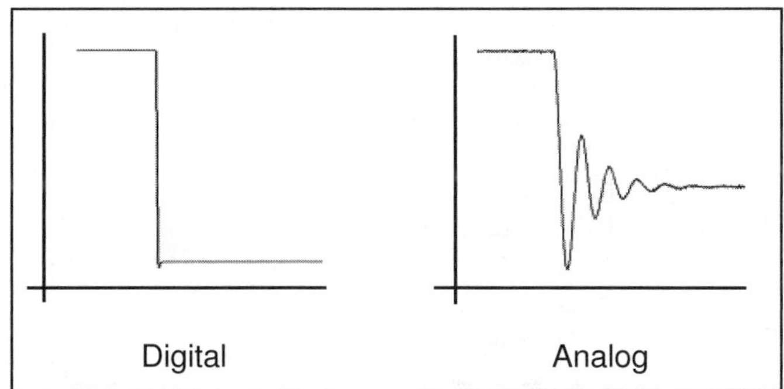

Figure 5 ***Digital vs. analog signal behavior***

The analog signal contains oscillations that can be caused e.g. by reflection or additional EMC protection circuits. Further, even if signal behavior is ideally digital, the CAN nodes are never running synchronously, as the oscillators have manufacturing tolerances and temperature dependencies. In order to compensate these effects every CAN controller has the following set of programmable parameters which are stored in the BTR (Bit Timing Register) memory:

- TSeg1 (Time Segment 1)
- TSeg2 (Time Segment 2)
- BRP (Baud Rate Prescaler)
- SJW (Synchronization Jump Width)

These parameters are used to define the CAN bit time and to control the synchronization process of the protocol engine. The CAN bit time is divided into three segments as shown in Figure 6. The SyncSeg (Synchronization Segment) is the area where the controller expects the edges of the CAN signal during a message frame. TSeg1 and TSeg2 are used to compensate the asynchronous behavior of the CAN nodes. The sample point of the CAN controller is placed between TSeg1 and TSeg2. Each of these segments consists of a certain quantity of time quanta (t_Q) whose length is derived from the oscillator frequency and the BRP. The size of SyncSeg is always one t_Q, whereas the number of t_Q for TSeg1 and TSeg2 can be defined by the user.

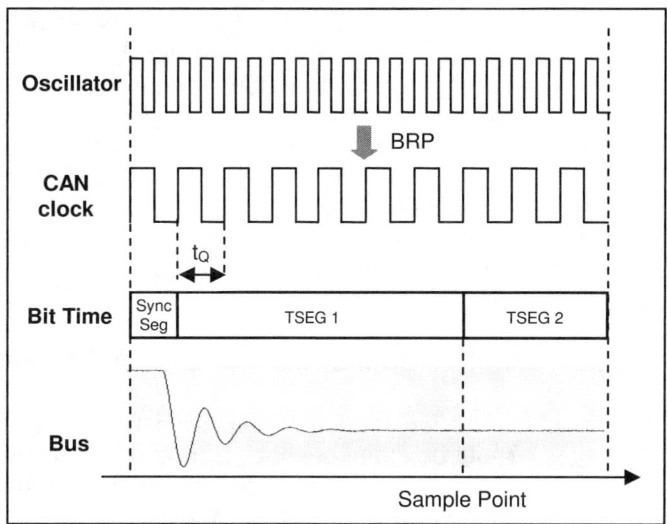

Figure 6 ***CAN bit timing segments***

The CAN controller expects the edges of the CAN signal within the SyncSeg period, but due to oscillator tolerances and propagation delays of the transmission lines and node internal delays (e.g. transceiver), the edges of the CAN signal can occur outside of this segment. The difference between the time quantum, where the edge is recognized, and the SyncSeg is denoted as phase error. In order to compensate this phase error, the CAN controller shifts the sample point, by increasing or decreasing the phase buffer segments TSeg1 and TSeg2 according to the phase error. The synchronization jump width is the maximum number of t_Q that the sample point can be shifted in order to correct the phase error.

CHALLENGE OF VERIFICATION

The verification of the physical layer of the CAN network must ensure that the worst case combination of parameters and tolerances assures sufficient signal integrity so that each allowed bit timing configuration leads to a correct sampled value. Verification by measurements on prototype vehicles is insufficient because the worst case configuration is usually not available during the early stage of the development process and the values of the tolerances are distributed randomly. Changing an existing prototype topology would significantly increase the development costs and time. Therefore the system simulation is a fundamental requirement for the verification of this kind of application in the early stages of a design process.

SIMULATION MODELS

SABER SIMULATION ENVIRONMENT

The complete CAN network and its components were modeled and simulated in the Saber Simulation environment. Saber is a analog/mixed signal simulator that provides a complete environment for modeling, simulation and post processing in order to analyze a wide range of applications. Designs can be created very rapidly via schematic entry. Saber provides both basic analysis types like transient (time domain) and AC (small signal) analysis as well as advanced analysis methods like Monte Carlo, which is very powerful for analyzing the effects of parameter tolerances. Saber's automation methods have also been used in this example in order to automate the simulation and post processing flow. The following sections describe the models required for the simulation.

OVERALL SIMULATION MODEL OF A CAN NETWORK

The overall simulation model contains five CAN nodes including all required components in order to simulate the physical behavior of the communication system. Every node includes EMC protection circuitry, transceiver and CAN controller. All nodes are connected via physical wires modeling the behavior of a twisted pair transmission line. Figure 7 shows the architecture of the overall simulation model.

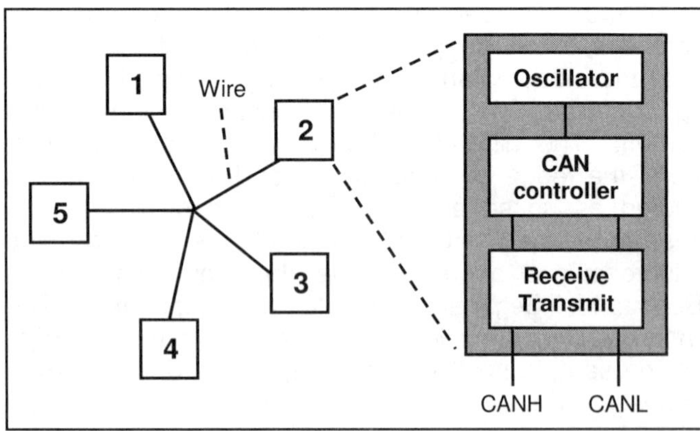

Figure 7 ***Structure of the CAN node model***

TRANSMISSION LINE

The transmission line is one of the critical parts in the simulation model. It must include effects like reflection and crosstalk but must also achieve good simulation speed as the overall CAN simulation model is intended to be used in analyses that are computationally intensive, e.g. Monte Carlo. The geometry for coupled transmission lines and the equivalent circuit diagram is shown in Figure 8. The parameters for this model (e.g. wave resistance, delay, coupling etc.) are determined via measurements and the definition of odd and even mode waves. Figure 9 compares the transient behavior of the simulated wire model with experimental measurements.

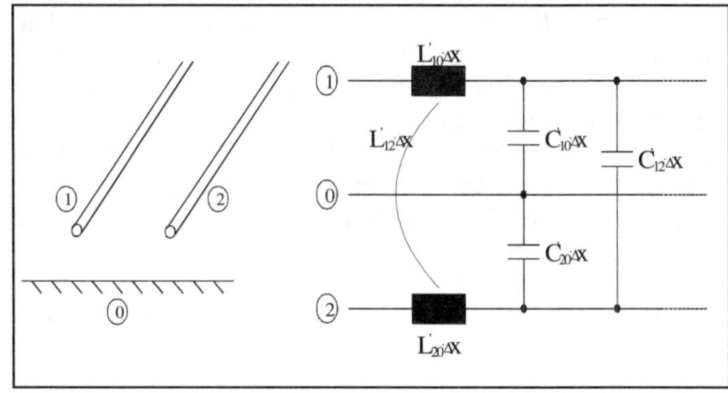

Figure 8 ***Model of a transmission line***

It can be seen that the difference between measurements and simulation is sufficiently small and the model maps very accurately the dynamic behavior of the transmission line.

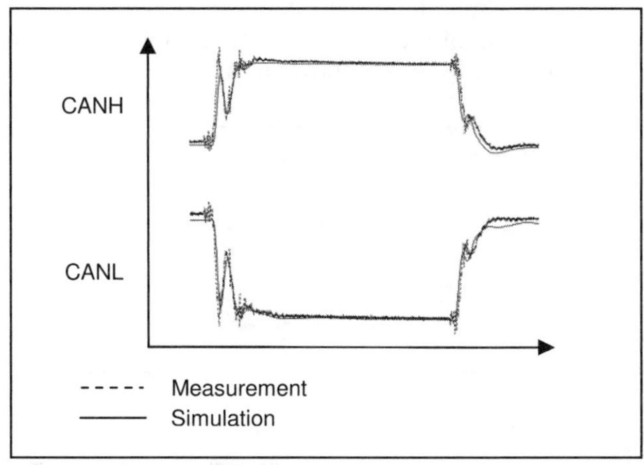

Figure 9 ***Simulation vs. measurement***

COMMON MODE CHOKE

The common mode choke is modeled hierarchically with coupled inductors and their resonance behavior.

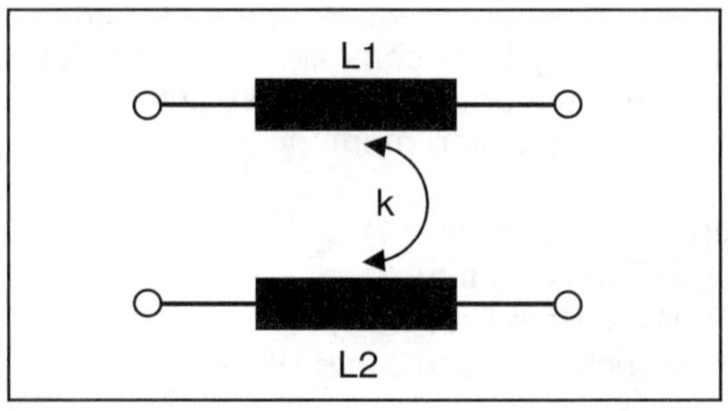

Figure 10 ***Model of the common mode choke***

Characterization of the model parameters is performed by measurements in the frequency and time domain. The input resistance (odd and even mode) input resistance (odd and even mode) was determined in the frequency domain by measuring the complex resistance values (magnitude and phase). Different common mode chokes can be modeled by characterizing this generic model using different parameter sets obtained from measurements. The model provides accurate AC and transient behavior while exhibiting excellent simulation speed.

TRANSCEIVER

The simulation model of the transceiver must be very accurate as it has a fundamental impact on the signal integrity. Therefore it is recommended to obtain this model directly from the semiconductor manufacturer. This application uses the TLE 6250 transceiver chip, a high speed CAN transceiver from Infineon. The model was especially developed for system simulation and is approximately 16 times faster than the transistor circuit model of the entire IC. Figure 11 shows the hierarchical architecture of the CAN transceiver model. The model considers all required functions like over temperature,

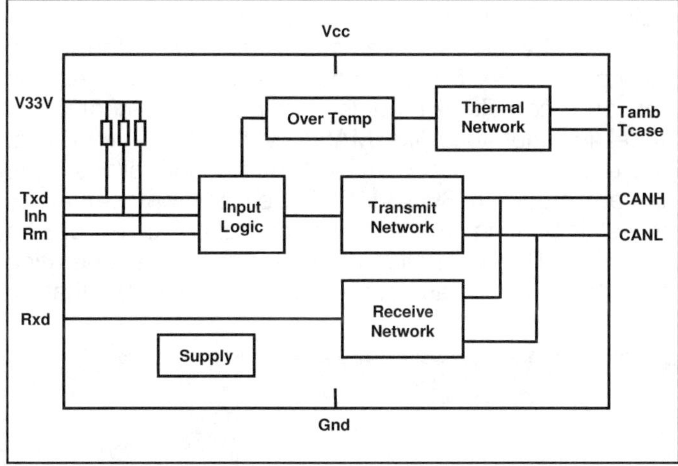

Figure 11 ***Architecture of the TLE6250 model***

low supply voltage, short circuit and real current consumption. It covers the complete range of input and output voltages, supply voltage and temperature limits specified in Infineon's data sheet for the TLE 6250. Applied in various test benches the simulation model has delivered both very accurate results and good simulation speed.

PARTIAL CAN CONTROLLER

Figure 12 shows the generic architecture of a CAN protocol controller including:

- BRP (Baud Rate Prescaler)
- BTL (Bit Timing Logic)
- BSP (Bit Stream Processor)
- AF (Acceptance Filter)
- EM (Error Management)
- Mailboxes
- IML (Interface Management Logic to μ-Controller)

The bit timing logic state machine computes the bit time sets the sample point and controls the

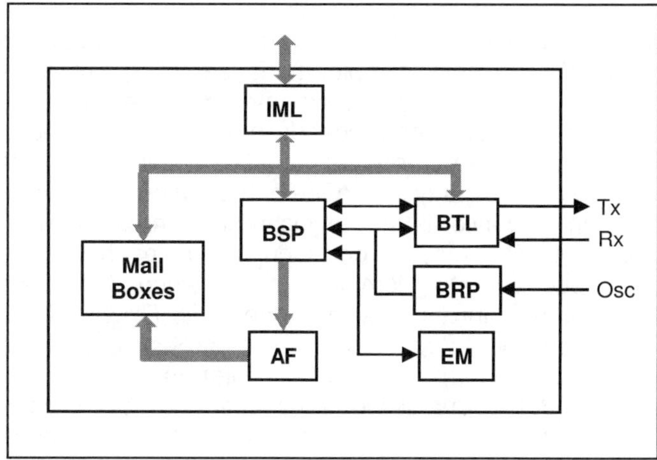

Figure 12 ***Architecture* of a *CAN controller***

resynchronization during a message frame. The BSP generates the message frames, inserts stuff bits and controls and verifies the check sum for every frame. For the verification of the physical layer only a reduced set of the CAN controller's functionality is required. The simplified model contains some functions of a CAN controller according to CAN specification 2.0 and ISO 11989 and is intended to simulate the timing and acknowledgement behavior of a CAN controller. Figure 13 shows the infrastructure of the simplified CAN controller model. The model has four connection pins:

- Osc (Oscillator)
- CAN_state
- Tx
- Rx

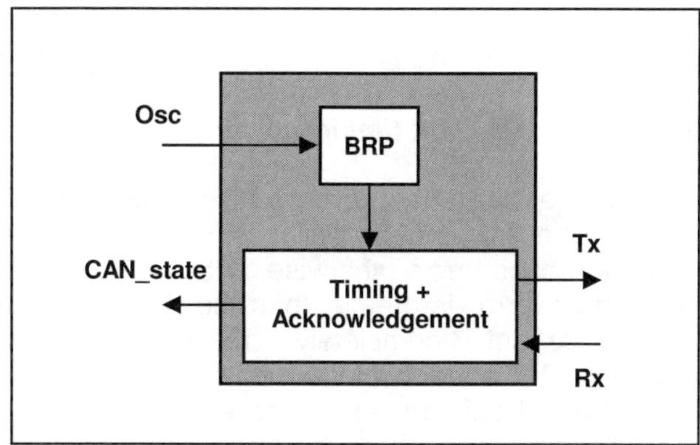

Figure 13 ***Simplified CAN controller model***

The pin CAN_state shows the state that has been sampled by the CAN controller at its Rx pin. This determines whether the correct value has been sampled or if the bit timing configuration is incorrect. The BTR parameters (TSeg1, TSeg2, Sample mode, BRP and SJW) can be specified by the user as model arguments of the controller model.

Timing behavior

The timing behavior determines the bit time (T_{Bit}), the sample point (SP), the sample mode (single or triple) and the SJW. In single sample mode sampling proceeds between two t_Q at the programmed value. In triple sample mode sampling proceeds in the previous three t_Q from the programmed value. The valid value is calculated by majority vote. One of the major functions of the timing behavior is the resynchronization as shown in Figure 14. The resynchronization occurs at the edges from recessive to dominant state when the CAN controller recognizes a falling edge at its Rx pin. If the edge occurs in TSeg1 (not in the SyncSeg, but before the sample point) the receiver interprets this as a delayed edge from a slower transmitter and TSeg1 of the receiver will be extended. If the edge occurs in Tseg2 (between sample point and SyncSeg), this is interpreted as early edge of a fast transmitter and TSeg2 of the receiver will be shortened. If the phase error is smaller than SJW, the relevant segment is corrected by the value of the phase error, otherwise by SJW. In the case that the phase error is greater then the SJW, the CAN controller cannot completely resynchronize the appropriate CAN node within a single bit timing cycle. These conditions define the necessary state machine for the synchronization. The following pseudo code describes the behavior of the state machine model:

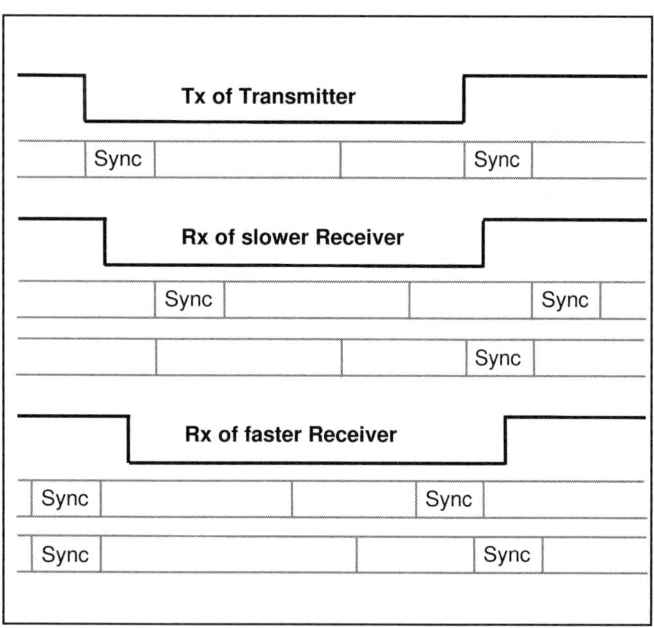

Figure 14 ***CAN bit timing***

```
when(falling edge on Rx)
   if(edge in SyncSeg)
      then set SP to default
   else if(edge in TSEG1)
      if(phase error<=SJW)
         then shift SP by phase error
      else then shift SP by SJW
   else if(edge in TSEG2)
      if(phase error<=SJW)
         then shorten TSEG2 by error
      else then shorten TSEG2 by SJW
```

Acknowledgement behavior

All receivers that receive a correct message acknowledge this by transmitting a dominant bit. The transmitter sends a recessive bit in the same time slot. The bits before and after the acknowledgement of the receiver are recessive.

State Machine Model of the Controller

The complete algorithm of the timing and the acknowledgement behavior of the CAN controller can be modeled as state machine. StateAMS enables graphical modeling of state machines containing analog and digital device behavior. The benefit of this technology is that it frees the user from dealing with any modeling languages as the entire behavior is described graphically in conjunction with analog equations and digital assignments. StateAMS creates the simulation model on-the-fly based on the state diagram information, making it easier for the model developer to alter and maintain complex models without hand-coding in modeling languages like MAST, VHDL-AMS or Verilog. Figure 15 shows a portion of the CAN controller's state diagram model in StateAMS. States are represented by circles indicating the current operating point of the controller. The controller changes from one operating state to another as soon as the transition that is

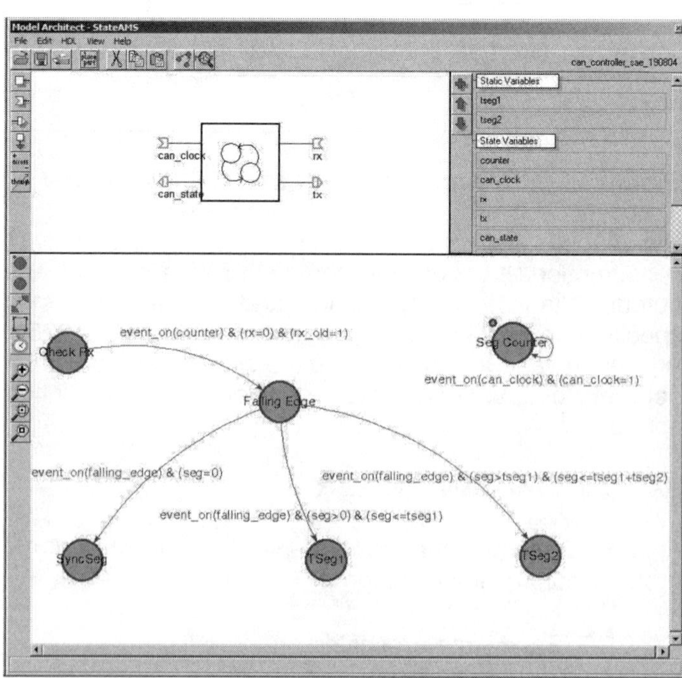

Figure 15 ***CAN controller model in StateAMS***

connecting these states becomes true. It is possible that one state is associated with more than only one transition. This means that the controller's decision as to which transition is taken depends on which of the associated conditions is satisfied. In the example above, the controller changes from the "Check Rx" state into the next state "falling edge", when a falling edge is detected at the controller's Rx pin. Three further conditions are associated with the "Falling edge" state. Depending on the segment in which the falling edge is detected, the controller selects the appropriate branch of the algorithm. Another state in the upper right corner and the other state machine are operating simultaneously. The state in the upper right corner sets the segment counter in order to track the time quantum the controller is currently working in.

SIMULATION OF THE CAN NETWORK

TEST BENCH MODEL

The required simulation described previously can be combined into a test bench for the purpose of verifying the behavior of an entire CAN bus network. Figure 16 shows the test bench including five CAN nodes

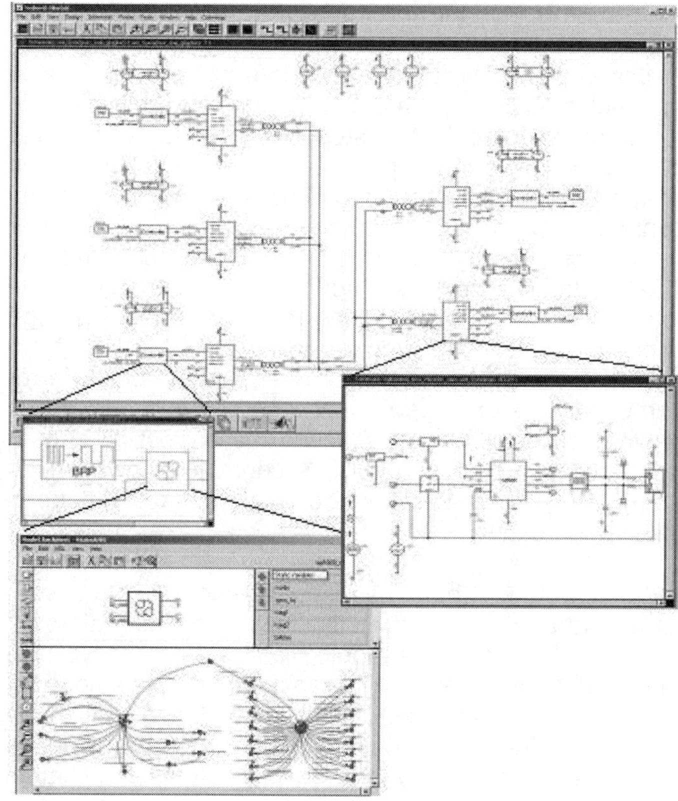

Figure 16 ***Overall simulation model***

connected together via transmission lines to form a star arrangement. Each CAN node is modeled hierarchically, consisting of the following components:

- CAN controller
- Receive/transmit network
- Oscillator

The hierarchical controller model contains the BRP and the BTL. The state machine of BTL has been modeled as a state diagram and the BRP has been implemented directly in MAST, Saber's modeling language. The receive/transmit network includes the CAN transceiver, connected to the voltage regulator and the appropriate termination circuits, consisting of stabilization circuit, choke coil and additional capacitors. The oscillator is modeled as a digital pulse source that samples the CAN controller. Model parameters are saved in a special configuration file called the Saber Command Script (SCS). The SCS enables the user to easily switch between different parameter configurations for the simulation model, and eliminates the need for the designer to maintain a different schematic for each configuration.

SIMULATING THE TEST BENCHES

The first test bench example illustrates how the synchronization of the CAN nodes works. ECU1 sends a series of 15 bits to the bus. The bit stream contains a series of falling edges (recessive to dominant) in order to show the synchronization activities of the ECUs. All ECUs are supposed to send an acknowledgement bit (dominant state) after receiving a series of 15 bits. The controllers are configured as shown in Table 1.

Parameter	Value
Frequency	9 MHz
TSEG1	5 tq
TSEG2	3 tq
BRP	2
SJW	3 tq
Sample mode	Single

Table 1

The entire bit time is divided into nine time quanta. In conjunction with an oscillator frequency of 9 MHz this results in a nominal bit time of $T_{Bit}=2\mu s$ and transmission baud rate of 500 kB. Figure 17 shows the simulated differential bus voltage of the CAN architecture measured at ECU5. ECU1, acting as transmitter, sends the bit stream "001010101010101" to the bus and the other ECUs acknowledge this bit stream by sending a dominant bit which causes an increase of the bus voltage. As shown in figure 18, these results contain information about the rising and falling time of the edges as well as settle time of the signals during oscillations for dominant to recessive bus level. The simulation results also allow the designer to analyze and verify the bit timing of the ECUs. Figure 19 illustrates the bit timing of ECU5. The upper signal "tq" indicates the time quantum of the bit time where the CAN controller is currently working. The middle signal is the receive signal "rxd" which is measured at the transceiver's digital receive pin connected to the CAN controller. It shows the bus

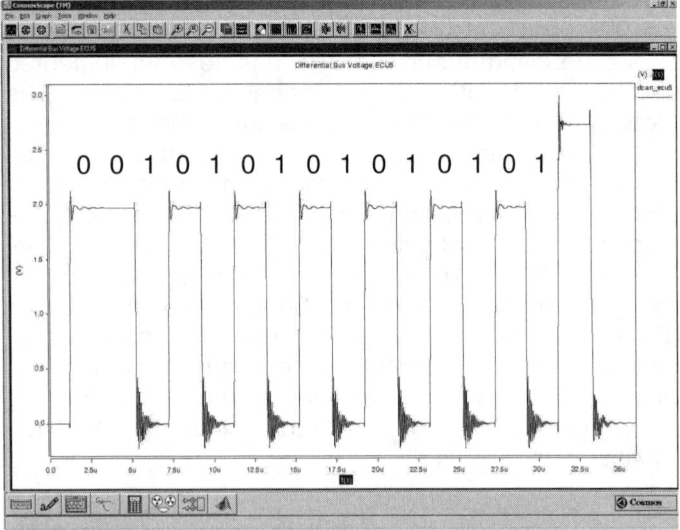

Figure 17 ***Simulated bus voltage***

status being detected by the receive network of the bus driver. The lower signal "can_state_ecu5" reflects the received bit sampled by the CAN controller at its receive pin connected to the transceiver output "rxd". These signals allow the designer to track the bit that is sampled on the bus and follow the synchronization of the protocol engine during a message frame. According to Figure 19, the controller detects a falling edge in TSeg1 (tq=5)

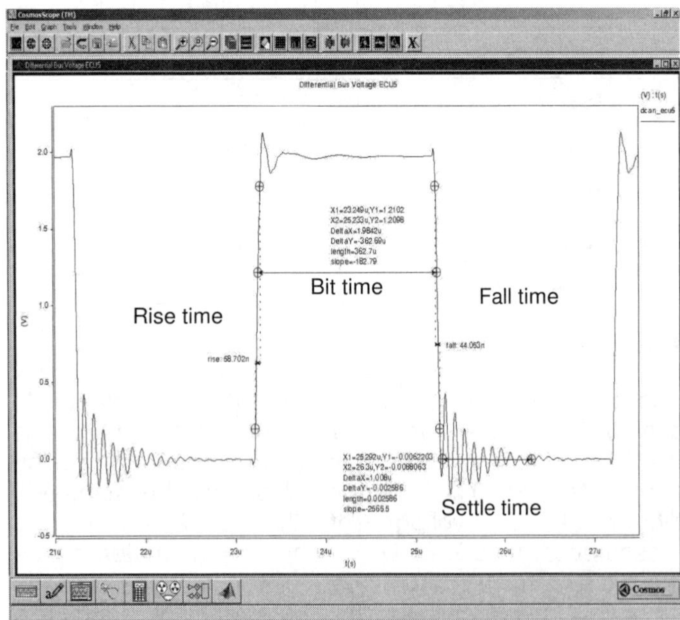

Figure 18 ***Simulation results***

which means it has to resynchronize as the falling edge has been detected outside of the SyncSeg. As the edge falls into TSeg1, TSeg1 is extended and the sample point moves automatically to the right on the time axis and the entire bit time is extended as well. The phase error is computed by Equation 1.

Phase error = tq-1. **Eq 1**

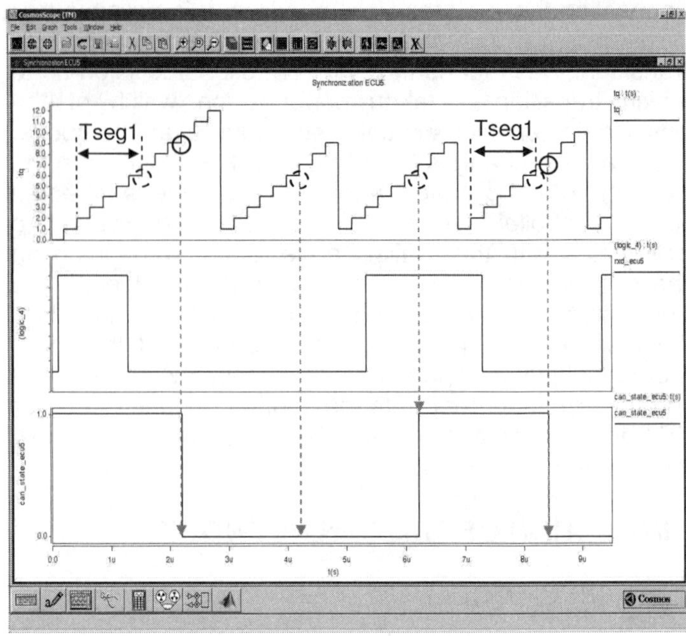

Default SP

Shifted SP

Figure 19 ***Simulated bit timing***

In this example the phase error is equal to 4 t_q. Due to the fact that the synchronization jump width limits the maximum synchronization step to 3 t_q, the CAN controller cannot completely compensate the phase error and a phase error of 1 t_q remains. The next two bits do not contain a falling edge, meaning that the CAN controller has no opportunity during this time to synchronize the CAN node. The next synchronization happens when the fourth bit is being sent. During this time the falling edge is detected in t_q=2 causing a phase error equal to 1 t_q. In this case the controller can compensate the phase error completely and the CAN node is completely resynchronized. For this scenario the correct bit stream has been sampled by the CAN controller, however the frequency tolerances of the oscillators have not been taken into account.

The following test bench applies the same CAN network architecture with two modifications. The oscillators of ECU1 and ECU5 are modeled with a tolerance of 2% that might be caused by manufacturing variations or temperature dependency. The oscillator of ECU1 is assigned a frequency of 9.18 MHz and the oscillator of ECU2 has a frequency of 8.82 MHz. Another situation that must be considered occurs when a series of five dominant and five recessive bits (0000011111) is being sent. This specific bit stream does not contain a falling edge that allows the controller to resynchronize. A series of five equal bits in a row is the maximum number as the controller automatically inserts a stuff bit after five identical bits. This bit has the inverted value of the previous bit in order to ensure that the controller has the chance to resynchronize during a message frame. Figure 20 shows the result of this scenario. The transmitter

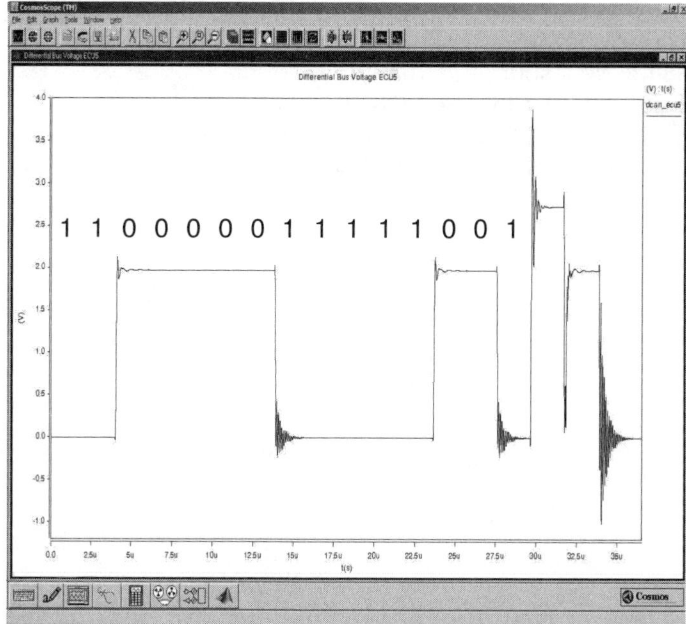

Figure 20 ***Simulated bit series***

sends the bit stream "110000011111001". The differential bus voltage of ECU5 shows an additional dominant status of the bus after the acknowledgement bit. This is not allowed as the bits prior and after the acknowledgment must be recessive. This indicates there is something going wrong in the system which seems to be related to the timing of the ECUs. Taking a deeper look into the timing of ECU5, shown in Figure 21, confirms this suspicion. The first falling edge of the bit

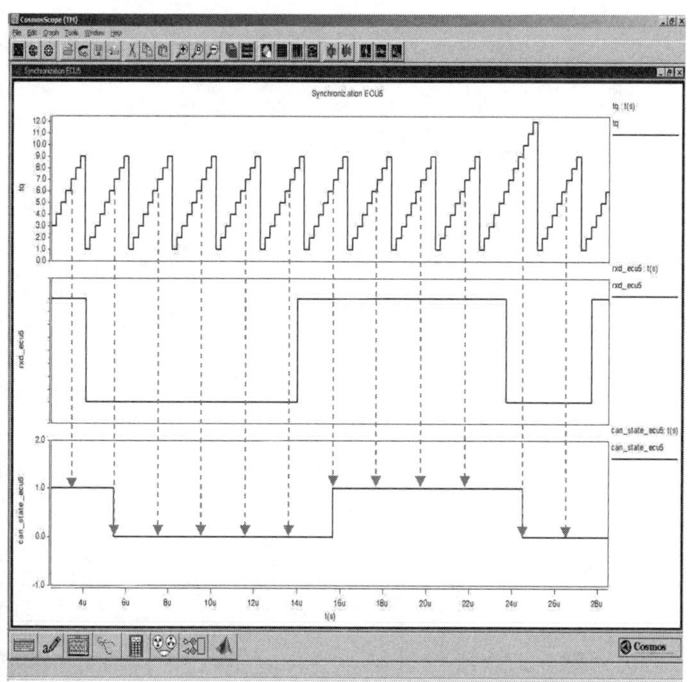

Figure 21 ***Simulated bit timig error***

stream sent by ECU1 is detected in the controllers SyncSeg of ECU5. This means that no synchronization activities are required as the receiver is in phase with the transmitter. During the next ten bits no synchronization happens as there is no further falling edge which can be applied by the controller in order to synchronize the appropriate node. The controller correctly samples five dominant bits after the falling edge. When the bus status changes from dominant to recessive, the controller detects four recessive bits and then a dominant bit. Even though the transmitter has sent five recessive bits, the receiver detects only four of them. The reason for this is the situation occurring after the detection of the fourth recessive bit, since the falling edge after the fifth dominant bit occurs prior to the sample point for this bit. This means that the controller drifted out of the synchronized mode as no_further synchronization was possible, which is required to compensate the oscillator tolerances and the asynchronous behavior of the oscillators. Figure 22 shows that the falling edge after the fifth recessive bit is detected in the sixth time quantum right before the sample point. The result is that the

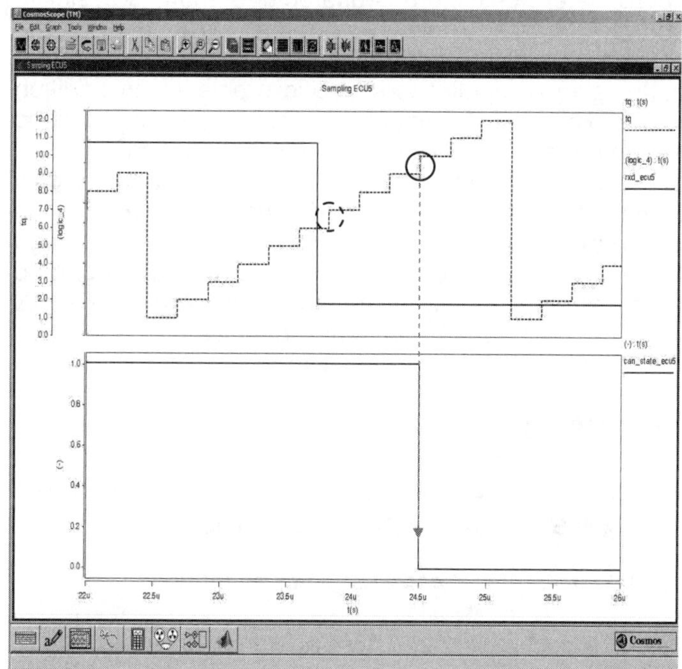

Default SP

Shifted SP

Figure 22 ***Incorrect sampled bit***

controller samples a dominant bit instead of a recessive bit, resulting in a bit error. Due to the fact that the falling edge is detected in t_q=6, the controller extends TSeg1 and shifts the sample point to the right on the time axis about the maximum synchronization jump width. This shift also explains the additional dominant bit after the acknowledgement, as the bit timing of ECU5 contains an additional phase error of approximately one complete bit time. This example clearly shows that detailed analysis is possible when simulating the physical layer of a communication system like CAN. Discovering a problem is only the first step during the verification of these communication architectures. In order to solve the problem properly a deeper look into the system is required. Simulation enables the system developer to understand and analyze the problem in detail and make appropriate corrections to the system.

CONCLUSION

This paper demonstrates simulation of the physical layer of a Volkswagen CAN bus network using the Saber simulation environment. It emphasizes the importance of simulation of this type of system at an early stage in the design process in order to reduce the number of prototypes. Simulation allows the analysis of different vehicle network architectures without having the hardware or the real vehicle network. Required changes are detected before the network architecture will be delivered to manufacturing and the simulation covers all tolerance limits and random variants. Beside early problem detection, a deeper understanding of the appropriate architecture is guaranteed and it is easier to analyze targeted network variants. This makes the network developer more flexible and allows faster addressing of application-specific problems. In addition to the examples shown in this article, further applications are important candidates for future investigation. The analysis of heterogeneous network architectures, e.g. a combination of high speed CAN and low speed CAN is important, in order to simulate latencies of message frames. The methodologies outlined in this paper can be used for other in-vehicle network technologies like LIN and FlexRay and will offer similar benefits.

REFERENCES

1. F. Hartwich, A. Bassemir, ***The configuration of the CAN Bit Timing***, Robert Bosch GmbH (1999)
2. Horst Engels, ***CAN-BUS***, Franzis' (2000)
3. Wolfhard Lawrenz, ***CAN Controller Area Network***, Hüthig (2000)
4. E. Jöhnk, K. Dietmayer, ***Determination of the Bit Timing Parameters for SJA 1000 CAN controller***, Phillips Application Notes (1997)
5. ***TLE 6250***, Infineon Application Notes (2002)

CONTACTS

Thorsten Gerke, Application Engineer (Synopsys Inc.)
Karl Hammer Schmidt Straße 34
85609 Aschheim/Dornach (Germany)
Tel: +49 (0) 89 99320-227
E-mail: thorsten.gerke@synopsys.com
URL:http://www.synopsys.com/saber

Carsten Schanze, Network Engineer (Volkswagen AG)
Mailbox 1784
38436 Wolfsburg (Germany)
Tel: + 49 (0) 5361 9-44218
E-Mail: carsten.schanze@volkswagen.de
URL:http://www.volkswagen.de

2005-01-1533

Authentication and Secure Communication for In-Vehicle Networks

Reza Jamasebi and Mohsin M. Jamali
Department of Electrical Engineering and Computer Science, The University of Toledo

ABSTRACT

A "*network*" has been defined in Webster as "*an interconnected or interrelated chain, group, or system*" and " *a system of lines or channels resembling a network*". Similar definition will also apply to in-vehicle networks as they connect hundreds of sensors and other electronic components inside vehicles. There are many standards exists for in-vehicle networks such as CAN, SAE J1850, SAE J1939, LIN, MOST, FlexRay and others [1-9]. However, these standards do not address security and reliable communication issues. With the growth in technology, there is a need for the communication between the in-vehicle network and remote services for safety, entertainment, assistance, etc. It seems that security for such systems still is an unanswered question. The questions such as "Do we trust the remote services?", "Are they the ones who claim?" and "Will our information remain confidential from unauthorized people?" need to be addressed.

Since the first step for a safe communication is authentication [10-13], we first explore the importance of authentication for in-vehicle networks. We propose an authentication method for CAN protocol for authenticating any remote services and establishing a secure communication using a secure key transmitted during the authentication. We use public key approaches for authentication to deal with the key distribution problem. Since this is a one-way authentication, we do not need a trusted third party and it is assumed that one of the parties is completely trustworthy. This work simulates an authentication method in exchanging a secure session key. First of all, authentication is implemented on main frame creating two processes representing two nodes and created bi-directional pipeline between processes representing the communication channel. Its hardware implementation uses two Phytecs boards (Infineon C505C Microcontrollers based) and communicates through a CAN bus.

INTRODUCTION

Transmitting the data across a network should be effective, accurate, error free and safe. Integrity is one factor of a safe communication. Integrity means the received data must be the same as the sent data with no duplication, insertion, modification reordering or replays. Integrity deals with reliable communication. In the case of an error during the transmission, a safe system has to detect the error, prevents any spreading of incorrect information and takes the necessary action to retrieve the correct data. Basically in the case of an error, two methods can be used to retrieve the correct data. In the first method, the receiver detects errors and asks the sender to retransfer the data. The Cyclic Redundancy Check (CRC) [13-14] is widely used for detecting errors. In the second method, the receiver detects errors and corrects them. Data correction is very complex and is used in the cases that retransmitting the data is very expensive or impossible. There are several methods proposed for error correction that varies from single bit correction to multiple bits correction [13].

Another important factor that must be taken into the account is confidentiality which means to prevent unauthorized people to access the information and detect any attacks. Confidentiality is a very important issue in today's computerized systems especially when the systems are distributed and communication is accomplished through a network. Cryptography is widely used to provide some confidentiality to the data. The encrypted information is not venerable even if unauthorized persons have access to that. Although protecting the information from unauthorized people are very critical but it is not the only security concern. Non-repudiation, access control and availability are the other concerns of a secure system.

In this paper, we first investigate the importance of security for in-vehicle networks and propose a mechanism to make the communication between the in-vehicle networks and remote services more secure. We justify the importance of authentication as a primary concern of network security and propose an authentication method for CAN protocol for authenticating any remote services and establishing a secure communication using a secure key transmitted during the authentication.

IN-VEHICLE NETWORK SECURITY

Although, the security was not an issue in the early in-vehicle networks, it is significantly important in today's systems. The vehicle network is not limited to inside the vehicle anymore. With the growth in the technology, we are seeing the connection from the vehicle to Internet, mobile phones, Global Position Systems (GPS), remote traffic control systems, navigators and many more remote services [15-18]. All these systems with the network inside the vehicle make a global network. We can not have the in-vehicle network isolated from the outside world anymore and this network would need interaction with the larger external networks. The network security deals with following issues:

- Data Confidentiality
- Authentication
- Data integrity
- Access Control
- Nonrepudation

EVALUATION OF SECURITY CONCERNS FOR IN-VEHICLE NETWORKS

There are five issues in network security as shown above. Data confidentiality means protecting the data from unauthorized persons. As far as in-vehicle network security is concerned, we do not want that the critical information about our vehicles to be received by intruders. Therefore, whenever we want to transfer the information between parties with the possibility of intruders' presence, we should encrypt that information to prevent any vulnerability.

Another concern of security is authentication. Authentication is the process of determining a user's identity, as well as determining what a user is authorized to access. One of the growing technologies in an automotive industry is remote communication between in-vehicle network and remote service providers where the authentication concern comes to the picture. We have to authenticate any service provider accurately to prevent malicious people to get to our network and cause problems or steal critical information.

Access control prevents unauthorized people from using certain resources. Basically for the in-vehicle network security, we can merge this concern to the authentication concern. In other words, first authenticate the people and then let them access a given resource.

Data integrity is another concern of security that means the received data must be the same as sent data. This concern mostly is solved by error detection schemes which are applicable for in-vehicle network as well. Nonrepudation means building a mechanism to prevent the parties' denial of participating in communication. Nonrepudation becomes critical in dealing certain transactions but at the present, it is not crucial for in-vehicle network security.

SECURITY AND CAN PROTOCOL

A computer protocol is a formal description of how computers talk to each other [11]. A set of formal rules describing how to transmit data, especially across a network is called protocol. OSI model is an open system protocol which allows any two different systems to communicate regardless of their hardware structures [7, 11]. The OSI model has following seven layers.

1. The Physical Layer (lowest layer)
2. The Data Link Layer
3. The Network Layer
4. The Transport Layer
5. The Session Layer
6. The Presentation Layer
7. The Application Layer (top most layer)

Each layer in this model does a certain function and communicates with the layers above and below directly. In this model, the upper layers deal with high level application whereas the lower layers deal with the transmission of raw data bits. The idea behind the layering of the protocol is to divide the tasks between the layers and make the implementation easier. The OSI model is a standard model that can be used as a reference for other protocols. During the communication, layers at the end nodes communicate directly through virtual links. However the physical link is just between the physical layers.

As far as security and integrity is concerned, different layers of this model take the responsibility of making a safe communication. Layer two which is the data link layer is responsible for a reliable communication between two adjacent nodes. This layer must detect the errors that might occur during the transmission of data from one node to another. Depending on application, this layer uses different methods to detect errors but the most commonly used method is CRC [14]. One of the tasks of the layer six in the OSI model is to provide the service for secure communication. Basically the information can be encrypted in this layer and the encrypted information will be transferred to secure confidentiality.

Controller Area Network (CAN) [1-9] is one of the protocols that are inspired from OSI standard model and is used in vehicles. This model has only three layers: physical, data and application layer of the standard model. Basically, there is no need for all seven layers for the in-vehicle network systems. For the sake of simplicity, the unneeded layers are eliminated. For example, the network layer in OSI model is responsible for routing and choosing the best path for transmitting the frames. As a matter of fact, routing is not an issue in in-vehicle networks which use single bus topology. As far as integrity is concerned, data link layer is responsible for the integrity of the data in CAN model. This layer checks the frames for errors. In this model, CRC is also a common approach for detecting errors.

One of the layers which is missing in the CAN model is presentation layer. This layer is primarily responsible for presenting the data in a form that its user can understand. Since the users for industrial networks and specifically for in-vehicle networks belong to a same system, presenting the data for different users is not an issue. Another responsibility of the presentation layer is to provide the secure communication.

Our proposal is to add security services to the application layer. This way, we will have mechanisms responsible for security issues and reliable communication. One of the applications of the added services will be an authentication process. In the next sections, we will investigate the importance of authentication for in-vehicle networks and how we can design the security layer to take the responsibility of authentication and secure communication.

REMOTE SERVICES AND SECURITY

Monitoring and diagnostic devices are needed to monitor and diagnose the problems of vehicle system through the network. Monitoring devices are used to determine the vehicle status and to check that the vehicle is in an appropriate condition. One obvious use of monitoring devices is for emission control. Each car has to follow the EPA [15] and/or CARB [16] regulation for emission control. It is possible to check these regulations continually and prevent any abnormality of system functionality with the use of monitoring devices and through the in-vehicle network.

Diagnostic devices on the other hand are used to find the problem with different parts of the vehicle. With the use of these devices, finding and fixing the problem becomes faster and easier. Growth in the wireless technology has raised the possibility of remote monitoring and diagnosing. Let's consider the following scenario. You are driving on a highway. All of a sudden your car breaks. You have no idea what happened. Using remote monitoring service, you can contact your 24/7 Service Provider Center (SPC) and ask for help. Each car has a unique ID number that you should provide to them. Using the information, they can contact to the network inside your car and use the diagnostic techniques to find the problem and even more they might be able to fix the problem remotely.

Another case may be that some fishing website sends information to your vehicle asking personal or vehicular information and directing to go to another site. If the vehicle happens to go to that website then any thing may happen similar to fraud involved in an identity theft.

Here is one unanswered question: "How can we make sure that we contact the legitimate SPC?" Furthermore, 'How can we make sure that an intruder does not intercept the communication?" This is where the security comes into the picture. We need to authenticate the SPC station before allowing it to access to the in-vehicle network and then establish a secure communication with the SPC to secure confidentiality of data. As a matter of fact, remote communication from the car to remote centers has been used for a while. This communication is called "Automotive Telematics" [17] or shortly "Telematics". Telematics refers to the mechanism of communication between vehicle and remote center for sending and receiving data both ways. The reason that we want to exchange data from vehicle to a remote center can lie into four categories:

- Safety and Security applications
- Personal applications
- Business applications
- Customer relationship management applications for manufacturers.

Our concern in this project is on safety and security applications. Some of the examples of these applications can be:

- Remote door unlocking
- Stolen car tracking
- Road side assistance
- Automatic collision notification
- Other applications

The example that we mentioned earlier is in the road side assistance application category. We need to have a SPC for this application. As a matter of fact, currently couple of service provider systems is in use. One of the famous ones is "OnStar" [18] system developed by General Motors Corporation. Our concentration for this work is on providing the authenticating system for the remote monitoring and diagnostic application to prevent any vulnerability and provide a mechanism for secure communication between parties. We want first to make sure that our service provider is the one who claims otherwise we may disclose some critical information about our vehicle to intruders. To prevent such a scenario to take place, we are going to design the authentication mechanism for the CAN protocol but first we should investigate what authentication means and which approach is the best candidate for this application.

AUTHENTICATION AND SECURE COMMUNICATION

Authentication is the process of determining a user's identity, as well as determining what a user is authorized to access, e.g. a military database. There are a lot of authentication approaches which are in use in today's computer networks. Authentication can be mutual or one-way. Mutual authentication protocols are used to satisfy communicating parties about their identities. The parties can exchange a session key and establish a private secure communication after authentication. One way authentication protocols are used in the case that one party wants to satisfy about the identity of another party. Basically two approaches are used for authentication:

1. Symmetric Encryption Approaches

2. Public-key Encryption Approaches

Symmetric Encryption Approaches [7] are based on the concept that the both parties share a secret key. Suppose that A and B are two parties that share a secret key K. If A sends a message encrypted using the secret key K to B, then B can decrypt the message using the same key. This way, B can be sure that the message came from A because nobody else has the secret key K to encrypt a message with. Basically, the symmetric approaches provide both confidentially and authentication. The problem associated with symmetric encryption approaches is that every two parties who want to communicate must share a secret key. Key distribution is an important issue.

One solution to this problem is using a third party called Key Distribution Center (KDC) [7]. Having KDC, each party needs to have a secret key with KDC who is responsible to provide a secret key between each two parties. Another approach to deal with this problem is using the public encryption approaches. In this section, we first introduce the public key encryption approach and then use this approach for authentication. Public key cryptography is an asymmetric approach because it uses two different keys (Public key and Private Key). The application for public key cryptography consists of encryption/decryption, digital signature, key exchange and authentication. One of the early algorithms for public key cryptography was developed by Ron Rivest, Adi Shamir and Len Adleman at MIT [10]. This scheme which is called RSA algorithm is described in the next section.

RSA ALGORITHM

In this scheme, the message is encrypted in blocks. Each block has a binary value less than some number n. Therefore, the block size is less than or equal to $\log_2(n)$. Suppose that M is the message block and C is the cipher block. Both sender and receiver must know the n. The sender holds the public key KU={e,n} and the receiver holds the private key KR={d,n}. The procedure of encryption and decryption is as follows:

Sender: $C=M^e \bmod n$

Receiver: $M=C^d \bmod n=(M^e)^d \bmod n$
$=M^{ed} \bmod n=M \bmod n$

As it is seen, the requirement ($M^{ed} \bmod n=M \bmod n$) must be satisfied. The mathematical justification to this requirement is as follows:

Based on Euler's theorem, the following relationship holds:

$$m^{k\phi(n)+1}=m^{k(p-1)(q-1)+1}=m \bmod n$$

Where p and q are two prime numbers and n and m are two integers such that n=pq and 0<m<n, and k is an arbitrary integer. As it is specified in Euler' theorem, $\phi(n)$ is the Euler Quotient function which is the number of positive integers less than n and relatively prime to n. Now, if p and q are two prime numbers then $\phi(pq)=(p-1)(q-1)$. Therefore we can make the following relationship:

$$ed = k\,\phi(n)+1$$

Where this is same as:

$$ed=1 \bmod \phi(n)$$

Therefore:

$$d=e^{-1} \bmod \phi(n)$$

Consider that this relationship is true only if the greatest common divisor of $\phi(n)$ and d is 1 ($\gcd(\phi(n),d)=1$). Figure 1 depicts how the RSA algorithm works. As it is shown in this figure, the sender has the public key which is KU={e,n} and encrypt the plain text using that key. The receiver on the other hand has the private key and can decrypt the cipher. Meanwhile if an intruder comes in between and see the transmitted message, he can not decrypt the message and figure out the content of the message because he does not hold the private key.

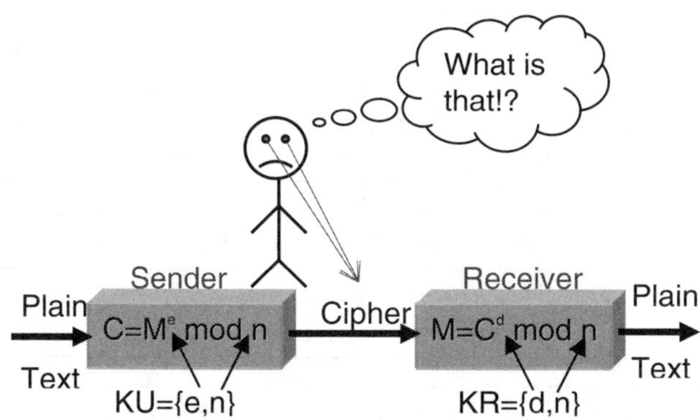

Figure 1: RSA Algorithm

SIMULATION AND IMPLEMENTATION

The approach that we used for authentication is based on RSA algorithm. What we want to achieve here is to authenticate the Service Provider Center (SPC) before letting it to communicate to the in-vehicle network and exchange a session key for establishing a secure communication. This kind of authentication is one-way authentication because the vehicle just wants to authenticate the SPC. If we want to implement the two-way authentication, we need a trusted Key Distribution Center (KDC) [7]. We know that each vehicle has a unique identification number such as VIN that is assigned by manufacturers.

Figure 2 shows the procedure of authentication and key exchange. Figure 3 and 4 shows the operation flowchart of Node1 and Node 2 respectively. This algorithm is simulated on the mainframe first. To build an appropriate environment to simulate this algorithm, we created two heavy processes (using fork() [19]) representing two nodes and made a bi-directional pipeline between the two processes (using socketpair [19]) representing the communication channel. Figure 5 depicts a snapshot of the simulation on main frame.

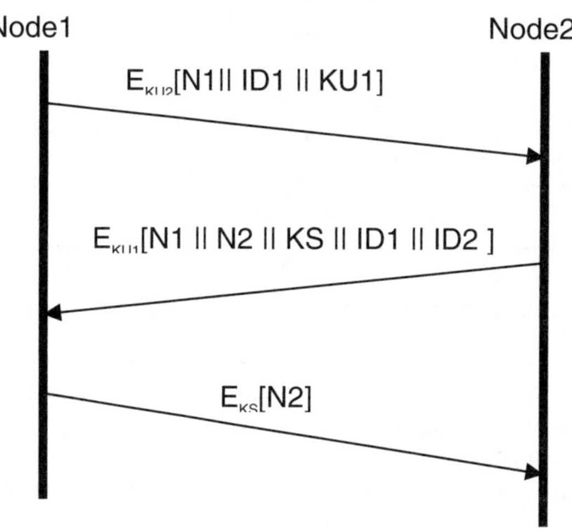

Figure 2: Authentication Procedure

To avoid the key distribution problem, we suppose, each vehicle has the public key of SPC and this is the legitimate SPC that holds the private key. In the first step, one of the in-vehicle network nodes which is in charge of security must generate a nonce (N1) and encrypt the ID number of the vehicle (ID1) combined with the nonce and its Public key (KU1) using the public key of SPC (KU2). Using the nonce, it makes the session unique and prevents the replays attacks [7]. Then, the node sends the encrypted block to the remote SPC. Upon receiving the block and after decrypting that using its private key (KR2), the SPC is notified the intention of the vehicle of establishing a secure communication. At this point, the SPC generates a session key (KS) and a nonce (N2). After that, the SPC will encrypt N1, N2, the session key (KS), the sender ID (ID1) and its own ID (ID2) using the public key of in-vehicle node(KU1) and sends the encrypted block back to the vehicle. Now, the security node can decrypt the block using its private key (KR1) and compare the nonce (N1) and its ID number (ID1) with the actual ones. If they are the same, then it can conclude that the message came from the legitimate SPC because nobody else is aware of the private key of Node2 (KR2). This way the vehicle network can continue the communication without worrying about disclosing the critical information to unauthorized people. In order to make sure that this is the valid session, the vehicle node must encrypt the nonce from SPC (N2) using the session key and send it back to SPC. Now, the two parties can establish a secure communication using the shared session key using any symmetric cryptography algorithm.

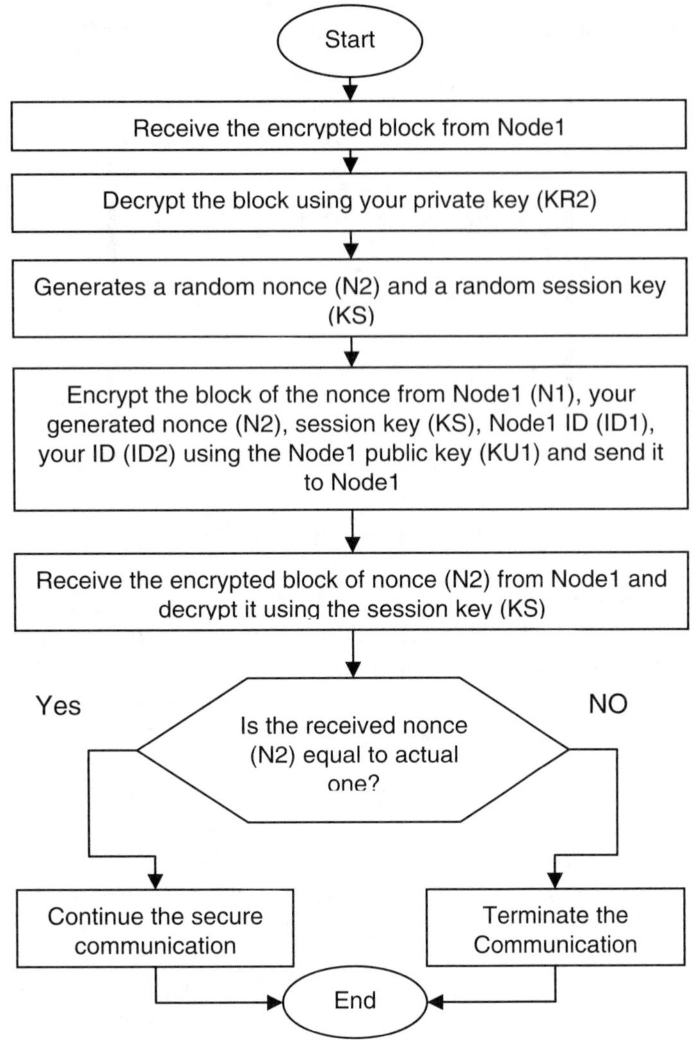

Figure 3: Node2 Operations

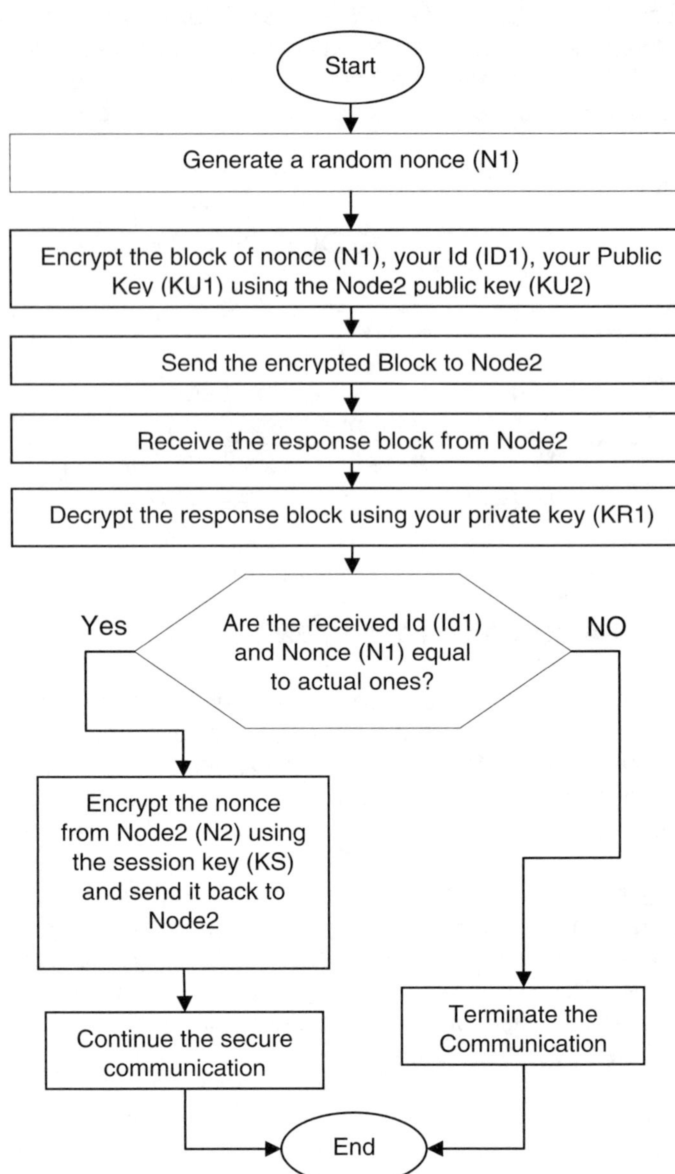

Figure 4: Node1 Operations

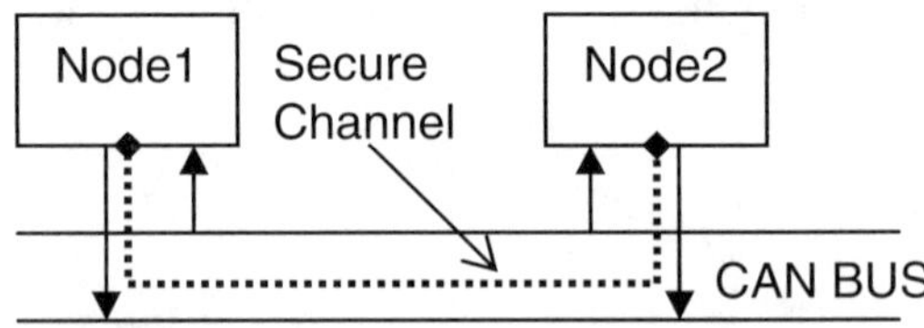

Figure 5: schematic of implantation

To implement the algorithm we use the two kitCON505C [20] boards representing the Node1 (the in-vehicle network node) and Node2 (SPC node).

C505C MICROCONTROLLER

The C505C microcontroller is a member of the Infineon C500 family of 8-bit microcontrollers [21]. It is fully compatible to the standard 8051 microcontroller. The C505C is an enhanced version of the C505 and incorporates a full CAN module with a top transfer rate of 1 M Baud. Additional on-chip peripherals are three 16-bit timers/counters, full duplex serial interface with programmable baud rate generator (USART) and an 8-bit A/D Converter.

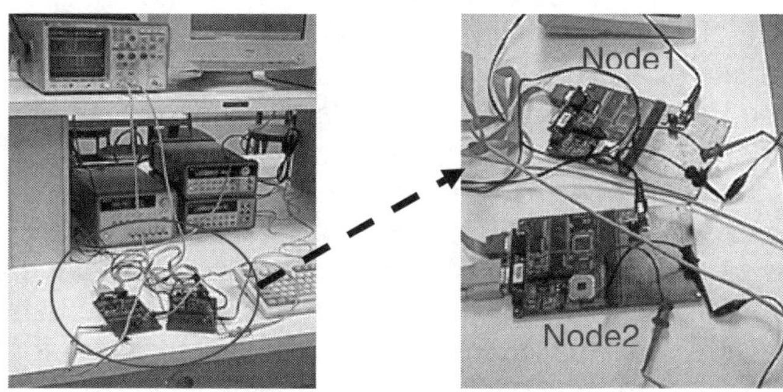

Figure 6: Hardware Implementation

NODES OPERARTION

Figure 5 depicts the schematic of the hardware implementation and Figure 6 shows the actual implantation hardware. In this implementation, Node1 encrypts its ID (ID1), a Nonce (N1) and its public key (KU1) using the Node2 public key (KU2) whenever it wants to establish a secure communication with Node2. Node1 represents the in-vehicle network node and Node2 represents the SPC node. Basically there is a function in each node (encDec function) that decrypts and encrypts the blocks of data. Node1 generates a random number using the rand() function and assigns it to N1. The first frame that is sent to Node2 by Node1 has three data bytes with the standard 11-bit identifier. After the Node1 generates the encrypted block of the three byte data, it will load the block to message object 5 using vLoadData_CAN function. Node1 then sends the encrypted block to Node2 via the CAN bus using the CAN_vTransmit function. Node2 receives the block using the CAN_vGetMsgObj function and loads it in message object 6. Upon receiving the block, Node2 decrypts that using the encDec function with its private key (KR2). Now, Node 2 is aware of Node1 intention for a secure commutation. Node2 then generates a random session key (KS) and a nonce (N2) using the rand() function. After that, Node2 encrypts a block of N1, N2, KS, ID1 and ID2 using encDec function with Node1 public key (KU1) and sends back to Node1 via the CAN bus. This frame will be five data byte frame with the standard 11-bit identifier which will be loaded to message object 5 and sent to Node1 using CAN_vTransmit. Node1 receives the block and decrypts the block using encDec function with its private key (KR1). It then compares the N1 and its ID (ID1) with the actual ones in an else-if statement. If they are the same, Node1 continues the communication by sending the encrypted N2 using KS to Node2. At this point, the two Nodes can continue the secure communication using the exchanged session key. If they are not the same, the loop will break and Node1 terminates the communication. In order to see the result of implementation, we monitored the TDXC and RDXC pins on the KitCon Boards. Therefore, we could see the transmitted and received data to and from the CAN bus by the microcontrollers. Based on the observation, whenever the Node2 uses the proper key and encryption algorithm, Node1 will respond properly and the communication will be established. Otherwise, if Node1 detects that the received data from the Node2 does not mach the original data, it terminates the communication and no activity is seen on the pins. Figure 7 depicts a snapshot of the simulation on main frame

CONCLUSION

Security is an open issue in automotive area. Although a lot of works have been done to physically secure in-vehicle networks, there is still need for development in the security arena. Especially when the communication between in-vehicle networks and remote services are applied then security becomes more crucial. This work provides an authentication mechanism for in-vehicle networks to authenticate any remote services and makes a secure communication. As it is shown, authentication is a very important aspect of in-vehicle network security. If we can provide a reliable mechanism for authentication, secure communication will be solved as well. When the in-vehicle network authenticates the remote party, they can exchange a common secret key and establish a secure communication. After exchanging a secret key, any cryptography algorithms can be used for a secure communication.

REFERENCES

1. M. M. Jamali, "A Comparative Study of Physical Layers of In-Vehicle Multiplexing Systems", *SAE Transactions, J. Passenger Cars-Electronic and Electrical Systems*, 108 (1999) 2315-2321
2. Christopher A. Luipini, " Multiplex Bus Progression," SAE Paper # 2001-01-0060.
3. Multiplexing and Fibre-optics, SAE International Congress and Exposition, SP-1012 1994.
4. Automotive Multiplexing Technology, SAE International Congress and Exposition, SP-1070, 1995.

5. Multiplexing Technology, SAE International Congress and Exposition, SP-1137, 1996.

6. Multiplexing SAE SP-1224, SAE International Congress and Exposition, 1997.

7. William Stallings, *Cryptography and Network Security: Principles and Practice*, Upper Saddle River NJ: Prentice Hall, 2003

8. http://www.can.bosch.com/

9. SAE Website www.sae.org

10. Rivest, R., Shamir, A., and Adleman, L. "A Method for Obtaining Digital Signatures and Public Key Cryptosystems." Communications of the ACM, February 1978

11. William A. Shay, *Understanding Data Communication & Networks*, Second edition, Brooks/Cole Publishing Company, 1999

12. Syed Masud Mahmud, Shobhit Shaker and Srinivas Reddy Morsa, "Secure Inter-Vehicle Communication", SP 2004-01-0204, SAE Special Publication, 2004

13. Peterson, W. W. and E. J. Weldon. Error Correcting Codes, 2nd ed. Cambridge, MA: MIT press, 1972

14. T. V. Ramabadran and S. S. Gaitonde, "A Tutorial on CRC Computations", *IEEE Micro*, Vol.8, No. 4, August 1988, pp. 62-75

15. http://www.epa.gov/

16. http://www.arb.ca.gov/

17. http://www.saic.com/automotive/

18. http://www.onstar.com

19. Keith Haviland, Dina Gray and Ben Salama, *Unix System Programming*, Second edition, Addison Wesley, 1998

20. www.phytec.de/

21. http://www.infineon.com

CONTACT

Mohsin Jamali received the B.Sc. from the Aligarh Muslim University, India in 1975, M.S. From the University of Saskatchewan, Canada in 1979 and Ph.D. degree from the University of Windsor, Windsor, Canada in 1984. He is a professor in the department of electrical engineering and computer science at the University of Toledo, Ohio. He teaches courses in the areas of microcontroller based digital systems designs, VHDLs, PLCs, and automotive electronics. His research interests are in application specific hardware design for real time applications. His e-mail address is mjamali@utnet.utoledo.edu.

Reza Jamasebi has received his B.S. degree in Electrical Engineering (Electronics) from Shiraz University, Iran. He has also received two master's degrees in Electrical Engineering (Control) from University of Tehran, Iran and Computer Science from Bowling Green State University, Ohio. He is currently pursuing his PhD at Case Western Reserve University, Ohio. The presented paper is part of his independent research collaboration with Mohsin Jamali in the Department of Electrical Engineering and Computer Science at the University of Toledo. His email address is r_jamaseb@hotmail.com.

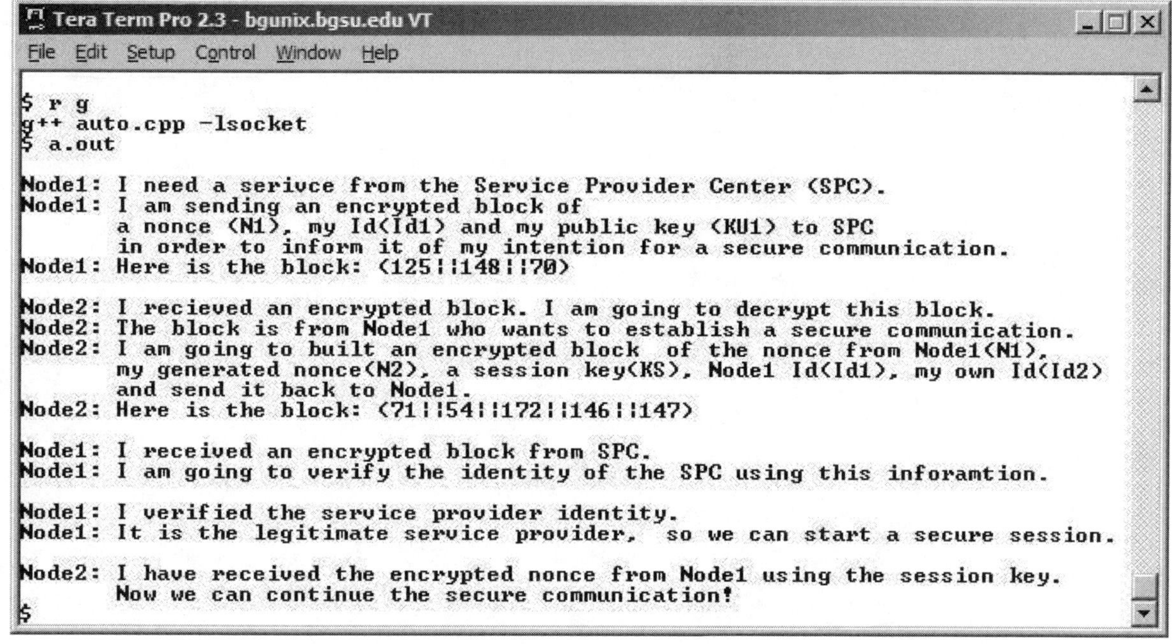

Figure 7: Snap shot of the authentication algorithm on main frame

2005-01-1531

In-Vehicle Network Architecture for the Next-Generation Vehicles

Syed Masud Mahmud
Department of Electrical & Computer Engineering, Wayne State University

Sheran Alles
Ford Motor Company

ABSTRACT

The demand for drive-by-wire, telematics, entertainment, multimedia, pre-crash warning, remote diagnostic and software update, etc. will significantly increase the complexity of the future in-vehicle communication networks. New types of communication networks will also be necessary to satisfy the requirements of safety and fuel efficiency, and meet the demand for new features. Different sets of vehicle electronic modules will require different types of networks. For example, drive-by-wire and active collision avoidance systems need fault tolerant networks with time-triggered protocols, to guarantee deterministic latencies; multimedia systems need networks with high bandwidth to transfer video files; and body control electronics need low-bandwidth networks to keep the cost down. As the size and complexity of these networks increase, ease of integration has become a major challenge for design engineers. In today's vehicles, there are mainly two networks: a high-speed network for the power train and a low-speed network for the body electronics. Since the complexity of the network is increasing and the demand for bandwidth is growing, future vehicles will require many partitioned networks. The partitioning of the networks will be done based on the locality as well as the functionality of the modules. One of the challenging issues will be the selection of topology to interconnect various in-vehicle partitions of the network. Interconnection among all in-vehicle partitions of the network is necessary for diagnostics and software updates in various modules. One logical approach for interconnecting various partitions of the network would be via a hierarchical bus. This paper shows various types of hierarchical connections among the partitions of in-vehicle networks. Different partitions may use different protocols. For example, one partition may use the CAN protocol, the second partition may use the TTCAN protocol, the third partition may use the LIN protocol, and so on. The hierarchical bus will be using intelligent switches to facilitate the translation of messages from one protocol to another protocol while the messages will be moving from one partition to another partition. This paper discusses the advantages and disadvantages of various types of hierarchical connections in terms of cost, bandwidth, latency, fault tolerance, and many other features. The paper also presents simulation models that can be used to determine the performance of various types of partitions and network topologies.

INTRODUCTION

Automakers are scrambling to implement advanced safety and engine management systems to make vehicles safer and more fuel-efficient, as well as meet growing consumer and government demands. Continuous demands for fuel efficiency mandate "drive-by-wire" systems that eliminate camshafts, power-sapping belt drives and pumps, and a great deal of unnecessary weight. The goal of x-by-wire is to replace nearly every automotive hydraulic/mechanical system with electronics. Electric brakes will replace hydraulics, increasing safety, lowering operating cost and eliminating the use of environmentally hazardous fluids. Steering columns will disappear and will be replaced by electric steering, improving driver safety and making it easy to provide left-hand and right-hand drive models.

The demand for drive-by-wire and many new features such as telematics, entertainment, multimedia, pre-crash warning, remote diagnostic and software update, etc. will significantly increase the complexity of in-vehicle communication networks. New types of communication networks will also be necessary to satisfy the requirements of safety and fuel efficiency, and meet the demand for new features. Different sets of vehicle electronic modules will require different types of networks. For example, drive-by-wire and active collision avoidance systems need fault tolerant networks with time-triggered protocols, to guarantee deterministic latencies; multimedia systems need networks with high bandwidth to transfer video files; and body control electronics need low-bandwidth networks to keep the cost down. As the size and complexity of these networks increase, ease of integration has become a major challenge for design engineers. Major studies are necessary to determine optimal topology for connecting all the in-vehicle networks; to figure out optimal bandwidth required from different types of in-vehicle networks for keeping latencies under certain bounds; and to select appropriate communication protocols for different networks.

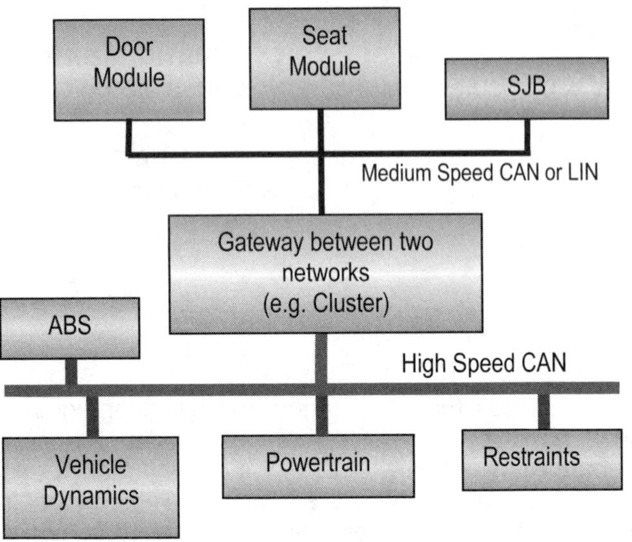

Figure 1: Schematic diagram of a current in-vehicle network.

In this paper, we present various types of in-vehicle network topologies that could be used with various types of networks and protocols to satisfy the requirements for safety, fuel efficiency, diagnostics, comfort and cost.

EVOLUTION OF IN-VEHICLE NETWORK ARCHITECTURE

For the last two decades, automotive companies have been using multiplexing networks in order to reduce wiring harness in vehicles [1-2]. The direct benefit of multiplexing is cost saving. Today's vehicles incorporate many different electronic modules, and have evolved into a distributed processing system. Serial buses are used for interconnecting the electronic modules of a vehicle. Serial buses have been selected due to many advantages of bus-based systems, over other interconnection systems [3]. The advantages of bus-based systems are low cost, lower complexity, greater reliability, better scalability, simpler communication protocols, ease of diagnostics, etc. Networks also enable the partitioning of the various electronic modules depending on function, feature or control location, further reducing cost by impacting the electrical distribution system and control signal (sensor/actuator) routing.

In today's vehicles, two serial buses are used. One bus is used for the powertrain system and the other bus is used for body electronics, as shown in Figure 1. Each bus can be considered as a partition of the in-vehicle network. Thus, today's vehicles have two partitions of networks. But, future vehicles will need many partitions of the in-vehicle network to provide services for various features such as drive-by-wire, multimedia, fuel efficiency, active collision warning/avoidance, etc.

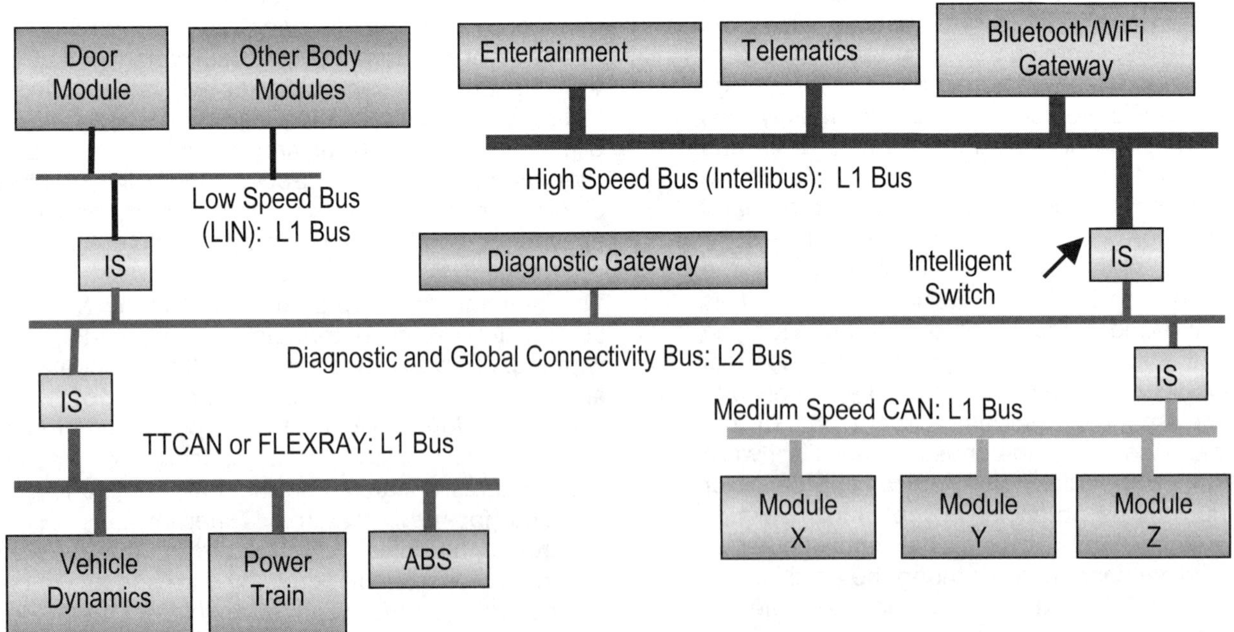

Figure 2: An in-vehicle network with four Level 1 buses, one Level 2 bus and four intelligent switches.

One of the challenging issues will be the selection of an appropriate topology to interconnect various partitions of the in-vehicle network. Interconnection among all partitions of the in-vehicle network is necessary for diagnostics and software updates. Since a bus-based system has many advantages over other interconnection systems, one logical approach would be to use another bus, a hierarchical bus, for connecting all other in-vehicle buses (partitions) together, as shown in Figure 2.

The system shown in Figure 2 has four partitions of the in-vehicle network. Each partition of the network uses a Level 1 bus to interconnect various nodes of the vehicle. Thus, the system shown in Figure 2 has four Level 1 (L1) buses: 1) a low-speed bus for body electronics, 2) a high-speed bus for entertainment, telematics, multimedia, etc., 3) a bus with a time-triggered protocol for the powertrain system and 4) a medium speed bus for other modules of the vehicle. The four L1 buses are connected using a Level 2 (L2) bus. Every L1 bus is connected to the L2 bus using an intelligent switch (IS). The intelligent switch will have a very low-cost microcontroller supporting two protocols: one for an L1 bus and another one for the L2 bus. An IS will act as a node on the L2 bus and also as another node on an L1 bus. The L2 bus, shown in Figure 2, has five nodes: four intelligent switches and a Diagnostic Gateway node. Dealers and mechanics can access different electronic modules of a vehicle via the Diagnostic Gateway module. The architecture shown in Figure 2 allows a very simple way of interconnecting various in-vehicle networks. It's also scalable. The intelligent switches are also simple. The number of intelligent switches, in the system, is equal to the number of partitions in the in-vehicle network.

Though the system shown in Figure 2 is scalable, the number of connections on the L2 bus will be too many if there are too many partitions in the in-vehicle network. The speed of a bus decreases as the number of connections to the bus increases. The speed of a bus also decreases, when its length increases. Figure 3 shows another variation of the system shown in Figure 2. There are only two intelligent switches in Figure 3 compared to four in Figure 2. But the switches of Figure 3 are more complex than those of Figure 2. The switches of Figure 3 make a star connection among three buses: the L2 bus and two L1 buses. Since the number of connections to the L2 bus is less in Figure 3 than in Figure 2, the speed of the L2 bus of Figure 3 will be higher than that of the L2 bus of Figure 2. However, one disadvantage of the architecture of Figure 3 is that it is not as scalable as the architecture shown in Figure 2.

The major problem with the architectures of Figures 2 and 3 is that neither one will tolerate bus faults. If any bus (L2 or L1) fails, then the communication among a group of modules will be disrupted. As a result, the vehicle system will fail to do its intended operations. Communication faults could be of two types: permanent faults and temporary faults. The breakdown of a bus is an example of a permanent fault. Temporary faults can occur due to the presence of momentary noise or high electromagnetic interference for a short time. The presence of a permanent fault will break down communications among many nodes.

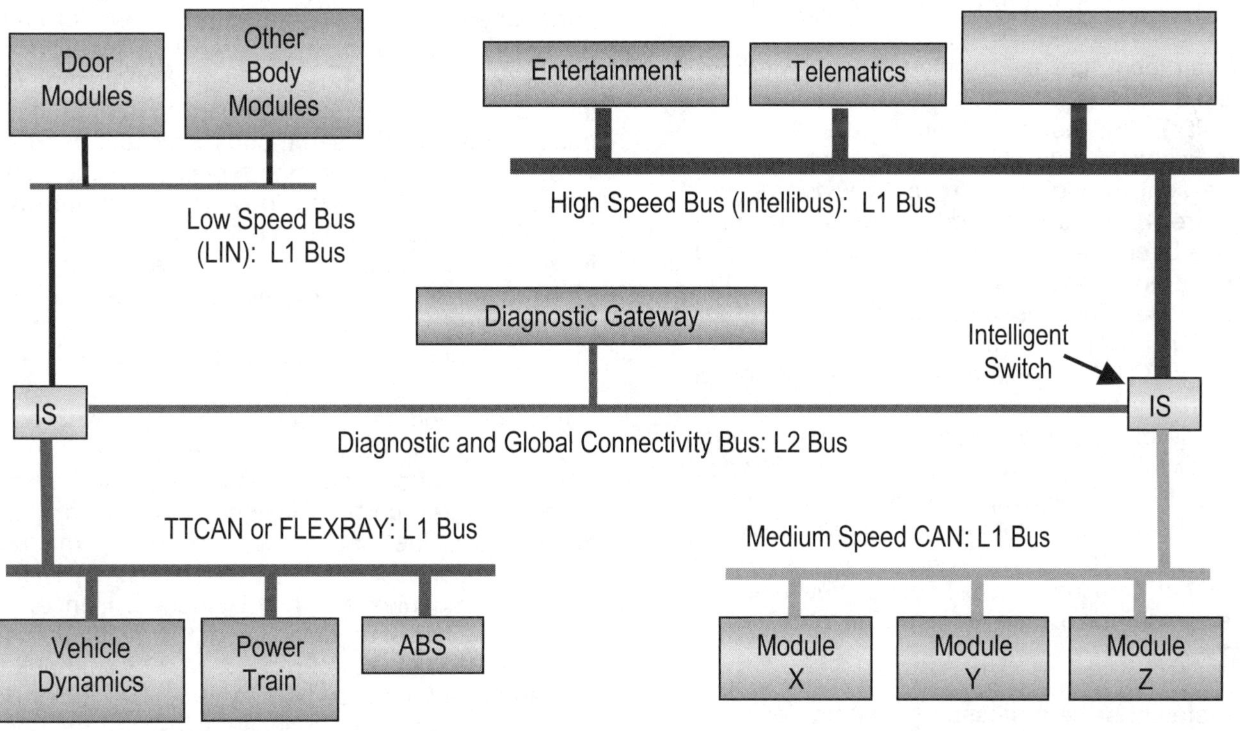

Figure 3: Schematic diagram of an in-vehicle network with four level-1 buses, one level-2 bus and two intelligent switches.

However, the presence of a temporary fault will increase the message latency. High message latencies could be acceptable for non-safety critical messages, but not for safety critical messages. One network partition of Figures 2 and 3 uses a bus with time-triggered protocol, for vehicle dynamics, power train and ABS systems. Since this network partition carries safety critical messages, on time delivery (within certain tolerance) of these messages must be guaranteed even if there are temporary faults.

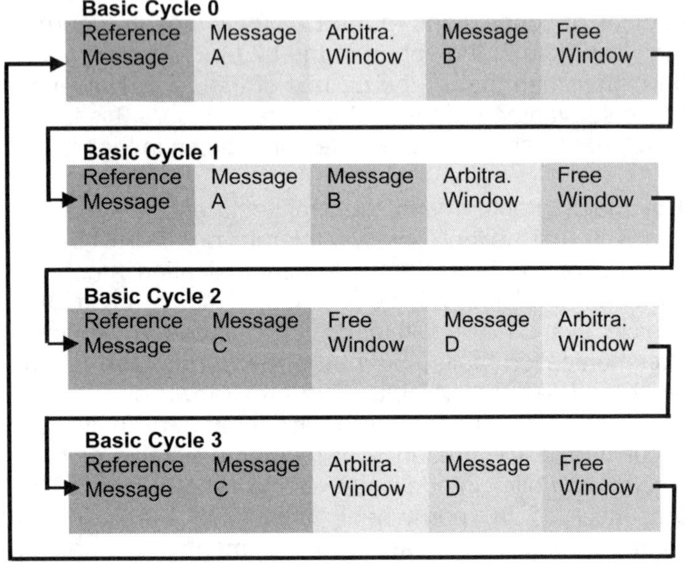

Figure 4: The system matrix of a TTCAN system.

The TTCAN protocol has three different time windows for messages: *exclusive window*, *arbitrating window* and *free window* [4], [5], as shown in Figure 4. Time-triggered messages, which require deterministic latencies, are sent through the *exclusive windows*. For example, Figure 4 shows that fixed windows (exclusive windows) have been reserved for messages A, B, C and D. Event-triggered messages are sent through the *arbitrating windows*. The *free windows* are reserved for future expansion of the system. The sequential flow of messages in a TTCAN system is represented by a matrix called the system matrix, as shown in Figure 4. A system matrix is divided into a number of basic cycles. The first window of a basic cycle is used for a reference message. In a TTCAN system, there is a master node, which is responsible for maintaining a global clock. At the beginning of every basic cycle, the master node sends the global time using a reference message. All other nodes synchronize their clocks after receiving a reference message.

In TTCAN systems, since a message must be delivered within the same time window in which it started, retransmission of the message is not allowed when errors occur within the message. Thus, if a safety critical message could not go through its Exclusive Window due to the presence of errors, it will have to wait until its next Exclusive Window. For example, if Message A could not go through its exclusive window of Basic Cycle 1 (see Figure 4) due to the presence of a temporary fault, then this message can not go until the time of its exclusive window in Basic Cycle 0. Thus, Message A will be delayed by three basic cycles. However, Message A can compete for the bus during an arbitrating window after it failed to go through its own exclusive window, but there is no guarantee that Message A will get the bus during an arbitrating window. If Message A is a safety critical message and if it is delayed by too long, then vehicle's safety will be compromised. Thus, it is desirable to have fault tolerant mechanisms for the transmission of safety critical messages with deterministic latencies.

One way of providing fault tolerant mechanisms is by maintaining additional paths among the nodes. Figure 5 shows a system that will tolerate permanent faults on L1 buses, but the system will work with degraded performance under such faulty conditions. Working with degraded performance may be acceptable for non-safety related systems, but not for powertrain and active collision avoidance/warning systems. In this architecture, if a Level-1 bus connecting a cluster of modules becomes faulty, then the modules of that cluster will have to communicate among themselves using the Level-2 bus. For example, if the TTCAN or FlexRay bus, shown in Figure 5, becomes faulty, then the Vehicle Dynamics, Powertrain and ABS modules will have to use the L2 bus for communicating among themselves. The architecture shown in Figure 5 is scalable and doesn't require any external switches. But, this architecture requires that every electronic module must have two ports: one for the L2 bus and another one for an L1 bus. Since all electronic modules of a vehicle will be connected to the L2 bus, the capacitive loading effect on the L2 bus will be much higher than that on the L1 buses. Thus, for the same communication media (single wire, dual wire, twisted pair, shielded twisted pair, etc.) using copper wire technology, the bandwidth available from the L2 bus will be much less than that available from an L1 bus. Another disadvantage of this architecture is that, since every module has two ports, the modules will be little bit more expensive than those modules that have only one port.

If two-port modules are going to be used to have fault tolerant capabilities for all modules, then Figure 6 shows a better way of connecting the modules at an expense of several three-port intelligent switches. In this architecture, the second port of every module of a cluster is connected by another L1 bus. Thus, every cluster of modules has two L1 buses. Hence, if an L1 bus of a cluster of modules becomes faulty, then another L1 bus of that cluster can be used for communication. If degraded performance from a particular cluster (for non-safety related cluster) is acceptable, then the second L1 bus and the corresponding port of each module of the cluster can be built using low-cost technology. But for safety critical modules, both ports and both L1 buses can be built using the same technology. The Level 2 bus (L2 bus) of the architecture shown in Figure 6 doesn't have too many connections. The total number of connections is equal to the total number of clusters plus another connection for the Diagnostic Gateway. Hence, the bandwidth of the L2 bus will not reduce significantly with the addition of new modules in the vehicle. This architecture is also scalable. Hence, the system can be easily expanded.

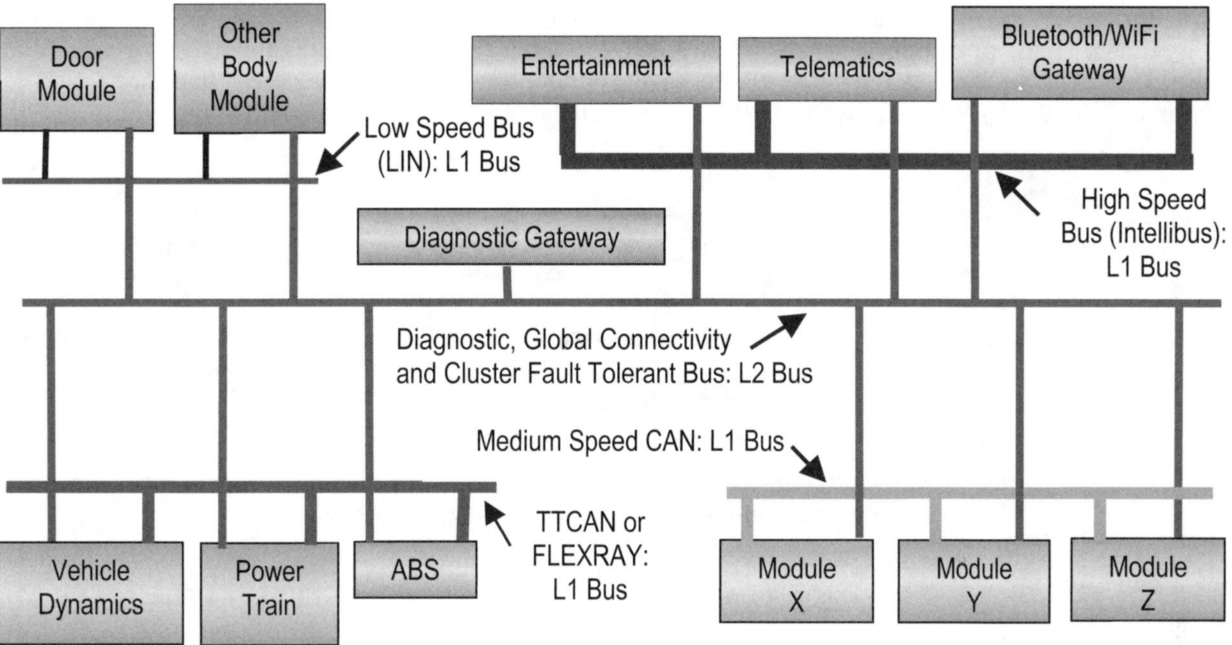

Figure 5: Schematic diagram of a fault tolerant in-vehicle network with four level-1 buses and one level-2 bus.

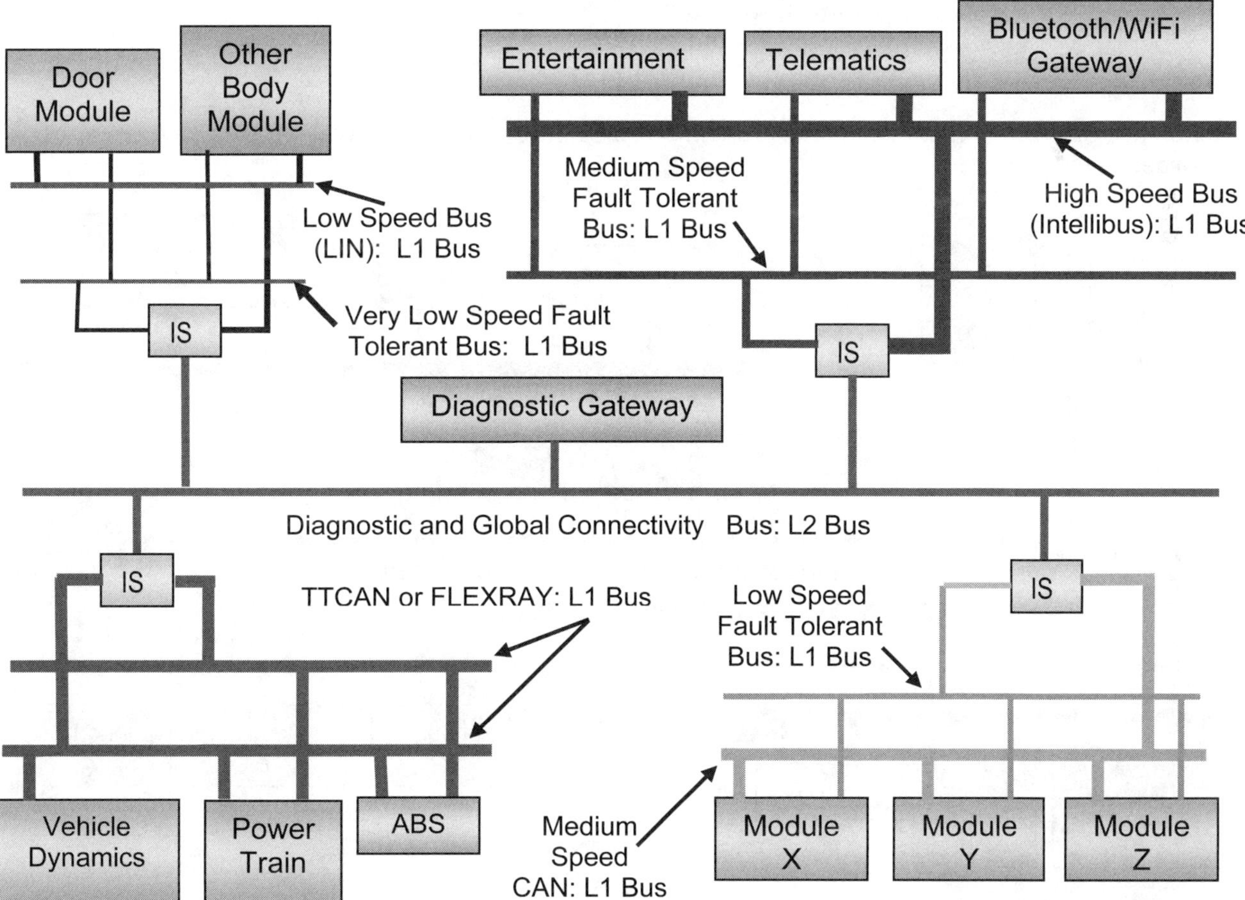

Figure 6: Schematic diagram of a fault-tolerant in-vehicle network with eight level-1 buses, one level-2 bus and four intelligent switches.

The major drawback of the architecture shown in Figure 6 is the cost of dual-port modules and three-port intelligent switches. Since all modules are not safety-critical modules. We can use dual-ports only for the safety-critical modules, and one port for all other modules. Figure 7 shows another architecture where dual-port modules are used only for the powertrain bus.

The architecture shown in Figure 7 is also scalable and doesn't have too many connections on the L2 bus. Thus, the system can be easily expanded, and good bandwidth can be obtained from the L2 bus. The number of intelligent switches, shown in Figure 7, can be reduced from five to two if we use three- and four-port intelligent switches, as shown in Figure 8.

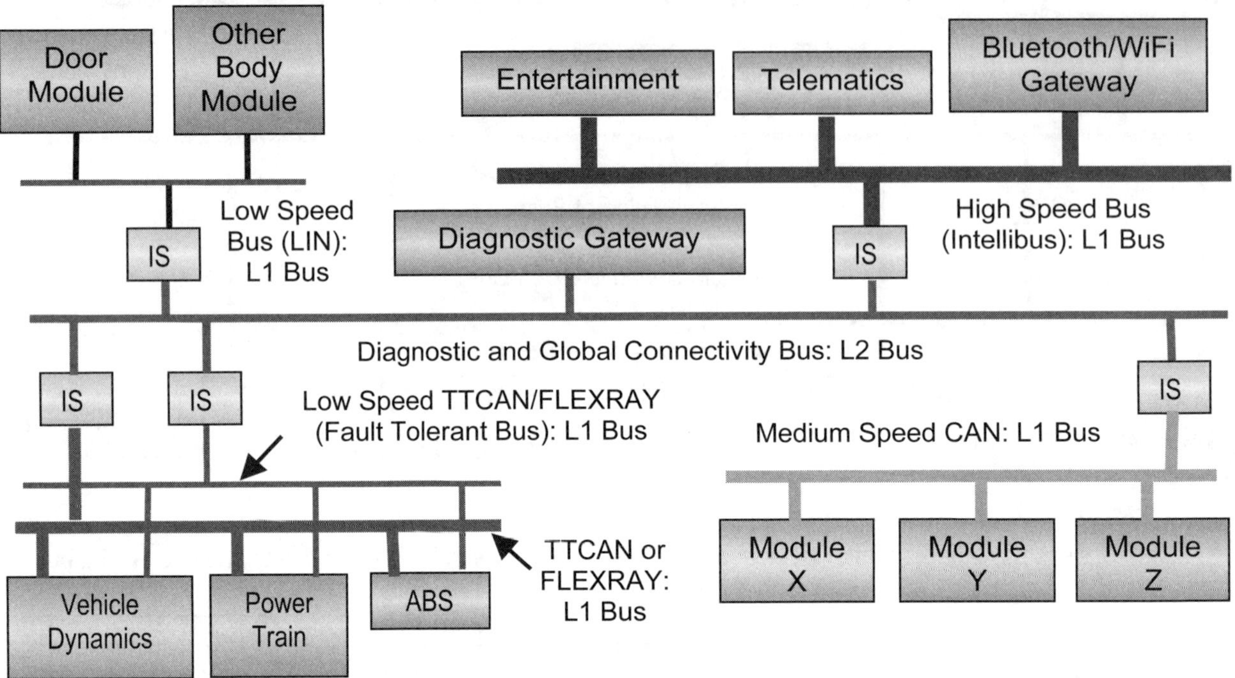

Figure 7: Schematic diagram of a partial fault-tolerant in-vehicle network with five Level 1 buses, one Level 2 bus and five intelligent switches.

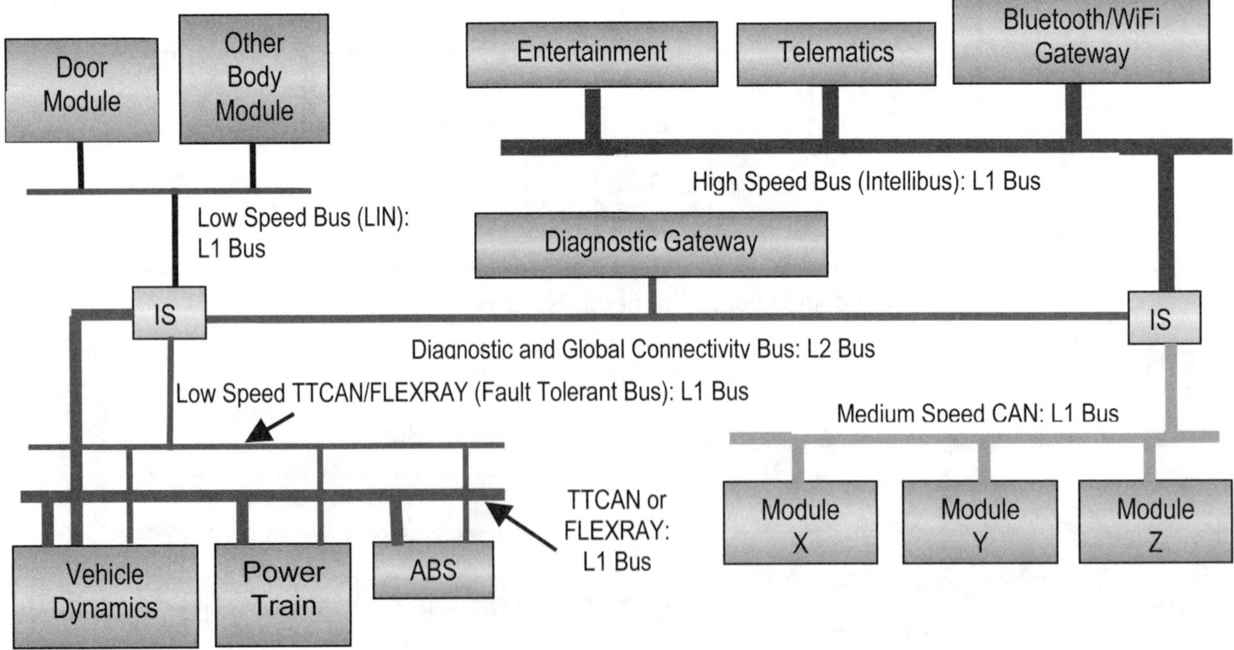

Figure 8: Schematic diagram of a partial fault-tolerant in-vehicle network with five Level 1 buses, one Level 2 bus and two intelligent switches.

FORMING CLUSTERS (GROUPS) OF ELECTRONIC MODULES

The electronic modules of a vehicle can be divided into several groups or clusters. The clusters can be formed based on functionality and locality. This means that the modules that do similar type of work and are located close to each other can be put in one cluster. Each cluster will be provided with at least one Level 1 bus. If there are similar electronic modules both at the front and rear of a vehicle, then the front modules can be put in one cluster and the rear modules can be put in another cluster. This way, other clusters can be formed depending on the locality and functionality of the modules. Then several clusters can be joined together by a Level 2 bus. If the clusters are formed the way it is described here, then each cluster will need a lower speed bus compared to the bus that would have been required otherwise. Since the inter-cluster communications may not be as much as the intra-cluster communications, even a low speed bus can be used as a Level 2 bus to connect the clusters. This approach of forming the clusters will save cost due to the fact that for the same length, a low-speed bus costs less than a high-speed bus.

PERFORMANCE ANALYSIS OF IN-VEHICLE NETWORK ARCHITECTURE

The performance of various partitions of the in-vehicle network as well as the entire network can be determined by developing simulation models. After executing the simulation models on computers, one can determine the minimum requirements for different partitions of the network architecture. Some of these requirements will include minimum processing powers needed from various electronic modules, minimum bandwidth needed from various buses, minimum size of buffers needed in various switches, etc. Computer simulations will also allow us to select the optimal network topology needed to meet the requirements of the next generation vehicles. The next section of the paper describes how simulation models can be developed to study various performance parameters of different partitions of the in-vehicle network.

TYPES OF SIMULATIONS:

Computer simulations can be divided into two types [7]: i) time-based simulation and ii) event-based simulation. In a time-based simulation, the program control loop is associated with time.

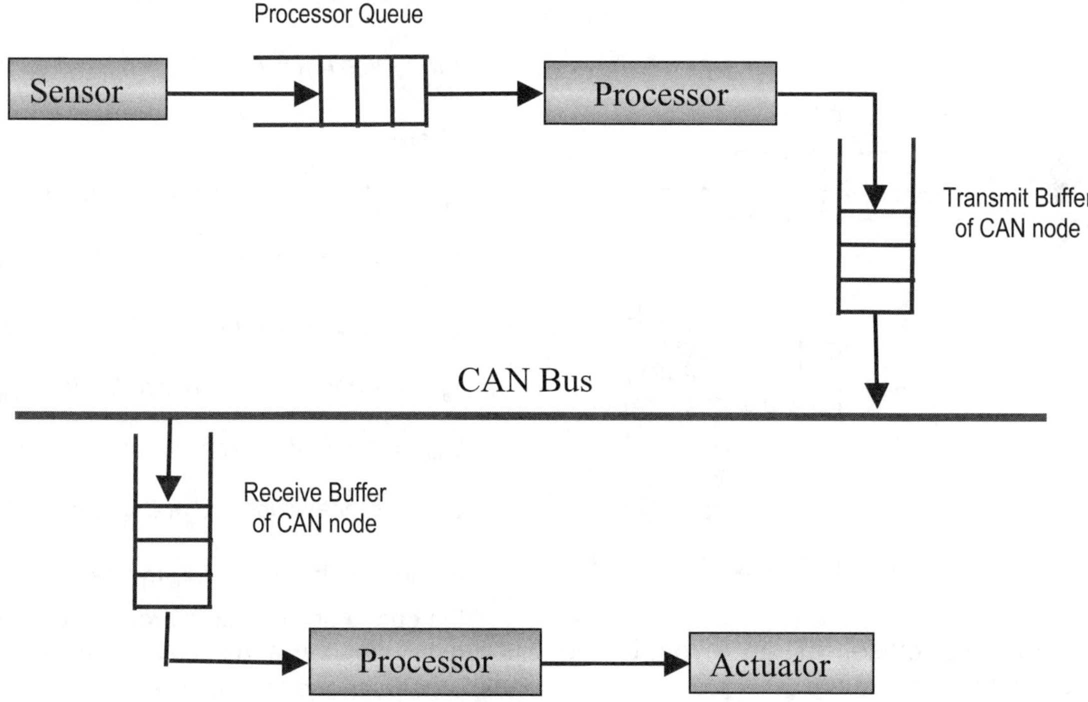

Figure 9: A diagram of information flow from a sensor to an actuator.

For each execution of the main control loop, the simulation clock advances by a fixed time unit. In the case of an event-based simulation, the execution of the main loop represents a single event. The simulation clock is simply advanced by the amount of time since the last event. For asynchronous systems, the event-based simulation is computationally more expensive and accurate than the time-based simulation. But, for synchronous systems, the time-based simulation is as good as the event-based simulation, and it is computationally less expensive than event-based simulation. CAN protocol is an event-based protocol. Thus an event-based simulation tool will be the most appropriate tool for analyzing various performance parameters of a CAN bus. Buses that use time-triggered protocols, such as TTCAN [4], [5] and FlexRay [6], carry both time-triggered and event-triggered messages. The time-based simulation can be used to simulate time-triggered messages and the event-based simulation can be used to simulate event-triggered messages. Thus, a combination of both time- and event-based simulations is necessary to simulate a bus like TTCAN or Flexray.

Various types of commercial tools are available to do different kinds of simulation. However, there could be some problems with commercial tools. For example, using commercial tools, it may not be possible to tune some of the simulation parameters the way we want to tune them. Thus, it might be a better idea to develop a custom simulation tool from the scratch. Using a custom tool we can do simulation in whatever way we want to do.

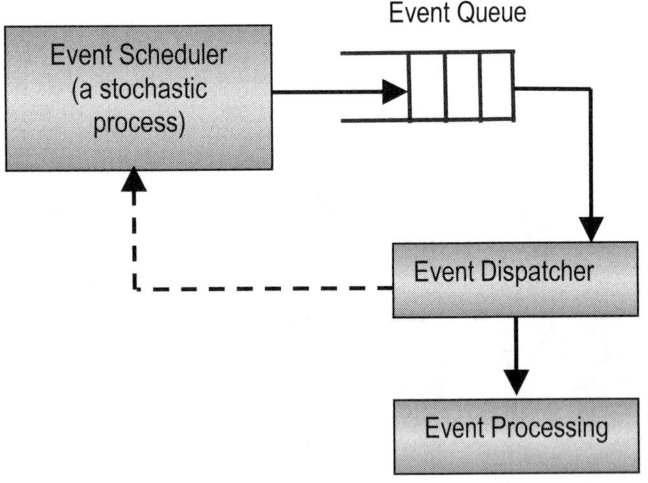

Figure 10: Software model of an event-based simulation.

DEVELOPING AN EVENT-BASED SIMULATION TOOL

Here we explain how to develop a custom event-based simulation tool to meet the requirements of our specific need for the next generation vehicles. In a vehicle system, an event is triggered by a sensor or by the driver's action such as pressing the brake or gas paddle. The event then goes to a processor queue, as shown in Figure 9. If the processor is busy or other events are waiting in the processor queue, then the event stays in the processor queue. Otherwise, the processor starts working on the event immediately. The event, queued in the processor queue, will stay in the queue until the previous events are taken care of by the processor. The processor spends some time (processing time) on an event. After that, the processor tries to send a message through the bus (say CAN bus) connected to the processor. If the bus is available, then the message is immediately sent to the bus. Otherwise, the message is queued in the transmit buffer of the CAN node. The message will go through the bus after the previous messages have been transmitted. After a certain time (transmit time), the message is queued to the receive buffer of the destination CAN node. If the processor at the receiving node is free, then it will immediately process the message. Otherwise, the processor will first take care of other queued messages and then it will process this new message. Figure 9 shows the entire process of information flow from a sensor to an actuator.

Components of the latency of an event:

There is a delay (latency) between the time an event occurs at a sensor or due to a driver's action, and the time an actuator takes an action. The latency has several components as shown by the following equation.

$$latency = t_{PQ} + t_{ps} + t_{TB} + t_{bus} + t_{RB} + t_{pd} \qquad (1)$$

where,

t_{PQ} = *delay at the processor queue*

t_{ps} = *processing time at the source node*

t_{TB} = *delay at the transmit buffer of the source node*

t_{bus} = *transmit time through the bus*

t_{RB} = *delay at the receive buffer of the destination node*

t_{pd} = *processing time at the destination node*

In the simulation model, the value of the delay, t_{PQ}, at the queue of the source processor can be determined by monitoring the arrival and exit times of the event in the processor queue. The value of the processing time, t_{ps}, depends on the type of the processor. This time can be expressed as

$$t_{ps} = T_s + k_s N \qquad (2)$$

Where T_s is a constant time, which represents the constant overhead of the processor at the source node in order to prepare a message. This constant overhead may include

- The time needed by the processor to get out of the main program,
- The time needed by the processor go to the interrupt service routine (assuming that the transmission of a message is interrupt driven),
- The time needed by the processor to check some status bits and set/clear some control bits of the CAN controller,
- The time needed by the processor for some other house keeping operations.

Thus, for a given processor, the value of T_s can be calculated based on its clock frequency and the number of instructions the processor needs to execute to do the abovementioned operations. The parameter k_s, shown in Equation 2, is another constant and N is the number of data bytes in the message. The value of t_{TB} can be determined by monitoring the arrival and exit times of the message in the transmit buffer of the source node. The value of t_{bus} can be expressed as

$$t_{bus} = \frac{M}{S} \quad (3)$$

Where, M is the total number of bits in the message, and S is the speed of the bus in bits/sec. For example, if the message is a CAN message, then M will include, the start bit, arbitration bits, RTR bit, control bits, data bits, stuff bits, CRC bits, all delimiter bits and the end of frame bits. The value of t_{RB} can be determined by monitoring the arrival and exit times of the message in the receive buffer of the destination node. Like t_{ps}, the value of t_{pd} can be expressed as

$$t_{pd} = T_d + k_d N \quad (4)$$

Where T_d is a constant time, which represents the constant overhead of the processor at the destination node in order to prepare a message, and k_d is the additional overhead per byte of data in preparing the message.

Simulation Model:

Figure 10 shows the block diagram of an event-based simulation model. In an event-based simulation model, an event is generated by a scheduler. The scheduler generates this event based on some kind of realistic stochastic process. We can develop a stochastic model for a particular event by collecting a large set of real data for that event. For example, the stochastic model of the brake event (pressing the brake paddle by the driver), can be developed by logging the driver's brake activity over a long period of time and collecting similar data from many vehicles.

After generating an event, the scheduler keeps that event in the event queue, as shown in Figure 10. When an event is dispatched from the event queue, another event is generated. This new event is then sent to the event queue. When a new event enters into the event queue, it is sorted within the event queue using the event-time as the sorting key. The new event is then placed at an appropriate point in the event queue. After dispatching an event from the event queue, the event is then sent to the event processing unit. The event processing unit then simulates the event in exactly the same way as a real system would process it.

The stochastic model of an event determines the interarrival time of the event, based on the behavior of the device that generates the event. A synchronous device, such as a time-triggered device, generates events after fixed interval of time. Hence, for a time-triggered system, the interarrival time is fixed. But, an asynchronous device doesn't generate events after fixed interval of time. Most physical asynchronous systems behave like a Poisson process. Thus, we can assume that a non time-triggered device will behave like a Poisson process. The stochastic model of an event will have the appropriate values of the parameters that define the characteristics of the Poisson process of the event. As mentioned earlier, these parameters of the stochastic model for an event can be determined by collecting a large set of field data for that particular event. The model shown in Figure 10 can be used to simulate an event-triggered system with an event-triggered bus (say CAN bus).

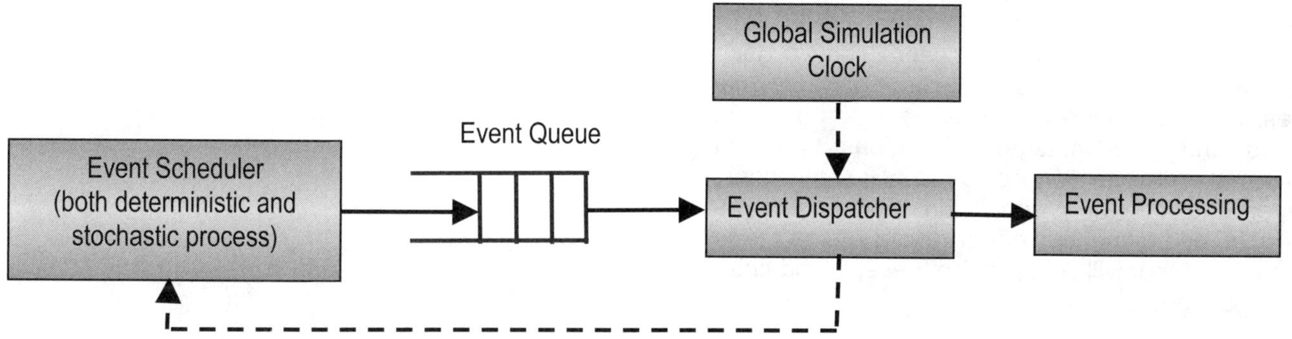

Figure 11: Software model of a combined time- and event-based simulation.

Since both TTCAN and Flexray support time- and event-triggered messages, we can develop the simulation models of these buses by building another layer on the top of the event-based simulation model. Figure 11 shows a software simulation model of a combined time- and event-based system. Here, the event scheduler is a deterministic as well as a stochastic process. In this case, a global simulation clock is maintained to keep the time-triggered events in sync. The frequency of this global simulation clock (software clock) should be at least equal to the highest frequency clock used in the in-vehicle network architecture. This requirement on the software clock will allow us to determine the latency and other performance parameters at a very high resolution (within a clock cycle of the highest frequency clock of the real system). At every global simulation clock pulse, the event queue must be checked. If the event-time of the event at the head of the event queue is less than or equal to the current value of the global simulation clock, then the event will be dispatched from the event queue. The dispatched event will then be checked to determine whether it is a deterministic event or a non-deterministic event. If it is a deterministic event, then the deterministic scheduling process will be used to schedule the next deterministic event. Otherwise, stochastic scheduling process will be used to schedule the next non-deterministic event. The scheduled event, whether deterministic or non-deterministic, will then be sent to the event queue. The event will be placed in the event queue after sorting it with other events in the event queue. The event-time will be used as the key to sort the events in the event queue.

By developing a simulation model, one can determine various performance parameters of the in-vehicle network. These parameters will include, but not limited to are the latency of different types of message, busload, bandwidth, and throughput.

CONCLUSION

In this paper, we discussed various types of topologies and protocols that could be used in the future in-vehicle networks. Due to the complexity of the future in-vehicle networks, many partitions of the network will be required. These partitions must be interconnected together for better diagnostic and software upload purposes. Since safety critical messages need fault tolerant mechanisms, we proposed how such mechanisms can be provided to the safety critical messages. The cost-effective way to compare the advantages and disadvantages of various types of topologies and protocols is by doing realistic simulations. This paper explains, how simulation models can be developed to determine the performance of in-vehicle network systems that will deal with both event- and time-triggered messages.

REFERENCE

1. R. K. Jurgen, "Coming from Detroit: Netwoks on wheel," IEEE Spectrum, pp. 53-59, June 1986
2. J. W. Tuska, "Multiplex wiring with microcomputer control," International Congress & Exposition, SAE paper 840495, Detroit, MI, Feb. 27 - March 2, 1984
3. C. R. Das and Laxmi Bhuyan, "Bandwidth availability of multiple-bus multiprocessors," IEEE Transactions on Computers, Vol. 34, No. 7, pp. 918-926, Oct. 1985.
4. Thomas Fuehrer, Bernd Mueller, Florian Hartwich and Robert Hugel, "Time-Triggered CAN (TTCAN)," Proc. of the SAE 2001 World Congress, Detroit, Michigan, March 5-8, 2001, paper number: 2001-01-0073.
5. Holger Zeltwanger, "Time-Triggered Communication on CAN," Proc. of the SAE 2002 World Congress, Detroit, Michigan, March 4-7, 2002, paper number: 2002-01-0437.
6. Christopher Temple, "Protocol Overview," Notes of FlexRay International Workshop, Detroit, Michigan, March 4, 2003.
7. Michael K. Molloy, "Fundamentals of Performance Modeling," Macmillan Publishing Company, 1989.

CONTACT

Syed Masud Mahmud, Ph.D.
Associate Professor
Department of Electrical and Computer Engineering
Wayne State University
Detroit MI 48202
Phone: (313) 577-3855
Fax: (313) 577-1101
Email: smahmud@eng.wayne.edu

Sheran Alles, Ph.D.
Technical Specialist
ECC Building
20600 Rotunda Dr.,
Ford Motor Company
Dearborn, MI 48124
Phone: (313) 594-0553
Email: salles@ford.com

2005-01-1279

Distributed Control System Development for FlexRay-based Systems

Pradyumna K. Mishra and Sanjeev M. Naik
General Motors Corporation

ABSTRACT

FlexRay is a new communication subsystem for future in-vehicle controls. There is a lack of mature model-based development methodologies to build complex FlexRay-based systems. In this paper we describe an end-to-end model-based development process for building a complex FlexRay-based distributed control system. We describe this in the context of safety critical x-by-wire systems for a realistic automotive application. This involves: control system modeling, functional simulation, and distributed software development. We first describe the process of functional and physical architecture design. Next we discuss the software development process dealing with software to hardware allocation, as well as scheduling of software and communication tasks on a time-triggered communication bus under stringent practical restrictions. We conclude by considering the integration issues relating to joint OEM/supplier development of distributed control systems. The above experience has been obtained during the model-based development of a FlexRay-based control system for a vehicle, which features by-wire steering, braking and propulsion.

INTRODUCTION

FlexRay is a new communication standard for future in-vehicle controls. This protocol provides flexibility and determinism by providing scalabale static and dynamic message[i] transmission. Due to FlexRay's time-triggered features and its possible use in safety critical applications, considerable software and developmental planning is required. Proper and optimal use of FlexRay in safety-critical applications requires construction of reliable embedded software. Model-based software development [2, 5, 9] can significantly increase the reliability and quality of software, as well as provide a proper development process. Some of the key benefits of model-based software development are "composability" and managing "complexity".

To develop reliable and efficient model-based software, one has to follow a rigorous software design process, given that the functional mathematical models are accurate. The functional models should capture the essential dependencies of the underlying physical architecture yet provide the abstraction to enable control system engineers to develop mathematical models without being overly concerned about the software and hardware implications. We believe that this is possible if the control system engineer assisting software development follows proper architectural and design guidelines. In this paper we intend to share our experience gained in the software development of a FlexRay-based control system for a complex X-by-wire vehicle[1] (Brake-by-wire, Steer-by-wire and Propulsion-by-wire). We also address issues faced by OEM and suppliers in the joint development of such systems.

In the development of our X-by-wire concept vehicle, we relied on a tool chain combining DECOMSYS[2], SIMULINK/STATEFLOW[3] and dSPACE[4] software tools for the basic controls software development. This tool chain can be used in a mechanized model-based developmental process for FlexRay-based rapid prototyping hardware. These tools automate part of the development process, yet significant development work has not been automated. We highlight the intricate and complex details of the automotive domain not yet captured by the above tool chain.

[1] This X-by-wire concept vehicle has a FlexRay network as a backbone and multiple CAN networks for communication.

[2] DECOMSYS provides a comprehensive set of tools for FlexRay-based software development.

[3] SIMULINK is a platform for multi-domain simulation and model-based design of dynamic systems. STATEFLOW is a design and simulation tool for event-based systems.

[4] dSPACE provides software and hardware products for rapid prototyping ECU development.

FLEXRAY-BASED SYSTEMS

INTRODUCTION TO FLEXRAY

FlexRay [1] is a new time-triggered communication system for high-performance in-vehicle applications. It supports both synchronous and asynchronous data transmission. Application-level tasks[ii] are executed and the related signals[iii] are communicated over FlexRay according to a predefined schedule. It combines the benefits of the familiar synchronous and asynchronous protocols. It supports data rates of up to 10 Mbits/sec per channel. FlexRay also supports fault-tolerant clock synchronization via a global time base. A fault-tolerant clock synchronization algorithm ensures the global time base. A modified version of the Welch and Lynch FT midpoint algorithm [10] is used to achieve this. This algorithm ensures that the global times of the different FlexRay controllers on each node do not differ by a significant margin, even in the presence of faults.

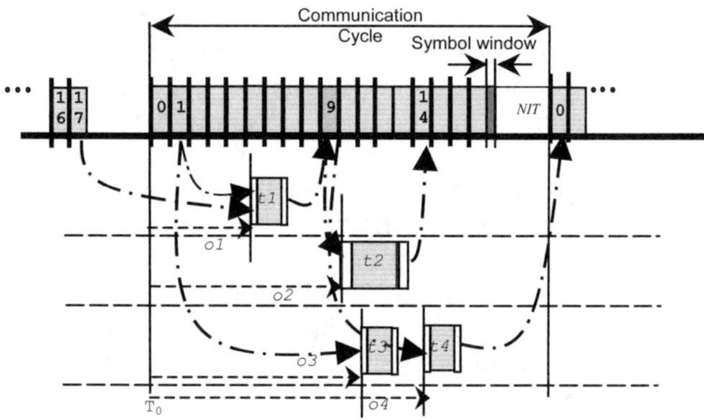

Figure 1: Example FlexRay task and communication schedule

In the above example (Figure 1), the FlexRay bus is configured for 18 static slots[iv] per communication cycle [v] (CC). In this example, we have the FlexRay bus configured for 10 Mbits/sec, a communication cycle of 1ms, a static slot size of 256bit (46μs), a dynamic segment of 0μs, a network idle time (NIT[vi]) of 163μs, and a symbol window of 9μs. Hence we have:

CC [1000μs] = Static slots [18] x Static slot length [46μs] + Symbol Window [9μs] + NIT [163μs]

This example consists of three nodes 1,2, and 3. Task *t1* executes on Node 1, task *t2* executes on Node 2 and *t3, t4* both execute on Node 4. Task *t1* reads data from Static Slot 17 of the *previous* communication cycle and Static Slot 1 of the *current* communication cycle. It performs computation based on that input data and provides the output to Task *t2* (on Node 2) and Task *t4* (on Node 3) via static slot 9.

All three nodes are synchronous at time T_0, which is the start of the communication cycle. Tasks in each node are triggered based on an offset relative to T_0. The offsets are o1, o2, and o3 for the tasks t1, t2 and t3 respectively. All tasks on different nodes agree on the time (are synchronized) and are able to communicate synchronously using FlexRay communication slots. Task *t2* collects data from Slot 9, hence Task *t2* cannot be allowed to start execution before Slot 9 is transmitted. If it starts executing before Slot 9 is communicated, then Task *t2* would use data communicated by Slot 9 of the *previous* communication cycle.

SOFTWARE AND PHYSICAL ARCHITECTURE

In a FlexRay-based system we define "host" as the part of an ECU where the application software executes. In this publication we will often use the term "node". We define a node as an entity that contains one host, one FlexRay communication controller[vii], two FlexRay bus drivers[viii], and other communication media like CAN transceivers, ADIO, PWM drivers etc.. A FlexRay node could also contain optional bus guardians. Each FlexRay physical channel is connected to one bus driver. The host interacts with the FlexRay controller via a communication handler interface (CHI) as defined in the FlexRay protocol specification [1].

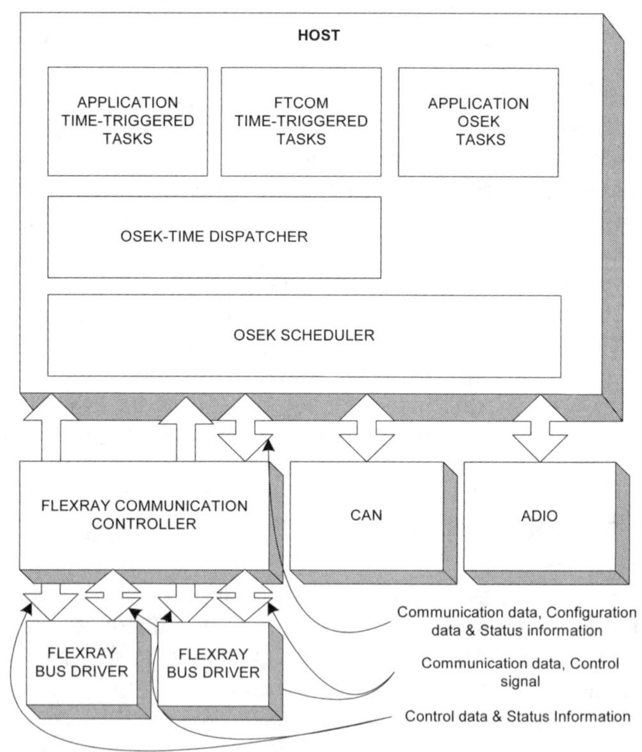

Figure 2: FlexRay based Software Architecture: Configurable by user

We will now describe the software architecture from an application developer's standpoint. At the highest abstraction of software design, we have time-triggered (TT) application tasks executing on the host. The host also contains a Fault Tolerant communication middleware layer that is compliant with the OSEKtime FTCom standard. This middleware layer is built on top of the FlexRay communication protocol, which provides standard API services like message exchange, integration and clock synchronization. Generally, the application TT tasks all have the same priority. The operating system uses a proprietary dSPACE kernel. This kernel is a pre-emptive "last come first served" scheduler. We permit pre-emptions in our system as long as they are all statically analyzed during design time. In this model, the OSEKtime dispatcher dispatches TT tasks based on a static schedule. However when two tasks are in contention for processing time, a "last come first served" scheduling strategy is used. A "first come first served" scheduling strategy is not used for the following reason: If one task runs unreliably and does not complete execution within its allocated time, this scheduling strategy will not allow any other tasks to pre-empt the unreliable one.

FlexRay distributed architecture consists of multiple nodes connected by dual FlexRay channels as shown in **Figure 3.** This FlexRay network is what we will refer to as a FlexRay distributed system. We use a linear passive bus topology, as shown here.

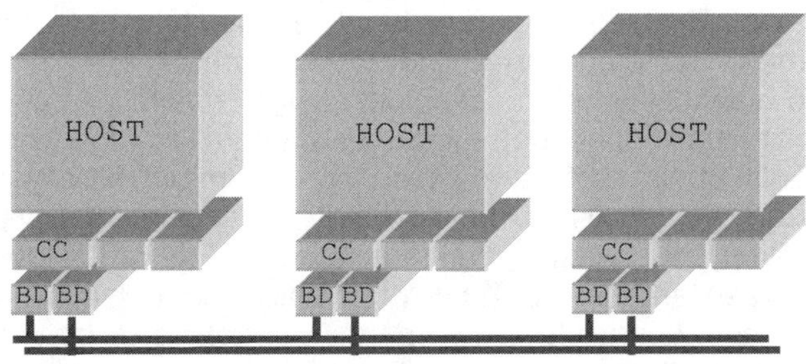

Figure 3: Three FlexRay nodes connected by a linear bus topology

We shall now describe the different functional architectures from the control system engineer's standpoint. **Figure 4** shows some of the basic different physical architectures for control systems. The centralized architecture is not well suited for fault-tolerant applications. The distributed architecture is very modular, but needs careful coordination between the different local controllers. In comparison, the hierarchical architecture offers benefits of both architectures. One of its shortcomings is that it involves more hardware. For our X-by-wire vehicle control system, a modified hierarchical physical and functional architecture was selected. The modification involves collocating different functionalities on each physical controller with the intent of reducing controller hardware. Even though the hardware architecture is distributed, the functional architecture is more hierarchical in nature.

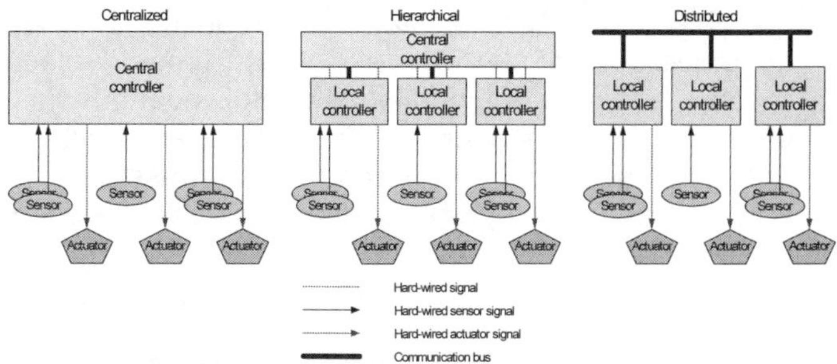

Figure 4: Different Functional and Physical Architectures

CHALLENGES IN MODEL-BASED SOFTWARE DEVELOPMENT FOR FLEXRAY-BASED SYSTEMS

Building reliable software for FlexRay-based systems involves building reliable controller models and then generating software from the controller models. In this section we list some challenges in building software from models:

- Providing end-to-end temporal guarantees under uncertain knowledge of execution times: While building a complex embedded system, it is difficult to predict the execution times of the SW components and the communication latencies. One has to make some educated guesses supported by analysis to ensure that end-to-end temporal guarantees are met. The models should be designed to be easily refinable once measurements are taken from the platform.

- Allocating software to hardware, global task scheduling and global message scheduling: Most previous work has approached this topic as multiple, isolated issues. While this leads to ease of handling, it results in sub-optimal solutions. Poor assignment of tasks to nodes causes unnecessary communication overhead. Inefficient communication is difficult to schedule, and middleware tasks have to perform extra packing and unpacking of signals. This consumes processor time, which directly impacts task schedules. Finding a good solution requires a unified approach where these "isolated" issues are targeted as one larger problem.

- Building an upfront global task and communication schedule with evolving functionality: FlexRay-based architectures might have software from different suppliers and OEM residing on the same host controller. Furthermore, different suppliers and the OEM may share the same Flexray communication network. Due to the nature of FlexRay, proper integration can only be guaranteed if computational resources (processing time) and communication resources (static slot identifiers) are distributed upfront between the suppliers. This distribution is possible only if application functionality is well-developed (e.g. known execution times, exact number and size of signals, task interdependencies etc.). This depends on the integrated architecture and how systems share resources, presenting a chicken and egg problem that requires iterative refinement.

MODEL-BASED FRAMEWORK FOR FLEXRAY-BASED SYSTEMS

In this section we will describe our design methodologies in terms of a model-based developmental process. It should be noted that it is not only a software development process, but also a process that touches control system functional design.

Various model-based processes have been proposed. The V process, which is quite popular, encompasses the entire development cycle. We shall limit the scope of our design to the left arm of the "V". DECOMSYS has proposed a model-based process called the "A" process in the publication "Model-Based System Development, An approach to Building X-by-Wire applications" [5]. This process has also been implemented as a tool chain within the V process, which has been used in our design.

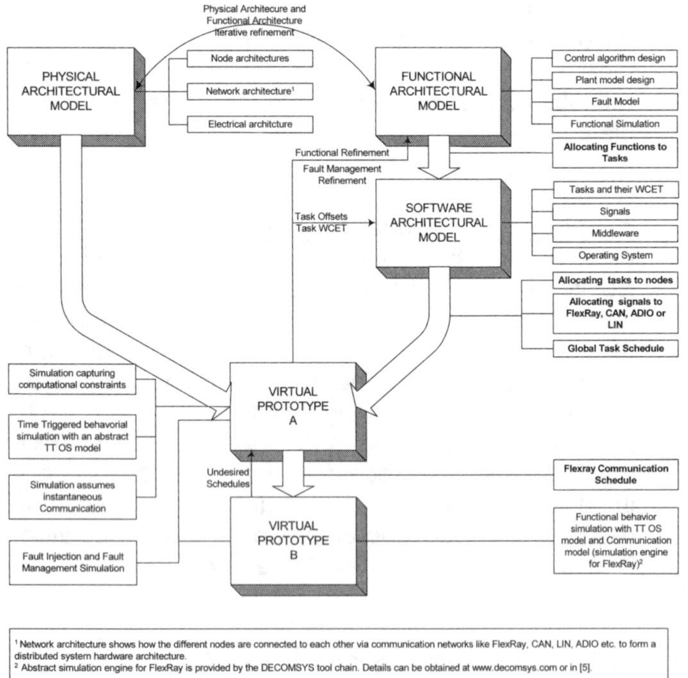

Figure 5: Distributed Systems Development Process

Figure 5 describes the steps involved in our design. We had to develop the functional architecture, software architecture and the physical architecture in modules. The fidelity of our design was verified and refined by simulations at various levels. The steps are highlighted in bold letters. Each 3-D box stands for an important design stage, while the associated boxes denote the properties. It should be noted that design was done in sequential steps from top to bottom. In subsequent sections, we describe the challenges faced in each of the design stages in detail and how they were resolved. Feedback arrows from the virtual prototype to the other design stages capture iterative design refinement.

Our design intent has been to use software tool based synthesis and analysis, which reduces the amount of testing performed during implementation.

FUNCTIONAL ARCHITECTURE

A functional architecture is an arrangment of functions and their breakdown along with interfaces (internal and external) that either defines the execution sequencing, conditions for control and data flow, and the relative performance levels of achievment for a desired outcome, or that provides a desired capability.

There are numerous well-known tools for modeling and simulation for the automotive domain like Simulink/Stateflow, Ascet-SD[5] and SCADE Drive for automotive[6]. We relied on Simulink/Stateflow for our development. In a modeling environment like Simulink/Stateflow, a functional architecture is used primarily for modeling and design of control algorithms and verification of functionality using simulation. This architecture does not model or capture the low-level details of the software executing on limited hardware resources, e.g. finite but non-zero execution time, pre-emption, and communication delays etc. Figure 6 shows a screen shot of an X-by-wire vehicle control system. The model consists of two parts: Controllers (X-by-wire vehicle control system) and Plant (Vehicle plant model). The vehicle control system contains controller models that will ultimately be software executing on computing nodes. The plant models are required for functional simulation.

Prior to simulation, SIMULINK orders all the blocks based on dependency constraints (i.e. topological dependencies) and execution rates. This involves flattening all hierarchical blocks into a single flat list grouped by execution rates. The execution order is extracted from this list. Any block where the output is directly dependent on its input (i.e., any block with direct feedthrough) cannot be executed until the block driving its input has executed.

[5] Ascet-SD is a rapid developmental tool for modeling and software development. Further details can be obtained at http://en.etasgroup.com/products/ascet_sd/

[6] SCADE Drive for Automotive systems has been developed by ESTEREL Technologies. Further details can be obtained at http://www.esterel-technologies.com/

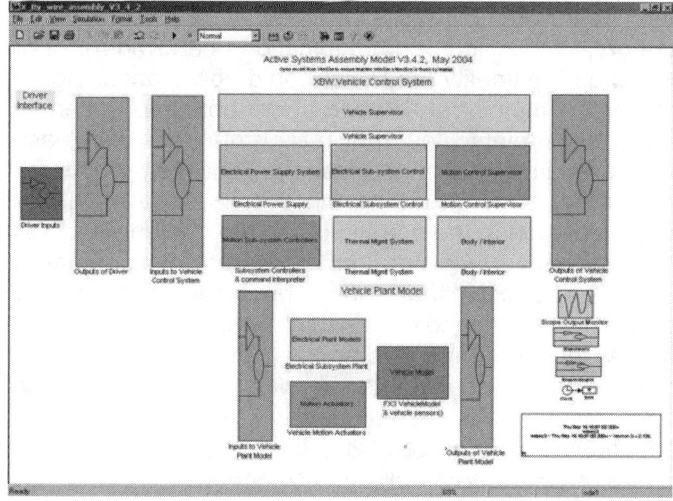

Figure 6: X-By-wire functional architecture in SIMULINK

The fidelity of this simulation in relation to the real execution behavior needs to be properly understood based on these important points:

- SIMULINK simulation block execution ordering might not reflect the true block ordering of tasks in a real-time distributed system.
- In SIMULINK all computations occur instantaneously and are not interrupted during their computation. This does not occur in a real system, where a task needs to be allocated a finite non-zero execution time which could be pre-empted during computation.
- All inter-block communication occurs instantaneously unless explicitly modelled otherwise.

The effect of the above three points needs to be accounted for with suitable analysis before generating code from the model. In order to verify the behavior of the control system accurately, we needed to capture some of the above constraints at the SIMULINK model level. In this section we briefly describe how we obtained a high fidelity simulation model in SIMULINK that captured software and hardware implications indirectly. This simulation model also provides the groundwork for proper iterative refinement.

The task schedule used in our development is a static schedule specified during design time. A static schedule is required for deterministic behavior. Preemption is sometimes disallowed in order to preserve determinism. We permit preemption as long as all preemptions are statically analyzed and fixed during design time. Hence, all tasks that get preempted are modeled as tasks that take a finite time longer than usual execution times.

If the task execution is unspecified, SIMULINK will determine the execution order of the subsystems (as explained above). In order to control the execution order, we built a separate scheduler using the SIMULINK "Functional Call Generator" . These blocks produce "task triggers" at prespecified rates, and are connected to "GOTO" blocks. A "Demux" block routes the trigger signals to the appropriate subsystems when it is connected to the output of the "Functional call generator". The subystem extracts its trigger signal via a "FROM" block. The topmost output signal from the "Demux" block triggers the first execution. The execution sequence then continues from top to bottom.

The details on how we obtain a static task schedule is described later.

Using this method, we simulate the functional architecture with subsystems having an execution order which is very similar to the final execution order. As mentioned earlier, this also lays the framework for iterative refinement, where the impact of changing task schedules on behavior can be examined in SIMULINK.

As mentioned in the introduction to this section (Points 2&3), SIMULINK assumes all computations to occur instantaneously without interruption and without any computational resource constraint. This is an abstraction from the real system, where a finite execution time needs to be allocated to a task which could be pre-empted during computation.

To model the finite computation time and communication delay, we used the Decomsys tool chain, which has an interface to SIMULINK. The computation tasks were annotated with "Worst case execution times" (WCET). Even though the tool does not model preemptions, we modelled pre-emptions as tasks with extended WCET. To elaborate further, each task that was preempted had a total execution time of its own added to the WCET of the task that preempted it. The Decomsys tools also provided simulation of communication synchronous time-triggered tasks and generic communication with or without delays. Further details on the process can be found in [5, 7].

In order to model real FlexRay communication delays, one has to obtain the FlexRay schedule. We shall address this problem in a subsequent section. However, once the static schedule has been determined, one can also simulate the functional architecture with real communication delays.

ALLOCATING FUNCTIONS TO TASKS

A functional architecture consists of functional blocks (which are hierarchical in nature) modeling the controller as well as the plant model (e.g., **Figure 6**). However, this architecture is used primarily for control system design and simulation. These functional blocks do not represent application software tasks[1]. We need to regroup "functional" blocks into "application task" blocks that symbolize "pieces" of software code. Essentially, we can now view each block at the model level as ultimately a "piece" of software with clearly defined inputs and outputs.

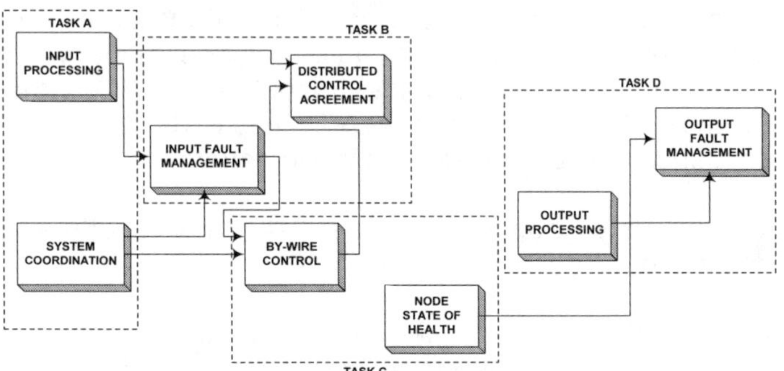

Figure 7: Allocating functions to tasks

The most effort-intensive part of collecting functions into tasks is to flatten the hierarchy. Hierarchy in SIMULINK is a visual organization to manage complexity, but the final execution is non-hierarchical. In our time-triggered system all software tasks that communicate over FlexRay have the same priority. The scheduler is a preemptive "last come first served" scheduler.

The functional architecture as shown in **Figure 7** consists of seven functional blocks. The functions are tagged to four tasks: A, B, C and D. The four tasks could be implemented on the same node or distributed on different nodes. Tagging two functions into one software task essentially implies one "piece" of software code where the two functions could be implemented as sequential blocks of software code. However, marking two functions as separate tasks essentially forms two "concurrent" entities.

The way in which functions are allocated into tasks greatly impacts the architecture and the performance of the system. In the above example it is also possible to have three different tasks, one for each subsystem. Having too much granularity increases the task and signal scheduling complexity. Composing functions into tasks was primarily based on experience and knowledge of the hardware architecture, however we can generalize some rules for allocating tasks to functions:

Rule 1: Any two functions which reside on separate computation nodes cannot be in the same task, i.e. only functions on the same computational node can be allocated to the same task.
Rule 2: Any two functions that act on the same inputs and have the same deadline for producing outputs can be combined into a task.

TASK ALLOCATION TO HARDWARE NODES

Tasks need to be allocated to nodes such that the resulting distributed embedded system satisfies all the temporal constraints of the design without exceeding the available resources. In addition to the temporal constraints, the allocation should be done in a manner that optimally utilizes the resources (computing, memory, I/O, and communication bandwidth). For example, optimality criteria could be "obtaining a solution", "obtaining a solution under bounded uncertain design constraints", "even utilization of nodes", or "ease of future integration of tasks". However, "optimal" assignment early on during the design stage might not be possible since the complexity of the design becomes apparent only during the final stages of development. It is this "complexity" that cannot be modeled accurately during the early stages of design. In our application, the criteria for allocating tasks to nodes were I/O and communication constraints as well as fault tolerance requirements. It is also important to ensure that the allocations do not exceed the computational resources and do not overburden any particular node.

Tasks that do not require direct I/O, e.g. *Subsystem coordination* as well as *Supervisor* and *Diagnostic tasks,* are allocated to nodes based on their proximity to other tasks (already allocated). Additional requirements for allocation could be to evenly spreads out the computation load based or based on fault tolerance requirements.

GLOBAL STATIC TASK SCHEDULE

The global task scheduling problem consists of determining the execution order of all the tasks (over all nodes) based on knowledge of the periodicity, WCETs, task dependencies, deadlines, and processing power of the nodes. The nodal task schedule is the outcome of the global task schedule. Different scheduling methods for embedded real-time systems have been adequately addressed in [4]. This publication reviews alternate approaches to scheduling methods

Two approaches exist for scheduling tasks for distributed systems: *Static* scheduling and *Dynamic* scheduling. With static schedules, the execution order of tasks is strictly determinstic and does not change during execution (if the design assumptions are not violated). Within dynamic schedules, the execution order is determined during run time.

For our design, we used a static schedule to achieve determinism. All time-triggered tasks (SBW, BBW, PBW, Vehicle dynamics supervisor) are of the same priority. Certain fault tolerant background application tasks that check the health of the processors are of higher priority than the rest of the application tasks. The real-time kernel implements a preemptive "last come first served" scheduling policy. However, there is an OSEKtime dispatcher that triggers tasks based on a static schedule. As mentioned earlier, in our design we permit pre-emption of tasks as long as we make sure that we statically analyze all possible preemptions during the design stage. Dynamically scheduled systems are extremely difficult to tune and to analyze for safety.

Once tasks are allocated to the nodes, the task execution times need to be scheduled on each node. Two tasks in a global schedule need to execute sequentially if they are on the same node. On the other hand, they can execute concurrently if they are executing on different nodes. Since we assume all nodes to be connected to each other via FlexRay, there is a global concept of time for all the nodes. The existence of the distributed clock synchronization algorithm in FlexRay permits all nodes to have a single concept of time. We relied on manual scheduling, because of the lack of mature scheduling tools targeting FlexRay-based applications. In this section we also highlight certain practical constraints in the realm of fault tolerant by-wire control systems which have not been captured in earlier work. These have been extremely critical in the manual schedules.

We have different tasks executing at different rates. As required in a time-triggered system, the rates must be harmonics of each other. In order to better understand the intricacies involved in scheduling tasks, one has to understand the events that take place when two tasks communicate over FlexRay. **Figure 8** shows tasks executing on three nodes. Each horizontal row denotes tasks executing on a single node and shows the starting and ending times of tasks and communications. **Table 1** describe the activities associated with each time event. We have Task A1 executing on Node 1 sending data to Task C2 on Node 3 via a FlexRay slot. We have **S** and **R** as the Send and Receive FTCom middleware tasks.

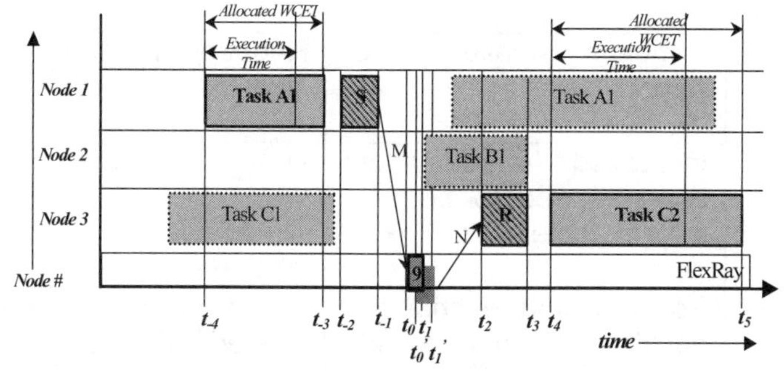

Figure 8: Time flow of tasks and messages in a FlexRay system

Timeline	Action
t_{-4}	Task A1 is triggered to start execution by the OSEKtime dispatcher.
t_{-3}	Task A1 is scheduled to complete execution.
t_{-2}	FTCom (middleware) *Send* task starts execution[7].
t_{-1}	FTCom (middleware) *Send* task completes execution.
M	Data (to be sent) transfer between the main memory and the FlexRay CC buffer.
t_0	Start time for the scheduled FlexRay Slot 9 to send the message across the bus.
t_1	End time for the scheduled FlexRay Slot 9 to send the message across the bus.
t_0'	Time after propagation delay where Node 3 receives the first bit of the frame.[ix]
t_1'	Time after propagation delay where Node 3 receives the last bit of the frame.
N	Data (received) transfer between the FlexRay CC buffer and the main memory.
t_2	FTCom (middleware) *Receive* task starts execution.
t_3	FTCom (middleware) *Receive* task completes execution.
t_4	Task C2 is triggered to start execution consuming the data sent by Task A1
t_5	Task C2 is scheduled to complete execution.

Table 1: Timelines when two tasks communicate via FlexRay

The static task scheduling problem consists of detemining the times t_{-4} and t_4 which are the triggering times of Task A1 and Task C2. However, we also have to determine the triggering times of the middleware tasks. Hence, the problem involves determining the time stamp offsets t_{-4}, t_{-2}, t_2, t_4 which are the starting times of Task A1, FTCom Send middleware task on Node 1, FTCom Receive task on Node 3, and the start time for Task C2 on Node 3. Sometimes, one triggers the Send (or Receive) FTCom task immediately after (or before) the task that sends (or receives) the data. This is typically not the case in our application, since the FTCom Send task multiplexes signals from a number of tasks (on the same node) and sends them over FlexRay in the same slot. A similar situation could occur on the receiving side. The timelines are actually offsets with respect to the start of the communication cycle, i.e. the start of the communication cycle in FlexRay is assumed as zero time. These offsets are tabulated in the OSEKtime dispatch table and the scheduler triggers tasks based on that.

In order to obtain the schedule we had to specify the WCETs of the tasks. We had to also determine the WCETs of the middleware tasks. There is significant difficulty in predicting the WCET of the middleware tasks. These WCETs depend on how many signals are packed into a slot and the sizes of the constituent

[7] Context switching time is modeled explicitly as an added WCET to the task that immediately follows the context switch.

signals. This, however, is not known before *we actually allocate signals into slots and schedule the communication slots*. Hence, we had to count on intiutive analysis, experience and iteratively refine our task schedules.

In the above example, we demonstrated the detail involved in scheduling two tasks involving two nodes communicating with each other over FlexRay. In our X-by-wire distributed vehicle we had over one hundred application and middleware tasks communicating with each other through numerous signals.

Fault tolerance can significantly limit the task-scheduling problem. As shown in **Figure 8**, replicated components need to be scheduled concurrently. It requires messages to be sent very close to each other for reasons of temporal message consistency. There are scenarios where voting occurs between nodes over multiple communication cycles.

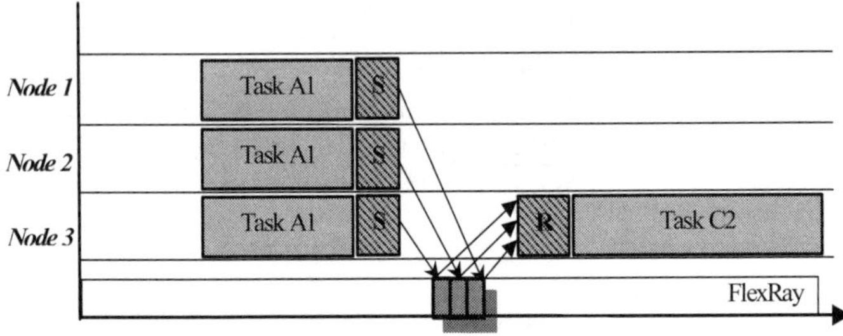

Figure 9: Effect of replicated fault tolerant tasks on scheduling

ALLOCATING SIGNALS TO FRAMES

In this section we shall discuss how we allocate signals into slots. Thus far, we have described the method of how signals need to be scheduled over FlexRay. We now determine how we actually allocate signals into the *same frame*[8]. In the subsequent section we shall schedule the frames and allocate FlexRay identifier numbers to the different frames.

FlexRay is a time-triggered fault tolerant communication bus. One complete instance of a communication structure that is periodically repeated in FlexRay is called the *communication cycle.* A communication cycle consists of a static segment, an optional dynamic segment, an optional symbol window and a network idle time segment. For the purpose of our analysis, the communication cycle shall consist of only a static segment and a network idle time segment.

We first had to choose the period of the communication cycle, which was a sub-multiple of the periods of all the tasks. The static segment of a communication cycle consists of *slots.* The size of each slot (**SS**= Slot size) can range from 0 to 254 bytes (0-127 two-byte words). In one communication cycle, only one node can own a communication slot. A slot consists of one message having only one *sender* and possibly many *receivers* (not the sender). A message contains multiple signals of varying lengths and types packed together.

Before packing signals into slots, one must decide on the optimum static slot size. The effect of the choice of static slot size is also dependent on the speed of the FlexRay bus. Even though the protocol specifies the maximum slot size to be 254 bytes, it is also limited by the available on-chip FlexRay buffer size. Our development buffers were restricted to 32 in number and 256 bits of memory each. **Table 2** summarizes the tradeoffs involved in selecting between different slot sizes.

	SMALLER SLOT SIZES	LARGER SLOT SIZES
1	Larger number of reads and writes required between host memory and FlexRay controller buffer ties up CPU time.	Fewer reads and writes required.
2.	More customized packing of signals into frames targeted to receivers[9].	Receiver might get many signals that it does not intend to use.
3.	Requires smaller buffer sizes	Requires larger buffer sizes
4.	Increased fragmentation: Signals need to be sent over multiple slots	Less fragmentation
5.	Possibly more economical packing of signals into frames.	Could possibly lead to wasted buffer space.

Table 2: Comparison of Smaller Slot Sizes with Larger Slot Sizes

FlexRay provides a great amount of flexibility in defining the size of the communication slot. Once the size of the communication slot is decided, it applies to all communication cycles and to all slots within a communication cycle. The granularity of the slot length depends on the Flexray communication configuration

[8] This is different from *actually scheduling a frame at a particular time,* i.e it is one problem to have 7 signals allocated to a frame and another problem to actually allocate the frame to FlexRay static slot number 9. It is the former that we are discussing.

[9] A node that receives a *static slot* must unpack all the signals and execute the Replica Determinate algorithm on them. If the slot contains signals that it does not need, it wastes resources trying to unpack them before discarding them.

parameters (e.g. bus speed, microtick[x] length, macrotick[xi] length), the signal list and properties. Various subsystems that share the FlexRay communication system may have a very different number and size of signals that need to be sent. Hence, agreeing on a unique slot size has an important impact on the design.

There are two key points in allocating signals to frames. All signals sent by one task to another at the same time may be allocated to the same frame. Signals that need to be sent at roughly the same offset (which might contain signals from different tasks on the same node) may be allocated to the same frame. Two signals that are meant for different tasks on different nodes should not be allocated to the same frame.

GLOBAL COMMUNICATION SCHEDULE

Once the global tasks are scheduled and signals are packed into frames, we need to schedule the frames into communication slots. This involves assigning a unique FlexRay identifier to each frame. The Decomsys tool chain has an automated scheduling wizard, but we found it unsuitable within the scope of our development (because of the scale of magnitude involved). One key problem is that the automated scheduling technique does not take into account task interdependencies when it comes up with its automated communication schedule.

Figure 10 shows Task A1 (periodicity ***p***) sending a frame via slot number 19 to Task C2 (periodicity ***p***). Ideally, we would want to send the frame in a slot between the end time of the middleware task S and start time of receiving middleware task R. If the frame is indeed sent in the time within this time frame, the reaction time will be simply the difference between the end time of Task C2 and the start time of Task A1. However, if we are unable to schedule the message within the desired time frame and we schedule the frame at a later slot, then the reaction time increases by the periodicity ***p***. Let us define the term *"Communication Miss"*, denoting a situation where a frame in not able to be scheduled in the desired time frame. Communication misses exist in our design (due to stringent temporal constraints) and so the impact of each miss on the control system has to be analyzed. They lead to increased phase lag in the control system. For cases where these are part of a feedback loop, they impact stability margins.

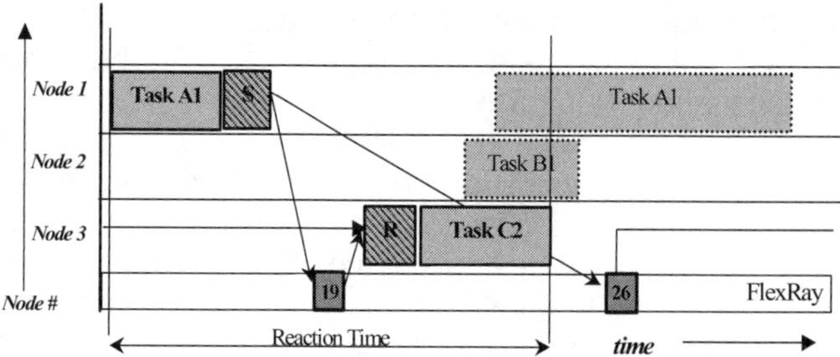

Figure 10: Effect of communication miss

The communication schedule needs to satisfy all the dependency constraints. Dependency violations could occur due to "Communication misses". In such cases, the effect of all such misses needs to be statically analyzed.

OEM/SUPPLIER SOFTWARE AND COMMUNICATION INTEGRATION

When it is used as a vehicle communications backbone, FlexRay has to be shared between electronic control units (ECU) from different suppliers. The situation becomes more complex when software from different suppliers shares the same ECU in addition to sharing the communication network. In this section, we shall highlight some of the integration issues related to FlexRay-based systems from the OEM-supplier co-development perspective. We will also outline how we dealt with them. **Figure 11** shows software from two suppliers, the OEM sharing three nodes and the FlexRay communication bus.

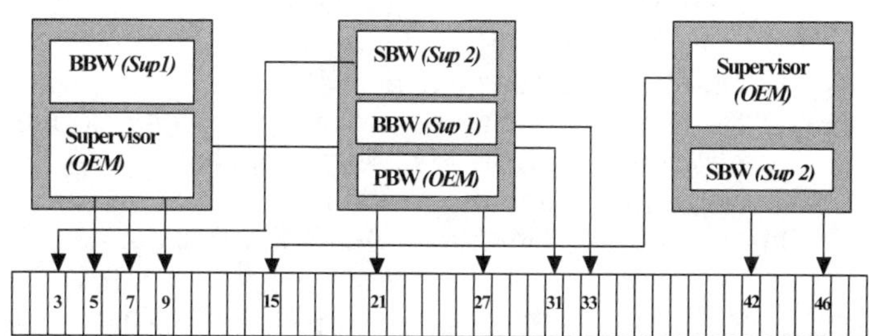

Figure 11: Supplier and OEM Software sharing nodes and the Communication subsystem

FlexRay being a time-triggered subsystem presents its unique set of integration constraints. In order to facilitate proper integration, one has to develop accurate models of the software and communication architecture during the earlier stages of the design. To be more precise, one has to determine the location of the supplier tasks on the nodes, the WCETs of the supplier tasks, the signal lists, and the task dependencies. The location of the software and WCETs is required to be able to divide the computational resources of each node. The signal lists and task dependencies are required to distribute the communication requirements.

The integration problem of the entire vehicle subsystem was solved hierarchically. First, a high level architectural model was developed and the constraints arising from this model were provided to each subsystem supplier. Each subsystem supplier developed their subsystem independently without violating the specified constraints. The constraints were developed by us (OEM) based on some front-end architectural analysis. During the different stages of development, the constraints were refined iteratively.

Next, we took each of the individual supplier subsystems as well as our own system and merged the entire architecture together. During this merge, we captured the inter-subsystem and OEM-subsystem interactions. We also tuned the architecture whenever conflicts arose. Proper development of constraints during the earlier stages of the design leads to proper integration and proper verification of the system during the final stages of development. Significant architectural analysis needed to be done while developing these constraints.

We now highlight the steps involved

<u>Step 1:</u> The OEM performs front-end analysis and provides constraints or models to the supplier. Some of the constraints provided to each subsystem supplier are

1. Communication constraints:
   - FlexRay bus speed.
   - Communication cycle time.
   - Slot frame size in bits.
   - Number of FlexRay slots available.
   - Network topology and other low-level communication-related parameters.
2. Processor constraints
   - Number of processors allocated.
   - Percentage of processing power of each node allowed to be utilized by each supplier.
3. Allowable loop rates (harmonics).
4. Other input/ouput interface (ADIO/CAN) constraints.

<u>Step 2:</u> Each subsystem supplier develops its subsystem independently adhering to the constraints. It then gives the integrator:

1. The number of nodes on which software tasks are going to reside .
2. The intertask dependency.
3. The WCETs for each task on a node.
4. The local offsets of each of its tasks within its subystem.
5. The signal list and signals packed into frames.
6. The frame identifiers for each frame used.
7. Other software architectural information.
8. The software models/object code which has the functionality hidden (which can also be used for functional simulation).

<u>Step 3:</u> The integrator merges the different supplier task and communication schedules with the OEM task and communication schedule:

1. Every task gets its share of computation time (modeled as WCET).
2. Every supplier message slot gets scheduled without violating any dependency.
3. Integration captures the intersupplier as well as supplier-OEM task dependencies.
4. Integration captures the intersupplier as well as supplier-OEM communications.
5. Integrator tunes the task and communication schedule of the entire system to resolve conflicts.

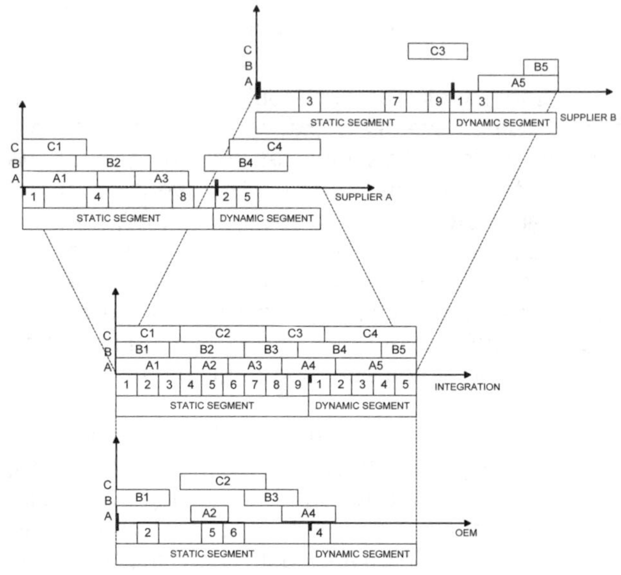

<u>Figure 12: Supplier subsystems being merged into a global system</u>

CONCLUSION

This publication describes a model-based software development approach for a distributed X-by-wire automotive control system utilizing FlexRay. Some of the challenges in this process are highlighted, including upfront integration, OEM/supplier collaboration, iterative hardware/software development, iterative communication and application software development. While several tools exist to enable different aspects of the overall process, the need remains for an end-to-end tool chain that addresses some of these real-world challenges in the automotive domain.

ACKNOWLEDGMENTS

The authors would like to acknowledge Thomas E. Fuhrman, Lawrence Peruski for their advice and the support of the management of GM R&D.

The authors would also like to acknowledge Mohan Sundar, Doug Cesiel, Arnold W. Millsap, Priya Narashiman and Tom. M. Forest for their assistance.

The authors would also like to thank our suppliers for joint discussions.

REFERENCES

1. FlexRay Consortium. FlexRay Communication System: Protocol Specification, 2004

2. Rajeev Alur, Thao Dang, Joel Esposito, Rafael Fierro, Yerang Hur, Franjo Ivancic, Vijay Kumar, Insup Lee, P. K. Mishra, George Pappas, Oleg Sokolsky. Hierarchical Modeling and Analysis of Embedded Systems, Proceedings of the IEEE, January 2003, Volume 91, Number 1.

3. Rajeev Alur, Thao Dang, Joel Esposito, Rafael Fierro, Yerang Hur, Franjo Ivancic, Vijay Kumar, Insup Lee, P. K. Mishra, George Pappas, Oleg Sokolsky. Hierarchical Hybrid Modeling of Embedded Systems. 1st International Workshop on embedded Software, October 2001 (LNCS 2211).

4. F. Balarin, L Lavagno, P. Murthy, A. Sangiovanni-Vincentelli. Scheduling for Embedded Real Time Systems. IEEE Design & Test, January 1998, pp. 71-82.

5. R. Nossal, R. Lang. Model-Based System Development- An Approach to building X-by-wire Applications. IEEE Micro, July/August 2002, pp. 56-63.

6. T. A. Henzinger, B. Horowitz, C. M. Kirsch. Giotto: A Time-Triggered Language for Embedded Programming, EMSOFT 2001, pp 166-184.

7. Roman Nossal. Meeting the Challenges in a collaborative OEM-supplier development of distributed embedded systems. SAE 2004 World Congress, 2004, SAE-2004-01-0278.

8. John Rushby. Partitioning in Avionics Architectures: Requirements, Mechanisms, and Assurances. NASA/CR-1999-209347, June 1999.

9. Edward A. Lee. Embedded Software- An agenda for Research, ERL Technical Report UCB/ERL No. M99/63, December 1999.

10. J. L. Welch and N. A. Lynch. A New Fault-tolerant Algorithm for Clock Synchronization, Information and Computation, vol. 77, April 1998, no. 1, pp 1-36

CONTACT

Please direct all questions to Pradyumna K. Mishra (Pradyumna.Mishra@gm.com) or Sanjeev M. Naik (Sanjeev.M.Naik@gm.com).

---

[i] *Message*: a collection of signals that is intended to fit the data payload segment of the FlexRay communication frame.
[ii] *Task:* piece of application software that can be executed as a concurrent unit.
[iii] *Signal*: application data produced and/or used by application tasks.
[iv] *Communication Slot*: an interval of time during which access to a communication channel is granted exclusively to a specific node for the transmission of a frame with a frame ID corresponding to the slot.
[v] *Communication Cycle* is one complete instance of the communication structure that is periodically repeated to comprise the media access method of the Flexray system. The CC consists of a static segment, an optional dynamic segment, an optional symbol window, and a network idle time segment.
[vi] *Network idle time* serves as a phase during which the node calculates and applies clock correction terms. It also performs implementation-specific communication cycle tasks.
[vii] A *Communication Controller (CC)* is an electronic component in a node that is responsible for implementing the protocol aspects of the FlexRay communication system.
[viii] A *Bus driver* is an electronic component, which consists of a transmitter and a receiver that connects a communication controller to one communication channel.
[ix] *Frame:* a structure used by the communication system to exchange information within the system. A frame consists of a header segment, a payload segment and a trailer segment. Application data is transmitted through the payload section.
[x] *Microtick:* an interval of time derived directly from the CC's oscillator. The Microtick is not affected by the clock synchronization mechanisms, and is a node-local concept. Different nodes can have microticks of different duration.
[xi] *Macrotick*: an interval of time derived from the cluster-wide clock synchronization algorithm. A Macrotick consists of an integral number of Microticks. The clock synchronization algorithm adjusts the actual number of microticks in a given Macrotick. The Macrotick represents the smallest granularity unit of the global time.

2005-01-0022

Analysis of the Communication Requirements of a Highly-Distributed Engine Control

Walton L. Fehr
Motorola, Inc.

ABSTRACT

Switch fabric communication networks have been proposed for use in automobiles as a means of reducing the physical complexity of communication and control systems. Such networks have proven very valuable in telecommunications and business computing applications. Similar advantages are foreseen in the automotive area. This paper begins to summarize the partitioning and communication requirements of a highly-distributed engine control system that would be part of a switch fabric network in a vehicle.

Engine controls have traditionally been constructed by connecting a large number of input and output devices to a large-scale control module. Most of the signal conditioning and output driving circuitry is combined with a microcontroller and other specialized integrated circuits in the control module. In a vehicle with a switch fabric network, some of the signal conditioning and drive electronics would be distributed out to the actual input and output devices. These devices would contribute their abilities to the engine control strategy running in some computing resource by using the switch fabric communication network. Two types of communication – event-based and periodic process – are used to illustrate the communication requirements of this kind of distributed control. A vehicle with a 4 cylinder engine is used in the analysis presented.

INTRODUCTION

ARCHITECTED VEHICLE

Motorola has been working on a concept that called The Architected Vehicle for some time. One scenario in this concept is based on two fundamental principles – strict layering of the software to allow for distributed control and a packet-based mesh-type network to connect the distributed elements together. This type of control implementation is sometimes called a Switch Fabric[1,2] because a two-dimensional representation of the network looks like a piece of woven fabric with packet switches at each of the intersections of the threads.

This scenario is being explored because it is hoped that by breaking the vehicle control problem down into smaller, distributed elements and by using standardized interfaces between the elements, the elements will become more generic. More generic elements can then be used in broader applications leading to the efficiencies of high volumes. The elements can become proven, qualified catalog items. Instead of having custom engineered subsystem control modules for every make and model as are used in automobiles today, the vehicle builder of the future will be able to choose generic control elements, connect them together with an industry-standard interface, and then add the top-level brand characteristics that make their vehicle unique.

STRICT LAYERING

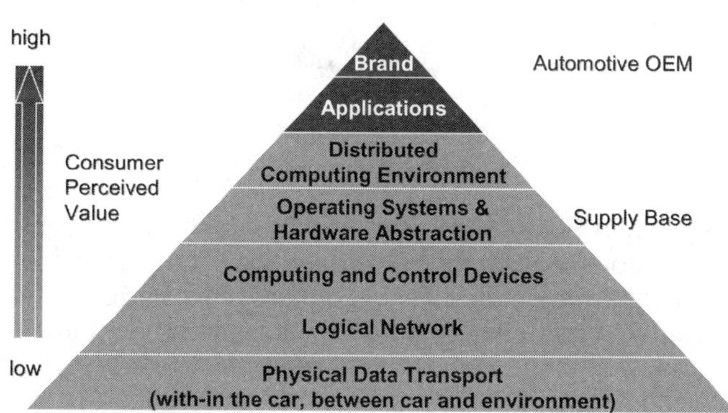

Figure 1. Software Layers[1]

Implementing control software with distinct layers with well-defined interfaces between the layers should help to separate the top two layers – brand and application – from the lower layers (see Figure 1). The lower layers could then become more generic and usable on a wider variety of installations. Having well-defined layers should allow vehicle builders to concentrate on the top layers while component suppliers provide the lower layers. Hopefully, all layers of the software will become more reusable since they will be running on more standardized hardware elements satisfying a long-standing desire of vehicle builders.[3]

PACKET-BASED MESH-TYPE NETWORK

The distributed control elements would be connected together by a mesh-type network made up of nodes with packet switches and point-to-point communication links. One of the main advantages of the switch fabric communication network is that there are multiple possible paths between any two of the nodes in the network. This gives the network redundancy that can be used if any one of the communication links should be disrupted and extra capacity because multiple communication packets can be traveling in the network at any one time.

The communication links between switch nodes would be implemented using a layered approach as well so that the actual payload of a packet would be independent of the medium in which it travels. Different media could be chosen for the different communication requirements within the network. The packet switches could be independent devices that would be located a places where a wire harness would naturally branch in a vehicle, or could be built into an input/output device or computing devices.

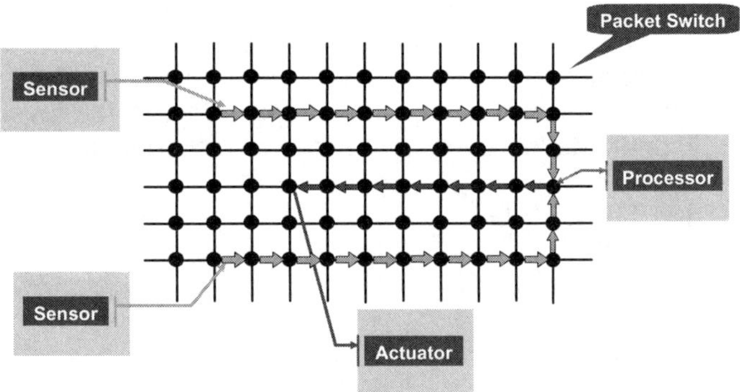

Figure 2. Switch Fabric[1]

As shown in Figure 2, an application might be running in a processor somewhere in the network. That application needs information from two sensors elsewhere in the network to decide when or how to activate an actuator at still another location in the network. Packets of information would be launched from the sensors when the phenomenon monitored by the sensor changes state or level (event based), or at some predetermined time (periodic). The packet would travel to an adjacent switch node in the network along a path determined by an overall routing strategy. The packet would continue to hop through the network form node to node until it reached the node where the application is running. The application would then use the new information to construct a control packet for the actuator which it would then launch out into the network toward the actuator. The actuator control packet would hop from node to node until it reached its destination where it would be used by the local intelligence in the actuator's node to properly activate the actuator.[1]

The fabric of communication links and switch nodes would uniformly blanket the entire vehicle as shown in Appendix A. The blanket would provide a unified communication and control infrastructure that would be used by all of the functional subsystems of the vehicle

MAIN SECTION

ENGINE CONTROL – GENERAL REQUIREMENTS

The engine control task can be summarized with the help of the drawing in Figure 3.[4] The shaded items between the driver of the vehicle and the engine itself make up the control. Traditionally, the entire control has been built as a set of software running in a specially designed electronic control unit (ECU). The ECU is connected to input and output devices by a wire harness.

The driver of the vehicle expresses a desire for how much torque should be applied to the vehicle's drive wheels by manipulating various user interfaces – accelerator pedal, brake pedal, etc. The Driver Interface segment of the control strategy in the ECU monitors the user interfaces and determines how much torque the driver is requesting. The Engine Controller segment of the control strategy then determines how to set the various actuators on the engine to generate the desired torque. Specific commands are given to the Actuator Controller segment of the control strategy which cause the actual actuators to operate. Information from sensors on the engine is fed back to the Engine Controller layer to modify its behavior.

ARCHITECTED VEHICLE IMPLEMENTATION

We are developing a proposal for how the engine control would be organized in a vehicle built with Architected Vehicle principles. We would start by breaking the physical components of the traditional ECU into small, intelligent, elements. Each of the input or output devices that are used by the control would be connected to a communication switch node in the fabric. We would then connect the elements with a fabric of communication.

Finally, we would separate the control software into elements with well defined layers which would be also distributed to the elements in the network (Figure 4). The Actuator Controller segment would be distributed to the input and output devices, and the Driver Interpreter and Engine Controller segments would end up in general purpose computing resources. The now-smart input and output devices would be connected to the general purpose computing devices by a switch fabric. There would no longer be a component in the vehicle called the Engine Control ECU.

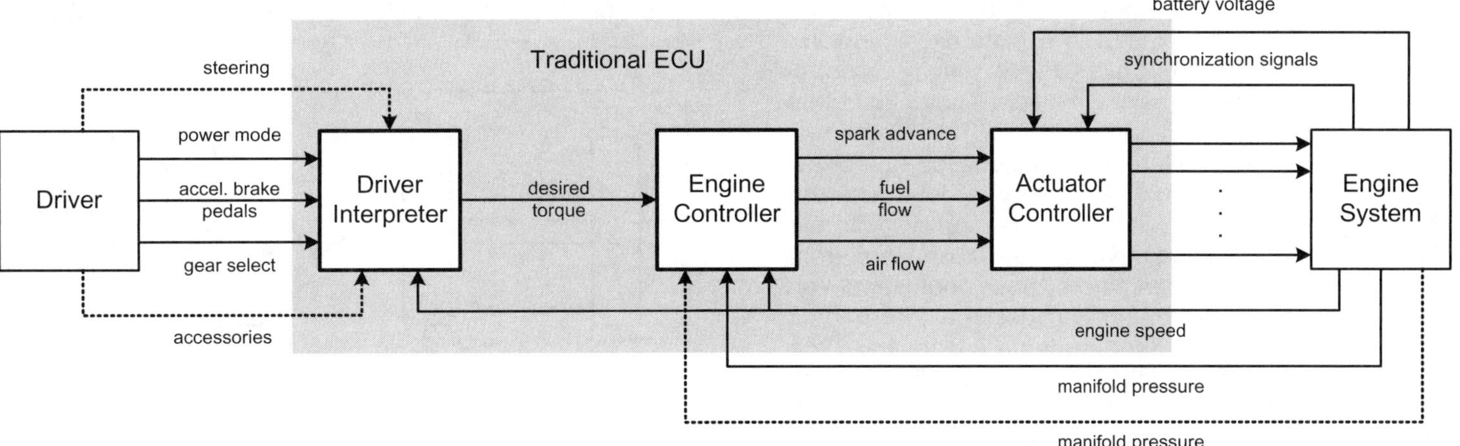

Figure 3. Engine control block diagram[4]

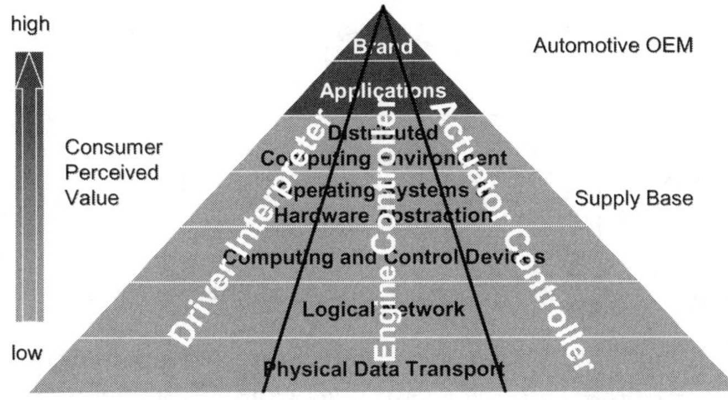

Figure 4. Software segments with layers

Table 1 gives a list of typical input and output devices monitored or controlled by the controller of a spark ignited engine that will be used as an example in this paper.

Table 1. Input and Output Devices

Input Devices	Output Devices
Crank Angle Sensor	Fuel Injectors (4)
CAM Phase Sensor	Spark Coils (4)
Air temperature	Purge valve
Coolant temperature	
MAP (or MAF)	Fuel pump
Accelerator Pedal Position	Coolant fan
Vehicle speed	Tachometer
Lambda Sensor (2)	Diagnostic port
Key position	Throttle Butterfly
Battery Voltage	
Diagnostic port	

Appendix B then shows how these input and output devices would be spread out within the communication fabric. Also shown are some elements of another control subsystem – exterior lighting – to illustrate that the fabric will be used as a unified communication medium for all control purposes in the vehicle.

Top Layers – Driver Request For Torque

The top two layers of the engine control software (Figure 4) would be isolated from the input and output devices. They could even be independent of the machine that they would run on. The brand-specific interpretation of the Driver Interpreter layer could be applied to any type of engine configuration that may be used in a particular model of vehicle. The vehicle designer could isolate those characteristics of the task of applying torque to the vehicle's drive wheels that would make the vehicle unique in the Brand layer. By doing this, all different engines (displacement, combustion type, number of cylinders, supplier, etc.) would behave the same to the vehicle driver.

The Application layer would calibrate the Brand layer to the individual nature of the engine being installed in the vehicle. For example, this layer would be used to account for differences in the overall performance of four cylinder spark-ignited engines from two different suppliers, or for the differences between the performance of a spark-ignited engine and a compression-ignition engine.

Atomistic Breakdown – I/O Devices, Software

As an example of how an input or output device used in the control system might look, we can look at a typical input device such as the accelerator pedal and an output device such as a fuel injector.

For the purposes of this paper we will assume that all of the input and output devices will be connected to a node of the switch fabric network. Each node will contain a packet switch so that the node can link to at least two other nodes. The accelerator pedal in located in under the instrument panel in passenger compartment of the vehicle so it would connect to neighboring nodes in the instrument panel.

Figures 5a and 5b illustrate some of the decisions that have to be made when an input device is separated from a traditional ECU and placed in a distributed network. Accelerator pedals for drive-by-wire engine control applications typically have multiple potentiometers connected to a rotating shaft. The individual potentiometers have different characteristics that allow some algorithm in the control strategy to determine the driver's intentions as well as the quality of the information from the input device. If the information from the independent potentiometers does not meet an expected pattern, the control can assume that one or more of them (or the wiring connecting the potentiometers to the controller) is faulty and use an alternate strategy.

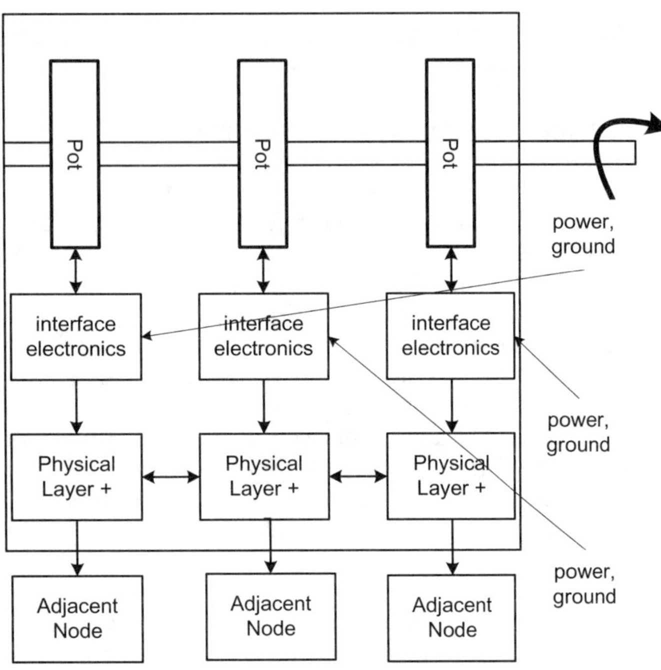

Figure 5a. Accelerator pedal node example

In order to preserve the uniqueness of the information form each potentiometer, the designer of the accelerator pedal could put independent interface electronics into the assembly for each of the potentiometers as shown in the Figure 5a drawing and provide independent power and ground feeds for each of the interface circuits. You would now have completely independent electronics to go along with the independent mechanical devices. Each independent subassembly would provide information to the network through different adjacent nodes providing path diversity for the accelerator pedal information.

Of course this would add complexity and possibly cost to the accelerator pedal assembly. A reasonable compromise might be to have a common set of interface electronics in the assembly as shown in the Figure 5b version of the drawing. Resources such as voltage regulators and logic devices could be shared by the three potentiometers. You would still have three independent physical layers with connections to three different adjacent nodes for information path diversity.

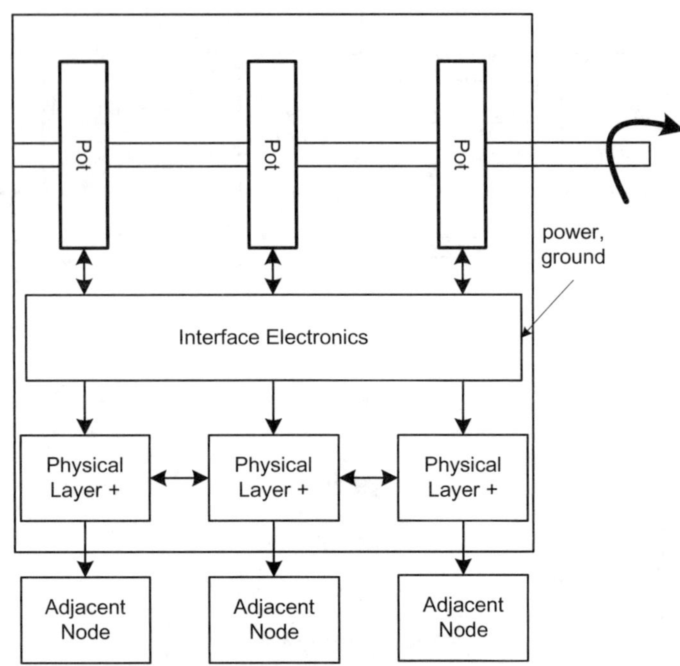

Figure 5b. Accelerator pedal node example

Note that both versions of the drawing show an internal connection between the physical layers. The connection is there because the physical layers would have the added task of providing an internal path for packets that travel through the node. The accelerator pedal will become a packet switch in the network as well as the input interface.

Also note that in both the highly independent version and the shared-resource version, a certain amount of information formatting would take place in the accelerator pedal assembly. The information reported to the rest of the network would be in an abstract, standardized form. Issues of supplier-to-supplier variation, unit-to-unit variation, supply voltage variation, temperature variation, etc. would be dealt with locally. The payload of information launched in the packets from the assembly might take the form of a value that represents the pedal position somewhere in the range from zero to full travel. The Driver Interpreter layer of software would look at the value from each of the three sensors to determine the pedal position and the quality of the information form the pedal assembly.

It is unlikely that all of the nodes in the network could be connected together in a neat checker-board pattern like shown in Appendix B. Components like fuel injectors might be connected to the network as shown in Figure 6. Because they are likely to be located in a line on a 4 cylinder engine, they may connect to adjacent nodes toward one end of the line. The additional links would then extend form injector to injector. With this pattern, the center adjacent node is only one or two hops away from any one of the injector nodes.

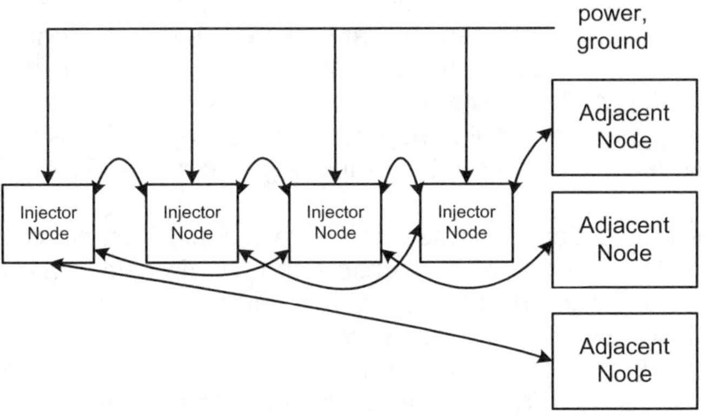

Figure 6. Fuel injector wiring

Parts of the Actuator Controller layer of the control strategy could be located at each of the injector nodes. Each node would have local knowledge of battery voltage from its connection to the vehicle power grid, and other information about the general condition of the vehicle such as air temperature, coolant temperature, and fuel temperature from its connections to the network. The application that controls the injectors could then send out more generic commands that would request a specific quantity of fuel be delivered.

Mesh-Type Packet-Based Communication Network

Information would travel through the switch packet network in the form of discrete packets. Each of the links in the fabric would be some type of physical communication medium that could transport a packet from one switch node to the next. As we will see in the analysis later in the paper a wide variety of communication speeds could be used in the individual links of the network. The point to remember is that the communication speed of each link in the fabric can be chosen for the message traffic that it will carry. Since each link is independent, the most cost effective medium can be chosen for the required communication tasks.

Packets that travel in the network would have appropriate header, and routing information for the medium that they travel in (Figure 7). The information payload would not change when a packet switch hands the packet from one medium to another. It would be preserved as it travels from its source to any of its destinations.

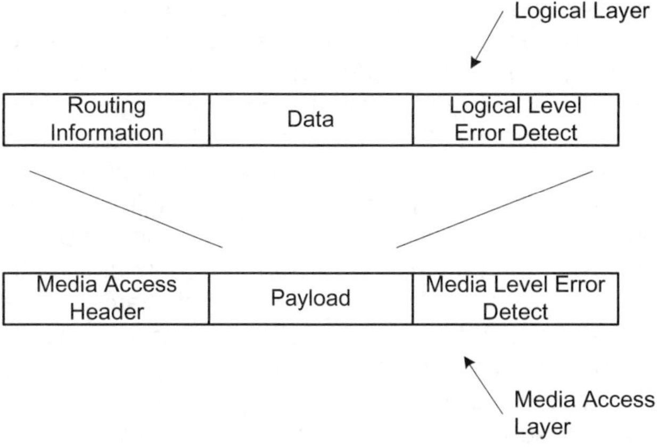

Figure 7. Packet frame with payload detail

Coordinated Universal Time, Angle

One problem often associated with packet-based communication through a mesh-type network is the lack of determinism. The example shown in Appendix B can be used to illustrate this issue. Suppose the Lamp Control application running in a node located in the passenger compartment wanted all of the turn lamps of the car to turn on simultaneously as you would if you were operating the 4-way flashers. It cannot issue a single command to turn on all lamps simultaneously like you would if all of the Lamp nodes were connected to a shared-access medium such as a J2850 or CAN bus.

In this case, the application would have to launch a command packet directed at each of the four corner Lamp nodes. Since each of the command packets would have to travel a different number of hops through a variety of communication media, it is unlikely that they would arrive at the Lamp nodes simultaneously. Packets may travel different paths each time the application desires to turn on the lamps since the route might be altered if a link is no longer available, or is being used by higher priority traffic. Also since the Lamp nodes may be provided by different suppliers using different control devices, running different software, you could not assume that even if the command was received simultaneously that it would result in the lamps turning on simultaneously.

Likewise, an engine control designer might want to have a process that samples the condition of the engine at a specific point in the rotation of the engine's crank shaft, and then update the state of actuators at another specific point in the rotation of the crank shaft. This is not an issue in traditional engine control ECUs since they usually have a crank shaft angle-of-rotation sensor feeding into the single processor inside of the ECU. The single processor can then set up a sampling schedule based on the angle of rotation of the engine and can also schedule actuator updates based on the angle of rotation of the engine.

Determinism would be less of an issue in the packet-based mesh network if there is a mechanism in place to set up a coordinated knowledge of time and angle of rotation of the engine's crank shaft throughout the network. Tasks can then be scheduled to occur at a certain time or angle. This approach is illustrated in Figure 8. In this example there is an engine control process (application) running in a computing resource somewhere in the network. The application would like to use information from three sensors that gather their samples at a specific angle of rotation after a firing event (with respect to a fixed reference angle). It would then make a decision about the state of the actuator that it controls and send a command so that the actuator will be changed at a certain angle of rotation before the next firing event.

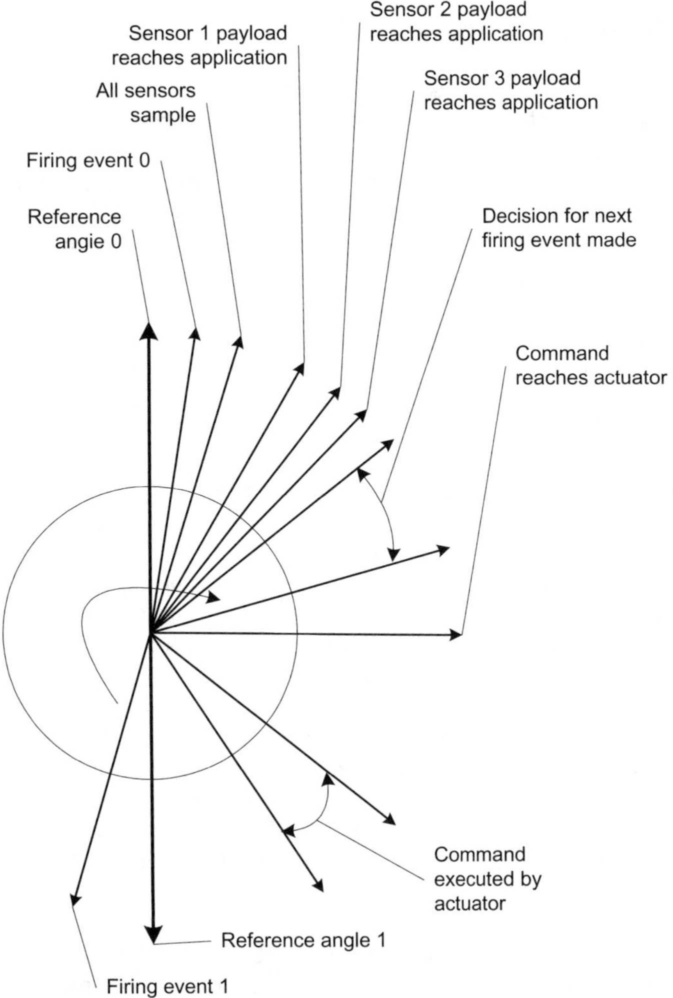

Figure 8. Angle example

For this scheme to work, all of the components of the process – the sensors, the computing resource running the application, and the actuator – would have to know the angle of rotation of the engine. Knowledge of angle of rotation could start from the node in the network connected to a crank angle sensor. These sensors typically look at a wheel with regularly spaced teeth attached to the engine's crake shaft. Often there is a special tooth pattern such as one or two missing teeth that can be used to determine the absolute angle of rotation. An application running in the crank angle sensor node could then update all of the other nodes in the network interested in crank angle every time that it senses the next tooth on the wheel. Each of the receiving nodes could have a local time-based model of the engine that would keep track of the angle of rotation between updates from the crank angle source node.

The application illustrated in Figure 8 could then send a schedule to each of the sensors that would cause them to gather a fresh set of data at a particular angle. The sensors would then each launch a packet into the network as soon as they had completed their task. Each of the packets from the sensors would contain the value sampled and the angle at which it was sampled. Some time later, the samples would arrive at the node running the control application. The application would always know which samples were associated with a particular sample event by the angle tag carried along with the sensor value. There might be a range of angle when the application might execute its decision making process if other applications are using the computing resource. When it finally runs, the application would then launch a packet toward the actuation in advance of when it is expected to be used. That packet would contain the new state of the actuator and the angle of rotation at which the actuator should be updated. Some time later, the command packet would arrive at the actuator. The actuator would then schedule the update at the requested angle of rotation.

RESULTS OF STUDY

Communication Requirements

The vehicle with a 4 cylinder engine and exterior lamps shown in Appendix B can be used to get a sense of the communication requirements for the links used in the switch fabric network. Communication rates between nodes in the network will depend on how applications need to behave.

For the event-based lighting part of the example, a good rule-of-thumb says that outputs that have a visual effect will be perceived to occur simultaneously if they occur within 100 milliseconds of each other and the event that initiated the activation. We will assume that the process starts when the driver actives the lamp switch and receives tactile feedback that the switch contacts have closed, and ends when hazard lamps begin to turn on at all four corners of the car. We also will assume that the Lamp application is running in the same node that the lamp control switch is connected to.

Keep in mind that at some time shortly after the vehicle was assembled, each application would have established a routing plan for packets from inputs and to outputs based on an overall routing strategy. They might also know which elements are closest and which are farthest either in distance or time. In the case of the Lamp application, it might also know a reasonable amount of time that it can expect the longest packet to travel to get to its destination so that it can include a coordinated time in the future for the lamps to activate. Also assume that the clocks in all of the nodes have been synchronized so that the lamp turn-on even can be scheduled to occur at the same time in all of the lamp nodes.

The following sequence of events will take place:

1. Switch contacts first close.
2. Switch debounce time period.
3. Lamp application execution.
4. Control packet launched to farthest target.
5. Control packet launched to next nearest target.
6. Control packet launched to next nearest target.
7. Control packet launched to nearest target.
8. The packet reaches the closest target and the command is scheduled.
9. The packet reaches the farthest target and the command is scheduled.
10. The scheduled turn-on time occurs and the lamps activate

Some time periods can now be assigned for some of the steps in the sequence. We can assume that a reasonable debounce time for a switch would be 30 milliseconds and that the application execution in step 3 and the turn-on process in step 10 might be 10 milliseconds each. That would leave 50 of the 100 millisecond budget for the communication to take place.

For the purposes of the example, we could assume that each packet is 150 bits long. This is in the same order as a CAN frame. We could also assume that the routing information in the frame would be contained in the first half of the frame and that each of the switches in each node could begin sending out a packet after they had received the first half of the packet. Therefore each hop through the network except for the last hop would take ½ of the travel time for a packet. In the example, the closest output node – the Left Front node – is 4 hops away and the farthest – the Right Rear node – is 11 hops away. The travel time from the node running the application to the farthest target would take the equivalent of 6 packet lengths to travel. Using the values of 150 bits per packet and a desire for the communication to take place within 50 milliseconds gives a minimum bit rate for the communication of:

6 frames * 150 bits/frame / 0.05 seconds =

18 Kilobits/second

A minimum operating rate of 18 Kilobits/second would be needed. A physical medium operating at 125 Kilobits/second would give almost an order of magnitude rate margin to account for other message traffic that might be in the network, clock synchronization uncertainty, etc. 125 Kilobits/second is a common rate for medium speed CAN busses used in vehicles.

A similar analysis can be made for the periodic process engine control part of the example. We can begin by making some assumptions about the process as shown in Figure 8. First, we can assume that we would like for sampling and actuator activation to take place within 0.1 degrees of the desired angle of rotation of the engine. If the maximum controlled operating speed of the 4 cylinder engine is to be 8,000 revolutions per minute (RPM), then the coordinated knowledge of angle of rotation of the crank shaft would need to be within:

8,000 rev/min * 360 deg/rev * 1/60 min/sec =

48,000 degrees/second

0.1 degree / 48,000 deg/sec =

2.1 microseconds

Engines of the type in the example often have 60 tooth wheels for their crank shaft angle of rotation sensor. At 8,000 RPM, new information for synchronizing the coordinated knowledge would be available at a rate of:

8,000 rev/min * 1/60 min/sec * 60 teeth/rev =

8,000 teeth/sec or

125 microseconds/tooth

At this rate the local model of the engine in each of the elements would have to be able to predict the angle of rotation of the engine to with 0.1 degrees between each refresh from the angle measurement source every 125 microseconds. Maintaining a model of the engine might be more difficult at slower operating speeds. If we assume that the minimum operating speed would be 100 RPM during cranking, the model of the engine in each of the elements would need to be able to predict the angle of rotation for:

100 rev/min *1/60 min/sec * 60 teeth/rev =

100 teeth/sec or

10 milliseconds/tooth

At cranking speed, the model would have to be accurate for 10 milliseconds until it would be refreshed by the angle measurement source.

For the example, we can use the MAP sensor, the accelerator pedal sensor 1 and oxygen sensor 2 as the three inputs to the application being run in the computing node, and the throttle butterfly as the output (Appendix B). From Figure 8, the sequence of events in this periodic process are:

1. Firing event 0 occurs after 0 degrees.
2. All sensors sample at 20 degrees.

3. The last sensor packet reaches the application at 45 degrees.
4. A decision is made by the application sometime between 55 and 70 degrees.
5. The command reaches the actuator at 90 degrees.
6. The beginning of the actuator event occurs at 135 degrees.
7. The end of the actuator event occurs at 155 degrees.

With the engine operating at 8,000 RPM, each degree of rotation would take:

1/(8000 rev/min * 1/60 min/sec * 360 deg/rev) =
21 microseconds/degree

The sensors would have to transmit their samples to the node running the application while the engine rotated 25 degrees. At 8,000 RPM, communication would have to take place in less than 525 microseconds. The packet from the MAP sensor would have to travel the farthest – 5 hops. Using the same assumptions as in the lighting example, the equivalent of three frames of bits would have to be transmitted in that 525 microseconds. In order to do that, each bit would have to be sent at a rate of:

(3 frames * 150 bits/frame) / 525 microseconds =
86 Kilobits/second

Likewise, the command sent from the node running the application to the actuator would have to travel while the engine rotated 20 degrees. Communication would have to take place in 420 microseconds. This message would take four hops to reach its destination at a bit rate of:

(2.5 frames * 150 bits/frame)/420 microseconds =
89 Kilobits/second

In this case, a minimum bit rate of 89 Kilobits/second would be needed to meet the requirements of the example. A communication medium running at 1 Megabits/second could be used to give roughly a one order of magnitude rate margin. Typical high speed CAN busses run at a 1 Megabit rate. The likelihood that packets would reach their targets could be improved by giving more critical engine control packets priority in the network so they would travel first ahead of other lower priority traffic. Also, the engine area and the links to the engine control sensors could be designated as a restricted zone in the overall routing strategy so other communication packets would not be routed through that area.

Message Packet Requirements

Analysis of the engine control problem lead to some observations about the requirements for the actual message packets that would travel in the network in order for efficient coordination of parameters such as time and angle of rotation throughout the network.

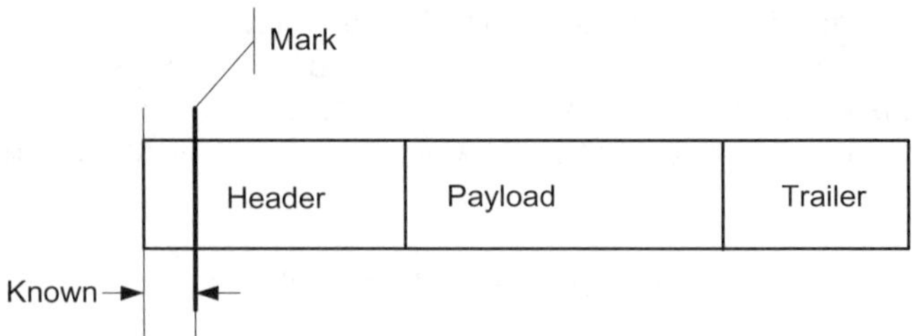

Figure 9. Message Frame

First, there should be a class of frames that is as short as possible to minimize the use of the communication links during parameter coordination. Typically a frame would have a header containing a start of frame pattern and routing information. Coordination frames would not need the routing information contained in other frames since their routing is implied. The start of frame pattern could be different from typical frames and would identify the frame type.

Also, the start of frame pattern could contain a mark that could be used by the coordination process. This mark would have to be identifiable regardless of the physical medium of the communication link. The mark would be used by the coordination process to indicate an exact time conveyed as the value in the payload of the frame. As the coordination frame is passed from node to node, each node would add an offset to the value in the payload that corresponds to the amount of time or the additional angle of rotation determined by the local clock or engine model in the node.

Physical Layer/Switch Requirements

The first likely requirement of the physical layers and packet switch that would be part of each node is that they be built to run as a deterministic process. The amount of time that a packet would need to travel through the switch would have to be predictable so that the time and angle parameter coordination process could take place. It is likely that the packet switch part of a network node would be built as a hardware state machine.

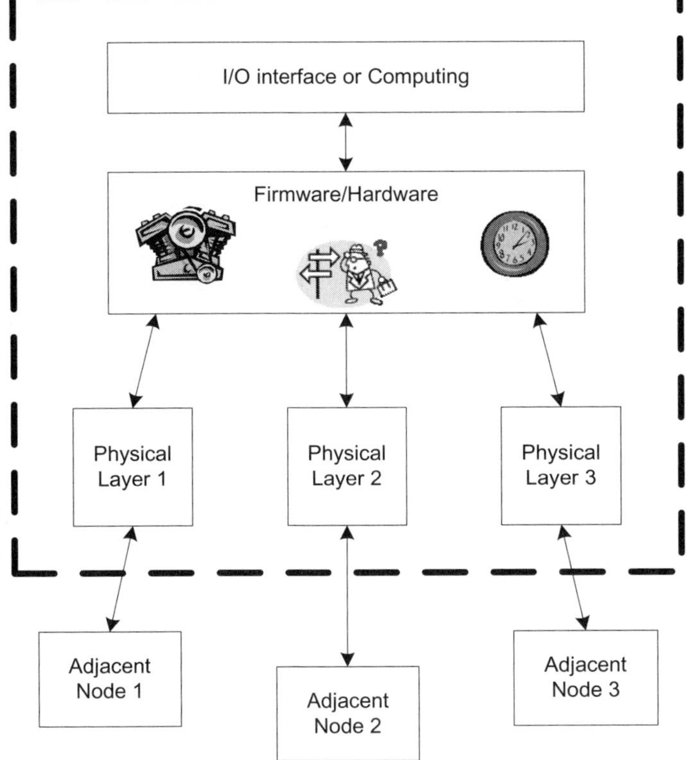

Figure 10. Physical layers and switch.

The second requirement of the switch would be that the real time clock and any parameter models would need to be part of the hardware state machine. This would be needed to support the parameter coordination process.

The last desirable feature of the switch would be that it would be able to start routing packet frames out as soon as the routing information has been examined if the appropriate output port is available. This would speed the travel of a packet form its source to its destination.

CONTINUATION OF WORK

A tremendous amount of work still needs to be done in this area before the idea is ready to try on an actual engine. Some of the open areas are outlined below.

Bigger Chunk Breakdown

The efficient communication in examples used in this paper depended on the idea of coordinated knowledge of an important operating parameter. If the technology to accomplish the coordinated knowledge is not available, control of the elements that depended on that knowledge could be collapsed into one node in the network. That node could still have the benefit of sharing other information with the rest of the vehicle. Also, you could still separate the higher layers of the control strategy – the Driver Interpreter and Engine Controller layers – so that they would be installation independent.

Communication Analysis – Fault Tolerance, Jitter

There would be uncertainty in any scheme developed to coordinate time and angle of rotation among the nodes of the network. That uncertainty would have to be understood so the proper level of margin could be built into the network.

Node Placement – Physical Wire Requirements

It would be unlikely that a uniform blanket of communication could be used in a vehicle as already shown in Figure 6. Physical barriers and asymmetric placement of input and output devices would interfere with the routing of the links. A compromise in the routing of the links will have to be reached, probably on a vehicle-by-vehicle basis.

Distribution of power and ground in the vehicle also has to be considered. Since the nodes in the network are now more self-contained with communication replacing individual signal wires, raw power and ground could be routed directly to them. The electrical distribution system would become more like a power and communication grid rather than bundles of random power and signal wires.

Need For Industry Standards

The ultimate cost effectiveness of the communication and control architecture described in this paper depends on components being built to industry standards. For example, the accelerator pedal used in the example above would have to become an industry-standard item. The vehicle builders and component suppliers would have to agree on mechanical, electrical, communication and validation attributes that would allow parts from different suppliers to be interchangeable. Once that is accomplished, the supply base would have the incentive to produce the devices at the lowest possible cost.

Economic Analysis

Before highly-distributed control systems will be adopted by a vehicle builder, they will need an economic justification for making the change. This approach to building the communication and control infrastructure in a vehicle can be viewed as disruptive technology. It is difficult to build a cost estimate of the disruptive technology using the cost models based on the technology that they are replacing. A new set of cost models will have to be developed and validated.

CONCLUSION

This paper set out to examine some of the communication requirements of a highly-distributed engine control system that is a part of a larger switch fabric communication network in a vehicle. The network would be built using the principles of Motorola's

Architected Vehicle. It was shown that the necessary communication could take place between the distributed control elements using media that are familiar to the automotive industry if there was coordinated knowledge of certain values – time and angle of rotation of the engine – throughout the elements in network. A great deal of work still needs to be done with this communication and control concept before it can be applied to an actual installation.

ACKNOWLEDGMENTS

The author wishes to thank his colleges at Motorola Jeurgen Reinold, Don Remboski, Sam Levenson, and Pat Jordan for their contributions to the basic work on the Architected Vehicle, and Des Hill and his colleges at Zytek for their assistance in preparing background material for this paper.

The author would like to dedicate this paper to the memory of his former college at Caterpillar Mike Moncelle whose early passing leaves a void that will be hard to fill. He always appreciated novel technology that could be applied to engine control.

REFERENCES

1. Switch Fabric – Communications Infrastructure for Next Generation Automotive Architectures, Motorola White Paper, March 2003.
2. Reinold, Juergen, Donald J Remboski; Vehicle Active Network Adaped to Legacy Architecture; US Patent 6,747,365; June 8, 2004.
3. Glielmo, Luigi, Francesco Vasca, Carlo Rossie; Architecture for Electronic Control Unit Taks in Automotive Engine Control; IEEE; September 25, 2000.
4. Costlow, Terry; Trends in Engine Control, SAE Automotive Engineering, May 24, 2003

CONTACT

The author is part of the Motorola Automotive Innovation Center and can be contacted by email at w.fehr@motorola.com.

APPENDIX A Switch Fabric Overlaying Entire Vehicle.

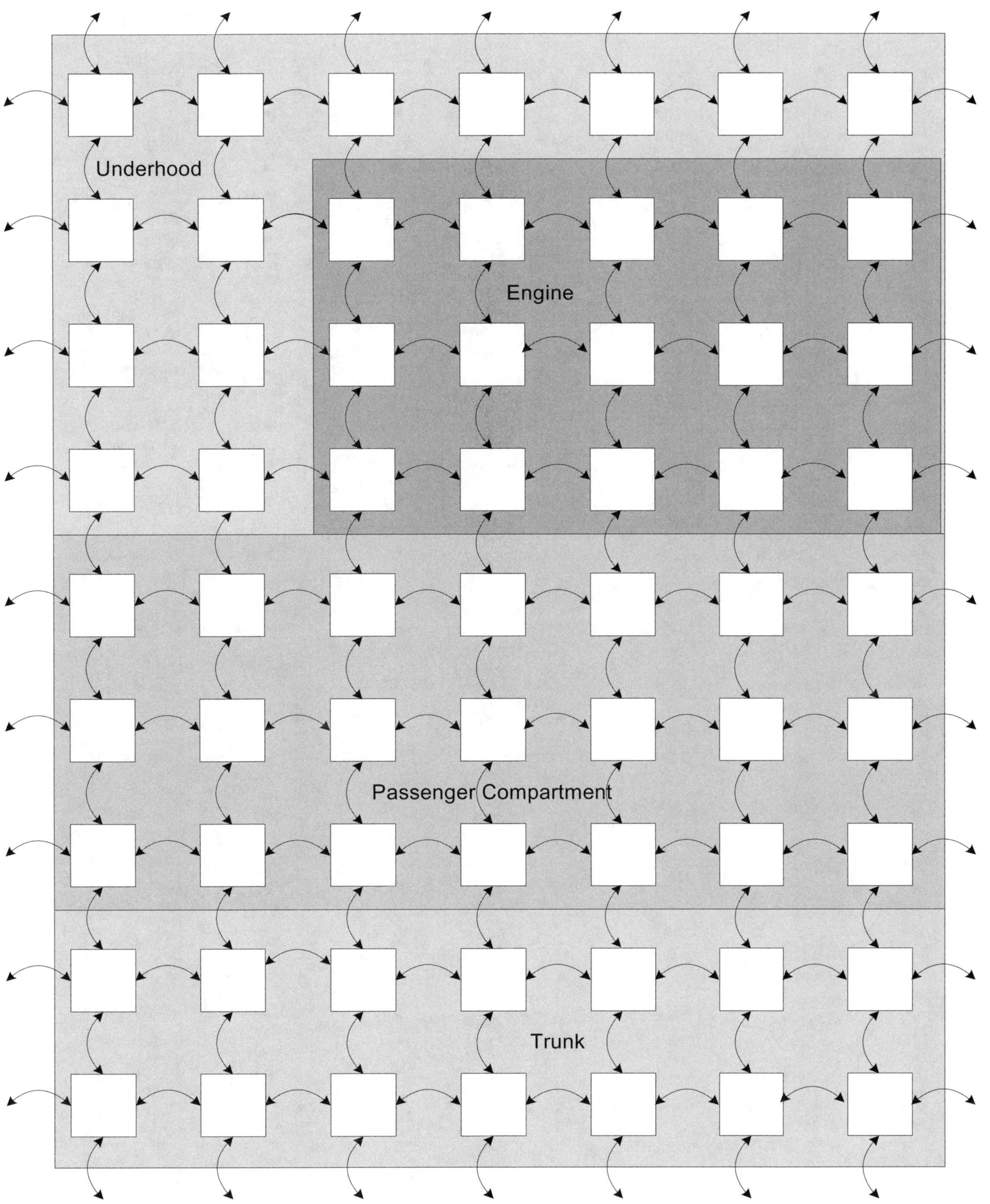

APPENDIX B Distributed Control Example.

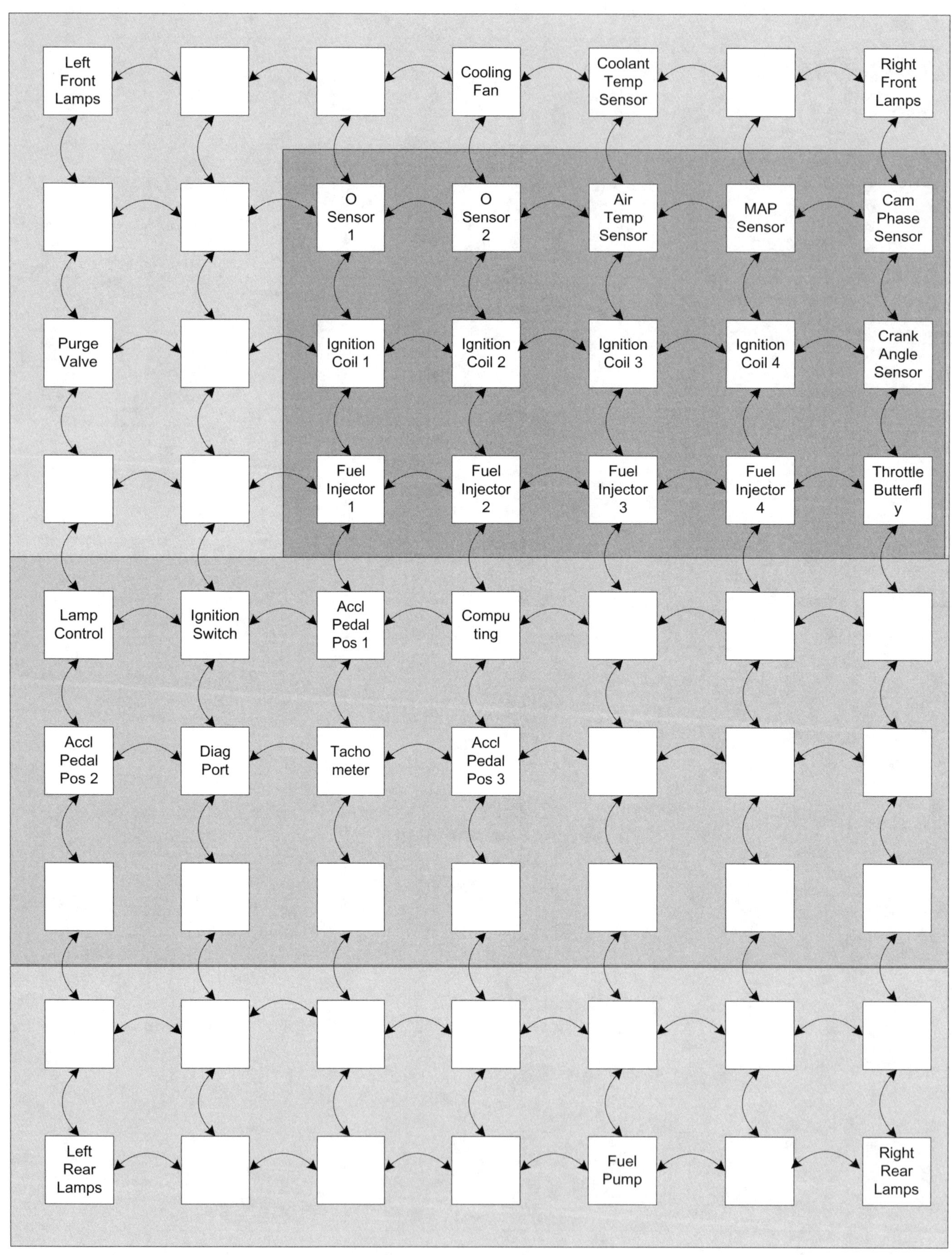

2004-01-1734

Virtual CAN Networks Over TTP – Integrating Legacy Systems Within the Time-Triggered Architecture

Christian Eder, Reinhard Maier, Martin Schwarz and Georg Stöger
TTTech Computertechnik AG

ABSTRACT

The next generation of cars will consist of a high number of networked electronic control units (ECUs) and significantly more complex software modules and control applications than today's models. Besides applications like engine control, air condition control and anti-theft systems, which are already available in today's cars, the first steps towards the introduction of safety-relevant steer-by-wire and brake-by-wire systems will be undertaken. Additionally, the demand for in-car entertainment and information systems (e.g. Internet terminals, video-streaming applications) will also increase. Since all these systems have conflicting requirements to the underlying network protocol (latency, predictability, throughput...), the straight-forward way would be to use autonomous busses and networks for every kind of distributed system within the car body (ultra-available safety-relevant systems, non-safety-relevant control systems, entertainment and media systems).

This adds extra unwanted complexity and cabling overhead (and therefore cost) to the overall car electronics. So it is legitimate to think about alternative architectures, e.g. a common backbone network which can be used by all ECUs. Nevertheless, the integration to a single in-car network must not impair nor compromise the service of any safety-relevant system.

This paper describes how a Time-Triggered Architecture (TTA), based on an underlying time-triggered communication protocol, can be employed to provide such an integration. In the first part the concept of virtual networks over the Time-Triggered Protocol (TTP) is presented and discussed. The idea is to provide "virtual" networks layers, like CAN or TCP/IP on top of a single TTP network. The advantage of these virtual networks is that existing legacy applications that rely on a certain network technology will be able to work almost unchanged. Most of today's in-car control systems are based on CAN. If these systems were reused in such an integrated scenario, this might open a migration path towards the introduction of next-generation electronic systems, largely reducing cost for the redevelopment of existing solutions.

In the second part, this paper presents an implementation for a CAN emulation over TTP in some detail and discusses characteristics and concepts of this solution.

INTRODUCTION

The Time-Triggered Architecture (TTA) is a distributed computing architecture, designed for building safety-relevant, fault-tolerant real-time systems. It has been developed at the Vienna University of Technology and has been brought to maturity in more than 20 years of research. The TTA therefore provides a stable communication and fault tolerance architecture for developing next-generation automotive applications, like steer-by-wire or brake-by-wire systems [1]. A fault-tolerant time-triggered protocol like TTP is the basis for a fault-tolerant TTA. TTP-based systems are already used in existing railway applications and the aerospace industry has also selected TTP for the development of new safety-critical, distributed applications like cabin pressure control systems and by-wire engine control systems.

However, in the automotive industry additional requirements have to be regarded if one considers introducing a new major communication network. Besides technical requirements, there are a lot of commercial arguments that influence the decision towards a specific system architecture. First, a strong point is the reusability of existing solutions and applications. Most of today's cars are equipped with CAN-based ECUs that provide services like engine control, air condition, theft warning, and many more. Since these systems have evolved over long years of development and are produced and deployed in huge numbers, they are both mature and very cost-efficient. Car manufacturers also have a strong interest in using these systems in next-generation cars. However, the step towards the introduction of safety-critical by-wire applications requires the usage of a new time-triggered communication system because an event-based protocol like CAN cannot provide the dependability and control-loop latency requirements of such applications [2].

In this paper, we will show that TTP can be used as a main communication backbone network that allows the deployment of such safety-critical applications as well as the use of existing legacy CAN systems by the concept of virtual networks that are provided on top of basic TTP.

The paper is organized as follows: The first section presents the basic terms and concepts of such virtual networks over TTP. We will investigate different approaches of implementing them, according to actual system requirements.

In the second part we will show a case study of an already existing CAN emulation layer. We will examine the performance of this solution and compare it to a "native" CAN implementation

VIRTUAL NETWORKS OVER TTP

TTP is a typical time-triggered real-time communication protocol. TTP uses a static predefined TDMA (time division multiple access) medium access strategy. Every node participating in TTP communication periodically sends state information of predefined size and content that is received by every other TTP node in the system (though not necessarily by the application). Communication between the TTP communication controller and the host CPU is realized via a communication network interface (CNI) that does not permit the exchange of control signals (a concept called "temporal firewall" [2]). The TTP approach allows the integration of event-triggered [2] communication within this concept.

These so-called "virtual networks" are implemented on top of the regular TTP communication as described below. This concept can be seen in figure 1.

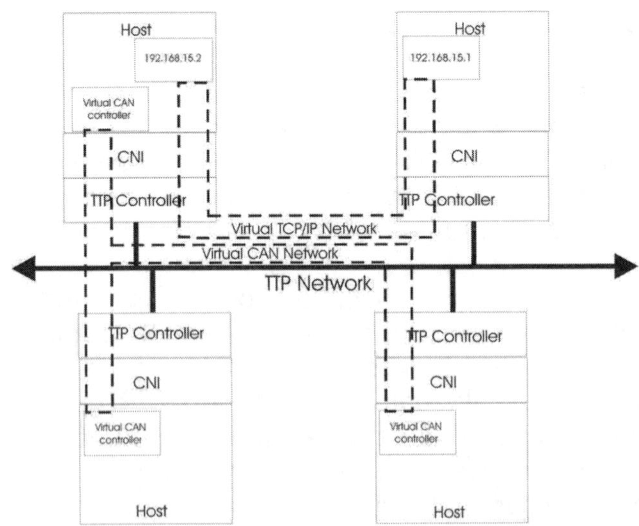

Figure 1: Virtual Network over TTP

By design, every node in a TTP cluster is allowed to send frames of predefined size during its assigned sending slot. If a node should participate in event communication on top of TTP, a part of its sending slot is allocated to event data (see figure 2).

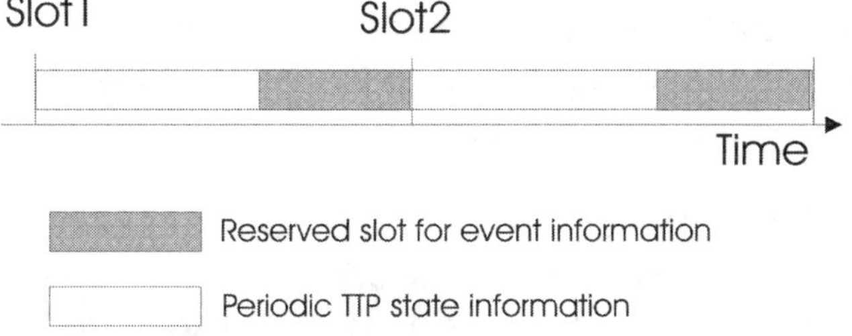

Figure 2: Event Slots within TTP Frames

As the contents of the frames sent are completely transparent to the TTP controller [3], the host has to provide a software layer the can be used by event-triggered communication tasks to send and receive this encapsulated event data.

This concept of event-triggered communication on top of time-triggered communication uses the following approach. If the application wants to send an event message over the virtual network, it uses the service provided by this software emulation layer. This event service takes event messages (e.g. CAN messages or TCP/IP frames) and forms a sequential event data stream out of these messages. Every TDMA round, a part of this data stream is then written to the CNI. This part is autonomously packed into a TTP frame and transmitted by the TTP controller. The amount of event messages that are transmitted in one TDMA round is limited by the bandwidth that is reserved for event-triggered communication. If the bandwidth is at least as high as the amount of event data waiting for transmission, all pending event data, and therefore all event messages, are transmitted. Otherwise the transmission of some of the pending event data is postponed to the following TDMA rounds (this is described in more detail below).

The event service layer at the receiver of the TTP frame has to unpack the event part of the frame and reassemble a sequential stream of received event data for every node that is sending such encapsulated event data. The original event messages can then be restored and provided to the application.

Since the sequence and the size of such sporadically transmitted event messages is not known a-priori, they have to contain a kind of ID that identifies the message ("native" TTP data is a-priori statically defined and can be identified based on the current time) and that can be used by the receiver to recognize the start of a new message in the event stream.

An ID can either identify the content of a multicast message as is the case in a CAN emulation where the ID maps to the concept of Message IDs in CAN (as shown in figure 3), or it can specify the receiver of the message (as would be the case in an internet protocol, IP emulation where the ID maps directly to IP addresses). In the latter case, the event service layer provides a message to the application only if the message is addressed to this node of the virtual network.

If the application polls for received event messages, the event service layer must provide them in a local software queue.

The size of a TTP frame is statically defined and is independent of pending event transmissions; so the event part of the frame cannot be omitted or shortened in a transmission if it is not or not fully used in a TDMA round. TTP sends two frames in every sending slot as it uses two redundant network channels. If the event data is not safety-critical and a loss of a transmission in the case of a transient channel failure can be tolerated, different event data can be transmitted in these two frames, therefore doubling the effective bandwidth that can be used by the virtual network.

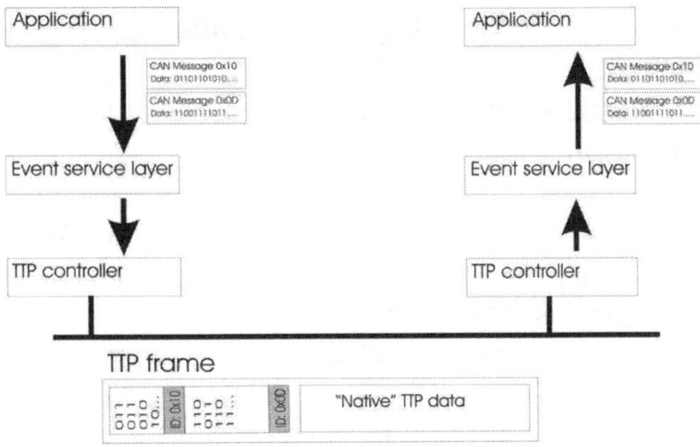

Figure 3: Packing of Event Messages

The latency for sending an event message from one host to another does not depend on the activity of other nodes, as is the case in "native" event-triggered communication. The latency for sending a message only depends on the activity of the CAN-based application on the node. If the amount of CAN data to be sent during one TDMA round is greater than the reserved bandwidth for event data, the emulation layer needs to decide which CAN messages are sent in this round and which are postponed to the following rounds. This decision can be made based on the priority of the CAN messages (a principle which is also used in "native" CAN as described below). We call this purely software-based process of selecting certain CAN messages for transmission in the next round "node-local arbitration". This arbitration is performed each round. Once an event message has made its way through the node-local arbitration, it is transmitted on the network with a latency of less than one TDMA round.

CASE STUDY: CAN OVER TTP

The Controller Area Network is an event-triggered communication protocol which is widely used in the automotive industry. It uses a CSMA/CA (carrier sense multiple access / collision avoidance) medium access strategy. Every message contains an identifier consisting of a number of bits. The identifier specifies the priority of the message. Concurrent medium access is resolved by monitoring the bus while transmitting, and allowing the highest priority message to be sent. Details can be found in [4]. There are a few properties of CAN that have to be taken into account [5] to allow a comparison with the presented emulation environment:

- The latency of a message depends strongly on the network load and the priority. A low priority message can experience an unpredictable long delay in high-load scenarios [6].
- The bit-arbitration logic of CAN limits the network throughput. The length of a single bit-cell must always be longer than the propagation delay of the network [6].
- The temporal properties of a CAN system change during system integration, as newly integrated nodes explicitly trigger the transmission of additional messages. Therefore communication behavior can not be analyzed and certified offline as it would be the case in a system that provides composability in the temporal domain [2].
- Communication errors are handled by transmission retries, which introduce additional network load and therefore latencies.
- CAN does not prevent babbling idiot failures [2]. A faulty node can monopolize the network by continuously sending high-priority messages.
- CAN does not provide a membership service at the protocol level.
- CAN does not provide clock synchronization at the protocol level.

What comes next is an examination of a specific CAN emulation layer on top of TTP. The introduction of the basic architecture will be followed by a discussion about why most of the impairments of "native" CAN (as presented above) can be reduced in this emulation environment.

BASIC ARCHITECTURE

Here is an overview of the basic architecture of a virtual CAN emulation that has been implemented at the TU Vienna. A more detailed description can be found in [5].

The emulation can be seen as a stack that consists of a number a software layers. On the highest level a virtual CAN controller is implemented that provides exactly the same programming interface to the application as a legacy hardware CAN controller, by emulating the corresponding register set. This allows for legacy CAN applications to be used almost unchanged. The application passes "CAN messages" to the virtual controller at arbitrary intervals. These messages form an event-triggered sequential data-stream. This stream is fragmented into packets that are transmitted during "periodic CAN slots". These CAN slots are reserved periods of a node's sending slot that are intended to be used for transmiting CAN data encapsulated within "normal" TTP frames. The time it takes to send a single CAN message depends on the size of the message and the size of the CAN slots of this node. Based on the requirements of the application, the size of the CAN slots can be defined in a way that it can be ensured that a single message can be sent within a certain number of TDMA rounds (once the node-local arbitration has been passed). What follows now is a brief examination of the software layers of the emulation environment:

First the task model of the CAN emulation environment will be presented. As the CAN emulation has to co-exist with the "normal" time-triggered service tasks of a node, the execution environment of the node is divided into a time-triggered and an event-triggered domain. If an OSEK/time [7] compatible operating system like ^{TTP}OS is used, the CAN emulation execution can be mapped to the background (idle) task of the operating system. The software-layers of the CAN emulation environment that are used by the CAN application can be integrated into the time-triggered environment as periodic time-triggered tasks that provide an interface which is capable of handling sporadic service requests from the CAN application. These software layers are:

1. **The Application Interface**: This layer provides the programming interface of a "virtual" CAN controller to the application. The application can sporadically read or write fields of a "virtual" CAN controller register set. The tasks of this layer periodically check the register set for service requests and update the status fields. This layer also stores fully received CAN messages until they are fetched by the application. Messages to be transmitted are also stored until they have become permanent at the receiver or been cancelled by the application.
2. **The Protocol Engine Emulation**: This layer basically implements the "core" of the CAN protocol. The features of the original CAN communication emulated by this layer are processing message transmission and cancellation, acknowledgment of reception, time-stamping of transmissions and ordering of incoming messages. Received messages are stored until they become permanent and then forwarded to the Application Interface layer. On the other side this layer takes send messages from the Application Interface layer and forwards them to the Event-Triggered Communication Channel layer if it signals readiness for the next transmission. This implies that the Protocol Engine Emulation layer has to perform node-local arbitration of outgoing messages. This can be done in a very simple way by storing them in a priority queue based on the "CAN message" priority. Furthermore, this layer uses the TTP membership information to detect whether their own frames have not been received by other

nodes and initialize re-transmission, which is a feature of the CAN protocol but not of time-triggered protocols.

3. **The Event-Triggered Communication Channel**:
   This layer takes a single CAN frame from the Protocol Engine Emulation layer and places it into the CAN slot of the outgoing TTP frames. If it does not fully fit into the CAN slot it is divided into multiple pieces. If the last piece has been placed, the next CAN frame is fetched from the Protocol Engine Emulation layer. In the opposite direction this layer assembles incoming CAN frames and forwards them if a complete frame has been restored. Since the length of a CAN message is not a-priori known by the receiver, the first byte of a CAN message always indicates the length of that message. This information can be used by receiver to assemble the CAN message out of subsequently transmitted TTP frames.

CAN PROPERTIES REVIEWED

We will now have a second look at the list of “native” CAN properties and discuss each of them with respect to the CAN emulation environment

- **Latency depends on network load and priority**: Since we have a TDMA medium access strategy, network latency does not depend the overall load. Anyway, message latency is still influenced by the priority, as every CAN message sent by a node has to pass through the node-local arbitration. To emulate a typical CAN controller, node-local arbitration orders pending messages based on their priority. Therefore the message latency still depends on the number of higher priority messages that are sent by the same host, but not on the message priorities of other nodes.
- **Bit arbitration limits network throughput**: Since there is no bit-arbitration in TTP, the network throughput is not limited by propagation delays. The throughput of a CAN-over-TTP emulation therefore can be better than ”native” CAN. Consider an example: A state-of-the art TTP network working at 25 Mbit, reserving only 2 percent net bandwidth for the CAN layer, allows the emulation of a 500Kbit virtual CAN controller. (which is regarded as a ”high-speed” controller in CAN terms). If CAN messages are not sent redundantly, a 500Kbit controller can be emulated by reserving only 1 percent net bandwidth. More than that, TTP does not have any limitations to the network throughput on the protocol level. The NextTTA project showed that TTP would even allow a network speed of 1Gbit [8] if suitable hardware could be provided.
- **Temporal properties change during system integration:** As discussed above, the CAN layer does not impair temporal properties of the underlying TTP system. TTP provides composability even in the temporal domain [9] and so does the CAN emulation environment.
- **Communication errors introduce additional latencies**: The re-transmission of CAN messages can only introduce additional latencies of messages of the same node. It does not influence the latency of other nodes.
- **Babbling idiot failures**: Since TTP uses independent bus guardians [10] to prevent babbling idiots, they are also prevented in the CAN emulation environment.
- **No membership service**: The virtual CAN controller can also provide TTP's membership information to the CAN application.
- **No clock synchronization**: The virtual CAN controller can also provide TTP's global time to the CAN application.

CONCLUSION

This paper has shown that emulation of CAN on top of a time-triggered network provides a feasible solution for the integration of legacy CAN-based functions within a single Time-Triggered Architecture. This allows introducing a fully time-triggered network as communication backbone bus while still using proven and well-tried CAN systems for non-safety-critical applications. This offers a clear migration path where experiences with a time-triggered network can be gained without introducing additional cost for parallel CAN busses. These experiences can be used to provide a smooth transition toward the next generation of cars, where safety-relevant electronic systems can be deployed within an already existing fault-tolerant technical infrastructure.

REFERENCES

[1] Reinhard Maier, Günther Bauer, Georg Stöger, Stefan Poledna, 2002, *The Time-Triggered-Architecture – A Consistent Computing Platform,* IEEE Micro Vol. 22/4

[2] Hermann Kopetz, 1997, *Real-Time-Systems: Design Principles for Distributed Embedded Applications,* Boston, Kluwer Academic Publishers

[3] Reinhard Maier, 2002, *Event-Triggered Communication on Top of Time-Triggered Architecture",* DASC (Digital Avionics Systems Conference), 2002, Irvine, California, USA

[4] C. Version and P. Philips. CAN specification version 2.0 parts A and B, 1992

[5] Roman Obermaisser, 2002, *CAN Emulation in a Time-Triggered Environment,* Proceedings of the 2002 IEEE International Symposium on Industrial Electronics (ISIE)

[6] Hermann Kopetz, 1998, *A Comparison of CAN and TTP,* Vienna University of Technology, Real-Time Systems Group

[7] OSEK/VDX, 2001, *Time-Triggered Operating System Specification 1.0,* http://www.osek-vdx.org

[8] Christian Eder, 2002, *Designing a High-Performant Real-Time Architecture based on COTS Components,* Vienna University of Technology, Real-Time Systems Group

[9] Hermann Kopetz, 2000, *Composability in the Time-Triggered Architecture,* SAE International Congress and Exhibition, 2000, Detroit, MI, USA

[10] TTA-Group 2003, *TTP Specification 1.1,* http://www.ttagroup.org

CONTACT

Christian Eder, TTTech Computertechnik AG, Schoenbrunner Strasse 7, 1040 Vienna, Austria, christian.eder@tttech.com.

2004-01-0211

A Sampling Period Decision for Robust Control of Distributed Control System using In-Vehicle Network

Kyunghan Chun and Myoungho Sunwoo
Hanyang University

ABSTRACT

This paper presents a preliminary study of a sampling period decision for robust control of a distributed control system based on an in-vehicle network with three types of data (real-time synchronous data, real-time asynchronous data, and nonreal-time asynchronous data). The architecture of automotive systems is currently changing from a number of standalone electronic control units (ECUs) to a functionally integrated distributed system which is linked by a network. The control performance of the integrated networked control system can be changed by the characteristics of time delays among the application ECUs. A basic parameter for a scheduling method of the networked control systems, a maximum allowable delay bound is used, which guarantees stability of the networked control system, and it is derived from the characteristics of the given plant using presented theorems. The presented theorems are derived from sliding mode technique for input-delay systems and a sampling period can be selected from the computed maximum allowable delay bound. The proposed method is shown to be useful through simulation examples.

INTRODUCTION

There are two alternative approaches for entering new control functions into an automotive electronic system: distributed or locally integrated (Figure 1). The distributed approach emerged with the first in-vehicle networks in the '80s. By this approach, different electronic control units (ECU) are connected by a communication link through equivalent network interfaces [1]. In addition, autonomous intelligent sensors [2] and actuators can be connected to other units through the network. Networking is the basis for new top-down control approaches, independent of local ECU platforms. Examples are traction control, vehicle dynamic control and electronic torque control.

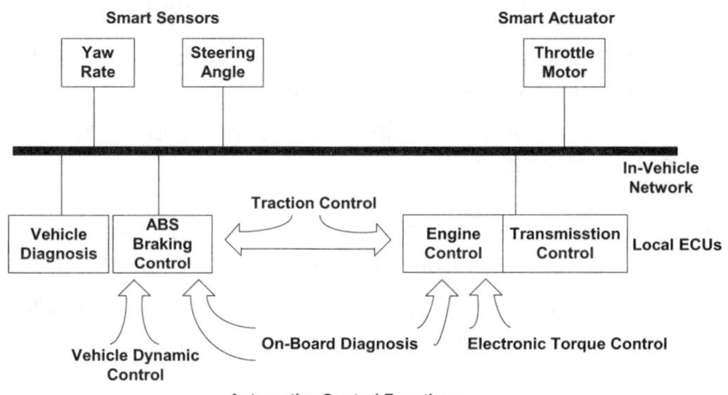

Figure 1 Distributed architecture of automotive electronics.

The introduction of control network "bus" architectures can improve the efficiency, flexibility, and reliability of these integrated applications, reducing installation, reconfiguration, and maintenance time and costs. The change of communication architecture from point-to-point to common-bus, however, introduces different forms of time delay uncertainty between sensors, actuators, and controllers. These time delays come from the time sharing of communication medium as well as additional functionality required for physical signal coding and communication processing. The characteristics of time delays could be constant, bounded, or even random, depending on the network protocols adopted and the chosen hardware. This type of time delay could potentially degrade a system's performance and possibly cause system instability.

This problem is related to input-delay systems. To tackle this problem, we suggest a sliding mode control. A sliding mode control has attractive features such as fast response and good transient response [3][4][5]. It is also insensitive to variations in system parameters, and external disturbances. Other sliding mode control schemes are proposed for uncertain linear systems with time delay [6][7][8][9]. Especially, sliding mode control with delay compensation are proposed for robust stabilization of uncertain input-delay systems [8] and the control law is derived to ensure the existence of a sliding mode and to minimize the effects of the delay and uncertainty in the sliding mode

This paper presents a sampling period decision method for the distributed control system in a vehicle network. Derived from sliding mode control for input-delay systems,

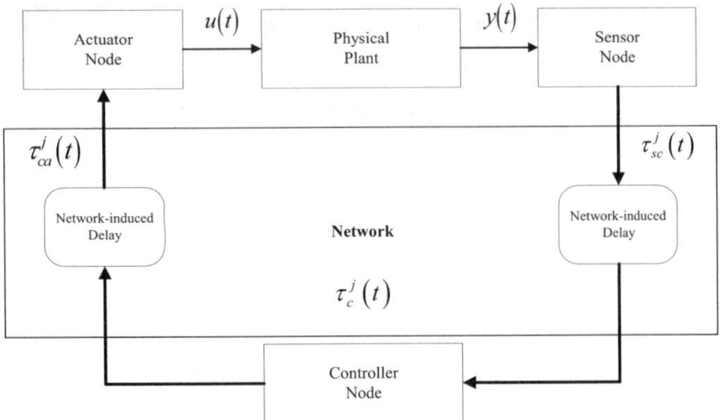

Figure 2 A feedback control loop with network-induced delays.

we suggest a guideline for the sampling period decision. A maximum allowable delay bound (MADB) is considered as a reference value of the sampling period, in which stability of the overall system could be guaranteed. A numerical simulation is given to illustrate the results.

A MAXIMUM ALLOWABLE DELAY BOUND

In Figure 2, many control loops can be connected using a single network medium. The MADB is defined as the maximum allowable interval from the instant when sensor nodes sample sensor data from a plant to the instant when actuators output the transferred data to the plant. If the sampling period in the j th loop exceeds the given MADB, then stability of the overall system could not be guaranteed. In this case, the output of the plant could deviate from the desired trajectory, or the controlled system could behave in an unpredictable manner. Hence it is necessary to derive the MADB from the parameters and configurations of the given plant and the controller.

Let us consider a linear input-delay system with uncertainties described by

$$\dot{x}(t) = Ax(t) + Bu(t-\tau) + f_0(x(t),t) + f_1(x(t-\tau),t) \tag{1}$$

where $x \in \Re^n$, $u(t) \in \Re^m$ and $\tau \in ([0,\infty),\Re)$ are the state vector, the input vector and the known delay time, respectively, and A and B are constant matrices with appropriate dimensions. The uncertainties, $f_0(x(t),t)$ and $f_1(x(t-\tau),t)$, represent the nonlinear parameter perturbations with respect to the current state and the delayed state of the system, respectively. In addition to equation (1), the initial conditions are given by

$$x(0) = x^0,\ x_0(\theta) = \phi(\theta),\ u_0(\theta) = \upsilon(\theta),\ -\tau \le \theta \le 0 \tag{2}$$

where $x_t(\theta) = x(t+\theta)$ and $u_t(\theta) = u(t+\theta)$. It is assumed that the pair (A,B) is stabilizable and the states are available for feedback. It is also assumed that the unknown functions $f_0, f_1 : \Re^n \times \Re_+ \to \Re^n$ satisfy the matching conditions, i.e.,

$$\begin{aligned} f_0(x(t),t) &= Be_0(x(t),t) \\ f_1(x(t-\tau),t) &= Be_1(x(t-\tau),t) \end{aligned} \tag{3}$$

where

$$\begin{aligned} \|e_0(x(t),t)\| &\le \rho_0 \|x(t)\| + k \\ \|e_0(x(t-\tau),t)\| &\le \rho_1 \|x(t-\tau)\| \end{aligned} \tag{4}$$

for $\rho_0, \rho_1, k > 0$. In sliding mode control, the matching condition is a suitable condition for which the system in the sliding mode is insensitive to uncertainty. Input-delay systems are not controllable by the control input for initial time, $t + \tau \le 0$. During the initial time, non-zero initial conditions and uncertainties can affect the stability of the system. In these types of systems, it is usually assumed that the initial condition $\upsilon(\theta) \in L^1((-\tau,0),\Re^m)$ exists.

DELAY BOUND BY USING A PREDICTOR

Consider a predictor (predictive sate), $\bar{x} \in \Re^n$, as

$$\bar{x}(t) = e^{A\tau}x(t) + \int_{-\tau}^{0} e^{-A\theta}Bu(t+\theta)\,d\theta \tag{5}$$

where $u_0(\theta) = \upsilon(\theta) \in L^1((-\tau,0),\Re^m)$. The sliding surface is defined as

$$\sigma(\bar{x}) = S\bar{x} = 0 \tag{6}$$

for $\sigma = [\sigma_1, \cdots, \sigma_m]^T \in \Re^m$ and the sliding matrix, $S = [S_1^T, \cdots, S_m^T]^T \in \Re^{m \times n}$. It is assumed that the matrix S is of full rank and the matrix SB is non-singular. The sliding matrix S is chosen so that the dynamics on the sliding surface have the desired closed-loop behaviors irrespective of input delay.

After selecting the sliding surface, the next step is to choose a control law such that it satisfies the condition for the existence of the sliding mode; $\sigma^T \dot{\sigma} < 0$. Consider the following control structure of the form:

$$u(t) = u_{eq} + u_N \tag{7}$$

where u_{eq} is an equivalent control for the nominal system of equation (1) without the uncertainty and u_N is a switching control to overcome the uncertainties of the system.

$$\begin{aligned} u_{eq} &= -[SB]^{-1} SA\left[e^{A\tau}x(t) + \int_{-\tau}^{0} e^{-A\theta}Bu(t+\theta)d\theta\right] \\ &= -[SB]^{-1} SA\bar{x} \end{aligned} \tag{8}$$

$$u_N = \begin{cases} -\dfrac{(SB)^{-1}\sigma S e^{A\tau}B}{\|\sigma\|}\hat{\delta}(x,t) & if\ \|\sigma\| \neq 0 \\ 0 & \text{otherwise} \end{cases} \tag{9}$$

$\hat{\delta}(x,t) = \rho\|x\| + k + \beta$, for $\rho = \rho_0 + \rho_1 q$, $q > 1$, $\beta > 0$, is the upper bound on the norm of the total uncertainty of the system. Theorem 1 ensures the existence of the sliding mode of system (1) for the controller (7) by using the Razumikhin's theorem [8].

Theorem 1 [8]: If the control law (7) is used for system (1), then the sliding mode always exists.

To estimate a maximum delay bound, theorem 2 is developed to guarantee the asymptotic stability of the system in the sliding mode.

Theorem 2 [9]: If the Lyapunov equation

$$P(A_{11} - A_{12}K) + (A_{11} - A_{12}K)^T P = -Q \tag{10}$$

and the following condition

$$\lambda_{\min}(Q) - 2\tau\rho\|PB_2\|\left\|T^{-1}\begin{bmatrix} I \\ -K \end{bmatrix}\right\| > 0 \tag{11}$$

are satisfied for the positive constant and positive definite matrix P and positive definite symmetric matrix Q, then system (1) under control law (7) is asymptotically stable.

From theorem 2 it is possible to estimate a maximum delay bound that guarantees the asymptotic stability of the system in the sliding mode as follows:

$$0 < \tau \le \tau_1 = \frac{\lambda_{\min}(Q)}{2\rho\|PB_2\|\left\|T^{-1}\begin{bmatrix} I \\ -K \end{bmatrix}\right\|} \tag{12}$$

Remark 1: the reduced order dynamics in the sliding mode are written as

$$\begin{aligned} \dot{z}_1(t) &= (A_{11} - A_{12}K)z_1(t) + \hat{f}_0(t, T^{-1}z_1(t+s)) \\ &\quad + \hat{f}_1(t, T^{-1}z_1(t+s-\tau)) \end{aligned} \tag{12}$$

by transformation

$$TB = \begin{bmatrix} 0 \\ B_2 \end{bmatrix}, \quad TAT^{-1} = \begin{bmatrix} A_{11} & A_{12} \\ A_{21} & A_{22} \end{bmatrix} \tag{13}$$

Remark 2: find K so that K assigns eigenvalues of the reduced order system to the left-half plane. Choosing $\bar{S}_2 = I_m$, leaves $\bar{S} = [K \quad I]$. Then, the sliding matrix is obtained as follows:

$$S = \bar{S}T \tag{14}$$

DELAY BOUND BY SMALL VALUE APPROACH

The aim of this subsection is to provide a time delay upper bound such that the asymptotic stability of system

$$\frac{dz(t)}{dt} = Ez(t), \quad E = A + B \tag{15}$$

ensures the asymptotic stability of the corresponding delay system

$$\frac{dz(t)}{dt} = Az(t) + Bz(t-\tau) \tag{16}$$

for any $\tau > 0$ less than this upper bound. An upper bound [10]

$$\tau_2 = \frac{\sqrt{\dfrac{\lambda_{\min}(P)}{\lambda_{\max}(P)}}}{2\|PB\|(\|A\| + \|B\|)} \tag{17}$$

is expressed in terms of the smallest and the largest eigenvalues $\lambda_{\min}(P)$, $\lambda_{\max}(P)$ of the real symmetric positive definite matrix solution of the Lyapunov equation

$$(A+B)^T P + P(A+B) = -I \tag{18}$$

with the identity matrix $I \in \Re^{n\times n}$.

DELAY BOUND BY LYAPUNOV-KRASOVSKII APPROACH

Suppose that

$$(A+B)^T P + P(A+B) = -Q \quad (19)$$

with $P, Q \in \Re^{n\times n}$ which are symmetric and positive definite.

Let Q_1 be the square root of the matrix Q

$$Q = Q_1^T Q_1 \quad (20)$$

Theorem 3 [11]: Let system (15) be asymptotically stable, then (16) is asymptotically stable for all $\tau \le \tau_3$.

$$\tau_3 = \frac{1}{2\sqrt{\lambda_{\max}(G)}} \quad (21)$$

where $G = Q_1^{-T} E^T PBQ^{-1} B^T PEQ_1^{-1}$.

To apply τ_2, τ_3, adding m integrators to the system (1), the system without uncertainties is written as

$$\begin{aligned} \dot{z}_1(t) &= Az_1(t) + Bz_2(t-\tau) \\ \dot{z}_2(t) &= \tilde{\upsilon}, \quad \tilde{\upsilon} \in \Re^m \end{aligned} \quad (22)$$

Consider the sliding surface

$$\sigma = z_2 + K_1 z_1 \quad (23)$$

where $K_1 \in \Re^{m\times n}$. And assume that

1. $rank(B) = r \le m$
2. (A, B) is controllable

Theorem 4 [11]: If the assumptions hold, then the control

$$\tilde{\upsilon}(t) = -K_1\left(Az_1(t) + Bz_2(t-\tau)\right) - g\,\mathrm{sgn}(\sigma) \quad (24)$$

with $g \in \Re_+$ makes the surface $s = 0$ attractive and invariant in finite time so that, for $\tau \le \max(\tau_2, \tau_3)$ where is given by (17),(21) applying to the system $\dot{z}_1(t) = Az_1(t) - BK_1 z_1(t-\tau)$, the system (1) with the control (24) is asymptotically stable.

Now we propose the maximum allowable delay bound, $\tau_{\max}$ for robust control as follows.

Theorem 5: If $\tau_{\max}$ is chosen as

$$\tau_{\max} = \max_{i=1}^{3}(\tau_i) \quad (25)$$

then the system (1) is asymptotically stable.

EXAMPLES

In order to illustrate the procedure, we consider an unstable plant

$$\dot{x}(t) = \begin{bmatrix} 0 & 1 \\ 3 & -2 \end{bmatrix} x(t) + \begin{bmatrix} 0 \\ 1 \end{bmatrix} \left\{ u(t-\tau) + e_0(x(t), t) + e_1(x(t-\tau), t) \right\}$$

where the initial condition, $x(0) = [-1.6 \quad 1]^T$ and the nonlinear parameter perturbations with model uncertainties are given by

$$\begin{aligned} e_0(x(t), t) &= 0.3x_2(t)\sin(x_2(t)) \\ &\qquad + 0.2\sin(2\pi\omega t), \quad \omega = 30 \\ e_1(x(t-\tau), t) &= 0.3x_2(t-\tau)\sin(x_2(t-\tau)) \end{aligned}$$

It can be easily seen that $\rho_0 = 0.3$, $\rho_1 = 0.3$, $k = 0.2$. Assigning -5 as the eigenvalue of the reduced order dynamics results in $K = 5$. Choosing $q = 1.1$, $T = I_n$ and $\overline{S}_2 = I_m$, yields $\overline{S}_1 = K$, $\|PB_2\| = 0.1$ and $\left\| T^{-1} \begin{bmatrix} I \\ -K \end{bmatrix} \right\| = 5.099$ for $P = 0.1$, $Q = 1$. Then, the sliding surface $S = [5 \quad 1]$ and the delay bound $\tau_1 = 1.1814$.

To compute τ_2 and τ_3, $K_1 = [8 \quad 4]$ so that $\dot{x}(t) = Ax(t) - BK_1 x(t-\tau)$ is asymptotically stable. $\tau_2 = 0.0089$ and $\tau_3 = 0.0791$ by equation (17), (21) for $P = \begin{bmatrix} 1.1 & 0.1 \\ 0.1 & 0.1 \end{bmatrix}$, $Q = I$. Therefore $\tau_{\max} = \tau_1 = 1.1814$ and it can be known that τ_1 is less conservative than τ_2, τ_3.

SIMULATIONS

For the verification of the proposed theorem, the plant used in the example is considered. The simulation results are shown in Figures 3 and 5. We show the output of the control system in which a controller, sensors, and an actuator are connected directly or connected by a network. The proposed controller and the conventional sliding mode controller [3] are compared by using parameters of the example.

Figure 3 shows the result of the proposed controller by direct connection (no input delay) which is same with result of conventional sliding mode control system (designed without consideration of input delay). In Figure 4, input-delay induced by network connection affects the stability of the conventional sliding mode control system. Figure 5 shows that the system is asymptotically stable against uncertainties in the sliding mode although there is input-delay because of network-induced delay.

Here, we assumed that the bandwidth being able to transmit all data packets in all MADBs of loops is allocated in the vehicle network with three types of data (real-time synchronous data, real-time asynchronous data, and nonreal-time asynchronous data) based on a scheduling method such as the earliest deadline first algorithm [12],[13] and the plant in the simulation is a distributed control system. This assumption ensures that all periodic data are transmitted within the respective sampling period to guarantee stability of control loops, while guaranteeing real-time transmission of real-time asynchronous data and minimum transmission of nonreal-time asynchronous data. That is, transmissions of three types of data should be allocated in the sampling period.

CONCLUSION

In this paper, the MADBs are obtained for the robust stability of a distributed control system in a vehicle network. Using the results of a sliding mode control with an input-delay system, we find the MADB which can be used for sampling period decision. The presented method is a guideline, as it provides a solution for determining the sampling period of each control loop. An example is presented to show the usefulness of the proposed method for the distributed control system.

The sampling period is obtained from the plant model independent of network protocols, while the network-induced delays depend on network configurations. In addition, a faster sampling is said to be desirable in sampled-data systems because the performance of the discrete-time system controller can approximate that of the continuous-time system. But in distributed control systems using in-vehicle network, the high sampling rate can increase network load, which in turn results in longer delays of the signals. Therefore finding a sampling rate that can both tolerate the network-induced delay and achieve desired system performance is important. This will be investigated in future studies.

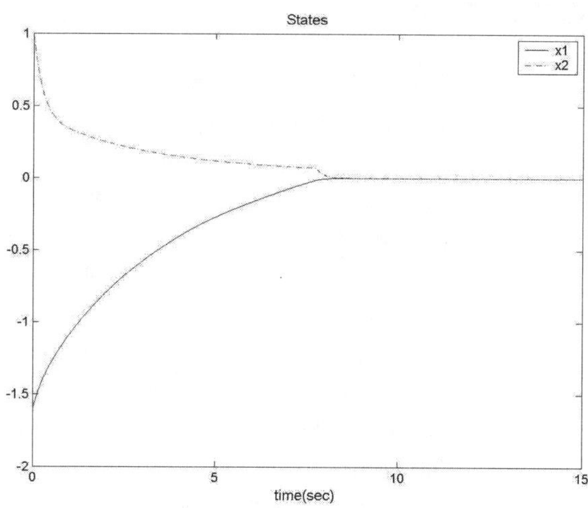

Figure 3 States (standalone controller with proposed SMC).

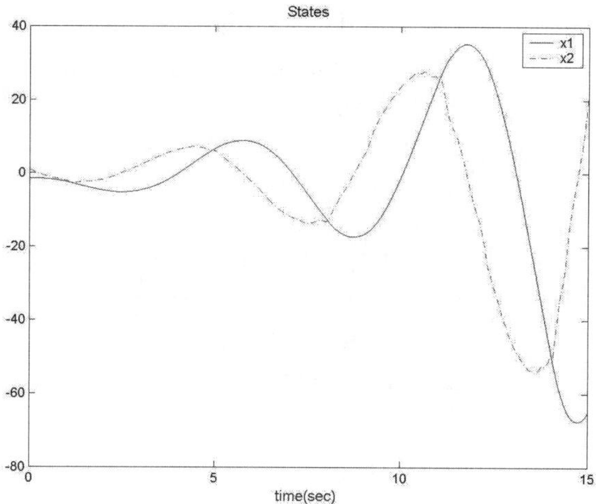

Figure 4 States (network based controller with conventional SMC).

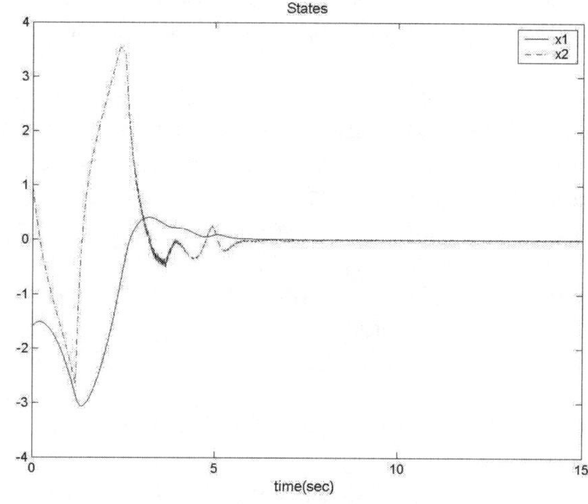

Figure 5 States (network based controller with proposed SMC).

NOMENCLUTURE

ECU	Electronic control unit
τ_{ca}^{j}	Communication delay from a controller to actuators of the j th loop
τ_{sc}^{j}	Communication delay from sensors to a controller of the j th loop
τ_{c}^{j}	computation time in the controller j
$\tau_{\max}$	Maximum allowable delay bound (MADB)
f_0, f_1	Nonlinear parameter perturbations
$\bar{x}$	Predictive state
σ	Sliding function
S	Sliding matrix
u_{eq}	Equivalent control input
u_N	Switching control input
$\hat{\delta}$	Upper bound on the norm of the total uncertainty of the system
P	Positive definite matrix
Q	Positive definite symmetric matrix
K	State feedback matrix
T	Transformation matrix
$\lambda_{\min}$	Minimum eigenvalue
$\lambda_{\max}$	Maximum eigenvalue
$\underline{S}$	Transformed sliding matrix
Q_1	Square root of the matrix Q
K_1	State feedback matrix
g	Switching control gain

REFERENCES

1. Mathony, H.-J., Kaiser, K.-H. and Unruh, J., (1994) "Serielle Kommunikation zwischen Steuergeräten", *Proceedings of Elektronik im Kraftfahrzeugwesen*, Vol. 437
2. Heintz, F. and Zabler, E., (1989) "Application Possibilities and Future Chance of Smart Sensors in the Motor Vehicle", *SAE Technical Paper No. 890304*
3. Hung, J.Y., Gao, W. and Hung, J. C., (1993) "Variable Structure Control: A Survey", *IEEE Transactions on Industrial Electronics*, Vol. 40, pp. 1-22
4. Ryan, E.P., (1983) "A Variable Structure Approach to Feedback Regulation of Uncertain Dynamical System", *International Journal of Control*, Vol. 38, pp. 1121-1134
5. Slotine, J.-J.E. and Li, W., *Applied Nonlinear Control*, Prentice-Hall
6. Koshkouei, A.J. and Zinober, A.S.I., (1996) "Sliding Mode Time-delay Systems", *Proceedings of the International Workshop on VSS*, pp. 97-101
7. Shyu, K.K. and Yan, J.J., (1993) "Robust Stability of Uncertain Time-delay Systems and Its Stabilization by Variable Structure Control", *International Journal of Control*, Vol. 57, pp. 237-246
8. Roh, Y.-H. and Oh, J.-H., (1999) "Robust Stabilization of Uncertain Input-delay Systems by Sliding Mode Control with Delay Compensation", *Automatica*, Vol. 35, pp. 1861-1865
9. Roh, Y.-H. and Oh, J.-H., (1999) "Sliding Mode Control with Delay Compensation for Uncertain Input-delay Systems", *Proceedings of American Control Conference*, pp. 309-313
10. Gopalsamy, K., (1992) "Stability and Oscillations in Delay Differential Equations of Population Dynamics", *Mathematics and Applications*, Vol. 74
11. Gouaisbaut, F., Perruquetti, W. and Richard, J.P., (1999) "A Sliding Mode Control for Linear Systems with Input and State Delays", *Proceedings of Conference on Decision and Control*, pp. 4234-4239
12. Levi, S.-T. and Agrawala, A.K., (1990) *Real Time System Design*, McGraw-Hill
13. Audsley, N.C., Burns, A. and Wellings, A.J., "Deadline Monotone Scheduling Theory and Application", *Proc. IFAC J. Contr. Eng. Practice*, Vol. 1, No. 1, pp. 71-78

2003-01-3738

Future Trends in Networking

Cyrilla Jane Menon
Dearborn Group, Inc.

Sergio Shimura
Dearborn Group Brazil

ABSTRACT

There are many changes occurring in the automotive industry regarding the usage of serial data communication, or networking. These changes are structural, technical and functional. Structural changes occur in the topology of the networks, technical changes focus on the adaptation of the existing networks, and functional changes incorporate new networks for specific applications. The progression of time, along with the desire to expand the functionality of networks in automobiles, has caused most car companies to realize that multiple independent networks are needed across a vehicle to handle specific functionality. Today there is strong agreement that there is no one single vehicle network that will fill all needs. This paper will address all the different networks and their proposed usages.

STANDARDS DEVELOPMENT

Knowledge of the standard development process is necessary in understanding network usage. Early networks were developed by individual companies trying to solve their specific need. But with the inclusion of legislation by goverments, networks began to be created by organizations.

Organizations in international venues are the Society of Automotive Engineers (SAE) and the International Standards Organization (ISO). The decision to standardize an SAE specification lies on the committee's members, comprised of individuals from various companies in the industry, who each have an equal vote; while the final vote for ISO specifications is done by member countries. There are other country-based organizations, such as DIN (Germany), that also create or work on standards as well; and some standards are formally created by one organization and adopted by another. An example of this is ISO 15765 (Diagnostics on CAN), which is also referred to as SAE J2480.

Working within a committee progress slowly, and can be delayed by outside political issues. The recent trend is to have interested parties create stand-alone organizations outside the formal SAE and ISO realm. The purpose for these groups is to quickly get an idea to market. After which, these groups may take their specification to an organization for "standardization".

INTRODUCTION

Transporting information from one electronic control unit (ECU) to another ECU on a vehicle is an ongoing challenge for vehicle manufacturers. In the early days, wires were connected point-to-point. These wire harnesses were vulnerable to high failure rate and added huge weight to the vehicle.

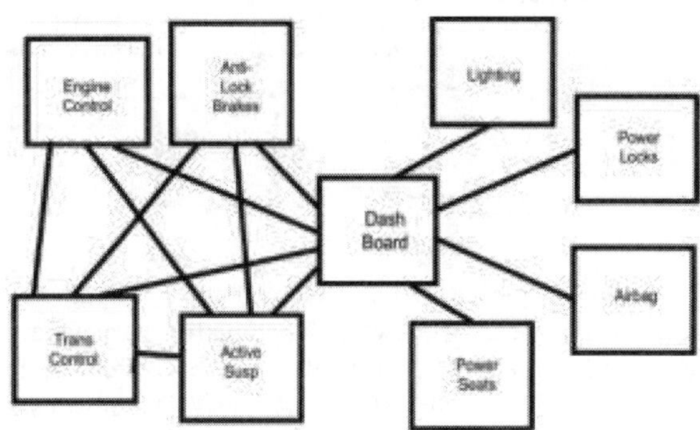

The networking, or multiplexing, of automotive electrical data onto communication buses began in the late 1970s. It was originally a single bus protocol primarily required for diagnostics, but was expanded to incorporate more functionality – a "one-size-fits-all" solution that included Class A, B, and C functions.

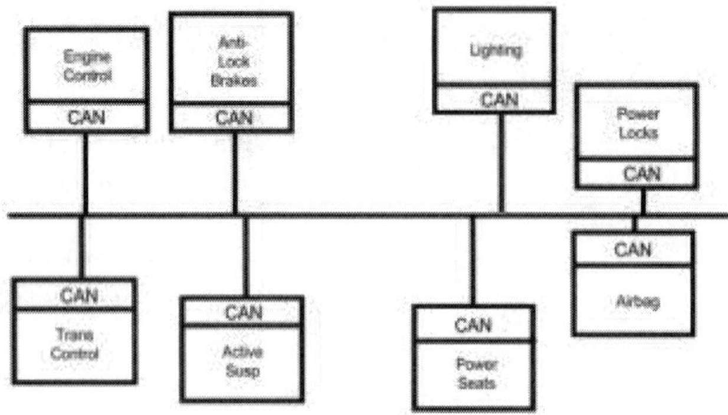

As time has progressed, along with the desire to expand the functionality of networks in automobiles, most car companies have realized that multiple independent networks are needed across an automobile to handle specific functionality. Today there is strong agreement that there is no one single bus that will fill all needs.

There are trade-offs for implementing these multi-tiered solutions - the costs of maintaining expertise on the several buses as well as the additional gateway functionality is a significant one. But the overall benefit to the consumer in achieving so many functions makes this implementation worthwhile.

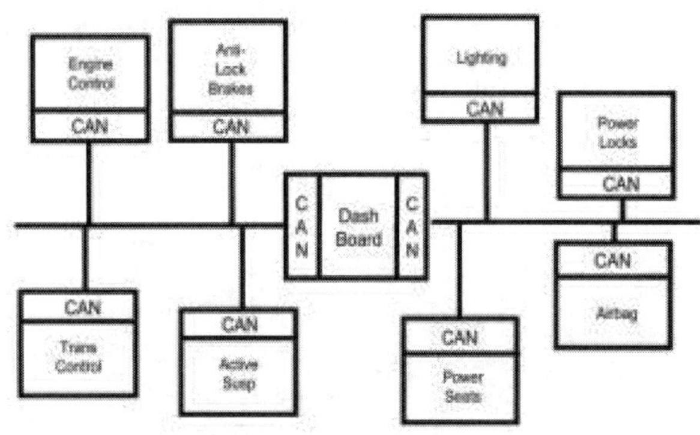

Chris Lupini, of Delphi Delco Electronics Systems, outlined six areas of network functionality in a paper presented at the 2001 SAE Congress. These areas are: Class A, Class B, Class C, Emissions / Diagnostics, Mobile Media, and X-by-Wire / Safety.

Some networks do not encompass just one type, but multiple functionalities. As an example, the most popular protocols being designed into car platforms today for Class A, B, and C functions is Controller Area Network (CAN).

CLASS A

SAE Specification J1213/1 describes Class A networks as "a multiplex system whereby vehicle wiring is reduced by the transmission and reception of multiple signals over the same signal bus between nodes that would have be traditionally accomplished by individual wires in a conventionally wired vehicle. The nodes used to accomplish multiplexed body wiring typically did not exist in the same or similar form in a totally conventionally wired vehicle." Although not officially adopted in any specification, the unofficial rule is that their data rate is less than 10 kps.

Earlier Class A networks were proprietary and used as low-end, non-emission diagnostic, general-purpose communication networks – with the emphasis on diagnostics. Some newer Class A networks are still proprietary, but are used more for information sharing applications. An example is GM's CAN network used in their body electronics application (LSCAN). This application is a single-wire CAN implementation that passes a lot of status information.

It is more popular to create Class A networks with UART-based hardware because of cost effectiveness. Ford's proprietary UART-based Protocol (UBP), is currently being used for body electronics for this reason.

A non-proprietary application under development and adoption is an international standard called Local Interconnect Network, or LIN. The LIN organization is independent and does not officially belong to ISO or SAE. LIN, utilizing an ISO 9141 physical layer, is typically referred to as the CAN subbus. Their website, www.lin-subbus.org, incorporates that terminology.

LIN's intended applications are short distance area control, like, roofing systems, steering wheel controls, a single door interface, etc. LIN is a master-slave network that allows only short packets of data of fixed length to be transmitted. These small local networks would be connected to a larger vehicle network.

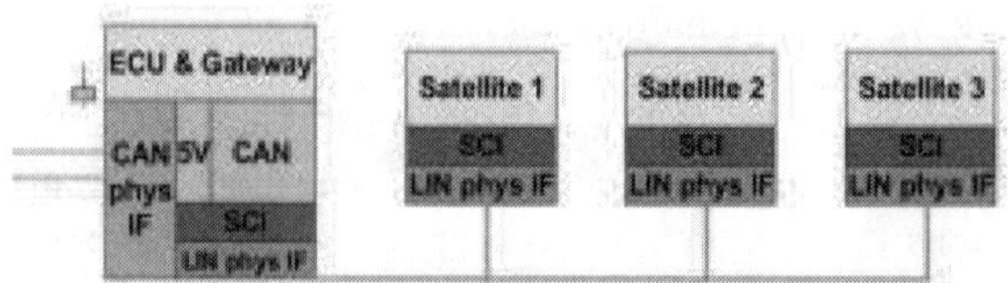

LIN's popularity is increasing. BMW released vehicles in 2003 using LIN. Currently, there is a SAE LIN committee that is attempting to work with the LIN organization to incorporate changes they have envisioned.

CLASS B

SAE J1213/1 describes Class B networks as "a multiplex system whereby data is transferred between nodes to eliminate redundant sensors and other system elements. The nodes in this form of a multiplex system typically pre-existed as stand-alone modules in a conventionally wired vehicle."

Class B networks are used primarily for non-diagnostic, non-critical communication. Their speeds unofficially range between 10 and 125 kbs. They support event-driven and some periodic message transmission in addition to sleep/wakeup.

In the US, SAE J1850 currently dominates this network type eventhough the industry is slowly adapting CAN. There are three flavors of J1850 – one for each of the major US automotive companies. GM refers to it internally as Class 2, Ford calls it Standard Corporate Protocol (SCP), and DaimlerChrysler uses the J1850 name. Ford uses the Type 2 physical layer, while the other two use Type 1. The basic messaging is outlined in SAE J2178. It is fairly easy to reference this specification to decode messaging.

Worldwide, however, CAN is the standard. With CAN defined simply as a Data Link Layer perthe ISO Open Systems Interconnect (OSI) model (ISO IEC 7498), implementators can add their own unique physical and application layer (messaging) to create a solution. ISO 11898-2, the most popular physical layer, is used in both the passenger car and heavy truck markets.

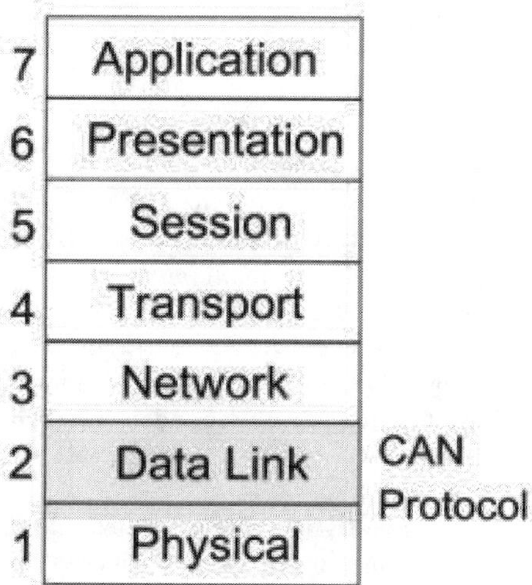

In Europe most car companies utilize CAN on one or more vehicle. Companies like Mercedes produce cars that have up to five separate CAN networks. CAN's expansion into the passenger car segment in North America and Asia is occurring. General Motors (GM), who released cars with CAN on their Saturn platform a few years ago, is gearing up to release many cars with their CAN-based GMLAN applications beginning in 2004.

Other changes for Class B networks are occurring because of new physical layers for CAN. The ISO 11519-2 "fault-tolerant" low speed 2-wire CAN interface is becoming popular in some car applications. This specification is being re-written as ISO 11898-3. Fault tolerant physical layers are slower and cost more than the traditional ISO 11898-2, but provide a more robust implementation.

Another CAN physical layer comes from GM as specification SAE J2411. This utilizes a single-wire interface with a much slower bus speed that normally operates at 33.3 kbps (and a high-speed mode of 83.33 kbps). Called SWCAN, or LSCAN, it captures similar properties as GM's version of J1850.

CLASS C

SAE J1213/1 describes Class C networks as "a multiplex system whereby high data rate signals associated with real time control systems, such as engine controls and anti-lock brakes, are sent over the signal bus to facilitate distributed control and to further reduce wiring."

Class C networks are fast networks used for applications that need high bandwidth such as real-time controlled powertrain implementations. Their speeds are typically 125 kbps to 1 Mbps. Because of their use in powertrain, these networks are typically used for diagnostics as well.

Many car companies have already or will be implementing Class C networks with CAN and ISO 11898-2 physical layers. The US car companies implement this under the specification SAE J2284. In these cases there is no standardization for messaging, because it is proprietary across car manufacturers.

Though there will not be any new Class C networks coming in the near future, there will be many changes or additions to existing implementations. For information regarding updates and additions, SAE J1939, Recommended Practice for Heavy Duty Trucks, and its sister specification, ISO 11783, Implementation for Agriculture, are good references. These CAN-based networks have added specific messaging to cover laser surfacing, navigation, and virtual terminal. Work has begun in Europe, and more recently the US, to commercialize ISOBUS as benefit to the enduser.

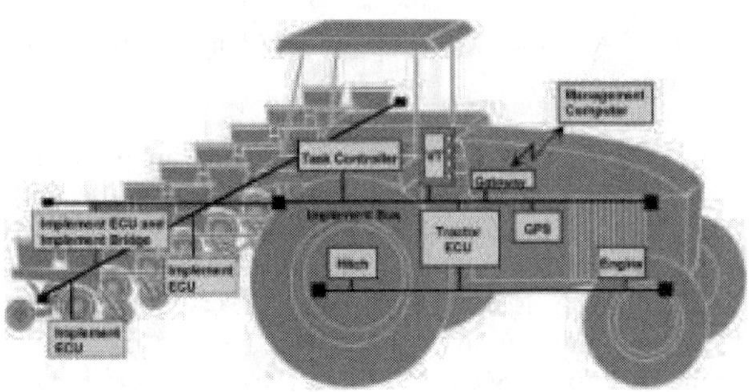

DIAGNOSTICS

Diagnostic applications have greatly influenced the development of networks within vehicles. Diagnostic can be divided into two components: legislated and non-legislated. The non-legislated diagnostics revolves around service repair applications, while legislated diagnostics is the emission-related aspects driven by individual governments for cars sold in their countries. Europe, US and other nations generally follow OBD-II, OBD-III, or E-OBD, but are not in sync with their implementation.

These networks typically use master-slave communication, with the off-board tool acting as the master, or the requestor. The messages that are used in these networks are referred to as services. As an example, a tool will use a specific service to request information from an ECU.

There are some physical networks used for diagnostics and normal communications while others are just exclusively used for diagnostics. These diagnostic-only networks include ISO 9141 and ISO 14230-4 (Keyword Protocol 2000). The latest network edition for the US in 2003 is CAN utilizing ISO 15675, referred to as Diagnostics on CAN. Europe legislated Diagnostics on CAN in the year 2000. Cross references of SAE and ISO standards is common and encapsulated in ISO 15031.

For the future, legislation has been accepted in Europe and the US to only allow passenger vehicles produced from 2008 and onward to use ISO 15765 as the diagnostic network. The debate as to whether or not the trucking industry in the US will be required to use ISO 15765 or remain with J1939-73 is still ongoing.

MOBILE MEDIA

Mobile Media network applications are sometimes referred to as telematics. Telematics is loosely defined as remote connectivity to a vehicle with an emphasis on consumer-driven applications. At least two different networks and protocols may be necessary.

Since this is a relatively new category, there are no networks that are dominant. One early CAN-based entrant that could not find a suitable market is IDB-C. CAN is an excellent choice for powertrain or body networks, because it allows short fast data packets. Unfortunately it does not allow transfer of large amounts of data efficiently – a critical requirement for these applications.

Fiber-optic based solutions seem to be the physical networks of choice for this area. The IDB Forum has added a newer network, IDB-F. This is a based on Firewire, or IEEE-1394. But the leader is MOST. BMW, DaimlerChrysler, and others established the MOST consortium. It is an object model solution that covers most mobile media applications.

For wireless applications, Bluetooth is already being installed in vehicles to interface with cellular phones. However, 802.11 also has it's proponents; and many groups and suppliers are studying a possible co-location so that the two standards can exist near each other. Ultrawideband (UWB) is the wild card that some think will "blow Bluetooth and 802.11 away". Approved by the Federal Communications Commission (FCC) in February 2002, it is essentially "white noise" communication. Using precise clocking, tiny amounts of information are transported across a very wide range of frequencies at very low power (perhaps 1/10000 that of a cell phone). Compared with spread spectrum which uses a small range of frequencies one at a time, UWB uses a wide range of frequencies all at once. UWB can be used for global position sensing, works indoors, and easily penetrates obstructions.

X-BY-WIRE / SAFETY

X-by-wire applications incorporate brake-by-wire, throttle-by-wire, steer-by-wire, etc. The typical bit rate is between 1 Mb/s and 10 Mb/s. and utilizes fiber optics due to high speed. The main concerns for these networks are reliability, performance, and real-time capability. The challenge to create a high-speed fault tolerant network remains. Most implementations utilize a dual bus topology for redundancy, thus cost becomes an issue.

The first drive-by-wire car was released this year using ByteFlight by BMW. Time-triggered Protocol (TTP) has a few applications too, but will be faced with the challenge by Time-triggered CAN (TTCAN), a new version of CAN that requires new silicon that was released this year.

Presently, the leading contender is FlexRay. It was established by DaimlerChrysler and BMW as a way to join ByteFlight and TTFlex. A decision was made that they could create one standard with mutual benefits.

The FlexRay consortium has more major automotive companies with GM signing up this year. BMW released a drive-by-wire car last year utilizing ByteFlight, but intends to produce future applications with Flexray. Flexray's current schedule for completion is within the 2003-04 time frame.

For safety-based networks, Safe-by-wire is an up-and-coming protocol. With companies such as Philips, GM, and TRW, this organization is creating a network that ties into the airbag deployment.

CONCLUSION

The use of multiple networks on a vehicle has been a reality for some time now. Primarily this has been due to the re-use, and carryover of existing networks and protocols. However, in the near future, new functions such as smart connectors, drive-by-wire, and mobile multi media will be forcing the need for additional protocols and networks. The need to provide better functionality to consumers will be the driving force in vehicle network innovation.

REFERENCES

1. ISO 7498 - Data Processing Systems, Open Systems Interconnection Standard Reference Mode.
2. www.lin-subbus.org
3. www.flexray.com
4. www.sae.org
5. www.iso.org
6. www.idbforum.org
7. SAE 2001-01-0060 "Multiplex Bus Progression" Lupini

CONTACT

Cyrilla Jane Menon
Marketing / Training Manager
Dearborn Group, Inc.
cyrilla@dgtech.com
http://www.dgtech.com

Cyrilla Jane Menon holds a master's degree in engineering from Wayne State University and a MBA from the University of Michigan. She has worked at Dearborn Group for over 9 years. Serving on many SAE and ISO multiplex committees, she has also co-chaired several CAN conferences. Mrs. Menon spends much of her time training engineers and technical personnel on vehicle networks, including in SAE's technical seminar.

Sergio Shimura
Dearborn Group Brazil
sshimura@dgtech.com

Graduated in 1987 from Escola Politecnica da Universidade de Sao Paulo in electronic engineering, Sergio Shimura holds a master's and doctor's degree from the same institution. With over 15 years of professional life, his experience includes embedded systems design, consulting and training. Recently Mr. Shimura joined Dearborn Group as its representative for Brazil.

2003-01-0114

TTCAN from Applications to Products in Automotive Systems

Patrick Leteinturier, Nico A. Kelling and Ursula Kelling
Infineon Technologies AG

ABSTRACT

This paper outlines the results of a study performed to analyze the mission of TTCAN from applications to products for automotive systems.

As commonly acknowledged communication is one of the key elements for future and even present systems such as an automobile. A dramatically increasing number of busses and gateways even in low- to midrange vehicles is putting significant burden upon the validation scenario as well as the cost. Accordingly, numerous new initiatives have been started worldwide in order to find solutions to this; some of them by the definition of enhanced or new protocols.

This paper shall have a look particular on the new standard of TTCAN (time-triggered communication on CAN).

This protocol is based on the CAN data link layer as specified in ISO 11898-1 and may use standardized CAN physical layers such as specified in ISO 11898-2 (high-speed transceiver) or in ISO 11898-3 (fault-tolerant low-speed transceiver). This particular property is beneficial when migrating towards time-triggered communication approaches.

Furthermore TTCAN provides a mechanism to schedule CAN messages either time-triggered or event-triggered. This feature opens new ways to partition, link and structure systems more efficiently in terms of cost and validation. Examples are implementation of a sensor bus, distributed or split control functionality and increased real-time performance in CAN-based in-vehicle networks without software overhead.

This paper will identify automotive applications and approaches that require or benefit from the TTCAN protocol. Strengths and limits of the solution are addressed for the domains of powertrain and safety vehicle dynamics. Partitioning will be proposed with the key advantages and system benefits for the applications. A new implementation of a level2 TTCAN node providing full TTCAN functionality with very low software overhead is presented as well.

INTRODUCTION

The increasing legal requirements for safety, the reduction of emissions, fuel economy and onboard diagnosis systems are driving the market for more intelligent systems. Therefore, the embedded systems that will have to control automobiles have grown to such an extent that they are now equivalent in scale and complexity to avionics systems, the requirements in terms of computational performance will even further increase by a factor 10 over the next 5 years.

Accordingly the automotive industry has to face a disruptive challenge with respect to validation possibilities as well as effort and – to complicate the matter – an increasing number of software components delivered from different sources to be executed on one common core. The introduction of x-by-wire, enabled by new communication protocols, in Powertrain and Chassis will offer new possibilities, such as:

1. Centralized systems can be distributed to control the right functions at the right places. Provided the right protocol features, this will allow to minimize hardware redundancy whilst at the same time increased system safety, reduce the validation complexity by encapsulation and to reduce cost, weight as well as electromagnetic emission by replacement of analog with digital links.

2. Greater flexibility and scalability at system level achieved by observable and well defined interfaces. New functions can more easily be introduced to satisfy the coming regulations.

3. Harmonization of control strategies. Loosely coupled control systems can become tightly coupled or even integrated. Local control can be migrated towards global control strategies.

4. Increased efficiency in resource management as well for processing performance, as for communication bandwidth and even cost of e.g. processing performance provided within the system implemented with different characteristics and in different technologies.

It is not, that some of these to a certain degree could not be realized with existing and established concepts – But beside the demand for highly sophisticated electronics, the demand on cost reduction (especially for small cars) is probably the number one driving factor for a smart system partitioning. Time-triggered system architecture is one commonly accepted approach as to manage the system complexity with respect to validation, predictability and safety. Hence, upcoming architectures are much supported with a new bus principle such as TTCAN as will be seen in the next chapters.

AUTOMOTIVE APPLICATIONS

Advantages of the application can be elaborated at various different levels. In this case we chose to distinct between design time and validation aspects on the one side and run-time benefits at the other side.

This section will concentrate first on architectural aspects, provide a description of four major categories with respect to control strategies in the context of smart partitioning and give reference to typical application use cases. This section will conclude with an application matrix that illustrates the capability and the limits of the TTCAN solution by exploring the applications where this bus can be used, relative to other emerging high-speed communication solutions on the market such FlexRay or TTP.

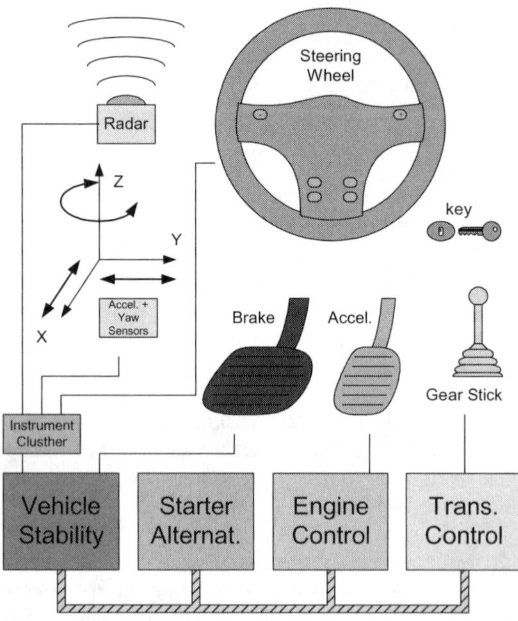

Figure 1: Connection between Powertrain and Vehicle stability

Credit to the runtime advantages will be given in subsequent chapters that exploit implementation aspects of the TTCAN module. Possibilities to improve available (usable) communication bandwidth without complex software strategies, the real time performance, and determinism of messages, fault detection and contingency action will be outlined.

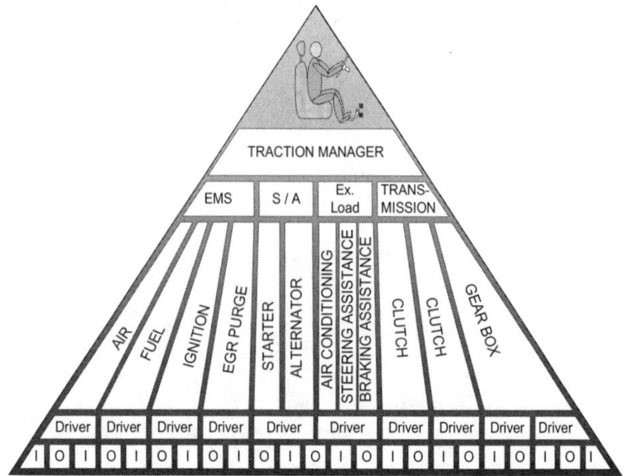

Figure 2: Control Pyramid of a Powertrain System

Powertrain and chassis systems are undergoing a huge evolution. Taking powertrain as an example, with early focus on engine management followed by transmission control and now advanced starter alternator concepts with the capability of energy recovery. Besides fuel efficiency that reaches very high values (40 to 45% with new diesel common rail), regenerative braking systems will even bring kinetic energy back into the system during braking.

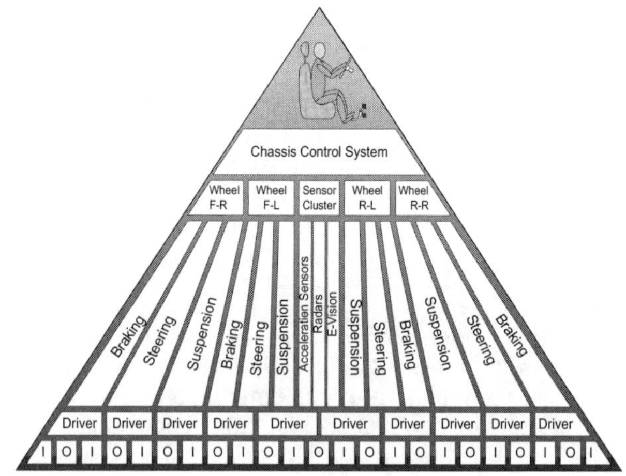

Figure 3: Control Pyramid of a Chassis System

On the other hand road safety is significantly enhanced by vehicle stability and traction control systems (ABS, ASR, ESP) that are further improved by integration of damping, suspension and steering control. More and more systems have to be linked, sharing sensor data and execute harmonized control over various actuators with the common target to optimize overall vehicle stability and wheel to road traction. Further harmonization of powertrain with chassis functions extents from unified chassis control towards unified drivetrain.

This trend is amplified by the introduction of x-by-wire that gradually replaces mechanical and hydraulic functions by electronic control. The technology of by-wire is particularly relevant in drive-by-wire applications. Step-by-step, comfort functions migrate to become warning functions, later driver assistance, emergency react and ultimately (eventually) autonomous driving functions. The revolution in automotive is to assist the driver on the top of a decision process with lots of electronics. The order coming from the driver is no longer transmitted by mechanical elements. This new approach allows to remove some constraints of previous architectures and to focus on the right function in the right place.

Application challenges & requirements

For drive-by-wire functions, powertrain and chassis systems are sharing numerous common information such as: key, acceleration pedal, brake pedal, gear ratio... The challenge of the new combined system will be to establish the right HMI (human machine interface), not only regarding correct interpretation of the driver's intention but also to provide him the right feedback. The second step will be to provide the information to the appropriate control unit in real- and deterministic time. The system has to be safe and failure tolerant. The last challenge but not the least is to ensure complete consistency in between the distributed and embedded systems. Figure 4 displays one possible, fully distributed safety architecture for electrical (dry) braking as it has been implemented within the European research project BRAKE (Delphi Systems, Infineon Technologies, Volvo Car Corporation, Wind River).

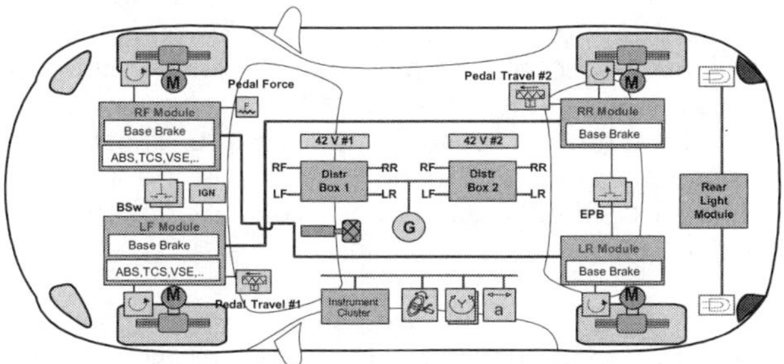

Figure 4: Distributed Safety Architecture for Electro-Mechanic Braking

Such application or architecture certainly marks the upper range in terms of safety- and bandwidth-requirements. In the given application, the used high-speed failure-tolerant, deterministic safety-bus operates as some sort of communication backbone to the entire system and encapsulates the different network nodes from each other.

Due to cost reason it is not desirable that each sub-system like engine management, starter-alternator, and transmission control or vehicle stability is measuring for itself the driver expectation (acceleration pedal, brake pedal...). In fact, this would even jeopardize the harmonization of various control functions towards global vehicle level control. Hence, most available information will have to be shared in between the sub-system.

In addition, not all applications have equivalently high bandwidth requirements compared to a complete and unified, distributed chassis controller. The most common closed-loop control scenarios for TTCAN suited partitioning are addressed in the following chapter.

Control Architectures

A typical, simple closed-loop control for a system is sketched in Figure 5. A sensor (S) measures the system, the controller computes how to modify the system and the actuator (A) performs the modification.

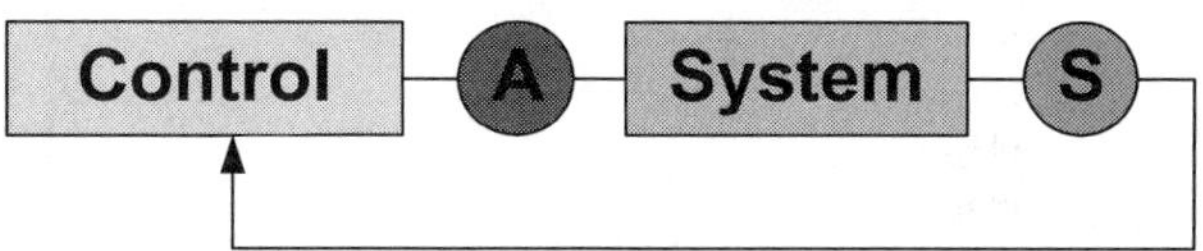

Figure 5: Control loop with (A)ctuator and (S)ensor

TTCAN exhibits multiple capabilities to change the partitioning of closed loop control. These can be clustered in the following four groups:

1 Sensor bus
2 Remote controlled sub-system
3 Split controlled system
4 Distributed System

<u>Sensor bus</u>

A typical situation particularly in chassis applications is a system with multiple sensors at various locations, where some or many of these have to be shared across multiple functions. An efficient approach based on TTCAN communication is as follows: The sensors are "smart" and able to communicate with the controller. A time window will be assigned to each of them.

For instance, for a chassis system with ABS, ASR, ... the sensors could include the lateral and longitudinal accelerometers, wheel speeds, yaw sensor(s), the radar sensor, and more. These sensor data have to be shared across different functions that control wheel traction, spin, braking, and overall vehicle stability such as roll, pitch and spin, that are also influenced by steering and damping.

Once the communication schedule is configured, the TTCAN communication controller will autonomously trigger the sensor if needed and communicate the sensor data at the configured rate and times. There is no need to provide additional software to establish timing correlation in between different sensor values, as all are sampled relative to the common network time. The control algorithm will be also able to run consistency checks, as well as some data fusion to improve the observation of the system. Some algorithms depend on the availability of a fixed number of samples from sensor A along with one or another fixed number of samples from another sensor B (e.g. filters). This can be inherently ensured by means of the communication schedule.

This application is opening new possibilities for a sensor cluster. The TTCAN inherent synchronization features allow for example cost efficient networked sensor nodes that provide their information at pre-defined and synchronized times.

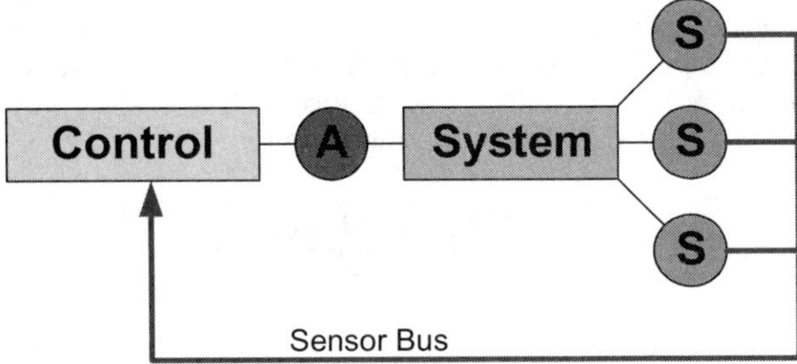

Figure 6: Sensor bus application

Fixed sample ratios between different sensors as may be used e.g. in various filter designs can easily be configured without need for software interaction. In addition, the complexity of a smart sensor can be reduced, as the sample triggering can be managed by means of the bus and no further controller is needed – a significant cost saver when looking at smart sensor modules.

Remote controlled sub-system

In this application the controller and the sub system are not located at the same place, the sub-system outsource the control algorithm to a central unit. As a consequence the sub-system has to communicate the value coming from the sensor and receive the new values for the actuator.

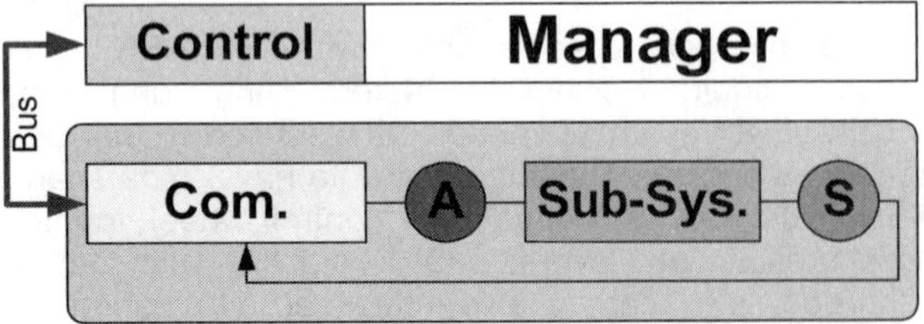

Figure 7: Remote controlled sub-system

This kind of control requires high bi-directional bandwidth. A time window will be reserved for the sensor value, another time window for the actuator value. This could be used for the electronic throttle in engine management.

Split controlled sub-system

This application is a variant of the remote control loop. Here, two control loops are identified: a fast one and a slow one. For example the fast control loop could be the control of the current and the slow control loop could be the control of the position. The benefit of this partitioning is to remove the need of high bandwidth to control the fast loop. In addition the local control can also guaranty some back-up scenario in case of communication fault. Further more, the complexity of the remote algorithm can take into account some adaptive control and learn the evolution of the sub-system during its life. Many applications can use this principle – for instance electronic turbo-charger, electronic throttle, electronic valves...

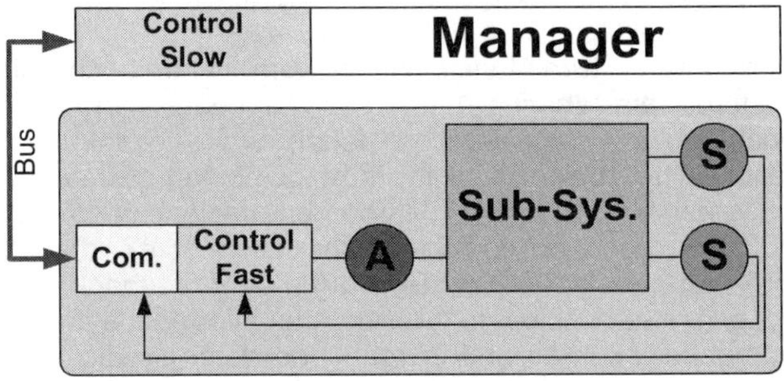

Figure 8: Split-Control sub-system

Distributed System

This application case is by far the most complex one. The control of the system is distributed, the actuators are distributed the sensors are distributed. To compute the values of the local actuators, each local controller requires access to the values of its local sensors and the values of the remote sensors and actuators. The system inherent controller redundancy can easily be used to establish a distributed safety case without adding costly redundancy to a central controller.

Many projects and activities among the automotive society have been analyzing the benefits, drawbacks and mechanisms of distributed versus centralized control architectures. A complete documentation could probably fill at least a book, and can therefore not be handled here. Nevertheless, studies have shown that distributed redundancy is increasingly efficient with higher system complexity. Part of the reason is the validation issue: The growth in system complexity is primarily limited by the ability to validate it, not by technological or physical limits. Distribution supports partitioning to cost, enforces clean and well-defined interfaces and consequently supports encapsulation and modularization. Ultimately, a transparent software design on top of a distributed architecture entirely abstracts control software from underlying hardware and network structures and finally will increase software reusability and scalability.

However, these studies have also shown that additional work has to be performed in the domain of development methodology and appropriate tool support. Model based design and model based system validation is only the first step. Existing design guidelines and interface definitions need thorough review. Besides that, the safety scenario can be greatly improved with communication protocol inherent features for replica determinism, such as configurable mutual exclusion algorithms. These are not part of TTCAN.

In summary, the approach of distributed system architecture is very efficient in cost and validation once fully transparent function design is established and well defined functional API interfaces are defined. On system level, this will initiate the transition from multi gateway architectures to common backbone topologies that enables further cost and flexibility advantages. Such will very soon demand high-speed communication. TTCAN is using the CAN physical layer and is limited to 1Mb/s and accordingly not well suited for this control architecture.

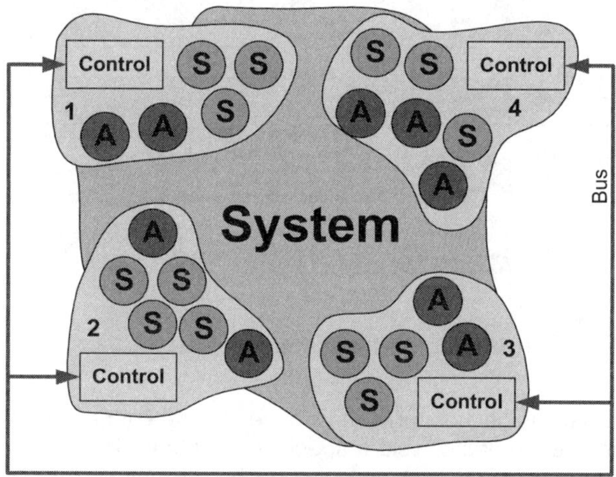

Figure 9: Distributed Control Strategy

Nevertheless TTCAN has very good opportunities in conventional gateway topologies to cover sub-applications like the intercommunication between engine management – transmission control – starter alternator and vehicle stability system. Most by-wire applications except fully distributed electrical braking indeed have relatively relaxed requirements that are well satisfied by the TTCAN protocol. Typical examples are rear electromechanical braking, parking brake, rear steering and some suspension functions. In this aspect, TTCAN can provide a convenient migration path until further harmonization and unification of control functions will demand high-speed safety communication.

ENHANCED CAN USABLE BANDWIDTH

Another application advantage is the capability of enhanced bandwidth utilization compared to standard CAN applications that do not implement a comparable application layer. Although some different application layers are used today that can feature similarly high bus utilization, these typically are implemented in software and therefore consume precious CPU load and are less efficient than a hardware solution. If no such application layer is used and sensitive messages have to be transmitted on the media, typical planned network load does not exceed somewhere around a third of the capacity. This is, as collisions on the media and automatic retransmissions will eventually load the bus up to a state where messages with lower priority may not come through any more. Typical planned CAN load cannot increase above approximately 40% without further provisions as the inbuilt collision mechanism may otherwise collapse the communication of messages with low priority. Using a software session layer, this planned load maybe extended up to eventually 80%. This is achieved typically by statistic based scheduling optimization for the network communication. Using TTCAN will allow the users to reach around 90% of the network load without further software provisions. Composability and testability can be improved implicitly by firstly deterministic scheduling and secondly by decoupling in time of the network from the CPU activities.

Application Decision Matrix

Summarizing the discussions about design benefits and applications that benefit from TTCAN communication, we present the following table (Figure 10).

Applications	TTCAN	FlexRay or TTP
Unified Engine Management, Transmission, Starter-Alternator, Vehicle dynamic	X	
Electronic Turbo-charger	X	
Electronic Throttle	X	
Sensor Cluster	X	
Parking Brake	X	
Electro-Hydraulic Braking	X	
Hybrid Braking	X	
Full Electro-Mechanical Braking		X
Rear Steering	X	
Basic Suspension System	X	
Full Active Suspension System		X
Full Chassis Control		X

Figure 10: Application's Requirements Matrix

The table compares, which applications can benefit from TTCAN communication compared to those, that have higher requirements e.g. in bandwidth such that a high-speed safety bus becomes mandatory. Certainly, in many cases TTCAN can be classified as a soft requirement depending on the system architecture, meaning that - especially when primarily point-to-point communication is required - other solutions can be applied. However, when targeting a migration towards harmonized control strategies, system unification and standardization in interfaces and protocols, TTCAN is a good option.

Limitations of TTCAN usage has been identified primarily with respect to total available bandwidth needed for distributed, full electro-mechanical braking, and the harmonized, unified global chassis control system.

TTCAN Protocol Implementation

Status

The upcoming TTCAN standard as an hardware layer extension to CAN has been implemented in a new module named "MultiCAN". MultiCAN is a more powerful scalable CAN, which is able to support two up to eight CAN nodes V2.b active. The current implementation of the MultiCAN module supports 4 CAN nodes, whereby one of these nodes is able to run TTCAN level one and two. The module supports 128 message objects flexible assignable to each CAN node. It also features a flexible, double-chained list management to enable list based FIFOs and gateway implementations.

Silicon will be available for open market as integrated part of the 32bit microcontroller devices in June 2003.

Protocol Overview

CAN itself is a completely event triggered system. To provide a possibility of a time-triggered system, TTCAN is specified as an additional layer, using the layers of the CAN standard. The CAN standard describes the conditions for synchronization of a CAN network. If the nodes are synchronized, any message may be transmitted at a specific point in time, without competing with any other message on the bus. By avoiding more than one message on the bus, a loss of arbitration is prevented and latency becomes predictable. This means, that TTCAN gives the possibility of a deterministic schedule on a TTCAN network with hard deadlines. Four different types of time slots are distinguished within TTCAN. One on a complete time triggered base is called exclusive time window, here two triggers define, the earliest starting point of a message, as well as the latest starting point of a message (so called Tx_Enable_Window.). In this window only a predefined message is allowed to be started, which leads to the fact, that no arbitration will take place. In case of a transmission error in an exclusive time window, no retransmission is allowed. To have the option of arbitration, so called arbitrating windows or merged arbitrating windows exist. In standard arbitrating windows messages are only allowed to be started if the bus is idle and the message does not violate the deadline of this time window, but no retransmission. In case of merged arbitrating windows, which consist out of several consecutive arbitrating windows, a retransmission due to an error or an arbitration loss is possible, as long as the deadline is not violated. The fourth and last window type is "free time windows". In these windows the bus idles. In case future extensions of the bus are needed, these windows can be used.

Scheduling, Matrix and Frame

The transmission schedule is predefined at design time and stored in a system matrix, which consists of transmission columns and basic cycles (rows). The columns of the matrix represent the transmission (time) windows that are sequentially processed and then repeated all over within each basic cycle.

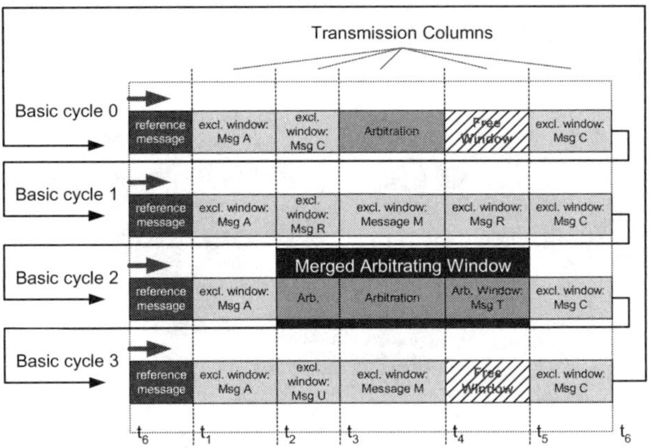

Figure 11: Example of a system matrix

Transmission columns may have different time spans, but in each basic cycle a special n^{th} transmission column has the same time span as in each other cycle. A basic cycle is a row inside the system matrix. Each basic cycle starts with a reference message, which includes global time. Basic cycles are identified by the cycle count number. Cycle count starts at zero and ends at 2^n-1. Within a basic cycle different time windows may exist. The shortest basic cycle includes a reference message. Inside a transmission column periodic messages may be defined by the repeat factor.

Figure 12 introduces a small example how the scheduler of MultiCAN works. MultiCAN has a linear scheduler, which has to be in increasing time mark order. The scheduler gets a start address. Starting from this address, predefined command sequences will be entered. A defined window is per default an exclusive time window. To change the default status an arbitration window has to be defined. The last part of an arbitration window and a single one close the arbitration window and are so called single or short arbitration windows. A window after short arbitration window is again an exclusive time window.

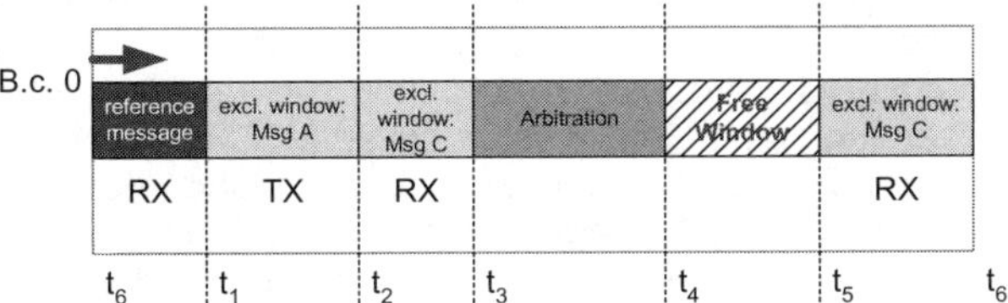

Figure 12 : Single basic cycle of a time slave

The scheduler knows eight different types of events (entries), which can be defined: Time mark, interrupt control, arbitration, transmit control, receive control, reference message, basic cycle end and end of scheduler memory. On every time mark, it is possible to generate an interrupt. A special interrupt is the interrupt on the reference message. This interrupt can trigger actions on other modules or give a regular timer event for the system. In the example of Figure 12, the TTCAN node shall transmit Message A and receive message C.

command	Arbitration mode	Interrupts	Event time
timer mark	No action	Here: none	t1
command	Check enable	Destination RX MO of interest	1st basic cycle / repeat factor
RX control	Yes	MO of ref msg	0 / 1
command	Alternative msg.	Transmission enabled	1st basic cycle / repeat factor
TX control	No msg., if destination object not valid.	Next TX trigger sends MO of msg A.	0 / 1
command	Arbitration mode	Interrupts	Event time
timer mark	No action	Here: none	t2
command	Arbitration mode	Interrupts	Event time
timer mark	No action	Here: none	t3
command	Check enable	Destination RX MO of interest	1st basic cycle / repeat factor
RX control	Yes	MO of msg. C	0 / 1
command	Arbitration mode	Interrupts	Event time
timer mark	short arbitration window	Here: none	t4
command	Arbitration mode	1st basic cycle / repeat factor	
Arbitration	short arbitration window	0 / 2	
command	Arbitration mode	Interrupts	Event time
timer mark	no action: excl time window	Here: none	t5
command	Gap mode	Event time	
basic cycle end	No	t6	
command	Arbitration mode	Interrupts	Event time
timer mark	No action	Here: none	t6
command	Check enable	Destination RX MO of interest	1st basic cycle / repeat factor
RX control	Yes	MO of msg. C	0 / 1

Figure 13: Scheduler example for Figure 12

The scheduler example in Figure 13 shows a way, how a schedule is defined on MultiCAN. Additionally, the scheduler has an error detection mechanism, which helps find, the following configuration errors: At the end of basic cycle, an arbitration window is still open. A slave device has a reference message scheduled. A time mark is missing during instruction collection. In a reference message window, another message window type is scheduled. A reference message is missing.

As all events refer to a time mark this schedule has a deterministic behavior. Only inside arbitration windows, it is not known, which message will be sent on the bus before the complete system is defined. A further feature that is not used in this schedule example is the so-called emergency message. In exclusive time windows, it is possible to transmit a scheduled message or – if that is not available - a message that is triggered by another object. The user has the possibility to configure, the message, which shall have higher priority. For example the message inside scheduler memory has higher priority. The exclusive time window starts and this message is not ready. In this case the user is sending the message of the message object, which has been defined backup. Maybe the user likes to get noticed in case measurements are not ready, here an emergency message will be sent.

Time Synchronization

In TTCAN the time synchronization takes place during synchronization phase and without synchronization losses after a gap. A gap has to be declared inside a reference message and takes place at the end of corresponding basic cycle. In a TTCAN network up to eight potential time masters exist. Every potential time master has a different priority, shown by the identifier, which is differing, in the last three significant bits. In case a potential time master wakes up, it waits for a predefined waiting time, listening to the bus. When no reference message of higher priority comes in, the device starts sending. In this stage arbitration takes place between potential time masters. A slave or a potential time master with lower priority will regard itself as synchronized as soon as it received two valid reference messages. During synchronization all potential time masters have Ref_Trigger_Offset set to Initial_Ref_Trigger as positive value. Ref_Trigger_Offset modifies the time mark, which determines the starting time of a reference message. In case a device with a positive Ref_Trigger_Offset sees a lower priority reference message on the bus, it will reset its Ref_Trigger_Offset to zero. In case a message with lower priority still starts its reference message first, the Ref_Trigger_Offset can be decrement until –127 or until it becomes time master. All potential timer masters who stop sending become backup time master. The new time master sets it Ref_Trigger_Offset to zero.

On MultiCAN the Ref_Trigger_Offset can be written during initialization phase, and will be transferred to a user write protected register. As soon as the synchronization phase starts, the potential time master takes part inside the protocol. The Ref_Trigger_Offset is taken care of, without any interaction with the user. As soon as the device is time master or a time slave (these are also potential time masters as long as the time master sends its reference messages) the scheduler controls the operation.

Outside the initial synchronization phase in strictly time-triggered systems the local time is adjusted to global time. In a level 2 TTCAN network NTUs are the time base of the system. One NTU is fraction of a second. The node view of an NTU usually differ slightly from the network view, which is caused by the local oscillators. After the network synchronization, the global time is known, sent out by the reference message. The time master provides the global NTU, which is valid for the complete system. A time slave get this global NTU by the reference message and adjusts is local time by the shift correction calculated from global time. The TUR is calculated as:

$$TUR = \frac{\text{local length of basic cycle}}{\text{global length of basic cycle}}$$

On MultiCAN the user does not have to take care of the adjustment of local time. The MultiCAN module takes care of this adjustment, so that the user is always sure, that local time and global time are almost identical.

Initialization

After reset the MultiCAN module is in configuration mode. To get the system running, the following steps have to be taken:

- The hardware sets local, global and cycle time to zero.
- Reception filtering is not possible, because it is not enabled.
- A TURADJ value has to be chosen. In case for automatic TUR adjust the corresponding enable has to be set. The TURADJ value will automatically transferred to TUR.
- The user has to setup the TTCAN schedule into scheduler memory.
- Further TTCAN register configurations have to be done.
- The bit for leaving configuration mode has to be set.
- The hardware starts local time.
- Synchronization mode is started automatically.
- The TTCAN protocol starts running.

Error Management

TTCAN contains four levels of error management. The protocol distinguishes between no error, warning, error and severe error. In case of no error, the TTCAN protocol runs without any restrictions. The second level is the warning state. Here a value called MSC is important. This value has the following functionality: Message status count (MSC) (range zero to seven) is an error counter, which provides a possibility to detect scheduling errors for exclusive time windows. It shall be remarked that each message object for exclusive time windows has its own MSC. The overall maximum and minimum MSC inside a matrix cycle is stored inside the MultiCAN module.

Three different root causes for a warning are possible:

- MSCMAX – MSCMIN > 2 at the end of a matrix cycle.
- A receive-message object reached an MSC of seven.
- Tx_Underflow: Not all transmit triggers got active.

A warning exceeds an interrupt flag.

The third stage is the event error. Reaching the error state, no transmit enable window will be opened, additionally the Reference_Trigger_Offset will be set on 127. The root cause of an error is:

- A transmit-message object reached an MSC of seven.
- Tx_Overflow, more than the number of specified Tx_Triggers has been taken.

An error interrupt flag is set.

The forth and last error type is a so-called severe error. Here all CAN bus traffic is stopped. The configuration phase of the MultiCAN module is entered again. There are four different types of root causes for a severe error:

- Application Watchdog, the application failed to service the watchdog. In this case it is not insured that the host is still working properly.
- Bus Off, a CAN bus error leads to bus off
- Config error, a merged arbitration window is not properly closed or a Tx_Trigger occurs in reference message time window.

- Watch_Trigger_Event, this trigger occurs if the reference message is missing, which means, that the time master stopped sending reference messages.

The INIT bit is set.

CAN Debug and Safety Concept

To avoid errors and to ensure to use the right error-handling MultiCAN offers a variety of mechanisms.
In case the device has two CAN modules, the following possibilities exist:

a) Two CAN modules, two CAN transceivers

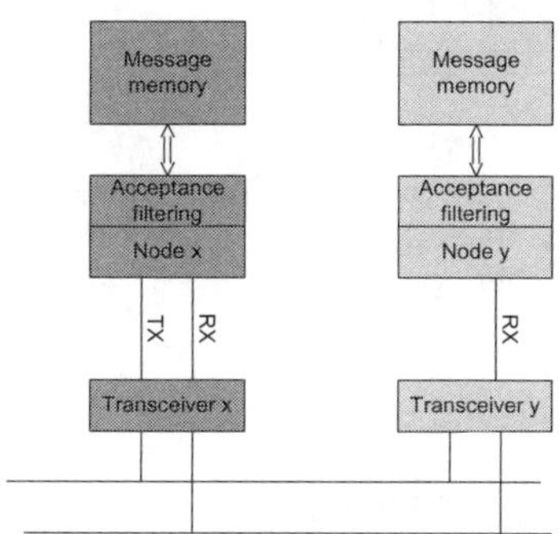

Figure 14: Two separate CAN nodes, two transceivers

Minus: This concept needs two CAN transceivers
Plus: Transceiver errors are detectable.

b) Two CAN modules, one CAN transceiver

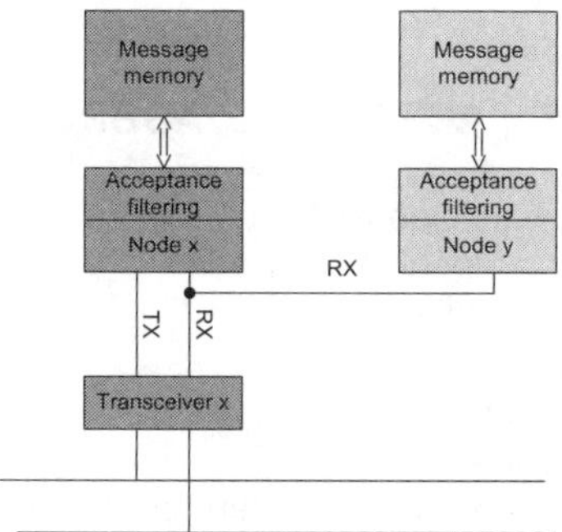

Figure 15: Two separate CAN nodes, one transceiver

Plus: This concept needs one CAN transceiver.
Minus: A transceiver error is not detectable.
Both concepts do have synchronized message access, which basically leads to the fact, that short time disturbances are recognized by both CAN nodes and lead to an error situation.

c) MultiCAN in Analyzer Mode

In Analyzer Mode the device listens to the bus, but it is not actively taking part of the protocol. The nodes are handled asynchronous as the protocol handler is requesting the information one node after another. Message objects are appended to a node. If the application shall test, that a received message is really correct, for each node a message object has to be setup and compared via software. A disturbance on the bus is seen in different states and has a different impact. It is even possible to find a problem between protocol handler and message memory.

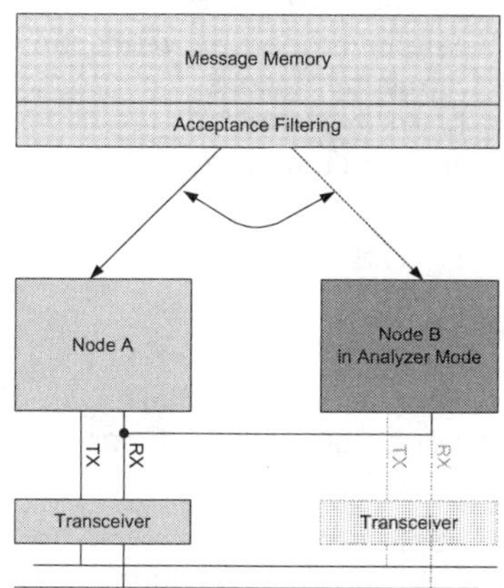

Figure 16: MultiCAN in Analyzer Mode

Beside the Analyzer Mode the MultiCAN module has additional features to avoid bus errors before they occur. The MultiCAN offers a synchronization analysis features as well as driver delay measurement feature, which help to make further extensions of the bus safer and small disturbances on the bus less critical.

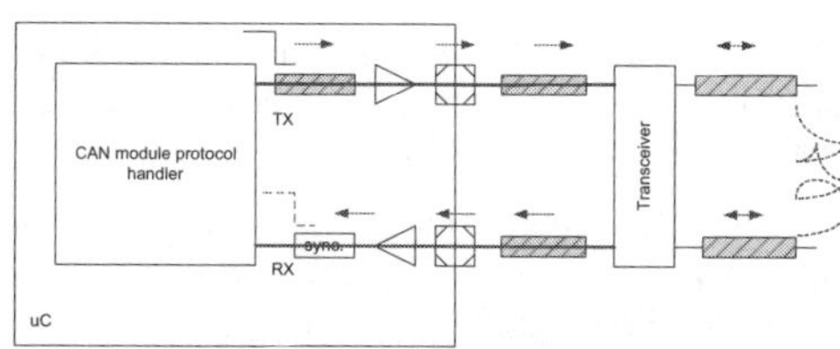

Figure 17: Schematic signal way, TX to RX

The synchronization analysis feature helps to prevent a possible bus error in case of slight changes or impacts on the bus. This feature monitors the time between the first dominant edge and the sample point measured a stored in a frame counter register. By using this feature it is easier to adjust the sample point to the actual sample point of the complete bus system.

The driver delay measurement feature helps to find a circuitry, where a sent edge is received time quanta before the sample point.
Both features help to find a configuration and circuitry, which is not fault-prone to slide changes or disturbances on the bus.

CONCLUSION

The usefulness of TTCAN besides competing high-speed safety communication protocols for automotive has been shown for different applications. Its benefit for more flexible system partitioning at improved cost levels has been outlined for common closed-loop control tasks. Finally, the description of Infineon's implementation of a full TTCAN level 2 protocol controller has demonstrated, how the supported mechanism ensure the positive runtime effects and consistency support without additional software overhead as would be needed with TTCAN level 1 implementations. The described protocol controller has been implemented in silicon and will be available in Infineon's 32bit microcontrollers.

REFERENCES

1 X-by-Wire: Opportunities, Challenges and Trends; Nico Kelling and Patrick Leteinturier; SAE 2003-01-0113

2 Integrated Self-test Technologies for Embedded Automotive; Wilhard Von Wendorff; SAE 2003-01-xxxx

3 New µController links: Micro-Second-Bus and Micro-Link-Interface; Klaus Scheibert and Jens Barrenschen, Hannes Estl; SAE 2003-01-xxxx

4 Real Time Data Fusion: a challenge for distributed intelligence; Patrick Leteinturier, Juergen Hoika and Claus Preuschoff; ATA 2002-01A4011

5 Seamless Solutions for Powertrain Systems; Juergen Hoika, Hannes Estl, Gunther Krall, Joachim Weitzel and Patrick Leteinturier; SAE 2002-01-1303

6 AUDO Architecture. A solution to Automotive µController Requirements; Patrick Leteinturier, Boris Vitorelli; SAE 2000-01-0145

7 TwinCAN A new milestone for inter-network communication; Jens Barrenscheen and Patrick Leteinturier; SAE 2000-01-0144

8 Semiconductor Technologies for the Automotive Electronics of the Future; Eschert, Hoika, Sirch Taeuber, Vennmann; VDA MICRO.tec 2000 EXPO Hannover

9 The Brake Project - Centralized versus Distributed Redundancy for Brake-by-Wire Systems; Nico Kelling, Worthy Heck; SAE 2002-01-0266

10 ISO/WD 11898-4: Road vehicles – Controller area network (CAN) – Part 4: Time triggered communication

11 MultiCAN Specification for AUDO-NG, Infineon Technologies AG, Jens Barrenscheen

CONTACT

Patrick Leteinturier
System Definition Automotive
Tel: +49 (89) 234-83828
Patrick.Leteinturier@infineon.com

Nico A. Kelling
System Marketing Powertrain Worldwide
Tel: +49 (89) 234-82218
Nico.Kelling@infineon.com

Ursula Kelling
Technical Marketing Serial Bus Systems
Tel: +49 (89) 234-83287
Ursula.Kelling@infineon.com

Address:
Infineon Technologies AG
Balanstr. 73
81541 München
Germany
http://www.infineon.com

DEFINITIONS, ACRONYMS, ABBREVIATIONS

ECU: Electronic Control Unit
HMI: Human Machine Interface
IC: Integrated Circuit
PCB: Printed Circuit Board
I/O: Input/Output
ASIC: Application Specific IC
ASSP: Application Specific Standard Product
DSP: Digital Signal Processor

2003-01-0112

New Serial Microcontroller Links - Micro-Link-Interface and Micro-Second-Channel

Klaus Scheibert, Jens Barrenscheen and Hannes Estl
Infineon Technologies

ABSTRACT

Trends in today's and future embedded powertrain systems show a strongly growing demand of communication between the functional units inside a car. A cost optimized system partitioning leads to several independent building blocks that have to be interconnected. Depending on the task of each building block, different classes of data exchange can be distinguished, differing in the required bandwidth, the tolerated latency and speed for real time critical tasks. In order to minimize the communication effort concerning time, chip size and overall costs, different communication requirements have been analyzed. The results lead to improvements of standard serial interfaces by application-oriented features.

This paper deals with two new approaches for serial interface modules:

- Micro Link Serial Interface (MLI) which creates a new way of low-cost inter-processor communication and
- Micro Second Channel (MSC) which has been developed in order to reduce the number of connections between a microcontroller and a power device

INTRODUCTION: REQUIREMENTS FOR DATA EXCHANGE WITHIN POWERTRAIN APPLICATIONS

Most modern powertrain systems are combining analog inputs with high performance calculating devices and power or transceiver devices. The individual requirements for all of these building blocks lead to a distributed system. As a result, the amount of data to be exchanged between the different functional units strongly increases. Different classes and characteristics of data exchange can be found in the system. They differ in the overall bandwidth, the tolerated latency and the data structure, varying from analog to digital. It has to be also taken in account that some data exchange only takes part between on-board components within an Electronic Control Unit (ECU) like e.g. between two microcontrollers, or it takes part between different ECUs coupled by a field bus (e.g. via CAN). Furthermore data exchange needs to be performed from some external mounted sensors (e.g. manifold pressure sensors) or to actuators (e.g. electronic drives). In order to optimize the overall system costs, the data transfer channels have to be adapted to their specific requirements.

The data paths between the main calculating units, such as the microcontrollers and associated peripheral units are characterized by a high data throughput and in most cases, a very short latency. For these data flows, high bandwidth channels have to be implemented. As a standard approach, two or more microcontollers can be connected to each other to multi-processor systems by their external parallel memory interfaces. This leads to problems if they operate in different clock domains or if they need to share a master–slave memory partitioning where the slave processor might stay in idle mode while the master gets access to the slave memory portions. Although the parallel access offers a high band width, it requires a large amount of signals and wiring effort (about 100 signals per chip). The new serial MLI approach (MLI = micro link) creates a new way for low-cost inter-processor communication.

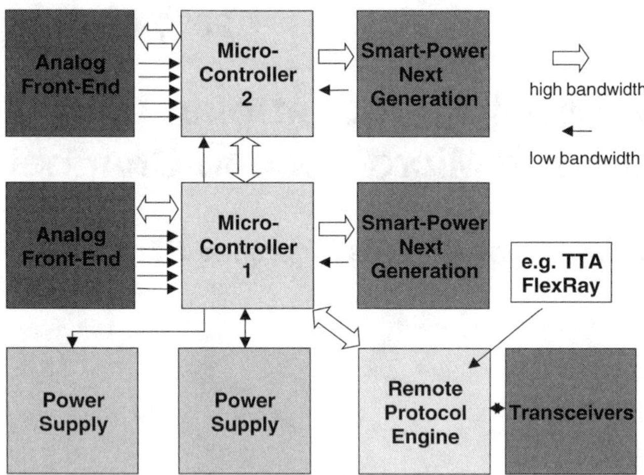

ECU Overview – Communication Channels

Another type of data transfer can be found between the control devices, such as microcontrollers, and the power devices. In modern ECUs, a large amount of power switches can be found which are mostly all PWM-controlled (pulse width modulation) by timer units on the microcontrollers. The main data direction is unidirectional from the controller to the power device. In order to reduce the number of connections between the devices, the data stream can be serialized and then transferred to the power device.

In most systems existing today, a serial communication between two devices depends on some CPU actions. In these cases, the data is packed in a certain format before being transmitted over the serial link. This packet structure is mainly done under SW control, before the automatic transfer is started. This leads to a base load of the CPU that increases significantly if the data throughput becomes more and more important. In order to avoid these additional tasks for the CPU, the data transfers should be independent from the running program. Only a fully autonomous data transfer can guarantee a high data rate without additional costs for computing power.

Driven by these needs, Infineon Technologies developed the next generation 32-bit powertrain microcontroller family, called AUDO-NG which is based on the 32-bit TriCore architecture. The AUDO-NG 32-bit microcontroller family incorporates two new serial communication peripherals with enhanced performance and dedicated feature sets:

- Micro Link Serial Bus Interface (MLI), which optimizes data exchange between a scalable amount of microcontrollers and

- Micro Second Channel Interface (MSC), which optimizes data exchange and pin count between Power ASSP/ASIC for e.g. Multi-Channel Switches.

MICRO LINK SERIAL INTERFACE (MLI)

MLI is a serial high speed link (up to 35 Mbaud in the first devices), which is based on a principle similar to the standard serial protocol. Due to its symmetrical structure, it supports full-duplex transmission. It only requires four signal lines in each data direction (downstream = transmit and upstream = receive). For each data transfer direction, there is one clock line (CLK), one data line (DATA) and two handshake lines (READY, VALID). One MLI transmitter might be connected to up to four scalable MLI receivers sharing the same Data and Clock line. An individual addressing of receivers is done by independent sets of handshake lines.

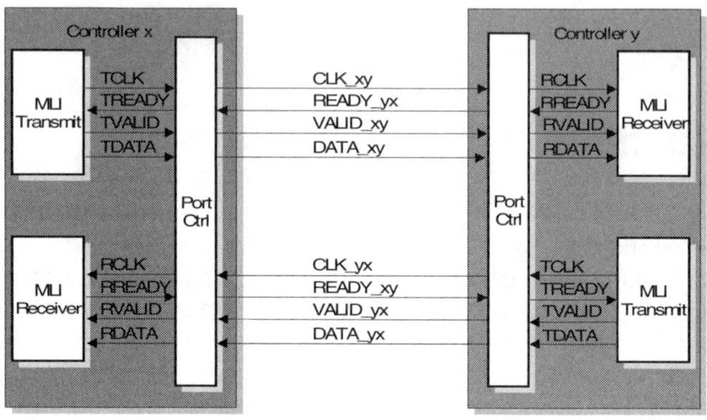

MLI Transmitter – Receiver Connection

The MLI interface has been developed to meet the following application targets:

- Data and program exchanging without intervention of CPU or PCP between microcontrollers of the AUDO-NG family. The MLI is connected to the system bus and can do data move operations independently from the CPU(s).

- The internal architecture of the block allows the communication between controllers in different clock domains.

- The read mode enables the desired data to be read from the other controller.

- Resources sharing between controllers.

- Capability of triggering interrupts in the receiving controller by sending a command.

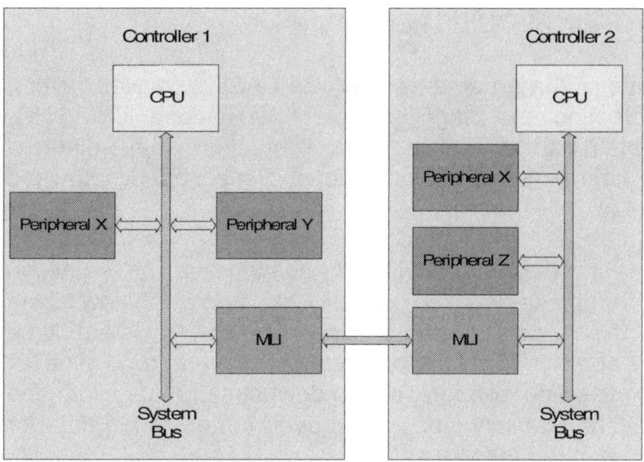

MLI in a Microcontroller

MLI I/O-pins are CMOS compliant, allowing microcontrollers from the AUDO-NG family to be mounted closely together on the same PCB. This target doesn't necessarily require cost-extensive LVDS drivers for better EMC behavior. Usage of CMOS MLI I/O drivers instead of LVDS drivers also has a beneficial impact on the absolute current consumption and requires less interface pins. Nevertheless there might be applications, where LVDS drivers are useful for MLI signals; e.g. for electronic valve train, where the ECU for the valves and the ECU for engine control are separated and need to communicate via longer MLI cable (up to more than 1 meter might occur). As a different cable length for the connection leads to a changing loop delay for transmitted or received messages, the timing of the MLI handshake signals can be adapted via programmming during the startup procedure.

The internal architecture of the MLI interface supports different clock domains for the transmitter or the receiver module. As the MLI interface is able to act as bus master on the system bus of the controller itself, it autonomously acts like a DMA controller and therefore might work in parallel to the CPU of the system. As a result, the MLI significantly reduces the CPU load for data transfer tasks. Remote control of peripherals located in the "other" controller is offered as a feature by this behavior; so calculation power or peripherals located in different sub-controller systems might be shared via MLI.

MLI connection is not necessarily restricted to a controller-to-controller connection. Other products, such as smart companion devices (ASSP) can also be connected easily. The advantage of these devices is their extended voltage range, so that they could incorporate e.g. a 5V analog sensor interface or other analog and digital data preconditioning circuits.

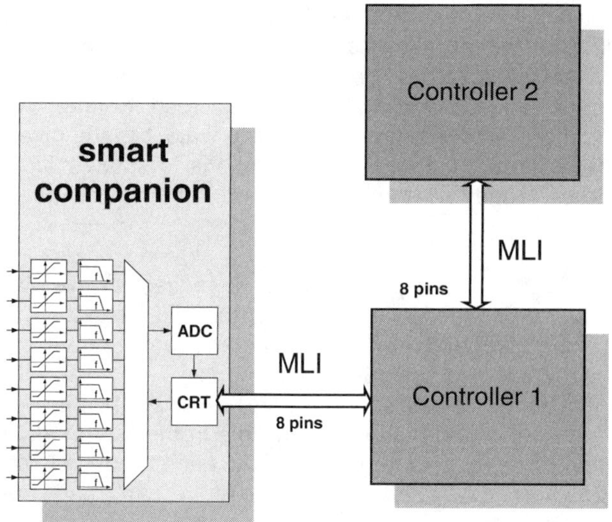

Smart Companion Device with MLI Connection

GENERAL DESCRIPTION OF MLI

The communication between two participants is based on a pipe structure. A pipe may be seen as a logical connection between a transmitter and a receiver. In each MLI module, 4 independent pipes are available. The pipes point to address areas in the receiver, starting at programmable base addresses. The MLI transmitter only sends a short offset relative to the base address instead of the full 32-bit address. Each pipe defines a buffer in the receiver's address map (defined by the base address, the offset and the length of the offset).

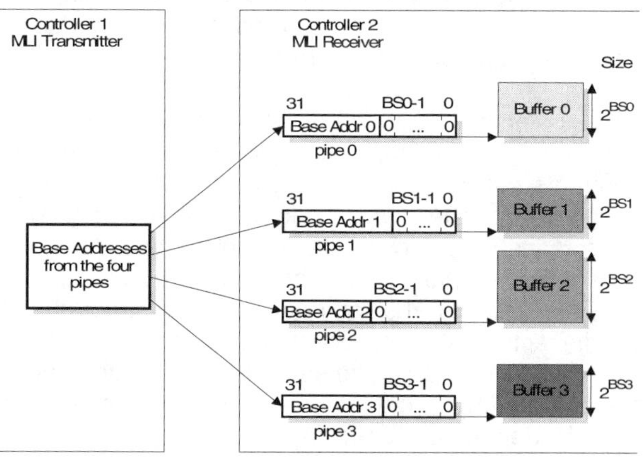

MLI Pipe Structure

In addition to the offset (its bit width defines the buffer size), the MLI transmitter sends a reference to the pipe in use. When the MLI receiver obtain this data it elaborates the absolute target address by simply concatenating the received offset to the base address of the selected pipe.

A data write access to a pipe in controller 1 leads to an automatic transfer from the MLI transmitter to the MLI receiver on controller 2. This transfer includes the written data, the offset address and the pipe number. The received information becomes available in the MLI receiver. The CPU of controller 2 can read it under SW control or the MLI can autonomously write it to the given address. In order to avoid write actions to safety-critical address areas, an access protection scheme has been added.

A read access to a pipe transfers a request to the MLI receiver on controller 2. If enabled, the MLI executes the read operation autonomously and the requested data will be sent back to the MLI on controller 1 (by the MLI transmitter on controller 2 to the MLI receiver of controller 1). When this information is available in the MLI module of controller 1, an interrupt can be generated and the CPU (or a DMA, etc.) of controller 1 can read the requested data.

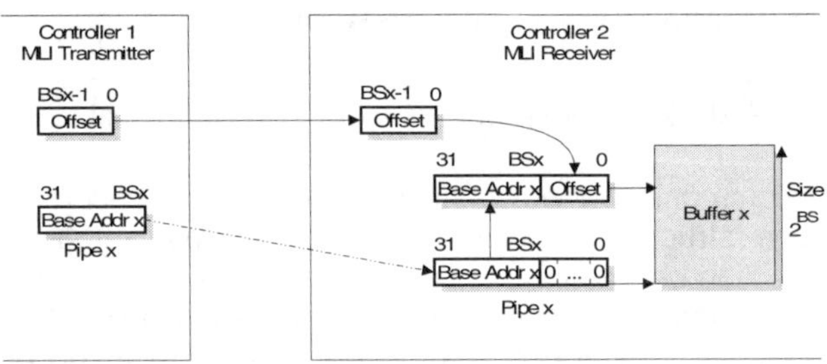

Target address generation

The kernel MLI includes an optimized mode to transfer data blocks. Whenever the MLI transmitter detects that the new address and the previous one follow a predictable scheme, it will send just the data reducing this way the number of transferred bits.

If the complete autonomous feature set of MLI connection is enabled, data transfers between two participants can take place without any CPU action for data handling. The transmitting MLI stores the write access to its pipes, does the complete encoding and transfers the complete move action to the receiving MLI. There, the address and the data are reconstructed and the write action is executed on the system bus. As a result, a MLI module can be seen as a fully autonomous module transferring data moves between the system buses of independent controllers.

MICRO SECOND CHANNEL (MSC)

The Micro Second Bus (MSC or µs Bus) is a natural evolution of the standard interfacing approach to Power IC / ASIC, which are used within today's powertrain applications.

SYSTEM REQUIREMENTS

State of the art smart power ICs / ASICs (power drivers, protection and diagnostic integrated in one IC / ASIC) contain three basic data domains with different requirements regarding latency time, bandwidth and speed.

- First the output switching domain, the main function of these ICs. To achieve the necessary switching frequencies and precise timings for "real time control", e.g. for proportional current regulation or gasoline injectors, a high downstream bandwidth and short latency time are required to deliver the data for all outputs "on time".
- Protection and diagnostic is the second. The upstream bandwidth, used to send diagnostic data or to read back programmed registers, can be low compared to the switching domain. Data transfer is not necessary permanently, only in case of a fault condition or on micro controller request.
- The last domain deals with configuration and programming of the smart power IC. Data transfer is done during start up and for changing the behavior of the IC in-between different operation modes. Medium bandwidth, but also short latency are necessary to react in real time for changing conditions or operations.

	switching	diagnostic	configuration
direction	downstream	upstream	downstream
bandwidth	high >10 MBaud	low <10 kBaud	medium 10 to 100 kBaud
latency	short (1µs range)	long (ms range)	medium (>1µs range)
operation	permanently	on request or on fault	startup or change of operation

MSC communication domains

Due to the fact that in an engine managenent system more than one smart power IC can be necessary, the scalability of a communication interface gives a big advantage. With only one interface at the micro controller different smart power ICs can be operated.

EVOLUTION OF THE COMMUNICATION

Evolution	Parallel Input parallel Status	Parallel Input SPI Interface	SPI + µs-Bus	Advanced µs-Bus
Pins / IO	16 + 16 = 32	16 + 4 = 20	4 + 3 = 7	6
performance	PWM	PWM configurability	PWM configurability	PWM configurabilit
diagnostic	1 bit / channel no memory	2 bit / channel fault memory	2 bit / channel fault memory	2 bit / channel fault memory
interface	parallel	parallel + duplex bus	duplex bus + point - point	point - point + async. upstream

time line

Evolution of the communication interface; e.g. for output 16 channels

Loads like gasoline injectors, ignition coils, oxygen sensor heater, purge valve, cooling fan relay and electro-hydraulic valves have to be switched. The first evolutionary step was the integration of multiple switches in one IC. That allows on one hand a reduction of PCB dimensions and therefore the reduction of cost, but also enables higher performance by integrated protection and diagnostic functionality. Today multi-channel switches with 2 to 18 channels are available. Depending on the specific application currents from 50mA up to 10A have to be driven. The loads could be either ohmic, capacitive or inductive in behavior.

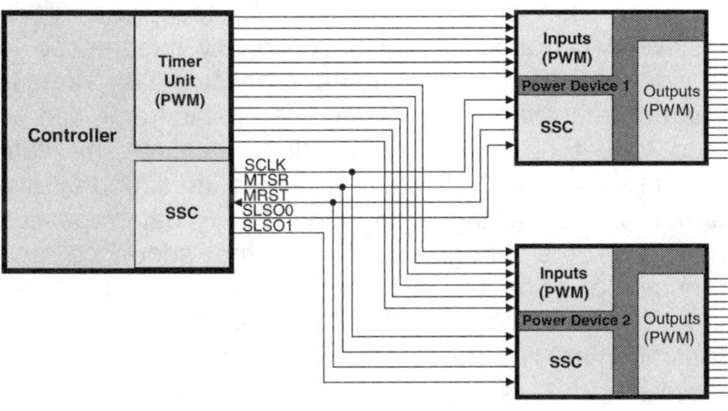

Conventional Interfacing with parallel I/O and SSC for low speed PWM and diagnostic Data

The common characteristic for all these power IC connections is the parallel interface for the high speed PWM channels coupled with the conventional SSC interface for transmitting configuration data, low speed PWM and receiving diagnostic data from the device. For cost saving reasons more than one power IC can be connected to the same SSC module and has to be selected by a separated Chip Select signal.

The next step in the direction of an optimized power IC interface is the introduction of the Micro Second Bus of the first generation, which replaces the parallel downstream approach by a serialized approach. Especially for devices with more than 8 integrated PWM power outputs this solution drastically reduces the amount of necessary pins on both, the power and µC sides.

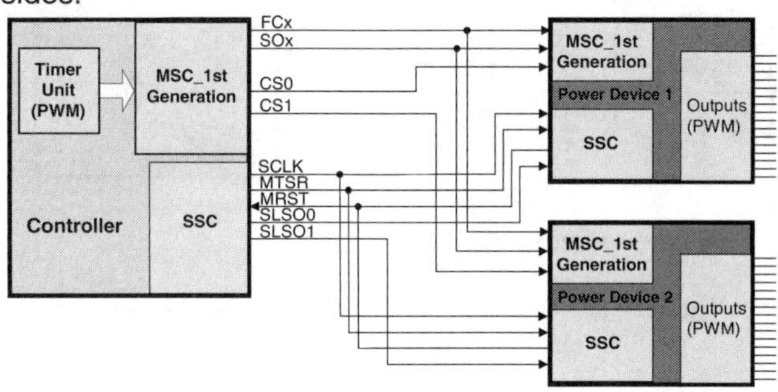

Enhanced Interfacing with MSC 1st Generation and SSC for low speed PWM and diagnostic Data

The latest evolution step towards an optimized interface for the power ICs is the introduction of the second generation Micro Second Bus, which integrates the initialization and configuration of the power device by sending dedicated command frames as well as PWM data frames to the same physical serial high speed channel (with up to 35 MBaud transfer rate in the first device). This combination of formerly separated functions (parallel channels and SSC channel) does not harm the requirement for sufficient downstream bandwidth due to the fact that power device initialization is normally only performed after power-on reset or after irregular emergency situation.

Upstream diagnosis from the power device has to be polled using the regular time base in conventional systems by the SSC interface of the controller with the drawback of additional system load. To prevent this additional system load, the next evolution step logically must be to simply upload diagnostic data from the power device if there is a change in the diagnostic data itself. To achieve this new goal, the power IC has to send asynchronously with lower speed (due to lower bandwidth requirement) only if there is updated diagnosis data available (e.g. in the case of a detected over-current situation). This split in the frequency domains between high speed for the downstream channel and the low speed for the asynchronous upstream diagnosis channel significantly lowers the demands for increased peripheral performance.

As power ICs often mounted in dedicated areas of the ECU where power dissipation could be conducted easily to the housing of the ECU, signal wiring for the high-speed downstream channel might get relatively long on the PCB and therefore might negatively affect the EMC behavior. Therefore it was decided to offer a LVDS approach for the critical downstream channel signals functional clock (FCLP, FCLN) and data shifted out (SOP, SON).

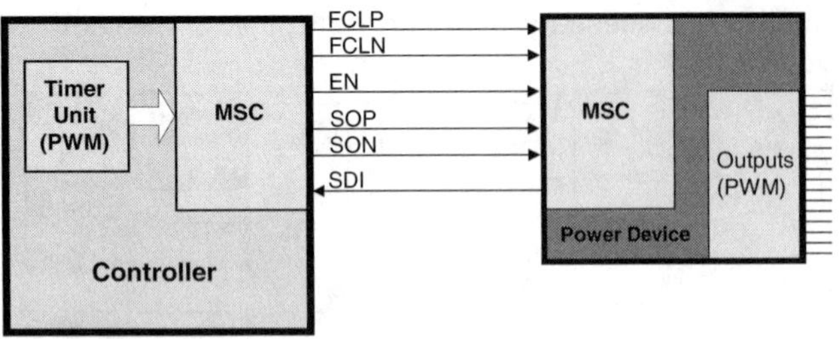

Standard MLI interface with 5 pins for high speed Downstream and 1 pin for low speed Upstream Channel

The MSC interface offers up to 32 high speed timer channels to be serialized for the downstream channel. The protocol supports as well 2x16 channels which offers wider flexibility. Furthermore, the MSC module on the controller side features up to four chip select signals for connecting up to four power ICs to one MSC module.

DESCRIPTION OF MSC DOWNSTREAM MODULE

The downstream connection to the power IC is realized by a high-speed synchronous interface which consists of SSC compliant programmable data stream format between 2 to 34 bits. The type of transmitted data might be distinguished between command frames which are used for initializing and configuring the power IC and data frames which transmits PWM information provided by the timer channels. The first bit (SEL bit) within a frame is used for the differentiation between command and data frames.

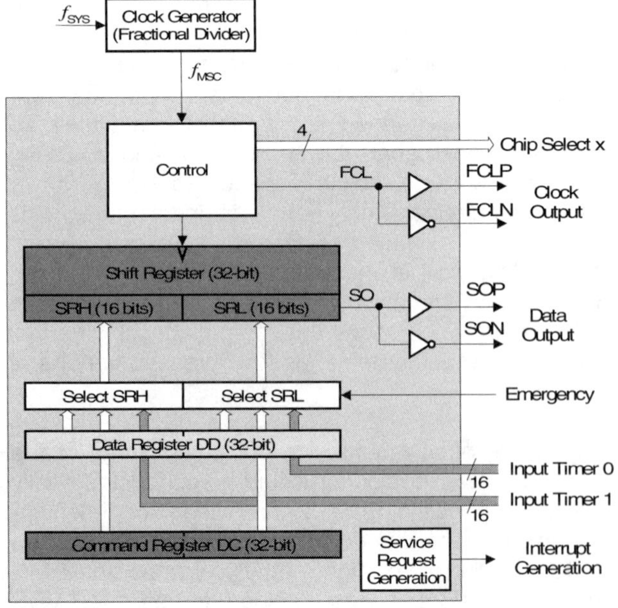

Downstream Channel Block Diagram

Furthermore, a dedicated 32-bit data register (DD) is introduced which might be used for the transmission of software generated channel switch activity or simply keeps the inactive level for each PWM channel which could be used for transmission in the case of an emergency event. For being able to connect more than one power IC to the MSC module, up to four chip select signals are supported. Each chip select signal generation is coupled to one of the two split shift registers SRH and SRL and therefore supports data frames up to sixteen PWM channels each.

MSC Downstream Protocol Layer

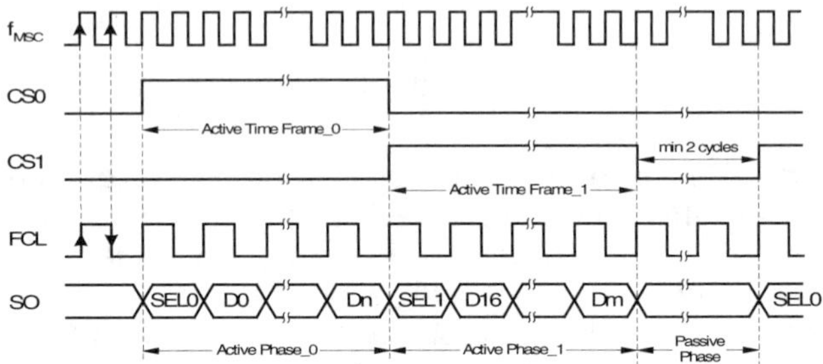

Serial MSC downstream protocol

Between the two active phases of a transmitted frame, at least two transmit clock shift cycles have to be regarded to maintain separation between two consecutively transmitted frames. The generation of the SELx bits and the generation of the transmit shift clock FCL within passive data frames might be optionally suppressed to provide an SSC compliant mode. A passive data frame is a data frame without any data content. This frame can be used to set up different repetition rates for the data transfer. The MSC downstream module supports two further settings, a "triggered mode" and a "data repetition mode". In the "triggered mode", the sequence and transmit period of data or command frames is completely under software control. In the "data repetition mode", the transmit intervals including optional transmission of 0-15 passive frames is autonomously managed by the MSC downstream module itself, therefore off-loading the CPU of this task. Nevertheless it is permissible to transmit command frames under software control within the automatically transferred data stream, where command frames have preference over data frames. The composition of selected active data/command frames plus the selected amount of passive frames is called time frames. The maximum repetition/switching time of a transmitted PWM timer channel is dependent on that value.

DESCRIPTION OF MSC UPSTREAM MODULE

The MSC upstream channel is an asynchronous serial receiver based on the standard asynchronous data transfer protocol. It is dedicated to receive a serial data stream from a peripheral device via its serial data input SDI using two specific data frame formats.

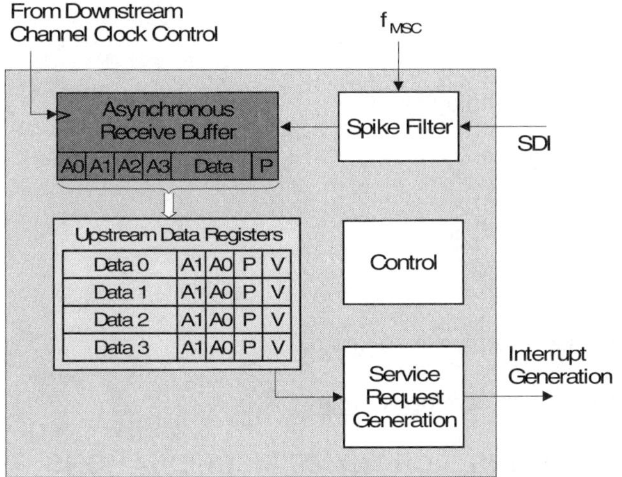

Upstream Channel Block Diagram

The incoming data at SDI (shift data input) is sampled after it has been filtered for spikes. The detected logic states of the serial input are clocked into a shift register. After the complete reception of the serial data frame, the content of the shift register is transferred into one of the four data registers and an interrupt can be generated optionally. The reception baud rate is directly coupled to the downstream shift clock and can be changed within a range of 1/4 up to 1/256.

MSC Upstream Protocol Layer

The received asynchronous data frames used by the upstream channel consists of four basic parts:

– one start bit, always at low level

– an optional 4-bit address field A[3:0] with LSB first

– an 8-bit data field D[7:0] with LSB first

– one parity bit and two stop bits, that are always at high level

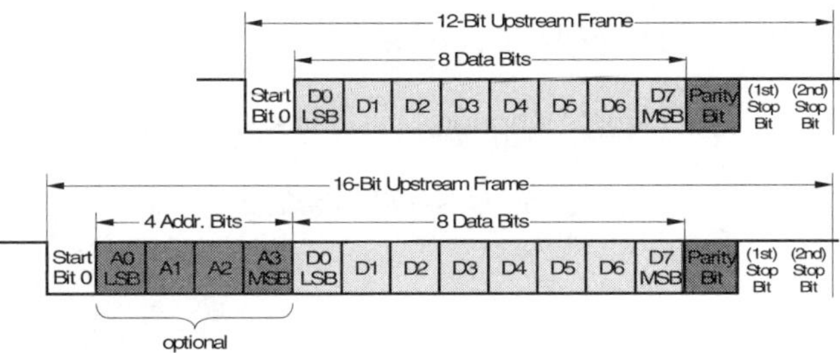

Upstream Channel Frame Types

If the optional address field is not enabled for transmission, the data format corresponds to the standard asynchronous protocol. In order to be able to distinguish different diagnostic messages of the power devices, 4 bits of address field can be added, leading to a 16-bit frame. The contents of the address bits can identify the source and the type of the received diagnostic data. When the content of the receive buffer for a 16-bit data frame has been received completely, it is transferred to one of the four upstream data registers UDx. The two most significant address bits A[3:2] of the received 4-bit address field select the number x of the upstream data register UDx in which the received frame content is stored. The upstream data register UDx is loaded with the two least significant address bits A0 and A1, the 8-bit data, the received parity bit, the calculated parity bit, and the parity checking result.

The MSC module supports four different kinds of interrupts: data, command and time frame interrupts for the downstream channel and a receive interrupt for the upstream channel. For safety reasons, the upstream channel allows the parity of the received data frames to be checked.

SUMMARY

The next generation Micro Second Bus offers chance for further improvement of modern automotive ECU's by:

- Handling the different data domains of smart power switches (output control, diagnostics, configuration) by only one physical communication interface. The significant reduction of pins on both sides, µC and power switches, leads to smaller packages, reduced wiring complexity and smaller necessary board space.

- The scalability of the MSC allows up to 4 smart power devices to be used with only one MSC module on the µC. This reliability reduces the load of the µC for communication with power devices as well as it decreases the required I/O and peripherals of the µC.

- The possibility to use the MSC with LVDS signals (as well as with CMOS compliant voltage levels) allows the µC to be placed further from the smart power ICs on the ECU without the need of additional means to reduce EMI.

- A significant CPU performance off-load due to autonomous function of the Micro Second Bus for downstream and upstream operation.

CONCLUSION

In today's powertrain systems a broad range of semiconductor technologies enable the design of electronics for signal sensing, control and actuation. The devices have to fulfill the special requirements demanded in powertrain applications and the data exchange between the several units have to be optimized to the required function and bandwidth. They have to withstand the harsh environment under the hood and they have to comply with maximum performance needs of a real-time system.

The introduced serial buses, Micro-Link Interface (MLI) and Micro Second Bus (MSC) within embedded powertrain application assist the customer within the development phase to scale down increased system complexity. Data exchange to external units now can be performed with optimized bandwidth and speed autonomously without contribution of further CPU load. Synchronization for the data flow is achieved by using the interrupt system with low impact on needed resources and calculation power. Furthermore, the introduction of MLI and MSC offers a smart way of saving system cost by smaller pin counts on the packages for the controller and for the pin count and the housing size for the power ICs. This reduced pin count also decreases the complexity of the whole module. Even “stand alone” controllers with embedded internal FLASH memory with cost optimized small packages due to the removed parallel external memory could now be easily connected to each other via MLI and share memory portions or even peripheral functions. This offers a smart way of software reuse in the case of a necessary “face lift” of an ECU which needs more performance due to increased application demands.

Last but not least the LVDS design for the high speed MSC interface helps to reduce EMI on PCB level and therefore saves additional effort for getting a fault tolerant system.

REFERENCES

1. "AUDO Architecture. A solution to Automotive µController Requirements"; Leteinturier, Vitorelli; SAE 2000-01-0145

2. “Seamless Solutions for Powertrain Systems”;Hoika, Estl, Krall; Weitzel; Leteinturier, SAE 2002-01-1303

CONTACT

Klaus Scheibert

Senior Staff System Engineer

Infineon Technologies AG

Balanstr. 73

81541 München

Germany

klaus.scheibert@infineon.com

www.infineon.com/powertrain

DEFINITIONS, ACRONYMS, ABBREVIATIONS

ASIC: Application Specific IC

ASSP: Application Specific Standard Product

AUDO-NG: Automotive Unified Processor – Next Generation

CPU: Central Processor Unit

ECU: Electronic Control Unit

EMI: Electro Magnetic Interference

IC: Integrated Circuit

I/O: Input/Output

LVDS: Low Voltage Differential Swing

MLI: Micro Link Serial Interface

MSC: Micro Second Channel

PCB: Printed Circuit Board

PCP: Peripheral Control Processor

PWM: Pulse With Modulated

SPI: Serial Peripheral Interface

SSC: Synchronous Serial Interface

2002-01-0443

Interoperability of Networked Components Requires Conformance Test of Communication Interfaces

Wolfhard Lawrenz
c&s group at University of Applied Sciences

ABSTRACT

Actually automotive industries is in a dilemma: Further customer satisfaction requires further features to be built into cars and this requires more electronics in cars. All this currently happens at a rapidly increasing pace and thus increasing networked cars electronic control systems complexity correspondingly. Networking obviously requires interoperable communication modules consisting of communication hardware and software. And here is the problem: As network protocols are specified mostly in natural languages such as English, no precise and non-ambiguous specification exists. As such implementers may understand the same specification differently. And as a result realizations of the same protocol may behave differently under certain operational conditions. As a consequence mixed suppliers control modules may not be able to communicate properly.

Conformance testing is the solution to this problem. The following paper explains the general procedure how to derive conformance tests under the constraints of verbal non precise device specification. All this is explained with the example of deriving and implementing tests for CAN protocol transceivers. Finally a more general c&s group developed procedure is outlined to derive tests and how to implement them on the basis of a standard ISO tester architecture. Last but not least a road map is given on the conformance tests implemented for various vehicle communication protocols by c&s group.

INTRODUCTION

Networking nowadays is a standard technology applied in cars. There are various kinds of communication protocols applied, which each meet the different application requirements as for safety, body electronics, power train, x-by-wire, etc. The goal of networking is to provide a means to exchange variables between distributed control applications. As such a door controller may read the position of a switch and exchange the proper value with the seat positioning controller thus moving the seat properly. Obviously controllers are provided by various module manufacturers containing communication modules which are supplied by various software and hardware manufacturers. Given that final user expectation would be that all these applications can communicate with no problems requiring that the underlying communication components all are "interoperable".

But interoperability of communication components may be a problem: Although standards exists in SAE and ISO very often these standards are not precise enough. Standards are mostly written in natural languages and thus contain specifications which are ambiguous, incorrect or contradictory. Taking this into account there is a high risk that mixed components networked systems may end up in communication problems. This is even more true today, as networks tend to integrate plenty of nodes such as 30 and more in one network branch.

A very effective countermeasure to this dilemma are conformance tests, checking the properties of components against a "well defined" set of test cases and thus ensuring that different suppliers' devices work are properly interoperable under operational conditions as specified by the tests.

Over recent years various efforts have been undertaken to specify, implement such kind of interoperability tests. c&s group has been working on such tests for various protocols such as CAN, eBUS, TTx, LIN, etc. Some of the specifications in the mean time have become standards such as ISO 16845 CAN (layer 2) Conformance Test.

LAYERED COMMUNICATION STACK

There is an ISO-OSI model structuring any communication path into 7 different layers. As such the various layers may be implemented by different suppliers. A complete communication path in a control module may then consist from different suppliers at the various levels.

A communication implementation not always fills all the 7 communication layers, if there is no need for certain functionalities. Figure 1 depicts a typical automotive scenario.
Layer 1 specifies the so called "Physical Layer". This comprises e. g. the actual wiring of the network and the

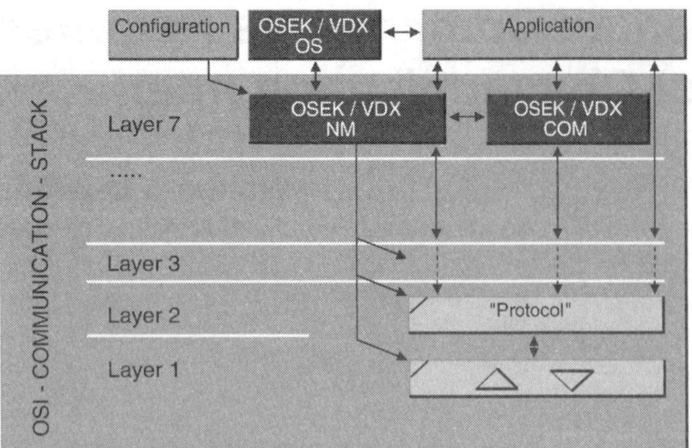

Figure 1: OSI Communication Stack

so called "Transceiver", serving as the interface between the wiring and the higher layer. Layer 2 very often is referred to as the protocol layer, which is CAN in this case. On top of CAN typically there are some further communication drivers in layer 2. These communication drivers typically adapt the various communication register structures of CAN to the next higher layers.

On top of layer 2 all the adjacent layers very often in in-vehicle communications are empty, no functionality like different data paths required. The final layer 7 – Application Layer – represents the interface to the user (software). In this case the OSEK/VDX implementation is depicted. As such OSEK/VDX specifies to blocks of interface. The NM – Network Management – continuously checks the health state of the whole communication path and reports it to the user application. The COM – Communication – module finally the services for the exchange of variables between the different user applications.

With regard to conformance tests all the implementations of the various layers must be checked, as discussed below.

CONFROMANCE TESTS SPECIFICATION – BASIC TECHNIQUE

Baring in mind the constraint of insufficiently specified components and the requirement that these components should be interoperable, one way out of this dilemma is to apply "sufficiently exhaustive" conformance tests to verify the desired interoperability of components. As no sufficiently detailed and formal description of the component exists a so called black box test technique is applicable. Test stimuli are applied from outside of the component – which is referred to as Implementation under Test IUT – to the accessible inputs, the responses are read from the outputs of the IUT and compared to what is understood from the specification.

In a first step in order to derive a first guess of a sufficiently exhaustive set of test cases an empiric driven selection of a set of test cases, representing practical conditions under which a component later on would work, is a recommendable practical approach. In a second step the individual elements of the above set are organized in such a way that they each would result as the parameterized product of a set of – mostly desired – orthogonal vectors. These vectors may be defined application driven. The parameterized product of the vectors defines the so called System Operational Vector Space – SOVS, comprising all so far known possible operational conditions under which IUT is expected to be functional in the specified way. In a third step a subset of the SOVS is selected empirically, driven from application experience, or even formally. This subset is then expected to be Sufficiently Exhaustive Minimal Set of (conformance) Test Cases SEMSTC on one hand while comprising not too many tests cases on the other hand resulting in a still acceptable test time.

Obviously the approach mentioned above is a practically viable procedure to derive a sufficiently exhaustive set of test cases. But this procedure of course incorporates the risk that the selected subset of tests does not cover sufficiently the behavior of the component. There are several ways to optimize the selection of test cases – see below:

- The selection of the of SEMSTC should be supported by formal methods
- The application of the SEMSTC in conjunction with the practically gained experience that in real application cases will be detected that tested components will show deficiencies in their desired interoperability will lead to an iterative optimization process influencing the re-specification of the test cases and the component. The newly detected problem is analyzed leading to:
  - A redefinition of the SOVS, their parameters and SEMSTC in such a way that the new case systematically is a member of the sets mentioned above.
  - A redefinition of the specification of the component, leading to a more precise, more detailed, more formal result, without necessarily being too stringent to the implementers. Based on that "more" formal methods could be applied to derive tests which would then lead to a better SEMSTC. The black box test method would then turn more into a gray box test technique.

CONFORMANCE TESTS SPECIFICATION – EXAMPLE: CAN TRANSCEIVERS

The Transceiver is the interface between the analog signal transmission over the physical communication media and the digital "world" towards the higher OSI-layers. The latter could comprise – as it is the case for CAN – lines for digital signals such as Receive_Data, Transmit_Data, Error_Signal, etc. Towards the physical media there may be analog lines such as CAN_High, CAN_Low, etc. The redundancy of these lines is used for differential mode signal transmission which provides a good means for high common mode noise injection immunity. In case of a failure – short circuit or broken wire – the redundancy is used together with the failure detection mechanism of the fault tolerant transceiver, to switch off the defect line, communicate with a reduced signal to noise ratio and signal the error to higher layers. Finally there are power supply lines for supplying the component with energy. There are means provided to switch the component from normal mode into low power or power off mode. For more details refer to [4].

SYSTEM OPERATIONAL VECTOR SPACE - As an example for the purpose of doing interoperability tests on standard transceiver components a SOVS is given, derived from experience, see table 1. This experience has been gained from practical applications at the automotive companies sites' and the experience in testing and organizing tests within the research work at c&s group. [1] For further details refer to [5], [6].

Transceiver-SOVS =	{ System Configuration } x { Communication } x { Power Supply } x { GND Shift } x { Op. Modes } x { Failure }

Table 1: Transceiver System Operational Vector Space

The individual vectors can be broken down into parameters as shown in table 2.

System Configuration	
Baud rate	.... 5 kBd ...... 125 kBd
Termination	Calculated total termination = ... 100Ω ......
Topology	Bus, ring, star, mesh, ...
Composition	Homogeneous, heterogeneous (ratio), ...
Number of nodes	1, 2, ...40, ...
Environmental conditions	Temperature (...20°C...), moisture, shock, ...
......	

Communication	
Nodes' interaction	▪ Logical ring: ▪ node x receives token ▪ node x transmits token to node x+1 ▪ after 1 cycle all nodes transmit 1 message leading to an arbitration conflict ▪ ... ▪ Arbitrary communication .... ▪ ....
Identifier	Any, special, ...
Data	Any, nodes reference, ...

[1] Funded to c&s group as a research grant by Audi, BMW, DaimlerChrysler, PSA, Volkswagen

......	

Power Supply ....

Ground Shift ....

Operational Modes ....

Failure	
Single bus failure	▪ no failure ▪ short circuit: ▪ CL_Vx(up)@Rx with: ▪ Vx = [.. -3V .. +18V ..] ▪ Rx = [.. 0Ω .. 50kΩ ..] ▪ CH_Vx(up)@Rx ▪ .... ▪ open circuit: ▪ CL_OW@Rx(up) ▪ CL_OW@Rx(down) ▪ ......
1,5 bus failures	▪ apply CL_BAT + CL_CH then remove CL_BAT ▪ apply CL_GND + CL_CH then remove CL_GND ▪ ...
2 bus failures	▪ apply CL_BAT + CL_CH ▪ apply CL_GND + CL_CH ▪ ...
n bus failures	▪ ...
Location of failure	At node 1, 2, ...
....	

Table 2: System Operational Vectors and their Parameters

SUFFICIENTLY EXHAUSTIVE MINIMAL SET OF TEST CASES - The individual test cases then would result from – theoretically – the combinatorial product of any set of values assigned to the parameters defining the vectors. Apparently this would lead to a very large number of test cases which would be difficult to execute in a reasonable amount of time. Therefore a reduced subset of vector ranges must be carefully selected, This selection is empirically driven from experience, reducing the combinatorial product to a "realistic worst case" test scenario SEMSTC. In this case the group of automotive companies funding the c&s research work agreed on the following reductions:

- System Configuration = constant standard network with 100 kBd, .. , 40 nodes, ..
- Communication = constant standard with a fixed functionality logical ring communication ....
- ....
- Failure = reduced parameter sets such as: single and 1.5 failure types only, location of failure between node 39 and 40, ...

In this case the number of combinations shrinks down significantly because the are only 4 of the 6 vectors to be varied combinatorial as 2 of the vectors are kept constant. Furthermore the numbers and the variation range of the parameters is significantly shrunk. All this led to the final specification of transceiver conformance tests; for more information see [5].

Table 3 shows a typical example for a tests case specification “Test case 4.3.6.7: CH_Vx(down)@Rx”. This case checks the behavior of the IUT in case of a short circuit failure. Therefore the IUT first is set into an initial state (repetitively) in which a specific condition is applied to the IUT: short circuit resistor and voltage against which the short circuit is applied. Then the actual test step is applied, which is a standard communication round, passing a token from one node to the next through out the standard test network. After each test step(s) the behavior of the network is checked, i.e. if an error is detected by the transceiver and into which state it is switched. The responses read are compared to the operational requirements and thus a decision is taken whether the test is passed or failed.

All the individual tests are specified to be carried out as so called homogeneous tests. This means that all tests as specified above are carried out on a homogenous standard network which consists of 40 nodes with all transceivers of the same brand. Then a second test run is performed with a first step inhomogeneous standard network is performed where the specific transceiver under tests is checked with regard to its interoperability against a so called “golden node transceiver”, which currently is a Philips 1054 type. Finally a third test run is executed in an inhomogeneous standard network, where the device under test is mixed with 3 other types of transceivers. This gives an additional higher degree of confirmation of interoperability of mixed systems proper operation.

Typically set up and execution of these tests takes approximately 2 months. In order to shorten the time for first feed back to the semiconductor manufacturer in 1 week time frame a first rough run through a shortened set of homogeneous tests is performed. As such some (mayor) deficiencies or malfunctions may be detected in an early phase and the semiconductor manufacturer may already very early work on corrections of the device.

TESTER IMPLEMENTATION – The principle of the realization of the tester then is shown in figure 2: A tester supervisor – typically a PC – holds all the software for the test cases and the software to perform check off line the test results with the required operation. Furthermore the supervisor controls the so called upper and lower tester which serve as the interfaces towards the device under test. These interfaces implement all the physical signal adaptation as well as the time buffering. As such they contain e.g. the programmable devices to provide the varying short circuit resistors, the correspondingly varying voltage generators, the memorizing

Constants	**Power Supply = 12V / GND Shift = 0V / Op. Mode = Normal**	
	Test procedure:	Short Circuit Failure (CL_Vx, CH_Vx)
	Operating area:	Short Circuit Operating Area
Initial State	System Configuration:	constant as specified in *Standard Net*
	Communication:	constant as specified in *Standard Net*
	Op. Mode :	Normal Mode
	Power Supply:	12V
	GND Shift:	0V
	resistor range for error generator R/U:	
	rx_start	: 0Ω
	rx_stop	: 50KΩ
	rx_next	: depending on steps

range		step
0Ω -	10Ω	1Ω
10Ω -	50Ω	5Ω
50Ω -	250Ω	10Ω
250Ω -	1.000Ω	50Ω
1.000Ω -	10.000Ω	1.000Ω
10.000Ω -	50.000Ω	10.000Ω

	voltage range for error generator R/U:	
	vx_start	: 16V
	vx_stop	: -3V
	vx_next	: depending on steps

range		step
16V -	-3V	0.1V

Test Steps	execution of communication as specified in *Standard Net*
Response	test results must match the operating areas as defined for short circuit failures

Table 3: Test Case “Short Circuit”

oscilloscopes, etc. The IUT finally is implemented through a standard network of 40 nodes. Each nodes contains one transceiver – IUT – which itself communicates with a CAN node and a micro controller. The micro controller runs part of the upper tester software which implements the token passing mechanism, the signal evaluation logics and the communication path to the supervisor.

All tests are executed fully automatic. This is a very important feature for any conformance tests as such tests do not depend on the actual condition of a tester person and his capability to observe and evaluate test measurement results. As such repeatability of tests is ensured any time any place. The results are all registered on the PC. If a problem is occurred the operator of the tester is alarmed to check the problem and communicate it to the supplier of the IUT. Along with that the actual test scenario is delivered which enables the manufacturer of the possibly faulty component to check for the problem and take countermeasures. At the end a final test report is produced by the tester which together with a summarizing Authentication Report is handed over to the manufacturer of the component.

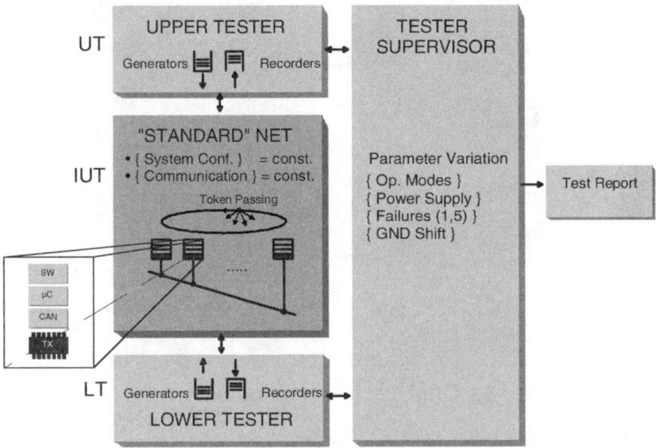

figure 2a: Transceiver Tester Architecture

figure 2b: Transceiver Tester Implementation

CONFORMANCE TESTS – FURTHER OSI-LAYERS AND PROTOCOLS

Specification of conformance tests and the design of the corresponding tester as it is done at c&s group follows a very straight forward well structured process.

CONFORMANCE TESTS SPECIFICATION – Given the constraints above that the specification of the device under tests – DUT – typically is given in a verbal manner, the following procedure is basically the c&s standard applied principle and process:

1. Definition of System Operational Vector Space
    - Preface:
        - All the definitions and specifications following are of course derived from the specification of the behavior of the device under test – DUT.
        - If this specification shows deficiencies, ambiguities, incorrectness's, contradictions, etc. additional specifications through SOVS must clarify the problems.
        - As the latter refinement/enhancement step is very essential to the interoperability of a "standard" component this critical procedure must be always done in consensus of a group of involved and competent partners – may be standardizations organization o corresponding group.
    - Definition of vectors of SOVS for DUT
    - Definition of relevant parameters for each vector
    - Definition of value ranges for all parameters
    - Definition of responses of DUT
2. Definition of Sufficiently Exhaustive Minimal Set of Test Cases
    - Definition of a reduced, practically "sufficiently" worst case value range of parameter values
    - Specification of granularity of steps "practically" sufficient to check variables ranges of parameters
    - Derive from there individual test cases and specify them in a (semi-) formal repetitive form based on a standard procedure:
        - Specify test environment constants
        - Specify set up step, which initializes the device under test into a well defined internal state
        - Specify a (or a sequence of) test step(s)
        - Specify the required responses of DUT
3. Update of test specification
    - Field experience typically observes special cases where the observed behavior may deviate from expectation and requirements. If these cases can be reproduced and if they can be considered relevant to the operational area of the devices then correspondingly modified and/or further test cases must be specified. As this procedure is very sensitive towards the mixed systems interoperability standards, a group's consensus – as said above – is a must before modifications are introduced.
    - Field experience typically is reported to the c&s group for further process by:
        - automotive manufacturers and suppliers systems experience
        - semiconductor manufacturers experience
        - c&s test executions and networked system design.

CONFORMANCE TESTS IMPLMENTATION – The conformance tester itself consequently realizes in a structured way the above mentioned specification of the tests

1. Analysis of the functional and performance requirements of all individual tests
2. Group the test cases into classes with
   - High time resolution requirements
   - Medium time resolution requirements
   - Low time resolution requirements
   - Off line parts of the tests. This typically comprises test case generation and evaluation of the observed results of the tests
3. Assume a standard tester architecture corresponding to ISO 9694 Coordinated Test Method to be applied for implementation of the tests. This consists of the following 3 levels – see fig. 2 and 3:
   - Supervisor, which typically is a PC. The PC typically can be considered as an off-line device as compared to the real time requirement given by the test cases' specification. As such the PC:
     - stores all the test cases
     - controls and downloads the test stimuli to the upper and lower testers
     - stores all the test results delivered by the upper and lower tester
     - evaluates the results of the test measured with the results required and thus prepares the final test record with the detailed and global results "test failed/passed".
   - upper tester, which is the "upper OSI layer" interface between the DUT and the supervisor. This interface must provide the correspondingly required electrical and real time capabilities.
   - lower tester, which is the "upper OSI layer" interface between the DUT and the supervisor. This interface must provide the correspondingly required electrical and real time capabilities.
4. Map the classes onto the above mentioned blocks of the standard tester architecture consisting. This process shall be guided by the constraints in order to facilitate the design and achieve optimal flexibility, minimum development costs and best quality:
   - Shift as much functionality as possible into software, running on standard hardware for the supervisor, the upper and lower tester
   - Apply standard off the shelf hardware for the implementation of the required features and real time constraints. Standard hardware typically is PC and measurement tools such as programmable data generator and analyzers, voltage generators, oscilloscopes, etc. Standard Communication between the blocks should be implemented on standard protocols such as Ethernet, IEC 488, etc.
   - Minimize the hardware to be designed especially for this purpose
5. All tests are executed fully automatic. This is a very important feature for any conformance tests as then such tests do not depend on the actual condition of a tester person and his capability to observe and evaluate test measurement results. As such repeatability of tests is ensured any time any place and a good quality is guaranteed.

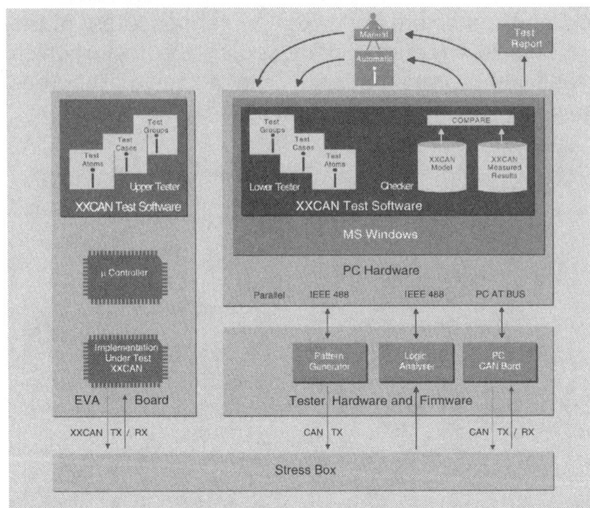

Figure 3a: c&s CAN Tester Architecture

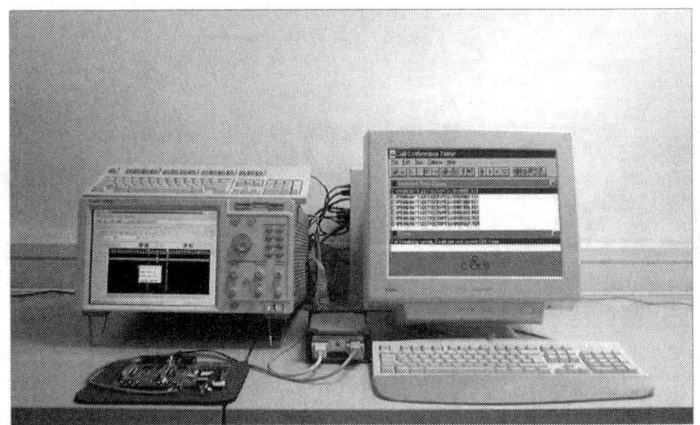

Figure 3b: c&s CAN Tester Implementation

CONFORMANCE TESTS REALIZED AT C&S – In 1995 c&s group was founded at the University of Applied Sciences in Wolfenbuettel, Germany. This was due to Motorola, charging c&s with a first research project to specify and implement the first time conformance tests for CAN OSI layer 2. This project lead together with especially Rober Bosch GmbH and Dassault Electronique finally to the actual ISO CAN test standard ISO 16 845. In the mean time c&s has evolved world wide to the mostly required test site world wide. Some automotive manufacturers do not accept CAN devices delivered by their module supplier except they have been tested by c&s. Furthermore c&s has been asked to re-use its communication protocol conformance test knowledge to apply it other CAN OSI layers and to other types of protocols. All of these activities have been done in very close cooperation either with automotive manufacturer and or semiconductor manufacturers.

Sciences in Wolfenbuettel, Germany. This was due to Motorola, charging c&s with a first research project to specify and implement the first time conformance tests for CAN OSI layer 2. This project lead together with especially Rober Bosch GmbH and Dassault Electronique finally to the actual ISO CAN test standard ISO 16 845. In the mean time c&s has evolved world wide to the mostly required test site world wide. Some automotive manufacturers do not accept CAN devices delivered by their module supplier except they have been tested by c&s. Furthermore c&s has been asked to re-use its communication protocol conformance test knowledge to apply it other CAN OSI layers and to other types of protocols. All of these activities have been done in very close cooperation either with automotive manufacturer and or semiconductor manufacturers.

As such for instance the Low Speed Fault Tolerant CAN Transceiver Tests have been developed in the ICT consortium under the support of Audi, BMW, DaimlerChrysler, PSA, Volkswagen; the High Speed CAN Transceiver Test have been sponsored by Ford_US, a further High Speed Transceiver Test will be specified in the ICT group. The TTx protocol tests are done in cooperation with semiconductor manufacturers. LIN tests are specified under the umbrella of the LIN Consortium and in special cooperation with car and semiconductor manufacturers. Further protocol tests have been developed for instance for eBUS protocol together with corresponding industries; others on request.

<table>
<tr><td colspan="7"></td></tr>
<tr><th colspan="7">C&S CONFORMANCE TEST IMPLEMENTATIONS</th></tr>
<tr><th>OSI</th><th colspan="3">CAN</th><th>TTx</th><th>LIN</th><th>Other</th></tr>
<tr><td>7</td><td colspan="3">OSEK/VDX NM, …</td><td></td><td></td><td></td></tr>
<tr><td>....</td><td colspan="3"></td><td></td><td></td><td></td></tr>
<tr><td rowspan="5">2</td><td colspan="3">c&s soft-com driver</td><td rowspan="2">c&s ..</td><td rowspan="5">c&s [2] ..</td><td rowspan="5">c&s [3] ..</td></tr>
<tr><td colspan="3">c&s robustness</td></tr>
<tr><td colspan="2">c&s Processor Interface</td><td>c&s Gateway</td><td rowspan="2">c&s TTx</td></tr>
<tr><td colspan="3">c&s ISO 16 845 enhanced</td></tr>
<tr><td colspan="3">ISO 16 845</td><td>~ ISO 16 845</td></tr>
<tr><td rowspan="3">1</td><td colspan="3">Transceiver</td><td rowspan="3">c&s [4] ..</td><td rowspan="3">c&s [5] ..</td><td rowspan="3">c&s [6] ..</td></tr>
<tr><td colspan="2">ICT-c&s [7]</td><td rowspan="2">Ford_US - c&s High Speed</td></tr>
<tr><td>Low Speed</td><td>High [8] Speed</td></tr>
</table>

Table 4: Overview on Existing Communication Protocol Conformance Tests

Tests are all performed in real time. That is why a high number of tests can be executed in rather a short time frame, typically in less than 2 months. This is the reason why simulation phases, which typically have been carried out at the semiconductor manufacturer's site and which are supposed to be quite exhaustive, can not cover so many test cases as if testing is carried out in real time. The difference is in the range of several tenth of orders of magnitude. As such the devices under test – DUT – must be provided as such that they can be run in real time. Therefore typically device manufacturers supply test modules either in an early design phase in an emulated form for instance in an emulator box – such as Quick Turn Box – or as an FPGA-based implementation. As testing includes a customer coaching process possible malfunctions are discussed with the supplier who then can rather easily modify his implementation and deliver an updated solution for the continuation of the test procedure. The final test though typically is carried out on (first) silicon.

The actual c&s capability in protocols conformance testing is shown in table 4.

CONCLUSION

Conformance testing is a good way – and may be the only way – to safeguard actually interoperability in networked systems with mixed suppliers' communication modules, as mixed suppliers' modules system is a must from the OEMs' point of view, because of their second source policy.

Although conformance tests specification and the related tester implementation are living from the engineering genius and practical experience, the back bone of the process is based on a very structured approach, the System Operational Vector Space. As such the overall procedure is a mix of an empiric and systematic process.

The reason to all this is due to the dilemma that there is no "precise" specification of the device to be tested, yet. The solution could be to require formal, executable specification from which in an automatic, formal process test cases could be derived. Although nevertheless this is a very desirable situation because of many reasons, it bears several problems. Very often first inventers of a new solution do not want to be to clear outside of their company. They want to maintain their advantage against their competitors as long as possible; by the way is a push-pull situation as standardization of communication interfaces of course requires an "open" standard as soon as possible. Furthermore formal specifications do not guarantee that some "clever" implementers would realize some features in an optimized way, resulting un-willingly in possibly interoperability conflicts. This has derived from special observations from practical systems applications.

As a result test specifications must be published as standard. Further more obviously these standards are “living” standards, as they tend to be updated, modified, enhanced by experience.

Looking at the test cases for a device from another view angle, they could be taken as another type of specification for the component itself. Whenever device manufacturers enter the design process they typically ask front up for the test specification. Baring this in mind test cases' specification should conform to the device specification itself. As such both ways correspondences should be maintained anytime. Consequently this implies that device standards would be “living” standards, too. How can we cope with that in our “traditional” standardization process ?!

REFERENCES

[1] W. Lawrenz: Networked Systems High Level Design & Test Philosophy and Tools; SAE Conference and Show Detroit, paper 950296, 27.03. - 03.03.95

[2] W. Lawrenz, editor: CAN - Controller Area Network from Theories to Application; Springer Verlag, 1997, ISBN 0-387-94939-9

[3] ISO 11898 Road Vehicle – Controller Area Network (CAN), part 1; International Standard ISO 11898, 1999

[4] Specification of a Fault Tolerant CAN Transceiver; GIFT Working Group (Audi, BMW, DaimlerChrysler, PSA, Volkswagen, Infineon, Motorola, Philips, STMicroelectronics), chaired by c&s group at Fachhochschule Wolfenbuettel, Germany, 2000, www.cs-group.de

[5] Test Specification for a Fault Tolerant CAN Transceiver; ICT Working Group (Audi, BMW, DaimlerChrysler, PSA, Volkswagen, Infineon, Motorola, Philips, STMicroelectronics), chaired by c&s group at Fachhochschule Wolfenbuettel, Germany, 2001, www.cs-group.de

[6] M. Scheurer: Entwicklung einer Methode zur systematischen Ableitung von Testfällen für Konformitätsprüfungen in der Informationstechnologie ; Diploma Thesis at Fachhochschule Wolfenbuettel, c&s group, Germany, July 2000

[7] Abramovici, M.A. Breuer, A.D. Friedman: Digital testing and testable design; Computer Science Press, 1990.

[8] A.L.Courbis, J.F. Santucci, N.Giambiasi : Automatic Behavioral Test Pattern Generation for Digital Circuits; 1st IEEE Asian Test Symposium, Hiroshima, Japan, November 1992, pp. 112-117

[9] S.J. Chandra, J.H. Patel: Experimental evaluation of testability measures for test generation; IEEE Trans. On CAD, Vol. 8, N°1, pp.93-97, January 1989.

[10] Z. Manna, A. Pnueli: How to cook a temporal proof system for your pet language; Report n°STAN-CS-82-954, Department of Computer Sciences, Stanford University , USA, 1982

[11] K.T. Cheng, A.S. Krishnakumar: Automatic functional test generation using the Extended Finite State Machine Model; 30th ACM/IEEE Design Automation Conference, USA, 1993

[12] M. Larnac, V. Chapurlat, J. Magnier, B. Chenot: Formal Representation and Proof of the Interpreted Sequential Machine Model; EUROCAST'97, LNCS 1333, Springer, Las Palmas de Gran Canaria, Spain, 1997

[13] J. Magnier: Représentation Symbolique et Vérification Formelle de machines séquentielles; State Thesis University of Montpellier II, France, 1990

[14] K. Hoffmeister: Applikations- bedingte Kommunikationsanfor-derungen im verteilten Kraftfahrzeug-Echtzeitsystem und deren Testbarkeit; Diploma Thesis at Fachhochschule Wolfenbuettel, c&s group, Germany, July 2000

[15] W. Lawrenz, Anne-Lise Courbis, Janine Magnier: Car System Conformance Testing, International Conference Systems Engineering and Information&Communication Technology, Nimes TIC 2000, September 2000

CONTACT

Prof. Dr.-Ing. Wolfhard Lawrenz
Director c&s group
at
University of Applied Sciences
Salzdahlumerstrasse 46/48
D-38302 Wolfenbuettel, Germany

Email: W.Lawrenz@FH-Wolfenbuettel.de
Web: www.cs-group.de

2002-01-0438

Development of Car Intranet Infrastructure

Rami Baroody and Nizar Al-Holou
University of Detroit Mercy

Salim Hariri
University of Arizona

ABSTRACT

The automobile currently has a number of processors to control different subsystems such as engine controller, transmission controller, ABS controller, lighting controller, entertainment controller, and airbag controller. These subsystems are connected as a single vehicle network. Different vehicle networks can run under different protocols such as CAN, VAN, SCP, DLC, ACP, and J1939. Controller Area Network (CAN) has become the standard for the automotive industry. However, CAN has limited speed to incorporate new applications, such as in-vehicle multimedia, entertainment, navigation, and computing. A new technology, Media Oriented Systems Transport (MOST), provides high bandwidth to accommodate such applications. Moreover, a trend exists to include other functionality, such as access to information in the car through wireless technology to provide Internet access that enables remote diagnostics, status update, roadside assistance, navigation, global positioning, infotainment, traffic monitoring, emergency, safety, and security service.

A system architecture approach to integrate CAN, MOST and wireless communication system into the car environment has been presented in this paper. Moreover, an open and universally accessible architecture of a Car Intranet infrastructure that includes three network technologies CAN, MOST, and Wireless communication has been proposed. This infrastructure can provide an entirely new type of service in addition to current services can be delivered to cars in an efficient and secure way through wireless data connectivity over the Internet.

INTRODUCTION

Electronics were introduced in automobiles with the advent of integrated circuits. The main application of electronics was found in the automotive engine's electrical system, with the next application of electronics found in the fuel ignition control, cruise control, ABS, and transmission control unit. Further, use of electronics was extended to the instrument panel, suspension control, air-conditioning system, and other body control systems.

With advances in (VLSI) and computers more electronics are being introduced in today's cars and trucks, providing many new features such as: navigation system, intelligent highway system support, automated collision avoidance system, etc [1]. Furthermore automotive electronics have been used to introduce other new features (e.g., accessing the internet, read newspaper, send e-email, search the net, listen to music, make phone calls, participate in video conferencing, and conduct remote diagnostics) with all services that are available to people through the Internet extended to the automobile [2].

As the application of automotive electronics increases to enhance exiting features and introduce new features in automobiles, the need for more electronic control units (ECU) becomes mandatory, fast communication links are needed [3]. As the number of node increase, associated costs also increase. To overcome this difficulty, multiplexing is used in automotive applications, with many signals transmitted over a single medium using a time-sharing basis. In multiplexing, a serial bus connects nodes inside a vehicle; allowing data transfer between sensors, actuators, switches, and processors over a common bus. A Controller Area Network (CAN) can be used as an embedded communication system for micro controllers, as well as an open communication system for intelligent devices. Also the extended version of CAN protocol (J1939) also can be used.

As electronics are used inside the car for multimedia applications, such as CD quality audio, surround sound, and high quality video, a high-speed network running protocols that satisfy the data rate requirements for those applications is needed. CAN have a limit speed, which is 1 Mbps [4], which is not sufficient for some Multimedia applications. A high-speed network, fiber-optic bus, known as Media Oriented Systems Transfer (MOST), is a high performance, low-cost multimedia network technology, created by the MOST Cooperation (Karlsruhe, Germany) that uses a 25-Mbit/second fiber-optic bus and is best suited for these applications.

While initial vehicle multiplex applications concentrated on single vehicle-wide networks running certain protocols, additional factors are causing a shift toward the use of multiple vehicle networks. Speed, application differences, costs, new emerging interconnection trends, and other influences are impacting the single network philosophy. The application of multiple vehicle networks is growing and methods for supporting this direction are required. Multiple vehicle networks may result in major changes in the meaning of vehicle diagnostics that may require the use of gateways. These changes may require modification of the original single network solutions to handle new requirements. From the industry perspective, a variety of vehicle network protocols exist, including CAN, MOST, VAN, LIN, etc. Each of these robust, powerful solutions represents a major technological investment in a single vehicle-wide network [5].

In this paper, an open, and universally accessible, architecture along with development of a car Intranet infrastructure that enables each vehicle to access and use Internet technologies for communication (voice, video), entertainment, monitoring traffic, emergencies, etc has been proposed. In Section II, classification of automotive communications, multiplexing protocols, CAN protocols and J1939 are presented. Section III, MOST is presented. In section IV the proposed System architecture and networks Gateways between CAN, MOST are presented. Finally, conclusions are discussed in section V.

CLASSIFICATION OF AUTOMOTIVE COMMUNICATION

The Society of Automotive Engineers (SAE) has defined three distinct protocol classifications, Class A, Class B, and Class C [6]. Class A is the first SAE classification and maintains the lowest data rate, a rate that peaks as high as 1Kbps and supports up to 100 nodes. Class A devices typically support convenience operations like actuators and "smart" sensors. The second SAE classification is Class B protocol. Class B supports data rates as high as 100Kbps and supports up to 50 nodes. Class B typically supports non-real time control and communications. Utilization of Class B can eliminate redundant sensors and other system elements by providing a means to transfer data between different nodes. Class C protocol is used for real time control applications with critical speed and accuracy and supports a data rate of up to 1Mbps.

MUTIPLEXING PROTOCOLS CONTROLLER AREA NETWORK (CAN)

Communication signals are transmitted and received by various network nodes according to a set of rules called protocols. Protocols set rules for coding, address structure, transmission sequence, error detection, and handling. The protocols also define the medium (copper wires or optical fiber), transmission speed, and electrical signal requirements. Protocols for automotive networking cover most of the Open System Interconnection (OSI) model [7]. In the harsh, noisy automotive environment, a multiplexing protocol should be optimized to meet technical and functional requirements of the application. Various network protocols have been developed for automotive multiplexing (e.g., controller area network (CAN), SAE J1939, vehicle area network (VAN), class2, etc.).

CONTROLLER AREA NETWORK (CAN)

CAN is an advanced serial bus system that efficiently supports distributed control systems. Robert Boost of GmbH, Germany initially developed CAN for the use in motor vehicles in the late 1980s. CAN is internationally standardized by the International Standardization Organization (ISO) and the Society of Automotive Engineers (SAE). The CAN protocol uses the Data Link Layer and the Physical Layer in the ISO - OSI model. CAN is most widely used in automotive and industrial market segments. Typical applications for CAN are motor vehicles, utility vehicles, and industrial automation. Other applications for CAN are trains, medical equipment, building automation, household appliances, and office automation. CAN is a protocol for short messages, with each transmission carrying 0 to 8 bytes of data, making it suitable for transmission of trigger signals and measurement values. CAN is a CSMA/AMP (Carrier Sense Multiple Access / Arbitration by Message Priority) type of protocol. The protocol is message oriented and each message has a specific priority according to which message gains access to the bus in case of simultaneous transmission. An ongoing transmission is never interrupted. Any node that wants to transmit a message waits until the bus is free and then starts to send the identifier of its message bit by bit. A zero is dominant over a one and a node loses the arbitration when it has written a one but reads a zero on the bus. As soon as a node has lost the arbitration, it stops transmitting but continues reading bus signals. When the bus is free again the CAN Controller automatically makes a new attempt to transmit its message. The CAN Controller chips complete this procedure, as well as error checking and retransmission of corrupted messages. The arbitration procedure requires that a limited number of identifiers (more than 500 million in Extended CAN) and that a specific identifier be sent only by one node. The only exception from this rule is when a message carries no data. As the amount of data that can be sent in one transmission is limited to eight bytes, the maximum latency time of the highest priority message can be calculated if the nodes are restricted to the use of the same message identifier, once transmitted, until a specified time has elapsed. Every CAN Controller in a network receives any message transmitted on the bus. Each node has to check whether a message is for him or not. Any CAN controller on the market offers some filtering capacity to reduce the processor capacity needed for this activity; with some more elaborate than others DO [8]. Figure 1 shows an example for CAN network within the car.

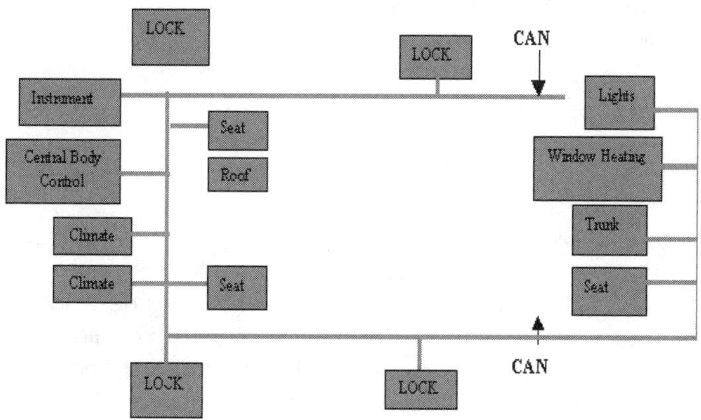

Figure 1 shows an example for CAN network within the car.

SAE J1939

CAN, introduced by Robert Boost, is a network protocol designed specially for in-vehicle networking [9]. The previous version of CAN version 1.2 has been successfully implemented in passenger cars, trains, and factory automation [3]. CAN protocol has been extended with a second message format called CAN V 2.0 [9]. The ASE has accepted this extended version of CAN protocol as the basis for in-vehicle networks in trucks and buses. The extended version protocol is called SAE J1939 [10].

J 1939 is a high speed, Class C type communications network designed to support real-time closed loop control functions between electronic control devices that may be physically distributed throughout the vehicle. SAE J1939 defines all relevant communication layers to support automotive multiplexing. Within J1939, a message is called the protocol data unit (PDU). There are two existing formats for the protocol data unit called PDU1 and PDU2. Format PDU1 includes source and destination address. Format PDU2 is used to send the data frames that are not destination specific.

MEDIA ORIENTED SYSTEMS TRANSFER (MOST)

Electronically controlled systems in automobiles are becoming increasingly dependent on rapid and reliable exchange of significant quantities of data. Within the communication and infotainment field, the secure transfer of high data volumes becomes more and more important. Apart from the data transfer for radio, CD players, telephone and navigation systems, the multi-channel usage of video data for TV-images, video games, DVD, voice-activated control for many functions, Internet accesses from the car, text-to-speech, and e-mail. These functions require a high bandwidth and reliability. These requirements can be met by the newly developed optical bus systems, which allow signal transfer via Plastic Optical Fiber (POF), combining advantages of a high bandwidth and insensitivity to electromagnetic interference with the weight-saving that can be compared to copper technology. This high-speed network, fiber-optic bus known as Media Oriented Systems Transfer (MOST), created by the MOST cooperation (Karlsruhe, Germany), uses a 25-Mbit/second fiber-optic bus is best-suited [11]. The topological structure of the MOST networks is a ring. Light signals are transported via POF from one connected apparatus to the next. In each apparatus, received light signals are transformed into electrical signals, which are then further processed by the MOST-processor. Generated signals are subsequently sent to an LED, which in turn converts this back into optical signals again. Figure 2 shows the MOST networks within the car.

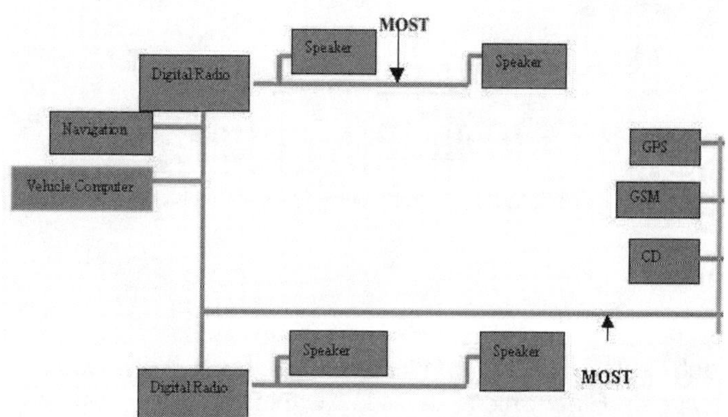

Figure 2 MOST Networks within the car

SYSTEM ARCHITECTURE

In automobiles, many subsystems need extensive interactions for information exchange. For example, an engine management system and transmission controller may work closely together for proper gear change. These kinds of interactions are becoming so numerous that the traditional view of vehicle electronics as independent sub-systems my not be adequate. The concept of local area network (LAN) has been introduced in automobiles to improve communications and interactions among different electronics systems. In applying a LAN to automotive electronics systems, an optimal protocol has been adopted for each system and each system may run different protocols that satisfy the data rate for their applications.

Multiple sub-networks are proposed in this section. Different groups of an electronics system may need different bus speeds. To accommodate this need, multiple buses can be introduced in automobiles, with these buses connected through Gateways. Figure 3 shows the proposed multiple networks scheme for automotive applications.

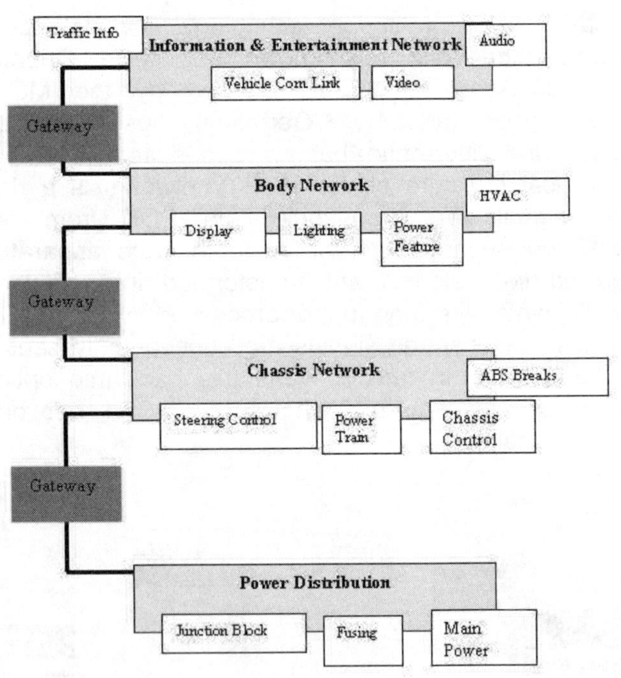

Figure 3. In-car network four Layers architecture

Each sub network consists of necessary electronics devices. Electronics devices within a sub network communicate with each through the local bus. For communications among various sub-networks, electronics devices can use Gateway. Because of the different requirement speed for applications running in these sub-networks, individual sub networks can contain individual protocols. In this scheme, no global bus has been used. This feature eliminates the bottleneck of global bus failure, and provides more reliability and bandwidth for multi-channel usage of video data for TV-images, video games, DVD; Voice activated control for many functions etc. Because the general trend today in vehicle development is to carry an increasing number of information and control messages via serial busses, we proposed system architecture inside the vehicle as we mentioned before in this section and as shown in Figure 3. For technical information and machine control, the CAN bus is dominating. For radio, CD player, telephone and navigation system, the multi-channel usage of video data for TV-images, video games, DVD, voice activated, control for many functions, Internet accesses, MOST Technology dominates. The proposed four basic sub-networks are:

- Information Network. Digital High Speed "Source Data" (MOST,)
- Body Network. Low / Medium Speed "Control Data" (J1939, CAN-B/C, LIN, etc. Multiplex).
- Chassis Network. Control of Critical Power train, Chassis & Safety Systems (CAN C)
- Power Distribution.

NETWORK GATEWAYS

Gateways between CAN, MOST

The Gateway between CAN and MOST provides connectivity from an automotive control bus (such as CAN or J1939) to MOST and is the emerging networking standard for in-vehicle multimedia and entertainment. The basic function of a data gateway is data translation and data routing. Figure 4 shows the network Gateway between Controller Area Network and Media Oriented Systems Transport. The Gateway functions are:

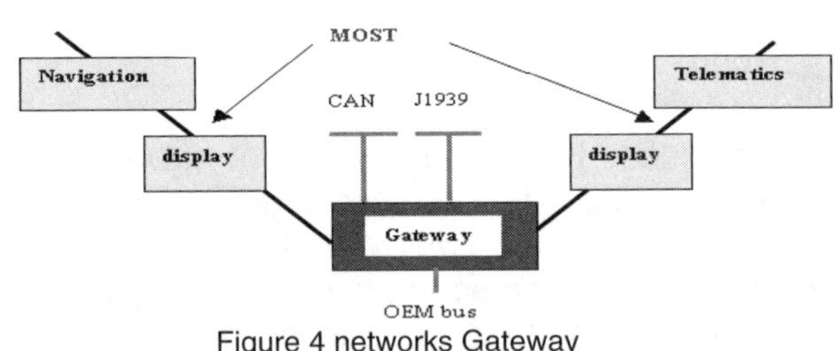

Figure 4 networks Gateway

Connecting two of the same or two different networks. Data from one or more input messages feeds in one or many output messages. The Gateway has the ability to connect networks with different baud rates and can provide a firewall for security of data between networks.

MOBILE IP

To provide access from automobiles to the Internet we consider the wireless communication aspect and the idea of Mobile Internet Protocol (IP), first, at the Home LAN (home, office), and then during travel time (foreign LAN). Standardization efforts have been made in this area already in the Internet community (e.g., the Mobile IP along with the IPv6)[2]. In summary, Mobile IP assigns temporary IP addresses to visiting hosts and directs Internet packets addressed to them at home locations to be forwarded to the point of attachment when a mobile IP (Car) moves from one sub-net to another. Figure 5 shows a mobile vehicle with services available on the Internet.

Networking can be carried out using a wireless technology, with satellite one of the most attractive technologies in USA for connectivity between the Internets from the road

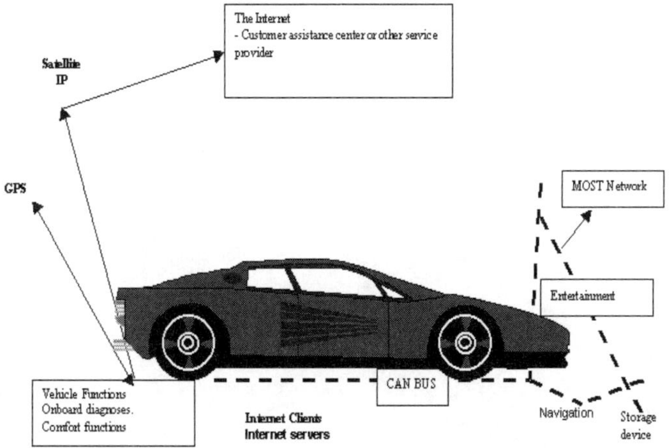

Figure 5 shows a mobile vehicle with services available on the Internet

CONCLUSION

As people continue to demand additional functions and features in their automobiles and technology continue to expand to meet these demands, developing the appropriate networks and connectivity protocols has become a priority for the automotive companies. Engineers and computer specialists need to work collaboratively to produce the types of systems and networks that will allow automobiles to be able to perform these functions at a reasonable cost and with good reliability.

REFERENCES

1. Ronal K.Jurgen, " The electronic Motorist," IEEE Spectrum, March 1995, pp.37-48.

2. Aktar Jameel, Axel Fuchs, and Matthlas Stuempfle " Internet multimedia on Wheels: Connecting Car to Cyberspace. " IEEE 1998, pp 637-642.

3. Tom Denton, "Automobiles electrical and electronics systems," 1995,SAE International, Warrendale, PA.

4. http://www.microcontroller.com/Learn Embedded/CAN1 sie/CAN1 files/frame.htm

5. Bruce D. Emaus " Aspects and Issues of Multiple Vehicle Networks. SAE 1995.

6. Friedrick H.Phail and David arnet, "In-Vehicle Networking-Serial Communication requirements and directions, SAE paper 8603901998.

7. http://www.nsi.fr/can2.html

8. http://www.kvaser.se/can/index.htm

9. Bosch, "CAN specification, ver2.0, Robert Bosch GmbH, Stuttgart 1991.

10. http://www.kvaser.se/can/hlps/index.htm

11. http://www.oasis.com/technology/technology.htm

12. Video and audio applications in Vehicles Enabled by Networked systems IEEE 1999.

13. Akihiro Tanaka, Masachika kamiya and kazunori Sakai " Gateway Application for Automotive Network System" "BEAN" SAE 1999.

CONTACT

Rami Baroody

Rbaroody@ecs.syr.edu

Professor: Nizar Alholou

Alholoun@udmercy.edu

2002-01-0264

The Application of Middleware to In-Vehicle Applications

Hasina M. Abdu and David H. Yoon
University of Michigan-Dearborn

ABSTRACT

With the increasing presence of the Internet in today's applications, ranging from legacy enterprise systems to handheld devices and home appliances, there is an increasing need for a generic middleware that can enable the interoperability between heterogeneous systems. In the specific case of in-vehicle networks, a generic middleware would enable the vehicle/driver to interact with a diversity of applications, including legacy enterprise systems, other embedded systems and wireless ad-hoc and ubiquitous applications. This paper is the result of an initial investigation into the requirements for such a middleware, and possible directions to be taken for its implementation.

INTRODUCTION

Recent advances in technology and the emergence of Internet-based applications have resulted in a distributed application environment that differs from the typical enterprise application scenario. Formerly independent applications must interact to access and share functions and data stored in heterogeneous database [13]. Collaborations with other enterprises, mergers, acquisitions, and the Internet further diversify this scenario. A variety of performance issues must also be considered: a fluctuating and unpredictable number of users, the need to satisfy increasingly demanding Quality of Service (QoS) requirements, and the need for interoperability between existing legacy applications and new web-based applications. To make the situation more complicated recent trends such as nomadic mobility, ubiquitous and ad-hoc computing, telematics and real-time applications impose an additional set of constraints on existing systems.

Middleware solutions such as CORBA [28], DCOM [31] and Java RMI, despite providing a framework to design and implement distributed applications, do not support the ever increasing set of requirements imposed by existing technology. In addition, these solutions are not interoperable, i.e., an application developed in a CORBA framework cannot communicate with an application under DCOM or Java RMI, unless a specialized bridge or gateway is used. What is needed is a generic middleware approach that is robust, flexible and scalable enough to support the rapidly changing trends in technology, without losing the interoperability with existing legacy applications. This *new-generation* middleware should enable the design, implementation and integration of heterogeneous applications, ranging from legacy enterprise systems to embedded in-vehicle applications. In addition, a varying set of QoS requirements specified by users and applications should also be satisfied.

This paper discusses the role of the *new-generation* middleware in enabling open and distributed in-vehicle applications. The following issues, along with possible solutions, are discussed:

- Need to satisfy QoS (fault-tolerance, real-time, etc.)
- Support for wireless communication with remote systems.
- Support for a programming model that enables the design and implementation of in-vehicle applications and integration with external applications.
- Need for efficient management of in-vehicle systems and applications

The rest of this paper is organized as follows. The next section justifies the application of middleware to in-vehicle applications, focusing on their main requirements. The *Related Work* section describes related work in applying existing middleware to in-vehicle applications, as well as approaches that focus on achieving interoperability between heterogeneous application frameworks. The *Proposed Approach* outlines the main issues that are being investigated by the authors and possible approaches to be taken. A summary of this initial investigation and future directions for this research are presented in the *Summary* section.

IN-VEHICLE APPLICATIONS: MOTIVATION AND REQUIREMENTS

One of the motivations for a framework for open in-vehicle applications is to efficiently communicate with external applications via the Internet. This would enable applications such as remote traffic control or remote fault detection and monitoring of the sensors in a car. Figure 1 illustrates an example in which the car driver can obtain information on traffic ahead of him/her through a wireless connection to the Internet. In Figure 2, sensors in the back of the car can detect objects when parking or backing-up. This information can be transmitted to the engine or break, slowing down or stopping the car if necessary. Remote management of in-vehicle networks is another application, as illustrated in Figure 3: management stations located at remote dealers can monitor and locate faults in different parts of the network, without being restricted to a given location, e.g., mechanic or dealer. The challenge does not lie on

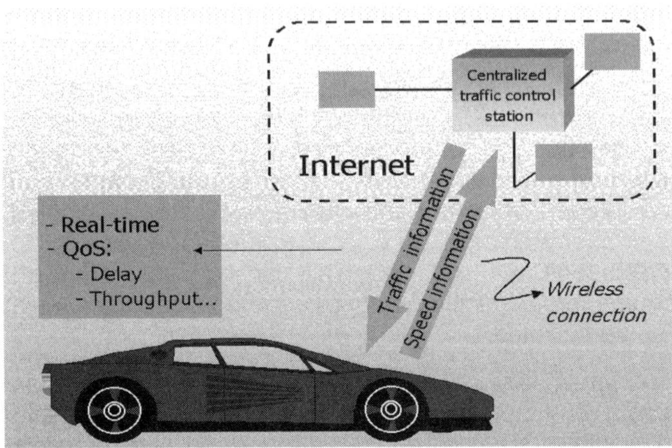

Figure 1 - Traffic control application

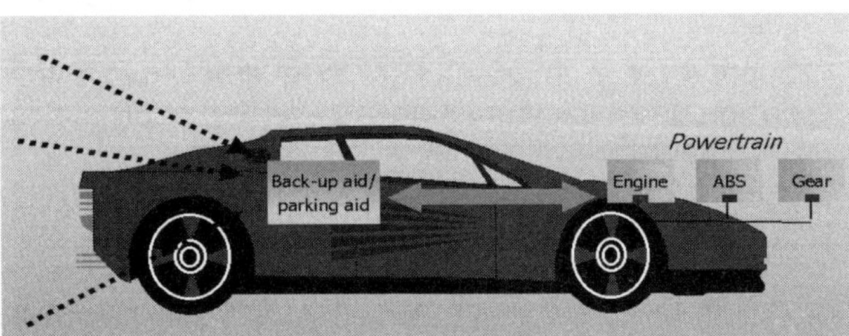

Figure 2 - Parking aid application

the applications themselves (in fact, some car manufacturers have implemented part of these applications), but in creating a framework that supports the modeling, implementation and deployment of a variety of applications. This framework will be the *middle tier* between the in-vehicle network and external applications, thus referred to as middleware. A generic middleware serves as a software bus connecting different application components, as illustrated in Figure 4. The main advantage of middleware approach over custom designed applications is that the former can free software designers from developing custom communication layers between processes. In addition, a middleware can provide a generic and structured approach to:

- Intranet/Internet connectivity
- Fault detection, isolation and recovery
- Satisfy Quality of Service (QoS) requirements, such as fault-tolerance and real-time constraints.
- Enable access to services under different framework/architecture/implementation

A properly designed solution offers additional benefits [24]: *composability*: large systems can be built in an incremental manner by integrating a set of well-specified and tested subsystems; *extensibility*: existing systems are open to incremental modification and extensible without some predefined upper limit; and *maintainability*: it is possible to implement well-defined error-containment regions and to achieve fault tolerance by replicating nodes.

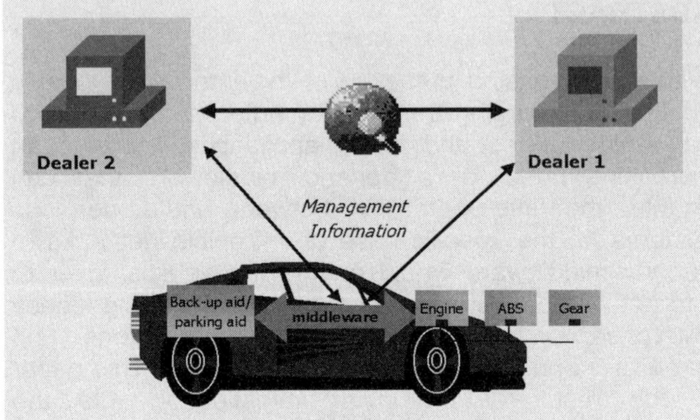

Figure 3 - Sample management scenario

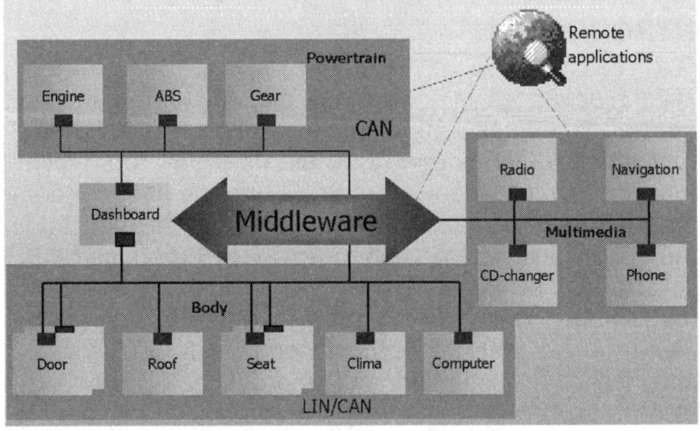

Figure 4 - A middleware for in-vehicle networks

The described functionality of a generic middleware cannot be achieved without software support. Due to the stringent conditions of real-time embedded systems, what is known as the embedded software crisis, open distributed frameworks cannot be employed as easily as in enterprise systems. In other words, middleware solutions such as OMG's CORBA, Microsoft's DCOM and Sun's Java RMI, cannot be directly integrated into embedded systems due the following:

- Most of these technologies assume a point-to-point, connection-oriented, transport protocol, whereas embedded systems are based on group communication.

- As opposed to enterprise systems, embedded systems have reduced resource footprint.
- Real-time embedded systems require predictable behavior, which is not supported by existing middleware solutions.

Another drawback of utilizing existing middleware solutions is that they are not interoperable, i.e., an application under a CORBA framework cannot communicate with an application under Java RMI or DCOM framework, unless specific bridges/gateways are deployed.

There have been attempts to tailor CORBA to CAN (Controller Area Network) systems used in cars. In addition, OMG has recently released a new version of CORBA for real-time systems [30], *Real-time CORBA*, which also supports the specification of QoS requirements. However, the suitability of CORBA to the restricted world of in-vehicle applications remains questionable, especially with the advent of more recent XML-based approaches that focus on interoperability and connectivity, and that consume fewer resources. Related work that address these issues are discussed in detail in the next section

RELATED WORK

We divide related work into two main groups: those that focus on tailoring existing middleware such as CORBA to embedded systems, and those that focus on creating new solutions that enable interoperability with heterogeneous applications.

TAILORING CORBA - Distributed object computing has been a promising approach to support the implementation of complex distributed applications. At the heart of contemporary distributed object computing models are *Object Request Brokers* (ORBs), which facilitate communication between local and remote objects. ORBs eliminate many tedious, error-prone, and non-portable aspects of creating and managing distributed applications. One of the widely used ORB models is the Common Object Request Broker Architecture (CORBA) [28], which is standardized by the Object Management Group (OMG).

Since 1991, CORBA has been the *de-facto* middleware used in building distributed enterprise applications. Language, platform and location independence enables the communication between objects implemented in different languages, running on different platforms and on different hosts in a transparent manner. To access a service offered by a remote server, a client only has to make a local method invocation and the ORB will take care of locating the server, transferring parameters and returning results. If client and server are located in different platforms, the ORB will also take care of any required conversions.

The interoperability between ORBs from different vendors is possible through the *General Inter-ORB Protocol* (GIOP). A specific example of GIOP is the *Internet Inter-ORB Protocol* (IIOP), that includes a mapping to TCP/IP.

CORBA's language independence is achieved through the *Interface Definition Language* (IDL). An IDL file contains the specification of attributes and operations that can be invoked by a client on a given server. The specification also includes exception values, type definitions, constants and operation signatures. The IDL compiler generates *client stubs* and *server skeletons* based on the specified information. Stubs and skeletons serve as the "glue" connecting remote application processes, and can be generated in various languages, including C, C++, Ada, Smalltalk and Java. Figure 5 illustrates the main components of a CORBA framework.

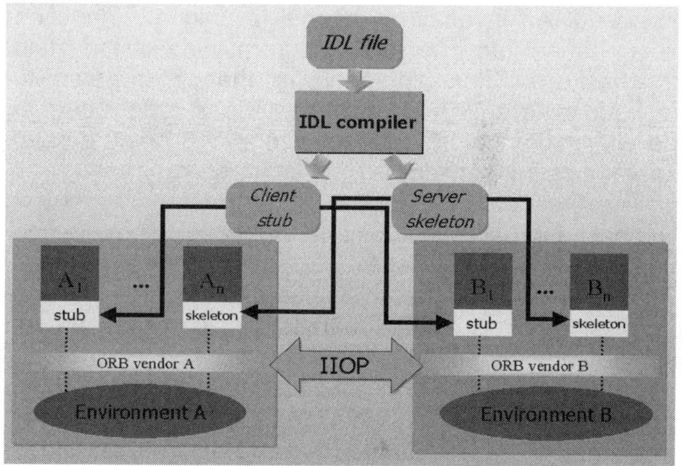

Figure 5 - Stubs, Skeletons, ORB, IDL and IIOP

CORBA was developed for enterprise systems that do not have the resource-constrained environment of embedded systems. In addition, group communication and real-time requirements need to be addressed. Some of the work that addresses these points are briefly described below.

<u>Group Communication</u> - CORBA is based on the connection-oriented transport model and an object reference denotes only a single CORBA object, thus resulting in a point-to-point communication. Embedded systems such as CAN offer a consistent broadcast mechanism in a straightforward manner via a serial broadcast medium and non-destructive priority-based bus arbitration. It also supports the producer/consumer model of data transmission, which is often referred to as the publisher/subscriber communication model [25]. In this context, a producer of a message is totally unaware of its consumers and simply broadcasts messages over the bus without specifying their destinations. Consider, for example, stopping a set of motors. When issuing a stop command, it is not of interest to address a specific motor, rather it must be ensured that all relevant motors

receive the command. Similarly, when reacting to a stop command, it is not of interest which controller has issued that command. On a more abstract level, a sensor object triggered by the progression of time or the occurrence of an event spontaneously generates the respective information and distributed it to the system. It can thus be considered as a producer. There have been different approaches towards including group communication and publisher/subscriber support to CORBA. In [24], a CAN-based transport protocol is designed to support group communication. This protocol makes use of the CAN identifier structure to implement a subject-based addressing scheme, which supports the anonymous publisher/subscriber communication model. [24] also proposed an abstraction scheme called *invocation channel*, which denotes a virtual communication channel connecting a group of communication ports and a group of receivers. A *conjoiner* object, responsible for group management, dynamic channel binding and address translation, is also proposed. An invocation channel is uniquely identified as a channel tag in an IDL program. One of the main drawbacks of this approach is that interoperability between different ORB implementations is lost due to the elimination of the connection-oriented point-to-point communication services.

Another approach, combining broadcast and filtering approaches, is proposed in [22]. In [7] an *Object Group Service* (OGS) aimed at facilitating the parallel processing of CORBA operation calls to a set of consumers is proposed.

Real-time support. The goal of real-time is achieving predictability in the behavior of some external attributes of a system, such as response time to inputs [10]. Obtaining this predictability (or ``end-to-end predictability'' of the system) requires that all the components in the system behave predictably. Thus, if CORBA is to be used in real-time systems, its behavior must be predictable. Making the CORBA component of a real-time system predictable means making the time of operations invoked on CORBA objects predictable.

There have been different approaches towards achieving predictability in CORBA and other frameworks [16,20]. In [21], a framework for invoking real-time objects on a CAN bus is proposed. The first byte of the arbitration field in a CAN message is used to define three levels of priority that can be assigned to any message: *hard*, *soft* and *no* real-time constraint. The deadline or scheduling of a message is done based on this priority value.

In [22] the use of asynchronous operations, as opposed to the synchronous request-response nature of CORBA and JAVA RMI is proposed. The motivation being the fact that synchronous operations result in blocking the caller until a response is obtained from the receiver, thus not resulting in a ``predictable'' behavior. An asynchronous or event-driven paradigm would not block the sender and would contribute in maintaining an end-to-end predictability.

In [23] an API for real-time Distributed Object Programming is proposed, which enables deadline imposition for arrival of results from an invoked object method, time-triggered actions and non-blocking invocation of object methods.

An extended IDL enabling the specification of timing constraints in a CORBA program, as well as ``fast-track messages'' used for time critical real-time traffic, are proposed in [19]. The ``fast-track messages'' can bypass layers of software and be sent to guarantee predictability.

Finally, we have OMG/s *Real-time* CORBA [30], with the goal of synchronizing the ORB operations with those of the underlying Real-time Operating system's environment in order to make operations predictable.

Reduced Resource Footprint - With the goal of reducing the resource footprint of CORBA, OMG has launched *Minimum* CORBA [29], primarily intended for embedded systems. The approach was to exclude dynamic aspects of standard CORBA, that are not required for embedded systems, e.g., the Dynamic Invocation Interface and the Interface Repository that supports it.

In [24], a resource-conscious customization of CORBA is proposed for CAN-based embedded systems, by reducing the size of data representation and by customizing GIOP with simplified message types and reduced headers.

FOCUS ON INTEROPERABILITY - The main drawback of existing middleware solutions is the lack of interoperability. For example, an application under a CORBA framework cannot communicate with an application under COM/DCOM, unless a specialized bridge or gateway is used. The lack of interoperability between existing middleware solutions is a challenge in achieving truly open distributed frameworks. This section outlines some of the work that has been done to address this problem.

One of the most recent approaches towards integrating existing applications over the Internet is the Simple Object Access Protocol or SOAP [11]. SOAP is a relatively new development born to meet the needs of developers who found DCOM and CORBA difficult to deploy in a world of the Internet and firewall requirements. SOAP is intended for ease of use and greater platform independence. Although DCOM and IIOP offer a broad range of services (albeit a bit complex) some developers consider that in 80 to 90 percent of potential applications they would gladly trade some features for a simpler technology that "guarantees the greatest interoperability in conjunction with simplicity" [11]. SOAP was developed to meet those needs.

In simplistic terms, SOAP is an open protocol specification that defines a method for using Remote Procedure Calls (RPC) with HTTP as the underlying protocol and XML as the data serialization format. The simplicity is introduced in that XML is the wire protocol, using its text-based format for data encoding. Every method call is translated into XML at run-time. To guarantee uniformity, the SOAP protocol requires adherence to a generic XML vocabulary. The data is parsed at the server side SOAP gateway. Information is encapsulated in an HTTP request in the form of a POST packet and then sent to a server. The calling browser utilizes a small number of HTTP headers that signal the target that a SOAP service is being transported by the HTTP packet. The text-based information makes developer comprehension and troubleshooting much easier. SOAP focuses on the familiarity of HTTP and XML systems to programmers and developers. Some of the main concerns/drawbacks with this approach are:

- Overhead - there is a high overhead associated with parsing ASCII requests. In addition, exchanging
- XML data can be a great toll on the limited bandwidth available in applications running in embedded/real-time systems.
- Simplicity - SOAP cannot perform the same variety of services DCOM or IIOP can perform. Instead, this component technology is evolving in response to immediate development needs in the current marketplace.
- Quality of Service and other requirements- it is not clear whether SOAP can support the specification of QoS or real-time constraints.

Others approaches towards interoperability include:

- XOIP (XML Object Interface Protocol)[26] – describes a way in which heterogeneous networked embedded systems can interface to a variety of distributed object architectures using XML.
- Generalized dispatch mechanism [17] – a flexible notion of dispatching is used to integrate objects belonging to different models, systems, and paradigms.
- OMG's Interworking Architecture [27] – specifies support for two-way communication between CORBA objects and COM objects. The goal is that objects from one object model should be able to be viewed as if they existed in the other object model. For example, a client working in a CORBA model should be able to view a COM object as if it were a CORBA object. Likewise, a client working in a COM object model should be able to view a CORBA object as if it were a COM object.
- Wireless applications for automobile applications [35] – the possibility of using Bluetooth with CAN systems for automobile applications is explored. However, the question is whether Bluetooth can offer the end-to-end predictability required for CAN systems.

SUMMARY – This section summarized two types of work: tailoring CORBA to support embedded real-time systems; and achieving interoperability between heterogeneous systems. The CORBA based solutions, despite attempting to address the needs of embedded systems such as in-vehicle networks, have the following drawbacks:

- They are not interoperable with other systems. For example, the management scenario illustrated in Figure 3 cannot be implemented if the management applications at the dealers are not running under a CORBA framework.
- The *Real-time* and *Minimum* CORBA versions, the only standard solutions, are still in early stages of deployment. Unless thoroughly tested with in-vehicle applications, it remains unclear if the complexity and overhead of CORBA is adequate for the resource-constrained environment of in-vehicle networks such as, for example, CAN applications.

The XML-based solutions and other approaches to interoperability, despite addressing the interoperability issue, present the following issues:

- QoS – The current XML-based approaches do not support the specification and enforcement of QoS requirements. In the case of in-vehicle applications, requirements include, for example, the specification of real-time constraints.
- Network bandwidth - The XML approach may be an overhead for the limited bandwidth available in in-vehicle networks as well as in wireless connections to external applications, such as the scenario illustrated in Figure 1.
- Programming model – as opposed to CORBA, SOAP and other XML based approaches do not provide a programming model to create distributed applications; being restricted to existing applications.

PROPOSED APPROACH

Unlike related work that propose a framework for in-vehicle applications based on tailoring CORBA to CAN systems, we investigate the use of an XML-based middleware to achieve interoperability between in-vehicle applications, legacy enterprise systems, other embedded systems and wireless applications such as ad-hoc and ubiquitous systems. We also investigate methods to include the specification and enforcement of QoS requirements, a programming model that will enable the design and implementation of new distributed applications and a framework for efficient management of in-vehicle networks and applications (Figure 6). The next sections will outline the main points being investigated in this work.

XML AND QOS – Future in-vehicle applications will consist of a combination of embedded systems, wireless and multimedia applications. For example, the future automobile may enable the passengers to view videos or join video conferencing through a wireless connection from an embedded browser. Despite the shortage of the underlying resources, such as network bandwidth, automobile drivers and passengers hope to receive consistent, predictable, timely and reliable services. Their hope can only be realized with the efficient specification and provision of Quality of Service (QoS). The term "QoS" involves [15] the specification and provision of *predictability*, *continuity* and *accessibility*. [15] defines *predictability* as the ability to maintain the contracted QoS and have minimum probability of QoS violations during the resource fluctuation period. *Continuity* is defined as the ability to degrade gracefully and adjust resource allocation distributions dynamically to tolerate transient resource scarcity. *Accessibility* is the ability to access the server from a wide range of devices, including PCs, workstations, cellphones, and PDAs.

A wealth of research work has been done to support the QoS specification for different types of applications. Recent approaches include solutions for setup and enforcement of QoS in middleware systems [8], [14], [15], [34]. An XML based QoS specification for multimedia applications is proposed in [15]. Figure 7 illustrates two examples of specifying QoS parameters for two in-vehicle applications: remote traffic control and remote video transmission. Delay (or response time), throughput and jitter are examples of QoS parameters.

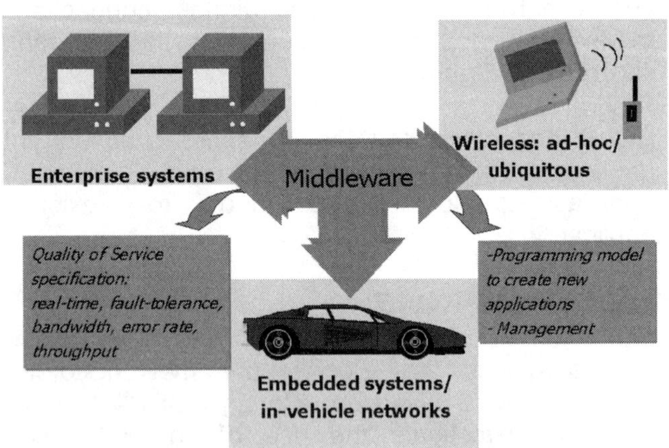

Figure 6 - Proposed framework

Our approach should include the following:

- A QoS enforcer that can detect illegal QoS specifications made by users.
- A QoS specification tool that facilitates the specification task, by relieving user from dealing with low-level system and resource information. This may involve the specification of *levels* of QoS, which can later be mapped to numbers, based on specific system parameters and low-level resource information.

```
<App name = "Remote traffic control">
    <QoS>
        <Delay> 10 </Delay>
        <Throughput> 230 </Throughput>
    </QoS>
</App>
```

```
<App name = "Remote Video TX">
    <QoS>
        <Delay> 10 </Delay>
        <Jitter> 30 </Jitter>
    </QoS>
</App>
```

Figure 7 - Using XML to specify QoS

DEALING WITH LIMITED NETWORK BANDWIDTH – One of the main drawbacks of using XML for in-vehicle networks is the overhead that it can have on network bandwidth. In-vehicle networks and embedded systems in general have serious bandwidth constraints. These constraints are also present when communicating with remote applications through a wireless connection.

We propose the use of a compressed format of XML, such as the Wireless Markup Language (WML) used by the Wireless Application Protocol (WAP). WML is a tag-based browsing language with screen management, data input and hyperlink capabilities. It is based on XML and inherits technology from HTML. It was designed to satisfy the resource constraints of wireless devices: small memory, limited CPU, small screen and limited input mode. These constraints are similar to the constraints found in embedded systems. WML's compressed and reduced format results in reduced network traffic and better caching. The use of WML can also be linked to the use of embedded browsers for in-vehicle applications.

The use of WML presents the same obstacle as XML: the need to specify and enforce QoS. We are currently looking into extending WML to support QoS specification and enforcement, based on the same requirements described in the previous section.

PROGRAMMING MODEL – Related work in interoperability with XML focus on communication between existing applications, but do not address the need of creating new applications.

Existing middleware frameworks are *process-oriented* methods based on a client server programming model, e.g., CORBA, COM, DCE [32], resulting in synchronous communication and tightly coupled systems. They are also based on point-to-point communication, instead of the publisher/subscriber interaction found in embedded systems.

XML, on the other hand, is a *data-centric* method for getting disparate systems to interoperate. Unlike, a client-server model, XML is message oriented, and promotes building loosely coupled systems.

The challenge in creating a programming model for a generic middleware is to give the user the choice of a programming model based on the application in question. For example, embedded systems are based on publisher/subscriber message oriented interaction, whereas many legacy enterprise applications are based on a client-server model. The proposed middleware should, therefore, support both communication paradigms. In this context, the authors are looking into the following question: how can XML be used to design and implement new applications under either communication paradigms?

MANAGEMENT OF IN-VEHICLE APPLICATIONS – Management consists of monitoring, analyzing and controlling the behavior of network components, to ensure that they behave as expected or specified by users. In this context, the proposed middleware should support two levels of management: internal management and remote management.

Remote management was illustrated in Figure 3: fault/failure of sensors and/or controllers in an in-vehicle network is detected at remotely located sites, without restricting the user to a given location, e.g., mechanic or dealer. This involves a wireless communication to a remote system, as well as satisfying QoS requirements such as the maximum delay time in obtaining a diagnostic or in locating a fault. Another issue to be considered is the choice of which remote location to connect to. This will depend on where the car is located, the type of diagnostic, the resource to be managed, and the requested QoS. The middleware should be equipped to locate the dealers or remote sites based on these requirements. We are currently examining previous work in management optimization ([1], [2], [3], [4], [5], [6]) to model this problem and include such specification in the XML/WML schema. For example, in addition to the desired QoS, an XML specification can include the type of diagnostics or resource being managed.

Internal management, on the other hand, involves management from within the in-vehicle network. In the particular case of CAN in cars, network management is implemented by CAN application layers ([9],[12], [18],[33]) following a master-slave configuration. The master node polls the slaves for a given set of information. If the information indicates a problem, the corresponding alert message is given to the user. Complex analysis or control functions that change the state of a component as a result of analyzing the monitored information are not implemented. In addition, most of the existing approaches are based on a master-slave format, being a centralized approach. We propose a distributed management approach, where one or more managers monitor, analyze and execute control functions on the different parts of the network. The number of managers and how their functions are distributed will depend on the network in question, the desired QoS and other requirements. Figure 8 illustrates a distributed management scenario.

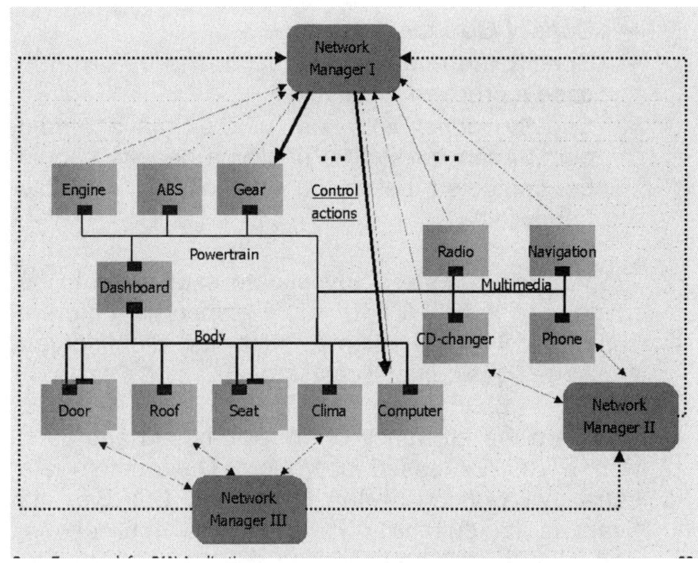

Figure 8 - Distributed management example

As in the case of remote management, the data to be collected, the analysis to be done and actions to be taken can be included in the XML/WML specification.

SUMMARY

This paper introduced the need for a generic middleware and its use in in-vehicle applications, enabling the seamless communication within the vehicle and with remotely located heterogeneous applications. Due to the stringent nature of embedded systems, there are many requirements to be satisfied. In addition, existing middleware frameworks cannot be easily adapted to the constrained world of in-vehicle networks.

We examined existing work on tailoring CORBA to CAN systems, as well as XML based approaches. We proposed the implementation of an XML based middleware that supports QoS specification and enforcement, satisfies resource constraints, supports multiple programming models and enables efficient management of in-vehicle network and applications. To achieve this goal, the following are the steps to be taken:

- Investigate the use of a compressed form of XML, such as WML, to address the problem of limited resources in embedded systems as well as wireless connections.

- Investigate existing work in QoS specification and enforcement, such as [15], to implement a framework for efficient specification, enforcement and execution of generic QoS specifications.

- Examine the author's previous work in modeling efficient management configurations based on a set of requirements. This will enable the user to:

  - Chose which resource to be managed
  - Specify QoS for management
  - Specify the management actions to be taken in case a problem is detected
  - Specify constraints on where management agents can be started or which dealers should be contacted based on location, or available bandwidth.

- Programming model – investigate extensions to be made to XML/WML to support different communication paradigms, such as client/server, message passing, multicast, etc.

- Compare the efficiency of an XML-based approach with a CORBA-based approach. The authors are currently working with *Real-time* CORBA, to evaluate its suitability for in-vehicle applications. The following will be examined:

  - How easily can QoS requirements be specified?
  - How is group communication implemented?
  - Is the overhead, if any, justifiable?

  Both approaches will be compared in terms of:

  - Resource consumption
  - Scalability
  - Interoperability
  - Flexibility
  - Complexity and ease of use

REFERENCES

[1] Abdu H., Lutfiyya H., Bauer M., *"Investigating Monitoring Configurations*", Proceedings of ACM Symposium on Applied Computing, Pennsylvania, pp 366-373, 1995

[2] Abdu H., Lutfiyya H., Bauer M., *"A Model for Adaptive Monitoring Configurations",* Proceedings of the 6th IFIP/IEEE International Symposium on Integrated Network Management, pp 371-384

[3] Abdu H., Lutfiyya H., Bauer M., *"Modeling Management Requirements in Distributed Systems",* Submitted to the Journal of Parallel and Distributed Computing, 2000

[4] Abdu H., Lutfiyya H., Bauer M., *"Towards Efficient Management of Distributed Systems,"* Submitted to the Journal of Computer Networks

[5] Abdu H., Lutfiyya H., Bauer M., "*A Model for Efficient Configuration of Management Agents in Distributed Systems,"* Submitted to the Elsevier Journal of Performance Evaluation

[6] Abdu H., Lutfiyya H., Bauer M., *"Towards Efficient Resource Management in Distributed Systems",* Proceedings of the IEEE International Parallel and Distributed Processing Symposium (IPDPS) 2001-April, 2001 - San Francisco

[7] Axel M. A., "*Design and Implementation of a CORBA-based Object Group Service Supporting Different Data Dispatching Strategies"*, http://citeseer.nj.nec.com/335099.html

[8] Becker C., Geihs K., *"Generic QoS Support for CORBA"*, Proceedings of the International Symposium of Computers and Communication (ISCC 2000), IEEE CS Press, Los Alamitos, Calif., pp. 60-65, 2000

[9] CAN in Automation (CiA), *"CAN Application Layer for Industrial Applications",* DS 201-201 Version 1.1, 1996

[10] Currey J., *"Real-time CORBA Theory and Practice*: *A Standards-based Approach of Distributed Real-time Systems"*, Embedded Systems Conference – San Jose, 2000

[11] DevelopMentor, IBM, Lotus Development Corporation, Microsoft, UserLand Software, "*SOAP: Simple Object Access Protocol*", http://www.w3.org/TR/SOAP

[12] Etschberger I. K., *"CAN-based Higher Layer protocols and profiles"*, http://www.ixxat.de/english/knowhow/artikel/hlp.shtml

[13] Geihs K., *"Middleware Challenges Ahead"*, IEEE Computer, Vol 34:6, pp 24-31, 2001

[14] Gill C. D., Levine D., Schmidt D. C., *"Towards Real-time Adaptive QoS Management in Middleware for Embedded Computing Systems"*, Fourth Annual Workshop on High Performance Embedded Computing, MIT Lincoln Laboratory, 2000, http://www.ll.mit.edu/HPEC/

[15] Gu X., Nahrtedt K., Yuan W. Wichadakul D. Xu D., "*An XML-based Quality of Service Enabling Language for the Web*", Journal of Visual Language and Computing, special issue on multimedia languages for the Web. Dec. 2001

[16] Hong S., *"Coping with Embedded Software Crisis using Real-time Operating Systems and Embedded Middleware"*, Invited for presentation at IEEE Asian Pacific ASIC (AP-ASIC) Conference, Korea, 2000

[17] Hurwitz B. *et al.*, "*Generalizing Dispatching in a Distributed Object System"*, ECOOP'94, pp. 450 ff, http://www.ifs.uni-linz.ac.at/~ecoop/cd/papers/0821/08210450.pdf

[18] J1939 Committee Draft, *"SAE: Recommended Practice for a Serial Control and Communication Vehicle Network", 1996*

[19] Jeon G., Kim T. H., Hong S., *"Seamless Integration of Real-time Communications into CAN-CORBA with Extended IDL and Fast-Track Messages"*, Proceedings of IFAC Workshop on Distributed Computer Control Systems (DCCS), Australia , 2000

[20] Jeon G., Kim T. H., Hong S., Kim S., *"A Fault Tolerance Extension to the Embedded CORBA for the CAN Bus Systems"*, Lecture Notes in Computer Sciences, 2000

[21] Kaiser J., Livani M., *"Invocation of real-time objects in a CAN bus-system"*, IEEE International Symposium on Object-oriented Real-time Distributed computing, 1998, http://citeseer.nj.nec.com/kaiser98invocation.html

[22] Kaiser J., Mock M., *"Implementing the Real-time Publisher/Subscriber Model on the Controller Area Network (CAN)"*, Proceedings of the 2nd Int. Symp. On Object-Oriented Real-time distributed Computing (ISORC99), France, 1999, http://www.infomatik.uni-ulm.de/rs/core/isorc99.ps

[23] Kim K. H., *"APIs for Real-time Distributed Object Programming"*, IEEE Computer, pp 72-80, 2000

[24] Kim K., Jeon G., Hong S., Kim S., Kim T., *"Resource-conscious Customization of CORBA for CAN-based Distributed Embedded Systems*", In the Proceedings of 2000 IEEE International Symposium on Object-Oriented Real-time Distributed Computing , Newport Beach, pp 34-41, 2000

[25] Kim H., Jeon G., Hong S., Kim T. H., Kim S., *"Integrating Subscription-based and Connection-oriented Communications into the Embedded CORBA for CAN Bus"*, Proceedings of 2000 IEEE Real-time Technology and Applications Symposium Washington DC, 2000

[26] Nielsen M. K., Jorgensen A. B., *"XOIP – XML Object Interface Protocol"*, Center for Object Technology, COT/3-34, 2000

[27] Object Management Group (OMG), "*Interworking Architecture"*, CORBA V2.3, 1999

[28] Object Management Group (OMG), *"The Common Object Request Broker: Architecture and Specification Revision 2.4"*, OMG Technical Document formal/00-11-07, 2000

[29] Object Management Group (OMG), *"Minimum CORBA"*, OMG Document formal/00-10-59, 2000

[30] Object Management Group (OMG), *"Real-time CORBA"*, OMG Document formal/00-10-60 edition, 2000

[31] Platt D.S., *"Understanding COM+"*, Microsoft Press, Redmond, Wash., 1999

[32] Rosenberry W., Kenney D., Fisher G., *"Understanding DCE"*, O'Reilly & Associates, Sebastopol., Calif., 1992

[33] Schofield M., "*An Introduction to CAN – The serial data communication bus"*, http://www-ife.tu-graz.ac.at/Local/Tech/Can-Bus/schofield.htm

[34] Vanegas R. *et al.*, *"QuO's Runtime Support for Quality of Service in Distributed Objects"*, Proceedings of IFIP International Conference in Distributed System Platforms and Open Distributed Processing, Springer-Verlag, New York, pp. 207-223, 1998

[35] Wunderlich H., Schwab M., "*The Potential of Bluetooth in Automotive Applications"*, Embedded Systems Conference – San Jose, 2000

.

.

2001-01-0672

The TTA Network - A Safe Yet Flexible Communication Architecture for Vehicle Electronics

Georg Stöger
TTTech Computertechnik AG

ABSTRACT

The paper presents a communication architecture for distributed embedded computer systems that require to transmit safety-critical real-time data - which must not be delayed - on the same bus as non-critical data. Such non-critical data can come from sources like sensors and event-based traffic, typically for on-demand diagnosis. This architecture utilizes the communication protocols TTP/C and TTP/A, and a software layer in the distributed nodes, to provide a fault-tolerant platform for reliable yet flexible communication over a multiplex bus.

INTRODUCTION

TRENDS - Probably the most prominent current trend in automotive electronics is growth - growth in numbers of modules as well as functions they provide. The number of ECUs in new car designs has steadily grown, exceeding 40 in current high-end vehicles, and probably 80 in next generation electronic systems. Accordingly the complexity of the resulting functions and their interfaces increased vastly, making system design or system integration (or both) an arduous task often containing an element of trial-and-error.

Another trend, which continuously gets high media coverage nowadays, is the - still rather timid - application of computer-controlled safety critical functions in the car, most notably "by-wire" applications. While promising a quantum leap in the area of active safety besides many other highly attractive features, such systems by their very nature must be extremely reliable - the requirement that faults, even very rare faults, must not lead to a failure of these systems. In other words, with the advent of by-wire applications, fault tolerance becomes a requirement for automotive electronics.

REQUIREMENTS - In order for such systems to maintain state-of-the-art reliability, automated *advance* warnings of component failures become necessary. This requires a diagnosis interface between a diagnosis point in the car (which could in turn be connected to the maintenance provider by wireless media like GSM) to each electronic component in the car -- be it an ECU or a small sensor. Data transmission over this interface can be initiated on a routine basis from the car's "diagnosis point" ECU, from a component registering a problem within itself, or directly from the maintenance provider.

A communication architecture that supports these requirements must

- allow for the definition of clear and comprehensible interfaces between ECUs and functions in a distributed system to help control the complexity of system design and test,
- support fault tolerance for building reliable safety critical systems,
- but also support on-demand communication for all, even very inexpensive and potentially unreliable, components in the system.

The first of these requirements goes beyond the scope of communication protocols and incorporates design strategy on a high level. However, not all communication protocols have the technical capabilities to support such a strategy once it has been defined, because they lack essential properties needed to support this approach, like composability (see Definitions) and predictability.

The second and third requirement are somewhat contradictory: If potentially unsafe components are allowed to use a shared communication bus that is also utilized for safety critical real-time traffic, a fault in any of these components could compromise system safety -- with a large number of such components in the system, the probability of a system failure might be unacceptably high.

This paper presents a communication architecture based on the *time-triggered architecture (TTA)* model. It describes how a combination of two multiplex protocols (TTP/C [1] and TTP/A [2]) can be used to design a fault tolerant distributed communication architecture that fulfils all of the abovementioned requirements, enabling the system designer to specify clear interface definitions for safety critical real-time traffic and on-demand traffic on the same network.

THE TTA NETWORK

SAFETY VS. FLEXIBILITY - The demand for event-triggered data transmission for the purpose of diagnostic functionality is not a hard real-time requirement. However, on the same bus there may be lots of carefully scheduled "hard real-time" messages which must not be delayed by the event traffic. So the flexibility for on-demand transmissions has to be subjected to the safety requirements and must not lead to delays of the real-time traffic under any circumstances, not even in case of faults (over-utilization of the bus, non-handling of the peak load) or errors in a transmitter (exceeding the maximum allowed retransmissions of a message).

This is done by scheduling bandwidth for both kinds of traffic, real-time and event traffic, and using a mechanism to safely prevent the bandwidth assigned to the real-time traffic to be "abused" by event traffic. But: the safeguard for this separation of bandwidth on the bus itself must be fault tolerant, otherwise a fault in the event message handling could lead to a failure of part of the real-time communication service, with catastrophic results.

The time-triggered communication protocol TTP/C has a fault-tolerant mechanism of securing the shared bus against excess bandwidth usage by any node: the system design allocates a fixed amount of the available bandwidth for each of the nodes or to 'reserved for later use'. This allocation is observed and controlled by two independent hardware units: the TTP/C controller and the bus guardian. No single hardware or software fault can make a TTP/C controller use more bandwidth on the bus than was statically allocated for it.

GUARANTEED TRANSMISSION FOR REAL-TIME DATA - The length of a TDMA slot represents the bandwidth available to the node assigned to this slot. Of the slot, one part is used for real-time messages only. In TTP, these are *temporal firewall* messages, which have a known update time and period. This allows to transmit them without any identifiers; they are identified by their time of transmission only. By eliminating identifiers, TTP/C systems can ideally utilize more than 90% of the gross bitrate, in realistic setups the efficiency is around 60-80%.

In another part of the slot, additional *temporal firewall* messages can be negotiated during system startup, e.g., depending on the current configuration of the system. These messages, once successfully negotiated, are known system-wide and have guaranteed transmission just as the messages scheduled off-line.

The remaining part of the slot can be used for event messages (which need explicit identifiers), reserved for additional real-time messages to be added in future design changes, or a mixture of the two. This partitioning of each slot is depicted in Figure "Real-time and on-demand slot part design".

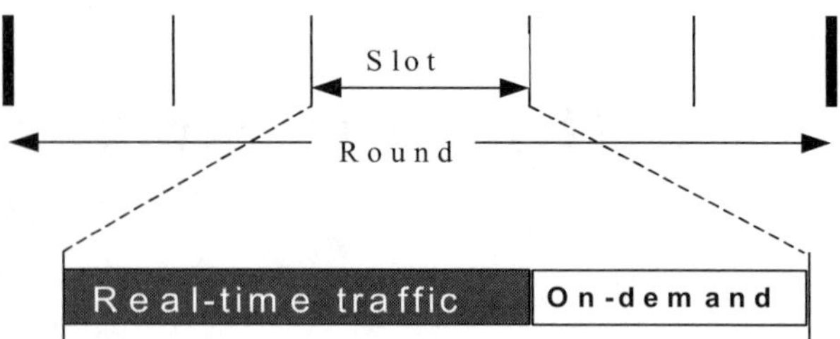

Real-time and on-demand slot part design

ALLOCATION FOR EVENT MESSAGES ON A PER-NODE BASIS - Within the static portion of bandwidth allocated to a node (e.g., 50 kbit/s) the node sends both real-time and event data. The distribution of the slot between real-time and event data is statically defined, e.g., the node sends 35 kbit/s real-time data, the rest is used for on-demand messages.

An important property of this scheme is that the bandwidth for on-demand transmission is arbitrated only among the event messages on each node, not between the event messages of all nodes in the system (as is typically the case for round-based event-triggered communication systems). This has several implications, which are illustrated with a simple example: three nodes A,B,C, each of which can send up to three independent event messages of equal size. The bandwidth allocation on the bus allows to transmit three event messages (shown as empty boxes) per real-time round, in addition to the regular real-time traffic (shown as dark boxes) which has guaranteed transmission. In the TDMA scheme assumed here, each slot allows for the transmission of just one event message per round.

Worst-case event bandwidth requirement:

A B C

Static (real-time) bus allocation:

Global:

Local:

As shown in the Figure "Peak load scenario", the worst-case transmission time is equal for node-local and system-wide arbitration: all nodes want to transmit all three of their events, this takes 3 rounds.

The average transmission time is longer for node-local arbitration: in the extreme case for our example, A wants at one time to transmit three event messages, while B and C have no events to send - this takes only one round with system-wide arbitration, but again the worst-case time of three rounds with node-local arbitration (see Figure: Unbalanced load scenario).

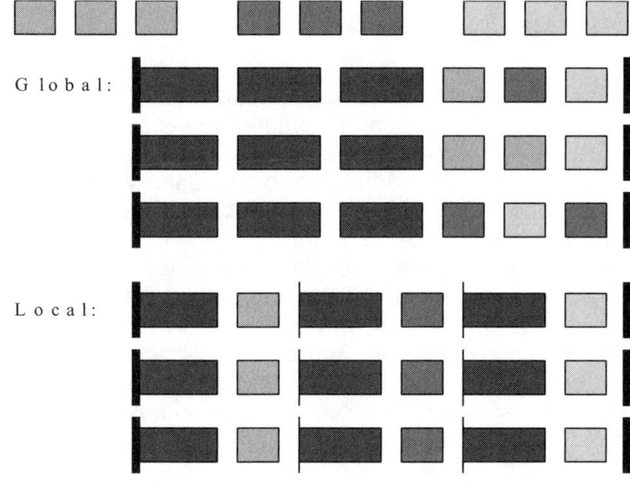

Peak load scenario

Event transmissions from one node do not change the timing of event transmissions from another node if arbitration is performed per node. This allows to (stochastically) analyze the timing properties of the event transmissions on a node without knowing the event timing on the other nodes. Also, changes made on one node (of software, hardware, etc) that modify the event timing of this node have no impact on the event timing of the other nodes. This allows to develop and analyze nodes separately, with no surprise effects from changed message timing at system integration (composability) - this is a general property of time-triggered systems.

The node-local arbitration is performed by the application CPU, based on any algorithm (e.g., priority-based, earliest deadline first) the node designer cares to specify. It is therefore possible to implement several such

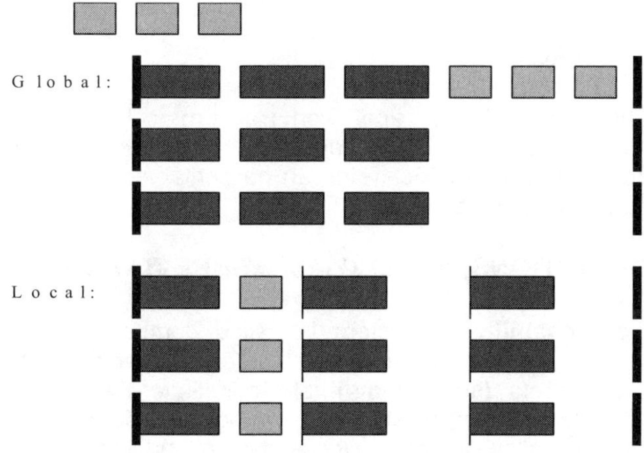

Unbalanced load scenario

algorithms (e.g., a priority-based protocol and a simple FIFO queue) to handle the event messages on a single node and assign a statically defined, or even dynamically determined, portion of the event data slot part to each of them. Each message that has "made it through the arbitration" then has immediate, guaranteed bus access.

In comparison, the cluster-wide arbitration is performed by the communication protocol, and is therefore limited to the specific mechanism offered by it (e.g., priority-based CSMA/CA as in CAN), and while different arbitration mechanisms can be implemented node-locally as well, the fact that a message has won the local arbitration does not guarantee that the message will get transmitted immediately or within a known time interval, because the node must still arbitrate against the other nodes on the bus in the system-wide arbitration for event data bandwidth.

Concluding, node-local arbitration based on TDMA is typically less efficient at utilization of bandwidth reserved for events than system-wide arbitration, but it provides composable analysis of node event handling, and allows to make guarantees for the transmission of event messages that have passed a node-local arbitration mechanism.

AN EXAMPLE BRAKE-BY-WIRE SYSTEM - This system runs a distributed control loop:

- The central brake ECU takes the brake_pedal_position (from the pedal sensors) and the current wheel_speed from each of the four wheels as input to produce brake_force messages to each of the wheels.
- Correction terms for the brake_force messages are issued from an Anti-lock brake ECU and considered by the wheel ECUs when applying the actual brake force to the wheels.
- Each of the wheel ECUs applies the computed brake force and reports back wheel_status and wheel_speed.
- The Diagnosis Point ECU does not send real-time data; it only becomes active when diagnosis is requested from the maintenance provider, then utilizing its slot to send diag_commands and requiring event transmissions from the other ECUs as well.

The real-time messages needed for the control loop are periodically transmitted every 5 milliseconds (200 Hz) and utilize a little more than 50% of the available net bandwidth of 400 kbit/s. These result from a 500 kbit/s physical layer and a TTP/C controller chip that delivers 80% efficiency at this bitrate and cluster design. The remaining bandwidth is distributed among the slots of the nodes according to the anticipated share of event traffic they are going to produce for on-demand diagnosis etc. or future extension of the real-time traffic.

The resulting bandwidth distribution looks like this:

	Real-time	On-demand
Wheel ECU (x4)	40 kbit/s	30 kbit/s
Central brake ECU	30 kbit/s	30 kbit/s
Anti-lock ECU	20 kbit/s	20 kbit/s
Diagnosis Point	---	20 kbit/s
Total	210 kbit/s	190 kbit/s

For the "real-time" data, the 40 kbit/s available for a wheel ECU amount to full 200 bits of data transmission per 5 ms control cycle, all messages contained in the 200 bits being known by all receivers without having to send identifiers.

Whenever an on-demand diagnosis command is sent, the result -- including an explicit identifier -- is sent back by the addressed node, by means of a simple queue that sends all event messages in a FIFO manner in the 'event part' of the slot. These event transmissions can utilize up to another 150 bits per control cycle (but this time including identifiers) and cannot interfere with the timing of any of the other messages in the system.

A TWO-LEVEL NETWORK FOR COMBINING FAULT TOLERANCE AND INEXPENSIVE I/O - Having discussed the handling of event messages in a safety critical TTP/C network, what benefits can be gained from such event messages in a system where all the critical functions and communications have been statically scheduled?

To allow for a flexible and scaleable architecture as well as the use of inexpensive I/O, only a set of 'backbone nodes' needs to be directly connected to the TTP/C bus. These backbone nodes can, in addition to performing computational tasks, act as gateways to one or several fieldbuses which connect smart sensors and actuators via a multiplex protocol. This protocol should be efficient but simple, so that it can be implemented on inexpensive sensors and actuators; and it must support on-demand diagnosis communication. One existing protocol that supports these requirements is TTP/A.

TTP/A is a time-triggered protocol with a master-slave architecture, and therefore integrates well into a fully time-triggered architecture with a fault-tolerant "backbone network" that allows to run point-to-point connections over a highly predictable and fault tolerant link, enabling full on-line diagnosis without endangering any real-time traffic on the same network.

Each of the nodes connected to the TTP/C "backbone" can be a gateway to TTP/A, acting as a master for one or several TTP/A buses, and coordinating the timing on these buses using the global time from the TTP/C bus. Thus, all I/O activity in the whole system can be globally scheduled, and the precision of the measurements is only limited by the precision of the TTP networks that carry the data, e.g., from a sensor over the gateway onto the TTP/C bus, over another gateway into a second TTP/A bus, and from there to a smart actuator.

Details on the TTP/A protocol are given in a separate paper (2001-01-0059); the technical protocol specification is available from www.ttpforum.org.

CONCLUSION

Using the communication architecture presented, guarantees for all off-line scheduled real-time traffic can be made in the presence of event-based traffic on the same bus. With this approach, composability for safety-critical and non-safety-critical functionality is possible with no compromise in safety or predictability of the communication. The underlying technology – the time-triggered architecture (TTA) and the time-triggered communication protocols TTP/C and TTP/A – is a leading candidate for future x-by-wire systems. It provides safety and predictability at reasonable cost. Combined with a software layer, most requirements for on-demand communication can be met without compromising these important properties.

ACKNOWLEDGMENTS

The concepts presented in this paper have partially been inspired by the ongoing tool development at TTTech Computertechnik AG, Vienna, Austria, and by feedback from TTP/C users in many companies and research groups.

REFERENCES

[1] H. Kopetz et al: Specification of the basic TTP/C Protocol, version 0.5, July 1999

[2] H. Kopetz, M. Holzmann, and W. Elmenreich. A universal smart transducer interface: TTP/A. In 3rd IEEE International Symposium on Object-oriented Real-time distributed Computing (ISORC 2000), 2000.

CONTACT

The author of this paper works as protocol expert for real-time systems and heads the training and support department at TTTech. He can be contacted via email: stoeger@tttech.com

DEFINITIONS, ACRONYMS, ABBREVIATIONS

Composability: A system is called composable with respect to a specific property, e.g., timing, if the components (subsystems) that constitute the system keep this property when they are integrated. Composable systems allow for constructive design and testing: if a property has been designed and tested for a subsystem, it does not change upon system integration. Therefore changes (even erroneous changes!) to other subsystems cannot invalidate this property of the subsystem.

TTA: Time-triggered architecture; in a TTA system, activities are based on the progress of real-time and globally co-ordinated schedules for communication and application. Therefore a TTA system is highly predictable and well suited for certification.

2001-01-0065

Seamless Solutions for LIN

Hermann Kern, Heinrich Gschloessl and Wilhard von Wendorff
Infineon Technologies

ABSTRACT

Today's body and convenience applications in general directly control actuators and sensors from a single central electronic control unit (ECU). Future systems will be made of subsystem-clusters communicating via a local Class/A communication bus. This enables modular system design to reduce system complexity. For these types of new distributed applications the LIN bus is currently the most promising communication protocol.

To allow a seamless migration from existing centralized to these next generation clustered system developers require software and hardware products for a homogenous and transparent LIN bus communication.

Within this paper Infineons presents its new LIN solution package:

- details on Infineons newly developed software building blocks allowing seamless customer specific LIN implementations;
- Infineon Technologies new family of LIN line drivers supporting smart wake-up from low power mode and smart power supply control;
- details on the line driver circuitries, configurable SW building blocks, EMC results, and achievable system performance are disclosed.

INTRODUCTION

The electronic system complexity of a car is currently growing extraordinary fast. The system and vehicle suppliers are therefore going through a process the personal computer industry went through several years ago.

The main issue to solve is setting up a development process:

- controlling the rapidly growing complexity of hardware and software;
- achieving the required quality to allow mass production with a low number of faults;
- shortening the development cycle;
- competitor differentiation by increasing or enhancing functionality;
- building up a network hierarchy covering the entire car within the road environment.

Today's centralized system use dedicated communication lines to pass analog/digital data from a central ECU to actuator and sensor units or vice versa. Each relevant state or event is coded analog to a dedicated channel. Being an analog system with a limited transmission delay, the time delay for communication is neglectable and deterministic. But the complexity grows fast with the number of sensors and actuators to be controlled. This growing number of analog links is increasingly sensitive to noise pick-up and emits electromagnetic radiation.

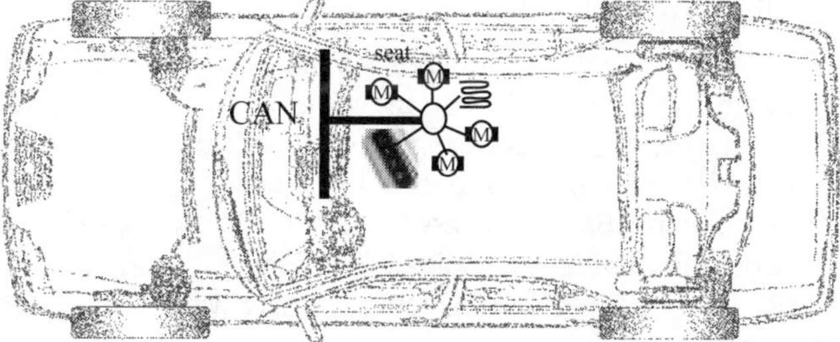

Figure 1: Central System Architecture

The automotive industry therefore follows the old rules of emperors: "divide and conquer".

To migrate a system from a centralized to a distributed system it has to be broken up into subsystems with common, standardized, and open interfaces.

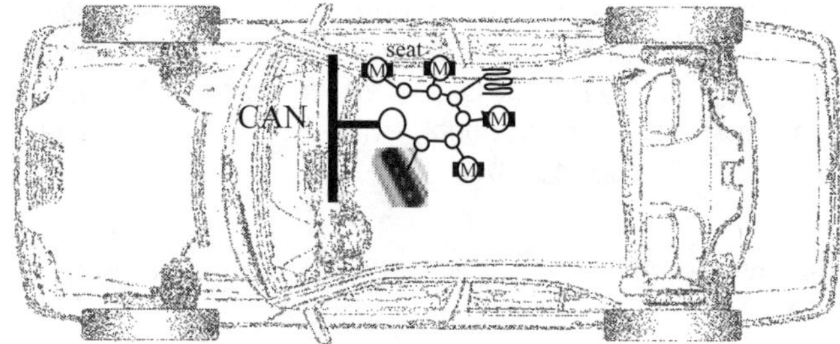

Figure 2: Distributed System Architecture

These newly introduced interfaces are a shared boundary between three or more subsystems. Rules (so-called communication protocol) of sharing this common resource have to be followed to allow proper communication of data across these interfaces. These protocols are implemented by dedicated hardware and communication software (hardware/software co-design)

The interfaces/protocols must support:

- transparent debugging, diagnosis, and maintenance during development and life cycle;
- flexible system distribution and assembly;
- synchronization of the asynchronous and de-tuned local clocks;
- easy to implement software and hardware interfaces;
- low cost interfaces;
- system composability (the ability to test a sub system and ensure the validity of these results within the overlaying total system);
- availability of devices supporting the interfaces;
- optimized wire harness (cost wise, space wise, and availability wise);

By breaking up such systems into smaller subsystems, the amount and length of the analog communication channels is decreased. Each of these subsystems communicates data to other sub-modules using the newly introduced multiplexed, commonly shared digital communication interface. Such an interface can be effectively implemented using an open standard field bus approach. The most promising field bus standard is currently the LIN bus, developed by an automotive industry consortium [2].

With the introduction of LIN bus as standard sub-bus the migration towards distributed systems will speed-up. LIN will open new system partitioning especially in the field of body and convenience applications. Door modules, Seat modules, and HVAC will be the applications using LIN first and the others will follow. But LIN is not going to replace CAN as communication path. LIN will be used as sub-bus below CAN.

The approach of distributed systems using sub-buses is not totally new but has not been realized so far because of cost reasons. Bus systems, which have been available, were high and low speed CAN, J1850, and K-Line. Now with LIN cost targets can be reached.

In contrast to CAN or J1850 the LIN requires no dedicated on-chip microcontroller communication module. LIN utilizes the standard serial communication interface (USART). That is one mayor point for the well-balanced cost/performance ratio of this recently introduced Class/A sub-bus.

LIN overcomes major issues when decentralizing a system:

- deterministic and real-time timeliness. CAN introduces a huge amount of jitter to the timeliness of communication due to a complex mechanism of error concealment and multi-master capability not mandatory required for intra-system communication.
- cost and complexity of a node is high. CAN requires complex communication circuitry and precise resources as a high precision clock, power supply etc.
- LIN provides more extended composability enabling scaling/configuring a system into a variety of configurations.
- LIN especially targets the needs of intra-system communication (communication within a single system/application) where else CAN targets inter-system communication (communication between independent systems/applications).

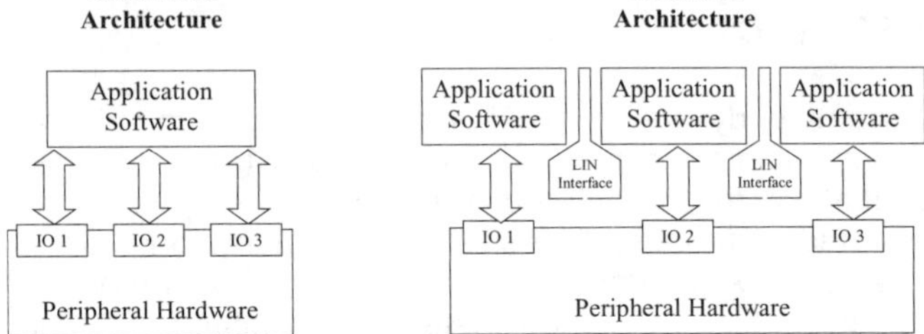

Figure 3: Structure of the LIN software driver

One of the challenges of the automotive industry is to be able to follow a smooth and clear road to migrate an existing centralized system to such a new decentralized field bus approach.

This migration requires:

- introducing new interfaces into the existing system (into hardware and software);
- distributing the single software to respective sub-systems;
- distributing the required “intelligence” (processing performance);

This touches all levels of design:

- the software design environment;
- the hardware building blocks (devices);
- the qualification and test environment;
- the debug and maintenance environment;
- the data for power and thermal budget calculations;
- the data for EMC requirement calculations.

Therefore exact knowledge of required communication resources (EMC, memory, bandwidth, power, and performance) is required. Infineon Technologies provides a toolbox to address the majority of these issues and to ease off the cumbersome path for system migration. This new toolbox simplifies the distribution of functions to a couple of electronic control units (ECU) hooked up by a system intra-communication bus (network within a single system/application) by providing flexible building blocks on different levels of system design:

- software modules supporting customer specific implementations;
- broad portfolio of integrated devices providing the respective resources of each sub-system;
- data on EMC, power, performance, memory requirements, etc.

So if a system developer has to migrate a conventional central system as sketched in Figure 1 into a distributed system, he has to identify and implement the new system internal interfaces. Infineon simplifies the task by providing software and hardware blocks ready to be used. These building blocks allow the decoupling and communication of the threads formerly running on a single ECU and after conversion running on different ECU. Designers no longer have to hassle around with the deep details of the LIN communication and partitioning, but can rely on the higher-level interfaces in software (application interface: API). The next step is to choose out of Infineon broad portfolio the appropriate hardware components. This hardware has to provide all the features used when designing centralized systems, e.g. synchronized power-up (smart power supply management), start-up synchronization etc. Therefore Infineon set up a family of different hardware to provide the respective features. Coming along with these new components are data as EMC behavior, power consumption etc. to fit the new distributed design to the given EMC, performance, and power budget.

Hopefully the last step of an engineer following this new seamless migration path is to head home early, because the system is running ahead of planned schedule. But wait, let's go through this flow and the respective components step for step.

LIN BASIC

LIN is a single master multiple slave bus system. According to that one master node and several slave build up the bus system. The master node contains a master task and a slave task, whereas slave nodes contain slave tasks only. Figure 4 illustrates the bus architecture.

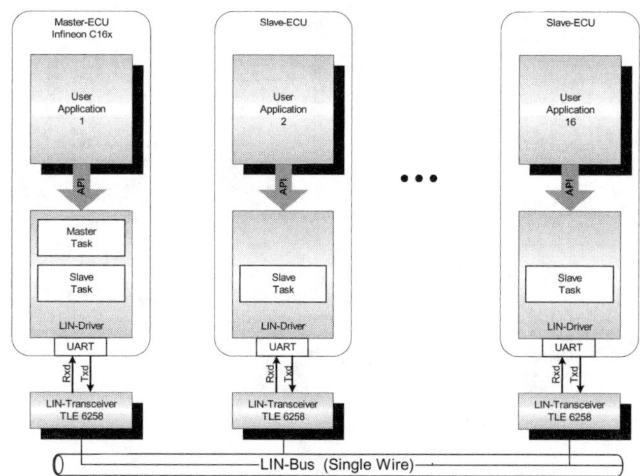

Figure 4: LIN bus architecture

A fixed message format is defined for the LIN protocol. Each LIN message starts with a header frame consisting of a synch break followed by a synch field and an identifier field. Only the master task may send this frame. Next 2, 4, or 8 bytes code the message data. A check sum field completes the LIN message (Figure 5). This response to the header is sent either by the slave task of the master node or by one of the several slaves nodes hooked up to the LIN bus.

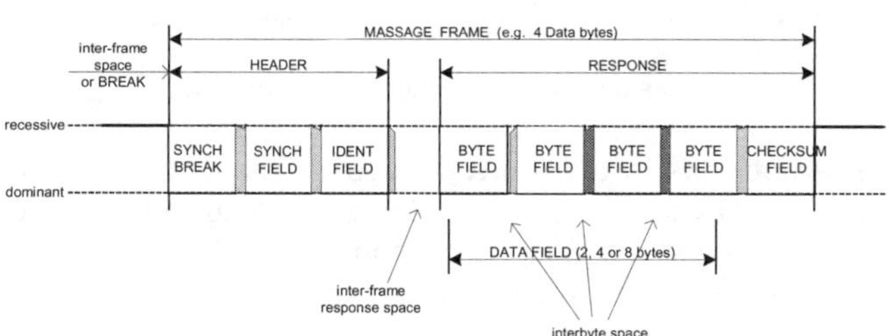

Figure 5: LIN message frame

Within a LIN bus system the master node initiates all message transfers.

Data exchange bases on a common hardware peripheral (serial communication interface) controlled by a dedicated LIN software driver. In opposite to CAN and J1850 the driver software handles the basic communication layers and takes care of message transfers, message filtering, and error detection (protocol handling). Two major modules, a master task and a slave task build up this driver software.

In general only the master task may send header frames and only a single slave tasks may reply a respective data field and check sum field. Certainly several slave tasks may receive one message. The master task controls the data exchange between master to slave, slave to master, and slave to slave. Figure 6 below illustrates the LIN communication paths.

Figure 6: LIN communication paths

The user has to configure the system as such, avoiding several slave tasks concurrently responding to the same ID. Moreover the user is responsible for arranging an application specific network management.

LIN SOFTWARE DRIVER

The domain of LIN will be local sub-bus systems. Most systems using LIN bus will have a gateway to CAN. Infineon Technologies has a strong involvement to CAN providing microcontrollers with on-chip CAN controllers, standalone CAN controllers, and a family of CAN transceivers (high, low speed, and single wire CAN). Moreover Infineon Technologies will also support LIN based designs with LIN transceivers, 8, 16 and 32-bit microcontroller families and LIN driver software.

Following the implementation concept of Infineons new LIN software driver is presented and details are given for the microcontroller hardware, software, and performance requirements.

Configurable software building blocks handle the LIN protocol. LIN message frame handling is done autonomously by the LIN software driver. Operations on LIN are at disposal of the user and are initiated by API-function calls.

The LIN driver entirely encapsulates hardware modules and exclusively handles all on-chip peripherals of the Infineon C16x microcontrollers, which support LIN. Doing that makes life easy for the designer and he can focus on his application. Figure 7 illustrates this approach.

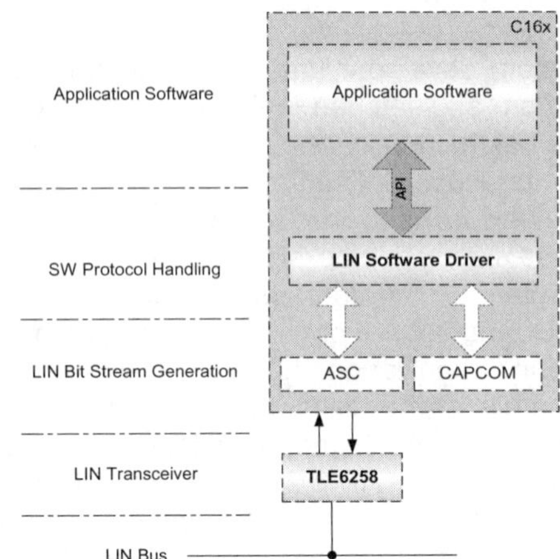

Figure 7: Structure of the LIN software driver

The LIN software driver builds on several state machines and functional blocks. Three main processes can be identified within the LIN software driver running as concurrent threads.

- a handler for message transfer that coordinates the correct generation of the message frame.
- a message filter that evaluates all received ID's within the slave task for their relevance and takes respective further actions if required.
- error detection process responsible for bus monitoring and detection of timing violations.

LIN SOFTWARE DRIVER PROPERTIES:

The message buffering will be discussed in detail hereafter to demonstrate the flexibility of the software driver architecture.

The LIN software driver provides a high amount of flexibility to the user in terms of LIN message buffering. The driver itself supports a single message buffer for all incoming and outgoing messages. It is up to the user to determine additional identifier specific message buffers, the respective location, and means of data integrity. Therefore the driver only requires a small amount of resources and provides a maximum of flexibility and applicability to the user. This concept of user definable message buffers allows e.g. receiving data objects directly from the LIN bus and transferring it to a CAN message buffer and vice versa.

LIN software driver properties are:

- LIN software driver and application code is cleanly divided into different libraries;
- strictly separation of specific application sections and LIN software driver data sections;
- enabling the user to handle interrupt service routine directly e.g. by a real-time operation system;
- allowing user definable message buffer;
- supporting LIN – CAN gateway functions.

A header file drives the configuration of the LIN driver. This allows a wide range of application specific configurations e.g. protocol and target specific settings. The workflow is illustrated in figure 8.

LIN protocol specific settings are:

- baud rate settings;
- configuration of Master or Slave LIN ECU;
- declaration of LIN Messages (ID allocation for send and receive messages).

Target specific settings are:

- allocation of Timer resources;
- allocation of serial interface resources;
- allocation of interrupt priorities.

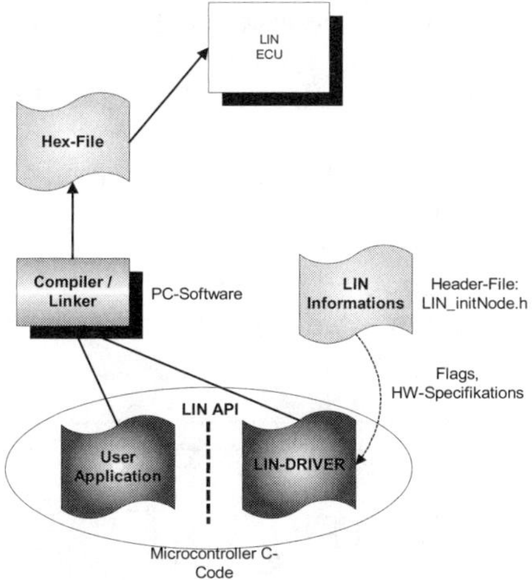

Figure 8: Configurable LIIN driver software

SOFTWARE DRIVER SERVICES

The Infineon Technologies software driver provides several services for a LIN implementation. All these services are under control of the user and invoked by service calls.

Two major categories of operations are provided:

1. Administrative services are used e.g. to configure or initialize the LIN software driver, respectively
    - LIN driver initialization
2. Functional services making use of services the LIN software driver provide.
    - Message transmission
    - Message reception
    - Message filtering
    - Connect/disconnect the LIN node to the LIN bus
    - Sending "*go to sleep mode*" command
    - Sending "*wake up*" command
    - Bus timeout detection
    - Frame monitoring
    - ID field calculation
    - Data length extraction
    - Check sum calculation
    - LIN message scheduler

SOFTWARE DRIVER PERFORMANCE

The LIN protocol uses hardware and software resources of a microcontroller. Like in real life nothing is for free. In this chapter the required on-chip resources, memory consumption and CPU load will be discussed to provide the system designer a reliable data base. The following absolute numbers relate to a C16x 16-bit microcontrollers of Infineon Technologies clocked with 20 MHz system clock and executing code from on-chip memory.

LIN utilizes the serial interface for message frame generation and additionally occupies one timer channel for LIN bus timing monitoring e.g. for detection of not responding slaves or no bus activity. Both peripherals require an interrupt handler and most of the LIN software driver is executed within the interrupt handler of the serial communication channel peripheral.

The introduced software driver occupies less than 3 Kbyte of code memory and less than 100 bytes of data memory. These numbers include all the basic LIN software driver functions. Only application specific user LIN message buffers require additional memory space.

Figure 9 sketches the signals on the LIN bus (CH2) and CPU load on the C16x (CH1). This microcontroller is configured as LIN Master and executes a LIN master and slave task. The master task transmits the header and the slave task of the same ECU attaches four data bytes and the corresponding check sum byte. During each spike on CH1 the CPU is involved in the LIN software driver. States 1, 2, and 3 are handled by the master task. The slave task is involved during states 4 to 9. Message filtering is done within state 4. Error detection takes place at every state of the LIN frame generation.

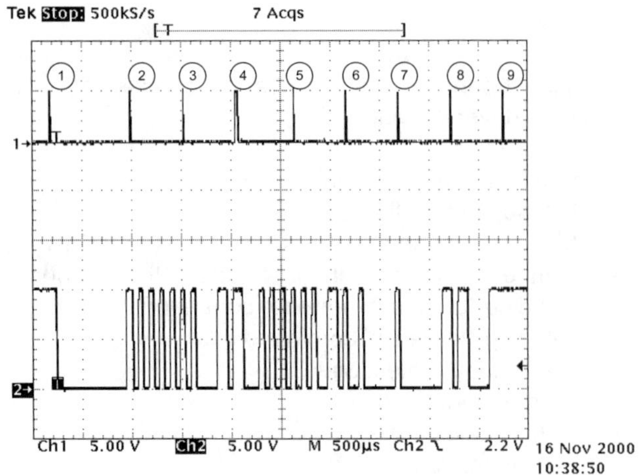

Figure 9: LIN buses signals

Master task:

1) Send-synch break
2) Receive-synch break and send synch field
3) Receive-synch-field and create / send ID-Field

Slave task:

4) Receive-ID-Field (message filtering), copy data to LIN transfer buffer and send first data-byte
5) Receive first data-byte and send second data byte
6) Receive second data-byte and send third data byte
7) Receive third data-byte and send fourth data byte
8) Receive fourth data-byte and calculate / send checksum-Field
9) Receive-Checksum

The LIN frame sketched in Figure 9 contains 4 data bytes and is running at baud rate of 19.2 kBaud. Its frame length is about 4.5 ms. The required CPU time for a LIN frame generation depends strongly on the number of declared ID's. In that example configuration 16 identifiers are defined. During the states 1 to 9 the CPU of the master LIN node is busy processing LIN driver operations. The overall processing time for the LIN software driver is 110 µs. While sending and receiving a LIN message frame the total CPU load of the LIN master node is below 3 %.

THE LIN TRANSCEIVERS

In general the physical layer of LIN is basing on an already well-known and approved standard: ISO9141 or also known as K-line or K/L-line. The ISO9141 network was mainly developed for transmission of diagnosis data within a garage. For that reason further improvement of the LIN physical layer performance respectively the transceiver is required in order to fulfil the requirements on a network that is operating while the engine is running but also during parking. Figure 10 sketches the main components of a typical LIN network.

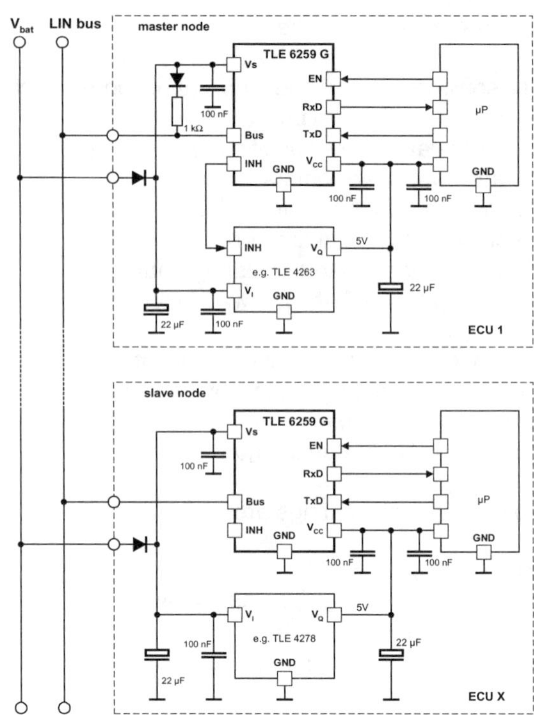

Figure 10: LIN network

To achieve a basic termination resistance for the recessive bus voltage level a 30kΩ pull up to the battery supply voltage is integrated in the transceiver ICs. Only the master node has an additional external termination of 1kΩ to achieve the required timings for the dominant to recessive edge of the bus signals. This only changes the total termination resistance negligible when the number of slave nodes changes due varying electronic equipment connected to the bus.

In case of an un-powered node (e.g. due to a blown out fuse) the bus is prevented from reverse currents by the diodes in the pull up path.

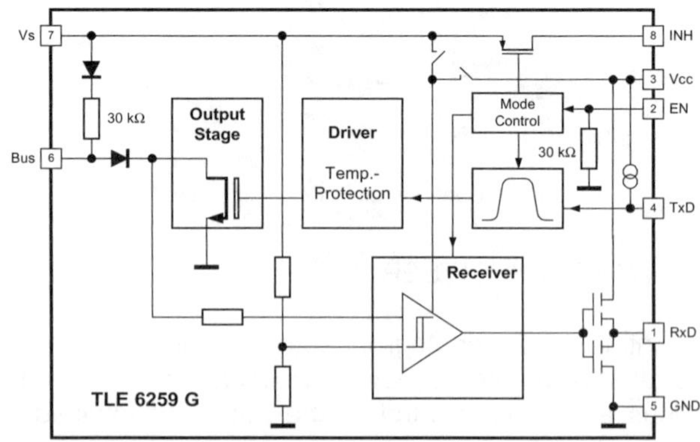

Figure 11: Block diagram of TLE6259

Infineon Technologies is going to offer two different stand-alone transceiver ICs for LIN applications: the TLE6258 and the TLE6259. Both are coming up in a P-DSO-8 package. The pin-out follows the proposal of the LIN consortium and represents the merger of the results of a pin FMEA as well as the requirements of EMC. In addition to the features of the TLE6258 the TLE6259 offers an inhibit output to control the voltage regulator that supplies entire ECU (Electronic Control Unit). When sending the TLE6259 to sleep mode via it's control input the inhibit output becomes high impedance by this switching off the voltage regulator. Now a wake-up of the ECU is only possible via a wake-up message on the LIN bus. During sleep mode the internal wake-up detection circuitry is supplied via the battery supply line. The current consumption is as low as 30µA in order to support the ever-decreasing quiescent current consumption requirements of today's and future cars. As soon a wake-up message is detected, the voltage regulator is enabled via the inhibit output pin and the wake-up is reported at the RxD output. The TLE6258 requires external 5V supply to detect bus wake-ups when switched to stand-by mode.

Compared to a differential mode as the CAN-system a LIN system is expected to have a much lower performance regarding EME (Electro Magnetic Emission). But the much lower maximum data transmission-rate in combination to limited slew rates of the bus signals is avoiding most of the problems arising in high-speed data transmission systems. Furthermore rounded corners of the signal edges also contribute to reduced emissions. To evaluate the EMC performance of the transceiver ICs on one hand the DPI method (Direct Power Injection) is used. RF interference is coupled into a LIN system to test the electromagnetic susceptibility. On the other hand the same test setup is used to investigate the electromagnetic emission performance. Figure 12 and 13 show test results for the first design step. Also the influence of additional capacitive bus-load is shown.

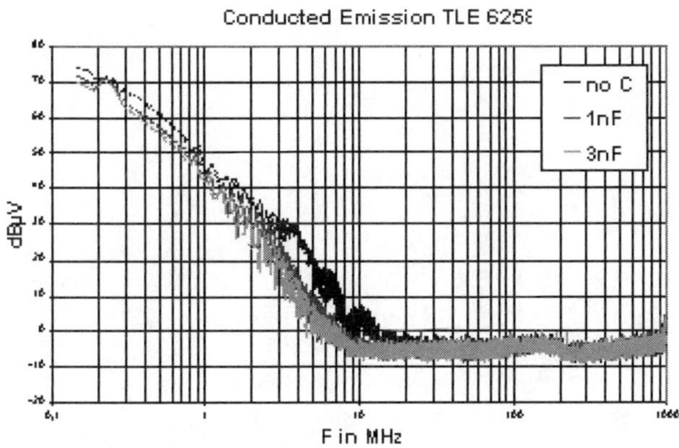

Figure 12: Electromagnetic emission TLE6258

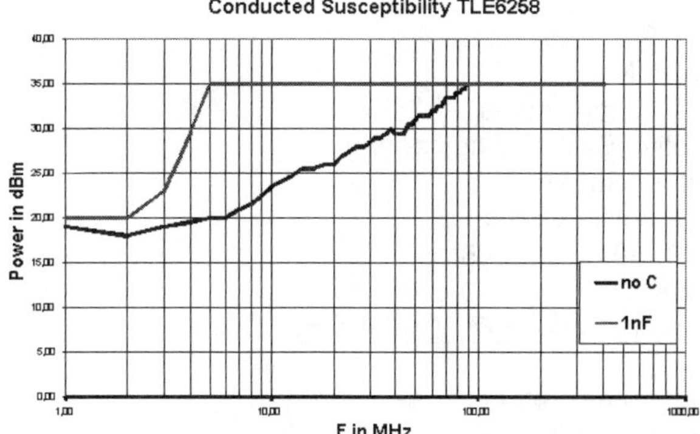

Figure 13: electromagnetic immunity TLE6258

CONCLUSION

Intersystem and intrasystem communication is evolving to one of the key technologies within future automotive systems. Infineon Technologies provides a broad portfolio of hardware, software, and application building blocks to reliably shorten the design cycle through robust network solutions, e.g. using CAN, J1850, ByteFlight, LIN, etc.

This paper presented the LIN family concept within Infineon Technologies portfolio. Software drivers allow a fast prototyping to investigate LIN architectures based on Infineon Technologies broad spectrum of integrated circuits. These modules allow power, EMC, and performance budget calculations to speed-up the migration from centralized systems to decentralized clustered system. So welcome aboard to Infineon's system world and make your sailing through the automotive communication highways a breeze.

REFERENCES

1. Murray, C. J.: "European carmakers get behind low-cost bus", EETimes, March 06, 2000.
2. von der Wense, H.-C.: "Introduction to Local Interconnect Network", SAE World Congress, Detroit, March 2000, Document No. 2000-01-0145, SAE Press.
3. von der Wense, H.-C.: "Introduction to LIN (Local Interconnect Network), http://www.lin-subbus.de/pdf/introduction_to_lin.pdf, March, 2000.
4. Web side of LIN: http://www.lin-subbus.org.
5. "LIN: Class-A Open Mux Standard Gains Momentum", Vol.13, No. 3, The Hansen Report on Automotive Electronics, Paul Hansen Associates, April 2000.
6. Web side of Infineon Technologies: http://www.infineon.com.

CONTACT

Hermann Kern
Infineon Technologies
Automotive System Engineering
St.-Martin.-Str. 76
81609 Munich, Germany
Tel.: (49) 89 234 83685
Fax: (49) 89 234 85150
Email: hermann.kern@infineon.com

Heinrich Gschloessl
Infineon Technologies
AI AP SYS PM
Balanstr. 73
81541 Munich, Germany
Tel.: (49) 89 234 22762
Fax: (49) 89 234 711898
Email: heinrich.gschloessl@infineon.com

Wilhard von Wendorff
Infineon Technologies
Automotive System Definition
St.-Martin.-Str. 76
81609 Munich, Germany
Tel.: (49) 89 234 83270
Fax: (49) 89 234 717830
Email: wilhard.wendorff@infineon.com

MODEL-BASED HARDWARE/SOFTWARE/ NETWORK DEVELOPMENTS

2007-01-1622

From Algorithms to Software – A Practical Approach to Model-Driven Design

Robert Baillargeon and Rick Flores
General Motors Corporation

ABSTRACT

The value of model-based design has been attempted to be communicated for more than a decade. As methods and tools have appeared and disappeared from a series of different vendors it has become apparent that no single vendor has a solution that meets all users' needs. Recently standards (UML, MDA, MOF, EMF, etc.) have become a dominant force and an alternative to vendor-specific languages and processes. Where these standards have succeeded and vendors have failed is in the realization that they do not provide the answer, but instead provide the foundation to develop the answer. It is in the utilization of these standards and their capability to be customized that companies have achieved success. Customization has occurred to fit organizations, processes, and architectures that leverage the value of model-driven design. From this opportunity, a practical solution to model-driven design has been created in the automotive domain that delivers on the promise of algorithmic expressiveness, process efficiency, and code generation fitness.

INTRODUCTION

Modeling activities in the automotive industry have typically followed a pattern: pockets of engineers across disparate technical departments discover the benefits of modeling functional requirements and creating executable specifications. Management recognizes the benefit of specifying algorithms more precisely and the potential to automatically generate code for production. The difficulties begin when attempting to scale the myopic view of a single algorithm development activity to a larger scope.

Once it is understood that code generation from models is as much of a process solution as it is a technical solution, the appropriate focus can be applied. It is from this concept of process focus, and problem space identification, that a practical method of transitioning from models to code can be achieved. Many foundational answers already exist in published methods and standards to reach this capability. What is new is their well-formed integrated application. With a focused task, and creative developers, the General Motors Software and Controls organization was able to develop and execute a pattern implementation for model-driven development. In the following we describe the critical methods and technologies. Additionally we will discuss the successful application of the concepts within General Motors.

MODEL-DRIVEN FOUNDATION

The model-driven foundation can be separated into two distinct categories that are critical to success. The first element is that the problem space must be identified and characterized. The second is the application of technology in the form of standards matured in the software industry.

IDENTIFYING THE PROBLEM SPACE

The problem space as a whole is that of automotive distributed embedded systems. More specifically, it is that of automotive body control systems. These systems are most typified as distributed reactive event-driven systems. The depth to which users explore and define the problem space typifies the success of implementing model-based methods. It is not simply the observed elements but also the relationships within the larger problem space, including organizational processes, which are critical.

The problem space of automotive systems has unique areas of expertise (serial communication, software architecture, hardware architecture, application/feature design ...) which collaborate in non-trivial manners to develop/define a system. It is often within these singular dimensions that processes and tools are defined as though they do not collaborate. However it is during the integration stage, the aligning of all dimensions, that issues are discovered. To address this issue, the problem space must morph to a broader concept of complexity management to align these dimensions. The resultant objective from problem space identification is the formulation of a solution that identifies which complexities can, and should, be managed to develop automotive systems. It is the characterization and understanding of these complex relationships which provides the opportunity to create the appropriate solution that fits the domain and the organization.

Each complexity provides a dimension which must be understood and elaborated to develop the appropriate solution. These complexities include inter-discipline relationships and dependencies. These inter-disciplinary dimensions include the technical elements that define automotive systems, such as serial communication, algorithms, and software. However, complexities are not restricted to the technical domain, but instead extend to the organizational domain and it's binding to technical assets. It is this organizational complexity which is often ignored or misunderstood while trying to apply solutions across industries or even across organizations within the same industry. While technical solutions are driven by concrete metrics of performance, organizational elements are driven by a value system which is enacted by behaviors and preferences to technical drivers. As such full understanding of the problem space, technical and organizational, must be discovered and documented to proceed to the next step of defining the solution.

While it remains an obvious and natural start to begin with the definition of the assets "required" in the development of an automotive embedded system, progressing to the next level of detail is critical. These asset types become the elements of the problem space. The next level requires the definition of relationships between elements that imply the process of asset creation and inherently data dependencies. The relationships describe the asset dependencies, activity inputs, and activity outputs which in turn formulate the foundation of the process. Ideally process elements are defined first, but in organizations where the process is implicit, starting with the assets is the only available path.

In our case, we found particular relationships of critical importance. These relationships described important process concepts that typically do not impact the implementation, but instead impact the efficiency and quality of the process we could create. Relationships which bind assets to particular roles of ownership allow responsibility of content and quality to be clearly defined. Relationships of asset dependencies allow the representation of prerequisites and natural flow of detail elaboration. Explicitly identifying these relationships enabled a mapping of technical constructs, assets, to organizational entities, roles. When this is performed the process and methods will collaborate to develop high quality products.

Capturing these relationships has required the proper set of abstractions. These have focused objectives on aligning intended behaviors. It has resulted in a capable and efficient organization and process. Additionally, by documenting the process it has provided the forum to improve and evolve the process.

As is true with many system identification efforts, it is critical to utilize the proper set of abstractions and objectives to prioritize the aspects that are critical to success. Some fundamental principles were established to guide progression from concepts to implementation. Our priorities were best defined as:

- Asset-to-asset relationships must be a natural progression
- All assets must establish a logical concept of ownership to roles
- Alignment of technical hierarchies and managerial/organization hierarchies must be enforced

What should be extracted from these concepts is that there are limitations to developing a "one-size fits all" solution that can be universally applied in all domains and organizations. But once the problem space is identified, including application and organization scope, characterized work in the solution space can be successful. It is the foundational concepts of problem space understanding that led to the solution implemented in General Motors Software & Controls organization.

THE PATH TO THE SOLUTION SPACE

Each organization is driven by its own unique set of value systems which are complemented by architectures and processes that support these value systems. While their specific solutions might be unique in form it does not necessitate unique tools and methods for an organization. Instead it is a viable belief that organizations can support their uniqueness through the application of methods and tools while leveraging the collective progress of the software industry.

The solution to managing the complexity of automotive embedded software space is the strategic, innovative employment of methods and tools that exist in the software domain. This is the path selected by the General Motors Software and Controls organization. Each element was evaluated on the contributions to the whole.

THE METHODS

Following is a collection of methods employed in development and deployment of the process. In various cases these methods were used either to define elements of the process or to implement the designs. These critical methods include meta-modeling, object orientated analysis, and patterns.

Meta-Modeling

Meta-modeling is the process of formalizing the elements and elemental relationships for a particular domain. It is this process which enables the definition and depiction of the process and asset relationships that define how products are created. Creation of meta-models requires a depth of knowledge that is typically only possessed by domain experts. The procedure of meta-modeling has two distinct values to the performing organization and individuals: understanding and communication.

The procedure of creating meta-models demands that the knowledge of the assets and process is known, or can be acquired. Many valuable insights can be obtained by creating and reviewing the meta-model. The visualizations, which demonstrate patterns and relationships, will identify points of confusion requiring further analysis. The resulting insight from the analysis of the meta-model is what drives change in the form of process improvement. These changes are typically due to inconsistencies and inefficiencies which become obvious via the rigorous method of description.

The other major value of a meta-model is in its capability to communicate. The richness of meta-models comes from their capability to succinctly describe elements and relationships. These relationships are expressive, providing mechanisms to describe commonalities, ownership and dependencies. The ability to describe these relationships can lead to the critical understanding of coupling and cohesion of assets. This enables the discussion of common process flow as well as the resulting effects of change in assets or process. The result of the creation of a meta-model is the formalization of a vocabulary and language that describes a domain.

Meta-models are often visualized by tools and built on standards such as EMF, MOF, or UML. Utilizing standards provides language foundation, and in several cases the desired graphical depiction and paths to implementation tools.

Object Orientation Analysis

While object orientated analysis is not a new concept to the software industry, it has typically been avoided in the automotive domain. This is because it is assumed that highly constrained devices cannot deal with the overhead implied by the expressiveness and flexibility of object oriented concepts. However, there are too many valuable elements of OOA to ignore its relevance and importance for description and analysis. The concepts of implementation are instead addressed though the use of alternative implementation formalisms which utilize the expressive description of OOA but do not incur an undue cost in static applications. The concept of implementation should be interpreted as an orthogonal concern to the description in the analysis space.

Software engineering practices have shown that OOA attributes of decoupling, generalization, and encapsulation provide important design characteristics. What was perceived, and later proven, is that these good design practices are valuable and important to developing and maintaining assets. With careful planning this can be done with little overhead as compared to the traditional forms of functional development. The critical elements for each of these three dimensions of object orientated analysis are as follows.

Decoupling is a critical property of any developed asset and is a common feature of careful use of object-oriented methods. Specifically, this is the concept of interfaces. What interfaces provide is a common contract between two, or more, assets that describe a formalism of interaction. This contract allows assets, both the providing and the requiring, utilizing the interface to change without directly impacting the other assets. This concept of "design-by-contract" is a valuable formalism which provides a foundation for a more stable asset base. It is the stability in the asset base which leads to more efficient process execution through direct reuse and stable extension points.

Generalization is the ability within the analysis space to describe the commonality of elements and provide vertical layers of relationships which refine their underlying type similarities. Generalization allows the segmentation of similar concerns of systems allowing for a single place to document behaviors which describe an entire class of objects. This improves maintainability by providing a single point in which changes can be managed. Additionally it provides a foundation in which elements can be extended without replicating behaviors or having the extended element be affected.

Encapsulation is a natural concept of object orientation which works well for both analysis as well as design. In its general form, encapsulation supports the isolation of internal decisions from external consumers. This is beneficial because the language itself prevents the users from depending on internal details, through usage. Instead, object collaboration requires the usage of explicitly exposed access points for data retrieval. Encapsulation complements the design-by-contract concepts by demanding the use of published contracts rather than the internals of a design which ideally remain hidden. Encapsulation inherently improves the robustness of designs by enforcing higher quality and explicit patterns of interaction.

Patterns

One of the benefits of using common industry practices is the ability to leverage methodologies that are well used and understood. The software industry has developed a formalism to describe the concepts typically referenced as patterns. These pattern descriptions are presented in process flow, tool usage, and design solutions. Fortunately the concepts of patterns are targeted to define the core characteristics of a concept such that it can be adopted and tailored for use.

Concepts of design patterns have been used in our applications. Concepts of process patterns (Software Product Lines) have been used in our process flows.

Concepts of tooling flow have been instituted in our code generation flow (Model Driven Architecture). Concepts of design patterns have been utilized in algorithm descriptions (Mediators). It is through the utilization of industry expertise that such advancement in process was rapidly achievable. The usage of these methods in combination can be proffered as an advancement to the state of the art.

THE TECHNOLOGIES

Technologies are critical to execute the intended processes and to achieve their desirable capabilities. However, it is critical that the tools are driven by the process; in the inverse case the assumptions are too burdensome in terms of syntax, semantics, and impacts on process flow. It is critical that the technologies leveraged are process independent, providing significant infrastructure foundation, and accommodating extension to a specific domain. These characteristics define the fitness of the tool to the purpose. Following are the set of technologies being leveraged by the Software and Controls organization.

UML

The Unified Modeling Language formulates a technology in standardizing the notation and semantics of a series of object orientated methodologies. What makes this an important technology to the software industry is in its localization of effort spent on object-oriented notations. It allows resources to be dedicated to extensions in related methodologies and tools, aiding the practice and industry as a whole.

It is this general applicability as the common language of object orientated expression that the UML provides an advantage to the practitioners. The standardization of language leverages a market for tooling that provides cost effective solutions for various industry applications. It also provides a technology where industry practices are exposed in a common manner, extending the capability of the whole with little cost of entry.

For reasons of economy and capability, the UML provides an enticing opportunity for any domain to express its constructs and should be considered. However, detractors, identifying the software-centric approach of the notation, say it limits the usage base. In addition, the general nature of the language allows the description of everything in general, but nothing succinctly leading to productivity and quality concerns. The UML in its base form provides only the generic constructs applicable in most domains, and yet, because of the generic form, it requires extensive detail and effort to construct models.

DSLs

While the UML provides a generic solution, the alternative is a specific solution tailored to a particular application. It has long been believed that domain-specific languages (DSLs) would provide the ideal answer to raise the productivity curve beyond that of General Purpose Languages (GPLs). The rationale is that when formalism can be attached to the natural language of a specific user base, then expressiveness of a language can be both more succinct in syntax and more detailed in semantics.

However, the development of DSLs has been curtailed due to the economics of the development. For most organizations the development of languages is not the core business in which they operate. As such, any development effort is considered a non-value added activity to a business. Additionally, it is difficult to quantify the gains attributed to such notations and it often has the countereffect of restricting the available tooling to support the language, which is available for most general purpose languages (GPLs). The end result of the gain of expressivity at the loss of availability of tooling can be considered a major deficiency of DSLs.

The ideal situation is the ability to rapidly develop a DSL with limited cost while still leveraging standard tools for economies of cost. This concept of DSL generation has been proffered and has continued to grow via such foundational models of MOF, EMOF, GME, and EMF. However the full realization of the vision on these platforms has yielded limited success, and additional research will be needed to achieve a complete and viable DSL platform.

Extending UML

The UML developers understood that a generic language was not suitable for all users, but would provide a foundation for extension. This capability allows UML concepts to be merged with those of DSLs. The result is a light-weight DSL which provides some of the objectives of DSLs with a greatly reduced cost of entry. The derivation of a domain-specific language from UML is through the concept of a UML Profile. A UML Profile provides the ability to document concepts of extending the language by creating additional behaviors and restricting the language by reducing behaviors.

Transitioning the UML from a generic language to a DSL utilizes a standard process. The first step defines the domain constructs and their relationships. Ideally this is presented as a traversable and formal meta-model. The next step requires the mapping of the domain constructs (meta-model elements and relationships) to specific UML constructs and applying identifiers, stereotypes, to identify the uniqueness of behavior. Lastly, the interpretation of the language must be formalized to allow the leveraging of the domain-specific expressions.

The extension of the behaviors within UML is achieved by utilizing stereotypes to extend behaviors of standard elements of UML types. This notation causes the elements to retain their previous behaviors and then achieve additional behaviors, including user-defined attributes, based on the newly derived types. These newly created elements are considered to have all of the same qualities of the original core elements, and the new elements should be considered first class elements on the same level as the base UML constructs. Most elements of a DSL can be achieved via the extension concepts.

A corollary to the extension mechanism for UML is that of restriction. Restriction is the lesser used of the modifications due to the implementation complexity in tools. In most cases restrictions are achieved by specifying a constraint language describing the restricted behaviors. Often these constraints are specified via the Object Constraint Language (OCL). The difficulty in implementing the constraint is to actively verify that a constraint has not been violated. Technical complexities result in constraints not being supported in commercial tools. Instead design guidelines, rather than more rigorously defined constraints, are often the solution.

A UML Profile in implementation is a bundling mechanism that contains the specialization of UML to a specific application/domain. All of the extensions and restrictions are described within the profile, and then a developer simply needs to use a usage relationship to the profile to enact its extensions and restrictions. It is this simple deployment of this DSL-like concept that makes it valuable and desirable to industry users. It resolves many of the issues that fault DSLs in their ideal forms.

The creation of the language is necessary, but not enough. The interpretation of the language is equally critical to its success and usability. This interpretation of the language provides the ability to transition the language from purely syntax to having semantic value. It is the semantics which provide foundations for expression and analysis of language constructs. Without this interpretation, reasonable uses of analysis and synthesis, such as code generation, cannot be performed. While such interpretation is not part of the UML standard, its support is both expected and desired.

MDA

As a formulation of the model interpretation flow a companion standard was developed which defines a particular path of interpretation and synthesis. Model Driven Architecture (MDA) is a pattern of the utilization of multiple models to derive implementations. Common to the MDA pattern is the definition of a Platform Independent Model (PIM) and a Platform Specific Model (PSM), which are combined with a set of rules to derive an implementation. The pattern of isolation of platform independence and platform dependence as collaborating concerns is an important concept that has been utilized and extended. This allows the separation of analysis and implementation concerns and later combined to create a specifically targeted construct, often code. It is this generalized pattern that has allowed the growth of tooling and supported the development of DSLs for application by reducing the cost of entry.

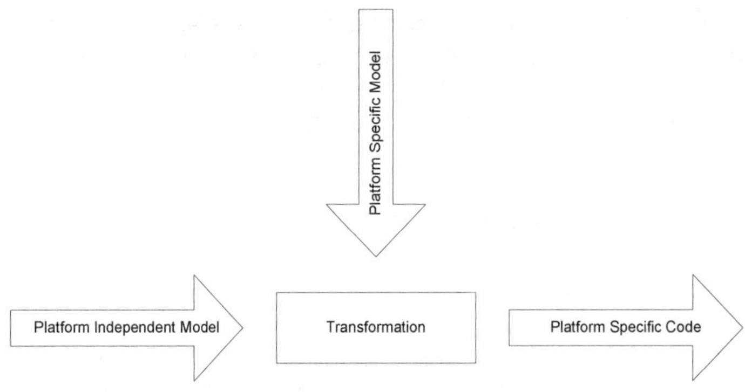

Figure 1: Generic MDA Flow

It is this conceptual flow of model manipulation transitioning the gap from platform independence, algorithms, to platform dependence, software, where value has been identified. It is these themes that have been leveraged, if not the full pattern of flow.

APPLICATION OF MODEL DRIVEN DESIGN

While the technologies are the enablers, it is in the application that proof is delivered that the concepts and objectives are realized. For this reason the following section details the utilization of technology in the development of the GM Software & Controls Process and Framework.

ORGANIZATIONAL FITNESS

The GM Software & Controls organization was formed to define methods, tools, and processes to enable the use of new business models for the development and procurement of GM's Body and Chassis embedded software. The desired business models ran the full spectrum: from GM specifying distributed systems through GM implementing full ECU software on a supplier's hardware platform. Among the strategic goals of the organization was the creation of a Software Product Line.

Software Product Lines is an evolving paradigm that is focused on the *planned* reuse of assets in the development of a *bandwidth* of products. The focus is on a two-tiered development process with separate release cycles (decoupled but dependent)

- Domain Engineering (Development) – Reusable asset development
- Application Engineering (Deployment) – Product development

This approach demands an integrated development framework of defined functional areas with clearly defined boundaries and interfaces between areas. A reality constraint is that the new methods, tools, and processes had to be tailored to work within the existing organizational framework. Without this technical-organizational binding, concepts of ownership could not exist and would result in impeding the assignment of asset ownership to individuals in the organization. Our approach was to begin by designing a meta-model that reflected our organizational structure.

FUNCTIONAL ARCHITECTURE MODEL

Deriving a meta-model based on the organizational entities, artifacts, and ensuing relationships has been instrumental in the creation of models that align with the higher-level process and deliverables. After defining this meta-model, a hierarchy was created that provided a development framework within which to accomplish the work of the business. This hierarchy ensures a match in the work of the functional requirement owners, modelers, software designers, and testers.

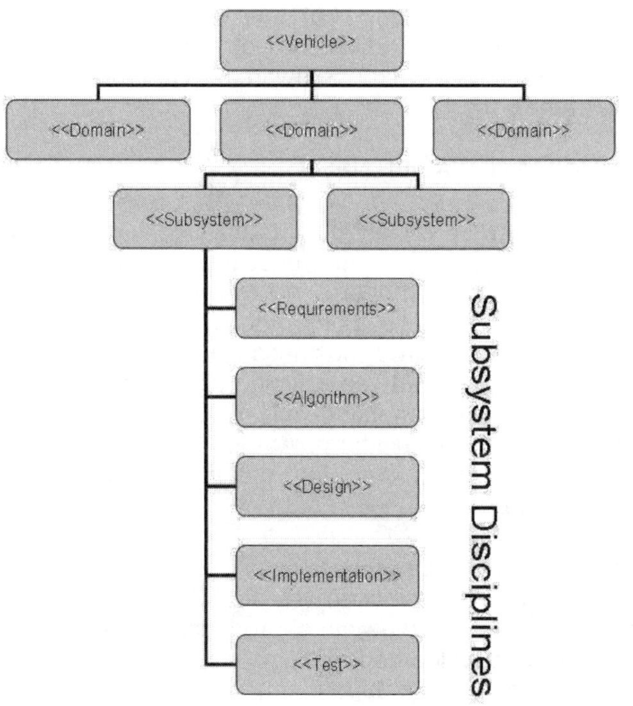

Figure 2: An Integrated Model Hierarchy

The artifacts of our process are developed within A UML design database reflecting this framework and managed within a matching Configuration Management project structure.

The 'model' is actually a collection of linked projects that can be viewed, communicated, and understood as an integrated whole. This view enables decision-making processes of assigning functional responsibilities to the <<Domains>> and <<Subsystems>> of the organization.

The Domains define the context for development of Subsystem requirements. Providing stable boundaries here is essential to allow the development of functional interfaces or contacts between Domains that persist over time. Subsystem areas are charged with developing and managing a whirlwind of new \ changing requirements facing today's automotive software system developers. In our environment, Workgroups are created at this Subsystem level and are responsible for the development of a technical specification for their area.

Subsystems are assigned ownership of <<Features>> and <<Devices>>. The concept of an electrical system feature is an interesting topic that in many cases tends to cross Subsystem boundaries. Nevertheless, specification of the functional intent and interfaces between Domains or Subsystems to accomplish a feature must be owned by a single Subsystem (e.g. InteriorLighting). Similarly, hardware I\O devices may be employed by many features (e.g. DoorAjar Switch) but input processing is owned by a single Subsystem (EntryControl). Ownership in this context is important, because a single point of contact is accountable for the correct functional operation of the feature.

The features are the threads that provide traceability from functionality implemented across the architectural framework back to requirements.

This framework is known as our Functional Architecture which defines the domains, subsystems, interfaces providing a context for the supported features of our software Product Line.

<u>Interfaces</u>

Establishing touch points and interfaces upon which the producers and consumers of system information can solidify their communication is a critical step toward managing the complexities of any large-scale design.

Interface management for electrical systems has typically focused on the creation of databases for each protocol (e.g. CAN, LIN) for communication between components. However, this relies on the physical implementation, which is not available when creating a Product Line.

Instead, we have used the more generic concept of Interface classes to define the formal interactions between domains and subsystems.

<u>Signals</u>

We define the term <<Signal>> to encompass the concept of a formalized interface between a producer and consumer(s) of data. An <<Interface>> class defines a signal accessor operation and return type. The unique interface becomes the Contract that can be realized to connect signal providers and consumers through an "explicit" link (drawing) or an "implicit" link (algorithmically).

Each <<Signal>> possesses the following:

- a <<Data>> attribute, defining type and default value
- a <<Status>> attribute providing failure operation if required.
- <<SignalAccessor>> operations for data and status
- <<SignalMutator>> operations to set data by proxy

The definition of signals used by the algorithms forms a Data Dictionary that can be extracted from the model in report form at any time during development. The <<Signal>> is a central concept used across levels of our process: from Algorithm to Software.

Figures 3 and 4 below show the usage of the signal concept as both Specification and Implementation for data communication. The <<Signal>> definition class in Fig. 3 specifies the data type of the signal and an associated status. The <<Interface>> class specifies the signal's accessor operation and return type. Now, the owning class of the signal data in Fig. 4 can allocate storage and provide the value to consumers through the signal accessor operation. A consumer only needs to use the specified accessor operation expecting the data type specifed by the return value.

An added benefit of this approach is the use of the signal class in Fig. 3 itself as a simulation stub during development. The class can provide its data as a proxy for the 'real' provider (e.g. signal owned by another Subsystem) using the <<SignalMutator>> Set operation().

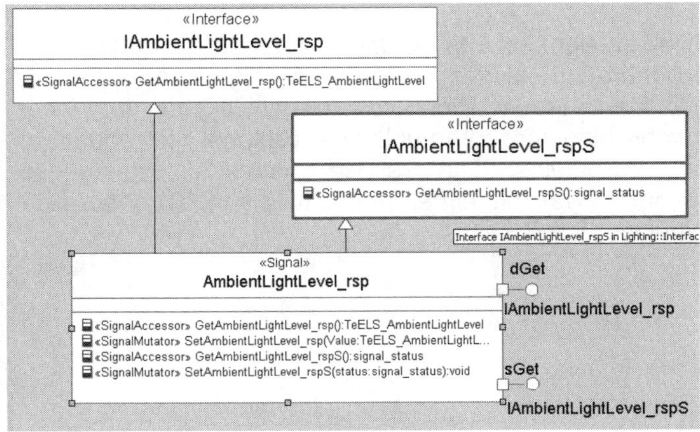

Figure 3 - Formal Interface for Ambient Light level Data and Status

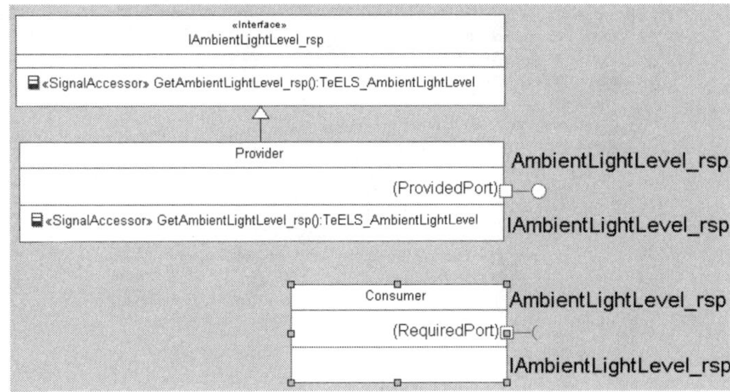

Figure 4 - Implementation of Formal Interface

ALGORITHM MODEL

The required behavior of each subsystem application is captured in the form of algorithm models. Algorithm modeling is the process of translating customer-based subsystem requirements into fully elaborated behavioral models.

The models capture applications with the intention of planned reuse through key abstractions. The models must be independent, to the maximum possible extent, of the physical allocation, the serial data protocol, the hardware platform, and the software platform implementation.

Our algorithm modeling development approach begins by creating an 'application architecture'. When creating a model, the modeler must make significant decisions regarding the organization of the application.

Ideally, the modeler organizes the application into logical design units based on

- Requirements
- Knowledge of the core \ optional aspects of the product line
- Existing modeling resources (toolbox)
- Personal experience

The screenshot below shows a slice of the integrated model hierarchy, expanding a section of the Interior Lighting subsystem application architecture. The subsystem behaviors are developed within a common framework of <<Domains>> and <<Subsystems>>. <<Signals>> reside in the <<Interface>> packages. The Interior Lighting application is organized into design packages based on the bulleted criteria described in the previous paragraph. A family of Cargo Lighting algorithms has been developed and can be deployed separately or jointly as a superset.

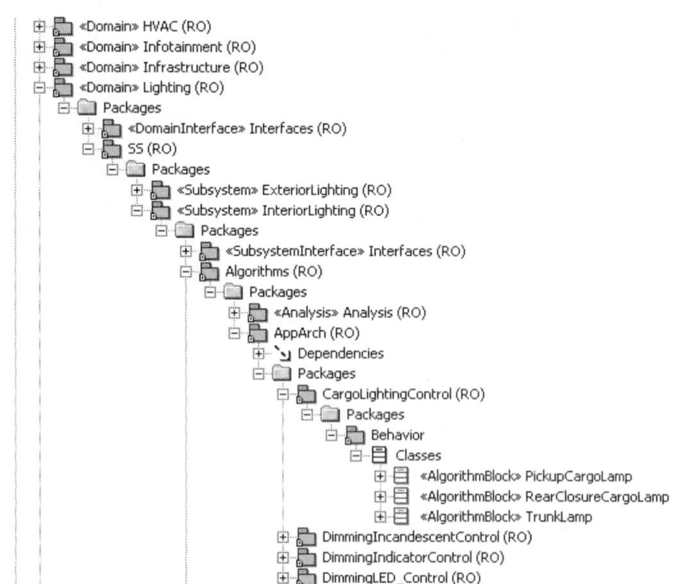

Figure 5: Integratated Model Hierarchy – InteriorLighting

An <<Algorithm Block>> is the elementary unit for building behavior, and is represented by a UML class utilizing concepts of composition or inheritance where appropriate for scalability. UML 2.0 Ports are used as the connection points on Algorithm Blocks to aggregate and expose required and provided data. The Ports allow flexibility in the Algorithm Block's context of usage.

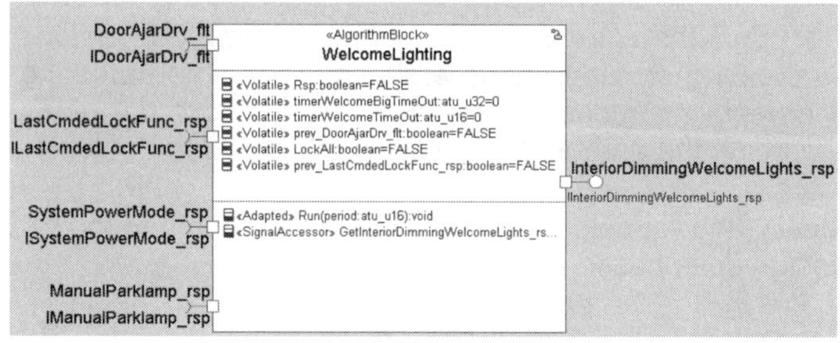

Figure 6: <<AlgorithmBlock>> Welcome Lighting

<u>Design Patterns</u>

Our methods have included leveraging some common design patterns found in the software industry adapted to meet our needs. Many of the patterns can be found in our modeling <<Toolbox>> and are applicable across all algorithm models.

<u>Template Pattern</u>

The **template pattern** defines the skeleton of an algorithm. Parts of the algorithm itself are made abstract, and the subclasses of the method override the abstract methods to provide concrete behavior. The general code resides in the parent class, and the variants are implemented in the subclasses. Thus the general algorithm is common, but the concrete steps may be changed by the subclasses.

As an example, our Toolbox includes an algorithm to drive a PWM output signal to either a value commanded by the main algorithm or a value commanded by an external test tool. If the value is commanded by the tool, a confirmation is reported back.

```
Osg.Frequency = GetFrequency();
if(GetStatus_cpid() == INACTIVE) {
  Osg.DutyCycle = GetDutyCycle();
}
else {
  Osg.DutyCycle = GetValue_cpid();
  Report_cpid();
}
```

The Get() operations in this code are all abstract as is the Report_cpid(). Each sub-classer of this algorithm implements the abstract operation with the parameters of the specific output being controlled by the sub-class.

<u>Mediator Pattern</u>

The **mediator pattern** provides a unified interface to a set of interfaces in a system. Classes send a message to the Mediator when needed, and the Mediator passes them on to any other classes that need to be informed. This promotes loose coupling between the sending and receiving classes, since only the Mediator need know of the internal methods of the receiving class(es).

As an additional example, a typical problem within our environment is that of competing requests for a shared resource. Our <<Open Service>> design pattern is an adaptation of the mediator pattern. An Open Service refers to a priority-based control strategy for a vehicle resource(s) (e.g. lamp) based only on incoming requests with no prior knowledge of specific requestors. This scalable approach allows adding requestors and re-arranging priority at a later date with no change to the Open Service provider.

The design of the Open Service includes two collaborating classes, a Service Mediator and a Service Provider, in addition to formal signal interfaces establishing the communication protocol for requestors of the service. The service makes a system-level resource available either internally to an ECU or across a network.

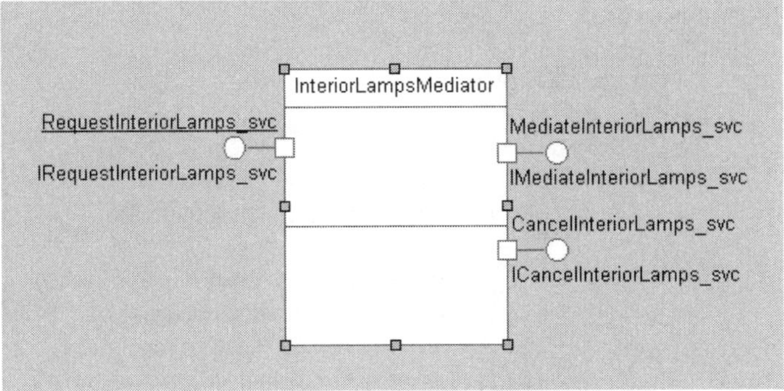

Figure 7: Interior Lamps Mediator

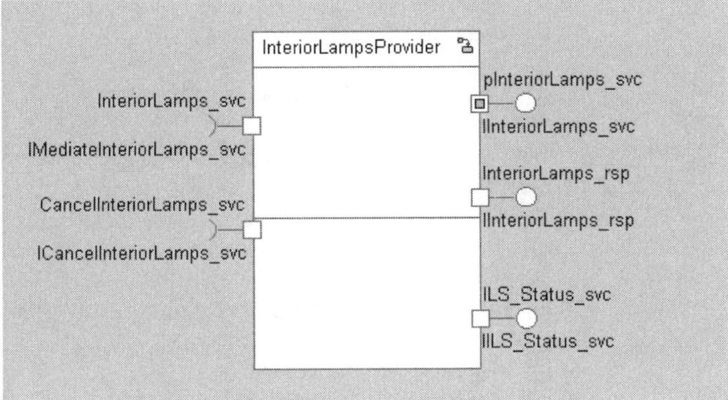

Figure 8: Interior Lamps Provider

Model Development Kit Pattern

This pattern was developed by our group as an improvement on our template-based pattern. The improvement lies in the realization that sub-classers of our toolbox parent classes know all the data required by the parents to accomplish their work. Therefore, the Don't-Call-Me-I'll-Call-You philosophy (e.g. parent calls on the sub-class to get each individual piece of data when needed), is inverted by having the sub-classer collect all required information and pass the data to a parent-defined concrete, parameterized operation. The new method improves efficiency by eliminating excessive transfers of control (calls and returns) between parent and sub-class. This form of parent-child relationship appears more like a library or function call rather than traditional generalization.

Revisiting the example above of the PWM Drive Output in Fig.9, the parent class logic is simplified to work directly with the parameters passed by the sub-class rather than using abstract operations to 'Get' the parameters one at a time. The sub-class' Run operation calls the inherited parent function passing parameters.

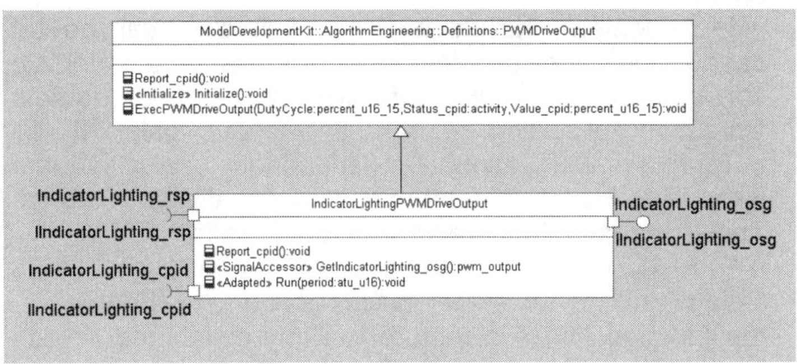

Figure 9 - PWM Drive Output

The pattern is also used to model diagnostic detecting\reporting behavior where the core logic in the toolbox uses simple Boolean enable, fail, and pass criteria and calibratable timers to determine when a diagnostic trouble code should be set. The determination of what enable, fail, and pass mean for a specific diagnostic is left to the sub-classer. This may involve the definition of a state machine or additional operations, as long as criteria are converted to the defined interface.

SOFTWARE DESIGN MODEL

Software Design is the process of composing behavioral elements to define the execution sequence and distributability in preparation for software creation. A separation from the Algorithm Modeling phase of the process is intended to allow focusing on:

- Execution Structure - support de-coupling of behavioral definition and structural composition. Also inhibit pollution of algorithm designs with software or vehicle architecture details.
- Allocation Constraints - provide system-level architects with software components that can be freely allocated. Dependencies have been comprehended within components.
- Variance Management - allow a variance strategy that includes\excludes behaviors based on deployment.

Execution Frames

At this point in the process, Execution Frames are created, which are schedulable entities that package a group of <<AlgorithmBlocks>>. These frames, stereotyped as <<Runnable>> blocks, provide an entry point to our real-time embedded Software Architecture. The data dependency of each Execution Frame is defined by its <<Agent>> port: a single port that exposes all externally required and provided interfaces of the frame's contained objects.

Each Execution Frame has the potential to define a dependency on an <<EnableCalibration>>. For optional vehicle content, the value of this calibration can be set based on the deployment choices (i.e. vehicle configurations) and will effectively ‘turn off’ a frame’s execution providing a net throughput gain. If no <<Enable Calibration>> dependency exists, the Execution Frame is understood to be always enabled. This is the case for core vehicle functionality.

Going back to an earlier discussion of a <<Feature>>, the functionality of a feature is likely distributed across several Execution Frames. The algorithm modeler knows which frames are involved in implementing a feature and sets the dependency as required for each Execution Frame. The <<EnableCalibration>> strategy allows multiple frames to be calibrated ‘Off’ with a single calibration. From a calibrator’s perspective, no knowledge of what frames constitute a feature is required; a single calibration will turn off execution for all frames involved in a feature.

The Design package screenshot below shows a subset of Interior Lighting subsystem Execution Frames. The expanded ExecutionFrame, EF_AutoInteriorIllumControl, contains Automatic Interior Lighting behaviors. The run-time scheduler will call the Execution Frame with the <<Ordered>> objects called in a sequence specified by an annotation (not shown) on the object. The objects are instances of the AlgorithmBlock classes defined in the Algorithm Modeling phase of the process. The Agent port exposes the architectural dependencies of the Execution Frame. An enable calibration is shown for the Execution Frame EF_FrontZnIntLamps_CtrlOut. The functionality in this frame is included\excluded based on the Boolean value of the calibration.

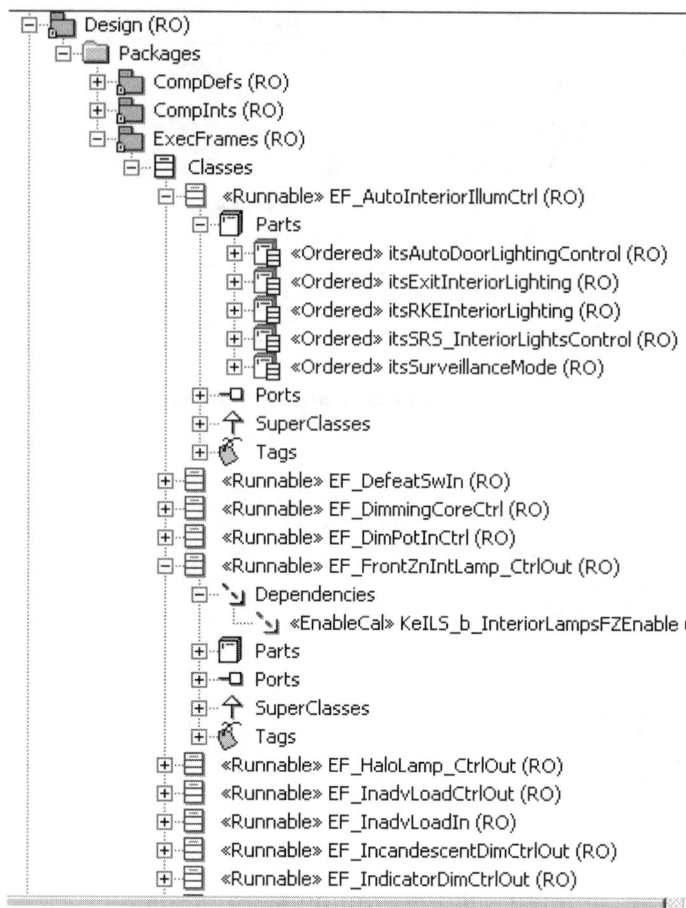

Figure 10: Design Model screenshot

Software Components

The next step in the process is to create distributable components. These components provide a mechanism to constrain the allocation of behaviors that should not be distributed across ECUs for functional or latency concerns. Once the behaviors are packaged to components, vehicle-level architects can analyze re-partitioning of these components across ECUs to optimize the system according to criteria such as latencies, wiring, and serial data bus bandwidth.

Using the terminology of our process, Execution Frames are packaged in Software Components for allocation across ECUs. The Software Component screenshot below shows <<Distributable>> Interior Lighting subsystem components. The content of the LGT_ControlInteriorLights component implies that a decision has been made to allocate the manual interior lighting switch debounce algorithm along with the automatic interior lighting algorithms. Every vehicle will have manual lighting and at least auto door interior lighting (e.g. lights illuminate when any door opens).

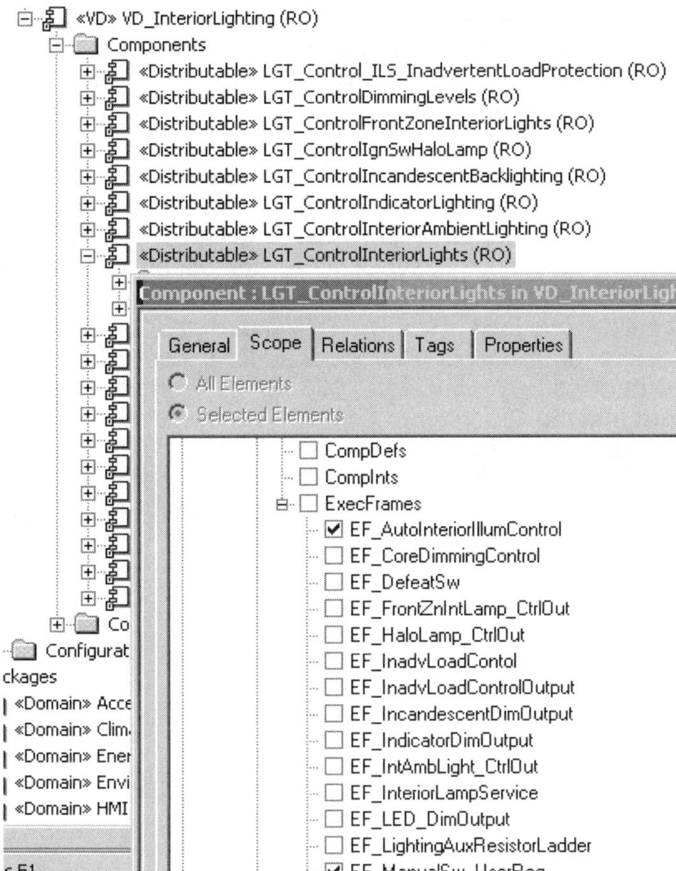

Figure 11: Software Component screenshot

SOFTWARE IMPLEMENTATION

Software implementation within the Software & Controls organization is an automated activity fulfilling the promise of "'models-to-code". The path to "models-to-code" remains unique within the industry by leveraging the MDA paradigm. It relies on our own custom set of translation rules to take a set of constraints, the models, impart a knowledge base, the rule, and generate the software.

The development of our own set of code generation rules provided freedoms and efficiencies that are not available commercially. These process and implementation efficiencies included such items as:

- Architecture fitness flexibility – Allowing change to the software architecture while retaining algorithm stability.
- Lazy Modeling – Allowing incomplete, yet precise, modeling of design constraints allowing automation of mundane and error prone tasks
- Optimizations – Allowing the ability to leverage more aggressive optimization due to fully known system characteristics unknown to commercial generators.
- Process Integration – Allowing complete adoption of the environment. including concepts of ownership, structure, and operational tasks that are specific to a particular organization.

The result from these capabilities and the usage our own translation rules is the achievement of the objective, from algorithms to software with full return on the investment of creating models. It is only through the rigorous support of process and integration with the design flow that these beneficial relationships can be achieved and the optimizations of design and process, which can return the investment cost.

TOOL REQUIREMENTS

The process requires a UML tool that can seamlessly link referenced projects from within a parent project allowing a view of a single integrated model.

This process requires a UML tool that can generate executable code allowing demonstrations of the subsystem requirements early in the design cycle. Multiple views of the system are supported by using container classes as the basis of prototype code generation. This capability has proven to be of great benefit in ensuring that the software ultimately meets the 'intended' requirements by obtaining buy-in from key stakeholders.

CONCLUSION

It can be concluded that there is a significant value in utilizing model driven approaches. This requires the concerted effort to focus on process. This process focus unifies the concepts of organizational and technical capabilities and can be realized concretely via models. The utilization of models provides the formalization of data which allows extended capabilities where informal methods have not been able to explore in the path. The application of the methodology and its foundations is proof of its viability and applicability in the automotive domain. It is through these collective methods and technologies that the true value can be extracted from models and achieve the concepts of transition from algorithms to software.

ACKNOWLEDGMENTS

The authors would like to thank the GM Software & Controls who execute this process on a daily basis, proving the capability and motivating the improvements.

REFERENCES

1. The Unified Modeling Language Users Guide (2nd Edition), Grady Booch, James Rumbaugh, Ivar Jacobson, Addison Wesley 2005
2. MDA http://www.omg.org
3. Software Product Lines: Practices and Patterns, Paul Clements, Linda Northrup, Addison Wesley 2002

4. Design Patterns, Erich Gamma, Richard Helm, Ralph Johnson, John Vlissides, Addison Wesley 1995
5. Rhapsody, http://www.telelogic.org
6. Model Driven Workbench, http://www.mdworkbench.com

CONTACT

Robert Baillargeon has over a decade of experience in electrical/electronic automotive systems. He has worked primarily in the Body Electronics domain performing algorithm development, process definition and tools creation for model-based development. He is currently a Staff Researcher at General Motors Research, where he is the Thrust Area Leader for Electronics, Controls, and Software Process, Methods and Tools. He has a BS in Electrical Engineering from Michigan Technological University and a MS in Information Technology-Software Engineering from Carnegie Mellon University. (robert.c.baillargeon@gm.com).

Through his career Rick Flores has been a key developer and advocate of General Motors' model-driven software development process. These processes are now being used to develop core components in GM's latest electrical architectures deployed on millions of vehicles annually. Rick was awarded the prestigious Society of Hispanic Professional Engineers' Junipero Serra Award in January 2006 for his efforts. He is currently the Algorithm Modeling Process Lead for GM Software & Controls Core Body Software group. He has a BS in Electrical and Computer Engineering from Wayne State University and an MSEE from University of Michigan.(rick.r.flores@gm.com).

2007-01-1620

A Generic Approach to Hazard Analysis for Programmable Automotive Systems

David D. Ward
MIRA Limited

Roger S. Rivett
Land Rover

Peter H. Jesty
Peter Jesty Consulting Ltd

ABSTRACT

With the increasing dependence on advanced electronic systems to control the functionality of road vehicles, the consideration of functional system safety as part of the design and implementation process for these systems is growing in importance.

An important part of such a process is to undertake a hazard analysis. Emerging standards and guidelines, such as ISO 26262 and MISRA Safety Analysis, contain a requirement to perform preliminary hazard analysis in order to identify unwanted events (typically at the vehicle level) that can result from technological causes, and to set safety requirements for the system under development to mitigate the risk associated with those events.

In this paper, a generic approach to automotive hazard analysis is described. The method is based upon a generalized model of the causal chain that leads from a low-level fault in an electronic system through to the potential for an unwanted event at the vehicle level. This model is used to derive a generic approach for hazard analysis. The paper demonstrates how an existing hazard analysis scheme, the MISRA Risk Graph for hazard classification, can be derived from the generalized model.

INTRODUCTION

The modern road vehicle is increasingly dependent on programmable electronic systems to deliver the functionality required or expected by manufacturers, legislators and consumers. As many of these systems control or influence vehicle functions that have a direct effect on the safety of the vehicle, its occupants and other road users, they are therefore safety-related systems.

There are many approaches to safety-related systems engineering, sometimes called functional safety, depending on the industry sector, but a common theme in all of these sectors is that the process contains the following generic elements:

- Identify what specific requirements are placed on the development of the system;
- Implement the system, taking these requirements into account
- Demonstrate that the final system meets these requirements.

As part of the process of identifying the specific requirements on the system, it is necessary to identify the ways in which the system could place its users, or other road users, in danger in the event of a malfunction or other deviation from the specified behavior. This leads to requirements for the way in which the system is designed and implemented to ensure that the danger is reduced to an acceptable level. Hazard analysis is the process of identifying the dangers and setting the requirements.

AUTOMOTIVE HAZARD ANALYSIS

The generic definition of a hazard is "a potential source of harm". In the automotive context the people that are potentially exposed to a source of harm arising from the vehicle typically include:

- The vehicle driver and passengers;
- Drivers and passengers of other road vehicles, e.g. passenger cars, motorcycles;
- Vulnerable road users, e.g. bicyclists, pedestrians;
- Service technicians;
- The vehicle manufacturing staff.

When a vehicle is operated it interacts with, or influences, things in its environment that may be stationary or moving. The environment includes not only the people potentially at risk above, but also other factors such as:

- The road;
- Road-side objects;
- The atmosphere.

Vehicle hazards arise at the interface between the vehicle and its environment. This interface is called the Vehicle Hazard Boundary, and the term hazard is only used for effects that occur at the Vehicle Hazard Boundary and not for the potential causes of those effects.

AUTOMOTIVE RISK MODEL

In many industry sectors, including those that generated the international standard IEC 61508 [1], the model of risk is as follows:

- There is "equipment under control" (EUC) which poses a risk to its environment, typically associated with a misdirected or uncontrolled release of energy (the hazardous event) (see Figure 1);
- The equipment is controlled by electrical, electronic or programmable electronic (E/E/PE) systems which normally run autonomously. Human responsibilities are mainly supervisory, and active intervention is only performed on rare occasions;
- This risk can be quantified, usually as a combination of the consequences of the hazardous event and the probability of it occurring due to a malfunction of the equipment or its E/E/PE controller;
- Measures need to be taken to reduce this risk to a level considered "broadly acceptable". A broadly acceptable risk is a level of risk commensurate with the risk associated with everyday life (see Figure 2).
- In the context of IEC 61508, these measures include safety functions, implemented in an electrical, electronic or programmable electronic system. The safety functions may either be implemented as a separate protection system or integrated into the EUC's control system.
- The safety requirements for safety functions are set in terms of a Safety Integrity Level (SIL) which covers:
    - Measures to avoid random hardware failures expressed as a design target for the probability of failure to operate on demand (for protection systems) or the maximum acceptable failure rate for dangerous failures (for functions which are part of EUC control systems);
    - Measures to avoid or eliminate systematic failures in the system, hardware and software design;
    - Measures to tolerate random hardware failures;
    - Measures to tolerate systematic failures.

This approach is summarized in Figures 1 and 2:

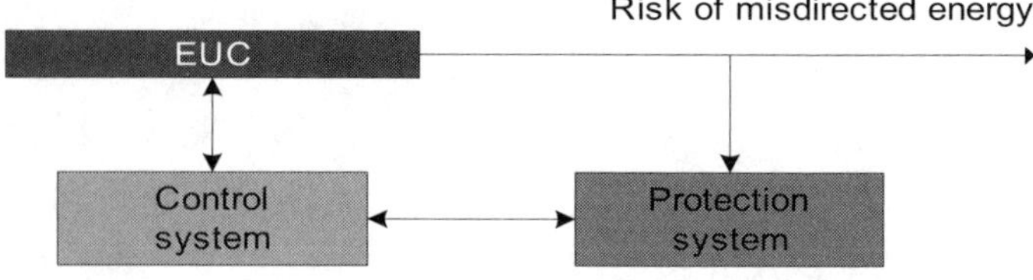

Figure 1: IEC 61508 model of system and safety functions [1]

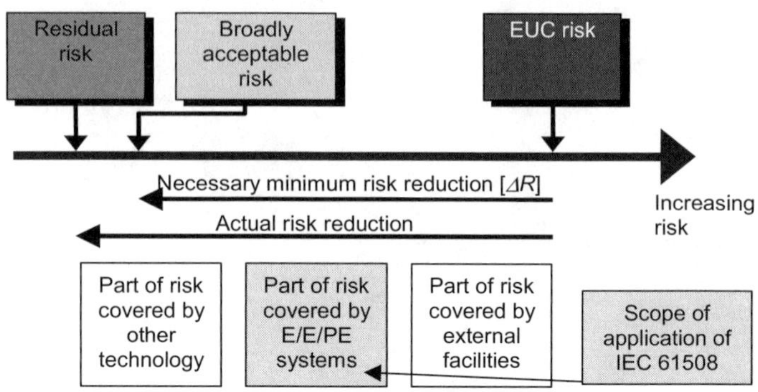

Figure 2: IEC 61508 model of risk reduction [1]

In road vehicles, there are only a few systems which conform to the IEC 61508 view of a protection system or safety function. The majority of vehicle systems are concerned with the control of the motion of the vehicle, and the safety of the situation depends on the correct, normal operation of these systems; not simply on the availability of a specific safety function. Hazards can arise from the failure of these systems to function as specified either through a fault leading to an incorrect state or failure, or through a dangerous function of the system. In addition, hazards can also arise through the interaction of the system with its environment. An example of such an interaction is electromagnetic interference.

There are several types of E/E/PE system, for example:

- Systems that allow the driver to control the motion and behavior of the vehicle (see Figure 3). It should be noted that the driver is normally "in the loop" in terms of vehicle control, and hence must be taken into account when analyzing vehicle system failures.
- Systems that provide information upon which the driver's strategy is devised.
- Systems to which a degree of autonomous control is delegated.

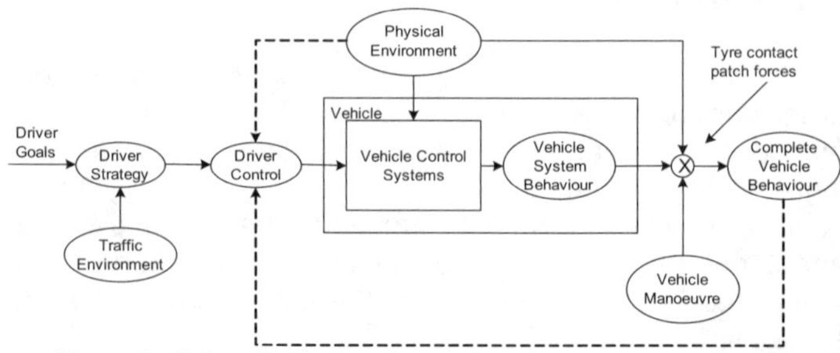

Figure 3: Driver "in the loop" model of vehicle control systems

In the context of a safety function such as those envisaged by IEC 61508, a fault in a technical system will generally lead to a failure to deliver the safety function (depending on the architecture and diagnostic schemes implemented). However, in the automotive context a fault in a technical system does not necessarily lead to a hazardous event. This will only occur if all of the following conditions are true:

- The fault is present in a technical system leading to the system being in an unwanted or potentially dangerous state (the hazard);
- The environmental conditions (including the scenario in which the vehicle is being driven) mean that the driver is exposed to a hazardous situation;
- The driver is unable to control the safety of the situation following the appearance of the hazardous situation.

This dependency may be represented by means of a state machine model, as shown in Figure 4. This model shows the state transitions between a failure occurring in a system and an accident occurring. It should be noted that a failure does not necessarily lead to an accident, and thus in order to perform hazard analysis it is necessary to identify the probabilities of the various transitions occurring.

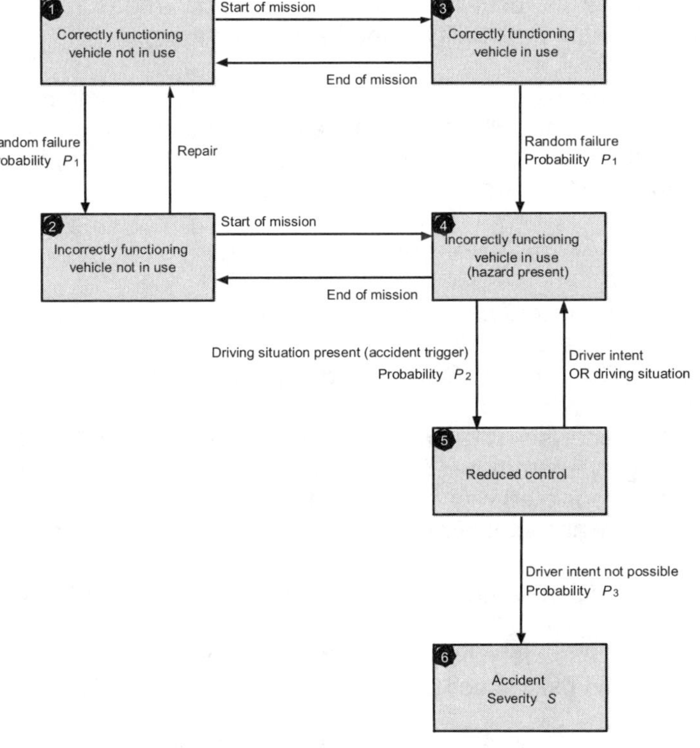

Figure 4: State-machine model of automotive risk

Thus, the risk associated with the hazard is represented by a function of the probabilities of the state transitions and the severity of the accident, and therefore *hazard risk* is defined as

$$f_{HR1}(P_1, P_2, P_3, S).$$

The probabilities are defined as follows:

P_1 = probability that the random failure occurs
P_2 = probability that the accident trigger is present
P_3 = probability that (driver) action to avoid the outcome is not possible

Note that in this equation, since P_1 ... P_3 are probabilities, they are therefore dimensionless. S is not dimensionless, and its units depend on the severity classification scheme chosen. For example, S may be defined in terms of the maximum expected number of fatalities, or it may be linked to an injury severity rating, such as the Abbreviated Injury Scale (AIS).

Based on this model, the following stages in a generalized hazard analysis process are identified:

- Hazard identification
- Hazard classification
- Risk analysis.

These stages are further discussed below.

HAZARD IDENTIFICATION

The hazard identification activity explores the possible hazardous states of the vehicle and/or its systems. Note that a vehicle driving on an empty road under good environmental and road conditions, in a good state of repair and with an alert driver does not constitute a hazardous state. A hazardous state occurs when a fault in a system leads to a failure of a system to perform to specification.

The goal of hazard identification is to identify the potential failure modes of a system that could lead to the vehicle being in a hazardous state. Thus, hazard identification is concerned with identifying the events that could cause a transition from State 1 to State 2, or from State 3 to State 4, in Figure 4.

There is also the situation where the complex interaction of several systems, all functioning as per their specifications, gives rise to unanticipated emergent behavior which is hazardous. In these cases the state transitions have effectively occurred before the vehicle is ever driven.

The hazard identification activity requires a clear definition of the system, its functionality and its boundaries. The detailed design of the system does not necessarily need to be known, as hazard identification techniques are available which can be applied to prospective (i.e. concept) systems. However, an analytical and rigorous method to perform hazard identification (such as HAZOP) is required.

A simple cause and effect chain which will apply under many circumstances is:

- Functions executing on a controller lead to outputs from electro-mechanical actuators which, if not to design intent, result in the vehicle being in a hazardous state.

If the functions are defined at a vehicle level, e.g. as textual descriptions, UML use cases, then hazard identification can be performed by considering "failures" of the ideal function.

Alternatively hazard identification may be performed by considering all possible behaviors of the electro-mechanical actuators without regard to any ideal functions that should be controlling their actions, and the consequent effects of these outputs on the vehicle. Often it is necessary to try both approaches to be sure that all hazards have been found.

Note that in this activity, driving scenarios are not considered, only "black box" failures of the system.

In practice it is usually necessary to consider factors which define a context for determining if a particular failure is indeed a hazard. These factors should not be specified in great detail; rather generalized descriptions should be used. These may include:

- Vehicle usage scenarios, e.g. high-speed driving, urban driving, parking, off-road
- Environmental conditions, e.g. road surface friction, side winds
- Reasonably anticipated driver use/misuse.

HAZARD CLASSIFICATION

Hazard classification is concerned with evaluating the parameters on which the hazard risk depends. In the generalized model these parameters are as follows:

- The probability that the random failure occurs. In Figure 4 this is the probability that a transition occurs from State 1 to State 2 or from State 3 to State 4.
- The probability of exposure to the hazardous situation. In Figure 4 this is the probability that a transition occurs from State 4 to State 5. It is the probability that, if the hazard is present, that there is an "accident trigger" – an external event or condition which means that the driver is exposed to the hazardous situation.
- The probability of failing to avoid the outcome of the hazardous situation. In Figure 4 this is the probability that a transition occurs from State 5 to State 6. It is the probability that if the driver is exposed to the hazardous situation he/she will not be able to exercise control over the situation and prevent an accident from occurring.
- The severity of the outcome (i.e. the severity of the potential accident).

Thus the goal of hazard classification is to determine the probabilities of the state transitions and combine them with the severity in order to allocate a "hazard risk" to the hazard. Note that while the first three parameters are shown as probabilities in the general model, the actual analysis in an instantiation of this model could be either qualitative or quantitative.

RISK ANALYSIS

Risk analysis is concerned with setting requirements for the system such that the risk associated with the hazard is at a broadly acceptable level. In general terms, this is done by identifying whether a hazard risk is greater than the broadly acceptable level; and if so, taking measures to modify one or more of the parameters in the risk equation such that the hazard risk is less than or equal to "broadly acceptable". Note that this analysis relies on the existence of some well-defined measure of broadly acceptable risk.

In general, for automotive systems, the values of "Exposure to hazardous situation", "Possibility to avoid outcome" and "Severity" are generally fixed, given that a decision has been made to implement a particular function using an electronic system. It is sometimes possible to alter these probabilities using "other technology safety-related systems" and/or "external risk reduction facilities" (see Figure 2). However the primary objective of this hazard analysis is to assess the requirements for implementing an electronic system for which it is usually necessary to apply measures to reduce the probability of the hazard occurring.

One means to achieve this is to set "safety integrity" requirements which can be aimed at addressing both random failures and systematic faults. In this case, it is possible to re-write P_1 as[1]:

$$P_1 = f_1(\textit{Safety Integrity})$$

and the *hazard risk* can now be defined as

$$f_{HR1}(f_1(\textit{Safety Integrity}), P_2, P_3, S).$$

Risk analysis is then a process of setting the "safety integrity" parameter for each hazard to ensure that the risk associated with that hazard is at or below the level of broadly acceptable risk, so that, for a particular hazard,

$$f_{HR1}(f_1(\textit{Safety Integrity}), P_2, P_3, S) \leq \textit{broadly acceptable}$$

Using this definition it is also possible to define the required risk reduction as $f_{RRR}(P_2, P_3, S)$ such that

$$\textit{Safety integrity} = f_{RRR}(P_2, P_3, S).$$

In this case the "required risk reduction" function incorporates the measure of broadly acceptable risk and results in the minimum safety integrity necessary to achieve the broadly acceptable risk.

---

[1] In this section the notation $f_X(\ldots)$ is used to denote a generalized function which maps the parameters

In practice a system will have several hazards and it is standard practice to set the initial safety integrity requirement for the system to be the highest of all of the safety integrity (SI) requirements of the individual hazards.

$$SI_{system} = \max(SI_1, SI_2, \ldots SI_n)$$

During design and implementation of the system it may be possible to allocate and/or partition these requirements to different parts of the system, provided that a rigorous means for doing so is defined, and that appropriate criteria for assessing the decisions are provided.

Once the system has been developed, it is necessary to demonstrate that the required safety integrity has been achieved for all hazards. In some cases, it may be necessary to apply a principle such as ALARP ("as low as reasonably practicable") if the required safety integrity cannot be achieved, and the effort required do so would be grossly disproportionate to the additional benefit that would be realized by achieving it.

HAZARD CLASSIFICATION USING A RISK GRAPH

As described above, hazard classification involves assigning values to most of the parameters on which the hazard risk depends. In the automotive context this means evaluating the expression:

$$\textit{broadly acceptable} = f_{HR1}(f_1(\textit{Safety Integrity}), P_2, P_3, S)$$

A common approach to evaluating such a function in a qualitative manner is to use a risk graph. In the automotive context, the probability of transition from State 4 to State 5 is evaluated using the "frequency of exposure" (E) parameter, thus $P_2 = E$; whilst the probability of transition from State 5 to State 6 is evaluated using the "possibility to avoid" (A) parameter, thus $P_3 = A$. The risk graph evaluates the required risk reduction and hence provides a partial evaluation of the hazard risk for each hazard.

Thus, in the automotive context:

$$\textit{required risk reduction (RRR)} = f_{RRR}(P_2, P_3, S)$$

which can be written as $f_{RRR}(S, E, A)$ with the parameters now listed in the order of their evaluation by the risk graph.

Each parameter of the required risk reduction function is assigned a number of values that it may take, e.g.

$S \cong [S_1, S_2, \ldots]$
$E \cong [E_1, E_2, \ldots]$
$A \cong [A_1, A_2, \ldots]$

The risk graph then allows the function to be evaluated by choosing a value for each parameter in turn, as shown in the following table:

S	E	A	RRR
S_1	E_1	A_1	RRR_X
		A_2	RRR_Y
		…	…
	E_2	A_1	
		A_2	
		…	
	…	A_1	
		A_2	
		…	
S_2	E_1	A_1	
		A_2	
		…	
	E_2	A_1	
		A_2	
		…	
	…	A_1	
		A_2	
		…	
…			

The value of each parameter is chosen in order {S, E and A} to arrive at the resulting required risk reduction. This can be thought of as replacing the base function, $f_{RRR}(S, E, A)$ with a series of curried[2] functions. Given the following definition of f_{RRR}:

$$f_{RRR}: (S \times E \times A) \rightarrow RRR$$

Replacing f_{RRR} with its curried version gives:

$$f_{RRR1}: S \rightarrow ((E \times A) \rightarrow RRR)$$

f_{RRR1} is evaluated by selecting the value for the S parameter and effectively produces another function:

$$f_{RRR2}: (E \times A) \rightarrow RRR$$

Replacing f_{RRR2} with its curried version gives:

$$f_{RRR3}: E \rightarrow (A \rightarrow RRR)$$

f_{RRR3} is evaluated by selecting the value for the E parameter and effectively produces another function

$$f_{RRR4}: A \rightarrow RRR$$

f_{RRR4} is evaluated by selecting the value for the A parameter and produces the final required risk reduction result.

[2] "Currying" in the mathematical context is the technique of transforming a function that takes multiple arguments into a function that takes a single argument

PARAMETER VALUE SELECTION

In constructing a risk graph it is necessary to consider two related issues:

1. How many values each parameter is allowed to take;
2. The actual values the parameters may take.

The number of values

The values in a risk graph are qualitative and the selection of the correct value is a judgment rather than a measurement.

The following general observations about this process may be made:

- The greater the number of values a parameter is permitted to take, the less likely it is that the analysis will produce a consistent result;
- Too few values for parameters will not allow necessary detail to be taken into account;
- Parameters should allow distinctions to be made that are necessary to affect the end result significantly, and that can be decided upon with sufficient confidence;
- In general a change of one step for a single parameter value will allow the outcome to change by one step, provided the other values remain fixed;
- The greater the number of values that a parameter is allowed to take, the more sensitive the final result is to that parameter. Therefore the greater the number of values a parameter is allowed to have, the greater must be the confidence that a value can be assigned in a repeatable manner, and that such numbers of values are necessary.

Severity parameter

The number of values taken by the severity parameter depends on the scope of the analysis, for example whether accidents are considered to be limited to outcomes involving a single vehicle or whether multiple vehicle outcomes are considered.

In general, injury does have a recognized severity scale, called the accident injury severity (AIS) scale. This scale is based on a medical assessment of injuries, co-incidentally derived from automotive accident victims. The AIS has 6 levels which can be conveniently condensed into three severity values, as shown in Table 1.

Severity	Maximum AIS	Description
S_1	1, 2	Minor injuries
S_2	3, 4	Major injuries
S_3	5, 6	Severe or life-threatening injuries (with the possibility of a maximum of one fatality)

Table 1: AIS-based severity definitions

Exposure parameter

This parameter represents the probability that the situation is such that the failure of the system (the hazard) is present in a hazardous situation.

For those failures where the driver's ability to maintain control of the vehicle has been reduced, then the issues that create a hazardous situation include:

- The environment (weather conditions) hot/cold, dark/light, wet/dry, hilly/flat;
- The road style: number of lanes, junction types, surfaces, signage;
- The status of the vehicle when the failure occurs (speed, direction);
- The density and status of other vehicles, or road users, in the vicinity.

When a value is being assigned to the exposure parameter it will need to be what can reasonably be assumed to be an average value taking into account:

- All markets into which the vehicle is sold;
- The possible driving styles of the customers;
- The possible vehicle usage patterns: urban, multi-lane, single lane, rural roads, towing.

Clearly, given so much diversity inherent within a global mass market product, it is difficult to be very precise in making this judgment, and therefore it would be prudent not to allow this parameter to have too many possible values. For those failures which do not affect the driver's ability to maintain control of the vehicle, the exposure is related to the time spent in the proximity to the hazardous system failure, for example the time spent working under the hood for vehicle repairers to be exposed to the un-commanded movement of mechanical parts, cooling fans, etc.

Avoidance parameter

This parameter represents the probability that the driver, and/or other people affected, can by their own actions contain the situation and avoid an accident occurring. This is assuming that the system failure has already occurred and that those affected are exposed to the hazardous situation and that without such actions the result will be an accident.

There are broadly 3 possible driver/participant actions:

1. Do nothing
2. Perform what could be considered to be a normal human action, based on the assumption that the driver has had appropriate training and experience to be driving the vehicle in the first place
3. Perform what could be considered an exceptional human reaction, either by design or by chance.

For systems which can be represented using the "driver in the loop" model (see Figure 3) the concept of "controllability" [2] is useful for assessing the possibility to avoid the hazard. In this case, controllability refers to the ability of the driver (or other traffic participant) to control the safety of the situation in the presence of the hazard.

When evaluating the controllability of a hazard, action (1) is not considered to be an appropriate response on the grounds that for this to occur one or more of the following would be true:

- The driver has not been trained to operate the type of vehicle and/or in the conditions being experienced;
- The driver is grossly inexperienced;
- The driver is under the influence of substances which can impair performance (alcohol, drugs);
- The driver's state of arousal is not conducive to normal reactions (e.g. extreme fatigue or stress, "jet lag").

These situations are considered to be outside the safety envelope. Similarly, action (3) is not considered acceptable on the basis that there is only a very small fraction of the driving population with these exceptional skills and it is inappropriate to rely on chance. Therefore action (2) is considered to be the norm.

For those failures where the driver's ability to maintain control of the vehicle has been reduced, the ability of the driver depends on:

- The level of system inter-dependency;
- The loss of authority or control due to the system failure;
- The provision of backup or other mitigation;
- The reaction time of the driver and/or other people affected.

For a particular application of a system to a vehicle most of these factors are known with a high degree of certainty, and it is only the reaction time that must be assessed. Based on the assessment of the loss of authority or control, the effort required by the driver (or other participants, but primarily the driver) to take actions that maintain the safety of the situation has to be assessed, taking into account the following reaction time factors:

- Recognizing the change of circumstances;
- Formulating a strategy to maintain the safety of the situation;
- Applying the corrective actions.

It should be noted that whether the failure to maintain the safety of the situation results in an accident is taken into account by the Exposure parameter.

The intuitive relationship between the loss of control and the mitigation effort required to maintain the safety of the situation is shown in Figure 5. This also shows the mitigation effort which it is reasonable to assume that the average driver can achieve.

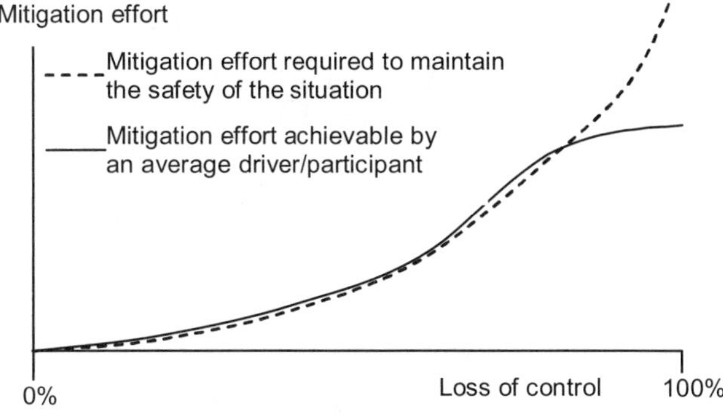

Figure 5: Model of mitigation effort

Figure 5 captures the intuition that the mitigation effort to maintain the safety of the situation increases in a non-linear manner from zero, for no loss of control, to a high value as more control is lost. Figure 5 also shows that it can be reasonably expected that the driver will provide the increasing mitigation effort up to a certain point but after that an accident is inevitable.

When deciding the number of parameters and their possible values the "Mitigation effort" is effectively being divided into a number of broadly equivalent regions. If the intuitive shape of the curve is correct, then if the regions represent constant changes in mitigation effort, they will not represent constant changes in loss of control.

When assigning a value of controllability it is necessary to make a judgment based on an average for the whole global driving population of the vehicle throughout its lifetime.

For those failures which do not affect the driver's ability to maintain control of the vehicle, the action to avoid the hazardous event is usually to physically remove oneself, or a body part, from the hazardous area. In these cases it is appropriate to consider only whether or not this is reasonably possible, and not to have a large number of possible values of the parameter.

Applying a risk graph

When using a risk graph for hazard classification it is necessary to employ a diverse team to perform the classification, including domain experts, systems experts and non-expert ordinary users. During the analysis, the rationale, and any assumptions, for the selection of values should be recorded along with the value chosen.

HAZARD CLASSIFICATION AND THE MISRA RISK GRAPH

In this section, the generic risk approach presented above is applied to the MISRA Risk Graph [2]. The MISRA Risk Graph itself is shown in Figure 6.

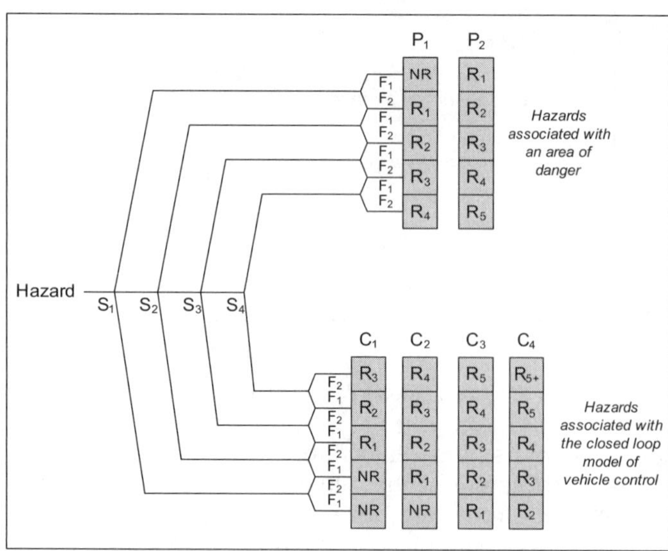

Figure 6: The MISRA Risk Graph

As stated above, the purpose of the Risk Graph is to produce a ranking of hazards in terms of their risk. Risk analysis then assigns Safety Integrity Requirements to the design such that the resulting risk associated with the hazard is "broadly acceptable".

The parameters in the MISRA Risk Graph are as follows.

SEVERITY PARAMETER

This is represented in the MISRA Risk Graph by the Severity factor (*S*), which is the severity of the outcome, and which is calibrated with reference to the accident injury severity (AIS) scale. The scope of the MISRA Risk graph includes systems which can affect more than a single vehicle, so an additional value for the severity parameter, S_4, is also used. See Table 2:

Severity	Maximum AIS	Description
S_1	1, 2	Minor injuries
S_2	3, 4	Major injuries
S_3	5, 6	Severe or life-threatening injuries (with the possibility of a maximum of one fatality)
S_4	5, 6	Severe or life-threatening injuries (with the possibility of multiple fatalities)

Table 2: MISRA Severity definitions

EXPOSURE PARAMETER

This is represented in the MISRA Risk Graph by the Frequency of Exposure factor (*F*), which represents the frequency of, and time of exposure in, the hazardous zone. Only two values are allowed, due to the difficulty of assessing this value with great precision. If F1 is chosen it means a significant risk reduction can be argued from reduced exposure.

Exposure	Description
F_1	Rare exposure in the hazardous zone
F_2	Frequent to permanent exposure in the hazardous zone

Table 3: MISRA Exposure definitions

AVOIDANCE PARAMETER

The MISRA Risk Graph provides two methods for representing this parameter, Controllability and Possibility to Avoid.

Controllability was first devised as part of the Drive Safely project in 1992 [4]. It represents the possibility that, for systems where the driver is "in the [control] loop", the driver can take action to control the safety of the situation following the failure and hence reduce the risk. Experience has shown that four different values are necessary and sufficient to properly distinguish the driver's ability to provide mitigation effort.

Controllability	Description
C_1	This relates to hazardous situations that produce operational limitations, but avoidance of an accident is normally possible with a normal human response.
C_2	This relates to hazardous situations where there is a reduction in the safety margin, and whilst avoidance of an accident is difficult, it is usually possible with a sensible human response.
C_3	This relates to hazardous situations that are not normally controllable, and avoidance of an accident is very difficult. However, under favorable circumstances, some control can be maintained by an experienced human response.
C_4	This relates to hazardous situations that are not controllable, and the outcome cannot be influenced by a human response.

Table 4: MISRA Controllability definitions

For example, this scheme has been used by chassis dynamics experts to assess failures of systems that affect a vehicle's handling characteristics based on the type of assignment shown in Table 5.

Controllability	Vehicle behavior	Driver intervention
C_1	Unimpaired precision in vehicle positioning	Readily controllable Minimal extra intervention required
C_2	Reduced precision in vehicle positioning	Controlled by expert Influenced by typical driver
C_3	Inadequate precision in vehicle positioning	Controlled by expert driver Favorable conditions
C_4	Total loss of precision in vehicle positioning	Total irretrievable loss of control

Table 5: Vehicle dynamics view of Controllability

In terms of the intuitive relationship between mitigation effort and loss of control shown in Figure 5, the MISRA use of controllability maps this relationship as shown in Figure 7.

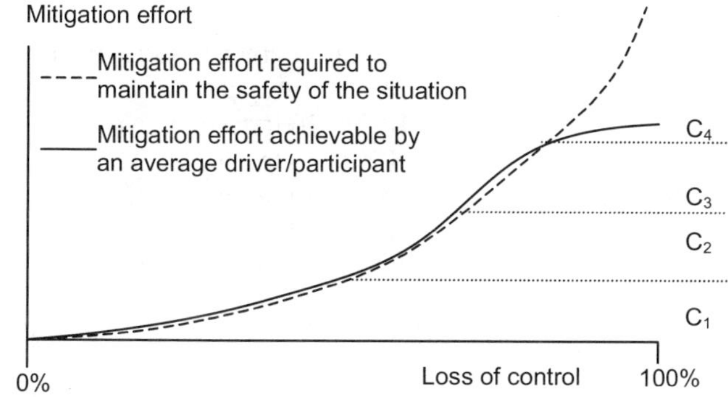

Figure 7: MISRA Controllability relation to mitigation

By definition, the MISRA C_4 classification applies at the point at which the driver is unable to provide the required mitigation.

The Possibility to Avoid parameter is also used because experience has shown that a "controllability" approach did not work well for hazards that are not associated with the closed loop model of vehicle control (see Figure 3), or that require classical protection systems in the sense envisaged by IEC 61508. Examples of such system failures include:

- Failure of an air bag to deploy in a crash event;
- Movement of the seats resulting in crushing or trapping the occupants;
- Movement of the vehicle body resulting in crushing or trapping the those working on a vehicle;
- The continued delivery of fuel after a crash;
- Doors being locked after a crash event;
- Production of smoke or fire;
- Ejection of hot fluid during crash events resulting in burns to vehicle occupants or rescue workers.

For these types of system failures the Possibility to Avoid (*P*) parameter is used, which represents the possibility that the person exposed to the risk can take an action to avoid it. Only two values of *P* are used, since it is not considered possible to distinguish between different situations with any greater precision than this. If P_1 is chosen, it means that a significant risk reduction can be argued from the action to avoid.

Avoidance	Description
P_1	Possible under certain conditions
P_2	Almost impossible

Table 6: MISRA Possibility to avoid definitions

In terms of evaluating the risk graph, P_1 is equivalent to C_2 and P_2 is equivalent to C_3. There is no equivalence to C_4, since these types of hazards are not associated with (high-speed) movement of the vehicle, and those that could produce multiple fatalities, due to scalding or burning, will always include additional mitigation to a E/E/PE system.

SAFETY INTEGRITY REQUIREMENTS

The result of evaluating the MISRA Risk Graph is the MISRA Risk Level (*R*).

The probability of a failure occurring is not directly evaluated, but instead the safety integrity requirements are used to ensure that the probability of failure is sufficiently low such that the level of risk is broadly acceptable or better, thus $P_1 = f_1(\textit{Safety Integrity})$.

That is, the Safety Integrity Requirements are allocated to the system such that:

$$f_{HR1}(f_1(R), F, C, S) \leq (\textit{broadly acceptable risk})$$

or

$$f_{HR1}(f_1(R), F, P, S) \leq (\textit{broadly acceptable risk})$$

The evaluation of $f_1(R)$ is described below in the section on MISRA risk analysis.

MISRA RISK ANALYSIS

Risk analysis is concerned with setting requirements for the system such that the risk associated with the hazard is at a broadly acceptable level. Standards such as IEC 61508 specify requirements in terms of four categories:

- Measures to avoid random hardware failures;
- Measures to avoid or eliminate systematic failures in the system, hardware and software design;
- Measures to tolerate random hardware failures;
- Measures to tolerate systematic failures.

The MISRA Safety Analysis Guidelines provide a proposal for those measures which can avoid random hardware failures. Measures to avoid or eliminate systematic failures in the software design can be found in the MISRA 1994 Guidelines [5]. The scope of the MISRA Safety Analysis Guidelines does not include measures to avoid or eliminate systematic failures in the system and hardware design, or measures to tolerate random hardware failures, or measures to tolerate systematic failures, but a mapping from the results of the Hazard Classification to other standards, e.g. IEC 61508 and ISO 26262, is provided. These standards can also be used as a source of measures to avoid or eliminate systematic failures in the software design.

USE OF STANDARDS TO DETERMINE SAFETY INTEGRITY REQUIREMENTS

MISRA supplies a mapping from the *R* parameter, produced by the MISRA Risk Graph, to common functional safety standards [1, 3] as shown in Table 7.

MISRA Risk Level	IEC 61508	ISO 26262
R_1	SIL1	ASILA
R_2	SIL1	ASILB
R_3	SIL2	ASILC
R_4	SIL3	ASILD
R_5	SIL4	NA
R_{5+}	See below	NA

Table 7: MISRA Risk Level mapping to systematic safety integrity requirements

Both standards specify Safety Integrity Requirements for all four requirement categories as expressed by SIL or ASIL.

MISRA PROPOSAL FOR MEASURES TO AVOID RANDOM HARDWARE FAILURES

The MISRA safety criterion is expressed as:

$$f_{HR1}(f_1(R), F, C, S) \leq (\textit{broadly acceptable risk})$$

or

$$f_{HR1}(f_1(R), F, P, S) \leq (\textit{broadly acceptable risk})$$

The MISRA proposal for the measures to avoid random hardware failures is expressed as a design target for the maximum acceptable failure rate for dangerous failures, *h*. Considering this parameter alone

$$f_{HR2}(h_n, F, C, S) \leq (\textit{broadly acceptable risk})$$

or

$$f_{HR2}(h_n, F, P, S) \leq (\textit{broadly acceptable risk})$$

The reference value of *h* is determined for the case where the severity includes a fatality, S_3, and where *F* and *C*, or *P*, are both set to unity, i.e. that an accident trigger has occurred and the driver is not able to avoid an accident (which implies a Risk Level of R_4), therefore

$$h_4 \leq (\textit{acceptable hazard occurrence frequency})$$

Using the Minimum Endogenous Mortality for technological causes it can be shown that:

$$(\text{broadly acceptable risk}) = 10^{-6} < P(\text{Fatality}) < 10^{-5} \text{ per person-year}$$

The probability of a fatality from an accident in the UK can be shown to be 1×10^{-3}. Assuming that there are 10^4 hours in a year and that there is a contribution from no more than 10 relevant vehicle-based systems, (therefore the system safety target is a factor of 10 lower than that of the hazard probability for the vehicle as a whole), it can be shown that the value of *h* for R_4, the worst case for a single vehicle, is:

$$h_4 = 10^{-8} \leq P(\text{Hazard}) < 10^{-7} \text{ per hour}$$

As is the convention with safety standards, the other values of *h* are produced by an order of magnitude change for each value of *R*. The full set of requirements is shown in Table 8.

MISRA Risk Level	*h* – Acceptable Hazard Occurrence Frequency per hour
R_1	$10^{-5} \leq P(\text{Hazard}) < 10^{-4}$
R_2	$10^{-6} \leq P(\text{Hazard}) < 10^{-5}$
R_3	$10^{-7} \leq P(\text{Hazard}) < 10^{-6}$
R_4	$10^{-8} \leq P(\text{Hazard}) < 10^{-7}$
R_5	$10^{-9} \leq P(\text{Hazard}) < 10^{-8}$
R_{5+}	See below

Table 8: MISRA Risk Level mapping to random safety integrity requirements

R_{5+} denotes a situation that is only considered to be acceptable on very rare occasions, and then only with the agreement of senior management. In addition, sole reliance should never be placed on E/E/PE systems to maintain the safety of the situation, and the acceptable hazard occurrence (see Table 8) should be at least an order of magnitude smaller than for R_5.

CONCLUSION

This paper has presented a generic risk model for automotive programmable systems, which takes into account the special characteristics of the automotive sector and the way in which safety-related systems are used in road vehicles. From this model, the distinct stages of hazard identification, hazard classification and risk analysis are identified.

An existing method for automotive hazard classification, the MISRA Risk Graph, was examined, and it was demonstrated that this method conforms to the generic risk model and therefore is highly suited for use as a means of classifying hazards in the automotive domain.

The generic model may also be used to describe other hazard classification schemes, and hence to provide a mechanism for comparing the results obtained from different approaches.

ACKNOWLEDGMENTS

The authors would like to acknowledge the contribution made to this work by other participants in the MISRA Safety Analysis activity, notably Richard Evans. The authors would like to thank the MISRA members and the management of their respective employers for giving permission to publish this paper.

REFERENCES

1. IEC 61508, *Functional safety of electrical/electronic/programmable electronic safety-related systems,* IEC, 1998–2005 (8 parts).
2. *Guidelines for the Safety Analysis of Vehicle-Based Programmable Systems*, MISRA, in preparation.
3. ISO 26262, *Road vehicles — Functional safety*, in preparation.
4. DRIVE Safely, *Towards a European Standard: The Development of Safe Road Transport Informatic Systems*, 1992.
5. *Development guidelines for vehicle based software*, (The "MISRA Guidelines"), ISBN 0 9524156 0 7, MIRA, 1994.

CONTACT

Dr David D. Ward
MIRA Ltd
Watling Street
Nuneaton
Warwickshire
CV10 0TU
UK

Tel: + 44 24 7635 5430
Fax: + 44 24 7635 8430

E-mail: david.ward@mira.co.uk
Internet: http://www.mira.co.uk/

Roger S. Rivett
Land Rover
Abbey Road
Whitley
CV3 4LF
UK

Tel: + 44 24 7620 7331
Fax: + 44 24 7620 4670

Email: rrivett@landrover.com

Eur Ing Peter H. Jesty
Peter Jesty Consulting Ltd
Warwick Lodge
Towton
Tadcaster
LS24 9PB
UK

Tel: + 44 1937 833640
Fax: + 44 1937 531579

Email: phj@peterjesty.com

2006-01-1498

Application Development for Safety Critical Distributed Embedded Systems with Model Verification

Marc Schanne and Andreas Judt
Forschungszentrum Informatik (FZI)

ABSTRACT

The increasing use of distributed applications in real-time and safety critical embedded systems results in the need for functional and non-functional system verification in the design process. This paper proposes model verification as solution to identify concept ional design failures in advance, and to verify model correctness in an abstract level.
With an extension to classical model checking environments like SPIN, or real-time model verification tools like UPPAAL, it is possible to analyze communication in distributed systems and verify design decisions compared to real hardware and system environments like network bandwidth or computing capabilities. With identification of communication points in distributed embedded systems and annotation of non-functional system requirements model verification can be adapted to support application development for safety critical systems in automotive or avionics.

1 INTRODUCTION

The use of distributed, object-oriented applications in the domain of safety critical systems requires a profound verification of used technologies and implementations. In recent years object-oriented technologies get more and more accepted in the field of safety critical and business critical systems [10]. Even if the discussion is controversial [19], the partner in the ongoing research project for High Integrity Java Applications[1] (HIJA) [1, 18] support the development of safety critical and business critical systems with object-oriented techniques and several verification tools.

The main focus in the project is the definition of Architecturally Neutral, high-integrity Real-Time Systems (ANRTS) with use of Java technology for the implementation of networked real-time embedded systems. The addressed application area requires the use of static verification to guarantee the implementation without any failures. To get a bird's eye view of the proposed tool chain section 3 introduces these with respect to the model checking tool presented later in this paper.

- The analysis of concurrent real-time threads for scheduling is provided for periodic and sporadic tasks with rate monotonic techniques;
- Worst-case execution time analysis provides upper bounds for method execution without interaction and blocking for single threads;
- Resource demands related to the different Java memory areas are analyzed for all application's tasks;
- Data-related assertions, pre-, post-conditions, and invariants are verified with a theorem prover adapted from the KeY project [3]; and
- Verification problems such as checking for misuse of RTSJ memory areas or potential null-pointer exceptions are checked with static data flow analysis based on the intermediate representation of the application in the Jamaica compiler [2].

The goal of model checking is differing and allows orthogonally the use of the other results and user annotations. With model checking non-functional timing requirements in networked high integrity systems are verified against real hardware and runtime environments. The proposed tool allows the verification of ANRTS implementations to assist the user in developing for the HIJA network model and his application protocol design.

The strength of model-checking is the verification of control flow with identification of unanticipated interleaving of concurrent threads, parallel execution, and communication. The following subsection discusses this for HIJA in an abstract way and provides a basis for the model checking tool design in section 4.

1.1 INTENDED BENEFITS OF MODEL CHECKING

Particularly for safety critical and business critical systems it is not enough to merely show that a system can meet its requirements (i.e., with extensive tests), it is necessary to show, that a system cannot fail to meet its requirements.

Model checking of finite state machines can verify critical system behavior. With careful simplification, model

---

1 IST-511718, partially funded by the European Commission in the 6th framework program

checking can identify non-pseudo errors in the implementation of networked safety-critical systems [13]. While formal verification concentrates on small programs due to its complexity, model checking provides a good compromise between testing and formal verification methods. Failures in a simplified program do not necessarily occur in the original: they indicate positions in the program where errors may cause a system failure. The challenge of code simplification is to avoid state explosion while errors in the model should assist the user to find errors in the original implementation.

The approach in the HIJA project simplifies a Java implementation of a distributed safety critical embedded system. The section 4.1 introduces the method used to parse and analyze Java source code with additional user's annotations. We concentrate on time constraints for real-time network communication and real-time method execution. With simplification and automated generation a set of timed automata, which describe the system's real-time constraints and communication patterns are identified. With additional descriptions of the used hardware these automata can be extended with assertions about the runtime environment with network bandwidth or computing capabilities. Section 4.2 specifies this mechanism and proposes a model generator for code simplification and generic identification of communication protocols. The adherence and feasibility of the complete system with respect to real hardware constraints can then be validated with model checkers for timed automata [17] like UPPAAL [7].

An error in the models can provide a hint for an error in the system's implementation or indicates potentially improper conditions for the used execution environments. In contrast, an error free checking cannot guarantee error-free execution, but this model checking approach can be used in software development tools to find errors in the development phase that have to be tested with prototype hardware. We believe that this approach reduces the number of iterations in the development process of high-integrity real-time systems. Compared to related work – introduced in the next section – the HIJA approach benefits from the integration in a full tool chain for the development of safety critical and business critical systems.

2 RELATED WORK

Software developers choose from three approaches for model checking. The first approach translates a program into a model checker's input language. The second approach is to develop language specific tools, while the third checks programs with a combination of both.

The Bandera project [8] addresses one of the major obstacles in the path of practical finite-state verification of software. Tools like SPIN use a simple programming language as formal description of finite state machines. Programs have to be simplified and translated into languages like PROMELA. The simplification causes the loss of program semantics, for example, computation with float numbers. Bandera uses a simplified Java language as formal description. The use of Java allows developers to concentrate on simplification rather than translation from an object-oriented to a functional language. Bandera integrates existing programming language processing techniques with techniques to provide automated support for the extraction of finite-state models that are suitable for verification from Java source code. Today, the Bandera system cannot extract a model automatically [14]. It requires guidance from a software analyst to simplify the original Java code.

Java PathFinder 2 (JPF) [5] is a system to verify executable Java byte code programs. In its basic form, it is a Java Virtual Machine that is used as an explicit state software model checker, systematically exploring all potential execution paths of a program to find violations of properties like deadlocks or unhandled exceptions. JPF reports the entire execution path that leads to a defect. JPF is enabled developers to find hard-to-test concurrency defects in multithreaded programs. JPF addresses the state explosion problem of model checking with a state collapsing mechanism that creates states on-the-fly. JPF calculates the states from a simplified and predicate-abstracted Java program. State sets are created with the included Bandera model checker. As SPIN used PROMELA as formalization, JPF used Java byte code. The JPF Virtual Machine is optimized for model checking, not for speed of execution. Predicate abstraction can lead to counter-examples that cannot occur from execution. These pseudo-errors have to be checked with the original program.

While JPF and Bandera try to use the full Java language as a formal description, the HIJA model checking approach reduces the Java implementation of safety critical distributed embedded systems to their points of communication. The result of our simplification is a set of timed communicating finite state machines which are checked with the UPPAAL model checker.

3 TOOL CHAIN

The proposed model checking tool is part of a tool chain developed in the HIJA project. The goal of high integrity applications is addressed with several verification tools described in this section. Based on the facility of real-time threads and networks distributed applications can be implemented. Hard real-time applications for safety critical systems need static feasibility analysis for scheduling and network utilization. The execution time for local, non-blocked of single methods can be bound to an upper limit by use of a Worst-Case Execution Time Analysis (WCETA) tool. With Worst-Case Memory Usage Analysis (WCMUA) the application's demand for stack and heap memory areas is analyzed. The KeY tool performs deductive verification of functional properties of the annotated code, and directly integrated in the byte code to native code compiler a static data flow analysis (DFA) based on the used intermediate program representation is provided.

3.1 SCHEDULING AND NETWORK ANALYSIS

The aim of scheduling analysis is the calculation of worst-case response time bounds for each schedulable object, it verifies if these periodic and sporadic threads meet their deadlines. The used standard response time analysis mainly includes three steps: assign priorities, calculate the blocking times, and calculate the response times.

For the addressed distributed applications the calculated blocking time results from local processor sharing and network usage and available bandwidth. For both measurement scenarios the analysis tool builds on the Modeling and Analysis Suite for Real-Time Applications (MAST) [4].

3.2 WORST-CASE EXECUTION TIME ANALYSIS

The WCETA concentrates on the execution time in a single thread. The HIJA analysis tool is build on top of the WCETA tool Gromit [11], which is adapted for the use with machine code in the form of ELF that is provided by the byte code to native code compiler.

3.3 WORST-CASE MEMORY USAGE ANALYSIS

WCMUA is used to calculate maximum stack use for all non-recursive method calls and the maximum amount of allocation in all heap areas. The tool verifies that the worst-case memory usage doesn't exceed the specified and available memory space. To verify the correctness of memory management using region-based allocation as provided by the RTSJ the static data flow analysis in section 3.5 is used.

3.4 THEOREM PROVER FOR FUNCTIONAL ANALYSIS

The KeY tool [3] performs deductive verification of an annotated Java code in order to statically prove its correctness according to its specifications. The specification of functional properties – verified by KeY – follow the design by contract paradigm, and assertions with pre-, post-conditions, and invariants are specified with the Java Modeling Language (JML) [15].

3.5 STATIC DATA FLOW ANALYSIS

Data-flow related verification is provided by a static data flow analysis integrated in the byte code to native code compiler of the JamaicaVM toolbox [2]. The DFA verifies the correctness of region-based memory area allocation rules by RTSJ, the absence of deadlocks in the local application, and the absence of Java runtime error conditions such as class-cast and null-pointer exceptions.

The application wide data flow analysis is basically a simple iterative algorithm that records for each variable in the system the set of all values that this variable may hold in the current implementation analyses only reference values. there is currently no representation of primitive types. The analysis iteratively adds elements to these sets as long as assignments are found that add new values to these sets. The algorithm stops when a fixed point is reached, this is, when there are no assignments left that would add values to a variable that are not yet recorded in the value set for that variable. The DFA has the difficulty of finding a compromise between the accuracy of the analysis and the efficiency of the analysis for non-trivial applications. The implementation avoids state explosion by managing complexity with less accurate analysis strategies.

4 MODEL CHECKING TOOL DESIGN

The proposed model checking tool differs from the other verification tools in the introduced tool chain. It is designed orthogonally and allows the use of the other results as input.

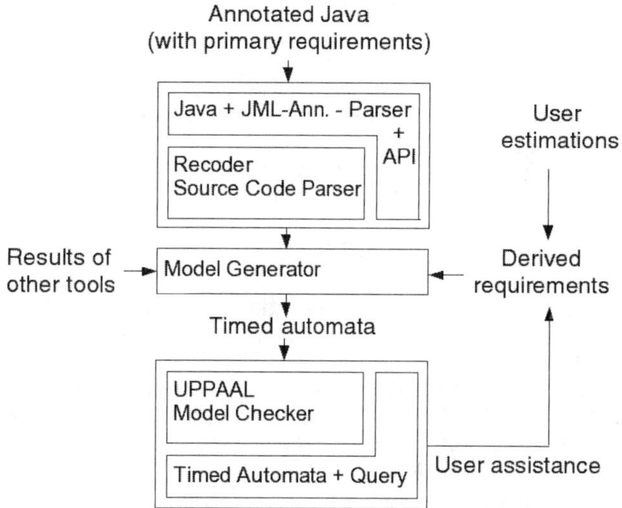

Figure 1: Design of the model checking tool

The figure 1 depicts the component structure of the model checking tool with its relationship to external inputs, that are, Java code with annotated primary requirements and results from other tools or estimations from the application developer.

This section introduces the model checking tool in the HIJA research project for verification of implicit protocols in distributed systems implementations. The design and usage of the tool is introduced by means of the component structure. The three main components are described in the following subsections with respect to their logical tasks and used external tools and APIs.

The tool verifies developer's design decisions by automatic identification of control-flow and interaction protocols out of the application source code. For the second level of use non-functional timing requirements in the ANRTS description are verified against real hardware and runtime environments. . In the first level of use the proposed model checking tool identifies control flow and communication points in the source code by parsing the application. An abstract execution of the control flow extracts a sequence of Java statements and in the second part this information is aggregated with parsed annotations to simplified timed automata. The last component encapsulates the external real-time model checker UPPAAL and provides generic queries to assist the developer for the implementation of integrity distributed applications.

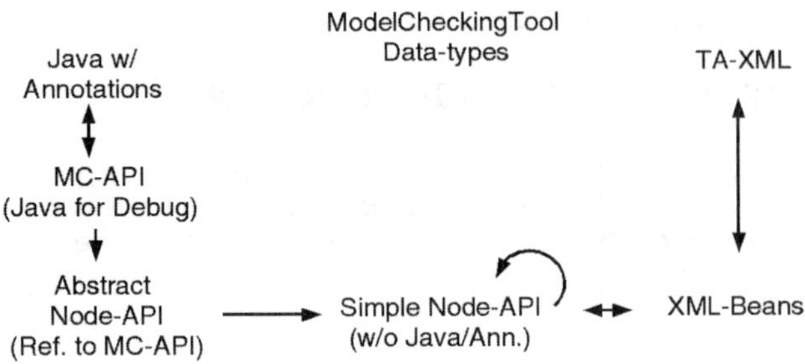

Figure 2: Data-types

A second overview of the tool components gives figure 2 with internal data-types for exchange. The annotated Java code is transformed in several steps into timed automata, encoded with TA-XML, for the model checker UPPAAL. With additional queries these can be checked for common protocol failures and timing problems.

4.1 PARSER FOR ANNOTATED SOURCE CODE

The entry component in the model checking tool represents a Java code and annotation parser (compare figure 1). This parser reads the ANRTS description and generates a sequence of statements, representing an abstract and simplified program execution. Figure 3 shows a fragment of the UML class diagram.

In the first level of use the proposed model checking tool identifies control flow and communication points for the Java RMI protocol as indicated in the class diagram.

With an abstract execution of the control flow the Parser extracts a sequence of Java statements relevant for remote communication.

Loops and conditional statements are returned without really execution and the state in local and instance variables are available over an context object. To avoid state explosion the generator in section 4.2 tries to extract only necessary values.
To support the automated extraction it is possible to annotate each statement with a special comment similar to tags of Java Modeling Language (JML) [15]. The following code fragment demonstrates some possible declarations:

```
04: //@ compoint id = "init";
05: s.init(remote_value);
06: //@ maxloopcount = 10;
07: while (true) {
08:    /*@ assert local_val == remote_val;
09:      @ compoint id = "sync"
10:      @ prev = {"init", "sync"};
11:      @ maxtime = 20;                 @*/
12:    remote_val = s.sync(local_val);
```

Line 05 shows a remote call, and the preceding annotation helps to identify this call and declares an id "init" for further model generation. The next while-loop contains a second communication point with a standard JML functional annotation (i.e., assert) and several protocol information in a non-formal manner. The whole source code, description and transformation of this example to synchronize local states in a client/server application can be found in section 5.

Another annotation in the code snippet shows the second level of use for the model checking tool. The remote call for synchronization is annotated with a required maximum execution time.

```
23:    //@ exec maxtime = $sym1;
24:    val = calcVal();
```

This annotation preceding a normal API method call estimates a maximum execution time for completion. The variable $sym1 is used to reference the used hardware profile with platform dependent values.

This second level of use for the model checking tool is verification of protocol execution under constraints depending on hard coded requirement in the application source code (i.e., line 11). These are called primary requirements and the generated model (compare the next section 4.2) verifies these requirements against platform specific guarantees and parameters.

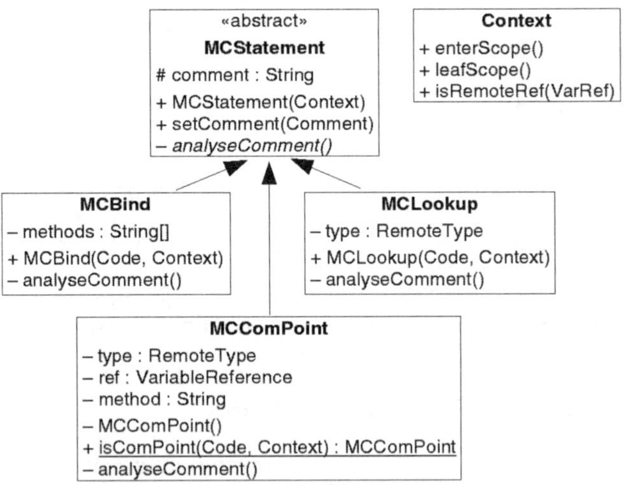

Figure 3: UML class diagram for parsed statements

The platform derived guarantees, parameters, and requirements are part of separate configuration files to allow the implementation of architecturally neutral systems (i.e., ANRTS). The UML class diagram fragment in figure 4 shows an MCAPIMethod class – returned by the ANRTS Parser – with a time value for worst-case execution time, that is annotated similar to example line 23/24.

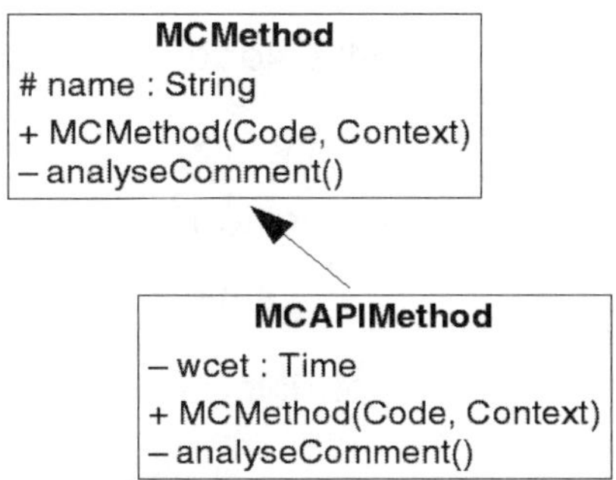

Figure 4: Statement for API method call with WCET

To avoid a state explosion at this point of analysis the application is parsed with main focus on distribution. The program parser identifies potential communication points (remote interaction methods) and simplifies the remaining control flow to statements related to this communication. The state of system variables are available but the following model generation step reduces the used context to communication relevant data, for example, control variables in relevant control flow or parameter and return variables for remote method calls.

To identify protocols in distributed high integrity applications the model checking tool parses the pure Java control flow and remote API use. For traversing and analyze of the source code Recoder [6], a Java framework for source code parsing and meta-programming is used. The supported annotations are similar to tags in the Java Modeling Language (JML) [15] and each statement class (compare figure 3) provides a comment parser to extract additional annotation data.

4.2 MODEL GENERATOR

Because it is difficult to identify the developer's design for a distribution protocol (i.e., correct sequence of method calls or event notifications) automatically, the model checking tool introduces simple annotation semantics to declare this information in an informal manner without huge implementation costs. The approach differs from other languages declaring semantics for concurrent objects [16]. The additional burden for the developer has to be minimized and in HIJA as much as possible results from other verification tools are used.

Each communication point (i.e., remote method call) can be annotated with an identifier and referenced for a simple sequence declaration. The following source code snippet shows two remote method calls from the example in section 5 with these annotations.

```
04: //@ compoint id = "init";
05: s.init(remote_value);

09:     @ compoint id = "sync"
10:     @ prev = {"init", "sync"};
12:   remote_val = s.sync(local_val);
```

The remote call in line 12 requires a preceding call of the initialization method in line 05 before its first execution.

This logic should also be extractable out of the pure Java source code but for more complex communication sequences in several conditional statements and loops – depending on calculations – that could be hidden for a syntax-driven parser.

This information is also used for the second level of verification usage introduced in the last section. This verification of application execution on real runtime environments itself is divided in two parts. Part 2A simplifies the application environment to optimal conditions, for example, blocking time depending on communication and scheduling of multiple threads, senders and receivers is ignored. In a subsequent analysis 2B with results from other verification tools (i.e., scheduling and networking analysis) this verification can be enhanced for almost realistic scenarios.

To build a suitable model for the system, the source code is transformed in a collection of abstract, state reduced automata. Figure 5 shows a UML class diagram fragment with elements of this graph, that are, several nodes for each kind of control flow or logic and transitions.

The proposed abstract interpretation of this tool is reduced on remote interactions. This generate finite state automata [12] representing the implemented protocol out of the annotated source code. By extending these automata with timing requirements and guarantees it is possible to verify these timed automata [17] with a suitable model checker, that is, UPPAAL [7].

The main class representing a remote method call with RMI is depicted in the UML class diagram in figure 6.

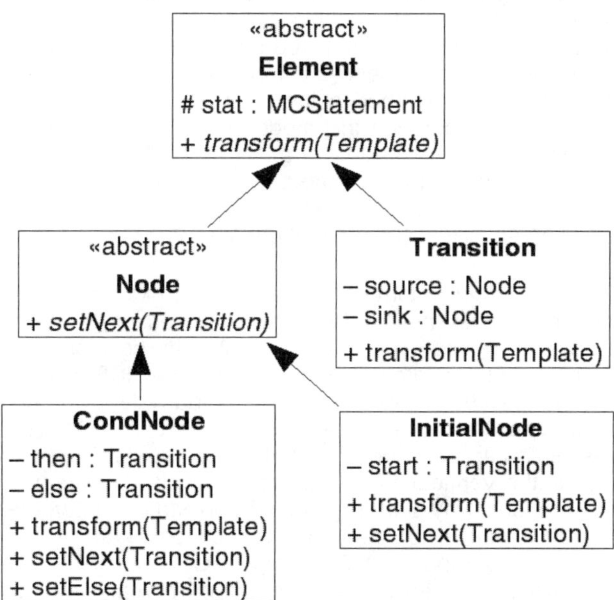

Figure 5: API for abstract node graphs

RMICallNode
– next : Transition – remote : ID – method : Name – maxtime : Time
+ transform(Template) + setNext(Transition)

Figure 6: Graph representation for RMI call

The RMI communication point is identified by an object id for the remote object and a method name. The object has to be obtained in a preceding RMI lookup statement and the introduced timing requirements are also saved in the RMICallNode object.

For better understanding figure 7 shows a fragment of the generated model in a simple graph notations with nodes and transitions. The elements can be complex structures represented by a single node as well as superfluous constructs not necessary for the protocol verification. For a RMICallNode in the final timed automaton two nodes and two transactions have to be created, and some of the created nodes could be merged with neighbor-nodes with standard graph and automata algorithms.

Figure 8 shows solely a client/server call, and this synchronous interaction is split in two parts represented with logical channels between two different automata, one for the client and one for the server control flow. The exclamation mark indicates the caller and the question mark the callee side. This concept of channels for finite state – or in this case timed – automata is used to map remote interaction in the collection of timed automata for all available threads.

Relating to figure 2 the model generator uses the sequence of Java statements to create different models of node/transition graphs. An abstract node model with complex or superfluous structures is transformed to simplified graphs, and these are transformed in an object representation for timed automata in XML, that is, TA-XML. After generation this model the TA-XML is serialized to an XML file and used as input for the integrated UPPAAL model checker, introduced in the next section.

4.3 MODEL CHECKER FOR TIMED AUTOMATA

To verify timed automata the proposed model checking tool integrates the UPPAAL model checker [7], and builds an easy to use graphical development environment by integration in the Eclipse IDE with a plugin. In HIJA Eclipse is used as standard development environment and the plugin has access to the ANRTS description and provides an interface for the developer to control the verification. Because the model is extracted in a generic way and is potentially wrong the interface only provides basic queries for verification. With use of the Timed Computation Tree Logic (TCTL) in UPPAAL it is possible to verify the absence of typical protocol failures. With, for example,

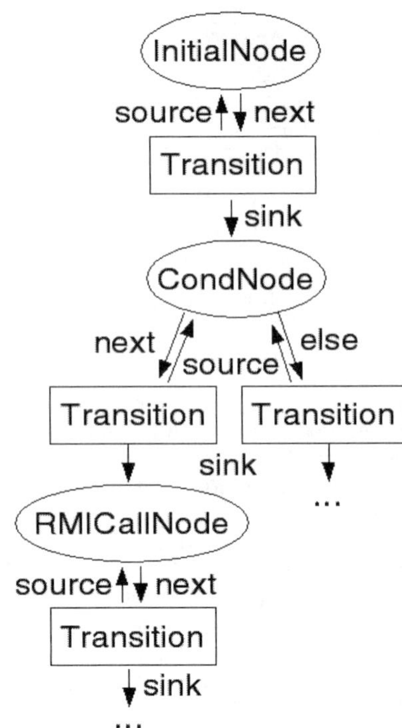

Figure 7: Example nodes and transitions

- `A[] not deadlock;`
- `E<> S.A;`
- `A[] S.A imply (B >= 2 and B <= 4)`

it is verified, that no deadlocks are possible for the whole system, the state A in system S is reachable, and state A implies, that state is reached in the timeframe 2 to 4.

More special, protocol related queries can be verified but that needs more sophisticated interaction with the developer and the plugin tries to limit this to a minimum.

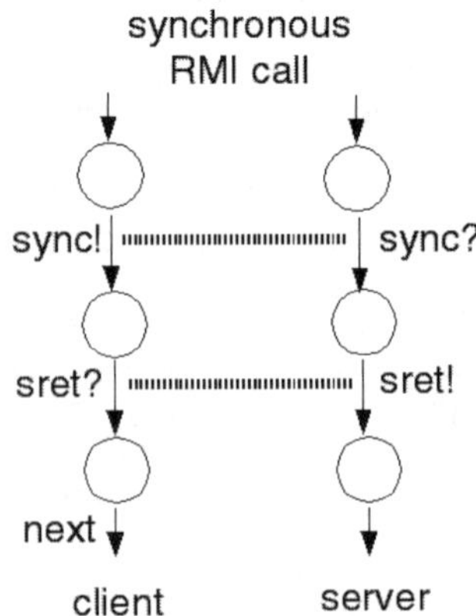

Figure 8: Transformed RMI call

5 EXAMPLE FOR PROTOCOL VERIFICATION

After this rough presentation of the proposed model checking tool in the research project HIJA this section gives a realistic test example to demonstrate the feasibility. In the first implementation step the tool supports RMI method calls, and the example builds a simple client/server application for synchronization of local states in client and server. For demonstration purpose the following Java source code uses simplified RMI and Java syntax.

```
00: // example application to sync
01: // states - client part
02: int local_val = 0, remote_val = 0;
03: Server s = Naming.lookup("server");
04: //@ compoint id = "init";
05: s.init(remote_value);
06: //@ maxloopcount = 10;
07: while (true) {
08:   /*@ assert local_val == remote_val;
09:     @ compoint id = "sync"
10:     @ prev = {"init", "sync"};
11:     @ maxtime = 20;                @*/
12:   remote_val = s.sync(local_val);
13:   local_val++;
14:   if (local_val != remote_val) {
15:     /*@ compoint id = "end";
16:       @ prev = {"sync"};           @*/
17:     server.destroy();
18:   }
19: }
20: // server part
21: //@ profile = file:url_to_profile
21: int val = -1;
22: public void init(int v) throws RE {
23:   //@ exec maxtime = $sym1;
24:   val = calcVal();
25: }
26: /*@ requires val == cval;
27:   @ exec maxtime = $sym2;          @*/
28: public int sync(int cval) throws RE {
29:   if (val != cval) {
30:     throw new RE("protocol error!");
31:   }
32:   incVal();
33:   return val;
34: }
```

Completing the example the following lines show an example hardware profile with platform dependent values on server side.

```
A0: // system description (e.g., capacity,
A1: // performance, throughput)
A1: // list of symbols and values
A2: $sym1 = 10
```

For the distributed example application, client and server implementations are known. The server provides remote methods (i.e., init, sync, and destroy) and the developer has annotated an intended execution sequence (i.e., possible prior ids in line 10). Figures 9 to 11 show fragments of the final TA-XML notation in a graphical representation. The graphs are reduced on basic parts for the distribution protocol.

The two fragments (figure 9 and 10) of server automata shows the main program logic to create and register a remote object and the remote method (i.e., init). Channels are used for local synchronization and remote method calls. The client fragment (figure 11) shows only the communication protocol.

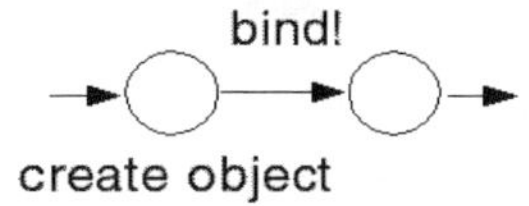

Figure 9: Server main thread

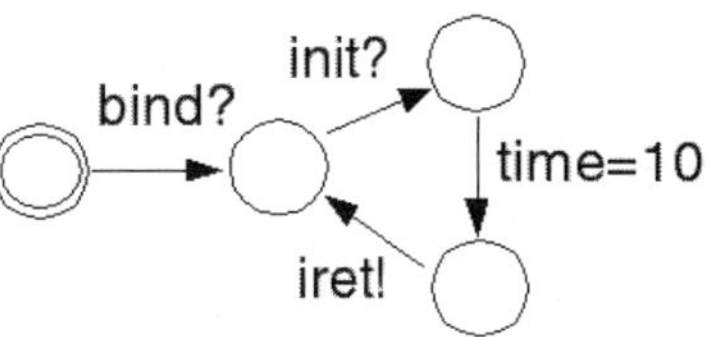

Figure 10: Remote method init

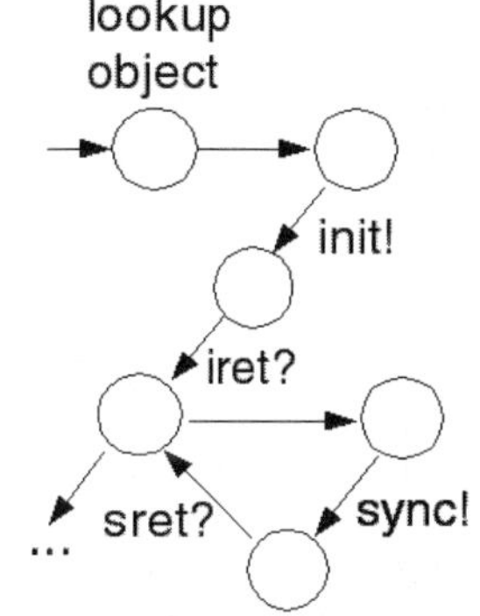

Figure 11: Client protocol fragment

6 CONCLUSIONS

This position paper about the use of model checking in the research project HIJA for verification of safety-critical embedded systems introduces tool design and demonstrates the benefits of model checking for high integrity systems. The verification in two different levels is introduced and the use of architecturally neutral real-time system descriptions with hardware profiles specifying the runtime environment is proposed. We believe that this approach reduces the number of iterations in the development process of high-integrity real-time systems, and by using of existing tools and APIs the development of a user-friendly assistance interface for application development predestinates the future research work in HIJA.

A ACRONYMS

ANRTS: Architecturally Neutral, high-integrity Real-Time Systems
DFA: Data Flow Analysis
HIJA: High Integrity Java Applications
JML: Java Modeling Language
JPF: Java PathFinder
MAST: Modeling and Analysis Suite for Real-Time Applications
RMI: Remote Method Invocation
RTSJ: Real-Time Specification for Java
TA-XML: XML for Timed Automata
TCTL: Timed Computation Tree Logic
UML: Unified Modeling Language
WCET: Worst Case Execution Time
WCETA: WCET Analysis
WCMUA: Worst Case Memory Usage Analysis

REFERENCES

1. HIJA. High Integrity Java Applications. Project Website. http://www.hija.info, 2004.
2. aicas GmbH. The Jamaica Virtual Machine. http://www.aicas.com/products/jamaica.html, 2001-2005.
3. The KeY Project. Project Website. http://www.key-project.org, 2005.
4. MAST. Modeling and Analysis Suite for Real-Time Applications. Project Website. http://mast.unican.es/, September 2005.
5. Java PathFinder. Project Website. http://javapathfinder.sourceforge.net, 2005.
6. Recoder V. 0.75. Project Website. http://recoder.sourceforge.net, 2005.
7. UPPAAL. Tool Website. http://www.uppaal.com, 2005.
8. Bandera. Bandera Tool Set. Project Website. http://www.bandera.projects.cis.ksu.edu, 2005.
9. UPPAAL2k: Small Tutorial, October 2002.
10. Gwinn, J. M. Object-Oriented Programs in Realtime. ACM SIGPLAN Notices 27 (February 1992), 47-52.
11. Hergenhan, A. and Rosenstiel, W. Static Timing Analysis of Embedded Software on Advanced Processor Architectures. In Proceedings of the Design, Automation and Test in Europe (DATE '00) (2000), p. 552.
12. Holzmann, G. J. Design an Verification of Computer Protocols. Prentice Hall, November 1990.
13. Holzmann, G. J. The SPIN Model Checker. Addison-Wesley, 2003.
14. Corbett, J. C. et al. Bandera: Extracting Finite-state Models from Java Source code. In Proceedings of the 22th International Conference on Software Engineering (2000), 439-448.
15. Leavens, G. T. et al. JML Reference Manual, July 2005.
16. Lerner, R. A. Specifying Objects of Concurrent Systems. PhD thesis, School of Computer Science, Carnegie Mellon University, May 1991.
17. Alur, R. and Dill, D. A Theory of Timed Automata. In Theoretial Computer Science. April 1994, pp. 183*236.
18. HIJA partners. D8.1 - HIJA White Paper. Tech. rep., The Open Group, June 2005.
19. Zalewski, J. Object orientation vs. real-time systems. Response to Alan C. Shaw's contribution. International Journal of Time-Critical Computing Systems 18 (2000), 75-77.

2006-01-0372

Architecture Design to Functional Modeling of Distributed ECU Networks

Gerhard Steininger
PROSTEP IMP GmbH

ABSTRACT

This article describes how to manage the increasing complexity of distributed electronic control systems and reduce time and costs at the same time. Included are the graphical modeling of function networks starting from a function database, building a technology independent design, simulation and continuous test and verification using Model-Based Design. The design process will finally highlight the deployment of those functions onto a target ECU network, as well as system analysis features like failure risk analysis and fault tracking. This process will be demonstrated with the standard tools for function design MATLAB and Simulink from The MathWorks and architecture design CAPE/C from Capeware Technologies GmbH.

INTRODUCTION

When starting a new vehicle project, one of the first problems is the definition of a reliable, cost efficient (production and warranty) ECU network to host the body electronics and safety functions needed. Functions are typically developed by many different suppliers and need to work together in a wide area of operation. In order to manage them, they are defined and tabulated with their inputs, outputs and properties, in a database.

FUNCTIONAL DESIGN

After the selection of a subset of those functions for a new vehicle project they are visualized in a hierarchical tree. The top node of the functional tree is the vehicle. Figure 1 shows a functional tree. The hierarchy is shown in the left window; the right window shows the data flow between the functions. The breakdown into sub-functions leads to small, easy-to-understand functional descriptions of what a function shall do and how it is implemented during subsequent steps of the engineering process.

Functions are objects which contain data like requirements, interfaces to other functions, simulation models, engineering and parts costs, MTBF-values, behavior in case of faults. Each node summarizes the sub-functions below the node. For example: a function calculates the costs of all sub-functions. The dynamic behavior of a function is defined using Simulink and Stateflow.

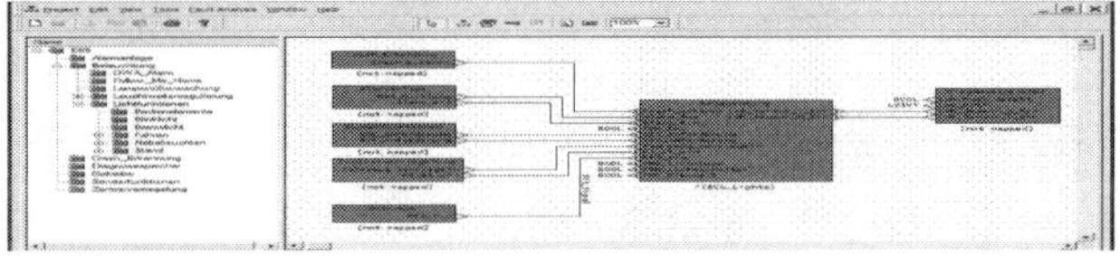

Figure 1: Functional tree and data flow

CREATION OF THE DATA FLOW BETWEEN FUNCTIONS

The data flow is defined by creating so-called "terminals". There are input terminals (on the left side of a function) and output terminals (on the right side of a function). The data flow is created by connecting input terminals with output terminals. Since it is not known yet on which ECUs the functions will be deployed, there is no need to define bus signals and messages at this time.

Terminals are objects with a lot of attributes such as data type, value ranges and signification. For reusability, it is important to know whether an information of type "bool" means "switch on" if it delivers the value "1" and switch off" if it delivers a "0" or vice versa. Otherwise, there is no chance to check for consistency if you connect inputs and outputs of different functions.

Terminals can be "propagated". If you have an output terminal at a function you can propagate it to another function; an input terminal is created automatically with the same attributes. A connection between the terminals is also created automatically. The auto routing mechanism draws the connection.

SIMULATION OF FUNCTIONAL NETWORKS

Functions are objects which can contain a simulation model. Every function on any level of the hierarchy can have its own model. It is possible to simulate a group of functions selected by the user. First, the functions are chosen and then the according simulation models are transferred to MATLAB-Simulink, including the connections between the functions. The sub-functions and its models are also transferred. This way, models can be created and stored behind functions. It is possible to simulate a complete vehicle on functional level if every level has a simulation model.

Since functions are objects under control of a multi-user-environment, with access rights, the simulation models can be handled under this control in a function type library.

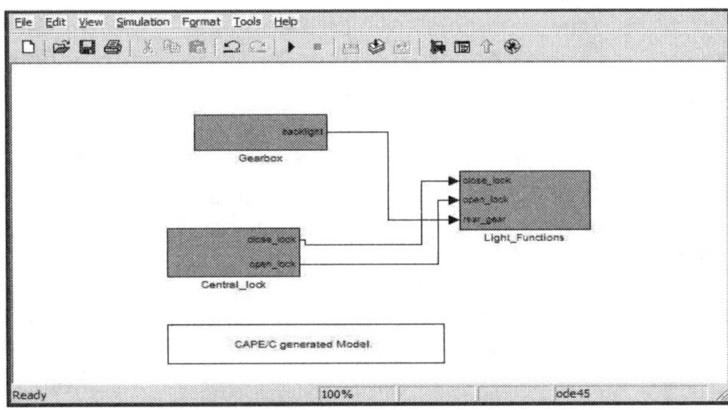

Figure2: Simulation with Simulink

VIRTUAL SOLUTION DESIGN – PROCESS CHAINS FROM SENSOR TO ACTOR

In the next step of the process the functions are to be partitioned in hardware and software parts. For this purpose an abstraction model is used called "virtual solution design" VSD.

The model needs only three basic elements:

- Process types: Sensors and actuators; Transformation of process values to electrical values and vice versa
- Hardware types: Input and output channels; transformation of electrical values to bits and bytes and vice versa
- Software types: Implementation of functionality in code

The three basic elements are used to design reusable, technology-independent solutions using a graphical model editor. Figure 3 shows the solution of the function "blink lights" from the direction switch down to the blink lights.

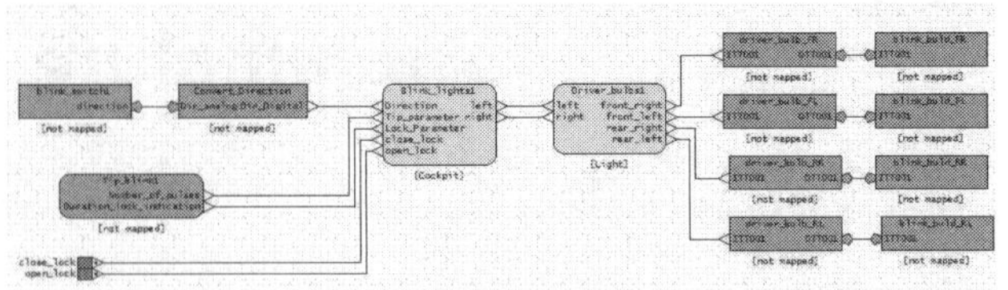

Figure 3: Virtual Solution Design (VSD)

SIMULATION OF VIRTUAL SOLUTIONS

All the solution model elements are objects which can contain simulation models, e.g. MATLAB-Simulink. The complete process chain can be transferred to Simulink for simulation purposes, e.g. calculation of worst case execution time when you start pressing the brake pedal until the brake lights flash on. The solution model elements are types which are handled in a library. The simulation models come with the instances of the types.

DEFINITION OF TECHNICAL ARCHITECTURE

The technical architecture is defined in a graphical editor (Figure 4). Devices and bus systems come from a type library and are instantiated into a vehicle project. Different technical architectures could be based on the same functional reference model.

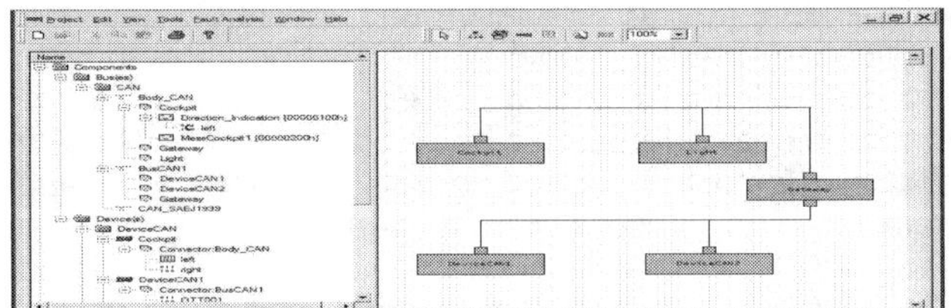

Figure 4: Technical Architecture

DEPLOYMENT OF HARDWARE AND SOFTWARE TO TECHNICAL ARCHITECTURE

Entire functions and single sub-functions, as well as single elements of a virtual solution model, can be manually mapped to different ECUs in the technical architecture view.

CONFIGURATION OF BUS SYSTEMS

The communication between ECUs resulting from this mapping is generated automatically. Messages can be defined according to the bus technology used (e.g. CAN), signals can be mapped into those telegrams.
Message catalogues can be created or read in and mapped to the functional network.

SIMULATION OF ECU'S

After mapping, it is known which functions run on which ECU. From an ECU, the simulation in MATLAB-Simulink can be started, all the simulation models from functions mapped to this ECU and their connections are transferred to MATLAB Simulink to simulate all the functions of this ECU.

FAILURE RISK ANALYSIS

Each object can have a description of the dependencies between inputs and outputs of the object. This information is used for several important checks already in an early phase of a project:

- What happens if a signal fails? What happens if several signals fail? Which functions are affected?
- What happens if a device fails? Which functions are affected?
- What happens if a cable or a bus segment fails? Which functions are affected?

These checks are absolutely to be done in case of security relevant functions. For other functions, they help avoid problems on the road, when the vehicle is already delivered.

TARGET IMPLEMENTATION

A developer does want to design the whole system target independent, and wants to be able to map the functions onto different targets, depending on the vehicle platform. The choices are size (centralized or multiple ECUs) or type of target (Microcontroller, FPGA, DSP etc.) The interfaces of every function are transferred and .c and .h-files are automatically generated. After the mapping of functions to ECUs it is known which software is running on which ECU. The code of the ECU can now be generated out of this information and downloaded into the ECU via online connection to the target system.

TEST AND DEBUGGING, FAULT BACK TRACKING

Testing the model on a desktop is preferable to deploying it on hardware for build and integration. Source-code-based testing has existed for many years, and recent methods enable model testing and structural coverage. Using simulation and coverage, developers can fully stress the functions and their communication to verify its design integrity.

Process values can be shown directly in the functional model, measured via bus interface or from logged data (e.g. CANalyzer). The information about the dependencies of inputs and outputs of a model object is used to perform fault back tracking. Any object can be marked as faulty, the possible causes calculated across the complete functional network, and the results presented graphically (Figure 5). Thus failures caused by functions distributed on several ECUs can be detected.

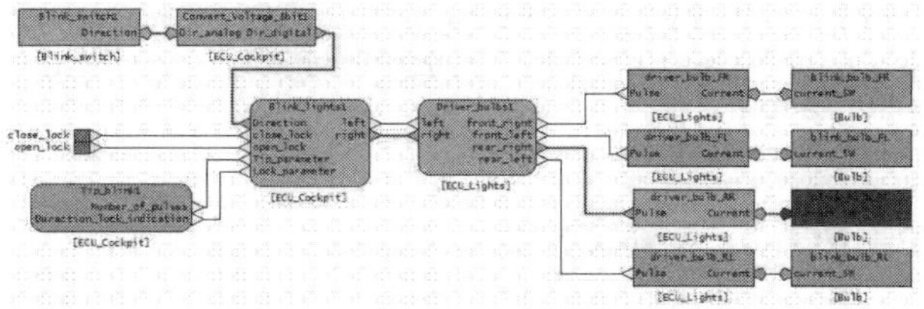

Figure 5: Fault back tracking

PRODUCTION CODE GENERATION

After that the model has been verified and validated, it is time to generate code. As with a compiler, this process is straightforward, with various optimization settings and user configuration options. The key is to keep the code efficient, accurate, and integrated with legacy code or other tools. It is also important for the code to be traceable to the diagram, so that it may be reviewed and verified.

AUTOMATIC GENERATION OF A SPECIFICATION

Documentation can be generated from the data of the functional reference model and the individual functions since it contains all information needed to describe the requirements of functions and ECUs. This way a “digital requirements document” is available at no additional costs.

OUTLOOK, RE-ENGINEERING OF EXISTING TECHNOLOGY

A lot of development has been done in the past in the automotive industry. If a new process and new tools are introduced, the question always will be: How can I switch, how can I reuse what I did in the past? It is desirable to incorporate existing knowledge into the new functional modeling.
MATLAB-Simulink. Simulation models, including hierarchies, can be transformed into functional networks and model object types.

CONCLUSION

Substantial function evolution requires support for the complete system engineering process. This pilot platform, was developed in close collaboration with customers, which is a key to success. It is an extensible and open-architecture environment that spans hardware and software development and connections to many different types of implementation targets.

The design platform is a foundation moving away from the single component or ECU view to the functional view in development of EE systems. It is possible to have a complete function with all its related HW and SW components in focus.

With the function centric view of the design platform, it also canbe used as a foundation for future architecture optimization.

ACKNOWLEDGMENTS

I would like to thank Joachim Langenwalter from The Mathworks and Jürgen Kaiser from Capeware Technologies. Without their help and their experience in the sector of design of distributed networks, this paper could not be completed.

REFERENCES

1. DATE 2005, Embedded Panel and Tutorial - Platforms and Tools for Automotive System Design (Automotive Special Day),9. March 2005; J Bortolazzi, DaimlerChrysler, DE ; A Sangiovanni-Vincentelli, UC Berkeley, US; H Brinkmeyer, IBB, DE; S Ortmann, Carmeq, DE ; J Langenwalter, The MathWorks Inc, US/DE; J-L Maté, SiemensVDO, FR, J Becker, Karlsruhe U, DE; C Morgano, Microsoft Europe
2. OMER3 Workshop, Object-Oriented Modeling of Embedded Real-Time Workshops. 12-14 October 2005, Architecture Design to Functional Modeling of Distributed ECU Networks, Gerhard Steininger

CONTACT

Gerhard Steininger, Dipl.-Phys., Head of PROSTEP IMP GmbH

Email: gerhard.steininger@prostep.com

2005-01-3133

Model Based CAE Technology for the Development of Automotive Embedded Distributed Control System

Zaimin Zhong and Jirong Li
Tongji University

ABSTRACT

Automotive embedded DCS is widely used to solve automotive control problems. This paper presents a model-driven development technology for such systems. Models of automotive embedded DCS are built up strictly complying with the four-layer-model architecture, which is presented by Model-Driven Architecture (MDA). Three kinds of models are used to describe the protocol data structure, the algorithm process and visualization aspects of automotive embedded DCS. Corresponding XML databases are created based upon these models. As a single data source, these databases play key roles in further development phases, including generating the protocol specification, MC&D systems and embedded programming, etc. Some demonstrative applications are presented in this paper.

INTRODUCTION

The traditional CAE approach for automotive embedded DCS development would focus on the process activities, which means a detailed study of the target application and introduces structured data modeling/databases only when necessary[1,2]. In this paper we present a new method of CAE approach for automotive embedded DCS, by which we focus on the architecture (or rather common models) of the whole system regardless of specific applications and/or implementations. Much attention is paid to the meta-model (the model of the model) of the studied target system, which is the key principle of MDA approaches. An open and standard database is deduced to be the instance of this model. Finally we build up some applications to demonstrate this based upon this acquired database.

REQUIREMENTS AND SOLUTIONS

REQUIREMENTS

Compared with computer aided development theories and tools for concentrated embedded control systems, development assistance facilities for automotive embedded DCS are quite underdeveloped to meet its increasing complexity. On the one hand, some existing solutions are quite restricted to different development teams and lack a consistent data exchange format. On the other hand, in some areas or development stages reasonable assistance techniques are still greatly needed to guarantee improving quality and efficiency. Therefore, it is very important and necessary for us to bring the CAE technology into the developing process of automotive embedded DCS. Our goal is to provide a general method and path for the development and maintenance of automotive embedded DCS and related toolsets based upon these methods and paths.

SOLUTIONS

To meet the above-mentioned requirements, this paper proposes a concept of a model-based CAE solution. This technique starts with the construction of the models of automotive embedded DCS according to MDA. These models are then converted into XML structured data description form, which acts as a database exchanged among different platforms and/or applications. Since an XML database can be processed easily with computers, such databases can be generated, edited, exchanged and transferred in every development stage of DCS (including development jobs, such as system description, publication of a network protocol, description and realization of a control algorithm, system debugging, measurement, calibration and diagnostics, etc.). On the basis of this database a set of software and hardware tools can be designed to facilitate design, implementation and run-time monitoring of DCS.

MDA BASED APPROACHES

This paper adheres to two key principles of MDA: layered architecture and platform-independent modeling. MDA comes from the well-known idea of separating the specific operation of a system from the details of how that system uses its platform.

"Model-driven" means that models are used to guide the course of understanding, design, construction, deployment, operation, maintenance and modification. The model is the starting point for the whole life circle of an application. The core concept of the MDA strategy is its four layer model structures[3] as instantiated in Fig. 1.

In the M0 layer, concrete elements (objects) are defined. These elements are actual prototypes of different applications. In the M1 layer, classes along with their attributes, operations and their interrelationships, which are common for object-oriented programming, are defined. MDA defines the M2 and M3 layer above M1 and M0: M2, which is called the meta-model layer, is the model of M1. In the M2 layer, the prototypes of types, operations and components are defined. UML is only in M2. As the model of M2, M3 is called the meta-meta model layer, as it defines the prototypes and rules of the meta model. MOF is the core of MDA strategy, which defines the basic concept aggregate of MDA and describes the system and MDA itself. In a word, MOF is a general meta-language, which we use to establish other languages. UML, which is used to describe object-oriented systems, is a kind of meta-language, that derives from MOF.

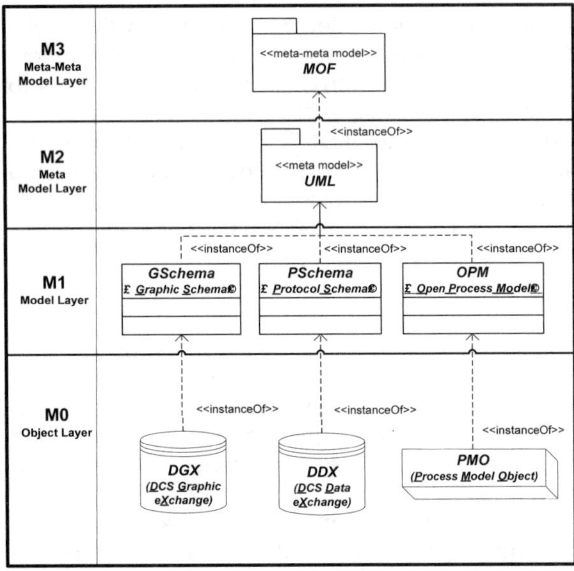

Fig. 1 Four-Layer-Model of DCS

Fig. 1 shows our models and their location in the four-layer-model architecture of MDA. We distribute our models in M1 and their object instances in M0. Our models in M1 are described mainly with UML class diagrams, but they could also be equivalently represented in other forms like XML DTD or XML Schema etc.. We use three kinds of models to describe the data structure, graphic instruments and algorithm & process aspects of automotive embedded DCS respectively. There are correspondingly three models within the M1 layer: PSchema, GSchema and OPM. The models built in the M1 layer can be instanced in the M0 layer as the following application databases:

- DCS Data eXchange (DDX)
- DCS Graphics eXchange (DGX)
- Process Model Object (PMO)

The format of the first two databases is an XML document (including XML and SVG), while the PMO is realized via UML dynamic object graphics, such as Sequence Diagram, Statechart Diagram, and Activity Diagram etc. for describing specific processes occurring during the whole life circle and its network nodes of automotive embedded DCS. UML graphics of the PMO consist of objects, which are instances of classes defined in OPM.

According to MDA, an application is divided into two basically different kinds of models: PIM and PSM.

A PIM is a platform independent viewpoint of a system. "A PIM exhibits a specified degree of platform independence so as to be suitable for use with a number of different platforms of similar type."[4] A PSM is a platform specific viewpoint of a system. A PSM combines the specifications in the PIM with the details that specify how that system uses a particular type of platform. Under the promise of not changing the PIM, a PSM maps it to a certain particular technique. All models described in Fig. 1 belong to PIM. All the applications (or all PSM possibilities) start from the databases located in the M0 layer.

MODELING TECHNIQUE

Some key solutions are described in this section, which are necessary to realize the concepts proposed in section 1. It includes data and process class definition using UML, XML Schema implementation and PIM visualization methods.

UML MODELING

Structure Data Modeling

In order to describe the structured protocol data used in fieldbus communication, we use PSchema and its instances DDX. PSchema models the structure of protocol data and governs the content of DDX documents. To clarify the technique used in the definition of PSchema, we take the Data Stream sub-model as an example to illustrate the most important aspects of a PSchema definition.

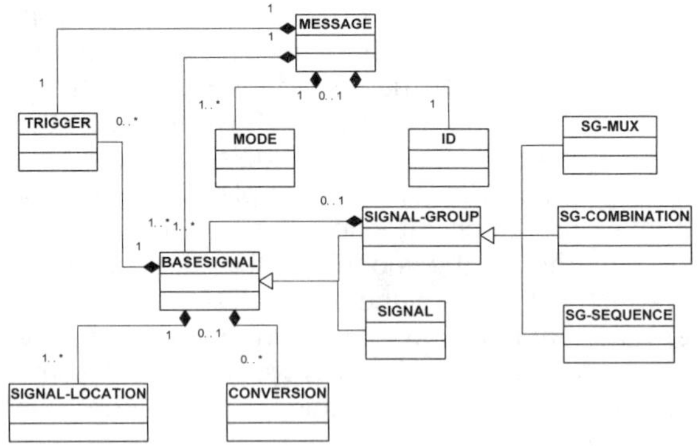

Fig. 2 The Data Stream Sub-Model

The Data Stream UML Class Diagram is shown in Fig. 2. We regard the essence of an automotive embedded DCS network as all of the information and its delivery. The main elements of the model are SIGNAL and MESSAGE. SIGNAL is the carrier of information, while MESSAGE is the carrier of SIGNAL. A SIGNAL, which is the basic element of a MESSAGE, is the minimum unit that constitutes the system.

Under the concept of SIGNAL, we use three classes to detail all of its variants: BASESIGNAL (parent class), SIGNAL (child class) and SIGNAL-GROUP (child class). SIGNAL is the original signal. Its attributes contain length, byte format, physical unit etc.. BASESIGNAL is an abstract parent class, which represents a signal unit of logical meaning. It summarizes attributes, which both SIGNAL and SIGNAL-GROUP have. BASESIGNAL is the basic element that can constitute either MESSAGES or SIGNAL-GROUPS. BASESIGNAL has three sub-elements: SIGNAL-LOCATION, CONVERSION (optional) and TRIGGER (optional). The SIGNAL-LOCATION sub-element denotes the location of BASESIGNAL in its container MESSAGE. The CONVERSION of BASESIGNAL explains BASESIGNAL. That means we can use the same conversion method to a SIGNAL-GROUP. The TRIGGER sub-element defines the trigger method and trigger time etc.. There is also a TRIGGER sub-element in MESSAGE. But the TRIGGER of SIGNAL is prior to that of its parent MESSAGE. A SIGNAL-GROUP represents relationships of BASESIGNALS. SIGNAL-GROUP is composed of BASESIGNALS, which means it can be constructed by SIGNAL and/or SIGNAL-GROUP itself. Theoretically SIGNAL-GROUP can have infinite layers of nesting. Three sub-elements of SIGNAL-GROUP are: SG-MUX, SG-COMBINATION and SG-SEQUENCE. SG-MUX is used to solve the problem of dynamic grouping of signals. SG-COMBINATION is used to resolve problems such as the ordering and combination of signals. SG-SEQUENCE is used for relatively long signals, which needs to be placed in several MESSAGES, to give the information of the number of MESSAGES and methods of splitting and assembling of such signals.

Algorithm & Process Modeling

According to the object-oriented principle, an OPM (Open DCS Process Model) builds up the basic process model of control algorithm logic of DCS mainly using a UML class diagram. Then we derive a series of UML use case diagrams, state machine diagrams, sequence diagrams or collaboration diagrams to model the process, e.g. download program code, upload target status and code update etc..

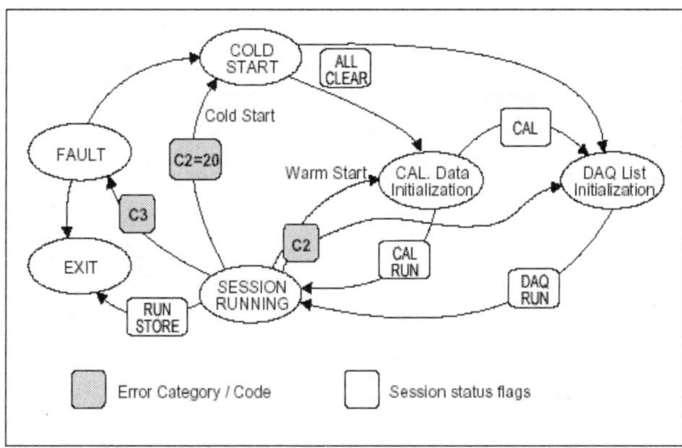

Fig. 3 An example of process modeling

Fig. 3 is an example of a state machine modeling the application of error handling. For protocol data units OPM makes reference to DDX elements.

Graphics Modeling

In addition to DDX we also model the graphics aspects of DCS, that is common tasks for a network application, like MC&D, test, verification, etc.. In order to divide the development process dealing with graphics also into PIM and PSM, we use UML class diagrams for abstracting the often-used graphics instruments of automotive embedded DCS, both the GUI instruments for testing, measurement and calibration, such as round dials and digital meters etc.

XML IMPLEMENTATION

In order to govern the grammar and name space of XML-formatted DDX and DGX, PSchema and Gschema based on UML must be translated to an equivalent XML glossary. This equivalent translation procedure must be accomplished by predictable rules. Independent of the rules used, the schematic result must be the same.

There are two choices that can be used to build up an XML glossary: XML DTD and XML Schema. The former is suitable for those files which consider the document as central, for example, reports of research or on-line publishing of books. But XML Schema is more suitable for documents which place data in the center. The network description of automotive embedded DCS deals with complicated content models and structure of data. In this case XML Schema will be therefore a better choice. Fig. 4 presents a XML Schema clip, which describes an element of MESSAGE as well as its attributes and sub-elements.

```
<?xml version="1.0" encoding="UTF-8"?>
<!-- edited with XMLSPY v2004 rel. 2 U (http://
www.xmlspy.com) by lijirong (tongji) -->
<xs:schema xmlns:xs="http://www.w3.org/2001/XMLSchema"
elementFormDefault="qualified"
attributeFormDefault="unqualified">
<xs:element name="MESSAGES">
        <xs:complexType>
            <xs:sequence>
                <xs:element name="MESSAGE" type="MESSAGE"
maxOccurs="unbounded"/>
            </xs:sequence>
        </xs:complexType>
    </xs:element>
<xs:complexType name="MESSAGE">
        <xs:sequence>
            <xs:element name="MODE" type="MODE"
maxOccurs="unbounded"/>
            <xs:element name="MSGID" type="ID"/>
            <xs:element name="MSGTRIGGER" type="xs:IDREF"/>
            <xs:element name="BASESIGNAL" type="BASESIGNAL"
maxOccurs="unbounded"/>
            <xs:element name="TRANSMITTER" type="xs:IDREF">
            </xs:element>
            <xs:element name="RECEIVER" type="xs:IDREF"
maxOccurs="unbounded"/>
        </xs:sequence>
        <xs:attribute name="NAME" type="xs:string"
use="required"/>
        <xs:attribute name= "XMI.ID" type="xs:ID"
use="optional"/>
    </xs:complexType>
†
</xs:schema>
```

Fig. 4 A Clip of Data Stream Schema

The syntax of the XML Schema obeys XML marking rules. There are quite a few research effort in standardization of the transfer rules from UML to XML Schema[2,7,8]. The most important rules used in this paper are listed below.

A UML class is mapped onto an XML element. The transformation of attributes has variations. When an attribute of a UML class has a prototype of <<attr>>, it is mapped onto the attribute of the XML element. When there is no prototype of the attribute of a UML class, it is mapped onto the sub-element of an XML element. When the attributes of a UML class have the prototype of <<content>>, it is directly mapped onto the content of an XML element. The aggregate and composition are mapped onto a sub-element. In cases where the target cardinality of the contained class is multiple, a wrapper element around the sub-elements is generated. The wrapper element is omitted if the {nowrapper}- constraint is defined in relation to the composition or aggregation. Associations in UML class diagrams are mapped onto references. "Element B is referenced in element A" means that Class A and Class B have a relationship of association. In cases where UML inheritances are mapped onto XML, two kinds of circumstances happen: <<impl-child>> and <<impl-parent>> are prototypes of inheritance, because XML does not natively support inheritance. When the <<impl-child>> prototype is adopted, all child classes are mapped in XML. When the <<impl-Parent>> prototype is adopted, both parent and child classes are mapped in the same element. This element takes an attribute named xsi:type, which includes the names of all child classes. When users build XML documents on the basis of this XML Schema, a different sub-element and its attributes can be accepted by choosing the xsi:type attribute.

APPLICATION OF PIM GRAPHICS USING SVG

Like PSchema, Gschema can also be represented via XML Schema. Users can design their own graphic instruments using GSchema, and that is the graphic database: DGX. DGX adopts the SVG format namespace, which is a kind of vector sketch description format that matches the XML standard and is independent of platform from the bottom up. DGX is a kind of secondary model, since some DCS model information (information about both graphics and data structures) is already represented in DDX. With the help of an SVG parser, such as Adobe SVG Viewer or Apache Batik, a robust and powerful GUI and/or a technical report can be generated.

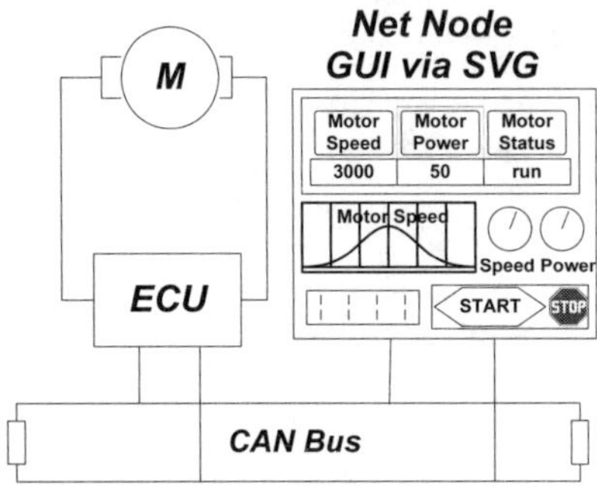

Fig. 5 GUI using SVG example

In Fig. 5 an ECU and a GUI equipment node are connected with a CAN bus. Signals defined in DDX can be received from the motor and displayed in the explorer supporting SVG. In the reverse direction parameters in the ECU can be evaluated and modified by controlling the motor. Furthermore, the technique of XSLT makes it possible to automatically create a GUI according to a given DDX. For example, a user adds a new message object and sets it to be calibratable. When the XSLT file is applied, a new graphic instrument (edit box, etc.) GUI including the visualization of messages will be added. The graphic instrument is definitely linked to the message object. It is easy to understand this concept, because DGX works closely with PSchema and the XML document DDX.

EXAMPLE APPLICATION WITH DDX, DGX AND THE PMO AS A CENTRAL EXCANGABLE DATABASE

Based upon the acquired models, the MDA principle can be applied in quite a few stages to assist the development of a DCS system, starting from the system analysis stage to the application tools design stage, including MC&D system, test equipment, implementation technique and signal visualization.

SINGLE DATA SOURCE EXCHANGE PROCESS

Starting from the databases in the M0 layer of the PIM procedure proposed above, various applications are possible, which are built up based on a concept of “Single Source Data Exchange Process”, see Fig. 6.

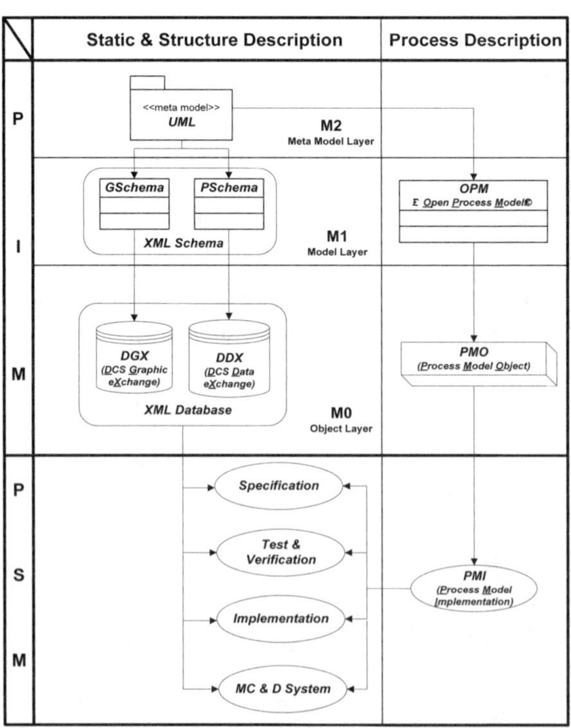

Fig. 6 Single Source Data Exchange Process

DDX and DGX act as the databases in the form of an XML document. They can work at the back end to support the following four applications: Specification, Test & Verification, Implementation, and MC&D System. Since we adopt an OPM and the instances of this model as the PMO, and they can finally be implemented as a Process Model Implementation (PMI) in Java or C code, which depends on whether the application is embedded in the target or runs on the host computer. A PMI describes the dynamic and process algorithm. That is what we need in the above-mentioned four applications. By means of that we build up an integrated CAE environment of automotive embedded DCS to realize functions of Protocol & Report Specification, Measurement Calibration & Diagnostics, Test & Verification and Embedded Program Implementation.

PROTOCOL & SPECIFICATION GENERALIZATION

DCS is usually a very complicated system, which means its protocol and field test reports are extremely complicated for a developer to deal with. To standardize the process of specification is the initial purpose of this research.

Fig. 7 shows the concept of computer aided specification generalization. As a widely accepted readable document format, there are lots of automatic format transformation techniques for XML. XSLT documents could be adopted to meet the requirements of transformation from XML into HTML, PDF and SVG, which makes it possible to automatically generate protocols and technical reports with test and view data. These XSLT documents are added to our databases. These XSLT documents only need to be changed when the models of the databases (GSchema, PSchema in the M1 layer) change.

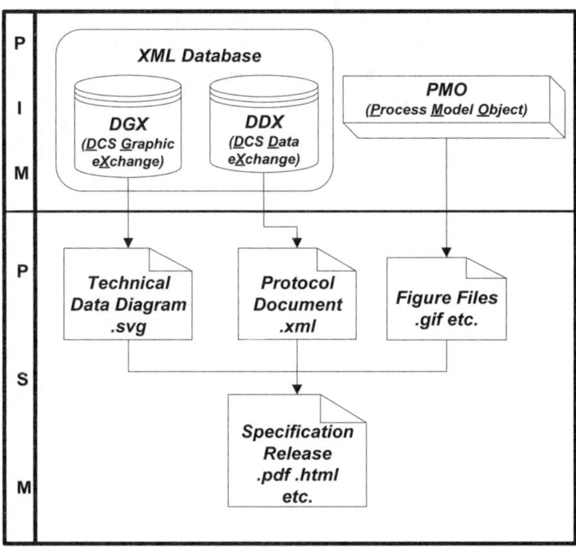

Fig. 7 Protocol & Report Specification

MC&D DEVICES

Java is one of the best implementation platforms integrated with XML. The parsing, creation and amendment of XML documents are all well supported by Java techniques, e.g. DOM and SAX. Many organizations also provide Java class libraries to process XML documents.

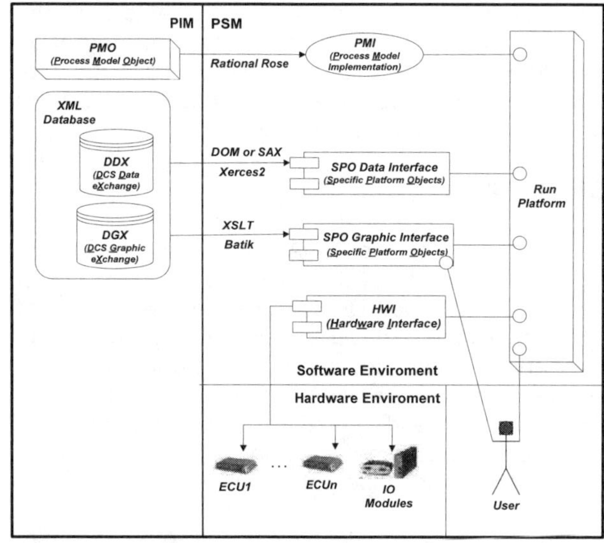

Fig. 8 Modular Structure for MC&D, Test & Verification Application

Fig. 8 presents an MC&D and Test & Verification system mostly based on a Java Implementation of XML. Firstly we have a Run Platform as the carrier of the whole system. By writing the Java processor of XML databases (one parser for the XML Document and one processor for the SVG Document) we build two kinds of interfaces: a Data Interface and a Graphic Interface to transform objects from DDX and DGX into a Specific Platform, by means of which we can easily use and operate our database in the Run Platform. A GUI based on DGX is built to trace input information from the user and hardware interface, which has functions of Graphics (for measurement signals) and Information Input (for calibration parameters). From situations of process modeling, we implement UML object graphics in Java and then integrate them into the Run Platform.

EMBEDDED CODING

As mentioned above, when the models are to be implemented with embedded targets, we could implement the PSM based on C. Two parallel ways to realize CAE of an algorithm of network nodes are shown in Fig. 9.

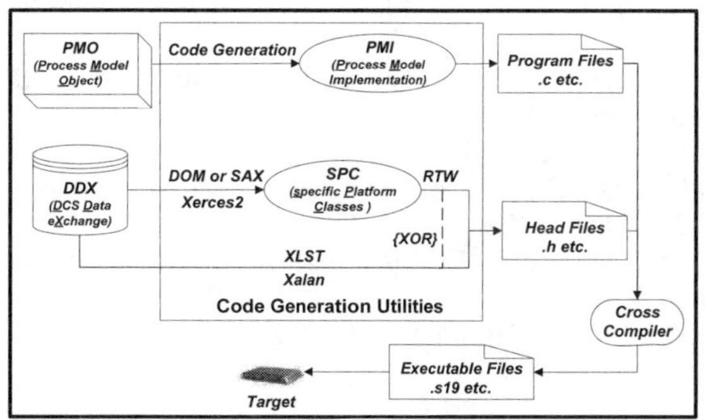

Fig. 9 Embedded code generation

C Program files are automatically generated from a PMI. The procedure is supported by several tools including Rational Rose[6]. C header files contain information about the definition of classes derived from an XML Schema Model via XSLT. The other way to create header files is to parse out elements from the XML document into a specific program and then generate header files using tools provided by that program. Finally executable files are generated from both kinds of files via cross compiler.

CONCLUSION

This paper adopts the MDA technique in software engineering assisting the developing process of automotive embedded DCS. It provides developers of DCS with a standardized development process and necessary computer tools, which not only enhances the quality and efficiency of development but also defines norms and standards of data and an information exchange format for distributed development among different teams.

DDX and DGX are introduced, which give a concept of the structural description of data. That makes it possible to exchange data based on a uniform database during the whole development process.

Moreover, we put forward the concept of OPM. Not just used to test and adjust or implement embedded applications, OPM can also combine logic and a sequence model with a target algorithm implementation, which makes it possible for automatic generation of target algorithm code.

It is certain, with the improvement of MDA, UML and XML techniques, that the CAE architecture proposed in this paper will make further progress.

REFERENCES

1. Dengel G., Dr. Krammer J., etc. MCD-2 [FBX] Ver 1.0 FIBEX-Field Bus Exchange Format, ASAM e.V., Jan. 2004
2. Dr. Augustin, Dr Hallermayer, etc. ASAM MCD-2D (ODX) Ver 2.0 Data Model Specification, ASAM e.V., May 2004
3. Pender T., UML Bible, Publishing House of Electronics Industry, 2004
4. Belaunde M., Burt C., etc. MDA Guide Ver 1.0.1, June 2003
5. Douglass B., etc. Real-Time UML: Developing Efficient Objects for Embedded Systems, Science Press and Pearson Education North Asia Limited, 2003
6. Gomaa H., Designing Concurrent, Distributed, and Real-Time Applications with UML, Pearson Education Inc. 2004
7. Valentine C., Dykes L., Ed., XML Schemas, SYBEX Inc. 2002
8. Birbeck M., etc. Professional XML 2nd Edition, Wrox Press, 2001
9. Horton I., etc. Beginning Java 2 SDK 1.4 Edition, Wrox Press, 2002

CONTACT

Dr. Zaimin Zhong,
College of Automotive Eng.,
Tongji University,
Siping Rd. 1239,
Shanghai, P. R. of China, 200092
zm_zhong@mail.tongji.edu.cn
Tel: 0086-13040631486

Mr. Jirong Li,
College of Automotive Eng.,
Tongji University,
Siping Rd. 1239,
Shanghai, P. R. of China, 200092
Jirong.li@163.com
Tel: 0086-13918289390

DEFINITIONS, ACRONYMS, ABBREVIATIONS

CAE: Computer Aided Engineering
DCS: Distributed Control System
DDX: DCS Data eXchange
DGX: DCS Graphics eXchange
DOM: Document Object Model for XML
DTD: Document Type Definition
GSchema: Graphics XML Schema
GUI: Graphic User Interface
MC&D: Measurement Calibration & Diagnose
MDA: Model Driven Architecture
MOF: Meta-Object Facility
ODX: Open Data eXchange
OPM: Open Process Model
PIM: Platform Independent Model
PMO: Process Model Object
PSchema: Protocol XML Schema
PSM: Platform Specific Model
SAX: Simple API for XML
SVG: Scalable Vector Graphics
UML: Unified Modeling Language
XML: Extensible Markup Language
XSLT: Extensible Stylesheet Language Transformation

2005-01-0320

Enabling Virtual Development for Practical Engine Control

Raymond Turin, John Mills, Steven Fowler and Christopher Myers
SimuQuest, Inc.

ABSTRACT

There is a clear sense of urgency among the automotive industry to cut the cost and time spent on all aspects of vehicle development, and move as much as possible towards virtual design practices. In the area of embedded engine control systems development this move requires that the industry gradually accept a paradigm shift towards a rigorously model-based design practice. This paper elaborates on current shortcomings in the development process and highlights key prerequisites that enable virtual design for engine control applications.

INTRODUCTION

The highly competitive market situation in the automotive business dictates that new products be developed and released at maintained or improved quality levels with increasingly competitive lead times. This is particularly true for the development of embedded engine control systems, as increasingly stringent emissions and safety standards demand ongoing algorithm improvements and the addition of new control features.

However, due to intrinsic limitations in the traditional product development approach, companies find it increasingly difficult to deliver fully tested and validated system upgrades in time, so that current lead times for control system development, calibration and validation are increasingly incompatible with the targeted overall vehicle development cycle times.

The intrinsic limitations have a variety of reasons. Most prominently, the traditional product development approach for embedded engine control systems is heavily focused on component development rather than system development. This is the legacy of the traditional art of engine tuning by means of mechanical devices, an art that also inspired the design of early electronic engine control systems. As newer generations of engine control systems inherited the proven and working functionality of their predecessors, a substantial core of heuristic and phenomenological control functions prevails to this day within engine control systems. The lack of a systematic control design not only gives rise to an increased amount of redundancy among the different control features, but it also ignores important characteristics of the overall control system early in the design stage, and it prohibits early system integration and validation. When combined with a manual software development process this approach can be disastrous, since production programs often encounter complications late in the development stage when necessary product modifications are increasingly expensive and time-consuming.

Another important limitation is the fact that product or control feature development evolves iteratively across intrinsically incompatible development platforms, from control design and simulation to rapid prototyping (with dedicated hardware and software) all the way to the production software development platform. Each transition across a development platform is characterized by efforts to interface the control feature with the available development infrastructure. This requires typically a significant amount of non value-added coding and debugging efforts.

Finally, the current process relies heavily on experimental software validation and algorithm calibration at the end of the development stage. Due to their mostly heuristic nature the control algorithms are often not amenable to a systematic calibration procedure and require instead the intuition of experienced calibrators.

However, the current process, albeit inefficient and arguably at the limits of improvements with regard to productivity, has three significant benefits: It is well understood and proven, it is compatible with the organization's resources and tools, and it is amenable to the incorporation of necessary legacy code. Thus, it is quite understandable that there is a natural inertia against a transition to entirely new practices, even if new practices appear to be the only solution to resolving the impending productivity deficiencies. How to overcome the potential pitfalls of introducing new technologies (even proven ones) in a production setting is a management issue and is beyond the scope of this paper. Any decision to introduce radically new production methods can have dramatic ramifications, and, therefore, must be carefully evaluated and planned at a strategic level. Once decided, however, it is absolutely necessary that appropriate resources in terms of personnel skills, tools, and finances be committed.

From a purely technical standpoint, an improved process has to make use of tools and methods that facilitate a systematic and methodical control system design, alleviate the need for experimental system calibration, and allow for system integration and requirements testing early in the development stage. A process concept that fits this description is by no means new. Over decades, the aerospace industry has been successfully applying model-based design practices and virtual algorithm validation to develop flight control systems for modern airplanes and spacecrafts. Of course, because of a lack of airborne proving grounds, that industry had no other choice than to do so. This paper reflects an attempt to formulate the necessary conditions, tools, and processes, which will establish virtual design in the automotive industry. The paper is organized as follows:

First, the concept of virtual development is defined and key enablers for such a concept are identified. Then, a detailed description of important features for each of the key enablers is given. The paper concludes with an outlook and final remarks.

VIRTUAL DEVELOPMENT CONCEPT

Considering the shortcomings of the current embedded engine control system development process, an improved process must specifically address the following technical issues:

- focus on systems-based rather than components-based algorithm development
- allow for early system integration and requirements testing
- seamlessly integrate all involved development platforms
- eliminate experimental validation

Systems-based algorithm development facilitates a systematic, methodical, and performance-oriented control design procedure. At the center of such a procedure is a thorough analysis of the plant physics and a rigorously model-based algorithm design paradigm. Understanding the physical nature of the plant helps to identify relevant plant characteristics, to minimize the number of heuristic calibration parameters and to optimize the control performance early in the design stage.

A prerequisite for early system integration and requirements testing is a model-based software development process. This process is based on a consistent and exclusive use of feature models (made from graphical modeling tools such as Matlab/Simulink, MatrixX, Stateflow, Statemate, etc.) throughout the different system development stages. The structure of feature models follows the principles of signal flow diagrams, which are the natural tools of control engineers to describe the mathematical nature of control algorithms. The integration of feature models at any given system level is relatively easy and extremely cheap compared to traditional software feature development and integration. Since feature models can be developed for any system functionality the system can be fully tested against the entire set of system requirements before any line of code is generated. Therefore, errors are detected early in the development stage when feature modifications are cheap and inconsequential.

The realization of a seamlessly integrated development environment requires that the control system architecture be redesigned such that it accommodates multiple targets in a seamless manner. The idea is that the main system functionality (what is commonly termed the Application Layer in a software architecture structure) is modeled from the feature models mentioned above in such a way that it can be implemented on different target systems, including a simulation target, without any need for modifications. To avoid manual software development the entire system architecture, including IO drivers and interrupt handling functionality, needs to be conceived in such a way that it is amenable to automated code generation.

Finally, eliminating or at least significantly reducing the need for experimental validation implies that the functionality of the control system can be validated in virtual reality using an accurate yet real-time capable plant model. Note that such a model also serves the need for a thorough plant analysis, and thus can be exploited to expedite and support the control algorithm design. The vision for such a virtual product development concept is summarized in Figure 1.

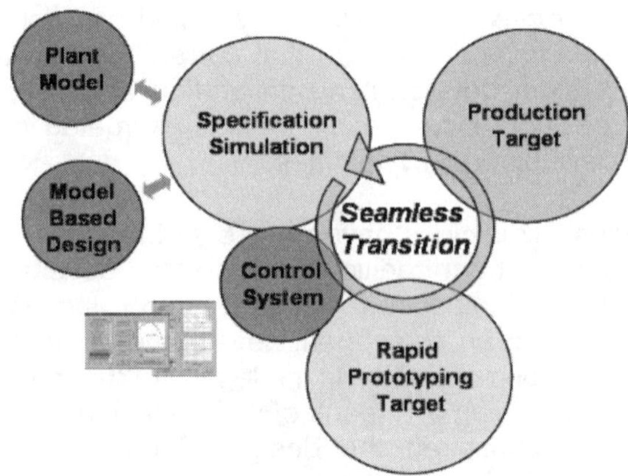

Figure 1 - Illustration of a virtual control system design process

ENABLING TECHNOLOGIES - From the illustration in Figure 1 it is clear that the realization of a seamless virtual design framework hinges on three enabling ingredients:

- a model-based system architecture that accommodates algorithm implementation and testing at any development stage and seamless platform transitions
- an accurate plant model for the target engine
- a suite of model-based control design tools

These complementing pieces need to be realized in such a way that they easily interface with each other. Ideally, to entirely avoid compatibility issues, they are all realized as an integral part of the primary modeling environment. In other words, if Matlab/Simulink is used as the primary modeling environment, it is highly advisable to design each of the key enablers in terms of native Matlab or Simulink functionality. The following paragraphs provide a detailed description of requirements and necessary features for each of the key enablers.

SYSTEM ARCHITECTURE - The control system architecture must be devised in such a way that it intrinsically accommodates different target hardware systems. This requirement implies a strict separation between the target-specific and the target-independent control system functionality. Clearly, the target-specific functionality is that portion of the system that directly interacts with target-specific hardware features, e.g., with I/O devices or with the interrupt system of the target micro. However, the interface between these two portions of the system architecture, in terms of data and task timing, must be identical for all potential implementation targets, i.e., a simulation target, a rapid prototyping target or a production target. Ideally, the feature model that comprehends the target-specific system functionality is realized as a configurable feature model. An example of such a configurable feature model is provided in Figure 2 in the form of a Matlab/Simulink architecture implementation. The target-dependent portion of the system architecture is realized in terms of a configurable subsystem. A configurable Simulink subsystem is a library block that can inherit the properties of any of a set of predefined blocks within the same library model (refer to Matlab/Simulink [1] for a detailed description of configurable subsystems). The example in Figure 2 illustrates an architecture realization involving three possible target configurations, a pure simulation target, a dSPACE Micro Autobox target [2] and production intent MPC5xx target [3].

To be consistent with a model-based software development process the entire functionality of the target-specific feature model should be assembled from dedicated hardware specific model blocks, such as trigger blocks, I/O driver blocks, etc. This minimizes the amount of manual coding and feature testing, but also permits the target-specific feature block to be structured to be largely identical for each of the different target applications.

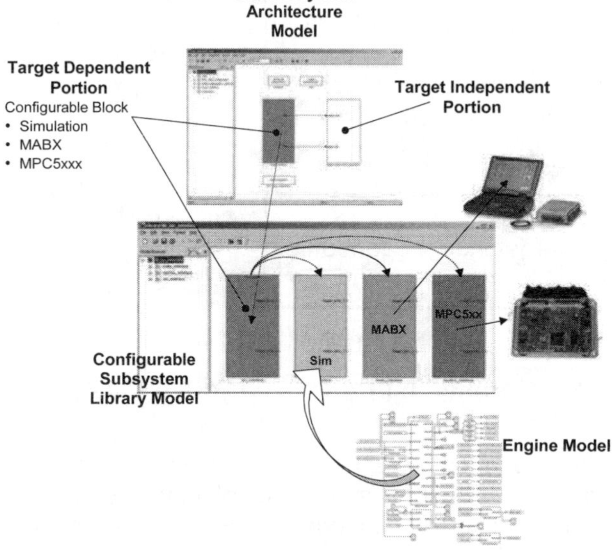

Figure 2 - Implementation of architecture configuration for different targets

A crucial step in crafting a system architecture that supports a virtual development concept is the design of an appropriate interface between the target-specific and the target-independent architecture portions. It is very important that this interface be designed in such a way that it accommodates different target applications without the need for significant changes. There are two major types of information that need to be exchanged between the target-dependent and the target-independent architecture unit across this interface: task timing (trigger) information and plant signal information. To implement the proper task execution it is imperative that the modeling-tool provide trigger signal functionality. Within the graphic signal flow context these trigger signals may seem very similar to regular signals, but the implemented functionality is entirely different. Since different applications typically have different numbers of tasks and different numbers of signals, it is important that both trigger signals and regular process signals be bundled for information propagation across the interface (see Figure 3). That way, the interface between the task-dependent and task-independent units has a consistent and application neutral design. The bundling and exchange of signal or trigger information can be implemented in various ways and using direct or indirect data transfer. However, because the bundled signals may contain large amounts of signal information, any implemented solution must be accompanied with a custom tool that makes the access to the elements of the bundled signals transparent and manageable to the user.

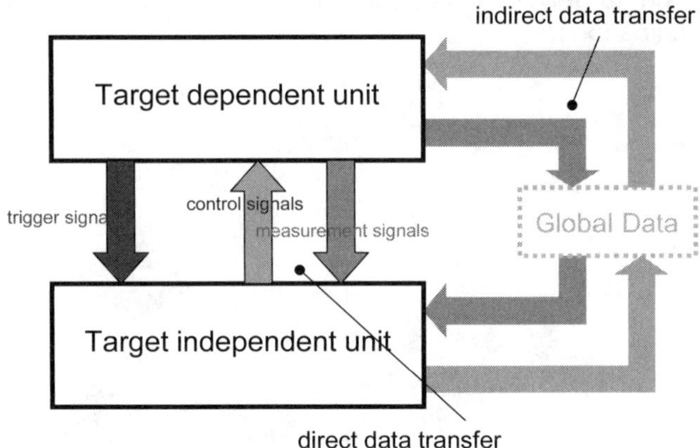

Figure 3 - Information propagation within the system architecture

Probably the most elegant way to implement the bundled signal concept is the use of global data and indirect signal transfer. An example of such a solution is SimuQuest's RPC++ [5], a Matlab /Simulink-based tool that features a data configuration GUI and a virtual bundling concept where each individual signal is associated with a hidden data store block [1]. This tool not only solves the interface issues, but also facilitates plug-and-play algorithm implementation within the system architecture, as it makes individual signal routing obsolete. Note that if the target application supports preemptive task scheduling it is imperative that the implemented signal transfer solution provide consistent data during execution of any of the existing tasks.

<u>Target Microcontroller Blocksets</u> - As already described, the control system architecture should be able to accommodate different target hardware systems. Following the virtual development and verification of an algorithm, final verification is required on test hardware. Off-the-shelf rapid-prototyping systems, such as those available from Opal-RT or dSPACE, are supported by compatible IO blocksets. However, many companies wish to use an ECU during the prototyping phase of development, which utilizes the same microcontroller as will be employed for production.

To support the production intent microcontroller the following are typically required:

- a Simulink blockset to support all of the microcontroller IO and available settings
- customized Simulink driver blocks to support special IO, e.g., CAM and crank inputs, and fuel and spark outputs for engine control

An example of a target blockset that is compatible with the RPC++ architecture is the SimuQuest MPC56x blockset. The MPC56x blockset supports all of the microcontroller configuration options. After integrating the MPC56x IO blocks into the model, production quality code can be generated that can be run on an MPC56x target prototyping module.

<u>Scheduler Blockset</u> – It is often desirable to emulate the scheduler that is to be employed on the production system. To facilitate scheduler emulation, scheduler blocks that accommodate arbitrary scheduling configurations of typical engine control applications are needed. Once such scheduler blocks are available the production intent scheduler can be simulated and production quality scheduler code can be automatically generated.

In summary, the target microcontroller blockset and scheduler blockset integrated into the RPC++ architecture enable a complete production software application to be automatically generated, without the need for any hand coding.

ENGINE MODEL - In a virtual control design setting the engine model takes the place of the target engine, both for algorithm design as well as for testing and validation purposes. Obviously, it is imperative that the model capture the performance characteristics of the target engine with high accuracy. However, the accuracy only has to go as far as it affects control system development. In other words, the model must capture all effects that implicate any of the sensors of the target engine. Similarly, the model must accommodate all inputs associated with the actuators of the target engine. Ideally, the model is architected in terms of reusable component model blocks representing real engine components. The component model blocks can then be used to rapidly assemble comprehensive engine models for any target engine configuration, i.e., single or dual bank, any number of cylinders, etc. Furthermore, it is desirable that the model be complemented with GUI-based tools that support rapid model tuning. Figure 4 provides an overview of relevant engine components.

While it is necessary that the engine model represent the characteristics of the target engine with high accuracy, it is also necessary that the model execute with reasonable speed so that control algorithms can be developed and tested expediently in an interactive manner.

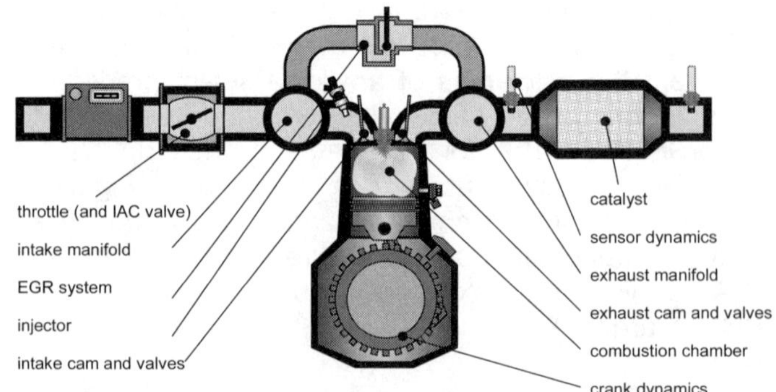

Figure 4 – Schematic of required component models for an engine model

Within the context of a virtual design framework it is necessary that the model be incorporated in the simulation target of the architecture structure outlined above (see schematic in Figure 2). Hence there is a need for basic compatibility between these two framework constituents. The inputs and outputs of the model must be connected to pertinent signal blocks that facilitate the exchange of all necessary data signals to and from the control algorithm functions. As mentioned above, the exchange of information across the interface between target-dependent and target-independent control functionality must be realized in a unified manner that accommodates all possible target configurations (see blocks within the configurable subsystem library model in Figure 2). In particular, the data transfer must be realized in such a way that the entire implementation of the target- independent control system functionality will not be affected if the target is changed.

ALGORITHM DESIGN TOOL SUITE - In order to expedite the development and calibration of engine control systems a systematic methodological design process is needed. At the core of such a process is an analytical appreciation for physical plant characteristics as part of the controller synthesis. This is precisely what model-based methods are based upon.

Model-based control design methods are technically mature, they are innately methodological, and, most importantly, they have been successfully applied in the aerospace industry for decades. This cannot be said for other so-called “intelligent” methods that also claim to solve current engine control development problems.

When they are properly complemented with computer-aided tools and graphic user interfaces, model-based design methods can be expanded into a general tool suite that covers every aspect of modern engine control applications. To be practical for generic engine control applications such a tool suite must accommodate the following controller design needs in an automated fashion:

- procurement of generic linear control design models for a given engine application in any arbitrary nominal operating point
- selection of sub-models of the generic design model involving arbitrary input-output pairings
- GUI supported controller synthesis for different design methods

The first bullet item means the automated derivation of linear design models (linearized around arbitrary nominal operating points) that capture the dynamics of the engine between every possible input and every possible output signal of an engine. The structure for the generic model must be derived from physical considerations. The model parameters must be derived from the sensitivities between relevant engine signals. For this purpose a comprehensive nonlinear model as described in the previous chapter can be used. Figure 5 illustrates the GUI-based model linearization as implemented in the SimuQuest tool suite LTI++. LTI++ is a tool suite that supports the design of linear, time-invariant controllers for arbitrary engine control applications.

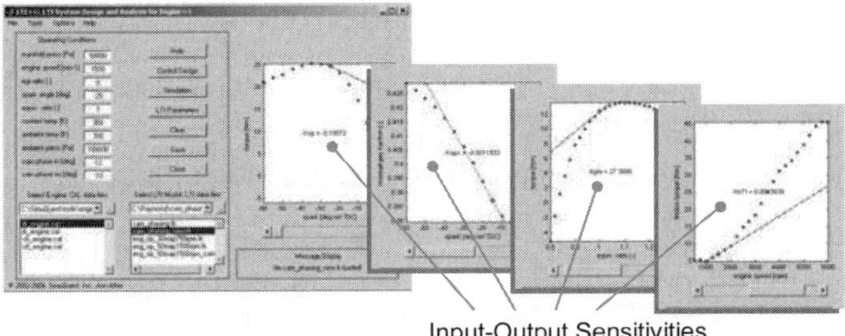

Figure 5 - Derivation of a generic linear engine model (LTI++)

The second bullet means the selection of arbitrary sub-models from a given generic engine model. Such a sub-model is defined by the dynamics between arbitrary input-output signal pairings, and addresses the need for a specific control application. For example, if the application is idle speed control, the selected input signals are spark and throttle position (or idle control valve position) respectively, the selected output signal is engine speed and the sub-model is that portion of the generic linear engine model that captures the interactions between these input and output signals.

Figure 6 illustrates the GUI within the LTI++ tool suite that facilitates the selection of arbitrary input-output signal pairings:

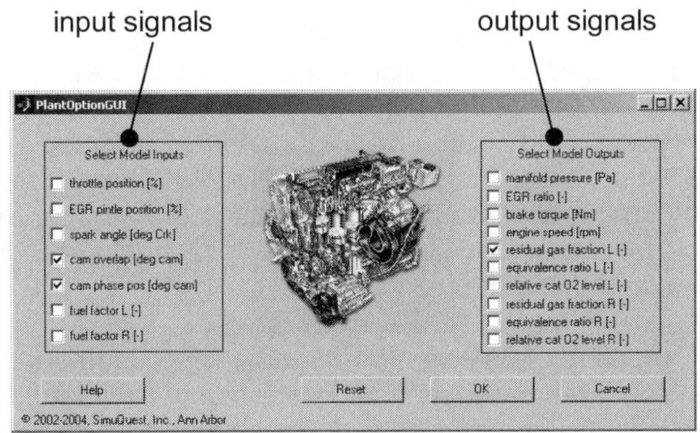

Figure 6 - IO selection for application specific sub-models

The third bullet means the provision of tools that accommodate different model-based controller synthesis methods. The tools need to be devised in such a way that they automatically adjust the display and processing of the available design parameters with respect to the order and the IO characteristics of a given design model and with respect to a selected design method. For example, an H-infinity design requires a weighting function for each of the generalized input and output signals [4]. A PID design, on the other hand, merely requires one PID element for each input signal. The tool must also provide the flexibility to make method-dependent modifications in the synthesis setup and to resolve ambiguities in possible feedback interconnections. For example, in the case of an H-infinity design it should be possible to configure each weighting function either as a high-pass, low-pass or band-pass element (see Figure 7). In the case of a classical design for MIMO applications each output of the plant must be assignable to the input of any of the PID elements. Finally, the tools should facilitate the rapid assessment of important controller characteristics both in the frequency and time domain (see Figure 7).

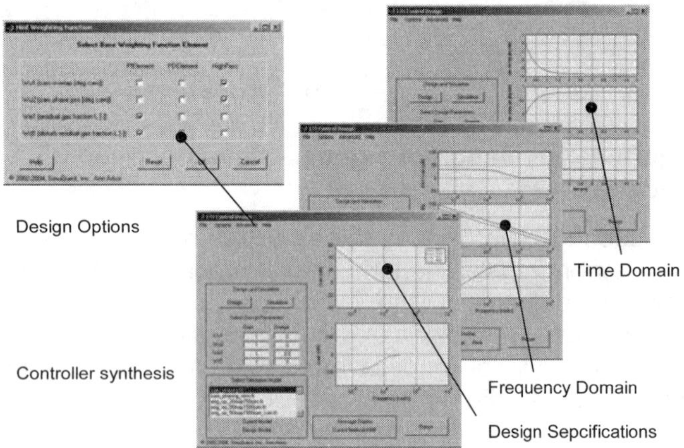

Figure 7 - LTI++ Controller Synthesis Tool

CONCLUSION

There are three key elements that facilitate virtual engine control design (including automated software development): an accurate plant model that can be widely used as a substitute for experimental tests, a suitable system architecture that seamlessly accommodates and integrates the relevant targets of prototyping and production platforms (including the simulation model) and that also facilitates rapid algorithm implementation and validation (plug-and-play), and a GUI-based tool suite for rapidly designing model-based control algorithms.

The industry has seen an increasing number of initiatives and products that are potentially useful for establishing a comprehensive virtual design framework, from model-based system architectures, to accurate engine models, to I/O blocksets for dedicated hardware targets, to tools that aid the control system design. While each of the products may be viable as a standalone entity, its ultimate usefulness in the present context depends on how it complements the other necessary parts and how it interfaces with the overall modeling tool. For example, the engine simulation model must be accurate enough to capture relevant engine performance characteristics in the entire engine operating-envelope. At the same time it must execute fast enough so that the entire control strategy can be evaluated in its ultimate form in simulation in real time.

The implementation architecture must accommodate automated code generation and portability of the control functionality across different hardware targets. Each enabler must seamlessly interface with the primary modeling tool (e.g., Matlab/Simulink). Thus, the key to successfully implement a virtual design practice lies in combining the enabling elements into a consistent, cohesive framework. Figure 8 highlights the ultimate virtual design process within this framework. It is an iterative process that expands into an experimental setting only twice: once at the beginning of the process to procure experimental engine data for adjusting the engine model, and once at the end of the process to download and validate the control system onto the target vehicle hardware.

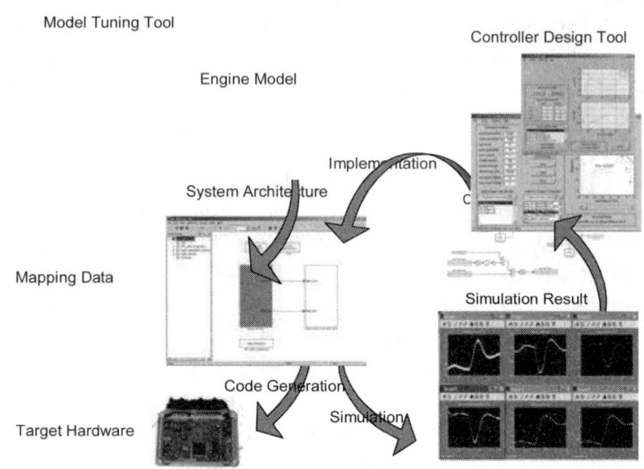

Figure 8 - Virtual control design concept

Of course, while the basic tools for virtual design are available, a number of open issues remain. For the virtual design process to be viable in a production setting it is important for the automotive industry to establish core competencies in each of the enabling areas, i.e., plant modeling, model-based control design, and model-based software development. Furthermore, the notion of calibration needs to be redefined, since most of the controller fine-tuning is done off-line, often as an intrinsic part of the controller synthesis. There will still be very little fine-tuning on the vehicle at the end of the design iterations. Lastly, the target-specific prototyping and calibration tools need to be aligned and consolidated so that they accommodate and support virtual design paradigms.

REFERENCES

1. The MathWorks, Inc., Using Simulink, Version 5.1.1, 2003
2. dSPACE, GmbH, MicroAutoBox Hardware, Online document, Available at HTTP: http://www.dspace.de/ww/en/pub/products/hw/micautob.htm
3. Freescale Semiconductor, MPC500 Micro-controllers, Online document, Available at HTTP: http://www.freescale.com/webapp/sps/site/taxonomy.jsp?nodeId=018rH3bTdG8648
4. Geering H. P., Robuste Regelung, IMRT Press, Institut fuer Mess und Regeltechnik, ETH Zuerich, 3rd ed., 2004
5. SimuQuest Inc., News/Updates, Online document, 2004, Available at HTTP: http://www.simuquest.com

CONTACT

SimuQuest, Inc.

734-426-8518

info@simuquest.com

www.simuquest.com

2004-01-1768

Supporting Model-Based Development with Unambiguous Specifications, Formal Verification and Correct-By-Construction Embedded Software

Wolfram Hohmann
Esterel Technologies

ABSTRACT

In this paper we will explore how 15 years after being introduced into avionics systems, "by-wire" technologies have entered the automotive world. The use of software within safety-relevant application areas like restraint systems, braking, steering and vehicle dynamics support and control systems, is requiring changes in the processes and methodologies used for embedded software development.

INTRODUCTION

Critical embedded systems in automotive applications must operate correctly under all circumstances. Erroneous behavior may not only cause increased costs and delay time to market, but also endanger the safety of passengers and put the business at risk through legal liability.

It is a well-known fact that software quality cannot be assured by system testing alone. The entire design process must also be defined by a "correct-by-construction" methodology and automation. Experiences from the avionics industry have shown that the use of a formal, deterministic and automated solution both reduces cost and improves quality.

This paper will describe a seamless development flow that combines design methodologies for dataflow and finite state machines with formal verification and correct-by-construction code generation.

The tool suite SCADE Drive™ from Esterel Technologies will be examined to illustrate a correct-by-construction methodology with safe automated implementation.

Conventional software development workflows typically follow this pattern: textual specification, manual translation of the specification into a design, review and verification of the translation, manual translation of the design into source code, manual generation of test cases and test pattern, and finally testing the product. The "conventional" method has no future for the development of critical embedded software in the automotive industry. Not only must the previously-mentioned safety objectives be achieved, but also the industry needs methodology and tools that improve communication between members of the project team, between departments within the automotive organization and between the automotive organization and its suppliers.

A model-based workflow, when automated with a correct-by-construction methodology, solves many of the aforementioned problems. "Correct by construction" means that the code produced is guaranteed to be a 100% match with the software specification. The remainder of this paper will explore this method, from creating the software specification to implementing it as embedded code.

SCADE Drive, Esterel Technologies' model-based programming tool suite uses two semantics that complement each other and result in a complete application-level system behavior description.

THE DATAFLOW SOLUTION

DATAFLOWS

The description of data flows connects internal and external data with logical, mathematical and combinatorial operations. Operations can be further combined into user-defined operators.

The graphical symbols used are well-known to electrical engineers from the areas of control engineering and digital signal processing.

Although the description is created using a graphical methodology, the basis for the models is the formal language Lustre, developed at the University of

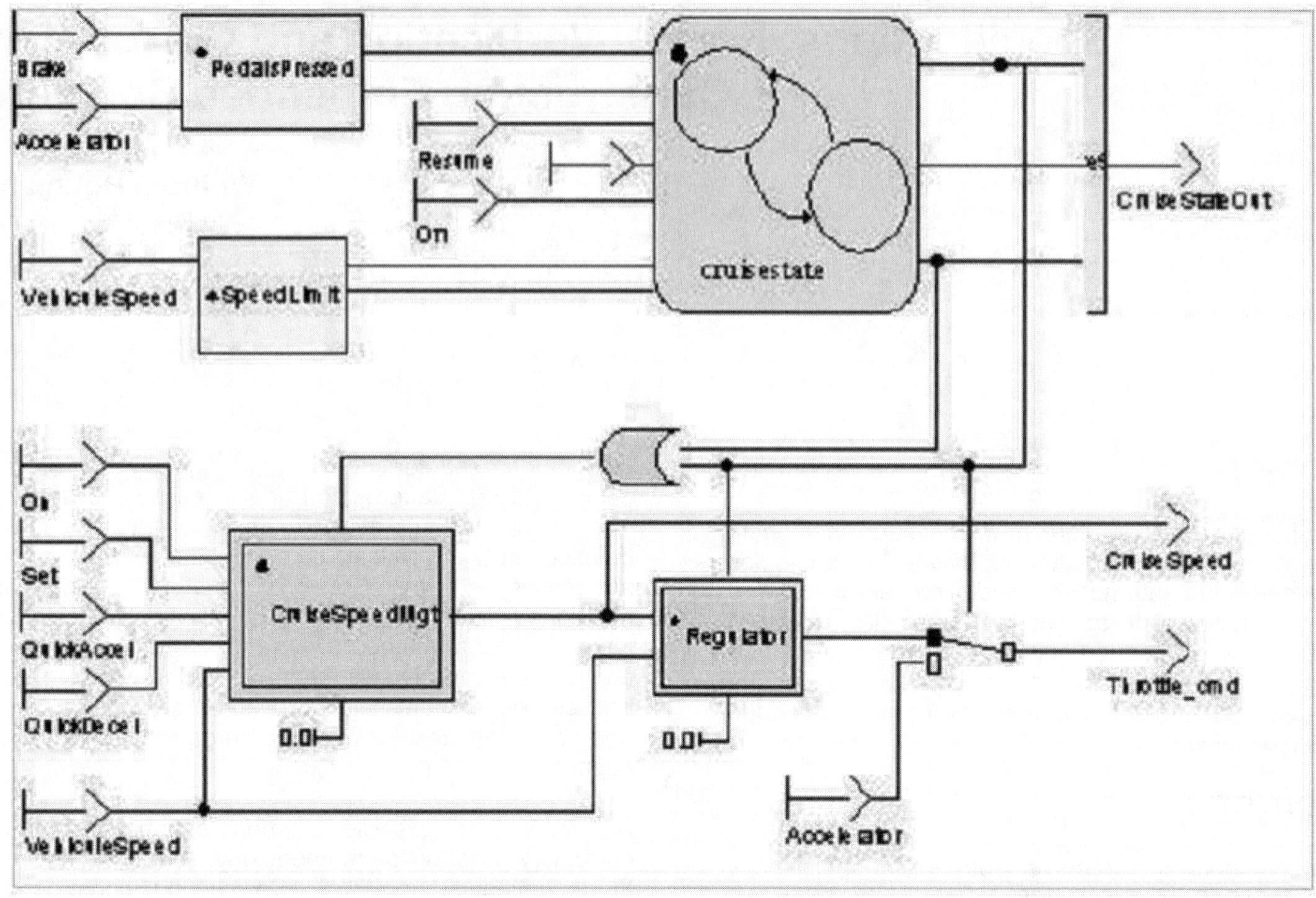

Figure 1 – Data Flows Connect Internal and External Data

Grenoble by Paul Caspi et. al. Data flow diagrams can also contain finite state machines.

STATE MACHINES

The description of finite state machines is accomplished using the formalism of "synch charts". Synch charts have been transformed by Esterel Technologies into a robust modeling method called "Safe State Machines". The finite state machines designed with this formalism can include hierarchies and true parallelisms.

Compared to other methods and tools, designers programming with Safe State Machines use a precise, unambiguous formalism, including the clear assignment of priorities in branched transitions rather than an automatic assignment of priorities based upon the graphical ordering of design elements. It is this level of formalism that assures that the eventually embedded software matches its specification 100%. Tools and methods that use informal processes cannot guarantee this.

Safe State Machines are based upon the formal, synchronous language Esterel originally defined at INRIA and Ecole de Mines by Gerard Berry, now Chief Technical Officer of Esterel Technologies.

DECLARATIVE LANGUAGES, DETERMINISM AND SYNCHRONICITY

The main technological difference between SCADE Drive and competing methodologies is not the look and feel of the tool or even its sophisticated use of symbols. The core of the differentiation is the underlying synchronous languages, Lustre and Esterel, that form the basis of the models. Only the use of these languages enables predictability of simulation, formal verification and correct-by-construction code generation. We will now highlight some of the important specific

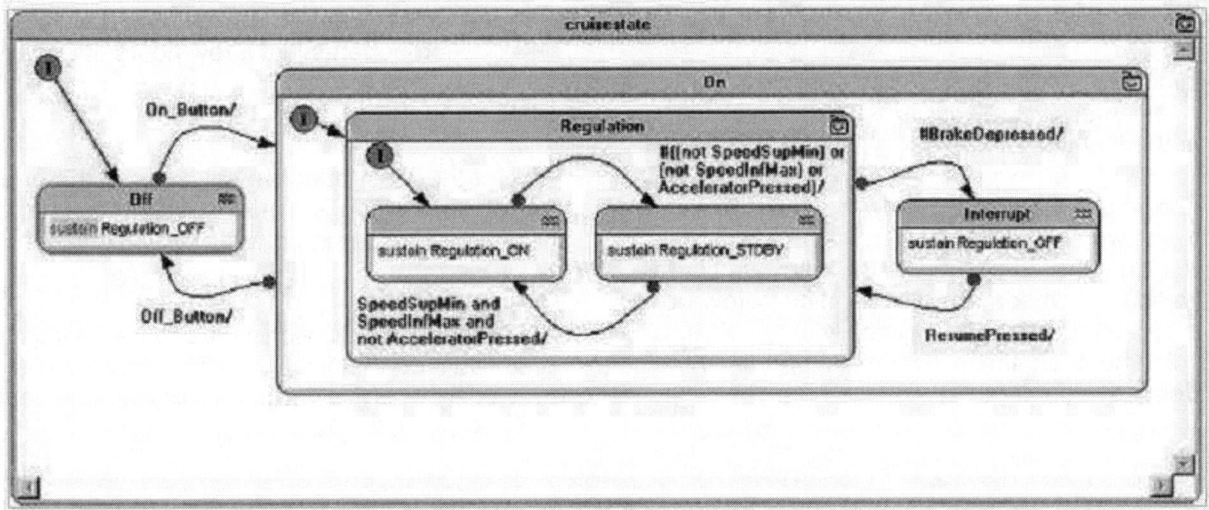

Figure 2 – State Machines

differences between these declarative languages and compare them to imperative languages.

Declarative Languages

Declarative languages differ from imperative languages (like C, C++ or Java) in that statements in declarative languages don't describe the sequence of the program flows such as *first add a to b, then if x <z add a to c.*

Instead, declarative languages describe a set of output values of a system $\underline{O}$ (t) and the set of the system state $\underline{S}$(t) by means of the set of input values $\underline{I}$(t) and the set of the previous state. $\underline{S}$(t-T). For example:

$\underline{O}$(t) = F1 ($\underline{I}$(t), $\underline{S}$(t-T)) and

$\underline{S}$(t) = F2 ($\underline{I}$(t), $\underline{S}$(t-T))

Synchronicity

Synchronicity is the basis of the computational model in the Esterel and Lustre languages. It is built upon the theory that all computations are executed at a certain logical moment and that **all** computations (calculating the outputs of all blocks by means of their inputs, determining the new state of **all** finite state machines) are executed in the **same** logical moment. Internal events that are generated from "firing" transitions are not inserted into event queues; they will be calculated in the same logical moment when they are generated. The same model is used for data flows that are generated by executing mathematical or logical operations. All operations are virtually executed at the same time, which implies that all feedback loops have to be explicitly calculated based upon the dataflow value that was valid at an earlier moment. This is one of the reasons why time-related operators like y= **Pre**(x) which assigns the value of x to y at a previous moment in time are so important in Lustre. In fact, all types of circular assignments in Safe State Machines will be detected by the tool in a similar way and the programmer notified of these errors.

It should be mentioned that circular event assignments as well as feedbacks lead to potential deadlock situations in asynchronous programming environments, especially if they use "event queues". As a consequence, customers using these tools have defined design guidelines that restrict many unsafe practices and forbid things these tools cannot do well, including parallel state machines and hierarchy. Because the SCADE methodology and tool handle both parallelism and hierarchy elegantly, no such restrictions are necessary.

Determinism

The **Determinism** of behavior is a direct result of synchronicity. Synchronicity guarantees that in a given system state the same sequence of input data always results in the same set of output data and new system state, respectively. Therefore it is possible to clearly predict the system behavior of the embedded software from the simulation results.

SIMULATION AND FORMAL VERIFICATION

SYSTEM AND SOFTWARE TESTS

An important objective of model-based methods for embedded systems is the earliest possible verification of the correctness. Simulation and formal verification are proven techniques that have a long and successful history in hardware development, saving time and effort for verification and preventing cost-intensive rework. Software development, including the development of critical embedded software, has lagged far behind.

Historically, the following issues have bedeviled software development:

1. Testing always starts late, compounded by the fact that massive rework is typically necessary after the first tests.

2. In the traditional flow, hardware development and software development remain sequential, which means that most of the software development work starts with the first hardware-software integration. This typically puts software development on the critical path of the entire system development.

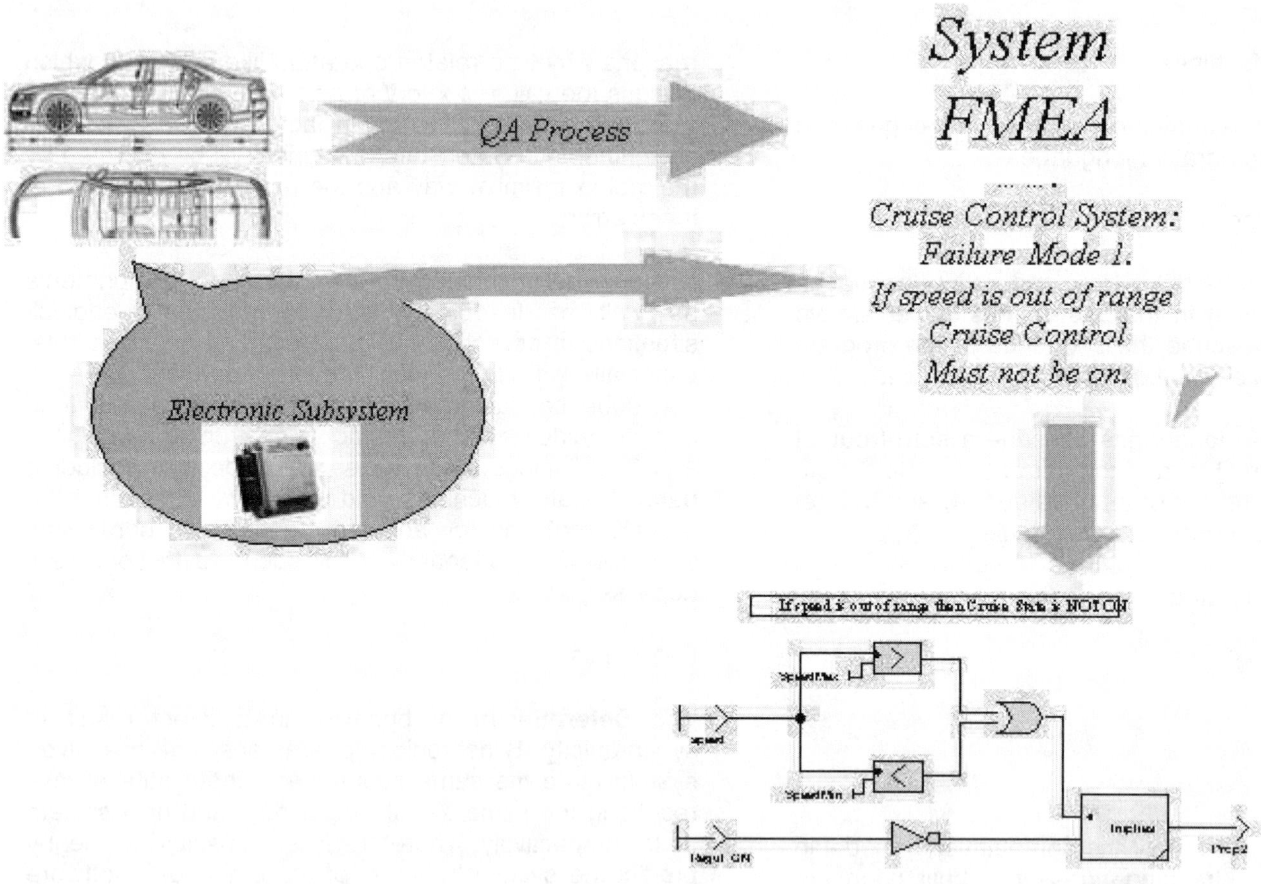

Figure 3 – FMEA System

3. The correct analysis of errors is very difficult due to the fact that during testing the software is embedded into the entire target system.

4. Test coverage measurement is very complicated, and absolute coverage may be nearly impossible to predict. History has shown that even months and months of traditional testing cannot prevent the failure of software components just a few hours after delivery.

SIMULATION

One of the most effective solutions to the need for early design verification is simulation. One basic aspect of this issue is especially important:

The simulated behavior needs to be a clear and unique prediction of the final system behavior. As discussed previously in this paper, this requirement can be achieved best through the use of deterministic models.

RAPID PROTOTYPING

Rapid Prototyping, defined here as simulating system behavior using a prototype version, is a good development strategy IF this same software can then be reused for the embedded code. Otherwise prototyping is a waste of resources and risks the introduction of new errors during the reimplementation of the code. The correct-by-construction methods described in this paper achieve the objectives of rapid prototyping but create embeddable code from the start.

FORMAL VERIFICATION

Traditional test methods define test cases in a positive and forward manner. This means they are based upon the system specification and are intended to prove that if certain paths of stimulation (forward) are followed, the function behaves correctly per the specification (positive). Test coverage is then estimated using various methods that have been created through theoretical and practical studies.

In addition to traditional testing, a quality assurance process based upon Failure Mode Effect Analysis (FMEA) is a de-facto standard in the automotive world and uses a "negative" and "backward" approach. First the application is analyzed from the outside and fatal situations that must be avoided under all circumstances are defined (negative). Next, tests are specified to determine that these situations never occur (backward).

Formal Verification offers an excellent method to fulfill the negative, backward approach of FMEA, creating also the real possibility of guaranteeing total test coverage. Instead of designing test cases by hand, executing them and then trying to estimate the test coverage afterwards, the mathematical correctness of the model itself is checked with formal verification. The fatal situation defined in an FMEA is then proven mathematically to determine if the situation to be avoided will ever occur.

An example: A cruise control system shall only regulate the speed if the speed itself is inside the bounds of minimum and maximum speed. This specific requirement derived from an FMEA can be modeled using an automated formal design and verification method such as the one provided by the SCADE Drive tool.

SCADE automates formal design and verification with Design Verifier*. Design Verifier allows the designer to detect specification errors and validate the design by proving that the required properties hold in all the possible cases and that:

The potential fatal situation can never happen. The test coverage of this result is 100 %, or under certain circumstances the fatal situation can happen. Design Verifier will give precise information about the erroneous scenario.

Formal verification is an excellent enhancement to a standard testing plan and can greatly improve the quality of testing. In fact, for safety-critical applications, formal verification provides such a large improvement in testing quality, it is very probable that we will see the continuation of today's trend where formal verification is defined to be a state-of-the-art process for automotive embedded software quality assurance.

AUTOMATIC CODE GENERATION

REQUIREMENTS FOR AUTOMATIC CODE GENERATION

The entire workflow can only be seen as being seamless if it is possible to generate portable C code from the designed, simulated and verified model. To reach this objective, the code generator has to fulfill certain requirements:

- The identicalness between the model and the generated code has to be proven.
- The generated code has to obey the highest quality standards.
- The generated code must not have too large an overhead with respect to code size.

In order to fulfill the first requirement, we decided to certify its code generator according to the avionics guideline DO-178B at the highest level of that guideline, Level A. The result is a "qualifiable" code generator. The customer using this code generator must produce a "qualification kit" for the specialists working on the project. The qualification kit is provided by Esterel Technologies. The code generator is qualified on the project and the resulting code can then be certified. Although this extremely strict guideline is not required in the automotive industry the automotive industry is moving toward these same types of guidelines and certification requirements for safety-critical embedded software.

We have been closely watching the automotive software development standard IEC-61508, and fully expect it to become the ubiquitous standard for safety-relevant software development in the automotive industry. In 2003, we began a certification project of its code generator with the German certification authority, TÜV. The goal is to achieve certification of the code generator as being certified for IEC-61508 SIL 4 (the highest level). We have already analyzed its generated C code relative to another emerging standard for development, MISRA, and found it to be in compliance. This analysis has been documented and is available from Esterel Technologies upon request.

One of the concerns sometimes voiced about automatic code generation is that the generated code has too much overhead. While this is true of older, primitive code generators, the latest benchmarks and comparisons of the SCADE code generator have shown that although the output of the code generator is dependent upon the design quality of the model (a model created using "brute force and ignorance" will always result in a suboptimal code), models designed with emphasis on design quality when generated with SCADE produce code that is absolutely comparable in size and performance to hand-coded software.

CONCLUSION

The proliferation of embedded software in safety and business-critical automotive applications, coupled with persistent cost and time to market pressures, has mandated new methods and tools for the development of embedded software.

Lessons can be learned from the Avionics industry, which began going through a similar transition more than 10 years ago and has pioneered the development of methods and tools that automatically produce embeddable code for even the most sensitive of safety-critical applications.

This paper has shown that model-based workflows, formal verification and correct-by-construction automatic code generation maintains or increases the quality and productivity of embedded software development and can enhance existing processes like FMEA.

REFERENCES

1. G. Berry and G. Gonthier. The Esterel synchronous programming language: Design, semantics, implementation. *Science of Computer Programming*, 19(2):87–152, 1992.
2. G. Berry. The foundations of Esterel. In G. Plotkin, C. Stirling und M. Tofte, Editors, *Proof, Language and Interaction: Essays in Honour of Robin Milner*. MIT Press, 1998.
3. Ch. Andre. Synccharts: A visual representation of reactive behaviors. Rapport de recherche tr95-52, Université de Nice-Sophia Antipolis, 1995.
4. N. Halbwachs, P. Caspi, P. Raymond und D. Pilaud. The synchronous dataflow programming language LUSTRE. *Proceedings of the IEEE*, 79(9):1305–1320, 1991.

* Design Verifier is powered by Prover Plug-In. Prover Plug-In is a trademark of Prover Technology AB in Sweden, the United States and other countries.

CONTACT

Wolfram Hohmann, wolfram.hohmann@esterel-technologies.com

2004-01-0720

Managing the Challenges of Automotive Embedded Software Development Using Model-Based Methods for Design and Specification

Mark Yeaton
The MathWorks, Inc.

ABSTRACT

This paper will discuss the issues associated with the creation of embedded software for automotive electronic control systems and show how these issues can be addressed using model-based methods to design, test and implement these systems. Model-based methods are already in use for many automotive applications, and there are potentially many more areas where they could be used, especially as the number and complexity of automotive embedded control systems increase. This paper will cite several examples of the successful use of model-based design.

AUTOMOTIVE EMBEDDED SOFTWARE

Embedded software will continue to be an important factor affecting the cost and development time of automotive electronic systems. In a recent article in *Automotive Engineering International* magazine, the president of a large automotive electronic components supplier states that the total value of software will more than triple, to 13% of a vehicle's cost, between 2000 and 2010. Because of consumer demand and heavy government regulation centered about environmental, safety, and performance issues, it is likely that a fair amount of this software will fall into the class of "control systems," with the remainder classified into other categories such as convenience, entertainment, and similar functions. The expansion of software applications will also be fueled by faster processor speeds and cheaper, more abundant memory. Design teams will need to increase in size and number as the amount of software continues to grow. Information exchange within and between these teams will need to occur rapidly and flawlessly.

Clearly, software development methods will need to keep pace so that vehicle, vehicle subsystem, and component delivery schedules and design budgets are not at risk of being compromised by software faults and failures. Well known research data (*Software Engineering Economics*, Dr. B. Boehm, Prentice-Hall 1981) has shown that the relative cost of fixing software defects increases one hundred times from initial requirements analysis to in-service use. In his book *Software Verification and Validation for Practitioners and Managers* (Artech House 2001), Steven Rakitin cites other supporting data that justifies the economic need to improve design and development techniques so that any defects that do exist are found and fixed as early as possible in the design effort.

EMBEDDED SOFTWARE DESIGN AND DEVELOPMENT CHALLENGES

The increased use of embedded systems in all types of products has challenged the ability of embedded systems software designers to successfully manage their design, development, and implementation. An article in the December 2002 issue of *Software Development Times* magazine cites a market study by Venture Development Corp., a technology market research and consulting firm that specializes in industrial and commercial electronics, computing, communications, software, and power systems markets. Their research data shows that over half (51.6%) of all embedded software design projects are late. Of the 48.4% of the projects that did not make it into the late category, almost one fifth were cancelled and almost one quarter were ahead of schedule, leaving only a small fraction that were judged to be on schedule.

The survey categorized the reasons for the projects being late into five responses: changes in specifications, complexity of the application, inadequate specifications, too few developers, and too few testing personnel. While this data did not specifically address the automotive industry or control system software, it is reasonable to assume that embedded control system software development in the automotive industry cannot be any less of a challenge than the norm in the embedded industry as a whole. This paper will examine how a "model-based design" approach can address the issues cited in the survey in the context of embedded control system software design and implementation.

THE NEED FOR MODEL-BASED DESIGN

Many manufacturers and component suppliers have already reached the point where their embedded control system projects cannot be undertaken using existing practices. These traditional methods typically require that designers write and implement software on prototype systems in order to understand the design. The need to begin the design before product prototypes and target hardware platforms are available has led to the adoption of model-based design methods. Model-based methods let designers construct detailed mathematical models of the product and software behavior. Using simulation, they evaluate their control system software designs on a desktop workstation, rather than in the lab or on a test track.

Historically, model-based design methods have been used in the aerospace industry for years, where the ability to construct working prototypes and test articles is severely limited by cost, safety, and security concerns. Early implementations of model-based design methods required engineers to create models using FORTRAN code and develop solution techniques for the equations that defined the models. While it is still possible that code could be written to implement a model of the physical product and the software itself could provide a model of the functionality of the final application, this is not the normal practice today.

A VISUAL DESIGN ENVIRONMENT AIDS IN UNDERSTANDING COMPLEX SYSTEMS

Today, most model-based design efforts are implemented in commercially available design packages that have the ability to abstract the product model and control system design information from a textual level to a visual level. Using shapes, color, size, and position, visual icons are used to describe the models of both the product itself and the embedded control system software. In addition, hierarchical design partitioning is a natural extension of the visual paradigm, and allows even the largest systems to be represented in a compact and meaningful way. As an added benefit, these hierarchical modeling elements can be easily reused in subsequent design efforts. The ability to visualize these complex software designs and the mathematical models of product behavior allows designers to easily understand and evaluate the design's correctness and performance.

Avoiding the need to write software early in the design process does not give designers free reign to create models and implement designs that are of no use to anyone but themselves. Successful implementations of model-based methods using visual design environments are carefully planned so that all team members adhere to standards and agree to certain practices for creating the models. This leads not only to efficiency within the design team itself, but also facilitates information exchange between vendors and suppliers.

THE EVALUATION OF SYSTEM SPECIFICATIONS BY MODEL SIMULATION

Model-based methods help to address the problem of inadequate specifications, since models can be simulated to determine if the design will meet requirements. Each hierarchical model element can stand on its own and design testing and evaluation can start very early in the model building process. The model becomes more complex and fully defined through the addition of more hierarchical elements or the substitution of "placeholder" or "stub" models with fully defined models. At every step in the construction of the model, simulation continues to give the designer confidence that the design is progressing as expected. This "build a little, test a little" philosophy reduces the likelihood of "surprises" at or near the end of the design effort.

THE MODEL IS THE SPECIFICATION

As visual methods for model-based design have matured, their ability to capture more than just mathematical and behavioral information about the system has improved. Very specific information that defines the actual software implementation, such as data typing, data structures, timing, and software structure can be defined and, where appropriate, evaluated by simulation. Most design tools provide the ability to capture textual information, which is used by members of the design team as a roadmap for design development and for formal documentation purposes. With these abilities inherent in the modeling environment, the model can become the specification for the design, allowing management of changes to be accomplished in the visual environment, rather than in a textual document.

Using the model information as a specification, the automatic creation of documentation and software becomes possible. With flexible and capable code generation tools, the automatically generated code can serve multiple purposes, such as prototyping, calibration, and even actual production implementation, all using the same model.

The ability to automatically generate code from the fully tested specification defined by the model frees software developers from the need to perform the manual task of creating code from a specification. They are able to use their time more effectively for more challenging systems integration tasks and to manually develop the code that is needed for hardware device drivers, communications, and operating system interfaces.

SOFTWARE TESTING CONSIDERATIONS

Since the complete system behavioral model, consisting of the physical product and the embedded software, is fully exercised by simulation very early in the design process, many errors are found and fixed long before final integration and testing takes place. Testing personnel will find fewer errors and will likely work more efficiently.

EXAMPLES OF MODEL-BASED DESIGN IN PROTOTYPE AND PRODUCTION APPLICATIONS

Automotive manufacturers and suppliers have largely adopted model-based design methods, but to different degrees. Each design situation is unique, with varying levels of legacy and opportunity for change that drive the degree to which a model-based design approach can be adopted.

Implementing a model-based design approach does not require complete reengineering of existing software development practices. Prudent business practices generally favor risk mitigation when adopting new technologies, and organizations can accomplish the insertion of model-based design into their existing environment in a staged manner. This can be as simple as "shadowing" a design effort or carving out a small project where model-based design can prove itself in a well-bounded and low-risk way. Then, as confidence is gained and the relationship of model-based design methods to existing practices is understood, full projects can be undertaken.

A key to the success of model-based design methods is the flexibility to integrate easily with existing design and implementation environments. Many well-known manufacturers have made considerable progress using model-based design techniques to the point where real-time prototyping and tuning of control system designs does not require the designer to manually develop any application-specific source code. Some manufacturers are currently using the model information to create software applications that are used directly in production vehicles. Others have built complete hardware-in-the-loop facilities where production embedded engine controllers can be tested without the need for real engines. The real-time software for these simulated engines comes directly and automatically from the models.

A few actual examples from the automotive industry are provided below, and many more are available. The range of automotive application areas where model-based design is used spans everything from the most basic to the most complex. In addition to the examples shown, model-based design methods have proved themselves in applications such as climate control, chassis control, transmission control, motorcycle engine control, and diesel engine control for heavy construction equipment. Even the design and production of equipment for automotive system testing, such as road simulators, has been aided with the use of model-based design.

With new technologies such as fuel cell power plants, engineers are taking advantage of a model-based approach to designing the embedded control and fuel production systems that make them practical for automotive use. Certainly, there will be no shortage of new technologies in the future of the automotive industry. Electric valve actuation, 42V electrical systems, and intelligent vehicles will require their developers to use model-based design approaches or face competitors who do.

EATON CORPORATION

Hybrid electric powertrains for trucks have the potential to reduce total cost and improve performance while also reducing emissions. They combine a traditional internal combustion engine, electric traction motors, a transmission, and energy storage devices that both propel the vehicle and extract and store energy during braking. The operation of these components is coordinated by a central powertrain control unit. Designing and building a prototype hybrid vehicle is a significant challenge. The internal combustion engine, electric motor, transmission, and energy storage devices can be connected in several different configurations, depending on how the vehicle will be used, and these components need to be sized for optimal performance over various routes.

A model-based design approach allowed Eaton to design the system before prototype hardware was available, then gradually integrate the real components and embedded control system using a real-time hardware-in-the-loop approach, where component models provided the specification for real-time software that could accurately simulate the behavior of the components that were not yet integrated.

JAGUAR

To meet demands for increasingly complex new vehicles while continuing to reduce costs, where possible, Jaguar develops and tests new functionality using existing production vehicles instead of building expensive prototypes.

Using general-purpose electronic control units (ECUs) and a model-based approach, Jaguar can support a variety of application areas including transmission, driver entertainment, and body system. The model-based design approach allows initial development to take place off-line on the designer's desktop computer, then easily transition to real systems, allowing more complete and accurate specifications to be sent to suppliers for them to develop the actual system.

MOTOROLA

The Motorola Automotive Group recently developed and optimized software for a battery management controller using a model-based design approach. Developing the controller was difficult because the interfaces among various system components were fluid and subject to change. A model-based design approach proved to be well suited to managing the changing requirements and providing fast design turnaround times. Code was automatically generated from the system model for the fixed-point HC12 microcontroller, using scaling factors that were automatically selected during model simulation.

RICARDO CONSULTING ENGINEERS

Gasoline direct-injection engines differ from other fuel-injected systems in that the fuel is injected directly into the combustion chamber, where it can form a stratified (non-uniform) mixture with the air. This system has the potential to give the engine improved performance and economy while still meeting emission standards. However, these advantages can only be realized with control strategies developed to optimize the appropriate fuel/air mixture.

Ricardo was able to model and simulate the six operational engine modes required, then design a control system for each one, plus manage the transition between each. The final design reduced emissions by approximately 50% and was completed with considerable cost savings.

TOYOTA

Engineers at Toyota needed an alternative to traditional design methods that were neither cost-effective nor efficient and that were hampered by costly or incomplete hardware prototypes and a design process that required re-engineering and re-programming at several steps along the way. A model-based design approach was selected as a way to bridge the gaps in their traditional automotive electronics development and create executable specifications to consolidate the work of spec writers, control designers, and programmers.

Using the model as an executable specification, real-time software for both hardware-in-the-loop testing and electronic control unit prototyping is automatically generated. When the system design was debugged and calibrated, software for the production control unit is automatically generated from the same model used to produce the code for prototyping and calibration. Toyota has shortened design cycles, reduced the amount of hardware prototypes required, and developed innovative new products as a result of adopting a model-based design approach.

SUMMARY

Designers of embedded system software in all industries face challenges as their designs progress from requirements to implementation. A model-based approach to embedded control system design is a proven technique for addressing challenges faced by automotive embedded systems engineers. This paper has shown how each challenge is addressed by the model-based design approach and has described actual usage of model-based design methods in commercial environments.

Born out of necessity in the aerospace industry, the concept of model-based design has fully evolved from a primitive, do-it-yourself endeavor to a well-accepted, commercial, off-the-shelf practice that can be used to the extent needed by a given project or organization. Today's modeling environments for embedded control systems are flexible, adaptable and can contain all the information necessary to define the complete embedded control system design and implementation. This gives organizations the immediate benefits of modeling and simulation, as well as the ability to fully exploit the model information for real-time software and documentation when they are ready.

Significant savings in time and cost over traditional design methods are possible. Model-based methods allow designers to begin design work earlier and confirm requirements and performance without the need to create hardware prototypes and write software. The ability to express the model in a visual environment lets designers easily share and reuse design information, avoiding the introduction of errors due to misinterpretation. The net result is that fewer errors are found during final testing and implementation of the software design and better products are produced.

2004-01-0713

Lessons Learned from Model Based Development of a Distributed Embedded Automotive Control System

Martin Törngren and Niklas Adamsson
KTH – Royal Institute of Technology

Per Johannessen
Volvo Car Corporation

ABSTRACT

Model based development promises to facilitate the development of embedded control systems, including design, early verification and validation as well as implementation. Existing tools are beginning to support the development of distributed control systems. There are however still challenges when it comes to integration with mechanics and methodologies for such interdisciplinary systems.

INTRODUCTION

This paper describes a joint project between Volvo Car Corporation and the Department of Machine Design at the Royal Institute of Technology (KTH), including the Division of Mechatronics and the Division of Integrated Product Development. The overall purpose of the project was to develop a suitable tool-chain environment that supports model based development of embedded control systems, and in particular Function and ARchitecture (FAR) integration. The tool chain development consisted of evaluating existing tools, choosing a suitable candidate and tailoring it for use in the project. A model car demonstrator and its distributed control system were developed as part of the project.

Engineers and senior researchers at KTH and Volvo Cars supported a group of students in their project within the Master of Science specialization in Mechatronics at KTH.

The structure of the paper is as follows: the remainder of Section 1 introduces automotive embedded systems and the FAR project. Section 2 briefly discusses challenges in model based development and Section 3 describes the results of the FAR project. Experiences obtained in the project are presented and discussed in Section 4, and Section 5 concludes the paper.

BACKGROUND - The use of automotive embedded systems is steadily increasing. Embedded control systems enable a wide range of innovative functionality and means to improve existing functions, including active safety functionality implemented in the chassis control system. An important step in this evolution is the drive-by-wire technology. These systems will have to handle high complexity and have high requirements on dependability.

Essential parts of the complexity challenge for these systems include making use of several disciplines at once and criticality. The interaction between disciplines in the systems on one hand provides new opportunities for design, but on the other hand also makes development much more complicated, since people with different backgrounds need well-established communication to work efficiently together. In addition, the new competencies and methods of working that are required for efficient development of mechatronical systems do not match how industry and academia are organized and work today [10, 16]. As a further obstacle, the development of automotive systems spans several companies.

When mechanical systems are replaced by embedded control systems, the software-based solutions need to be at least as reliable as their mechanical counterparts. This is a challenge, since computer control systems add new types of complexity. Examples thereof include new types of system entities, interrelations between entities and the introduction of new faults [5].

The current methods of system development invariably lead to (see [15] for an overview on design practices in automotive development):

- long turn-around time, since the complete vehicle behavior can only be tested late in the integration phase

- lack of continuity between requirements definition, system design and distributed system implementation; typically involving different people and with little formalized communication (e.g. handing over textual specifications)

- sub-optimal solutions, because of the lack of formal models and holistic (co-)design approach

To meet these challenges, requires new competencies, new approaches of organizing work and new tools. As a mean to improve this situation, model based development is strongly pushed in both industry and research.

THE TASK OF THE FAR PROJECT - During 2002 when the project was formed we wished to develop an environment for rapid prototyping of automotive functionality with support for evaluation of electrical design concepts. The development environment should consist of a tool chain for automatic code generation from Simulink models to executable C code for a distributed computer environment. As a target for the C code and a demonstrator of new functionality, a prototype car was planned. The target environment should also support fault injection for validation and verification of the systems, electrical design concepts such as allocation patterns and redundancy techniques. The overall budget for the project was limited to 350 kSEK and should cover all material and software development costs, KTH and Volvo Cars covered man-hours. [3]

PROJECT IMPLEMENTATION - The project was implemented as part of a final year project course at KTH. The division of Mechatronics at KTH has been conducting such courses since 1983. The overall aim of the course is:

After the course the student will have knowledge and skills to develop mechatronic products in small or large development teams.

The projects are organized as development projects typically developing a prototype. The FAR project included 10 students and three supervisors from KTH and Volvo Cars. The total effort of the project is estimated to be approximately 7 man-years. The project started in November 2002 and ended early June 2003.

MODEL BASED DEVELOPMENT OF AUTOMOTIVE CONTROL SYSTEMS

CONCEPT OF MODEL BASED DEVELOPMENT - As mentioned in the introductory section, complexity management calls for new development approaches in order to meet requirements on time-to-market, product quality and product optimization. The last item is essential for large series production, where especially production cost must be kept low. However, today, development and maintenance costs related to software and electronics are also becoming significant [9].

These requirements call for a more mature engineering approach that employ models that can be used to support design, analysis and synthesis, in early as well as late development stages.

We define model based development as:

Systematic use of modeling throughout the life cycle to support product development and maintenance.

The following aspects are central to MBD:

- *Modeling language(s) providing appropriate levels of abstraction in system.* The languages are based on well defined modeling syntax and semantics, and support the specific system aspects or qualities such as timing and reliability of interest in design.
- *A modeling framework (or meta-model) that relates different models (e.g. through refinement) and aspects (e.g. functionality and timing behavior) to each other – providing a systems perspective.*
- *Design methodology providing guidelines for modeling as well as for design in terms of principles, heuristics and known solutions.*
- *A process, defining design tasks and their dependencies for implementing MBD.*
- *Tools, for implementing and automating MBD.*
- *Usability support including suitable graphical representations and separations of concern such as multi-view modeling.*

The need for an increase of the abstraction level follows directly from the need to cope with the system complexity. Model based development intends to ease communication within the development organizations, as well as between different companies, since product data is embedded in the different models that are used. One holistic goal for model based development is to replace written specifications.

One very important aim of MBD is to carry out verification and validation of concepts and solutions in very early development stages. The ultimate solution is to explore a virtual car.

There are several initiatives striving towards MBD, including domain specific and more general ones including East-EAA - MBD for the automotive industry [6], Model driven architecture proposed by OMG [11], and Control system development, see for example [2].

These and other approaches differ in that they represent different traditions, focus on different system aspects/qualities and to what extent they take domain specific constraints into account.

ISSUES FOR MBD OF EMBEDDED CONTROL SYSTEMS - There are multitudes of challenges with MBD that must be dealt with. Over the past decades a large number of efforts have been made to increase the efficiency of embedded systems development. A strong continuing trend is that of trying to raise the level of abstraction at which systems are specified and designed, and to provide tools that assist in transferring such designs to operational systems. Related to this trend, embedded systems programming has been progressing from the use of assembly languages to high-level programming languages, and more recently the use of graphical system representations such as Matlab/Simulink and UML. Concerns about efficiency and reliability of the tools continue to be raised as this process progresses. However, no one questions the use of high level programming languages anymore. One reason for this is that they have a reached a satisfactory level of maturity. Further, guidelines are available, such as the ones developed for automotive systems by MISRA [12].

The same level of maturity has not yet been reached for the corresponding graphical programming languages. Although tools supporting UML and Simulink are capable of generating C code, the following problems exist:

- *Different conceptual approaches and computational models*: UML is based on object-oriented concepts while Simulink is based on functional decomposition. Both these approaches are used in the same projects today. However, there is still poor integration between the tools, which complicates system development.

- *Efficient implementation of distributed systems*: Embedded systems typically have limited resources and are used in distributed computer systems. Resource optimization is being tackled, but improvements are still required. It is essential that peculiarities of the implementation can be recognized in the early stages of development. Approaches for configuration of and code generation for distributed systems are only recently being developed, see e.g. [2] for an overview of some of these approaches.

- *Shortage of methodology*: Programming at higher levels of abstraction does not automatically lead to improvements. There is a need for methodologies and guidelines addressing issues including readability, reusability, tool-related constraints, and efficient and reliable implementation.

Even greater challenges face researchers and developers when it comes to the development of mechatronic systems such as vehicles. Mechatronic systems come with a need to represent information of requirements and constraints, functionality, and their realizations in mechanics, electronics and software – a software perspective only is obviously not sufficient. Relations between entities (e.g. components) at the same, and between different levels and disciplines need to be maintained to ensure that products will fulfill requirements and be maintainable.

Within the company organizations there is a high competence level; however the competence is usually domain-specific, and there is a gap between the so-called module-suppliers and system integrators [13]. Even though one purpose of model based development is to close the gap between the domains, new competence is needed within the organizations to be able to utilize the full capacity of model based development.

Another issue is the variety of modeling languages and tools, [8]. These languages and tools are not always inherently compatible with each other. Most of the tools and languages are developed for specific domains. There is a risk that the organizations get caught in a tool environment, as there are high costs involved in both procuring and adapting new tools.

It is clear that introducing MBD requires a fundamental change in that way that work is performed, and will require a significant initial development effort. This relates both to staff training, costs for tools, and to initial model development.

RESULTS OF THE FAR PROJECT

DEVELOPMENT PROCESS - The project was structured into four main phases as outlined in Figure 1. The initial phases combined a top-down and bottom-up perspective. The goals and constraints (e.g. budget and timing) of the project were identified and assessed. Available technology was studied to get input as to feasible solutions. The choices of technology and tools were to a large extent limited by the budget and availability of technology. In addition, the system specification phase addressed overall solution approaches. Structures for functionality, mechanics and electronics hardware were also developed. The final phases of the project focused on module development and stepwise incremental integration. The models developed during the project are illustrated in Figure 1 with text in Italic font.

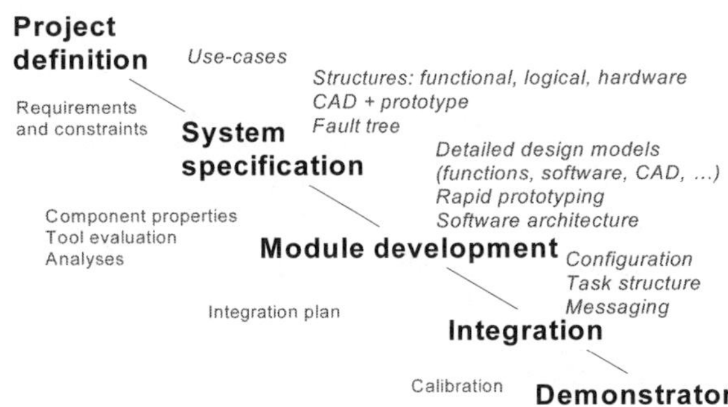

Figure 1. The different phases of the project and the specific models that were developed.

DEMONSTRATOR AND TOOLS - The project developed a model car demonstrator with four-wheel steering, individual braking and four-wheel drive, thus basically with three actuators per wheel. The car can be programmed into several modes of operation, including manual driving, driving with adaptive cruise control and driving with collision avoidance. Figure 2 shows the car.

Figure 2. The developed demonstrator.

Use Case Diagrams - The UML "Use case" [4] can be used to model requirements in early design phases. It describes the functionality that the system should provide to the user. In Figure 3, the Use case diagram that was given as an input requirement to the project is shown. It details three main users and their purposes in the project.

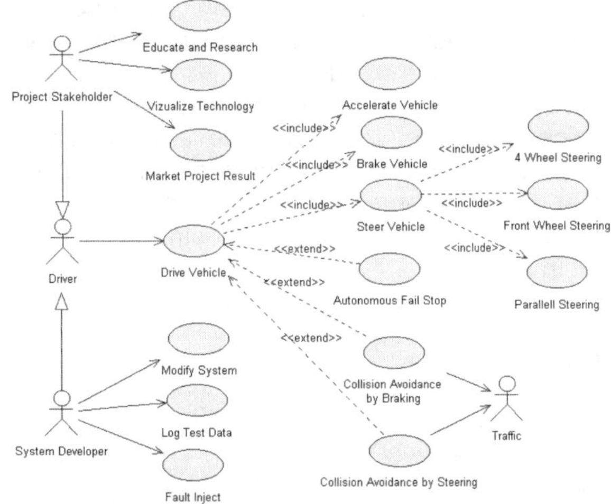

Figure 3. The Use Case Diagram for the project.

Functional View - The functions to be implemented in the vehicle were modeled in UML class diagrams. Figure 4 shows the overall structure of the class diagrams. The HMI and actuators are physical instances, while global and local control are functionality to be implemented in software. Global control handles the vehicle as a complete system while local control handles individual actuators. This separation of global and local control supports a high degree of reusability and separation of concerns.

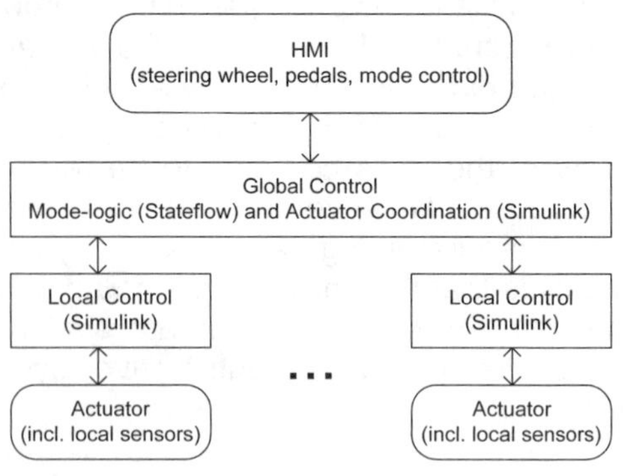

Figure 4. Functional view of the application.

Hardware View - To separate the driver's HMI and the car, two radio links are used, as seen in Figure 5. The HMI consists of one node, one video receiver, and a joystick or steering wheel with pedals. On the car there are six nodes connected through a TT-CAN network. One of the nodes is the central node, connected to the driver's HMI. Another node is the radar node used to measure distance to adjacent objects. The four wheel nodes control the local actuators at each wheel.

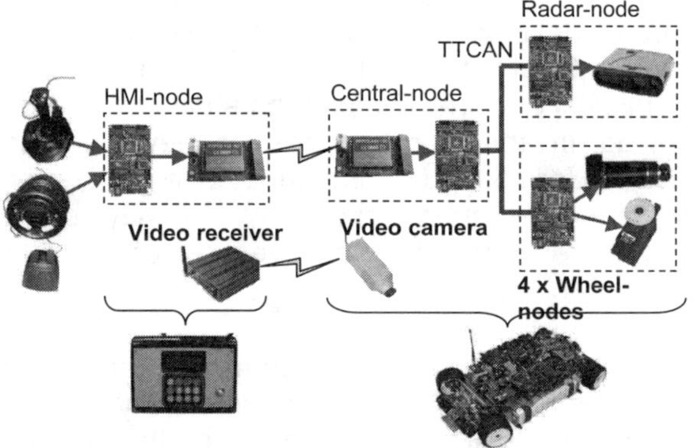

Figure 5. Hardware systems in the project.

Software View and Tool chain - The software platform was developed using the Rubus real-time operating system, Rubus RTOS [14], and Time-triggered CAN (TTCAN). Rubus, TTCAN and basic I/O drivers form the framework to which the application software is downloaded. This is shown in Figure 6. This framework supports a high degree of separation from the development of application software.

Rubus Visual Studio, Rubus VS, is the graphical development environment used for the off-line scheduler for Rubus. The off-line schedule is synchronized with TTCAN in the nodes. TTCAN provides a global clock that is used to synchronize all nodes via Rubus.

The application functionality was developed in the Matlab tools Simulink and Stateflow from Mathworks. Stateflow models mode logic for global control and Simulink models actuator coordination and local control, as shown in Figure 4. C code is automatically generated from Simulink and Stateflow using the Targetlink code generation tool from dSPACE.

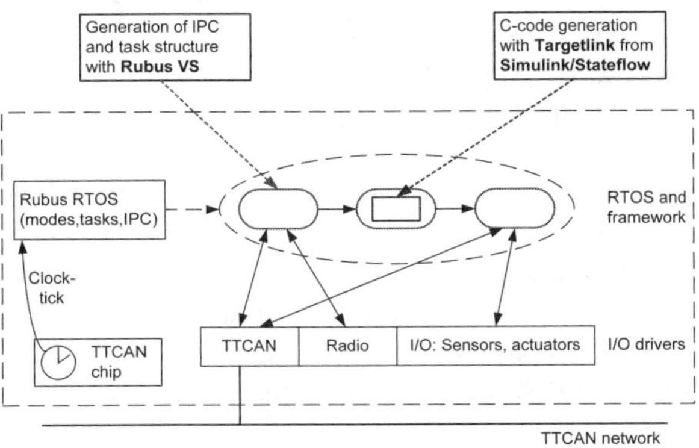

Figure 6. Software view for one computer node illustrating the tools used and how functionality is integrated in the tasking structure.

EXPERIENCES AND DISCUSSION

The FAR project had two main purposes. One purpose was the educational goal that was to provide the students with the knowledge and skill to develop mechatronic products in both small and large teams. Sometimes this aim is to some degree in conflict with the project's scope, the other aim within the course, to deliver the final product. Here a careful balance between the two is necessary.

Halfway into the project, a dependency matrix was introduced by the supervisors. The purpose of the matrix was to illustrate interdependencies between system components and required functions and solutions. This matrix showed the students the opportunities that the design presented, but also the complexity issue, i.e. the connection points between the sub-systems.

The students were to some extent a bit naive regarding integration of the different systems, so they tackled isolated time-consuming engineering problems and postponed the system integration work. This led to deadline pressure at the end of the project when integration problems arose.

Model based development was one major part of this project. The models developed within the project, as shown in Figure 1, were mainly used for communication purposes. Some models, including the detailed functional design models and the task structure were also used directly for design automation by chosen tools. The approach used for software and function development also directly supports early architecture evaluation. Although we did not have time to automate such a connection, the timing obtained in the software design through scheduling, or alternatively from the implementation, can be modeled in Simulink using for example the KTH developed X-in-the-loop simulation tool [7]. In the end, the final solution did not support a completely automatic tool chain from model to realization. This partly depended on the limited duration and resources of this project, but also indicates that there is still much work to be done before a virtual car is achieved. However, we believe that a project like this is essential for educational purposes, both from an academic and industrial point of view.

We also believe that the project was successful in identifying and highlighting both advantages and challenges for model based development.

In parallel with the FAR project a multiple case study was performed in the Swedish vehicle industry. The purpose with the study was to explore and describe how modeling affects integration within multidisciplinary product development from the perspective of the product developers [1]. The conclusions in the study were that model based development is one of many integrating mechanism that can be used, but it requires certain enablers before an organization can fully utilize it. The conclusions are in line with the lessons learned in the FAR project; model based development has great potential but still it is rather immature and there are many factors (organizational, processes) that must be considered to achieve a satisfactory technical integration.

CONCLUSION

This has been a very interesting and successful project from both academia's and industry's point of view. One aim of the project was to create a general platform for research of by-wire technology. We wish to invite other companies and universities to recreate this environment to support joint research. This project will continue to be used in joint academic research projects between academia and Volvo Cars.

ACKNOWLEDGMENTS

This project has only been possible thanks to the students' great achievements and commitment to develop the tool chain and car on time and according to the given specification.

This work has been supported by funding from the Program Board for the Swedish Automotive Research Program and the Program Board for IT in the Engineering Industry Research Program both at VINNOVA, the Swedish Agency for Innovation Systems.

Further we wish to thank our partners in this project; Arcticus systems, Chalmers Lindholmen, dSPACE and GMV-Microlf. We have also received valuable support from the staff at the Dept. of Machine Design at KTH.

We also wish to acknowledge DeJiu Chen from KTH for valuable comments and discussions.

REFERENCES

1. Adamsson, N (2003). Modellbaserad mekatronik-utveckling och kompetensintegration - En komparativ fallstudie inom svensk fordonsindustri. Dept. of Machine Design, KTH. ISSN 1400-1179. ISRN KTH/MMK – 03/40 – SE.
2. Artist roadmap on Hard Real-time Systems: http://www.systemes-critiques.org/ARTIST/ Roadmaps/A1-roadmap.pdf
3. Backstrom et al. (2003), Project FAR – Project report. Dept. of Machine Design, KTH. ISSN 1400-1179, ISRN KTH/MMK – 03/28 – SE.
4. Booch G., I. Jacobson and J. Rumbaugh (1998). The Unified Modeling Language User Guide, Addison Wesley Publishing Company.
5. Chen DeJiu and Törngren Martin (2001). Towards a Framework for Architecting Mechatronic Software Systems. Proc. of the 7th IEEE Int. Conference on Engineering of Complex Computer Systems, Skövde, Sweden, June 11-15, 2001
6. East-EAA – an ITEA project: http://www.east-eea.net/
7. El-khoury Jad, Törngren Martin. Towards a Toolset for Architectural Design of Distributed Real-Time Control systems. Proc. of IEEE Real-Time Systems Symposium – RTSS, London, December 2001.
8. El-khoury Jad, DeJiu Chen and Martin Törngren. A Survey of Modeling Approaches for Embedded Computer Control Systems. Technical Report. TRITA - MMK 2003:36, ISSN 1400 –1179, ISRN KTH/MMK/R-03/11-SE. Department of Machine Design, KTH 2003
9. Freund Ulrich, Alexander Burst, Graphical Programming of ECU Software – An Interface Based Approach, white paper, ETAS GMBh, 2001.
10. Gausemeier, J., Flath, M. & Möhringer, S. (2001). Conceptual design of mechatronic systems supported by semi-formal specification. International conference on advanced intelligent mechatronics proceedings, Como, Italy.
11. OMG. (2003b). MDA Guide Version 1.0. Object Management Group. Version 1.0. May 2003. Available at www.omg.org. Accessed 2003-05-21.
12. MISRA - The Motor Industry Research Association (1994). Development Guidelines for Vehicle Based Software, ISBN 0-95241-560-7. MISRA, the United Kingdom.
13. Reilhac, P., Bavoux, B (2002). Vehicle E/E Architecture: A New Paradigm for Collaborative Product Creation? A Case Study. SAE Convergence 2002: Transportation Electronics. Detroit, USA.
14. Rubus: Arcticus Systems AB: www.arcticus.se
15. Sangiovanni-Vincentelli Alberto, Automotive Electronics: Trends and Challenges, Convergence2000, Detroit (MI), USA, October 2000
16. Yan, X.T., Sharpe, J.E.E. (1994). A Comparative Study of Simulation Techniques in Mechatronics. Int. Conf. on Control ´94, vol. 2, page 934 –940.

CONTACT

Martin Törngren, Martin@md.kth.se

Web-page: http://www.md.kth.se/RTC

2004-01-0358

Designing Embedded Real-Time Systems (ERTS) With Model Driven Architecture (MDA)

Subra Ganesan
Oakland University, and HTC Inc.

Venkat Alladi and John (Jian) Wei
Ciber Inc.

Kamalesh Alladi
University of Michigan, Ann Arbor

ABSTRACT

Today, in a typical car, electromechanical components contribute roughly 30% to the total vehicle cost with Embedded Real Time Systems (ERTS) responsible for roughly 80% of major controls functions. ERTS units influence the quality of the end product, and thus customer satisfaction. Quality means conformance to requirements in terms of functionality, usability, reliability, performance and supportability. In software design terms, it means traceability, portability, interoperability, and reusability.

This paper introduces a MDA approach for building portable, interoperable, and reusable software systems. Through architectural separation of concerns, MDA addresses quality from the perspectives of the customer and software design. To illustrate the effectiveness of MDA, we present a software design of an Engine Idle Speed Control Unit.

INTRODUCTION

The number of ERTS in a vehicle has steadily increased over the past thirty years. A typical mid-range luxury vehicle today (e.g. Volvo S80) can easily have upwards of 20 ECUs (Electronic Control Units), interconnected through multiple networks. This trend will continue as consumers expect more and more entertainment, safety, convenience, and environmentally friendly features in a vehicle.

Automotive ERTS is so complex today, in terms of number of control units, complexity of algorithms, networking options, hardware and software solutions, that software modeling has become a necessity in the ERTS development process. The old "Build-Break-And-Fix" approach simply cannot scale anymore. With the ever-increasing complexity, software engineers have to rely on models to provide verification points, in order to improve quality of design.

Cost pressure is another long-term trend. A U.S. Department of Transportation study found that from 2002 to 2003, price of cars adjusted by content has decreased by 1.2%. In this competitive market environment, software engineers are under pressure to deliver more quality functionality with fewer resources.

Software engineers have known the basic ingredients of effective management of complexity, cost, and quality relationships for decades. These ingredients are reuse, interoperability, portability and traceability. Reuse is the idea of repeated use of work artifacts. Interoperability is the idea of systems built on different platforms (e.g. C++, or Java) working with each other seamlessly. Portability is the idea of developing once and deploying multiple times in different run-time environments. Traceability is the discipline of relating system artifacts.

Models play a critical role in achieving effective reuse, interoperability, portability and traceability as models simplify our view of the problem domain and allow verification of solutions before the final system is built.

In the automotive industry today, modeling is often concentrated in the Control Law Design activities using tools such as MatLab. A number of tools can also generate code from Control Law Design models, in effect bypassing the analysis and design activities in the software development process. From the perspective of software development, this approach is analogous to the failed "Build-Break-And-Fix" method, which has proved to be costly and of low quality. A more rigorous approach to modeling is needed in the ERTS software development process.

One of the major challenges of promoting modeling in ERTS has been the notation of object-orientation (OO) in the prevailing modeling languages (e.g. UML) and approaches (e.g. OOAD-Object Oriented Analysis and Design), whereas C, a non-OO language remains the predominant language in the ERTS world for performance and resource reasons. AJACS (Applying Java to Automotive Control Systems) project has however closed this gap by allowing Java, an OO programming language, to be used as an intermediary development language between the OO models and the non-OO low level C or native machine code. Further closing the gap, the to be released OMG (Object Management Group) UML 2.0 standard will likely incorporate ERTS specific concepts such as Capsule, Port, and Protocol, as many tool vendors are already supporting these concepts (e.g. IBM Rational Rose Real Time). A large number of UML models are being popularized ranging from class diagrams for static view to state diagrams for dynamic views. Many of these UML models will become, or in some development shops, have already become standard practice in the ERTS development process.

Model Driven Architecture (MDA) is an open, vendor-neutral approach to using UML models to direct the software development activities for the purpose of achieving reuse, interoperability, portability and traceability, by separating computation independent business domain logic, platform independent application logic, from the underlying platform specific technology. The result is preservation of investment in business and application logic while maintaining the flexibility of adapting to the evolution of technologies.

MDA is a generic standard managed by OMG. In this paper, we present an interpretation of the MDA standard specific to the processes, algorithms, programming languages and deployment platforms in the ERTS development environment. We developed models for the Engine Idle Speed Control as an example of this interpretation.

In the MDA and UML section, we describe the overall relationship between UML and MDA, and the principle approaches in MDA. We then describe the integration of MDA into the existing ERTS development methodology. The Engine Idle Speed Control section presents models that are developed following the MDA standard.

MDA AND UML

The following 3-Layer Model illustrates the relationship between the MDA, UML, and ERTS Models:

Layer 3	System Model Layer
Layer 2	MDA Standard
Layer 1	UML Standard

Figure 1. The 3-Layer Model of MDA Approach

Layer 1 is the UML Standard layer, under the OMG UML standard, provides a rich graphical language for specifying, visualizing, constructing, and documenting the artifacts of software systems, as well as for business modeling and other non-software systems.

Layer 2 is the MDA Standard layer, built on the layer 1 UML standard, defines an approach to IT system specification that separates the specification of system functionality from the specification of the implementation of that functionality on a specific technology platform.

In the MDA approach, UML models are categorized into Computation Independent Models (CIM), Platform Independent Models (PIM), and Platform Specific Models (PSM). CIM models are also referred to as domain models. CIM model in general describes the domain requirements (e.g. use case functionality) and it does not specify the structure of the systems. PIM model describes the structure of the system, but does not show details of its use of the chosen platform. For instance, a PIM model could be a UML Collaboration Diagram describing the interactions and the sequence of interactions among timer, sensor, actuator, and controller, without elaborating how timer is to be implemented in a particular platform (e.g. hardware vs. software solution). PSM specifies how the model makes the use of the chosen platform. A PSM may provide more or less detail, depending on its purpose. A PSM becomes an implementation, if it provides all the information needed to construct a system, and to put it into operation.

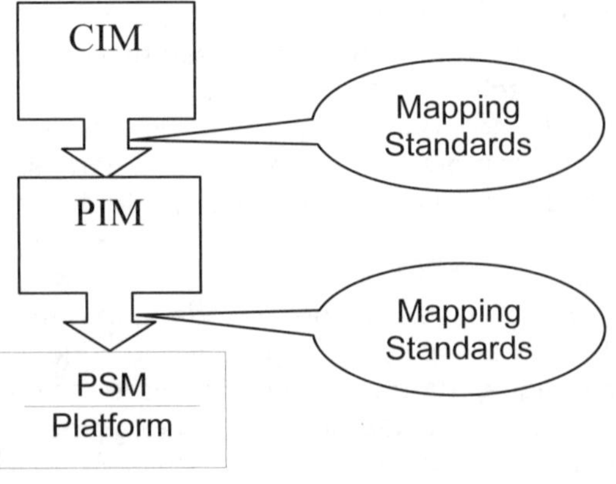

Figure 2. MDA Principle Models

Through mapping and translation standards, MDA approach allows the CIM and PIM models to specify system functionality and system structure, and to be realized on multiple platforms, enabling different applications to be integrated by explicitly relating their models at the CIM, PIM or PSM level, thus ensuring reuse, interoperability, and portability as technology evolves.

Layer 3 is the System Model layer, built on UML and MDA generic standards and guidelines, defines an application domain specific interpretation of MDA, in terms of specific UML models that are characteristic of MDA CIM, PIM and PSM models. For example, UML sequence diagram is a suitable PIM model for the E-Commerce domain. For the ERTS domain, given the number of concurrent computing threads, UML state diagram is a more suitable interpretation of the MDA PIM model.

DEVELOPMENT PROCESS WITH MDA

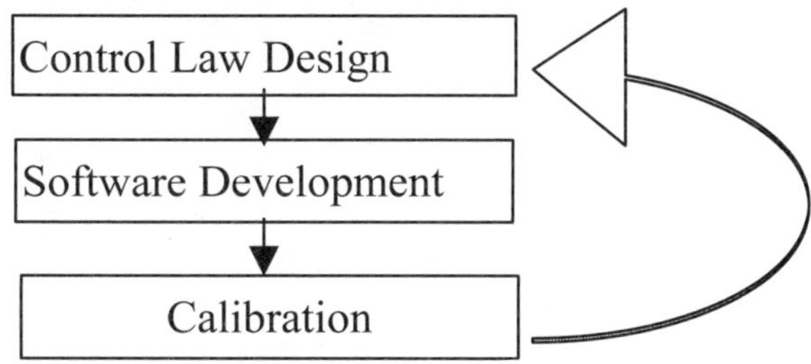

Figure 3. Simplified View ERTS Development Process

ERTS development process in general consists of three phases, namely Control Law Design, Software Development and Calibration. For the discussions in this paper, we view MDA as primarily applicable to the Software Development phase.

ENGINE IDLE SPEED CONTROL

The electronic engine control system (Figure 4) consists of sensing devices (or sensors), which continuously measure the operating conditions of the engine, an electronic engine control unit (ECU) that evaluates the sensor inputs using data tables and calculations, and determines the output to the actuating device. The actuating devices are commanded by the ECU to perform an action in response to the sensor inputs. The goal of the ECU is to ensure that the engine operates at near optimal conditions at all times. Optimum conditions are often defined by mixture composition (fuel, air and burned products), density and temperature. The basic functions of an engine control systems are fuel injection control, exhaust gas re-circulation (EGR) control, ignition or spark timing control and idle speed control.

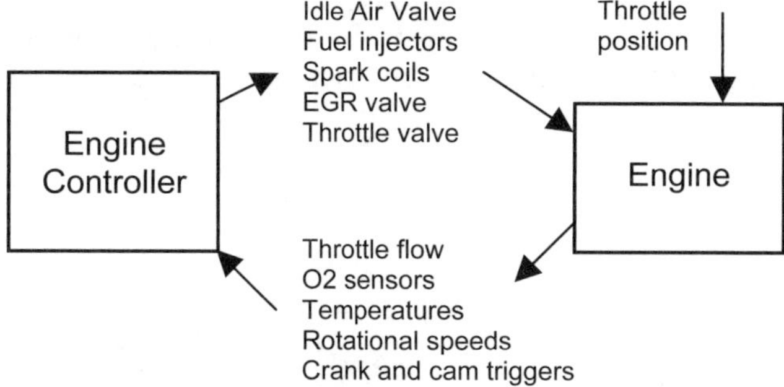

Figure 4. Engine Control Module

Idle speed control (ISC) - represents one of the most generic and basic automotive control functions. On the average, vehicles consume about 30 percent of their fuel in city driving during idling. It is therefore important to optimize vehicle and power train operations at idle. In general, the engine idle speed as measured in revolutions per minute (rpm) should be as low as possible for improved fuel economy. However the low vehicle speeds should not unduly compromise vehicle noise, vibration and harshness (NVH), accessory (e.g. alternator, air conditioner) performance, and engine combustion quality.

The primary goal of the ISC is to maintain a desired engine speed despite the torque disturbances occurring due to accessory loads such as air conditioning, power steering, alternator, and engagements of automatic transmission. Another goal of ISC is to achieve smooth transition between idle and open throttle operations.

Functional requirements of the ECU include constant monitoring of the operating conditions of the engine such as engine speed, throttle position, engine coolant temperatures and barometric pressure and other factors such as ambient conditions and the indicators of loads due to the accessories. Based on these inputs, the ECU should control the air fuel ratio, the spark advance and the airflow through the idle speed bypass valve (ISBV)

Non-Functional requirements of the ECU include maintaining the lowest idle speed that allows smooth running to achieve the lowest exhaust emissions and fuel consumption. The control should be effective and robust for large production volumes of engines operating in different idle speed regimes (loads, temperatures), with different aging history.

ISC Simulation Model - With the possible exception of neural networks and fuzzy-logic based controllers, most control technologies used for the ISC design require models of the relevant plant dynamics. This paper uses a non-linear engine model (Figure 5) available in the Matlab/Simulink toolbox. The engine model incorporates idle speed bypass valve dynamics, manifold filling dynamics, intake to power stroke delay, torque generation or combustion characteristics and engine rotational dynamics.

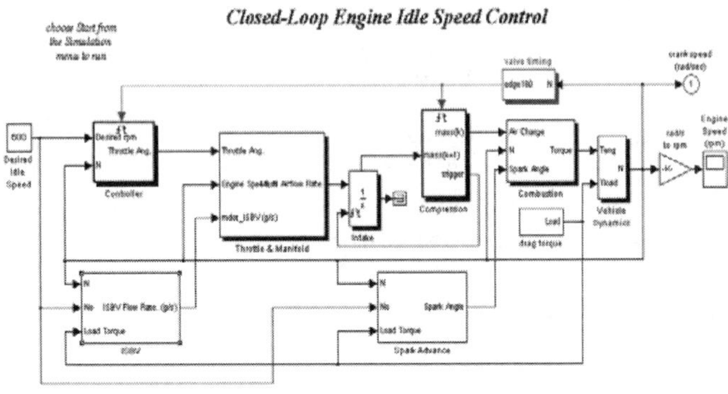

Figure 5. Idle Speed Control Model

This model assumes steady state sonic airflow through the air bypass valve, a uniform pressure distribution throughout the manifold, a constant stoichiometric air-fuel ratio and no intake manifold leaks. Exhaust gas recirculation (EGR) is not included in the model since EGR is not used at idle. Also the fuel path wall wetting has been ignored.

The control task is triggered by crank angle events. A trigger is sent when the piston is at the top dead center (TDC) or the bottom dead center (BDC) of the cylinder. Coordinated control of air bypass valve and spark advance is used for idle speed regulation. A PID control is used for the airflow loop and a proportional feedback control for the spark advance loop.

SOFTWARE ARCHITECTURE

Software architecture describes the structure of a system from static and dynamic viewpoints. The static viewpoint shows what the key elements of the system are and how they are arranged within the system. The dynamic viewpoint describes the interactions among static elements and the interactions between static elements with its environment. In this paper we demonstrate the static and dynamic viewpoints of ISC using MDA. The following sections describe the CIM, PIM, and PSM views of the ISC system.

Computation Independent Model (CIM)

CIM represents the system architecture from a domain perspective. This view represents the functional features and the key entities of ISC system independent from its implementation details. Both Figure 3 and Figure 4 is ISC CIM.

Figure 6. CIM - Problem Space

Figure 6 represents the dynamic view of CIM from a domain perspective. This view is also called as a Use Case Model [UML]. The actors of the Use Case Model represent the internal subsystems of the ISC. This viewpoint clearly identifies how the subsystems interact among themselves at a domain level.

Figure 7 represents the static view of the ISC domain. In this view, the key entities represented in the Matlab/Simulink model are shown as classes. This view shows the rules and relationships among different ISC entities. This view is also called as the domain model.

The CIM has many advantages. The most important one is that it provides representation of the domain/problem space, which is easily understood by a software engineer or a control engineer. Thus CIM acts as a tool to bridge the gap between the software team and domain experts.

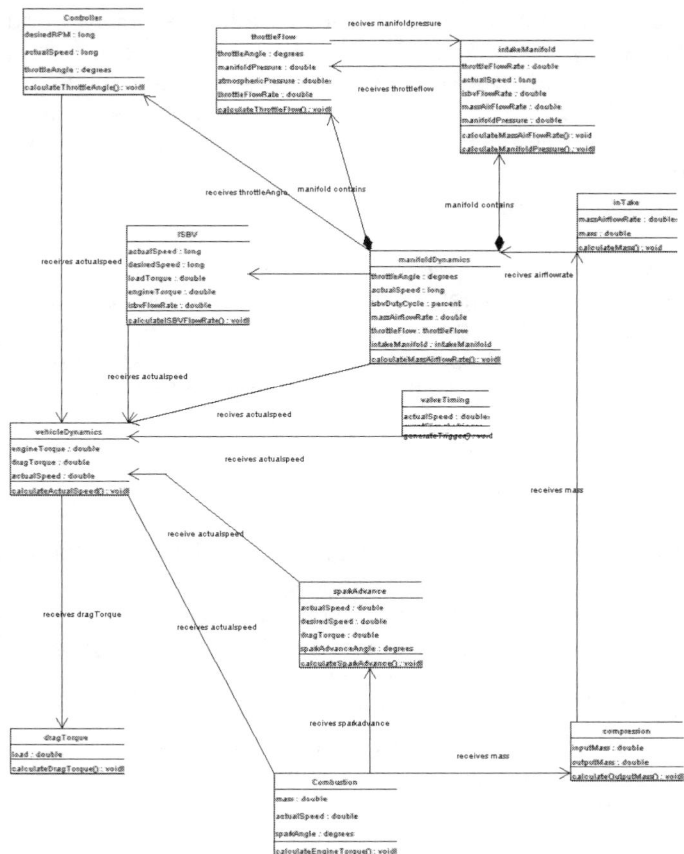

Figure 7. CIM - Domain Model

Platform Independent Model (PIM)

PIM represents the ISC system architecture from an operation perspective. PIM can be depicted at various levels of abstractions. It could be a state transition diagram that shows the lifecycle of a key entity or a sequence diagram that shows the interactions among entities within a subsystem or a view that shows separation of responsibilities. The inputs for the ISC PIM view are the CIM and the non-functional requirements.

Figure 8 segregates the responsibilities of the system into 3 packages – the model, the controller, and the view consistent with the MVC pattern.

The PIM has many advantages. The most important one is that it allows for design constraints to be represented as part of the model. This allows software engineers to validate key constraints, such as timing, against the model. Typically, the response time for real time embedded systems is in microseconds. A software engineer, who is responsible for addressing the constraint, can verify whether the system would meet the needs with the help of PIM. One another use of PIM is to verify the operations view with the requirements itself. Using PIM, a software engineer can easily trace the PIM elements to CIM and verify the functionality that is delivered.

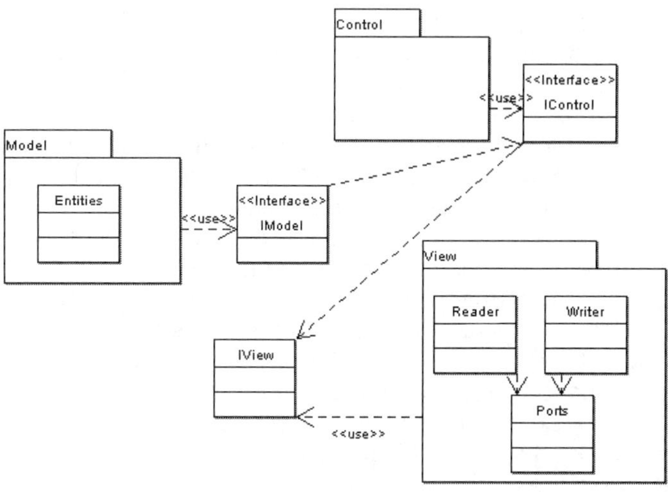

Figure 8. PIM – Operations View

Platform Specific Model (PSM)

The PSM represents the deployment view of the system architecture. The PSM can be shown at different levels of abstractions. A simple PSM, which could be a static layer view, details the composition of each layer that is part of the system. One other view of PSM can be a component diagram that depicts the platform specific components (software) that will be deployed on nodes (hardware), which represent the platform.

Embedded Application Java Code				
Logging	Security	Timing	Messaging	Error Handling
Java Embedded Server Engine				
Native Application Code				
RTOS – OSEK-VDX/JavaOS				
Motorola/IBM Power PC Controllers				

Figure 9. PSM – Static Layer View

Figure 9 represents a static PSM. This view is specific to Java platform. The view depicts the organization of hardware and software at different layers to represent the entire system.

CHALLENGES WITH MDA

This paper proposes the use of MDA for Automotive ERTS. Automotive ERTS has been around for long time now. But the application of MDA for Automotive ERTS is very new. Unlike UML, which has been a modeling standard for many years, MDA is an emerging standard for modeling architectures. OMG is conducting research in MDA with its core members. Although OMG has published a MDA specification guide, there is still a lot of information that has to be hashed out. For example, the guidelines for mapping between CIM-PIM and PIM and PSM are very rudimentary. One other example is the CIM, PIM and PSM. According to the current specifications, the models can be represented at various levels of abstractions without much clarity on what level of abstraction should be used when? We plan to address these challenges as we conduct more research in MDA. We also intend to develop detailed specifications for our interpretations on the usage of MDA models for Automotive ERTS by working with established tool vendors.

CONCLUSION

MDA is the natural progression to the next level of higher abstraction in ERTS development. MDA separates UML models into CIM, PIM, and PSM models. MDA promotes quality, reuse, interoperability, and portability by introducing model-driven analysis and design, and verification points at three levels of abstraction during the software development life cycle. Through use of UML, MDA promotes effective visualization, specification, construction, and documentation.

Beyond the conceptual interpretation of MDA as discussed in this paper, we aim to implement the models by building the actual Engine Idle Control software following AJACS specification in 2004. We also intend to collect metrics to evaluate the overall effectiveness of MDA.

REFERENCES

1. D. Hrovat and J. Sun (1997). Models and control methodologies for IC engine idle speed control. In: Control Eng. Practice, 1997, Vol. 5, No. 8
2. Ronald Jurgen, Automotive electronics handbook
3. K. Butts, N. Sivashankar and J. Sun (1996). Feedforward and feedback design for engine idle speed control using ℓ_1 optimization. Proceedings of the American Control Conference (ACC), Seattle, Washington.
4. AJACS, http://www.ajacs.org/
5. OSEK/VDX, http://www-osek-vdx.oeg/
6. MDA, http://www.omg.org/
7. UML, http://www.omg.org/

2004-01-0300

Model-Based System Development – Is it the Solution to Control the Expanding System Complexity In The Vehicle?

Roland Jeutter and Bernd Heppner
ETAS GmbH

ABSTRACT

Already today the car is a complex embedded system with a multitude of linked subsystems and components. In future these distributed systems have to be developed faster and with high quality via integrated, optimized design process. Scalable systems with an increased maintainability can be generated, if an agreement on a standardized technical architecture (hard- and software) is made at the beginning of the development. The challenges in the design of such distributed systems can be met through advanced automotive systems and software engineering in conjunction with suitable processes, methods and tools. Because the designers that must collaborate are distributed in different divisions or companies, it is essential that an overarching model based design methodology is used.

INTRODUCTION

The automotive industry is undergoing a technological change, and technical innovations. Especially electrical and electronic systems and software will continue to characterize the next 15 years. The trend from hardware to software solutions will continue. 90% of innovations depend on software. Software design allows a greater degree of freedom than any other technology. Software also provides enormous benefits and potential regarding cost reduction, reduced weight, reduced space requirements, improved reliability, etc..

The following constraints govern electrical/electronic systems design [1]:

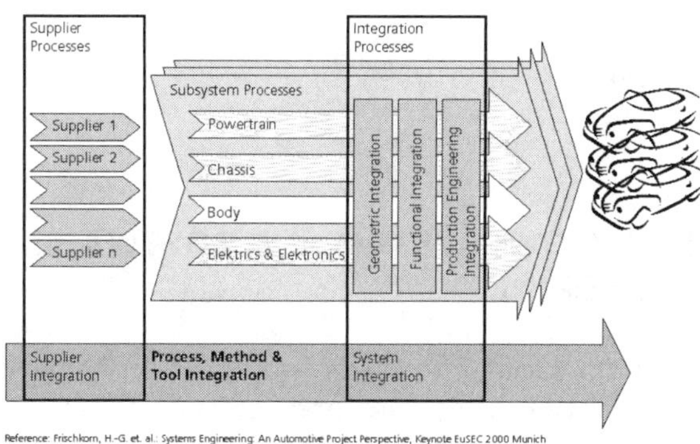

Figure 1.

- The design of complex functionality with tight requirements on safety and correctness.
- The design of distributed architectures consisting of several subsystems
- The mapping of the functionality onto the components of a distributed architecture with tight real-time and communication constraints.
- High-cost pressure restricts the usage of control unit resources in the components of a distributed architecture; SW implementations must be very efficient (performance, memory).
- Since system and component hardware and software have different product life cycles than the vehicle, it is necessary to standardize the technical system architectures (HW and SW) in the distributed system to enable maintainability, service and re-use.

- The high-time pressure and growing complexity of electronic systems conceal high risks in quality thus adequate system and software engineering process need to be implemented.

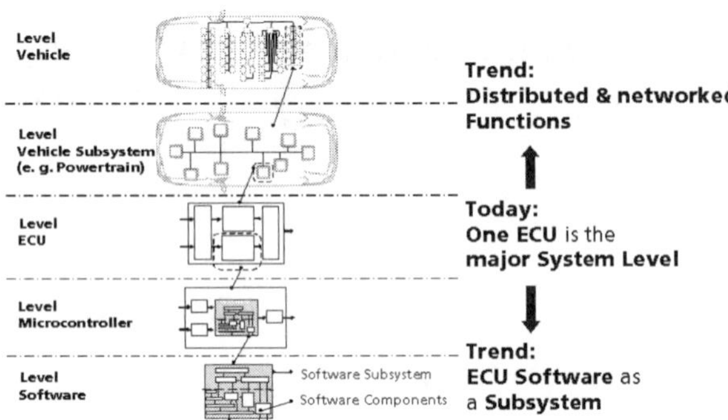

Figure 2.

AUTOMOTIVE SYSTEM AND SOFTWARE ENGINEERING

Vehicle functions can be defined as something that the customer perceives as and considers as valuable. Today, vehicle functions are typically implemented through systems that consist of electronics, software, sensors, and actuators [2].

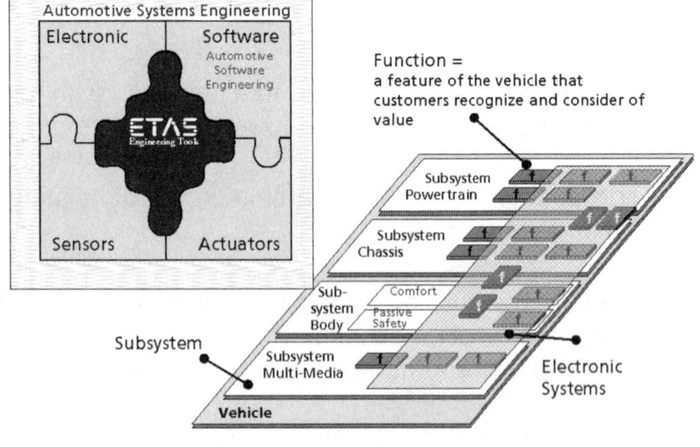

Figure 3.

In practice, a separate development process exists for each of these areas, and these different processes must be integrated into the systems engineering process.

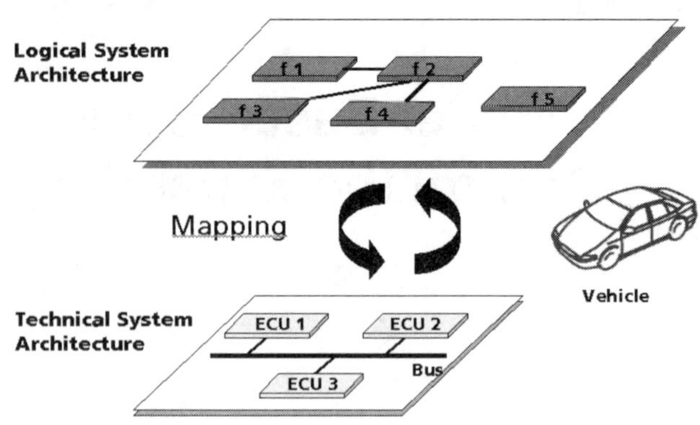

Figure 4.

The set of functions and the interoperability of the functions are called the Logical System Architecture.

The Technical System Architecture must fulfill all requirements derived from technical, economical, organizational as well as production constraints.

The development steps required to define the Technical System Architecture and to implement the Logical Architecture is called Automotive System Engineering.

The implementation of software on the Technical System Architecture is called Automotive Software Engineering [2].

MODEL BASED SYSTEM DESIGN

The Model Based System Engineering Process is the technical oriented core process embedded in the overall design process of a vehicle. It needs to be extended with the understanding of the organizational structures in the industry. Today the intellectual property required for the design , development and production of electrical/electronic systems is distributed between Tier2, Tier1 and OEM. The competencies, know-how and expertise in the automotive industry in distributed system design methodologies, system engineering and embedded realtime software engineering need to be improved in a very short time and the engineers have to systematically become trained and supported in new methodologies. In addition infrastructures and IT systems for collaboration, information sharing and distributed project management are required to achieve a consistent flow of information and expertise. Best in class management processes (e.g. CMMI, SPICE,..) have to be put in place to achieve high quality results and to control the risk in technical and financial areas.

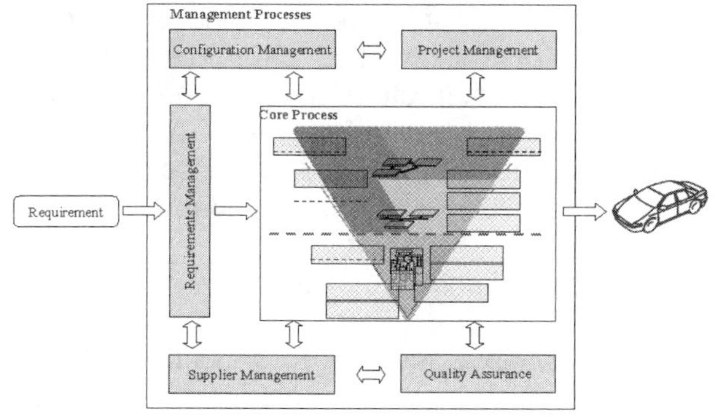

Figure 5.

The need to re-use functions throughout all levels of the design hierarchy to meet time-to market requirements, to assure the high requirements in safety and reliability and to cope with the increasing variety of car-platforms and models will directly lead to Standardized Technical System Architectures.

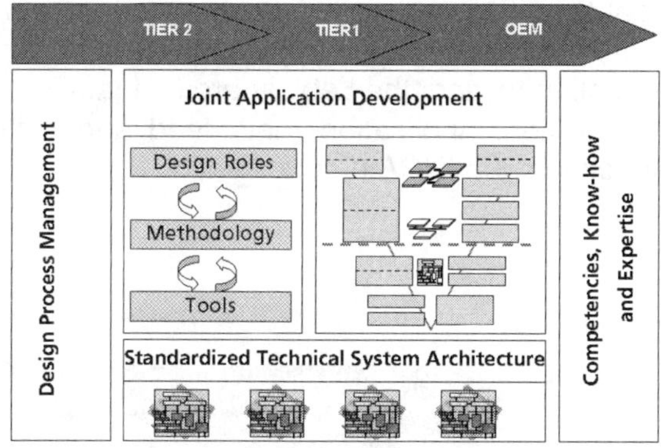

Figure 6.

Model Based System Engineering - In Model Based Engineering, the model is the central artifact and is used and systematically refined throughout the entire development process. The model contains continuous and/or discrete elements that capture the behavior of the system under development. Its structure reflects the functional decomposition of the system as well as the technical architecture in hardware and software. Furthermore the model must be executable and can be simulated. Tools exist to also animate the model to explore the behavior of the system to support recursive and iterative development style through the different levels of abstraction.

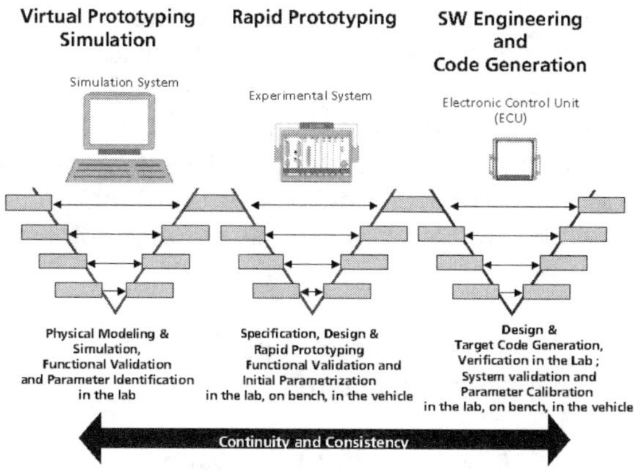

Figure 7.

The V-Model - The V-model visualizes the core process in the development of vehicle functions. It contains the following major development steps (excerpt from [1]):

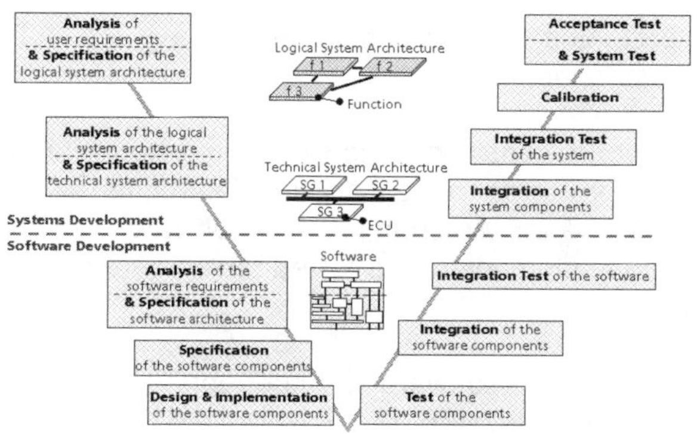

Figure 8.

- Analyzing user requirements and specifying the logical system architecture:Based on the user requirements to be considered, the goal of this process step is to specify the logical system architecture, i.e., the function network, the function interfaces, and the communication between the functions for the entire vehicle or for a subsystem. No decisions for the technical implementation are made yet during this step.

- Analyzing the logical system architecture and specifying the technical system architecture:

The logical system architecture forms the basis for specifying the actual technical system architecture. Various methodologies from the technical disciplines involved are used to analyze the alternative implementations that are based on a uniform logical system architecture. The technical system architecture also determines what functions or sub functions will be implemented by software. These are also referred to as software requirements

- Analyzing the software requirements and specifying the software architecture:

The next step is to analyze the software requirements and specify the software architecture, i.e., determine the boundaries and interfaces for the software system, software components, software layers and operating modes.

- Specifying the software components:

It is now possible to specify the software components. This is initially based on the assumption of an "ideal world." This means that implementation details, such as implementation in integer arithmetic, are neglected at this stage.

- Designing, implementing and testing the software components:

"Real world" aspects are now taken into consideration in the design. It is necessary to determine all details pertaining to implementation. The software components are then implemented and tested based on these design decisions.

- Integrating software components and software integration testing:

Developing and testing the software components, which is frequently done by separate employee teams, is followed by the integration of the software components into the software system, and subsequent integration testing of the software.

- Integrating the system components and system integration testing:

This step consists of combining the software with the control unit hardware to obtain a functional electronic control unit. The electronic control units must then be integrated with the other components in the electronic system, i.e., set-point adjusters, sensors and actuators, so that a system integration test can be performed.

- Calibration:

The calibration of the software functions of the control units consists of setting the parameters of those software functions that often have to be determined individually for each type and variant of a vehicle. The parameters may be implemented in the software in the form of characteristic values, curves and maps.

- System test and acceptance test:

At this point, it is finally possible to conduct a system test against the logical system architecture and an acceptance test against the user requirements.

A number of tool vendors provide Computer Aided Design Tools for the different development stages in the V-model. E.g. ETAS offers tools and services that assist systems and software development in a consistent way. The model-based function development process is supported by the different product families in ETAS' portfolio as follows [2]:

- Analysis and specification of functions: the ASCET-SD product family
- System design, implementation and integration of functions (software engineering): ASCET-SD target code generators, DDS data management, OSEK operating system, realtime Architect, the ERCOSEK real-time operating system and Automotive Services
- Function testing: the LabCar product family
- Calibration, application (data feed and testing) of functions: the INCA product family

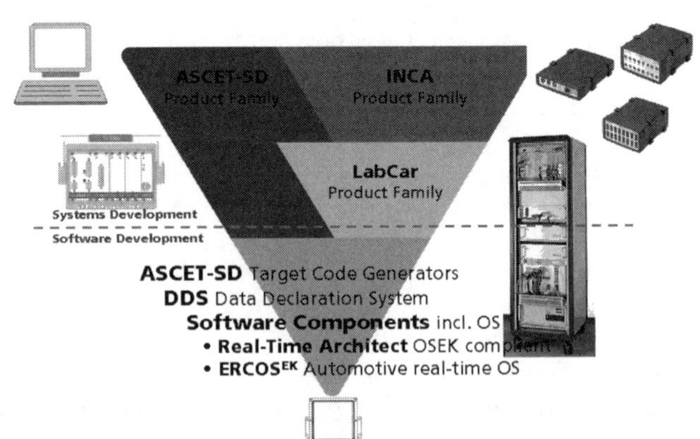

Figure 9.

Standardized Technical Architectures for Reusable Software Functions - The Logical System Architecture describes the complete functional and logical behavior of a system.

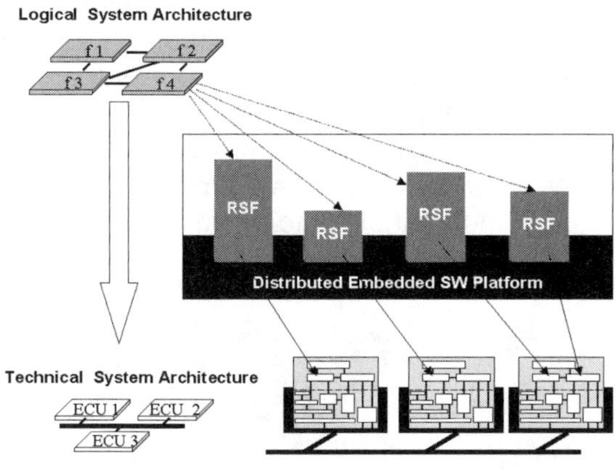

Figure 10.

It consists of functions with inputs and outputs and communication relationships between each other independent from the technical realization. The functions of the Logical System Architecture get realized in various SW modules (Reusable Software Functions RSF) that interact in a given order.

The Technical System Architecture is the real physical network of ECU's, that is supposed to provide the execution power for the Logical System Architecture. It is based on standardized hardware components and provides the physical interface between the ECU's and between the ECU's and the vehicle. Components of the Technical System Architecture are e.g. micro controller, input and output devices, memory, network components (CAN, LIN, MOST, FlexRay, ..) , sensors and actuators.

The Distributed Embedded Platform Software separates the RSF from the hardware and enables a standardized interoperability between the RSFs. The RSF must be developed in isolation from the final hardware and the RSF must interface, in the end, to real inputs and outputs. The RSF must therefore be written against abstract hardware, the inputs and outputs must be hidden behind an Standardized Application Programming Interface. The Distributed Embedded Platform Software is a layered SW architecture and is based on the standardized operating system OSEK, software components that abstract the network and hardware architecture and service routines, that allow the administration and maintenance of the distributed system. The top level of the platform software often called middleware enables the hardware independent communication between the RSFs and the hardware with real inputs and outputs. Enabling re-use and interoperability are driving the agenda of AUTOSAR, a newly formed consortium of automotive OEMs and Tier 1 suppliers [3].

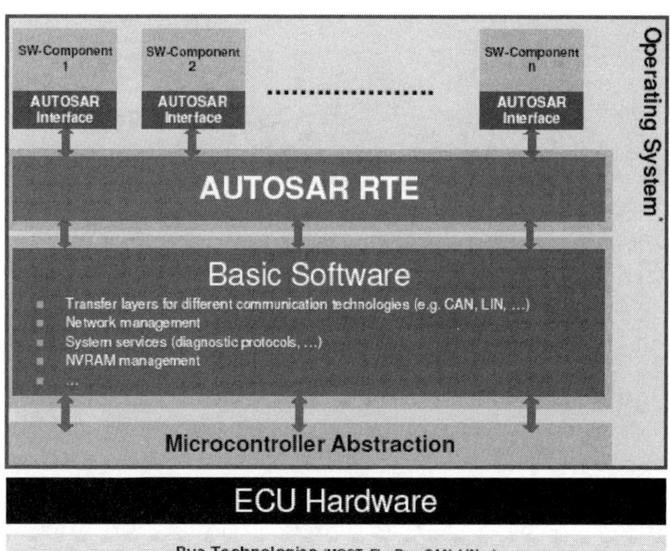

Figure 11.

RSF Component Based Design Process - To meet-time-to market requirements, to increase reliability and to cope with the increasing variety of car-platforms and models the re-use of the Logical System Architecture refined by RSFs is a proven approach. With reusable, interoperable RSF components, the entire industry can then share commodity functions while concentrating on novel, high-value added competitive hardware and software parts.

The Big Goal is to support Reusable Software Functions (RSFs) that allow functions to be developed once, put in a library and used again and again without changes.

The Standardized Distributed Embedded Software Platform must be defined and specified at the beginning of the design process and provides the stable foundation for the RSF Component Based Design Process.

Required New Roles

- RSFSuppliers - People who write RSFs against a requirement using a Specification Contract.
- ECU Integrators - People who take a set of RSFs and put them into an ECU, mapping abstract I/O to physical I/O.
- System Integrator - The person responsible for managing the ECU Integrators to connect all the ECU's in the car.

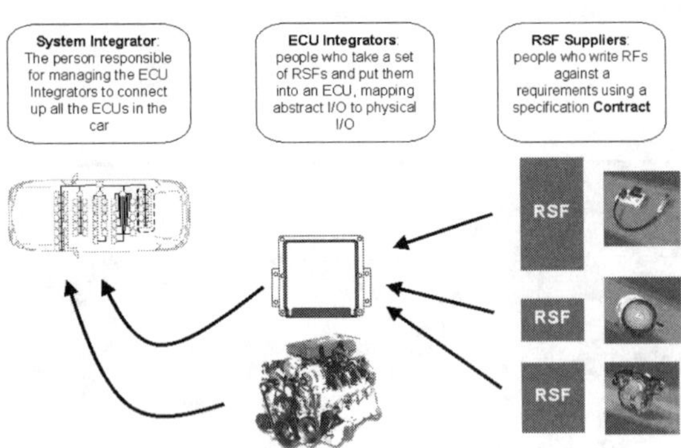

Figure 12.

New Processes - There needs to be a new way of managing the specification, test and integration of RSFs.

- RSF Development - The developer of an RSF doesn't know what other RSFs are running on the ECU. He doesn't do the integration work, the ECU may not exist yet. The developer must therefore make assumptions about the amount of CPU time and resources available to his RSF.

This leads to the idea of a Specification Contract for RSF that states what the specified behavior is and what permitted resource usage is of the RSF.

- Specification Contract for RSFs - The Contract is a promise that the RSF will do certain things, e.g. it promises to produce outputs with a certain timeliness, to have a certain functional behavior, to take only a certain CPU time, to take only a certain amount of memory.The Contract also contains obligations on the person using the RSF, e.g. they must give the tasks in the RSF certain CPU times, they must make sure the inputs have a certain timeliness.

The person integrating RSFs into a single ECU (i.e. the ECU Integrator) must respect these assumptions. The ECU Integrator can use this assumptions in selecting RSFs and designing the system by contract and building the system based on RSF components.

MANAGEMENT OF THE SYSTEM DESIGN PROCESS

The efficient use of distributed architectures implies that functions do not necessarily correspond one-to-one with technical architecture components. This implies that a much tighter relationship among design teams of different companies of the design supply chain must be established. Because designers that must collaborate are distributed in different companies, it is essential that an overarching design methodology be devised with the adequate support of tools and modeling techniques . The underlying premise of Design Process Management is that the quality of the final product is largely determined by the quality of the process used to develop and maintain it. An effective process ties together people, tools and methods into an integrated whole [4].

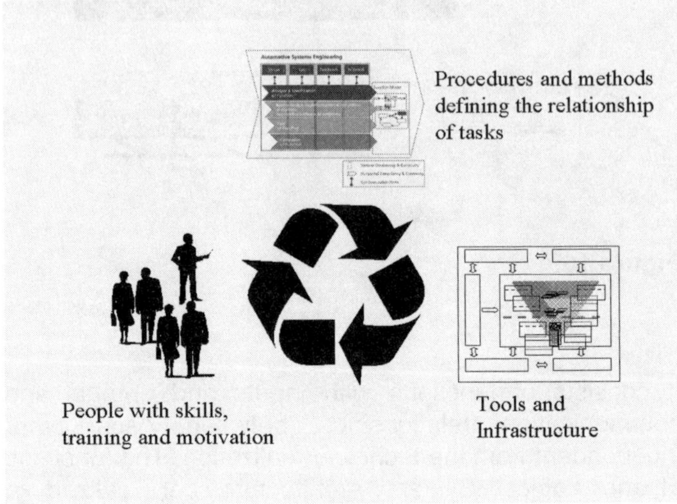

Figure 13.

<u>Key Management Processes and Ability to Perform</u> - The purpose of Requirements Management is to establish a common understanding between the customer and the system design project of the customer's requirements that will be addressed [4]. The requirements management incorporates the task [1]

- Collection of requirements
- Tracking of change requests

It is important that the applied requirements management process addresses the specific needs in the Automotive System Design:

- Cooperation between companies
- Co-working between teams
- Refinement of the requirements because not all requirements can be fixed at the start of the project
- Long Lifecycle of the final product with requirements for service, maintenance, recycling ,...

Configuration Management involves identifying the configuration of the system (e.g. selected components, their descriptions, specifications, implementations, ..) at given points in time, systematically controlling changes to the configuration and maintaining the traceability of the configuration throughout the life cycle. It addresses the different life cycles of the system components as well as the generation of the components, artifacts/results by different teams, e.g. specification, behavior models, RSFs with their Contracts, the integration and validation plans and experiment results.

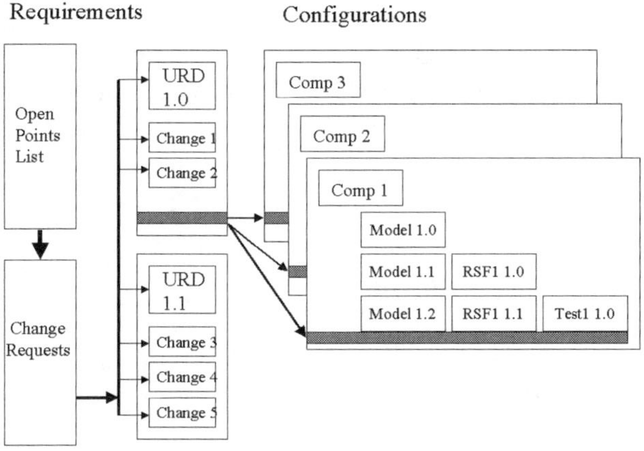

Figure 14.

The Project Management consists of 2 important tasks: the planning and the controlling of the individual projects to achieve the objectives in terms of Quality, Cost and Time. Planning is the most important task, because it incorporates the constraints in organizational structures and in available resources (people, money and technologies) by setting individual work packages, that contribute to the overall success of the project. Controlling on the other side consists of tracking the progress of the work packages and analyzing the differences. Immediate definition of countermeasure to minimize the risk for the quality, cost and time objectives is the most difficult job and leads to successful and not successful project results.

The work packages in the design of distributed systems are executed in different teams and across company boundaries. Thus the above described challenges in the Design Process Management can only be controlled by an integrated approach of Requirements, Configuration and Project Management based on standardized communication interfaces and a common understanding of the project management model.

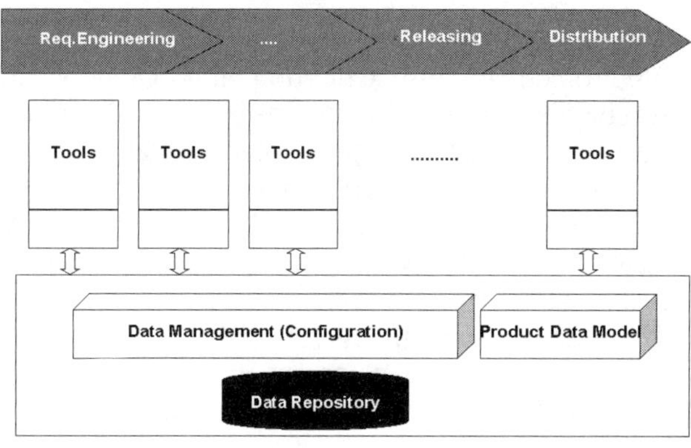

Figure 15.

At any time of the project the actual valid state of the requirements needs to be accessible for all members of the design project team. Changes need to be collected, analyzed for the impact and released in a systematic way. Beside the tracking of changes a consistent link from requirement to the realization/implementation in functions and components needs to be established to allow efficient and consistent co-working and collaboration.

In addition specific training programs be put in place to develop the skills and knowledge of individuals so they can perform their roles effectively. For each role the future skills needs are identified and how these skills are obtained. Some skills might be developed through informal vehicles (e.g. on-the-job training and mentoring), whereas other skills need more formal training vehicles (e.g. classroom training) to become effectively established .

CONCLUSION

We are convinced that the challenges to design distributed systems for vehicles can be met through advanced Automotive Systems and Software Engineering in conjunction with suitable processes, methods and tools. Standardized Technical System Architecture and on standards based infrastructures for collaboration and co-working become as important as the mature management of the System Design Process. Design in the past was treated as an art but needs to be managed as a consistent design process in future. The solutions to those challenges will have a great impact on the way how the vehicle's electrical and electronic architecture are designed.

REFERENCES

(1) AlbertoSangiovanni-Vincentelli Integrated Electronics in the Car and the Design Chain: Revolution or Evolution? - Electronic Systems for Vehicles, 25 and 26 th September 2003Type any references over these paragraphs.

(2) Zurawka T., Schäuffele J., ETAS GmbH - Automotive Software Engineering, ATZ/MTZ technical book

(3) AUTOSAR, www.autosar.org

(4) Carnegie Mellon University Software Engineering InstituteThe Capability Maturity Model, Addison-Wesley

CONTACT

Roland Jeutter
Vice-President
German Operations
ETAS GmbH, Postfach 30 02 40, 70442 Stuttgart,
roland.jeutter@etas.de

Bernd Heppner
Director Business Development
German Operations
ETAS GmbH, Postfach 30 02 40, 70442 Stuttgart,
bernd.heppner@etas.de

2003-01-0863

Auto-Generated Production Code Development for Ford/Think Fuel Cell Vehicle Programme

C. E. Wartnaby, S. M. Bennett and M. Ellims
Pi Technology

R. R. Raju, M. S. Mohammed, B. Patel and S. C. Jones
Ford Motor Company

ABSTRACT

Pi Technology and the Ford Motor Company are using MATLAB Simulink/Stateflow model based design and automatic code generation in C, for the main software development for three electronic control units targeted at the Ford Focus fuel cell vehicle.

The automatic generation of code for embedded automotive applications offers a number of potential advantages over traditional methods. These include faster development, the avoidance of coding errors and avoiding inconsistencies with the design specification. However, the use of automatically generated code in production-intent safety-related systems requires at least the same standard of validation and verification. If code generation were perfect, one could validate only the design. However, it is impractical to require that the code generator must be validated for all possible input designs. Furthermore it must be assumed that the compiler and the hardware can also introduce faults. Therefore we adopt the approach of testing output code for the particular designs we wish to implement, in the same manner as we would test hand-written code for production systems [1]. This retains the additional benefits of exposing the design to further detailed scrutiny in test preparation, and encouraging designs that are straightforward to test.

This paper discusses the development lifecycle employed on this project, highlighting the particular benefits, issues, and challenges surrounding the use of automatically generated code for these production-quality safety-related automotive controllers.

INTRODUCTION

The Ford Focus fuel cell vehicle (FCV) is targeted for limited production in 2004. It is a hybrid vehicle with a hydrogen fuel cell providing primary power for an electric drivetrain. Around a dozen electronic control units (ECUs) must interact via CAN to manage the vehicle systems correctly. Of these, three are being developed by Pi Technology to meet Ford's requirements.

They are: the vehicle system controller (VSC), energy management module (EMM) and thermal system controller (TSC). Building three brand new applications and knowing that system requirements were likely to evolve during the lifetime of the project, Pi has attempted a new and powerful development philosophy for these controllers, based on automatic code generation.

Modified versions of an existing Motorola MPC555-based ECU with identical processor cores are used to support the three applications. Pi has taken advantage of this common hardware by writing a custom set of Simulink library blocks, tailored for automotive use, to provide input/output, communications and diagnostic services. The ECU and libraries together make a reusable *platform* for application development[1].

The platform software is a mix of Simulink and traditional C code, and is entirely generic. Any of the three applications can be built on it, as all application-specific functionality resides in the high-level Simulink model. This allows rapid application changes to be made, or entirely new applications to be built and run: one mouse-click turns the whole application model into an executable ready for download.

THE VEHICLE CONTROL APPLICATIONS

The functions of the three ECUs under development for this project are briefly described here.

The VSC is the key supervisory controller in the vehicle. It coordinates the complex startup and shutdown sequencing of the vehicle systems necessary to bring the fuel cell up to a working state and return it to a state suitable for being entirely switched off. It is also

[1] The platform software has been reused and extended in Pi Technology's OpenECU™ project.

responsible for balancing electrical supplies and demands at all times. This central rôle requires that it often acts as a communications hub, with very high CAN message throughput. The VSC also reads key driver inputs such as the three-track accelerator pedal sensor, ignition key inputs, brake pedal inputs and cruise control switches. It computes the driver-requested torque and coordinates the electric motor and regenerative braking control modules to achieve this. Finally, it contains extensive fault mitigation logic to maintain the vehicle in the optimum safe state should any of a variety of faults occur.

The EMM has responsibility for managing the vehicle energy stores. It maintains the high voltage battery state of charge during driving and manages the "sinking" of surplus electrical energy during regenerative braking. It also oversees the hydrogen refuelling and optional electrical recharging operations, and monitors hydrogen levels and leakage sensors. It has a significant number of digital inputs and outputs to support those functions as well as some miscellaneous vehicle device control. It supports a significant amount of CAN messaging on two independent buses, and acts as a gateway between them.

The TSC has responsibility for thermal management. Cooling a low-temperature automotive fuel cell is more challenging than cooling a comparable combustion engine as there is little heat rejection to atmosphere by the exhaust, and a relatively small temperature difference between the heat source and ambient. Heating can also be required for fuel cell start-up. To achieve all this the TSC actively controls a number of fans and pumps, requiring digital and pulse-width modulated outputs, based on numerous analogue temperature sensor measurements. It communicates with the VSC via the main CAN bus.

The VSC is the most demanding of the three applications in terms of computational resource requirements, and so provides the key challenge for the autocode process we have adopted.

I. AUTOMATIC CODE GENERATION: BENEFITS, CHALLENGES AND SOLUTIONS

Our goal was to not only use automatic code, but to do so in an effective way consistent with safety-related automotive systems. This requires both good technical solutions, and good process. In this section we discusses the technical solutions.

WHAT IS AUTOCODE?

Automatically generated code or "autocode" here consists of C language source files that are derived from a higher-level design by a software program. These source files are compiled and linked using a normal compiler to produce an executable software application which can run on target hardware.

The action of the code generator on the models to produce C code is analogous to the action of a C compiler on C code to produce assembly language files. Just as we hope that a C compiler will produce technically perfect assembly files that require no editing by hand, given correct C source, so we hope the code generator to produce technically perfect C files from the design models, if those models are error-free. In each case the human designer is liberated from working in low-level code in favour of using higher-level constructs closer to the application engineering level (though the choice of high-level constructs may be influenced by the lower-level code that results). And in each case we test the output code, to verify that it actually works as intended.

ADVANTAGES OF AUTOMATIC CODE GENERATION

In the formal software development of safety-related systems, Pi produces a detailed design model using some methodology (such as Simulink modelling) even if the code is to be written by hand. So the automatic code generation step saves some labour (and hence time and cost) in translating models to code. Coding is a small but very significant component of a traditional hand-coded development.

The real gain comes when many iterations of design and coding are made, especially in prototyping work, when the proportion of time that would have been spent hand coding increases and so the cost saving of automatic code generation is increased. Many design iterations and extensions have indeed been necessary for the ECUs described here, due to the novelty of the applications and the vehicle system in general.

Furthermore the effects of design changes can be much more quickly assessed and fed back to further design changes using automatic code generation; this is rapid prototyping. The size and complexity of these applications precluded thrashing out a complete design using rapid prototyping techniques alone at the model level, but has allowed quick experimental work on some features at this level by building on the stable base of the formally specified and systematically tested main development work.

There are benefits beyond time saving and cost reduction, however. The automatic generation of code from the design removes the error-prone process of maintaining design and code in synchronicity; we can be sure that the code always corresponds exactly to what is in the design models, with nothing left out and no obsolete code left in.

A further great benefit on this particular project is portability: the application models can be run on different target hardware, so long as a compatible Simulink block library is provided for that hardware. On this project the first prototype applications were run not on the MPC555-based final target hardware, but on PC-based systems using MathWorks' xPC product and our own I/O drivers.

Once the MPC555 target hardware and software platform was available, porting the applications was straightforward. Most of the work involved (e.g. data type changes and multitasking support) was not specific to the hardware, but was required for production code efficiency.

DISADVANTAGES OF AUTOMATIC CODE GENERATION

Using an automatic code generator removes our ability to write the C code exactly as we wish, just as using a C compiler takes away our control of the assembly output (and hence machine code) it produces. Disadvantages include:

- the code may be inefficient in terms of ROM, RAM or CPU consumption;
- the code may not be structured to facilitate unit testing, static analysis or inspection, which are recommended [2][3] for safety-related work;
- the constants and variables may be named or declared in a way that makes the use of a calibration or diagnostic tools to access them difficult, yet such access is vital for automotive development and service;
- the code may make calls to unvalidated library functions which we do not wish to include in the build;
- the difficulty of performing low-level I/O and communications operations;
- significant work may still be involved in combining automatically generated code sections with each other and hand-written code;
- the danger of being "locked in" to particular tools.

These are all problems we have had to address on this project, as detailed in the following sections.

AUTOCODE APPROACH

For this project we have not chosen to autocode sections of functionality and combine these through manually-written "glue" code to interface them to each other and the hardware. To do so would require the storage and maintenance of the resulting autocode, removing much of the advantage in automatically generating it.

Instead we have adopted a fully-blown autocode structure, similar in convenience and power to commercial rapid prototyping systems, yet running on the actual production target hardware with all of the advantages of its low unit cost, production hardware dimensions, connections and signal conditioning, low power consumption etc. Our approach is to carry this "rapid prototype on production target" code through to production by the application of suitable process and controls, so that no porting or conversion exercise is required for production.

The MPC555 microcontroller, running at 40 MHz, is a relatively powerful embedded platform with native floating-point support. This removes the need for processor-specific arithmetic optimizations which have been performed by others [4].

CHOICE OF TOOLS

Pi chooses tools for particular projects on a case-by-case basis. For this project we chose The MathWorks' MATLAB version R12 with its Simulink and Stateflow toolboxes.

By designing application software in Simulink and Stateflow, we can (with some care) achieve several things simultaneously:

- considering it as a CASE tool, we have a formal detailed design from which software can be written by hand if necessary;
- as a code generator specification, target code can be derived from it automatically;
- as an executable design, offline simulation can be performed as part of the design process, increasing the chance that it will work first time;
- as documentation for the software and calibration work, given suitable structure and commenting.

Other than the ability to run simulations, Simulink has the particular advantage over a traditional Yourdon CASE tool of allowing reusable library blocks, which is important for minimising complexity and maximising maintainability. It is also sufficiently mainstream that we are unlikely to be left using an obsolete format, and if necessary could port from it to tools from other vendors.

Several code generators are available for Simulink or similar modelling tools, including TargetLink [4][5], MatrixX SystemBuild [6], ADI Beacon and AscetSD [7].

For this particular project, Real-Time Workshop was selected for the following reasons:

- Pi already had in-house expertise with it, including customisation of the code generation process and adding new library blocks using Target Language Compiler (TLC) code;
- it allowed reasonably straightforward early prototyping work using MathWorks xPC target, before the production target hardware was available;

- after some experiments it was found to be adequately efficient with RAM, ROM and CPU, if not necessarily the best in class;

- it allowed the use of quite "natural" Simulink models for code generation, without extra configuration information or custom block libraries (other than to perform I/O).

We have chosen to keep using the MATLAB R12 release versions of MathWorks tools, as available at the start of the project, even though more recent versions would provide significant benefits for autocoding (using the now separate Embedded Coder product). This is because the R12 version of RTW is adequate for these applications and the production hardware they must run on. However, to port our platform code to a newer release would involve a significant amount of work due to changes in the core scheduling scheme and some changes in TLC code interfaces, which would consume unnecessary project effort. But for future projects we might well adopt a newer release of MATLAB tools.

HARDWARE INTERFACE: THE PLATFORM CONCEPT

The three different ECU applications (the VSC, EMM and TSC) have been implemented on essentially the same hardware, with only minor I/O differences. This hardware is little changed from a previous Ford/Visteon powertrain control module used for a different production vehicle programme.

Pi's *platform* is the combination of this hardware, and software libraries, that allow any of the supported applications to operate. This is similar to a rapid prototyping system. The software libraries take the form of Simulink library blocks which provide access to hardware inputs, outputs and configuration options, together with support code to run a given autocode application. An example library block is shown in Figure 1.

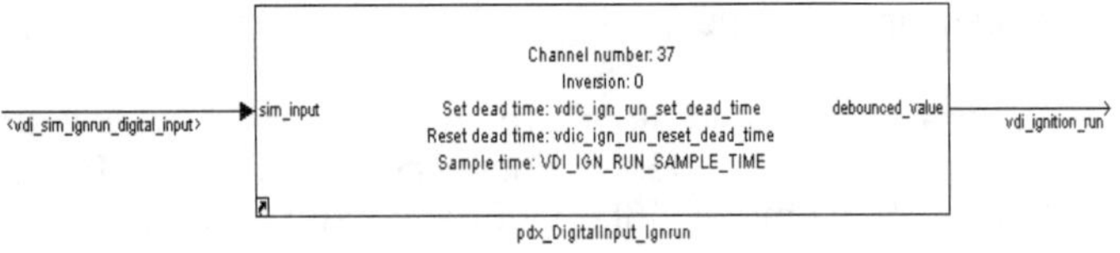

Figure 1: an example platform Simulink library block; this one is used to read a real digital input value into a Simulink-based application.

To take full advantage of the common hardware, and to allow as yet unknown future applications to be supported in the same way with little or no additional investment, a strict partitioning has been adopted between each application and the platform: the platform is entirely generic, with no special knowledge of any of the applications, while all application-specific information is contained only in the Simulink models that constitute that application. Necessary application-specific information such as channel numbers and message ID values is supplied to the platform only via Simulink block parameters as seen in Figure 1.

Currently each application consists only of Simulink/Stateflow models and textual data dictionaries; there is no application-specific hand-written code (though this could be used to optimize portions if necessary). Real-Time Workshop is used to convert each application into C code, and as part of this process calls to hand-written C functions are automatically inserted where platform library blocks were used. Those calls depend on Target Language Compiler (TLC) files which define the automatic code details for our custom blocks. The hand-written platform functions called perform actual hardware input and output activity by accessing microcontroller special function registers. This structure is shown in Figure 2.

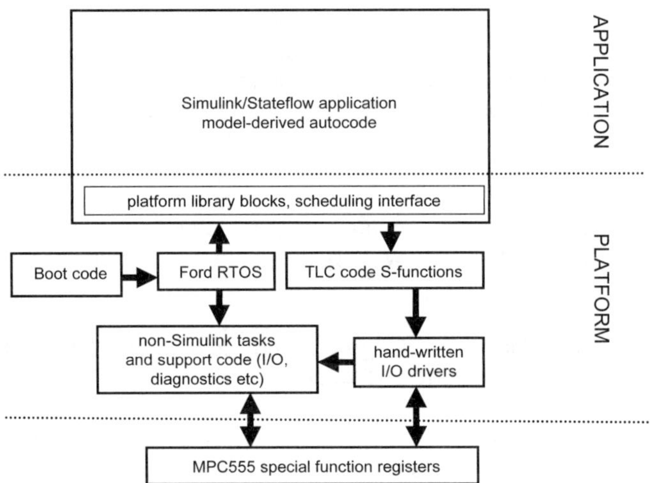

Figure 2: application/platform architecture

Pi decided to use automatic code generation only for the application part of each ECU; that is, validation, control algorithms, high-level decision logic etc. We consider that many lower-level operations, though feasible in model-derived autocode, can be handled far more effectively by hand-written C code. C code is notably stronger than Simulink in any work driven by tables of data or involving bitwise operations, hardware registers or requiring operating system primitives. Note that other authors [8] have attempted to combine application and device driver autocoding, but not using Simulink for the device driver part.

Deciding the boundary between what is done in Simulink and what is done in C code was a delicate balancing act considering code efficiency, design details, and how often each facility was expected to be reused amongst the supported applications.

CAN messaging is particularly important for these applications, so special care was taken in this interface. The platform CAN library blocks are implemented entirely in C code. They perform all transmission, reception, bitfield packaging and unpackaging, and expose convenient message-dependent inputs and outputs at the Simulink level which can be simply written to or read by other blocks. These inputs and outputs are given Boolean, integer or floating-point types as appropriate, to optimise CPU and RAM utilization.

Other operations which we felt should not be attempted at the Simulink model level include responding to diagnostic and calibration tool communications protocols, parsing a serial data stream from a global positioning service (GPS) receiver, and coordinating access to non-volatile memory.

A notable weakness of the Real-Time Workshop R12 release[2] is that it presently generates multiple copies of code corresponding to multiple library block instances, instead of generating several calls to a single function as would be natural and obvious in hand code. This has been tolerated generally but has influenced our implementation in some cases. For example, we have defined a library block which takes an integer value from a CAN message, checks it against special 'error' values, range-checks it, and scales it to floating-point form in engineering units. This was initially implemented as a pure Simulink library subsystem, but had to be re-implemented as C code because the large number of code instances generated by the Simulink version led to excessive ROM consumption. In general any library block that is used tens or hundreds of times has required implementation in C to reduce code size.

On the other hand, some work within platform blocks is actually implemented in Simulink; for example, the validation and filtering of analogue input values is well-suited to Simulink, and the number of block instances in any one application is reasonably small. So while hand code is called to actually read the analogue to digital converter result, autocode is used to process that value, within the platform library block.

CODE STRUCTURE AND SIMULINK/STATEFLOW STYLE GUIDE

A style guide is used to control modelling with the aim of improving code efficiency, maintenance, clarity, consistency and testability.

The style guide directs engineers to adopt certain modelling practices and ban constructs which are deemed unsuitable for some reason. This encourages the bulk of processing, including decision logic, to be performed in Simulink, but using Stateflow charts where appropriate for state-based or complex combinatorial logic. Overall, the modelling style is chosen to coincide as closely as possible with the natural strengths of Simulink and Stateflow, keeping the models as simple as possible overall. This tends to lead to the generation of efficient code, and models that are as maintainable and straightforward as possible.

We have avoided adopting a suggested modelling style which mandates the separation of "control" and "processing", by performing all decisions in Stateflow charts, as this dramatically increases model complexity without any apparent advantage. Nor have we adopted a style which encourages the implementation of most equations and logic in Stateflow chart code. While providing an efficient translation to C code, the latter obviates much of the advantage of using model-based design because the design is almost C code already.

A style is also chosen such that our models could be used, as a fallback position, as designs for hand code should that ever become necessary. The style guide is updated as new issues are found; it provides a distillation of our experience in generating good models.

Particular Simulink blocks that are known to generate unwanted library function calls, which depend on absolute time or which generate particularly inefficient code are banned. For example, the Simulink "initial condition" block is useful for performing special action at the first iteration of the model. However, it generates automatic code with unnecessary function calls and makes use of a problematic 'minus infinity' constant. Using a discrete unit delay (1/z) block fed by a constant (e.g. 0), but with some different initial value (e.g. 1), can usually be used instead, with efficient and straightforward code generated.

Simulink, Stateflow and Real-Time Workshop options are set to improve code efficiency and testability; sometimes there is a trade-off between these aims. For example, the 'atomic subsystem' option is applied to Simulink subsystems to break the generated code into separate functions of a size suitable for unit testing. However, this results in a deeper call tree and limits local variable reuse, increasing stack consumption.

The 'Boolean logic signals' option is selected to represent flags as small integers instead of floating-point numbers, dramatically improving RAM and CPU use. Where appropriate, integers are used for other quantities such as enumerations and "raw" CAN values. Floating-point signals are used for "engineering units" quantities, but single-precision (32-bit) format is used instead of the default double precision.

Other options to control the storage of signals are carefully chosen to minimize RAM consumption. The RTW code is structured such that the same routines are

[2] Later releases of RTW allow "code reuse", but we have stayed with R12 for this project to avoid significant porting work to other core code.

called from different rate tasks, with only part running in each task. With a multi-tasking system this effectively means that any stack space required for local variables is multiplied by the number of rate tasks, each of which has its own stack. It is therefore preferable to encourage RTW to statically allocate storage for signals, rather than using stack (temporary) variables as would be intuitive. Statically allocated signal variables are also essential for unit testing and convenient for access using the calibration tool or debugger. The simplistic and repetitive nature of the generated code makes the effect of compiler options very predictable and their careful selection important.

TASK SCHEDULING

In a typical powertrain control application, a number of tasks must be performed at various periodic rates, while other processing must be done in response to events. Internal combustion engine controllers typically have to perform calculations at particular engine angles, usually by means of interrupt-triggered processing based on a crankshaft position sensor signal. The three applications considered here are simpler than combustion engine controllers in this respect, because all of the required application processing is periodic, linked to the requirement to send outputs as periodic CAN messages. This lack of event-based processing is a very useful simplification for applying automatic code generation, because Simulink models naturally run on a periodic tick or multiples of that period. (Note however that event-based processing is quite possible in Simulink-derived code.)

To allow fast periodic tasks to run on time even in the presence of lengthy slower tasks, a pre-emptive multitasking model was adopted. The existing and well-proven Ford proprietary "PTEC" real-time operating system was used as the basis. Custom code was written to automatically generate a different operating system task for each Simulink-derived model task rate, with priorities descending with increasing period length (rate monotonic ordering) [9].

As it happens, present chronometric data indicate that a single-tasking model would suffice, as the work of all 'slow' tasks is completed sufficiently fast to be inserted between invocations of the fastest (10 ms) code. Adopting a non-preemptive approach would reduce model complexity and RAM consumption. However, a multi-tasking model is maintained to guard against slow tasks growing to the point at which they must straddle invocations of the fastest tasks as development proceeds. See also "Code Performance" below.

The standard Simulink mechanism of specifying sample rates for data source blocks (typically hardware or CAN inputs), with other downstream blocks generally inheriting those sample rates, is used to control which processes are performed at what rates. No custom configuration is used to specify tasks. This ensures that the application, with its various periodic tasks, executes on the target hardware in just the same way as it does in Simulink simulation.

Simulink conventions were also used to ensure data consistency across rate transitions, and indeed are enforced by Simulink.

Non-autogenerated tasks and interrupt-driven processes within the platform are also set up to handle necessary background work and serial communications, as for any comparable hand-coded project.

CALIBRATION SUPPORT

To support development work, the ATI/Vision CAN calibration tool is used. While later versions of MATLAB provide some support for ASAP2, this was not available early in the project. Pi therefore wrote a custom tool to generate an ASAP2 description file. RAM variables (signals) and adjustable calibration constants to which the calibration tool must have access are explicitly named in the model and identified in the data dictionary. At build time the Pi tool parses the data dictionary to produce a template ASAP2 file, the storage type of signals or constants identified as displayable or calibratible in the data-dictionary are set to "exported global", and finally after the model is compiled the tool extracts the addresses from the linker output and completes the ASAP2 file. Adopting this route enables Pi to include other data into the ASAP2 file such as a description, min-max range and resolution.

DIAGNOSTIC SUPPORT

Particular platform library blocks are provided to represent elements that should be accessible to Ford's standard Worldwide Diagnostic System service tool. This interrogates ECUs via CAN to discover which diagnostic trouble codes (DTCs) might be set and to inspect variable values accessible as Parameter Identifiers (PIDs), using a Keyword Protocol 2000 based protocol. This is a specific automotive facility that no ordinary rapid-prototyping system provides.

The platform has no prior knowledge of what DTCs and PIDs are to be included in each application. Instead the application designer includes DTC block instances in the Simulink model, specifying the identifier number as a parameter and feeding in a suitable Boolean flag representing the fault. Similarly PIDs are handled as library blocks. An additional library block allows the application designer to specify the CAN message identities which should be used for diagnostic communication.

CODE PERFORMANCE

It is difficult to compare the resources used by these autocoded applications with hand-coded versions, as they are completely novel, and no hand-coded equivalent versions exist. However, as an indication of resource utilization, some data are presented here for the most demanding of the three applications: the VSC. As explained above, this is the most demanding of the three applications; as an indication, it processes the values of some 1300 CAN messages per second.

The available hardware resources are as follows on the MPC555-based ECU:

Internal flash memory (ROM) for code	448 KB
Off-chip flash memory for calibration data, and future expansion of the code	1024 KB
TOTAL ROM AVAILABLE	**1472 KB**
Internal RAM	26 KB
Off-chip RAM	32 KB
TOTAL RAM AVAILABLE	**58 KB**
PowerPC CPU core with native floating-point support operating at	**40 MHz**

The actual size and timing statistics for two particular releases of the VSC application are as follows; the first is a comparatively early build, while the latter is closer to full production functionality:

	Software Version	
	V1.4	V1.9
Application periodic tasks	7	7
Application features (some rather large)	16	16
Simulink blocks	4715	~8000
Non-trivial subsystems	700	1200
Code size	232 KB	330 KB
Calibrations and Constants	23 KB	26.5KB
TOTAL ROM REQUIREMENT	**250 KB**	**356.5KB**
Application/platform RAM	11.5 KB	18KB
Stack/RTOS RAM	15 KB	20KB
TOTAL RAM REQUIREMENT	**25.9 KB**	**38KB**
Approximate average CPU load	**30%**	**45%**
Approximate peak CPU load in worst 10 ms 'tick'	50%	60%

The hardware modules here are specified with plentiful RAM and ROM to allow some contingency, but these data show that quite demanding applications based on this platform could fit in only the on-board MPC555 resources. For our applications and modules, we have headroom to allow for future expansion due to new functionality or changes in build procedures or options to aid testing.

From informal code inspection, we acknowledge that at least some automatically coded portions of these applications would consume somewhat less RAM and fewer CPU cycles if coded by hand; however, the advantages in automatic code generation for this project easily outweigh any potential savings in terms of reducing available hardware resources in production, and we cannot say that RAM would be saved if *all* the code were written by hand. RTW's active re-use of storage may actually give it an edge over handwritten code.

Some preliminary static analysis of the RTW code (using PCLint) did not reveal any significant issues with the code produced, but formal static code analysis remains to be done on this project.

II. DEVELOPMENT PROCESS FRAMEWORK

This section describes how the Simulink modelling and autogeneration of code described above fits into the complete development process for this project. We require not just autocode that runs in production, but autocode which we are confident is suitable for use in a safety-related production system. The development process, and in particular the testing, is vital in achieving this.

Pi Technology projects for safety-related software-based systems generally follow a V-model formal development lifecycle. However, the detailed processes and tools employed at each development stage are tailored to suit the circumstances, safety integrity level [2] and customer preferences of particular projects, as documented by a project-specific quality plan [13]. The FCV project is no exception in this regard. The major difference from traditional Pi projects is the automatic generation of C code from application design models; the usual steps of requirements capture, specification, design and various levels of testing, together with formal change and configuration control, are all present, as appropriate for a safety-related software product. The platform consists to a large extent of hand-written code, for which the development process is comparable with other projects within Pi Technology.

The work for all stages is maintained under configuration control, changes are coordinated through a formal change control system, and all work is peer reviewed.

See also [14] for a general discussion of process and tools as applied to model-based design and automatic code generation.

REQUIREMENTS CAPTURE FOR EACH ECU

Vehicle-system-wide requirements documentation and communications protocol specifications are maintained by Ford in a dedicated DOORS database. For the particular control modules under development by Pi, Ford provided requirements documents early in the project. Subsequently, requirements have been received as written or verbal requests, subsidiary requirements documents addressing particular functional areas, and as Ford change requests. All Ford-requested changes are captured in the Pi change control database and then scheduled for incorporation into phased software releases. Ultimately, requirements are incorporated into the subsystem design specification (SDS) for each ECU.

SUBSYSTEM DESIGN SPECIFICATION (FUNCTIONAL SPECIFICATION)

In the SDS for each ECU, the customer requirements are decomposed (where necessary) into small statements of required functionality which are:

- clear and unambiguous;
- assigned a unique alphanumeric tag to allow subsequent traceability;
- related to their source (person, change request, document reference);
- testable from the external interface to the ECU (including communications messages).

The SDS is largely a textual document, but with tables and diagrams where appropriate. Its main purpose is to provide detailed requirements for design work and functional testing. However, it is also a key component of end-user documentation in that it specifies the externally observable functionality of the ECU.

Pi's Pixref tool [12] is used to automatically generate traceability matrices linking each functional requirement in the SDS to the Simulink model location where it is implemented, and the test script location where it is tested (see 'system testing' below). It works simply by searching for and correlating the incidence of requirement tags in different files to generate each matrix, highlighting any requirements that have not been referenced or obsolete ones that are still present in error.

A separate SDS is written for the platform in isolation, defining what services it provides and the detailed functionality of the library blocks it makes available. This is used to design and test against, and as a user manual for engineers working on the application models.

ARCHITECTURAL DESIGN

A *feature* on this project is a software module relating to some functional area, whose boundary is chosen to keep the content logically consistent, reasonably self-contained and of a size manageable for a single engineer to work on at one time.

For the platform, which is responsible for all hardware interaction and is largely hand-coded, the architectural design document contains detailed explanations and policies spanning a number of areas relating to hardware interfacing, naming, build process, the memory map, etc., as well as partitioning the software into features.

For each ECU application however, the architectural design consists of two components, each of which is brief. Firstly, a textual document describes any overall design policies or the way in which key application-specific problems are solved, and the functional requirements of the SDS are allocated to features. Secondly, an application model is constructed in Simulink which links together the (initially empty) subsidiary models corresponding to each feature. The "wiring" of this model defines the data interfaces between feature models, which is subsequently refined through data dictionary entries for the data flows. See Figure 3.

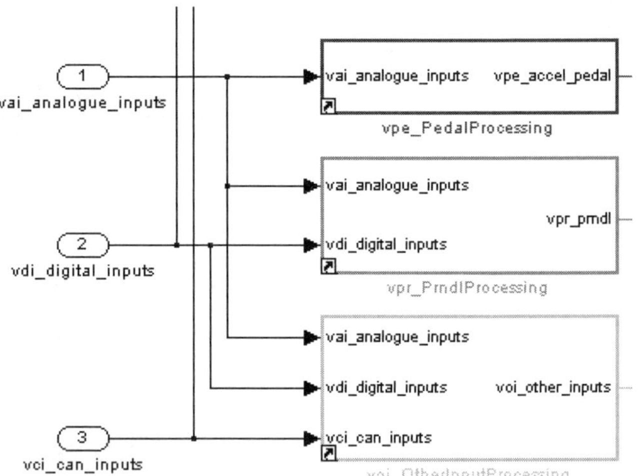

Figure 3: a fragment of the application model showing three feature blocks

A generic application architecture document explains how and why to structure an application in general, to avoid repetition in the architecture documents for the three applications considered here (and any additional applications in the future).

DETAILED DESIGN (FEATURE MODELLING)

Each application feature is constructed as a separate Simulink library model. This is to facilitate configuration management and parallel working within the team, simply by making each model a separate file in the version control system. These are all linked to from the application model, which allows the entire application to be navigated as a whole though the component parts are constructed as separate entities. As explained previously, the style guide is used to give a consistent and effective modelling style. Software requirement tags are included in comments to provide traceability to the SDS, which can be checked using Pi's Pixref tool. See Figure 4.

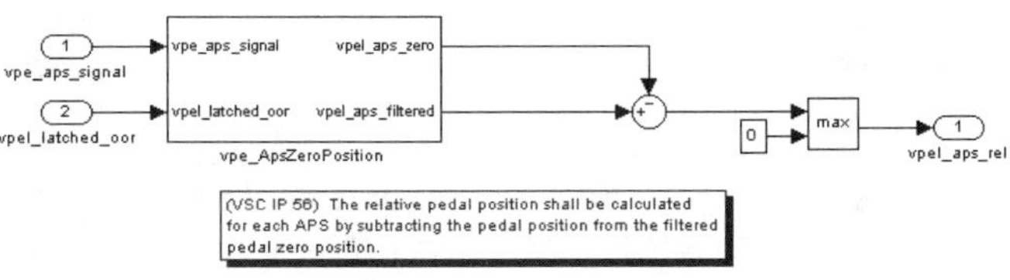

Figure 4: an example model fragment using standard Simulink blocks, subsystems and comments for traceability and understanding

For the platform software a detailed design document is written for each feature, containing a structure chart, an explanation of the design considerations, and pseudocode of (just) sufficient detail to allow subsequent coding and unit testing.

CODING

The process of generating code from the application model is entirely automatic. No modification or integration of the Real-Time Workshop code is performed by hand. The entire application model is simply loaded in Simulink and the 'Build' menu item selected, resulting in a downloadable file in a few minutes. This is of paramount importance in prototyping, development and testing work, where changes can be made at the model level and run on the production-intent target hardware almost immediately. This ensures that all implementation changes are made at the model level, with which the code is rigorously consistent; there is no temptation to "tweak", and then have to maintain separately, the derived code.

Simulink parts of the platform are built at the same time as the application that uses them. Hand-coded C files are written and maintained by hand in the traditional way.

TESTING

As with other Pi software development projects, testing is divided into different activities with different complementary aims and strengths. These are explained in turn below.

UNIT TESTING

To unit test in Pi's terms is to exercise thoroughly small *units* (typically C functions) of implementation, meeting certain structural and data coverage goals, to ensure that those units operate correctly over a wide permutation of input data [1]. The purpose is twofold: to ensure that the code operates in all cases in accordance with the design, but secondly (and perhaps less obviously) to ensure that the design behaviour is reasonable for all cases. Unit testing finds both design problems and coding errors. Where automatic code generation is used, we expect few coding errors, but still expect to find detailed design errors.

Unit testing uncovers errors of detail that are unlikely to be identified in higher-level testing; however, it will not uncover problems that depend on the successful integration of different areas of software, and the actual hardware.

The code generator and compiler are not *trusted*. At present, validated code generation and compilation tools do not exist for Simulink and the MPC555 processor and in any event are not even theoretically possible[3]. Indeed during development some examples of erroneous auto-generated C code have been found. Some issues occur which prevent models building or generated code compiling. However, we have experienced issues in the code including the details of the precise behaviour of enabled subsystems in multirate code and the silent non-support for some bitwise operations.

Our approach therefore is to test the generated code, rather than relying on model-level testing and assuming 'perfect' translation by the tools. This code testing differs little from software unit testing on Pi's hand-coded projects, using Pi's test harness generator (THG) to exercise code units in a test harness automatically derived from an input spreadsheet which lists test vectors and provides expected output values. The application models provide an executable detailed design for the code, defining its proper operation. In preparing test vectors and expected results, which are compared with the actual results generated by the implementation, unexpected outcomes from that design are encountered and fixed.

Only a small trial amount of unit testing has been performed so far on this development project, but full unit testing is required for the production releases.

---

[3] We can never be sure that the specification is correct. No verification system can verify every correct program. We can never be certain the verification system is correct [10].

FEATURE (MODULE) TESTING

The bulk of functional testing is performed at a hardware-in-the-loop level (see "System Testing" below). Many of the system tests are targeted at specific areas of functionality rather than overall system validation, as they must be to achieve high functional coverage. However, simulation-based testing in MATLAB has also employed informally as part of the model-based design process, and sometimes formally to validate small areas of functionality that are inaccessible at the hardware level in a production-intent software build. This fills the potential gap between unit testing and system testing, by detecting defects that depend on the interaction between smaller units but which would still be difficult to detect from the external hardware interface.

Formal simulation tests take the form of spreadsheets which list the feature inputs (including calibration "constant" values) and expected outputs as a function of time. A custom Pi tool, the Simulink Harness Generator (SHG) automatically runs some arbitrary model subsystem through the specified input regime and checks whether the observed outputs are within the defined expected tolerances.

This form of testing allows inputs to be set to combinations that would be difficult or impossible to achieve when running the feature embedded in the whole application, including different calibration value permutations, while allowing time-dependent behaviour to be exercised. The bulk of code and data coverage is achieved through code unit testing, however, as code testing is required anyway to meet safety-related process and coverage goals.

For platform code, feature tests are used to exercise otherwise inaccessible behaviour (e.g. CAN error handling), sometimes requiring intrusion on the code under test using the debugger.

INTEGRATION TESTING

Integration testing here is limited to performing checks that CPU load and memory usage is within acceptable limits such that the application executes reliably on the target hardware. The other testing stages are relied upon to show the proper execution of algorithms and translation of inputs to outputs.

Additional facilities have been included in the platform software to allow the run-time accumulation of statistics relating to task execution times and maximum achieved stack depths. These are vital for application/platform integration testing, as the platform has no prior knowledge of the computational demands of the application, and an application might be specified that exceeds the available CPU resources.

SYSTEM TESTING

The SDS for each application, which provides the definition for system-level testing, does not intrude into the internal software architecture of each ECU. It is written specifically to define only behaviour that is observable at a hardware level. As a result, system testing for these autocoded applications does not differ from that of hand-coded systems, and so this level of testing is entirely conventional for Pi.

System testing detects defects that stem from any software or hardware issues resulting in an ECU failing to meet its functional requirements. Its great strength is that it builds confidence that the ECU actually meets its requirements in real-world conditions, when all of the software and hardware is integrated as a whole. However, system testing can never achieve full code or data coverage as unit testing can. Qualitatively, system test coverage is actually greater for these applications than for a typical combustion engine controller, because of the large number of CAN data interfaces which expose much of the detailed internal processing to relatively direct test scrutiny.

A Pi AutoSim hardware-in-the-loop (HIL) simulator [11] is configured to mimic the rest of the vehicle from the perspective of the ECU under test. It provides 12V digital signals and simulated loads, voltage and resistance inputs, and most importantly for these applications, a full simulation of the vehicle CAN traffic. The system of CAN inputs and outputs is derived automatically from the vehicle protocol specification using a custom software tool written for this project.

In the same way that modelling effort is divided into features to allow parallel working, so system tests are divided into a number of automatically executed *scripts*, each written to test some collection of functional requirements detailed in the SDS. The test scripts set both hardware and CAN inputs, and test hardware and CAN outputs, and also control the ECU power supplies. Traceability to the SDS is ensured by commenting the requirements tags in the test scripts. Pixref is again used to generate a traceability matrix showing where each requirement is tested in some script, and that no obsolete requirements are tested for.

A brief overall test plan explains general testing strategy, documents the procedure for formal test execution and the recording of results, and explains the hardware set-up and organisation of files. However, the detailed thinking behind each test is contained only in the test script itself (and the resulting output files), to minimise maintenance problems and allow parallel working by different engineers. All test scripts are run automatically in sequence before any formal software release as regression tests.

For the platform, special test applications are devised which map inputs to outputs (both hardware and communications signals) in a predefined way. These are then built and tested in the same way as the "real" applications.

For prototype development work, only system tests and model review are employed. Unit testing is generally omitted due to the high rate of requirements change on such a novel project. This achieves acceptable quality for the limited scope of development work by the customer.

CONCLUSION

Together Pi Technology and Ford have successfully developed three novel and challenging production-intent control applications using model-based design and automatic code generation from MATLAB/Simulink. The resulting code currently consumes only a modest proportion of the available RAM, ROM and CPU cycles available on the target Motorola MPC555-based production hardware.

Key elements in the success of the project so far are:

- formal controlled development of requirements, models and tests;
- the use of a modelling *style guide* which encourages consistent, structured and yet straightforward use of Simulink and Stateflow and constructs which lead to efficient generated code;
- investing in the development of a generic *platform* to support these and possible future applications;
- implementing low-level driver functionality using hand-written code, not autocode;
- completely embracing fully automatic code generation for the applications, with no hand-coded adjustments or fixes to the application code;
- automated hardware-in-the-loop system testing.

The development of these applications is presently still in progress, but successive versions have been running successfully on target hardware in a number of test vehicles for many months.

REFERENCES

1. Michael Ellims and Richard P. Parkins, "Unit Testing Techniques and Tool Support", SAE 1999-01-2842.
2. "Development Guidelines for Vehicle-Based Software", Motor Industry Software Reliability Association (MISRA), available from http://www.misra.org.uk.
3. IEC 61508, Functional Safety: Safety Related Systems . Parts 1 to 7.
4. Giuseppe Amato and Lutz Köster, "High Performance Code Generation for Audo, an Automotive micro-Controller from Infineon Technologies", SAE 2000-01-0393.
5. Lutz Köster, Thomas Thomsen and Ralf Stracke, "Connecting Simulink to OSEK: Automatic Code Generation for Real-Time Operating Systems with TargetLink", SAE 2001-01-0024.
6. Walton Fehr, Todd Martin, Robert Lapkass and Danilo Viazzo, "Graphical Modeling and Code Generation for Distributed Automotive Control Systems", SAE 2000-01-3061.
7. Andreas Greff and Torsten Günther, "A New Approach for a Multi-Fuel, Torque Based ECU Concept using Automatic Code Generation", SAE 2001-01-0267.
8. George Saikalis, Shigeru Oho and Steffen Zunft, "Zero Hand Coding Approach for Controller Development", SAE 2002-01-0142.
9. C.L. Liu, James, W. Layland, “Scheduling algorithms for multirogramming in a hard real-time environment”, Journal of the ACM, 20(1) January 1973, pp 46-61.
10. Beizer, B, oftware Testing Techniques international Thomson Computer Press 1990.
11. Ellims, M. “Hardware in the Loop Testing of Embedded Control Software”, ImechE Symposium on Engine Control Systems, IEE Control 2000, University of Cambridge 6 September 2000. Available at http://www.pitechnology.com.
12. The Pixref tool will be available for download from http://www.pitechnology.com.
13. Mike Ellims and Keith Jackson, "ISO 9001: Making the Right Mistakes", SAE 2000-01-0714.
14. Scott Ranville, "Practical Application of Model-Based Software Design for Automotive", SAE 2002-01-0876.

CONTACT

The authors can be emailed at charlie.wartnaby@pitechnology.com. See also http://www.pitechnology.com.

DEFINITIONS, ACRONYMS, ABBREVIATIONS

ASAP: Arbeitskreis zur Standardisierung von Applikationssystemen (workgroup for the standardization of application systems, see http://www.asam.net/) (calibration tool description file format)

CAN: Controller Area Network

DTC: Diagnostic Trouble Code

ECU: Electronic Control Unit

EMM: Energy Management Module

FCV: Fuel Cell Vehicle

GPS: Global Positioning Service

HIL: Hardware-In-the-Loop

IEC : International Electrotechnical Committee.

PID: Parameter IDentifier

SDS: Subsystem Design Specification

SHG: Simulink Harness Generator

THG: Test Harness Generator

TLC: Target Language Compiler

TSC: Thermal Systems Controller

VSC: Vehicle System Controller

Practical Application of Model-Based Software Design for Automotive

Scott Ranville
New Eagle Software

ABSTRACT

A number of factors are driving a change in how the automotive industry develops software. Some of these factors include: increasing complexity of the software; increasing quantity of software in the vehicle; reduced resources of development time, engineers, money; and the emergence of software-based safety-critical systems. To address these issues, the automotive industry, as well as a number of other embedded industries, are moving to a model-based software design process. The goals of the model-based process are to reduce the overall cost and time of the development process while increasing the quality of the software. These goals will be accomplished by re-aligning the emphasis of the engineering effort to earlier in the design process and by automating as much of the design process as is possible.

This paper will present a number of the key steps in the software design process, describing the objective of each step and listing a number of issues that need to be addressed. This should provide a good overview of a model-based software design process with enough detail to provide a sense for the scope of the problem.

Some of the particular steps that will be described include: modeling style guides, automatic code generation, model checking, automatic test vector generation, rapid prototyping/hardware-in-the-loop, schedulability analysis, networked applications, and configuration management.

INTRODUCTION

A popular development process for embedded software is the so-called "V" development process. [10]

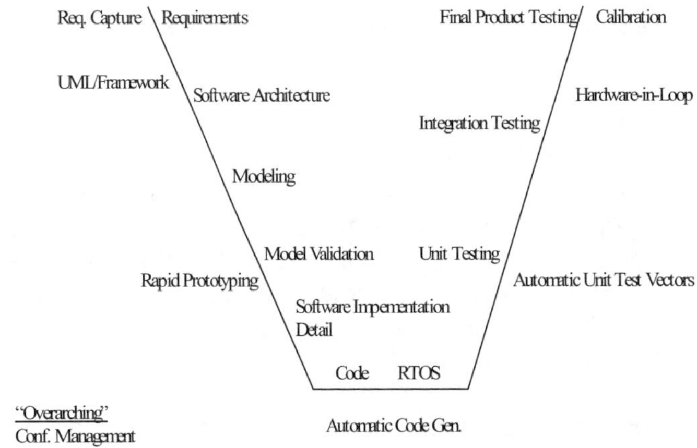

Figure 1 "V" Development Process

Figure 1 shows a generic "V" development process. Inside of the "V" are the general steps that compose the "V" process. The outside of the "V" are general technology areas and tools that can be applied to the process steps.

This paper will provide an overview of these steps and technology areas, some of the issues for each, and some tools that exist for each.

TECHNOLOGY AREAS AND TOOLS

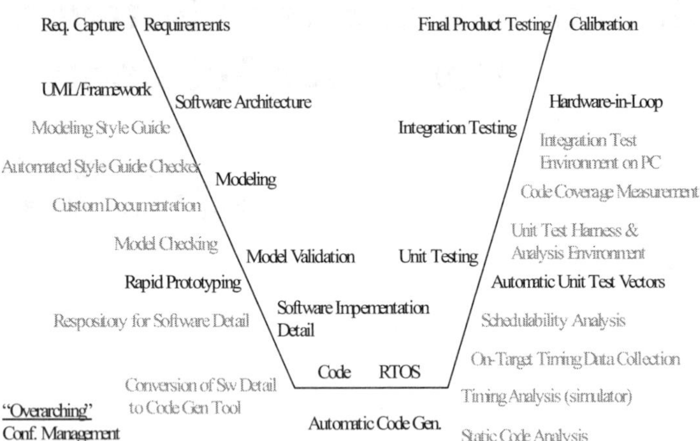

Figure 2 Tools Needed for Software Development

Figure 2 Lists some tools that will help form a complete software development environment. Frequently no organization will use every tool but only those that make sense for their particular situation.

REQUIREMENTS CAPTURE - As with many industries, high-level requirements are not overly common in the automotive field. However, the industry trend is towards more requirements capture and use in the development process. The goal is to make sure that the software meets all customer requirements. This will also help improve the software development process for standard metrics such as CMM.

Historically, requirements have been in written prose and are "linked" to a particular element in the design. However, this does not facilitate automated use in the rest of the development process. One of the challenges now is to have requirements from which analysis can be preformed automatically, but yet, are easy enough for a "layman" to enter.

Requirements capture, analysis, and efficient linking to other tools in the process is an open research area as not many tools or methodologies exist to facilitate their effective use. Some existing tools that help along these lines include: Telelogic DOORS, Slate, Requisite Pro.

UML/FRAMEWORK TOOLS - Historically, the overall software architecture has been kind of an ad hoc byproduct of the software design process. As software systems become larger and more complex, tools are needed to help facilitate establishing and analyzing this architecture and understanding all the complex interactions of the component pieces.

UML tools appear to be addressing this need as well as some other tools that are being classified as framework tools. One of the current limitations with these tools is that they do not interface well to the lower level design tools where the software algorithms are being modeled. There are also limited analysis tools for this class of design tools.

Some of today's tools that do help in this area include : Rational Rose, I-Logix Rhapsody, RTI ControlShell, Kennedy Carter xUML, Telelogic DOORS.

MODELING STYLE GUIDE - Many of the modeling tools offer a vast array of modeling constructs. Depending on the purpose of the model, these constructs may not be optimal. For example, when the models are used for generating code, it is sometimes necessary to avoid constructs that are known to produce inefficient code. Another popular use of a Style Guide is to help promote a common look and feel of models developed by different engineers, thereby making it easier to understand another's model.

While not a problem, one item of concern for leveraging existing Style Guides, is that many companies will have a different set of constraints on the software and how the tool is used. In some cases companies in the same industry segment will have exactly opposite established procedures. This, then, mandates different Style Guides.

In regards to the The Mathworks Matlab tool, the automotive industry has gotten together to create a publicly available style guide. Many companies have internal style guides or are developing one.

AUTOMATIC STYLE GUIDE CHECKING TOOL [7] – Developing a Style Guide does not help improve the software process unless it is used and enforced. Depending on the style guide rules that are developed, checking that these rules are enforced can be a laborious task. Frequently, these rules can be automatically checked by a tool, which saves a significant amount of time in the model preparation stage.

For Matlab models, the only known commercially available tool for automatically checking compliance to a Style Guide is the Tarragon MINT tool.

DOCUMENTATION TOOL - Very frequently, the models that are developed need to be passed on to another group, either within the company or outside the company. Often, this other group is only interested in the algorithm contained within the model and does not want to run the model in its native environment. Thus, a tool is needed to create a document that can be passed on, either electronically or in printed form. Most all modeling tools have a print mechanism (to paper, but not necessarily to an electronic file format such as PDF), but this is usually insufficient. Often the desired documentation needs to be in a specific format (Word, PDF, etc.) and contain extra information that is not directly in the model, for example text from the requirements capture tool. Also, many groups want to customize the organization of how the model is presented. Thus, a custom documentation tool outside of the modeling tool is often needed.

For the Matlab environment, The Mathworks provides a DocGen tool that does allow for customized documents to be generated.

MODEL CHECKING [4] - A common question when models are created is how to "prove" that the model is correct. While proving that the model matches the requirements and provides intended functionality is an open research topic, model checking can help to ensure that the model itself is consistent. This helps to guarantee that there are no inherit errors before proceeding down the rest of the development process, and thus, that the end product will be of higher quality. Some modeling tools have built in model checking, but many do not. Thus, a separate model checking tool is needed, along with an automated translation to this tool from the original model.

Some of the existing model checking tools include: Siemens VALID, Reactive System Reactis (to be released end of 2001), ADI AUTT, I-Logix, IAR, visualSTATE.

RAPID PROTOTYPING - The trend in industry is towards reducing the cycle development time and overall cost. One technology for this is rapid prototyping. Rapid prototyping allows for the algorithm to be tested with hardware without taking the timely step of developing production intent software. Tools exist that take the model and run it on a computer with "unlimited" resources. This allows the model developer (who is probably not a software person, but rather a controls person) to test directly without the need to use the software part of the company. The model developer can observe how his algorithm works, modify it if needed, and, when satisfied, pass it on to the software people.

Some of the existing companies that provide solutions for this include: dSPACE, Opal-RT, ADD2, The Mathworks, ADI, PI Technologies, and ETAS.

REPOSITORY FOR SOFTWARE DETAIL - A common practice in the industry is to develop a model for one component (feature) at a time. In automotive, and other embedded domains, a common practice is to use global variables due to limited resources. The components are often developed independently from one another, and are often reused on different projects. To help facilitate this dispersed development environment and reuse, a database of the parameters and the associated properties are often stored in a central repository. This then facilitates easier integration of these components into a complete application.

Commercially available tools such as Oracle can provide the framework for these databases, but these repositories of information usually involve custom tools for each company.

CONVERSION OF DATA REPOSITORY TO CODE GENERATION TOOL - When generating code from a model, the coder (be it a person or tool) needs to reference the software repository to determine the characteristics of the software parameters. This can be a laborious task, so a tool to automatically reference the repository and convert it to a form needed by the automatic code generation tool, will save a significant amount of time during the code generation stage and prevent translations errors (typos) that will occur when this step is done manually.

Because the databases usually involve custom solutions, the translation of this information usually also involves custom tools.

AUTOMATIC CODE GENERATION [1-3] - Many organizations take the time to develop models for the purpose of automatically generating code, as this can save time and produce consistent code. Once the automatic code generation tool is "certified" as correct, the generated code can always be assumed to faithfully duplicate the functionality defined in the model. Thus, automatic code generation is viewed as a significant time saver and enabler to produce higher quality code.

A number of issues exist for this, as the code generation tools require a large amount of information that usually is not modeled. For example, Matlab is widely used in the automotive industry to model the control algorithm. However, this tool was not originally designed to allow the software information to be easily defined. Also, with Matlab as an example, some of the code generation tools do not support all the modeling constructs that exist. Matlab is somewhat unique in that there exist 3rd party tools that produce code for Matlab models. For many of the tools, there are no 3rd party add on tools involved, and the modeling tool is less likely to not support one of its own modeling constructs.

Some of the existing modeling tools with code generation capabilities or 3rd party add on code generators include: The Mathworks RTW, dSPACE TargetLink, ADI BEACON, ETAS ASCET-SD, MatrixX SystemBuild, Cadence VCC, I-Logix Rhapsody in MicroC, and IAR visualState.

STATIC CODE ANALYSIS - For hand written code and until automatically generated code is trusted, static code analysis is a good quality step in the software development process. Static code analysis can help to automatically detect errors and standard violations (example, Safer-C, MISRA) without executing the code. Static analysis can also provide quantifiable metrics, and help to facilitate understanding the code.

A number of tools exist for this, and a couple of them include: LDRA, Programming Research QAC, and Les Hatton Safer C.

AUTOMATIC GENERATION OF UNIT TEST VECTORS [5-8] - Generating test inputs to drive a test of the software is a very hard, time consuming, and imprecise activity. Once generated, the test vectors can be used to validate that the code and model produce the same outputs for the same set of inputs. The test vectors can also be used to drive the software for the collection of timing data. Using a tool to generate the test vectors will significantly reduce the development time and most likely produce a set of higher quality test vectors that cover more of the model specification.

Some of the existing or forthcoming tools for this include: ATTOL, T-VEC Technology T-VEC, Siemens VALID, Reactive System Reactis, ADI AUTT, and EDAptive Computing VectorGen.

UNIT TESTING HARNESS AND ANALYSIS ENVIRONMENT [8] - Once test vectors are generated, a harness is needed to execute the test vectors. One environment can be an off-line tester. This environment will input the test vectors to both the model and the code and capture the resulting outputs. A good harness tool will also provide an easy to use environment to allow the user to detect differences in the model and code output and to track down exactly why this difference occurred. Another useful variant of this tool is to download the code to an embedded target so that the output from this target can be compared to the model output.

TIMING ANALYSIS – As applications grow in size, the throughput of the code may become more important. Also, within the automotive industry, the introduction of more full featured RTOSs [11-12] is a relatively new increase in the software complexity. It will become increasingly important to be able to predict and measure the code execution time. This will allow up front analysis to be done to ensure that a somewhat abstract case that will occur in the field, but does not occur in the testing is found and fixed before final customer deliver.

There are some tools such as Diab RTA Suite and AMC Code test that will measure the execution time of code on hardware. These tools are good for measuring existing performance, but do not help to do this earlier in the design process where fixes are easier and less costly.

There are also some tools such as Tri-Pacific Rapid RMA that will take execution times, and scheduling policies and analyze this to prove if the system is schedulable or not. These tools are good if timing data exists, but this data is often hard to come by. One tool that will help get this data is a "timing vector" generator tool. This is similar to a tool that produces unit test vectors, except that instead of trying to achieve a certain level of code coverage, the vectors are designed to produce "typical" timing paths and worse case execution paths. This is currently only a research topic.

Another class of tool that is starting to emerge that will help with the upfront analysis is timing accurate simulators. There are some of these tools that exist, for example from WindRiver, however, they are not yet widely used, in part because the tools do not cover a broad spectrum of microprocessors.

One interesting scenario is to use a modeling tool with automatic code generation, collect execution times from a timing accurate simulator that is driven by automatically generated timing vectors, and then run this timing data through a schedulability analysis tool. This will allow the designer to know ahead of time that the design meets its allocated timing budget.

NETWORKED APPLICATIONS – As the systems become more complex, the automotive industry is moving towards a networked environment. This may also help in other areas such as reducing the total weight of the vehicle. This will present a new set of challenges for the automotive industry. Some of these challenges will include being able to simulate the network environment, and analyzing it. Another challenge is to be able to download the code to each of the network nodes at one time for a rapid prototyping type of application.

Some tools are becoming available in this area such as from Vector CANtech and TTTech.

CONFIGURATION MANAGEMENT – Configuration management is another item that has been around for a while and is necessary for helping with version control. This is a well-established practice with a number of tools. However, these tools are not yet well integrated with the newer modeling tools. Increased integration will be needed before the entire software development process can become a smooth process.

Some of the tools for this include: PVCS and Rational Clearcase.

CONCLUSION

There are a number of steps and tools in the modern software development process. Some of these tools and technologies are well established, such as Configuration Management and Rapid Prototyping. A number of the tools and technologies are receiving significant research attention and industry pull, in particular automatic code generation and unit test vector generation. Some of these, especially automatic code generation are getting close to being introduced into the process as mainstream tools.

One of the biggest outstanding issues is that many of the tools only help in a small part of the entire process. This is not a problem in itself; the problem lies in that seamless tool interaction is very limited at this time.

The automotive trend is towards the use of model-based tools with a high degree of automation. While not there yet, as the modeling experience increases and the tool vendors provide better solutions, modeling will become more mainstream and should significantly improve the software development process. [9]

REFERENCES

1. Toeppe, S., Ranville, S., Bostic, D., "Automating Software Specification, Design and Synthesis for Computer Aided Control System Design Tools", 2000, Proceedings of the 19th AIAA/IEEE/SAE Digital Avionics System Conf.
2. Toeppe, S., Ranville, S., Bostic, D., Wang, C., "Practical Validation of Model Based Code Generation for Automotive Applications", 1999, Proceedings of the 18th AIAA/IEEE/SAE Digital Avionics System Conf.
3. Toeppe, S., Ranville, S., Bostic, D., Rzeimen, K., "Automatic Code Generation Requirements For Production Automotive Powertrain Applications", 1999, IEEE International Symposium on Computer Aided Control System Design
4. Sims, S., Butts, K., Cleaveland, R., Ranville, S., "Automated Validation of Software Models", 2001, Automated Software Engineering Conference
5. Black, P., Ranville, S., "WINNOWING tests: GETTING QUALITY COVERAGE FROM A MODEL CHECKER WITHOUT QUANTITY", 2001, 20th AIAA/IEEE/SAE Digital Avionics System Conference
6. Ranville, S., Black, P., "Automated Testing Requirements – Automotive Perspective", 2001, The Second International Workshop on Automated Program Analysis, Testing and Verification
7. Toeppe, S., Ranville, S., "An Automated Inspection Tool For a Graphical Specification and Programming Language", 1999, QualityWeek Conference
8. Toeppe, S., Ranville, S., "Model Driven Automatic Unit Testing Technology : Tool Architecture Introduction and Overview" , 1999, Proceedings of the 18th AIAA/IEEE/SAE Digital Avionics System Conference
9. Patel, S., Smith, P., Sun, W., Ramanan, R., Donald, H., Toeppe, S., Ranville, S., Bostic, D., Butts, K., "CACSD in Production Development : An Engine Control Case Study", 2000, Global Powertrain Conference
10. Butts, K., Toeppe, S., Ranville, S., "Specification and Testing of Automotive Powertrain Control System Software using CACSD tools", 1998, Proceedings of the 17th AIAA/IEEE/SAE Digital Avionics System Conference
11. Ranville, S., Butts, K., "Single-Stack RTOS for Deeply Embedded Applications", TBD date, Embedded Systems Programming Magazine
12. Toeppe, S., Ranville, S., "RTOS Evaluation and Selection Criteria For Embedded Automotive Powertrain Applications", 1999, Embedded Systems Conference – Europe and Embedded Systems Programming Magazine, July 2000, p 108-123, "Commercial RTOSes for Automotive Applications"

The author, Scott Ranville, graduated from the University of Michigan with a Bachelors of Science of Engineering in Electrical Engineering in 1992, and a Masters of Science of Engineering with a major in Control Theory in 1993. After college, Scott started work at Ford in the Electrical Fuel and Handling Division developing in-vehicle battery charging algorithms. In 1995 Scott transferred to the Scientific Research Laboratory researching computer aided control system design tools and methodologies. In 2001 Scott became a consultant for New Eagle Software where he consults on model-based embedded software design tools and processes. Areas of specialty include discrete controller models, automatic code generation, model checking and automated generation of unit test vectors, and RTOSs.

sranville@neweagle.net, www.neweagle.net

2002-01-0875

Automotive Software Development: A Model Based Approach

Martin Rappl and Peter Braun
Munich University of Technology

Michael von der Beeck
BMW Group

Christian Schröder
Telelogic AB Germany

ABSTRACT

This article focuses on model based development of electronic control units (ECUs) in the automotive domain. The use of model-based approaches solves requirements for the fast-growing integration of formerly isolated logical functions in complex distributed networks of heavily interacting ECUs. One fundamental property of such an approach is the existence of an adequate modeling notation tailored to the specific needs of the application domain together with a precise definition of its syntax and its semantics. However, although these constituents are necessary, they are not sufficient for guaranteeing an efficient development process of ECU networks. In addition, methodical support which guides the application of the modeling notation must be an integral part of a model-based approach.

Therefore we aim at developing a so-called ‘system model’ which comprises all of these constituents: the modeling language AML its mapping to the Unified Modeling Language (UML) which represents the modeling language standard for object-oriented system development as well as a system of abstraction levels which will help the AML user to achieve a well-structured development process. Within this methodical framework we outline the use of the AML in this article by illustrating a case study which comprises parts of the body car electronics within a car. Used model concepts are discussed in detail by showing its correlation to the UML representation and its counterpart in the metamodel.

Long term goal of the project Automotive is to establish the AML as a de facto standard for the specification of embedded systems. The accompanying realisation of an integrated tool chain, comprising the tools Telelogic UML Suite /28/, ETAS ASCET-SD /27/ and Telelogic DOORS /28/ as well as the validation of the methodology by the different project partners facilitate this goal.

INTRODUCTION

Within the automotive industry model based specification techniques are becoming more and more popular allowing the complete, the consistent, and the unambiguous specification of software and hardware for car specific networks of control units. In this context model based approaches provide methodical support to manage the integration of logical functions as interactive compounds within distributed networks of electronic control units. In addition well founded models are the source for analysis, validation, and verification activities.

The basis for the design of a model based specification methodology is a precise knowledge of the architecture of the targeted system class. In our opinion a good modeling approach regards different kinds of information which are necessary to implement a domain specific system. In Automotive our notion of the system architecture is centered around different kinds of information classes and their relationship among each other. During modeling all this information is stored in an integrated and consistent system model. To cope with the complexity of this model a system of domain specific abstraction levels provides an appropriate structuring mechanism for the specification of systems on different technical levels. Within the system of abstraction levels, the specification of functions on a logical level is counted more and more among the core competences of car manufacturers.

Further a precise notion of a systems architecture and its model based representation is fundamental for the transition from textual requirements specifications to first models and on the refinement of these models to an implemented system. The underlying model theory has to provide different kinds of modeling concepts to regard the different kinds of information to be modeled and the model theory has to support refinement relationships between every kind of information. Beyond the notion of a version and the notion of a configuration has to be an integral part of the theory.

Further the model theory also forms the basis for the use of different kinds of notations. The presented work is related to the work the OMG /15/, the U2 Partner group /24/, and the pUML group /6/ are carrying out. In contrast to their approach we believe, that a more rigorous mathematical theory is necessary for a realistic model based development process. Nevertheless the representation of abstract model concepts is done by specifically adapted notations from the UML 1.3 /16/, the ASCET-SD modeling language /27/, and textual specification techniques which stem from the tool DOORS /28/.

STRUCTURE OF THE PAPER – The paper introduces central terms used in this article and in the context of model based systems development. Thereupon the concepts for a seamless and integrated development methodology with the focus on logical functions and on the functional network are illustrated.

- In the first section the principles of model based development are described. Therefore, central terms like *system model*, *Automotive Modeling Language (AML)*, *metamodel*, *semantics*, *abstraction levels*, *notation* as well as *mathematical foundation* are introduced.

- Following a system of abstraction levels is presented which provides a mean of structuring the system model as well as the development process.

- The subsequent section focusses on two of these abstraction levels to provide insights into the modeling theory. At first the functional level is described. On this level (complete) building blocks of the system under development are modeled. In the subsequent section, the network level is presented which first deals with the tailoring of functions to particular functional variants and second specifies the interaction and communication pattern among them. In both cases the usage of the UML notation artifacts is demonstrated by the application to a case study example from the automotive domain.

- In the final section we draw our conclusions and provide an outlook to future work.

THE PROJECT AUTOMOTIVE – The work presented in this paper represent results of the research project FORSOFT Automotive – Requirements Engineering for embedded systems /25/. The partners of this project are the Munich University of Technology, the tool providers Telelogic and ETAS, the car manufacturers BMW and Adam Opel as well as the suppliers Robert Bosch and ZF Friedrichshafen.

PRINCIPLES OF A MODEL BASED DEVELOPMENT

In contrast to conventional structured programming methods model based methods provide a comprehensive support for all kinds of issues imposed by modern system development processes. This support comprises activities ranging from the modeling task itself to requirements tracing as well as version, configuration, and change management. Furthermore the produced models constitute the basis for applying formal verfication and validation techniques.

But unlike the existence of the Backus Naur Form (BNF) used for the syntax definition of textual programming languages, there exists no commonly accepted standard for the conceptual design of model based development languages and methods. In Automotive we use an algebraic specification approach for the definition of the model based specification method. In Figure 1 all relevant concepts and their interrelationships are shown. These concepts are constituents for the definition of the automotive specific development process, which is the focus of our research. The highlighted concepts of Figure 1 are discussed in detail in the following sections of this article.

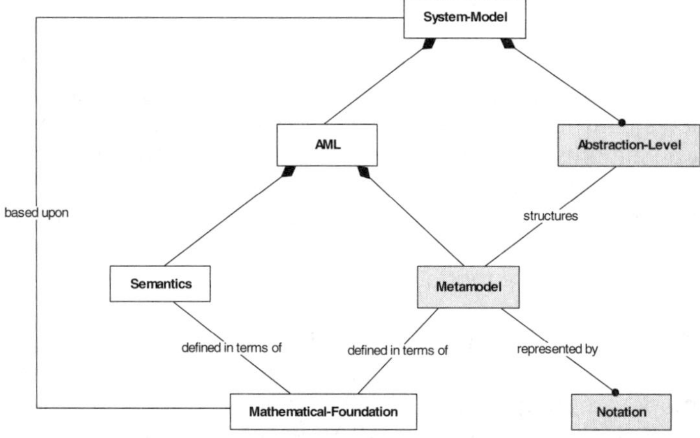

Figure 1: Basic Modeling Concepts

System Model – The system model contains all theoretical foundations necessary for the development of models within the specific domain of Automotive. The system model itself is based upon a mathematical foundation and consists of the Automotive Modelling Language (AML) and the Automotive specific system of abstraction levels. As this paper presents current work in progress, Figure 1 has to be completed by the specification of a corresponding development process. This affects future work of the project Automotive.

Automotive Modeling Language – The AML consists of a metamodel part and a semantic part. In the context of the project Automotive the terms *abstract syntax* and *metamodel* are used as synonyms. The AML defines a language which is specific for the development of embedded automotive systems. The AML itself contains the abstract modeling concepts used in this language as well as their meaning.

Metamodel – The definition of a clear and unambiguous metamodel of the AML constitutes a main purpose within the project and is primary addressed in this paper. The metamodel is defined in terms of a mathematical foundation and is structured by a system of Automotive specific abstraction levels. The metamodel represents abstract modeling concepts which are used to build an integrated model. A model contains all necessary information about the functional logic, the distributed network of electronic control units, the actors, the sensors, and the environment. The metamodel structures this information and describes the possible interrelationships. For representing the metamodel of the AML a restricted subset of UML class diagrams is used together with metamodel patterns as a rationale. Besides pure class diagram constraints are defined to ensure a basic consistency level.

Semantics – One big advantage of model based development methods shows up when one needs to handle complex system specifications and wants to reason about it. The semantic part describes the static and dynamic semantics of models. It is defined in terms of the mathematical foundation and by using the metamodel, at least theoretically. However, a complete and precise semantics defintion is not a main focus of the project Automotive. Only some fragments of this definition will be worked out within Automotive. Rather for the use of the AML the defined semantics and their mathematical foundation won't be visible.

Abstraction Levels – The information gathered during the development process is structured and stored using different levels of detail. The abstraction levels precisely define which sort of information is stored at which level. Beyond this the abstraction levels are used to structure the metamodel which in turn allows to specify dependencies among the information defined in an actual user model. The definition of appropriate abstraction levels and their usage is a core activity of the project Automotive (see next section).

Notation – Textual and graphical notation elements are used to model specific parts of a system. The concrete syntax of those notational elements has to conform to the metamodel. Within Automotive a restricted subset of the current UML notation standard is used to represent some parts of a model. The other parts are represented by a subset of notations offered by ASCET-SD, a tool for the design and prototyping of embedded systems. Also textual notations like structured (hyper-)text and tables are used especially in the earlier phases of the system development process.

The main reason for using UML within Automotive is the growing importance of this language as a modeling standard within the area of software engineering. We make use of UML model elements to represent parts of the concrete graphical syntax of the AML. To be aligned to the actual language standard we first define a UML profile. The resulting modeling concepts will be revised with respect to their applicability, efficiency, and expressiveness in the realm of automotive software development.

However, examining the expressiveness of the UML with respect to its application to the development of embedded systems one already realizes fundamental weaknesses which consequently have an impact on the expressiveness of the AML representation as a UML profile /9/. There are several approaches addressing that issue, e.g. the merge of UML and SDL 2000 /2/. These approaches are currently being elaborated and evaluated by the U2 partners group /24/ during the ongoing UML 2.0 standardization.

Mathematical Foundation – The mathematical foundation contains formal definitions of some terms which are used to describe metamodels. Furthermore definitions and operations are defined here to be used in the semantic part of the AML. With these definitions in mind also a formal definition of the abstraction levels could be given. The mathematical foundation contains work currently in progress and only some fragments of this foundation will be defined within the project Automotive.

ABSTRACTION LEVELS OF EMBEDDED SYSTEMS

To cope with the complexity of system models, abstraction levels are introduced. Abstraction levels have been successfully applied in the field of hardware design /13/ and in the field of protocol design (ISO/OSI reference model /23/) For the design of a systems engineering methodology abstraction levels can be utilized in several ways. First, abstraction levels act as means of structuring and integrating large information sets. Thereupon rests the construction of a seamless development processes. Second, abstraction levels structure the definition of activities within the development process and therefore they provide methodical advise. Third abstraction levels can be utilized to structure the model theory in an uniform manner. This facilitates the design of a model based specification methodology. In the next sections the role of abstraction levels is discussed from a mathematical, model oriented point of view as well as from a methodical, process oriented point of view. Subsequently the system of automotive relevant abstraction levels is sketched.

Abstraction levels define restrictive views upon the system model. A view within an abstraction level shows the system on a uniform technical level. For the development of networks of control units six different abstraction levels are defined /Figure 2/.

From a mathematical point of view a system model defines a collection of sets containing all necessary information to derive an implementation for control units. Each abstraction level provides a certain view as well as a certain accessibility on a subset of these information sets. The defined levels build upon themselves. Model information and logical dependencies defined in higher abstraction levels are accessible in the lower ones. The information is successively refined by adding more technical information of new modeling concepts within lower abstraction levels. Those modeling concepts introduce new information as well as relationships to existing information of higher abstraction levels. To assure consistency of the complete system model a set of consistency constraints is defined.

From an engineering point of view, the abstraction levels guide the analyst through the process of requirements elicitation and requirements structuring. They facilitate the process of writing down ideas and visions an engineer (or an other stakeholder) has in mind for the functioning of the system under development. The system of abstraction levels gives assistance for the structuring process of ideas. Rather it follows requirements engineering principles for a successive refinement of informations. Starting with abstract models which just provide a minimum set of technical details, at each abstraction level new, more technical oriented concepts are introduced which explicate the afore modeled information. The specification starts with the definition of signals and their ordering and ends with the specification of the central processing unit, the communication infrastructure, and the realtime operating system /Figure 2/.

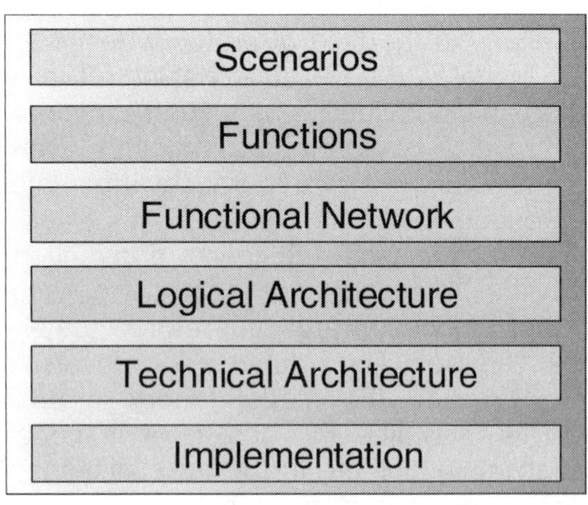

Figure 2: Automotive Relevant Abstraction Levels

The division of the system model with the help of abstraction levels determines different semantic properties which are characteristic for each level /Table 1/. These semantic properties depend on the used modeling concept and define the dynamic semantics of the used notation. So for example in higher abstraction levels, systems are event driven and triggered by a global system time frame. In lower, more technical oriented levels systems are clock triggered and data driven. The global time is split into a set of local times each related to a control unit. The same is true for the transition from asynchronous to synchronous communication principles.

	Execution	Communication	Time
Semantic Properties	clocked/ event driven	synchronous/ asynchronous	synchronous/ asynchronous
Scenarios	event	synchronous	synchronous
Functions	event	synchronous	synchronous
Functional Network	event	synchronous	synchronous
Logical Architecture	data	synchronous	asynchronous
Technical Architecture	data	asynchronous	asynchronous

Table 1: Semantic Properties of the System Model

In the following paragraphs each abstraction level is described separately to show its role in the development process. In the subsequent sections, the functional level and the functional network level are explained explicitly in terms of concepts, UML representation and the underlying metamodel.

Scenarios – The abstraction level scenarios contains model information about the system with the lowest amount of technical details. At this level there is a big universality in enriching the model with technically oriented information. The core modeling concept at this stage is the concept of a signal and operations on signals (actions). This concept provides in addition to an ordering mechanism enough modeling power to describe scenarios. Scenarios are ordered sequences of actions which are necessary to achieve a determined goal in a certain context. Scenarios describe exemplary use cases, 'not use cases' showing how a system must not be used, possible exceptions or test cases.

One intuitive way to interpret this model is to observe the occurences of actions. There is no mechanism to restrict the visibility of signals and there is no need for exchanging actions. These also holds for the time. Therefore both, the communication mechanism and the (global) time can be regarded as synchronous.

Functions - Functions define building blocks of the to be developed system. In contrast to scenarios functions describe complete sequences. The view upon the function at this high abstraction level is independent of later used implementation techniques or target languages. Particularly functions are considered which behave as abstractions of the later used control units, actors, sensors or the environment.

The set of functions is structured to allow easy navigation between the usually great number of different functions of a system. Therefore several different hierarchical structures have been defined to locate functions for a deeper understanding and easier modification. Each structure shows at least a clipping of the functions of the whole system. Different hierarchies of functions result from different levels of experience or different views upon a system by different developers.

As mentioned above each function divides the systems behavior into manageable pieces. For reuseability each function restricts the scope of signals and requires a mechanism for exchanging signals. By exchanging signals the overall systems behavior is achieved through interaction. A communication mechanism can be realized without great expense by a synchronous communication pattern between subfunctions. Due to the high abstraction level at this stage, a global time ensures the synchronous execution of the observed functions.

Functional network – The purpose of the functional abstraction level is to define generic and reusable building blocks so that they can easily be adapted to different system development contexts. The formed functions serve as a framework for the definition of functional variants. At the abstraction level of the functional network, the tailoring of functions to specific functional variants is considered. Therefore required functions are selected and variants are formed. This generally leads to an enlargement of the namespace. The different variants are connected to gain information about their signal dependencies. Mutual dependencies between different functions within these variants are displayed at this stage.

The introduced modeling concepts at this stage facilitate the use of functions in different contexts and do not add new technical information. The introduced modeling concepts do not influence the semantic properties inherited from the functional level.

Logical architecture – By developing the logical architecture the model is enlarged with information belonging to orthogonal modeling concepts. Concurrently gained information from the functional network is now refined. The new, orthogonal modeling concepts deal with the logical distribution (information about logical control units) and the information about actors and sensors of the environment. The different variants defined at the functional network level are instantiated and deployed on the different logical control units.

At this stage the system is treated to be clocked instead of being event driven. For the communication of architectural entities a signal exchange has to be assured at each clock. Furthermore each clock enables the system to perform operations on the state space. The actions of the higher abstraction levels can now be interpreted as an operation on the state space at each step under the premise of the occurrence of the action. It is important that time is split into a real time part (universal time) of the environment and into a system time part which has its own clock. The adjustment of those different times is crucial for proper operation of the system. The adjustment is not done continuously. Instead it takes place at certain peaks. The peaks depend on the tolerance which is valid in weak real-time systems. Hard real-time systems do not permit tolerances at all.

Due to the abstraction of technical informations at this level, the communication among different logical control units and the communication within function instances deployed on logical control units are regarded as synchronous. At a more technical level this perfect synchrononity has to resolved by an asynchronous communication model.

Technical architecture – The technical system architecture offers further modeling concepts describing concrete technical information. So the model is enriched with information about concrete bus-realisations and conrete control units. Further information describes control unit specifications and operating system descriptions. So it is possible to gain first performance estimates.

Comprehensive experience from the development of electronic control units reveals that a clear separation within a logical system architecture level and a technical system architecture level is very helpful when it comes to the partitioning of functions on electronic control units. On the logical architecture level only a subset of partitioning criteria is applied in order to achieve a clear view of the functional structure - without identifying the set of functions which constitutes an ECU. However, finally the complete set of partitioning criteria (e.g. also those which consider geometric requirements) has to be applied. This will be done on the technical architecture level and results in the identification of the set of electronic control units. To each of them a set of to be realized functions is assigned.

Since control units as well as a detailed technical model is regarded at this stage, the synchronous communication mechansim is replaced by a asynchronous one. This is done due to the fact of the model robustness. As each control unit can be replaced by a physical one, the failure of a control unit must be considered at this stage. With a synchronous communication model the overall system would be blocked or would malfunction.

Implementation – At the implementation level the realization of the model is done in hard- and software. This goes beyond the first prototypes which could be generated from the models gained above. For example often code has to be optimised for performance and size reasons. Beside this often adoptions to existing systems have to be made.

THE FUNCTIONAL LEVEL

CONCEPTS – The core modeling concept at this abstraction level is the concept of the function /Table 2/. A function provides an encapsulation of behavior at a logical level. Functions act as basic building blocks for further development activities such as tailoring of variants, instantiation, deployment and so on. Each function can be regarded as a single service which has to be fulfilled by the whole system. For structuring functions, uniform structuring rules are applied to ensure a uniform decomposition process. Therefore, modeling concepts like signal delegation resp. propagation and coordinator functions are introduced.

The role of these concepts is similar to the concepts of order, request and inquiry known from the CARTRONICS /10/ approach. A more general view is given regarding the concepts of the recursive control pattern /19/. This architectural pattern can be applied in the following context: a complex system shall be divided into subsystems containing a significant amount of control. The recursive control pattern provides the following solution: Control parts and functional parts are decoupled within each component. More concrete, within each hierarchically structured function *f* a coordinator function exists which gathers all signal flows

- outside *f* before each of them is delegated to one of the (other) subfunctions of *f*, or
- of the (other) subfunctions of *f* before they are propagated outside *f*.

The first case is called *delegation*, whereas the second case is called *propagation*. Both cases are subsumed under the term *vertical communication*.

In contrast to another well-known architectural pattern used in software-engineering technology (namely the subsystem controller pattern /20/) the recursive control pattern allows that two subfunctions of a hierarchically structured function can be directly connected by signal flows in order to achieve horizontal communication. However, we do not require the application of the recursive control pattern for each hierarchically structured function.

We now come to the concepts for structuring functions and displaying the mutual data dependencies between two of them. At this point we follow recent work on architectural languages which recommend the use of ports and connectors.

Abstraction Level: *Functions*	
Hierarchically structured functions	**Diagram Type:** *Class Diagram*
Modeling Concept	**UML Representation**
Functions	Classes
Hierarchical Structure	Decomposed Classes
Environment	Stereotyped classes
Inports	Interface classes resp. Lollipops
Outports	- no appropriate construct available -
Signal Dependency	Dependency arrow
Propagation	Dependency arrow between function and environment
Delegation	Dependency arrow between environment and function

Table 2: UML Representation of Functional Concepts

Functions – Functions are basic building blocks which structure the total amount of behavior into manageable pieces which are reusable. In UML functions are represented as classes. For clarity reasons classes are shown in a folded state. Hence this kind of class visualization hides information about attributes and methods.

Hierarchical Structure – Each defined function can be decomposed into a set of subfunctions. To each decomposed function a coordinator may be bound. A coordinator resolves functional dependencies between functions on the same hierarchical level. Furthermore the coordinator function has some responsibility for controlling the signal flow via vertical communication /Figure 3/. For representing the functions in UML we use hierarchically structured classes. For the representation, one clearly has to distinguish between an external view and an internal view. The external view shows a function from the outside. An internal view shows all included subfunctions and the decomposed function as a class with the stereotype <<environment>>. This enables one to represent all vertical communication relations in symmetry to the horizontal communication relations.

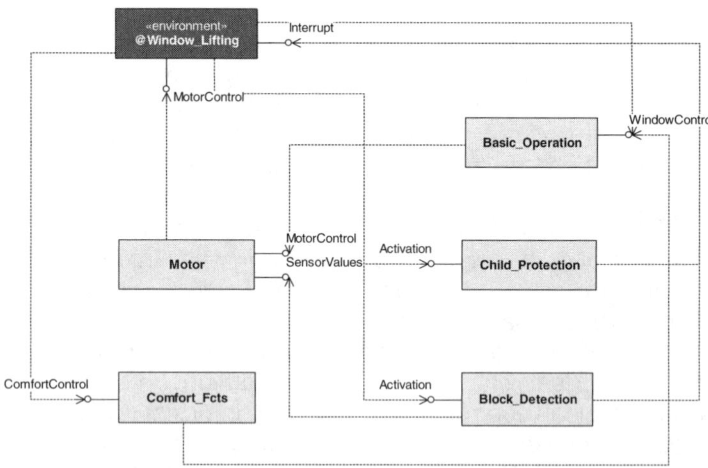

Figure 3: Hierarchically Structured Functions

Environment – In contrast to the listed concepts /Table 2/ the environment takes up an exceptional position. The environment represents the compliment of the function itself. That means it contains all specified functions except the function itself and all composd subfunctions. The environment is used for the definition of the vertical signal flow. It is represented in UML as a regular class. That ensures the binding of an interface class (lollipop). By that a perfect symmetry can be reached between the vertical and the horizontal signal flow. In the metamodel the environment does not have a counterpart. That's due to the fact, that all informations can be calculated from the external view. In the UML the environment is displayed as a class, attached with the <<environment>> stereotype. For qualification reasons the name is prefixed with an '@' character.

Inport – The communication between functions is handled via signal exchange. A set of signals is combined to a port. The set of specified and used ports can be classified into inports and outports. Inports aggregate signals that the function is offering to other functions to provide some services. Outports in contrast aggregate signals that the function is requiring from other functions for operation. The ports themselves are represented as lollipops which are attached to classes. In the UML the lollipop is a shorthand for an abstract class which contains interface information and is inherited to the class, where the interface is realized. In the automotive methodology the definition of the signals is done by interface classes /Figure 4/. This ensures a reuse of ports. Each attached interface class represents an instance of a port definition.

Outport – In the Automotive methodology outports are not stated explicitly. This limitation depends on the expressiveness of the current UML standard which is not offering an appropriate modeling construct. Of course we could use colored lollipops to distinguish between in- and outports, as some work suggests /17/, but in our opinion this leads to a lot of confusion by misinterpreting the meaning of familiar symbols. For a further discussion of an appropriate representation of outports please refer to the documentation of architecture description languages like UML/RT /19/ or AutoFocus /21/.

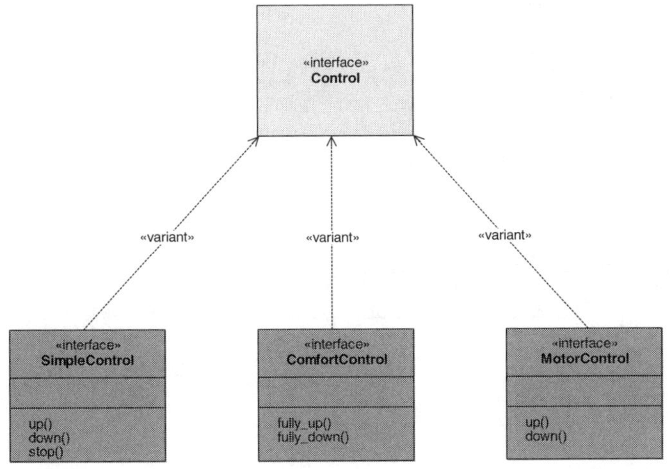

Figure 4: Exemplary Signal Definition

Signal Dependency – Within the modeling concepts of the AML a horizontal and a vertical signal flow are differentiated. The horizontal signal flow denotes the communication of functions within one functional level. The vertical signal flow denotes the communication between two levels of functions (as stated above). Due to the symmetry of modeling concepts and due to the introduction of an element depicting the environment, the horizontal and vertical flow of signals can be identically represented as UML dependency arrows.

Delegation/Propagation – Depending on the direction of the communication the vertical signal flow, the flow is distinguished between delegation and propagation, respectively. Delegation denotes the flow of signals from a function down to the composed subfunctions, whereas propagation denotes the opposite direction of the signal flow.

EXAMPLE – In Figure 3 a simplified model of the window lifting functionality is sketched. This function is part of the body car electronics within a car. It is modeled by the element *Window_Lifting* and is further decomposed into five subfunctions. The diagram shows an internal view of this function. An external view of the function *Window_Lifting* is included in Figure 6.

The class *@Window_Lifting* attached with the stereotype <<environment>> denotes the environment of the function *Window_Lifting*. The environment is composed of all specified functions except the function itself and its composed subfunctions. The role of the model element environment is to visualize the vertical signal flow between the environment and the function resp. subfunctions. So for example the interface *MotorControl* of *@Window_Lifting* shows the communication of the function *Window_Lifting* with some functions outside of *Window_Lifting*, by exchanging signals which are compatible with the interface specification of *MotorControl*. By using an explicit model element for the representation of the environment, a symmetric port concept can be realized within the AML.

The inports attached to the specified functions are defined explicitly by interface classes. Figure 4 shows the interface *Control*, which is called a signal in terms of the AML. The definition comprises a set of signals which can be exchanged. *Control* is the composition of the signals: *up*, *down*, *stop*, *fully_up* and *fully_down*. Note that those signals are not shown explicitly in the picture. Figure 4 shows some variants of *Control*, which use subsets of these signals. So for example the signal *MotorControl* includes the signals *up* and *down*. The definition of those signals and their corresponding variants is used for a complete specification of functions. *Basic_Operation* /Figure 3/ uses the interface *MotorControl* of the *Motor* by sending signals to it.

METAMODEL – As stated above the metamodel provides abstract modeling concepts of the AML. Again the system of abstraction levels is used at the meta level as a structuring mechanism. Figure 5 shows the static part of the metamodel at the functional level. For the representation of the metamodel a restricted subset of the UML class diagram notation is used. For the description of the metamodel used keywords are written in *italic* to ease reading and navigation.

To provide a more fine granular and uniform structuring mechanism, metamodel patterns are used for the definition of modeling concepts on every abstraction level. The metamodel of the AML is defined by the help of three different patterns. A very simple pattern is the hierarchy pattern. The hierarchy pattern is used for the definition of arbitrary hierarchical structures. In Figure 5 this pattern is applied for the definition of the metamodel element *Function*. The other two patterns are called variant pattern and instance pattern. Their application is shown at the network level.

The introduction of hierarchical structures, variants and instances as modeling concepts implies a general mechanism of how to proceed with any hierarchical structures. The process itself starts with the definition of hierarchical structures, continues with the tailoring of variants, and ends with the instantiaton of variants. The instances serve as an input for the lower abstraction levels. At the functional level /Figure 5/ *InstantiableSignals* are taken as an input of the higher abstraction level scenarios. *InstantiableSignals* denotes the set of signals which have passed the variant formation and instanciation process. Within the AML this mechanism is applied at several abstraction levels. Its application to the functional structure is explained in the network level section in more detail.

For a better understanding we have chosen different colors to distinguish between model elements, variants and instances. Classes which define model elements on the modeling level are shown in yellow[1]. Classes which define variants on the modeling level are shown in red[2]. Classes which define instances on the model level are shown in cyan[3].

The modeling concept of the function is represented by the class *Function* including the attribute *Name*. A *Function* composes an abitrary number of *Subfunctions*. In Figure 3 the function *Window_Lifting* represents an instance of a function. This function is hierarchically structured and can be decomposed into five subfunctions. The modeling concept of the function is represented as a class in UML. The class name shows the name of the function.

Corresponding to UML classes, AML functions have local attributes. In terms of the AML, these attributes are called *Variables* /Figure 5/. A *Variable* is a specialization of an *InstantiableSignal* and therefore inherits its name and type. The metamodel element *InstantiableSignal* is defined in the upper metamodel part belonging to the abstraction level scenarios. The related diagram is not outlined in this paper. *InstantiableSignal* is used to represent a constant, a UML class-attribute, a UML class-method, or a UML interface class. The AML concept of a signal facilitates to model even more complex structures which go far beyond the simple definition of attributes and methods. But note, in UML these structures can not be specified adequately. Next to the definition part of signals, the metamodel of the upper section also provides concepts for tailoring signals to variants whereas another part deals with the formation of instances. At the functional level only the set of *InstantiableSignals* are taken as an input, which are instances of signals.

While taking a look at the functions shown in Figure 3 we can see the explicit specification of their interfaces. In

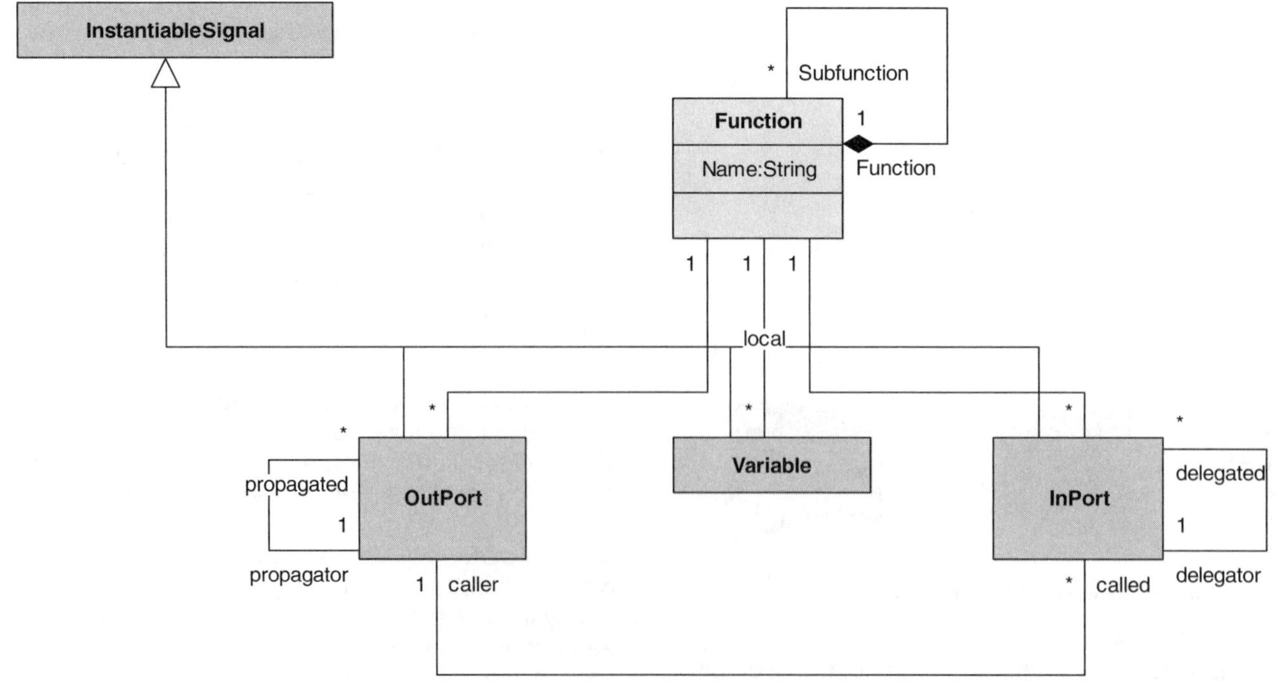

Figure 5: Metamodel for Abstraction Level Functions

UML-class diagrams the port concept is represented by interface classes (lollipops) to show at least an unidirectional interface specification which is provided by each function. So for example the function *Motor* provides *MotorControl* and *SensorValues* as *InPorts*. An *InPort* is an *InstantiableSignal*. In Figure 4 the definition of *MotorControl* is derived from the more complex *Control* signal by the formation of a variant. In the model /Figure 3/ *MotorControl* already acts as an instance. This facilitates the direct use of *MotorControl* on the functional level. The process of building variants and instances can be shortened in order to restrict the namespace and of course to keep the diagrams lean.

In the metamodel the call relation as well as the delegation and the propagation of signals are modeled by one-to-many associations. For representing mutual functional dependencies on the same hierarchical level, dependency arrows are used to model call relations between the function and ports. For example the *MotorControl* interface is called by the *BasicOperation*. As described above delegation and propagation are call relations between functions at different hierarchical levels. For representation dependency arrows are taken as well. For example the *WindowControl* signal of *Window_Lifting* is delegated to *Basic_Operation*.

THE NETWORK LEVEL

CONCEPTS – The set of defined functions is building up a framework for further development activities. Within this framework, the elaborated functions are basic building blocks which can be put together in various combinations. Due to the plurality of similar control activities within a car, a great number of variants exists for each single function. These are made up of various combinations of their subfunctions. When defining variants, new signal dependencies arise /Table 3/. These signal dependencies emerge from the specified variants and are not contained in the model of the previous abstraction level. After tailoring functions to functional variants we can construct their instances. These instances can be deployed on logical control units at lower abstraction levels.

Abstraction Level: *Functional-Network*	
Definition of functional variants	**Diagram Type:** *Class Diagram*
Modeling Concept	**UML Representation**
Functions	Classes
Variants	Classes
Tailoring	Functional Structure (see Table 2)
Inports	Interface classes resp. Lollipops
Outports	- no appropriate construct available -
Signal Dependency	Dependency arrow

Table 3: UML Representation of Functional Network Concepts

Variants – Using variants of general functions allows to specialize common functional behavior according to the particular subsystem needs /Figure 6/. From a methodological point of view the relation between functions and variants allows to manage complexity by abstracting specialized behavior to general needed mechanisms. In contrast to the concept of inheritance in object orientation building variants just means to select subfunctions from the (sub-) function pool of a general function (see metamodel). A Variant has a name and consists of a list of Variant Interfaces (similar to Function Interfaces).

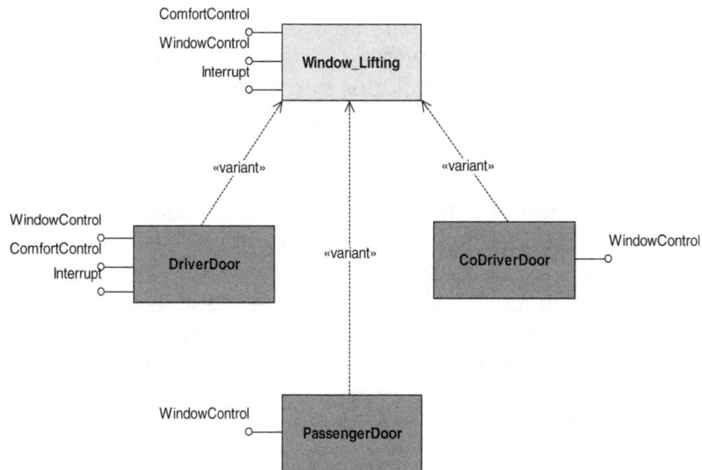

Figure 6: Definition of Functional Variants

Tailoring – The process of tailoring functions to variants takes place within two steps. In step 1 the set of variants associated with a function is stated explicitly. In step 2 subfunctions and subvariants are selected for each specific variant. Variants are displayed in UML as arbitrary folded classes marked in red color. These variants are bound to the derived function by a dependency arrow attached with a <<variant>> stereotype. For the specification of the selected subfunctions and the selected subvariants the same modeling concepts are used as they are used for the specification of subfunctions at the functional level. Therefore all specified concepts such as inports, signal dependencies (horizontal + vertical communication) are used at this stage as well.

Inports – Analog to the representation of functions, inports are attached to variants. Here again interface classes are used. The collection of inports attached to variant primarily depend on the selected subfunctions resp. subvariants. As variants select a subset of functions of the original functional decomposition, the collection of inports attached to a variant is a subset of the original inport collection as well. In Figure 6 three variants with differing interface specification are stated.

Signal Dependency – At the functional network level new signal dependencies arise between different variants. These signal dependencies are displayed in the same way as on the functional level by using dependency arrows. The associated diagram is called functional network in terms of the AML.

EXAMPLE – As described above tailoring of functions to variants is one essential step. Figure 6 shows the definition part of three variants of the function *Window_Lifting*. Each of the defined variants selects a certain subset of subfunctions. The diagram also shows the interface provided by a variant. The set of offered ports of each variant is a subset of the ports attached to the corresponding function. The same is true for the subfunctions of *Window_Lifting*. For example the *DriverDoor* doesn't include the *Child_Protection*. The explicit declaration of subfunctions of a variant looks similar to the diagram shown in Figure 3.

On the network level inter-functional dependencies between the defined variants will be described. Figure 7 shows an example where the dependencies between the variants of Window_Lifting are described. In this example the DriverDoor has some advanced functionality for the remote operation of other windows. The meaning of the dependency arrows is exactly the same as it is at the functional level.

METAMODEL – Figure 8 shows the modeling concepts for the network level. This part of the metamodel deals with the definition of variants and instances of functions. As stated above we use patterns to build up the AML metamodel. At the functional network level we make use of the variant and the instance pattern. We instanciate them to provide modeling concepts for the formation of variants and for the definition of instances. The particular combination of elements, variants, and instances is not only used at this stage it is also used in other parts of the metamodel, e.g. within the definition of signals or in more technical oriented levels.

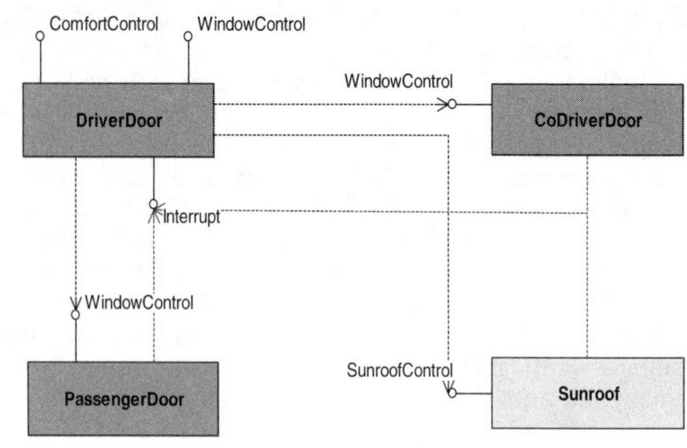

Figure 7: Signal Dependencies Between Variants

For the definition of functional variants the set of functions which stems from the functional level is taken as an input. In the instance of the variant pattern each *Function* can be tailored by many *FunctionVariants*. For example the function Window_Lifting is tailored by the functions *DriverDoor*, *CoDriverDoor* and *PassengerDoor* /Figure 6/. *FunctionVariants* may not exist without the *Function* they are tailored from. Each *FunctionVariant* selects functionality provided by its corresponding *Function*. For example the *DriverDoor* selects all subfunctions of *Window_Lifting* except *Child_Protection*,

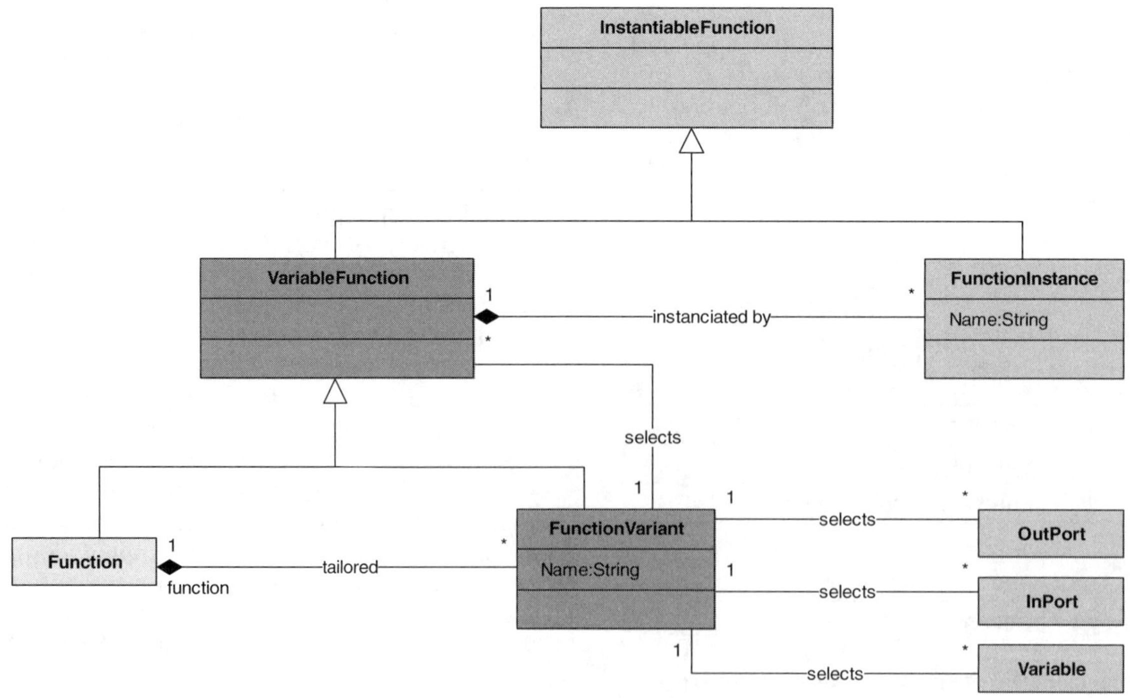

Figure 8: Metamodel for Abstraction Level Functional Network

as the *DriverDoor* provides no such functionality. This select relation is only valid for direct subfunctions of the tailored *Function*. *FunctionVariants* can be defined hierarchically that means a *FunctionVariant* can contain further variants of functions. On the other hand *Functions* may be used within the definition of variants at the same time. This is a necessary ‘shortcut’ to describe the situation that every function may be used as a variant itself holding all of its subfunctions. To avoid a blow-up of the namespace we make use of the superclass *VariableFunction*. In this context a function may play the role of a variant. Besides the selection of functions, also the *OutPorts*, *InPorts*, and *Variables* of the tailored *Function* have to be selected. So for example the PassengerDoor only provides the interface *WindowControl* of all possible interfaces of *Window_Lifting* /Figure 6/.

The last pattern used for the construction of the metamodel /Figure 8/ is the instantiation pattern. Every *VariableFunction* can be instantiated in an arbitrary number. Taking *VariableFunction* as an input for the instanciation pattern, variants as well as functions can be instantiated. Here again a ‘shortcut’ is introduced to ease the specification. *InstantiableFunction* is the superclass of *VariableFunction* and *FunctionInstance*. So *Function* and *FunctionVariants* act as *FunctionInstances*. Again no auxiliary name has to be introduced for the instantiation of a variant resp. function.

CONCLUSION

Motivated by the aim to meet the challenges of developing complex networks of heavily interacting electronic control units (ECUs), we have presented a system model comprising all necessary constituents for a model-based software development in the automotive domain. Three essential ingredients of this system model have been presented in this article:

- A system of abstraction levels to structure the metamodel as well as the user model and
- the meta model resp. abstract syntax of the AML (Automotive Modeling Language) as well as
- the representation of the AML by means of the UML aligned to the current UML standard.

Whereas the AML establishes the basis for an adequate modeling of software in the automotive domain - especially for ECU networks – the system of abstraction levels additionally provides means for structuring the development process according to different domain-specific categories. Our application of these concepts to a common realistic example, a window lifting control system, reveals the benefits of applying our approach.

Future work will cover the following two directions:

- First of all, we plan to complete the automotive specific system model: On the one hand this comprises the formal and complete definition of up to now informally and insufficient described parts. For example consistency dependencies between two adjacent abstraction levels have to be defined in an unambiguous way. On the other hand the concrete development process has to be defined based on the system of abstraction levels by providing rules and heuristics, how to use these levels.
- Second, the tool supported transformation from non-executable models to executable, target-dependent code will be explored in order to achieve the long-term objective of a seamless, complete software development process for automotive applications.

ACKNOWLEDGMENTS

We thank Jianjun Deng for carefully reading draft versions of this paper. We are much obliged to our colleages of the project Automotive for many fruitful discussions and we thank Manfred Broy for directing this research. This work has partially been funded by the Bayerische Forschungsstiftung (BayFor) within the Forschungsverbund für Software Engineering II (FORSOFT II).

REFERENCES

1. Jesper Andersson: Die UML echtzeitfähig machen mit der formalen Sprache SDL, OBJEKTspektrum 3, 1999.
2. Morgan Björkander: Graphical Programming Using UML and SDL, IEEE Computer, Vol. 24, 2001.
3. Peter Braun and Martin Rappl: Model based Systems Engineering - A Unified Approach using UML, Systems Engineering - A Key to Competitive Advantage for All Industries Proceedings of the 2nd European Systems Engineering Conference (EuSEC 2000), Herbert Utz Verlag GmbH, München, 2000.
4. Peter Braun, Martin Rappl and Jörg Schäuffele: Softwareentwicklungen für Steuergerätenetzwerke – Eine Methodik für die frühe Phase, VDI-Berichte, Nr. 1547, S. 265 ff., 2000.
5. Michael von der Beeck, Peter Braun, Martin Rappl and Christian Schröder: Modellbasierte Softwareentwicklung für automobilspezifische Steuergerätenetzwerke, VDI-Berichte, Nr. 1646, S. 293 ff., 2001.
6. Brodsky, Clark, Cook, Evans and Kent: Feasability Study in Rearchitecting the UML as a Family of Languages Using a Precise OO Meta-Modeling Approach, The pUML Group, 2000.
7. A.-P. Bröhl and W. Dröschel: Das V-Modell – Der Standard für die Softwareentwicklung mit Praxisleitfaden, R. Oldenburg Verlag München Wien 1993

8. Manfred Broy ++: The Design of distributed Systems, An introduction to FOCUS – Revised Version, Technical Report, TUM-I9202, Technische Universität München, 1993.
9. Manfred Broy, Michael von der Beeck, Peter Braun and Martin Rappl: A fundamental critique of the UML for the specification of embedded systems.
10. Pio Torre Flores ++: Integration of a Structuring Concept for Vehicle Control Systems into the Software Development Process using UML Modeling Methods, SAE Technical Paper Series 2001-01-0066, Detroit, 2001.
11. Maximilian Fuchs and Dieter Nazareth: Ein BMW-Experiment zur Verbesserung des Steuergeräte Entwurfprozesses mit ASCET-SD, In Proceedings Industrielle Software Produktion,13/14 November 1997, Messe Stuttgart International, Stuttgart,1997.
12. Bernd Gebhard and Martin Rappl: Requirements Management for Automotive Systems Development, SAE Technical Paper Series 2000-01-0716, Detroit, 2000.
13. C. Hansen, O. Bringmann and W. Rosenstiel: A VHDL Component Model for Mixed Abstraction Level Simulation and Behavioral Synthesis, Proceedings of Forum on Design Languages (FDL'99), Lyon, Frankreich, September 1999.
14. Derek Hatley and Imtiaz Pirbhai: Strategies for real time system specification, Dorset House Publishers, New York, 1988.
15. Object Management Group: OMG Unified Modeling Language Specification (draft), Version 1.3 alpha R5, March 1999.
16. OMG: XML Metadata Interchange (XMI), Proposal to the OMG OA&DTF RFP 3: Stream-based Model Interchange Format (SMIF), OMG Dokument, Oct 20th, 1998.
17. Bernhard Rumpe and Andy Schürr: UML + ROOM as a Standard ADL?, Engineering of Complex Computer Systems, ICECCS'99 Proceedings, IEEE Computer Society, 2000.
18. Christian Schröder and Ulf Pansa: UML@Automotive - Ein durchgängiges und adaptives Vorgehensmodell für den Software-entwicklungsprozess in der Automobilindustrie, Praxis Profiline, IN-CAR COMPUTING, 1. Auflage 2000, Vogel Verlag, ISBN 3-8259-1909-9, 2000.
19. Bran Selic, Garth Gullekson and Paul T. Ward: Real-Time Object Oriented Modeling, John Wiley, 1994.
20. Desmond F. D'Souza and Alan C. Wills: Objects, Components and Frameworks with UML – the CATALYSIS approach, Addison-Wesley, 1998.
21. Oscar Slotosch ++: Tool supported Specification and Simulation of Distributed Systems, Proceedings International Symposium on Software Engineering for Parallel and Distributed Systems, pp. 155-164, IEEE Computer Society, Los Alamitos, California, 1998.
22. Richard Stevens ++: systems engineering – coping with complexity, Prentice Hall Europe, Hertfordshire, 1998.
23. Andrew S. Tanenbaum: Computer-Netzwerke, Wolfram's Verlag, 2. Auflage, 1992.
24. U2 Partner Group (http://www.u2-partners.org): Unified Modeling Language 2.0 Proposal, Initial Submission to OMG RFP ad/00-92-02, 2001.

URLS

25. Homepage Automotive (FORSOFT): http://www.forsoft.de/automotive/
26. Homepage BMW AG: http://www.bmw.de/
27. Homepage ETAS GmbH: http://www.etas.de/
28. Homepage Telelogic AB: http://www.telelogic.de/

CONTACT

The authors' addresses:

Dipl. Inf. Dr. Michael von der Beeck
BMW Group – Function Development Process
Knorrstr. 147
D-80788 Munich
michael.beeck@bmw.de

Dipl. Inf. Peter Braun
Munich University of Technology
Department of Computer Science
Chair of Software und Systems Engineering
Arcisstr. 21
D-80333 Munich
braunpe@in.tum.de

Dipl. Inf. Martin Rappl
Munich University of Technology
Department of Computer Science
Chair of Software und Systems Engineering
Arcisstr. 21
D-80333 Munich
rappl@in.tum.de

Dipl. Phys. Dr. Christian Schröder
Telelogic AB - Germany
Gadderbaumerstr. 19
D-33602 Bielefeld
christian.schroeder@telelogic.de

KEYWORDS

Abstraction Level, Automotive, Electronic Control Unit (ECU), Metamodel, Requirements Engineering, Systems Engineering, System Model, Unified Modeling Language (UML)

2002-01-0872

The Embedded Cake: A Layers Model of Embedded Systems

Larry Leveille, Patricia M. Gary and James Brown
Pacific Information Design, Inc.

ABSTRACT

Embedded systems cover a wide variety of devices and applications. Seemingly, each embedded system is different from other embedded systems. After all, the system controlling a microwave oven has virtually nothing in common with the system in a calculator, an airplane flight controller, or a car's engine controller.

However, is there a way to look at embedded systems from a generic viewpoint? Put another way, are there parts of all embedded systems that are common whatever the purpose or function of the individual devices? What exactly do the microwave oven controller and a vehicle's engine controller have in common?

The design of a "layers-type" model representing embedded systems development arose from asking just such questions. Starting with the background of the OSI Network Model, where all functions of network communications fit within one of seven layers, we began to ask if a similar structure could serve to describe embedded systems.

INTRODUCTION

WHY A MODEL?

The question of whether a layers model of embedded systems could be constructed leads to the question of "Why do it?" What would the value of such a model be to the engineers involved in the design and production of embedded systems?

In answering this question, we were led to several issues that arise when discussing embedded systems. One of these issues is the requirement for 'domain experience' in the project's engineers. Domain experience refers to a background in the real-world specialty the system is addressing. For example, for a microwave oven, we like the engineers to already understand the microwave oven, how it works, what its quirks are, and so on. The same is true of any specialty involving embedded systems, such as factory machine controls, vehicle engine controllers, or a cellular telephone.

It is a nearly universal assumption that the people who work on embedded systems must have a background in the particular device being created. The engineers are hired in part because they may have such expertise. Conversely, it is seen as difficult to use engineers on an embedded system project who do not have direct domain experience.

Suppose we can answer the questions "What parts of the embedded system are specific to my project?" and "What parts are similar between projects?" Like any engineering project, there are portions of embedded system projects that are specific and some that are general. It is the aim of the model to separate these portions in a logical manner.

A second issue is the relationship of the model to the development process of an embedded system. Are there tasks or sets of tasks in the development of embedded systems that are common to all embedded system projects?

Finally, when we construct the layers model of an embedded system, what are the inputs and outputs that are required and produced by the model's layers? What will be needed within each layer; what will result from each layer? What components will have to be revisited repeatedly throughout the project's development cycle and how will knowing this enable the participants to better manage the development process?

Basic Model

Figure 1 shows the Embedded System Model. The model is comprised of seven layers and describes both the physical system and the development process by which it is built. The paragraphs below give brief descriptions of each layer. In the following sections, we discuss each layer in detail.

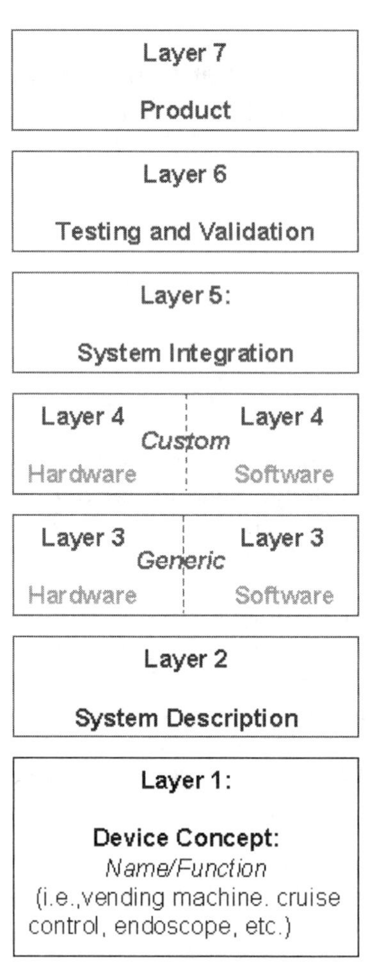

Figure 1. Embedded system model.

Layer 1

Layer 1 is called the Device Concept. In this layer, the embedded system is conceived in real-world terms. The questions *"What is the name of the device?"* and "*What is the device's function?"* are answered at this layer.

Layer 2

Layer 2 enters the engineering disciplines. It is called the System Description. In this layer, the real-world concerns of the Device Concept layer are converted into engineering language. It reflects and builds on the preceding layer's activities.

Layer 3

Layer 3, the Generic Hardware / Software layer, reflects the general hardware and software concerns of the system. The Generic layer addresses the non-specific parts of the system, detailing such things as the processor and the programming language.

Layer 4

In Layer 4, Custom Hardware / Software, the hardware and software issues specific to the device are addressed. Here we are concerned with things directly affected by the device itself.

Layer 5

The next layer, layer 5, is System Integration. Here, the hardware and software are combined to produce the embedded system.

Layer 6

This is the final "engineering process." In layer 6, Testing and Validation, the system is shown to perform the specified function(s) correctly.

Layer 7

And finally, in layer 7, Product, the system is placed in use. "In use" may mean production of large quantities for sale, or the installation of a single device to perform its designed function.

Detailed Discussion of Each Layer

The following sections describe in detail each layer in the model. The items used in each layer (Inputs) are discussed and the Outputs of each layer are described.

Layer 1 – Device Concept

The Device Concept Layer (see Figure 2) is where the idea for the embedded system begins. At this point, the system is only a developing concept. The source of the idea may be engineering, marketing, management, or customers. Once the idea is roughly in place, several decisions must be made at this layer.

Layer 1:

Device Concept:
Name/Function
(i.e.,vending machine. cruise control, endoscope, etc.)

Figure 2. Layer 1: Device concept.

Inputs

The Device Concept layer receives as much external input as any of the layers. It is here that strong 'domain experience' is usually required, either in the engineering staff, or in the people responsible for specifying the device. At this layer, the embedded device is envisioned, named and planned.

The primary input to this layer is the decision to develop the system. The decision implies several other inputs to the layer as well. An analysis of the advisability of buying rather than making the system is generally performed, helping in the decision to develop the system.

Further, the resources available for the project should be identified at this layer. An analysis of the feasibility of the system is next on the list. The system is something that should be made, not bought, but does the organization have the resources to pull it off? Feasibility issues to address are cost, technology available, schedules (both desired and achievable) talent and skills available for the project, and finally, preliminary identification of the resources needed. Outside inputs to the model provide all the data necessary for the feasibility study.

Outputs

From the Device Concept layer, a number of outputs are generated that are used at higher layers of the model:

- Function
- Name
- High-level functional requirements

First, the device is assigned a function. (Strictly speaking, this is a part of the original concept definition.) At this point, a name for the device is usually coined. In addition to name and function, the high-level functional requirements are established.

High-level functional requirements, in the *ideal* form, provide a detailed description, in real-world terms, of how the device will work. For example, suppose that the decision has been made to develop a vending machine using embedded software to control it. The functional requirements for the vending machine would specify the following basic information: how many slots; the type of product to be vended; hot / cold / room temperature, etc. Other questions to address for the vending machine might include its capability to make change, network capability / Internet access, and the user interface.

At this time we also make a preliminary determination of the number of systems to be built. The projected volume will help us make system decisions later. For example, a piece of specialized test equipment, where only a few units will be built will have economic constraints that do not apply to a system such as a vehicle engine controller, where the volume is in the hundreds of thousands.

As one example, the incremental cost of additional memory is insignificant in the test equipment, while it is a significant ongoing cost in the engine controller. The amount of memory has a bearing on the programming language selected, the software design methodology, and other decisions relating to the availability of memory resources.

Layer 2 – System Description

The system description layer (see Figure 3) enters the engineering realm of the project. In this layer the decisions all revolve around the system as a whole. The 'real-world' description that exists from the Device Concept layer must be transformed into an engineering quality description that becomes the basis for the design and implementation of both the software and hardware.

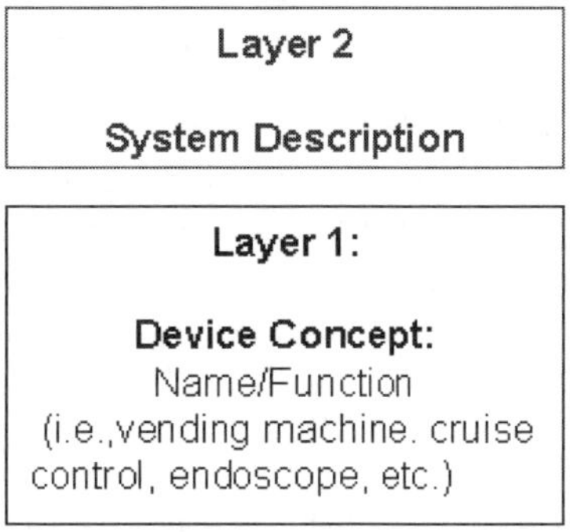

Figure 3. Layer 2: System description.

While the domain expertise is critical at the Device Concept layer, at the System Description layer it is not as important. The high-level functional requirements generated in the Device Concept layer are used in this layer to produce system requirements. The transformation of the high-level functional requirements to engineering system requirements can be more of an engineering exercise, with input from domain expertise.

Inputs

The main input to this layer is the set of high-level functional requirements from the Device Concept layer. Other inputs are the basis for the decisions that are made here. For example, what are the organization's policies on how the project is conducted? What are the standards, if any, that must be followed? What development resources are available for the project? The answers to these and other questions provide the basis for generating the layer's outputs.

Outputs

From the System Description layer, we will generate a set of system requirements. These requirements are the basis for the software and hardware requirements in later layers.

The user interface for the system is constructed or documented at this layer. The definition may take the form of a prototype, a specification, or some other form. The model does not prescribe any particular methodology, so the interface definition may use whatever form is suitable to the project.

A further result of this layer is the ROM (Rough Order of Magnitude) cost estimate. The estimate includes an estimate of development cost, establishment of a budget, schedules, and planning of development resources.

Finally, this layer produces the project management regime, procedures, standards, and practices. Procedures are defined to cover, in the software portion of the project, Requirements Management, Configuration Management, Software Quality Assurance, Coding and Documentation Standards. Note again that the model prescribes no particular processes to be used, but does recognize that these procedures are necessary. Indeed, they are present on any project, but may be only informal practices rather than formal procedures. Likewise, for the hardware, formal or informal procedures cover such things as logic type, hardware design aids, design practices, and standards to be followed, and so on.

For the documentation, this layer should produce a definition of the documentation package for the project. Specifications to be written are listed, user manuals (if any) defined, and the design documentation to be produced is defined for both the hardware and software. One possible concern regarding the documentation is the need for specific documentation procedures by regulatory oversight. The documentation plan should address any specific requirements arising from regulatory issues.

Layer 3 – Generic Hardware and Software

In the Generic Layer (see Figure 4), we continue the process of engineering the system. In addition, a variety of issues are settled in this layer regarding both hardware and software. At this layer, however, the decisions are 'generic', in that they must be made for any embedded system, regardless of the device envisioned.

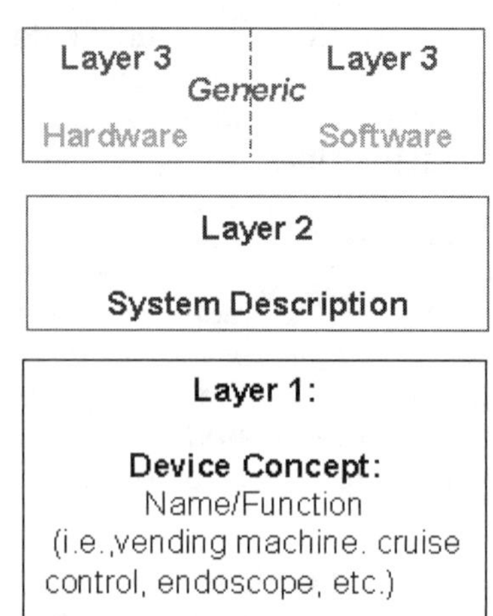

Figure 4. Layer 3: Generic hardware/software.

Domain expertise is not as important at this layer. Little that is decided at the Generic layer is directly related to the specific system under consideration.

Inputs

Again, the primary input to the Generic layer is the output of the previous layer. The System Requirements produced earlier fill that role in this layer.

Other inputs are the information about the decisions to be made. For example, one generic decision for the hardware side is the selection of the processor to use. To make this choice, we must have the information that tells us the power of the processor, its possible configurations, and so on. On the software side, the programming language to be used must be chosen. The background information that we use to help us make these decisions is the input to this layer.

Outputs

From the Generic layer come many decisions or choices about the system. Until now, we have dealt only with the complete system. In this layer, we are separating the system into its hardware and software components, and making initial choices about both.

The development tools to be used on the project for both hardware and software are chosen in the Generic layer.

On the hardware side, the hardware to be used is chosen. One of the more critical items chosen is the processor. Related decisions are the speed of the processor, and whether a RISC or CISC processor is selected. (Processor choice has implications for the software decisions, as well.) Other hardware items to address are what communications (Serial (RS-232, RS-422), Ethernet, CAN, etc.) are necessary.

We investigate the possible availability of COTS (Commercial Off-The-Shelf) components for the hardware design. For example, if a certain type of communications is required, is there a commercially available product that can be used in the project hardware to provide the communications function? Ideally, we could purchase a commercially available board for communications and use it in our system, rather than having to design the function from scratch for our system.

Finally, for the hardware, the input and output necessary to the system is defined. Will discrete I/O be sufficient, or are analog inputs necessary? If they are, what accuracy is needed? What I/O besides discrete and analog is required?

For the software side of things, the processor choice leads to some more decisions. What operating system will be used – an off-the-shelf Real-Time Operating System (RTOS), a custom operating system, or some other alternative? What languages are available for the processor and what development tools can be supported?

An important subject for the software is the establishment of real-time requirements. What are the performance requirements for the software in the areas of interrupt latency, input/output update frequencies, priority of functions, and so on?

The decisions regarding hardware and software are intimately related in several cases. At this layer, we are still dealing with engineering the *system*, and part of the process is our increasing understanding of the relationships between the parts of the system.

Layer 4 – Custom Hardware and Software

Engineering specific to the particular project is performed at the Custom Layer (see Figure 5). The Custom layer comprises the application of the decisions made in the Generic layer to the specific system information developed in the System Description layer.

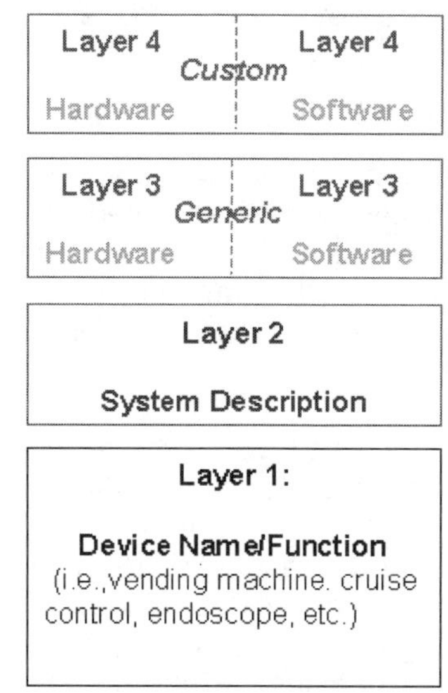

Figure 5. Layer 4: Custom hardware/software.

The System Requirements resulting from the System Description layer are analyzed, and used to create two more sets of requirements: the hardware requirements and the software requirements. From those requirements, the hardware and software designs are developed and other decisions are made relating to the hardware and software designs. Finally, the hardware and software designs are implemented at this layer.

Domain expertise is useful in this layer during the implementation phase, although not strictly necessary. The quality of the system requirements generated in the System Description layer affects how much domain expertise is necessary. The goal of the system requirements from the System Description layer should be to contain as much of the domain expertise in the requirements as possible, thus reducing the need for domain expertise in the Custom layer. If the system requirements are not complete and fully detailed, it will be necessary for more domain expertise to be available in the Custom layer.

Inputs

The System Requirements from the System Description layer are analyzed, as mentioned above. This analysis provides us with two results: a set of hardware requirements and a corresponding set of software requirements. These two sets of requirements are then used to develop the hardware and software designs for the device.

Remaining inputs at this layer are the hardware and software design techniques available through the engineering staff. Regulatory information, if any, about the particular system provides further input.

As part of the Custom layer, test plans for both the hardware and software are developed in this layer.

Outputs

From this layer, we produce the hardware and software requirements for the system, which are used as further input to create the hardware and software designs for the system. These designs then are implemented to produce the initial hardware and software for the new system.

Another item developed in this layer is the test strategy for unit test. How can the hardware and software engineers show that their designs have been implemented according to the respective requirements? Test software (separate from the operational software) may be developed to assist the system and hardware engineers in testing their designs. At the completion of the Custom layer, the hardware and software are working together, at least at the component level.

In this layer, software algorithms are developed. General algorithms may be used, such as a task-scheduling scheme, or proprietary algorithms may be developed, such as a specific control strategy for the device.

Finally, it is at this layer that regulatory concerns are directly addressed. For a medical device, for example, there are the stringent FDA requirements regarding testing of the software and the associated documentation required. Similarly, on systems used in aircraft, the testing requirements of DO-178B may be applied to the software. An organization may be subject to policies relating to CMM (Capability Maturity Model) requirements, or the organization may have their own documentation scheme.

Hardware documentation is important as well. While there are few regulatory requirements addressing hardware documentation, engineering practice calls for documentation sufficient to allow reproduction of the system. In some cases, regulatory requirements do exist regarding how the hardware can affect the environment. RFI (Radio Frequency Interference) emissions, for example, must be controlled.

Layer 5 – System Integration

In the System Integration Layer (see Figure 6), the hardware and software are put together and tested in the 'real world.' This is where the system is measured against the System Requirements from the System Description Layer. Does the system perform the intended function?

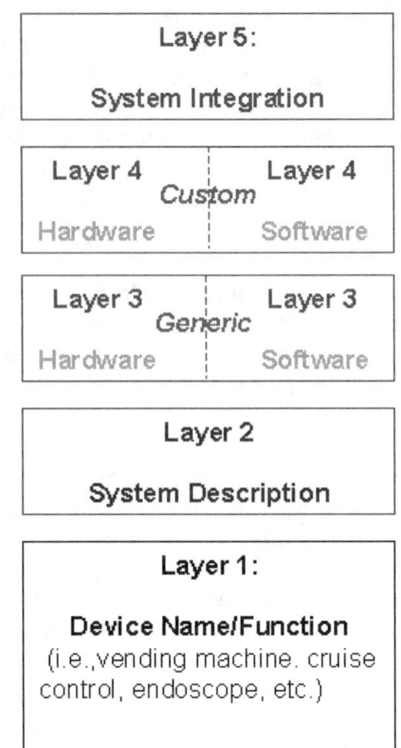

Figure 6. Layer 5: System integration.

It is the first exposure of the developed system to the problem space. In the previous layer, the software and hardware were developed with a focus on correct operation according to the hardware and software designs. Preliminary integration of hardware and software at the component level was performed, but the System Integration layer focuses on the system as a whole, in the environment in which it is intended to operate.

Inputs

The first inputs to the System Integration layer are the hardware and software that were developed in the previous layer. Test plans are developed from the System Requirements to use in planning the integration and testing process.

Outputs

A successful integration will give us an embedded system, operating according to the System Requirements. Formal integration test results may be generated, depending on the policies of the organization. The system is ready to be tested against all its requirements to demonstrate that the system has been developed correctly.

Layer 6 – Testing and Validation

In the Testing and Validation Layer (see Figure 7), we use the System Requirements developed earlier, and the test plans based on those requirements, to show that the system has been developed correctly. Verification that the system meets all its requirements and validation that the system performs the intended function are the activities at this layer.

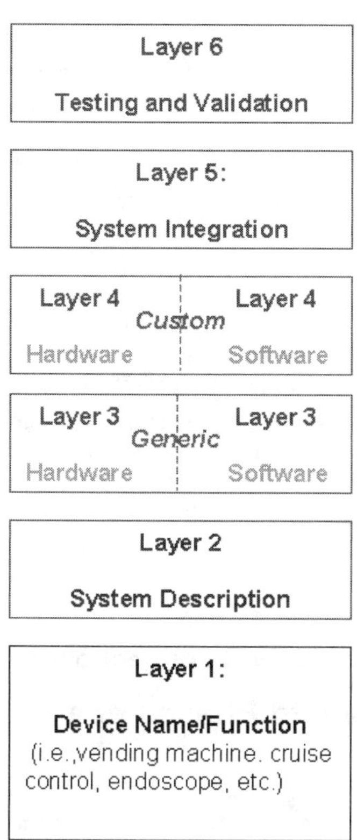

Figure 7. Layer 6: Testing and validation.

It is at this layer that domain expertise becomes important again. Domain expertise is needed to allow the engineers to understand that the system is performing the intended function or to identify problems with the system.

At this layer, testing is entirely an engineering activity. The eventual user of the system is not yet involved in testing the system. The Testing and Validation layer, upon completion, shows that the system is ready for the user.

Inputs

The developed system resulting from the activities of the earlier layers is, of course, the main input to the Testing and Validation layer. Detailed test plans based on the System Requirements are used in the testing activity.

Outputs

After this layer, the embedded system is complete, and ready for the user. The system has been shown to operate according to requirements and to perform the desired function.

From the testing procedure, test logs and reports are produced. Any problems found in the testing, and the associated corrective action, should be recorded as part of the test reports. A formal method should be established to keep track of any problems with the system discovered after release as well as the actions taken to correct them.

Layer 7 – Product

The Product Layer is where the emphasis changes from the engineering process of developing the system to the eventual user of the system. At this point, the system has become a product. The system is provided to the users for another round of testing. Their testing will be based on the high-level functional requirements developed back in the Device Concept layer. The users must verify the system does its job properly.

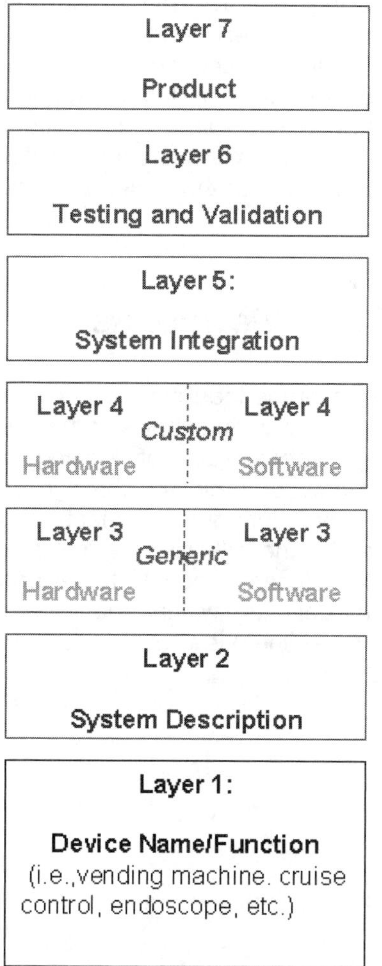

Figure 8. Layer 7: Product.

Often, at this layer, the system is provided to users as a specified test system, called an Alpha Test, or Beta Test. This allows the users to record observations about the system and identify possible problems. The information is returned to the engineering staff, which makes corrections and fixes, and returns the system to the users.

Inputs

The completed embedded system is the input to this layer.

Other inputs to this layer include the Alpha & Beta test feedback, if the system undergoes that procedure, and the System test log from the Integration layer.

Outputs

The desired output is a validated, customer-accepted product. Other outputs are the records of the Alpha and Beta testing, if performed, and of any changes made to the product.

As part of the Product layer, procedures are put in place to maintain and possibly improve the system in the future. Because virtually every system will contain problems (bugs) that will be discovered by the users, these procedures provide the basis for corrections and fixes during the system's life span. In addition, the information recorded is used as a basis for deciding on and planning any upgrades or improvements to the system.

Layers from Other Viewpoints

The layers model of an embedded system provides us with an understanding of the various parts of the system. There are, of course, other ways of looking at an embedded system. Some of these are through project phases, issues that arise during the project, and the development process. In the following paragraphs, we relate the embedded layers model to alternative viewpoints. The model fits within the alternative viewpoints, giving a baseline view of any embedded system (see Figure 9, below).

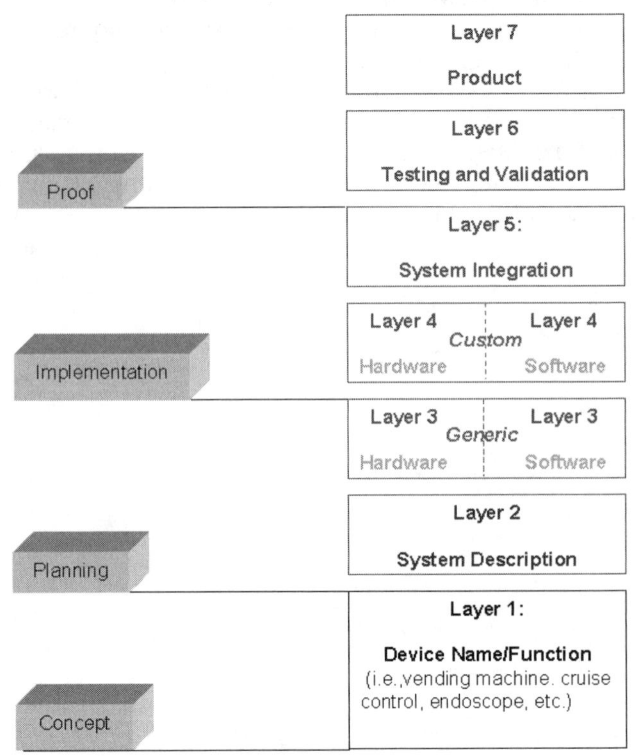

Figure 9. Entire layers model with project phases.

Relationship of Layers to Phases of a Project

Development of an embedded system is a project that goes through several basic phases. As shown in Figure 9, these phases are Concept, Planning, Implementation, Proof, and Release.

The first phase, the Concept phase, is where the idea for the system is conceived. This phase of the project corresponds to the Device Concept Layer.

The Planning phase corresponds to layers 2 and 3, System Description and Generic Hardware and Software. In this phase of the project, the decisions are made that guide the development of the system.

The Implementation phase of the project corresponds to Layer 4, Custom Hardware and Software, and Layer 5, System Integration. In this phase, the system is developed into a working device, based on the concept developed and the decisions made in the planning phase.

The project phase of Proof corresponds to Layer 6, Testing and Validation. In this layer, the system is shown to perform its intended function. Note that, while testing activities may be performed in the Product layer, those activities are customer- or user-related, and their aim is to improve the system, not show that it has been developed correctly.

Release is more of an event than a project phase. At the completion of the project, the system is 'released' to the users. This corresponds to Layer 7, Product.

Relationship of Layers to Target, System and Project Issues

The layers in the model progress through three sets of issues during the development of the embedded system. These issues are shown in Figure 10. Initially, the focus is on the target system – the system we are going to build. Layer 1, Device Concept, and the first part of Layer 2, system description, are specifically concerned with target system issues.

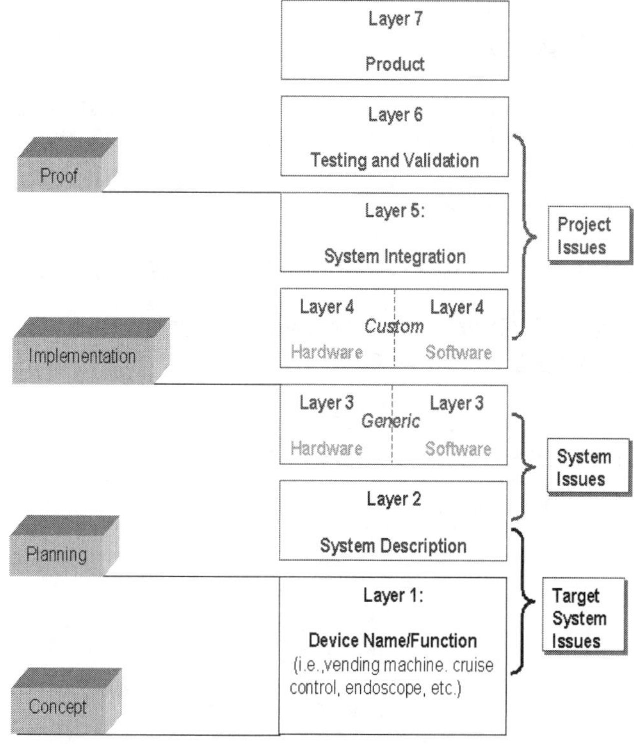

Figure 10. Entire layers model with project phases and issues.

Beginning in the System Description layer, and continuing into Layer 3, Generic Hardware and Software, the project is addressing system issues. Here the engineering of the system is begun and decisions are made that will guide the development of the system. The system issues tend to be general, and, while they are related to the particular system, they are similar between most embedded system projects.

Layers 4 through 6, Custom Hardware and Software, System Integration, and Testing and Validation, all address issues specific to the project. These issues are concerned with the decisions and questions that arise from the specific device.

Relationship of Layers to Development Process

In the detailed discussion of the layers of an embedded system, we explored the activities undertaken within each layer, as well as the inputs and outputs to each layer. The model addresses the development of the embedded system, and relates directly to the development process. The table below lists some typical project activities and results generally seen in a development project and the model layer in which it occurs.

Development Process Item	Layer Where Found
System Requirements	Layer 2 – System Description
Software / Hardware Requirements	Layer 4 – Custom Hardware / Software
Test Definitions – System	Layer 6 – Testing and Validation
Test Definitions – Hardware / Software	Layer 4 – Custom Hardware / Software
Design	Layer 4 – Custom Hardware / Software
Implementation of System	Layer 4 – Custom Hardware / Software
Unit Test	Layer 4 – Custom Hardware / Software
Integration	Layer 5 – System Integration
Verification / Validation – System	Layer 6 – Testing and Validation
Verification / Validation – Software / Hardware	Layer 6 – Testing and Validation

How Can the Model be Used?

Recall that the construction of the model was based on the questions "What parts of the embedded system are specific to my project?" and "What parts are common to any project?" The model, as constructed, gives us the answers to these questions.

Layers with content specific to the particular system under development are Device Concept, System Description, System Integration, and Product. (Layers 1, 2, 6 & 7) In these layers, as identified above, there is a need for domain expertise for at least some of the activities within these layers. To properly complete these layers, we need engineers with skills specific to the industry, product, or system type.

Conversely, the Generic Hardware / Software, Custom Hardware / Software, and System Integration layers (layers 3, 4, & 5) are not specific as to the skills required. The activities in these areas require skills that are general rather than industry- or product-specific.

Therefore, one part of the answer to the question of how the model can be used is in assessing what skills are necessary for an embedded system development project. By understanding where in a project's lifecycle domain knowledge is needed, and where it is not, we can better staff the project and therefore make better use of engineering resources. Thus, for any given project, the skills necessary to a particular stage of development can be more easily identified.

Further, the information can be used to plan personnel assignments. Engineers with particular skills or expertise can be assigned where their skills are needed and will be most valuable. Using skill levels of various engineers wisely enables planning assignments such that the proper person is assigned the proper tasks. For example, an engineer with good design skills, but little domain knowledge of the particular system, can be assigned to the design tasks in Custom Hardware with confidence. Likewise, an engineer with detailed domain knowledge is more valuable in the activities within the System Description layer.

Finally, the information can help an organization recognize where there are gaps in its skill sets, either for a specific project or for the organization as a whole. Having that information allows planning workarounds and actions, such as hiring/contracting the requisite skills, to fill any gaps.

CONCLUSION

We have constructed a model appropriate for an embedded system, describing the parts of the system, and the process by which the system is developed. Where there are other ways of viewing the embedded system, the layers in the model correspond to the different perspectives.

The model provides us with a framework for identifying the particular skills needed in the different stages of an embedded system development project. With this information, we can plan personnel assignments and either allocate or acquire the skills we need for a particular project.

Typically, each embedded system has been viewed as *unique*. The model helps us visualize embedded system projects as a genre of engineering projects, which enables us to see that all types of engineering projects have many "layers" in common.

ACKNOWLEDGMENTS

The authors wish to acknowledge their employer, Pacific Information Design, Inc., who encouraged them in the construction of the model and the writing of this paper.

CONTACTS

Pacific Information Design, Inc., 411 East Canon Perdido Street, Suite 16, Santa Barbara, CA 93101

www.pacinfosb.com

Larry Leveille, President; larry.leveille@pacinfosb.com

Patricia M. Gary, Vice-President, Marketing; patty.gary@pacinfosb.com

James Brown, Software Engineer, jim.brown@pacinfosb.com

SYSTEMS TESTING/DIAGNOSIS

2006-01-1679

The Armageddon Device Part II

Ronald P. Brombach
Ford Motor Company

ABSTRACT

Applying good engineering practices to software-intense automotive systems can save automakers millions of dollars in warrantee costs, lost customer loyalty and lawsuits. Carefully crafted development testing could expose non-robust software that fails intermittently when the customer activates the function.

The chances are very good the service technician will replace the ECU when the customer brings the vehicle in for repair of the intermittent behavior. These electronic parts are sent to the supplier for analysis. Upwards of 60% of all ECUs analyzed are TNI (Trouble Not Identified) related.

This paper elaborates on a method of developmental testing that provides these cost savings. This paper continues to build on concepts discussed in the SAE paper, "*The Bus Crusher and The Armageddon Device Part I"*. [1] The experiment of subjecting an ECU to several electrical disturbances is explained in detail.

The objective of an embedded system is to have a predictable output for any combination of input sequences. If the operation of the embedded system is viewed as a big state diagram, testing verifies that the embedded system operates in acceptable states and that transitions between states are all known and predictable. The stress-testing concept described in this paper generates sequences of stimuli that can't normally be planned for (the number of combinations is massive). The embedded system must always remain in a known acceptable state, regardless of the stimulus. The testing techniques described allows for the creation of a stimulus to verify the robustness of the embedded system.

Experiments were conducted on electrical breadboards, which were subjected to RF (Radio Frequency) noise, periodic network initialization, communication bus failures, intermittent ground open, and repeated cycling of the locking function. The hypothesis of the experiment was to stress the ECU's operating environment by causing events that seldom occur, and make them happen with high regularity. The electrical noise level is below the ECU design limit, e.g., the task monitoring the ECU voltage range will ignore voltage drops of less than 15 msec (milliseconds). Subjecting the ground circuit to an interruption of less than 15 msec should result in no humanly perceivable behavior change.

Methods to stress the software are the focus of this document. Described are:

1. Building the RF Blaster
2. Building the Armageddon Breakout box
3. Introducing new noise factors; ground lift and periodic network initialization
4. Lock-Unlock Cycle test
5. Results of the tests

INTRODUCTION

Software is one of the biggest challenges facing the automotive industry. A few years ago, Mercedes and BMW both claimed they were having trouble with software. Their action to resolve the problems was to remove some of the difficult to implement features: basically, software that is too complex to specify and test. This masks the short-term issue with automotive software development. It only mitigates the issue. This strategy does not address the long-term desire to develop software that performs flawlessly.

Software-driven designs will continue to grow and play an important role for the future of the industry. Ford's experience has been far from painless. Software issues discovered late in the development cycle cause the software team to explain what went wrong and get a lot of "management help ".

We can't simply apply the same engineering tools we are so familiar with and get high quality results. Can a product be "over engineered"? Possibly. But if it fails to meet customer expectations, is it still "over engineered"? No. There are many reasons a product could fail. Software must not be the reason the product failed.

How do we guarantee the product is defect-free? This has been a challenge not only for embedded software but also for all products that need software to operate correctly. No one likes issues with the software. Software is not based on the fundamental laws of physics, like various laws of nature that drive our standard engineering practices. That's why it is both a huge opportunity and a challenge for the industry.

The quality of the product is directly related to the number of issues in the software. As the software is developed and tested, defects are driven out, but no one will guarantee 100% defect-free software. Software is too complex to make that claim. Other methods must be employed to wring-out non-compliances.

How should the product be tested to make sure issues are identified? Exposing the product to an extreme environment is a good method for robustness testing in the physical world. An electro-mechanical system is affected by: wear out, humidity, temperature, vibration, fluctuating battery voltage, EMC (Electro-magnetic Compatibility), etc... In a pure sense, software is immune to these environmental conditions. (There can be poorly designed hardware-software interfaces that are sensitive to noise.)

The goal of this type of stress testing is to find issues early. Also, have a test suite to verify the level of robustness in the design. When software is modified, these test suites can be used to assess if the software is performing better or worse.

The Armageddon Device Part 1 [1] discussed noisy environments and their effect on ECU behavior. The following summarizes and explains the original paper:

1) **Bus Crusher** – was originally a “chattering” relay connected to the MSCAN bus wires. A modified setup uses the MSCAN bus shorting technique, but is now controlled by the Netway box.

2) **RF Blaster** - a 315 MHz transmitter connected to a CD Player.

3) **New test: Lock-Unlock Cycle Test** – Cycle the lock and unlock while the noise factors are present. This test is the main goal of the paper. It describes in detail this test procedure.

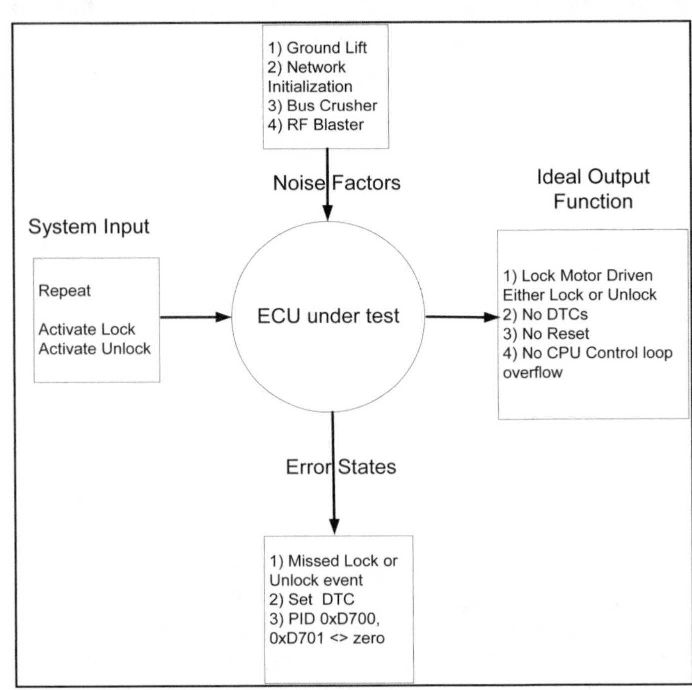

Figure 1 Process Diagram for the Lock-Unlock Cycle test

TESTING MINDSET

The goal of a test engineer is to develop and conduct tests. The mantra should be, “I'm not happy until I can break the software.” The person developing these tests needs to review the design, identify possible weaknesses, and develop tests to push the limits of the design. Interrupt service routines (ISRs) are a great place to look for these weaknesses.

Questions the test engineer should ask as the engineering documentation is being reviewed:

1) What is the ECU's ideal function?
2) How can I break the design?
3) What are the lessons learned from previous vehicle programs?
4) What are the standard and customary tests that are currently conducted?
5) Are there any “unusual” conditions the vehicle may be subjected to?
6) What are the boundary conditions for correct operation of the subsystem?

BEHAVIOR ASSUMPTIONS

The process diagram for the Lock-Unlock cycle test is shown in **Figure 1**. This diagram helps to understand the ECU being tested and the environment it is tested under.

1) Repetitive cycling of the same function should have the same behavior over and over again. For example, Missing too many RKE (Remote Keyless Entry) FOB unlock requests would be unacceptable. (~1% miss rate)

2) Software itself has no known wear out mechanism. A side effect could be excessive write cycles to NVM (Non-Volatile Memory). For example, RKE rolling code requires NVM or the backlighting dimmer potentiometer calibration continuously updates NVM.

EXPECTATIONS

All designs have limits. As long as the noise factors are below the design limit or tolerance, the ECU should have predictable and expected behavior. Subjecting the ECU to noise that is small or intermittent should have little effect on its behavior.

Based on Ford requirements and customer perceived behavior, the following test conditions/criteria are introduced:

1) Meeting requirement #72 - The ECU shall respond to a RKE FOB packet when there is 15 msec of no noise present. Based on Ford's RKE specification #72.

   The ECU should have some level of noise tolerance. ECU behavior should not be affected if the noise level is below the design intent. RF noise should not cause the ECU to become "RF deaf" once the noise is removed.

2) No false DTCs (Diagnostic Trouble Codes) - Exercising these tests should not introduce any unexplainable DTCs. False DTCs shall not be reported. Customer operation should not set DTCs, e.g., cycling the ignition switch quickly.

3) Interrupts are Inherently Evil – Most RF data reception, MSCAN reception and MSCAN transmit algorithms use ISRs (Interrupt Service Routines). The network initialization message was sent while clocking in the RF data bits. This will increase the probability that ISRs will run concurrently. Network initialization should be completed within 9 msec or approximately 10 messages. Feature content is directly related to the number of initialization messages.

4) Short power interruption - A 13 msec ground interruption was generated while the RF bits were being clocked in. This short power interruption should not trigger the software shutdown procedure. (Voltage drop out detect time is between 15 to 20 msec, based on 4 samples every 5 msec). The software should always react to a 21 msec voltage drop but not 13 msec. For some of the tests, opening the ground circuit was too difficult. The ECU power fuse was opened instead.

5) RF Blaster - RF noise is generated with a CD player and a modified RKE FOB transmitter.

6) Bus Crusher - Shorting the MSCAN bus wires to ground. Crushing the bus for 50 msec should not cause any functional behavior anomalies. All of the missing message strategies for MSCAN (Medium-Speed Controller Area Network) are greater than 1 second. The Bus Crusher is energized 5 msec after the Network initialization message is sent out.

HEADLAMP FLICKER PROBLEM

An ECU with a headlamp flicker problem was tested using the RF Blaster. The ECU periodically wakes up and checks for a RF signal. The headlamps flickered when the ECU came out of sleep. The RF Blaster detected the headlamp flicker problem.

An unknown logic error in the software would turn on the headlamp circuit for 10 msec each time RF noise is present. If the bit timing matched the Ford RKE specification, the duty cycle was 10 msec every 400 msec. (Observable with an oscilloscope.) However, with a non-Ford RKE protocol transmission, the headlamps turned on every 10msec for every 120 msec. This duty cycle is noticeable to a person testing the vehicle or breadboard. The headlamps glowed.

CONTINUING THE ARMAGGEDON EXPERIMENT

Not all of the equipment or test set-ups were developed in "*The Bus Crusher and Armageddon Device Part I.*"[1] More experimenting was needed to develop the test equipment. The RF Blaster, the Armageddon breakout box and the Netway box software needed to be built and verified.

The RF Blaster was the first piece of equipment to be developed. The original design is shown in **Figure 2.** It requires a RF transmitter, which weighs 30 pounds, is large and very expensive. A "hand-me down" RF generator was discovered in the EMC (Electro-Magnetic Compliance) lab, however, it did not operate above 160 MHz. An alternative method was needed.

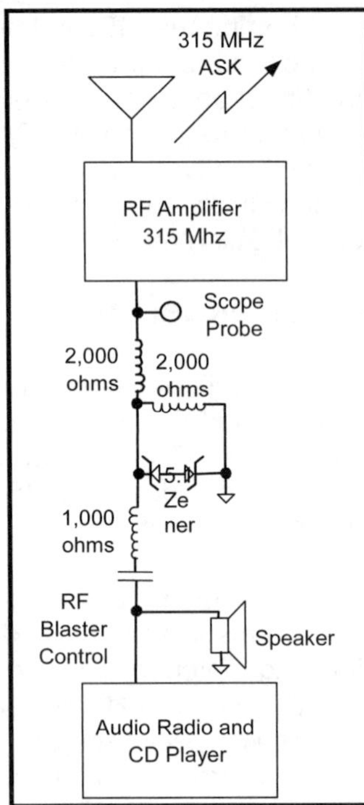

Figure 2 Proposed RF Blaster

One RKE FOB supplier had a very simple transmitter design. There were many engineering samples in the office that could be used in the experiment. If the experiment burned out a unit, there were many more that could be modified and used. It may work.

A resistor divider network was connected to the output of the CD player to protect the input transistor of the transmitter. No RF signal was generated when the system was turned on. Maybe connecting the CD player output directly to the base resistor of the transmitter circuit would generate a signal. (Signal Input in **Figure 3**) Now a 315 MHz signal is being generated as sown in **Figure 4.**

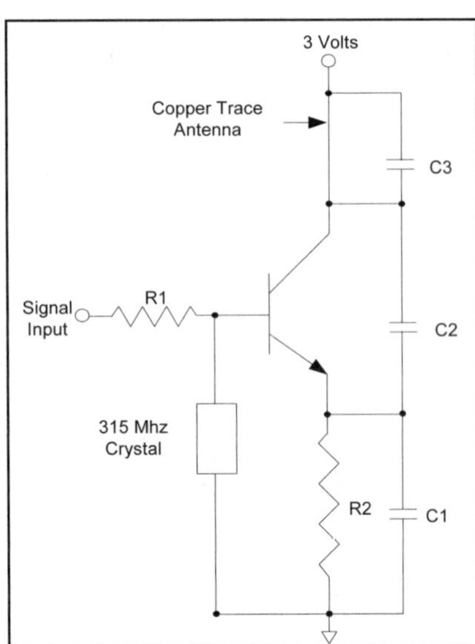

Figure 3 RF Transmission section of the RKE FOB

To make the circuit work, the CD player's volume had to be turned up all the way. The left channel had a speaker connected, (**Figure 5)** and the balance had to be turned all the way to the right channel. The volume was too loud if the balance was not changed. The transmitter would work as seen on the scope shown in **Figure 4.**

"HIGHWAY TO HELL" TEST

There was a problem with a high power audio amplifier that entered thermal overload. The overload condition was not identified using classical music. If the audio volume was turned up to the maximum limit when "Highway to Hell" by AC/DC was played, the amplifier went into thermal overload. Why not try using the "Highway to Hell" CD as the noise source?

A high-speed digital scope with a simple loop antenna was able to capture the RF Blaster noise. The loop antenna was achieved by connecting the ground cable of the scope probe to the probe tip. The gain on the scope was turned to 20 mv/div (millivolts/division). The noise pattern shown in **Figure 4** was observed.

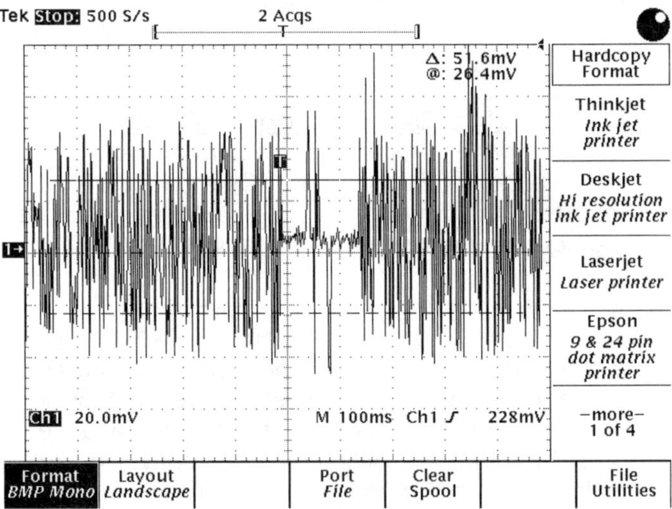

Figure 4 Scope plots of RF Blaster noise

Could the noise wash out a valid RKE signal, as was hoped? The RF Blaster was moved to the electrical breadboard room where they are many breadboards to test on.

The first step was to power up the breadboard and verify that the learned RKE FOB worked. Pressing the unlock button caused the lock motor to cycle when the RF Blaster was turned off. The RKE FOB operation is verified. Pressing the RKE FOB unlock button when the RF Blaster was turned on resulted in no unlock event. The RF Blaster was distorting the signal. It worked!

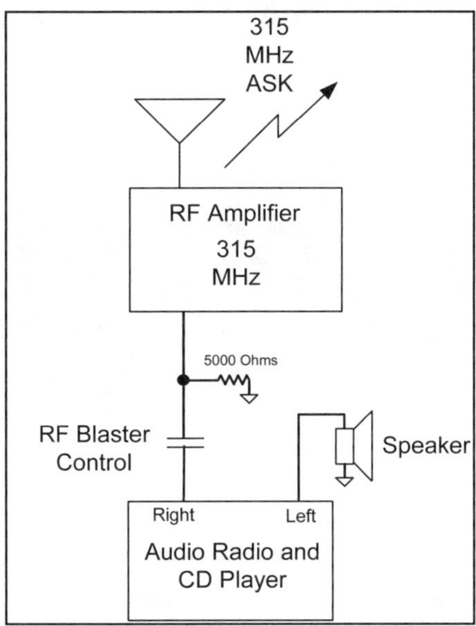

Figure 5 Simplified RF Blaster

Figure 5 shows the CD player connected to the RF transmitter with relay contacts in series. This allows the Netway Box to control the RF Blaster operation within a few milliseconds and achieve electrical isolation. The RF Blaster is designed to play music through the RF transmitter. It generates a random noise spectrum from 20 Hz to 17 KHz.

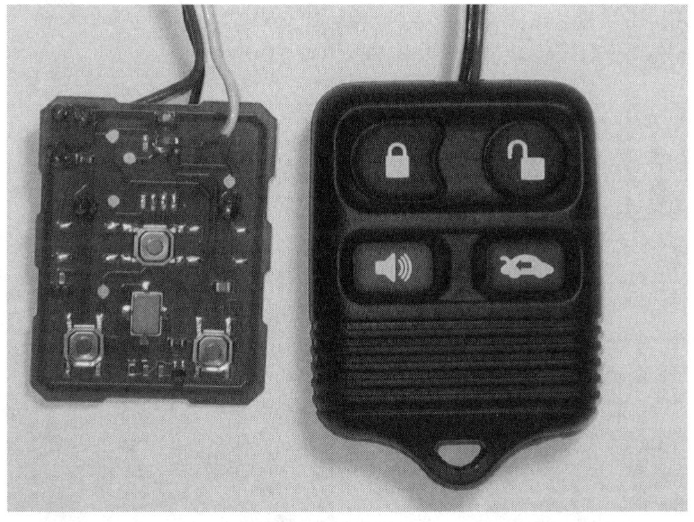

Figure 6 Modified RKE FOB

Figure 6 shows two modified RKE FOBs. The device on the left has three wires connected: 3 volt power, ground and the input signal. It is connected to the output of the CD player via normally open contacts. (Note: the microcontroller is removed to have a solder point.

Another RKE FOB was modified with four wires: 3 volt power, ground, lock and unlock. When connected to the Armageddon breakout box, energizing the lock or unlock relay closes the button (Emulating the user pressing the button). This allows the Netway box to control when a valid lock or unlock RF signal is transmitted.

UNEXPECTED SIDE EFFECT

The durability of the RF transmitter's electrical circuitry was uncertain when driven directly by the CD player output. Would the circuit burn out? How long would it last before it burned out? The duty cycle was much higher than the device was intended for. The RF transmitter's component values were unknown. Testing was needed to make sure this unorthodox usage of the RF transmitter continued to function over many hours. The experiment ran during days when it could be checked on in the lab. The experiment ran 5 hours for 3 days.

The range of the RF Blaster was undetermined. The focus was to ensure the drive transistor would not fail. Determining RF range was secondary. An engineer at a bench near the RF Blaster testing station asked what kind of experiment was being conducted. I explained the RF Blaster concept to him. He looked at me, chuckled a little and said," That explains everything." The engineer was testing newly released software and thought he encountered a problem. Was the problem with the new ECU software or the HIL (Hardware in the Loop) software? He asked other engineers for help. They spent several hours scratching their heads trying to troubleshoot the problem.

These engineers were unaware of the experiment that was being conducted 3 meters away. The durability experiment had interfered with their RKE testing. The engineer continued, "We ran a RKE cycle test and had intermittent behavior. We thought we were getting possible interference from the adjacent parking lot. We looked through the test software. Then the RKE system functioned correctly after 2:00pm." Now I had to chuckle, because 2:00pm happened to be the time that the durability experiment was shut down. By running these experiments in the lab, I have been titled "The Mad Scientist."

BUILDING THE ARMAGEDDON BREAK-OUT BOX

To be able to take the setup from the lab to a vehicle environment, a test box needed to be built. Physically testing in a vehicle environment requires the tester to be durable, reliable and simple to use. The development started off simple. Battery voltage, Ground, MSCAN bus wires were connected to the breadboard via the J1962 OBD-II diagnostic connector.

Banana jack connectors allow reliable and quick connections. The relays allow the control circuits to be isolated, avoiding interference with other circuits.

BASIC RKE TRANSMITTER AND RF BLASTER INTERFERENCE

When a RKE FOB button is pressed, the basic operation of the RKE transmitter is as follows: (rounded values)

1) 50 msec input debounce
2) 50 msec of 315 MHz ASK signal output
3) 50 msec inter-packet gap or idle time.
4) A 100 msec button press generates 4 packets per message.

The RF Blaster and the RKE FOB were wired to the Armageddon breakout box. The Auxiliary relay controlled the lock relay and the RF Blaster relay. The normally open contacts were connected to the lock relay. The normally closed contact was connected to the RF Blaster relay. When the Auxiliary relay was energized, the lock relay contacts closed for the RKE FOB and the RF Blaster was turned off. The intent was to synchronize turning off the noise and turning on the RKE signal.

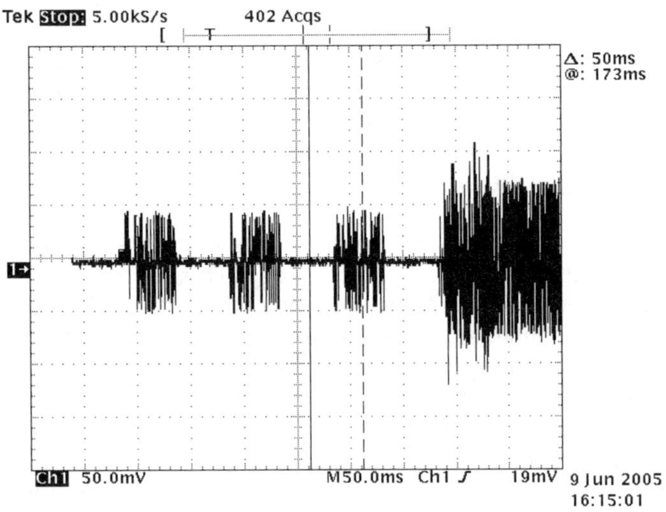

Figure 7 Three valid RKE packets transmitted

The Netway box generated two signal pulse widths: 50 msec and 350 msec.. The result of generating a 350 msec pulse is shown in **Figure 7.** It shows three valid RKE signals. The fourth signal was distorted by turning on the RF Blaster. Portions of the fourth packet can be seen riding on top of the RF Blaster noise.

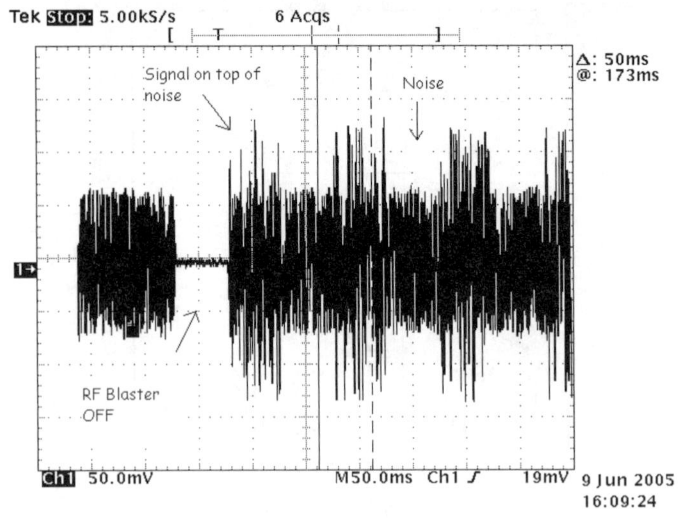

Figure 8 Zero Messages are transmitted

Figure 8 shows a 50 msec period with RF turned off. The Netway box reasserts the RF Blaster noise after 50 msec, which distorts all four packets of the RKE FOB transmission.

This worked, but there was too much RF off time. There was always a 50 msec RF off time (button debounce time for the RKE FOB) . The Netway box was needed to reduce the RF off time to 15 msec.

Any number of packets can be distorted by controlling the RF Blaster with the Netway Box. The ECU will not decode RKE signals that are too noisy.

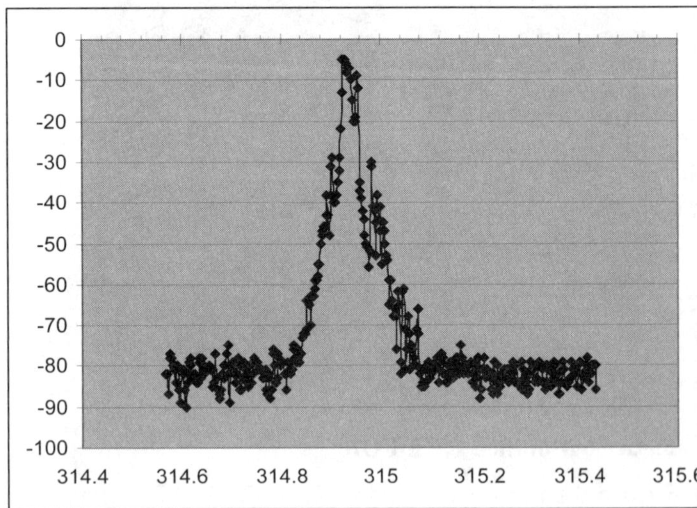

Figure 9 RF Blaster spectrum analyzer

Figure 9 shows the output of the RF Blaster with a spectrum analyzer. The expectation is that with a crystal in the transmitter circuit, the output frequency would be very close to 315 MHz. ECUs are designed to have –90 db sensitivity.

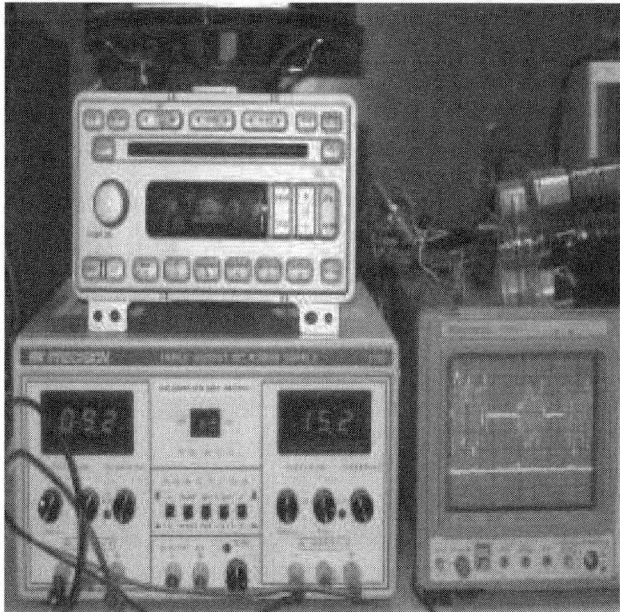

Figure 10 RF Blaster with power supply

Figure 10 shows the durability experiment with a CD player, an RF transmitter and an oscilloscope trace on the right. The song playing on channel #3 of the "*Highway to Hell*" CD is *"Walk All Over You"*. The RF Blaster is walking all over the ECU's RF receiver.

MORE POWER

A new experiment was designed to determine if the RF signal could be strengthened. The 3-volt connection was replaced with a power supply. Increasing the voltage did not increase the field strength of the RF Blaster as expected. The transmitter output seemed to be the same regardless of the supply voltage. No further experimentation was done because the RF Blaster interfered with RKE reception. With a 3 volt power supply it distorted the valid RKE signal.

BETTER RF EARS

A detection mechanism was needed to see what type of 315 MHz signal is being generated. The problem rekindled a memory of working in Germany with a supplier on an issue. We needed to measure the sleep current of the ECU. The very weak current was less than 500 microamps. An oscilloscope was the equipment that was available.

The supervisor coiled the ground circuit several times around the probe loop. Relative current was now visible on the oscilloscope. Could this simple idea work for increasing the detection capability of the oscilloscope?

A plastic peanut butter jar was wrapped with 18-gauge wire and connected to the oscilloscope. Could multiple wire loops "amplify" the transmitter signal? (Assumption: coils of wires would be cutting more lines of flux) These coils of wire did not increase the detected signal.

Diagnosing why the peanut butter jar wire coil did not improve the sensitivity was not worth the effort. The wire coil was not needed, because a simple loop antenna worked. A signal was seen on the oscilloscope when the ground wire and probe accidentally shorted.

LOCK-UNLOCK CYCLE TESTING

The base Lock-Unlock cycle test was developed on the Netway box for a previous project. The software was modified to control the Armageddon breakout box. (Cycling of the Lock, Unlock, RF Blaster, Bus Crusher, Network Initialization and Ground Lift.) This allowed the project to move quickly, since the base feature of cycling was completed.

The expectation is that the lock-unlock motor should cycle correctly under this test. The RF Blaster is used to block any packet the ECU can receive. The battery voltage is set to 13.6 volts for 5,000 cycles. The Lock-Unlock cycle test is graphically shown in **Figure 11.**

The Netway box also monitors the lock and unlock motor circuits. The software uses a simple counter that counts the number of missed lock or unlock events. Software monitors are: Continuous DTCs, Self-test, PID 0xD700, PID 0xD701 and clearing of continuous DTCs. Data is retrieved after each series of tests.

The data returned in PID 0xD700:

- BYTE 1: Power on reset
- BYTE 2: Illegal op code
- BYTE 3: Watchdog timer reset
- BYTE 4: Data Range Failure

The data returned from PID 0xD701 in byte:

- BYTE 1: Stack overflow
- BYTE 2: Loss of idle time
- BYTE 3: Minimum Idle–Time
- BYTE 4: Not used

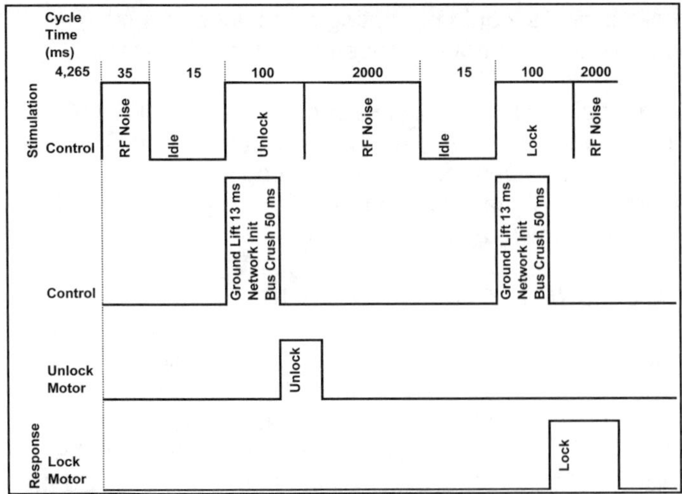

Figure 11 Lock-Unlock Cycle Test (not to scale)

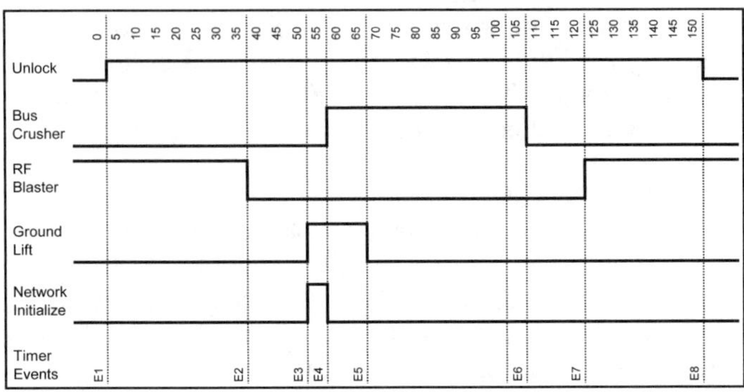

Figure 12 Detailed timing for the Lock and Unlock cycle test

Figure 12 details **Figure 11,** starting at Time = 0. The detail shown in **Figure 12** applies to the unlock request. The lock part of the test has the same timing sequence.

E1: Unlock event = ON (T=0)
E2: RF Blaster = OFF (T=35)
E3: Send Network Init and Ground lift = ON (T=50)
E4: Bus Crusher = ON (T=55)
E5: Ground Lift = OFF (T=63)
E6: Bus Crusher = OFF (T=105)
E7: RF Blaster = ON (T=120)
E8: Unlock event = OFF

Figure 13 Netway Box sequence of events

Figure 13 specifies the time at which events occur. The Netway box does not measure the response time of the system. The software uses a simple counter to record each lock/unlock activation.

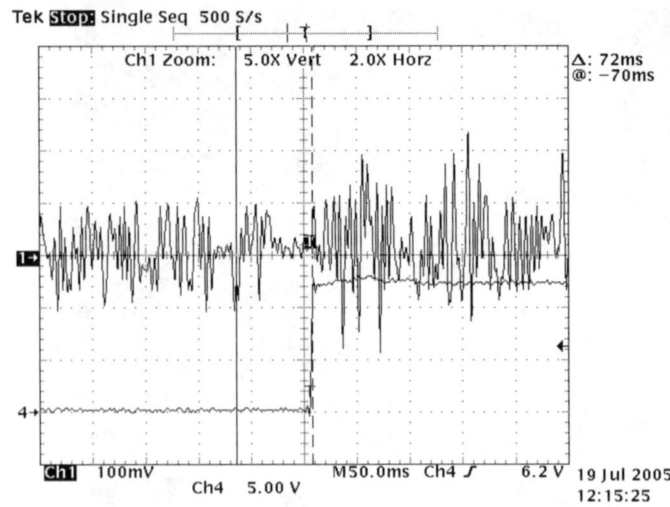

Figure 14 Time measurement between the bits being clocked in and edge of unlock motor

Figure 14 shows the time between the first bit of the RKE packet and the rising edge of the unlock motor voltage. It took 72 +/- 5% msec with the ignition switch in the RUN position with all noise factors present. Five other measurements were conducted with the ignition switch off and noise factors off; the average response delay was 66 msec.

A normal distribution would be expected by collecting many data points. This could be used to determine if the software is relatively stable. This test measurement and analysis could be derivative work for a future project. This time delay measurement is an indicator of system stability. RKE response time should be very consistent, under the noise factors defined in this paper.

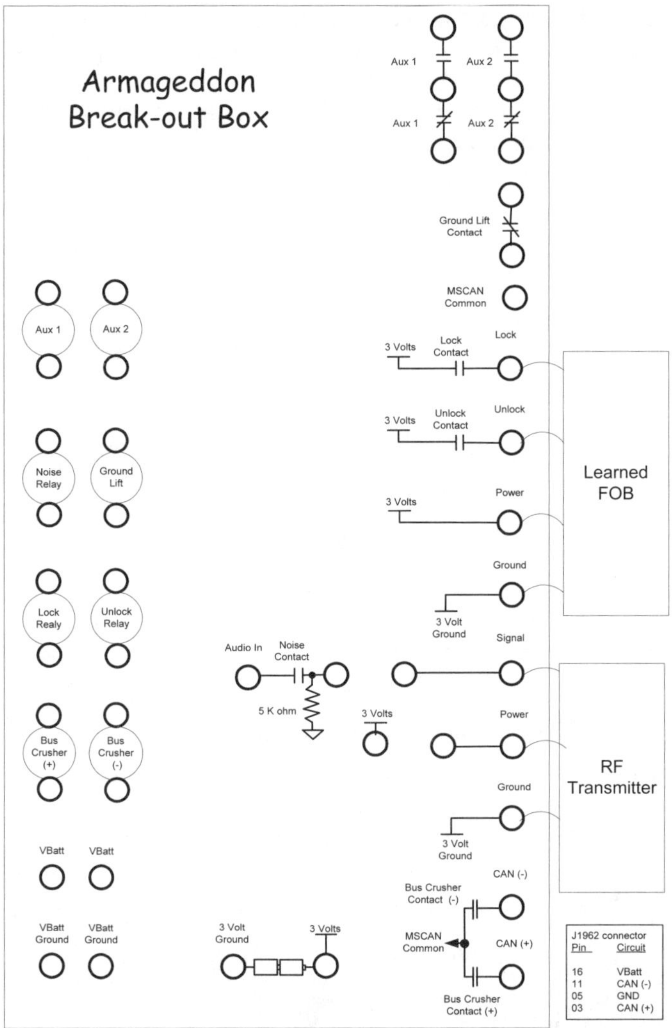

Figure 15 Layout for the Armageddon break-out box

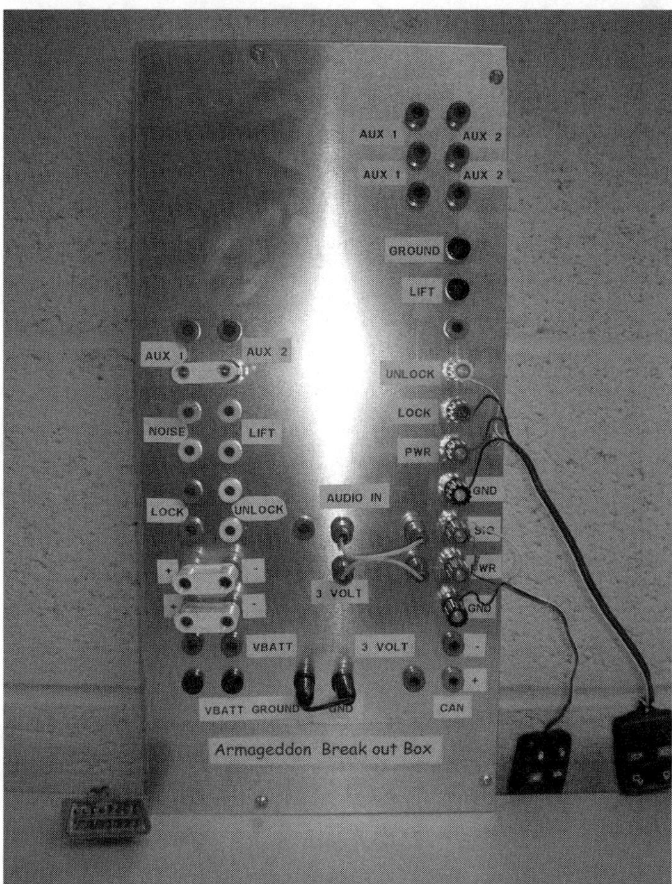

Figure 16 Armageddon breakout box

Figure 15 shows the schematic of the Armageddon breakout box.

Figure 16 is a picture of the Armageddon break out box. Vehicle battery, Ground, MSCAN (+) and MSCAN (-) are connections to the J1962 OBD-II diagnostic connector. The connector is located on the lower left of the picture. The RF transmitter is located next to the box on the right. The RKE FOB is pictured at the far right.

#	Trigger	Command	Description
1		Enable log; SET digout1 = 1h; SET timer1 = 100; SET x0 = 00h; SET y0 = 0000h; SET digout2 = 0h; SET digout5 = 1h; LOGEVNT;	1) Turn on MS CAN data logging based on the filters; 2) Turn off outputs, digout1 = lock, digout2 = unlock, digout5 = 3) x0 is for counting locking events 4) y0 is for counting total lock/unlock iterations
2		SET x1 = 00h;	1) Initialize x1 to zero it is number of counts between asking for DTC's
3		SET y1 = 0000h; SET y2 = 0000h; SET y3 = 0000h;	1) y1 is number of cycles for entire test, 2) y2 is number of missed Locks, 3) y3 is number of missed unlocks
4	timer1	SET digout1 = 0h; SET timer2 = 10; SET timer3 = 1000;	1) Set digital output for locking to 0 for not locked. 2) Set timer2 for sending user message and timer3 to start locking.
5	timer2	QUE usermsg3; SET timer2 = 1000;	1) Send User Message (Vehicle Speed) 1 every second to create network traffic
6	timer3	SET timer8 = 1000; SET x1 + 01h; IF x1 > 0Ah; CL 10; ENDIF; SET timer4 = 2000; SET digout1 = 1h; SET digout2 = 0h; SET timer10 = 35; SET timer12 = 50; SET timer11 = 120; SET timer5 = 150;	1) Lock then start timer4 for unlock activation and start timer8 which is the timer to wait for lock event to occur. 2) Increment counter to read DTC's 3) Check counter to see if 10 events have occurred, if so goto line 10 to read DTC's. 4) Else set timer4 to delay time before unlocking starts 5) Turn locking on (digout1) and unlocking off (digout2) 6) Set timer10 to 35 ms for time to turn noise off 7) Timer12 to 50ms delay before sending Network Init and Ground Lift start 8) Timer11 to 120ms for RF niose back on again 9) Timer5 to 150ms for time to keep lock actuated
7	timer4	SET timer9 = 1000; SET y1 + 0001h; IF y1 == 2710h; CL 11; ELSE; SET timer3 = 2000; SET timer10 = 35; SET timer11 = 120; SET timer12 = 50; SET digout1 = 0h; SET digout2 = 1h; SET timer6 = 150; ENDIF;	1) Unlock and set timer9 for timer to wait for unlock event to occur and then start timer3 for lock activation. 2) Check total iteration counter, if at max iterations goto line 11 to end program, if not then 4) Set timer10 to 35ms for time to turn noise off 5) Set timer11 to 120ms for RF noise back on again 6) Set timer12 to 50ms delay before Sending Network Init and Ground Lift start 7) Turn locking off (digout1) and unlocking on (digout2) 8) Set timer6 to 150ms for time to keep unlock actuated
8	timer5	SET digout1 = 0h; IF analog1 > 0h; SET digout3 = 1h; ELSE; SET digout3 = 0h; ENDIF;	1) Turn lock output off 2) Read Analog input for Lock motor 3) If Lock Motor input is high, then lock has been actuated, so turn on the lock LED (digout3) on Netway box
9	timer6	SET digout2 = 0h; IF analog2 > 0h; SET digout4 = 1h; ELSE; SET digout4 = 0h; ENDIF;	1) Turn unlock output off 2) Read Analog input for unlock motor 3) If unlock Motor input is high, then unlock has been actuated, so turn on the unlock (digout4) LED on Netway box
10		QUE usermsg1; SET x1 = 00h;	1) Read DTC's every 10 cycles 2) Reset counter back to zero
11		SET digout2 = 1h; SET digout1 = 1h; DISABLE timer4; DISABLE timer5; DISABLE timer2; DISABLE timer8; DISABLE timer9; DISABLE timer10; DISABLE timer11; DISABLE timer12; DISABLE timer13; DISABLE timer14; DISABLE timer15; LOGEVNT;	End of Program
12	filter1	QUE usermsg5; SET timer7 = 500;	1) Number Of DTC's is greater than 0, log and clear DTC's 2) Set timer7 to 500ms for sending PID read message
13	timer7	QUE usermsg4;	1) Send user message to read PID
14	inp1(0->1)	DISABLE timer8	1) Input 1 (Lock) has transitioned to high, so stop the timer no need to monitor input
15	timer8	SET y2 + 0001h; LOGEVNT;	1) Missed Lock Event, increment Missed Lock counter 2) Write it to the log
16	inp2(0->1)	DISABLE timer9	1) Input 2 (Unlock) has transitioned to high, so stop the timer no need to monitor input
17	timer9	SET y3 + 0001h; LOGEVNT;	1) Missed Unlock Event, increment Missed Unlock counter 2) Write it to the log
18	timer10	SET digout5 = 0h;	1) Timer10 controls the RF noise off
19	timer11	SET digout5 = 1h;	1) Timer11 controls the RF noise on
20	timer12	QUE usermsg6; SET digout6 = 1h; SET timer13 = 15; SET timer14 = 5;	1) Start Ground Lift, 2) Send INIT message, 3) Set timer13 to 15ms to Start Ground Lift 4) Set timer14 to 5ms for Bus Crusher On timer
21	timer13	SET digout6 = 0h;	1) After 15ms turn Ground Lift off
22	timer14	SET digout7 = 1h; SET timer15 = 50;	1) Turn on Bus Crusher 2) Set timer15 to 50ms to turn Bus Crusher off
23	timer15	SET digout7 = 0h;	1) Turn off Bus Crusher after 50ms

Figure 17 Netway box software program

Figure 17 shows the program that controls the Netway box. The sequence of evaluating starts at the top of the program, then executes the timers. The software architecture is event-based. The Netway box performs the action when the timer expires.

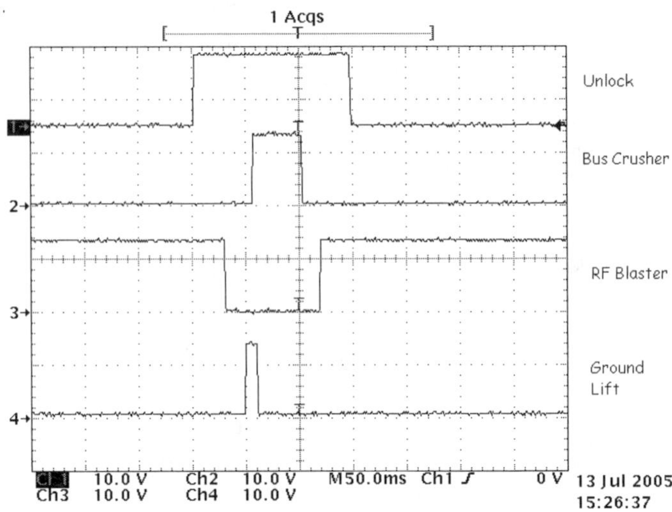

Figure 18 Netway box output verification

Figure 18 shows a four-channel high-speed digital oscilloscope connected to the output of the Netway box. This confirms the programming sequence is correct.

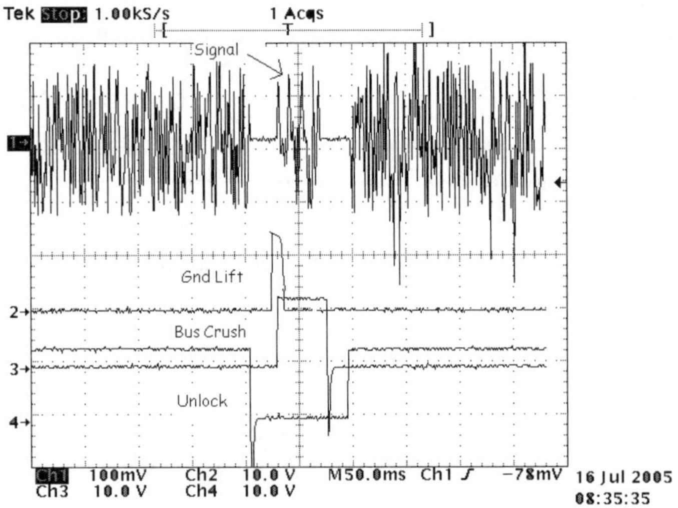

Figure 19 Scope trace with all noise factors on

Figure 19 shows the noisy environment with:

1) One RKE packet.
2) 13 msec ground lift.
3) MSCAN bus being crushed.
4) Unlock control signal of 150 msec.

DETAILED TEST PLAN

The battery voltage was set to 13.6 volts. The ignition switch is either in the "run" or "off" position. Before each test cycle is executed one needs to:

1) Clear continuous DTCs
2) Retrieve continuous DTCs
3) Run Self-test and report results.
4) Clear the software monitor PIDs.
5) Retrieve the software monitor PIDs

After each test cycle is executed:

1) Retrieve continuous DTCs
2) Run Self-test and report results.
3) Retrieve the software monitor PIDs

Three ECUs from different suppliers were evaluated on electrical breadboards. To protect the identity of the suppliers, the ECUs were titled "**A**", "**B**" and "**C**".

TEST RESULTS SUMMARIZED

Number of Cycles
The three ECU setups were cycled at least 5000 times on an electrical breadboard. Half of the tests were conducted with the ignition switch in the "run" position and the other half were conducted with the ignition switch in the "off" position. Each test cycle activated the lock and unlock once.

Evaluation Rule: If the number of misses exceeded 50 (reliability of 99%. (50/5000)), the test was modified. The 150 msec lock/unlock pulse was changed to 250 msec, allowing two valid RKE packets to be transmitted instead of one.

Another variation on the basic test was to move the RF Blaster transmitter 2 meters from the receiver's antenna (All ECUs had internal antennas). The valid RKE FOB was kept near the ECU. In some cases both variations were taken.

Power interruption: Only ECU "**A**" passed this element of the test. Interrupting the ground circuit for 13 msec is part of the basic test. It was difficult to interrupt the ground circuit unless an ECU breakout box was used. No breadboards were equipped with such a device. The alternative was to use the ECU power feed.

DTC logging: ECU "**A**" and "**C**" had incorrectly set bus fault conditions during this test. The documentation that is sent to the supplier must also include requirements pertaining to logging MSCAN bus fault criteria.

A 50 msec short on the MSCAN bus wires must not set a DTC. Current documentation does not explicitly state the conditions for which a bus fault DTC should be set.

ECU "A" Test Performance

ECU "**A**" performed best under the noise conditions. With the ignition switch in the "run" position there were 2 missed lock events and 3 missed unlock events. No modification of the basic test was needed.

When the ignition switch was in the "off" position 109 missed lock events and 113 missed unlock events occurred. The test was modified to allow 2 valid packets to be transmitted. The miss rate went to 16 missed lock and 14 missed unlock events.

Three DTCs were set during these tests:

1. 0xC073: "Control Module Communication Bus A Off"
2. 0xD900: "MSCAN Bus fault - receiver error",
3. 0xA026: "Incandescent backlite output circuit failure"

The first 2 DTCs could be expected due to the type of MSCAN bus faults being introduced. However, a 50 msec bus fault should not set either of these two codes. A review of the fault strategy is needed to determine if the fault detection was done correctly.

DTC 0xA026: "Incandescent backlite output circuit failure", was a surprise. A review of the fault detection strategy with the supplier is needed to understand why the DTC was being reported.

ECU "B" Test Performance

The ground lift was not included in the test because the ECU had a 2 msec voltage drop out detection strategy. ECU "**B**" was designed before the voltage range monitor functionality was defined. The suppliers designed their own voltage range detection. A 2 msec voltage drop was enough to cause the lock/unlock motors to not actuate.

With the ignition switch in the run position there were 1619 missed lock events and 2089 missed unlock events. The test was modified so that two packets are transmitted, and the RF Blaster transmitter was moved 2 meters away from the ECU receiver. The miss rate went to 5 for lock and 8 for unlock.

Two additional experiments were conducted to further characterize the misbehavior:

1. The RF Blaster transmitter was moved 2 meters away from the receiver.
2. The 15 msec quiet time was changed to 50 msec. This improved the lock miss rate to 899 and the unlock was 869.

With the ignition switch in the off position there were 636 missed lock events and 635 missed unlock events. The test was modified so that two packets were transmitted, and the RF Blaster transmitter was moved 2 meters away from the ECU receiver. The miss rate went to 9 for lock and 6 for unlock.

It is suspected that the AGC (Automatic Gain Control) of the receiver is turning down the gain of the RF receiver in the presence of noise. There is not enough time for the correct gain to return when the valid RKE data bits are being transmitted. However, when two packets are transmitted the hit rate is significantly improved.

No DTCs were set during any of these tests.

Strange behaviors were observed on the electrical breadboard for ECU "**B**". Lock or unlock missed events occurred when standing near the breadboard. Walking near the breadboard and moving away influenced the missing lock/unlock events. The Armageddon test should be run on a vehicle with ECU "**B**" before declaring this a test failure. We were unable to re-run the test on a vehicle before publishing this document.

ECU "C" Test Performance

We were unable to isolate the power to the microcontroller without affecting the behavior of other functions. The power interruption portion of the testing was removed for this module.

With the ignition switch in the run position there were 469 missed lock events and 465 missed unlock events. The test was modified in two ways:

1. The RF Blaster transmitter was moved 2 meters away from the receiver. This improved the lock miss rate to 216 and unlock was 208.

2. The RF Blaster transmitter was moved 2 meters away from the receiver and two packets were sent. This improved the lock miss rate to 50 and unlock was 38.

With the ignition switch in the "off" position there were 500 missed lock events and 502 missed unlock events. The test was modified to have two packets transmitted. This improved the lock miss rate to 100 and unlock was 104.

Two DTCs were set:

1. 0xC073: "Control Module Communication Bus A Off"
2. 0xD900: "MSCAN Bus fault - receiver error."

CONCLUSION

The project took more effort than expected, but was worth it. However, the value of this work is immense. There are a number of robustness requirements that are more important than the functional / behavioral product requirements. In fact, if these requirements are not met, the product will fail with the customer in the loop. The real engineering challenge to Ford is knowing and compensating for lessons learned.

Developing functional tests is generally a straightforward process. Look at the requirement and design the test. How do you test for unknown software logic dependencies or temporal linkages? This is done with developing unique tests described in this paper. It is important to understand the weakness of a design and develop tests that stress the limits without exceeding the design intent.

Test variations

Several test setups required modifications to get the ECU to pass the 99% hit rate. For example, with ECU "B" the ground lift could not be used because the software will detect a voltage drop of 2 msec. Also, the lock/unlock pulse width was changed to 250 msec from the defined test of 150 msec, because too many events were lost.

The ECU fuse was used instead of the ground circuit for ECU "**A**". The location of the ECU ground circuit was difficult to locate and connect. The fuse was replaced with the A spade connector to the Armageddon device.

Generating noise

RF generators are expensive, bulky, and require 110 volts to operate. A low-cost approach was devised that accomplished similar results. The approach was inexpensive and compact. The parts to build the Armageddon breakout box and the RF Blaster were easily available in the lab.

Unintended interference

The ECU's RF receiver can have gains exceeding 90 db. Small amounts of noise can wash out other RF signals in the lab. Care/coordination must be taken not to disturb other experiments going on the in the lab.

The Armageddon test was halted when other engineers needed to test RKE performance on different breadboards in the lab. If the Armageddon test had not been stopped, several behaviors would have been observed:

1) They would observe the RKE being non-functional.
2) Or their breadboard lock motor would start cycling without the RKE FOB being pressed. (This ECU learned the Armageddon's RKE FOB.)

Stand-alone RF Blaster

A RKE FOB was modified to continuously transmit a 315 MHz signal as long as the unlock button was pressed. This did not distort the signal 100% of the time. Sometimes the valid RKE FOB signal could be received by the ECU. The hypothesis is the AGC in the ECU receiver was adjusting the signal strength so the "data slicer" could receive the incoming signal. The AGC could not adjust the signal strength to compensate for the random noise that is generated by the RF Blaster.

NEXT STEPS (PART III)

Derivative projects

Many derivative tests can be developed by controlling the noise factors with the Netway box. The Armageddon Device Part III will detail the development of the Software Key-Life test and Reset Cycle test. It will utilize repetitive cycling of the same function to see if the ECU behaves the same over and over again.

A TPMS (Tire Pressure Monitoring System) uses the same frequency as the RKE system, 315 MHz. The first step is to develop inexpensive TPMS stress test equipment; a learned TPMS sensor that can transmit on demand. This allows synchronization with the RF Blaster.

The Armageddon Device can be incorporated into a standard DV (Design Verification). Test for all products that use 315 MHz receivers once a base line is established. It can be used to determine the relative robustness of the design.

Reset Cycle test

Cycle the ECU power, making sure the headlamps turn on at the same time after reset every time. This will be completed for Armageddon Device Part III.

Software Key-Life test

Cycle door lock, door ajar, ignition switch and check for interior/exterior lighting and door lock motors. - This will be completed for Armageddon Device Part III.

Unlimited opportunities

Experience has shown that ECU transitions are one of the biggest software issues (e.g., entering sleep, waking up from sleep, ignition switch transitions from OFF to ON or ON to OFF, battery voltage in and out of range, etc.).

Many key life cycle tests can now be developed such as:; Double Unlock Cycle test, a Reset Cycle test, Sleep/awake Cycle tests, Battery voltage dips, etc... The key is the repetitive cycling of the function. Most tests only test these events once. Now questions can be asked and results tested for:

1) What is the effect of noise on the RKE system when the ECU is in sleep mode or entering sleep mode?
2) Will the ECU enter sleep mode with noise active?
3) Will the ECU wake up in a noisy environment?
4) Will it take longer to wake up and activate the feature?
5) What is the effect of the noise on quiescent current load? KOL (Key Off Load)

Stimulate more I/O

Modify the Lock-Unlock cycle test such that the Ground Lift, Bus Crusher and Network Initialization are more randomly distributed. Add cycling of customer-controlled functions: ignition switch position, door ajar and headlamp control to the Netway box control. The turn signal for the ECU shall also be activated. Cycling the lock motor is still the core test. The number of events/stimulations to the ECU is limited due to the Netway capacity of 8 inputs and 8 outputs

Table 1 below shows the noise factor name, how long the event lasts, the range of time the event is inactive and how much the inactive time is incremented. This means that if the ground lift inactive time is 130 msec, the next time the 13 msec pulse is generated it will be 131 msec. This inactive time is incremented by 1 msec until it reaches 200 msec. When the timer value reaches 200 msec., the next inactive time is 130 msec.

Noise Factor	Active time (msec)	Inactive time (msec)	Inactive increment time value	Percent Duty Cycle
Ignition switch cycling	1,000	1,000 to 2,000	100	33 to 50
Door Ajar	1,000	1,000 to 2100	150	32 to 50
Head Lamp	1,000	1,000 to 2000	200	33 to 50
Ground Lift	13	130 to 200	1	6.5 to 10.0
Bus Crusher	10	100 to 200	2	5.0 to 10.0
Network Init[1]	1	30 to 102	3	8.8 to 33

Table 1 Noise and Customer Activated functions

[1] Each initialization message generates approximately 10 messages, or 9 msec of time.

TONGUE IN CHEEK

The ability to generate RF has been established. What other noise sources can be used? How about connecting the RF transmitter to the RS-232 output port on a PC. Data files could be piped to the port with selectable baud rates. A document like the MISRA-C [2] could be piped to the port. If the ECU passes the test can we say it is "RF MISRA –C" compliant?

CONTRIBUTORS

Many thanks go to the three people that helped make this project successful:

Joe Iaquinto is my technical mentor and has provided valuable feedback on the development of the document. Joe has over 30 years experience in the system's engineering community.

Chris Gee is a Ford electrical technician who built the Armageddon Break out box and the CD player connections.

Darrell Howson is a Ford engineer who wrote the Netway box program, captured oscilloscope wave shapes, ran combinations of tests and collected data.

ABOUT THE AUTHOR

Ron Brombach has 24 years of experience in the computer field. He has worked in the steel, and industrial automation industries. For the past 19 years, Ron has been at Ford. Ron has been an active member of SAE since 1992. Ron has earned a B.S.E.E. from Oakland University in Rochester, Michigan and a M.S. in Computer Control Systems from Wayne State University in Detroit, Mi. Ron's current assignment is a supervisor in the body module software area and holds three patents. Ron's email is rbrombac@ford.com

REFERENCES

[1] SAE paper 2004-01-1762 ***The Bus Crusher and The Armageddon Device Part I*** March 2004 by Ronald P. Brombach P.E. Ford Motor Company Dearborn, MI

[2] *MISRA –C Guidelines For The Usage Of The C Language In Critical Systems.* Published in October 2004 by MIRA Limited. ISBN 0 9 9524156 4 X PDF

2006-01-1499

Static Memory and Execution Time Analysis of Embedded Code

Christian Ferdinand and Reinhold Heckmann
AbsInt Angewandte Informatik GmbH

ABSTRACT

Failure of a safety-critical application on an embedded processor can lead to severe damage or even loss of life. Here we are concerned with two kinds of failure: stack overflow, which usually leads to run-time errors that are difficult to diagnose, and failure to meet deadlines, which is catastrophical for systems with hard real-time characteristics. Classical validation methods like code review and testing with repeated measurements require a lot of effort, are expensive, and do not really help in proving the absence of such errors. **AbsInt**'s tools **StackAnalyzer** and **aiT** (timing analyzer) provide a solution to this problem. They use abstract interpretation as a formal method that allows to obtain statements valid for all program runs with all inputs.

INTRODUCTION

Failure of a safety-critical embedded system may result in the loss of life or in large damages. Also for non-safety-critical applications, software failure may necessitate expensive updates. Therefore, utmost carefulness and state-of-the-art machinery have to be applied to make sure that an application is working properly. To do so lies in the responsibility of the system designer(s).

Classical software validation methods like code review and testing with debugging are very expensive and cannot really guarantee the absence of errors. Formal verification methods provide an alternative, in particular for safety-critical applications. One such method is *abstract interpretation* [2], which allows to obtain statements that are valid for all program runs with all inputs. Such statements may be absence of violations of timing or space constraints, or absence of runtime errors. For example, stack overflow can be detected by **AbsInt**'s **StackAnalyzer**, and violations of timing constraints are found by **AbsInt**'s **aiT** tool [4] that determines upper bounds for the worst-case execution times of the tasks of an application. Among other things, these tools perform a *value analysis* as the principal source of information about the values manipulated by the analyzed program.

VALUE ANALYSIS

Value analysis tries to determine the values stored in the processor's memory for every program point and execution context. Often, restricting value analysis to the processor registers suffices, but sometimes, it is useful to get information about main memory as well.

Value analysis is a static analysis method producing results valid for every program run and all inputs to the program. Therefore, it cannot always predict an exact value for a memory location, but determines *abstract values* instead that stand for sets of concrete values. More precisely, it computes for each program point and execution context an *abstract state* that maps memory locations to abstract values. Each machine instruction is modeled by a transfer function mapping input states to output states in a way that is compatible with the semantics of the instruction. At control-flow joins, the incoming abstract states are combined into a single outgoing state using a combination function. Because of the presence of loops, transfer and combination functions must be applied repeatedly until the system of abstract states stabilizes. Termination of this fixed-point iteration is ensured on a theoretical level by the monotonicity of transfer and combination functions and the fact that a memory location can only hold finitely many different values. Practically, value analysis becomes only efficient by applying suitable widening and narrowing operators as proposed in [2].

There are several variants of value analysis depending on what kinds of abstract values are used. The simplest form of value analysis is *constant propagation*: an abstract value is either a single concrete value or the statement that no information about the value is known. A more elaborate form of value analysis computes safe lower and upper bounds for the possible concrete values, i.e. abstract values are intervals that are guaranteed to contain the exact values.

All the value analysis variants described above determine sets of possible values for individual memory locations without any relationship between these sets. Yet if an unknown value is moved from register `r1` to `r2`, then both registers contain unknown values afterward, but these values are known to be equal. So a possible extension of value analysis may record known equalities between values, or more generally, upper and lower bounds for their differences, or even more generally, arbitrary linear constraints between values.

Value analysis, even in its simple form as interval analysis, has various applications as an auxiliary method providing input for other analysis tasks. Some of these applications are listed in the next few sections.

STACK USAGE ANALYSIS

A possible cause of catastrophic failure is stack overflow that usually leads to run-time errors that are difficult to diagnose. The problem is that the memory area for the stack usually must be reserved by the programmer. Underestimation of the maximum stack usage leads to stack overflow, while overestimation means wasting memory resources. Measuring the maximum stack usage with a debugger is no solution since one only obtains a result for a single program run with fixed input. Even repeated measurements with various inputs cannot guarantee that the maximum stack usage is ever observed. Some, but not all compilers provide information about stack usage, but this requires the availability of the source code, and the information becomes invalid when the generated code is optimized by hand or by some automatic tool.

AbsInt's tool **StackAnalyzer** provides a solution to this problem: By concentrating on the value of the stack pointer during value analysis, the tool can figure out how the stack increases and decreases along the various control-flow paths. This information can be used to derive the maximum stack usage of the entire application.

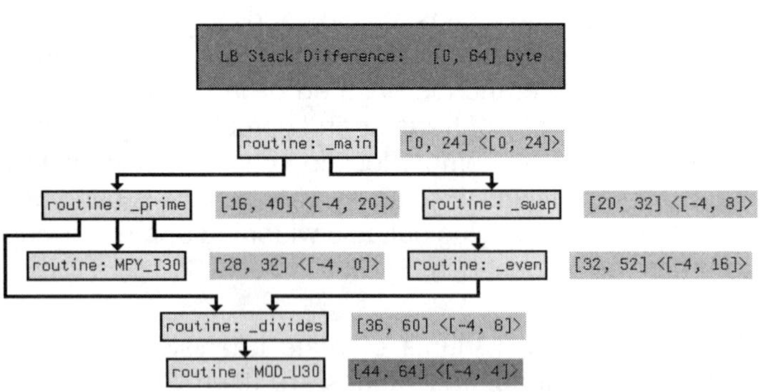

Figure 1: Call graph with stack analysis results

The results of **StackAnalyzer** are presented as annotations in a combined call graph and control-flow graph. Figure 1 shows the call graph of a small application, with stack analysis results at routines and for the entire application (at the top). On this level, the results of stack analysis are displayed in boxes located to the right of the boxes representing the routines of the application. Each result box carries two results: a *global result*, coming first, and a *local result*, following in angular brackets. Each result is an interval of possible stack levels.

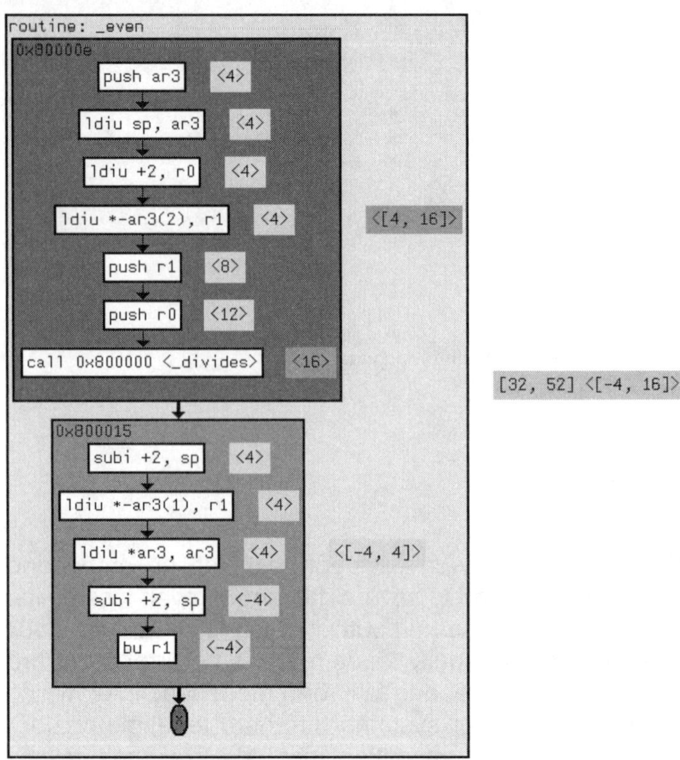

Figure 2: Individual instructions with stack analysis results

The local result at a routine R indicates the stack usage in R considered on its own: It is an interval showing the possible range of stack levels within the routine, assuming value 0 at routine entry. The local result for a routine is derived from the results at individual instructions, which are shown in Figure 2 for one of the routines of this example.

The global result for routine R indicates the stack usage of R in the context of the entire application. It is an interval providing bounds for the stack level while the processor is executing instructions of R, for all call paths from the entry point to R. Thus, the global result at routine R does not include the stack usage of the routines called by R.

The predicted worst-case stack usages of individual tasks in a system can be used in an automated overall stack usage analysis for all tasks running on one Electronic Control Unit, as described in [6] for systems managed by an OSEK/VDX real-time operating system.

WCET ANALYSIS: WORST-CASE EXECUTION TIME PREDICTION

Many tasks in safety-critical embedded systems have hard real-time characteristics. Failure to meet deadlines may be as harmful as producing wrong output or failure to work at all. Yet the determination of the Worst-Case Execution Time (WCET) of a task is a difficult problem because of the characteristics of modern software and hardware [14].

Embedded control software (e.g., in the automotive industries) tends to be large and complex. The software in a single electronic control unit typically has to provide different kinds of functionality. It is usually developed by several people, several groups or even several different providers. Code generator tools are widely used. They usually hide implementation details to the developers and make an understanding of the timing behavior of the code more difficult. The code is typically combined with third party software such as real-time operating systems and/or communication libraries.

Concerning hardware, there is typically a large gap between the cycle times of modern microprocessors and the access times of main memory. Caches and branch target buffers are used to overcome this gap in virtually all performance-oriented processors (including high-performance micro-controllers and DSPs). Pipelines enable acceleration by overlapping the executions of different instructions. Consequently the execution behavior of the instructions cannot be analyzed separately since it depends on the execution history.

Cache memories usually work very well, but under some circumstances minimal changes in the program code or program input may lead to dramatic changes in cache behavior. For (hard) real-time systems, this is undesirable and possibly even hazardous. Making the safe yet – for the most part – unrealistic assumption that all memory references lead to cache misses results in the execution time being overestimated by several hundred percent.

The widely used classical methods of predicting execution times are not generally applicable. Software monitoring and dual-loop benchmark modify the code, which in turn changes the cache behavior. Hardware simulation, emulation, or direct measurement with logic analyzers can only determine the execution time for some fixed inputs. They cannot be used to infer the execution times for all possible inputs in general.

In contrast, abstract interpretation can be used to efficiently compute a safe approximation for all possible cache and pipeline states that can occur at a program point in any program run with any input. These results can be combined with ILP (Integer Linear Programming) techniques to safely predict the worst-case execution time and a corresponding worst-case execution path.

STRUCTURE OF WCET COMPUTATION

AbsInt's WCET tool **aiT** determines the WCET of a program task in several phases [4] (see Figure 3):

- **CFG Building** decodes, i.e. identifies instructions, and reconstructs the control-flow graph (CFG) from a binary program;
- **Value Analysis** computes value ranges for registers and address ranges for instructions accessing memory;

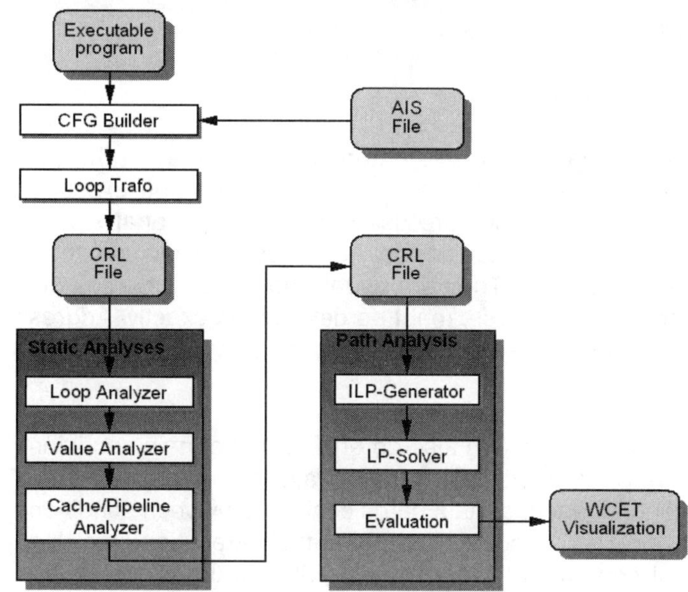

Figure 3: Phases of WCET computation

- **Loop Bound Analysis** determines upper bounds for the number of iterations of simple loops;
- **Cache Analysis** classifies memory references as cache misses or hits [3];
- **Pipeline Analysis** predicts the behavior of the program on the processor pipeline [7];
- **Path Analysis** determines a worst-case execution path of the program [13].

Separating WCET determination into several phases makes it possible to use different methods tailored to the subtasks [13]. Value analysis, cache analysis, and pipeline analysis are done by abstract interpretation [2]. Integer linear programming is used for path analysis.

RECONSTRUCTION OF THE CONTROL FLOW FROM BINARY PROGRAMS

The starting point of our analysis framework (see Figure 3) is a binary program and a so-called *AIS file* containing additional user-provided information about numbers of loop iterations, upper bounds for recursion, etc.

In the first step a parser reads the executable and reconstructs the control flow [11]. This requires some knowledge about the underlying hardware, e.g., which instructions represent branches or calls. The reconstructed control flow is annotated with the information needed by subsequent analyses and then translated into CRL (Control-Flow Representation Language) – a human-readable intermediate format designed to simplify analysis and optimization at the executable/assembly level. This annotated control-flow graph serves as the input for microarchitecture analysis.

VALUE ANALYSIS

Value analysis tries to determine the values in the processor registers for every program point and execution context. Its results are used in loop bound analysis and in cache analysis (possible addresses of indirect memory accesses). They are usually so good that only a few indirect accesses cannot be determined exactly. Address ranges for these accesses may be provided by user annotations.

Value analysis can also determine that certain conditions always evaluate to true or always evaluate to false. As consequence, certain paths controlled by such conditions are never executed. Therefore, their execution time does not contribute to the overall WCET of the program, and need not be determined in the first place.

LOOP BOUND ANALYSIS

WCET analysis requires that upper bounds for the iteration numbers of all loops be known. **aiT** tries to determine the number of loop iterations by *loop bound analysis*, but succeeds in doing so for simple loops only. Bounds for the iteration numbers of the remaining loops must be provided as user annotations.

Loop bound analysis relies on a combination of value analysis and pattern matching, which looks for typical loop patterns. In general, these loop patterns depend on the code generator and/or compiler used to generate the code that is being analyzed. There are special **aiT** versions adapted to various generators and compilers.

CACHE ANALYSIS

Cache analysis classifies the accesses to main memory. The analysis in our tool is based upon [3], which handles analysis of caches with LRU (Least Recently Used) replacement strategy. However, it had to be modified to reflect the non-LRU replacement strategies of common microprocessors: the pseudo-round-robin replacement policy of the ColdFire MCF 5307, and the PLRU (Pseudo-LRU) strategy of the PowerPC MPC 750 and 755. The modified algorithms distinguish between sure cache hits and unclassified accesses. The deviation from perfect LRU is the reason for the reduced predictability of the cache contents in case of ColdFire 5307 and PowerPC 750/755 compared to processors with perfect LRU caches [5].

PIPELINE ANALYSIS

Pipeline analysis models the pipeline behavior to determine execution times for sequential flows (basic blocks) of instructions as done in [9]. It takes into account the current pipeline state(s), in particular resource occupancies, contents of prefetch queues, grouping of instructions, and classification of memory references by cache analysis. The result is an execution time for each basic block in each distinguished execution context.

PATH ANALYSIS

Using the results of the micro-architecture analyses, path analysis determines a safe estimate of the WCET. The program's control flow is modeled by an integer linear program [13, 12] so that the solution to the objective function is the predicted worst-case execution time for the input program. A special mapping of variable names to basic blocks in the integer linear program enables execution and traversal counts for every basic block and edge to be computed.

ANALYSIS OF LOOPS AND RECURSIVE PROCEDURES

Loops and recursive procedures are of special interest since programs spend most of their runtime there. Treating them naively when analyzing programs for their cache and pipeline behavior results in a high loss of precision.

Frequently the first execution of the loop body loads the cache, and subsequent executions find most of their referenced memory blocks in the cache. Because of speculative prefetching, cache contents may still change considerably during the second iteration. Therefore, the first few iterations of the loop often encounter cache contents quite different from those of later iterations. Hence it is useful to distinguish the first few iterations of loops from the others. This is done in the VIVU approach (virtual inlining, virtual unrolling) [8].

USAGE OF aiT

The techniques described above have been incorporated into **AbsInt**'s **aiT** WCET analyzer tools. They get as input an executable, user annotations, a description of the (external) memories and buses (i.e. a list of memory areas with minimal and maximal access times), and a task (identified by a start address). A task denotes a sequentially executed piece of code (no threads, no parallelism, and no waiting for external events). This should not be confused with a task in an operating system that might include code for synchronization or communication.

The WCET analyzers compute an upper bound of the runtime of the task (assuming no interference from the outside). Effects of interrupts, IO and timer (co-)processors are not reflected in the predicted runtime and have to be considered separately (e.g., by a quantitative analysis).

The task WCETs predicted by **aiT** can be used to determine an appropriate scheduling scheme for the tasks and to perform an overall schedulability analysis in order to guarantee that the application meets all timing constraints (also called *timing validation*) [10]. Some real-time operating systems offer tools for schedulability analysis, but all these tools require the WCETs of tasks as input.

VISUALIZATION OF aiT'S RESULTS

In addition to the raw information about the WCET, several aspects can be visualized by the **aiSee** tool [1] to view detailed information delivered by the analysis.

Worst Case Execution Time: 2389 cycles = 53.089 us

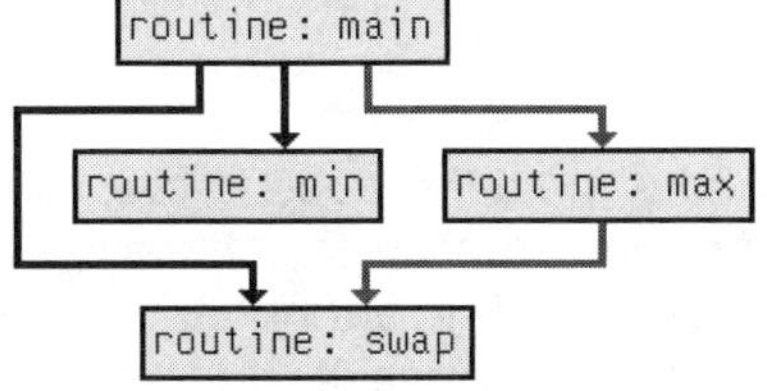

Figure 4: Call graph with WCET results

Figure 4 shows the graphical representation of the call graph for some small example. The calls (edges) that contribute to the worst-case runtime are marked by the color red. The computed WCET is given in CPU cycles and in microseconds provided that the cycle time of the processor has been specified.

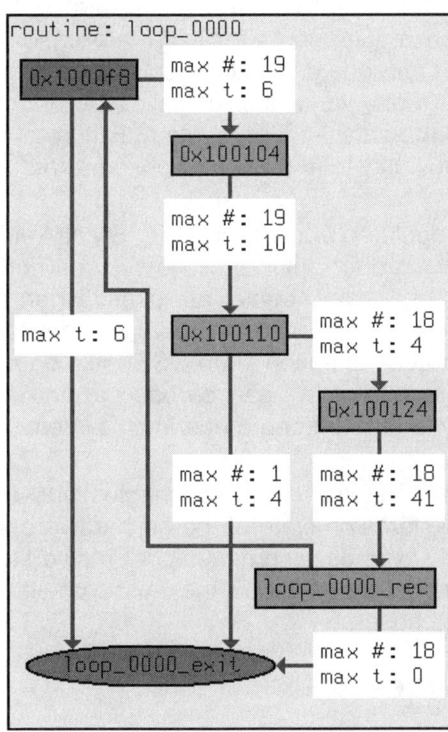

Figure 5: Basic block graph in a loop, with timing information

Figure 5 shows the basic block graph of a loop. The number `max #` describes the maximal number of traversals of an edge in the worst case, while `max t` describes the maximal execution time of the basic block from which the edge originates (taking into account that the basic block is left via the edge). The worst-case path, the iteration numbers and timings are determined automatically by **aiT**.

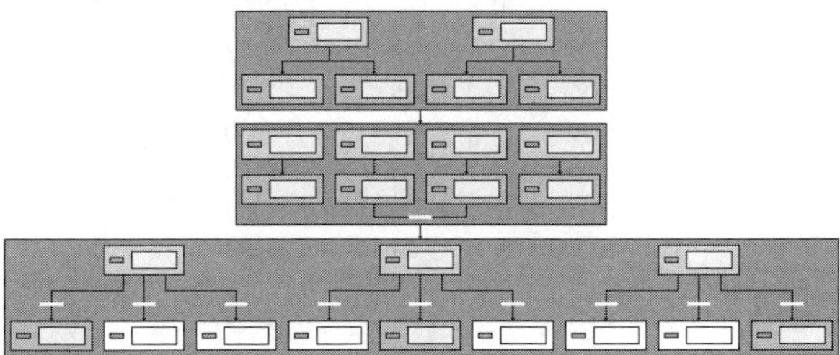

Figure 6: Possible pipeline states in a basic block

Figure 6 shows the possible pipeline states for a basic block in this example. Such pictures are shown by **aiT** upon special demand. The large dark grey boxes correspond to the instructions of the basic block, and the smaller rectangles in them stand for individual pipeline states. Their cyclewise evolution is indicated by the strokes connecting them. Each layer in the trees corresponds to one CPU cycle. Branches in the trees are caused by conditions that could not be statically evaluated, e.g., a memory access with unknown address in presence of memory areas with different access times. On the other hand, two pipeline states fall together when details they differ in leave the pipeline. This happened for instance at the end of the second instruction, reducing the number of states from four to three.

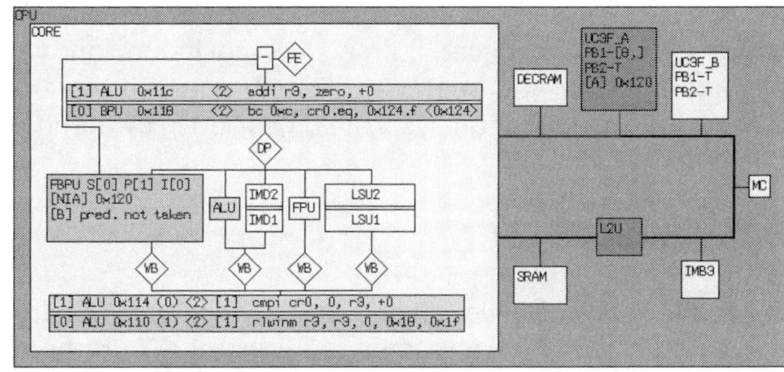

Figure 7: Individual pipeline state

Figure 7 shows part of the top left pipeline state from Figure 6 in greater magnification. It displays a diagram of the architecture of the CPU (in this case a PowerPC 555) showing the occupancy of the various pipeline stages with the instructions currently being executed.

DEPENDENCE ON TARGET ARCHITECTURES

There are **aiT** versions for PowerPC MPC 555, 565, and 755, ColdFire 5307, ARM7 TDMI, HCS12/STAR12, TMS320C33, C166/ST10, Renesas M32C/85 (prototype), and Tricore 1.3 (under construction).

Decoders are automatically generated from processor specifications defining instruction formats and operand meaning. The CRL format used for describing control-flow graphs is machine-independent. *Value Analysis* must

Example		from external RAM			from flash		
Program	Size	measured cycles	predicted cycles	over-estimation	measured cycles	predicted cycles	over-estimation
fac	2.9k	949	960	1.16 %	810	832	2.72 %
fibo	3.4k	2368	2498	5.49 %	2142	2228	4.01 %
coverc1	16k	5670	5672	0.04 %	3866	4104	6.16 %
coverc	4.3k	7279	7281	0.03 %	5820	6202	6.56 %
morswi	5.9k	17327	17332	0.03 %	8338	8350	0.14 %
coverc2	24k	18031	18178	0.82 %	12948	14054	8.54 %
swi	24k	18142	18272	0.72 %	13330	14640	9.83 %
edn	13k	262999	267643	1.77 %	239662	241864	0.92 %

Table 1: Precision of **aiT** for some C166 programs

interpret the operations of the target processor. Hence, there is a separate value analyzer for each target, but features shared by many processors (e.g., branches based on condition bits) allowed for considerable code sharing among the various value analyzers.

There is only one cache analyzer with a fixed interface to pipeline analysis. It is parameterized on cache size, line size, associativity, and replacement strategy. Each replacement strategy supported by **aiT** is implemented by a table for line age updates that is interpreted by the cache analyzer.

The pipeline analyzers are the most diverse part of **aiT**. The supported target architectures are grouped according to the complexity of the processor pipeline. For each group a common conceptual and coding framework for pipeline analysis has been established, in which the actual target-dependent analysis must be filled in by manual coding.

PRECISION OF aiT

Since the real WCET is not known for typical real-life applications, statements about the precision of **aiT** are hard to obtain. For an automotive application running on MPC 555, one of **AbsInt**'s customers has observed an overestimation of 5–10% when comparing **aiT**'s results and the highest execution times observed in a series of measurements (which may have missed the real WCET). For an avionics application running on MPC 755, Airbus has noted that **aiT**'s WCET for a task typically is about 25% higher than some measured execution times for the same task, the real but non-calculable WCET being in between. Measurements at **AbsInt** have indicated overestimations ranging from 0% (cycle-exact prediction) till 10% for a set of small programs running on M32C, TMS320C33, and C166/ST10. Table 1 shows the results for C166. The analysis times were moderate – a few seconds till about 3 minutes for edn.

CONCLUSION

Tools based on abstract interpretation can perform static program analysis of embedded applications. Their results are determined without the need to change the code and hold for all program runs with arbitrary inputs. Employing static analyzers is thus orthogonal to classical testing, which yields very precise results, but only for selected program runs with specific inputs.

aiT allows to inspect the timing behavior of (time-critical parts of) program tasks. It takes into account the combination of all the different hardware characteristics while still obtaining tight upper bounds for the WCET of a given program in reasonable time. **StackAnalyzer** and **aiT** are used among others by Airbus in the development of various safety-critical applications for the A380. They will be used as verification tools in the sense of DO178b. The qualification requirements for such verification tools are lighter than for code generation tools. In contrast to code generation tools, verification tools cannot introduce any errors into the safety-critical system. Failure of a verification tool may only lead to an overlooked error.

In a less regulated application area, **StackAnalyzer** and **aiT** can be used for optimizing the system. For instance, the results of **StackAnalyzer** are useful when optimizing the assignment of priorities to tasks in order to minimize the memory consumption in an OSEK-like operating system. The results of **aiT** can be used to find an optimal schedule in a time-triggered operating system.

The usage of static analyzers enables one to develop complex systems on state-of-the-art hardware, increases safety, and saves development time. Precise stack usage and timing predictions enable the most cost-efficient hardware to be chosen.

REFERENCES

[1] AbsInt Angewandte Informatik GmbH. *aiSee Home Page*. http://www.aisee.com.

[2] Patrick Cousot and Radhia Cousot. Abstract Interpretation: A Unified Lattice Model for Static Analysis of Programs by Construction or Approximation of Fixpoints. In *Proceedings of the 4th ACM Symposium on Principles of Programming Languages*, Los Angeles, California, 1977.

[3] Christian Ferdinand. *Cache Behavior Prediction for Real-Time Systems.* PhD thesis, Saarland University, 1997.

[4] Christian Ferdinand, Reinhold Heckmann, Marc Langenbach, Florian Martin, Michael Schmidt, Henrik Theiling, Stephan Thesing, and Reinhard Wilhelm. Reliable and precise WCET determination for a real-life processor. In *Proceedings of EMSOFT 2001, First Workshop on Embedded Software*, volume 2211 of *Lecture Notes in Computer Science*, pages 469–485. Springer-Verlag, 2001.

[5] Reinhold Heckmann, Marc Langenbach, Stephan Thesing, and Reinhard Wilhelm. The influence of processor architecture on the design and the results of WCET tools. *Proceedings of the IEEE*, 91(7):1038–1054, July 2003. Special Issue on Real-Time Systems.

[6] Winfried Janz. Das OSEK Echtzeitbetriebssystem, Stackverwaltung und statische Stackbedarfsanalyse. In *Embedded World*, Nuremberg, Germany, February 2003.

[7] Marc Langenbach, Stephan Thesing, and Reinhold Heckmann. Pipeline modeling for timing analysis. In *Proceedings of the 9th International Static Analysis Symposium SAS 2002*, volume 2477 of *Lecture Notes in Computer Science*, pages 294–309. Springer-Verlag, 2002.

[8] Florian Martin, Martin Alt, Reinhard Wilhelm, and Christian Ferdinand. Analysis of Loops. In Kai Koskimies, editor, *Proceedings of the International Conference on Compiler Construction (CC'98)*, volume 1383 of *Lecture Notes in Computer Science*, pages 80–94. Springer-Verlag, March /April 1998.

[9] Jörn Schneider and Christian Ferdinand. Pipeline Behavior Prediction for Superscalar Processors by Abstract Interpretation. In *Proceedings of the ACM SIGPLAN Workshop on Languages, Compilers and Tools for Embedded Systems*, volume 34, pages 35–44, May 1999.

[10] John A. Stankovic. *Real-Time and Embedded Systems.* ACM 50th Anniversary Report on Real-Time Computing Research, 1996. http://www-ccs.cs.umass.edu/sdcr/rt.ps.

[11] Henrik Theiling. Extracting Safe and Precise Control Flow from Binaries. In *Proceedings of the 7th Conference on Real-Time Computing Systems and Applications*, Cheju Island, South Korea, 2000.

[12] Henrik Theiling. ILP-based interprocedural path analysis. In Alberto L. Sangiovanni-Vincentelli and Joseph Sifakis, editors, *Proceedings of EMSOFT 2002, Second International Conference on Embedded Software*, volume 2491 of *Lecture Notes in Computer Science*, pages 349–363. Springer-Verlag, 2002.

[13] Henrik Theiling and Christian Ferdinand. Combining abstract interpretation and ILP for microarchitecture modelling and program path analysis. In *Proceedings of the 19th IEEE Real-Time Systems Symposium*, pages 144–153, Madrid, Spain, December 1998.

[14] Reinhard Wilhelm. Determining bounds on execution times. In R. Zurawski, editor, *Handbook on Embedded Systems*, pages 14-1 – 14-23. CRC Press, 2005.

CONTACT

Reinhold Heckmann
Christian Ferdinand

AbsInt Angewandte Informatik GmbH
Science Park 1
D-66123 Saarbrücken
Germany

Phone: +49-681-38360-0
Fax: +49-681-38360-20
e-mail: info@absint.com
Web: `http://www.absint.com`

2006-01-1331

Verification and Validation Methods for TDMA Based "by Wire" Systems

Daniel R. Barbour, Samuel R. Jarrell, II and Phillip R. Ward
CertTech, L.L.C.

ABSTRACT

This paper addresses techniques and tools used for verification and validation (V&V) of safety critical systems that utilize Time Division Multiple Access (TDMA) bus technology to communicate between subsystems. Presentation of an example solution for safety critical systems and software will include descriptions for use of the solution at multiple stages of product development. Stages include:

- Software or model verification and validation
- Prototype evaluation
- Hardware and software integration
- System testing
- Software regression testing
- Data collection during stress, exploratory, or field testing

In the process of implementing the above V&V process goals, we found it was necessary to create simulations of certain software subsystems. These simulations allowed for the implementation of V&V strategies prior to the actual completion of the system software itself. Substituting a test resource for one or more elements on the bus solves two problems. These bus based simulations relieve some project schedule dependencies and allow testing of subsystem elements prior to the availability of the other system elements on the TDMA bus. The simulations also allow injection of data that is typically impossible to evoke from a properly functioning subsystem element. These simulations are sometimes a simplification of the real subsystem they represent but are still extremely useful because they allow the bus to function exactly as it would in the target system and allow total control of the data consumed by the subsystem under test.

The solution is scalable from a single computer deployment to a distributed system that allows significant abstraction in defining tests, scenarios, or exploratory algorithms and flexibility in software and hardware implementation of the abstractions. Flexibility in integrating with other technologies is achieved through coupling to a scripting environment that supports controlling other physical or electronic stimuli and collecting data from instrumentation.

INTRODUCTION

In 2002, CertTech, L.L.C. began working with an avionics manufacturer to provide Validation and Verification (V&V) support for a new "glass cockpit" avionics system to be installed in Business and Regional aircraft. The avionics system design incorporated a dual-redundant TDMA data bus based on the TTP™/C Time Triggered Communications protocol [1] to transport both Safety Critical and non-Safety Critical data between avionics subsystems.

This paper focuses primarily on the tools and methods CertTech developed to demonstrate that each avionics subsystem conformed to its requirements within the TTP™/C bus environment. While the activities described in this paper specifically pertain to the TTP™/C data bus, the tool concepts and the methods utilized during testing are considered broadly applicable to any system utilizing a TDMA-based data bus architecture.

Not covered by this paper is any discussion pertaining to validation activities for proving either the correctness of the TTP™/C protocols or its advantages for use in satisfying the safety critical requirements of the system. These areas were not part of CertTech's scope of work for the avionics manufacturer. The tools and methods CertTech developed were compliant with the FAA recognized verification standard for airborne systems. The DO-178B is an industry standard developed by the RTCA organization. This standard addresses verification of the requirements. The validity of the safety related elements of the requirements are addressed in a separate and independent safety assessment. Numerous papers already cover those topics in depth.

CHALLENGES

While the majority of CertTech's staff had many years of experience in verifying federated avionics systems that were interconnected via ARINC 429 data interfaces, and some staff also had experience in testing Boeing 777 avionics utilizing the ARINC 629 data bus, no CertTech staff had any prior experience with the TTP™/C architecture or its protocols. In addition, the customer's project presented some interesting challenges:

Lack of Commercial Tools

No commercial tools (hardware or software) existed to monitor data messages on the bus *in the manner the avionics manufacturer planned to encode the data*. The customer's implementation included additional data content to achieve desired data integrity assurance. Correspondingly, no tools existed to inject properly formatted data messages on the bus in place of an absent bus member.

Staggered Avionics Subsystem Development Cycle

At the time the project began, no avionics subsystem had yet been developed to use the TTP™/C data bus, and each of the subsystems was going to be developed by different teams with subsystem deployment activities occurring over a 24+ month period. This staggered cycle required methods to test each subsystem on the data bus anywhere from a standalone basis (with no other avionics subsystems attached) up to a complete (whole) avionics system.

Evolving System Data Bus Message Definitions

When CertTech began working with the avionics manufacturer, only a limited set of the data bus messages had been defined. The number, type, and complexity of the data messages were expected to increase significantly over the course of the system/subsystem development period. Additionally, some discussions with the system and software engineering team members hinted at the possibility of introducing encapsulated message-streaming protocols between subsystems at a later stage in the project development (or as part of future system upgrades). This reality prompted the need for a highly flexible tool set that could be adapted in response to the changing needs of the project.

Constraints Imposed on the Electrical Bus Loads

Test resources connected to the data bus were required to impose the same loading characteristics as the "real" avionics subsystems to ensure that the presence of the test resources did not mitigate (or exacerbate) the response of an any attached avionics subsystem during Radio Frequency Susceptibility (Radiated and Conducted) testing (per DO-160D Section 20) as well as Lightning Induced Transient Susceptibility testing (per DO-160D Section 22) [2].

Capabilities Required for Verifying Safety Critical Attributes

Verification of the Safety Critical aspects of the system software required the ability to (1) inject erroneous or out-of-range data, (2) independently inject differing data values for each message instance supplying the same information on the redundant data busses, (3) selectively disable either (or both) of the redundant data bus channels, and (4) monitor for, and log, the occurrence of any bus protocol errors during system operation.

Support for Automated Test Execution

In order to support automated system requirements testing, as well as regression testing following system software changes, the tools needed the ability to be configured and controlled in a test script execution environment.

TEST TOOL DEVELOPMENT STRATEGY

Early discussions with the customer exposed the fact that while various groups at the customer's site had expressed needs for TTP™ test "capabilities" being available to support their activities "at some future time," no two groups shared a common vision of the capabilities such tool(s) should support. Furthermore, due to the staggered development cycle, some groups had yet to be fully formed and had, therefore, a very limited understanding of both "TTP™" per se, of the manner in which their implementation was expected to differ from that defined by TTTech for a standard TTP™ implementation, and of the capabilities they would require from supporting test tools.

To avoid a later contentious relationship with one or more groups at the vendor's site (after the tools were considered "complete" by the majority of users), CertTech deemed it prudent to approach the TTP™ custom tool development as if it were an internal subsystem development project. This entailed collecting as much input from the various user groups as possible and then developing a detailed Tool Requirements Document. The document was then distributed for review to the same user groups to clarify misunderstandings, obtain customer buy-in, and (ultimately) to establish a clearly defined basis for bounding the customer's expectations.

Note: New tool users invariably wanted additional tool features that were not explicitly described in the original requirements document. The flexibility incorporated into the tool's design permitted accommodating the majority of those requests.

CUSTOM DATA BUS TOOLS – Overview

Implementation of the Tool Requirements resulted in the development of a custom TTP™ data bus test resource panel and numerous software applications to accomplish the system requirements verification objectives. These tools incorporated the following attributes or capabilities:

Multi-node TTP™ Test Resource Panel

Each TTP™ Test Resource Panel incorporated a Motorola PowerPC-based processor, independent power supplies (AC and DC operation supported for Bench and Flight Testing), and up to three TTP™ bus nodes (i.e., circuitry required to connect to a TTP™ data bus). Also included was a 100 Mbps Ethernet Interface for attachment to a Test Control Computer or Simulation platform (see Figure 1)

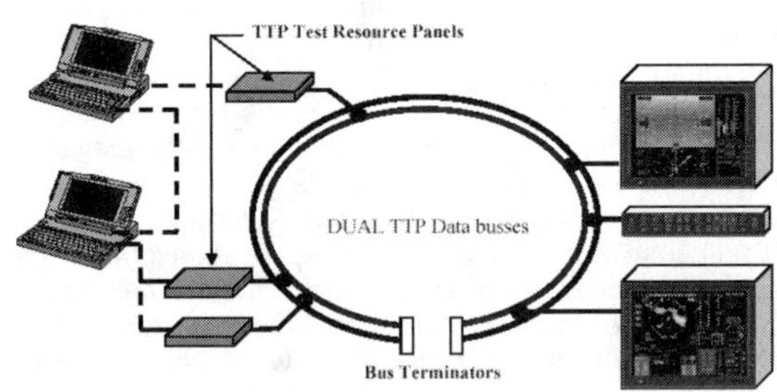

Figure 1. – Example TTP™ Test Resource Panel Utilization

[A three nodes per panel design was selected to support a potential future Triple-Redundant data bus network, but each node could also be used independently in accordance with information supplied by a selected test configuration file.]

To maintain consistent electrical characteristics (i.e., "look like" another avionics subsystem on the bus from an electrical perspective), the <u>same</u> interface circuit design used by the avionics subsystems was incorporated into the TTP™ Test Resource Panel. (The interface circuitry utilized TTTech's AS8202NF TTP™

Communication Controller [3] with custom bus driver circuitry to support the desired bus length, system loads, and DO-160D RF and Lightning Transient Susceptibility protection goals.)

CUSTOM TTP™ Software Test Applications

TTP™ Data Bus Monitor Application – The capability to (only) observe the data messages being transmitted by any (or all) avionics subsystems in real-time was provided via a custom bus monitor application that would run on a PC or laptop. This application was indirectly coupled to the data bus via the Ethernet interface incorporated into the TTP Test Resource Panels. It parsed the raw data messages (encoded per the customer's definitions) into a presentation format (in appropriate engineering units) suitable for use by System Engineers, Software Developers, and Flight Test Engineers. The application also supported time-tagging and logging all "raw" data bus message traffic for later analysis or playback.

TTP™ Data Simulation of Avionics Subsystems - A generic/configurable TTP™ data message simulator was developed to support the data bus I/O emulation of any avionics subsystem for which hardware was still under development. The simulator was designed to be distributable across multiple PC's, and each simulator instance could be interfaced to the bus via one or more selected nodes in a designated TTP™ Test Resource Panel. Multiple simulations could therefore be launched at a time, with each simulation independently configured to represent the data traffic provided by a different avionics subsystem with its unique data I/O characteristics.

In addition to coupling the simulation applications to the physical bus via the TTP™ Test Resource Panel's Ethernet interface, the data I/O design for the simulators was abstracted and isolated via a Data Bus Server application that facilitated coupling the simulators to an internal "virtual" data bus. This capability supported early software integration testing of avionics subsystem software in a pure software environment (i.e., without first loading the avionics software in a physical device or subsystem and then connecting that subsystem to a physical bus).

Like the TTP™ Data Bus Monitor tool, each simulator could also be configured to log data; however, (unlike the TTP™ Data Bus Monitor application) the logged data was limited to the data applicable to the avionics subsystem *"that"* simulator instance was emulating.

Support for Interactive Behavioral Emulation – As noted previously, a "generic" data simulator application was designed that could be instantiated multiple times with each instance independently configured to operate in place of a different avionics subsystem. This approach was satisfactory for replacing subsystems that did not interact with other subsystems (i.e., where the data transmitted by the simulated subsystem was *not* dependent upon dynamic bus data received from a "real" avionics subsystem).

Custom simulation applications could have been built using the same base simulator design to support complex behaviors. However, the need for such simulations was never actualized, and the generic design proved sufficient to accomplish the verification objectives placed before CertTech.

It was found, however, that the capability for supporting the simple *echoing* of data values was useful for integration and development testing in some cases. One example of such a case was during the emulation of a radio transceiver subsystem whereby the transceiver subsystem normally reported its current frequency setting (among other data) and a separate controller subsystem would command new frequency settings based on pilot control inputs. A "real" transceiver would change its reported frequency to match a controller-specified command value (if operating properly). By incorporating a configurable "echo-pair" behavior in the generic simulator design, it was possible to have the radio transceiver simulation automatically respond with a new tuned value upon receipt of a tune command, or to disable the echoing in order to behave as if the communication link were broken and thereby verify the error handling operations of the controlling software. This capability was utilized in multiple instances for several different subsystems.

The provision for "echo-pair" strategy behavior in the simulator design was useful for exercising Human-Machine Interface (HMI) software in a "real" controller subsystem and have it appear that the controlled device was attached to the data bus when, in fact, it was replaced by a suitably configured simulation.

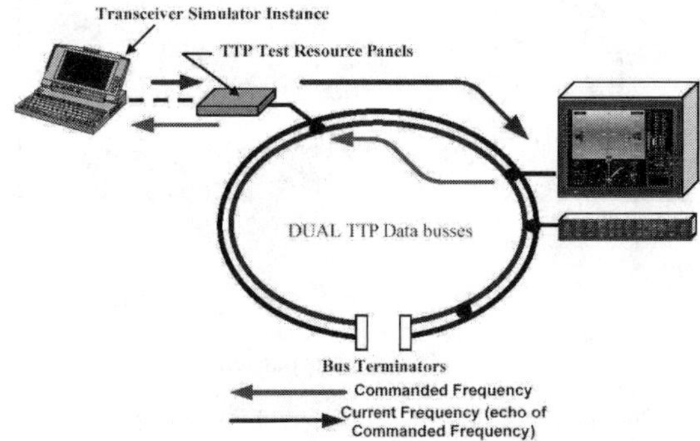

Figure 2. – Demonstration of Echo-Pair Behavior usage

INHERENT SUBSYSTEM DESIGN SUPPORT FOR TESTING

The previous sections addressed CertTech's response to the lack of applicable tools for monitoring and/or injecting messages transported on the TTP™ data bus. However, the ability to verify that an avionics subsystem transmits the "correct" data messages requires control of the source data from which the subsystem derives or creates the data bus messages. Verifying that an avionics subsystem correctly receives all applicable data messages is also necessary and is not always a trivial task, especially when observations and control of a subsystem under test are limited to physical subsystem I/O (black-box) boundaries.

The ability to accomplish the avionics system verification activities (including the verification of correct data bus I/O processing) was greatly facilitated through the inclusion (by design) of low-level data monitoring and control capabilities within the software installed in the avionics subsystems. This capability not only aided in the testing of software used for encoding and decoding data bus messages but also greatly supported systems requirement verification and allowed testing elements of the software in isolated stages as noted below:

Verifying Correct Data Propagation - For "existing" avionics subsystems (e.g. subsystems for which the design activities have been completed and units have been built) verifying correct message transmission can be accomplished by supplying known test signals at the sensor interfaces of the subsystems. For instance, a data concentrator unit that couples to engine sensors (engine temperature, engine rotational speed, fuel flow, fuel level, switch states, etc..) and subsequently publishes the sensor values on the data bus can be verified by attaching an appropriate mix of thermocouple or Resistance Temperature Device (RTD) stimulus sources, waveform signal generators, switches, and other test stimuli as needed.

By applying a sequence of controlled resistance values to an RTD input – the signal chain between the sensor and the data bus (including the sensor's Analog to Digital conversion (ADC), resistance to temperature conversion algorithms, and data message encoding software) can be verified by observing the resulting temperature values that are reported on the data bus.

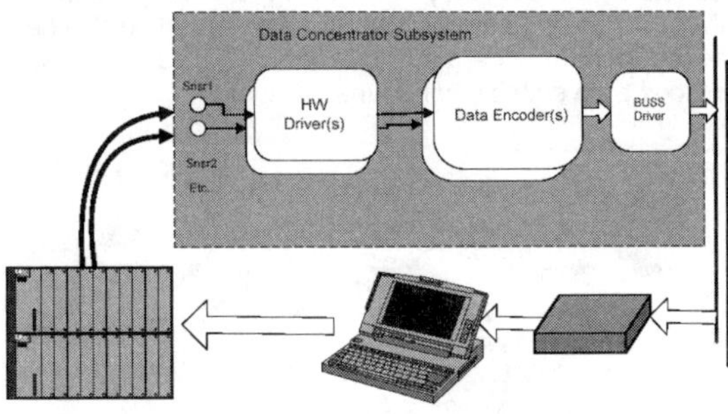

Figure 3. – Testing the Input Data Conversion Chain (Classical approach)

This approach, however, requires the subsystem under test to be "built" and the physical inputs stimulated appropriately before the data chain can be tested. If a deviation from expected values "is" observed, a non-trivial amount of effort may need to be expended to isolate the source of the discrepancy (Is the problem in the Test Stimulus?, Electronics? HW Driver? Data Encoder? All of the above?)

The built-in test support for directly observing and controlling data *internal* to each subsystem facilitated testing data bus message encoding without simultaneously stimulating the physical sensor inputs is represented in Figure 4..

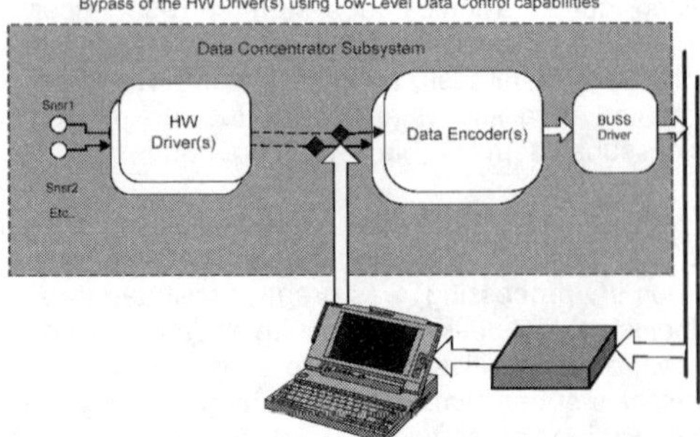

Figure 4. – Testing the Data Encoder(s) in isolation

In combination with the ability to monitor the low-level data in any subsystem, the correct propagation of data across the system as a whole, as well as the operations performed upon that data during, could be easily verified by simply moving the test observation points throughout the system.

Bypass of the HW Driver(s) using Low-Level Data Control capabilities

Correct End-to-End Decoding Directly Confirmed using Low Level Data Monitoring

Figure 5. – End-to-End Data Flow Testing

Likewise, testing of sensor electronics and HW Drivers was simplified by decoupling the data bus (and the rest of the data chain) from the data flow path:

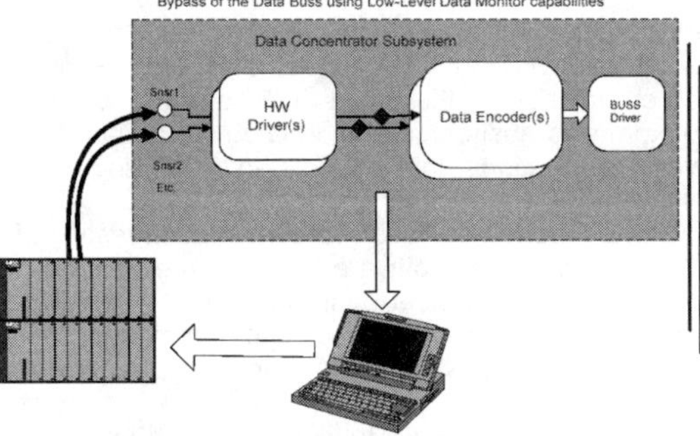

Figure 6. – Sensor Circuitry Verified in Isolation

Virtual System Environment Testing

The previous paragraphs outlined test methodologies that were applied with avionics subsystems "in-the-loop" and that took advantage of built-in test capabilities provided by the subsystem software. However, due to the staggered development cycles, the software development teams for the subsystems were frequently waiting on hardware design and fabrication to be completed to exercise their software with other subsystem in-the-loop in an integrated fashion.

This lack of subsystem hardware also stymied the prove-in of system test scripts that were written against system and subsystem requirements in parallel with the software development activities.

A solution that would accommodate the needs of both the software developers and test script developers early in the development cycle was deemed to be highly desirable by the customer. Even a low-fidelity emulation of the system was viewed as beneficial, as long as the time-sequential nature of the data interactions was maintained. That is, in exchange for earlier integration of the software and test scripts, the users were willing to trade the time deterministic attributes of the system and reserve verification of the system's time determinism for a later phase in the project when all of the subsystem hardware became available.

The approach taken was to model the bus' full TDMA cluster-cycle data in shared memory and then adapt the existing software to read/write the bus data via the shared memory space, as shown in Figure 7:

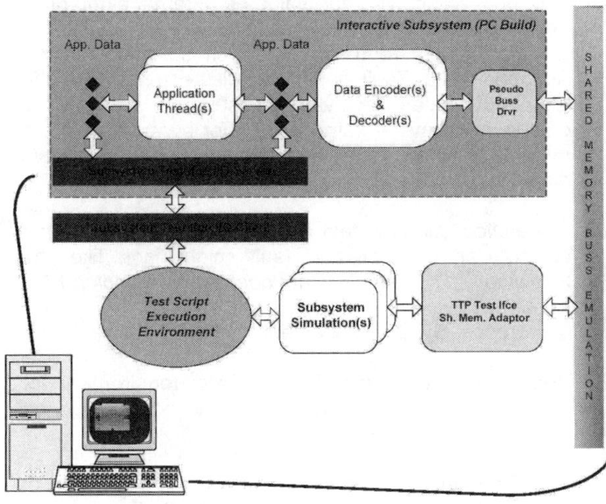

Figure 7. –Application Testing in a Virtual System Environment (with Simulations)

The adaptations to the software for both the subsystem code and the test tools proved to be relatively minor in nature since the software designs for each were based on a layered architecture. The subsystem software modifications were effectively limited to the Bus Driver module while the Test Tool modifications were limited to the driver used for interfacing the tools to the TTP™ Test Resource Panel.

From the perspective of the test script execution environment, the system appeared no different when operated in either the virtual environment or with "real" avionics subsystems attached to the data bus. Both teams (application developers and test script developers) benefited immensely from these changes by allowing the earlier testing and debugging of the subsystem software by the software developers (at their desks) and earlier prove-in of the system test scripts.

A follow-on advantage of this approach was that it permitted a portion of the test script development and prove-in to be delegated to off-site test teams where full integration test benches were not available.

As noted previously, however, this approach provided only a low-fidelity emulation of the normal TDMA bus driven data interactions. Migration of subsystem software (that would later run on dedicated embedded processors) to a Microsoft Windows™ PC environment resulted in longer process execution cycles and unpredictable data update times. For the types of software being tested (data encoders/decoders, status displays, user interfaces, and control panels) these side effects were not critical. Testing applications that depended upon precise timing of data updates (such as control algorithms for an aircraft autopilot system, or adaptive speed control in an automotive environment) would require an alternative test solution or wait upon the availability of the target hardware.

"Mixed" System Environment Testing

One of the alternative test solutions used for early testing of the aircraft flight control software was to migrate the software to run in one of the TTP™ Test Resource Panels. As noted in the paragraph titled "**Multi-node TTP™ Test Resource Panel,"** the panels used a Motorola PowerPC processor. In fact, the processor card selected for use in the Test Resource Panel was intentionally chosen by the development team to be a processor card that was designed and built for use in one of the avionics subsystems.

The rationale for using one of the avionics processor cards, though more costly than a Commercial Off The Shelf (COTS) option, was that any Test Resource Panel could potentially be used as a host-platform for avionics software while waiting on the avionics subsystem hardware to be completed. For flight control software, which only interacted with the external environment via the data bus interfaces included in the test resource panels, this flexibility proved to be beneficial.

Testing of the flight control software evolved throughout its development. Initially, a mixed simulation plus hosted-code environment was used wherein external aircraft flight model simulation algorithms were used to supply the aircraft's speed and body orientation data that was interfaced to the data bus via one (or more) Test Resource Panel(s), and the flight control software was hosted in the processor card of a separate Test Resource Panel. During later developmental stages, the flight control software was executed in the processor card of its own avionics subsystem, actual digital servos used for flight surface control were also included on the data bus while the aircraft flight model simulation algorithms continued to provide the environmental data. Once sufficient confidence was obtained by testing in the latter environment, actual performance of the flight control software was evaluated on a test aircraft with data collection performed, in part, by the TTP™ Data Bus Monitor Application.

LATENCY LIMITATIONS WHEN USING SUBSYSTEM SIMULATIONS

As noted in the previous section, system test activities for the avionics system still included actual flight testing. While the simulation of avionics systems on the data bus were highly beneficial and permitted meeting the software testing objectives for each of the avionics subsystems, they still have different timing behavior than the "real" avionics subsystems. In general, the simulations were slower to respond to data written to the bus than the actual avionics subsystems. For the test environment developed by CertTech, several sources contributed to this fact:

(1) The simulation applications are indirectly coupled to the data bus via the TTP™ Test Resource Panel(s) via an Ethernet link. The communication layer between the simulators and monitor applications (running on

Microsoft Windows PC platforms) and the data bus activity incurred an observed latency on the order of 80 to 120 m/sec. This was down from an original 500-600 m/sec latency after tuning the TCPIP layer for small packets by disabling the Nagle algorithm. While some additional improvements on this could have been made, this latency was deemed acceptable to meeting the required test objectives at the time.

(2) The simulation applications were built to run in a Microsoft Windows environment for ease of use and portability to the desktop PC systems used by the System and Software engineering team members. Due to resource sharing activities performed by the Windows OS, the simulator timing event activities incurred an additional variability that typically fell within a range of +/- 25 mSec but that could exceed these values under high PC load conditions.

[Note: during formal testing activities the PC systems were decoupled from the company intranet, and all applications unrelated to the test activities (such as email, virus protection, background "messenger" services, scheduled software update checks, etc.) were terminated.]

A closer match between the performance of the simulation environment and that of the avionics subsystems they emulated could have been achieved by migrating the simulations to run on the PowerPC processor of the Test Resource Panels. However, such an approach would still not have eliminated the need to perform field testing with the actual subsystems. Since the required software testing objectives were being satisfied, this alternative approach was not pursued.

DOMAIN-CENTRIC TEST SCRIPT DEVELOPMENT TOOLS

In the aviation environment, system requirements must be traceable to their applicable verification tests, and the test procedures themselves must be documented with details defining their purpose, test setup, and input values to be applied to satisfy required software coverage objectives and the pass/fail criteria for each of the input data sets [4].

For safety-critical aviation software (Levels A and B), the procedures must be independently developed; for Level A software the procedures must also be independently reviewed for correctness. In order to facilitate this independent review objective, and also support the creation of executable test procedures by domain-knowledgeable staff (who, many times, are not test programmers), CertTech developed custom test scripting tools for the client.

These tools permitted system engineers and/or test staff to *directly* define the executable test procedures using high level language constructs. It was not necessary for test staff (or system engineers) to first create detailed test procedures for later implementation in a test language because the scripting tools, themselves, automatically created descriptive document files from the executable procedures. The output documents were readily reviewable by independent staff familiar with the requirements. Furthermore, following execution of the test procedures, the test result files could also be directly converted to English-sentence formatted report documents with the results directly traceable to the applicable System Requirement(s).

A simplified example of this approach is outlined below:

Let us suppose that an avionics subsystem is replicated on the bus network and each replicate (SysA_1; SysA_2) provides Air Speed data (data range of 35.0 – 200.0 m/Sec) on each of the redundant data buses in the system as indicated below:

- **SysA_1:Bus_A:Airspeed**;
- **SysA_1:Bus_B:Airspeed**;
- **SysA_2:Bus_A:Airspeed**,
- **SysA_2:Bus_B:Airspeed**

The above data is consumed by a second avionics subsystem (SysB: the system under test), which performs a verification cross-check on the Airspeed data prior to applying the values to internal algorithms. For the sake of this discussion, we will define an *artificial* system requirement, which specifies that an Airspeed Data Fault condition will be reported if the Airspeed values received on separate buses (but originating from the same unit) differ by more than 0.1 m/sec and when values originating from separate units differ by more than 0.5 m/sec for any bus.

A detailed manual test procedure for verifying the correct reporting of this fault might look like the following: *(this example is not necessarily complete)*

"Reference: SysB Requirement XXX

Verify that the Airspeed Data Fault requirement for SysB is correctly implemented by performing the following tests:

Test Boundary Conditions: Tests will be performed at the edges of the valid Airspeed values of 35 m/sec and 200 m/sec as well as a set of tests at a nominal airspeed value of 125 m/sec.

"The following tests are performed at the 35 m/sec boundary:

Apply initial simulated airspeed values of 35.0 m/sec for all four bus parameters **SysA_[1|2]: Bus_[A|B]: Airspeed** and verify that the Airspeed Data Fault is <u>not</u> reported (see Test#1 in the table below).

Modify the Airspeed values for each of the remaining test numbers in the test matrix table below and verify that SysB generates the indicated Fault Condition status:

Airspeed Data Fault Requirement
Test Matrix: [35 m/sec Lower Boundary]

Test #	Parameter: **Airspeed**				**Fault?**
	SysA_1		SysA_2		
	Bus_A	Bus_B	Bus_A	Bus_B	
1	35.0	35.0	35.0	35.0	No
2	35.0	35.1	35.5	35.4	No
3	35.1	35.0	35.4	35.5	No
4	35.5	35.4	35.0	35.1	No
5	35.4	35.5	35.1	35.0	No
6	**35.5**	**35.3**	35.0	35.0	**Yes**
7*	35.5	35.4	35.0	35.0	No
8	35.5	35.4	**35.0**	**35.2**	**Yes**
9*	35.5	35.4	35.0	35.1	No
10	**35.6**	35.5	**35.0**	35.1	**Yes**
11*	35.6	35.5	35.1	35.1	No
12	**35.6**	35.5	35.1	**35.0**	**Yes**
13*	35.5	35.6	35.1	35.1	No
14	35.5	**35.6**	**35.0**	35.1	**Yes**
15*	35.5	35.6	35.1	35.1	No
16	35.5	**35.6**	35.1	**35.0**	**Yes**
17	35.5	35.6	35.1	35.1	No
Etc.					

*Note: These table entries ensure that the fault is cleared between conditions that would create a new fault condition

The remaining tables for 200 m/sec and 125 m/sec would look essentially the same (e.g., by copying the table and then substituting "200" for "35" and "125" for "35" in the respective copies)

Providing detailed written test procedures for later implementation by a test programmer is, of course, a perfectly valid and common approach. However, if the same effort required to write the detailed procedures can instead be applied in a fashion that is directly executable and is still readable (thus verifiable) by independent domain experts, then one process step is eliminated. This not only reduces the overall project work load but also eliminates a potential bottleneck wherein test programmers are inefficiently waiting for procedures to be written.

An example for setting the value of a bus parameter in the High Level Script Syntax would look like the following,

SET_BUSSDATA ECU=SysA_1, Bus=A, Data=Airspeed, Value=35.5, Units=m/Sec

where "SET_BUSSDATA" represents the Command ID for a function to be performed and the remaining fields represent the parameters (the "ECU=" field identifies the Simulator Name for the subsystem simulation activities; the "Data=" field identifies the Bus Parameter to be modified; the "Value=" field represents the data value to be applied; and the "Units=" field [when present] was sometimes used by a transformation algorithm in the test resources when the Bus data was carried in different units than specified at the system level; it was also occasionally used to facilitate the readability of the documentation.)

When the above script line was processed by the test tool's documentation generator, the following output would be produced:

"Set the [Airspeed] data for [SysA_1] on Bus [A] to a value of [35.5 m/Sec]."

Likewise, when checking the value of the Airspeed Data Fault status, the High Level Script Syntax would be entered as:

GET_ECU_DATA ECU=SysB, Data=AirspeedDataFault, Limits=True

This line would be processed by the documentation generator to produce the following:

"Read the value of the [AirspeedDataFault] reported by [SysB] and verify that it is set to [True]."

The following additional test script elements assisted the test developer in generating full test description reports from their executable procedures that satisfied the objectives of DO-178B:

- System Requirement Trace Field
- Test Procedure Description Field
- Test Case Description Field
- In-Line Comment Fields

Data-Driven Test Support

Obviously, the original textual procedural document (though not executable) is more "compact" in format since it is presented in a tabular fashion. The tabular format also allows a reviewer to quickly determine if sufficient test scenarios have been specified to achieve the necessary test coverage objectives.

In recognition of the advantages provided by table specified test inputs applicable to many test scenarios, the test tools also supported writing "Data-Driven" test procedures. For these procedures the source information for the test commands (including any expected results) could be extracted from a comma separated variable (.csv) text file or directly from a Microsoft Excel spreadsheet. The tests would execute until all rows of the selected table/file were processed.

The downside when using the Data-Driven approach was that the generated test reports were more obscure in nature, since the actual test values used at runtime were not embedded in the test procedures. This obfuscation of the report was sufficiently offset through the liberal usage of in-line commenting and comments directing the reviewer to the external data files containing the actual test parameter and result lists.

Menu Driven Environment

Expecting the test developers to specify the required [Command][Parameter...] test command lists by hand based on the contents of a test dictionary was not a viable approach. Even in the case of a simple system with only a few avionics subsystems, a large repertoire of test command options was required to fully test each of the subsystem elements. Furthermore, each of the numerous test command options had their own unique parameter control lists yet many re-used common parameter names. The value ranges of every overloaded command-parameter name would vary greatly from its usage in one command to that of another, however, and this would contribute to user confusion and frustration.

This test-space state explosion problem led to the development of a "guided" menuing system for entering and editing test commands. Included were context sensitive options for assisting the user when entering parameter values that were appropriate for the currently selected Command ID (refer to Figure 8 below).

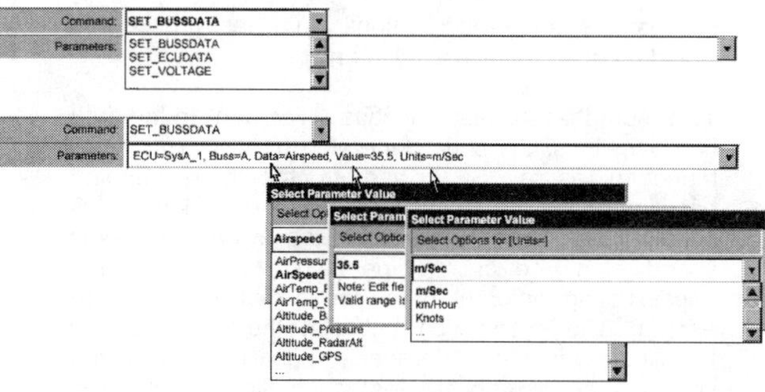

Figure 8. – Example Menu Driven Test Development

System Engineering team members at the client site who used this test development environment found it very intuitive to use and were quickly able to begin writing executable test procedures with only a short introductory session covering the tool options.

Subsystem software developers also found the flexibility of the script development environment to be extremely beneficial in creating short (ad hoc) integration test scripts to exercise their software at an early stage of its development.

MANAGING THE "AVALANCHE" OF BUS PARAMETERS

One of the additional challenges faced by CertTech dealt with the large number of data bus parameters that were exchanged in the system. To provide support within the test tool environment described previously, each of the existing parameters (and all future "To Be Developed" parameters) required their own test command handler. At the beginning of the project, several hundred parameters had already been defined with an additional 500+ to be defined over the course of the project. Furthermore, as the avionics system development proceeded, the specifications for some parameters were expected to change, and others were simply eliminated.

Faced with the prospect of a large amount of on-going development and support work, CertTech elected to develop a code-generation wizard for automatically creating the required test tool command handlers for each of the data bus parameters. This wizard acquired type and description data for each of the parameters from a Microsoft Access database in which the avionics manufacturer managed the data bus parameter definitions. Baselining of the data bus parameters was accomplished by saving an instance of the database in a configuration management system; upon each baselining event CertTech regenerated all of the test tool command handler test software via the code-generation wizard.

For new data bus parameters, this approach was highly efficient. Additions did not affect previously created test scripts, and the availability of the new command handlers permitted users to proceed with creating test procedures that utilized the newly added bus parameters. Not surprisingly, however, modifications to existing parameters, or deletions of parameters, would typically require manual rework to any previously developed test procedures that referenced the affected parameters. Since the parameters were typically changed (or deleted) in response to modifications made to requirements for one or more of the avionics subsystems, such modifications to the test procedures would have been necessary in any case.

To ensure that the test tool capabilities tracked the data bus baselines, the code generated by the wizard was managed as a "SET" tied to the corresponding baseline(s) for the Access database definitions. This coupling was essential because the avionics systems varied from one aircraft-type installation to another, necessitating different data bus definitions for each aircraft. The association between the software tool baselines and the database baselines permitted selecting an appropriate test code file set that was suitable for the aircraft installation to be tested.

RELATIONSHIP TO SAFETY ANALYSIS

The tools and processes described here were developed for requirements based testing per a RTCA DO-178B compliant verification plan. All the safety related statistical analysis and the resulting system requirements are generated by domain experts with appropriate training and credentials. Validation occurs at the system level.

The goal of this approach is to verify that the documented requirements are being met. Determination of the validity of requirements is a separate issue. However, requirements errors and omissions are routinely discovered as a result of the independent scrutiny that occurs during development of verification test cases.

PORTABILITY OF APPROACH

This approach was developed by CertTech to accomplish a specific set of goals for a specific system software verification activity. However, this approach is used for other safety critical systems with components that share critical data on both bus and point to point architectures. The details of bus communications hardware, differing protocols, and data formatting may impact the test system infrastructure significantly but the test system software architecture and techniques remain the same.

Each new circumstance requires adaptations, but we have not encountered a circumstance which prevented implementation of this approach. Our expectation is that implementing this same approach for testing systems using other buss architectures such as FlexRay™ would have similar benefits.

CONCLUSION

This paper outlined the test methodologies used by CertTech to accomplish system software verification of an avionics subsystem that utilized a TDMA data bus. It points out the need for integrated test tools supporting data bus monitoring and data injection for replacing absent subsystems with simulations thereof. Furthermore, this example demonstrates that highly flexible test tools are essential when addressing test problems for which limited prior experience exists.

REFERENCES

1. Hermann Kopetz and Günter Grünsteidl. TTP—a protocol for fault-tolerant real-time systems. *IEEE Computer*, 27(1):14–23, January 1994.

2. DO-160D/E, Environmental Conditions and Test Procedures for Airborne Equipment. Published by RTCA, Inc. 1828 L Street NW, Suite 805, Washington, DC 200306 (www.rtca.org)

3. AS8202NF TTP-C2NF Communication Controller from TTTech Computertechnik AG (Vienna, Austria)

4. DO-178B, Software Considerations in Airborne Systems and Equipment Certification. Published by RTCA, Inc. 1828 L Street NW, Suite 805, Washington, DC 200306 (www.rtca.org)

2006-01-1328

Tester4MOST: A New User-friendly Testing Tool for MOST

Ji-Hoon Yun, Jun-Sik Lee and Seung-Woo Seo
Seoul National University

Seong-Jin Lee, Hyoung-Uk Kim, Jung-Bum Suh and Jang-Dong Choi
Hyundai Motors Company

ABSTRACT

MOST (Media Oriented Systems Transport) is the in-vehicle network technology for multimedia devices and it has been already adopted by many major car companies. To test MOST devices and networks, several testing tools are currently available in the market. However, most of the tools require programming based on their own languages to configure a user-specific test scenario. This makes the test difficult and unclear because test engineers should learn new programming language and the scenario code itself can have bugs. In order to provide easy and clear configuration of custom test scenarios, we develop a new MOST testing tool, called *Tester4MOST*. For the scenario configuration through GUI, we propose a scenario model which can deal with a variety of tests in the aspects of application and network. On the other hand, in a MOST network, there can be multiple controlling nodes and controlled devices which interact with each other. To test MOST devices and networks under that condition, we need to operate multiple testing nodes simultaneously in a test. For this purpose, we introduce the test head and client, each of which can be either a control point or a controlled device. Using this functionality, Tester4MOST can perform tests in more realistic situations. In addition, the test log is recorded in a specific format and its analysis is separated from the testing so that test engineers can obtain the test results in many diverse ways.

INTRODUCTION

In recent years, the demand for diverse multimedia services including data communication in vehicles has been increasing. So, more components are being installed and connected with each other in each vehicle. However, current technologies face two problems for multimedia services: wiring harnesses and bandwidth limitation. Increasing number of multimedia components and interactions between them result in complex and huge amount of cabling. This increases costs and volume of required cable connections. On the other hand, the bandwidth required for multimedia applications is also increasing. However, current electrical cabling is reaching its physical limits due to the increasing electromagnetic emissions in a vehicle. To solve these problems, the MOST (Media Oriented Systems Transport) technology has been proposed and standardized by the MOST Cooperation [1] and many car companies.

MOST is the in-vehicle network technology for multimedia devices and it has already been adopted by many top-level cars from major car companies (*e.g.* BMW, Audi, Daimler Chrysler). In a MOST network, multimedia devices are connected with each other using Plastic Optical Fiber (POF) in a ring topology. Thus it can reduce the required cabling connections and provide high-speed data transmissions. To enable networking of multimedia devices and manage the network in a vehicle, MOST defines the mechanisms of channel access, connection management, resource management, etc. So, the test of a MOST system should be performed in the aspects of network-related functionalities as well as application-specific functionalities. This makes the test of MOST systems different and complex compared to the conventional multimedia systems.

To test MOST devices and networks, several testing tools are currently available in the market (*e.g.* Testerlyzer [2], CANoe.MOST [3], 4CS [4]). However, most of the tools require programming based on their own languages to configure a user-specific scenario. This makes the test difficult since test engineers should learn a new programming language. Furthermore, this sometimes makes the test unreliable because the test results can depend on how the test scenario is coded, and the problems found through the test can be due to the fault of the scenario code itself. Considering those disadvantages of the existing tools, a test tool needs to be easier to configure custom scenarios without its own programming language and GUI (Graphical User Interface)-based scenario configuration can be a good alternative.

On the other hand, each of the nodes in a MOST network can communicate with any other nodes in the same network. Due to the networking of multimedia devices in a vehicle, there can be multiple control points and each control point may control multiple controlled devices. For example, there can be two HMIs (Human-to-Machine Interface) for front and rear seats, respectively, in a vehicle. In that case, devices in the network are controlled by two control points and their interactions are different from the case of single control point. In such a sense, a testing tool needs to consider the interactions between multiple control points and multiple controlled devices in a test, which we refer to as *networked test* in this paper. To perform the networked test, multiple testing nodes should be able to cooperate for the test, *e.g.*, role assignment, synchronization, result collection, etc. Otherwise, it is difficult to control the test.

In order to support easy and clear configuration of custom test scenarios and the networked test, we develop a new MOST testing tool, named *Tester4MOST*. With our tool, users configure their custom test scenarios through the user-friendly GUI. For that, we propose a scenario model which can deal with a variety of tests in the aspects of application and network. Basically four types of test can be performed using Tester4MOST, i.e. multimedia function test, delay test, accuracy test and compatibility test. To support the networked test, we introduce the test head and clients in the test, each of which can be either a control point or a controlled device. The test head and clients exchange the test scenario and logs through TCP/IP [5] communication. After the test, the test head analyzes the collected logs and generates the test result automatically. In addition, Tester4MOST provides more freedom in result analysis. The test log is recorded in a specific format and its analysis is separated from testing. Tester4MOST uses Awk [6] for the result analysis, which is a well-known script language for log analysis. So, test engineers can obtain the test result in many diverse ways by writing their own script for the result analysis in Awk.

The rest of this paper is organized as follows: Section 'MOST' briefly explains the MOST technology. We explain our testing tool Tester4MOST in detail in Section 'TESTER4MOST'. Section 'TYPES OF TEST' shows the types of test supported by Tester4MOST. In Section 'EXPERIMENTS', we present some test examples and experimental results using Tester4MOST.

MOST

MOST is the data network technology for multimedia applications in the automobile environment [7][8]. To support the multimedia applications, MOST can transfer audio, video, generic data packets and control messages. The MOST technology adopts POF as transmission media so that it enables high-speed up to 24.8Mbps and robust transmission at lower cost replacing the old wiring harnesses. In MOST networks, devices are connected forming a ring topology. One of the devices, called the timing master, generates the MOST frames at a given frame rate (typically 44.1kHz). The frame structure is shown in the figure below.

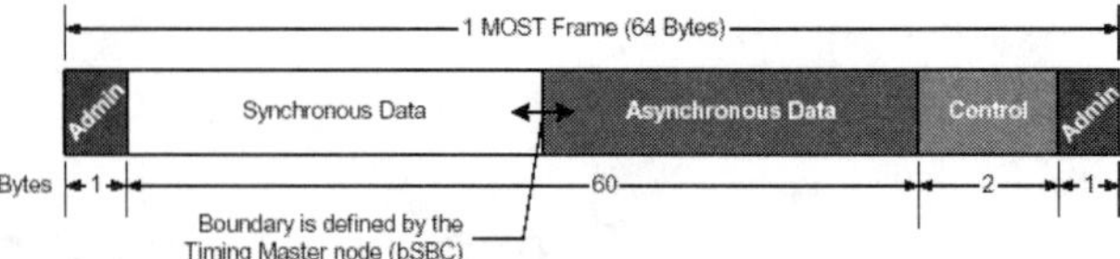

Figure 1. MOST frame structure

The length of a frame is 64 bytes. 60 bytes are reserved for transporting synchronous source data (*e.g.* audio and video) and packet data, 2 bytes are available for control messaging. For dividing up the 60 bytes between synchronous source data and asynchronous data, there is a boundary descriptor value which is transported in the administrative sections. A MOST device accesses the synchronous channel, which is allocated by the connection master, in a Time Division Multiplexing (TDM) manner. The bandwidth for such a channel can be adjusted by allocating any number of bytes to one logical channel. The maximum number of bytes available in a synchronous channel is 60 bytes / frame, which corresponds to 60 x 8 bits or 15 stereo channels of CD quality audio.

From the logical point of view, as shown in the figure below, a MOST device consists of several function blocks, an interface level providing a standard interface (NetServices, Basic Layer) for communication between the function blocks and a unit providing MOST functionality (*e.g.* a MOST transceiver chip), and the physical interface to the MOST network.

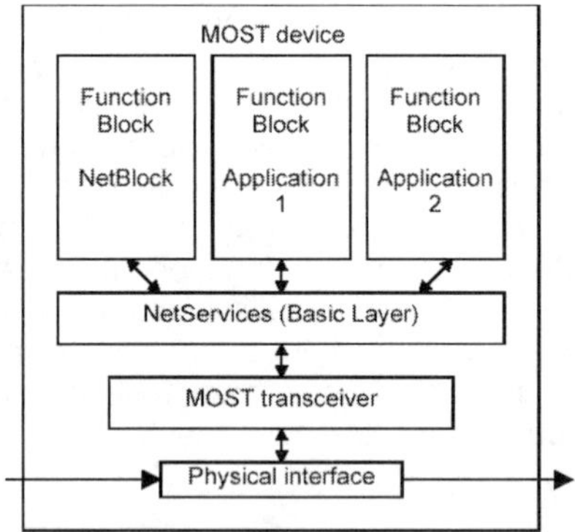

Figure 2. Logical structure of a MOST device

A function block represents an application *e.g.* a tuner, an amplifier, or a CD player. There is one special function block, called NetBlock that handles functions related to the entire MOST device. NetBlock is mandatory for all MOST devices. Each function block contains a set of functions which are accessible from the external MOST world. There are two types of functions: properties and methods. Properties and functions that provide determining or changing of the current status of the function block. Methods are functions that are started, and return a result after a certain time. For being able to distinguish between the different function blocks (FBlocks) and functions (Fkt) of a device, each function and function block has a name, or an identifier (ID) respectively. When accessing functions, certain operations are applied to the respective property or method. The kind of operation is specified by the OpType. For distinguishing function blocks of the same type in a MOST network, there is another identifier called instance ID (InstID). So a protocol that gives access to a certain property in a function block looks like:

FBlockID.InstID.FktID.OPType(Data)

The standard function blocks and their functions for multimedia applications (*e.g.* CD player, radio tuner) are defined in the function catalogs [9].

TESTER4MOST

In this section, we describe our testing tool, named *Tester4MOST*. Tester4MOST is implemented in C++ using the MOST NetServices libraries from OASIS [10]. Tester4MOST is designed to satisfy the following goals:

- Users can configure custom test scenarios through GUI without programming.
- User can operate multiple testing nodes in a test.
- Users can customize the result analysis of test logs.
- All the test procedures including result analysis are performed automatically.
- All the information (*e.g.* scenario, optional configuration) is stored in XML (eXtensible Markup Language) [11].

Consequently, test engineers can accomplish desired tests easily and flexibly, and obtain the test results in diverse ways using Tester4MOST.

Before explaining the scenario model of Tester4MOST, we present its software architecture first in the following subsection.

ARCHITECTURE

Figure 3 shows the software architecture of Tester4MOST in UML (Unified Markup Language) [12]. Each box in the figure corresponds to a software component which is a C++ class. It shows the component name, member variables and member functions. The role of each component is explained as follows:

- Scenario: Scenario corresponds to a test scenario. It consists of states which are contained in a list structure (state_list).
- State: State contains the message (MOST event) to send and the message (MOST event) to expect in the corresponding state.
- MostIF: It is the interface between Tester4MOST and a MOST network. Since Tester4MOST can send and receive messages (MOST events) only through this interface, it can be easily extended to test CAN [13]-cum-MOST networks by changing this component.
- Logger: Logger logs sent and received messages (MOST events) during a test in a specified format.
- Analyzer: Analyzer analyzes the log file after the test according to the analysis configuration.
- NetAgent: NetAgent distributes test scenarios and collects logs using TCP/IP sockets in the networked test.
- XMLParser: Test scenarios and tool configurations are stored in XML format. Tester4MOST stores and loads them through XMLParser.

Options and AnalysisConfig implement the general and analysis-related configurations.

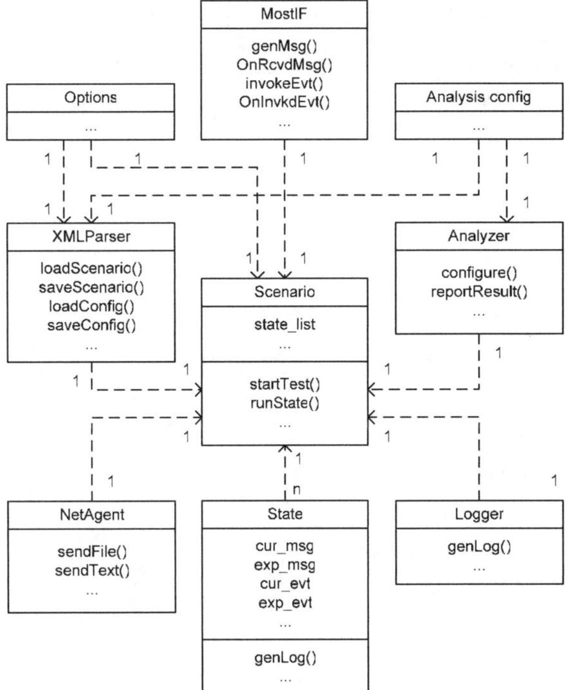

Figure 3. Tester4MOST architecture in UML

SCENARIO MODEL

In order to configure a test scenario via a simple user interface, we propose a scenario model for generic test scenarios. Then, a user specifies blank parameters of the model through the user interface. The figure below depicts the scenario model.

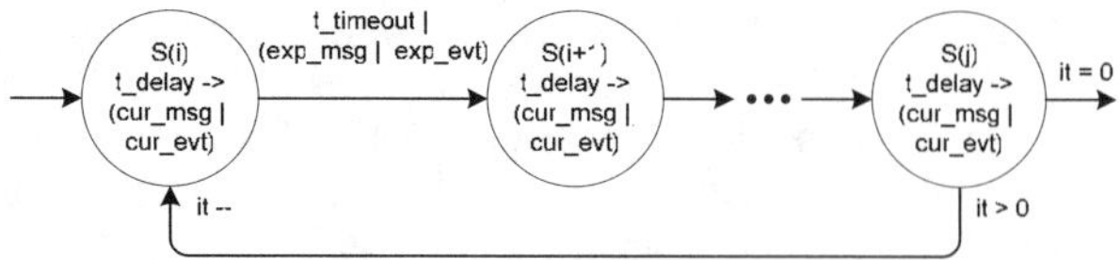

Figure 4. Scenario model

As shown in the figure, the scenario model consists of states and the states are stored in a list structure in a sequential order. Tester4MOST performs a test according to the configurations of the states sequentially. Each state contains a control message to send, called *current message* (cur_msg), and control messages which are expected to receive, called *expected message* (exp_msg). Users can configure one of them or both, but it is not allowed for a state to have none of them. The users can configure multiple expected messages. This is for the case of the notification matrix registration in which a control point requests the notification registration for several properties and the controlled device notifies the control point of the status of the properties by sending multiple control messages simultaneously. For each state, Tester4MOST operates as Figure 5.

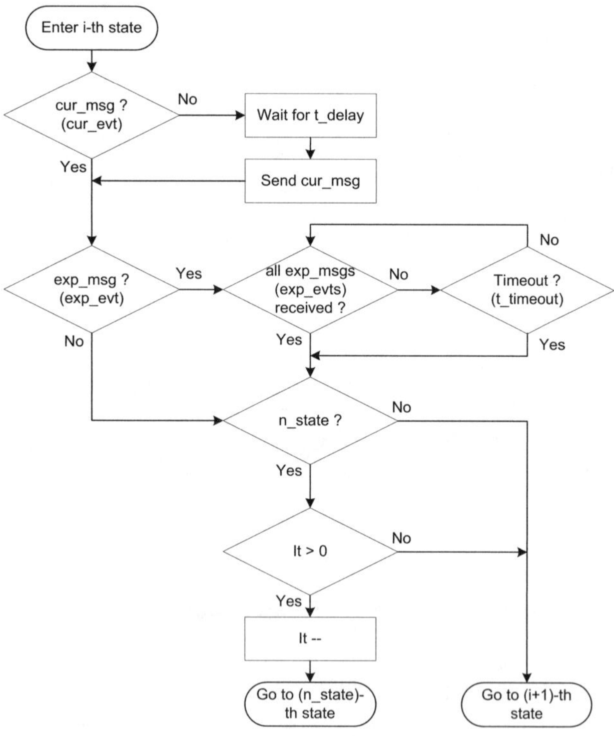

Figure 5. Flow chart of state processing

In a state, Tester4MOST sends a current message in a delay time (t_delay in the figure) and waits for the expected message(s) for a timeout time (t_timeout). If all the expected messages are received or the timeout timer expires, Tester4MOST moves to the next state. If the next state (n_state) and the number of iterations (It) of the state are larger than zero, Tester4MOST moves to the specified next state (n_state) and decreases It by one. Otherwise, it moves to the very next state. In this manner, Tester4MOST can repeat a series of consecutive states for a specified number of times. According to this operation, the status of a state can be presented in four phases, as shown in the figure below.

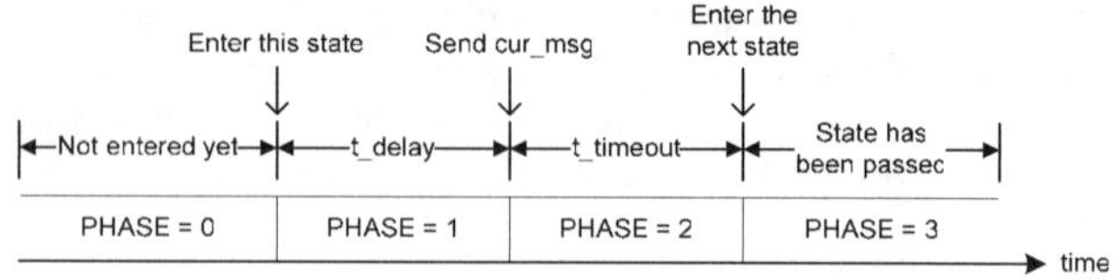

Figure 6. Four phases of a state

Using the scenario model, we can operate and test the network in the following ways:

- Control MOST device(s) with specified time intervals.
- Check whether the target device(s) responds correctly.
- Check how fast the target device(s) responds.
- Repeat the operations above automatically.

Users can derive their test scenarios from the combinations of the behaviors above. Figure 7 shows an example of the scenario configuration in Tester4MOST. It is a simple test in which all the functions of the MPEG decoder are invoked sequentially. A row corresponds to a state and each column specifies the corresponding parameter of the states.

I..	N	Name	cur_(msg, evt)	exp_(msg, evt)	D	Timeout	N..	I..
0	0	FktIDs	0x200.0x6F.0x00.000.1..	0x200.0x6F.0x00.000.C..	0	100	-1	0
1	0	Notification	0x200.0x6F.0x00.001.1.02.0113	0x200.0x6F.0x00.001.C..	0	100	-1	0
2	0	SourceInfo	0x200.0x6F.0x00.100.1.01.01	0x200.0x6F.0x00.100.C..	0	100	-1	0
3	0	Allocate	0x200.0x6F.0x00.101.2.01.01	0x200.0x6F.0x00.101.C..	0	100	-1	0
4	0	DeAllocate	0x200.0x6F.0x00.102.2.01.01	0x200.0x6F.0x00.102.C..	0	100	-1	0
5	0	SourceName	0x200.0x6F.0x00.104.1.01.01	0x200.0x6F.0x00.104.C..	0	100	-1	0
6	0	SinkInfo	0x200.0x6F.0x00.110.1.01.01	0x200.0x6F.0x00.110.C..	0	100	-1	0
7	0	Mute	0x200.0x6F.0x00.113.1.01.01	0x200.0x6F.0x00.113.C..	0	100	-1	0
8	0	SinkName	0x200.0x6F.0x00.114.1.01.01	0x200.0x6F.0x00.114.C..	0	100	-1	0
9	0	SyncDataInfo	0x200.0x6F.0x00.116.1..	0x200.0x6F.0x00.116.C..	0	100	-1	0
10	0	OutputStandard	0x200.0x6F.0x00.200.1..	0x200.0x6F.0x00.200.C..	0	100	-1	0
11	0	OutputFormat	0x200.0x6F.0x00.201.1..	0x200.0x6F.0x00.201.C..	0	100	-1	0
12	0	VideoStatus	0x200.0x6F.0x00.F10.1..	0x200.0x6F.0x00.F10.C..	0	100	-1	0

Figure 7. Example of scenario configuration

A state can have a MOST event to invoke (cur_evt) instead of a current message and MOST events to expect (exp_evt) instead of expected messages. In Tester4MOST, MOST events are classified into two categories: events to invoke and events to be invoked. MOST events which Tester4MOST can invoke by changing the status of the MOST Network Interface Card (MNIC) are as follows: zero power mode, bypass mode, ring break diagnosis (RBD), etc. MOST events which Tester4MOST can detect but cannot invoke by itself are as follows: Net_ON, Net_Off, end of RBD, network change event (NCE), lock, unlock, critical unlock, etc.

All the necessary information to specify a test scenario is configured through GUI of Tester4MOST. The proposed model can describe broad range of scenarios. We present the types of tests which Tester4MOST can support, later in the paper.

NETWORKED TEST

In a MOST network, there may be multiple control points and each control point may control multiple controlled devices. In this case, those controlled devices may notify of the status changes of their properties to the multiple control points. Therefore, to test MOST devices and networks in more practical situations, we need to test the interactions between multiple control points and multiple controlled devices, which we refer to as *networked test*. In order to accomplish the networked test, the testing tool should be able to operate multiple testing nodes according to multiple test scenarios simultaneously in a test. Despite of the importance of the networked test, it is not typically supported by existing MOST testing tools.

Furthermore, a MOST device can access only every third message propagated through the network so that a single MOST device cannot occupy the whole control channel. For this reason, a single testing node cannot fully overload a MOST device. To accomplish stress test upon the device, at least three testing nodes need to induce control messages to the single target device and thus the testing tool should support the networked test.

To support the networked test, Tester4MOST introduces the *test head* and *client*. The figure below shows the network configuration for the networked test with Tester4MOST.

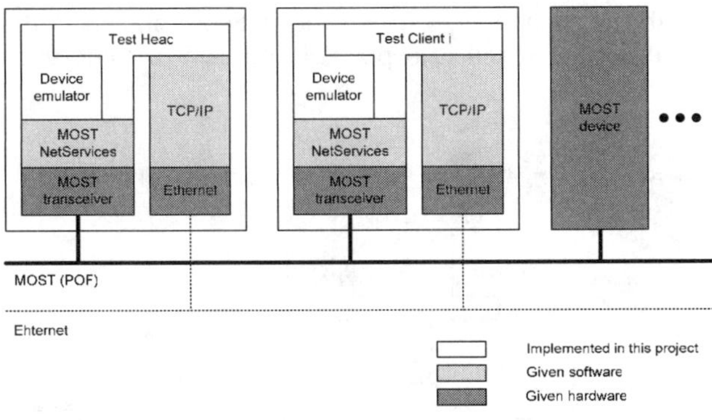

Figure 8. Network configuration for the networked test

A node which is running Tester4MOST can be either the test head or client. There should be only one test head in a network. All the control signals including scenario files and log files are transmitted through TCP/IP communication. For this reason, the test head and all the test clients should be connected to LAN (Local Area Network). The test head and clients can operate as legacy MOST devices during the test using the device emulator. The device emulator emulates a multimedia device and has corresponding function blocks.

The procedure of the networked test is shown in Figure 9. First, the user configures the test scenario in the test head. The original test scenario contains all the scenarios for the test head and each test client. When the user starts the test, the test head divides the original test scenario into multiple scenarios for test clients according to the node ID. Then, the test head distributes those scenario files to each test client. After the test head signals the test start to all the clients, the test head and clients start the test simultaneously. Over the test, the test head and clients control and interact with other MOST devices and each other according to their own test scenarios. When a test client finishes its test, it transfers its log file to the test head. After all the tests of the head and clients are finished, the test head merges its log file and the uploaded log files, and analyzes the merged log file automatically. The user needs to configure only the test head. The test clients are controlled by the test head. Here, we assume that the transmission delay through LAN is negligible.

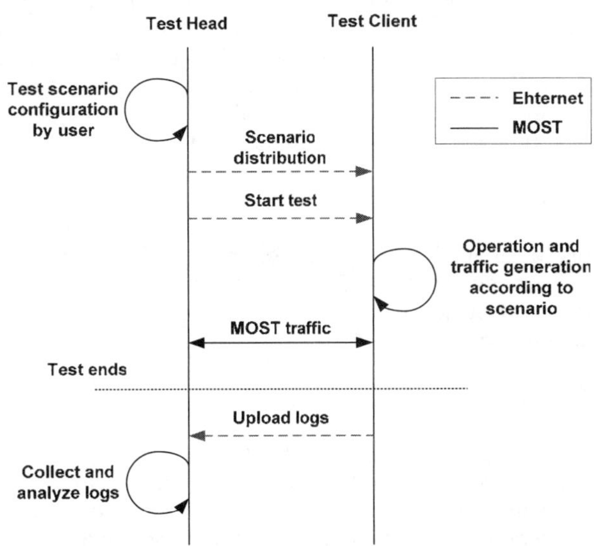

Figure 9. Procedure of the networked test

LOGGING AND ANALYSIS

Tester4MOST records test logs in the specified formats. It records a line of log when t he testing node sends or receives a message (or MOST event). It also records a line of log when a state transition occurs. Each log specifies the time when it occurred so that it can be utilized to obtain meaningful results.

In order to provide more freedom in result analysis, the analysis is separated from testing and described by Awk, which is a well-known script language for log analysis. When the test is finished, the Analyzer component of Tester4MOST triggers the analysis by executing the analysis script. The inputs of the analysis script are the log file and the analysis configuration. Tester4MOST provides diverse types of analysis basically, i.e., compatibility, throughput, delay and accuracy. For each item, the user can configure the detailed analysis options.

If the user wants to analyze the log in a new aspect or generate the result in a new format, the user writes a new analysis script and uses it instead of the default script. The custom analysis script can be used with Tester4MOST without recompilation of Tester4MOST because the analysis is performed by the separate program.

TYPES OF TEST

In this section, we present four types of tests which can be conducted using Tester4MOST.

MULTIMEDIA FUNCTION TEST

In this test, test engineers test the multimedia functions (*e.g.* audio, video) of devices. To check the validity of device output in various operation sequences, Tester4MOST controls the target device(s) according to the configured scenario automatically. Then, the test engineer checks whether the device plays the expected audio or video in a specific state.

DELAY TEST

This test investigates the response time of a device. For this purpose, Tester4MOST sends a control message to the target device and measures the response delay for expected messages.

ACCURACY TEST

In the accuracy test, we check the accuracy of the operations of a device typically in the heavily overloaded condition. For this, Tester4MOST controls the target device and check how accurately the device responds to the controls in time.

COMPATIBILITY TEST

In the compatibility test, Tester4MOST checks whether the target device implements all the required functions. Those functions consist of the mandatory function in the corresponding function catalog and the custom functions required by car integrators. This test is accomplished by checking the output messages when Tester4MOST invokes the required function.

EXPERIMENTS

In this section, we perform test examples for each type using Tester4MOST. A test using Tester4MOST is accomplished in the procedure shown in Figure 10. First of all, the user configures the test scenario and performs the automatic scenario verification. In the scenario verification, Tester4MOST checks whether the scenario is complete. For example, each state of the scenario should have at least one of the current and expected messages. If the verification fails, the user completes the scenario according to the errors notified. After the verification finishes successfully, Tester4MOST performs the test according to the test scenario. When the test finishes, Tester4MOST analyzes the log file according to the analysis configuration. The analysis configuration specifies which items to analyze (*e.g.* throughput, delay, accuracy). The analysis configuration can be configured before test or analysis.

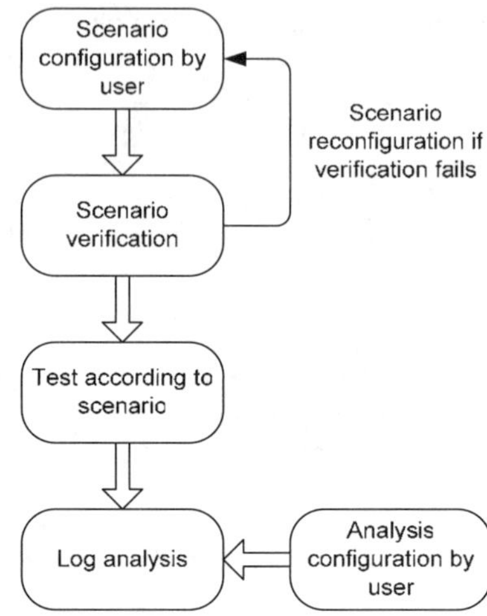

Figure 10. Procedure of a test

EXPERIMENTAL SETUP

For the experiments, we use the network shown in the figure below, which is a possible network configuration of a car.

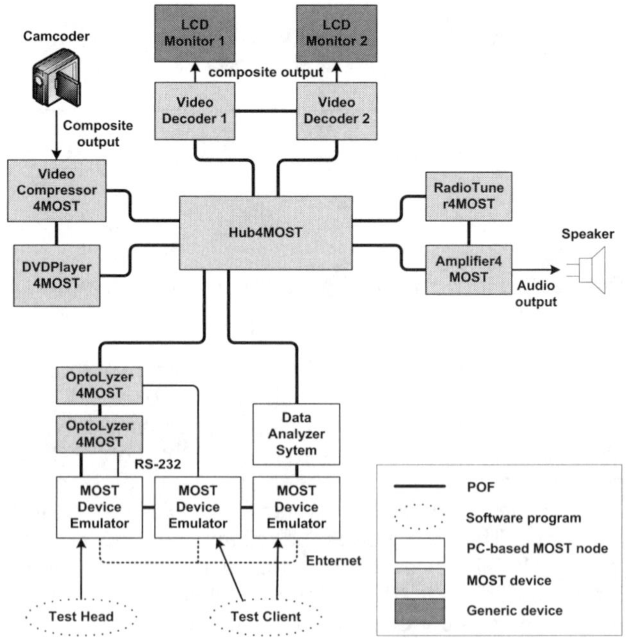

Figure 11. Experimental setup

The network consists of a MOST hub, several multimedia devices and PC-based MOST nodes. The network forms a ring topology through the hub. The PC-based MOST nodes use the PCI-type MOST transceiver from OASIS. One of the PC-based MOST nodes emulates a CD changer. The internal structure of the CD-changer emulator is shown in Figure 12.

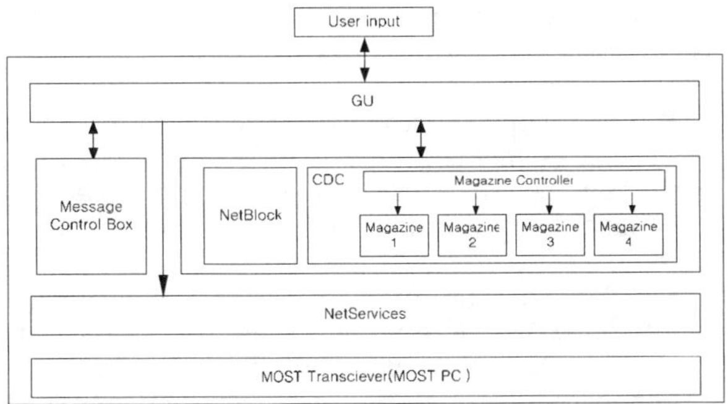

Figure 12. Structure of CD-changer emulator

The CD-changer emulator has the mandatory NetBlock and CDC function block for CD-changer functionalities. In the emulator, a MP3 file corresponds to a track of a disc and the directory which contains MP3 files corresponds to the disc. Although the audio stream of the emulator is from MP3 files, the emulator is seen as a CD changer by the other nodes in the network.

MULTIMEDIA FUNCTION TEST OF CD CHANGER

First, we test the multimedia functions of the CD changer. This test corresponds to the first type of test, multimedia function test. As mentioned above, the CD changer is implemented as a device emulator and one of the PC-based MOST nodes behaves as the CD changer. For the test, we control the CD changer in the following procedures.

1. Stop the player.
2. Play the player.
3. Increase the track number twice.
4. Increase the magazine number.
5. Increase the track number.
6. Decrease the magazine number.
7. Go back to the step 1.

When Tester4MOST controls the CD changer in this manner, the user should be able to listen to the third track of the first disc when the step 3 is finished and the second track of the second disc when the step 5 is finished if the CD changer works well. The user can tune the time intervals (t_delay) to test the CD changer delicately. To repeat the steps above, the next state and the number of iterations of the state which corresponds to step 7 are set to appropriate values.

When we tested our CD-changer emulator with this test scenario, we could not hear the second track of the second disc. Instead, the first track of the second disc was played. When we increased t_delay of the step 5 to 100ms, it worked well. From the test result, we can conclude that the MP3 files of the second disc are somewhat big and it takes relatively long time to load all the files when the magazine number is set to 2. Consequently, before loading is finished, all the control messages for the CD changer are ignored. Through this multimedia function test, we could find the bug of the CD-changer emulator. In this manner, we can test multimedia functionalities of a MOST device and find potential problems before production.

RBD DELAY TEST

The timing master can detect link disconnections by invoking RBD. In this test, we investigate the RBD delay time. The test scenario is configured as below in Tester4MOST. In this test, we configure the current and expected MOST events as RBD and RBD_END, respectively. Then, Tester4MOST invokes RBD and waits for RBD_END event. We repeat RBD 50 times. The result analysis shows the average, minimum and maximum delay time with the variance. In our experiment, RBD takes about 251 ms on the average.

AMPLIFIER4MOST RESPONSE DELAY TEST

In this test, we investigate the response time of the Amplifier4MOST for the function 'Volume'. Because 'Volume' function is the most frequently invoked functions among the functions of the amplifier, the amplifier needs to respond as fast as possible in various situations. For this reason, the response time of 'Volume' function is one of the most important functions to measure the performance of the amplifier. The scenario configured is similar to the previous test. Instead of MOST events, we configure the current and expected messages as 'Volume' function with appropriate data values. Tester4MOST provides the dynamic view of the measured delay in real time. Figure 13 shows the response time dynamically during the test. From this graph, the user can check the response time dynamically during the test. The result analysis also shows the average, minimum and maximum delay time with the variance. In our test, it takes about 3 ms on the average to retrieve the status of the property 'Volume', which is much shorter than the RBD delay. From the results, we can conclude that this amplifier can process consecutive invocation of 'Volume' function appropriately.

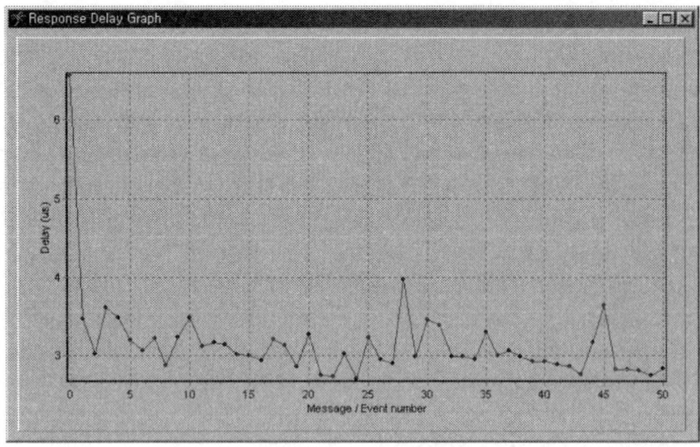

Figure 13. Dynamic view of measured delay

MOSTVIDEO DELAY AND COMPATIBILITY TEST

In this test, we investigate the compatibility of MOSTVideo with the corresponding function catalog. MOSTVideo is the video decoder which decodes a MPEG-1 stream to analog video. Simultaneously, we can also measure the response delay for each function. In the test scenario, Tester4MOST invokes the functions of MOSTVideo sequentially and waits for the expected messages which should be received if MOSTVideo has the corresponding functions.

If we configure the type of result analysis as compatibility test, the result analysis shows whether the functions considered are implemented appropriately. Our test showed that MOSTVideo had all the mandatory function defined in the corresponding function catalog. Here, we can also see the measured delay for each function. From the result, it takes more time to allocate (25ms) and deallocate (22ms) the synchronous channel than the other functions (around 15ms). It takes the longest time to retrieve the function ID list from the MOSTVideo (36ms) because the response message is longer than the other response messages.

CONCLUSION

In this paper, we introduced a new MOST testing tool Tester4MOST, which supports custom scenario configuration through GUI and the networked test. Since Tester4MOST does not need to use its own programming langue in scenario configuration, test engineers can accomplish test more easily and rapidly. Moreover, through the networked test, we can consider realistic network environments and interactions between devices. In addition, the test engineers can obtain the test results in their own aspects by writing a new analysis script.

In the future, we plan to conduct further implementation to enhance Tester4MOST as follows:

(1) Although the scenario model adopted by Tester4MOST covers various types of test, it needs to be extended to be able to express more delicate scenarios. For that purpose, we plan to introduce branch in our scenario model.

(2) We also plan to introduce randomness in sending messages in the scenario model. By considering randomness in a test, a scenario can cover more situations and consider more realistic interactions.

(3) Finally, we plan to support CAN messages in Tester4MOST. In a lot of cars in the market, some HMIs (e.g. control panel on steering wheel) are connected to a MOST network via CAN-MOST gateway. In other words, some HMIs generate CAN messages to control MOST devices. For this reason, it is necessary to support CAN and MOST in a single testing platform. This also makes it possible to test CAN-MOST gateways.

REFERENCES

1. MOST Cooperation, http://www.mostcooperation.com
2. Testerlyzer, Ruetz Technologies, http://www.testerlyzer.com/.
3. CANoe.MOST, Vector Informatik, http://www.vector-informatik.com.
4. 4CS, GADV mbH, http://www.4cs.de.
5. W. Stevens, "TCP/IP Illustrated Volume 1: the Protocols", Addison-Wesley Professional, 1993.
6. Awk, http://www.gnu.org/software/gawk/gawk.html
7. MOST Cooperation, "MOST Specification Framework Rev 1.1", Version 1.1-07, 1999.
8. MOST Cooperation, "MOST Specification Rev 2.3", Version 2.3-00, Aug. 2004.
9. MOST Cooperation, "MOST Function Catalog Rev 2.3", Version 1.0, 2001.
10. OASIS Silicon Systems, http://www.oasis.com.
11. W3C, "Extensible Markup Language (XML)", http://www.w3.org/XML/.
12. Object Management Group (OMG), "Unified Modeling Language (UML)", http://www.uml.org/.
13. Robert Bosch GmbH, "Controller Area Network (CAN)", http://www.semiconductors.bosch.de

2005-01-1040

Next Generation Test Automation

Christopher Anhalt, Klaus Lebert and Frank Tränkle
ETAS GmbH

ABSTRACT

This paper presents ETAS GmbH research and product development activities related to test automation for embedded systems in the automotive industry. We propose a structured approach to flexible, systematic and efficient test automation.

This research is based on several years of experience with test automation processes, products and solutions. Current research and development activities are closely linked to a pilot customer, implementing unified and automated test processes across several divisions.

Central aspects of our research include a precise definition of various tasks and roles in an overall test process, the flexible connection of test case development tools, and test bench independence.

Our research helps create test solutions which offer improved reusability of test cases and better manageability of test processes.

INTRODUCTION

Automated embedded system testing in the automotive industry can be characterized by the following requirements:

- Test processes shall be manageable, efficient, and produce reliable, comprehensive test results.
- A standardized approach shall create synergies. For example, it shall support the reuse and exchange of test cases.
- Test systems shall enable the efficient testing of single ECU variants as well as networked ECUs.
- Test systems shall have open interfaces to connect to different test benches, units under test, and test case design tools.
- Test systems and processes shall provide an integrated approach to Model in the Loop (MiL), Software in the Loop (SiL), and Hardware in the Loop (HiL) test scenarios.

Test automation procedures largely determine how efficiently test systems can be used and how well these requirements are met. Test automation is a key element of test systems, becoming strategically important. Therefore, OEMs as well as suppliers benefit from standardized approaches to automated testing.

On the other hand, standardization is not a simple task. Or, as Broekman and Notenboom write, *"there is no point in looking for the ONE test approach for embedded systems."* [1]. On a more detailed level, process-related as well as technical requirements for embedded systems tests may differ a lot.

Hence our research has been aimed at the following two central goals:

- Analysis of current test procedures and processes, description of roles and tasks which provide a generic, flexible model for embedded system testing activities.
- Design and development of a commercially available next generation test automation tool, based on the insight we gained about roles and processes, and meeting the requirements listed above.

The next two sections introduce core concepts and a role model for test automation. Then we explain our tool architecture and product features in greater detail. Finally we provide some information about a pilot customer tool roll-out, and potential areas of future R&D activities.

CONCEPTUAL OVERVIEW

Test cases are important artifacts for embedded system testing processes. In order to introduce some structure to test processes, we took a closer look at the handling of test cases. As a key result of our analysis, we distinguish between

- Test case development
- Test case management, and
- Test case execution.

This distinction is fundamental for what follows.

TEST CASE DEVELOPMENT

Test case development activities include the development of "abstract" test cases: These are test cases which do not include parameter definitions and test bench specific information, and which are independent from the unit under test. On the other hand, abstract test cases can contain test case parameters that control test execution flow and connection to the test bench for later adaptations in the test case management phase.

Obviously, there is some trade-off between independence (and hence reusability) and development effort of test cases. The system shall let the user choose which degree of abstraction he or she would like to work with.

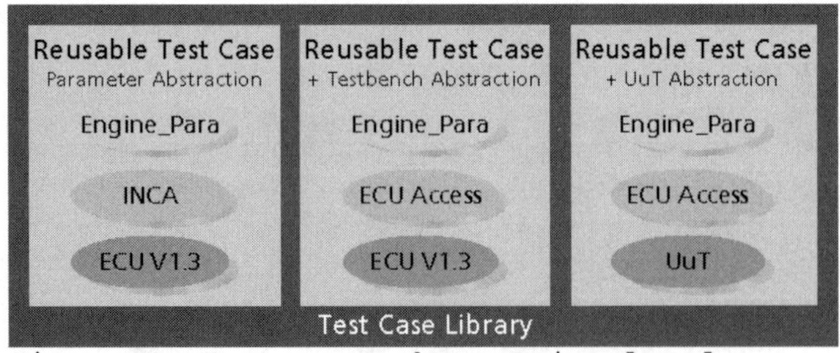

Figure 1: Test case abstraction levels

Abstract test cases are collected in a test case library.

TEST CASE MANAGEMENT

Test case management includes all activities required to create an executable test case sequence.

Test case management starts with the definition of a test project. A test project comprises a set of unit under tests and test functionality, i.e. test cases selected from the test case library. The selected test functionality is called "master set" of test cases.

Next comes a definition of test case parameters, matching the requirements of this test project.

Finally the user defines "test campaigns". These are precise definitions of test case sequences which can be started and executed automatically. For example, by selecting test cases from a master set, a user may define three separate test campaigns for a complete functionality test, for a shorter plausibility test, and for a test covering special functionality only.

The result of test case management is an executable test project, i.e. a defined set of unit under tests to be tested with specific test functionality, organized in test campaigns.

TEST CASE EXECUTION

So far, test campaigns do not contain any test bench specific information. Rather, they may run on different test benches. For example, in a hardware-in-the-loop scenario, a test campaign may be executed on two different test benches from different hardware vendors.

Therefore a user selects a test bench and a configuration for this test bench. Then a test campaign can be executed. Finally the user reviews the results.

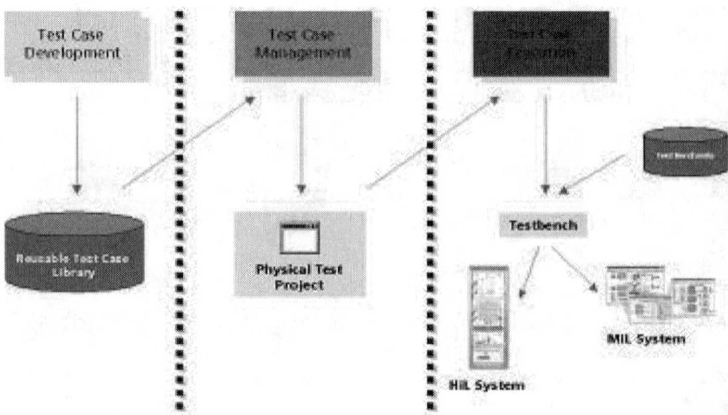

Figure 2: A new process for managing test cases

The tool architecture and the role model described later on follow this overall structure. It offers significant advantages, such as:

- Test case reusability: While the initial test case development effort for reusable test cases may be higher than in conventional scenarios, improved reusability shall decrease test case development efforts in the long run.
- Test bench independence: The definition of a test project without test bench specific information helps to integrate Hardware-in-the-Loop testing with testing effort earlier in the development cycle, for example Model-in-the-loop testing. When a company decides to introduce new tools and processes, test bench independence helps to protect past investments into test bench hardware and software.
- Reduced dependency on single technical experts: The distinction between test case development, test case management, and test case execution lets employees focus on what they know and can do best. For example, a test design expert for test case development does not have to understand test bench configuration issues. Or a person executing a test run does not have to be able to work with a test design tool, or understand details of test project parameterization. Procedures and responsibilities are more transparent.

ROLE MODEL OVERVIEW

Our conceptual approach makes it possible to divide the test case development and deployment process into distinct roles so that different people (or even companies) can perform different parts of the process. Each step in the procedure outlined above requires one or more distinct sets of skills.

While test case development matches a test case developer role, test case management may be split further into roles for test project definition, test parameter management, and test campaign management.

A test bench configuration manager role requires expert knowledge and is separate from a test handler role, executing predefined test campaigns with predefined test bench configurations.

The following table summarizes how we refer to each skill set as one of the following roles:

Role	Task
Test Case Developer	Develops reusable test cases and puts them into test case library
Test Project Manager	Sets up test project by selecting Unit under Tests and test cases
Test Parameter Manager	Defines test case parameters for given Unit under Test
Test Campaign Manager	Defines test execution runs
Test Handler	Tests specific unit under tests by selecting predefined test bench configuration and executing predefined test campaigns
Test Bench Configuration Manager	Defines test bench configurations

Figure 3: Roles and tasks in a test process

Role models are commonly used for the definition of standardized yet flexible IT system architectures and tool landscapes. For example, the industry standard J2EE [2], which defines interfaces for server architectures, includes a description of roles and tasks involved in the development and deployment of distributed applications.

In real world scenarios, one user may work in more than just one role.

AUTOMATION TOOL SET ARCHITECTURE

GENERAL VALIDATION SYSTEM

An automation tool is part of a larger test system, or "general validation system". Key elements of such a general validation system are:

- The Unit under test (UuT)
- The driver-vehicle-environment (DVE), which may consist of simulated and real parts

- Diagnostics and measurement & calibration tools, in order to access the UuT or part of the DVE

- An experiment environment, which lets the user execute a test case manually

In addition to these runtime system components, there are components required for the development system:

- A test design tool for the development of test case functionality

- A modeling tool for the development of DVE simulation models

The automation tool is part of the runtime environment, connecting test design tool and manual experiment environment.

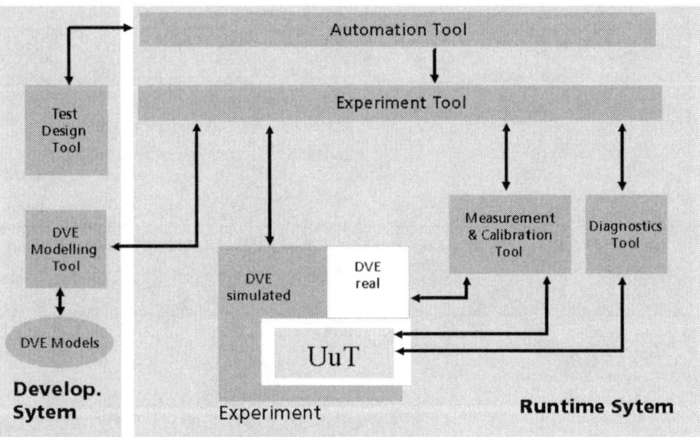

Figure 4: General validation system

TEST BENCH INDEPENDENCE

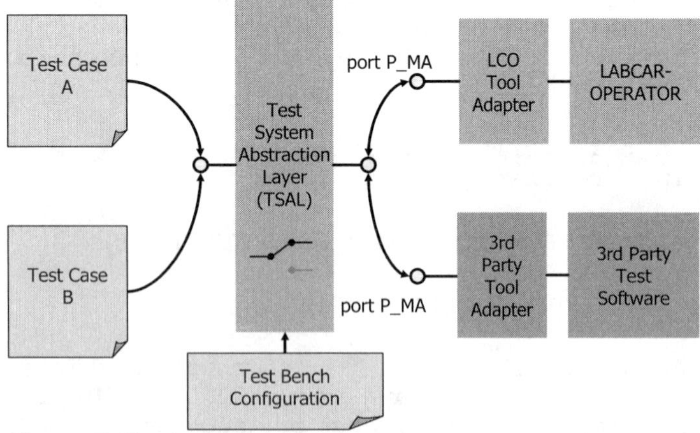

Figure 5: Tool architecture overview

In order to be test bench independent, test cases must be implemented along the following guidelines:

- Test cases access the test bench and the Unit under Test only via abstract ports.

- Test cases reference variables of the DVE or UUT only by symbolic identifiers.

Ports are abstract interfaces to test bench tools. They provide sets of function signatures to invoke test bench tool functions. Examples for ports are P_MA to access the DVE simulation model, P_DIAG to access the ECU diagnostic interface, P_EAM and P_EAC to access the ECU measurement and calibration interfaces. All ports are independent from the concrete implementation of the function signatures in test bench tools.

For executing test cases on test benches, the ports are connected to tool adapters that convert abstract signature calls to concrete test bench tool API calls. These connections are part of the test bench configuration. Thus, the decision on which test bench the test shall be executed can be made during the test execution phase.

The Test System Abstraction Layer is the test execution master. It dispatches the signature calls invoked by the test cases to the connected tool adapters. It further converts symbolic variable identifiers (e.g., "nengine") to tool-specific variable addresses (e.g., "vehicle.engine.nengine").

TEST DESIGN TOOL CONNECTION

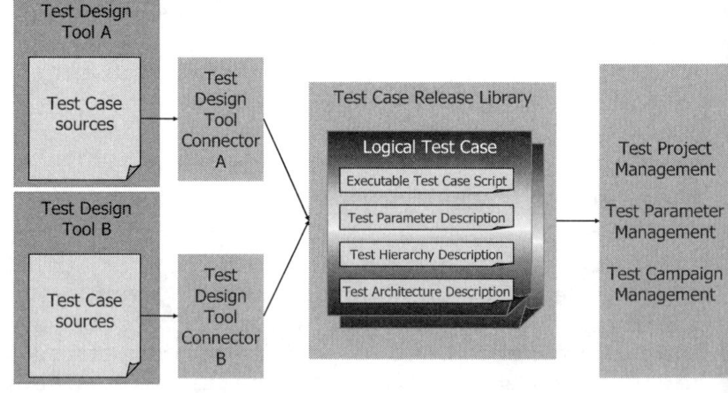

Figure 6: Test design tool independence

The automation tool not only provides interfaces to implement tool adapters, but also interfaces to connect to test design tools such as Telelogic TAU/Tester and National Instruments TestStand or test scripting languages such as Perl and Python. Connections to test design tools or scripting languages are realized by implementing Test Design Tool Connectors.

Next to the executable test case script, a Test Design Tool Connector extracts the following information from a abstract test case:

- The test parameter specification lists all test parameters that have been specified for the test case in the test design tool. This information is later used in the test parameterization phase.

- The test hierarchy description represents the aggregation hierarchy of the test case, i.e., from which test entities the test case has been composed. This information is later used both in the test project management and parameterization phases.

- The test architecture description lists all ports and signatures that are invoked by the test case. This information can be later used in the test execution phase to check if the test case can be executed on a pre-configured test bench.

All three information items are generated into XML files. Together with the test case script, they form the abstract test script that is inserted into the test case library. In the test project management phase, test projects are built by retrieving abstract test cases from this library.

LABCAR PRODUCT

DESIGN TOOL INTEGRATION TELELOGIC TAU/TESTER

The first version of a commercially available product, LABCAR-AUTOMATION V2.0, includes a component for the integration of Telelogic's TAU/Tester test design tool.

With TAU/Tester, test cases are developed using TTCN-3. TTCN-3 (Testing and Test Control Notation version 3) is a language used to write detailed test specifications. The latest version of the language, TTCN version 3, is standardized by ETSI (ES 201 873 series) and the ITU-T (Z.140 series) [3].

In order to simplify and speed up the development of test cases with the LABCAR-AUTOMATION tool, a "TTCN-3 framework" is part of the integration package.

AUTOMATION TOOL USER INTERFACES

User interfaces are closely related to the role model outlined earlier. They are separated into the following set of LABCAR-AUTOMATION tools: Test Manager, Test Handler, Test Report Viewer, SUT Mapping File Editor.

Test Manager

Test project managemenet, test parameter management and test campaign management roles share some common properties: Each of these roles deals with the same test project structure and the same test case functionality selected for this test project.

Hence these three roles are integrated into one GUI tool, offering a test project window, a test functionality window, and three different work panes (one for each of the three roles).

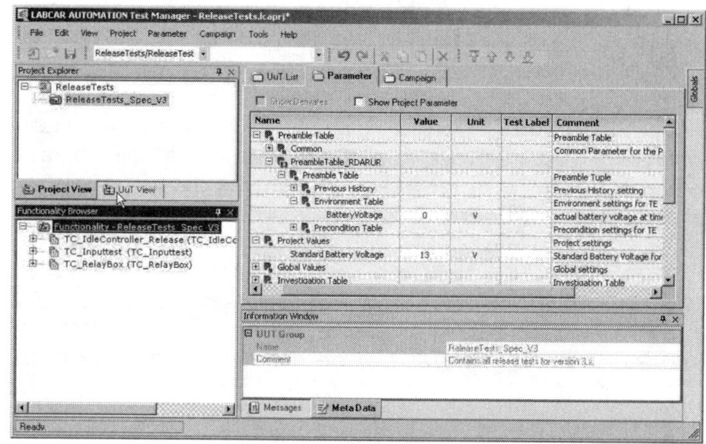

Figure 7: Screen shot Test Manager GUI

The GUI takes reusable test cases and a list of Unit under Tests as starting point, in order to deliver an executable (still test bench independent) test project, testing specific UuTs with specific test campaigns.

Test Handler

A Test Handler GUI tool lets users select a specific test campaign and test bench configuration and start the automatic test execution.

IMPLEMENTATION OF PORTS

For LABCAR-AUTOMATION V2.0, three different ports have been implemented:

- Simulation model access

- Diagnostics access

- ECU measurement and calibration access

Corresponding tool adapters access the manual experimentation software LABCAR-OPERATOR, the diagnostics tool Softing DTS, and the measurement and calibration tool INCA.

LABCAR-AUTOMATION provides documented APIs to implement tool adapters to other test bench tools, to register new ports, and to implement test design tool connectors.

PILOT CUSTOMER ROLL OUT

The research described in this paper has been done in close cooperation with Robert Bosch GmbH. Robert Bosch's goal is to standardize their test processes and tool architectures for their Chassis Systems, Gasoline Systems, and Diesel Systems divisions.

During 2003, each division executed more than 1000 fully automated system test. Each test run took between several minutes and several hours.

The roll-out of the new LABCAR-AUTOMATION tool started during September 2004 in all three divisions. Development for TTCN-3 based test cases to be used in production environments started soon after in October 2004.

A roll-out of the new tool and automated tests in production environments is currently being prepared.

AREAS OF FUTURE RESEARCH

PORT STANDARDIZATION

Ports are an important abstraction layer between test case code and physical test bench properties. A standardization of ports will help increase test case reusability and portability of test bench components.

TEST MANAGEMENT INTERFACES

Future versions of LABCAR-AUTOMATION shall add test management features, in order to allow for more efficient ECU variant handling, and further reduced parameterization efforts. Usability is a key requirement.

TTCN IN THE AUTOMOTIVE INDUSTRY

As a standardized test design language, TTCN-3 clearly offers important benefits. Further propagation of TTCN-3 in the automotive industry may well go hand-in-hand with participation in TTCN-3 (and related) standardization activities. Interestingly, the current UML Testing Profile Specification contains a TTCN-3 mapping [4].

CONCLUSION

Our research led to the conclusion that a clear separation between test case development, test case process management, and test case execution provides a useful framework for systematic test automation.

The introduction of abstract test cases and a role model associated with the handling of such test cases offers significant benefits for practically all areas of embedded systems testing in the automotive industry.

The first version of a next generation automation tool is successfully used in pilot projects.

REFERENCES

1. Bart Broekman, Edwin Notenboom; "Testing Embedded Software"; Addison-Wesley, 2002.
2. For more information about J2EE, see http://java.sun.com/j2ee/. At the time of writing, more detailed information about its role model could be found at http://java.sun.com/j2ee/1.4/docs/tutorial/doc/Overview6.html#wp79888
3. http://www.etsi.org/ptcc/ptccttcn3.htm
4. http://www.omg.org/docs/ptc/04-04-02.pdf

CONTACT

christopher.anhalt@etas.de

2005-01-0750

Evolutionary Safety Testing of Embedded Control Software by Automatically Generating Compact Test Data Sequences

Hartmut Pohlheim and Mirko Conrad
DaimlerChrysler AG

Arne Griep
IAV GmbH

ABSTRACT

Whereas the verification of non-safety-related, embedded software typically focuses on demonstrating that the implementation fulfills its functional requirements, this is not sufficient for safety-relevant systems. In this case, the control software must also meet application-specific safety requirements.

Safety requirements typically arise from the application of hazard and/or safety analysis techniques, e.g. FMEA, FTA or SHARD. During the downstream development process it must be shown that these requirements cannot be violated. This can be achieved utilizing different techniques. One way of providing evidence that violations of the safety properties identified cannot occur is to thoroughly test each of the safety requirements.

This paper introduces Evolutionary Safety Testing (EST), a fully automated procedure for the safety testing of embedded control software. EST employs extended evolutionary algorithms in an optimization process which aggressively tries to find test data sequences that cause the test object to violate a given safety requirement.

A compact description formalism for input sequences for safety testing is presented, which is compatible with description techniques used during other test process stages. This compact description allows 1) an efficient application of evolutionary algorithms (and other optimization techniques) and 2) the description of long test sequences necessary for the adequate stimulation of real-world systems. The objective function is designed in such a way that optimal values represent test data sequences which violate a given safety requirement. By means of repeated input sequence generation, software execution and the subsequent evaluation of the objective function each safety requirement is extensively tested.

The use of EST for the safety testing of automotive control software is demonstrated using safety requirements of an adaptive cruise control (ACC) system.

The EST approach can easily be integrated into an overall software test strategy which combines different test design techniques with specific test objectives.

INTRODUCTION

Many of the innovations in the automotive field are results of the use of software-intensive systems in vehicles. The proportion of functions which are activated for regulatory or controlling purposes when the vehicle is in motion has risen steeply in the last few years. Especially in the case of safety-relevant functions, the quality of the control software is of the utmost importance.

Software development is not yet at the stage at which the quality of embedded control software can be ensured using constructive procedures alone. Their use must be supplemented with analytical procedures which detect errors in the software. Since there are currently no universally recognized measurement procedures for software quality, measuring is often replaced with dynamic testing [HV98]. Functional (black-box) test design techniques are mainly used for testing embedded control software, i.e. testing that focuses on demonstrating that the implementation fulfills its functional requirements. The test cases or test scenarios are predominantly created manually. In some cases, the functional test design techniques are also complemented with structural (white-box) test methods in order to demonstrate the structural integrity of the software.

For safety-related systems this approach is not sufficient. In this case, the control software must also meet application-specific safety requirements. Such safety requirements typically arise from the application of hazard and/or safety analysis techniques, e.g. Failure Mode and Effect Analysis (FMEA) [IEC60812], Fault Tree Analysis (FTA)

[IEC 61025] or Software Hazard Analysis and Resolution in Design (SHARD) [FMN+94]. During the downstream development process it must be shown that these safety requirements cannot be violated. This can be achieved utilizing different techniques. One way of providing evidence that violations of the safety properties identified cannot occur is to thoroughly test each of the safety requirements. As is the case for any other test problem, the search for suitable test cases/test scenarios and their appropriate description is of decisive importance.

Being universally applicable strategies for improvement and optimization, Evolutionary Algorithms (EA) have become widespread in a broad range of searching problems. Their application is based on a seemingly simple and easily comprehensible principle, namely 'Darwin's evolution paradigm' or, in other words, the principle of the 'survival of the fittest'. Like in nature, solutions are improved step-by-step, and optima are identified or approximated by applying variation and selection to a population of alternative solutions [VDI/VDE 3550].

Prerequisites for the application of EA are the definition of the search space, in which solutions are searched for and of an objective function, with which the fitness of the solution proposals found can be evaluated.

The interpretation of the search for suitable test scenarios, which violate a given safety requirement, as an optimization problem and the subsequent use of EA to solve this problem leads to the concept of Evolutionary Safety Testing (EST) [Weg01]. Thereby, the search space is defined by a compact description formalism for possible input sequences.

In principle, the EST approach can be applied to different embedded control software development stages. In order to be able to incorporate the results of evolutionary safety testing early in the development process, it is, however, advisable to already apply the procedure to the executable model of the future software.

Here, EST should not be the only test design technique which is employed but rather it should be used together with others as part of an overall test strategy for automotive control software developed in a model-based way.

The remainder of the paper is structured as follows: Section 1 explains why sequence testing is necessary for cyclic software components which are typical for embedded automotive controls. Section 2 shows how evolutionary algorithms can be used to automatically generate real-world input sequences for the safety testing of embedded automotive control systems. An example is used to illustrate the entire process. In Section 3 we show how the evolutionary safety testing is incorporated into a model-based test strategy. Related work is presented in Section 4.

1 CYCLIC SOFTWARE COMPONENTS AND SEQUENCE TESTING

1.1 CYCLIC SOFTWARE COMPONENTS

As embedded controls mostly interact with the outside world continuously via sensors and actuators, they must be able to process time-variable sensor signals and produce time-variable outputs.

When analyzing the software of those systems, a large class of implementations can be identified which use a implementation scheme whereby the control algorithm is triggered at regular time intervals by its environment to compute output values and an internal state from given inputs. This class is referred to as cyclic software components (cf. [GHD98], [MK99]). In the world of automotive controls it is very common for a software function to be based on an initialization and step function. Whereas the initialization function is only called once at the beginning, the step function is executed periodically e.g. every 10 ms. An adaptive cruise control system (ACC) which checks the velocity and distance to a preceding vehicle at regular intervals to find out if a safe distance is maintained, is an example of this system class.

<u>Example ACC</u>

If the driver so desires, the ACC system controls the speed of the vehicle whilst maintaining a safe distance from the preceding vehicle. The activated system monitors the section of road in front of the vehicle. If there is no preceding vehicle ('target') on this section, the system regulates the longitudinal vehicle speed in the same way as a conventional cruise control system. As soon as a preceding vehicle is recognized, the distance control function is activated which makes sure that the vehicle follows the vehicle in front at the same speed and at a safe distance.

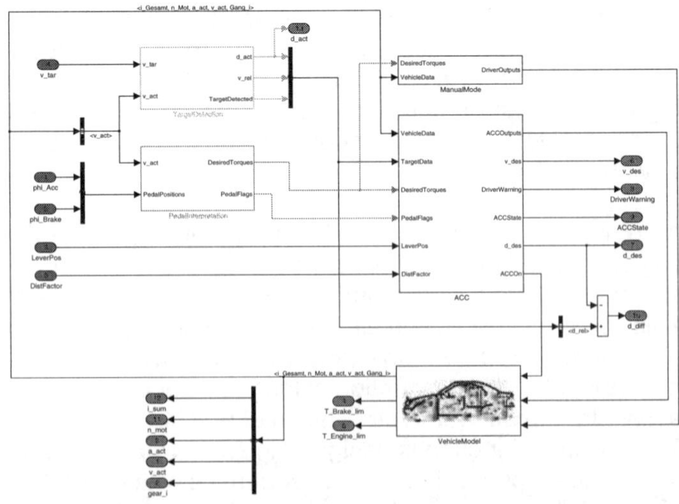

Figure 1. Simulink/Stateflow model of the ACC system

In the model-based development process [Rau03], [KCF+04], the ACC is first described using an executable Simulink/Stateflow [SLSF] model. The structure of the overall system is presented in Figure 1. Besides the actual ACC system, there are two preprocessing systems for the recognition of preceding vehicles (TargetDetermination) and the evaluation of the current pedal values (PedalInterpretation). A system for parts of the plant model (VehicleModel, ManualMode) also exists. These make a closed loop test of the entire system, including the vehicle and the vehicle in front, possible. A more detailed description is contained in [CH98] and [Con04].

If a cyclic software component such as the ACC is to be simulated with realistic input data during the test and if a system reaction is to be induced, the test inputs must be given as time-variable signal waveforms.

1.2 SEQUENCE TESTING

In principle, the testing of cyclic software components can be performed in different ways.

Single input-state-pairs

The approach traditionally used is to generate pairs of internal states and input situations as shown in Figure 2. This means that a test case represents a certain point in time within a test sequence. For this, internal states have to be set directly. This approach works well for simple software components but raises several problems.

The direct setting of internal states is not possible in all cases and requires changes to be made to the test object. When generating the internal states, the test environment has to make sure that the states produced are valid according to the specification. Forcing the system into a generated state is, in most cases, not useful for the tester. This is because the tester has to use the test data generated to analyze software bugs. He first needs to ascertain how to produce the initial state which caused the problem. In other words, he has to manually reconstruct the initial part of the relevant sequence. This information is not provided by the test environment.

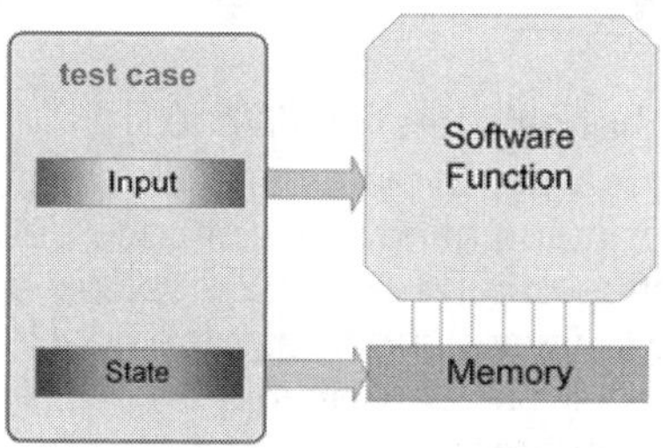

Figure 2. Automatic testing by generating (state, input) pairs

Input sequences

For complex systems it is necessary to provide real input sequences.

(a) Extensional input sequences: Within this group, one approach is to create lists of inputs for sequential calls of the function under test. This means that a test sequence is formed using a list element for each point in time in the test sequence. In other words, the test sequence is represented by enumerating / listing all of its elements (Figure 3).

As a rule, this approach leads to long and low-level test descriptions, but is often sufficient for software components based on pure state models.

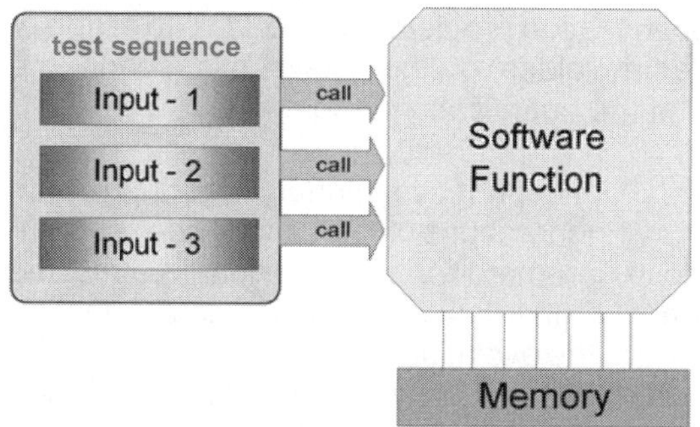

Figure 3. Automatic testing by generating list of inputs

(b) Intensional input sequences: For control systems requiring long 'real world' input sequences, an abstraction from the extensional sequence description is indispensable. Test sequences are described by their main characteristics. One way of doing this is to describe only selected points in time in a test sequence (time tags) and to specify transition functions for those values in between. This leads to an intensional or encoded sequence description (Figure 4).

Intensional descriptions can be very compact and comprehensive and are also often easier to understand for humans. A test sequence can be described using substantially less parameters than is the case for extensional input sequences.

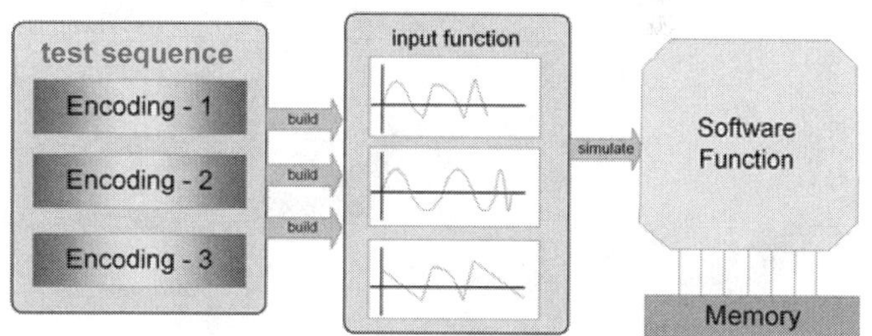

Figure 4. Automatic testing by generating input sequences from encoded input functions

The two variants for describing tests with input sequences are, from the tester's perspective, the better solution, since they guarantee that the software component is tested in the same way as it will later be used.

Test approaches which use test sequences (as opposed to single input-state-pairs) in order to stimulate the actual test object will be referred to as sequence testing (approaches) from here on. Within sequence testing, test inputs and system reactions are not considered to be static values but rather time-variable signal waveforms.

2 EVOLUTIONARY SAFETY TESTING

Evolutionary algorithms (EA) have been used to search for data for a wide range of applications. EA is an iterative search procedure using variation and selection to copy the behavior of biological evolution. They work in parallel on a number of potential solutions, the population of individuals. In every individual, permissible solution values for the variables of the optimization problem are coded. The range of possible variable values of the individuals spans the search space of the optimization problem.

The fundamental concept of evolutionary algorithms is to evolve successive generations of increasingly better combinations of those parameters which significantly affect the overall performance of a design. Starting with a selection of good individuals, the evolutionary algorithm achieves the optimum solution by exchanging information between these increasingly fit samples (recombination) and introducing a probability of independent random change (mutation). The adaptation of the evolutionary algorithm is achieved by the selection and reinsertion procedures used because these are based on the fitness of the individuals. The selection procedures control which individuals are selected for reproduction depending on the individuals' fitness values. The reinsertion strategy determines how many and which individuals are taken from the parent and the offspring population to form the next generation. The fitness value is a numerical value that expresses the performance of an individual with regard to the other individuals in the population so that different designs may be compared. The notion of fitness is fundamental to the application of evolutionary algorithms.

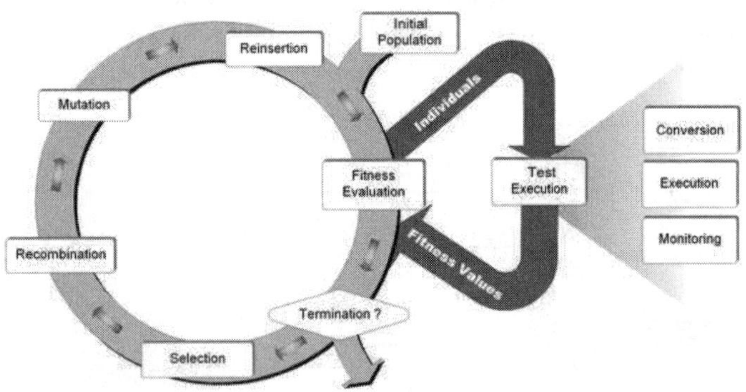

Figure 5. The structure of Evolutionary Testing

Figure 5 gives an overview of a typical procedure for evolutionary algorithms. First, an initial population of guesses as to the solution of a problem is initialized, usually at random. Each individual in the population is evaluated by calculating its objective value. Afterwards, the fitness of each individual is calculated by ranking the objective values of all the individuals of the population. The remainder of the algorithm is iterated until the optimum is achieved, or another stopping condition is fulfilled. Pairs of individuals are selected from the population according to the pre-defined selection strategy, and are combined in some way to produce a new guess in an analogous way to biological reproduction. Combination algorithms are many and varied. Additionally, mutation is applied. The new individuals are evaluated for their objective value (and fitness), and survivors into the next generation are chosen from the parents and offspring, often according to fitness though it is important to maintain diversity in the population to prevent premature convergence to a sub-optimal solution.

For the optimization we employed extended evolutionary algorithms. This includes the use of multiple subpopulations, each using a different search strategy. We also used competition for limited resources between these subpopulations.

For a detailed discussion of evolutionary algorithms and the extensions used see [Poh99]. The algorithms employed are implemented in the widely used MATLAB based 'Genetic and Evolutionary Algorithm Toolbox for use with Matlab – GEATbx' [Poh05]. It consists of a large set of operators e.g. real and integer parameter, migration and competition strategies.

When using EA for a search problem, it is necessary to define the search space and the objective (fitness) function.

2.1 EVOLUTIONARY ALGORITHMS FOR SEQUENCE TESTING

Evolutionary Testing uses EA to test software automatically. The different software test objectives formulate requirements for a test case / test sequence to be generated. Until now, the generation of such a set of test data usually had to be carried out manually. Automatic software testing generates a test data set automatically, aiming to fulfill the requirements in order to increase efficiency and resulting in an enormous cost reduction.

The general idea is to divide the test into individual test objectives and to use EA to search for test data that fulfills each of the test objectives.

In the past, evolutionary testing has proven itself to be of value for different testing tasks:

- Evolutionary temporal behavior testing [Weg01]
- Evolutionary structural testing: Evolutionary Structural Testing has the goal of automating the test case design for white-box testing criteria [BSS02]. Taking a test object, namely the software under test, the goal is to find a test case set (selection of inputs) which achieves full structural coverage

Depending on the task and test objective, both single input-state-pairs and test sequences can be created by the evolutionary test as stimuli for the test object.

Since complex dynamic systems, like the ACC, must be evaluated over a long time period (longer than the highest internal dead time or time constant), such systems must be tested by using input sequences. Furthermore, they must not be stimulated for only a few simulation steps, but rather the input signals must be up to hundreds or thousands of time steps long. Long input sequences are therefore necessary in order to realistically simulate these systems. As a consequence, the output sequences to be monitored and evaluated have the same duration.

Example ACC

In order to check the correct reaction of the ACC system with regard to speed changes of the vehicle in front, the length of realistic test sequences has to be in the magnitude of some 10s. Assuming a sampling rate of 10ms for the cyclic ACC software component, this results in input (and subsequently) output sequences which are some 1000 time steps long.

Several disadvantages result from the length of the sequences necessary: using extensional sequence descriptions, the number of variables to be optimized and the correlation between the variables is very high. For this reason, one of the most important aims is the development of a very compact, intensional description for the input sequences. Such a description has to contain as few elements as possible but, at the same time, offer a sufficient amount of variety to stimulate the system under test as much as necessary.

Moreover, possibilities for automatically evaluating the system reactions must be developed, which allow differentiation between the quality of the individual input sequences.

The generation of test sequences for dynamic real-world systems poses a number of challenges:

- The input sequences must be long enough to stimulate the system realistically.
- The input sequences must possess the right qualities in order to stimulate the system adequately. This concerns aspects such as data type of the signal, speed and rate of signal changes.
- The output sequences must be evaluated regarding a number of different conditions / properties. These conditions/properties are often contradictory and several of them can be active simultaneously.

In order to develop a test environment for the functional test of dynamic systems which can be applied in practice, the following steps must be completed:

- definition of the test objective, i.e. the safety property to be violated,
- description of the search space, i.e. the description of the input sequences,
- description of the objective (fitness) function in order to evaluate output sequences regarding the test objective,
- assessment of counter examples generated

2.2 DEFINITION OF THE TEST OBJECTIVE

In order to utilize evolutionary sequence testing for safety testing, the test objective is to violate a safety requirement resulting from a hazard and/or safety analysis.

Example ACC

A major requirement for the ACC system is to maintain a 'safe' distance to the vehicle in front. More precisely the desired distance d_{des} between one's own and the target vehicle is defined according to the German 'Tacho-halbe-Regel' by:

$$d_{des} [m] = v_{act} [m/s] * 3.6/2 * DistFactor$$

For normal road conditions the distance factor is 1, for wet or icy roads >1.

A derived safety requirement could be that the actual distance d_{act} is not allowed to go below the d_{des} by more than 10m. In other words:

$$d_{act} [m] > d_{des} [m] - 10$$

2.3 DESCRIPTION OF THE SEARCH SPACE

In order to define the search space, we have to deal with a number of descriptions. At the beginning, there is the compact description of the search space given by the safety tester (compact search space description). Finally, we need the individual (sampled) signals, which are used as inputs for the simulation (extensional test sequences). In between, there are the boundary descriptions of the variables to be optimized (optimization variable boundaries) and the instantiation of the individual sequences (intensional test sequences). These different sequence description levels are illustrated in Figure 6.

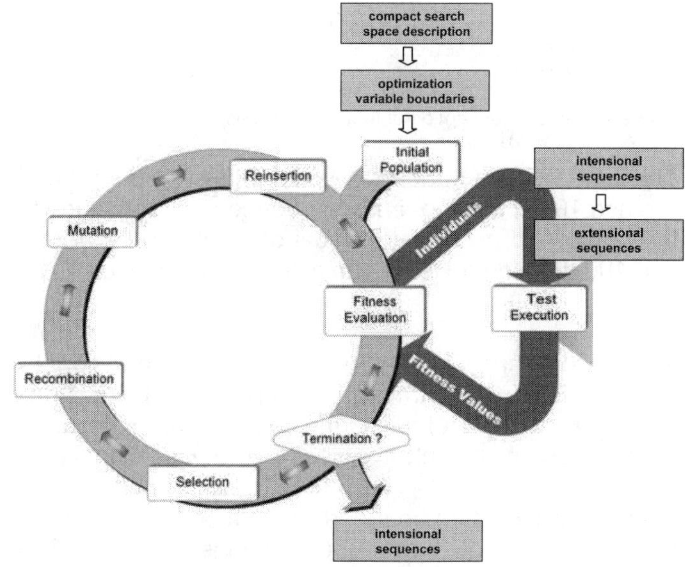

Figure 6. Different levels of input sequence description

For an intensional sequence description, each signal of a long simulation sequence is subdivided into consecutive sections. Each section is parameterized by the variables: section length, signal amplitude (at the beginning of the section) and interpolation function. Typical interpolation functions are, for instance, step, ramp (linear), impulse, sine and spline.

Only the admissible ranges for these parameters are specified for the optimization. In this way, the boundaries are defined, within which the optimization generates solutions which are subsequently evaluated by the objective function with regard to their fitness.

The signal amplitude of each section can be defined absolutely or relatively. The length of the section is always defined relatively (to ensure the monotony of the signal). The interpolation functions are given as an enumeration of possible types. These boundaries must be defined for each input of the system. For nearly every real-world system these boundaries can be derived from the specification of the system under test.

Example ACC

An example of an input sequence description in the MATLAB .m scripting language is provided in Figure 7. Figure 8 provides an example of an extensional sequence generated by the optimization based on the settings given in Figure 7.

```
% Input settings

% input names and order: 'phi_Acc', 'phi_Brake', 'Lever-
Pos', 'v_tar', 'DistFactor'

% number of sections / base points for each input signal
BasePoints = [10 10 10 10 10];

% relative section length
BasisBounds = [ 1  1  1  1  1; ...
               10 10 10 10 10];

% min. / max. amplitude for each input signal
AmplitudeBounds = [0 0 0 20 1; ...
                   0 0 2 45 1];

% possible interpolation functions for each input signal
TransitionPool = {{}; {}; {'impulse'}; {'spline'}; {}};
```

Figure 7. Textual description of input sequences

The ACC system under test has 5 inputs (see Figure 1). We use 10 sections for each sequence. The amplitude for the brake and accelerator pedal can change between 0 and 100, the control lever can only have the values 0, 1, 2 or 3.

In real-world applications the variety of an input signal is often constrained with regard to possible base signal types. An example of this is the control lever in Figure 7. This input contains only impulses as the base signal type.

To generate a further bounded description, it is possible to define identical lower and upper bounds for some of the other parameters. In this case, the optimization has an empty search space for this variable – this input parameter is a constant. An example is the distance factor in Figure 8. This input signal is always set to a constant value of 1. Thus, it is not part of the optimization (but is used as a constant value for the generation of the internal simulation sequence).

The different descriptions ensure that the requirements for an adequate simulation of the system and a very compact and comprehensible description by the tester are fulfilled. The compact description is used for the optimization, ensuring a small number of variables.

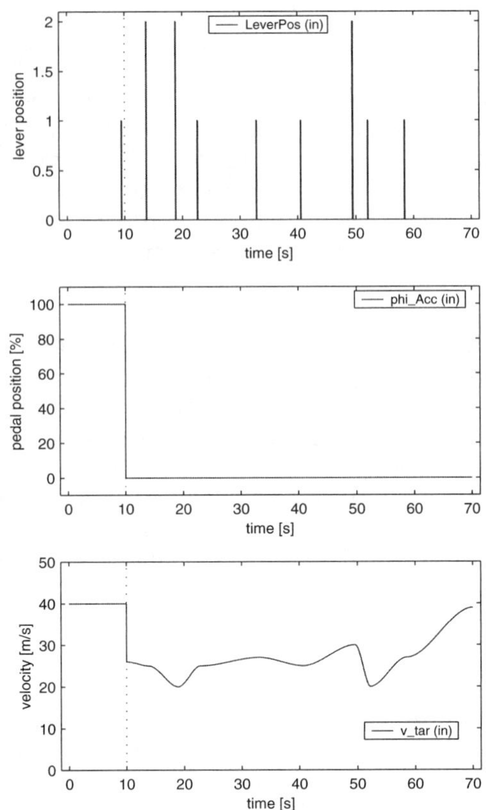

Figure 8. Simulation sequence generated by the optimization based on the textual description in Figure 7; top: throttle pedal, middle: control lever, bottom: velocity of target car

Example ACC

When comparing the size of both descriptions for the example dynamic system used (5 inputs – 3 of the inputs are constant, 10 signal sections, 2 variable parameters for each section (section length and amplitude), 60s simulation time, sampling rate 0.01s) the differences are enormous:

$$NumParameter_{Extensional} = 5 \cdot 60 \cdot (1/0.01) = 30000 \qquad (1)$$
$$NumParameter_{Compact} = (5-3) \cdot 10 \cdot 2 = 40$$
$$CompressionRatio = \frac{30000}{40} = 750$$

Only this compact description opens up the opportunity to optimize and test real-world dynamic systems within a realistic time frame.

2.4 DESCRIPTION OF THE OBJECTIVE FUNCTION

The test environment must perform an evaluation of the output sequences generated by the simulation of the dynamic system. These output sequences must be evaluated regarding the optimization objectives. During the test, we always search for violations of the defined requirements. Possible aims of the test are to check for violations of:

- signal amplitude boundaries,
- maximal overshoot or maximal settlement time.

Each of these checks must be evaluated over the whole or a part of the signal lengths and an objective value has to be generated.

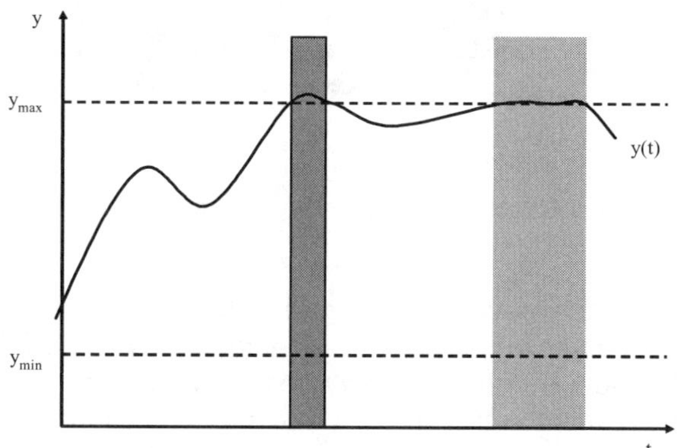

Figure 9. Violation of maximum amplitude

An example of the violation of signal amplitude boundaries is given in Figure 9. A minimal and maximal amplitude value is defined for the output signal y. In this example the output signal violates the upper boundary. The first violation is a serious violation as the signal transgresses the bound by more than a critical value y_c (parameter for this requirement). In this case, a special value indicating a severe violation is returned as the objective value (value -1), see equation (2). The second violation is less severe, as the extension over the bound is not critical. At this point an objective value indicating the closeness of the maximal value to the defined boundary is calculated. This two-level concept allows a differentiation in quality between multiple output signals violating the bounds defined. The direct calculation of the objective value is provided in equation (2).

$$signal_{max} = \max(y(t)) \qquad ObjVal_{max} = \begin{cases} -1 & signal_{max} \geq y_{max} + y_c \\ \left(\dfrac{signal_{max}}{y_{max}}\right)^6 & signal_{max} < y_{max} + y_c \end{cases} \qquad (2)$$

Example ACC

Equation (3) shows the objective function for the test objective defined in Section 2.2.

A similar assessment is used for calculating the objective value of the overshoot of an output signal after a step in the respective reference signal. First, the maximal overshoot value is calculated. Next, the relative height of the overshoot is assessed. A severe overshoot outside the specification returns a special value (again –1). This special value is used to terminate the current optimization. The test was successful, as we were able to find a violation of the specification and thus reach the aim of the optimization. In all other cases, an objective value equivalent to the value of the overshoot is calculated (similar to equation (2)).

$$d\_act_{min} = \min(d\_act(t)) \qquad ObjVal = \begin{cases} -1 & d\_act_{min} \leq d\_des - 10 \\ \left(\dfrac{-d\_act_{min}}{-10}\right)^6 & d\_act_{min} > d\_des - 10 \end{cases} \qquad (3)$$

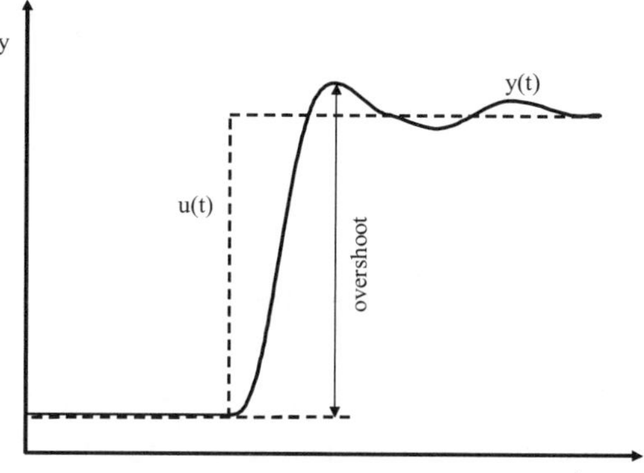

Figure 10. Assessment of signal overshoot

Each of the requirements tested produces one objective value. For nearly every realistic system test we receive multiple objective values. In order to assess the quality of all objectives tested we employ multi-objective ranking as supported by the GEATbx [Poh05]. This includes Pareto-ranking, goal attainment, fitness sharing and an archive of previously found solutions.

Example ACC

With an active ACC, the car can be accelerated only by pushing the control lever upwards (the respective input value is 1). The car is decelerated by pushing the control lever downwards (input value: 2). Besides the amplitude of the input control lever, the relative length of the signal sections could be changed between 1 and10. The results of a successful optimization are shown in Figures 11 and 12.

The optimization process is visualized in Figure 11. The left graph presents the progress of the best objective value over all the generations. The optimization continually finds better values. In the 83rd generation a serious violation is detected and an objective value of –1 returned. The middle graph presents the variables of the best individual in a color quilt. Each row represents the value of one variable over the optimization. The graph on the right visualizes the objective values of all the individuals during the optimization (generations 1 to 82).

The graphs in Figure 12 provide a much better insight into the quality of the results, visualizing the problem-specific results of the best individual of each respective generation. The input of the control lever is shown in the two top most graphs. The resulting velocity of the car is presented below. The graphs are taken from the 3rd (left) and 83rd generation (right). At the beginning the actual distance d_{act} (bottom graph left) is far above the critical boundary. During the optimization, the velocity is increased (the control lever is pushed up more often and at an earlier stage as

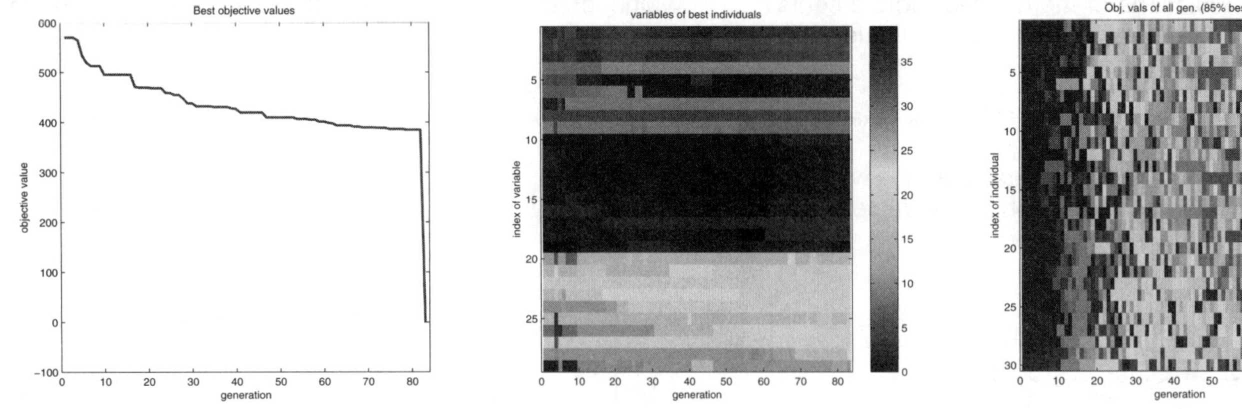

Figure 11. Visualization of the optimization process, left: best objective value; middle: variables of the best individual; right: objective value of all individuals

well as being pushed down less frequently). Additionally, the velocity of the target car is low (nearly the whole time at the defined lower boundary) during the whole scenario (3rd graph from the top). At the end an input situation is found, in which the actual distance d_{act} is smaller than the bound specified (bottom graph right). By looking at the respective input signals the developer can check and change the implementation of the system.

During optimization we employed the following evolutionary parameters: 20 individuals in 1 population, discrete recombination and real valued mutation with medium sized mutation steps, linear ranking with a selection pressure of 1.7 as well as a generation gap of 0.9. Other tests with a higher number of relevant input signals and thus more optimization variables employ 4-10 subpopulations with 20-50 individuals each. In this case, we use migration and competition between subpopulations. Each subpopulation uses a different strategy by employing different parameters (most of the time differently sized mutation steps).

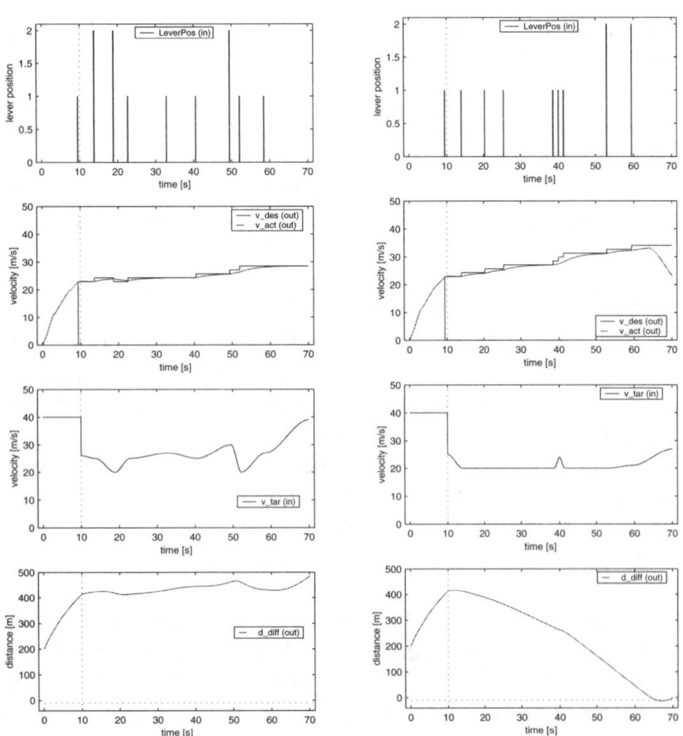

Figure 12. Problem-specific visualization of the best individual during the optimization, left: 3rd generation, right: 83rd generation; from top to bottom: input of the control lever, vehicle velocity (desired and actual), velocity of target, distance

2.5 ASSESSMENT OF COUNTER EXAMPLES

In the context of an automatic safety test it is of central importance that the test sequences which were generated automatically (counter examples) undergo an intensive analysis (assessment) carried out by human experts. Therefore, it is useful to provide a graphical notation for the generated input sequences which caters for the human tester [Con01]. Moreover, for the seamless integration of the test sequences resulting from EST with test sequences generated by other test design techniques, it is desirable to have input sequences depicted in the same way as other functional test scenarios.

For this purpose, one possibility would be to apply the extended classification-tree notation, which is used in the context of the Classification-tree Method for Embedded Systems (CTM_{EMB}) [Con04], [Con04a].

The CTM_{EMB} notation allows a comprehensive graphical description of time-dependent test sequences by means of abstract signal waveforms that are defined stepwise for each input.

The classifications of the tree represent the input variables of the functional model. Its classes are obtained by dividing the range of each variable into a set of non-overlapping values or intervals. Based on the input variable partitions, the test scenarios describe the course of these inputs over time in a comprehensive, abstract manner.

Time dependent behavior, i.e. changing the values of a model input over time in successive test steps can be modeled by marking different classes of the classification corresponding to that input. Continuous changes are defined by transitions (solid connecting lines) between marks in subsequent test.

Example ACC

Figure 13 shows an example of the visualization of the counter example given in Figure 12 by means of the CTM_{EMB} notation. The manual assessment shows that the input sequence which leads to the violation of the given safety requirement could occur in reality too. This means the algorithms or parameters of the ACC function must be modified and the evolutionary safety test has to be repeated.

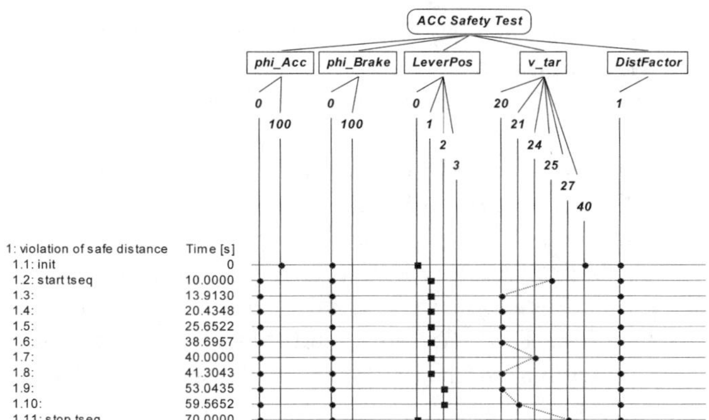

Figure 13. Visualization of a counter example generated by the EST

3 MODEL-BASED TEST STRATEGY

A singular testing technique does not generally lead to sufficient test coverage. Therefore, in practice, the aim is for complimentary test design techniques to be combined in the most adequate way to form a test strategy. The aim of an effective test strategy is to guarantee a high probability of error detection by combining appropriate testing techniques. An effective model-based test strategy must adequately take into account the specifics of model-based development and especially the existence of an executable model.

A model-based test strategy which integrates evolutionary safety testing is outlined in the following. The systematic functional model test based on the functional specification, the interfaces, and the executable model forms the focal point of such a model-based test strategy. In addition, an adequate structural test criterion is defined on model level, with the help of which the coverage of the tests thus determined can be evaluated and the definition of complementary tests can be controlled [Con04a]. If sufficient test coverage has thus been achieved on model level, the model should be mature enough to start safety testing.

Based on the safety requirements, the EST approach should be applied to every given safety requirement in order to aggressively try to generate counter examples.

If the EST process leads to one or more counter examples, those examples have to be assessed carefully. If the counter examples are impossible in practice, the search space description has to be adapted in order to avoid those scenarios in future. If scenarios described by the counter examples could happen in practice, the model or its parameter has to be corrected. After that, the model test has to be repeated: all existing model tests have to be repeated. By doing this, the tester has to ensure that the structural coverage is still sufficient and that all the tests lead to valid system reactions. Finally, the EST process has to be repeated. If no new counter examples are generated, the code generation can be started. All model test sequences can be reused for testing the control software generated from the model and the control unit within the framework of back-to-back tests. In this way, the functional equivalence between the executable model and derived forms of representation can be verified ([BCS03], [CSW04]).

The proposed model-based test strategy can be tool supported by integrating the different tools for creating test sequences into the model-based testing environment MTest ([LBE+04], [MTest]).

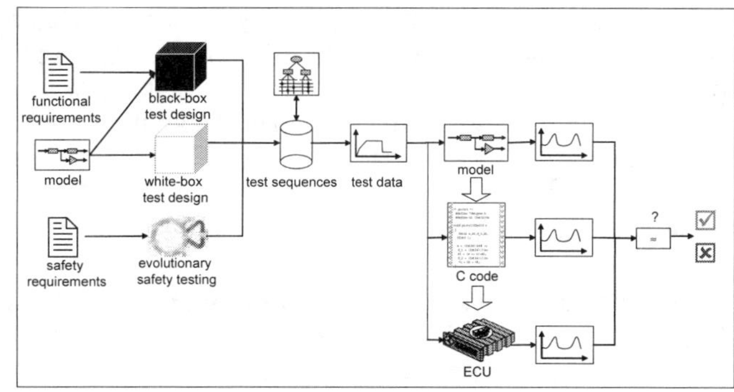

Figure 14. Model-based test strategy

4 RELATED WORK

Within the framework of model-based development, the derivation of safety requirements on model level can be supported by special model-based hazard/safety analysis techniques ([GC04], [PMS01]).

The instrumentation of the executable models with watchdogs/assertions (see e.g.[Rau99], [Reactis], [SL-VV]) or model checking of safety properties (cf. [EmbVal]) are alternative or supplementary techniques for checking the fulfillment of safety requirements.

Test design techniques which can be applied to black-box model testing are described in [HPP+03], [CFS04], [Con04], [Con04a], [HSM+04], and [LBE+04]. [HSM+04]White-box test design techniques for models are discussed in [Ran03], [Lin04], and [HSP05].

An approach for safeguarding the transformation from the tested model into code, i.e. the code generation, is described in [SC03].

CONCLUSION

In this paper we have presented the use of evolutionary sequence testing for the safety testing of embedded automotive control systems.

We have presented a small selection of the results. The results show the new test method to be promising. It was possible to find test sequences, without the need for user interaction, for problems which could previously not be solved automatically.

During the experiments a number of issues were identified which could further improve the efficiency of the test method presented. It is necessary to include as much of the existing problem-specific knowledge in the optimization process as possible.

A systematic approach for the selection of test scenarios and a notation for their appropriate description must therefore form the core elements of a safety testing approach for automotive control software. In order to allow testing to begin at an early stage, test design should build upon development artifacts available early on, such as the specification or an executable model.

ACKNOWLEDGMENTS

The work described was partially performed as part of the IMMOS project funded by the German Federal Ministry of Education and Research (project ref. 01ISC31D), http://www.immos-project.de

REFERENCES

[BCS03] Baresel, A., Conrad, M., Sadeghipour, S.: The Interplay between Model Coverage and Code Coverage. Proc. 11. Europ. Int. Conf. on Software Testing, Analysis and Review (EuroSTAR 03), 2003.

[BPS03] Baresel, A., Pohlheim, H., Sadeghipour, S.: Structural and Functional Sequence Testing of Dynamic and State-Based Software with Evolutionary Algorithms. Proc. Genetic and Evolutionary Computation Conf. (GECCO 03), pp. 2428 – 2441, 2003.

[BSS02] Baresel, A., Sthamer, H., Schmidt, M.: Fitness Function Design to improve Evolutionary Structural Testing. Proc. Genetic and Evolutionary Computation Conf. (GECCO 02), pp. 1329-1336, 2002.

[Bei83] Beizer, B.: Software Testing Techniques. New York: Van Nostrand Reinhold, 1983.

[CFS04] Conrad, M., Fey, I., Sadeghipour, S.: Systematic Model-Based Testing of Embedded Control Software: The MB3T Approach. Proc. ICSE 2004 Workshop W14S on Software Engineering for Automotive Systems (SEAS 04), pp.17-25, 2004.

[CH98] Conrad, M., Hötzer, D.: Selective Integration of Formal Methods in the Development of Electronic Control Units. Proc. 2. IEEE Int. Conf. on Formal Engineering Methods (ICFEM 98), IEEE Computer Society, pp. 144-155, 1998.

[Con01] Conrad, M.: Beschreibung von Testszenarien für Steuergerätesoftware - Vergleichskriterien und deren Anwendung. VDI Berichte, Vol. 1646, VDI Verlag, pp. 381-398, 2001.

[Con04] Conrad, M.: A Systematic Approach to Testing Automotive Control Software. Proc. Convergence 2004, SAE paper 2004-21-0039, 2004.

[Con04a] Conrad M.: Modell-basierter Test eingebetteter Software im Automobil – Auswahl und Beschreibung von Testszenarien. PhD thesis, Deutscher Universitäts-Verlag, 2004.

[CSW04] Conrad, M., Sadeghipour, S., Wiesbrock, H.-W.: Automatic Evaluation of ECU Software Tests. Proc. SAE World Congress 2005, SAE paper 2005-01-1659, 2005.

[EmbVal] EmbeddedValidator (product information). OSC – Embedded Systems AG, www.osc-es.de/products/en/embeddedvalidator.php

[FMN+94] Fenelon, P., McDermid, J.A., Nicholson, M., Pumfrey, D.J.: Towards Integrated Safety Analysis and Design. ACM Computing Reviews, Aug. 1994, pp. 21-32, 1994.

[GHD98] Grieskamp, W., Heisel, W., and Doerr, H.: Specifying embedded systems with statecharts and Z - An agenda for cyclic software components. Proc. Formal Aspects of Software Engineering (FASE 98), LNCS 1382, Springer-Verlag, 1998.

[GC04] Grönberg, R., Conrad. M.: Werkzeugunterstützung für Sicherheitsanalysen von Hardware- und Software-Systemen. Technical Report FT3/A-2000-007, DaimlerChrysler AG, Forschung und Technologie 3, Berlin, Germany, 2000.

[HH+01] Harman, M., Hu, L., Munro, M., Zhang, X.: Side-Effect Removal Transformation. Proc. IEEE Int. Workshop on Program Comprehension (IWPC), Toronto, Canada, 2001.

[HPP+03] Hahn, G., Philipps, J., Pretschner, A., Stauner, T.: Prototype-Based Tests for Hybrid Reactive Systems. Proc. 14. IEEE Int. Workshop on Rapid System Prototyping, San Diego, US, 2003.

[HSM+04] Horstmann, M., Schnieder, E., Mäder, P., Nienaber, S., Schulz, H.-M.: A framework for interlacing Test and/with Design. Proc. ICSE 2004 Workshop W14S on Software Engineering for Automotive Systems (SEAS 04), 2004.

[HSP05] Hermes, T., Schultze, A., Predelli, O.: Software Quality is not a Coincidence - A Model-Based Test Case Generator. Proc. SAE World Congress 2005, SAE paper 2005-01-1664, 2005.

[HV98] Hohler, B., Villinger, U.: Normen und Richtlinien zur Qualitätssicherung von Steuerungssoftware. Informatik-Spektrum, 21, pp. 63-72, 1998.

[IEC60812] IEC 60812:2003: Analysis techniques for system reliability - Procedure for failure mode and effects analysis (FMEA)

[IEC 61025] IEC 61025:2004: Fault tree analysis (FTA), 2004.

[JSE96] Jones, B.-F., Sthamer, H., Eyres, D.: Automatic structural testing using genetic algorithms.

Software Engineering Journal, vol. 11, no. 5, pp. 299–306, 1996.

[KCF+04] Klein, T., Conrad, M., Fey, I., Grochtmann, M.: Modellbasierte Entwicklung eingebetteter Fahrzeugsoftware bei DaimlerChrysler. Lecture Notes in Informatics (LNI), Vol. P-45, Köllen Verlag, pp. 31-41, 2004.

[Kor90] Korel, B.: Automated Test Data Generation. IEEE Transactions on Software Engineering, Vol. 16 no. 8, pp.870-879, 1990.

[LBE+04] Lamberg, K., Beine, M., Eschmann, M., Otterbach, R., Conrad, M., Fey, I.: Model-based Testing of Embedded Automotive Software using MTest. Proc. SAE World Congress 2004, SAE paper 2004-01-1593, 2004.

[Lin04] Linder, P.: Modellbasiertes Testen von eingebetteter Software - Ein Ansatz auf der Grundlage von Signalflussplänen. Proc. Automotive Safety & Security 2004, Stuttgart, Germany, 2004.

[MK99] Mackenthun, R., Kelling, C.: An Agenda for the Safety Analysis of Cyclic Software Components. In: ESPRESS: Final Reports, Berlin, Germany, June 1999.

[MTest] MTest (product information), dSPACE GmbH, http://www.dspaceinc.com

[PMS01] Papadopoulos, Y., McDermid J., Mavrides, A., Scheidler S., Maruhn, M.: Model-Based Semiautomatic Safety Analysis Of Programmable Systems In Automotive Applications. Proc. Int. Conf. on Advanced Driver Assistance Systems (ADAS 01), 2001.

[Poh99] Pohlheim, H.: Evolutionäre Algorithmen - Verfahren, Operatoren, Hinweise aus der Praxis. Berlin, Heidelberg: Springer-Verlag, 1999. http://www.pohlheim.com/eavoh/index.html

[Poh05] Pohlheim, H.: GEATbx - Genetic and Evolutionary Algorithm Toolbox for Matlab. http://www.geatbx.com/, 1994-2005.

[Ran03] Ranville, S.: MCDC Unit Test Vectors From Matlab Models – Automatically. Proc. Embedded Systems Conference, 2003.

[Rau99] Rau, A.: Verwendung von Zusicherungen in einem modellbasierten Entwicklungsprozess. It+ti 3/2002, pp. 137-144, 2002.

[Rau03] Rau, A.: Model-based Development of Embedded Automotive Control Systems. PhD thesis, http://dissertation.de, 2003.

[Reactis] Reactis Tester / Validator (product information). Reactive Systems Inc., http://www.reactive-systems.com

[SC03] Stürmer, I. and Conrad, M.: Test Suite Design for Code Generation Tools. 18. IEEE Int. Conf. on Automated Software Engineering (ASE 03), 2003.

[SLSF] Simulink/Stateflow (product information). The MathWorks Inc., http://www.mathworks.com/products.

[SL-VV] Simulink Verification and Validation Toolbox (product information). The MathWorks Inc., www.mathworks.com/products/simverification

[Sth96] Sthamer, H.: The Automatic Generation of Software Test Data Using Genetic Algorithms. PhD Thesis, University of Glamorgan, Pontyprid, UK, 1996.

[TCC+98] Tracey, N., Clark, J., Mander, K., McDermid, J.: An Automated Framework for Structural Test-Data Generation. Proc. 13. IEEE Conf. on Automated Software Engineering, 1998.

[VDI/VDE 3550] Computational Intelligence, Evolutionary algorithms - Terms and definitions. VDI/VDE guideline VDI/VDE 3550, Part 3, Verein Deutscher Ingenieure, 2003.

[Weg01] Wegener, J.: Evolutionärer Test des Zeitverhaltens von Realzeit-Systemen. PhD thesis, Shaker-Verlag, 2001.

[WSB01] Wegener, J., Sthamer, H., Baresel, A.: Evolutionary Test Environment for Automatic Structural Testing. Special Issue of Information and Software Technology, vol. 43, pp. 851–854, 2001.

[WSJ+97] Wegener, J., Sthamer, H., Jones, B., Eyres, D.: Testing Real-time Systems using Genetic Algorithms. Software Quality Journal, vol. 6, no. 2, pp. 127–135, 1997.

CONTACT

Hartmut Pohlheim received a Diploma in Systems Engineering in 1993 from the University of Technology Ilmenau (Germany). In 1998 he earned his PhD at the University of Technology Ilmenau with a dissertation titled “Development and Engineering Application of Evolutionary Algorithms”. Since 1995 he has been a research scientist at the Software Technology Lab of DaimlerChrysler Research & Technology in Berlin.

In 1995 Mirko Conrad earned a Diploma degree in Computer Science from the Technical University Berlin (Germany). In 2004 he received his PhD from the TU Berlin for his work on model-based testing of embedded automotive software. Since 1995 he has been a project manager and research scientist at the Software Technology Lab of DaimlerChrysler Research & Technology. He is member of the Special Interest Group for Testing, Analysis and Verification of Software in the German Computer Society (GI TAV) and the MathWorks Automotive Advisory Board (MAAB).

Arne Griep received a Diploma in Systems Engineering in 2002 from the University of Technology Ilmenau (Germany). Since 2003 he has been a software developer at IAV GmbH (Germany).

2004-01-1593

Model-based Testing of Embedded Automotive Software using MTest

Klaus Lamberg, Michael Beine, Mario Eschmann and Rainer Otterbach
dSPACE GmbH

Mirko Conrad and Ines Fey
DaimlerChrysler AG

ABSTRACT

Permanently increasing software complexity of today's electronic control units (ECUs) makes testing a central and significant task within embedded software development. While new software functions are still being developed or optimized, other functions already undergo certain tests, mostly on module level but also on system and integration level.

Testing must be done as early as possible within the automotive development process. Typically ECU software developers test new function modules by stimulating the code with test data and capturing the modules' output behavior to compare it with reference data.

This paper presents a new and systematic way of testing embedded software for automotive electronics, called MTest. MTest combines the classical module test with model-based development. The central element of MTest is the classification-tree method, which has originally been developed by the DaimlerChrysler research department. The classification-tree method exists for several years now and is mostly used for C-code testing. Now, it has been adopted to the needs of a model-based development process for embedded systems.

MTest opens a new way of assuring quality for embedded software, that is especially designated for automotive software developers.

This paper demonstrates, how MTest is used to test automotive software from model-in-the-loop over software-in-the-loop down to processor-in-the-loop testing. Additionally, test scenarios once developed using MTest can be reused in a hardware-in-the-loop environment. Thus, MTest provides a means to automatically test automotive software within the whole development process.

MODEL-BASED SOFTWARE DEVELOPMENT

Within automotive electronics development, a model-based development process has been established over the last years. Using modelling, simulation and code generation tools is a common way to develop and implement new vehicle functions.

Therefore the control function to be developed is described by the means of simulation tools like MATLAB/Simulink/Stateflow (function design). Such tools provide a graphical way of describing functions and systems. This includes block diagram notations as well as state charts. Using Rapid Control Prototyping (RCP) systems, the new functions can be proven in the real vehicle or on a dynamometer. Therefore, automatic code generation is used to generate C code from the function model. This code is run on powerful real-time systems. Such systems are connected to the real plant by special I/O. Changes can be made directly to the function model and tried out immediately by generating code once again.

Implementation of the function on a production ECU is done by automatic production code generation. However, the requirements on a production code generator are much higher then for RCP. The generated code must be highly efficient, error-free, reproducible, and well documented. An example for a production code generator is TargetLink [1].

MODEL-BASED TESTING

Today's way of automotive function and software developing using RCP is characterized by an experimentational way of working. Systematic and automated testing doesn't play an important role so far. Additionally, testing tools are missing today, which provide special methods for the testing tasks in the specific process stages. This is true especially for the early stages of function and software development. The model-based testing process as described in the following lays a major focus on systematic and automated testing in the early stages. It also includes ECU testing activities which are typical for the later development stages.

THE MODEL-BASED TESTING PROCESS

The model-based testing process (Figure 1) describes the different activities within the whole automotive electronics development process from a testing point of view. This includes testing in the early function development as well as ECU testing later in the process.

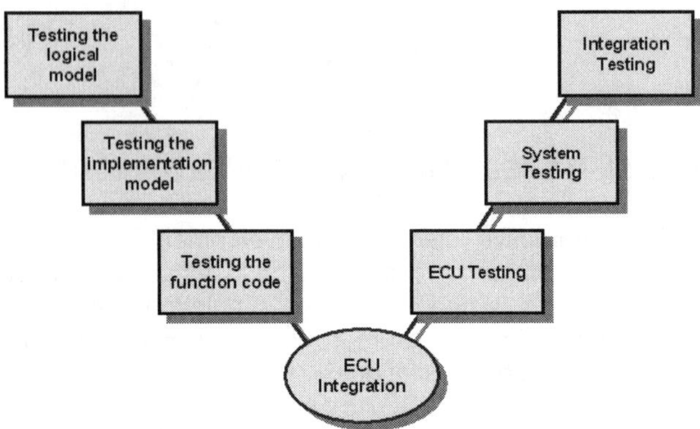

Figure 1: Model-based testing process

Testing the Logical Model

Testing the logical model means systematic and automatic testing of an executable model of the function or controller to be developed. This model is the test object or unit under test (UUT). The test can be done open loop or closed loop using a model of the plant (model-in-the-loop, MIL).

Testing the Implementation Model

The functional model has to be prepared for implementation. Software design information has to be added. Functional models are usually floating-point models whereas the implementation in C is often realized using fixed-point arithmetic. Thus scaling information, implementation data type, LSB and offset, is to be specified for each block output signal and parameter. The behaviour of the fixed-point implementation has to be compared with the behaviour of the functional model. It has to be checked if the quantization effects introduced are acceptable. This verification is done by simulation since the equivalence between the two representations can not be formally proved. The implementation model can also be tested in a closed loop environment (MIL).

Testing the Function Code

The next step is testing the actual function code. This can be done on a host PC (software-in-the-loop, SIL) or on the target processor (processor-in-the-loop, PIL).

ECU Integration

The generated function code has to be integrated with the overall ECU software. ECU integration means integration with other function modules, the operating system and I/O drivers. Although, this step isn't a test step in the sense of the model-based test process, the integration is already to be taken into consideration and prepared when creating the implementation model. Special focus is laid on functions and global variables that are defined or to be called and re-used outside of the implementation model. Their definitions and declarations must match the ones in the external code.

The operating system integration depends on the scope of the model. If the model only describes a single feature that will be part of one task in the ECU then the call of the generated function is usually manually implemented in the OS frame. If the model has a wider scope and consists of multiple functions and tasks then operating system objects are already specified in the model. For example, dSPACE offers a special module for its production code generator TargetLink to support and automate the integration with OSEK operating systems. Task distribution, intertask communication and other OS properties can be specified directly in the model. The generated code then already contains the corresponding OSEK keywords and can be integrated with the OSEK OS without any further manual integration work [2].

ECU Testing

ECU testing typically is done using hardware-in-the-loop simulation (HIL). Therefore the ECU prototype is connected to a real-time simulation system simulating the plant. Corresponding ECUs are also simulated rest bus simulation). Almost always, ECU testing is black box testing where the inputs are stimulated and the outputs are monitored.

System Testing

System testing means to test the ECU in its direct technical environment using HIL simulation. Therefore the ECU is at least partially integrated with other ECUs and its behavior is tested in conjunction with other ECUs.

Integration Testing

Finally, all ECU of a single vehicle are integrated and the whole network system is tested. This is called integration testing. HIL simulation is used more and more also for integration testing.

The testing tasks described above are different from each other. In the following, a testing methodology is described, which supports especially the early phases, i.e. testing the logical model, testing the implementation model and testing the function code. Additionally, test data once developed using this methodology can also be used in hardware-in-the-loop simulation.

THE MTEST APPROACH

The MTest (MTest = "Model-based Testing") methodology complements model-based development with a method for systematic test definition. The starting point of the MTest testing process is a model of the function or controller to be developed, implemented in Simulink or TargetLink. Based on the interface of the logical model, and by using the classification-tree method, the function developer can derive test scenarios systematically and describe them graphically. With the graphical representation the user gets visual information about the test coverage. Test coverage indicates, how well the test cases cover the range of possible test input combinations and is therefore the most important test metrics.

The MTest process consists of different testing activities building the base for systematic testing and therefore support for a systematic testing procedure. The testing activities are shown in Figure 2 schematically. They are described more detailed in the following paragraphs.

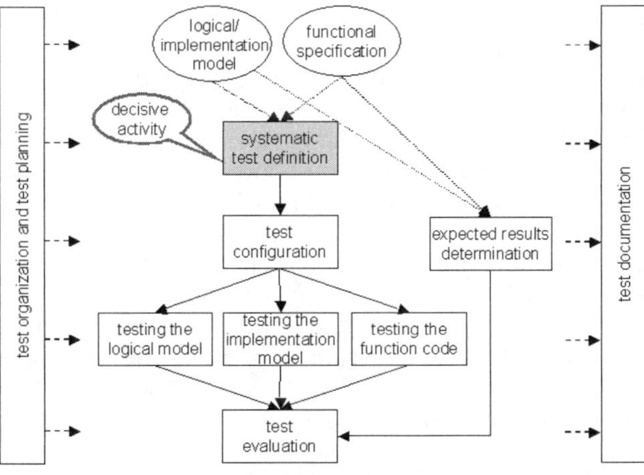

Figure 2: Model-based testing activities

As an alternative to using the classification tree method, it is possible to use existing data as test data. This is called "direct testing".

To illustrate the MTest approach to model-based testing we use the example of a vehicle dynamics control (VDC) system that controls the vehicle motion in physical limit conditions (cf. [3]).

SYSTEMATIC TEST DEFINITION

The MTest approach to model-based testing utilizes a specific instance of the classification-tree method with extensions for embedded systems (CTM/ES) for the systematic test definition, [4], [5]. The classification-tree method is a black-box partition test design technique, where the input domain of the test object is split up under different aspects usually corresponding to different input data sources. The different partitions, called classifications, are subdivided into (input data) equivalence classes. Finally different combinations of input data classes are selected and arranged into test sequences.

SELECTING THE TEST INTERFACE

A subsystem within an .mdl file is to be selected first in order to be able to subsequently relate the test scenarios to the respective units under test (UUT), i.e. Simulink or TargetLink model subsystems.

The interface of the subsystem to be tested will then be analyzed automatically, and the information relevant to testing will be extracted (model extraction).

The input of the subsystem to be tested forms the potential input variables for the test. It is consequently called a 'potential test interface'. There is no necessity, however, of using the potential test interface for the test object stimulation on a one-to-one basis: Fed back values, for example, do not need to be predetermined as they are generated by the system environment. On the other hand, it is often easier to describe a complex input signal by means of (additive or multiplicative) superposition of two sub-signals. In this case, instead of the potential interface signal the two sub-signals would be described. The values actually used for the simulation are referred to as 'effective input interface'. If there are differences between the potential and the effective interface for a certain test object they have to be mapped onto each other.

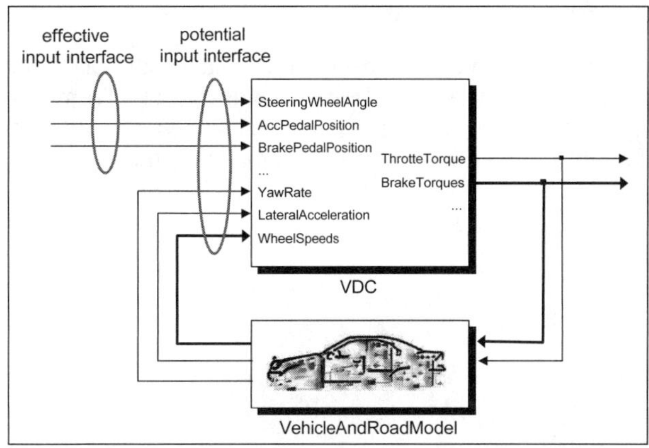

Figure 3: Potential and effective test interface

The VDC-software's behavior is determined, among other things, by the steering-wheel angle, the accelerator and brake pedal positions, the yaw rate, and the four-wheel speeds. These signals form the example's input interface. If a closed loop test with typical driving maneuver is to be performed, however, only the driver inputs SteeringWheelAngle, AcceleratorPedalPosition and BrakePedalPosition have to be stimulated. These values form the effective input interface. The remaining input values are implicitly determined by the vehicle/road model. (Figure 3).

CREATING THE CLASSIFICATION-TREE

Based on the effective test interface MTest automatically outputs a first, incomplete instance of a classification-tree called basic tree (Figure 4): The name of the unit under test itself forms its root node (here: "VDC"), the signals of the effective input interface (e.g Steering-WheelAngle) are denoted as classifications below the root node. In a second step, the generated classifications must be disjointedly and completely partitioned into (equivalence) classes which are suitable abstractions of individual input values for testing purposes.

The partitioning aims to achieve a selection of the individual classes in such a way that they behave homogeneously with respect to the detection of potential errors. That is, the unit under test behaves either correctly or erroneously for all the values of one class (uniformity hypothesis).

An heuristic procedure has proved successful in approaching this ideal partitioning as much as possible in practice. The inputs' data type and value range provide first valuable clues to partitioning: Where real-valued data types with minimum and maximum values established are concerned, it is possible, for example, to create a standard class each for the boundary values, for the value of zero and for those intervals in between. Alternatively, real-valued data types could be partitioned into same size sub-intervals. Similar data-type specific standard classifications can also be utilized for different data types.

As soon as information on the data types or value ranges of the input variables is available to MTest, the data-type specific standard classifications for different data types can be generated automatically (cf. [6]).

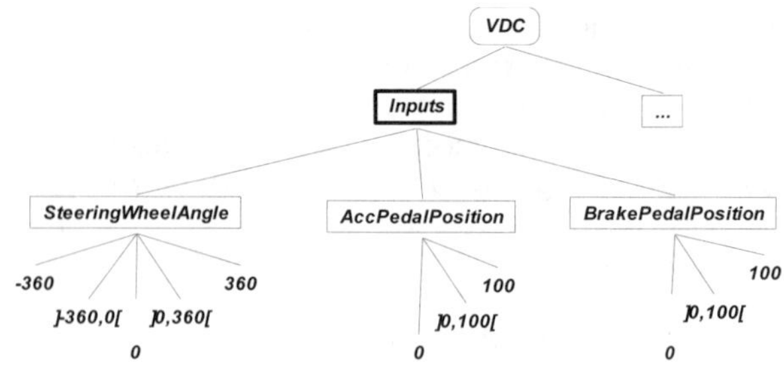

Figure 4: Basic classification-tree

Figure 4 depicts the automatically generated basic classification tree for the VDC example: It contains the automatically generated standard partitioning for real-valued signals for the 3 effective interface input signals. The following five classes arise for the signal Steering-WheelAngle, which can take on values from the range of –360° to 360°: –360,]-360, 0[, 0,]0, 360[and 360. In this case,]x, y[denotes an interval, open on both sides, with the boundary values x and y.

As a rule, the data-type specific standard classifications are not detailed enough for a systematic test. They have to be refined or modified manually in order to approach a partitioning according to the uniformity hypothesis. The quality of the specification and the tester's experience are crucial in this respect.

The evaluation of the pedal positions (described as percentages in the VDC software) recognizes a pedal as depressed only if it is activated above a certain threshold value PedMin. The pedal values above and below the threshold should therefore be considered separately because behavior is expected to differ. As the acceleration force also influences the system behavior, there has to be an additional distinction between light (pedal position< 50%) and strong (pedal position ≥ 50%) pedal operation. The result is a final partitioning of the pedal positions into the classes 0,]0, PedMin[, PedMin,]PedMin, 50[, [50, 100[and 100. In this case, [x, y[denotes an interval which is closed on the left side and open on the right side. The partitioning of SteeringWheelAngle has been refined as to subsume all 90° sections in one class respectively (Figure 6).

DEFINING TEST SEQUENCES

Based on the input partitions, test sequences can be determined. These sequences specify how the behavior of the regarded unit under test should be tested. The domain for the description of test scenarios is provided by the completed classification-tree. The tree is used as the head of the combination table. Each sequence captures a data abstraction of the unit under test's inputs. Hence, it describes – largely independent from detailed or precise data – what is to be tested. In order to represent test sequences in an abstract way, they are decomposed into individual test steps. According to their temporal order, the steps build the rows of the combination table. Such a sequence of test steps is called a test sequence. Each test step defines the inputs of the UUT over a certain time span. The time spans are listed in a separate column on the right-hand side of the combination table. The beginning and end points of these time intervals are called synchronization points, since they synchronize the stimuli signals at the beginning and end of every test step.

The description of the values of the single stimuli signals for each test step takes place by marking a class defined for this signal in the classification tree. This is indicated in the middle part of the combination table. The stimulus signal in the respective test step is thus restricted to the part-interval or single value of the marked class. The combination of the marked input classes of a test step determines the input of the UUT at the respective synchronization point.

The values of the stimuli signals between the synchronization points are described by basic signal shapes. Different signal shapes (e.g. ramp, step function, sine) are represented by different arrow types which connect two successive markings in the combination table. In this way stimuli signals can be described in an abstract manner by the means of parameterized, stepwise defined functions [4].

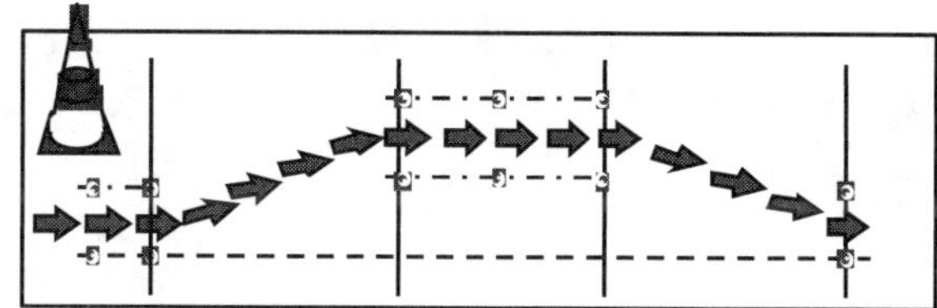

Figure 5: Driving maneuver "lane change"

Figure 6 shows the lane changing maneuver of Figure 5 as a test sequence in the combination table. After an acceleration phase the steering-wheel is first turned in a 90-degree angle to the left, then, the steering wheel is turned to 90-degree in the opposite direction and back into the original position. After a hold phase the wheel is turned by 90-degrees to the right, back to the left and back into the neutral position. Here, a solid line as arrow type means a ramp shaped change of the signal value, no (visible) transition means a skip of the signal value at the end of the interval.

The accelerator pedal ramps up during the acceleration phase. The adjusted pedal position is held and at the end of the test sequence the pedal is released again. At the same time, the brakes areactivated. A dashed line as an arrow type denotes a change of the signal value in the form of a sine half-wave.

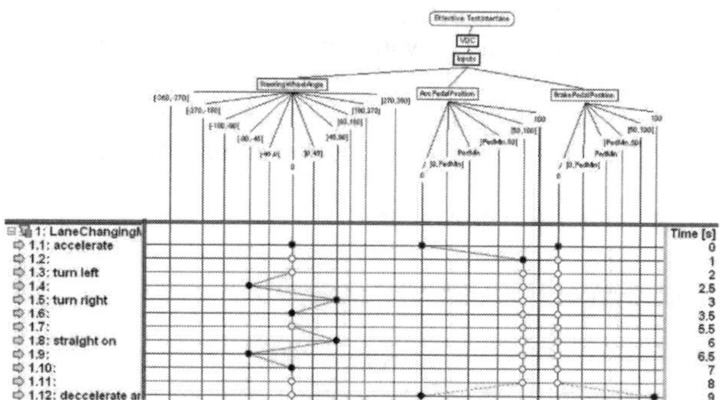

Figure 6: Classification-tree with test sequence

Further test sequences can be described underneath the classification tree by using the procedure above mentioned.

After the determination of test sequences has been completed, it is necessary to check if they ensure a sufficient test coverage. At this early stage of the testing process, the CTM/ES already allows the determination of different abstract coverage criteria based on the classification tree and the test sequences:

A requirements coverage analysis can verify whether all requirements of the requirements specification are covered sufficiently by the test sequences. In general, a n:m-relationship exists between requirements and test scenarios. In the course of the analysis it is necessary to prove that every requirement is being checked by at least one test scenario and that the existing test scenarios are adequate to test the respective requirements.

Furthermore, the CTM/ES supports a range coverage analysis. This analysis checks the sufficient consideration of all equivalence classes defined in the classification tree in the test sequences. This check can be executed, according to the respective application case, by using different, so-called classification-tree coverage criteria (CTC) (cf. [5]):

- The minimum criterion (CTC_{MIN}) requires every class of the tree to be selected in at least one test step. The minimum criterion is usually accomplishable with a few test sequences, the error detection rate, however, is rather low.
- The maximum criterion (CTC_{MAX}) requires every possible class combination to be selected in at least one test step. The fullfillment of the maximum criterion should bring a high error detection rate. Because of the combinatorical "explosion", this criterion is only practicable when having a small number of classes.
- The n-wise combination criteria (CTC_n) present a compromise. Here, it is necessary to ensure that every possible combination of n classes is selected in at least one test step. For example, a pair-wise combination of classes (CTC_2) is practicable.

The selection of appropriate criteria has to take place in a problem-specific way within the frame of the test planning. If the criteria defined beforehand are not sufficiently fulfilled, additional test steps / test sequences need to be added until the required criteria are fulfilled.

TEST CONFIGURATION

TEST DATA REFINEMENT

The test scenarios gained by using the classification method only contain abstracted stimulus information, because only equivalent classes have been used, but no specific data. Thus, in a second step, the test data is instantiated by the means of definite numbers. The borders of the classes of the classification tree are used as signal constraints, wherein the actual signal traces can vary.

Instantiating the test data is done using the signal editor shown in Figure 7. The borders of the equivalent classes form the constraints of the value ranges at the respective sample points. By default, MTest uses the mean values of the intervals in the classification tree. In this example at the sample point *3 sec*, the value has been edited within the constraints (cf. the marked cell at the bottom).

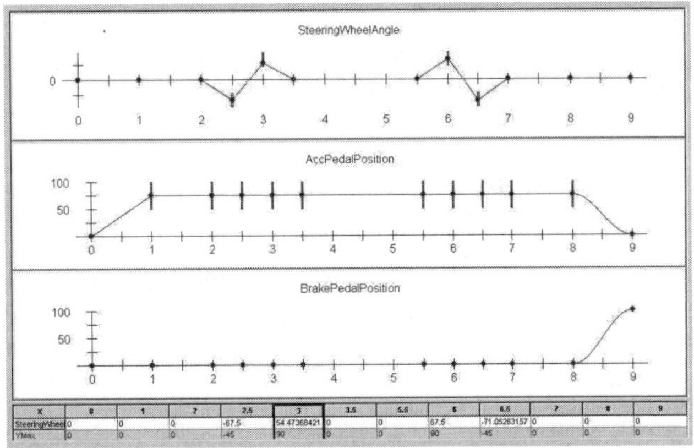

Figure 7: Signal editor with interval borders

As an alternative to the classification tree method, MTest allows to use real data as test data. This is called "direct testing". Using direct testing, it is possible to import real measurement data, gained e.g. from a driving or a dynamometer experiment. This data can be used to stimulate the UUT (Figure 8).

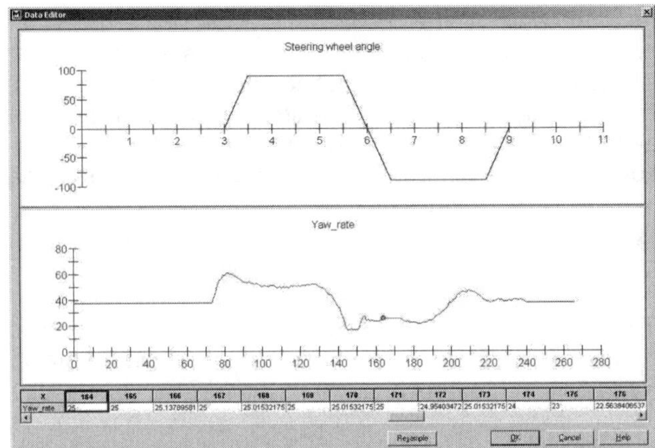

Figure 8: Editing imported test data

ASSIGNING TEST DATA TO THE MODEL INTERFACE

When using the classification tree method, the assignment of the generated test data to the inputs of the UUT is done automatically. Using direct testing, the data must be explicitly assigned to the inputs of the UUT (Figure 9).

Once the assignment has been defined by the user, MTest checks for the consistency in terms of signal type, signal complexity and signal dimension.

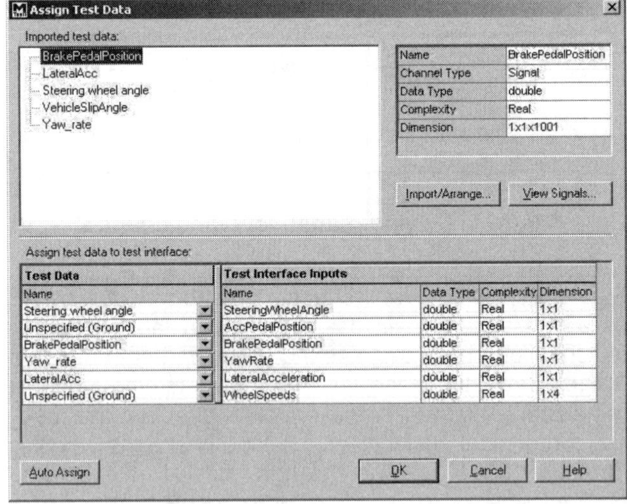

Figure 9: Assignment of test data

DEFINE REFERENCE DATA AND EVALUATION CRITERIA

Test and simulation results can also be compared to reference data. Reference data can be a result of former test runs, or even be any kind of measurement data which can be imported.

In a further configuration step, the user can define the evaluation rule, i.e. how the results shall be compared with reference data. Therefore the user can select out of a set of evaluation criteria, including absolute and relative difference. This set can also be extended by the user.

TEST EXECUTION AND EVALUATION

GENERATE TEST HARNESS

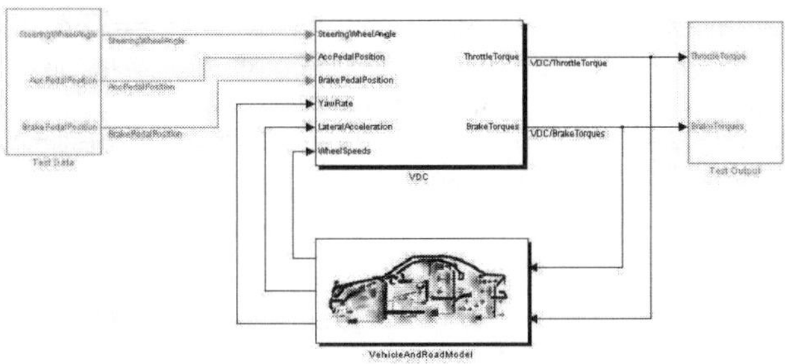

Figure 10: Generated test harness in Simulink

The test scenarios which have been defined using the classification tree method or by importing data can be applied to all of the three representation forms of the UUT: to the logical model, to the implementation model and to the function code. Therefore, MTest supports executing the tests in Simulink and in the different TargetLink modes. For the execution, a test harness in generated automatically in Simulink (Figure 10) and a copy of the Simulink or TargetLink model of the UUT is inserted into it.

MTest can activate the required TargetLink simulation mode – floating-point simulation on the host PC („TargetLink MIL"), production code simulation on the host PC („TargetLink SIL") and production code simulation on the target processor („TargetLink PIL") – and if necessary start the TargetLink production code generation.

Figure 11 shows, how the desired modes in which a test sequence is to be executed, can be selected by the user. Figure 12 shows how the different modes are represented in an MTest project tree.

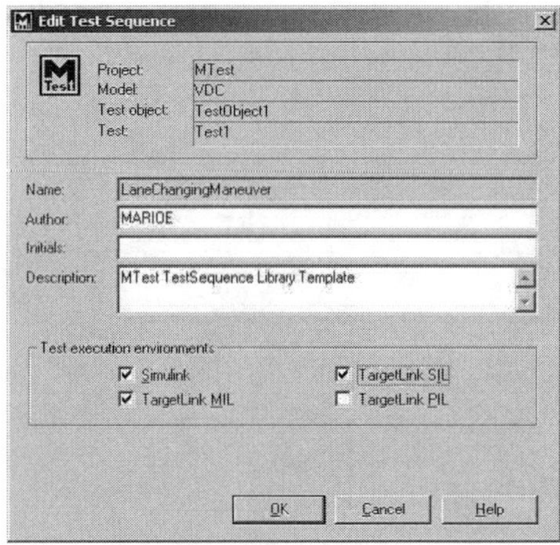

Figure 11: Dialog to define the simulation modes

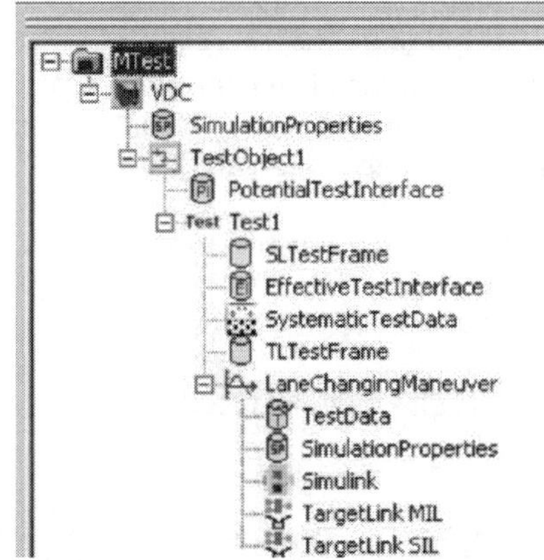

Figure 12: MTest project tree with different simulation modes

RESULT MANAGEMENT AND REPORT GENERATION

Once the test has been executed, the test results are collected automatically and displayed instantly. The amount and the depth of result information can be adjusted by the user.

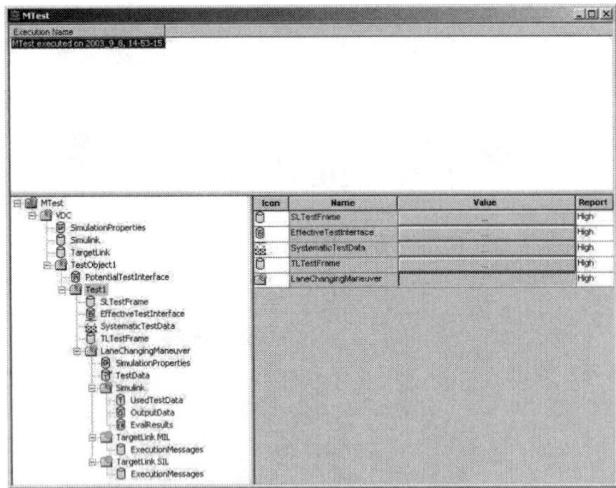

Figure 13: Result browser

The results are structured hierarchically and displayed as a tree (cf. Figure 13). The result tree can include any data item and any test which has been done in the different simulation modes. The user can navigate through the tree and view all details. For signal traces, the user can also generate plots immediately.

Finally, it is possible to generate test reports based on the result information. Test reports can be produced in different formats, e.g. HTML or PDF.

MTEST IN AUTOMATIONDESK

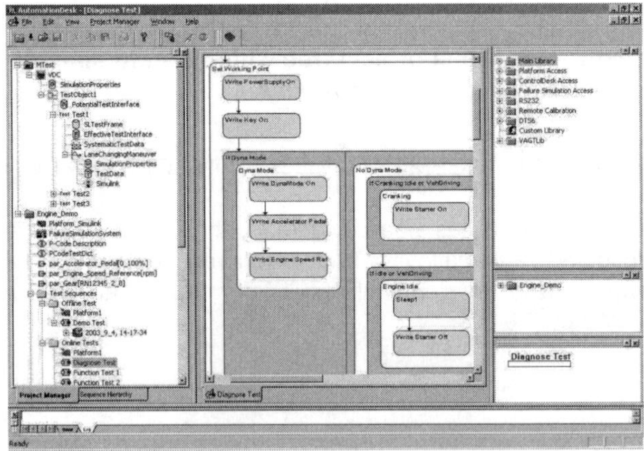

Figure 14: AutomationDesk

Although the testing tasks and activities within the different process stages vary from each other very much, a testing environment must combine and integrate all these approaches under one common roof. this can be achieved, if all the necessary elements of the process are provided by one testing tool. An example is the tool AutomationDesk, [7], [8] (Figure 14).

The enormous number of tests for a single function or ECU is not only to be developed and executed. All the tests must be stored and administrated consistently, so that they can be performed repeatedly ("regression testing") and reproduced at any time. The large amount of test results – each test run produces a new result instance – must be stored persistently. Storing, maintaining and administrating this large amount of tests together with the test data and the test results require powerful means to manage test projects.

Figure 15 shows an example of a test project structure in AutomationDesk. The test data and the test results together with the test sequences are displayed in project trees. The upper part of the tree contains an MTest project, the lower part contains a typical HIL project. It is obvious that test data which have been gained e.g. by using MTest can be reused in an HIL simulation.

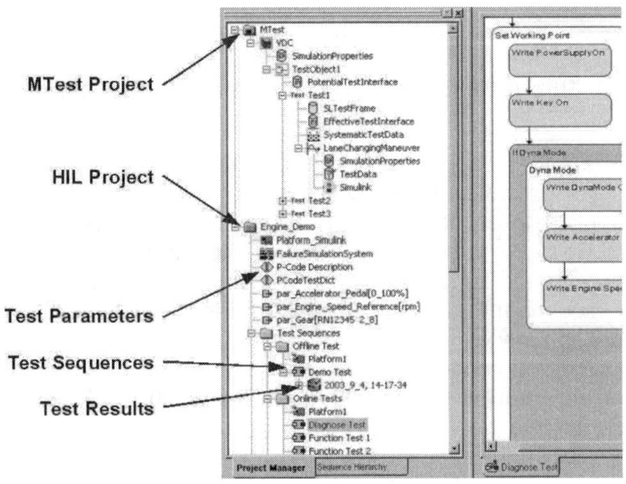

Figure 15: Test project examples in AutomationDesk

CONCLUSION

This paper describes a method and a tool for systematic and automated testing, called MTest. Based on a model-based testing process, MTest especially allows for model-based testing in early function and software development. The core of MTest is the classification-tree method, providing a systematic way of developing test scenarios graphically. Since MTest is an integral part of the test automation environment AutomationDesk, test scenarios once developed using MTest can be reused in later development stages, e.g. when testing real ECUs or ECU prototypes by the means of hardware-in-the-loop simulation. AutomationDesk together with MTest therefore build a testing environment supporting the whole model-based development process.

REFERENCES

1. dSPACE TargetLink poduct information: http://www.dspaceinc.com.
2. Köster, L.; Thomsen, t.; Stracke, R.: Connecting Simulink to Osek: Automatic Code Generation for Real-Time Operating Systems with TargetLink. SAE 2001,March 5-8,2001,Detroit, Michigan, USA Technical Paper 2001-01-0024
3. v. Zanten, A.; Erhardt, R.; Landesfeind, K.; Pfaff, G.: Stability Control. In: R. K. Jurgen (Ed.): Automotive Electronics Handbook. 2nd edition, Mc Graw-Hill, 1999
4. Broekman, E.; Notenboom, E.: Testing Embedded Software. Addison-Wesley, 2003
5. Grochtmann, M.; Grimm, K.: Classification Trees for Partition Testing. Software Testing, Verification and Reliability, 3, 63-82, 1993
6. Conrad, M.;Dörr, H.; Stuermer, I.; Schuerr, A.: Graph Transformations for Model-based Testing. Proc. of Modellierung 2002, Tutzing (D), März 2002
7. Lamberg, K., Richert, J.; Rasche, R.: A New Environment for Integrated Development and Management of ECU Tests. SAE 2003-01-1024, 2003.
8. dSPACE AutomationDesk product information: http://www.dspaceinc.com .

CONTACT

Dr. Klaus Lamberg is responsible for the product strategy, product planning, and product launches of test and experiment software at dSPACE GmbH, Paderborn, Germany.

E-mail: klamberg@dspace.de
Web: http://www.dspaceinc.com

2003-01-1035

Real Time Calibration and Debug Techniques of Embedded Processors with the Nexus 5001 Interface

Ronald W. Stence
Motorola Semiconductor Products Sector

ABSTRACT

Recent technology improvements in the area of embedded processors have changed the methods of debugging and calibration with instruction reconstruction and data collection. This transition has come about in part, due to the System-on-a-Chip (SoC) methodology from silicon vendors and the encapsulation of significant portions of the system on a single piece of silicon. The result is the removal of the external address and data bus and higher performance. Motorola is a leader in the SoC methodology with the integration of Flash memory technology that allows the application to function without an external memory bus. The requirements in real time applications such as engine management and transmission systems have brought on a new requirement for the embedded processor vendor to provide real time information. The IEEE-ISTO Nexus 5001 Consortium has been working to provide a real time debug and calibration specification and standard to address these issues.

INTRODUCTION

The embedded processors and the applications that use them have evolved dramatically over the past decade. Often current embedded processors are highly integrated devices with a staggering number of on-chip peripherals, smart I/O, SRAM, Flash, ROM, cache, co-processors, and external bus interface logic. Unfortunately, the debug interfaces have not made the same dramatic improvements during that period. The integration of memory and I/O systems on-chip are resulting in embedded processors that no longer have an external address or data buses. Embedded processors with this level of system integration will force changes in the design and debugging of microcontroller based systems. The encapsulation of the system into a single chip is not new, the 8-bit microprocessors have been doing this for years. The ability to fully integrate an embedded system in to 32-bit microprocessors at speeds of 50MHz and higher, is the current state of the art for silicon vendors delivering into the automotive requirements. Motorola will bring an increased level of performance and integration into the vehicle with new PowerPC ISA compatible MPC5500 devices to a level above 100MHz.

Motorola continues to lead in the development of the real time debug and calibration with the Nexus 5001 Consortium while delivering Nexus 5001 based debug ports on multiple architectures. Motorola pioneered the use of run control debug ports such as OnCE, BDM and JTAG for more than 10 years ago; however, traditional run control is an intrusive debug technique that relies on the external address and data bus for instruction and data tracing.

The integration of on-chip memory systems such as DMA, cache, flash and RAM can make the external address and data bus ineffective in providing the necessary visibility to the internal bus activity. The run control debug ports can make tracking down a run time bug very difficult or impossible without specialized debug busses and considerable expense. To overcome these and other debug issues, a consortium of companies was formed to address this difficult issue on multiple architectures. The Global Embedded Processor Debug Interface Standard consortium, now part of the IEEE-ISTO under the project name Nexus 5001, originated from a 1998 working group of 5 companies. The Nexus 5001 consortium is focused on developing an open real time development tool interface standard to be implemented across multiple embedded controller architectures. The Nexus 5001 consortium currently consists of 20 companies consisting of silicon vendors, automotive suppliers, hardware and software calibration and development tools vendors from across the globe.

One of the largest issues facing the embedded controller market today is the ever-shortening development time, with small focused teams developing multiple generations of products in parallel. To enable the engineering teams to hit the shorter cycle times and reduced development cost a new tools methodology is required. The development tools methodology used in designing and debugging microprocessor-based systems of today will have to improve to become more effective. Over the last decade the embedded controller market has seen a proliferation of new microcontrollers from 8-bit MCUs to DSPs to high performance RISC processors. The development tools used to debug embedded control applications are not capable of providing non-intrusive visibility into the highly integrated embedded processors being deployed today. This problem is further exacerbated with the ever-increasing frequency and complexity of 32-bit processors.

TRADITIONAL DEBUG TECHNIQUES

The traditional debug techniques found on virtually all embedded processors over the past decade depend on visibility to the address and data bus to perform real time debugging. These traditional debugging techniques include in-circuit emulation, special bond out chips, logic analyzer preprocessor probes and intrusive run control debug ports (BDM, OnCE, JTAG and others).

IN-CIRCUIT EMULATORS

In-circuit emulation often removes the target processor from the system logically if not physically. In-circuit emulators suffer from a limitation in the clock speed of around 30-50MHz due to loading and transmission delays. In-circuit emulators or expensive and often have difficulty keeping current silicon in the emulator which can result in tracking down bugs that aren't there anymore. Additionally, an in-circuit emulator might not be able to emulate on-chip features such as floating point units, caches, on-chip peripherals and on-chip memory.

BOND OUT CHIPS

The bond out chips have several issues, including: out of date silicon, limitations such as clock speed and bus loading, difficulty in full test and characterize relative to the production versions of embedded processors, expensive to maintain.

LOGIC ANALYSIS

The standard approaches used by logic analyzer companies are clip-on probes or solder down adapters to gain access to the external address and data buses. These techniques were reasonable for most embedded processors several years ago. Improvements in on-chip integration have made it possible for 32-bit embedded processors to become fully integrated. Once the external bus is removed, debugging or even probing the embedded processor difficult if not impossible.

RUN CONTROL DEBUG PORTS

Run control debug ports have been on embedded processors for nearly 15 years. One of the first run control debug ports was the BDM on the M68332 from Motorola. Run control debug ports provide an engineer the ability to run, stop and interrogate registers and memory while in the system. The common characteristic is these debug ports is that they require the embedded processor to be halted or stopped before the port can transmit the requested information. Some of the more recent run control debug ports have moved to cycle stealing to allow for some limited information to be sent over the debug port while the embedded processor is running. The difficulty with this technique is the limited amount of information, reliance on the external address and data bus for information and the impacts to the processor performance during run time. The debug ports can satisfy some of the needs of the engineering team as long as real time during debugging was not a concern. One major advantage of these tools was the relatively low cost and the simplicity of the interface.

REAL TIME DEBUG AND CALIBRATION

Motorola and the Nexus 5001 consortium are working to make dramatic improvements in the debug and calibration interface and to generate a standard across multiple embedded processor architectures. The Nexus 5001 standard will specify common connectors, low level protocols and on-chip features such as debug registers, pins and signals.

The Nexus 5001 specification includes standard features for setting breakpoints and watchpoints on data and instructions for the intrusive and non-intrusive run control debugging. The specification will deploy several unique features for tracking down the toughest bugs. Some of these new features include ownership trace messaging, data trace, memory substitution, port replacement, program trace, overrun and error messaging. While many of these features have been deployed on microprocessors over the years, none have implemented all of these and a real time debug interface.

The Motorola MPC565 was the first Nexus 5001 Class 3 embedded processor designed for the automotive market place. Tool venders, module suppliers and car companies are using the Nexus 5001 interface on the MPC565 to debug and calibrate engine management systems. Figure 1 is a picture of the die with the two major nexus blocks highlighted. The Nexus debug logic is known within

Motorola as the READI block. The Overlay SRAM is used to overlay other SRAM, internal flash, or external memory. The Overlay SRAM logic will match the number of clock cycles to access the memory being overlaid. This allows the system to have the exact bus performance characteristics during calibration and debug of the system. The Motorola READI block contains the internal bus snooping control, watchpoints & breakpoint logic, TCODE translation logic, the transmit FIFO and several other functions.

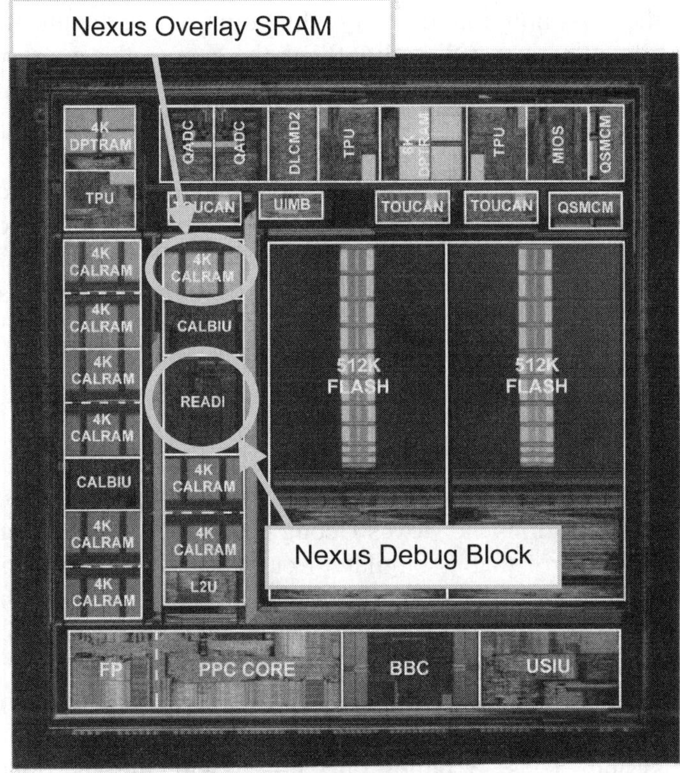

Figure 1: Current MPC565 Nexus 5001 Implementation

The current calibration and debugging methodology deploys a "must see every cycle" mindset towards debug and calibration of a powertrain system. The Nexus 5001 methodology makes four assumptions about the debugging scenario that frees it from the "must see every cycle" mindset.

1. The source code and object code are available to the debugging tools. This allows the host based tools to track or make calculations as to the program flow without any direct address or data bus visibility.
2. The only change of flow instructions required from the target system to the host based debugging tool. When the host calibration/debugging tool has access to the object code, proper synchronization can be maintained between the embedded processor and the host tool with just change of flow instruction addresses being transmitted over the debugging interface. The Nexus 5001 specification will send out a synchronization message if a change of flow has not forced a synchronization address within 255 instructions. This would be a rare event since most C compiled programs generate a change of flow once every 5 to 10 instructions for virtually all embedded processors.
3. Third, only a limited number of the data locations have to be displayed in real time, while most can be examined during a halted condition or updated due to a special event. The ability of the Nexus 5001 interface to trace on data values will be new for many engineers. Often this is accomplished with a powerful logic analyzer tracing the address bus and triggering on the data bus writes to a specific memory location. This is a very cumbersome task that is made nearly impossible with the advent of large data caches and system SRAM on-chip.
4. Fourth, if or when an error occurs, the user must be informed by the debugging environment. The Nexus 5001 specification provides for a variable sized FIFO buffer in the transmitter section. If the FIFO overflows, the interface will transmit an error condition. The user has the option to specify that when an overflow error condition occurs, to enforce a stale of the embedded processor or to continue with a new synchronization message.

The Nexus 5001 debug interface is a standard debug methodology across multiple architectures and development tools. The protocol implements a standard packet messaging interface that allows each architecture to remain unique while still communicating with common commands and debug information. This will allow the engineer to debug multiple architectures with very similar capabilities and tools.

Figure 2 is the interface protocol and the physical pin interfaces. The interface is based around the JTAG pins for the basic functions. For higher bandwidth and dedicated communications, the auxiliary port can be added with variable widths. To reduce the information being sent over the interface three features were added. These features were designed to increase the performance of the debug interface without significantly impacting the system cost.

1. First, the optional auxiliary pins can be removed by the silicon vendor to minimize the cost of the interface when the application can tolerate a reduced bandwidth debug port. The lower pin count implementation might be found on 8-bit and 16-bit devices or in market segments where real time debugging is less critical. The JTAG interface is to slow for high performance 32-bit microprocessors, so an optional auxiliary port has been added to the Nexus 5001 standard to address the high performance and full duplex needs of some applications.
2. Second, a packet based messaging scheme has been developed to minimize the overhead of the information

between the target microprocessor and the host debugging tool. The packet information is called a Transfer Code (TCODE) and is used in conjunction with the auxiliary port pins.

3. The third method of reducing the information from the debug port to the host development tool is to limit transmissions to sending the required addresses to trace the instruction flow. For example, if the target processor does not have a change of flow, then the 32-bit address is not transmitted. When a change of flow such as an interrupt or branch occurs, the Nexus 5001 development interface would send the new beginning address. In this environment it is a requirement that the source code and the linked code is available to the host tool at the time of the debugging session. Also, if the debugging session must be real time, then some information must be derived by the development tools. For example, not all data values have to be visible at all times, so if the data trace option is used, only the data that the engineer is concerned about would be sent to the Nexus port during run time.

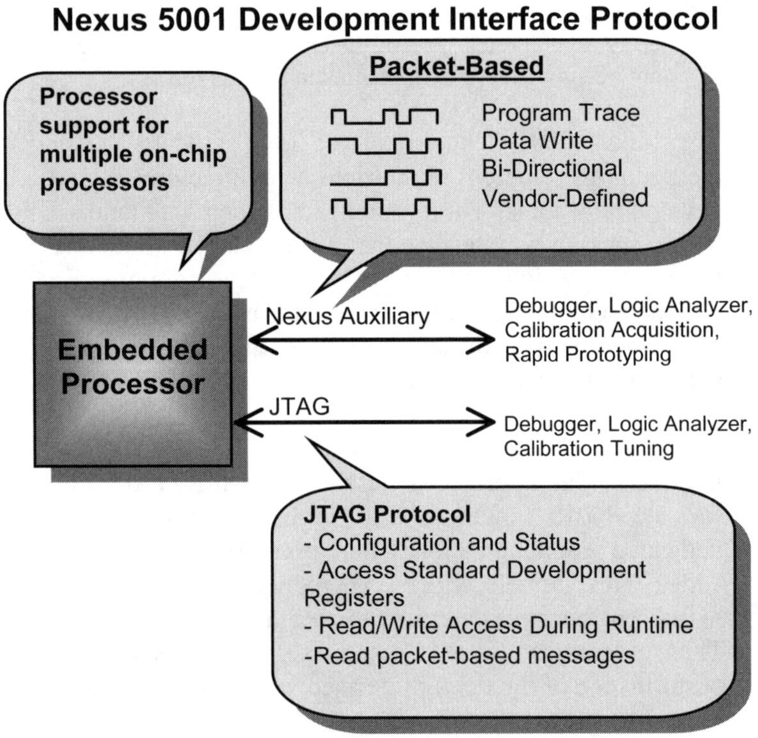

Figure 2: Nexus 5001 Development Protocol and Pin Interface

NEXUS 5001 FEATURES

The Nexus 5001 feature set is a mixture of the best practices in debug interfaces from the past 15 years of industry experience. Each feature has proven its worth on one or more processors in the past. The difference occurs by bringing them all together in a single industry standard debug interface to provide the industry with distinct advantages such as: run control, real time instruction and data trace information, RTOS support, memory substation, breakpoints and watchpoints to name just a few features. The philosophy was to create the maximum functionality while minimizing the pin and silicon area that directly affects the cost of the interface to the end user. Some of the technology advancements include smaller transistor geometries, resulting in smaller devices and less space for the address and data bus pins. The natural migration to the integration of system memory on-chip is results in reduced visibility of the embedded processor. Higher clock and bus speeds are making traditional debug techniques, such as emulators, very expensive and limited in capabilities. The Nexus 5001 consortium is changing the debug methodology with several new approaches to simplify debugging in the future for engineers.

Figure 3 provides a high level view of the 4 areas or classifications the Nexus Debug port. Class 1 is the basic run control that is similar to current BDM, OnCE and JTAG based debug interfaces. Class 2 contains all of the features and functions of Class 1 with the additional features of watchpoint messaging, ownership trace and program trace messaging. Class 3 provides many of the functions required to perform calibration of a powertrain system. Class 3 builds on Class 2 with the additional features of read-write memory access while the processor is running and data trace messages. The highest level of real time debug capabilities is reserved for Nexus Class 4 with memory substitution and port replacement capabilities. The Nexus 5001 specification directly outlines these capabilities for each Class.

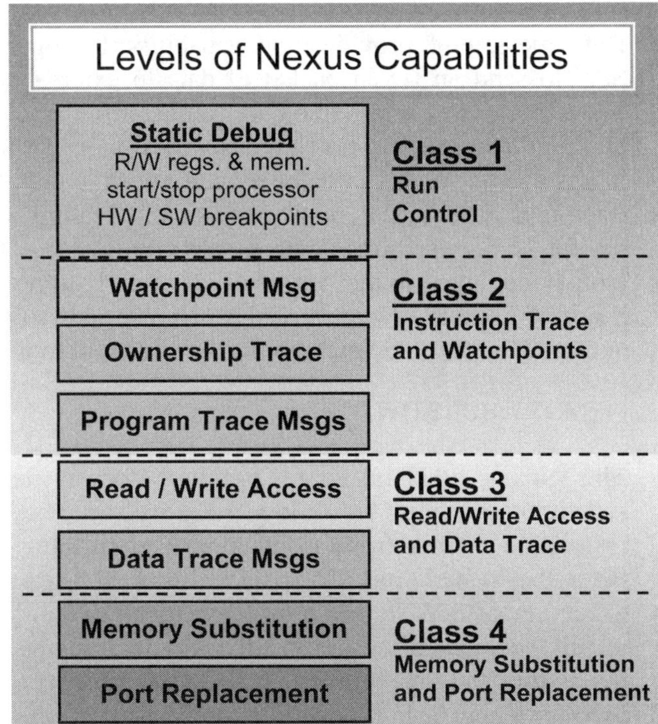

Figure 3: Nexus 5001 Development Protocol and Pin Interface

RUN CONTROL

Architecture specific Run control features are very unique to each processor's architecture but the basic types of capabilities are fairly universal and have been for many years. These include the ability to halt and start the processor, read and write the processor registers, single step the processor and modify memory.

READ-WRITE ACCESS

Read-Write access is where the debugging tool is able to access, read and write registers and memory without impacting the processor's execution of instructions. The Nexus 5001 standard goes beyond what has historically been made available in the area of read-write access, by allowing access while the processor is running. The Nexus 5001 standard requires that memory accesses be allowed while the core processor is running, which is along the approach of a debug DMA channel.

BREAKPOINTS

The breakpoint features facilitate the software development process by allowing the developer to halt the processor core at a specific processor state. If there is internal ROM or flash or if a breakpoint or trap instruction does not exist in the vendor's architecture then this feature becomes a valuable tool for development. The Nexus 5001 requires at least 2 address comparison and 2 data comparison registers be implemented in silicon which can be programmed as breakpoint registers, with up to 8 of each.

WATCHPOINTS

The watchpoint features are very similar to the breakpoint features. They use the same address and data comparison registers as the breakpoints do. The difference is that watchpoints do not halt the processor core but instead send a watchpoint message to the external tools monitoring the Nexus 5001 trace pins. This is very useful in sequencing and triggering external logic analysis collection, both of Nexus 5001 trace information and external I/O signals.

INSTRUCTION TRACE

The Nexus 5001 standard defines a standard protocol for instruction trace visibility that is processor independent. This is accomplished in such a way as to significantly reduce the amount of information bandwidth needed to transmit the information off chip. The instruction trace feature implements a Program Flow Change Model in which instruction trace is synchronized at each program flow discontinuity. The address information is compressed to further reduce the bandwidth needed. A program flow discontinuity occurs at taken branches and exceptions. Development tools can interpolate what transpires between program flow discontinuities by correlating information from Instruction Trace information and static source or object code files.

DATA TRACE

The Nexus 5001 specification defines a standard protocol for data trace visibility of accesses to memory locations and memory mapped device-specific internal peripherals. The standard defines a minimum of 2 data trace range resources which can be controlled to emit data trace messages on reads, writes or both within a specified address range. As in the Instruction trace feature, the address information is compressed to reduce bandwidth requirements. Additionally, data trace can be globally enabled and disabled by using watchpoint features to further reduce required bandwidth of the Nexus port.

The Nexus Class 3 requirement for Data Trace information allows a host tool to reconstruct the target's data based on data visibility. A properly configured Nexus Class 3 tool will send data write information over the Nexus port and allow the host tool to reconstruct the total data image. With only Data write information, the host tools can display to the user all of the modified data during a program run. Figure 4 is a screen shot from an Ashling Tool showing the MPC565 data trace for write only. When the Nexus port is configured to send all data access the Nexus port can more easily be overrun or force a stall, depending on the configuration by the user. In addition to data trace information, time stamping, address and actual values can be attached to the data trace stream and the host tool can attach the global or local variable name for ease of debugging and calibration by the engineer.

Data Trace (39043 data frames acquired)

Frame	Time	Address	Symbol	Value	Access
00000164	17.8500000us	3FC03C	__exitptr	00000000	Write
00000166	18.0000000us	3FC040	_exitfreefp	00000000	Write
00000168	18.1500000us	3FC044	environ	00000000	Write
00000170	18.3000000us	3FC048	_cleanupfp	00000000	Write
00000172	18.4500000us	3FC04C		00000000	Write
00000174	18.6000000us	3FC050	szDisplay	00000000	Write
00000176	18.7500000us	3FC054		00000000	Write

Figure 4: Data Trace Screen-shot

OWNERSHIP TRACE

The Ownership trace feature is a mechanism for allowing the S/W that is currently executing, to send messages to external development tools. In its typical usage, Ownership trace is used to provide a macroscopic view into the S/W running. An example would be for task or procedure flow reconstruction when debugging software written in a high level language. Ownership trace offers the highest level of abstraction for tracking software execution. Ownership trace is especially useful for embedded processors with a memory management unit, in which all processes can use the same logical program and data spaces. Ownership trace offers development tools a mechanism to decipher which set of symbolic and sources are associated with lower level program instructions. It is expected that a Real Time Operating System (RTOS) would be the primary users to enable external tools to determine what is transpiring in the operating system.

DATA MESSAGING

Data messaging provides the capability for operating S/W to send an ID-ed packet of data to external tools. These packets of associated data can be arbitrarily large. Due to the construction of the Data messaging protocol, it is a much more efficiently packed message than Data trace messages. A common usage of this feature would be for communicating with Rapid Prototyping tools already deployed in the Automotive industry, to perform a sort of Remote Procedure Call to an external H/W tool and send all the parameters to the development tool.

MEMORY SUBSTITUTION

The Nexus 5001 standard provides for a memory substitution feature to allow memory accesses and instruction fetches from a development tool rather than from the system memory. This allows non-real time execution of S/W before a system's memory subsystem is fully debugged. Additionally, single stepping with instruction and data fetches via the auxiliary port can be used for a non-real time ROM monitor.

The feature can also be activated upon the occurrence of a watchpoint. This can support easy run-time patching for portions of ROM memory, with the patch provided via the auxiliary port running at a reduced rate. Another option is to activate memory substitution upon the occurrence of a data access or an instruction fetch from a device-specific address range.

PORT REPLACEMENT AND SHARING

In embedded applications, the embedded processor vendors scrutinize the use of every physical pin. Inevitably there are never enough pins available on the embedded processor to meet both the application and development needs. Port replacement and sharing support is intended to solve this dilemma by using common embedded processor ports for a secondary development support function.

The first approach is a Port Replacement strategy. This approach provides a mechanism for low speed I/O pin functions to be emulated by the development tool. This is accomplished using port replacement messages via the Nexus 5001 port. Whenever the processor wants to change the value on the Low speed I/O port, the new output value is routed to the development tool for presentation to the signal pins. Similarly, when inputs change, the new values are routed through the development tool to the Nexus 5001 debug port.

The second approach is a Port sharing strategy. This allows Nexus 5001 data out signals to be shared on an existing bus such as a high speed L2 cache bus. The development tool only pays attention to the data out pins when the control signals indicate Nexus 5001 data is present. This allows for very wide Nexus 5001 data out ports to be implemented without requiring additional physical pins.

VENDOR DEFINED EXTENSIONS

The developers of the Nexus 5001 standard understand that there is no way to perfectly predict all of the possible needs for development features for unique processors or future processor features. This allows for additional functionality or optimization without disrupting the ability of standard tools to support the standard features. If a tool does not support a vendor specific feature, it at least knows how to safely ignore it without disruption of normal functionality.

MULTI-CORE DEBUGGING

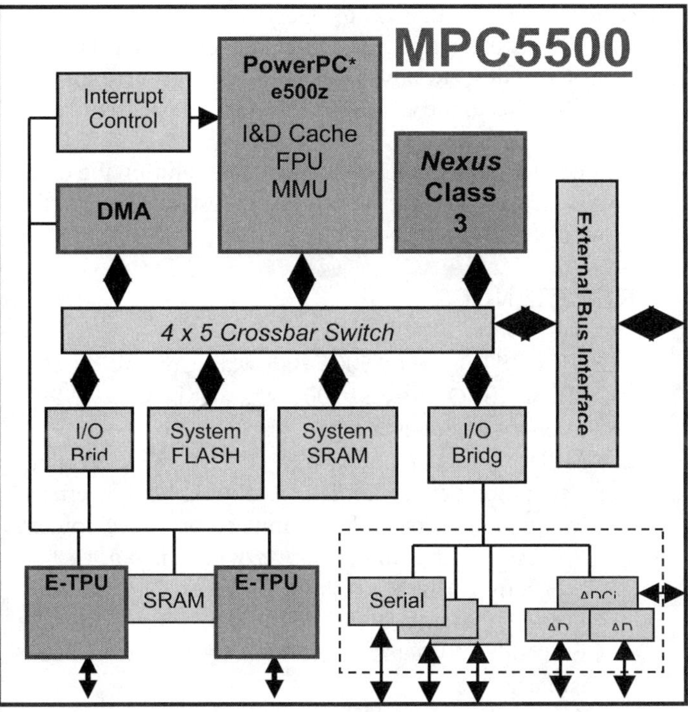

Figure 5: Motorola MPC5500 Multi-Processor Nexus Implementation

Within the next few months, Motorola will offer a PowerPC ISA compatible architecture that will allow multi-core debugging with the MPC5500 products designed for powertrain applications. The first version will allow for a debug port to be enabled for four processing elements. The four processing elements are the e500z PowerPC ISA compatible core, the dual Enhanced Timer Processor Units (E-TPU) and Direct Memory Access (DMA) unit. With the single connection over the Class 3 Nexus 5001 interface, the host tool can collect data from any or all of the four elements simultaneously. In addition, the debug and calibration tool could establish breakpoints and/or watchpoints on any of the four processing elements. An example where this would be used is when the engineer is tracking an issue between a timed event over the E-TPU and the code running on the PowerPC ISA compatible Book-e processing core.

NEW DEBUG AND CALIBRATION METHODS

The hardware & software engineer and calibration engineers will have to adopt a new debug and calibration strategies with the advent of a fully integrated embedded processor. These changes will be analogist to the transition from assembly language to high level languages such as C. The feeling that the experienced software engineer often noted in the mid 1980's during the transition was "a loss of control."

The visibility of an embedded processor's data bus and instruction bus will be different in several ways. First, the amount of raw data that is available is significantly less. Figure 3 shows the amount of data that a 32-bit data bus and address bus can provide. The Nexus 5001 Interface does not require as much raw data to perform instruction reconstruction. The Nexus 5001 standard reduces the amount of instruction data by only requiring the change of flow information, which is typically 1 out of every 6 to 10 instructions. Thus reducing the required bandwidth by 1/10th on the Nexus 5001 port.

Second, the address information is reduced to only transmit the difference in the address between the current instruction location and the updated location. Analysis of embedded applications, most applications remain local in execution patterns. Furthermore, by sending only the change of flow information significantly reduces the address information required to track the instruction execution flow.

Third, the data trace information can be focused to specific memory regions with the Nexus 5001 standard. By reducing and focusing the information over the Nexus 5001 Interface to only data writes the requirement for bandwidth can be further reduced by half or even more. Figure 6 is a Motorola MPC5500 device with the Nexus Class 3 port. The MPC5500 may require 2 clocks to transition the Nexus port pins above 150MHz at automotive temperature with the effects clearly showing in the bandwidth calculations showing a step function at 200MHz. The Figure 6 chart demonstrates the effects of the increased clocks at higher frequencies on the available bandwidth of the port vs the full address and data buses. The impact of instruction trace provides the largest performance improvement. Instruction trace can be disabled when the bandwidth is required for the calibration tables during a calibration session. The data trace messages can provide improvements in available Nexus port bandwidth by only tracing highly specific data locations and data writes. The Data Messaging mode is useful for tables or blocks of data that need to be transferred to the host tool during calibration or debug sessions as a single block. The address bus is assumed to require additional clock cycles at higher clock frequencies and can be seen by the lower line labels "Sustained Address/Data Bus Debug Bandwidth" in Figure 6.

The data in Figure 6 uses the basic assumption that a minimum of 24 address signals, 32 bit data signals and another 10 control signals are required for a traditional real time trace. A BDM run control port can be implemented with as few as 2 signals, but often required 4 to 6 as a minimum. The Nexus port can utilizes the JTAG port for the basic run control and a variable width auxiliary port for the high-speed data.

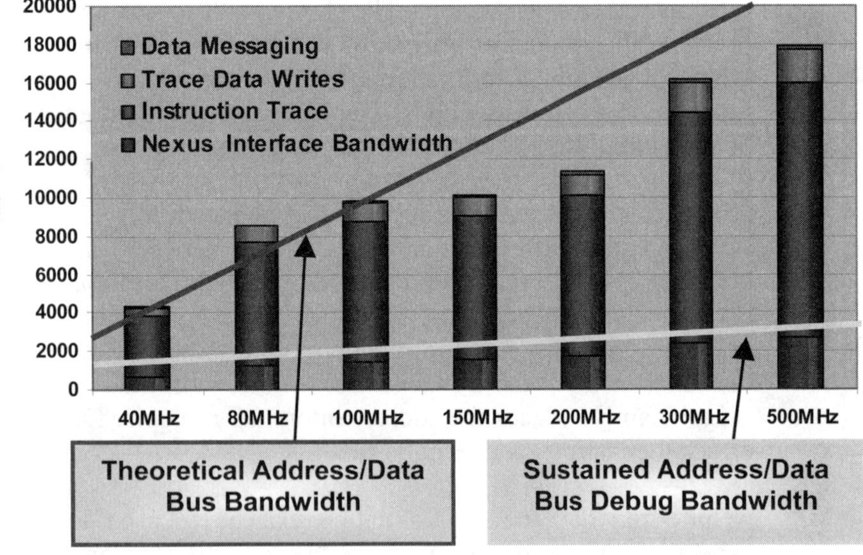

Figure 6: Nexus 5001 Port Bandwidth Calculations

The Nexus auxiliary port can transfer data on both clock edges for high-speed applications. Another feature of the Nexus auxiliary port is that it can be various port widths depending on the amount of throughput required. The maximum auxiliary port width is 16-bit wide.

CONCLUSION

The embedded processors already in the market and coming to market over the next 12 months will make the traditional run-control debug methodology obsolete. The external address and data buses have virtually disappeared from the 8-bit processors of today. The 16-bit and 32-bit processors are reducing in many cases the external buses in favor of more specialized I/O functions while integrating the memory on-chip leaving little room for the external buses.

The Nexus 5001 consortium has published the current revision of the specification (version 1.0 1999) on the consortium Web site (www.ieee-isto.org). The current revision is available on the consortium Web site.

ACKNOWLEDGMENTS

The author wishes to thank the members of the Nexus 5001 Consortium. Special thanks to Gary Miller, Kevin Hall, Wayne Willis, Martin Elbs, Rudan Bettelheim, Alan Hutton, David R. Gonzales, Randy Dees and Richard Collins for contributions to the development of the Nexus standard.

A special thanks to Gerrie Stence for tolerating the extra hours needed to get a worldwide standard off the ground.

REFERENCES

1. IEEE-ISTO Nexus 5001 Hardware Committee, etal, "IEEE-ISTO Nexus 5001 Standard, v1.0 1999", http//www.ieee-isto.org
2. Miller, G. (Motorola), Hall, K. (Agilent Technologies), etal, "The Evolution of Powertrain Microcontrollers and it's Impact on Development Processes and Tools", http//www.ieee-isto.org
3. O'Keeffe, Hugh (Ashling), "The Nexus 5001 Forum™ Standard providing the Gateway to the Embedded Systems of the Future", http//www.ieee-isto.org
4. Allen, James (Delphi), "Calibration Development with Production Intent Electronic Control Units" SAE Paper 00P-487, 2000

CONTACT

The author has worked in the electronics industry for 21 yea Most of this time he spent working in the semiconduc industry with Motorola. Prior to working for Motorola, M Stence worked for Advanced Micro Devices (AMD) a Tellabs.

Mr. Stence has made significant contributions toward establishing the IEEE-ISTO Nexus 5001 Debug Interface as an industry wide standard and currently serves on the Steering Committee and as the Vice Chairman of the Nexus 5001 Consortium. He has received 3 Motorola Corporation awards for his contribution to the Nexus 5001 standard.

Mr. Stence currently holds 7 U.S. Patents in the area of embedded processors and graduated from Texas A&M University in 1986 with a BS in Computer Science.

Email: ron.stence@motorola.com

DEFINITIONS, ACRONYMS, ABBREVIATIONS

SOC – SYSTEM-ON-A-CHIP

A highly integrated embedded processor that is focused at a single market. Often contains the part or all of the system memory.

DMA – DIRECT MEMORY ACCESS UNIT

Capable of transferring data from one location to another location without requiring intervention form the main CPU processor.

NEXUS

Name of the IEEE-ISTO Nexus 5001 Consortium and Specification. The charter of Nexus is to develop a real time debug and calibration standard for multiple embedded processor architectures. More information and the specification are available on the web site (`www.ieee-isto.org`).

JTAG – JOINT TEST ACCESSS PORT

Orginally defined as a boundary scan port under the IEEE 1149.1. Extended use as a slow speed run-control debug port by the Nexus 5001 Specification.

BDM – BACKGOUND DEBUG MODE

A debug port that was deployed on Motorola embedded processors in the late 1980s. Provided run control and memory & register visibility with the processor in a halted mode.

RUN CONTROL DEBUG

The basic run control (run, halt, download and upload data to and from memory and/or registers while the processor is stopped) debug mode found in many embedded processors. Operates over a dedicated debug port to provide basic run control and static memory, register information. Data is often serialially transmitted from the target to a host developemnt tool. Examples of Run Control ports include: BDM, ONcE and JTAG debug.

RISC – REDUCED INSTRUCTION SET COMPUTER

A processor Architecure that has many attributes that defines it as a different type of processor core (i.e. DSP, CISC). The major attributes of a RISC processor are: 1) fixed length instructions, 2) load/store architecture, 3) single cycle execution of instructions 4) hard coded instructions, 5) high-level language support.

TCODE – TRANSFER CODE

Defined by the Nexus 5001 Specification as a defined command used to communicate between the target processor and the host tool.

E-TPU – ENHANCED-TIMER PROCESSSOR UNIT

A complex timer orginally desinged to handle angle and time based systems on the M68332. The Enhanced TPU has new extensions and is assembly code compatible with the TPU found on multiple devices and architectures.

2002-01-1169

Embracing the Systems Approach to Automotive Diagnostics

Mark Jensen
Vector CANtech, Inc.

ABSTRACT

Perhaps more than any other automotive discipline, diagnostics has been the source of fragmented and redundant efforts. Diagnostic test tools are frequently reinvented for engineering, manufacturing and dealership service activities. Embedded software to support diagnostic functions is uniquely and manually created for each ECU. Uncoordinated databases storing duplicate protocol information are common. The absence of a comprehensive diagnostic data model has prolonged these inefficiencies and prevented diagnostic activities from realizing a unified system. A systems approach, based on a comprehensive data model, can eliminate redundant and parallel efforts across diagnostic activities and improve reliability by integrating previously uncoordinated applications. A proposed structure and the benefits of such an approach are the focus of this paper.

INTRODUCTION

Traditional diagnostic data models define bus messages and request/response transactions. These data models promote data entry tools with user interfaces that are organized by message and transaction structure. While this design is necessary and appropriate for the diagnostic data administration activity, it is not sufficient to satisfactorily support the other diagnostic activities that use the data. Activities that produce test tools, vehicle ECU software and service manuals require not only message definition data, but also a great deal of relational data. This relational data defines diagnostic objects that combine data and message-based functions into self-sufficient packages. Relations also define classes that organize objects by their structure, groups that organize objects by vehicle system and groups that organize objects by operational states.

Historically, data models and tools have ignored most relational data, as it tends to be too abstract to easily support. Without this relational data, each diagnostic activity is left to define, implement and validate its own relational data. These parallel and redundant efforts are the direct result of an insufficient data model and are obvious indications of a fragmented approach to diagnostics.

A system-based strategy that considers the use cases of all diagnostic activities can avoid these inefficiencies. Such an approach requires a comprehensive data model that defines both message content and relational structures. Data from this model is sufficient to not only eliminate parallel efforts supporting redundant data, but support automation in areas that rely on human expertise and labor to overcome data limitations.

AN OBJECT-ORIENTED DATA MODEL

The first step in creating useful relations between pieces of diagnostic data comes in the form of objects. Objects are self-contained packages that can stand on their own. Objects contain everything necessary to access and work with a particular item. By packaging diagnostic information into objects, a data model with real potential begins to take form.

DIAGNOSTIC OBJECTS

Diagnostic objects group pieces of data together with the diagnostic services that access and manipulate them. Object-oriented software activities often refer to objects as having fields and methods. Fields are pieces of information contained in an object. Methods are functions an object can perform. These abstract concepts require further definition and working examples to understand.

Object Fields (Data)

Diagnostic objects contain fields of data. The information in the fields uniquely identifies the object. Some fields hold data that must be sent or received in diagnostic messages (bits and bytes). Some fields hold data that help define the object conceptually, like names and descriptions (text strings or images).

Object Methods (Services)

Diagnostic objects contain methods that are the functions the object can perform. Some methods perform the bus messages transactions that are diagnostic services. Some methods perform queries on or assign values to the data fields.

Example Use Case: The VIN Object

The simple definition of a VIN (Vehicle Identification Number) is the 17-digit alphanumeric string that uniquely identifies every vehicle built. A diagnostic object that encapsulates the VIN must include not only a field for the 17-digit string, but also methods and additional fields. For instance, a method to read the VIN from the ECU is required, as is a method to write the VIN into the ECU. Additional data fields might contain the name and description of the object. Protocol identifiers for services, data, byte lengths, byte positions and decoding methods are also valuable fields.

Fields
- Name: VIN
- Description: vehicle identification number
- ID: 01
- Length: 17
- Type: ASCII
- Data: 1B3HM6SC90T234567

Methods
- Read: readDataByLocalIdentifier
  - Request Message: 21
  - Response Message: 61
- Write: writeDataByLocalIdentifier
  - Request Message: 3B
  - Response Message: 7B

Objects as Puzzle Pieces

The concept of objects brings data and message transactions together into self-contained independent packages. These neatly packaged objects have value of their own, but their full potential is not realized until they are applied in a systems approach. In a systems approach, objects must be looked at like pieces of a jigsaw puzzle. Each piece in the puzzle is unique and self-contained, but has no real value until correctly placed as a part of the big picture.

Relational data can bind diagnostic objects together like interlocking pieces in a puzzle. Just as puzzle pieces have attributes that allow them to be arranged into a coherent picture, diagnostic objects have data and services that allow them to be related to each other to form a complete diagnostic system.

While assembling a puzzle, it is natural to sort and organize the loose pieces according to the task at hand. Depending on the situation (or use case, as it is referred to in software development) there will be different sorting criteria. It may be useful to sort by color, like when finding all the blue pieces for the sky. Sorting by shape may be helpful, like when finding all of the pieces that go along the puzzle edges. Perhaps sorting first by color and then by shape is necessary to find one critical piece. Diagnostic systems also have different use cases that require different methods of organizing objects. Relational data defines these associations and provides the means to sort and organize objects in useful ways.

OBJECT CLASSES

Object classes organize objects by their structure. Objects in a class all have the same structure. The class defines the fields and methods the objects contain.

Common Methods and Fields

Every object class defines a set of methods that every object in the class must support. The VIN object in the previous section has methods named 'Read' and 'Write'. Every object in the same class as the VIN object must also have these same methods.

Every object class defines a set of fields that every object in the class must support. The VIN object in the previous section has fields named 'Name', 'Description', 'ID', 'Length', 'Type' and 'Data'. Every object in the same class as the VIN object must also have these same fields.

Unique Data

If objects in a class must all have the same fields and methods, they can only be unique in terms of the information kept in the fields and methods. While every object in a class may have a 'Name' field, they will each have a unique name stored in that field. Likewise, every object in a class may have a 'Read' method, but each will return a different value when executed.

Example Use Case: I/O Control Class

Suppose a set of solenoids all work in the same way to implement a set of various vehicle functions. It makes sense for these solenoids to have diagnostic objects that are members of the same class. Every solenoid object will have the same set of fields and methods as every other solenoid object. In fact, every output that can be controlled with diagnostic messages may belong to the same class, which can be collectively referred to as the 'I/O Control' class.

Fields
- Name
- Description
- ID
- Length
- Type
- State

Methods
- Monitor: IOControlByID - getCurrentState
  - Request Message: 30 01
  - Response Message: 70 01
- Override: IOControlByID - overrideECUControl
  - Request Message: 30 07
  - Response Message: 70 07
- Release: IOControlByID – returnControlToECU
  - Request Message: 30 00
  - Response Message: 70 00

VEHICLE SYSTEM GROUPS

Vehicle system groups organize objects by the vehicle system(s) they are associated with. Objects in a vehicle system group are all related to the same vehicle system, but need not have anything else in common.

Protocol-independent Relations

The relations that exist between the objects in a vehicle system group are subjective and can not be inferred through automated processing. Human intuition is necessary in deciding what vehicle system groups should exist and what objects should belong to each group. Consequently, each object must support a means of identifying the vehicle system group(s) it belongs to. Likewise, each group must support the ability to list the objects it contains.

Up until now, it has been easy to assume that all object relations exist just within the domain of a single ECU. Vehicle system groups may cross ECU boundaries and relate objects associated with physically distributed systems.

Example Use Case: A/C System

Most air conditioning systems combine electrical and mechanical components from more than one ECU. For instance, a climate control module on the dashboard usually handles the thermostat activities, while an engine control module usually handles the compressor. It is useful and intuitive to group objects from both ECUs together into a single vehicle system group.

A/C System Group

- Current Cabin Temperature (climate)
- Desired Cabin Temperature (climate)
- Outside Temperature (climate)
- A/C Compressor Pressure (engine)
- A/C Compressor Clutch (engine)

OPERATIONAL STATE GROUPS

Operational state groups organize objects sequentially by time. Objects in an operational state group are all available for use while the ECU is in that operational state. Objects that do not belong to an operational state group are not accessible while the state is active.

Sequential Relations as State Diagrams

Operational states can be thought of as the nodes of a state machine flow diagram. In these diagrams, each state group is a bubble with arrows connecting it to other state group bubbles. Inside each bubble is a list of objects that are available for use in that operational state.

Some objects will have methods that cause a new operational state to replace the current operational state. In terms of the state diagram, these methods provide the means of traversing the arrows from one bubble to another. With this structure, the pre-conditions necessary for using any object can be satisfied through an automated process that navigates from the active bubble to the bubble containing the object. Likewise, the post-conditions caused by using an object can be mapped directly onto the state diagram.

Example Use Case: Security Level

Some diagnostic objects are available for use at all times. Other objects may not be available for use until some security check has been passed. This situation can be thought of as two state bubbles. The first bubble contains the objects that are always available. The second bubble contains the same objects as the first, plus a few more that are available only after a security check has been passed. The security check is implemented as a method of one of the objects in the first bubble.

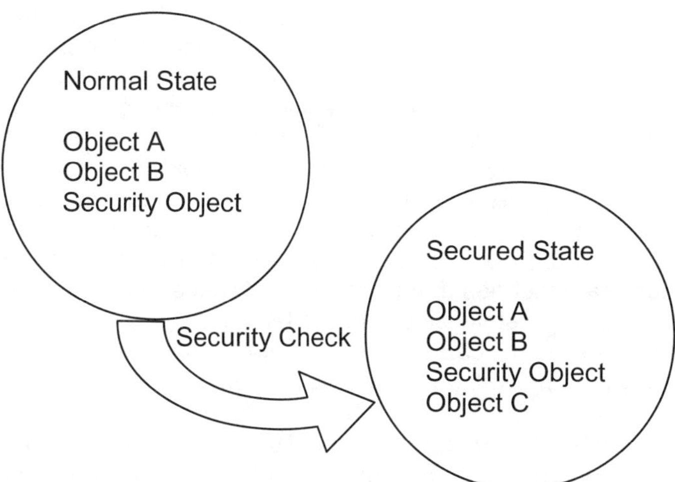

If 'Object C' in the 'Secured State' bubble is needed, but the 'Normal State' bubble is active, executing the 'Check' method of the 'Security Object' will change the current operational state to the 'Secured State' bubble and make 'Object C' accessible.

THE RELATIONAL DATA PROBLEM

Relational data, like that described above, is easy to conceive and understand. The use cases that point out the need for relational data are obvious. Unfortunately, as is the case with many abstract concepts, creating a software structure that can support diagnostic relations is not trivial. Further, recognizing the impact of relational data on other areas in the diagnostic system poses an equally involved task.

MODELING DIFFICULTIES

Modeling relational data and implementing it in software presents several issues. Some issues are technical in nature and some are cultural. The technical issues can be resolved with expertise and knowledge. The cultural issues can only be resolved by considering the overall diagnostic system and embracing a systems approach.

Technical Issues

The most obvious technical issue facing developers is how to model relational data and implement this model in software. An unusual, but manageable, combination of common software architectures can address all aspects of the task.

Object-oriented software is a common tool employed to solve many complex problems. Many languages, like C++ and Java, are designed explicitly for this purpose. Even without these ideally suited languages, object-oriented concepts are well understood and can be applied in most any situation. The diagnostic object and class concepts defined above use simple hierarchical and rule-based relations. These concepts are a natural product of an object-oriented approach.

The relational data that defines vehicle system groups and operational state groups is neither hierarchical nor rule-based in nature. As a result, these groups frequently elude automated sorting and categorizing techniques. Defining these groups and intelligently processing their members requires the use of discrete mathematics. Discrete math defines set theories that provide a foundation for defining groups (or sets) by directly enumerating members. These theories also define operations that compare and manipulate the contents of sets. Discrete math also defines finite-state automata theories that provide structures and processing methods for state diagrams. State diagrams and state machines are commonly used in embedded control software and well understood by software developers.

Hierarchical structures and discrete math are not common partners. Fortunately, objects tend to work very well in discrete math. Combining the two concepts provides an opportunity for a unified solution.

Cultural Issues

If established and accepted disciplines are suitable for working with diagnostic data, then why is a systems approach to diagnostics still a goal and not a reality? The answer is as abstract as the systems approach itself and resides in the cultural structures of the organizations responsible for diagnostic systems.

The tasks of developing graphical object-oriented software and automotive diagnostic systems are distinctly different. Software developers assigned to design and create diagnostic data administration tools usually do not have sufficient diagnostic expertise to recognize or define valuable diagnostic relations. Diagnostic engineers usually do not have sufficient software experience to design or implement their own data administration tools. Further, as the diagnostic world covers many activities and applications, few engineers are aware of all the possible use cases.

It is very likely that a team comprised of both software and diagnostic experts is necessary to design a sufficient system. By gathering and describing all use cases, diagnostic engineers can imply functional requirements and formulate a system goal. By analyzing the use cases, software engineers can design a data model that supports the objects and relations necessary to meet the goal. By analyzing this data model and identifying the use cases of the data administration activity, software engineers can design software that meets the team goal. Calling on the diagnostic engineers to verify that the system design adequately supports all use cases closes the design loop.

Such an approach is common in the data processing world. The results and successes of this collaborative design strategy are well published. Yet, in the world of automotive diagnostics, where embedded software and electrical engineering reign, this approach is relatively obscure. The organizational distances that separate the data processing and diagnostic activities of most automotive companies have prolonged this lack of awareness. Even today, organizations proficient in some disciplines, but not all, try to tackle these problems alone and miss the benefits of a systems approach.

SYSTEM IMPACT

A single data source that provides all information required by all other diagnostic activities has many benefits. Simply listing these benefits as 'obvious' reasons for adopting a systems approach is subjective and leaves room for arguments that favor existing practices. Instead, a review of the common fragmented approach provides insight into these benefits by presenting use cases that generate redundant data, parallel efforts and introduce opportunities for inconsistencies.

ECU Software

Most diagnostic systems today start with the ECU software. Here, the diagnostic messages are implemented directly in source code on an as needed basis. The software is manually created and based on application-specific logic and data. The diagnostic information defined by this embedded software is manually documented and transferred to the data administration activity.

Had the data for the diagnostic messages been defined first, it would be possible to automate the generation of some ECU software. Certainly not all ECU software relates to diagnostics or is suitable for automated generation. However, a considerable amount of highly repetitive and error prone source code could be generated from a diagnostic data source. Generating ECU software can increase efficiency and reliability as human interpretation is eliminated.

Data Administration

As the data model is ignored in the ECU software development activity, the first application of the data model and the tools that implement it will be in the data administration activity. Here the main concern is to define all diagnostic messages for use in other activities. The bits and bytes that make up these messages are easily entered and maintained without relational data. The data administration activity is content they have met their requirements and pass the data down to other activities.

The data is now set and any problems associated with not having relational information are pushed downstream where the data can not be changed. This incomplete view of the data model and its use cases will produce fragmented and inefficient processes downstream.

Downstream Activities

Downstream diagnostic activities that receive this data include diagnostic tool development and service manual authoring. These activities have use cases that require relational data. Test tools need to present all diagnostic objects related to a vehicle system in a single view. Service manuals need to list all possible fault codes objects as well as associating them with vehicle systems. Without relational data from the data administration activity, these activities must provide their own relations.

In the end, each downstream activity creates local relational data to supplement the supplied data. This local relational data is redundant across the downstream activities and requires parallel efforts to support. Worse yet, the human interpretation necessary to define the local relational data is likely to vary from one activity to another. Inconsistent interpretations lead to inconsistent diagnostic applications.

A central data model that supports all diagnostic applications can avoid these parallel, redundant and inconsistent practices. Further benefits are possible as comprehensive data enables automated generation of software and documentation that previously required human expertise and effort to make.

Restructuring the Data Flow

Understanding the data flow from ECU development to data administration to the downstream activities is essential in realizing the full impact of a systems approach. By changing this flow to start with the data administration activity and moving the ECU development downstream, a significant savings in product cycle time is possible. Diagnostic test tools and service manuals could be produced in parallel with the ECU software, rather than in series as is done today.

IMPLEMENTATION STRATEGY

A comprehensive data model that includes relational data requires starting with an equally comprehensive data administration tool. This tool must support all use cases for entering and maintaining the data. The tool must also support the ability to export the data for use in downstream activities. Designing and implementing such a tool requires an understanding of the data model and a means of mapping the model structure onto an intuitive graphical user interface and useful file formats.

MULTIPLE USER INTERFACE VIEWS

As stated earlier, a comprehensive data model will combine multiple organizational structures. No single user interface is likely to merge these structures into a single intuitive view. For that matter, no single use case is likely to require the simultaneous use of multiple views. A user interface that allows the operator to alternate between different views is a highly effective design. The splitting of these views into separate implementations dramatically reduces the complexity of the software, both for the user and the developer. By ignoring the relations that are not of value in a particular view, each view remains manageable to use and implement.

MULTIPLE DATA EXPORT UTILITIES

A variety of downstream applications will take data from the central data administration system as input. The data administration tool must provide this data in the form of exports.

One approach to minimize the complexity of the data administration tool is to export all data to a single comprehensive format. Such an approach allows each downstream activity to process the exported data in their own way.

The complexity of this local processing can be minimized through the use of local translation utilities. These translation utilities allow activities to exchange data in a common format, but still provide the local formats necessary in each activity. Managing changes in the data model seems to point to centralized development of these translation utilities. Having each activity create and maintain its own translation utility can be difficult to coordinate at times of change. If the translation utilities are the responsibility of the data administration tool developers, changes in the data model can be centrally and reliably deployed.

CANDELA

CANdela is an object-oriented data administration tool from Vector. The philosophy of CANdela is consistent with the systems approach to diagnostics outlined in this paper.

Current Capabilities

CANdela defines diagnostic data in the object structure described above. All CANdela objects must be instances of pre-defined object classes. By pre-defining the possible classes, the complexity of the user interface is dramatically reduced, but the flexibility of the data model remains intact.

CANdela's user interface aims to be intuitive and familiar. Employing a design similar to the Windows Explorer and Windows Help software from Microsoft, CANdela minimizes the user interface aspects of the learning curve. This self-explanatory interface allows users to organize data by class and navigate the object hierarchy structure.

CANdela stores data in files according to the XML language syntax. This highly flexible language is ideal for modeling diagnostic objects and relational data.

CANdela offers an export utility to the standard RTF (Rich Text Format) file format. These exports can be used in a variety of documentation activities that produce hardcopy manuals and online information.

Next Steps

Features to support vehicle system and operational state groups are currently under development. A multiple view user interface will structure these concepts in an intuitive, but separated, format.

Diagnostic test tools that use CANdela XML data files directly are scheduled for development and will begin to appear downstream in the coming year. These test tools will employ a common diagnostic communication driver that understands the CANdela data model and will use it to its fullest capabilities. These test tools will provide plug-n-play diagnostic support for ECUs modeled with CANdela.

In combination with CANdela, CANdelaDESC is a project to support automated source code generation for diagnostic functions in ECU software. This generated source code will integrate directly into Vector's industry standard CAN-based software components. CANdelaDESC (Diagnostic Embedded Software Components) completes CANdela's systems approach to diagnostics.

ASAM

ASAM (Association for Standardization of Automation and Measuring Systems) is a global consortium of automotive OEMs and suppliers of test equipment. ASAM sponsors the development of standards for defining and using automotive test data. The MCD (Measurement, Calibration and Diagnostics) activity of ASAM addresses diagnostics directly. Activities that adopt the ASAM standards have the opportunity to interchange diagnostic data and software solutions. Such interchangeability is extremely valuable in a systems approach.

MCD-2D

MCD-2D is an ASAM-sponsored standard that defines a diagnostic data model implemented in the open format of SGML. MCD-2D provides object-oriented data structures and relational data to organize the objects. MCD-2D is a work in progress, but already offers substantial stable content. Industry evaluation and adoption of MCD-2D is in the early stages.

MCD-3D

MCD-3D is another ASAM-sponsored standard that defines a diagnostic communication interface for test tools using MCD-2D data. The interface is object oriented and supports many of the concepts of a systems approach. MCD-3D is also a work in progress.

INDUSTRY POSITION

As stated earlier, most automotive companies employ a fragmented approach to diagnostics. Most organizations must reconsider their current structures and charters in order to adopt a systems approach. Despite these organizational concerns, as the concept of a systems approach gains exposure, the level of interest is increasing rapidly. The technical attraction of the systems approach is clear in engineering activities. However, the real move towards a systems approach is driven by business reasons. As a result, a support base of suppliers is quickly moving to meet the demand.

Changing Organizational Structure

In order to adopt a systems approach, existing diagnostic organizations may need to be restructured. Some expertise that typically only exists in the downstream activities must be moved up into the data administration activity. Some manually supported activities will be displaced by automation. This displaced manpower will likely possess exactly the kind of expertise that must be relocated.

Perhaps the biggest cultural hurdle will come in the form of specifying diagnostic information prior to implementation in ECU software. The notion of automated source code generation based on data received from an outside source is not a comfortable one for most ECU developers. ECU software development has long been considered the starting point of diagnostic data. In fact most ECUs have few, if any, diagnostic data requirements and are free to implement protocol and data definition on the fly. Reversing this flow of data presents a change in the ECU development process that may be harder to implement than the software itself.

Business Driven

The benefits of a systems approach to diagnostics all revolve around increasing consistency and reliability while reducing development time and duplicated effort. These benefits all represent process improvements that provide direct business benefits. Reuse of relational data across downstream diagnostic activities improves efficiency and improves consistency. Automated generation of software reduces manpower resource requirements for software development. Data reuse, automated source code generation and the parallel development of ECU software and test tools all reduce product development cycle times.

Support Readiness

Diagnostic suppliers see the impending move by OEMs to the systems approach. Tools like CANdela and standards like ASAM MCD-2D/3D are well underway. Partial support for the systems approach is already in place. A complete set of off-the-shelf products will be ready soon. Look for systems based diagnostics to appear in vehicle development programs during calendar year 2002. Given the current pace of tool development, first releases of complete systems solutions should be available in 2003. Acceptance of these solutions will be gradual, but steady. Systems with a chance to rapidly succeed will start with a comprehensive data model and an administration tool to support it. The downstream use of the data from this system can be phased in over time. The rollout of a systems approach need not happen in one sweeping action.

CONCLUSION

A comprehensive data model can enable a systems approach to diagnostics. By implementing such a model, a single database can feed data to all other diagnostic activities and integrate them into a unified process chain. This integration eliminates the redundant and parallel efforts that are common across the diagnostic activities of today. System reliability and consistency are improved through the reuse of data from a single source. Manpower requirements are reduced through the automation of systems that currently depend on repetitive software development. As proof of this concept, tools such as CANdela and standards such as ASAM MCD-2D/3D are already laying the foundation for such diagnostic systems.

ACKNOWLEDGMENTS

I would like to thank my colleagues, Christoph Raetz and the CANdela development team, of Vector Informatik, whose vision and work serve as the foundation for this paper.

CONTACT

Mark Jensen
Vector CANtech, Inc.
Suite 550
39500 Orchard Hill Place
Novi, MI 48375
(248)449-9290 x247
mark.jensen@vector-cantech.com
www.vector-cantech.com

APPENDIX

ASAM:
Association for Standardization of Automation and Measuring Systems, a global consortium of automotive OEMs and suppliers of test equipment

CANdela:
An object-oriented diagnostic data administration tool from Vector

ECU:
Electronic Control Unit, a vehicle control module implemented as an embedded system

MCD:
Measurement, Calibration and Diagnostics, a work group within ASAM

MCD-2D:
An ASAM-sponsored standard that that defines a diagnostic data model implemented in the open format of SGML

MCD-3D:
An ASAM-sponsored standard that defines a diagnostic communication interface for test tools using MCD-2D data

IMPLEMENTATION EXAMPLES

2007-01-1617

A Prototype Distributed Architecture for Safety Critical Automotive Systems

Peter Miller
Ricardo Plc

ABSTRACT

This paper describes a prototype distributed architecture which is suitable for future safety-critical automotive systems like brake–by-wire (BBW) and steer–by-wire (SBW). It includes a description of a multiple ECU HIL system that was used to validate the implementation. This architecture is analyzed in terms of safety, reliability, cost and communications requirements. A "dual duplex" system is also proposed as a potential solution for more complex applications.

INTRODUCTION

Technology trends are showing that the demand for more processing power and more electronic control units (ECUs) in the vehicle is growing at a significant rate [Figure 1]. This trend is a consequence of the speed at which new applications are being developed to support the driver, where each associated sensor or function typically uses a dedicated ECU.

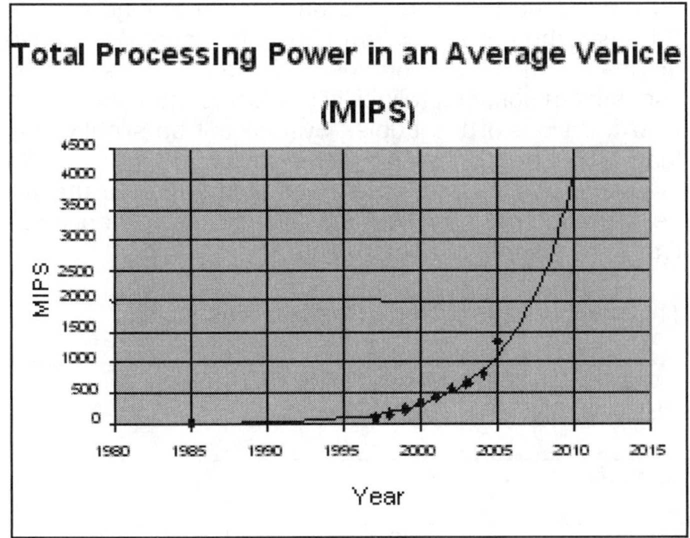

Figure 1 – Projected growth in processing power per vehicle.

DRIVE-BY-WIRE

Brake-by-Wire and Steer-by-wire in particular offer significant opportunities for vehicle "branding" as well as environmental (no hydraulic fluid) improvements. They are also enablers for many "integrated safety" applications. However, the sub-systems themselves are extremely safety-critical. Electrical system integration for all these applications is a complex task. New approaches, technologies, tools and processes are needed, and the electrical architectures will need to change to meet the challenge.

IMPACT FOR ELECTRICAL ARCHITECTURES

Vehicle electrical architectures will naturally evolve from the existing systems mainly due to the number of legacy control systems and the need to manage risk. New Drive-by-wire systems can replace existing vehicle dynamics control sub-systems on a functional basis, provided that the sub-system safety requirements are met, similar to the way that today's ABS/ESP controller meets the vehicle dynamics safety case.

FUTURE CONTROL UNIT NEEDS

A key requirement for new architectures is to ensure that they are cost-effective while at the same time meeting both current and future needs within the vehicle lifetime.

Figures 2 to 5 illustrate basic system architectures with varying amounts of redundancy (higher redundancy means higher safety in a well-designed system).

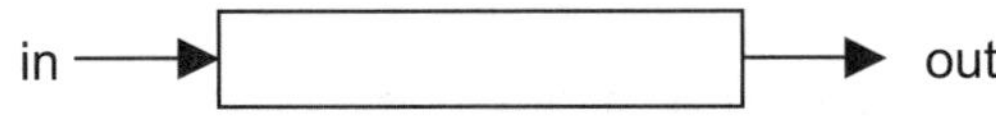

Figure 2: No fault tolerance

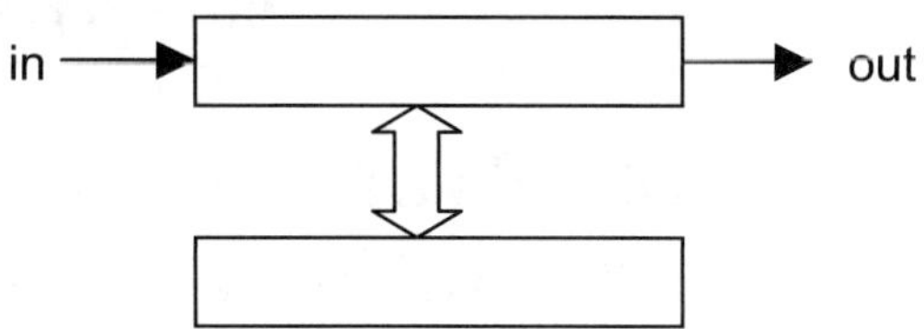

Figure 3: Watchdog, attempts to fail silent

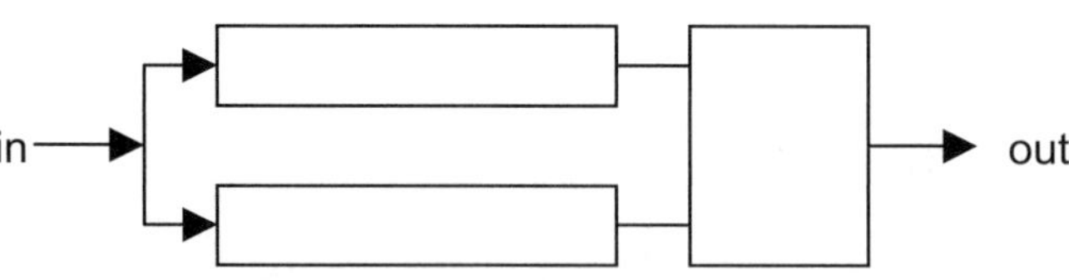

Figure 4: Duplex – Fail Silent

The simple implementation of the triplex system shown in Figure 5 does not solve the problem of faults in the input (in), the voter or the output (out). A more comprehensive system uses multiple sensors/actuators and a distributed voting system to avoid such single point failures, as shown in Figure 6. In this case the individual control units use a separate and redundant communications network over which to share data for the distributed voting protocol. Basic system functionality is still provided by the individual control units, while the system protection against faults will need redundant network links from multiple control units to the actuators and the addition of redundant power sources etc. [1,2]. It should be noted that distributed voting normally uses a synchronous system, with the high-speed communication network also having to be used to provide time synchronization.

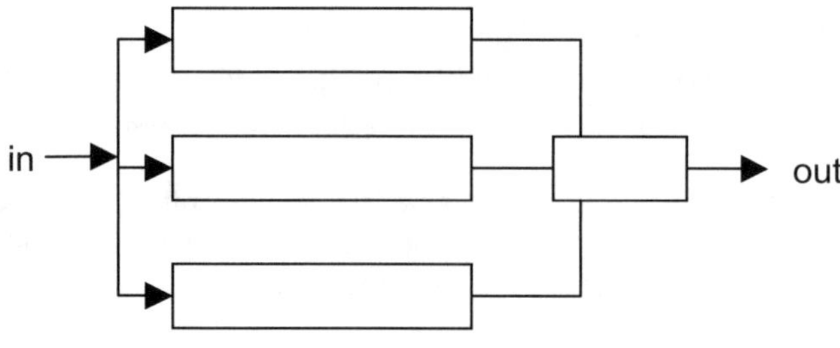

Figure 5: Triplex – fail operational on a single fault

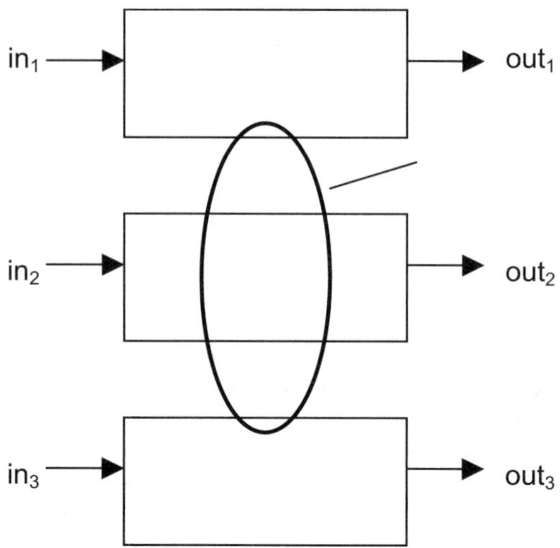

Figure 6: Distributed voting via a redundant network

In redundant systems, common mode failures occur when a single failure affects more than one module at the same time [3]. Design mistakes (in the specification, hardware or software) are potentially the worst type of common mode failures.

RELIABILITY AND COST

If we take the mean time to failure of a basic system with no redundancy, such as the one shown in Figure 2, as "M", then the duplex system shown in Figure 4 will have at least twice the number of components. Thus, assuming a constant reliability rate/component, the mean time to failure of the duplex system will be slightly less than M/2. For the triplex system shown in Figure 6 with the same assumptions, the mean time to first failure will be slightly less than M/3 (as slightly more than three times the number of components are required).

This can be summarized in the following table.

AMOUNT OF REDUNDANCY	MEAN TIME TO FAILURE	COST
Simplex	M	C
Duplex	<M/2	>2*C
Triplex	<M/3	>3*C

The table above clearly shows that as the "safety" is improved, the reliability is reduced and the cost increases. This means it is important to identify an appropriate level of safety for the system. The approach of "over killing" the safety is not viable, as the cost will not be affordable - and even if it was, the reliability is unlikely to be acceptable in an automotive application (where components are expected to last the life of the vehicle, e.g. 10-15 years).

EXAMPLE IMPLEMENTATION – BRAKE-BY-WIRE

As an example, consider a brake–by-wire system as shown in concept in Figure 7.

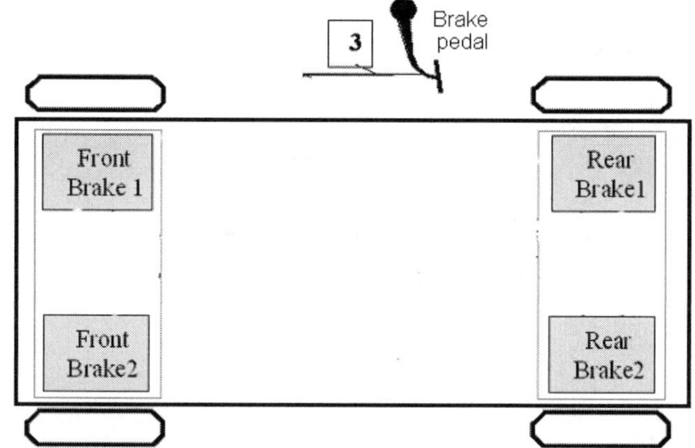

Figure 7: Basic brake-by- wire architecture.

A brake pedal is the user input to the system, measured by a number of redundant sensors on the pedal. The actual brake actuation is via electrical actuators on each wheel. (Rear) brake lights also have to be activated whenever the brake pedal is pressed. The presently accepted architecture uses a hydraulic linkage between the brake pedal and the wheels, with diagonal redundancy on the connections to the brakes. This is shown in a very simplified form in Figure 8.

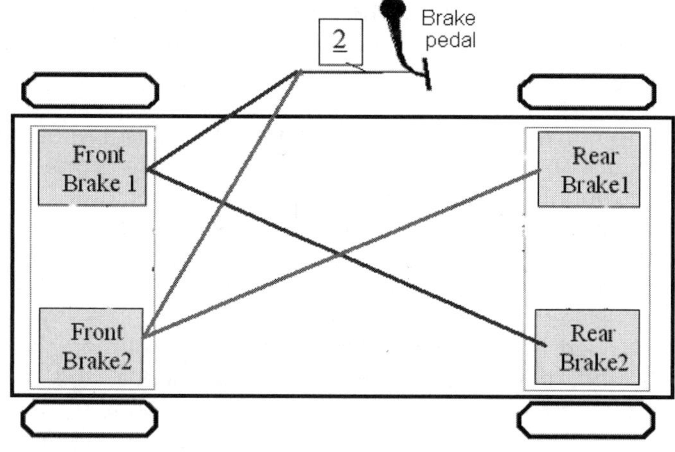

Figure 8: Basic layout of today's dual redundant hydraulic braking system.

Using the hydraulic implementation shown in Figure 8 as a basis the architecture shown in Figure 9 was developed.

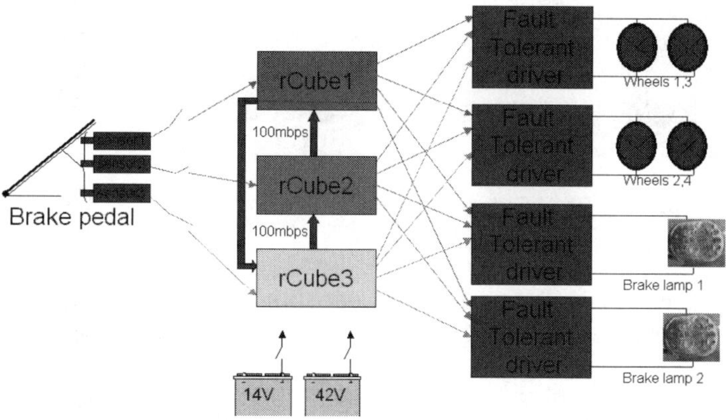

Figure 9: Potential brake–by-wire architecture

The boxes marked "rCube" are an advanced ECU called the rCube [4] developed by Ricardo especially for use in prototyping safety related systems, and Figure 9 shows three of these units in a distributed network configuration. This architecture was selected bearing in mind the normal development process, which is shown in Figure 10 below.

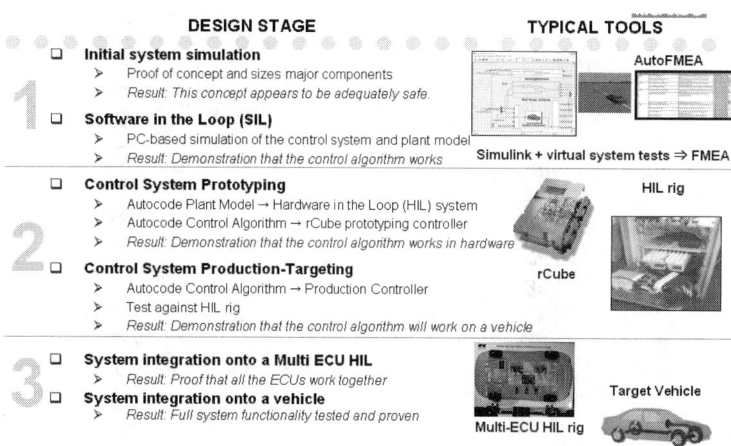

Figure 10: Typical design process for safety related systems.

The difference here was that this process was intended to design the final (demonstration multi ECU HIL) system with flexibility in the amount of redundancy present, so it is easy to demonstrate the trade-off between system complexity (and thus cost and reliability) and safety.

Ricardo would typically implement Design Stage 1 using Simulink and then a tool called AutoMEA [7] to do the safety analysis. However, as we wished this system to be easy to switch between different levels of redundancy, a prototype implementation of the control system was created in C and a simple GUI added - see Figure 11.

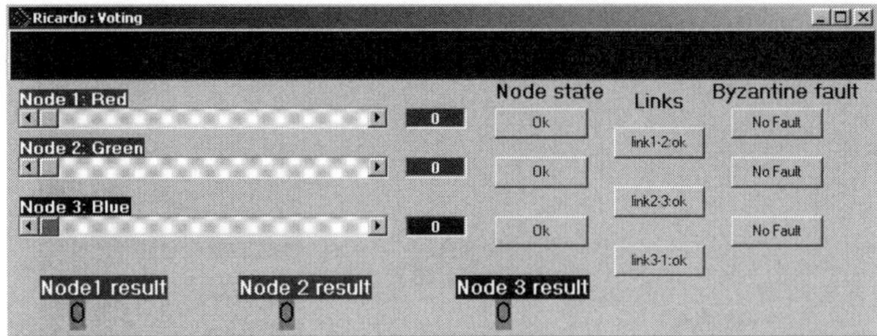

Figure 11: Basic GUI around brake by wire core code

This GUI allows up to 3 sensors on the brake pedal (shown as sliders to the left of the screen) and shows the amount of braking force applied from the rCubes to the fault-tolerant drivers (with the capability to inject various faults in the system and instantly see the results). When this system worked correctly it was expanded to model the whole system of Figure 9.

Normally the next step would be to implement a single ECU and test this in a HIL system (see Design Stage 2 in Figure 10). However, in this system all ECUs are identical (as are the fault-tolerant drivers), so the next step actually undertaken was Design Stage 3 of Figure 10 – a multiple (3) ECU HIL system, a photograph of which is shown in Figure 12.

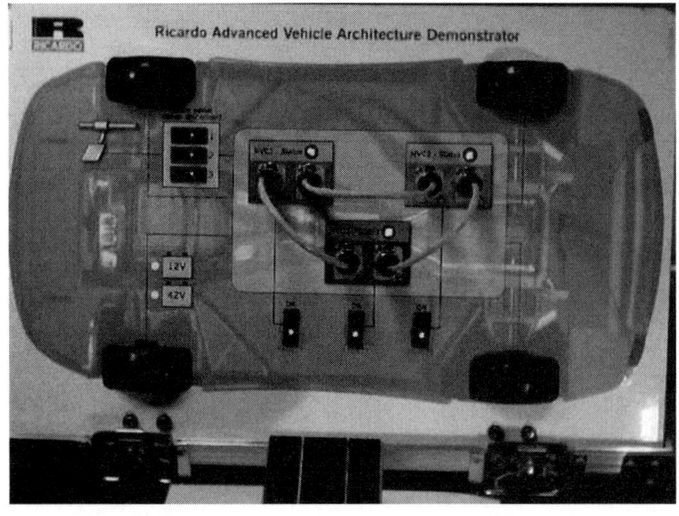

Figure 12: Multiple ECU HIL implementation for BBW.

MULTIPLE ECU HIL SYSTEM – TEST RESULTS

The multiple ECU HIL shown in Figure 12 can be configured into a simplex, duplex or triplex configuration.

A simplex configuration is shown in Figure 13. Here only rCube 3 (blue) is operational.

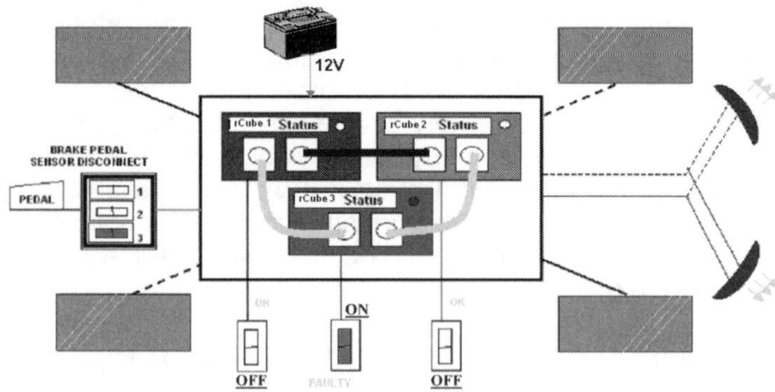

Figure 13: The system set up for single ECU (simplex) operation

In this case no redundancy is present, so many faults will cause a complete loss of braking, which is clearly an unacceptable situation.

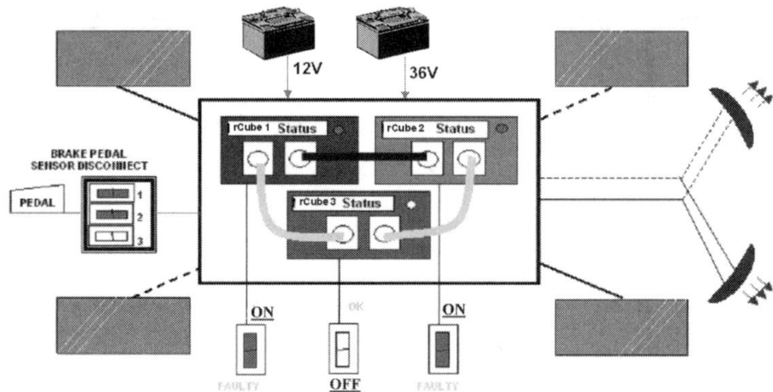

Figure 14: The system setup for duplex operation

For a duplex system (Figure 14) , rCube's 1 and 2 (red and green) are both communicating via a single communication link. The behavior is then very similar to today's dual circuit hydraulic braking systems. One fault may cause partial loss of braking (1 diagonal pair). Note that to get a true duplex system, redundant power (e.g. 12/42V) is needed to allow the system to continue to operate with "any" one fault. In this implementation the loss of 42V is similar to loss of power assist with today's brakes, in that only 12V is available for the brake actuators rather than 42V, so maximum braking force may be reduced.

The implementation of the fault tolerant driver shown in Figure 9 for the duplex case can be quite simple, as shown in Figure 15. In the left implementation of Figure 15 it is assumed that each "switch" (eg MOSFET controlled by one of the microprocessors) is designed to fail off, or the safe state for the load is ON. It is clearly possible to put the switches in series if the safe state for the load is OFF and the outputs are not guaranteed to fail off. If two switches are used in series, the most robust solution is to use one low side and one high side switch (right hand solution of Figure 15), as this allows the load to be turned off even with any one point shorted to either ground of Vbat.

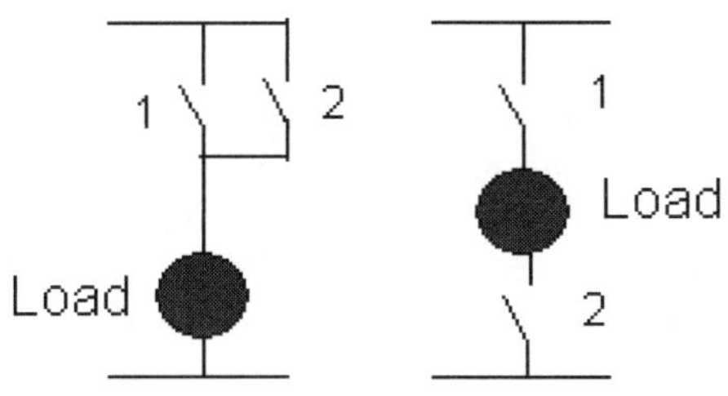

Figure 15: 2 simple fault tolerant driver implementations

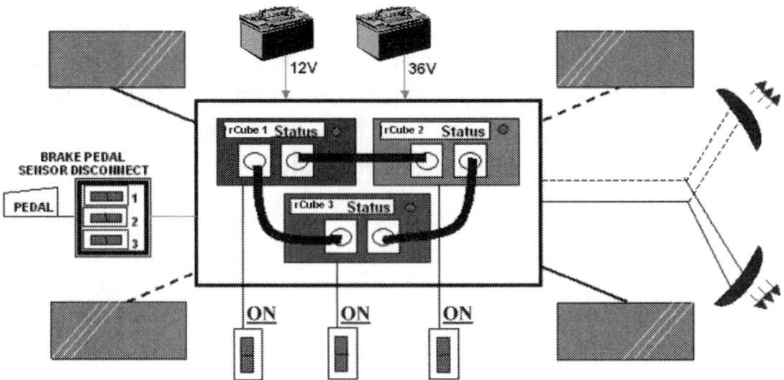

Figure 16: System set up for Triplex operation

For triplex operation (Figure 16) , all 3 rCube's are used. They communicate via 2 network links to give redundancy. In this case the 1st failure has no effect ("reduces to 2 ECU system"). The 2nd failure in all except one case (loss of both 12 & 36V power) still leaves the capability to brake.

WHAT IS AN APPROPRIATE LEVEL OF REDUNDANCY FOR A BRAKE–BY-WIRE SYSTEM ?

The HIL system confirmed what a basic system analysis and the SIL system had shown: a simplex solution is clearly not safe enough for a brake–by-wire system. A duplex system (configured as shown in Figure 14) is effectively as safe as today's dual circuit hydraulic braking systems in that it is resilient to a single fault. A triplex system would offer improved safety, but at a significant increase in system cost and complexity (and thus a lower reliability).

Controllability Categories	Definition	SIL
Uncontrollable	This relates to failures whose effects are not controllable by the vehicle occupants, and which are most likely to lead to extremely severe outcomes. The outcome cannot be influenced by a human response.	4
Difficult to Control	This relates to failures whose effects are not normally controllable by the vehicle occupants but could, under favourable circumstances, be influenced by a mature human response. They are likely to lead to very severe outcomes.	3
Debilitating	This relates to failures whose effects are usually controllable by a sensible human response and, whilst there is a reduction in the safety margin, can usually be expected to lead to outcomes which are at worst severe.	2
Distracting	This relates to failures which produce operational limitations, but a normal human response will limit the outcome to no worse than minor.	1
Nuisance Only	This relates to failures where safety is not normally considered to be affected, and where customer satisfaction is the main consideration.	0

Figure 17: MISRA definitions for SIL levels.

Given that you can stop the car by using engine braking and the handbrake, you could argue that, using the MISRA definitions of Figure 17 [8], brakes were SIL-2 "Debilitating". A duplex system as shown in Figure 14 can be shown to meet the requirements of SIL-2, so this re-enforces that this is an appropriate solution.

COMMUNICATION SPEED

So far this paper has not considered any requirements for the communication links between the ECUs. In the HIL system 100Mbps links were used, with the protocol and actual communication speed being set by software within the rCubes. For a review of potential automotive communication networks see [6].

The actual amount of data that needs to be sent via the communication link is actually very low. One CAN frame (which is transmitted as <= 117 bits including possible bit stuffing) can contain up to 8 bytes of data. At CAN's maximum data rate of 1MBps one frame is transmitted in <=0.117ms. The voting system used [4] only needs 4 messages to be transmitted (on point-to-point links so that CAN adds no additional latency), so a 1ms loop time is quite practical (but really unnecessary from a practical viewpoint; 10ms updates would be quite adequate in practice, as this is still much faster than the human brain-eye response time). A more advanced system that also implements ABS, brake assist, ESP, etc., will increase the amount of data that has to be sent (e.g., wheel speed information is also required) but we believe it would be quite possible to still use (point–to-point) CAN links. The reason for proposing CAN links is that the hardware is very readily available (and thus very low-cost) while meeting the required data rate. The reliability of the CAN network is quite adequate for this application , as the whole system reliability is guaranteed by the overall architecture.

WHAT ABOUT THE SITUATION WHERE THE BRAKE ACTUATOR NEEDS A MICROPROCESSOR ?

In some brake–by-wire implementations (e.g., those described in [5]), a microprocessor is actually required to control the brake actuator (eg the "fault tolerant drivers" shown in Figure 9 would themselves contain microprocessors). In this case the duplex solution proposed earlier would actually contain at least 6 microprocessors (in fact possibly 10, as each fault tolerant driver would presumably need at least 2 microprocessors).

In this situation a "dual duplex" solution could be adopted (which requires 4 microprocessors) as shown in Figure 18.

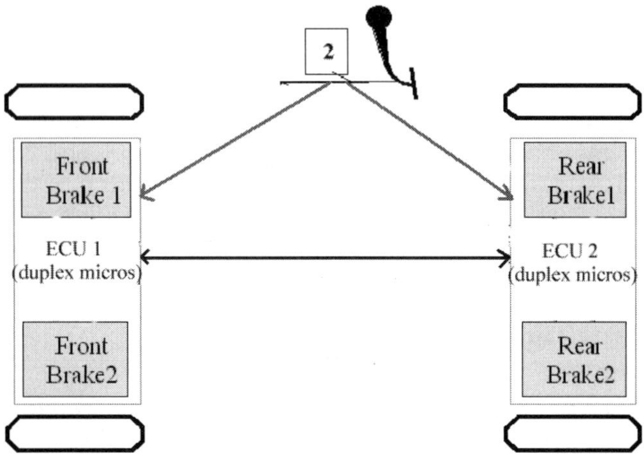

Figure 18: potential solution where a microprocessor is required to control the brake actuators ; "dual duplex".

Figure 18 shows a front-rear split, but a diagonal split (as used earlier in this paper) could be used if required. The concept here is that ECU 1 and ECU 2 each implement a "fail silent" braking system on a pair of wheels. They are used in a duplex arrangement (as in Figure 14). Both ECU 1 and 2 internally have 2 microprocessors to guarantee the "fail silent" requirement on the brake actuation.

It may be possible to implement a system of adequate safety with just one duplex pair of microprocessors (rather than the double duplex system shown in Figure 18), but the large number of additional wires necessary (which must travel the length of the vehicle – wires to the actuators and sensors are needed for each brake actuator) will have such a significant cost and reliability impact that the author does not believe this will be a viable solution.

CONCLUSION

This paper has presented a prototype distributed architecture for safety-critical automotive systems. As an illustrative example it has used a brake-by-wire system, and the architecture has been implemented for this in both software in the loop (SIL) and a multi-ECU hardware in the loop (HIL) system. Using this example it was shown that a duplex implementation appears to offer adequate safety while minimizing cost and maximizing reliability. The communication requirements for this architecture were shown to be compatible with a CAN network. A brake-by-wire system that requires complex (microprocessor) control of the brake actuators was then discussed. In this situation it was shown that recursively using the proposed architecture (to create a dual duplex system) was a viable solution and one that may actually minimize cost and maximize reliability.

REFERENCES

1. R. Johansson, P, Johansson, K. Forsberg, H. Sivencrona, J. Torin, "On Communication Requirements for Control-by-wire applications", Proceedings of the 21st International System Safety Conference 2003.
2. R. Essermann, R. Schwarz, S. Stolzl, "Fault Tolerant drive by wire systems", IEEE Control Systems magazine Oct 2002 pp64-81.
3. S. Mitra, N. Saxena, E. McCluskey, "A design diversity matrix and analysis of redundant systems", IEEE Trans on Computers May 2002 Vol. 51 no. 5 pp498-510.
4. S. Channon and P. Miller, "An advanced Network Vehicle Controller (NVC) to support future technology applications", AMAA2003, Berlin, Germany
5. Henry Hartmann, Martin Schautt, Antonio Pascucci, Bernd Gombert , "eBrake® – the mechatronic wedge brake", SAE 2002 Brake Colloquium, paper 2002-01-2582
6. C. A. Lupini, "Multiple Bus Progression 2003", SAE Technical Paper Series 2003-01-0111.
7. P.Miller, B.Sewell, A.Dominguez-Garcia, "Automatic Model-based Reliability Analysis", FISITA 2006 conference, paper F2006V043, October 2006.
8. "Development Guidelines for Vehicle Based Software", MIRA, November 1994. Also available as ISO/TR 15497:2000.

CONTACT

Peter Miller
Ricardo UK Ltd, Cambridge Technical Centre,
Block 5, The Westbrook Centre, Cambridge, CB4 1YG.
peter.miller@ricardo.com

www.ricardo.com

2006-01-1657

Rapid Prototyping of Production Vehicle Control Systems

Denis Eberhard
AUDI AG

Simon Brewerton
Infineon Technologies UK Ltd

ABSTRACT

Developing automotive chassis applications is becoming increasingly complex due to cross-functional system interactions and the inherent safety critical nature of the systems involved. One consequence is the need for a rapid prototyping platform, targeted and tailored to meet the specific needs of the chassis domain.

This paper describes an example of such an architecture for a chassis rapid prototyping system incorporating several Infineon TriCore embedded microcontrollers and Emulation Devices (ED), networked together by the Micro Link Interfaces (MLI). It also discusses how using such a development platform can lead to a significant reduction in the overall development time of a production intent chassis system.

INTRODUCTION

The use of rapid prototyping techniques is becoming more and more important to automotive software development process due to the desire to shorten the development cycles and have a faster time to market. In parallel, automotive manufactures are increasingly implementing proprietary software as an enabler to deliver unique selling points, features and function which differentiate their products from those of their competition. One solution to this conflict of increasing function and decreasing engineering time available is to use a fast and easy rapid prototyping system which is adapted to specifically fulfill the special needs of automotive software development. These needs can roughly be classified by the functional automotive domains. The functional automotive domains include:

- Powertrain
- Chassis
- Body/Comfort
- Multimedia/Telematics
- Safety (active/passive)
- Man Machine Interface

Different requirements of the production systems (and therefore also the rapid prototyping solution) have to be met depending on the particular functional automotive domain. The focus of this paper will be the chassis domain which includes:

- braking systems
- electromechanical parking brake systems
- damping control systems
- suspension control systems (see Figure 1)
- electrical steering systems
- adaptive cruise control systems
- tire pressure monitoring systems
- new future systems

Figure 1: Adaptive Air Suspension in the Audi A6 Avant quattro

These systems are highly safety critical and have to meet hard real time requirements. This must be considered when developing solutions using a rapid prototyping system as these rapid prototyping platforms could be used in a test vehicle. As a person might drive such a vehicle, the platform itself becomes safety critical, so should already be able to detect and survive under hardware faults and errors.

Future chassis systems will show a growing degree of cross-linking between today's systems. By linking existing systems together and sharing information between them it is possible to implement new functionalities which have not been feasible before.

This paper describes new technologies which are enabling rapid prototyping in the automotive chassis domain. An example system implementing these technologies is shown and the associated benefits are illustrated.

RAPID PROTOTYPING OF CHASSIS APPLICATIONS

Commonly the system development process is like shown in Figure 2. The requirement specification describes the concept and the main behavior of the system. After that the functional description is agreed with a 1st tier supplier. This supplier designs the software and the hardware of the system, which covers the lower part of the V-model. The implementation of the hardware and software is verified by the right branch of the V-model.

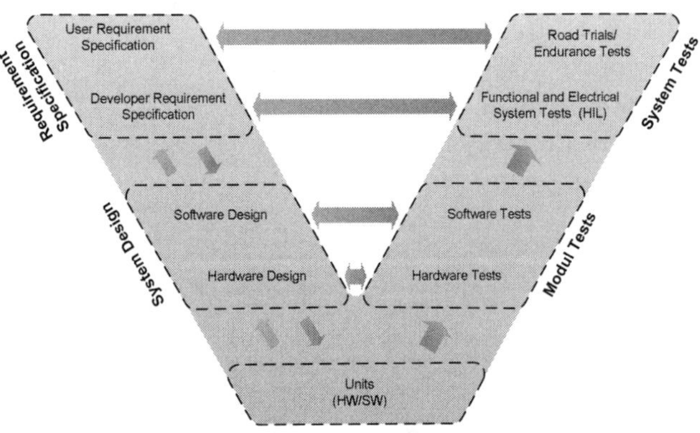

Figure 2: General development process shown in a V-model

However, problems can arise when the delivered implementation is not correct or does not fit the requirements, as a large loop back to the upper level of the V-cycle had to be done. These correction cycles contribute a substantial amount of extra time to the development cycle, leading to costly re-engineering and delays. For these reasons only very few correction cycles are possible.

To reduce the total development time these iteration loops need to be shortened. Switching to a series-like hardware platform during the rapid prototyping process can substantially reduce the added time of the correction cycles. The time saved allows an increased number of possible correction cycles, enabling the system developer to easily change the model and instantly test it in the car. The second advantage is that of the omitted development step of porting the software from an off-the-box rapid prototyping system to a production bases series electronic control unit (ECU). The available resources of the target production system can be taken in account during the first development steps, with a series processor which is able to hook to a rapid prototyping synthesizer.

Certain provisions must be included to allow the early integration of a series-like rapid prototyping system. These systems have to provide some special features, such as powerful main processor as well as special interfaces to support development tools. An implementation of such a feature set is provided by the TriCore processor family, for example.

In addition a new trend in automotive system development is observable. Future systems will abolish the hard connection between a software-functionality and its hardware. Software becomes more and more modular, so generic hardware platforms come in view. Software is developed and tested increasingly independent from the hosting electronic control unit. For this reason slightly different ECUs can be used for the functional tests and verification in the later development steps, too. The architecture of such a system using modern interfaces and technologies is described below.

MICROCONTROLLER AND INTERFACES FOR RAPID PROTOTYPING

THE TRICORE PROCESSOR

The processor used in the rapid prototyping system is a 150MHz TC1796 32 bit TriCore. It has a triple issue superscalar Harvard architecture, supporting many native data types, including packed arithmetic and a mixed 16 and 32 bit instruction format. The rich instruction set combines arithmetic, control, SIMD and DSP instruction subsets into a unified architecture, making it suitable for numerous applications in the automotive space. For rapid prototyping of applications this processor also provides a high speed serial communication channel (MicroLink Interface) which allows pipes to be established between the main processor and a number of slaves. The main processor can run the real-time application and the slaves can be used for data acquisition, tool hosting, function bypassing and safety monitoring.

THE MICROLINK INTERFACE (MLI)

The MicroLink interface is a fully duplex, high speed serial interface which allows a master node to map shared memory regions between itself and up to 3 slaves, under hardware control. The advantage of this interface over traditional memory mapping using an external bus is that there are only 8 pins required for MLI (Figure 3), whereas a full 32bit external bus interface would require around 70 pins. As the TC1796 has a 2MByte internal flash, the external bus interface is normally not required for an application and would have to be routed specifically for a prototyping interface if MLI were not used.

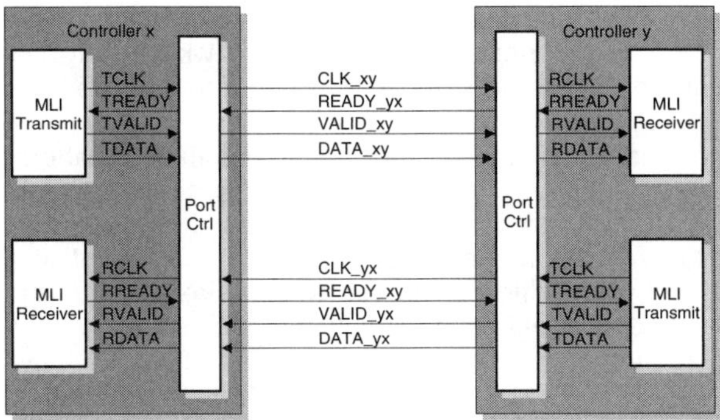

Figure 3: Topology of Micro-Link Interface connecting two AUDO-NG Microcontrollers

The MLI allows up to 4 independent channels or pipes to be formed from an address space within the local MLI peripheral to a corresponding space within the remote processor. The remote address space is accessed via the remote MLI peripheral via a DMA in the remote processor. This mechanism allows the remote processor to set the access permissions of the local host, and once set, the link can run autonomously without software support in the remote device. The link is fully duplex, so each device can be both a master and a slave on the link at the same time, allowing memory and peripheral sharing from one device to another. An interrupt mechanism is also provided in the protocol to allow a remote device to raise an interrupt in the local device and vise versa if required.

THE ED-DEVICE

As microcontrollers become faster and more integrated it becomes harder and harder to build suitable debug interfaces that cover all of the use cases where software and systems are tested and developed. The state of the art is typically to use a external memory expansion on a series control unit to allow the software and calibration tables to be run from a volatile memory (SRAM). The purpose is to use the same step of silicon as the production intent hardware, and run the same software without the need to re-compile the code for a new memory mapping. This extra calibration hardware has two major drawbacks. Firstly it requires that an external bus exists on the production silicon, requiring around 60 pins for a 32 bit wide external bus with control signals. The cost of these 60pins is carried into every device although not actually used in the production vehicle. Secondly the external SRAM does not normally have the same data path and program execution timing as the actual device with wide internal buses, prefetch mechanisms and embedded flash memories. Real-time system response therefore can only be approximated in the development system and has to be re-validated on the actual production system. It is also sometimes impractical to bring out a high speed trace connection to an external debug / trace tool due to cable capacitance, length and physical environment (temperature, package, etc)

The TriCore processors overcome many of these issues by providing an emulation device for the purpose of prototyping and calibration. The existing production silicon design is embedded in a monolithic construction with an Emulation Extension Chip (EEC).

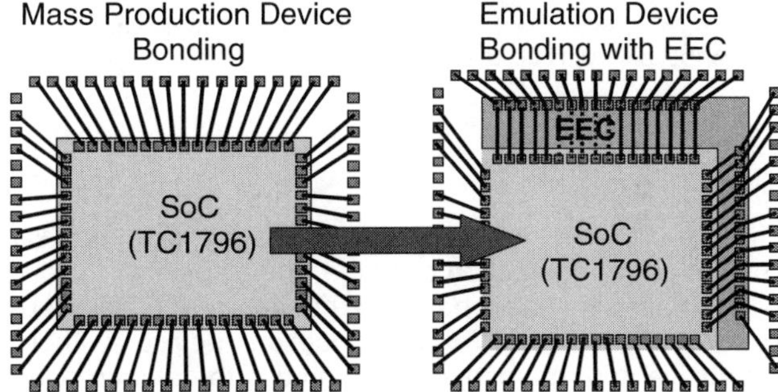

Figure 4: Bonding of Production Device and Emulation Device with Emulation Extension Chip

The EEC allows a very large number of connections to be made on a metal layer at the die level which permits a large number of internal signals to be traced internally by the EEC. The EEC also houses a trace buffer block (SRAM) which can be used as calibration overlay for internal flash memory, data logging for program data and code trace, and for code execution for algorithm development and debugging.

The Emulation Device (ED) with the EEC allows a thin connection to the host PC to be realized, as all the time critical trigger, timestamp, data acquisition and processing happens locally, embedded in the device, so only data viewing and configuration is made over the external connection. The complex trigger mechanisms also allow for an embedded ‘logic analyzer’ to be realized to align program and data trace with external hardware events and I/O states.

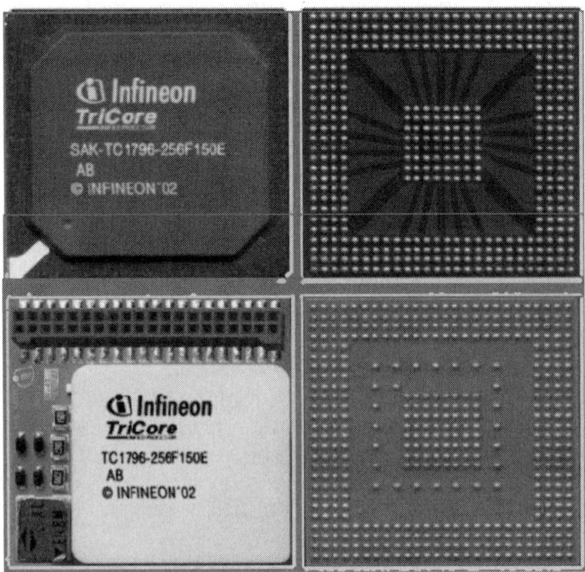

Figure 5: TC1796 Production Device (top) and TC1796ED Emulation Device (bottom) with built in USB interface

The Emulation Device (ED) is packaged in a special version of the production package of the specific TriCore device, allowing it to be soldered into a development system in place of the production device without expensive and real-estate consuming external memories and connectors. Connection to the device is made via a USB connection, directly to the top of the package via the black high density connector. For deeply embedded designs the same signals are also available via the internal pad ring and centre balls so connection can be made through the host PCB if desired.

HARDWARE AND SOFTWARE IMPLICATIONS

COMPARISON HARDWARE PLATFORMS

Typical complex system development starts with a simulated model for the associated systems which interact with the desired application function. These models are typically very computationally intensive, using the double precision floating point representation of all signals by default, unlimited RAM and unlimited non-volatile memory, together with simulated input and output signal test vectors. Whilst these are excellent systems for investigating functionality and algorithm development they are very far away from what could actually be installed in a production vehicle, and lack the real-time system response which is available on the target processor. The limited resources of the target system mean that the models and simulations have to be restricted to fit into the number representation of the target. This can lead to rounding and truncation errors, underflows and divide by zero errors which can be difficult to find when the model is ported to the embedded device by the automatic code generator. RAM and ROM usage can also sometimes be a problem depending on the complexity of the model and the skill of the modeler. The model must be constructed in such a way that the sub-functions do not dissect the problem into too many nested function calls, which not only require more stack depth but take longer to execute.

In summary, being close to the final computing platform as soon as possible within the design cycle prevents many of the porting issues and keeps the modeler in contact with the actual production system, so creating a compact and efficient model which already has the correct data formats and resolutions.

HARDWARE PLATFORM FOR CHASSIS SYSTEMS

The connectivity advantages provided by the TriCore processors allow for a whole new range of possible architectures of rapid prototyping hardware platforms. Figure 6 shows an example architecture of such a rapid prototyping system using the MLI and the Emulation Devices for embedded development support.

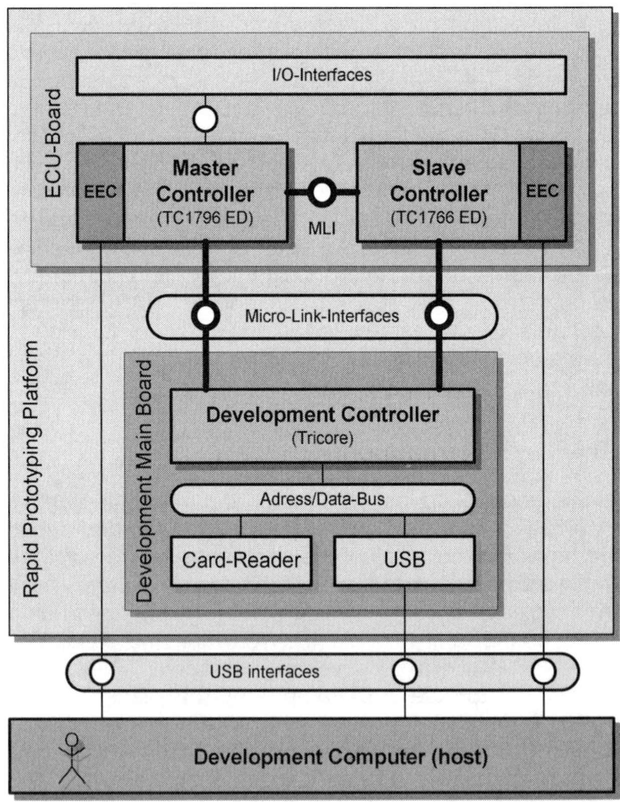

Figure 6: Overview of the chassis rapid prototyping system

The upper block shows an implementation which is close to a production ECU board, incorporating a master controller and a slave controller connected by the MLI. All the I/O of the ECU board is shown by the generic I/O-Interface block. This block depends on the target system under development.

The development platform is complemented by the Development Main Board. This incorporates a development controller which is used as a host interface to the outside world. This device is also from the TriCore processor family so provides MLI connectivity. The ECU Board and the Development Main Board are connected by these MLI Interfaces, one from each target processor to the development (host) controller. This way the development controller has access to both the address spaces of the Master Controller and the Slave Controller. The connection to the outside world is made by the Development Main Board by implementing several possible high speed serial connections, such as USB and Ethernet. USB is also used to communicate between the external PC host and the embedded Emulation Devices. This flexible choice of high-speed serial interfaces allows the easy connection of remote PCs and networks without the need of expensive proprietary interface solutions such as CAN or Flexray adapter, etc. The MLI backbone allows this single serial entry point to gain access to any of the inter-connected peripheral controllers without an unacceptable increase in system loading or loss or real-time performance.

In addition the Development Main Board can be equipped with a card reader for logging and storing data. This feature extends the Development Platform as an intelligent data logging unit, allowing further use cases during the whole verification and testing process.

Calibration of the system is done by using the equivalent Emulation Device of the Master Controller and the Slave Controller. Each Emulation Device provides further USB interfaces for control and uploading data processed by the 'embedded logic analyzer' features of the devices, in addition to the USB interface of the development controller.

ECU PROTOTYPING PROCESS

When using the close-to-production rapid prototyping system the development process shown in Figure 2 can be further expanded. The expanded development process is illustrated in Figure 7.

When specifying the requirements of the system, a model is created describing the behavior of the system. This model can be used as living requirement specification later on.

Because the rapid prototyping system is a close-to-production device the System Design steps can be skipped in the early development state and the first actual practical tests can be done. This is a very short cycle to align the specification of the system with the system requirements. The more often this cycle is repeated the greater detail and accuracy of the Requirement Specification. It is possible to sit in the car and do road trips while adjusting and developing the algorithm of the system. This short development cycle can be done several hundreds of times. Without a series-like rapid prototyping system less then 10 correction cycles can be done (see above).

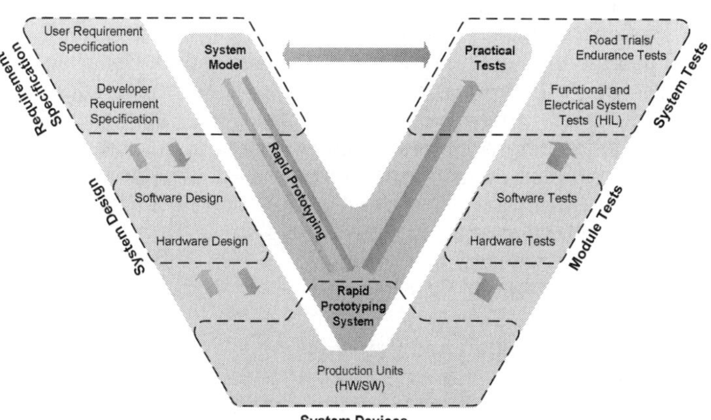

Figure 7: Process of evolutionary rapid prototyping using close-to-production hardware

Once the Requirement Specification is complete the detailed System Design can be developed. In this development step the software design is done and the algorithm of the model is supplemented by all the required basic software such as operating system, diagnostics, error management etc. Furthermore, optimization of the software code can also be performed.

The production hardware units are designed in parallel to the rapid prototyping developments, as the production hardware is a subset of the development system. Maybe a smaller processor within the same processor family could be substituted, or some specific input or output interface circuits could be included in the Production Units. The decision to use a smaller processing device can be easily reached by analyzing the rapid prototyping system running the system model, to see if it would be capable. In general there should be no need for a major change to the hardware architecture of the prototyping unit to get to that of the production units.

The Module Tests, which also have been skipped in the first rapid prototyping steps, have to be applied to the Production Units. These tests cover (for example) ambient tests and functional software module tests. But all of these tests are applied only to particular parts or modules of the system and not yet to the complete system.

The System Tests are done in the next testing and verification steps. For example, hardware-in-the-loop tests (HIL) are used to prove the complete system functionality and the compliance to all the specified electrical and electromagnetic requirements. The interaction with all the other systems in the car is also tested in this phase, where the real Sensors, actuators and systems are used, rather than previous phase where recorded or generated stimuli were used instead.

The results of the practical testing of the rapid prototyping system are incorporated in the test and verification process on the right branch of the V-model. Thus the verification process is also shortened. Because the rough tests have already been passed during rapid prototyping phases, no great problems during the detailed testing would be expected. Some of the practical tests can also be performed using the ED version of the processors in the rapid prototyping, allowing calibration and limit testing of the developed system.

SYSTEM CALIBRATION

Once the algorithm and the structure of the software has been developed the loop can be closed by connecting the prototyping ECU to a real vehicle system. This creates the necessity to calibrate the system to operate with the particular set of sensors and actuators that the vehicle platform provides. Often there are many kilobytes of calibration tables in a prototype software release, as the software engineer does not know the parameters which have the most influence on the system dynamics or those which a systems engineer might want to tweak, so typically they include them all. The industry has grown in the calibration area over the past 5 years as vehicle manufactures and tools providers have collaborated to make some common standards for tool interoperability and interfaces.

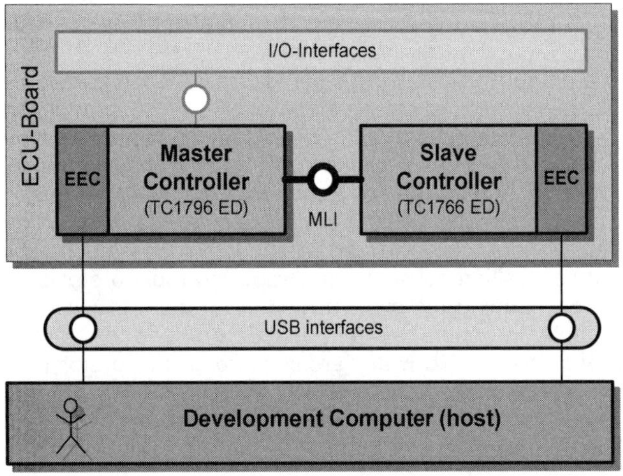

Figure 8: Calibration an 'instrumented' production ECU using the Emulation Devices (ED)

The common calibration interface is currently the CAN bus, and on top of the CAN bus a protocol known as XCP. Tools such as Vector CANape, ETAS INCA, and many others all support this XCP protocol. The advantage of XCP is that it is independent of the physical transfer layer, so works over CAN just as well as it does over JTAG, Nexus, or indeed USB. The ED devices used in the example system also support the XCP protocol to allow interconnectivity. The physical transfer layer of USB is also unique that it provides multiple pipes over one USB link to allow a single PC to host multiple tools at once and concurrently connect via a single USB cable to the target system (similar to the principle used in the USB hubs).

Blocks of SRAM are implemented in the ED together with a hardware addressing overlay mechanism which allows internal flash memory sectors (where the static calibration data is normally kept) to be redirected to a page of SRAM. The SRAM can be read and written by the external tool over XCP to allow data to be viewed and changed. Then the entire SRAM page can be copied back to the embedded flash of the ED to make the changes non-volatile. No special hardware except the placement of the ED in a production ECU is required to make a regular ECU into an 'instrumented' ECU. It is also possible to use a regular production ECU and the MLI interface as the overlay mechanism and a slave controller connected to the MLI as the host for the calibration tables and XCP interface. This allows even ECUs without ED to be calibrated without hardware changes.

DATA LOGGING FOR USAGE DATA

Another advantage of the chassis rapid prototyping platform is the support for logging and processing debug data. This way additional logging hardware is not required. The amount of data is effectively reduced, because the necessary data can be filtered in the electronic control unit and only the relevant data is selected. Two main logging methods are possible.

1. external logging to a host connected via USB
2. internal logging to memories (SRAM, memory card)

<u>Logging to external host</u>

During the first development states an external host is connected to the chassis rapid prototyping platform via the USB interface. The Development Controller is configured to act as a gateway and send predefined information from one or both of the target processors to the development host computer. The MLI is the central technique to be able to access all internal memories without having to add special software code to the target system software. This way the real production software code can be examined.

The Development Controller on the chassis rapid prototyping platform can also filter the data forwarded to the host. Complex trigger events can be realized to reduce the amount of data to be logged.

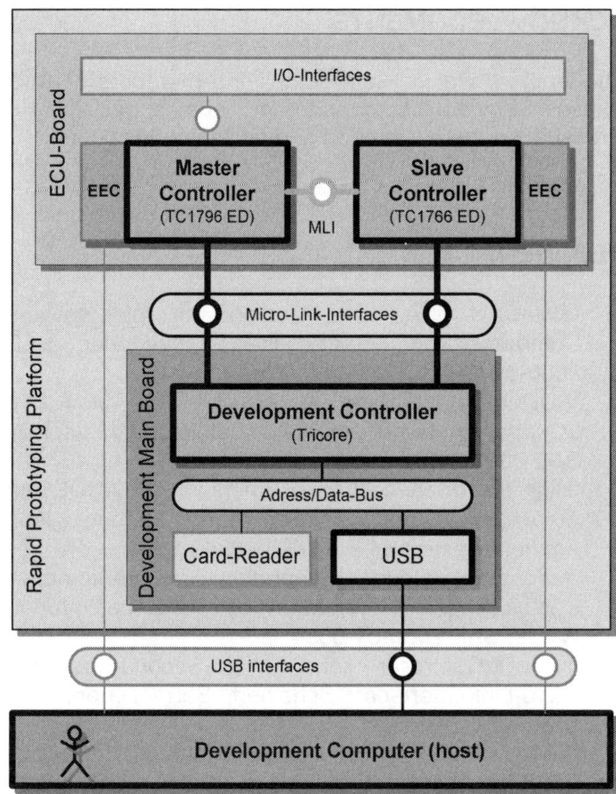

Figure 9: Chassis rapid prototyping system with focused elements for external logging

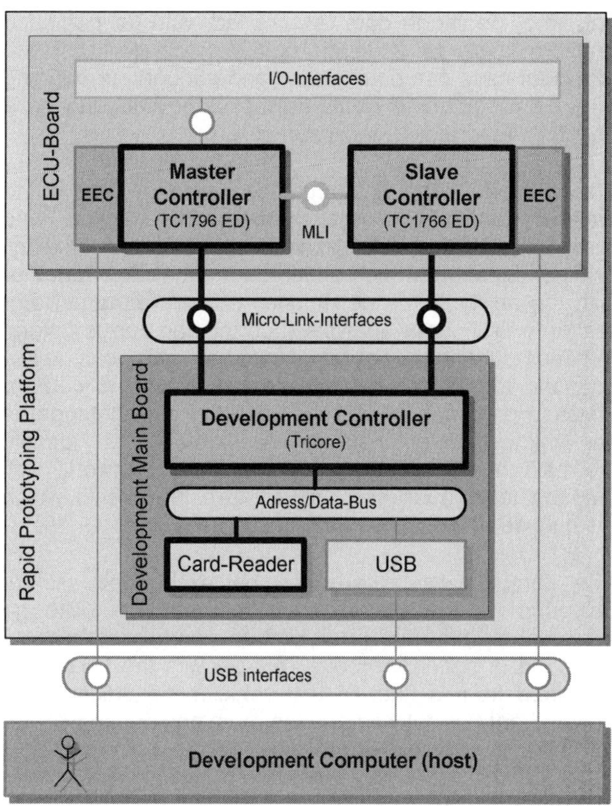

Figure 10: Chassis rapid prototyping system with focused elements for internal logging to the Card-Reader

There are several different options for the underlying protocol of the communication between the Development Controller and the host. For example XCP is a common protocol layer which is compatible with current development tools used for calibration. Proprietary protocols are also possible but require more effort to develop the corresponding software running on the development host computer.

Logging to internal memories

In the later development states an external host is often not present any more. Then the Development Controller stores pre-selected data on the internal memory card or in other internal memories like EEPROM, SRAM or Flash. The trigger events have to be set quite restrictively due to the limited memory size.

For example internal system states and counters could be monitored. Counters which might cause an error memory entry can be monitored and logged. This way the threshold of the counters can be adjusted to the desired value or critical counting close to the threshold can be detected and corrected.

Logging of statistical data is possible too, such as usage of different software functions or drive cycle counters, etc. This kind of usage data can help improve the performance of the system.

Code coverage analysis in the real environment is also possible. Timings and occurrence can be stored on the memory card for later analysis.

ADVANCED DATA LOGGING

The deep embedded nature and production quality of the development controller lends itself to being used for longer term reliability testing of pre-production systems as well as laboratory use in test environments.

The internal non-volatile memory and the availability of a local development controller permit the long term 'intelligent' logging of the running system, without compromising the overall real-time performance. This could, for instance, allow the capturing of events which lead to a certain error being logged, or log all the worst cases for a set of internal variables for bounds testing, or recording the number of times a certain function meets a particular condition or exception. With the extended trigger mechanism and the ability to selectively record only the pertinent data associated with a particular problem there is a much better probability that the particular case can be captured and enough surrounding data be recorded to re-create the same scenario on a bench in laboratory conditions.

This powerful logging feature can also be applied to capture data about other networked controllers and systems, connected for example by CAN or FlexRay. The combination of high speed data acquisition together with the ability of the development controller to perform real-time DSP data analysis (Fourier transforms, filters, matrices, artificial neural networks, etc) can allow scenario trigger mechanisms to be created to capture possible problems even if the extent of the full trigger is yet unknown. For instance the system can identify 'normal' operation by artificial neural network self learning techniques and only capture the events which fall outside of the top 98% of these cases.

The compact flash card can be exchanged without powering off the system by a test engineer with no electrical training and in all kind of environment without the need of specialist tools. This permits the files to be uploaded from a fleet of test vehicles periodically and emailed or physically sent to the main engineering centre for offline post-processing.

CONCLUSION

An example of the aforementioned rapid prototyping system using TriCore processors has been a key enabler for Audi to take a more streamlined approach when engineering their world renowned, complex, real-time chassis control systems. Using engineering hardware early on in the design phase of the systems allows a fully executable specification to be generated, even before a system supplier has been chosen or any production hardware has been built. This maturity of the specification clearly impacts the delivered prototypes for the application and enables a much earlier quality maturity level to be achieved. Engineering effort is also minimized because the only errors which need to be fixed are those of the implementation phase of the project and not those due to an error in the system design or specification. Although using a close-to-production prototyping environment limits the system engineer in the scope of what can be actually implemented it does mean that that is being specified is correct and achievable in volume production and low-cost electronic control units.

The rapid prototyping system may not be the answer to every advanced development scenario or applicable to every chassis system which could be imagined, but it does have a significant advantage when compared with today's state-of-the-art development racks which typically take up the whole trunk of the vehicle and do not accurately reproduce that environment in which the system expert and software developer will eventually have to engineer their system.

ACKNOWLEDGMENTS

The Authors would like to thank the members of Audi Chassis Electronics department, and especially Hr. Grosshauser for his support and editing of this paper.

REFERENCES

1. "TwinCAN – A New Milestone for Inter-Network Communication"; Barrenschen, Leteinturier; SAE 2000-01-0144
2. "AUDO Architecture. A solution to Automotive µController Requirements"; Leteinturier, Vitorelli; SAE 2000-01-0145
3. "High Performance Code Generation for AUDO, an Automotive µController from Infineon Technologies"; Amato, Koester; SAE 2000-01-0393
4. "Automatic Code Generation for Automotive Configurable I/O System"; Westerholz, Leteinturier, Weiss; SAE 2000-01-0554
5. "New µController links: Micro-Second-Bus and Micro-Link-Interface"; Scheibert, Barrenschen, Estl; SAE 2003-01-0112
6. "TTCAN from Applications to Products in Automotive Systems"; Leteinturier, Kelling, Kelling; SAE 2003-01-0114
7. "Embedded System Tool to Support Debugging, Calibration, Fast Prototyping and Emulation "; Mayer, Siebert, Leteinturier, Qual; SAE 2004-01-0304
8. "Rapid Gasoline Powertrain System Design and Evaluation"; Brewerton; Leteinturier; SAE 2005-01-0062

CONTACT

Dipl.-Ing. Denis Eberhard
AUDI AG
Development of Chassis Electronics
85045 Ingolstadt
Tel.: +49-(0) 841-89 33183
Fax: +49-(0) 841-89 84 33183
Email: Denis.Eberhard@AUDI.de
URL: http://www.audi.com

Simon Brewerton
Infineon Technologies
Automotive Application Engineering
Infineon House, Great Western Ct
Hunts Ground Rd, Stoke Gifford
Bristol, BS34 8HP, England
Tel.: +44 (0) 117-952 8744
Fax: +44 (0) 117-952 8777
Email: Simon.Brewerton@Infineon.com
URL: http://www.infineon.com

DEFINITIONS, ACRONYMS, ABBREVIATIONS

CAN: Controller Area Network
CPU: Central Processing Unit
DAS: Device Access Server tool interface
DMA: Direct Memory Access
DPRAM: Dual Ported Random Access Memory
DPSRAM: Dual Ported Static Random Access Memory
DSP: Digital Signal Processing
ECU: Electronic Control Unit
ED: Emulation Device
EEC: Emulation Extension Chip
HIL: Hardware in the Loop
HW: Hardware
I/O: Input or Output
JTAG: Joint Test Action Group (Standard for debugging)
LIN: Local Interconnect Network
MCDS: Multi-Core Debug Solution
MLI: Micro Link serial bus Interface
PC: Personal Computer
PCB: Printed Circuit Board
PCP: Peripheral Control Processor
PLL: Phase Locked Loop (module in GPTA)
PSI: Package Sized ICE (In-Circuit Emulator)
PWM: Pulse Width Modulation
RAM: Random Access Memory
SIMD: Single Instruction Multiple Data
SPI: Serial to Peripheral Interface
SRAM: Static Random Access Memory
SW: Software
UART: Universal Asynchronous Receiver Transmitter
USB: Universal Serial Bus
XCP: X (any physical layer) Calibration Protocol

2006-01-1173

Development of a Steer-by-Wire System for the GM Sequel

Douglas Cesiel and Michael C. Gaunt
General Motors Corporation

Brian Daugherty
Visteon Corporation

ABSTRACT

Steer-by-wire systems (SBW) offer the potential to enhance steering functionality by enabling features such as automatic lane keeping, park assist, variable steer ratio, and advanced vehicle dynamics control. The lack of a steering intermediate shaft significantly enhances vehicle architectural flexibility. These potential benefits led GM to include steer-by-wire technology in its next generation fuel cell demonstration vehicle, called "Sequel."

The Sequel's steer-by-wire system consists of front and rear electromechanical actuators, a torque feedback emulator for the steering wheel, and a distributed electronic control system. Redundancy of sensors, actuators, controllers, and power allows the system to be fault-tolerant. Control is provided by multiple ECU's that are linked by a fault-tolerant communication system called FlexRay.

In this paper, we describe the objectives for fault tolerance and performance that were established for the Sequel. An overview of the system design and development process is presented. The resulting component layout and control system architecture is discussed. We conclude that it may be possible for a steer-by-wire system to meet certain objectives for fault tolerance and performance. It can also provide design flexibility that enables new vehicle architectures such as the Sequel fuel cell vehicle.

INTRODUCTION:

The goals of the Steer-by-Wire system are to support the GM Sequel vehicle requirements as well as learn more about the performance attributes and safety considerations of a full steer-by-wire system.

Steer-by-wire systems replace the conventional mechanical linkages with electronic sensors, controllers and actuators. The style of driver interface selected for the Sequel vehicle is a conventional steering wheel. Non-conventional driver interfaces, such as a joystick, are technically feasible, but require the driver to adapt to an unfamiliar method of vehicle control.

Depending upon the design, a steer-by-wire system can offer several benefits compared to conventional mechanical steering systems. Elimination of the mechanical linkage between the steering wheel and the steering gear can provide an enhancement to design flexibility. The steering "feel" (driver feedback) can be tuned electronically. This can help reduce the traditional tradeoffs between ride and handling. In theory, the desired steering feedback can be obtained without being linked to other design decisions, such as tire selection, suspension caster, scrub radius, bushing stiffness, or steering gear and linkage friction. Packaging flexibility can also be enhanced because steering gear location is not critical to obtain desired ackerman correction or tie rod load gradient. Steer-by-wire may enable or enhance vehicle control technologies related to collision avoidance, lane keeping, and enhanced stability control.

There are several significant challenges associated with the commercial application of steer-by-wire technology to automobiles. Safety and security objectives must be met. A SBW system contains electrical components that have lower reliability than the mechanical components found in conventional steering systems. Redundancy of electrical components may be an effective method to assist SBW systems in meeting safety objectives. However, component redundancy may also have a negative impact on cost and reliability. Despite the continuous cost reduction of electronic sensors, controllers, and actuators, the SBW system cost remains a significant obstacle to application in passenger cars.

This paper will discuss the design of the SBW system used in GM's Sequel vehicle. The Sequel is a fuel cell powered demonstration vehicle. The authors begin by reviewing the safety approach, the system layout, and the key performance objectives that were selected for the SBW system. Next, the SBW control system architecture is presented. Then, an overview of the algorithms that provide the desired performance and fault detection and management capability is presented. Finally, concluding remarks and references are provided.

SYSTEM SECURITY AND AVAILABILITY APPROACH:

The system security and availability requirements for SBW have a significant influence on the hardware, software, and communication designs. The initial step in designing a SBW system is to develop objectives for system security and functional availability. It is clearly desirable that SBW systems provide secure operation comparable to today's mechanical systems. It is also desirable to provide high system availability so that, if a failure occurs, the driver will still be able to operate the vehicle and will not be stranded. Electro-mechanical systems have not yet achieved the reliability of mechanical systems, so it is necessary to include redundancy in the steer-by-wire system. The use of either fail-safe or fault-tolerant architectures to achieve safety objectives has been described by Heitzer and Seewald [1]. A fail-safe architecture includes a mechanical backup system so that steering control is maintained in the event of an electrical failure. A fault-tolerant architecture includes redundant electrical components so that the system can continue to function in the event of a single failure. The approach used in the Sequel vehicle combines benefits of both architectures to achieve the desired security and system availability.

Two objectives were established for the GM Sequel SBW system that significantly influenced the system architecture. The first objective was to provide a level of operational security comparable to mechanical steering systems. The second objective was to maintain "near normal" performance after the first failure while maintaining secure operation. The continued availability of SBW in the presence of a single fault would provide the driver with flexibility to schedule service at a convenient time.

To achieve fail-safe operation, the SBW system retains a mechanical linkage between the steering wheel and the road wheel actuator. This mechanical backup system is only employed when multiple faults have occurred that would make it impossible to continue secure operation of the system in by-wire mode. One consideration that led to use of a mechanical backup was the difficulty of ensuring secure by-wire operation in the event that the vehicle is struck by lightning while in motion. Current automotive electrical components, connectors and wire harnesses can not be relied upon to function after a lightning strike or other catastrophic event.

In addition to fail-safe operation, the Sequel SBW system also provides fault-tolerant operation. The system design contains sufficient redundancy so that it can continue secure operation with near normal performance levels in the event of certain single point failures. Depending on the failure type, the system can be configured to continue functioning in by-wire mode even after three failures. To ensure that the design met the fault-tolerance objectives, several standard analysis techniques were used. The Hazard Analysis and Design Failure Mode & Affects Analysis (DFMEA) were created. Since the SBW system's redundancy prevents single point failures from affecting performance, standard DFMEA analysis proved to be difficult. Only multiple failures produce significant performance effects, and there are an extensive number of fault combinations to consider. Fault tree analysis (FTA) was an effective tool to analyze the system to ensure that it met the security objectives.

SYSTEM CONFIGURATION:

The SBW system consists of three main electromechanical subsystems: Front steer actuator, a driver interface system (DIS) with a mechanical back-up, and independent rear steer (Figure 1). Not shown in Figure 1 is the FlexRay distributed controls network.

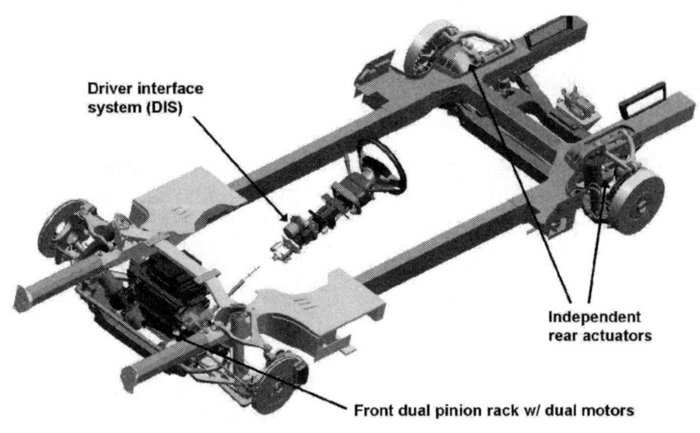

Figure 1: Sequel Steer-by-wire configuration

FRONT STEER ACTUATOR:

The front steer actuator (Figure 2) is in a dual pinion electric power steering configuration. There are two 42V brushless motors; each capable of providing full steering performance. The motors drive a common worm gear shaft, which drives a worm wheel and the assist pinion. A rotational sensor called a "resolver" is used with each motor. For redundancy and start-up initialization, the front steer actuator contains two full range absolute position sensors located at the primary pinion.

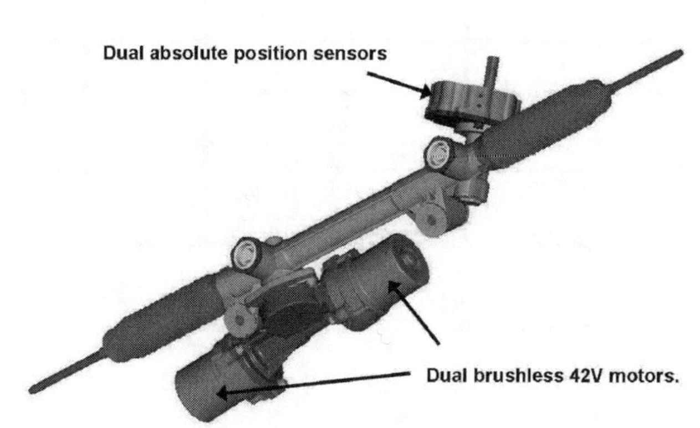

Figure 2: Front steering actuator

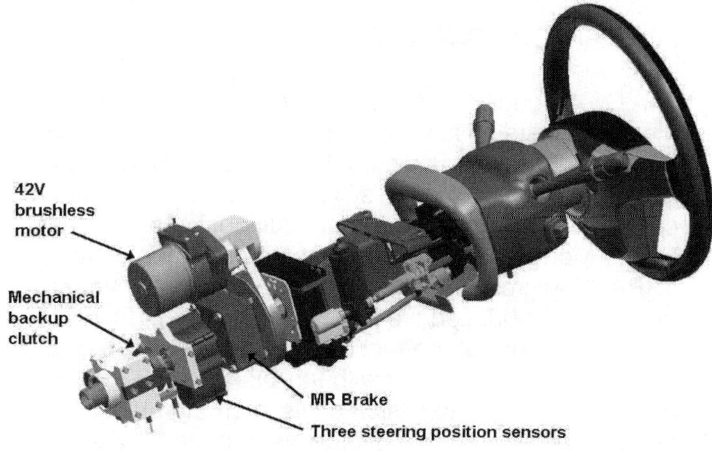

Figure 3: Driver interface system location

DRIVER INTERFACE SYSTEM:

Figures 3 and 4 depict the Driver Interface System (DIS) and the mechanical back-up mechanism. A 42V brushless motor provides the feedback torque to the driver through a 4:1 ratio belt. The end stop function is provided by the 42V motor and the magnetorheological (MR) brake. The MR brake, which can provide up to 10Nm of torque, provides passive handwheel torque in the event of motor failure. This gives some driver feedback torque and prevents the handwheel from free spinning. Three absolute position sensors are used to measure steering wheel angle.

The mechanical backup device is a solenoid driven clutch. The normally closed solenoid slides the clutch over a 20 spline column shaft. There are two clutch position sensors. One senses engagement and the other senses disengagement. The solenoid current is also used for redundant sensing. The intermediate shaft attaches to the mechanical backup device and spins freely with the front steering actuator's primary pinion when the clutch is disengaged.

INDEPENDENT REAR STEER ACTUATORS:

The GM Sequel has rear steering to reduce the turn circle and improve vehicle handling (Figure 4). To package the fuel cell battery and other components, it was necessary to have independent left and right actuators. They can provide +/- 5.7 degrees of road wheel angle. The 42V brushless motor drives a worm shaft and sector gear to move the pitman arm. The selected gear ratios make the system non-backdrivable. In certain failures, the actuator will maintain its position and the non-failed actuator will move to the same angle and hold its position.

Each actuator has two absolute position sensors and one motor resolver sensor. This sensor set provides the proper level of redundancy. Rear steering functionality is not as critical as front steering. Therefore, the SBW system is designed to shut down rear steering when certain single point faults are detected.

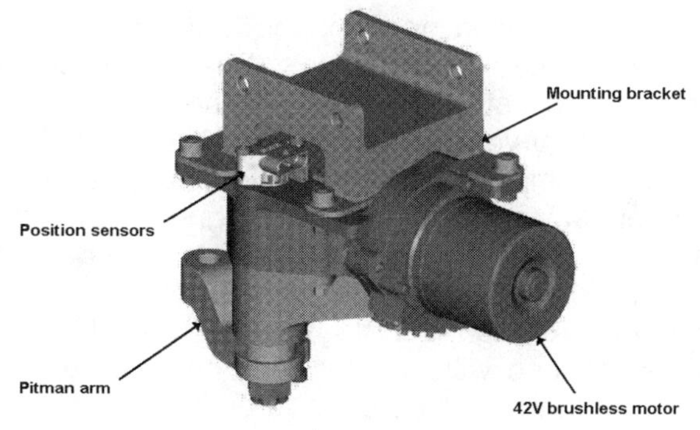

Figure 4: Rear steer actuator

POWER CONFIGURATION:

The GM Sequel's 14V and 42V power configuration for the SBW system is shown in Figure 5. It can be seen that the 42V power is distributed between two buses so if one bus fails, SBW can still function. The 36V battery can provide up to 2 minutes of additional power if both Power Modules fail. The SBW control system uses dSPACE Micro-autoboxes (MAB's), which receive power from the 14V bussed electrical center (BEC). In case there is a failure of the fuel cell 14V power supply, the 14V BEC communicates with the Diode Battery Switch Assembly (DBSA) to switch on its internal 42V to 14V DC/DC converter and provide power to the MAB's.

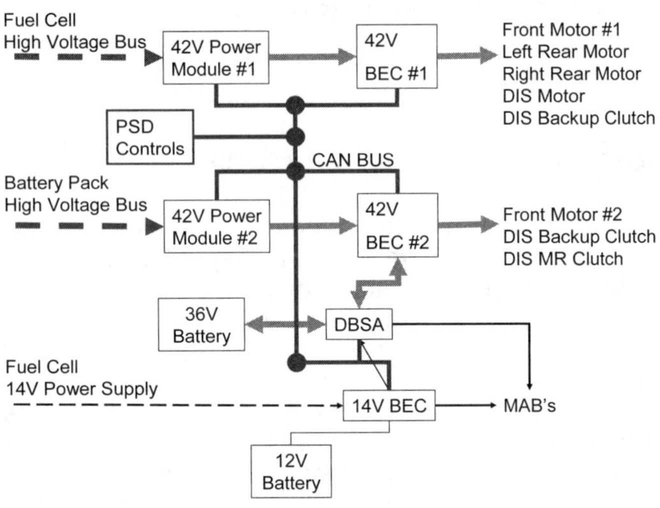

Figure 5: Redundant electric power supply

PERFORMANCE OBJECTIVES:

FRONT STEER ACTUATOR SUBSYSTEM

Table 1 shows the main performance requirements for the front steer actuator subsystem. One of the goals was to improve the steer response of the GM Sequel over a conventional vehicle. An important feature SBW provides, to accomplish this goal, is variable steering ratio. The front steering system was designed to provide an overall steer ratio range of 10:1 to 18:1. At low and moderate vehicle speeds, the ratio is near the lower end of the range. At high vehicle speeds, the steering sensitivity is reduced with a steer ratio near the upper range. Vehicle tuning will be done to optimize the front steer ratio vs. speed curve and the rear to front steer ratio vs. speed curve.

The front steer actuator subsystem was also designed to support aggressive hand wheel velocities.

Condition	Hand wheel Speed	Hand wheel Turn Range	Steer Ratio	Max Rack Load
		deg	n:1	N
Drastic steer event at medium to high speeds	Aggressive	0 to 180	up to 18:1	2700
Steering while rolling at low speeds	Moderate	360 to stop	11 to 16	5900
	Aggressive	0 to 360	11 to 16	5600
Steering while standing	Moderate	0 to 360	10	8500
	Moderate	360 to stop	10	8500

Table 1: Front steer performance requirements

REAR STEER ACTUATOR:

In Table 2, the rear steer performance requirements are presented. The negative rear/front steer ratio indicates the rear wheels are out-of-phase with the front.

The rear steer actuator was designed to track the front steer actuator position and the specified rear-to-front steer ratio. Using a method similar to what was proposed by Zara [2], the rear-to-front ratio vs. speed curve is shown in Figure 6.

Condition	Hand wheel Speed	Hand wheel Turn Range	Rear/Front Steer Ratio	Desired effective overall steer ratio	Max Tie Rod Load
		deg	R/F	n:1	N
Drastic steer event at medium to high speeds	Aggressive	0 to 180	0.1 to 0.3	up to 25:1	1400
Steering while rolling at low speeds	Moderate	360 to stop	-0.162 to 0.1	10 to 18	1800
	Aggressive	0 to 360	-0.162 to 0.1	10 to 18	1700
Steering while standing	Moderate	0 to 360	-0.162	9	4000
	Moderate	360 to stop	-0.162	9	4000

Table 2: Rear steer performance requirements

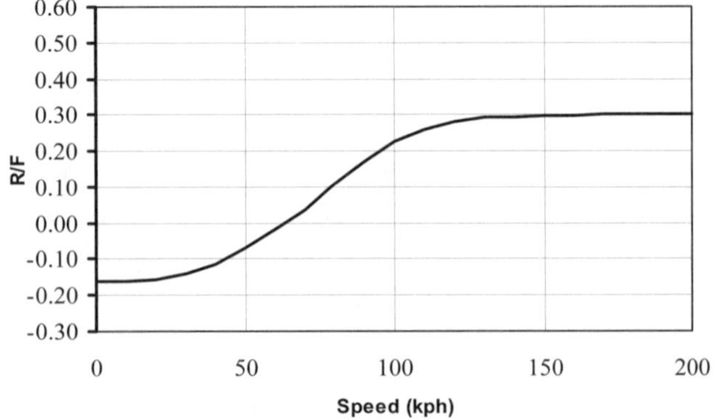

Figure : Rear-to-Front Steer Ratio vs. Speed

STEERING END STOP FUNCTION:

Since there is no mechanical connection between the front steer actuator and the DIS during normal driving, the steering end stop must be simulated. Based on experience with mule vehicle testing, the end stop needs to develop 15 - 20Nm of resistive torque within 5 degrees of steering wheel rotation. This is accomplished by ramping up the DIS motor current and activating the MR brake. Figure 7 shows steering wheel angle vs. steering wheel torque for the end stop function.

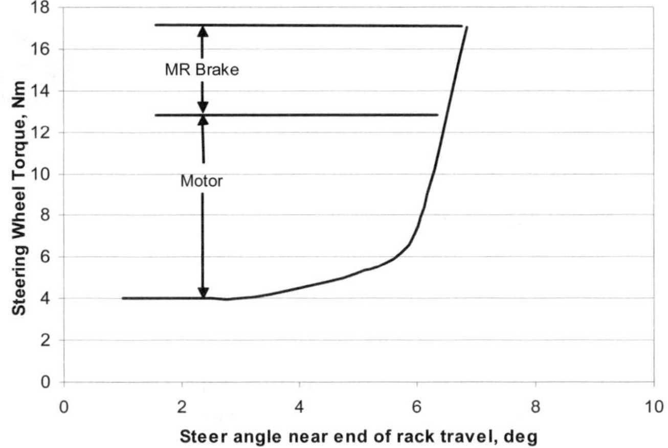

Figure 7: Steering wheel end stop torque

CONTROL SYSTEM DESIGN

The SBW control system architecture was designed to satisfy the security and fault tolerance objectives. The design process started with an analysis of the required functions of the SBW system. Then, subsystem (i.e. front steer subsystem, feedback torque subsystem, rear steer subsystem) functions were identified. A hazard analysis was performed to examine certain potential failures (loss or degradation of the required system functions). The identified hazards formed the top level of a fault tree. Preliminary designs were developed in which the functions were partitioned into control modules, actuators and other building blocks of the system. The fault tree method was used to analyze the design. Iteration occurred until a design was created that satisfied the security and fault-tolerant objectives.

Two types of controller architectures were considered to meet security and fault tolerance objectives. The first architecture required two or more fail silent units (FSUs). The second architecture required three or more non-secure controllers that would compare output commands and use a voting strategy to shut off any controller that issued commands that did not match the majority.

The FSU is a controller that has the ability to diagnose itself and automatically terminate output commands if an internal failure occurs. Using two FSU's for SBW control would increase the potential for continued system operation if one FSU fails. However, it would be necessary to put the vehicle into a "limp home" mode in the event that only one FSU is controlling the SBW system. By "limp home" we are referring to a low speed driving mode to allow limited vehicle mobility. The experimental SBW system developed for Sequel used rapid prototyping controllers (dSPACE micro-autoboxes). These controllers are not FSU's, so a decision was made to use these non-secure controllers and a voting strategy to improve security.

The actual SBW control system architecture that was chosen for the Sequel vehicle uses four dSPACE micro-autoboxes, although three would have been enough to implement a voting strategy. The decision to use four controllers was made because of hardware IO limitations that required the use of more than three controllers.

The four controllers are linked by a FlexRay [3] bus. This type of communication network allows high speed, deterministic, and fault-tolerant transmission of data between the control modules. FlexRay allows the controllers to share all input signals, output commands, and fault conditions in real time.

Figure 8 shows how the SBW actuators are connected to the controllers. Each actuator receives its control signal from a specific controller. The controllers are connected to the actuators in such a way as to increase the potential that steering control is maintained in the event of a failure of a single controller or actuator. The rear steer system is not required for directional control. Therefore, as currently configured, if it fails it maintains its last position until the system is repaired. The rear angle is limited to 5.7 degrees and the vehicle can continue to be driven with minimal impact on handling with the wheels held at that angle.

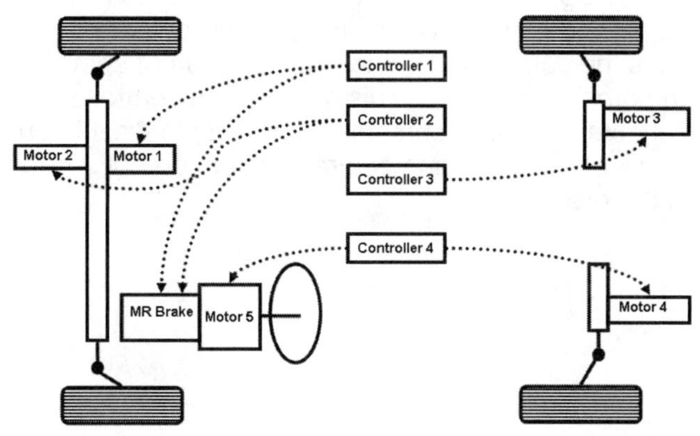

Figure 8: SBW controller connections to actuators

Figure 9 shows how the SBW sensors are connected to the controllers. The redundant signals are routed to different controllers in such a way as to increase the potential that steering control is maintained in the event of a failure of a single controller or sensor.

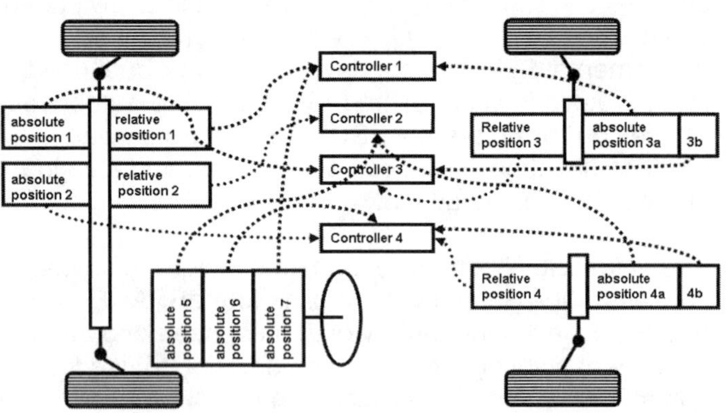

Figure 9: SBW sensor connections to controllers

Use of redundant sensors allows fast diagnostics through direct signal comparisons. This allows faults to be detected and managed within 40 ms. Fault management involves reducing the potential for incorrect commands to reach an actuator. When a fault occurs, the system transitions to a backup mode of operation. Rapid response is required so that the driver can maintain directional control.

Each sensor is hardwired to a separate controller. Sensor signals are distributed to the other controllers via FlexRay.

Figure 10 shows the FlexRay connections between SBW controllers. Since FlexRay provides a means for real time sharing of data [3,4], the four SBW controllers form a distributed control system in which all controllers access the same input signals and the output commands of the other controllers. This allows each controller to watch over the other controllers and vote to disable any controller that is sending commands that do not agree with the majority.

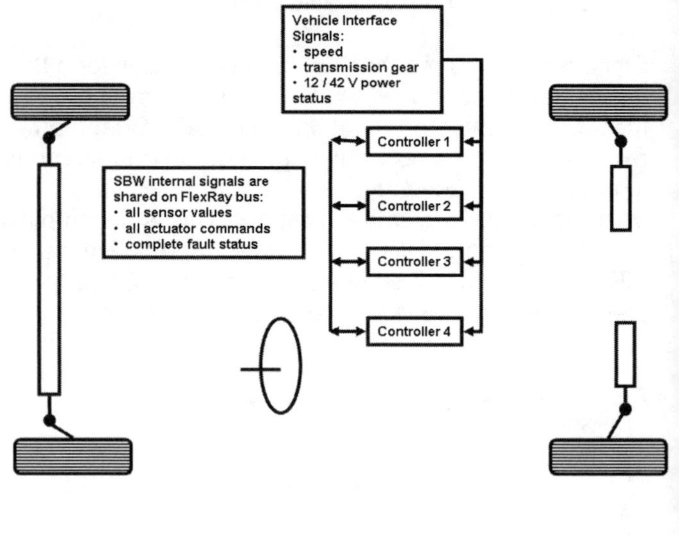

Figure 10: Distributed control FlexRay signals

Figure 11 illustrates how the voting is implemented. An external voting strategy was required since the controllers are not FSU type devices. The output command of each controller passes through a relay switch. Each relay switch is controlled by voting commands from the controllers, which are capable of shutting off the relay. This reduces the potential that incorrect control signals will reach an actuator motor. The voting signals are binary "on / off" commands. The relay will default to the "off" position. To turn the relay "on," at least two of the four controllers must vote to turn it "on." Thus, a single controller cannot shut off the output from another controller. If two controllers vote that the relay should be "off," the relay will be turned "off."

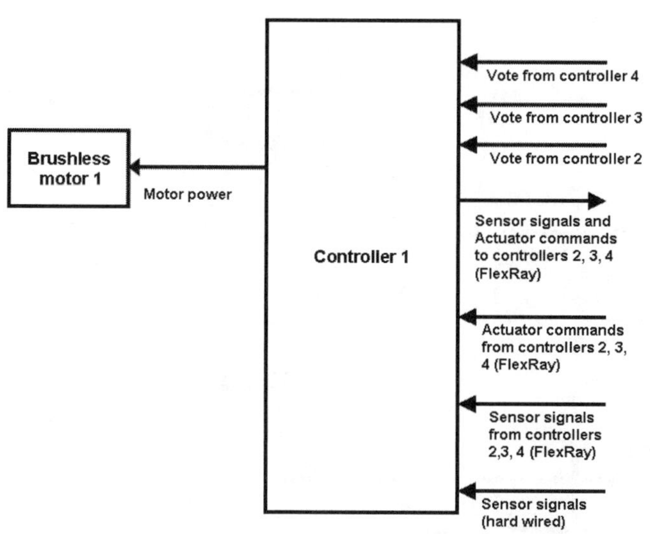

Figure 11: Voting mechanization

ALGORITHM DESCRIPTION

Figure 12 shows the control structure of the SBW system. The SBW control system can be divided into three parts: 1) DIS torque control subsystem, 2) front wheel position control subsystem, and 3) rear wheel position control subsystem.

The DIS controls steering wheel feedback torque and transmits steering wheel angle to the front wheel position control subsystem. The DIS does not include a torque sensor. Closed loop control is used for the DIS motor current, but there is no direct measurement of the steering wheel torque.

Steering wheel torque control is a function of front road wheel position, vehicle speed, and the front rack force estimate that is received from the front wheel control subsystem. Vehicle speed is needed to allow the feedback torque to simulate a conventional variable assist steering system. The rack force estimate is needed to ensure that the steering wheel torque provides realistic feedback of road conditions. It allows feedback to vary as the vehicle transitions between lower and higher friction surfaces, or as a result of bumps in the road. However, this signal alone does not provide a sufficient basis for DIS torque control. It is necessary to use the position signal to increase the potential that the correct phase relationship is maintained between the steering wheel torque and road wheel angle. The road wheel position feedback influences the steering wheel torque felt by the driver. By modifying the DIS control transfer function, the steering feedback can be varied over a wide range. It can be tuned to provide equivalent or improved feel and returnability when compared to conventional steering systems.

The front subsystem controls the front road wheel angle and transmits road wheel position and estimated rack force to the DIS torque control subsytem. There is no sensor that directly measures rack force. Estimated rack force is critical to achieve acceptable steering wheel feedback torque.

The rear subsystem controls the rear road wheel angle. A speed dependent mapping of rear / front ratio is used. Rear steer angles are out-of-phase with the front angle at low speeds for improved maneuverability. The rear angles are in phase with the front at high speeds for improved vehicle stability.

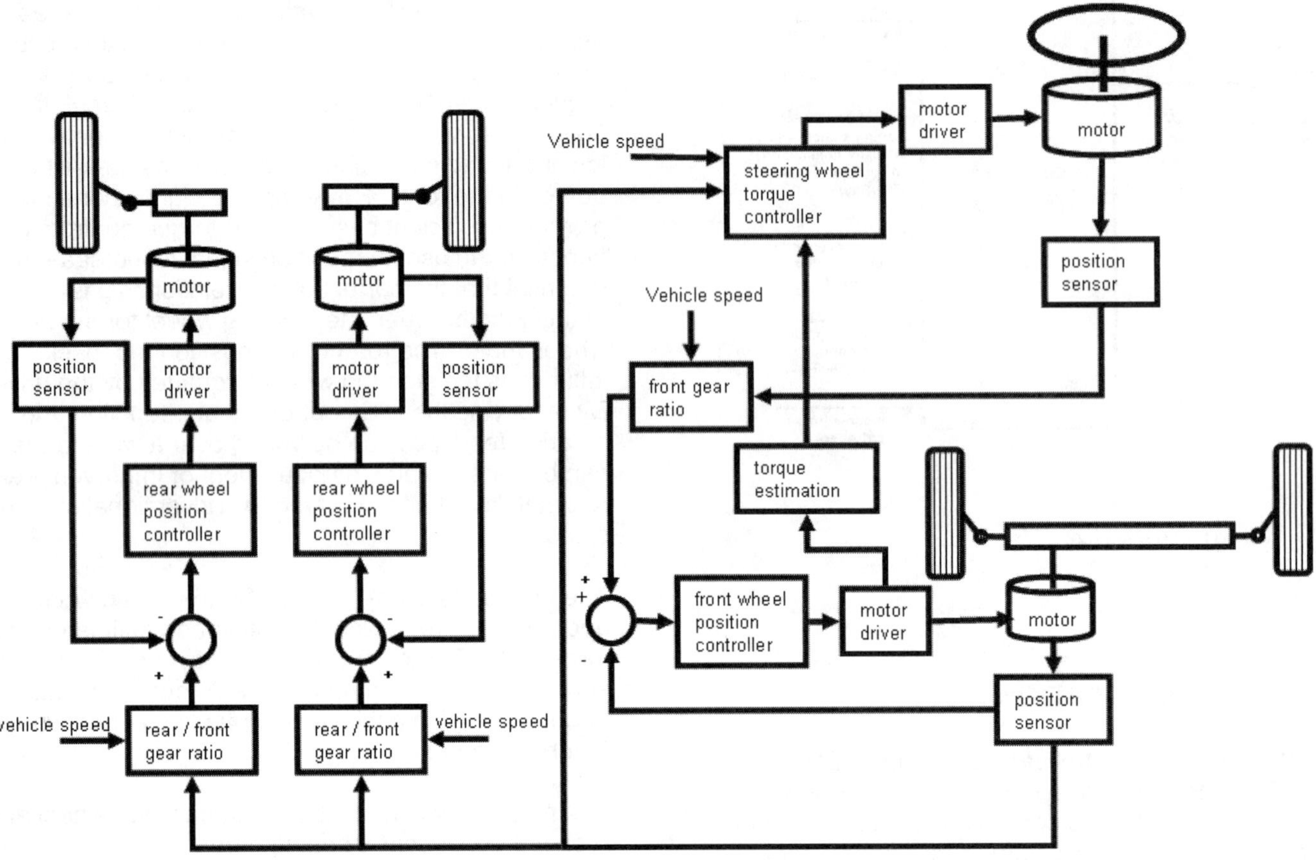

Figure 12: SBW control structure

FUTURE EXPANSION:

The SBW system was designed to allow it to be integrated with other by-wire chassis systems that are included in the Sequel vehicle. To accommodate future integration plans, the SBW software includes an interface for a Supervisory Control Module (SCM). This interface provides the capability to augment steering control. The SBW control system will provide the base steering control. The SCM will be able to modify the front and rear wheel angles and DIS feedback torque that is commanded by the SBW system.

Higher level control features will be implemented in the SCM. The SCM interface will facilitate integration of by-wire systems to enable future vehicle control technologies (i.e. lane keeping, semi-autonomous parking, stability control) and driving dynamics (i.e. lead/pull compensation, Ackerman correction). Also, by having individual control of the road wheels and the driver torque, many of the control features can be enhanced over what is currently possible with electric power steering or active front steering systems.

CONCLUSION

A SBW system was developed for the GM Sequel that provided packaging flexibility for its unique architecture. An acceptable level of security and functional availability was achieved through a use of fault-tolerant and fail-safe architectures.

Testing and subjective evaluation of a mule vehicle has indicated that the SBW system performance was similar to existing hydraulic and electrically assisted steering systems.

Substantial redundancies are required to achieve fault-tolerant operation. Even with electrical redundancy, mechanical backup may be needed to protect against possible loss of function in the event that the vehicle experiences a significant electrical disruption.

The redundancies required to achieve an acceptable level of steer-by-wire fault-tolerant operation result in a significant cost penalty compared to current mechanical systems. This extra expense will restrict the application of steer-by-wire technology to unique vehicle designs which draw significant benefits from this technology.

ACKNOWLEDGEMENTS

The authors would like to acknowledge Visteon Corporation for it's significant contributions to the steer-by-wire system design. We recognize Behrouz Ashrafi, Bruce Bowling, John Balint, Steve Gable, Mary Huang, Muqtada Husain, Chris Myers, Doug Oliver, John Oynoian, Larry Peruski, Stan Seely, Steve Stachowski, Yixin Yao, and Bing Zheng.

The authors also want to acknowledge Steve Opiteck from General Motors for his contributions to the performance and tuning of the SBW system.

REFERENCES

1. D. Heitzer and A. Seewald, "Development of a Fault-tolerant Steer-By-Wire Steering System," SAE 2004-21-0046.
2. N. Zara, "Rear-to-Front Steer Algorithm for Four-Wheel-Steer, Full-Size Trucks- Analytical Assessment, " SAE 2005-01-0405.
3. FlexRay homepage: http://www.flexray.com
4. P. Mishra and S. Naik, "Distributed Control System Development or FlexRay Based Systems," SAE 2005-01-1079.

2006-01-0308

Advanced Development of Speech Enabled Voice Recognition Enabled Embedded Navigation Systems

Kenneth White, Harvey Ruback and Jan Sedivy
IBM Corporation

Koichi Kojima and Keisuke Kondo
Honda R&D Co., Ltd

ABSTRACT

This paper will focus on the technology improvements and development effort required to enable human sounding system responses and voice enablement for destination entry for automotive navigation systems. Honda and IBM have been working together since around 1999. The first product to reveal the fruits of this relationship was the 2003 Accord. Voice enablement consists of speech recognition of a Radio/Audio, Climate Control, or Navigation related command, and providing voice responses using a combination of prerecorded messages combined with Text-To-Speech (TTS) generated outputs.

The Accord in 2003 used a combination of high quality prerecorded prompts with occasional use of TTS synthesis. The 2005 Acura RL and Odyssey introduced use of Concatenative (human sounding) TTS. This paper will discuss the trade-offs and design considerations for the use of Concatenative TTS as opposed to Formant TTS technology.

Figure 1: Acura 2005 RL

In 2005, the Acura RL and Odyssey navigation systems allowed selection by voice of a street name for the United States market. This was an innovative breakthrough in embedded speech technology usage due to the number of street names that at any one time could be stated by the user. This paper will describe the embedded speech technology enhancements that where required for this support and discuss the design and system consideration for destination selection by voice.

INTRODUCTION

In 2002, Honda released its first voice enabled Navigation system as an option for the 2003MY Accord that uses technology provided by the IBM Embedded ViaVoice (EVV) product. IBM voice technology is provided as a software developer's kit (SDK) that enables an embedded (automotive) application to perform voice recognition and/or perform speech synthesis (Text-to-Speech or TTS). Since then, Honda and IBM have continued to improve the speech capabilities provided by the Honda Navigation System and have introduced the Navigation System as an option for more car lines.

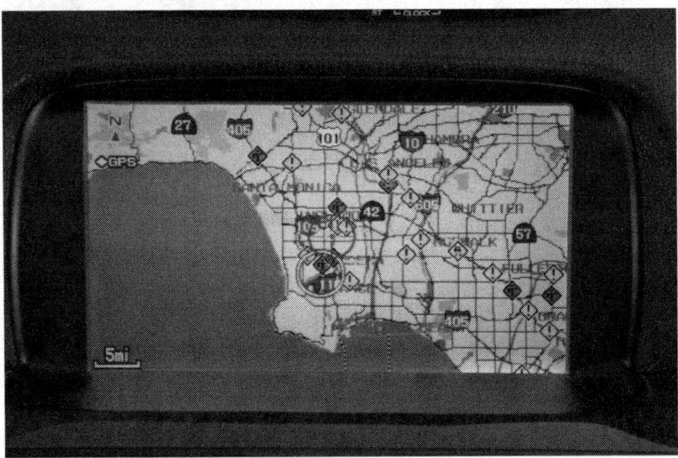

Figure 2: Honda Navigation Map

There are three fundamental aspects for voice enablement. First, the core speech technology must be robust. This is defined as being able to deliver high accuracy for speech recognition within a resource-constrained environment and TTS support that is state of the art (intelligible and human sounding). Second, the voice dialog must be intuitive and match the other methods (touch screen or Jog Dial) of user input. Third, the core technology must continue to improve without necessarily a proportional improvement in platform resources!

Continual improvement is a key element in Honda's design process. What is acceptable for one model year is often insufficient for the next revision. Given the cost constrains of embedded platform development CPU and memory resources are often limited and do not increase dynamically from year to year. However, underlying technology must continue its improvement in order to provide better support to the end users and enable better solutions.

The purpose of this paper is to explore voice technology in detail from this perspective and explain some of the issues and solutions that have been developed in order to voice enable an automotive application.

Problem Statement

As technology progresses, so does the number and complexity of the applications available to the driver in the vehicle cabin. The radio has additional features - settings, bands, presets, etc... The climate control systems have additional settings – zones, fans speeds, temperature controls, etc... In addition, new applications such as navigation systems are becoming more prevalent in vehicles as demonstrated by Honda vehicles since 1996. As the number of tasks and the complexity of each task increases, so does the cognitive load of the driver. This increase in the driver's cognitive load increases the amount of driver distractions in the vehicle. Since driver distraction directly affects the safety of the driver and passengers, a solution is needed to enable simple access to these new applications.

Challenges for Speech Technologies in the Automotive Environment

Even prior to the integration of speech recognition, Honda navigation systems provided, user-friendly operation. To enhance usability and safety, Honda deployed speech recognition and text to speech solutions from IBM (IBM Embedded ViaVoice) as an integral part of their navigation application user interface. Using this technology, Honda allows the driver to speak commands to activate system functions. It also utilizes text to speech and pre-recorded prompts to notify the driver of events. The result is a user interface that simplifies the driver's access to vehicle functions while reducing the driver's cognitive load, and providing a safe in vehicle cabin interface.

The environment represented by vehicles is very challenging for speech recognition. The vehicle environment is both noisy and unpredictable. In addition, unlike server based systems, embedded systems in vehicles have limited system resources such as memory and processing power that can be dedicated to speech recognition processing. As a result, creative and efficient speech processing algorithms are required in order to obtain high speech recognition accuracy in this difficult noise environment.
The accuracy of speech recognition is highly dependent on the quality of the input audio. There are many environmental factors in the vehicle which can degrade the quality of the input signal used for speech recognition. Signal to noise ratio (SNR) is a major contributor to speech recognition performance. SNR is the ratio of the speech energy in the input signal compared to the energy of the ambient noise in the input signal. High SNR is obtained when the speech energy is significantly more powerful then the noise energy for the input signal. High SNR is the optimal case for speech recognition since the speech can clearly be distinguished from the noise. High SNR is not often achieved in the vehicle due to the nature of the environment. In the vehicle, road noise, wind noise, and climate control noise reduce the SNR of the input signal used for speech recognition. In addition, the noise is dynamic and constantly changing. This condition adds significant complexity to the speech recognition processing since the non-speech signals are neither predictable nor constant. Transient or burst noise sources also add to the complexity of in vehicle environment. These noise sources typically consist of short, high energy events that are similar in make up to speech sounds. Examples of transient noises are clicks from buttons, bumps, horns, and wipers. All of these noises create a harsh environment that greatly reduces the SNR of the input audio for speech recognition in vehicles.

The selection and placement of the microphone can help improve the SNR of the input signal. Directional or noise reducing microphones provide a level of noise reduction based on their pick up geometry and design characteristics. The basic design of directional microphones allows them to be more sensitive to input signals from a given area relative to their position than to other signals. Therefore, by properly positioning these microphones in front of the intended speaker some of the environmental noise can be reduced, thus increasing the SNR for the driver. This leads to a challenge for the automotive manufactures. Due to physical constraints of the cabin, wiring, and production, it can be difficult to place microphones in their optimal location for the driver.

Another challenge for speech recognition processing in vehicles is the diversity of the user population. In the past, speech applications were typically created and used by people familiar with computers and the specific application domain. In the vehicle, the user domain becomes very diverse, essentially anyone who drives a car. This diversity results in a variety of speaker characteristics such as dialect, accent, volume, speaking style and speed. In addition, since people use spoken communication as a part of their daily lives, it is very difficult for them to adapt their speaking characteristics in order to improve the accuracy of speech recognition performance. As a result of these factors, the speech recognition system must be able to achieve a high level of accuracy for a large and diverse population of users.

Speech recognition processing is similar to most other computing intensive tasks in that improved results can be achieved with more advanced algorithms, but these algorithms require addition computing resources. In the vehicle, increasing the available system resources is not usually a simple or feasible option due to cost, space, and reliability constraints. Therefore, the application of more advanced microphone technologies utilizing multiple microphones with advanced digital signal processing or increasing the memory size and CPU requirements for higher recognition accuracy are not always possible. The challenge of finding the optimum balance between the available system resources with the most advanced and efficient speech processing algorithms is the goal of the speech engine designers and system integrators.

Text to speech, or TTS, has similar challenges for the in vehicle environment. The TTS voice that is generated must be easy to understand or intelligible. Some manufacturers insist on a defined “corporate voice”. In addition to intelligible, the voice must be natural sounding. Natural sounding refers to human-like vs. mechanical in nature. This is critical because the TTS voice reflects on the quality of the vehicle. In order to achieve the highest possible voice quality, pre-recorded prompts are often used for the fixed, non-dynamic phrases that need to be spoken. The challenge here for TTS is the generation of a voice that when spoken along with these pre-recorded prompts sound natural and smooth. As with speech recognition, TTS quality can be improved with additional system resources, but again, this is not always a feasible solution. Therefore, advanced techniques are required to meet the challenges of TTS for the in vehicle embedded environment.

TECHNOLOGY OVERVIEW

The kernel of the speech enabled automotive applications is the Embedded ViaVoice (EVV) speech recognition engine, which has been designed for embedded applications with constrained resources. The engine is implemented in C/C++ and is highly portable and scalable to 32 bit CPU’s and architectures. It requires minimal support from the underlying operating system, and it provides a simple and efficient API.

The engine is a result of IBM’s 30 plus years of experience in speech recognition. The EVV uses the standard Hidden Markov Models technology for modeling speech. This technology enables speaker independent (no training required) recognition of medium to large size vocabularies. The latest engine enables grammar based as well as language model recognition. The grammar based applications require the designer to produce lists of all words or phrases used at each state of an application. The dictation feature is aimed at free form applications, where the user is not limited by a list of commands but addresses the system in free speech. The engine also supports recognition of very large lists of words required for applications such as selecting street names. The engine is carefully tuned to recognize digits and short commands, which are very important for many applications, such as dialing phone numbers. During recognition the engine informs the application not only about the recognized word but provides a list of the N best words along with their confidence score. This information can be used by the application to improve the user interface. When the confidence score is low, the application can ask the user for confirmation, or if it is high the application proceeds immediately. Another challenging part of the engine is the silence speech detector, which is required to support the push to activate or the push to initiate operational modes. Silence speech detector decides where the end of utterance is and this is essential for carrying dialogs with open microphone. The user does not need to push the button before each interaction. Voice recognition in the Honda Navigation application is designed to use the recognition engine in Push to Activate mode where the use presses a button to signal the start of recognition and the system opens the microphone, captures and processes what the user says, and then automatically returns a result.

The EVV is highly optimized for noisy environments, it adapts to different speakers and different noise conditions while it is used. The rule of thumb is that the larger the acoustic model, the better various conditions can be compensated for in the car. However, a large model has negative impact on the memory and the CPU requirements. To keep the resource requirements low it was necessary to develop a set of sophisticated adaptive algorithms enabling high recognition accuracy under various conditions and for many different speakers. For non native speakers, who may not have standard pronunciation, an enrollment procedure is available which improves the accuracy after dictating several short phrases. In some applications, a nametag can be assign to a phone number. To support this feature the EVV has Acoustic Baseform Service. This allows generation of the pronunciation pattern from an utterance. Once the pronunciation pattern is stored, the phone number can be recalled by stating the nametag. The EVV has Acoustic Distance Measure which enables it to recognize if a nametag is acoustically similar to an existing nametag. The application can then prompt for entry of a different nametag.

The selection and recording of various speakers and numerous noises in the car is required to ensure robustness in many different environments and to tune the speech recognition engine for the highest possible accuracy. Extensive collection of databases and sophisticated training technology enables continuous improvement or the recognition accuracy and robustness. (here we may use a picture)

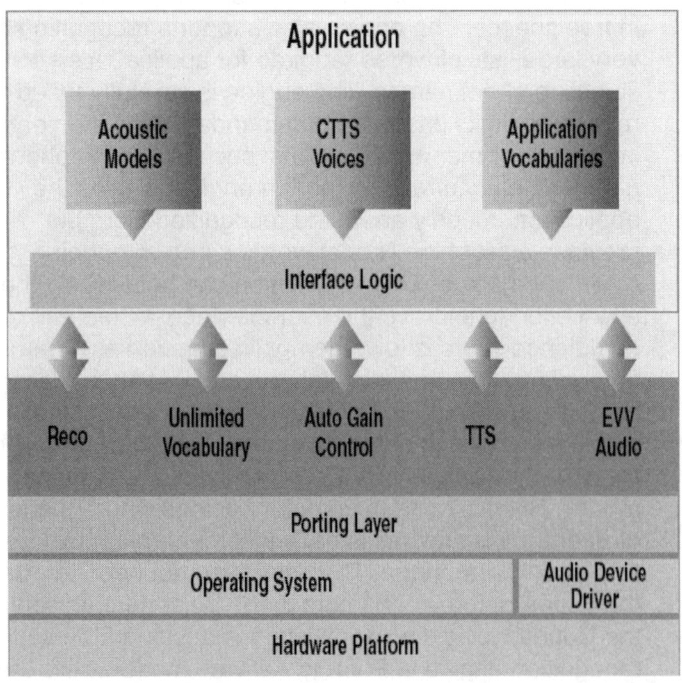

Figure 3: Embedded ViaVoice Architecture

HONDA'S APPROACH TO SPEECH TECHNOLOGIES

Honda introduced its first voice enabled Navigation system in the 2003MY Accord supporting US English for North America. The 2004 update included application to the Acura TL and added support for Canadian French.

Honda typically does not schedule major system updates every model year but prefers a two year update period with the following model year to provide incremental improvements and application to additional models. This is important so that the original design and validation work can be limited to a more constrained set of design considerations.

The IBM EVV voice technology continues to be updated and improved every calendar year. Normally, IBM provides one major release per year with incremental releases multiple times a year based on unique customer requirements.

The design of the Honda voice enabled Navigation system is state of the art from a Human Machine Interface (HMI) prospective. Voice enablement is only one aspect of the overall HMI design. There are several physical system design aspects that must be considered: microphone type and position, talk button placement, AC vent design/placement and screen design.

In all Honda voice enabled cars the microphone is placed in the overhead console positioned usually with the head of the microphone oriented towards the driver. This usually results in a 12 to 16 inch distance between the microphone and the driver. The system design is focused on the driver as the primary operator of car functions. This microphone positioning is fairly optimal since the height of a driver usually doesn't dramatically affect distance since shorter drivers move their seats forward offsetting their lower height. Microphone type is usually a standard automotive grade omni directional microphone.

Figure 4: Microphone placement in overhead console

Several alternate locations where considered and rejected for microphone placement: dash board, rearview mirror, and steering well. The position of the AC center console vents is very important when deciding on microphone location. The center vents are designed so that when pointed at their maximum upward direction, the flow of air misses the primary sensitive path of the microphone as it is oriented towards the driver. The vent should be designed with consideration for microphone placement since center vent airflow can dramatically affect recognition performance.

A talk button is used to signal to the system to open the microphone and start feeding audio to the voice recognition system component. The user is not required to repress the talk button to close the microphone since the system can determine this itself. Talk button placement is usually on the dash with a second alternate button on the steering wheel so that it is easy for a driver to use while not precluding passenger use of the voice capabilities of the navigation system. Physical design of the system focuses on the driver as primary user but Honda found out that often the passenger would often use the system and normally had no problems using the system given how it was designed.

When designing the system the voice commands that are active at any point in time must match the screen design and layout. For example, if the user is deciding on how to define a route and is at the destination input menu, the tab on the screen is "Address". The voice command would be the same, "Address" so that as menus are navigated by a user the primary set of voice commands matches what is displayed on the screen. This illustrates that voice commands need to be intuitive and match the other button names, menu names, and audio prompts.

The 2003MY Accord saw the introduction of the 1st generation of a Honda voice enabled navigation system. In 2005 this was dramatically improved from three perspectives. First, the speech synthesis component was changed from Formant Text to Speech (FTTS) which is more machine sounding to Concatenative Text to Speech (CTTS) which is more human sounding. Text to speech enables a system to take text and generate audio that is played so that a user can hear what the text says. Since TTS is used to provide direct feedback to the user, all aspects of the TTS voice quality reflect heavily on a user perception of the vehicle. Also, users expect to understand what the TTS system says every time, whereas with speech recognition, periodic misrecognitions are expected and tolerated. Given these high expectations for TTS and that it's a central focus of the user interaction with the vehicle, providing TTS technology is actually more complicated than providing voice recognition tends to be. FTTS technology has the advantage of being fairly intelligible and requires minimum system resources (usually 1 to 2 MB of RAM/Flash with less than 25 MIPs of CPU resources are more than sufficient). CTTS can be less intelligible and requires significantly more system resources (usually between 9 to 16 MB of RAM/Flash with between 75 to 95 MIPs of CPU). Even though FTTS is more intelligible than CTTS users much prefer human sounding TTS. It is more important that TTS sounds good than its ultimate understandability.

Honda has placed great emphasis on high quality system prompts. Many people where auditioned to select the voices used within the Honda car lines. TTS is used when it is impractical to prerecord a prompt for play back. Prompts are played in the car at 22 kHz mono audio. It was found that when using TTS that it was better to synthesize TTS at the same frequency and channel specification of the prompt so that the resulting audio has the same quality.

CTTS technology relies on prerecorded voice segments that are kept in a database used by the TTS engine during speech synthesis. This database is compressed so that its memory foot print can be minimized. Compression does help with memory size but affects CPU utilization. The maximum CPU utilization rate must be understood when deciding the amount of compression. IBM has been producing high quality CTTS voice for its server based voice products (produced at IBM Boca Raton and IBM Yorktown) for many years and has a research center in Haifa that specializes in compression. These centers cooperated on producing embedded CTTS technology that is state of the art.

There are several additional considerations when using CTTS. Honda and IBM found that it was very important to generate a CTTS voice that matched the voice of the prerecorded prompts. In 2005 this was done primarily for the Honda US English female voice. In surveying its user community Honda found that over 80% of its users preferred the female voice over the male voice in the US. Therefore, focus was given on maximizing the performance of the female CTTS. The volume of the CTTS synthesis must match that of the prerecorded prompts. When a CTTS voice is generated it often must be customized so that it can be matched to the volume of the prerecorded prompts. The speed of the CTTS synthesis must also be matched.

In the 2005 Navigation system Honda and IBM dramatically increased the number of voice commands and enabled the selection of street names. From a voice command prospective for example, the "Find nearest categories" function increased to around 90 from less than 40 in the 2003 Navigation system. The find nearest function is one of the more popular voice commands. Points of Interest (POIs) can be displayed or selected as route destinations. The POIs are organized in categories. For example, "Find Nearest Italian Restaurant" lists the Italian Restaurants in order of distance from the car for a user to select one as a destination. Increasing the number of categories effects voice recognition accuracy since the complexity of the voice commands is usually a factor of the number of active commands and the ambiguity between these commands. The core voice technology provided by IBM kept pace with Honda's system requirements so that the underlying accuracy provided by the system being used in 2005 is actually higher than that being used in 2003 even though the voice command complexity often doubled.

The second major voice recognition function provided in 2005 was that of street name recognition. This was provided for US English of US road names. IBM provided technology had to be revised during development of this function. Initially the technology enabled recognition of lists of up to 32,000 street names. These lists would be arraigned as flat lists and combined with the use of N best support within the navigation system. N best support is a voice recognition function that returns the top N results. When performing street name recognition N best support should be used since the number of potential results increases as the size of the list increases. Within a list it is possible that the same pronunciation maps to multiple street names.

The Honda street name voice recognition function enables selection of a street name either by city or by state. Within the US no single city exceeds 16,000 entries. Only four states exceed 64,000 entries. The largest is Texas with around 140,000 entries. The IBM voice capability being used for this had to be modified since its initial 32,000 list recognition capability did not scale to implementation of voice selection of a street name within a state. Memory and CPU requirements had to scale to the automotive embedded space with a high degree of accuracy being provided. Honda screen design typically shows 6 entries per screen. For this capability multiple screens are support with every attempt being made that the correct result for what the user said is displayed on the 1st screen. Screen design is important when deciding on N when enabled N best support. During testing of this function Honda actually timed several people using the system manually as opposed to using voice when selecting an address as a route destination and it was found that using voice was much faster and more enjoyable for the user.

THE FUTURE

The future for speech recognition technology is bright. Today, it has been proven that speech recognition technology is an effective technology to simplify the in vehicle user experience as demonstrated by Honda vehicles. As more advanced functionality is integrated into the vehicle and as vehicles are connected to remote servers providing even more services, speech recognition will play a key role in enabling these functions for the drivers and passengers. In the future as hardware costs reduce, more advanced microphone will be used to improve the SNR, thus increasing the overall accuracy of the system. Also, new techniques, such as audio visual processing will be integrated to augment the speech recognition process using visual cues or lip reading techniques to improve the overall recognition performance. Services will also be provided to the vehicle occupants via connected services. With these connections, speech recognition processing will be performed on remote servers where system resources constraints are more easily overcome. Finally, how the user interacts with the system will become more natural. The systems will be able to understand free form speech and the user will not be required to speak from a predetermined set commands. Also, the user interface will include interaction with the user, guiding the user through tasks and asking them questions to assist the user in completing their goals. The result will be a conversational system, where users interact with the system in a natural manner, as if they were talking to a live person. This is the end goal, to create a system that interacts with the user just like another person would include comprehending complex commands, asking for clarification, and providing a comfortable, natural user interface that requires no learning or training to be fully utilized.

CONCLUSION

Honda and IBM have been working together on delivering leading edge voice solutions for over 6 years. Innovation and providing exciting new functions to our customers is a core component in its design philosophy. IBM has been a leader in providing voice-enabling solutions for over 30 years. Voice enablement technology is a key component in the automotive space. IBM focuses on delivering core technology that enables its partners, like Honda and its tier 1 suppliers, to provide to the end user exciting new technology that simplifies user tasks while improving the user experience.

2005-01-1479

On Automatic Collision Avoidance Systems

Thorsten Brandt, Thomas Sattel and Jörg Wallaschek
L-LAB: Public Private Partnership of University of Paderborn and Hella KGaA Hueck & Co.

ABSTRACT

In future automotive collision avoidance systems (CAS) collision-free path planning will be required. For this reason, two possible path planning techniques are compared. The first method is based on the mathematical theory of differential games, the second method focuses on so-called elastic bands. However, the method of elastic bands is essentially modified to provide solutions in complex driving situations. Furthermore, it is shown how path planning, path following control and driving condition estimation can be embedded in a possible overall CAS-setup. Therein, driving conditions are estimated based on the characteristic velocity. Finally, simulation results for an emergency maneuver are presented.

INTRODUCTION

The future development of today's driver assistance systems strongly depends on the efficiency of automotive actuators and environmental sensors such as radar, lidar, laser scanners, video systems and appropriate image processing software. However, sensor fusion of these systems promises a prolonged innovation thrust [1]. Thus, in the most far-reaching scenarios future vehicles will become completely autonomous. These intelligent vehicles require collision avoidance systems (CAS) to handle unexpected emergency situations.

Within this framework it seems reasonable to consider technological extensions of already existing driver assistance systems, for example lane departure warning or emergency braking, in order to provide evasion functionalities. For the time being, these CAS can take over the driving task in emergency situations that a human driver cannot handle.

If the estimated collision risk exceeds a prescribed threshold value the CAS initiates an emergency maneuver. Depending on the complexity of the situation, different actions can be taken: braking, evading or evading in combination with braking or accelerating. Today's emergency systems are only capable of sheer braking. This work mainly focuses on evading maneuvers at constant velocity to provide the foundation for systems that combine evasion maneuvers with velocity changes.

Besides further developments in sensor and actuator technologies as well as in the identification of emergency situations, the following fundamental problems have to be solved and are addressed in this paper:

1. Path planning: generation of possible collision-free evasion paths,

2. Path following: determination of control signals such as the steering angle to guide the vehicle on the planned evasion path,

3. Driving condition estimation: model based prediction whether the planned path is drivable or not.

First, a possible overall CAS-setup is suggested. Next, two methods for collision-free path planning are presented and compared. The first method is based on the mathematical theory of differential games. Path planning in situations with *one* oncoming vehicle can be accomplished by numerically solving the "*Modified Game of Two Cars*" as shown by Lachner et al. [2,3] in the *1990*s. The second approach employs so-called elastic bands which were introduced for robotic path planning by Quinlan and Khatib [4] in the *1990*s and recently adapted to automotive applications by Gehring and Stein [5] and Hilgert et al. [6]. Therein, the main focus lay on vehicle following and lane change maneuvers. However, for collision avoidance further modifications need to be implemented. It is shown how the borders of the road and moving obstacles can be incorporated in the framework by use of repulsive potential fields.

Subsequently, path following control and model based driving condition estimation are discussed. An adequate vehicle model and driving condition estimation based on the *Characteristic Velocity Stability Indicator* are mentioned. Finally, simulation results for an emergency maneuver incorporating a static obstacle, an oncoming vehicle as well as the borders of the road are presented.

CAS: AN OVERALL SYSTEM SETUP

An overall setup of CAS combining, among others, the detection of emergency situations, path planning, path following and driving condition estimation, respectively, is illustrated in Fig. 1. The connecting lines between the blocks symbolize transferred sensor data as well as logical values. Therein, logically true values are signified by bold face tags.

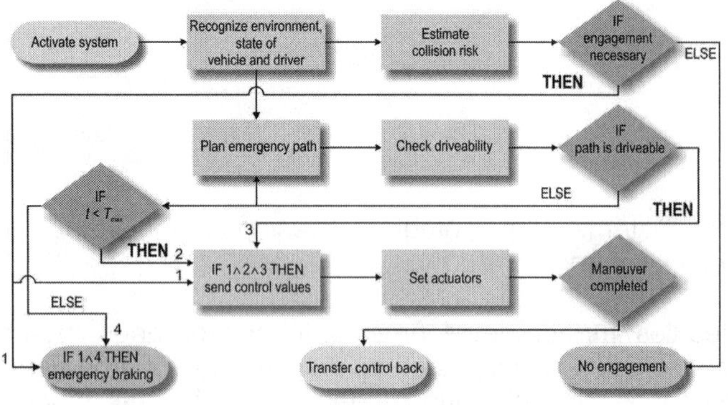

Fig. 1: Possible overall CAS-setup: logical framework of an initiated emergency maneuver

Once the CAS is activated it permanently evaluates environmental sensor data, the driving conditions of the CAS-equipped vehicle and eventually the state of the driver to identify emergency situations. Thereby, emergency situations are characterized by a high *collision risk* with other vehicles, pedestrians or any kind of obstacle, respectively. If the estimated collision risk exceeds a prescribed threshold value, the CAS initiates an emergency maneuver as shown in Fig. 1.

In doing so, possible emergency paths are planned based on the available sensor data. Then, the planned emergency paths are checked for drivability, for example by the *Characteristic Velocity Stability Indicator*. This iterative procedure searches for a drivable emergency path until a valid solution is found or the time limit T_{max} is exceeded. In case that no valid solution can be found within the given time limit emergency braking without steering should be initiated, as depicted in Fig. 1.

However, if in a detected emergency situation a drivable emergency trajectory is generated fast enough, the necessary control signals to guide the vehicle on that trajectory are sent to the actuators of the vehicle. In this, *x-by-wire* technology seems suitable. When the emergency maneuver is finished the control is transferred back to the driving instance. This can be a human driver or a system that autonomously controls the vehicle.

PATH PLANNING

Since path planning is an essential feature of future CAS two promising automotive path planning techniques are presented. The first is based on differential games. Second, a method using elastic bands is outlined and a comparison of both methods is given.

DIFFERENTIAL GAMES

A possible method to generate emergency trajectories that avoid collisions with *one* oncoming vehicle is to formulate the collision avoidance problem as differential game. This section gives a path planning approach incorporating the *Modified Game of Two Cars* based on the work of Lachner et al. [2,3].

The basic idea of the *Modified Game of Two Cars* is to consider the CAS-equipped vehicle *E* (Evader) and an oncoming vehicle *P* (Pursuer) as parts of one dynamical system, bounded by the borders of the road.

The configuration of the system is depicted in Fig. 2. The states of this system are the lateral distances of the centers of mass to the middle of the road x_E and x_P, the distance between the two vehicles in road direction y, the orientations of the velocity vectors ϕ_E and ϕ_P and the velocity v_E of the CAS-equipped vehicle *E*. For clarity, the states can be combined in a state vector

$$\mathbf{z} := (x_P, x_E, y, v_E, \phi_P, \phi_E)^T .$$

The velocity of the oncoming car, v_P, is assumed to be constant.

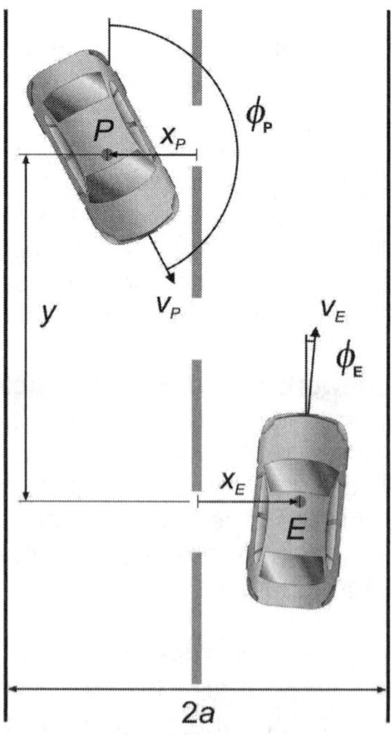

Fig.: 2: Modified Game of Two Cars

Lachner et al. [2,3] modeled both vehicles as rigid bodies with normalized mass in the plane of the road, neglecting the rotational moment of inertia. Therein, it is notable that the rotational motion is kinematical constrained

$$\dot{x}_P = v_P \sin\phi_P \ , \qquad (1)$$

$$\dot{x}_E = v_E \sin\phi_E \ , \qquad (2)$$

$$\dot{y} = v_P \cos\phi_P - v_E \cos\phi_E \ , \qquad (3)$$

$$\dot{v}_E = b_E \, \eta_E \ , \qquad (4)$$

$$\dot{\phi}_P = w_P \, u_P \ , \qquad (5)$$

$$\dot{\phi}_E = w_E(v_E) u_E \ . \qquad (6)$$

The maximum deceleration is marked by the constant value b_E. After normalization, the control variables consist of the nondimensional steering-wheel deflections u_P and u_E of both vehicles as well as of the nondimensional drive or brake force η_E of E.

The scaling factors are the velocity depending maximum angular velocities

$$w_P = \frac{\mu_0 g}{v_P} \ , \qquad (7)$$

$$w_E = \frac{\mu_0 g}{v_E} \ . \qquad (8)$$

Therein, g denotes the gravitational constant and μ_0 the friction coefficient between the tires and the surface of the road.

Inequality constraints result from the requirement not to leave the road of width $2a$,

$$-a \le x_P \le a \ , \qquad (9)$$

$$-a \le x_E \le a \ , \qquad (10)$$

as well as from the bounds of the nondimensional control variables

$$u_{P,\min} \le u_P \le u_{P,\max} \ , \qquad (11)$$

$$u_{E,\min} \le u_E \le u_{E,\max} \ , \qquad (12)$$

$$\eta_{E,\min} \le \eta_E \le \eta_{E,\max} \ . \qquad (13)$$

The characteristic property of this coupled nonlinear state space model is that not all control variables are accessible. E only has control over the variables u_E and η_E, while P can only access u_P. Combining the control variables of E in a control vector $\mathbf{u_E}$, the state space model (1)-(6) can be written as

$$\dot{\mathbf{z}} = \mathbf{f}(\mathbf{z}, u_P, \mathbf{u_E}) \ . \qquad (14)$$

The objective of E is to avoid a collision with P. Therefore, a minimum distance between E and P has to be maintained over the time period of the evasion maneuver

$$d_{\min} := \min_{0 \le t \le \infty} \sqrt{(x_P(t) - x_E(t))^2 + y(t)^2} \ . \qquad (15)$$

In order to design a control strategy for collision avoidance for E, maximization of d_{min} is desired. It is assumed that E and P cannot communicate. Thus, E has no knowledge about possible driving strategies of P and vice versa. For this reason no common strategy can be planned.

However, a frequently used approach to solve differential games is to assume a worst-case scenario: for the oncoming vehicle P an optimal strategy for hypothesized collision intension is presumed. In doing so, the task is to identify the corresponding strategy of the collision avoiding vehicle E, that is the normalized steering angle, $u_E(t)$, and the nondimensional drive or brake force $\eta_E(t)$.

In order to solve this maximization problem of the minimal distance between both vehicles, Lachner et al. [2,3] simplify the problem by considering the squared lateral distance between both vehicles at the instant of mutual passing ($t=t_f$)

$$d_{final} := (x_P(t_f) - x_E(t_f))^2 \ . \qquad (16)$$

The applied numerical technique is very time consuming and needs a sufficiently accurate estimate of the start solution because convergence cannot be guaranteed for all start solutions. Furthermore, the numerical procedure is very complex and the time consumed for the solution varies for different initial conditions. For this reason, the method of differential games can only be used offline for path planning. For real time synthesis, e.g. neural networks can be trained with solutions, which are generated offline for different initial conditions as illustrated in Lachner et. al [2,3].

ELASTIC BANDS

Another possible approach to generate emergency trajectories for vehicle collision-avoidance maneuvers is given by the concept of elastic bands. The basic idea how this concept can be employed for vehicle path planning is illustrated in Fig. 3. An elastic band consists of nodes connected by springs. One of the terminating nodes is fixed to the host vehicle, the other can arbitrarily be placed on the road along the planned path. The elastic band moves virtually with the host vehicle and follows the planned path. For autonomous path planning, information about the environment solely rely on sensor data of the host vehicle. Hence, the configuration of the nodes of the elastic band is described with respect to a reference frame (x_V,y_V), fixed to the host vehicle.

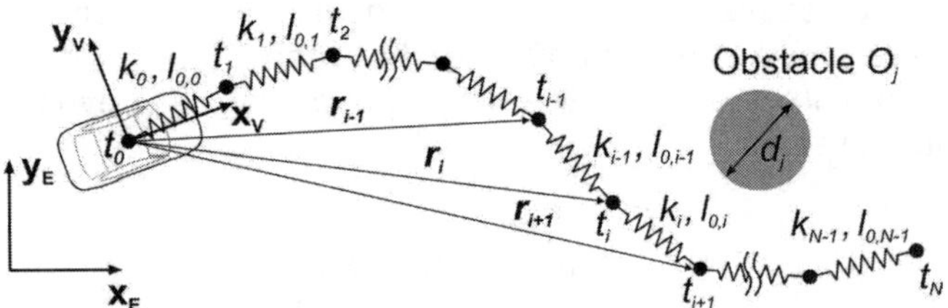

Fig. 3: Elastic band described in a vehicle fixed reference frame (x_V,y_V), earth fixed reference frame (x_E,y_E) and obstacle O_j

Without environmental disturbances the elastic band is in its initial equilibrium configuration. Environmental changes cause external forces acting on the nodes. These external forces shall repel the elastic band from environmental borders or obstacles. This enforces a new equilibrium configuration of the nodes of the elastic band, resulting in a deformed shape, as shown for example in Fig. 3. When the path planning procedure is finished, the elastic band is detached from the CAS-equipped vehicle at time t_0. Then, the elastic band virtually lying on the road is driven through by the CAS-equipped vehicle. Noteworthy, that a copy of the vehicle fixed reference frame (x_V,y_V) remains on the surface of the road at time t_0 and is denoted (x_P,y_P).

Compared to the original concept, applied by Gehring and Stein and Hilgert et al. [5,6], two modifications are introduced. First, the influence of the borders of the road on the equilibrium configuration of the elastic band is incorporated. Second, the influence of moving obstacles is taken into account. Both effects are described by suitable virtual potential fields.

In the following, the internal and external forces acting on each node are described based on internal and external potentials, respectively. Subsequently, force equilibrium is formulated and some comments on the computation of the equilibrium solutions are given. Finally, an interpolation method for smoothing the transition between the nodes of the elastic band is mentioned.

Internal Potentials of an Elastic Band

Adjacent nodes of the elastic band are coupled by linear springs. The nodes are numbered in temporally ascending order with $i=0,\ldots,N-1$: $t_{i+1} > t_i$, as they are successively driven through by the CAS-equipped vehicle. Using the position vectors $\mathbf{r}_i$ to each node, as illustrated in Fig. 3, the linear coupling between neighbouring nodes can be formulated by internal potentials

$$V_i^{\text{int}} := \frac{1}{2} k_i \left(\left\|\mathbf{r}_{i+1} - \mathbf{r}_i\right\| - l_{0,i}\right)^2 \quad , \tag{17}$$

where $l_{0,i}$, k_i denote the length of the undeformed spring i and the corresponding spring stiffness, respectively. The distance between adjacent nodes is given by the Euclidean norm

$$\left\|\mathbf{r}_{i+1} - \mathbf{r}_i\right\| = \sqrt{\left(r_{i+1,x} - r_{i,x}\right)^2 + \left(r_{i+1,y} - r_{i,y}\right)^2} \quad . \tag{18}$$

The total internal potential, governing the behavior of the elastic band, is

$$V^{\text{int}} := \sum_{i=0}^{N-1} V_i^{\text{int}} = \frac{1}{2} \sum_{i=0}^{N-1} k_i \left(\left\|\mathbf{r}_{i+1} - \mathbf{r}_i\right\| - l_{0,i}\right)^2 \quad . \tag{19}$$

The directional derivative of the total internal potential with respect to the position vector of the corresponding node yields the internal forces

$$\begin{aligned} \mathbf{F}_i^{\text{int}} &= -\frac{\partial V^{\text{int}}}{\partial \mathbf{r}_i} = -k_{i-1}\left(\left\|\mathbf{r}_i - \mathbf{r}_{i-1}\right\| - l_{0,i-1}\right)\frac{\mathbf{r}_i - \mathbf{r}_{i-1}}{\left\|\mathbf{r}_i - \mathbf{r}_{i-1}\right\|} \\ &\quad + k_i\left(\left\|\mathbf{r}_{i+1} - \mathbf{r}_i\right\| - l_{0,i}\right)\frac{\mathbf{r}_{i+1} - \mathbf{r}_i}{\left\|\mathbf{r}_{i+1} - \mathbf{r}_i\right\|} \end{aligned} \tag{20}$$

acting on each node.

External Potentials of the Borders of the Road

Likewise, the influence of the borders of the road on the nodes of the elastic band is described by repulsive external potentials

$$V^{B_q}(\mathbf{r}_i) := -k^{B_q} \ln\left\|\mathbf{r}_i - \mathbf{r}_i^{B_q}\right\| \quad \text{with} \quad q \in \{l, r\}, \tag{21}$$

where the potential of the left and right border are defined separately. The effect of the borders of the road on the elastic band can be illustrated by springs, having spring stiffness k^{B_q} , acting between the borders and the nodes of the elastic band, as shown in Fig. 4.

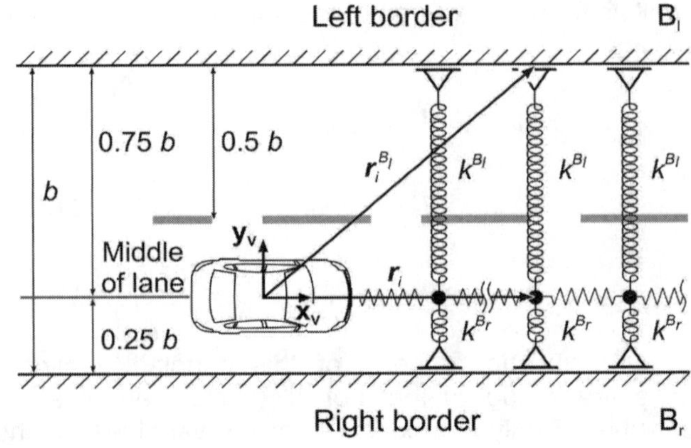

Fig. 4: Neutral position of an elastic band

The position vector $\mathbf{r}_i^{B_q}$ marks the point of the border, having the shortest distance to the corresponding node i. According to (21), the external potentials decay logarithmically towards the center of the road. Analogously to the procedure carried out to derive the internal forces, the external forces, acting on the nodes of the elastic band become

$$\mathbf{F}_i^{B,q} = -\frac{\partial V_i^{B_q}}{\partial \mathbf{r}_i} := \frac{k^{B_q}}{\left\|\mathbf{r}_i - \mathbf{r}_i^{B_q}\right\|} \cdot \frac{\mathbf{r}_i - \mathbf{r}_i^{B_q}}{\left\|\mathbf{r}_i - \mathbf{r}_i^{B_q}\right\|} \quad . \tag{22}$$

To adjust the neutral position of the elastic band, the spring stiffnesses k^{B_l} and k^{B_r} in Fig. 4 must be chosen appropriately. This is accomplished by assuming force equilibrium at each node in the neutral position of the elastic band. As a consequence a relation between the spring stiffnesses and geometric parameters of the road, see Fig. 4, follows

$$\mathbf{F}_i^{B_l} = \mathbf{F}_i^{B_r} \quad \Rightarrow \quad \frac{k^{B_l}}{k^{B_r}} = \frac{0.75b}{0.25b} = 3 \quad . \tag{23}$$

For finding equilibrium solutions of the elastic band at small distances to the borders of the road limited external forces

$$\mathbf{F}_i^{B_q} = k^{B_q} e^{-\left\|\mathbf{r}_i - \mathbf{r}_i^{B_q}\right\|^2} \cdot \frac{\mathbf{r}_i - \mathbf{r}_i^{B_q}}{\left\|\mathbf{r}_i - \mathbf{r}_i^{B_q}\right\|} \tag{24}$$

turned out to be useful.

External Potentials of Moving Obstacle

To meet the requirements of a collision-avoidance approach, it is important to incorporate the influence of moving obstacles on the deformation of the elastic band. As sketched in Fig. 3, obstacles are modeled by safety circles having diameters d_j being larger than the sum of the maximal extension of both the obstacle and the CAS-equipped vehicle. It is presupposed that information on position and velocity of obstacles are provided by the sensor system of the CAS-equipped vehicle at the beginning of the path planning, t_0. In a first approach, the velocity of obstacles during the evasion maneuver is assumed to be constant. Thus, the path of the obstacle during the evasion maneuver is linearly extrapolated as illustrated in Fig. 5.

Assuming that the CAS-equipped vehicle drives through the emergency path, given by the elastic band, at a planned longitudinal velocity $v_x(t)$, the time t_i when the vehicle passes through the corresponding node i can be determined.

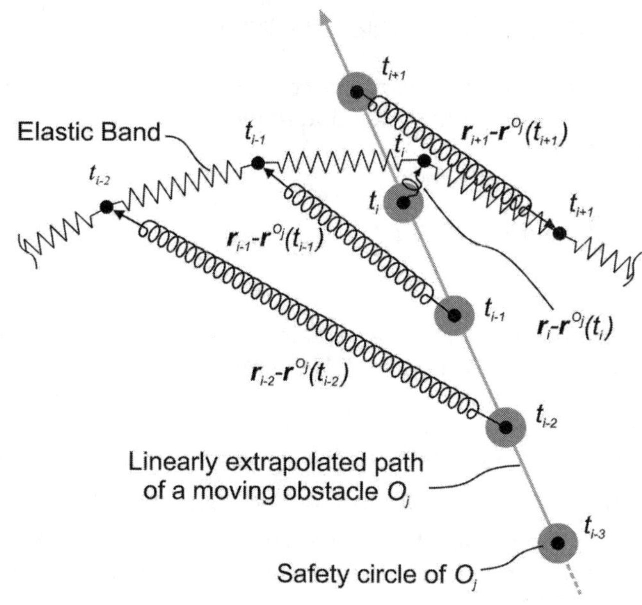

Fig. 5: Incorporation of a moving obstacle O_j

The key idea behind the construction of potentials for the moving obstacle is as follows. To each node i at time t_i along the elastic band corresponds a position of the obstacle along its own path. The correlating nodes of the elastic band and the positions of the obstacle O_j at times t_i, $i = 1,\ldots,N$ are coupled by a repelling potential field

$$V^{O_j}(\mathbf{r}_i) := -k^{O_j} \ln\left(\left\|\mathbf{r}_i - \mathbf{r}^{O_j}(t_i)\right\| - \frac{d_j}{2}\right) \quad , \tag{25}$$

where k^{O_j} denotes the stiffness parameter and $\mathbf{r}^{O_j}(t_i)$ is the position vector to the obstacle at time t_i. The coupling of the elastic band with the obstacle is illustrated in Fig. 5 by coiled springs. The external forces repelling the elastic band from the obstacle are given by

$$\mathbf{F}_i^{O_j} = -\frac{\partial V^{O_j}(\mathbf{r}_i)}{\partial \mathbf{r}_i} := \frac{k^{O_j}}{\left\|\mathbf{r}_i - \mathbf{r}^{O_j}(t_i)\right\| - \frac{d_j}{2}} \cdot \frac{\mathbf{r}_i - \mathbf{r}^{O_j}(t_i)}{\left\|\mathbf{r}_i - \mathbf{r}^{O_j}(t_i)\right\|} \quad . \tag{26}$$

Also for the moving obstacles bounded external forces

$$\mathbf{F}_i^{O_j} = k^{O_j} e^{-\left(\left\|\mathbf{r}_i - \mathbf{r}^{O_j}(t_i)\right\| - \frac{d_j}{2}\right)^2} \cdot \frac{\mathbf{r}_i - \mathbf{r}^{O_j}(t_i)}{\left\|\mathbf{r}_i - \mathbf{r}^{O_j}(t_i)\right\|} \tag{27}$$

turned out to be useful.

Determination of Equilibrium Solutions

The collision-free equilibrium configuration of the nodes of the elastic band is determined from the force equilibrium

$$\mathbf{F}_i^{\mathrm{sum}} = \mathbf{F}_i^{\mathrm{int}} + \mathbf{F}_i^{B_l} + \mathbf{F}_i^{B_r} + \sum_j \mathbf{F}_i^{O_j} = 0 \quad , \qquad (28)$$

resulting in a nonlinear algebraic equation which can for example be solved using a Newton-Raphson method. It is noteworthy that at each iteration step of the numerical solution procedure, the coupling of the elastic band with the obstacle must be updated since the position vector $\mathbf{r}^{O_j}(t_i)$ changes with the deformation of the elastic band. In doing so, it is suggested to vary the stiffness parameters k_i in order to prevent the elastic band from start twisting.

Smooth Transition of the Equilibrium Solution

After determining the equilibrium configuration of the elastic band, the transition between adjacent nodes is smoothed by a time-parameterized cubic-spline interpolation. The time-parameterized emergency path expressed in the road fixed reference frame is then given by $(x_P(t), y_P(t))$.

COMPARISON OF DIFFERENTIAL GAMES AND ELASTIC BANDS

A comparison of the two given path planning methods is summarized in Tab. 1. It can be followed that elastic bands are more suitable for automotive collision avoidance. The major drawbacks of the method based on differential games are the restricting assumptions about the vehicle model and the fact that only one obstacle can be incorporated in a 2-player-zero-sum game. Furthermore, collision-free maneuvers can only be guaranteed if the oncoming vehicle acts exactly as assumed in the differential game.

Table 1: Comparison of differential games and elastic bands for path planning

	Modified Game of Two Cars [2,3]	Elastic bands
Vehicle model	The vehicles are modeled as particles with kinematic constraints.	The method does not require a particular vehicle model.
Velocity of CAS-equipped vehicle	Changes in the velocity of the CAS-equipped vehicle are part of the solution.	The velocity of the CAS-equipped vehicle is not part of the method yet.
Return to the initially planned path	Path planning terminates at the instant of mutual passing.	The last node of the elastic band can arbitrarily be placed on the road.
Number of obstacles	The method is limited to one oncoming vehicle.	The number of obstacles is variable.
Assumptions on the obstacles	Worst-case behaviour for the oncoming vehicle is assumed. Collision avoidance cannot be guaranteed in case of different behavior!	The path of a moving obstacle is linearly extrapolated yet.
Real time capability	This method is not real time capable. Real time synthesis can for example be performed by training of neural networks with solutions that are generated offline.	The method of elastic bands is real time capable in case of limited velocities. At higher velocities, real time capability can be gained by limiting the number of iterations or by training of neural networks as well.

PATH FOLLOWING

Having planned the final emergency path, a path following procedure is required that brings out the steering angle of the CAS-equipped vehicle along the emergency path for the planned longitudinal velocity $v_x(t)$. In Hilgert et al. [7] a least-square procedure is used to compute the steering angle along planned paths for lane change maneuvers. It turned out that this method is computationally cost intensive. The path following procedure outlined here, is based on a closed-loop control system. The components of the control system consisting of a vehicle model, combined with a linear lateral guidance model and a PID-controller are described in the following.

The used reference frames are depicted in Fig. 6.The equations of motion of the CAS-equipped vehicle are formulated in the vehicle fixed reference frame (x_V,y_V). The emergency trajectory is described in the reference frame (x_P,y_P) which was detached from the vehicle at time t_0. Furthermore, a reference frame $(\tilde{x}_V, \tilde{y}_V)$ moving on the emergency trajectory is introduced for the lateral guidance procedure. As a global reference the earth fixed reference frame (x_E,y_E) is used.

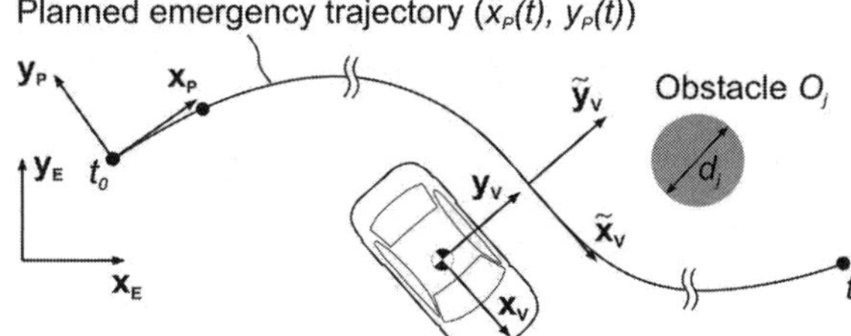

Fig. 6: Reference frames with unit vectors

VEHICLE MODEL

For performance reasons, the complexity of the vehicle model should be as low as possible. However, an appropriate level of accuracy must be retained. In collision avoidance maneuvers the lateral vehicle dynamics are of most interest. A widely used model in lateral vehicle dynamics is the bicycle model, see Fig. 7.

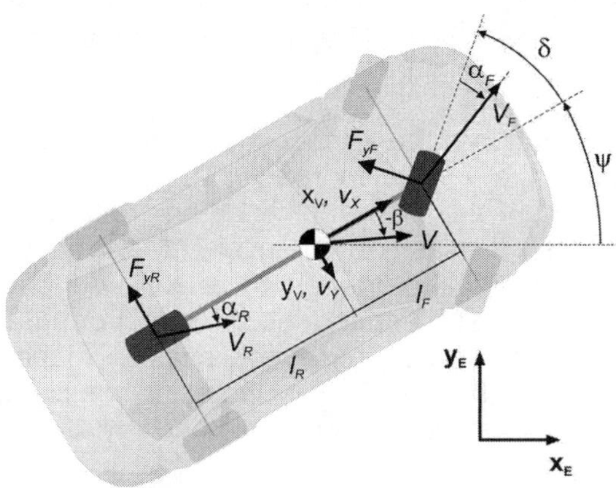

Fig. 7: Bicycle model

This planar model combines the left and right track into a single one. Often the equation of motion are linearized assuming constant velocity V of the center of gravity c.g.. Up to lateral accelerations of approximately 4 m/s^2, the linear model provides reliable results. The linear equations of motion can be written as [8]:

$$\begin{bmatrix} \dot{\beta} \\ \ddot{\psi} \end{bmatrix} = \mathbf{A} \begin{bmatrix} \beta \\ \dot{\psi} \end{bmatrix} + \mathbf{B}\delta \qquad , \qquad (29)$$

with

$$\mathbf{A} = \begin{bmatrix} -\left(\dfrac{c_{\alpha F} + c_{\alpha R}}{Vm}\right) & \left(\dfrac{-c_{\alpha F} l_F + c_{\alpha R} l_R}{V^2 m} - 1\right) \\ \left(\dfrac{-c_{\alpha F} l_F + c_{\alpha R} l_R}{J_z}\right) & -\left(\dfrac{c_{\alpha F} l_F^2 + c_{\alpha R} l_R^2}{V J_z}\right) \end{bmatrix} \qquad (30)$$

and

$$\mathbf{B} = \begin{bmatrix} \dfrac{c_{\alpha F}}{Vm} \\ \dfrac{c_{\alpha F} l_F}{J_z} \end{bmatrix} \qquad , \qquad (31)$$

where ß and $\dot{\psi}$ denote the state variables *side slip angle* and *yaw rate*, respectively. The control variable δ indicates the steering angle. The parameters of the model are described and quantified in Tab. 2.

However, it should be noted that for higher lateral accelerations than 4 m/s^2 or changing velocity the nonlinear bicycle model should be employed. Equations of motion including a simple power train model can for example be found in [9].

Table 2: Vehicle parameters [9]

Symbol	Description	Value	Unit
m	Vehicle mass	1280	[kg]
J_z	Moment of inertia about z_V-axis	2500	[kgm^2]
l_F	Distance of front axle to c.g.	1.203	[m]
l_R	Distance of rear axle to c.g.	1.217	[m]
c_{aF}	Front tire cornering stiffness	100000	[N/rad]
c_{aR}	Rear tire cornering stiffness	100000	[N/rad]

STEERING ANGLE DETERMINATION

For the determination of the steering angle $\delta(t)$ along the planned time-parameterized emergency path $(x_P(t), y_P(t))$ a lateral guidance model is used, as depicted in Fig. 8. Its state variables are the lateral deviation *y* and the angular deviation $\Delta\psi$. The lateral deviation *y* describes the shortest distance between the center of gravity of the vehicle and the path.

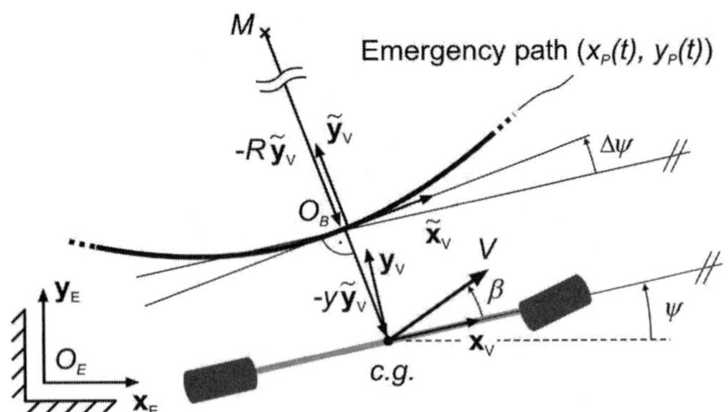

Fig. 8: Guided bicycle model with emergency trajectory

The projection of the velocity V of the vehicle onto the unit vector $\tilde{\mathbf{y}}_V$, pointing towards the instantaneous center of curvature M, describes the lateral deviation rate $\dot{y} = V\sin(\beta + \Delta\psi)$. For small angles the following relation holds for the lateral deviation rate

$$\dot{y} = V(\beta + \Delta\psi) \quad . \tag{32}$$

For small angles, the angular deviation rate is given by

$$\Delta\dot{\psi} = V\kappa - \dot{\psi} \quad , \tag{33}$$

where κ denotes the curvature, which is evaluated by

$$\kappa(t) = \frac{\dot{x}_P \ddot{y}_P - \dot{y}_P \ddot{x}_P}{\left(\sqrt{\dot{x}_P^2 + \dot{y}_P^2}\right)^3} \quad , \tag{34}$$

for the planned time-parameterized emergency path $(x_P(t), y_P(t))$. The coupled equations of the laterally guided bicycle model are

$$\begin{bmatrix} \dot{\beta} \\ \ddot{\psi} \\ \dot{y} \\ \Delta\dot{\psi} \end{bmatrix} = \begin{bmatrix} A_{11} & A_{12} & 0 & 0 \\ A_{21} & A_{22} & 0 & 0 \\ V & 0 & 0 & V \\ 0 & -1 & 0 & 0 \end{bmatrix} \begin{bmatrix} \beta \\ \dot{\psi} \\ y \\ \Delta\psi \end{bmatrix} + \begin{bmatrix} B_1 & 0 \\ B_2 & 0 \\ 0 & 0 \\ 0 & V \end{bmatrix} \begin{bmatrix} \delta \\ \kappa \end{bmatrix} \quad , \tag{35}$$

with A_{ij} and B_i according to (30) and (31), respectively.

This model is embedded into a simple closed-loop structure with a PID-controller, where the lateral deviation *y(t)* is regulated at zero and the curvature $\kappa(t)$ acts as disturbance function, which is prescribed by the planned path. The steering angle $\delta(t)$ is the control variable. The controller parameter are adjusted to avoid oscillatory behaviour of the closed-loop system.

DRIVING CONDITION ESTIMATION

The driving condition estimation can for example be performed based on the characteristic velocity

$$v_{ch}^2(t) := \frac{v_x^2(t)}{1 - \dfrac{\delta(t)\, v_x(t)}{\dot{\psi}(t)\,(l_F + l_R)}} \quad . \tag{36}$$

A suitable method is the so-called *Characteristic Velocity Stability Indicator* CVSI [10]. In this method the longitudinal and the characteristic velocity of the CAS-equipped vehicle are compared. The advantage is that only few data are needed, which are uncomplicated to compute or measure. The corresponding driving conditions to the CVSI values are given in Tab. 3.

Table 3: Interpretation of CVSI values

CVSI	Driving condition
1	Under-steering, stable
2	Neutral-steering, stable
3	Over-steering, stable
4	High-over-steering, indifferent
5	Braking away, unstable

SIMULATION RESULTS

In the following simulations, the path planning is performed in presence of two obstacles. Therefore, the method of differential games cannot be applied and the method of elastic bands is employed. The initial setting is as follows:

The CAS-equipped vehicle drives in the middle of the right lane on a *7* m wide road at a speed of *15* m/s. Then, at time t_0 the CAS detects an emergency situation and initiates an evasion maneuver. At that time a non-moving obstacle appears *67* m ahead. An oncoming vehicle travels at a speed of *25* m/s from an initial distance of *65* m. The performed evasion maneuver is depicted in Fig. 9. Therein, the oncoming vehicle and the non-moving obstacle are represented by their safety circles.

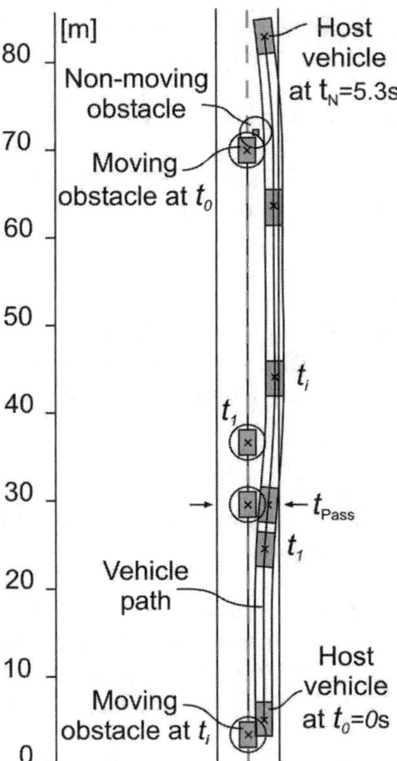

Fig. 9: Simulation result of the evasion maneuver

The parameters that are used in the path planning are summarized in Tab. 4. The forces of the borders of the road and the obstacles were modeled according to (24) and (27), respectively. The computation of the steering angle for the path following was performed by use of a PID-controller. The steering angle, the lateral acceleration as well as the yaw rate, computed based on the linear bicycle model are given in Fig. 10. It can be seen that the lateral acceleration for this maneuver stays below 4 m/s^2. Therefore, the use of the linear bicycle model is sustainable. Furthermore, the CVSI is displayed and indicates that the vehicle moves stably on the planned evasion path.

CONCLUSIONS

An overall setup for CAS was suggested. Especially, it was shown how path planning, path following and driving condition estimation can be embedded in this framework. Subsequently, a method for emergency path planning based on differential games was compared to a method based on elastic bands. Therein, the method of elastic bands was modified for automotive collision avoidance problems. The comparison showed that the latter method seems to be more suitable for automotive path planning. Furthermore, an adequate vehicle model was extended by a guidance model. The CVSI was used for model based driving condition estimation. Finally, sample simulation results for an emergency maneuver employing the described setup were given.

Table 4: Path planning parameters

Symbol	Description	Value	Unit
d_1	Safety diameter of oncoming vehicle	4	[m]
d_2	Safety diameter of non-moving obstacle	3.6	[m]
k^{O_1}	Force scaling factor of oncoming vehicle	8	[-]
k^{O_2}	Force scaling factor of non-moving obstacle	6	[-]
k^{B_l}	Force scaling factor of left border	10	[-]
k^{B_r}	Force scaling factor of right border	$10 \cdot e^{-24.5}$	[-]
k_i	Internal spring stiffness of interval i (Initial value equal for all intervals)	53	[N/m]
$l_{0,i}$	Initial length of internal spring of interval i (equal for all intervals)	0.77	[m]
n	Number of nodes	53	[-]

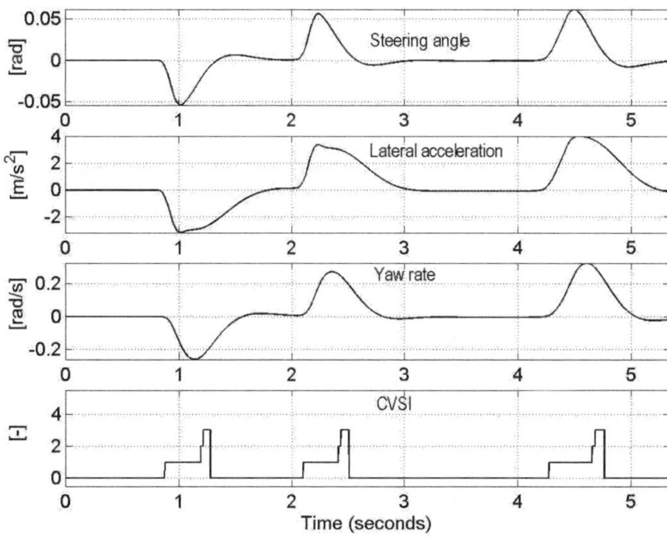

Fig. 10: Steering angle, yaw rate, lateral acceleration and CVSI of the CAS-equipped vehicle following the emergency trajectory based on a linear bicycle model

ACKNOWLEDGEMENTS

Many thanks to the *L-LAB* and the *International Graduate School of Dynamic Intelligent Systems* in Paderborn for supporting this work with facilities and a research scholarship.

REFERENCES

[1] Vukotich, A., Kirchner, A.: *Sensor fusion for driver-assistance-systems*. Elektronik im Kraftfahrzeug, Baden-Baden, Germany, 2001 (in German)

[2] Lachner, R.: *Echtzeitsynthese optimaler Strategien für Differentialspiele mit schneller Dynamik mit Anwendungen bei der Kollisionsvermeidung*. PhD Thesis, University of Clausthal-Zellerfeld, Germany, Papierflieger, 1997

[3] Lachner, R., Breitner, M.H., Pesch, H.J.: *Real Time Computation of Differential Games with Applications to Collision Avoidance*. International Series of Numerical Mathematics, Vol. 124, Birkhäuser, Basel, 1998

[4] Quinlan, S., Khatib, O.: *Elastic Bands: Connecting path planning and control*. Proceedings of the IEEE Conference in Robotics and Automation 93, 1993

[5] Gehring, S.K., Stein, F.J.: *Elastic Bands to Enhance Vehicle Following*. IEEE Intelligent Transportation Systems Conference Proceedings, Oakland (CA), USA, 2003

[6] Hilgert, J., Hirsch, K., Bertram, T., Hiller, M.: *Emergency Path Planning for Autonomous Vehicles Using Elastic Band Theory*. IEEE/ASME Conference on Advanced Intelligent Mechatronics AIM, Kobe, Japan, 2003

[7] Hilgert, J., Bertram, T., Hiller, M.: *Path Planning for Autonomous Driving from a Vehicle Dynamics Point of View*. 4. VDI Mechatroniktagung Innovative Produktentwicklungen, Frankenthal, Germany, 2001 (in German)

[8] Isermann, R.: *Diagnosis Methods for Electronic Controlled Vehicles*. Vehicle System Dynamics 36, No. 2-3, pp. 77-117, 2001

[9] Smith D.E., Starkey, J.M.: *Effects of Model Complexity on the Performance of Automated Vehicle Steering Controllers: Model Development, Validation and Comparison*. Vehicle System Dynamics 24, 1995

[10] Börner, M. Andreani, L., Albertos, P., Isermann, R.: *Detection of Lateral Vehicle Driving Conditions Based on the Characteristic Velocity*. IFAC World Congress 2002, Barcelona, Spain, 2002

2004-01-3039

Improving the Efficiency of Production Level Algorithm Development for an SUV HEV Powertrain

Fazal Syed and John Czubay
Ford Motor Company

ABSTRACT

Recent events in the world have refocused auto manufacturers to design and produce more fuel efficient and environmentally friendly vehicles. One method to improve the fuel efficiency of vehicles is the hybridization of the vehicle's powertrain. Ford Motor Company is developing a hybrid electric powertrain for the Escape SUV. To quickly develop a control system to smoothly manage two propulsion systems as if it were a conventional powertrain is a difficult challenge. To meet that challenge, extensive use of Computer Aided Engineering simulation and analysis is necessary to quickly design, develop and verify control algorithms ready for production. This paper will present the design and development methodology for the production control algorithms to seamlessly move from the simulation environment to the embedded microcontroller.

INTRODUCTION

Automotive companies are under increasing pressure to provide vehicles that improve fuel economy and still provide increasing levels of performance. Environmental responsibility is becoming a factor to many people who wish to purchase a vehicle. People desire a vehicle that uses less fuel, produces lower emissions and still has the same performance attributes of a conventional vehicle. To provide a "no compromise" solution that will provide those desired attributes, Ford Motor Company is developing an SUV fitted with a hybrid electric powertrain. The development and integration of the two propulsion units into a seamlessly functioning powertrain requires significant change in the hardware and an even greater change in the controls required. There are several architectures for integrating multiple propulsion units together into a hybrid powertrain. These architectures are typically referred to as the series, the parallel and the series/parallel configurations. The series/parallel configuration is also known as a "split" hybrid as it provides characteristics of both a series and a parallel configuration. The "split" hybrid is the configuration selected for use in the Escape SUV and is presented in figure 1.

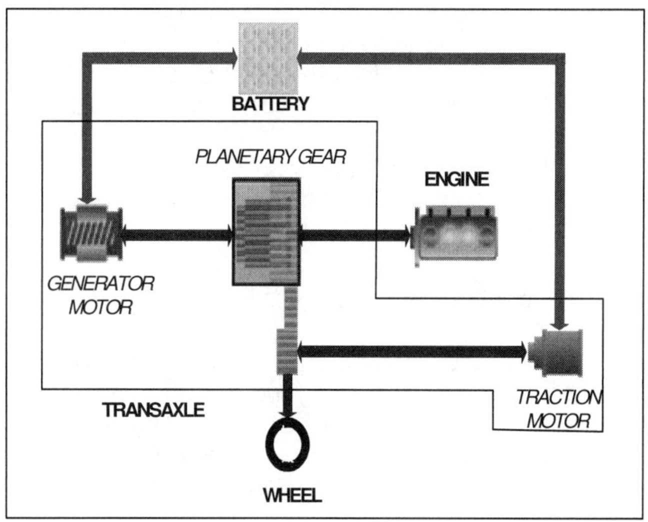

Figure 1: "Split" Hybrid Architecture

This architecture has the spark ignition petrol engine coupled to a planetary gearset, which can directly transmit torque to the wheels with the proper reaction torque of the generator, as in a parallel hybrid configuration. The engine is also coupled to the generator, which can generate electricity for the traction motor, as in a series hybrid configuration. This configuration with two electric machines in this "split" hybrid architecture requires a highly coordinated control system. Newly developed control algorithms are needed to perform the blending of torque from multiple power sources through this series-parallel hybrid configuration.

Along with the traditional engine and transaxle controllers, additional subsystems involved in controlling a split hybrid powertrain are the high voltage battery controller, a regenerative braking system and a higher-level Vehicle System Controller, or VSC, that coordinates those functions. The controller hierarchy is shown in Figure 2.

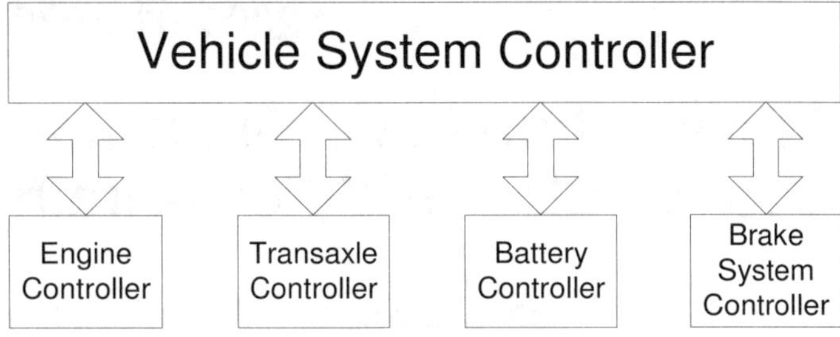

Figure 2 – Hierarchy of Subsystem Controllers

The vehicle system controller (VSC) communicates with each of the subsystems to manage and coordinate the drivetrain functions to satisfy the driver's request and balance the energy flow to and from the multiple torque units. The VSC must balance the energy flow through the planetary gearset to provide the function for the unique hybrid operating modes such as:

- Electric Vehicle (EV)
- Engine Start/Stop
- Regenerative Braking

With the added complexity of several additional controllers and the all new hybrid specific functionality, newer methods for designing and validating the control algorithms for production are necessary to improve the efficiency of the design and development cycle.

DESIGN AND DEVELOPMENT METHODS

The traditional path to the development of production algorithms is typically: a requirement is generated, some limited modeling is performed and a detailed design is created for software implementation.

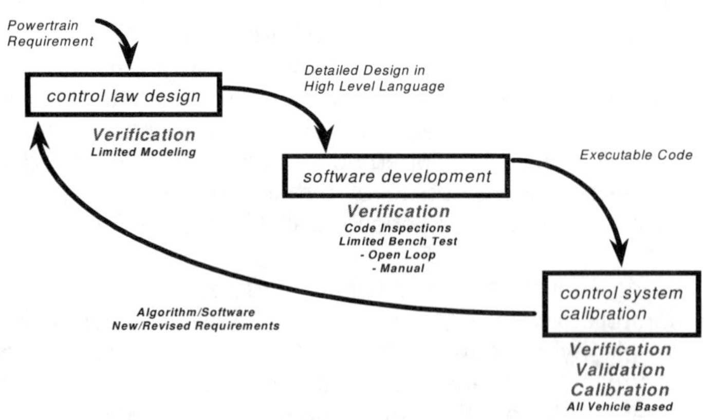

Figure 3: Traditional Algorithm Design Process

The production software is then written to meet those detailed design requirements and the software is bookshelved and released for calibration development. Software bookshelving is a rigorous process that contains many steps including design reviews, code inspections and testing that ensures the software meets certain standards. This traditional process is shown in Figure 3.

This process may be sufficient for the maintenance of legacy code or for the implementation of minor algorithm enhancements. However, this process is not efficient for the development of major new algorithms. The time from when the powertrain requirement is generated to the verification of the executable code in the target microcontroller can be on the order of several weeks. If revisions are desired, such as adding more calibration "knobs", then the entire process may stretch out into months of development. This traditional process is not effective to efficiently develop all new algorithms and the subsequent software implementation for a hybrid powertrain.

A newer process utilizing techniques for Computer Aided Control System Design (CACSD) is applied to facilitate the development and generation of the production software. This process, shown in Figure 4, follows the Systems Engineering V-model in which the requirements are cascaded down the left side of the V to the Algorithm Design phase. When the algorithm design satisfies the requirements, the design is then passed down to the software design phase. After the software design is completed the functional verification process begins, as represented by the right side of the V. This phase is used to ensure the production algorithms are coded properly and that they meet the initial requirements.

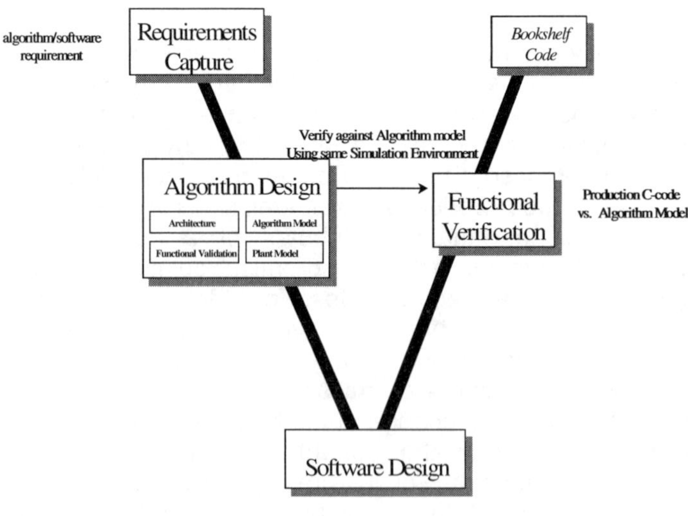

Figure 4: Development Process using CACSD

One major advantage comes from being able to iterate the design in the Algorithm design section using the simulation environment. It is often during this stage that the requirements may be identified as being insufficient and may require further development. In an ideal environment, the requirements would be captured, the algorithms designed and the software developed and released for calibration development. However, in dealing with an all new hybrid technology, the ability to capture all the requirements up front is limited by an individual's knowledge of the system. That knowledge grows over time and the quality of those requirements improves with the improved understanding of the hybrid powertrain's capabilities and limitations. Hardware design tradeoffs are made early in the design process and the control algorithms must be designed with those constraints in mind. As such, the development of the requirements and the algorithms turns out to be an iterative process.

Another advantage of this process comes from performing the simulations against a plant model. This process allows the algorithm design engineer to develop a better working knowledge of the system in a shorter amount of time. The simulation runs also allow the algorithm designer to verify the algorithm's function against the requirements. The control system design occurs using the Matlab®/Simulink®/Stateflow® environment, which are a suite of commercial simulation tools produced by The MathWorks Inc. that facilitate improved design times. Many design iterations may occur in the simulation domain before the software design phase even begins.

Finally, the functional verification process provides the ability to verify the software coded algorithms against the original detailed design. This functional verification occurs using the same simulation model as in the Algorithm Design phase. The same test case scenarios used to verify the modeled algorithms can be reused on the production software. The outputs of the production software can be directly compared against the Algorithm model and differences can be easily identified. If the software design is not satisfactory or bugs are discovered, then the C-code can be easily changed and the simulation rerun. This iteration of the C-code takes place before any of the software is bookshelved, saving a lot of time going through a rather formal and intensive process.

SIMULATION ENVIRONMENT

A vehicle model with the subsystem models of the various hybrid specific systems was created for the development of the Vehicle System Controller (VSC). This vehicle development model as developed in the Matlab®/Simulink®/Stateflow® environment and is shown in Figure 5.

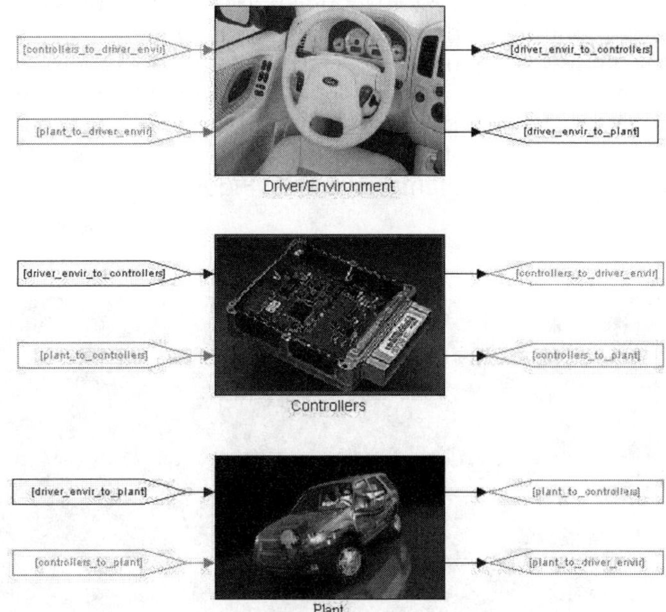

Figure 5: VSC Vehicle Development Model

This model, shown at its highest level, is a complete vehicle model that consists of three major systems, which include:

- Driver/Environment System
- Controllers System
- Plant System

The Driver/Environment System has the typical driver inputs such as, the gear lever position, the accelerator pedal and the brake pedal. These inputs may be controlled manually or through the use of an automated driver. During manual driver operation, the driver's inputs are controlled by the person running the simulation through on-screen GUI controls. This is especially useful for testing the algorithm for driver inputs not typically seen during predefined drive cycles or even just investigating limitations of the algorithms. The automated driver can be configured to follow a wide selection of standard drive cycle traces representing urban, highway or even mountainous terrain. The Environment portion of the model may be configured for such conditions as ambient and cabin temperatures, barometric pressure, grade of the road or even the friction coefficient of the road surface.

The Plant System contains the models for the physical subsystems that make up the traditional vehicle components, as well as, the hybrid powertrain specific components. Some of the models that exist in this system are the brake system, driveline (4x2 or 4x4), planetary gearset, engine, high voltage battery and electric machines. Some of the other characteristics of the vehicle that are also modeled are the drag coefficient, rolling resistance of the tires and the vehicle weight.

The Controllers System contains the models of all the microcontrollers that are contained within the VSC realm as shown in Figure 2. This system represents the controllers for the different functions required on a hybrid vehicle. This includes the actions of the brake controller, the transaxle controller and the engine controller. The Controllers subsystem is shown in Figure 6.

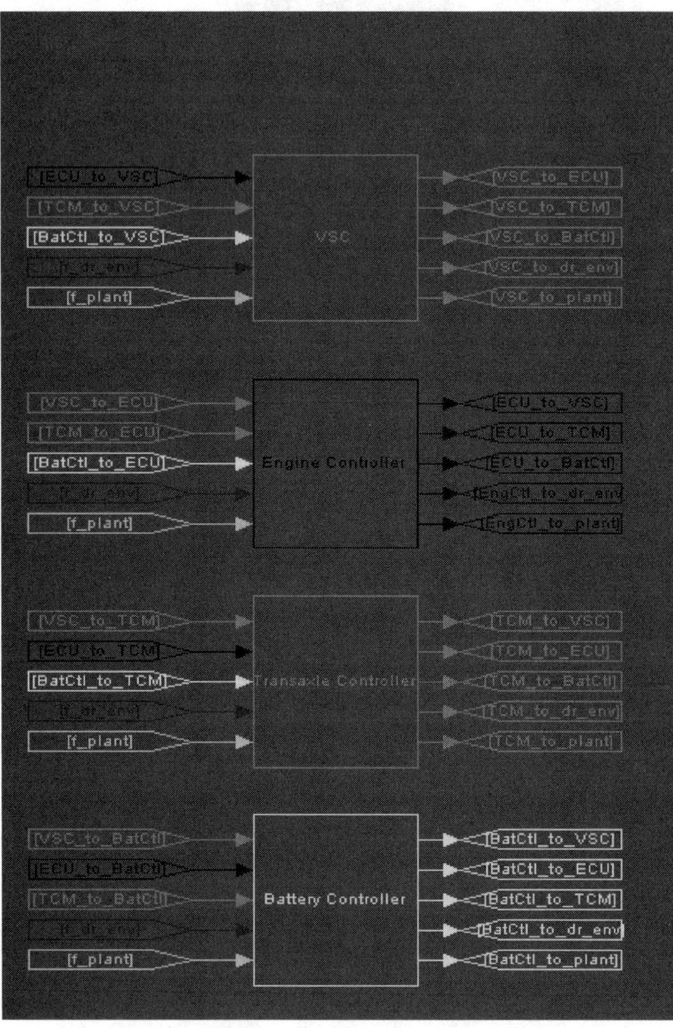

Figure 6: Generic Hybrid Controllers Model

The generic hybrid controller configuration allows easier management of the interfaces between the multiple controllers. This makes it possible to have several individual groups, including suppliers, to jointly specify the interfaces and then independently develop the controller models. The Vehicle System Controller is further decomposed into smaller functional entities called features. These features interface with each other within the VSC in a very similar way the microcontrollers interface with each other at the Controller Subsystem level. This generic method helps to simplify the management of the interfaces within the VSC model.

Simulations using a representative vehicle model are useful for examining the steady-state and the transient behavior of the system using the designed algorithms. With the complexity of the system and the dependence of communications between the multiple microcontrollers, this environment "closes the loop" and provides the feedback necessary for development. The model can be scheduled to run a variety of drive cycles to ensure the algorithms are robust.

The complete system development model also has the benefit of examining the algorithms sensitivity to noise factors. The noise factors may be anything from actual noise being coupled onto an input signal to having variability in one of the characteristics in a subsystem component. The methods to test the Controllers robustness to noise using the actual hardware would be very expensive to create with some custom test equipment developed to inject and measure the noise and system response. It would also be a very time consuming proposition in the setup and execution of the tests. Varying a subsystem characteristic such as variation in engine torque output or changes in the battery resistance with age are very useful methods to understanding the systems sensitivity to these factors. Also, the tolerance in the signal accuracy may be examined under this environment. Finally, system response and stability can be studied by introducing time delays between the Controllers and Plant. All of these factors may be studied within this environment, which not only enhances the person's knowledge of the system but more importantly, enables the robust development of algorithms in a timely manner.

MICROCONTROLLER CONSIDERATIONS

The production software for the hybrid powertrain control algorithms are implemented in a microcontroller system and it is very important to be able to simulate the same production code in a simulation environment. In order to accurately simulate that code in that simulation environment, the models must account for some for the same execution behavior that would be seen in the production embedded controller. Typically, most of the production software for embedded control systems is designed around a selected microcontroller along with on-chip program memory, random access memory (RAM), timers, capture compare inputs/outputs, electrically erasable programmable read only memory (EEPROM), and communication units. Some of the special developments that must be done in the model to incorporate the similar behavior seen in an embedded microcontroller are:

- General Purpose Timers

- Real-time Operating System (RTOS) task rate scheduling
- Digital & Analog Inputs/Outputs

These functions must be incorporated in the simulation environment to provide a value-added vehicle test system where production code can be simulated. Figure 7 shows a microcontroller environment block.

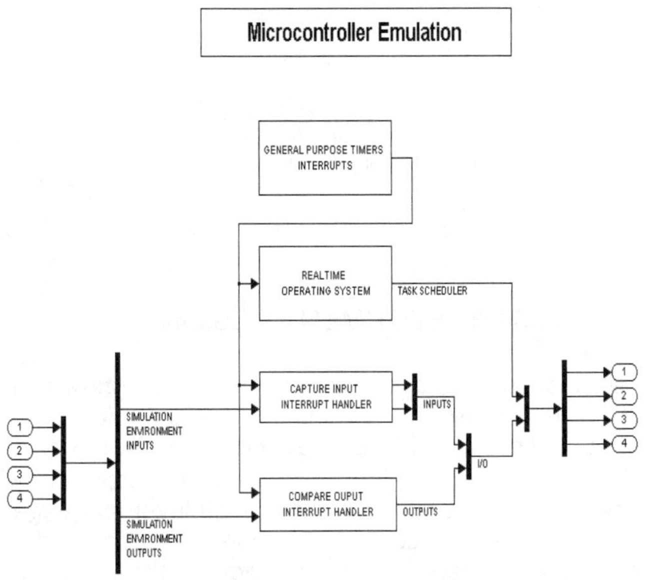

Figure 7. Microcontroller Environment Block

The General Purpose Timers (GPT) in our simulation environment consisted of both a high-resolution clock and a low-resolution clock. The high-resolution clock is used for generating timer interrupts and free running high resolution timer. This free running high-resolution timer can be used in the functions that require high-resolution timers, such as injector pulse width modulation. The low-resolution clock is used for scheduling the real-time operating system (RTOS). Figure 8 shows the block diagram of the General Purpose Timers (GPT).

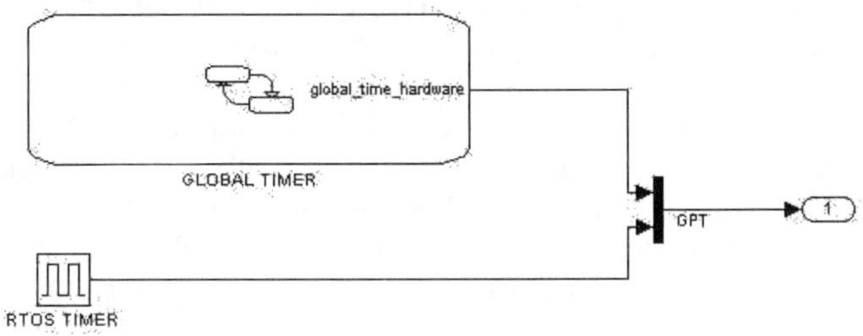

Figure 8. General Purpose Timers Emulation

The Real-Time Operating System (RTOS) task scheduler is the heart of most of the automotive embedded control systems. The Real-Time Operating System calls various tasks in the embedded software at various times based on their priorities. The Real-Time Operating System in our simulation environment is implemented using the low-resolution clock, since embedded RTOS schedulers don't require high-resolution timers. In our particular system, we chose a resolution of 2msec for our clock since it represented the lowest common denominator for our desired execution task rate scheduler and it allowed us flexibility for future studies. Task events are generated at multiple intervals of the rising and falling edge of this clock. These events generated at the multiples of the low-resolution clock calls the respective tasks at their desired task rates. By using a simple counter, tasks may be called at rates of as low as 2ms and as high as several hundred milliseconds. This wide range allows us to study the impact of changing the execution rates of certain algorithms to gage the impact that it may have on functionality. This is critical to ensuring the embedded microcontroller maintains a safe chronometric level while running in the vehicle. Figure 9 shows such an implementation of a generic RTOS interface to the simulation environment.

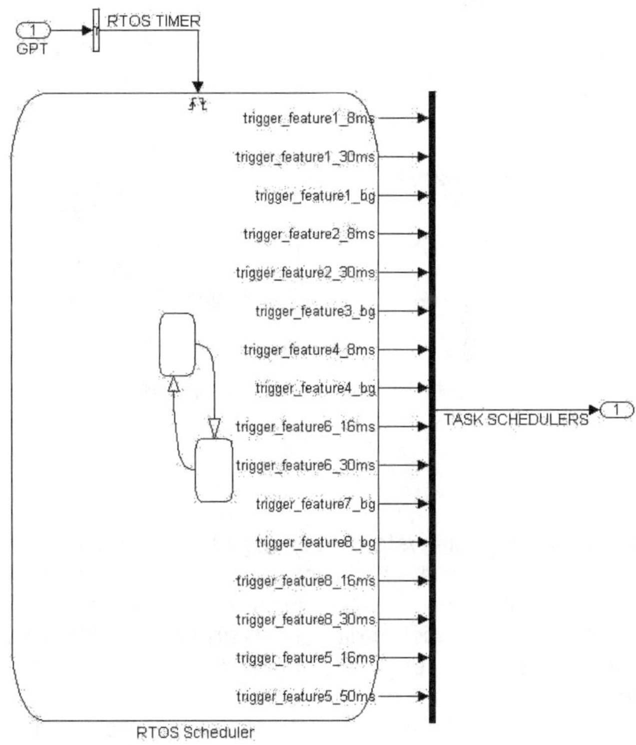

Figure 9: General RTOS Scheduler Model Interface

The features are designed at the architecture portion of the Algorithm Design phase to have the algorithms executed at certain task rates. The portions of the algorithm that are to be executed are placed in the appropriate portions of the RTOS scheduler. The simple counter set up in Stateflow® provides this function and only makes the function call to the feature's task rates at the appropriate time. The implementation of the RTOS scheduler is shown in Figure 10.

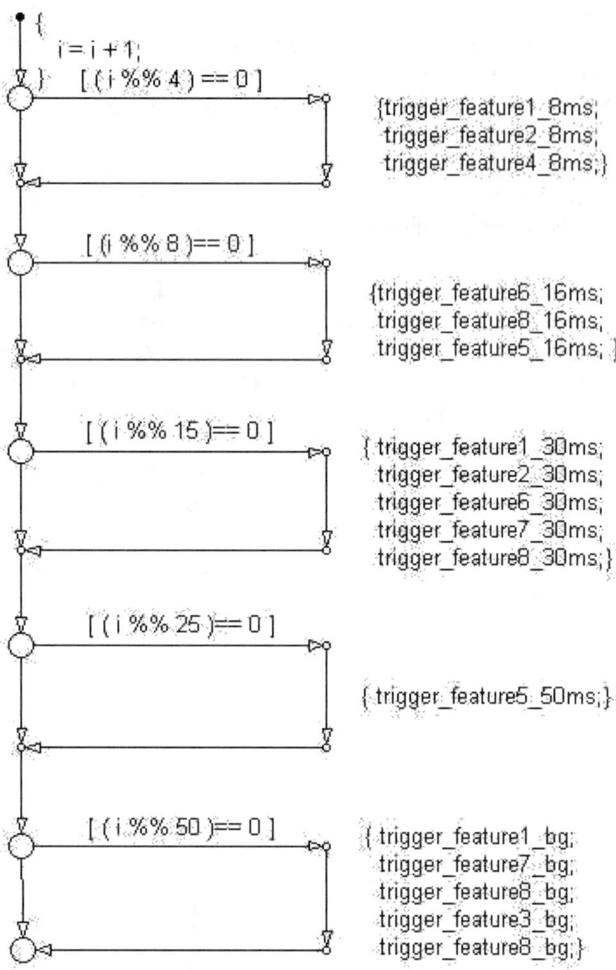

Figure 10: Generic RTOS Scheduler

A microcontroller system consists of various inputs and outputs that must be simulated in the simulation environment to run the production software code. The simple inputs consist of digital and analog signals. These signals, such as engine coolant temperature, airflow, throttle position and etc, are simulated as simply a gain and an offset signal coming from the plant system and driver/environment system. Other inputs like capture inputs, such as crank position sensor, cam position sensor, and PWM inputs, make use of General Purpose Timers to generate inputs for simulation environment. Similarly, simple outputs consist of digital ON/OFF signals. These signals, such as transistor-transistor logic (TTL) switch, are simulated as TRUE/FALSE type signals. Other outputs like compare outputs, such as pulse width modulation (PWM) signals, injector signals, coil signals, and etc, make use of General Purpose Timers (GPT), along with the event triggers, to generate outputs for the simulation environment. Figure 11 shows the basic block diagram for Inputs/Outputs.

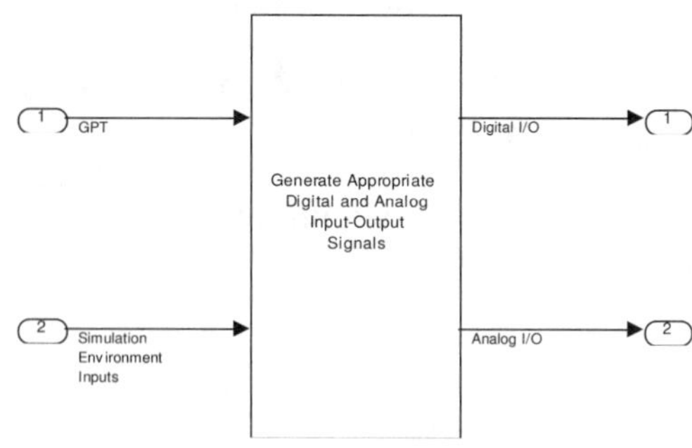

Figure 11: Input/Output Block

ALGORITHM DEVELOPMENT DESIGN

The left side of the systems engineering-V, shown in Figure 3 is where the algorithms for the VSC are developed. The algorithms may be developed using Simulink® blocks, Stateflow® representations, or they may even be programmed using a high-level language such as C. The choice for the representation of the algorithm may depend on several factors. If the design engineer is trying to convey a controls based algorithm to their team, then a Simulink® representation may be selected. If the design engineer is looking to implement a state machine based algorithm, then a Stateflow® representation may be preferred. The modeling environment is flexible enough to enable the design engineer to choose the representation that will allow them to more quickly develop and verify the designed algorithms.

The design of the VSC is done at a functional level in what is referred to as a "feature". A "feature" is composed of a related set of functions for the purpose of one person, the subject matter expert, to design, implement and maintain for production.

The simulation environment allows the algorithm design engineer to have an improved "feel" for how their design interacts within the system. This method of designing in a virtual vehicle removes some of the constraints in dealing with the actual hardware. It avoids the time delays and the expenses in bookshelving the C-code, which includes C-code development, documentation and verification processes. The time delays in the bookshelving process are avoided by compiling C-code into a target application and then testing it on the actual hardware. This leads to an increased understanding of the system as a whole, in a shorter amount of time. Algorithms experts are developed quicker without as much expensive in-vehicle or dyno time.

FEATURE SOFTWARE VERIFICATION

Once the algorithms are designed and tested and the software is written, it must then be tested for functionality. The C-coded implementation of the feature can then replace the model representation in the VSC Development model. The interface to calling the C-code from within Matlab®/Simulink®/Stateflow® may be done through known and published methods of S-function calls [4] from within Simulink® or the in-line function calls from within Stateflow®. This allows the code to be debugged in a closed-loop environment. This is a greatly improved advantage over traditional methods where the C-code was written and compiled onto the target processor and open-loop testing occurred on a software bench by poking input variables and then monitoring the outputs through the use of debuggers. Until autocode generation becomes as widely accepted and trusted as C compilers, the C-code development is going to be an iterative process.

The C-code is tested using the same set of test scenarios as was developed for the model representation. This ensures that the C-code behavior is identical to the model representation. Post processing data scripts can be used to compare the model representation outputs with the C-code outputs and have the differences automatically highlighted. This enables quick verification of the C-coded algorithms and provides for an automatic verification of C-code even when minor changes are implemented.

Once the C-coded algorithms meet the requirements, then this code is officially released for production and made available for application builds to be compiled for the target microcontroller. Because the iterations happens sooner in the design cycle, it avoids the time delays and the expense in bookshelving the C-code, having it compiled and released for a target application and then tested on the actual hardware.

SUPPLEMENTAL MODELING EXAMPLES

The algorithms for the feature may be designed and tested using a simple open-loop model. This type of modeling allows close interaction by being able to invoke specific input values. This helps to determine if the appropriate output values were calculated by the designed algorithm. The inputs may consist of switches, slider bars and values that are swept across the range of the input variables. Calibration functions may also be verified at this level to ensure proper functioning calibration "knobs" are developed. This open-loop approach is extremely useful for testing state machines. While it is a relatively simple task to create a state machine design using Stateflow®, translating that design into production C-code representation is a challenging task since it has to be translated to state variables. By keeping the model simple, inputs can be changed one at a time and the outputs can be directly compared against the Stateflow® model. A generic open-loop feature model is shown in Figure 12.

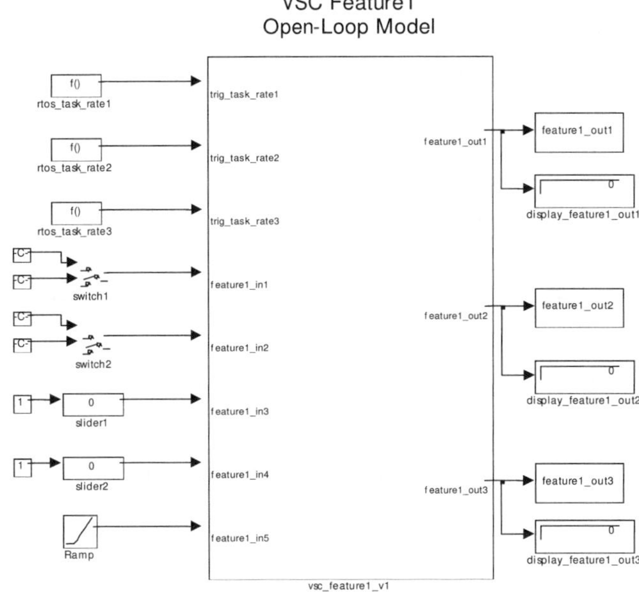

Figure 12: Open-Loop Feature Model - User Inputs

The design engineer is then able to directly interact during the simulation with the designed algorithm. This has the advantage of being able to develop and verify the algorithms at a much lower and focused level where complete control over the feature inputs is easily accomplished through the use of standard Simulink library blocks. It also allows the algorithms to be tested against a wider range of input values that may not be seen with predefined drive cycles.

The feature can also take vehicle data as the inputs to verify against the output values seen in simulation vs. vehicle data. An example of a generic open-loop model with vehicle or dyno data driving the inputs is shown in Figure 13.

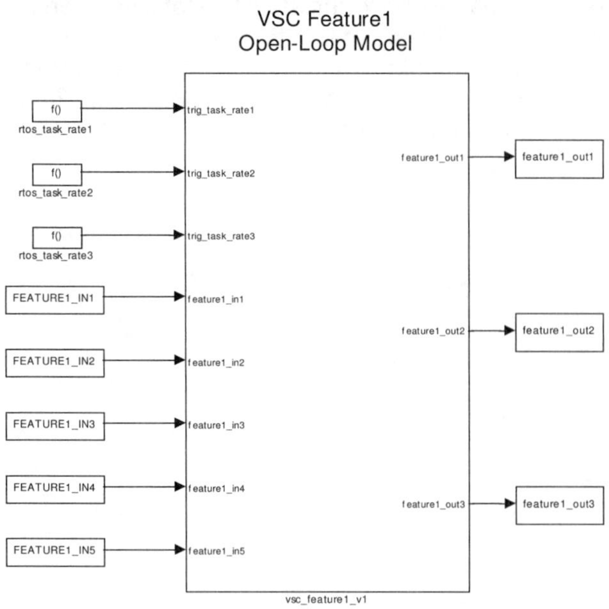

Figure 13: Open-Loop Feature Model - Data Inputs

This ability greatly improves the algorithm debugging times and allows greater understanding of the algorithms. It provides the algorithm design engineer another method to help resolve any design discrepancies that are reported in development. Data that has been captured during a unique test in a vehicle or a powertrain dyno may then be used to recreate the condition exhibited using the simulation environment. These data sets can be used to create unique test case scenarios that are not seen under typical drive conditions, which are then used for all future algorithm functional verification phases.

The ability to use vehicle data in the open-loop simulation also is a great tool for the algorithm design engineer and the calibration engineer. By using the simulation environment, the design engineer can explain the function of the algorithm and also how to calibrate the algorithm to achieve the desired function. Actual vehicle data may be imported into this environment and it provides both engineers an interactive tool to discuss the calibration parameter values that may be chosen and also how acceptable tradeoffs can be made. Since the behavior of a function can typically be calibrated within a wide range from full functionality to being calibrated "off", it becomes very important to be able to import the calibration that was being used during the time the data was collected, directly into the model. A series of scripts and custom C-code functions were created to "pull" the calibration parameter values from a "Cal" file used by the production calibration tools and then import them directly into the model.

CONCLUSION

An efficient algorithm development methodology was presented in the development of all new HEV specific production algorithms. Some of the benefits of this process include:

- Modeled algorithms are tested against requirements using a simulation environment that has a vehicle model.
- Improved algorithm robustness through modeling of identified noise factors.
- Improved software development debugging times and fewer software re-releases due to software "bugs".
- Improved software quality by testing the production C-coded algorithms against the model representation and the requirements.
- Reduced dependence on expensive prototype hardware.

The development methods and the simulation environment presented all decrease the overall time and the total cost of vehicle development.

ACKNOWLEDGMENTS

The following people have contributed to the work discussed in this paper:

- Vincent Fryermouth: Ford Motor Company. Simulation Development.
- Shailesh Kozarekar: Ford Motor Company. Simulation Development.
- Ming Kuang: Ford Motor Company. Plant model development.
- Ryan McGee: Ford Motor Company. Simulation Development.
- Deepa Ramaswamy, Supervisor of HEV Controls development.
- Joe Supina: Ford Motor Company. Simulation Development.
- Chris Teslak: Ford Motor Company. Calibration Script Development.

REFERENCES

1. Walters, J., Husted, H., Rajashekara, K., "Comparative Study of Hybrid Powertrain Strategies", SAE Paper 2001-01-2501.
2. Butts, K., Cook, J., C. Davey, C., Friedman, J., Menter, P., Raman, S., Sivashankar, N., Smith, P.,

Toeppe, S., Automotive "Powertrain Controller Development Using CACSD," Perspectives in Control: New Concepts and Applications, Tariq Samad (ed.), IEEE Press, 2000.

3. Butts, K., Smith, P., Toeppe, S., et al, "CACSD Presentation", Internal Ford Motor Company Communication, Jan 2000.
4. The MathWorks, Inc., 1998. *Simulink: Writing S-Functions,* 3rd edition, Chapter 1. Natick, MA: The MathWorks, Inc.

CONTACT

John Czubay is an HEV Controls System Engineer at Ford Motor Company. He can be reached by email at jczubay@ford.com.

Fazal Syed is an HEV Controls System Engineer at Ford Motor Company. He can be reached by email at fsyed@ford.com.

DEFINITIONS, ACRONYMS, ABBREVIATIONS

CACSD: Computer Aided Control System Design

CAE: Computer Aided Engineering

EEPROM: Electrically Erasable Programmable Read Only Memory

GPT: General Purpose Timer

GUI: Graphical User Interface

HEV: Hybrid Electric Vehicle

PWM: Pulse Width Modulated

RAM: Random Access Memory

RTOS: Real Time Operating System

SUV: Sport Utility Vehicle

TTL: Transitor-Transitor Logic

VSC: Vehicle System Controller

2004-01-0711

Embedded System Development of an Electric Power Assisted Steering System Using MATLAB/SIMULINK/Real-Time Workshop

Auto Lin, Go-Long Tsai and Bo-Chiuan Chen
National Taipei University of Technology
Institute of Vehicle Engineering, Taiwan

ABSTRACT

Electronic Control has been widely used in automotive systems, such as Vehicle Dynamics Control, Anti-Lock Braking Systems, Active Suspension and Steering System control, etc. The rapid prototyping development of an embedded controller for an electronic power assisted steering system (EPAS) will be presented in this paper. A steering model is established in MATLAB/SIMULINK to verify the proposed EPAS in this paper. This model includes the effects of kingpin inclination, caster, camber and lateral offset to calculate the total steering torque. The EPAS control strategy has considered the driver commands and vehicle speed to provide multiple stages of steering torque assistance. TMS320F240 DSP is used as the embedded controller of EPAS. EPAS Control algorithms have been designed using MATLAB/ SIMULINK/Real-Time Workshop and Input/Output of Blocksets of TMS320F240 DSP have been developed in SIMULINK. Owing to the controller design, done by drag-and-drop blocks in SIMULINK, it can avoid the risk of hand-coding error. This process allows automotive engineers to develop EPAS control strategies easily under the GUI environment in SIMULINK. Auto-Code generation techniques are introduced to transform the SIMULINK model into ANSI C code. The machine code is loaded into TMS320F240 DSP after compiling the C code. TMS320F240 DSP would operate as a standalone embedded system for controlling the EPAS. This "Model to Chip" technique can greatly reduce the effort of control strategy development, and achieve the goal of rapid prototyping.

INTRODUCTION

In the past, the Hydraulic Power Assist Steering system (HPAS) has been widely used as the steering auxiliary device in automotive vehicles. Most of its power is provided by the engine. Due to the advantages of the system control strategy and EMS system, it works well when the vehicle is being operated in parking and low speed conditions. While the vehicle is being driven at high speed, it will not be appropriate to provide the assist ratio, and the hydraulic pump is running all the time. These cause engine power consumption and less safety at high speeds. The development of a Hybrid car, fuel cells and electric cars made the EPAS system catch more attention [1]. Vehicles equipped with an EPAS system could not only be improved as to fuel economy, but also provided different assist ratios in different driving situations. The power output from EPAS is adaptable, and depends on the installed steering subsystem. The controller installed on the steering column will capture the signals of steering position, torque and speed, and then determine the optimal assist ratio such as a higher assist ratio at low speed and a lower ratio at high speed. That will significantly improve the drivability and safety [2]. In addition, EPAS can reduce the vehicle weight by getting rid of the power steering pump, hoses, hydraulic fluid, drive belt and pulley compared to the HPAS, which will simplify the engine body configuration and reduce the amount of space needed for engine room. According to researches [3-4], the EPAS can save 2~5% of the fuel consumption. Malsbury[5] concluded that the EPAS will completely replace the traditional HPAS in the future.

Aknan [6] brought up the concept about using the embedded controller TMS320F240 DSP in EPAS. For some reason he didn't apply the concept in a real application. This paper will illustrate the concept and apply rapid prototyping to the embedded controller used in EPAS. The I/O blocksets of TMS320F240 were set up in MATLAB/SIMULINK via the MATLAB/SIMULINK/Real-Time Workshop development software. Then the use of the auto-code generation will transform EPAS SIMULINK model into ANSI-C code.

Because the processes of creating block and simulation system were done by a GUI method, it avoided the risk of trivial processes in artificial coding. Whenever the control strategies are modified, only the upgrade of relative function blocks and parameters is necessary. This "model to chip" method can greatly reduce the development work of control strategy design, and achieve the rapid prototyping goals.

MODEL-BASED PLATFORM

The MATLAB/SIMULINK[7] and STATEFLOW[8] are not only tools for system model design, simulation and analysis, but also are powerful tools for developing a real-time system in combination with auto code generation technology. That makes a computer model easily put into application. The development platform is called "Model-Base environment". From the Model-Based kernel, the development environment can be divided into three parts, as shown in Fig. 1. The main sections in the illustration about the Model-Based environment are: (a) System Level design in Host PC, (b) Real-Time Simulation and (c) Model to Chip.

As to the system level environment, instead of the hand coding method, the visualization function block of SIMULINK or flowchart of STATEFLOW were used, which let the dynamic model be built up and the control strategy applied more efficiently with less time consumption. What's more, it was easy to change the simulation parameters.

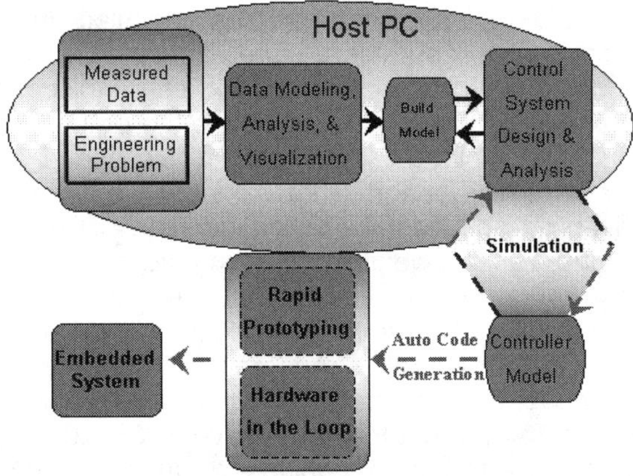

Figure 1: Sketch of Model-Based Development Environment

When the model is built up in the environment of MATLAB/ SIMULINK/STATEFLOW, then the automatic C code generated directly from the model via the Real-Time Workshop complements SIMULINK. It can transfer a model from Real-Time Workshop Embedded Coder and STATEFLOW Coder into ANSI C code. That will load the C code to target after compiling and debugging. The results obtained from control system simulation and performance will be confirmed in the PC environment. By doing so, it will be guarantee that the Model To Chip method is applicable and that Rapid Prototyping or Hardware in the Loop will work well. The development process mentioned above can avoid the risk of trivial processes in artificial coding and make the design of control strategy easier. However, the DSP chip performance and efficiency depend on the code size. The Mathworks Inc. have offered the trend of auto code generation efficiency of Real-Time Workshop [9] (Fig.2). It shows that the Real-Time Workshop Version 4.1 with MATLAB Version 6.1 is almost as efficient as hand coding.

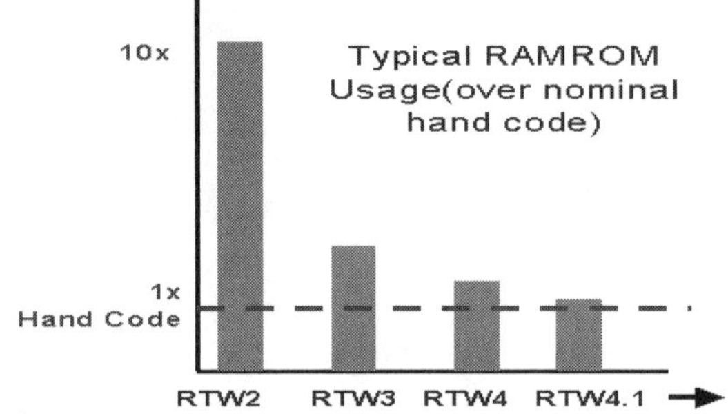

Figure 2: Trend of auto code generation efficiency of RTW diagram

EMBEDDED SYSTEM DESIGN OF TMS320F240

The system level concept was used to develop the embedded system software of TMS320F240. The design of the TMS320F240 input/output block was done in SIMULINK. The software used in the system design is shown in Fig. 3. It included MATLAB, SIMULINK, STATEFLOW, Compiler Toolbox[10], Real-Time Workshop, Real-Time Workshop Embedded Coder, STATEFLOW Coder and Code Composer of Texas Instruments. The hardware requirement includes a TMS320F240 Evaluation Module and an XDS510PP PLUS Emulator.

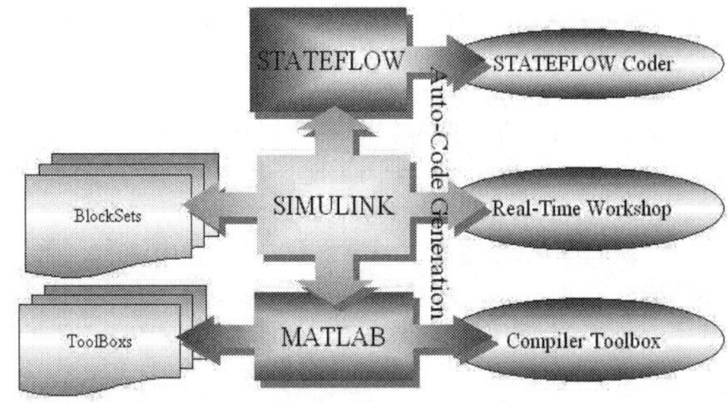

Figure 3: Structure of MATLAB

SPECIFICATION OF TMS320F240 DSP - The TMS320F240 [11] has a performance of 20 MIPS. Almost all instructions are executed in a single cycle of 50 ns. It is manufactured using submicron CMOS technology, with a low power dissipation rating. The related input/output functions are shown in Fig. 4. It consists of the Event Manager (Pulse Width Modulation (PWM), 16-bit general-purpose timer, compare units, capture units, etc.), dual 10-bit analog-to-digital converter (ADC), Serial communication interface (SCI), 28 individually programmable and multiplexed I/O pins, six external interrupts and Watchdog (WD) timer module with real-time interrupt (RTI) etc.

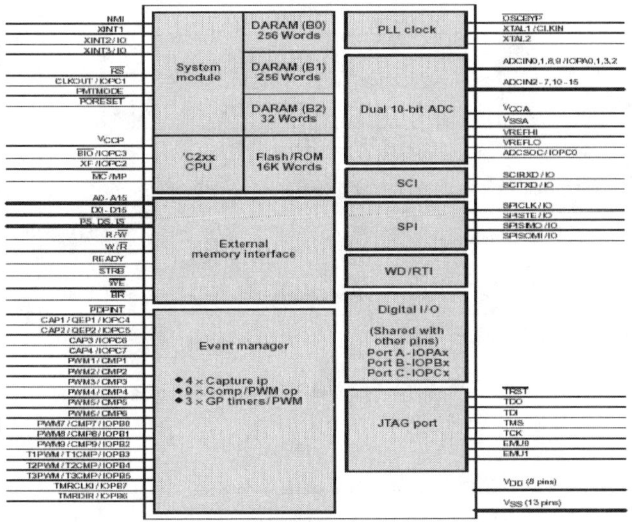

Figure 4: TMS320F240 Block Diagram

BUILDING SIMULINK INTERFACE FILE - MATLAB dose not provide the I/O function library for TMS320F240 yet, so the coding for the interface program is needed to make TMS320F240 active in MATLAB environment. The specific function is build based on the chip and be carried out in MATLAB/SIMULINK.

S-Function - S-function [12] can be used to create the I/O function library whenever the control algorithms are not sufficient or unavailable in the SIMULINK function library. Attention should be paid to the performance and compatibility with the combined effect on S-Function and embedded system. Among all the programming languages, the C language is acceptable and supported by MATALB in developing the embedded system controller . (Table1).

Table1 S-Function support languages

S-Function	Noninlining Support	Inlining Support
M-File	No	Yes
Fortran MEX	No	Yes
Ada	No	Yes
C	Yes	Yes

Target Language Compiler File (TLC) - The target language compiler file [13] can be divided into two parts. The first part, as shown in Fig. 5, is a block that can combine with the S-Function for some specific purposes on the target chip. The other one will take over the communication with the Real-Time Workshop system and control the progress of automatic code in MATLAB, as illustrated in Fig. 6.

```
%selectfile NULL_FILE

%assign CodeFormat = "Embedded-C"

%assign AutoBuildProcedure = 1
%assign TargetType = "RT"
%assign Language   = "C"

%include "codegenentry.tlc"
```

Figure 5: TLC structure for Block

```
%implements "ntutve" "C"

%% Function: Outputs ==========================================================
%%
%function Outputs(block, system) Output

  /* %<Type> Block: %<Name> */
  %%
  /* Multiply input by two */

  %assign rollVars = ["U", "Y"]

  %roll idx = RollRegions, lcv = RollThreshold, block, "Roller", rollVars

    %<LibBlockOutputSignal(0, "", lcv, idx)> = \
    %<LibBlockInputSignal(0, "", lcv, idx)> * 2.0;

  %endroll

%endfunction

%% [EOF] ntutve.tlc
```

Figure 6: TLC structure for system

Template Makefile - To ensure that the program can be correctly executed on the embedded system, each target of the embedded system has its own specific compiler tool. Texas Instruments provides a compiler tool, Code Composer Studio, for TMS320F240. The model was built up by some coding processes in SIMLINK and the auto code generation in MATLAB should automatically link to Code Composer. After that, Code Composer will take over the Compiler and debug work and then throughput the project to the target.

Make Command File - The Make Command file is used to control the performance of Real-Time Workshop. It will also determine the timing to launch the Code Composer.

TMS320F240DSP Blocksets - Using the concept mentions above, TMS320F240 I/O function library could be built in SIMULINK. This I/O block includes the system setting, LED display, ADC, step motor, brush less DC motor (BLDC), General purpose I/O, Interrupt Serve Routine (ISR) and communication of RS232 (Fig. 7).

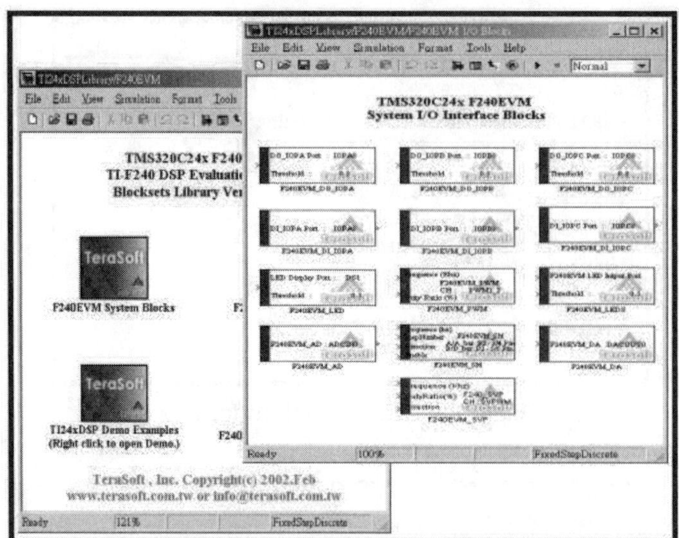

Figure 7: TMS320F240 Blocksets of SIMULINK (http://www.terasoft.com.tw/)

The BLDC block shown in Fig. 8, offering the ISR setting for a Hall sensor, consisted of three input signals for motor actuation and one user-defined parameter. They are signals for motor operation speed, duty ratio and rotation direction, and a parameter for dead band. Then the inverter will turn on the MOSFET at the optimum delay time (Fig. 9).

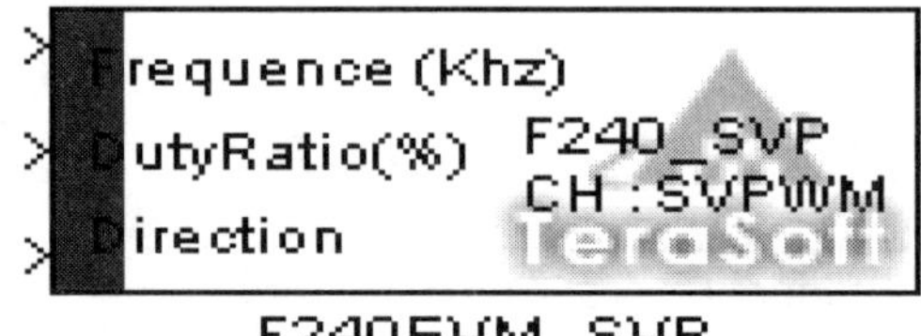

Figure 8: BLDC SIMULINK Block

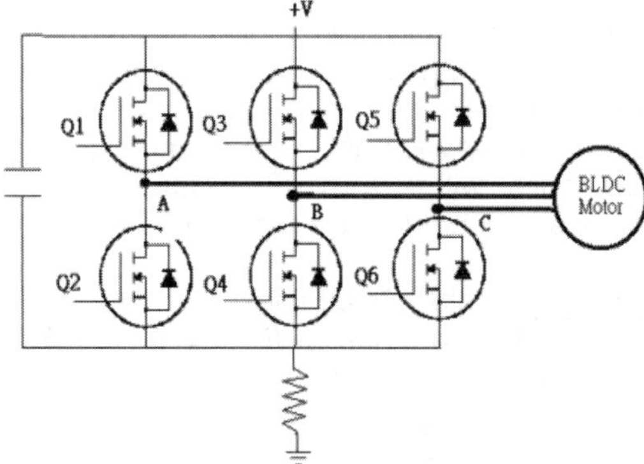

Figure 9: BLDC Three-Phase Inverter

The ADC block provides sixteen channels for an analog-to-digital converter. It can change the output channel in SIMULINK optionally, as shown in Fig.10.

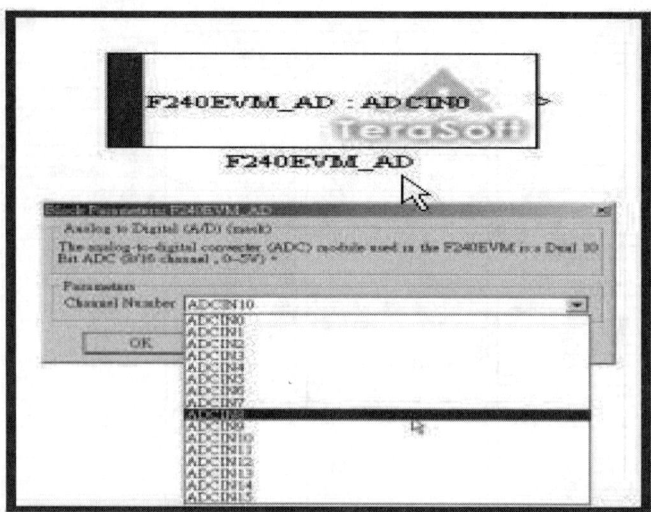

Figure 10: ADC SIMULINK Block

The LED display block showed in Fig. 11, provides eight optional digital LED output channels. The LED channel active or not depend on the option function or the threshold voltage values.

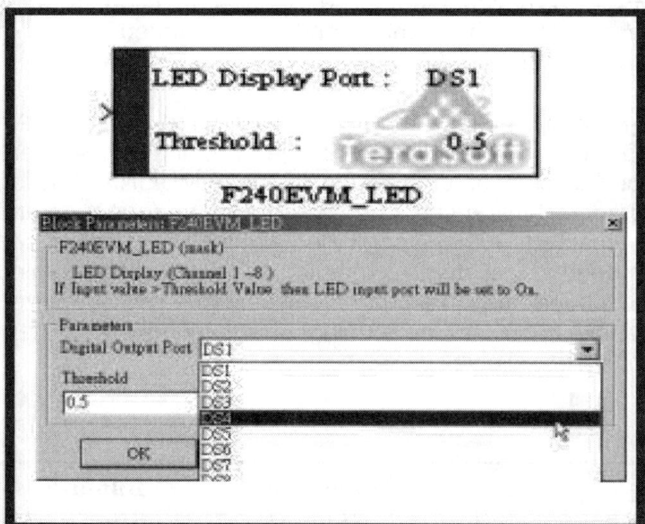

Figure 11: LED Display SIMULINK Block

The others function block of TMS320F240 will not be described in depth in this paper.

REAL-TIME WORKSHOP START-UP PROCEDURE - The TMS320F240 I/O library has been developed in SIMULINK. The EPAS control strategy is constructed using the TMS320F240 I/O library and SIMULINK library. In addition, the EPAS control strategy was completely modeled in SIMULINK by Real-Time Workshop TLC to build the control model. It will transfer the model into "filename.c", "filename.h", "filename.asm" and "filename.obj", etc., and MATLAB will launch the Code Composer. The file is saved by the auto code generation process and sent to Code Composer. It will be executed by the compiler and debugged to produce a "filename.out". Then this file will download to TMS320f240 (Fig. 12, 13).

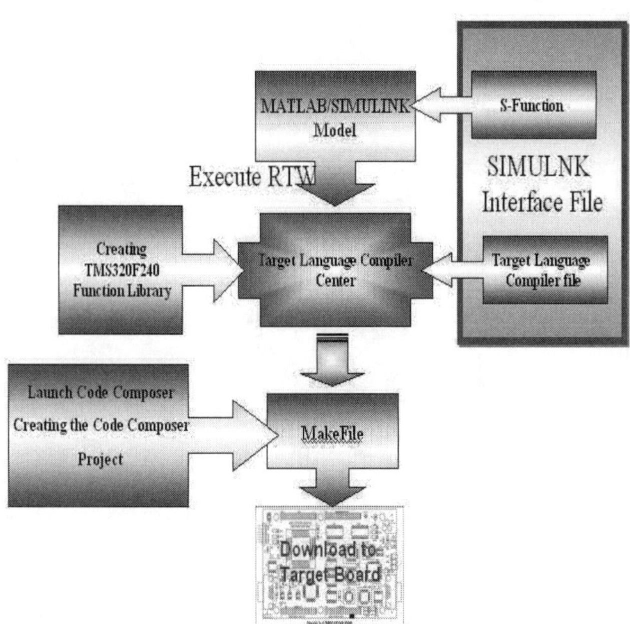

Figure 12: Real-Time Workshop execution process

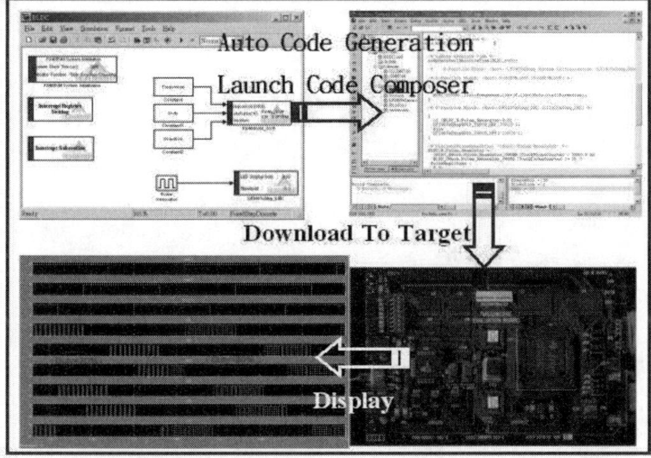

Figure 13: Concept of Auto-Code Generation flowchart

The EPAS control strategy (Fig. 14) model is of input signals which include the steering position, steering torque, current of motor, speed, ignition switch, battery voltage, engine RPM and driver mode etc., while the output signals include Space Vector Pulse Width Modulation (SVPWM) for the control motor. The RS232 communication port will be used for parameter observation and tuning. The functions discussed above are all included in the TMS320f240 function library in SIMULINK. In the future, it will be unnecessary to design the TMS320F240 I/O function again. The program will remain the same for the development of EPAS control strategy in SIMULINK on the same DSP chip.

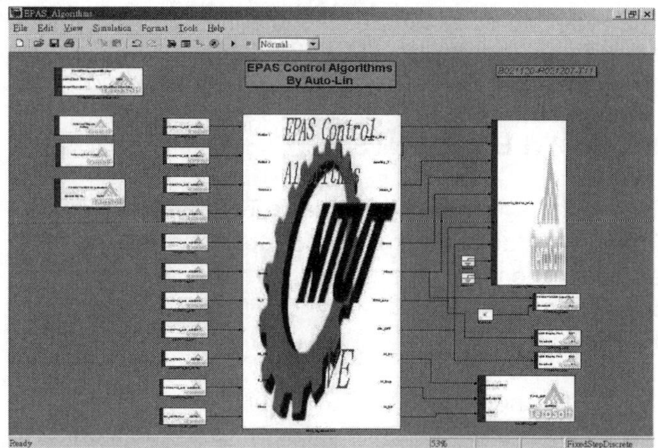

Figure 14: EPAS Control strategy with TMS320F240 Blocksets

Using the model-based platform combined with SIMULINK and STATEFLOW is more efficient, and less time is needed to develop the control strategy for an embedded system. After an initialization scheme work on the DSP chip, performed later for similar control concepts and strategies which have the same input/output configurations, it is easy to apply and no other works are needed. Furthermore, a block diagram is used in SIMULINK instead of hand coding to perform the strategy or embedded I/O function. When the control strategy is modified, the only thing that the user or designer should do is change the parameters or block functions to achieve difference target purposes. The real-time simulation development environment for EPAS (Fig. 15) showed that the real-time simulation was combined with the embedded controller. It can verify the performance, time and cost, and can provide good results.

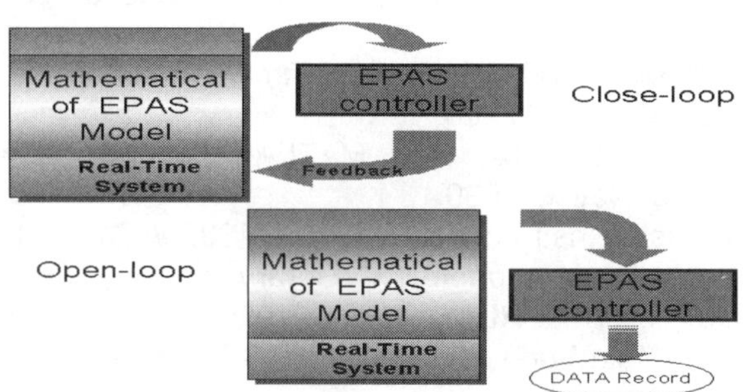

Figure15 Concept of a Real-Time System

CONCLUSION

We were able to develop an embedded system with TMS320F240 using the platform of Model-Based and combined with the SIMULINK and STATEFLOW . This development is more efficient, and less time is needed than the traditional manner of developing the control strategy.

The real-time simulation environment for EPAS with the embedded controller TMS320F240 verified the performance, and reduced development time and cost.

ACKNOWLEDGMENTS

The authors would like to thank TeraSoft Inc. Taiwan (http://www.terasoft.com.tw/) for providing the technical assistance in rapid prototyping.

REFERENCES

1. E. g. Chowanietz, "Automobile electronics in the 1990s Part2: Chassis electronics," Electronics & Communication Engineering Journal, April 1995
2. Werner Harter, Wolfgang Pfeiffer, Peter Dominke, Gerhard Ruck, Peter Blessing, "Future Electrical Steering Systems: Realizations with Safety Requirements," SAE Technical Papers No.2000-01-0822.
3. P. Köpf, "Trends and Alternatives in Power Steering Systems with Particular Emphasis on Energy Consumption," SAE Technical Papers No.945039.
4. Dominke Peter and Ruck Gerhard, "Electric Power Steering – The First Step on the Way to Steer by Wire," SAE Technical Papers No.1999-01-0401.
5. Ronald K. Jurgen, Electronic Steering and Suspension Systems, Society of Automotive Egineers, Inc. 1999 PT-77, pp.43-49.
6. M B Akhan, M. J. Byatt, G.Toqut, I Munro, "ELECTRIC POWER ASSISTED STEERING (EPAS)," DSP Chips in Real Time Measurement and Control (Digest No: 1997/301),IEE Colloquium on , 25 Sep 1998
7. The MathWorks, Inc., Using SIMULINK, Natick: 2000.
8. The MathWorks, Inc., Stateflow User's Guide, Natick: 2000.
9. The MathWorks, Inc., Real-Time Workshop User's Guide, Natick: 2000.
10. The MathWorks, Inc., MATLAB Compiler User's Guide, Natick: 1999.
11. Texas Instruments, " TMS320/L240 DSP Controllers-Peripherals Library and Specific Devices," SPRU161C, June 1999.
12. The MathWorks, Inc., Writing S-Functions, Natick: 2000.
13. The MathWorks, Inc., Target Language Compiler Reference Guide, Natick: 2000.

2004-01-0517

Digital Knock Signal Conditioning using Fast ADC and DSP

Patrick Leteinturier and Mark Nuchimowicz
Infineon Technologies AG

ABSTRACT

The increasing legal requirements for safety, emission reduction, fuel economy and onboard diagnosis systems is pushing the market for more innovative solutions with rapidly increasing complexity. Hence, the embedded systems that will have to control the automobiles have been developed at such an extent that they are now equivalent in scale and complexity to the most sophisticated avionics systems. The former analogue filter design is now replaced by digital signal processing. This paper will demonstrate the key elements to provide a powerful, scalable and configurable solution that offers a migration route to evolve and even revolutionize automotive electronics.

To illustrate this migration toward digital processing the knock function has been developed. A simple RC filter is used as external anti-aliasing. To get the maximum flexibility the signal is very early converted and processed digitally. The micro-controller has been developed using a three-layered solution. The lowest layer "peripheral layer" is having a programmable differential amplifier, a very fast A/D converter which can sample the signal up to 3,5 Mega-sample per second, this layer use a decimation filter to compress the flow of information. The second layer is the "transport layer", it allows moving and preprocessing the data to reduce the load of the main processor. The highest layer is the "application layer", it runs the very sophisticate DSP algorithm in real time to measure the energy of the knock phenomena and to decide the appropriate correction. A very effective interrupt engine supports this architecture for high real time performance. The high data throughput has been enhanced by the optimization of this three-layer architecture. This implementation is providing an improved Knock Detection functionality and enhances the flexibility across a large platform of engines and vehicles.

INTRODUCTION

Knock detection capability is expected in all modern gasoline engine systems. In most cases a companion chip provides today the necessary functionality.

This paper presents new approach, which extends the main micro-controller functionality with knock detection capability without any additional component.

The general knock detection signal processing will be described and the appropriate architecture identified. It is not the objective of this paper to suggest any specific knock detection solution, but to demonstrate the relevance of the architecture to provide a cost effective high performance and high flexibility knock detection platform.

ENGINE KNOCK PHENOMENA

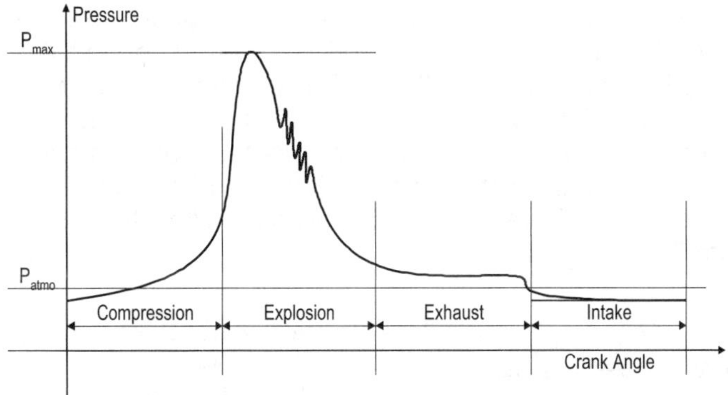

Figure 1: Knock signal

To accomplish the proper combustion, it is necessary to work with high pressure in the combustion chamber. In this condition, high temperatures will be reached in the cylinder. The direct consequence is an abnormal combustion propagation that will quickly damage the chamber. The system must sense and correct this behavior.

Since the knock is a random phenomena due to the dependencies of many parameters (fuel quality, manifold design, air temperature, compression ratio, air density), the system is obliged to observe each combustion cycle on a cylinder basis.

This analysis is assuming knock detection is using a piezoelectric sensor mounted on the engine block. Many mechanical vibrations are recorded. The system has to be able to separate the vibrations caused by abnormal combustion from the normal mechanical vibration of the engine.

STATE OF THE ART

Knock detection is in most cases implemented using a companion chip to the main micro-controller. We can observe three types of companion chips:

- ASIC: Application Specific Integrated Circuit
- ASSP: Application Specific Standard Product
- DSP Standalone: Dedicated DSP implementation

In case of ASIC and ASSP the detection principle is fixed. The user can influence few parameters but not the essential detection principle. Usually some external components are required. In the case of a dedicated DSP standalone the user has some freedom of implementation and configuration but needs lot of additional components whish increase dramatically the cost. In addition very quickly this solution shows some communication bottleneck with the main micro-controller.

The engineers have very quickly recognized the potential to run the knock detection on the main micro-controller. Two major obstacles have been identified, the first is the availability of a micro-controller with enough data throughput and DSP performance, and the second is a cost-effective solution. In order to limit the sampling frequency in the 100 kHz range some first implementations were using active anti-aliasing filters. Using lot of components this filter has been always seen as a compromise with a clear objective to be reduced to the simplest form of the anti-aliasing filter the "RC-Filter".

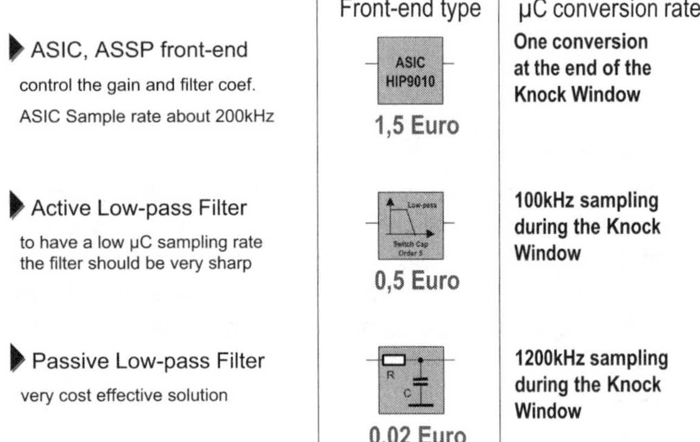

Figure 2: Solution clusters

REQUIREMENT & SYSTEM BENEFITS

FLEXIBILITY

The car manufacturers and the system suppliers are facing more than ever the difficult task to manage the large variety of engines and vehicles. Each engine behave in its specific manner, the more commonly used are 1, 2, 3, 4, 5, 6, 8, 10, 12 cylinder engine. The knock is also depending on the fuel, intake manifold, the air/fuel mixture preparation, the cam diagram, the compression ratio, the presence or not of a turbo-charger, the engine cooling system... In order cover the large platform of engine and vehicle a flexible solution is needed. The previous ASIC or ASSP are covering just a part of the complete family, new development are made every year with the difficulty of design, redesign, qualification. Using specific solution lower the volumes reduce the reliability of a device it is also the reason to push for the integration of the digital knock function into the main-processor.

SELF CALIBRATION

The knock phenomenal has been modeled to cover the large family of engine system. It is the duty of modern electronic to run these algorithms in real time. It remains an important task to calibrate the knock algorithm. The calibration data could be partitioned in different classes. The parameters that can be calibrated by embedded algorithm, these are called "self-calibrated parameters". The parameters that must be calibrated by an operator during the calibration phase, these are called "calibrated parameters". The parameters that must be programmed for each individual system, these are called "trimmed parameters". The last are the parameters the system must learn and adapt during the entire life of this one, these are called "adaptive parameters". A very important part of the cost of an engine management system is coming from the calibration, it is also the duty of modern electronic to optimize the overall cost then to reduce the calibration effort by running more model based algorithm using self-calibrated parameters.

SELF TEST

The on board diagnosis regulation is pushing engineers to test the complete sensor loop, the sensor, the wires, the connector, the signal conditioning. A closed loop control is in most cases recommended. The ASIC and ASSP solutions are very inflexible in this respect. An analysis of the signal spectrum provides a complete diagnosis of the sensor and its connection to the ECU. The solution to run the knock filters on the main processor is very mush appreciated, the vibration of the engine can be completely processed the fundamental and harmonics. It is possible to compare the phase and amplitude at various places in the spectrum, and to correlate this information at different speed and load of the engine.

DATA FUSION

As the information is process on the main micro-controller it is now possible the merge information together. For example the crankshaft signal can be analyzed using DSP algorithm at the same time as the knock in order to correlate the two information. This technique is called data fusion. New gasoline engines could have soon in standard a proportional lambda sensor, the three-information lambda, engine vibration, engine speed can fuse and open the door for an enhancement of misfire detection. This new capability also opens the door to virtual sensing.

KNOCK DETECTION PROCESS

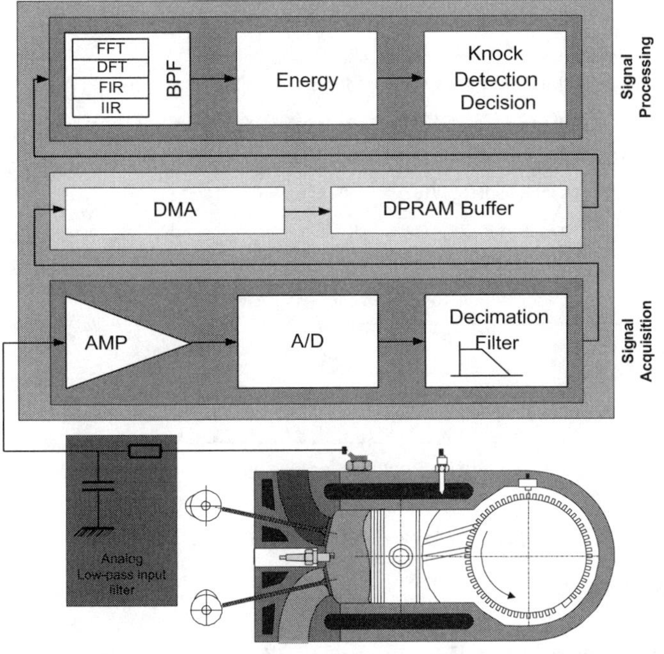

Figure 3: Knock detection process

The new AUDO generation extends the architecture to enable complete knock detection functionality with only simple RC external filter.

Figure 3 shows the essential element necessary for generic knock detection functionality. The detection process is split to two main parts

- Signal acquisition
- Signal processing

SIGNAL ACQUISITION IMPLEMENTATION

Motivation behind the implementation

- Minimum of external components
- Relative small constraint on usable signal bandwidth
- Minimum constraints on Knock Detection implementation details
- Reasonable usage of CPU resources
- Support of synchronic signal processing

Overview

The Signal Acquisition part receives the sensor signal, converts it to digital representation and stores it in memory. This is very rough functional description. By detailed study we can recognize the following components:

- AMP
- Fast A/D
- Three types of AAFs (Anti-Aliasing Filters)
- DMA
- Dual Port RAM (DPRAM)

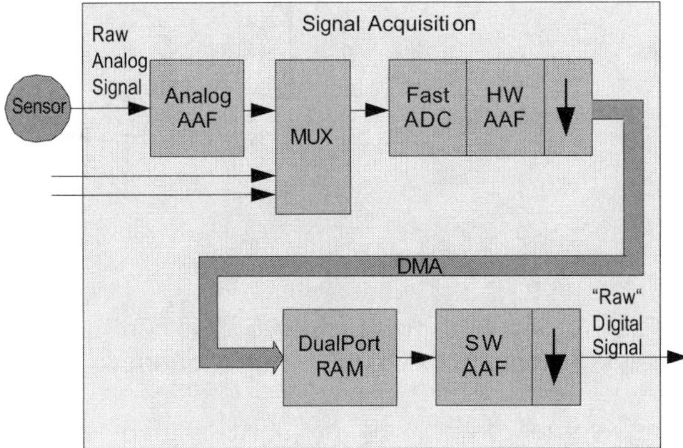

Figure 4: Signal Acquisition

Anti-aliasing filter (AAF) implementation strategy

Figure 4 shows signal acquisition part which includes three types of anti-aliasing filters (low-pass filter).

- Analog AAF: external analog low-pass filter
- HW AAF: hardware digital low-pass filter
- SW AAF: software digital low-pass filter

ANALOG AAF

The desire to use minimal of external components and its impact on the design details is the effect of some of the signal processing constraints which must be fulfilled in the implementation.

Nyquist theorem

A sampling frequency Fs will permit signals of interest to be reconstructed at one-half the sampling frequency. If sampling rate is 100 kHz, for example, then signals below 50 kHz can be reconstructed and analyzed reliable

Usually the sensor signal spectrum can't be predicted so to prevent the aliasing effect into the band of interest (i.e. 0-35 kHz for knock detection), the signal has to be filtered by a low pass filter (anti-aliasing filter AAF) with sufficient damping before being analyzed. This analog filter could be specified i.e. with the following anti-aliasing conditions:

maximal -3dB at 35 kHz
minimal -25db at 50 kHz

Limiting the spectrum to 50 kHz will allow working with sampling frequency of 100 KHz without aliasing effects.

If the evaluation is made in opposite direction then the question is which sampling frequency for a given minimal hardware of a simple RC filter is required.

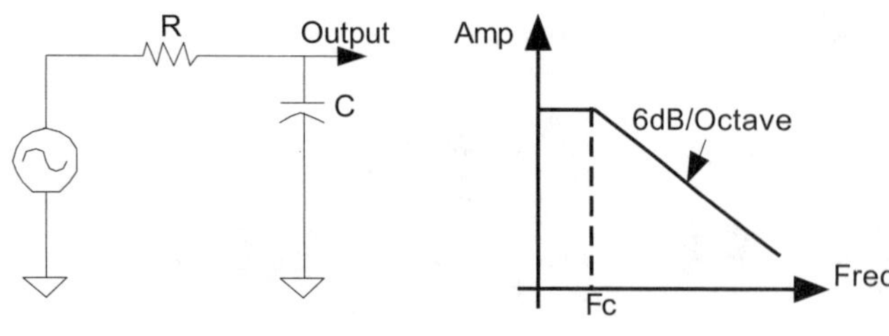

Figure 5: First Order Filter

The First order filter in Figure 5 has 6dB/Octave attenuation relative to the 3 dB corner frequency.

Assume corner frequency of 35KHz than 25 dB attenuation will be achieved after about 4 octaves which means 16 times the corner frequency or 16*35 = 560kHz. To prevent aliasing effect the sampling frequency should be 1.12 MHz. We can say to have the option to work with a simply external filter the A/D converter should be able to work in MHz range!

Implementing the Knock Detection algorithms in software with Fs above the 1MHz will be very inefficient and waste of CPU resources. The same algorithms working with 1/10 of Fs will require 1/10 of resources. It is clear that some additional AAF and sampling reduction (decimation filter) is necessary.

HW AAF

Decimation or data reduction filtering of a source input of data samples is often done in hardware. This is advantageous because of the reduced load of the subsequent signal processing.

Normal digital filtering uses 3 operations, these are delay and multiplication of the samples with certain predefined weights and the summation of the intermediate results to gain final results.

However for the implementation of these structures on silicon the application of a multiplier is too sumptuous in terms of chip area and therefore too expensive. For this reason solutions are needed which only use the delay and the summation operation.

There is one possible solution that uses the summation of equally weighted samples. Such a FIR filter with all N coefficients equal to one is called comb filter. There is efficient recursive form that made the number of additions independent of filter size.

Two comb filters with programmable order and decimation factors have been implemented. Cascading of both filters provide high flexibility of implementing various filter characteristics (see Figure 6).

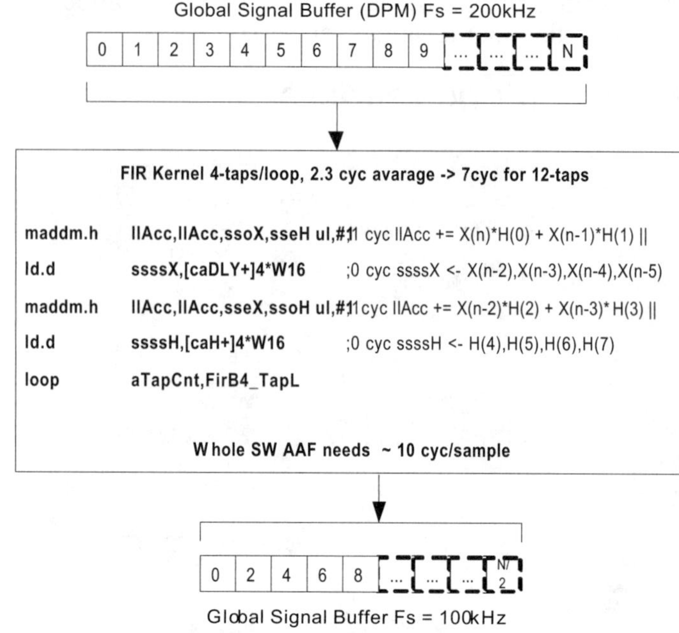

Figure 6: SW AAF implementation

SW AAF

The implemented FIR filter doesn't have its own delay-line but works directly on the Global Signal Buffer which makes the processing more efficient. As only every second sample is required for further processing (down sampling by 2) each second output will be calculated. So effectively the filter is processing the signal in 100 kHz rate.

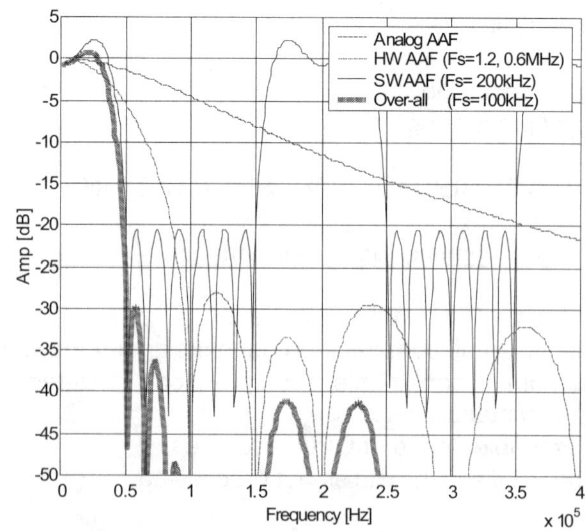

Figure 7: AAF Frequency Responses

When working continuously the filter requires 10*100kHz = 1 Mcyc/sec. Assuming AUDO working with 150 MHz clock frequency -> (1/150) * 100 = ~0.7% of the CPU resources will be used.

AMP and the Fast A/D converter

The AMP and the A/D converter have direct impact on characteristic of the conversion process from the analog domain to the digital domain. AMP differential input allows a better noise reduction

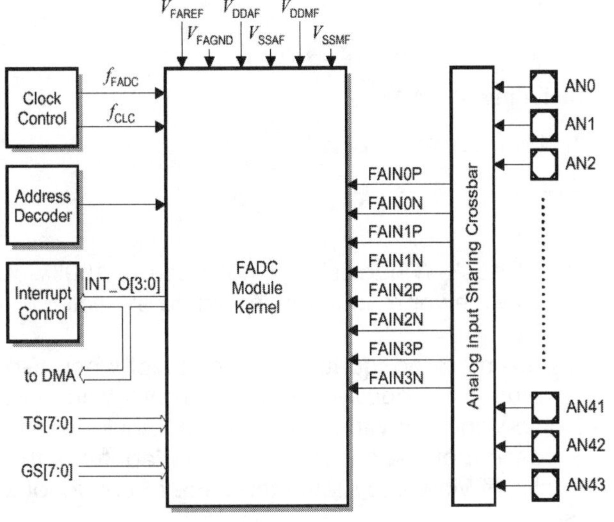

Figure 8: Fast A/D converter (FADC)

The speed of the A/D converter together with the decimation filter either has an influence on the sampling rate or indirectly decides about available frequency range. In theory the available frequency bandwidth is ½ of the sampling rate but in a real application it is dependent on the anti-aliasing filter characteristic. High sampling rate guarantees high frequency bandwidth which in some cases includes valuable information. Usually selecting the correct frequency is a very important factor which can have a crucial impact on the quality of the detector. It should be clear that high sampling rate has a direct impact on the required resources. AUDO has a flexible sampling rate setting which allows selecting the optimal sampling rate. The output of the decimation filter is a stream of digital data which is managed by the DMA unit.

The A/D converter features

- 10 bit resolution
- Fast conversion of min. 280nsec (3.5 Msamples)
- 4 differential inputs channels
- Differential input amplifier with programmable gain of 1, 2, 4, 8 for each channel
- Free running (channel timer) or trigger conversion modes
- Trigger and gain control for external signals
- Built-in channel timers for internal triggering
- Channel timer request periods independently selectable for each channel
- Selectable, programmable anti-aliasing and data reduction filter block

DMA, DPRAM: Zero overhead data transport

Knock detection processing modules (software algorithms) working typically with sampling frequencies in range of 100kHz consume a very big amount of data which must be transported from the A/D converter to the internal data memory.

AUDO will get all the conversion results in no load and no idle. The DMA will transfer the samples into the Dual Ported RAM. An interrupt will be issued at the of the block transfer.

Signal Processing (Knock detection), complete digital domain solution

The main job and the intelligence is included in this part of the detector. All the implementation is made in software so in principal unlimited design flexibility is provided! To some degree is also true in the real implementation. We can say unlimited flexibility but with limited complexity. As in each software implementation there are limited processor resources are available. As real-time performance should be assured some limit on complexity is expected. The blocks included in the diagram presents the expected processing blocks which are used in the dedicated knock detection product. It is very probably that each solution will include energy measurement in selected frequency bands. FFT DFT FIR IIR or any other algorithms will be adequate for this. Based on available products and research it is known that typical DSP algorithms will consume most of the resources. Very powerful AUDO DSP capability allows high complex implementation for the current and future knock detection designs.

Implementation example

To make some estimation of the necessary CPU resources a much known Knock Detection principal will be evaluated [2]

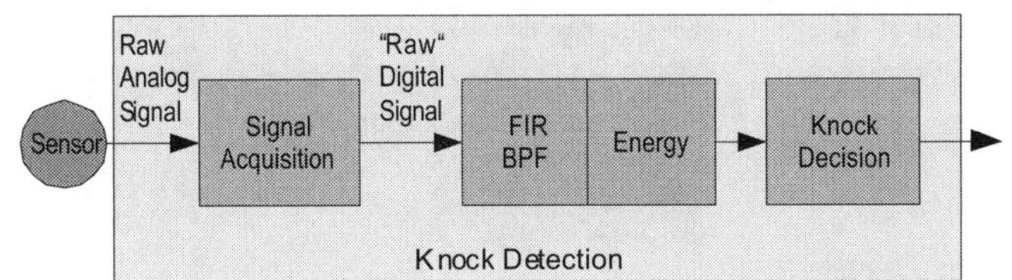

Figure 9: Knock Detection

The sensor signal converted by A/D converted will be processed by band-pass filter with frequency of interest. Finally the signal energy will be calculated and compared to a selected reference value. The filtering and energy evaluation will be synchronic to the knock-window that is managed by the signal acquisition unit and provided to the FIR/Energy unit [3].

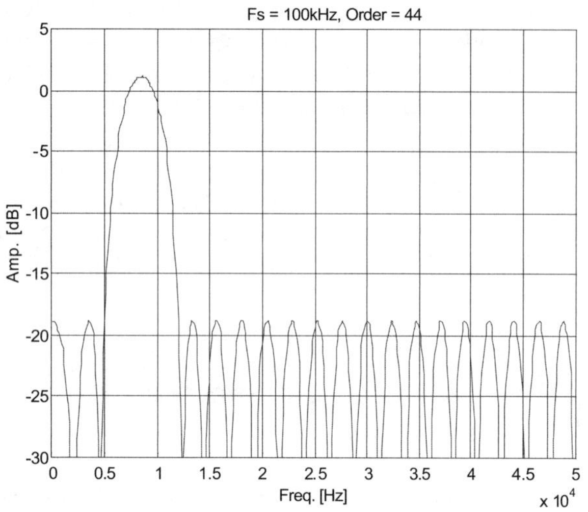

Figure 10: Frequency response of FIR BPF 44-taps

Filtering of the signal should be made synchronically to the "Knock Window". Using FIR filter which works directly on the "Global Signal Buffer" without internal delay-line allows fine synchronization without transient effects (same as SW AAF but using the output of SW AAF) . Figure 10 shows the starting point of the filtering which is using directly first 44 samples (0..43) and providing stable output [5]. The real processing will be not evaluated directly on the received signal but first buffered and then processed.

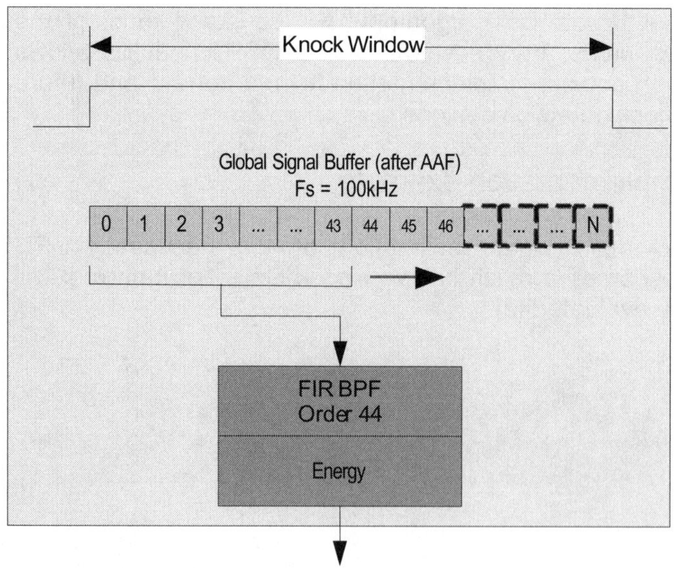

Figure 11: Synchronic Signal Processing

The kernel implementation is very similar to the SW AAF so the expected performance is directly proportional to the evaluation showed in Figure 11. Some additional processing is required for the energy measure but it is small relative to the filter implementation.

Over-all required resources for the filter (FIR, size = 44) including energy measure are 38 cyc/sample. If the processing is continuous then

> Assume: Fs = 100 kHz, Fclk = 150 MHz
>
> 100kHz x 38 cyc = 3.8 Mcyc/sec
>
> 3.8 M/150M x 100 = **2.54%**
>
> Including SW AAF
>
> **2.54% + 0.7% = 3.24%**

Usually the "Knock Windows" will not occupy 100% of the time so even fewer resources should be expected.

The 3.24% are more adequate to the concept when two types of evaluation windows are used Knock-Windows and the Noise-Windows windows in which knock doesn't occurs. In case both windows don't overlap from the resource point of view this match the case of continuous filter processing.

ADDITIONAL IMPLEMENTATION ASPECTS

<u>Knock-Detection one of many tasks</u>

Knock detection is one of many tasks that should be processed in real time and parallel to other tasks. Powerful multitasking support is crucial for properly functioning system

The Following AUDO features can be identified

- Flexible multi-master interrupt system (Interrupt serviced by CPU, PCP or DMA)
- Hardware controlled context switching
- Hardware Interrupt Priority arbitration with 255 priority levels
- very fast interrupt response time < 180 nsec @150 MHz

<u>The relation of efficient algorithms AND detection quality</u>

The knock detection requires DSP algorithms like filtering and FFT calculations to be implemented along with the other algorithms. The DSP algorithms are the most resource consuming, as they perform a lot of calculations on the input data. The strong architectural support for DSP algorithms combined with the creativity of the developer leads to efficient implementation. Such an efficient implementation leads to effective usage of resources. The resources gained by efficient implementation provide the user with the flexibility to extend the complexity of algorithm for better quality of the application. Therefore it can be concluded that the strong architectural support of the processor for DSP algorithms leads to a better quality of knock detection.

The above explanation can be represented pictorially as in Figure 12.

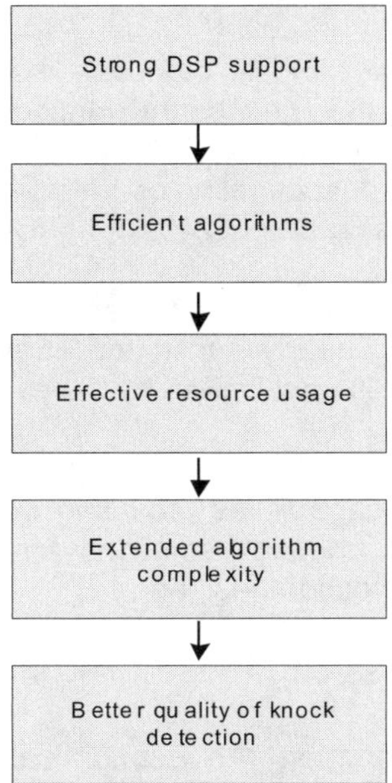

Figure 12: Quality in relationship to the AUDO architecture

Most of DSP algorithms require multiply and accumulate operations to be performed repeatedly. The AUDO architecture has 32 bit hardware MAC which performs a single 32 bit MAC, two 16 bit MAC's and 16-32 mixed MAC in a two, one and one cycle respectively. The options supported by MAC are listed below.

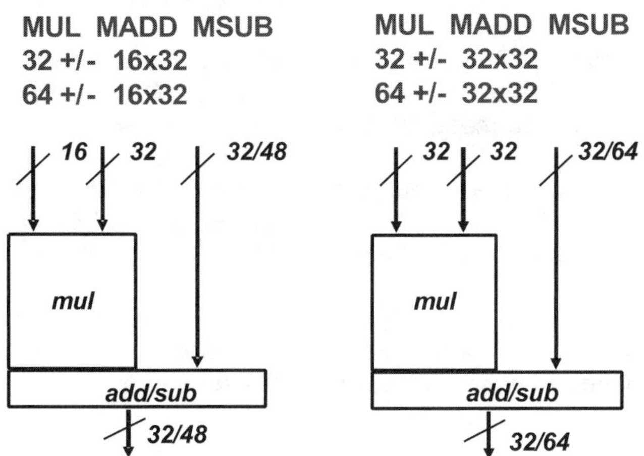

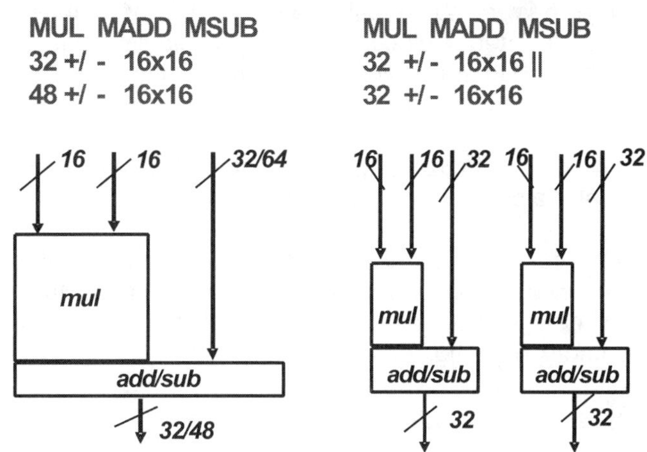

Figure 13: DSP operations

The MAC instruction also supports rounding, saturation and shift operations in the same cycle that increases the numerical accuracy of the calculations without consuming additional cycles. The shift operations are useful while handling Q format data.

The core support load, store and arithmetical calculations on Q format data directly with special instructions.

Most of the DSP algorithms contain group of instructions to be executed repeatedly. The zero overhead loop support of the architecture enables execution of groups of instructions without any additional overhead to test and decrement the loop each time.

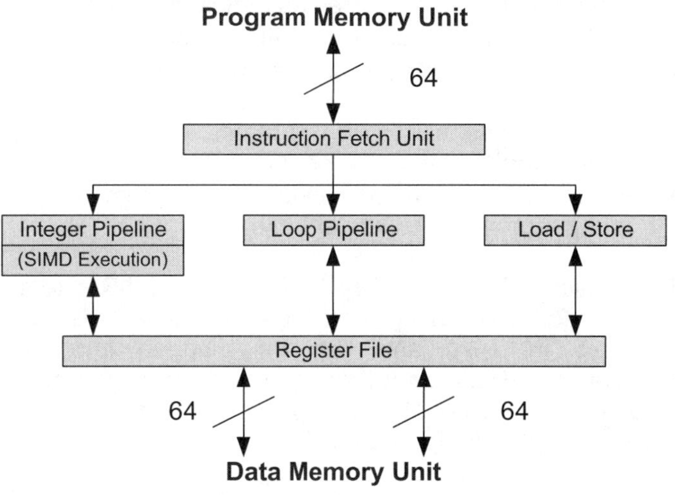

Figure 14: AUDO Pipeline

The circular buffer addressing supported reduces a lot of computations in filter implementation as there is no need to check for the end of delay line buffer each time in the filter loop. The bit reverse addressing enables the developer to compute the FFT without rearrangement of data.

The core has a superscalar architecture with three pipelines: an integer pipeline, load/store pipeline and a zero over head loop pipeline, allowing execution of up to three instructions in parallel.

The following diagram gives a simplified view of superscalar pipelined architecture

Hence we can conclude that the AUDO architecture with its strong DSP support and a super scalar architecture provide designer a platform for implementing high quality knock detection algorithms.

Fast Algorithms implementation

The processor architecture should be complimented with the best implementation of algorithm to make the most efficient use of all its architectural features. Even the best architecture is wasted if the efficient mapping of algorithms is not done. There are two ways in which the fast and efficient implementation of the application can be done on AUDO.

- DSP library – Trilib
- Code generator – TargetLink [6]

Trilib, the DSP library for AUDO contains a collection of ready-to-use DSP functions which are optimally mapped to the AUDO architecture. The salient features of Trilib which help in application development are

- It covers the common DSP algorithms with Source codes.
- Hand-coded and optimized assembly modules.
- C/C++ callable functions on different compilers.
- Efficient implementation should be properly validated for its correct functionality. The assembly implementations in Trilib are tested for bit accuracy against the Matlab and model C codes.
- Proper documentation about the implementation and performance issues of Trilib

The basic building blocks (FFT, FIR and IIR filters) needed for the knock detection routine is already available in Trilib and can be plugged into the application with ease. It reduces the development time by a significant amount and help to reap the full benefits of being quicker to the market.

TargetLink automatically generates the C or AUDO assembly code from the block diagrams used as executable specifications for the application. This method offers the benefits of generating the optimal code for any executable specification and requires minimal testing. The testing of the code generator tool is sufficient. The disadvantage with the TargetLink is that the final generated code may not be as optimal as hand coded assembly.

CONCLUSION

Ever growing embedded processor capabilities allow integration of more and more functionality continuously eliminating external dedicated components and making the system more reliable, flexible and less expensive.

The new embedded processor has been demonstrated with extended capability that allows efficient implementation of knock detection functionality with only simple external RC filter.

A representative knock detection solution has been explored and the necessary functionality has been mapped to the processor architecture. In the evaluated example main functionality of the detection could be implemented using only 3.24% of the CPU resources,

Pure digital domain implementation provides the designer with nearly unlimited flexibility and the complexity that is only limited by the available processor resources.

Powerful DSP capabilities providing efficient algorithms allowing highly complex solutions for the current and future knock detection designs.

REFERENCES

1. E. B. Hogenauer, “An Economical Class of Digital Filters for Decimation and Interpolation.” IEEE Trans. On Acoustic, Speech, and Signal Processing, Vol. ASSP-29, April 1981, pp. 155-162

2. Intersil FN4371.1 November 1998, Data Sheet ,"HIP9011 Engine Knock Signal Processor”

3. 2001-01-1216 - Knock Detection Algorithm and its Implementation in a Full Chip Simulation Environment;
David D. Putti, Pascal Renard, Motorola Sps

4. Application Report- “Engine Knock Detection Using Spectral Analysis Techniques With a TMS320 DSP” Texas Instrument, 1995

5. A.V. Oppenheim and R.W. Schafer, "Discrete-Time Signal Processing" Prentice Hall, Englewood Cliffs, New Jersey 07632, 1989. ISBN 0-13-216292-X

6. 2000-01-0393 High-Performance Code Generation for AUDO, an Automotive µController from Infineon Technologies; Amato Giuseppe

CONTACT

Patrick Leteinturier
Infineon Technologies
Automotive System Definition
Balanstrasse 73
81541 Munich, Germany
Tel.: (49) 89 234 83828
Fax: (49) 89 234 81029
Email: patrick.leteinturier@infineon.com

Mark Nuchimowicz
Infineon Technologies
Automotive Technical Marketing
Balanstrasse 73
81541 Munich, Germany
Tel.: (49) 89 234 82935
Fax: (49) 89 234 81785
Email: mark.nuchimowicz@infineon.com

DEFINITIONS, ACRONYMS, ABBREVIATIONS

DMA: Direct Memory Access
DSP: Digital Signal Processing
FIR : Finite Impulse Response
Fs: Sampling Frequency
AAF: Anti-aliasing filter
SW: Software
HW: Hardware
ASSP: Application Specific Standard Product
ECU: Electronic Control Unit
RC filter: Resistance & Capacitance Filter
A/D: Analogue to Digital Converter
DPRAM: Dual Ported Random Access Memory
ASIC: Application Specific Integrated Circuit

The Requirements of Future In-Vehicle Networks and an Example Implementation

Stephen Channon and Peter Miller
Ricardo Consulting Engineers

ABSTRACT

Electronics is driving 90% of the functional innovation in vehicles which is generating a demand for more (single function) control units to realise the new feature content. Adding such extra ECU's cannot be supported without limit due to packaging space on the vehicle and the significant increase in electrical system complexity. Also, the need for functional integration (between ECU's) is necessary to satisfy key market trends for improved vehicle safety and drive-by-wire capability. This need would not be met by lots of single function ECU's which is leading to a demand for new in-vehicle network architectures. At the same time, the OEM's are looking to define the vehicle "brand image" through advanced software applications which need to be integrated with supplier software within multiple ECU's.

This paper describes the impact on vehicle electrical networks of the multiplying ECU problem (driven by the multiple sensor and vehicle control system technologies) and describes possible system architectures to support the increasing demand for functional integration. An approach to support the evaluation of network architectures shall be illustrated using the development of a prototype network vehicle controller that provides a high performance microprocessor (>500MIPs) and high speed network interfaces.

INTRODUCTION

Technology trends are showing that the demand for more processing power and more electronic control units (ECU's) in the vehicle is growing at a significant rate [Figure 1]. This trend is a consequence of the speed at which new applications are being developed to support the driver where each associated sensor or function is typically demanding a dedicated ECU. The application areas driving this trend are increased safety and infotainment.

SAFETY - New active safety applications are making use of the capabilities of radio frequency, laser and digital video sensors to monitor the local external environment around the vehicle. In order that these sensors work effectively they need to be located around the vehicle perimeter. Many of these locations already have some electronics, however the additional sensors are increasing the complexity of the installation, for example requiring dedicated communications busses in the interior headlining, door mirrors, front and rear bumpers.

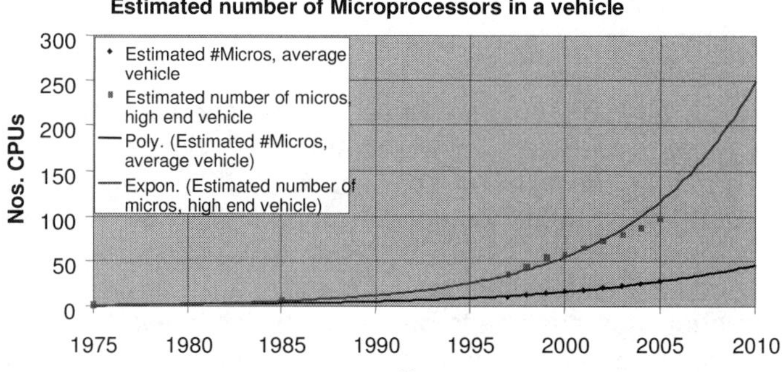

Figure 1 – Projected growth in number of processors/vehicle

INFOTAINMENT - Infotainment is rapidly developing to become a standard installation requirement at vehicle build to include provision for mobile phone and navigation features alongside the CD/DVD. Most of the associated ECU's interconnect using a dedicated communications bus and link into the overall vehicle electrical architecture via a gateway. More advanced feature content is being developed by considering what extra information could be made available by using the positioning and communication systems as sensors to enhance vehicle safety and control.

DRIVE-BY-WIRE – Brake-by-Wire and Steer-by-wire in particular offer significant opportunities for vehicle "branding" as well as environmental (no hydraulic fluid) improvements. They are also enablers for many "integrated safety" applications however the sub-systems are themselves extremely safety critical. Electrical system integration for all these applications is a complex task. New approaches, technologies, tools and processes are needed and the electrical architectures will need to change to meet the challenge.

FUNCTIONAL INTEGRATION - Enhanced safety and additional features can be provided by combining the functionality of the individual sensors. This functional integration needs significant processing power and there are several options as to how and where this could be provided. Further functional integration with the vehicle dynamic control systems offer future applications such as autonomous collision avoidance.

IMPACT FOR ELECTRICAL ARCHITECTURES

Vehicle electrical architectures will naturally evolve from the existing systems mainly due to the number of legacy control systems and the need to manage risk. New Drive-by-wire systems can replace existing vehicle dynamics control sub-systems on a functional basis, provided that the sub-system safety requirements are met, similar to the way that today's ABS/ESP controller meets the vehicle dynamics safety case.

DEMAND FOR NEW BUS PROTOCOLS

Functional integration requiring interaction between the sub-systems is driving the need for new network requirements:

- Interaction between Drive-by-wire sub-systems will require a deterministic communications protocol to replace the existing high speed CAN bus and there are a number being developed [1] that include Flexray, TTP/C and TTCAN. To ensure the most cost effective approach for the whole network the challenge shall be to determine which network nodes need to have a deterministic communications bus connection, as the new protocols will initially have an associated cost premium.
- Integrated safety applications requiring detailed information from the wide range of new sensor systems will need much higher communications bandwidths than provided by existing bus protocols. The functional partitioning of the sensors and safety applications is thus crucial to be able to fit in with the existing bus structure. For example, it would be a radical departure to suggest that the external monitoring sensors link into the (higher capacity) MOST bus protocol that is typically used for the Infotainment features, given the respective locations of the control units and the need to translate information through a gateway to access either the Body control bus for driver warning or the vehicle dynamics control bus for autonomous vehicle control. Safety considerations may also rule out the use of MOST, even though it's speed is attractive.

FUTURE CONTROL UNIT NEEDS

A key requirement for new architectures is to ensure that they are cost effective while at the same time meeting both current and future needs within the vehicle lifetime. As well as providing the right network topology and communications busses, the control units technology will need to provide significantly enhanced processing power to support the range of new control algorithms. Design of a more capable electronic control unit (ECU) will also need to consider

- Hardware partitioning between application and safety checking microcontrollers and circuits and the protection of interfaces
- Real Time Operating Systems for scheduling and management of complex tasks and data memory
- Software partitioning between the application level code and the low level driver software and programming structures to enable integration of both supplier and OEM control applications
- Safety strategy for hardware fault tolerance and how redundancy can be built in
- Which network links are needed and thus which communications busses, so as to access the appropriate control functions.

Such considerations will already have been made for existing control systems. As the new requirements of the advanced drive-by-wire and integrated safety are captured, so a value analysis will be required to assess whether to introduce a new ECU for the required function or to integrate the function into an existing controller with expanded capability.

NETWORK CONFIGURATIONS

In particular, value analysis is required when looking at the higher level vehicle control systems that require a combination of and interaction between existing sub-system controllers. Should a combined vehicle control function (e.g a command to brake and steer at the same time) be integrated between existing ECU's (a distributed approach) or should a separate controller (a centralized approach, which may be a modified existing sub-system controller) be provided purely to implement the higher level functionality? Combination of integrated safety and drive by-wire for collision avoidance is a good example of a representative feature set.

Consider the case of integrating a new function onto an existing controller, an approach towards centralized network control. While the concept may be quite straightforward, the implementation will be significantly affected by the impact on overall system safety and the need to avoid single points of failure. Equally the system and ECU need to be designed for scalability such that there can be a graceful degradation in performance. It will be possible to design an ECU to meet such criteria, however the controller will be large, dedicated and may lack flexibility to cope with future system expansion.

In comparison, an approach towards distributed network control shifts the emphasis for vehicle system safety from a single sub-system/centralized controller to a network concept. The network will need to enable the synchronization, fault tolerance, redundancy and checking processes that are necessary and for this case are managed and operated between a number of nodes to provide the system scalability.

The core requirements for a controller to satisfy either a centralized or distributed network approach are very similar:

- More processing power
- More memory capability
- Multiple communications protocols (some of these might be internal for the centralized approach)
- Operating systems and software partitioning

Yet the approach to meet the vehicle safety case can differ according to which network topology is chosen. The safety requirements will demand that there is a robust level of checking between microcontrollers, whether a single centralized ECU comprises multiple microprocessors or whether the processing and checking is distributed between processors in a number of network nodes. The diagrams below indicate some techniques to increase the level of safety in ECU systems:

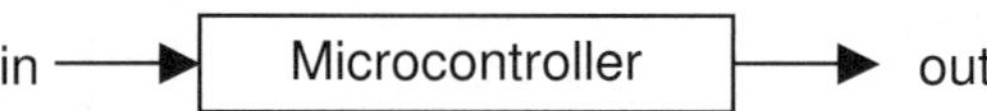

Figure 2: No fault tolerance

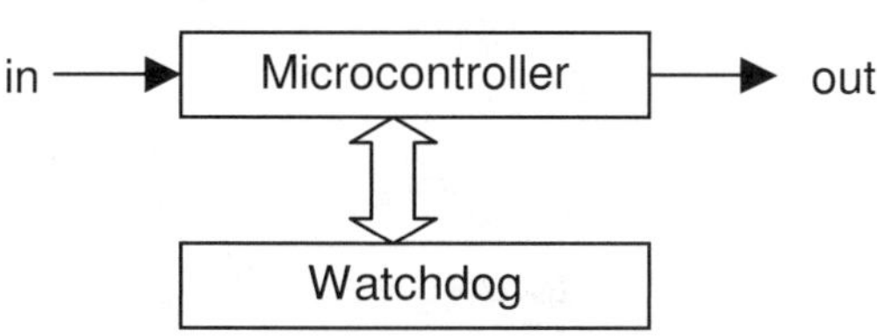

Figure 3: Watchdog, attempts to fail silent

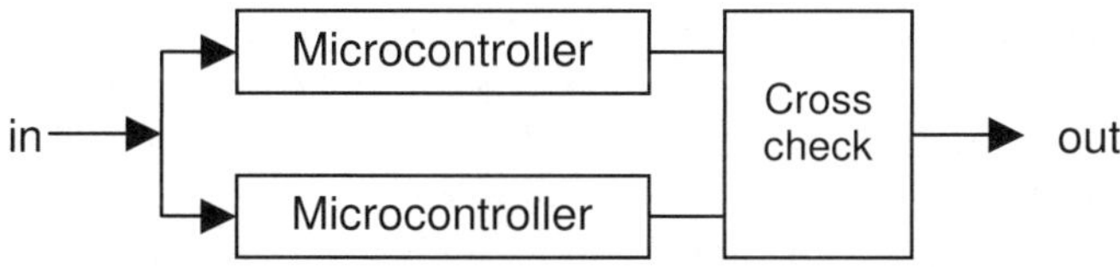

Figure 4: Duplex – Fail Silent

A simple implementation of the triplex system as shown in Figure 5 does not solve the problem of faults in the input (in), the voter or the output (out), where the system configuration is not protected against a single fault in either the input or the output. A more comprehensive system uses multiple sensors/actuators and a distributed voting system to avoid such single point failures, as shown in Figure 6. In this case the individual control units use a separate and redundant high speed communications network over which to share data for the distributed voting protocol. Basic system functionality is still provided by the individual control units while the system protection against faults will need redundant network links from multiple control units to the actuators and the addition of redundant power sources etc. [2]. It should be noted that distributed voting implies a synchronous system, with the high speed communication network also having to be used to provide time synchronisation.

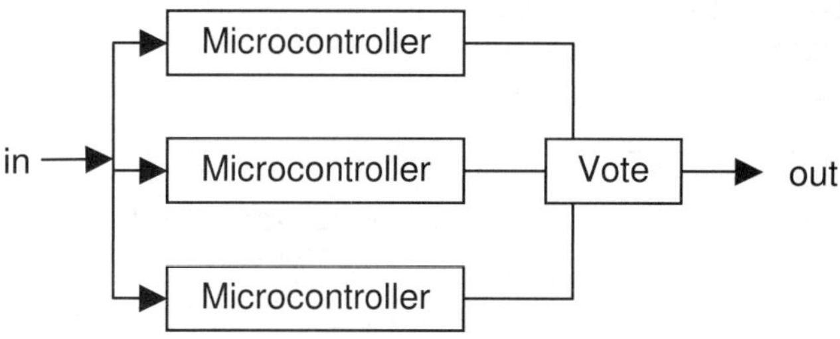

Figure 5: Triplex – fail operational on a single fault

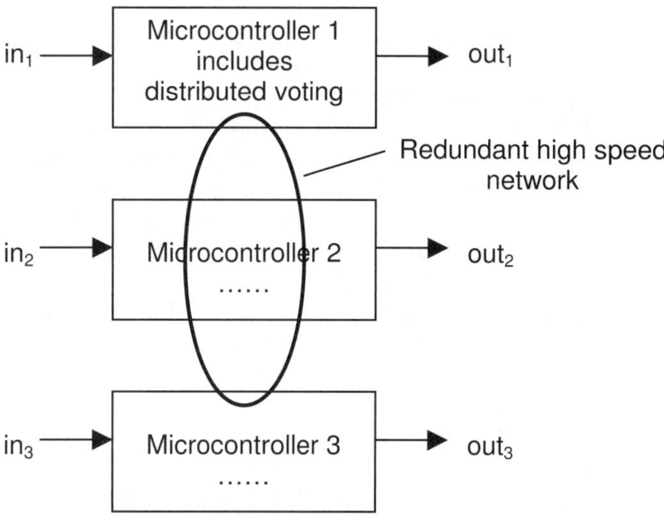

Figure 6: Distributed voting via a redundant network

In redundant systems, common mode failures occur when a single failure affects more than one module at the same time [3]. Design mistakes (in the specification, hardware or software) are potentially the worst type of common mode failures.

In a distributed network, the voting and time synchronisation need to be implemented over high speed communication busses between the network nodes. In a centralized network, the data sharing between the processors can be implemented using different hardware solutions, such as shared memory or dual port RAM instead of the (serial) bus communications. Therefore the additional ECU requirements for a centralized controller design could be said to be a specific case of an ECU that meets the distributed network requirements i.e. a design for a distributed system would work in a centralized system, but the converse is not true.

EXACT AND INEXACT VOTING

In a distributed system, each microcontroller in a single node has to reach the same decision as all the other nodes, using only data available to it via the network (Figures 6). This approach avoids a separate "voter" which would become a single point of failure (Figure 5).

Exact voting can be used for example on digital inputs (just 0/1), or data that is the result of calculations done on previously voted data. Inexact voting is used for analog inputs, etc, which may not be exactly identical. Table 1 below illustrates the results that a distributed voting system would need to achieve.

Case	In 1	In 2	In 3	Out 1,2,3	
				Exact Vote	Inexact Vote
1	1	1	1	1	1
2	0	1	1	1	1
3	0	1	2	Error	1
4	0	1	200	Error	0.5
5	0	100	200	Error	Error

Table 1: Examples of Exact and Inexact Voting results

Case 1 shows the simple voting case when each input is identical. For case 2 when one of the inputs is different, the vote can still be determined on a straightforward majority basis. However in case 3 when all three inputs are different, an exact vote will return an error while an inexact vote could still return a result agreed on a consensus basis. In case 4, one input value is significantly different to the other two (different) inputs, so the exact vote will return an error while an agreed result could similarly be returned for an inexact vote on a consensus basis. However in case 5, no result can be returned from either exact or inexact voting as each of the three input values are significantly different to the other two such that no output value can be agreed.

Ricardo used this approach to voting in the distributed example implementation, where the inexact voting is used to achieve the time synchronisation.

EXAMPLE IMPLEMENTATION

Ricardo have developed an advanced Network Vehicle Controller (NVC) [4] and have used three of these units in a distributed network configuration to demonstrate the concepts of

- Time synchronisation between network nodes and
- Distributed voting algorithm implemented in software

over high speed communication links. The concepts implemented as part of the development of the network controller are not intended to represent the architecture for every vehicle node, rather to suggest an approach to satisfy the safety requirements of future vehicle integrated dynamic control between relatively fewer high power nodes. The diagram in figure 7 shows the high level topology of the network, where an NVC has been used for each node and the indicated functions represent the potential ECU's which might contain the future applications and algorithms.

NETWORK PERFORMANCE

So as to assess the needs for the synchronisation and voting algorithms in the network, two key performance criteria are required in a prototype distributed network node:

- Higher processing power
- High speed inter-processor communications.

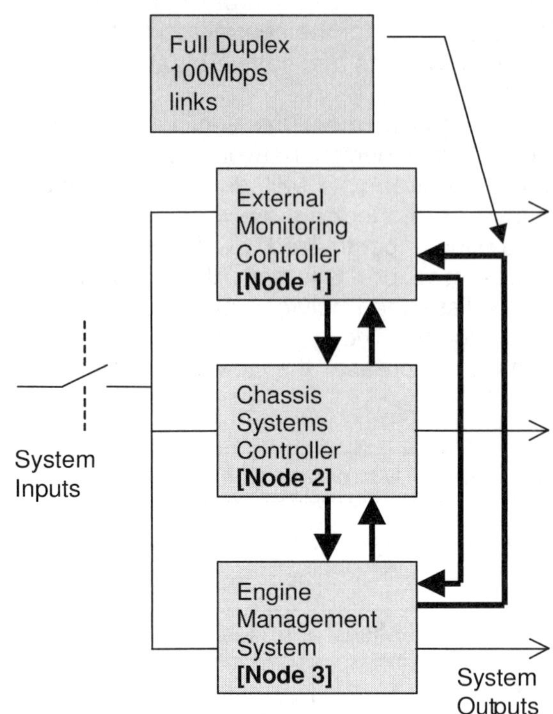

Figure 7: High level distributed network topology used in example implementation

ECU Processor performance

A high performance processor is required to provide the raw computing performance and also to manage the overhead associated with data handling and data memory. Existing state-of-the-art microcontroller performance is typically found in powertrain ECU's, one of today's most widely used devices being based on the Motorola Power PC Oak family. The NVC uses a much more powerful processor from the Power PC family. Table 2 compares the typical processing power performance (based on manufacturers data of performance in MIPs) of the NVC prototype to a typical powertrain ECU today:

Description	NVC	Powertrain ECU
Microcontroller performance	500MIPs	50 MIPs
Average time per instruction	2nsec	20nsec

Table 2: Comparison of microcontroller performance

It should be noted that three NVC units provide the equivalent processing power to the 20+ ECU's found in a typical vehicle today. Figure 8 illustrates the trend toward the demand for increased processing power in vehicles.

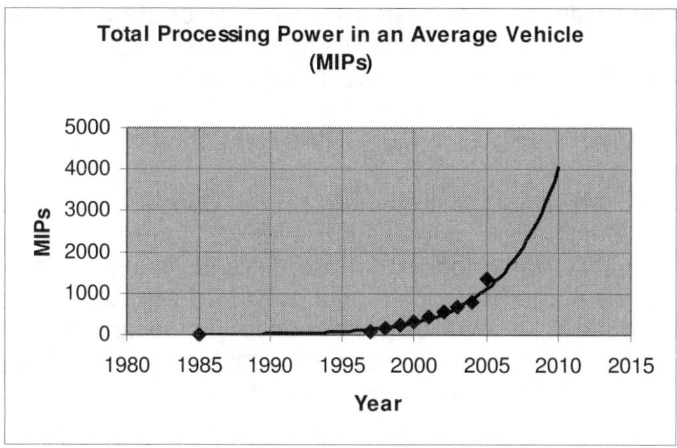

Figure 8: Increase in processing power/average vehicle

Communications bus speed

So as to assess the overhead of data checking between network nodes, a bus speed greater than the widely used high speed CAN bus in powertrain applications was used on the prototype example implementation. Although the NVC includes CAN bus capability, the data checking between network nodes is conducted via dedicated links using 100Mbps Ethernet. Here the Ethernet is configured as point to point between nodes for full duplex operation. Table 3 compares these data transmission rates:

Description	Ethernet	High Speed CAN
Max. Communication speed	100Mbps	1Mbps
Data byte transmission speed	10Mbyte/s	0.1Mbyte/s
Data transmission time/byte	100ns	100µs

Table 3: Comparison of data transmission speeds

The transmission time will be longer than suggested by the network rate due to the protocol overheads and cable propagation delays of ~6ns/m etc. Ethernet was chosen because of it's wide availability (even integrated into microcontrollers), high performance and also as it has been subject to rigorous analysis, including formal proofs [5].

Why is this important?

A comparison of the ratios of processor speeds (instructions per second) against data transmission speed (bytes/sec) is of interest in that the lower the ratio, the less time the processor is waiting for data transfer to take place before further (relevant) tasks can be performed. For the NVC the ratio is $500*10^6:10*10^6$ or 50:1 and for a powertrain controller it is 500:1. Thus the combination of NVC high performance processor and 100Mbps Ethernet gives an order of magnitude improvement in "throughput".

This becomes important when considering data transfer over a network that is managing a regular task at 1msec intervals. A 1ms task represents 500,000 instructions of a 500MIPs processor and 50,000 instructions at 50MIPs, both allowing a significant amount of data processing to be undertaken. The available time for "real work" is, though reduced for distributed network nodes as time synchronisation and voting tasks to validate system safety and fault tolerant checks first need to performed, as illustrated in figure 9

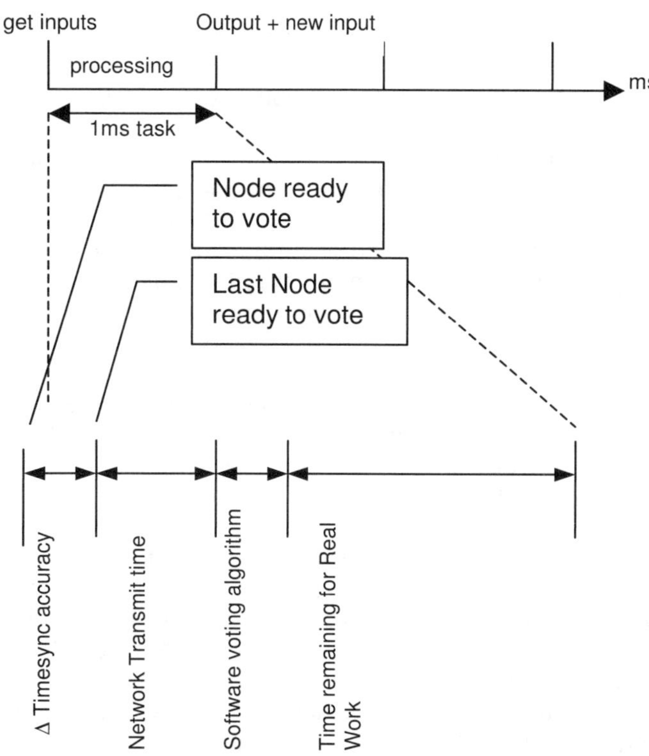

Figure 9: Synchronisation and voting timing during 1ms task

The Network Transmit Time period shown in Figure 9 is the time taken for each node to receive the data for voting from the other two nodes. To achieve this the network transmit time period is split into two separate stages. Stage 1 is when each node sends out its own data to the other 2 nodes (Figure 10). The notation D1 is the voting data for node 1 etc. and each node transmits and receives data in parallel.

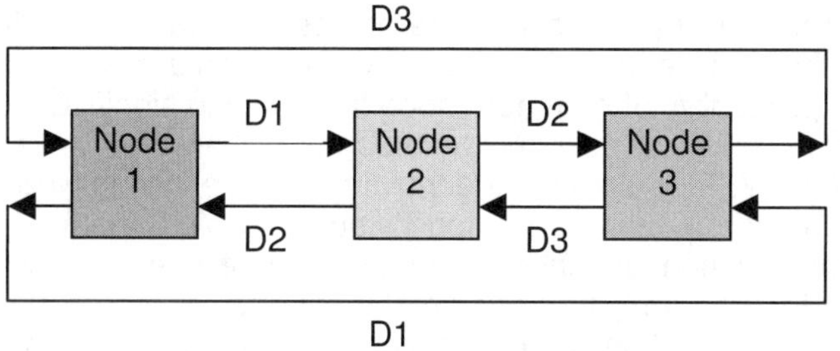

Figure 10: Stage 1 transmission of voting data

Stage 2 is when each node retransmits the data received from each other node and passes it forward *in the same direction*, Figure 11.

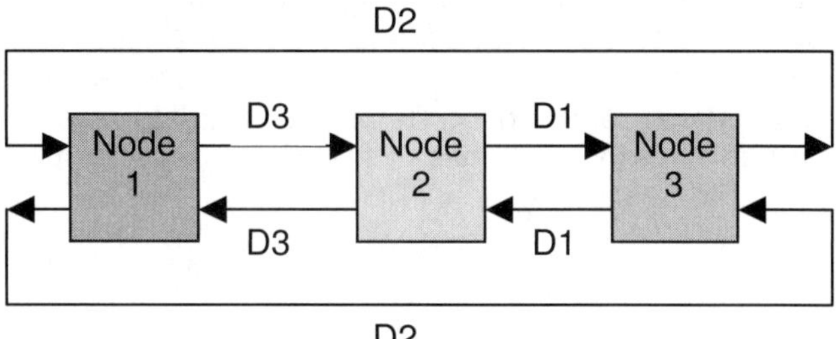

Figure 11: Stage 2 re-transmission of voting data

Thus at the end of each transmission stage, each node has received the voting data from the other two nodes twice, once from each direction around the network ring. This means that the voting data transfer is tolerant of any single network link fault and further, the faulty link can be identified by comparison of data transmission time and direction.

The data to be voted on has been organized into 2 bytes from each node. Thus the total number of bytes to be transmitted during the Network Transmit Time is four which takes 400ns across the 100Mbps Ethernet links.

The time synchronisation accuracy at the start translates into a number of "lost" instructions. This lost time is typically a fraction of the Network Transmit Time period, as too is the time taken for the processor to calculate the voting algorithm. Therefore it is not unrealistic for the total overhead timing associated with the synchronisation and voting to be less than 1µs, giving a ratio of overhead to real work of 1:1000 for a repetitive 1ms task.

Assuming the same task and data voting procedures but using the processing performance and communications bus speeds based on today's powertrain controllers, the Network Transmit time becomes 400µs over a 1Mbps high speed CAN bus. The further overhead from time synchronisation and software voting on the CAN means that very little processor time would be left for real tasks, a typical ratio of overhead to real work being significantly reduced to around 1:2.

It should be noted that while inaccuracies in time synchronisation cause wasted processor time, the extreme of "cycle locking" the processors (which is only really possible in a centralized system) would mean that the probability of common mode faults would significantly increase with a possible adverse impact on the system safety. With a small (random) time difference between processors, common mode faults (which normally happen when an unlikely combination of events occur together) will only be seen on at most one processor at a time, a situation which is corrected by voting. This concept potentially allows the use of (well designed and tested) common hardware and software in each node which dramatically reduces the costs of creating such systems. As an example of suitable testing, the NVC voting software was tested for every possible condition, as well as ensuring that the test case covered every possible executable statement in the code.

COMPARISON TO INDUSTRY DEVELOPMENTS

The example implementation described used microprocessors and higher speed communications busses available today that are not specifically targeted at the automotive industry, yet provide a significant step up in the next level of performance. There are several parallel developments currently that are specifically targeting higher power processors and higher speed networks for the automotive industry. However, the levels of performance are still an order of magnitude lower than provided in the example implementation. Next generation automotive microcontrollers being introduced in 2004 from Motorola in the Power PC family will provide up to 150MIPs (e.g. MPC5554) with 500MIPs forecast to be available around 2008. Flexray [6], a protocol proposed for drive-by-wire systems is only designed to work up to 10Mb/s.

CONCLUSION

This paper has presented an approach toward meeting future requirements in vehicle networks using redundant high speed communications busses with software voting and time-synchronisation. The example implementation demonstrates true distributed control, a target that many OEM's are seeking, to provide the levels of advanced functionality with a minimum number of high performance ECU's.

This approach will have a significant impact on the architecture of future vehicle networks. These are still evolving and there is currently no one standard approach to meet the varied demand for functional integration and vehicle safety requirements. It is, however, clear that both processing performance and communication bus speed in the future networks need to step up significantly from today to meet the requirements. What is less clear is whether the current industry developments provide a sufficient step up in performance to facilitate such a change in architecture as described in this paper, or whether the roll out of architecture changes and integrated features and functions will take longer.

The levels of processing power and communications bandwidth available in 2004 may not support true distributed control that meets the vehicle safety requirements. The question then is; will the OEM's be forced down a centralized network architecture route?

REFERENCES

1. R. Johansson, P, Johansson, K. Forsberg, H. Sivencrona, J. Torin, "On Communication Requirements for Control-by-wire applications", Proceedings of the 21st International System Safety Conference 2003.

2. R. Essermann, R. Schwarz, S. Stolzl, “Fault Tolerant drive by wire systems”, IEEE Control Systems magazine Oct 2002 pp64-81.
3. S. Mitra, N. Saxena, E. McCluskey, “A design diversity matrix and analysis of redundant systems”, IEEE Trans on Computers May 2002 Vol. 51 no. 5 pp498-510.
4. S. Channon and P. Miller, “An advanced Network Vehicle Controller (NVC) to support future technology applications”, AMAA2003, Berlin, Germany
5. F. Wang, Pao-Ann Hsiung, “Efficient & User friendly verifications”, IEEE Trans on Computers, Jan. 2002 Vol. 51 no.1 pp61-83.
6. C. A. Lupini, “Multiple Bus Progression 2003”, SAE Technical Paper Series 2003-01-0111.

CONTACT

Stephen Channon
Ricardo UK Ltd,
Bedford Heights, Manton Lane, Bedford MK41 7PA
stephen.channon@ricardo.com

Peter Miller
Ricardo UK Ltd,
Bedford Heights, Manton Lane, Bedford MK41 7PA
peter.miller@ricardo.com

www.ricardo.com

2002-01-0266

The BRAKE Project - Centralized Versus Distributed Redundancy for Brake-by-Wire Systems

Nico A. Kelling
Infineon Technologies AG

Worthy Heck
Delphi Automotive Systems

ABSTRACT

This paper presents the objectives and preliminary results of the BRAKE project – a joint effort of Delphi Automotive Systems, Infineon Technologies, Volvo Car Corporation and WindRiver. The objective of this project is to use microelectronics technologies to design a **distributed** Brake-by-Wire system including:

- A distributed fault tolerant system for enhanced safety
- An extension of the OSEK based operating system for a distributed time triggered architecture
- An open interface between vehicle control, and brake system control

The results comprise the requirements, interface specification (see [1]), a full simulation model, a hardware-in-the-loop bench, and a demonstration vehicle. The application has been developed using advanced automatic code generation for Infineon's TriCore based automotive microcontrollers.

INTRODUCTION

Today, many system vendors develop complete chassis systems. The characteristics of each system are determined by both hardware and software. In the future, software will play a greater role in defining the character and brand of the vehicle, and the vehicle manufacturer, as system integrator, will have to define the behaviour of the total vehicle in terms of function, performance, comfort, endurance, safety, etc to differentiate with respect to competitors. The driver will no longer experience the characteristics of the "real car", so much as the characteristics of a virtual car model the carmakers want to brand. The system vendors will provide modules that plug into this vehicle-level system. Interfaces allow the integration of these modules at the vehicle level. Car manufacturers jointly with the ECU suppliers and electronic device vendors, supported by tool suppliers, must innovatively expand their system development to meet this new challenge of complex automotive "super-systems".

This paper presents the achievements of a project partially funded by the European Commission under the ESPRIT program to leverage the application competencies for automotive safety related chassis control systems by means of:

- Distributing vehicle control over multiple subsystems from different vendors
- Enabling vehicle control by defining open interfaces between chassis control systems
- Providing a safety architecture based on system distribution
- Enhancing the OSEK operating system to create a distributed operating system

- Developing safe communication schemes to link distributed systems

The scope of the project is to design and implement a distributed system as a cost-effective approach for a safer braking system. This includes the design and implementation of a communication controller to implement the communication of multiple control units executing a distributed brake control (Fault-Tolerant Deterministic Automotive Protocol), and a distributed deterministic operating system. The final system will be verified using fault injection techniques using hardware-in-the-loop and vehicle demonstrator platforms.

This paper presents the advantages of distributed systems in terms of overall safety, fault tolerance and cost. The implementation of braking control on multiple distributed control units, and the integration of different brake control functions from different suppliers through an open distributed time triggered interface is discussed. In particular, the benefits of time triggered scheduling and support for distributed systems, along with enhanced node encapsulation are explored. The paper finishes with a brief overview of the model based and system level validation process.

THE PARADIGM SHIFT OF AUTOMOTIVE EMBEDDED SYSTEMS

The automotive industry continues to use mechanical subsystems with electronic control because:

- Electronically supervised systems increase the reliability by continuously testing the system components
- Features can be introduced into the car more quickly and more easily than mechanical systems
- Digital communication between vehicle subsystems enables new and greater authority vehicle level functions

Until recently electronic control has mainly been used to control and to supervise the functionality and to adapt the behavior of mechanical systems. In case of an error within the electronic control, the performance of the mechanical system is reduced, while still providing minimum functionality. This is known as fail-safe operation.

System requirements in the future can no longer be met with fail-safe operation. X-by-wire systems will no longer have mechanical backup and in the presence of an error, the electronic system will have to provide minimum functionality, and ensure that errors are confined.

In addition, as vehicle systems transition to X-by-wire, it will no longer be the mechanical design that defines the character of the vehicle (comfort, handling, and performance), but software function. This means that the interface between customer and supplier becomes more complex including mechanical, electrical, and software interfaces. Since the character of the vehicle ultimately forms part of the OEMs' brand differentiation, then many OEMs will want to become more involved in the control software definition.

Today, the responsibility for software development for X-by-wire systems and the subsystem knowledge commonly resides with the suppliers. Furthermore, the suppliers have greater knowledge of how to control their actuator, whilst the OEM determines how it will control the vehicle. This creates the need for software partitioning and OEM-Supplier interfaces.

INNOVATION

The BRAKE project explores important innovations in the emerging market of safety critical applications. These include:

- Dynamic allocation of control tasks to multiple electronic control units
- Time-triggered scheduling of the tasks enabling task encapsulation
- Design of safety architectures that exploit the inherent redundancy of braking systems to significantly lower the system cost while at the same time increasing system fault robustness.

By working on an appropriate methodology and tool infrastructure the project enables the development of a distributed control algorithm and the subsequent allocation of the resulting control tasks to a network of distributed control units. The BRAKE architecture consists of four such control units, each of which is located at or near one of the vehicle's wheel brakes. Having sufficiently powerful electronic control units to run the necessary software components, and an appropriately designed operating system, centralized control schemes will become obsolete.

A key part of the software running on an ECU is the proposed operating system that is designed according to the time-triggered concept for deterministic system behavior, which allows complete separation of tasks (task encapsulation). In case of a faulty task, the operating system is able to enter a "silent state" (fail-silent).

Error detection exploits the fact that the brake system has 4 wheels. Each wheel brake control unit computes the required braking torque for itself and each of the other wheel brake control units. A fault tolerant communication system is used to communicate the real time image of each of the wheel brake units. In contrast to the more conventional approach with central master and local redundancy the total number of required individual electronic control units is significantly reduced.

The BRAKE project also contributes to the definition of open interface standards, using open system concepts to reduce the dependency on specific suppliers and products. In particular the focus is on:

- the interface between the brake actuator's control circuitry and the brake's electronic control unit
- the interface to the communication system,
- the interface between upper control layers

The project began by establishing a brake system architecture that meets the automotive requirements for safety and reliability, utilising the inherent redundancy of a braking system. In order to leverage this inherent redundancy, each brake actuator is able to function with some level of independence. This means that the control software is no longer centralized, but de-centralized. Significant challenges arise in the implementation of such architecture, specifically:

- Global time synchronization between component ECUs and processes to ensure accurate calculation of vehicle states from sensor inputs
- Deterministic actuation of wheel brakes with the respect to brake demands
- Composability of brake system elements
- Encapsulation of sub-systems and faults
- Acceptable vehicle performance in the presence of fault through redundancy, including:
  - Dynamic reconfiguration and redistribution of brake function
  - Optimisation to minimise number of redundant subsystems
  - Extended and optimised degraded modes to achieve full potential of vehicle performance

This distributed approach specifically applies to the base brake function such that driver demand can always be interpreted and vehicle deceleration can always be achieved through brake actuation. This is the most critical function to ensure a safe and reliable brake system. Advanced braking functions such as anti-lock braking, traction control, vehicle stability and chassis control allow optimization of vehicle braking and stability but are not required for basic deceleration performance. These functions may remain centralized with fail-safe behavior allowing maximum integration with other chassis systems, for example in a vehicle supervisory role. The scope of this project is to ensure base brake functionality, whilst at the same time identifying the interfaces required to allow communication between distributed subsystems and vehicle level systems

SAFETY CONCEPT

As more and more automotive systems can no longer rely on mechanical backup, they have to provide deterministic behaviour even in the presence of faults. Today's approach for fail-safe operation is to build each system unit (ECU) redundant in order to achieve safety. The requirements and rules for proper partitioning and validation concepts for such systems with local redundancy have been addressed in several research projects (e.g. EU X-by-wire project).

As systems grow in complexity and previously separate systems share information and start to interact, they become hard to verify and even more difficult to ensure fail-safe operation.

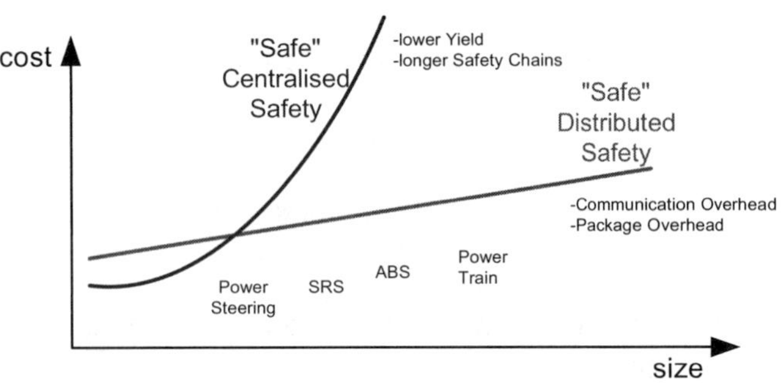

Figure 1: Cost for safety concepts relative to system complexity

This project uses the inherent distributed redundancy of the brake system in order to provide fail-safe/fault tolerant operation instead of adding redundancy to particular nodes.

Many automotive systems are naturally distributed for the following reasons

- Actuator location (e.g. physical location, multiple devices to reduce power/size etc..).
- Sensor location (e.g. due to low signal levels)
- Number of Connectors
- Complexity
- Modularity
- Power dissipation

BRAKE-BY-WIRE SYSTEM – CENTRAL VS. DISTRIBUTED ARCHITECTURE

A conceptual brake-by-wire is shown in **Figure 2**. The basic system contains:

- A pedal module that interprets driver intent and provides driver feedback
- A dependable power system to ensure power availability
- A computer system to control the complete system
- Four actuators to brake the vehicle
- Interfaces to other on board vehicle systems.

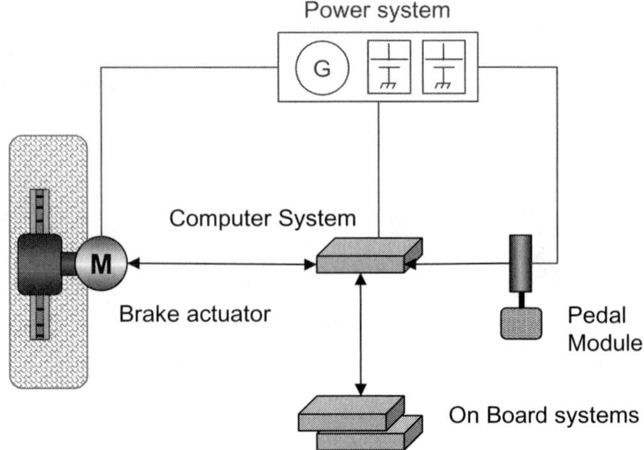

Figure 2 - Conceptual brake-by-wire system

The pedal module contains a device that emulates the desired force versus displacement characteristics as well as the force and travel sensors required to interpret driver demand. These signals are sent to the redundant computer system that processes and sends output signals via phase converters to the brake actuators. Phase converters represent the power electronics and convert high level signals into low level signals that drive the motors/solenoids that generate the clamping force at each wheel.

An outline of a Brake-by-Wire system using a traditional centralized redundancy concept is sketched in Figure 4.

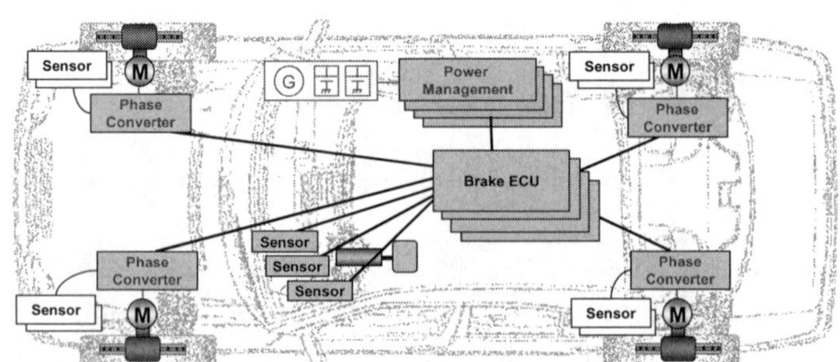

Figure 3 - Brake-by-Wire system with traditional centralized redundancy

This system ensures each ECU is fail-safe, (using redundancy). The centralized system requires:

- Fault tolerant Pedal Module (tolerating 1-2 errors). 3 complete subsystems (microcontroller, sensor, power supply, communication link etc.).
- Fault tolerant Electronic Brake Module (tolerating 1-2 errors) by having 2 fail-safe systems. Each of the fail-safe systems are made up of 2 microcontrollers, two control paths to deactivate the ECU.
- Fault tolerant Power Management Module (tolerating 1-2 errors) by having 2 fail-safe systems. Each of the fail-safe systems are made up of 2 microcontrollers, two control paths to deactivate the ECU.
- Phase Converter for each actuator (this could be fault tolerant if 4 wheel braking is required after a single fault has occurred)

Considering the resource requirements, the following resources are required to build the safety concept when applying symmetric redundancy for the individual ECUs:

- 4 High End Microcontrollers (incl. RAM, ROM, IO), 4 for the Brake Module
- 3 Low End Controller for the Pedal Module (incl. Sensor, Power Supply, RAM, ROM)
- 8-16 Midrange Microcontroller/DSP for the Phase Converters, Power Management (incl. Power stages, sensors, RAM, ROM)

These resources add up to a total of 15-23 microcontrollers, 11 separate electronic control units, 9 communication links. The respective conventional safety chain is sketched in Figure 5:

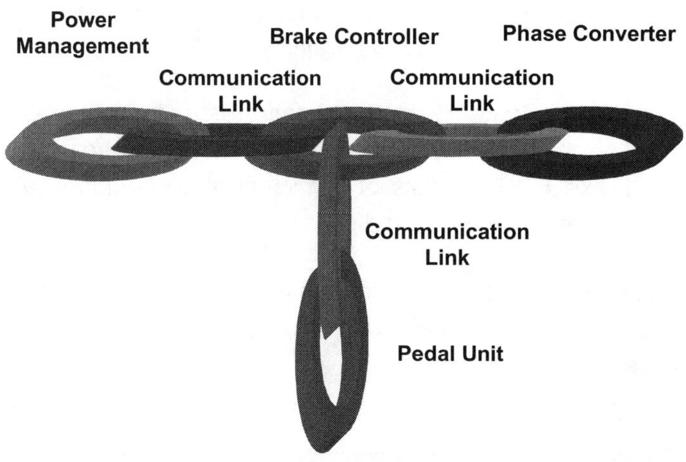

Figure 4: Dependencies of a Brake-by-Wire system with traditional centralized redundancy

A total of 4 ECUs and 3 communication links must be operational to allow braking on one wheel.

The BRAKE project proposes a distributed brake-by-wire architecture where the control units are distributed to shorten the safety chain, and redundant fail-silent ECUs are only included where there is no inherent system redundancy (e.g. pedal module). The resulting distributed architecture is illustrated in Figure 6.

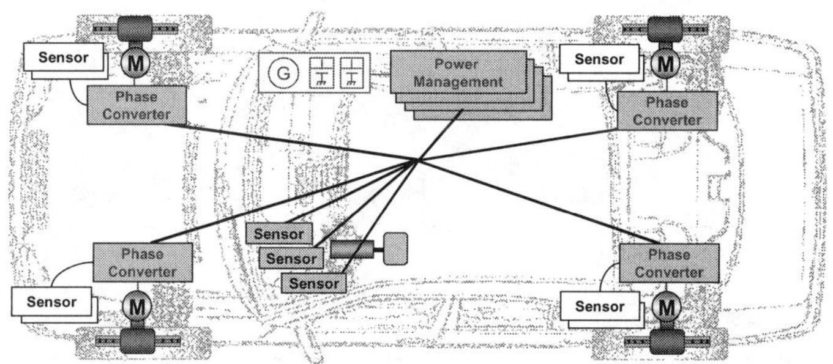

Figure 5: Brake-by-Wire system applying advanced distributed redundancy

The total requirements for the system are:

- Pedal module tolerating 2 errors. This translates to 3 complete subsystems (intelligent sensor) including microcontroller (low end), sensor, power supply, and communication link
- Power Management Module tolerating 1-2 errors. The power management system is made up of 2 fail-silent subsystems. Each fail-silent subsystem is

made up of 2 microcontrollers (midrange), two control paths to deactivate the ECU

- Wheel Brake ECU that integrates both the brake control and the phase converter functions. The wheel brake ECU consists of 1 microcontroller (high end), power electronics, and sensor I/O

This gives a total of 11 microcontrollers (incl. resources), 9 separate electronic control units, 8 communication links.

The safety chain is now shortened and only 3 ECUs and 2 communication links must be operational to allow braking at one wheel. (see figure 7).

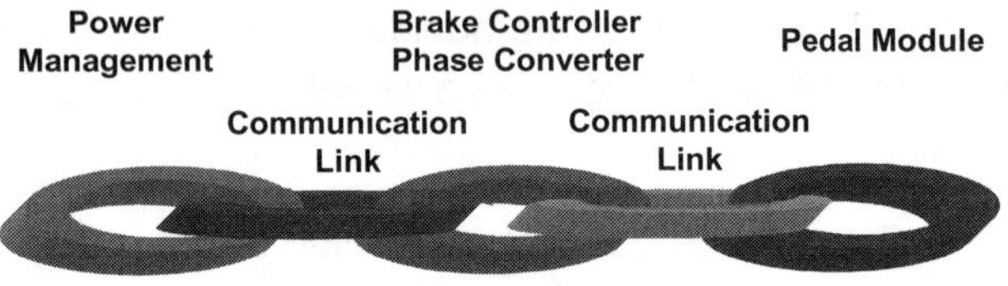

Figure 6: Dependencies of Brake-by-Wire system with distributed safety architecture

The comparison of required resources as characterized before is given in tabular form in Figure 8:

	Micro-Controller		Electr. Control Unit (ECU)	
	Existing	BRAKE	Existing	BRAKE
Pedal Module	3	3	3	3
Brake Module	4	-	2	-
Phase Converter	4-12	4	4	4
Power Module	4	4	2	2
Total	**15-23**	**11**	**11**	**9**
Links			8-9	7-8
Number of required working ECU to allow Brake operation			4	3

Figure 7: Resource Consumption for a base Brake-by-wire application for local centralized versus a distributed safety concept.

The benefits of distribution may become greater for more complex applications. Furthermore, the architecture provides the scalability, flexibility, extendibility and testability that is needed for highly safety critical applications at reduced system cost. Higher-level functions can be added at designer's choice of fault tolerance. They can be executed on one or more nodes depending on the level of redundancy that is ordered by the criticality of the application. The redundancy control, i.e. the detection of node failure is supported by the communication protocol. As described in various different reports, the time triggered protocol provides a temporal firewall between attached nodes on the communication channel(s). In addition, higher-level network features are specified for the distributed safety protocol that supports the node failure detection in the value domain. These features include a distributed mutual exclusion protocol. Assuming a malicious host controller failure that disallows the host controller to properly verify his own sanity. In such case outputs can be protected against erroneous commands from host controllers through independent communication controller features.

COMMUNICATION

The communication between the distributed components of the system is an essential element of the system architecture. It is more than information exchange, as it is the one key medium that connects and correlates the distributed control units in the control path and encapsulates them at the same time to prevent fault propagation in the time and value domain.

Hence, stringent requirements are defined for a suitable communication system, including application level features, synchronised and distributed global time synchronisation, failure tolerance, encapsulation at the protocol and at the physical level, compatibility with other systems already in production, aspects of migration to the new architecture and more. These coupled with the economical aspects can only be satisfied with a true open standard for deterministic failure-tolerant communication protocol.

Today's leading bus system "CAN" is used for event triggered information transfer. Microcontrollers (8bit/16bit and 32bit) are equipped with on chip CAN protocol engines and stand-alone protocol controllers are available.

Existing CAN systems are not deterministic (i.e. the timing of messages is not predictable). This behavior is not acceptable for fault tolerant safety critical applications like brake-by-wire. In such applications, messages must be transferred at predictable times (deterministic). Several system suppliers as well as vehicle manufacturers have identified this problem and therefore intend to use other bus systems. Provisional versions of the TTP-Bus and the byteflight-Bus have already been developed and implemented. Time triggered CAN and several others bus systems are under development. Today there is no clear and mature industry standard for safety critical busses that also satisfies the full feature profile in technical and economical terms. A new protocol architecture that offers high-bandwidth, scalable and fault tolerant communication with the safety related features of pure time-triggered communication and the flexibility to support event-triggered communication for other applications is under development. The goal is to provide a basis that respects the ideas and requirements of different global players to make it an open standard for automotive industry. A number of vehicle manufacturers, system, silicon and tool suppliers are involved in this development. The protocol can be configured from purely event-triggered up to purely time-triggered communication and any mixture in between to optimally reflect the application specific needs in terms of safety versus flexibility. Within this project, prototype implementations and demonstrators for in-vehicle evaluation have been developed and evaluated in the application. A number of further requirements that have not been sufficiently covered elsewhere, have been worked out and implemented in a FPGA based prototype implementation for in vehicle, real application development and evaluation. Figure 9 shows a picture of the evaluation platform for the safety-bus communication controller that was developed within the BRAKE project.

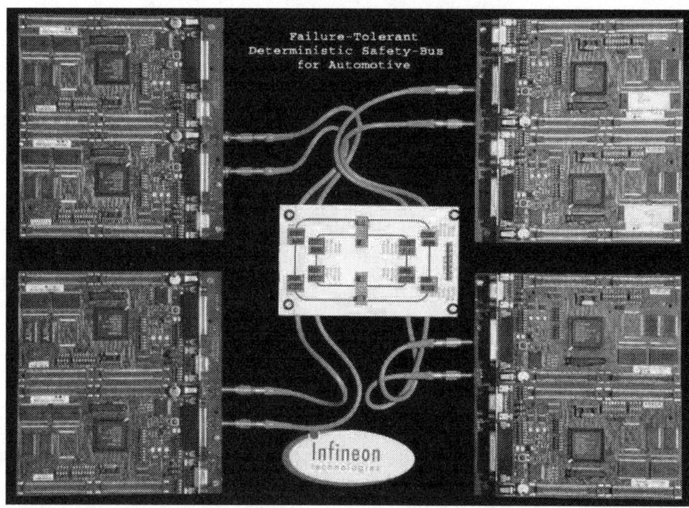

Figure 8: Lab-Setup for Four-Node fault-tolereant deterministic communication validation with FPGA-based prototypes

SYSTEM ARCHITECTURE

The complete system architecture has been developed in conjunction with a system safety program plan (described in [4]). The first stage was to specifically identify the safety requirements, as well as the functional and performance requirements. The brake system was then broken down into key subsystems, including:

- Computer System
- Sensors
- Actuators
- Dependable Power
- Dependable Communication
- Bus topology

Alternative approaches that met the safety requirements were then identified and evaluated in terms of safety, performance, cost.

The safety concept of the architecture builds on the inherent system redundancy as opposed to adding resources to achieve fault tolerance. The communication system, being failure tolerant, becomes a key element in connecting and encapsulating the distributed sub-systems from each other. With the help of network features, the encapsulation is performed in the time domain and additionally to some extent in the value domain.

A number of different network topologies and routing alternatives have been evaluated with regards to their safety properties for a brake-by-wire architecture. The two key candidates – distributed star topology and an unidirectional redundant ring structure are depicted in figures 9 and 10.

The distributed star topology offers valuable properties to the network with respect to media access control via redundant bus-guardians and further encapsulation of different sub-modules, but it remains an element with single point of failure. Consequently, the central star coupler is required to be absolutely dependable and protected against any fatal failure, which might be caused by mechanical events

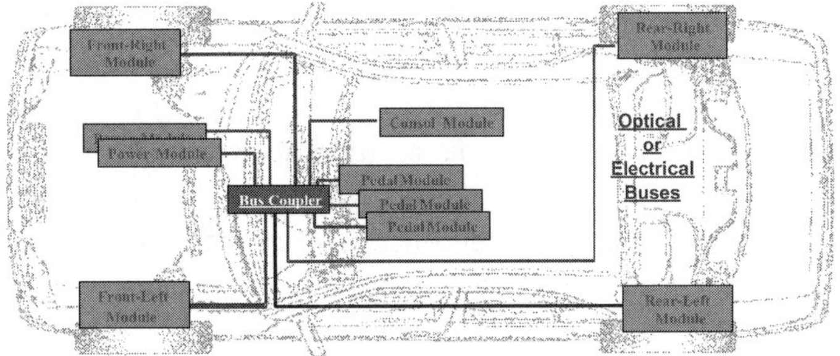

Figure 9: Distributed Safety-architecture with distributed star topology

Alternatively, a ring structure offers very high robustness against local, mechanical or electrical failures. Uni-directional wires can be routed separately, such that a loss of any single connection and many combinations of multiple cuts do not cause any loss of information.

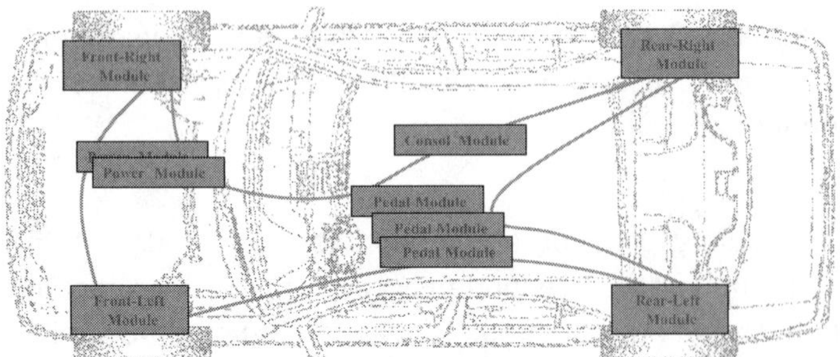

Figure 10: Distributed Safety-architecture with distributed star topology

The actual implementation as performed within the BRAKE project, uses a variant of the uni-directional ring toplogy

The overall system architecture is depicted in figure 11.

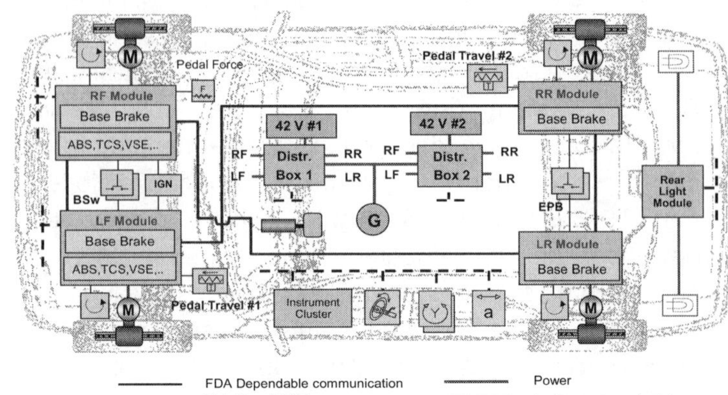

Figure 11: Distributed Safety-Architecture as implemented in BRAKE

Driver intent is established using 2 travel sensors and one force sensor – each sensor is connected to a different wheel node, and consistency checks are performed once the sensor values have been communicated over the network.

Each wheel node calculates the actuation commands for all four wheels. These commands are communicated via the network so each of the four wheel nodes can compare their own actuation commands with those calculated by the other wheel nodes. The voting mechanism in the network layer of each wheel node can then disable the power to individual actuators in case of a fault. If a node needs to be shut down the brake force is re-distributed to prevent the vehicle from yawing.

The advanced brake functions are executed in the two front wheel nodes. If the front wheel nodes do not calculate the same output commands for these advanced brake functions, the function will be deactivated. This provides fail-safe operation.

The dependable power supply is provided by two 42 V batteries. Each battery is connected to a distribution box that protects the 42 V net from short circuits. Each wheel node is connected to each distribution box providing redundant power supply.

The communication system is designed to be failure tolerant in itself. The computation and control is distributed to the available resources that verify against each other over the network with appropriate network support. Value domain encapsulation using a mutual distributed exclusion protocol feature is one further measure to allow detection of failures in the value domain across the network and without further software interaction. As the software modules are calculating actuation commands in redundant manner, that will be exchanged via the network, the protocol allows to have the incoming data-sets to be compared against a reference data-set provided by the attached host and to determine the majority agreement within the network. In case of failure of one ECU that cannot detect its own faultiness, this network feature allows to prevent the commanding of actuation with data from such faulty node.

SYSTEM SIMULATION & VALIDATION

The full system has been modelled in the Simulink environment. It comprises of the following sub models:

- Scenario (including driver and road inputs, initial values, e.g. battery state of charge and brake temperatures)
- Sensors (converts physical values to voltage signals before they enter the computer system model. The brake pedal sensors comprise one force sensor, two travel sensors and two brake switches.)
- System inputs (pedal feel emulator, the batteries and the generator)
- Actuators (includes the dynamics of the components of the actuator: the actuator motor, the reduction mechanism, the ball screw and the brake calipers)
- Vehicle (comprising a power train model and a vehicle dynamics model; the transmission model is configured as a front wheel drive 5 speed manual transmission with automatic clutch control, 15 Degrees Of Freedom model with x, y, z, roll, pitch and yaw, the four wheel speeds, the vertical displacement of the four unsprung masses and one DOF for the steering rack position)
- Computer system (including the four wheel nodes, scheduler of the operating system, network system, distribution boxes for power supply with three layer node application)
- Fault injection (configurable and scriptable fault injection such as signal timing (delay), change to signal offset (fixed or drift varying with time), saturation, signal noise, "stuck" signal (i.e. fixed value), random signal)

One challenge in the modelling approach was to generate a clear partitioning in the system by means of clear interface definitions that have been the basis for parallel development and evaluation of the sub models. The approach taken was to create vectorized signals in between the Simulink sub-models that need to exchange signals.

Results of the fault Injection Simulation and hardware in the loop simulation can be found in [1].

The application code is largely generated from the "computer system" sub-model within the Matlab/ Simulink model. The TargetLink tool [6] from dSPACE generates the optimised production code for the target embedded system. The code is then executed on a TriCore [7] based AUDO TC1775 [8] micro controller. This tool supports the development and verification by means of comparative simulations on host and or target platform. The pure algorithm's behaviour and results can be compared to target code execution on the host computer and to the embedded target real-time execution.

CONCLUSION

This paper has described the concepts and development approach of a new distributed safety architecture for highly safety critical applications, applied to a brake-by-wire system within the BRAKE project. Safety and cost-advantages have been rationalized and an effective, model based development approach has been outlined to cut down overall system complexity into manageable units, that are testable and verifiable.

At the time of the writing, the final integration into the vehicle is ongoing and further system validation is being performed on the hardware-in-the-loop and simulation platforms. Results will be reported once available.

ACKNOWLEDGMENTS

The contents and concepts presented herein are the result of the contributions of all BRAKE project partners. Namely, these are Delphi Automotive Systems (Paris, France), Infineon Technologies AG (Munich, Germany), Volvo Cars Corporation (Gothenburg, Sweden) and Wind River (Swindon, UK).

REFERENCES

1. EU-project BRAKE, development of a distributed brake by wire system, Per Olsson, Nico Kelling, Pascal Chaumette, 10. Internationaler Kongress, Elektronik im Kraftfahrzeug, 27-28 September 2001
2. Distributed Automotive Safety System, Technical report, Nico Kelling, *SAE2001-01-0027*
3. New Deterministic Automotive Bus System, Wilhard v. Wendorff, Patrick Leteinturier, *SAE2001-01-0057*
4. A Comparison of Hazard Analysis Techniques for A System-Safety Process For By-Wire Automotive Systems, Sanket Amberkar, Joseph G. D'Ambrosio, Brian T. Murray, SAE-2001-00PC-102
5. Mathworks homepage (2001), http://www.mathworks.com
6. dSPACE homepage (2001), TargetLink - Automatic Code Generator for TriCore, http://ww.dspace.de
7. Infineon TriCore (2001), http://www.infineon.com/TriCore
8. Infineon AUDO TC1775, http://www.infineon.com/AUDO

CONTACTS

Nico A. Kelling
Infineon Technologies AG
System Competence Center Automotive
Balanstraße 53
D-81541 Munich, Germany
phone: +49 (89) 234-82218
fax: +49 (89) 234-715308
email: nico.kelling@infineon.com

Worthy Heck
Delphi Automotive Systems
Group leader, Advanced Braking Systems
Centre Technique – Paris
117, avenue des Nations
ZAC Paris Nord II – B.P. 60059
95972 Roissy CDG Cedex, France
phone: +33 (0)1 49 90 45 16
fax: +33 (0)1 49 90 49 30
email: worthington.heck@delphiauto.com

2001-01-0691

Embedded Electronics in Electro-Mechanical Systems for Automotive Applications

Bruce A. Myers, Jeff H. Burns and Joseph M. Ratell
Delphi Delco Electronics Systems

ABSTRACT

The extensive use of electronics has revolutionized the implementation and scope of many of the features and functions in a modern automobile. This automotive electronic revolution has significantly improved the performance, reliability and comfort of the automobile. In some cases, electronics have also simplified component fabrication and automotive assembly. However, the full potential that electronics have for reducing the assembly complexity of the automobile has yet to be realized. More extensive use of electronics embedded into mechanical components and mechatronic systems will significantly simplify automotive assembly in the future. This paper examines three current and future applications of embedded electronics in automotive applications. These examples illustrate the advantages and challenges associated with embedded electronic concepts. Future applications, new technology development needs, and changes in automotive component sourcing, are discussed. Given the significant advantages of embedding electronic functions into automotive system enclosures, it is clear that this trend will gain momentum in the future. The end result will provide significantly higher value and higher reliability transportation for the consumer.

INTRODUCTION

The features and functions of a modern automobile are becoming increasingly dependent on the use of electronics. Electronic modules are used today to perform most of the control functions in the typical automobile that 25 years ago were performed by mechanical mechanisms. Many new requirements for the automobile, which utilize electronic controls, have also evolved during this time. Among these are emission control, improved fuel efficiency, new safety features, enhanced engine and drive train performance, and improved ride and handling performance. In addition, many of the electronic functions that the consumer has grown accustomed to using at home and work, such as entertainment and communications systems, are being integrated into his/her car or truck. Consequently, the automobile is becoming an integrated electronic and mechanical system. In many cases, the major functions that an automobile performs are implemented with a combination of mechanical and electronic devices. Historically, most of these combined electronic and mechanical functions have been designed as a combination of mechanical parts and electrical modules independently purchased and assembled into the automobile at the assembly plant.

The automotive electronic revolution has significantly improved the performance, reliability and comfort of the automobile. In some cases, electronics have simplified component fabrication and automotive assembly. However, the full potential that electronics have for reducing the assembly complexity of the automobile is just now starting to be realized by embedding electronics into mechanical components and systems. In addition to reduced assembly complexity, embedded electronics can generate a number of other advantages for both the automobile manufacturer and the end consumer. These include lower costs, improved system performance, size and mass reduction, improved quality and reliability, and improved aesthetics.

A typical application of embedded electronics is shown in Figure 1 where sensors, power switching, control electronics, associated electrical interconnects and a motor are incorporated into an integrated electro-mechanical module.

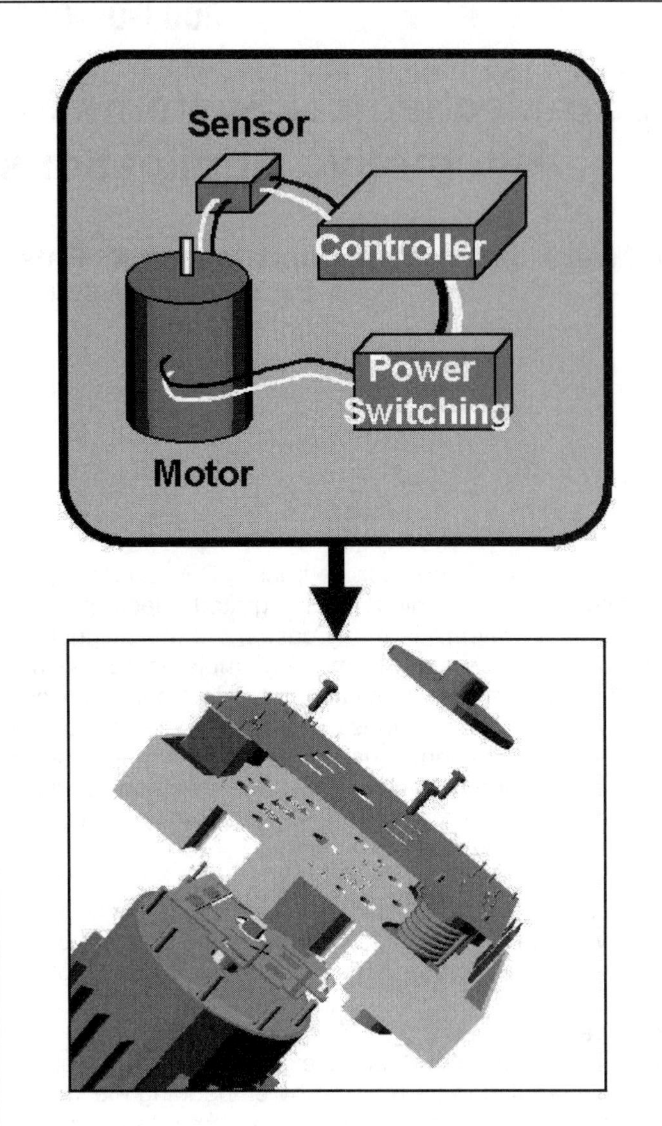

Figure 1. Integrating Many Functions Into One Module

Embedded electronics introduce a number of challenges to the automotive parts supplier as well as the automobile manufacturer and dealer. These include packaging the electronics for potentially more severe environmental conditions, the need for simultaneous design of the electronic and the mechanical parts for complete systems, and the need for integrated electrical-mechanical automotive parts suppliers. Embedded electronic modules also generate significant serviceability and reparability issues. This paper focuses on the technical issues associated with embedded electronics using case studies of a few embedded electronic designs past, present and future.

MAIN SECTION

CASE 1: THE AUTOMOTIVE ALTERNATOR - The automotive alternator is an example of an electronic function embedded into an electro-mechanical device that has been in production for many years. The modern automotive alternator consists of a rotating electro-mechanical generator, a diode rectification bridge and an electronic module for voltage regulation. The diode bridge and the voltage regulator module are mounted inside the alternator housing. The mechanical and electronic functions of the alternator are tested and then assembled into the car as a single unit. Figure 2 shows the interior assembly of a typical alternator.

Figure 2. Electronics Embedded in an Alternator

In this application, referring to Figure 2, the electronic voltage regulator module (4) is mounted on the generator housing (1) under the top cover (3). The rectifier diode bridge (not shown) is also mounted on the housing under the cover. The module including the electronic content is cooled by air forced through the module (2).

This application is typical of the many challenges that an embedded electronic application imposes on an automotive supplier. The challenges and solutions used to address them in the alternator are listed in Table 1.

REQUIREMENT FOR ELECTRONIC CONTENT	TECHNOLOGY/FEATURE USED TO ADDRESS REQUIREMENT
Small Size Needed For Mounting Inside Alternator	Flip Chip ICs, Printed Resistors, Unpackaged Power Devices
Module Power Dissipation	Electronics Cooled by Forced Air Generated by the Alternator Rotor
High Ambient Temperature (125C)	Thick Film Hybrid Circuits, High Performance BeO Based Thermal Stacks, High Temperature Capable Si Devices, High Temperature Solder and Other Materials
Severe Thermal Cycle (-40/125C)	Compliant Adhesives, Material CTE Matching, Compliant Flip Chip Solder
Corrosive Fluid and Gas Exposure (NOx)	Sealed or Overmolded Electronics, Silicone Gel Potting Materials, Sealed Connectors
Simplified Electrical Interconnect	Combination of Small Wire Harness, Mounting Screws and Lead Frames
Serviceability	Failed Alternators Disassembled and "Rebuilt" with Replacement Components
Modular Assembly	Generator with Integrated Electronics Tested and Assembled Into Car as a Single Unit

Table 1. Requirements & Solutions for Alternator

In this example, the solutions used to solve the packaging issues evolved as a result of the relatively small electronic content and the technology that was available 30 years ago. The longevity of this implementation of embedded electronics is indicative of how successful embedded electronic concepts can be in the automotive environment.

CASE 2: ELECTRONIC STEERING SYSTEMS - Electric motors used in systems such as electric power steering applications commonly consist of a separate electric motor and an electronic motor controller. There are several disadvantages to this approach. First, the mounting of two separate components requires extra room and increases assembly complexity. The interconnect wires between the two units also introduce additional electrical resistance and can act as antennae that both receive and radiate electromagnetic interference.

To solve these problems, it is desirable to integrate the motor, power switching, and electronic control functions into one package. The resulting embedded electronic design concept places the power switching section of the controller directly on the end of the motor. The motor control board is also placed on the end of the motor such that sensors for measuring the angular position of the motor can be placed directly on the PCB board. This results in a small package with a minimum number of electrical connections.

This design approach, illustrated in Figures 3 and 4, mounts the power semiconductor switches, normally MOSFET's, on a power distribution bus that is mounted between the motor and the motor control board. In addition, motor position sensors are mounted directly on the motor control board.

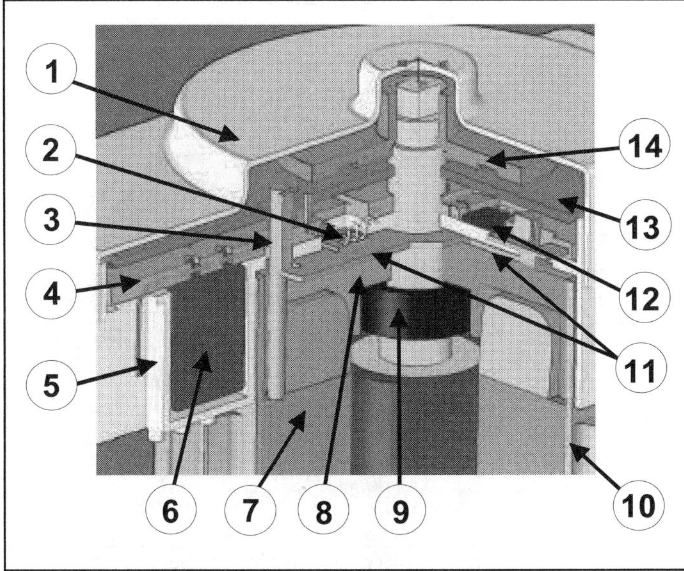

Figure 3. Embedded Electronics Motor – Cutaway View

Referring to Figure 3, inside the case (5) an interconnect board (4) is used to connect various electrical parts (6) and the power distribution bus/lead frame (11) together to form electrical circuits. The semiconductor power switches (2) are connected to the interconnect board (4) with wire bonds through windows in the case (5). Above the interconnect board (4) the motor control board (13) is mounted. This control board (13) contains various electronic devices that together control all motor functions. Also mounted on the control board are sensors that together with the encoder wheel (14) monitor the angular position of the motor.

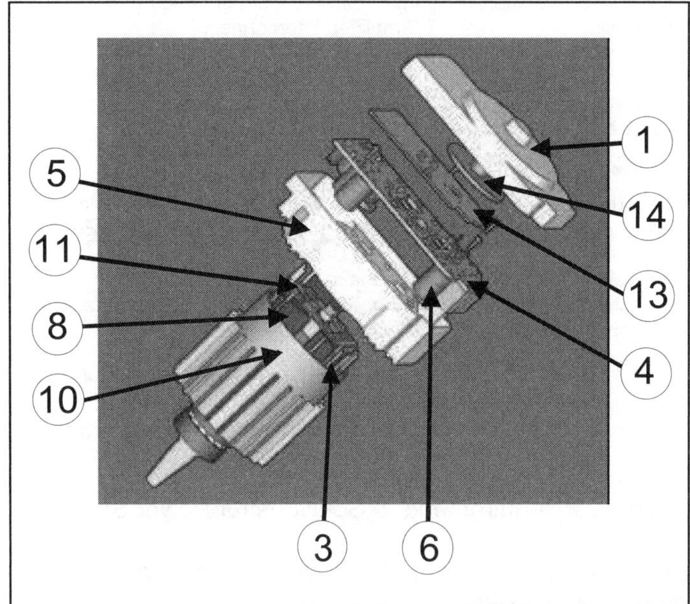

Figure 4. Embedded Electronics in Motor-Exploded View

Referring to Figures 3 and 4, the motor winding terminations (3) pass through the motor end cap (8), the case (5), and the system control board (4). The power distribution bus (11) has tabs that are bent upward and connect to the motor winding terminations (3). This connects the motor to the power switches. Parts that dissipate a large amount of heat (12) may be mounted to the inside of the case. Some of the parts of the motor include the outer sleeve (10), end cap (8), bearing (9), and motor core (7). The motor control electonics unit is enclosed with a cover (1).

This design achieves a tight integration between the electric motor and its controller, which generates a very small system package. Problems associated with interconnecting wires are minimized and the viability of the novel thermal management approach has been verified by finite element analysis. Table 2 summarizes the challenges for this embedded electronic application and the solutions used to resolve them.

REQUIREMENT FOR ELECTRONIC CONTENT	TECHNOLOGY/FEATURE USED TO ADDRESS REQUIREMENT
Small Size Needed For End of Motor Mounting	Flip Chip ICs Unpackaged Power Devices
High Power Dissipation	Power Devices Cooled By Direct Conduction Into Motor Housing and Motor Mount
High Current Switching Capability	Insert Molded Copper Lead Frame, Simplified Interconnect
Reduced Emitted Electro/Magnetic Noise	Elimination of High Current Wire Harness
High Ambient Temperature (125C)	145C Capable PCB, High Performance Copper Frame Thermal Structure, High Temperature Capable Si Devices, High Temperature Solder and Other Materials
Severe Thermal Cycle (-40/125C)	Compliant Adhesives/Interfaces, Material CTE Matching, Flip Chip Underfill Epoxy
Corrosive Fluid Exposure	Sealed Case, Silicone Gel Potting Materials, Sealed Connectors
Simplified Electrical Interconnect	Integrated Copper Lead Frame Attached Directly To Motor Windings
Serviceability	Requires Replacement of Entire Integrated Motor/Electronics Unit
Modular Assembly	Motor with Integrated Electronics Attached to Steering Linkage Which Is Tested and Assembled Into Car as a Single Unit

Table 2. Requirements & Solutions for Power Steering

Figure 5 shows a production intent implementation of this embedded concept.

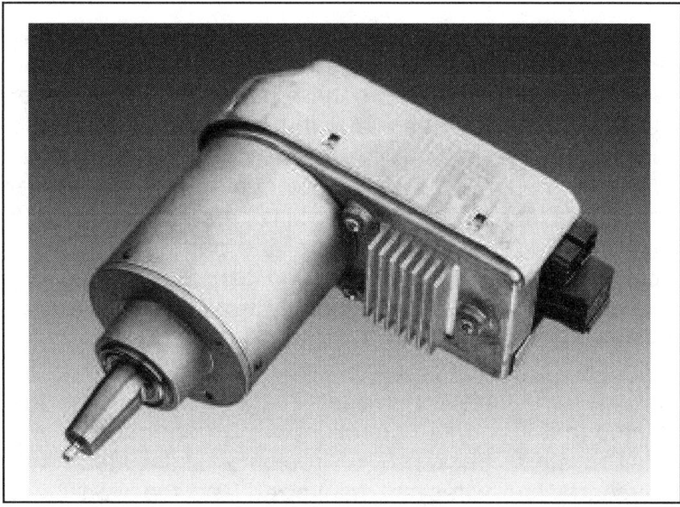

Figure 5. Embedded Power Steering Application

CASE 3: ELECTRONIC CONTROLLED TRANSMISSION - Embedding the electronics required for transmission control inside the transmission case has the potential to significantly reduce the complexity of the current wire harness and allow modular test and assembly of the transmission function as a single unit. The integration of the electronic transmission control module (TCM) into the transmission case requires packaging technologies capable of higher temperature operation and capable of operation in a very harsh environment. As shown in Figures 6, 7, and 8 a ceramic hybrid substrate containing the electric control function can be integrated with the transmission solenoid lead frame. Figure 6 shows a cut away view of the assembly structure. In this figure, the electronic control module (5) is mounted directly to the transmission channel plate (11). The control module is electrically interconnected to the fluid control solenoids (2) with a lead frame using lap joints (4) and pressure contacts (3). The lead frame and connector (7) are insert molded into the solenoid module (1). The resulting module controls the transmission fluid (10) through the channel plate. All of the materials used in the module must be capable of withstanding continual exposure to hot transmission fluid. Many of these materials including the controller module passivation (6), the connector plating (8), and the assembly adhesives (9) will likely be materials not normally used in current automotive electronic applications.

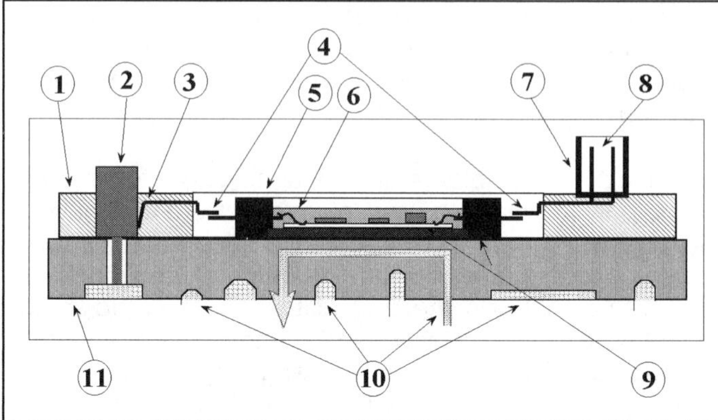

Figure 6. In-Transmission Electronics – Cross Section

External electrical interconnection is provided by a wire-harness with a pass through (the transmission case) connector body. Subsystem assembly of the TCM into the transmission case occurs during transmission assembly. In the implementation shown in Figure 7, the lead frame lap joints have been eliminated by the use of a single piece lead frame.

Figure 7. In-Transmission TCM

Figure 8. Embedded TCM Utilizing Ceramic Substrate

Although the TCM can use existing thick film hybrid circuit technology, several enhancements to the external TCM package must be implemented to enable the unit to withstand the severe temperature and transmission fluid exposure environment seen inside the transmission case. This includes the use of non-silicone based adhesives, high temperature and transmission fluid resistant plastics, and a sealed connector. The solutions used to address these and the other challenges of this embedded electronic application are summarized in Table 3.

REQUIREMENT FOR ELECTRONIC CONTENT	TECHNOLOGY/FEATURE USED TO ADDRESS REQUIREMENT
Small Size Needed For Mounting Inside Transmission	Flip Chip ICs, Printed Resistors, Unpackaged Power Devices
Module Power Dissipation	Electronics Cooled by Conduction Into Transmission Channel Plate
High Ambient Temperature (140C)	Thick Film Hybrid Circuits, High Performance BeO Based Thermal Stacks, High Temperature Capable Si Devices, High Temperature Solder and Other Materials
Severe Thermal Cycle (-40/140C)	Compliant Adhesives, Material CTE Matching, Flip Chip Underfill Epoxy
Continuous Corrosive Transmission Fluid Exposure	Sealed Module Case, Non-Silicone Potting and Sealing Materials, Sealed Connectors
Simplified Electrical Interconnect	Combination of Small Wire Harness, Mounting Screws and Lead Frames
Serviceability	Failed Transmission Disassembled and "Rebuilt" with Replacement Components
Modular Assembly	Transmission with Integrated Electronics Tested and Assembled Into Car as a Single Unit

Table 3. Requirements & Solutions for Transmission

DISCUSSION

Advantages - The advantages of using embedding electronics in systems with both electrical and mechanical function are: reduced size, reduced cost as assembled in the car, improved initial quality, and improved systems level performance. Size and mass savings are realized through reducing the number of individual components and interconnects. A shared case for both the electronics and mechanical functions can allow shared thermal management, seals and mechanical structures, which in turn reduces the number of components and fabrications steps.

Significant cost savings can be gained not only by the reduction in the number of individual components and the fabrication steps, but also by testing complete systems at the component assembly plant. Rejected units are much more easily identified and corrective action can be more effectively taken at the module assembly plant rather that at the vehicle assembly plant. Fully integrated and tested electro-mechanical modules can easily be assembled into the automobile with high initial quality and low final assembly costs.

The elimination of electrical interconnects and wiring harnesses also generates improved initial quality and can significantly improve system performance. This is especially true where high currents are required. Shorter conductor paths reduce the voltage drop in high current lines. When high currents are switched; shorter conductor paths can substantially reduce emitted electromagnetic noise. Noise sensitive electrical circuits are also benefited by shorter conductor path lengths by reducing the amount of electrical noise induced in low current wires.

Challenges - The design and assembly of embedded electronics into automotive modules generate a number of technical challenges. Many embedded electronic applications require high operating temperatures. In some cases, these temperatures can reach as high as 140C or more. The maximum ambient temperature for most automotive electronic applications today is 125C. The power generated in electrical circuits at this ambient temperature typically results in up to 140C circuit board temperatures and 150C silicon device junction temperatures. Since these internal temperatures are the maximum application temperatures for many of the circuit materials and silicon devices available in the commercial market today, increased application temperatures require either the use of non standard, higher cost materials and devices or the development of low cost higher temperature alternatives. Since one of the major drivers for embedded electronics is to reduce system level costs, low cost high temperature circuit materials and components must be developed to make embedded electronics viable for many applications.

The need for constant automotive fluid exposure and immersion for applications such as the in-transmission controller described in Case 3, will require new materials that can withstand the chemical degradation that these fluids can cause to many types of organic materials such as plastics, adhesives, and seals. Robust and low cost materials are required to protect the sensitive electrical circuits inside the electronic enclosure. In many cases materials that are insensitive to fluid exposure are currently considerably more expensive than the material they replace in non-immersed applications. These material costs will need to be reduced or lower cost alternatives will need to be developed to make many fluid immersed applications viable.

Figure 9 lists in more detail technology areas that will require additional development to enable wider application of embedded electronics.

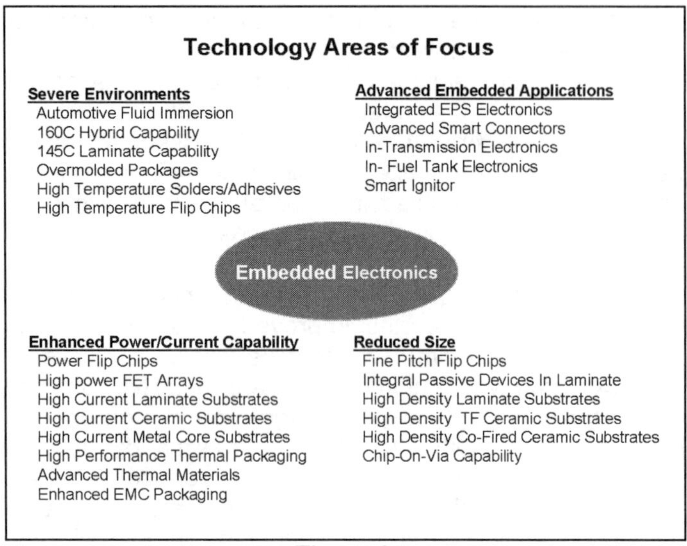

Figure 9.

Serviceability of modular systems is an issue that is likely to have three different solutions. These solutions are: replacement of the entire electronic/mechanical module, replacement of the entire module which can then be rebuilt/repaired, or individual replacement of major components in the module at the service facility. The solution used for a specific application will depend on the cost of the module and its individual components, the reliability of these components, and the extent that the module design will allow component replacement. The lowest cost option for high reliability and high manufacturing yield systems will be a throwaway non-repairable design. These designs will be "hard wired" and will use common enclosures for both mechanical and electronic components. As a result, they will be inherently lower cost to manufacture due to reduced component counts and lower interconnect costs. The lower manufacturing costs of these "hard wired" systems will drive many to adopt hard wire designs into currently repairable systems. This, in turn, will drive suppliers to make significant improvements in manufacturing yield and to improve component reliability.

The system level cost savings associated with embedded electronics can only be fully realized if the electrical and mechanical functions of the completed module are designed in an interactive manner. This is most easily accomplished if the systems, electrical, and mechanical design tasks are performed in a single organization or alternatively, in a very close partnership between two companies. This is a departure from standard automotive supply practices where different components of the same electronic/mechanical system are individually quoted and sourced from several suppliers. Effective utilization of embedded electronics will require that systems be quoted and sourced as complete modules. This requirement will give a significant competitive advantage to full service suppliers

As these technology and sourcing issues are resolved, a large number of automotive systems will be able to achieve higher levels of integration using embedded electronic solutions. Figure 10 lists many such systems.

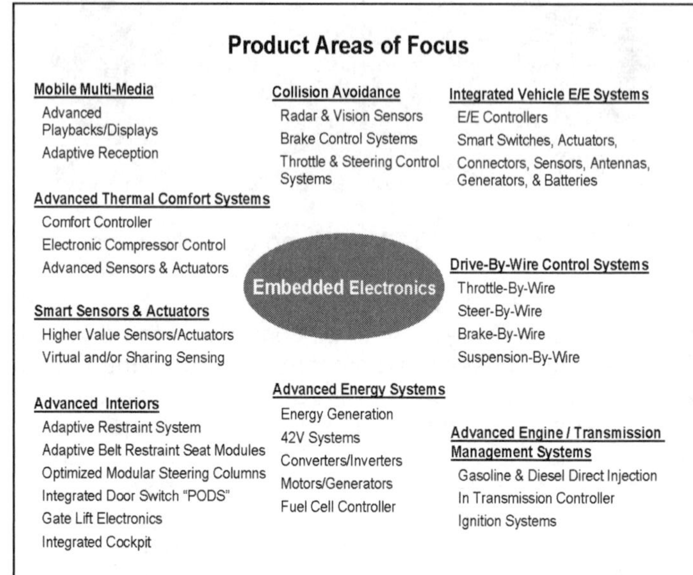

Figure 10.

CONCLUSION

The cost, size, quality, and performance benefits to be gained by embedding electronic content into existing automotive electro-mechanical modules will drive significant technology improvements in several areas. These improved technologies will allow electronics to be applied in higher temperature, smaller size, and higher current applications. Complex electronic functions will also be more capable of withstanding harsh environmental conditions such as immersion in automotive fluids.

The extent that electronics will be embedded into complex modules will be tempered, however, by system complexity and serviceability issues. The development of high yield and high reliability component and module assembly designs will, over time, allow the migration of lower cost non-serviceable embedded electronic designs into ever more complex automotive systems.

Major consolidation and cooperation in the automotive supplier base will be required to enable suppliers to meet the demand for modular system level solutions. Automotive sourcing will focus less on parts sourcing and more on modular systems sourcing from a limited range of full service tier-one suppliers.

The end result will be cars and trucks that provide significantly higher value and higher reliability transportation for the consumer.

ACKNOWLEDGMENTS

The authors wish to thank Daniel Ward, Harold Fields, Dan Schroeder, DHR Sarma and Jim Spall for their assistance and contributions.

REFERENCES

1. Jeff Burns and Suresh Chengalva, “Integrated Motor Drive Unit, A Mechatronics Packaging Concept for Automotive Electronics”, SAE 2000-01-0132
2. Glen W. De Vos, “Physical Integration Strategies for Distributed Powertrain Electronic Control Systems”, Engine Expo ’99 Proceedings

CONTACT

Bruce A. Myers – Staff Research Engineer, Jeff H. Burns – Advanced Project Engineer, Joseph M. Ratell – Senior Project Engineer

Advanced Packaging Processes and Materials, MS-D16, Delphi Delco Electronics Systems, P.O. Box 9005, Kokomo, IN, 46905-9005, Tel: (765) 451-3086, Fax: (765) 451-3115, bruce.a.myers@delphiauto.com

FUTURE TRENDS

The Enabling Path to Future Distributed Automotive Embedded Systems

Patrick Leteinturier
Infineon Technologies AG

ABSTRACT

The increasingly stringent requirements for safety, fuel economy, emissions reduction, and onboard diagnostics are pushing the automotive industry toward more innovative solutions and a rapid increase in electronic performance.

This paper will list the key factors necessary to increase overall data throughput and to provide the right features to satisfy future drivetrain requirements. The paper will address different aspects such as microcontroller architecture, cores, memories, power, sensor technologies, assembly/packaging, and development tools. It also will present techniques to improve modularity, scalability, and configurability that will offer a migration path to permit the evolution and even revolution of drivetrain electronics. Because quality and reliability requirements are among the most stringent of any application fields, the paper will outline the path to reach zero-defect products.

Other factors that will be addressed include technology evolution: The shrink path beyond 130 nm will be analyzed to identify advantages, constraints, and costs. A comparison of new solutions will be presented for future nonvolatile memories. The architecture trade-off using embedded versus standalone memory will be examined.

The automotive microcontroller industry faces the enormous challenge of bringing together high performance, harsh environment, quality, safety, reliability, durability, long-term delivery, scalability, configurability, and evolution at low cost. This challenge can be met only through close collaboration among OEMs, Tier 1s, and microcontroller manufacturers.

INTRODUCTION

The recent barrel price increase has shown that crude oil will not be the energy source forever. On one hand, we must conserve it as much as possible; on the other hand, we must prepare for its replacement. The challenge is not only energy availability but also the effect of exhaust gases on our environment. It is not only vital to reduce emissions such as CO, NOx, HC, and PM; we also must combat CO_2 to limit global warming. The Kyoto treaty and the CAFE (Corporate Average Fuel Economy) regulations are working in this direction. The ACEA target is to reduce emissions to 140 g/km of CO_2 by 2008 and to achieve a further reduction (to 120 g/km) by 2012. Engineers from all countries are working on this challenge, and different steps are required: improve engine efficiency, improve transmission for fuel economy, save further fuel by using hybrid solutions, regenerate energy during braking, and introduce high-performance battery management. The ultimate step will be to migrate toward the hydrogen economy.

To achieve this powertrain revolution, the control electronics will need a tremendous increase in performance and features. This paper will describe the key factors for the success of the mission.

MAIN SECTION

AUTOMOTIVE TRENDS

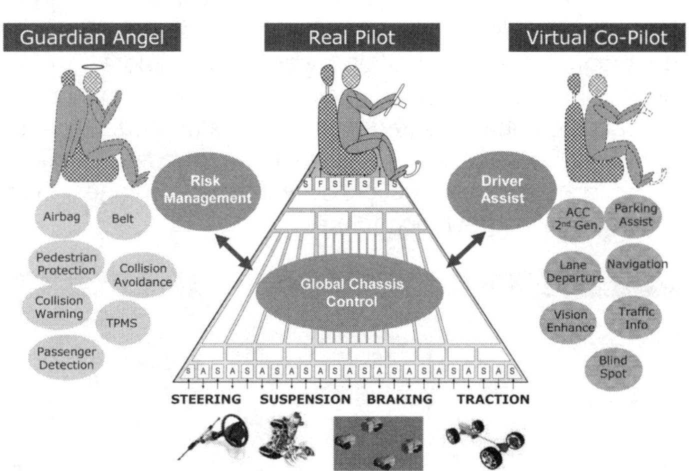

Trend 1: Global control replaces local control

Car innovation is characterized by the convergence of subsystems, with previous local controls such as engine management, braking, steering, and suspension harnessed to work together as coherent systems. The real driver or "pilot" benefits from global chassis control that is able to keep the car on the best trajectory according to the driver's expectations. To travel safely, the real driver needs assistance from a "virtual co-pilot." This assistance could be passive, such as traffic information, or active, such as a substitution of the real pilot (e.g., in the form of cruise control). To improve safety further, it is important to have a virtual guardian angel looking out for dangers such as possible collision, tires with the wrong pressure, and so forth. Again, the guardian angel will be able either to inform the pilot or to perform actions to protect people.

Trend 2: Distributed systems in vehicles

Global controls are pushing engineers to break through the limits of previous systems. Sensors, actuators, and controls are distributed to the best locations to guarantee the best implementation. Even the mechanical limitations are being redefined to give way to new forms of partitioning such as x-by-wire and mechatronic integration. Systems will be linked with new communication and power networks. The new networks will have to reduce communication dependability and interface complexity. This revolution opens new horizons for system scalability, flexibility for options, evolution, reusability, and composability.

Trend 3: Software will play an increasingly important role

Continuing from the previous observation, "drive and feel" will become increasingly defined by algorithms and software. The major part of OEM brands will be written in software, and it will continue to increase over the years. Software complexity also will increase, and software development will need to be split among a number of software producers. A revolutionary change in software development methodology will occur. Software development and validation must become more model-based. To allow easy maintenance and maximum reusability, software interfaces will be standardized. The software will have to be hardware-independent to allow multiple hardware suppliers to introduce changes over time as well as new technologies.

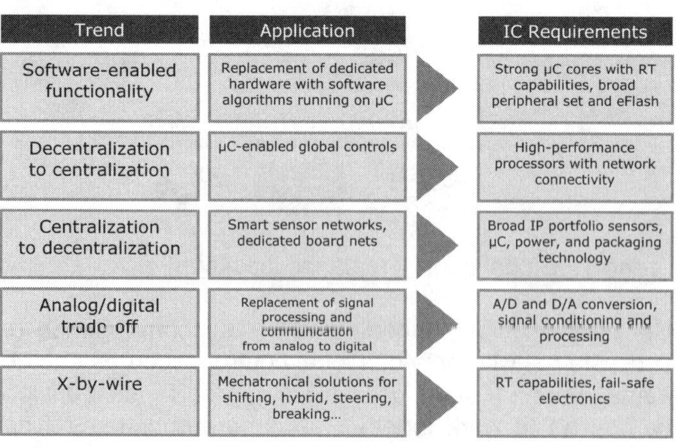

Trend	Application	IC Requirements
Software-enabled functionality	Replacement of dedicated hardware with software algorithms running on µC	Strong µC cores with RT capabilities, broad peripheral set and eFlash
Decentralization to centralization	µC-enabled global controls	High-performance processors with network connectivity
Centralization to decentralization	Smart sensor networks, dedicated board nets	Broad IP portfolio sensors, µC, power, and packaging technology
Analog/digital trade off	Replacement of signal processing and communication from analog to digital	A/D and D/A conversion, signal conditioning and processing
X-by-wire	Mechatronical solutions for shifting, hybrid, steering, breaking...	RT capabilities, fail-safe electronics

CHALLENGES AND APPROACHES

The challenge we have in front of us is to solve multiple equations simultaneously. Managing increasing system safety and reliability, achieving an improvement in quality targets, improving design flexibility, reducing system cost and time to market, and finally managing the increasing system functionality and complexity all require the system architecture, design and verification methods, and performance and technologies to be implemented concurrently.

Approach: System architecture

Today's high-end vehicles run up to 80 separate ECUs. These ECUs are mostly the legacy of previous systems. Communication between ECUs originally was point-to-point. The increasing need for information requires an increase in in-vehicle networking. Data traffic was quickly forcing a split into multiple subnetworks with an exponential increase in the number of gateways. If continued, this strategy will result in an unavoidable increase in costs.

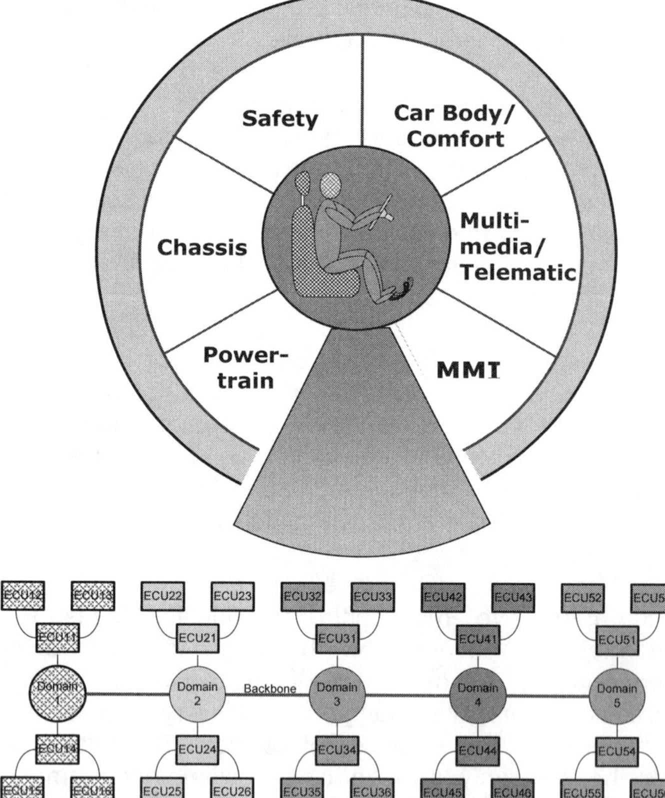

With the globalization of vehicle controls, a new approach must be applied, with a common backbone able to offer substantial benefits for the entire system. A backbone requires a sufficiently fast and safe communication channel that operates transparently and deterministically with the communication layer of the software. High-speed safety bus protocols such as

FlexRay appear to be well suited. New components must be invented to allow smart sensors and actuators using mechatronic techniques. ECU design itself is moving toward smarter and more integrated components able to run safety features: fail-safe, fail-silent, and fail-functional. New processors for controlling the vehicle will not only need to be real-time-embedded but also will have to host robust software.

Approach: Performance and technologies

The semiconductor industry delivers a 30% to 60% annual performance increase for the same cost. This performance has to be used not only to increase functionality but even more so to manage the complexity and lower the system cost by offering the software platform, with reusable software modules across applications and even customers. One key element toward realizing the software platform is the creation of hardware-independent software. To lower costs, hardware functions such as knock signal conditioning for engine management are being migrated into software. Software development is becoming more critical, and automatic code generation is offering a huge potential for faster implementation and for more efficient algorithm verification and for getting out legacy code easily. This performance increase opens new horizons for standardization of application interfaces, e.g., AUTOSAR, development of transparent software with encapsulation, and software self-test. As semiconductor technologies move rapidly, it is important to run a microprocessor family concept with, of course, performance increases and an easy migration path to allow upward compatibility.

Approach: Design and verification methods

As system complexity increases, developers must find new design and verification methods. The amount of information is increasing at an exponential rate, and, at the same time, there is a growing need for visibility. At all levels—sensors, controls and power actuations—new techniques must be deployed to allow model-based development with simulation at multiple levels such as architecture mapping, functional performance, or cycle accuracy. Verification must be applied at different stages in the development process: during simulation, fast prototyping, debug, calibration, system validation, qualification, and certification. The silicon must provide the right hooks to allow the tools to get the information needed for all the verifications and for all the components, sensors, controls, and power actuations. These links must remain inexpensive and easy to handle in the difficult car environment. Furthermore, concurrent tools should be used at the same time, and total transparency must be applied between production and instrumented devices.

Application concerns

The systems that will control our future cars will have to provide the right HMI (Human/Machine Interface), will have to be safe–deterministic–real-time, and will need to be distributed–embedded in the car. To achieve this performance, three types of dependability will have to be solved: dependable computation, dependable communication, and dependable power.

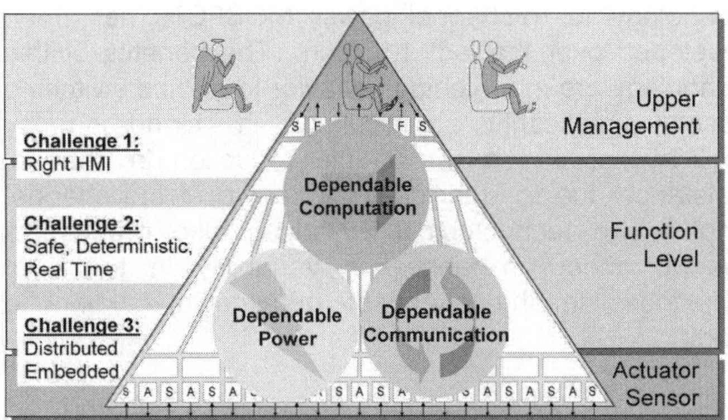

THE SEMICONDUCTOR TECHNOLOGIES

Microcontrollers are manufactured in logic technologies—after DRAM, the technology with the highest integration. The increasing integration, which results in smaller structure sizes, allows the implementation of powerful processors and peripherals. It can fulfill the performance demands of upcoming applications. The trend to integrated DSP functionality will allow the introduction of more complex and precise software algorithms for signal processing, which allows software replacement of functionality that formerly was realized in hardware. In the embedded control area, the highly integrated CMOS 130 nm and 90 nm are running millions of fast switching transistors at more than 200 MHz. This technology allows analog measurement and flash memory integration.

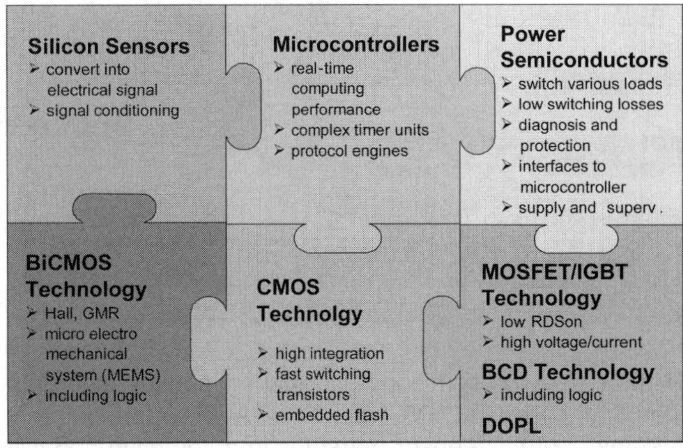

The development of power semiconductor technologies over the last several years has concentrated mainly on optimizing existing systems in terms of costs and partial integration. The resulting hybrid technologies (BCD technologies), which allow the integration of power output stages (DMOS or bipolar), analog circuits (e.g., band gap, target/actual measurement and comparison), and digital logic (e.g., diagnostic, simple error memory, serial interface, tristate output), led to products that permit a significant reduction in the components needed in a control device. The MOSFET technologies are following the trend of minimization of costs for the same functionality, which leads to smaller silicon area for the same RDS(on). A new generation of so-called SFET technology for n-channel power MOSFETs has been developed over the last 1.5 years. The benefits of this technology are in switching behavior to reduce switching losses significantly, particularly in high-frequency applications, and a remarkable reduction in channel resistance due to significant shortening of the channel length. The technological advances also produce a positive effect on fabrication variability in terms of robustness in the event of breakdown (avalanche mode).

Powertrain applications require multiple sensors to connect the "real" environment to the electronics. Semiconductor-based sensors are dedicated to measure speed, position, temperature, and pressure. The change from passive sensors to active ones by integration of sensor elements and the signal conditioning are a major trend for powertrain and chassis. This trend is motivated by the fundamental need for more precise measurements and more relevant physical values of the system. In the sensor area, the mixed signal BiCMOS technologies are able to manage Hall effect, GMR, and MEMS microelectromechanical system including logic.

Sensors

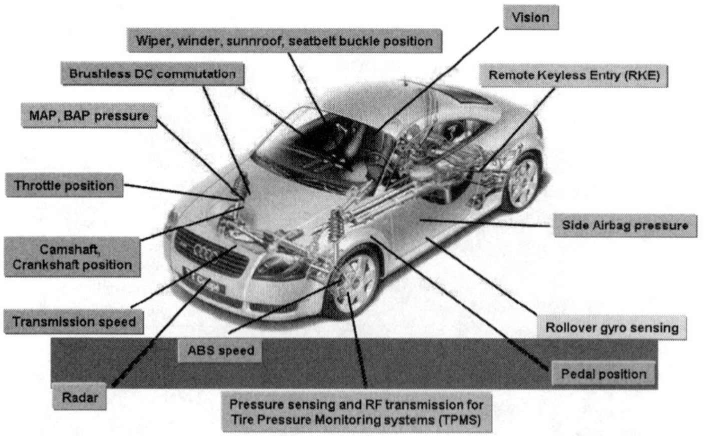

Market size for semiconductor-based sensor elements was $1.6 billion in 2005, with 15% CAGR. Approximately two-thirds of this sensor market is in automotive and will remain the key growth driver for sensors. The share of active sensors in automotive use increased from less than 30% in 1999 to more than 75% in 2006 due to requirements for more accurate and reliable measurements. The physical values to be sensed are distance, position, speed, acceleration, pressure, temperature, humidity, magnetic field intensity, current, and quantity of chemical components. New applications such as adaptive cruise control require new sensors for obstacle detection such as radar and camera-based vision. Silicon technologies are not only able to sense these multiple physical values but also to integrate signal conditioning, diagnosis, and wired or wireless communication-based analog or digital information.

REPLACEMENT OF PASSIVE SENSORS BY ACTIVE SENSORS

Multiple sensors are used in the vehicle to measure position or the speed of translating or rotating elements. The use of variable reluctance sensors and potentiometers is limited in many fields because the applications often require better accuracy over lifetime for improved power-up strategies.

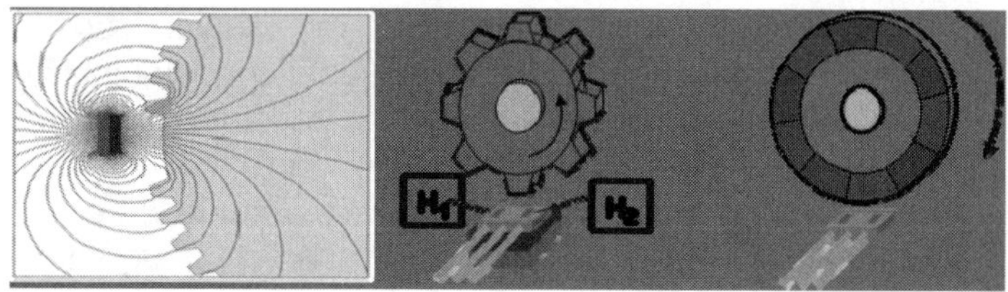

The challenge also is to reduce the hardware components to keep the sensor and ECU as small as possible. All these features are now available on active sensors with, in addition, the possibility to improve electronic safety such as self-diagnosis, self-calibration, and the implementation of digital communication.

MICROCONTROLLER PERFORMANCE

A number of different criteria should be taken into account when selecting a microcontroller. Most people still measure performance in MIPS, millions of operations per second, or simply use static C benchmarks. We can classify the benchmarks into four categories.

The first obviously is the static benchmark relating to the algorithms that the application will have to execute. In automotive, we can identify three main subcategories: the filters (e.g., FIR, IRR, DSP), the state machines (e.g., conditions, switch case), and the controls (e.g., PID, H-infinity, Kalman+LQG, vectors, statistics, trigonometric, table look-up and interpolation, neural networks).

The second is the dynamic benchmark relating to task arbitration, context switch, parameter encapsulation, memory management, and so forth. This is closely linked to the operating system support.

The third is the functional driver benchmark. This relates to the performance of a complete driver such as AUTOSAR (e.g., CAN driver, LIN driver, PWM driver,

ADC driver). This is a system benchmark including peripherals, a bus system, DMA, co-processor, and processor.

The final benchmark is autocoding technology. The target is to measure the efficiency of the chain: code generator, C compiler, and the target microcontroller.

In its new setting, the EEMBC is aiming to develop the four benchmark types and to provide the automotive community a measurable attribute of performance.

MICROCONTROLLER ARCHITECTURE

Overall architecture

Powertrain processors have sophisticated architectures. The ones ramping up today contain up to 40 million transistors. The microcontroller has the mission to acquire inputs, to compute this information, and to provide outputs. The inputs and outputs could be analogs or digital at the pins of the device, or events could come from buses such as FlexRay, CAN, LIN, and SPI. The microcontroller architecture is the clever assembly of cores, buses, memories, caches, and peripherals to achieve the best system performance to cost.

Microcontroller core

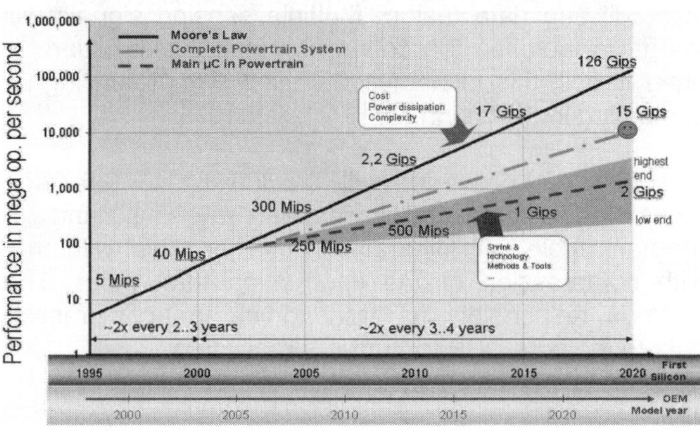

The microcontroller core has been designed to lead the most aggressive technology roadmap of embedded systems. Some 130-nm versions are already available on the market, 90-nm versions are already in the hands of designers, and 65-nm versions are scheduled. It will be reasonable to run this powerful core at 500 MHz in automotive conditions.

High-end cores are superscalar machines running up to three instructions in parallel: load store, arithmetic, and loop management. Cores also use multiple-step pipelines to perform instruction fetch, decode, execution, and write-back.

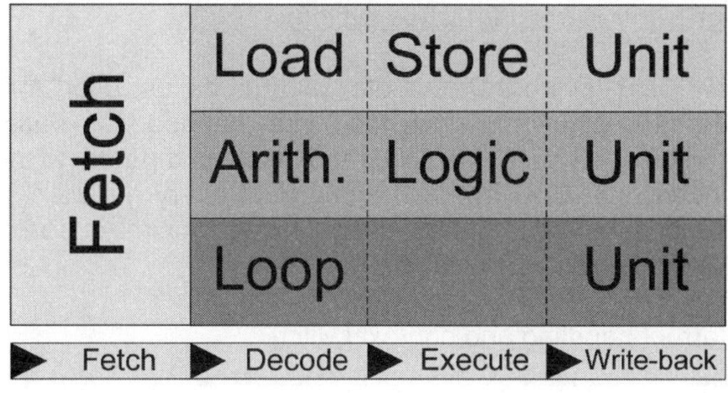

To further improve performance, next-generation cores will incorporate multithreading functionality. Multithreading is an innovative technique for utilizing the existing microprocessor hardware resources more efficiently, while adding almost negligible overhead to the chip area. Instead of waiting for instructions coming from slower nonvolatile memories, other already available instructions will be executed instead. It's like having two virtual CPUs. Automotive real-time criteria will be met using specific advanced scheduling techniques.

Three-layer architecture

The wish of all microcontroller architects is to develop the maximum performance for the minimum gate count and to provide a chip in which all the transistors are delivering the best benefit at every clock. One way to meet this challenge is to partition the computation so that conflict is not possible and modules are not waiting for the results of others. A precondition is the availability of clean interfaces.

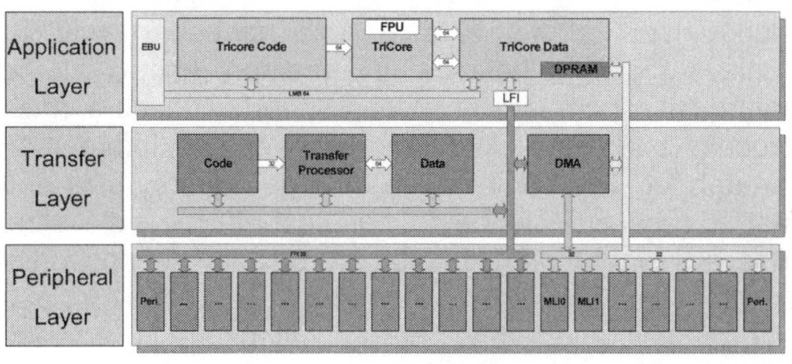

The three-layer architecture has been developed for this purpose: one layer to run the application, one for the peripheral modules, and one to manage the transfers between application and peripherals without conflict. A scalable implementation has been realized to suit different requirement levels in terms of performance and bandwidth. The first is having as transfer layer a DMA (Direct Memory Access) with a multi-master bus able to manage all possible conflicts. The second step replaces the DMA with the PCP (Peripheral Control Processor). It is a full 32-bit processor optimized for transfer management. The third step adds the strength of the DMA and the PCP.

Microcontroller external bus system

New DDR (Double Data Rate) bus interfaces, used for external flash, minimize the time needed for data transfers between the CPU and flash compared to a conventional EBU by transferring data every half-clock. Reduced pin-count and voltage levels minimize cost, EMI, and power consumption.

Interrupt handling and context switch

Unlike a PC application, automotive is a real-time embedded system. Hardware mechanisms must be built to conserve processing performance for arbitration and to reduce the task service latency. A service request node has the capability to arbitrate up to 510 tasks in only four clock cycles. When the task is identified, the working context is saved automatically. In such a case, the hardware mechanism also will save on microcontroller performance.

Memories

The memory requirement is growing at the rate predicted by Moore's law, that is, roughly a doubling of memory size every 18 months, or in a more automotive period, it is equivalent to multiplying the memory size by a factor of 10 every five years. The following graph represents memory growth in powertrain applications. In 1998, the nonvolatile memory requirement was only 128 Kbytes; in 2005, it was 2 Mbytes. At this rate of growth, powertrain will reach 32 Mbytes by 2010. In fact, the single EMS engine management system will not reach this value, but the sum of powertrain sub-applications (i.e., engine, transmission, battery management, starter, alternator) will not be far away. To achieve the right balance, the memory should at the same time increase in access speed. The core must process code and data quickly to ensure information throughput. The combination of large memory size and fast access time leads to non-cost-effective die size. This is why new architectures are developing innovative solutions to run with high performance and high flash size but cost effectively. These solutions are called wide access, burst memory, double data rate, caches, and multithreading.

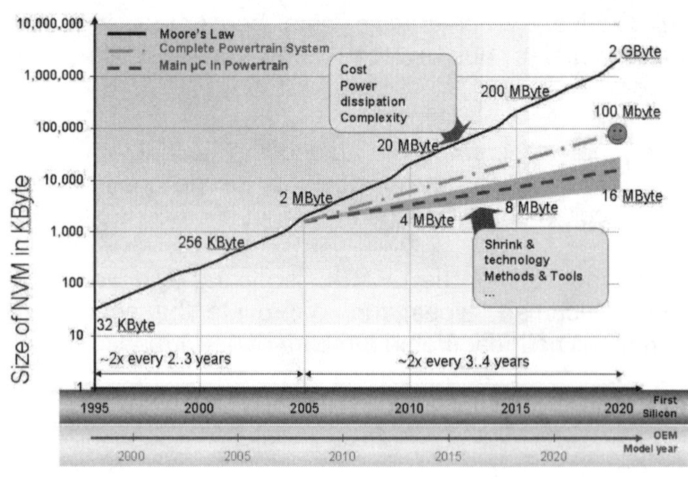

Code and data cache

Caches minimize bottlenecks between the high-speed CPU and slower internal and external nonvolatile memories. The right caching strategy tuned for automotive applications is the key to reaching maximum efficiency. This comes with separate instruction and data caches, designed for maximum predictability.

DMA (Direct Memory Access)

In most applications it is useful to transfer information from A to B with minimum overhead. That is the function of the DMA direct memory access; this move engine copies information without stopping the cores to process the data.

Peripheral fast AD converter

The tremendous increase in microcontroller performance together with fast analog acquisition has allowed the migration of functions from hardware to software implementations. This approach has the benefit of reducing system cost and improving functionality. The knock function in software provides more design flexibility across multiple sensors, engines, and vehicles. It also is more robust against hardware tolerances and aging. It allows the evolution of the function and better diagnosis. On the same principle, future developments also will see data fusion. Multiple sensing signals will merge to increase the coherence of the information. In other cases, this technique will allow virtual sensing by computing indirect signals.

The fast AD converter will provide up to 3.5 mega samples per second, with anti-aliasing and a programmable gain differential amplifier. This will come with compression of the information throughput. The DMA is responsible for transporting the compressed data to the core DSP for further processing.

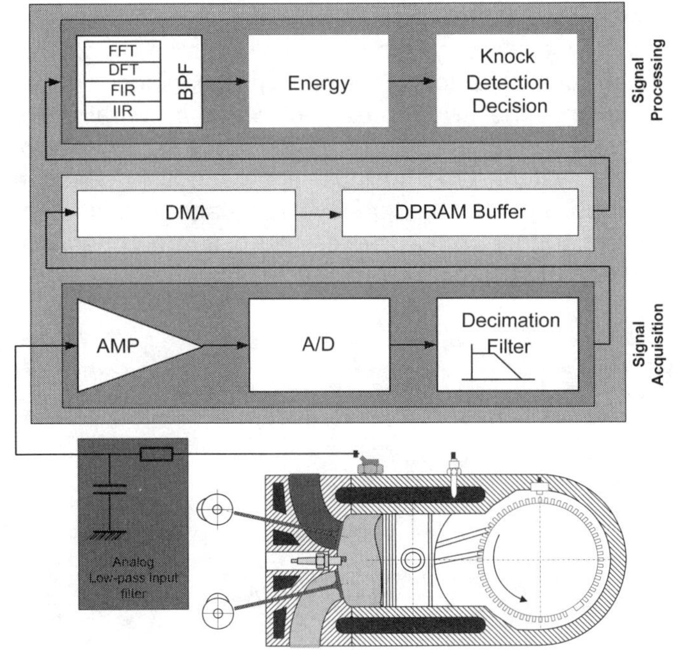

μC connectivity

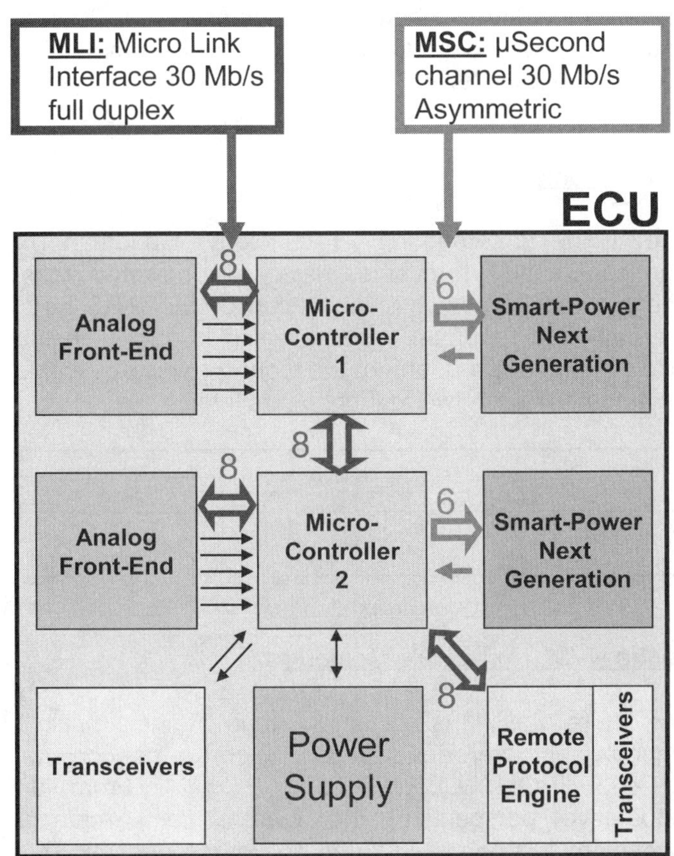

In times when everything has to be fast and cost effective, the design and fabrication of an ECU also must follow the same rules. The answer to the problem is partitioning and mapping of components that can be reused. The principle is called ASSP (Application Specific Standard Product). The component is generic and offers the advantage of allowing higher volumes at lower cost. In addition, quality and reliability often are better than specific ASICs. The precondition for the success of an ASSP is connectivity to the rest of the system. As communication among components increases, new internal buses must be developed. The SPI (Serial Peripheral Interface) reached its limits at about 5 megabits per second. The challenge is more in the range of 30 megabits per second. In collaboration with key customers, a new bus has been developed to fulfill the need for high-bandwidth connectivity.

It is now possible to connect processors of the same ECU like transputers, but also to link the processors more efficiently to the next smartpower generation as well as the analog front end. For example, if a new protocol engine emerges, this can be implemented on a standalone device and can be connected easily to the processors. The new connectivity allows the previous point-to-point connection to be replaced by high-speed serial communication and in this way reduces the cost of the ECU.

ECU communication and network

The level of networking in modern production vehicles is increasing steadily. The number of control units and the amount of shared data transferred among them has enabled some degree of distributed functionality to be achieved. However, the move to full distributed real-time systems requires a higher bandwidth and more deterministic buses than the LIN or CAN, which currently are the state of the art. One such next generation of automotive bus system is FlexRay. It provides a guaranteed signal latency, composability, error detection, and bandwidth up to 10 Mbit/sec. The microcontroller will have to integrate buses according to the communication requirements. The following table gives a relative comparison among the three buses. LIN, CAN, and FlexRay are not competing with each other.

Relative System Cost	Speed	Effective Efficiency	Common Uses
LIN	19.2 Kb/s	~25%	Body, Periphery
HS CAN	1 Mb/s	~30%	Engine, Chassis, Safety, Body
FLEXRAY	10 Mb/s	~70%	Future Real-time

Memory protection and management

To develop safety software, it is important to guarantee protection of the processor resources in terms of memory, I/O access, control access, and CPU performance. It is one step toward the certification of software. It also is essential to be able to develop software at multiple locations, by multiple teams, and even by multiple companies. The work of the integrator will facilitate and sometimes enable by using hardware solutions for memory management unit and multiple user mode with given privileges. The operating system that will schedule the application also will need new features to guarantee execution in a given time, signature watchdog, and even multi-core redundancy.

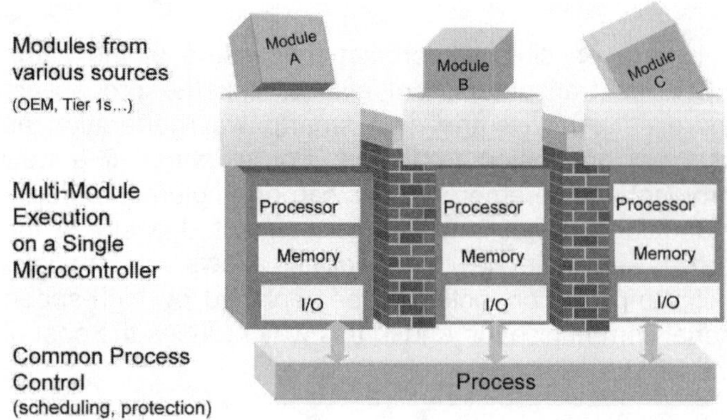

Redundancy

In safety-critical applications, redundancy is a must. In powertrain, the electronic throttle control is a typical example. In the future drive-by-wire, more applications will become safety critical and will follow clear guidelines such as IEC61508, ISO-26262, and the SIL (Safety Integrity Levels) classification. The redundancy can be shared between the symmetrical and asymmetrical architectures, one using the same core and the other using different cores. The cores could be on the same or different die(s), but also on the same or different package(s). We also can identify the need or not for independent supply, oscillator, or reset system. The redundancy could be spatial, temporal, or functional. Some self-test/auto-test could be mandatory.

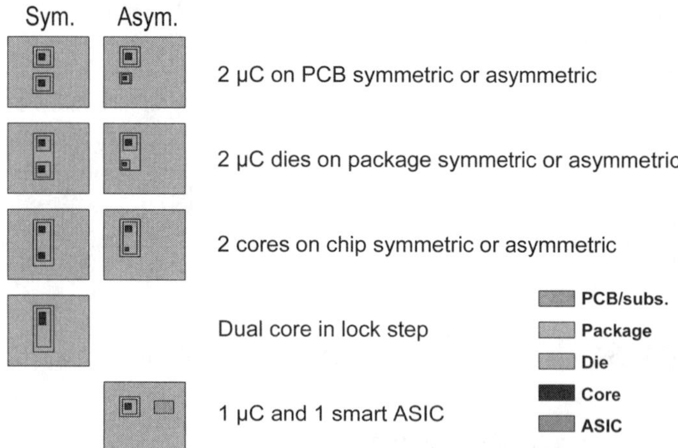

Parallel processing

The powertrain performance requirement is increasing. The megahertz battle is a great challenge, and the PC market is stagnating at about 3 GHz. At this frequency, the processor is consuming very high power. This requires an expensive cooling system. An alternative to the increase in megahertz is parallel processing. This solution brings a lot of flexibility, depending on the application. The two cores can work in parallel for increased performance or for redundancy in the case of a safety system. One possible approach is to describe the control algorithm in high-level language; two different code generators could develop two different codes that will run on the two cores and check each other.

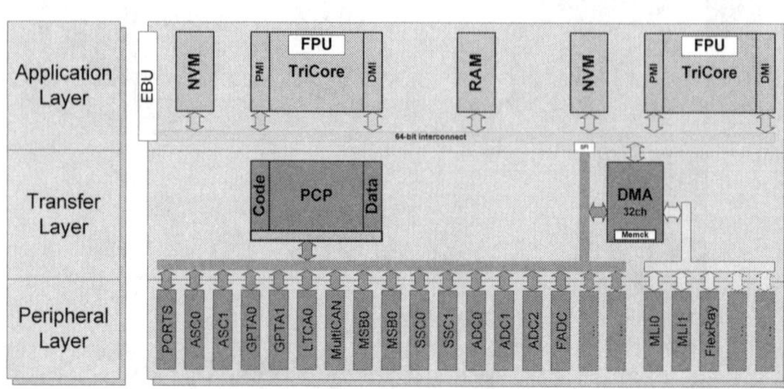

If a multiprocessor is now well established in the PC industry, it is only at the starting point for automotive with stringent real-time embedded requirements. Much work needs to be done to create parallel computation software architecture. This work also will impinge on software processes, methodology, and, of course, tools.

ITRS roadmap

The ITRS (International Technology Roadmap of Semiconductors) forecasts major silicon innovations. The automotive sector is influenced by the ITRS MPU M1 half-pitch roadmap variant, which is shown in the following table. On average, the technology is applicable for automotive use two to three years later.

Year	2000	2002 2003	2005	2007 2008	2010	2013	2016	2019
Technology (nm)	180	130	90	65	45	32	22	16

Future NVM (Nonvolatile Memory)

The future of NVM is not set in stone. Rather, multiple technologies are envisaged: high-K, nanocrystal, MRAM, NROM, CBRAM, and PCRAM. From an automotive perspective, the current flash memory technology will persist until the end of the decade. This does presuppose the need for a "universal memory." The ovonic unified memory (OUM), also known as phase-change memory (PCRAM), is the most promising of the nonvolatile memory alternatives, more so than magnetic RAM (MRAM) or ferro-electric RAM (FeRAM), which likewise are being studied as potential replacements.

High-K: This technology replaces the conventional tunnel oxide and ONO with Al_2O_3. The expected benefit is significant reduction in programming voltages, leading to area reduction.

Nanocrystal: This technology envisions the replacement of a single floating gate by many nanofloating gates (1E12/cm^2). The advantages are that thinner tunnel oxide is possible, and a single leakage path is not fatal.

MRAM: Data storage is achieved within magnetic material. The programming is realized by current-induced magnetic fields. The advantages are fast programming, high endurance, and high compatibility with standard CMOS.

	Cell Size	Cell Efficiency	Module Cost	Read Speed	Retention	Endurance	Temperature Behavior	Power Consumption	Shrinkability
High-K	+	+	0	0	0	0	0	0	+
Nano-crystal	+	+	+	0	-	0	0	0	+
MRAM	0	0	+	0	+	+++	-	0	+
NROM	+	0	+	0	-	-	-	-	+
CBRAM	+++	++	++	0	0	++	0	++	++
PCRAM	++	+	++	0	0	++	0	0	+++

NROM: This technology replaces the floating gate with charge-trapping nitride. The write function is realized by channel hot electrons, and erase by hot-hole injection. The advantages are a smaller cell size (however, 2 bits per cell option is not possible for automotive) and that a single leakage path is not fatal.

CBRAM: Data storage is achieved by forming/removing a conductive path of Ag precipitates within a solid electrolyte located in a via hole. The advantages are good scalability, low voltage, low power, fast programming, high endurance, and high compatibility with standard CMOS.

PCRAM: Data storage is effected using chalcogenide material. Write/erase is achieved by switching between amorphous and crystalline phases. The advantages are good scalability, fast programming, high endurance, and high compatibility with standard CMOS.

EMBEDDED SOFTWARE

The AUTOSAR partnership is an alliance of OEM manufacturers and Tier 1 automotive suppliers working together to develop and establish a *de facto* open industry standard for automotive E/E architecture that will serve as a basic infrastructure for the management of functions within both future applications and standard software modules.

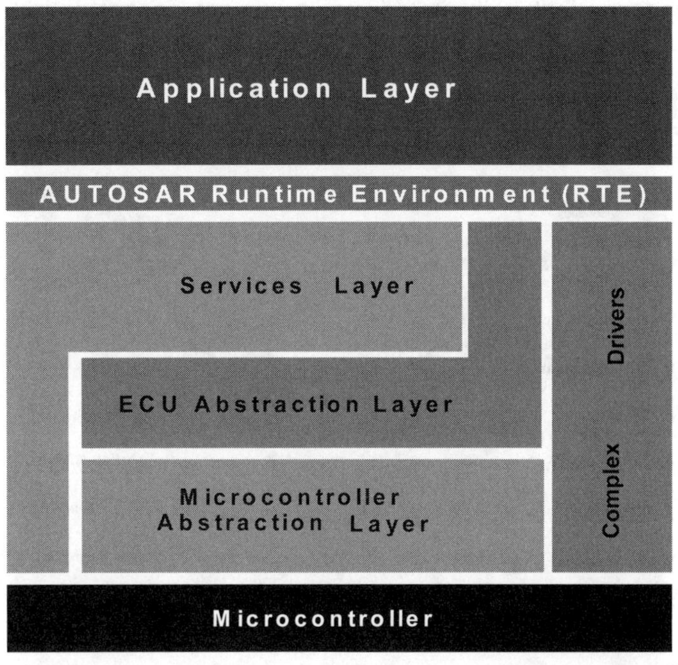

The objective of the partnership is the establishment of an open standard for an automotive E/E architecture. It will serve as a basic infrastructure for the management of functions within both future applications and standard software modules. The goals include the following:

- Implementation and standardization of basic system functions as an industry-wide "standard core" solution
- Scalability to different vehicle and platform variants
- Transferability of functions throughout the network
- Integration of functional modules from multiple suppliers
- Consideration of availability and safety requirements
- Redundancy activation
- Maintainability throughout the whole "product life cycle"
- Increased use of "commercial off-the-shelf hardware"
- Software updates and upgrades over the vehicle lifetime

The AUTOSAR scope includes all vehicle domains. More information is available at http://www.autosar.org/.

The impact of AUTOSAR on microcontroller architecture will be important in the long run. AUTOSAR obliges our automotive society to rationalize the software architecture to optimize reusability, testability, validation, quality, and so forth. The first implementations often demand more CPU performance and bigger memory size, but the hardware architecture must learn how to implement well-structured software in a cost-effective manner. The migration is already in progress; the microcontroller suppliers are taking the microcontroller abstraction layer more into account and are constrained into optimizing the hardware and software implementation at the same time. This is, for example, achieved by adding features to allow the development of independent software layers, argument encapsulation, creating different user modes to give the right privilege—no more, no less.

DEVELOPMENT TOOLS

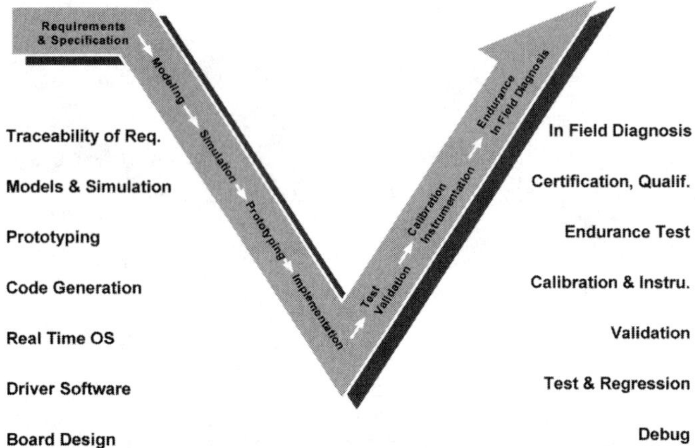

The automotive system development cycle is characterized by a great deal of interaction among OEMs, Tier 1s, silicon vendors, and third-party tool vendors. New technologies such as automatic code generation are becoming efficient. This has an important impact on the microcontroller architecture. The development of optimized libraries is essential. These libraries use the best of the cores, the buses, the memories, the cache, multithreading, multicores, and all features that appear complex to the non-expert community.

With the growing amount of information inside the microcontroller, new tools have been created. The previous emulators (at a price level of 20k) are now implemented on-chip. This new approach allows debug prototyping and calibration to take place in the difficult vehicle environment. Function partitioning enables cost-effective development, with even more cost efficiency during mass production. The behavior of the ECU is identical during development and in mass production. A further requirement is communication using standard interfaces such as USB to reduce the cost of tools. To enable these requirements to be met, the microcontroller integrates on-chip debug and calibration mechanisms.

POWER DEVICES

In powertrain applications, loads such as the injectors, oxygen sensor heater, purge valve, cooling fan, and several relays must be switched. The integration of multiple switches in one IC allows the reduction of the dimensions of PCBs and therefore the reduction of cost. Today, multi-channel switches with 2 to 18 channels are available. Depending on the specific application, currents from 50 mA up to 50 A have to be driven. The loads could be ohmic, capacitive, or inductive.

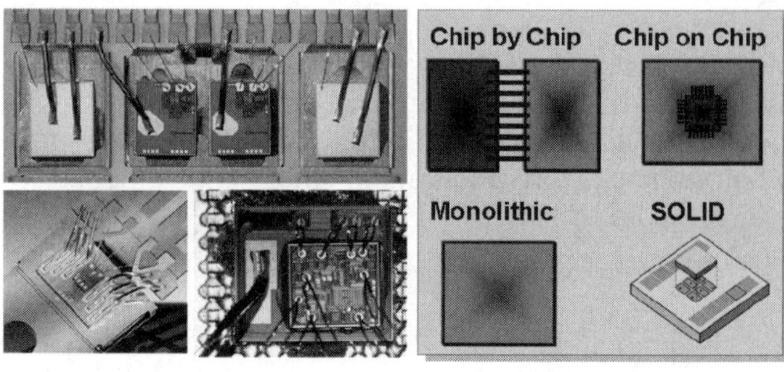

Multi-Channel Switches

More and more digital logic can be implemented beside the power output stages, thanks to the mentioned BCD technologies. This enables the introduction of new features previously done by special ASICs or the microcontroller.

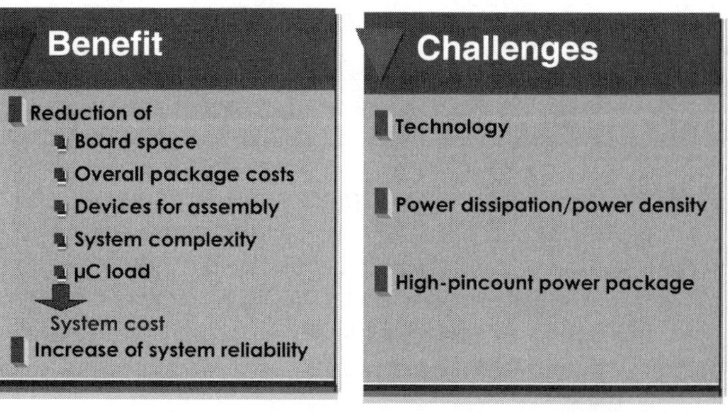

For example, loads such as injectors can actuate in a peak and hold current regulation mode and are driven by external pulse width modulation (PWM). Today's multi-channel switches can incorporate circuitry to run such advanced functions autonomously without further external control.

In addition to this control functionality, today's switches incorporate protection and detection features such as for short circuits, overload, over-temperature, over-voltage, open loads, Electro-Static Discharge (ESD), and reverse current. Additionally, fail-safe modes such as shutdown after detection of an overload, limiting the current, or a "limp home" mode can be implemented to increase system reliability. The multi-channel switches usually can be controlled by a standard communication interface

(SPI). Diagnostic information is transferred via SPI back to the microcontroller. High-speed point-to-point communication interfaces have been developed. On one hand, they increase the data bandwidth for future time-critical applications (e.g., current regulation by PWM); on the other hand, they reduce the number of necessary I/O ports at the microcontroller and the power switch (e.g., for ≥8 channel devices).

Switching processes, especially at high frequencies, cause electromagnetic emissions. Therefore, shaping of the switching signal can help to reduce these emissions to a minimum. This is realized in multi-channel switches with so-called soft edging, slew rate control, or soft clamping.

Power Bridges

Power Bridges' main application in powertrain is the control of DC motors. Those motors move throttles and flaps. Today's Power Bridge ICs contain the following features. The DC motor is driven by a fully protected H-bridge. The motor is controlled by PWM with frequencies exceeding 20 kHz. This leads to reduced reaction time and causes no mechanical resonance and less current ripple. Active freewheeling is implemented to reduce power losses.

Also, the integration of digital logic allows accurate control of the H-bridge and enables functionality regarding protection and diagnosis. The programming of the H-bridge can be performed with two input pins. The modes are "running," "freewheeling clock," and "counterclockwise." An additional serial interface (SPI) is used to set the following operation modes:

a. **Slow decay**: Conventional freewheeling, current decreases due to resistance of motor winding and power stages only
b. **Fast decay**: Active break by full supply voltage, fast response, smooth transition around neutral position

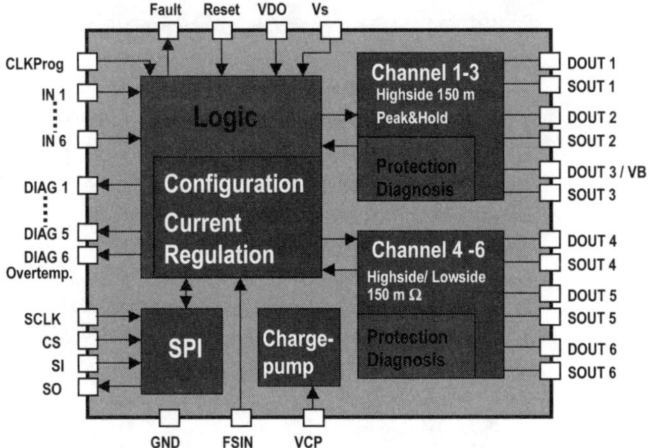

Configuration of a multi channel chip for powertrain (e.g., TLE6288R)

Furthermore, the SPI allows programming the current limit and the chopper-off-time. The SPI interface also enables diagnostic functions to detect short-circuit cases, open loads, and to limit the current. A three-step temperature monitoring (pre-warning, warning, and shutdown) enables more safety functionality. The detailed failure mode can be communicated to the micro-controller via the SPI.

SMART HIGH-SIDE SWITCHES

For high-current applications, smart high-side switches can drastically reduce the number of necessary components and can increase powertrain performance. These fully protected high-side switches can drive static currents up to 100 A and can incorporate additional protection and diagnosis functions such as current limitation over-voltage and over-temperature protection, open load diagnostic, and current sensing. Therefore, a single high-side switch can replace four electrical/mechanical components—the power-relays, the relays' driver, diagnosis/protection circuits, and the fuse—and in this way reduces the wiring harness, board space, and system complexity. The ability to perform PWM up to 1 kHz gives an additional advantage over mechanical solutions.

Typical applications for high-side switches are the starter (up to 1000 A peak), cooling fan (PWM required to reduce power consumption), pressure pumps (PWM for pressure regulation), and glow plugs for diesel systems (PWM and current sensing necessary for normal operation).

TRANSCEIVERS

The main function of transceivers is to transmit the communication signals of the microcontroller on the communication line in the car. In powertrain applications, high-speed CAN is the standard bus protocol. High bus bandwidth up to 1 MBaud enhanced EMC behavior is demanded. Therefore, high-speed transceivers that are optimized for EMC have been developed, manufactured in a BCD process that enables the integration of logic and power components on the same die. This results in an excellent EMC behavior of the transceiver. In addition, such devices are designed for ESD protection and can withstand up to 8 kV for contact and 15 kV for air discharge. For improved driving functionality, an integrated slew rate control enhances the EMC behavior. Such devices can be switched off during a reset of the micro-controller and provide a receive-only/silent mode to prevent so-called babbling idiots in the network. This characteristic ensures that the transceivers maintain the communication on the network to transmit important engine data from ECU to ECU within the powertrain system and to body and safety networks.

In addition to CAN, the LIN protocol becomes the standard for a bus for diagnosis. Single-wire transceivers that are compatible with the LIN specification and ISO9141 functions can transmit up to 20 kBaud and incorporate a short circuit to ground and battery control and over-temperature protection. Furthermore, such transceivers have been designed for very low current consumption in standby mode.

POWER SUPPLY

The sensing, control, and actuation functionality can be granted on an ECU only if power is supplied in an appropriate way. The requirements for the supply of the mentioned components demand new power supply architectures far removed from traditional solutions. In previous systems, single linear regulators were adequate. With lower voltages, higher currents, and special sequencing requirements, multi-voltage power supplies become state of the art.

The new concept consists of a step-down pre-regulator and three post-linear low drop voltage regulators (LDOs) on one single chip. The asynchronous Buck-converter provides a bus voltage that acts as the source of the three linear regulators. The purpose of the concept "Buck and Linear" is to reduce the total power loss in the chip in case of driving high currents at the output of the linear regulators. Considering a powertrain system with a total current consumption of more than 1 A, this concept is very attractive for 12 V systems.

SMART PARTITIONING/EMBEDDED POWER

To conquer the coming challenges, low-cost electronic distributed solutions are needed. A distributed module will have to manage its own power supply, reset, communication, control, sensing, and actuating. To manage the right assembly, different partitioning can be explored.

μC and power in one package

The different functions must be mapped to technologies, and then these technologies to the chip, and the chip to packages. We can identify three families of solution: the monolithic, the multi-chip, and the discrete. The following figure shows the multi-chip solution, where the power functions are made on the base chip and an 8-bit microcontroller is the top chip, with the two chips mounted flip-chip/chip-on-chip.

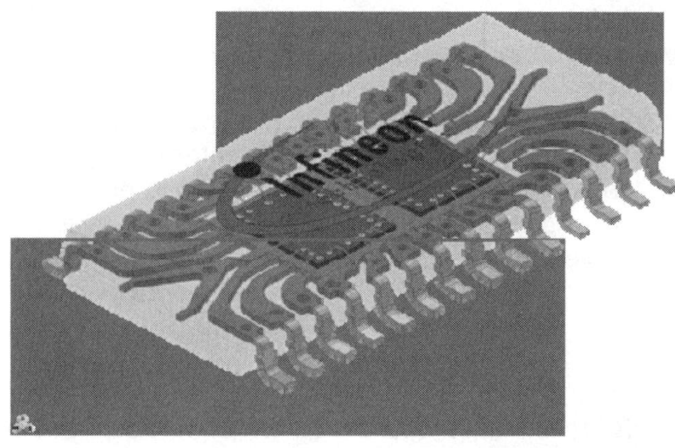

POWER MODULES

In the race for energy efficiency, hybrid vehicles are gaining momentum. In this field, electric motors and generators vary from 10 kW to 100 kW, with voltage from 200 V to 600 V. The challenge is to assemble high-performance trench IGBT inside a power module to allow proper cooling of the electronics. Here, the three phase inverters are mounted on the HybridPACK1 designed for the main inverter of a mild HEV application with a power range up to 20 kW, 420 V, and HybridPACK2 designed for full HEV application with a power range up to 80 kW, 420 V. All these modules use the most advanced 600 V IGBT3 technology.

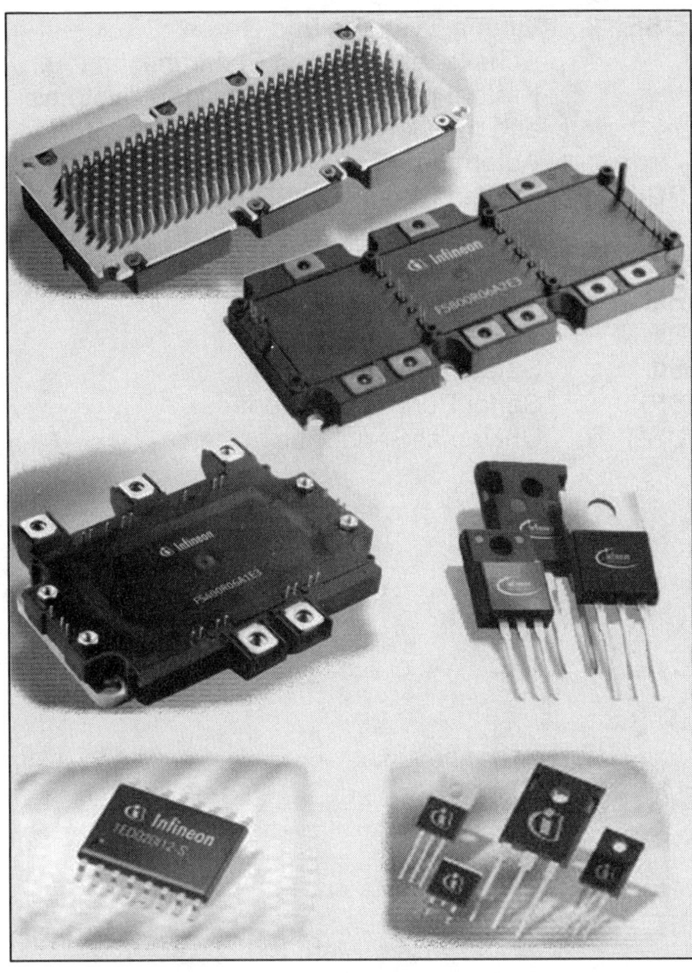

CONCLUSION

In today's powertrain systems, a broad range of semiconductor technologies enables the design of electronics for signal sensing, control, and actuation. The devices must fulfill the special requirements demanded in powertrain and chassis applications. They must withstand the harsh environment under the hood, and they must comply with the maximum performance needs of a real-time system.

Sensing speed, position, temperature, and pressure can be realized in silicon today. Microcontrollers grant the real-time control of a powertrain and chassis system. The performance of today allows the implementation of torque-based control algorithms. A broad range of power devices is available to switch the loads, to transmit signals to communication lines, and to supply power to the electronic devices of the ECU. These devices incorporate logic functionality for safety and diagnostic reasons.

Owning all the technologies previously mentioned enables innovative and smart partitioning of future devices: smart sensors, smart power devices, and devices that sense and actuate. In this smart partitioning, the strength of each technology can be deployed from high computing performance to switching high currents.

In addition to silicon technology, advanced packaging technologies can answer tomorrow's questions regarding an electronic solution. Power modules could push the integration of semiconductors in one package to place them close to the actuator.

The mission for the semiconductor industry for future devices is clear. Semiconductors must fulfill the requirements in terms of quality, reliability, and performance with a reasonable price. In close cooperation with the automotive industry, the cost optimization for the semiconductors within the whole powertrain and chassis system can be found by applying the mentioned smart partitioning. This also could incorporate the reduction of development efforts while the complexity of the systems is increasing.

CONTACT

Patrick Leteinturier
Tel: +49 (89) 234 83828

Patrick.Leteinturier@infineon.com

Infineon Technologies AG
Am Campeon Building 1-12,
85579 Neubiberg, Germany
http://www.infineon.com

DEFINITIONS, ACRONYMS, AND ABBREVIATIONS

ACEA	Association (des) Constructeurs Europens (d') Automobiles [association of European car makers]
ADC	Analog to Digital Converter
ALU	Arithmetic Logic Unit
ASIC	Application-Specific IC
ASSP	Application-Specific Standard Product
BIST	Built-In Self Test
CAFE	Corporate Average Fuel Economy
CAN	Controller Area Network
CPU	Central Processing Unit
DDR	Double Data Rate
DMA	Direct Memory Access
DSP	Digital Signal Processor
EBU	External Bus Unit
ECU	Electronic Control Unit
EEMBC	EDN Embedded Microcontroller Benchmark
EMI	Electro-Magnetic Interference
FFT	Fast Fourier Transform
FIR	Finite Impulse Response
HCCI	Homogeneous Charge-Compression Ignition
HMI	Human/Machine Interface

I/O Input/Output
IC Integrated Circuit
IIR Infinite Impulse Response
ITRS International Technology Roadmap of Semiconductors
LD/ST Load/Store
LIN Local Interconnect Network
LQG Linear Quadratic Gaussian
MAC Multiply and Accumulate
MIPS Millions of Operations Per Second
MLI Microlink Interface
MSB Microsecond Bus
NVM Nonvolatile Memory
OEM Original Equipment Manufacturer
OSEK Offene Systeme und Deren Schnittstellen für die Elektronik im Kraftfahrzeug (English: Open Systems and the Corresponding Interfaces for Automotive Electronics)
PCB Printed Circuit Board
PCP Peripheral Control Processor
PID Proportional Integral Derivate
PM Particulate Matter
PWM Pulse Width Modulation
SIL Safety Integrity Level
SPI Serial Peripheral Interface
USB Universal Serial Bus